The Cambridge GED Program

Consulting Editors

Mary Ann Corley
Supervisor of Adult Education
Baltimore County Public Schools

Del Gratia Doss
Supervisor, Adult Basic Education
St. Louis, Missouri

Ron Froman
Administrator of Adult Education
Orange County Public Schools, Orlando, Florida

Dorothy Hammond
Coordinator
New York State Writing Project

Lawrence Levin
KNILE Educational & Training Association
Former Director ABE/ESL/HSE Services
New York City Board of Education

Noreen Lopez
Adult Educator
Illinois

Arturo McDonald
Assistant Superintendent—Adult Education
Brownsville, Texas

Cheryl Moore
Curriculum Director, Windham School System
Texas Department of Corrections

Carrie Robinson Weir
Director, Adult Education Resource Center
Jersey City State College

Harold Wilson
Director of Adult Basic Education
Indianapolis Public Schools

Jane Zinner
Director of Grants and Curriculum
Association for California School Administrators

Contributing Editors

Gloria Cohen, Ed.D.
Consultant, Curriculum & Gifted Education
New York Metropolitan Area

Carole Deletiner
Adult Basic Education Teacher
Formerly, New York City Technical College

Don Gerstein
Academic Educator
Wyoming State Penitentiary 1981–1986

Nathaniel Howard
Senior Training Representative
Consolidated Edison, New York City

Joan Knight
Former City-wide Supervisor of Staff Development
New York City Board of Education Adult Program

Bonnie Longnion
Dean of Continuing Education
North Harris County College, Kingwood, Texas

Joe Mangano
Research Associate
State University of New York at Albany

Ada Rogers
Adult Education GED Program
Broward County, Florida, School System

Ann Rowe
Education Specialist
New York State

Elois Scott
Reading Specialist
University of Florida, Gainesville

Stephen Steurer
Correctional Academic Coordinator
Maryland State Department of Education

Dr. Jay Templin
Professor of Biology
Widener University, Delaware Campus

Jeffrey Tenzer
Auxiliary Services for High Schools
New York City

The Cambridge GED Program

Writers

Gary Apple
Owen Boyle
Jesse Browner
Phyllis Cohen
Carole Deletiner
Randee Falk
Don Gerstein
Peter Guthrie
Alan Hines
Jeanne James
Lois Kasper
Rachel Kranz
Gloria Levine
Amy Litt
Dennis Mendyk
Rebecca Motil
Susan Muller
Marcia Mungenast
Thomas Repensek
Ada Rogers
Ann Rowe
Richard Rozakis
Elois Scott
Sally Stepanek
Steve Steurer
Lynn Tiutczenko
Tom Walz
Willa Wolcott

Executive Editor

Jerry Long

Senior Editor

Timothy Foote

Project Editors

James Fina
Diane Maass

Subject Editors

Jim Bedell
Diane Engel
Randee Falk
Scott Gillam
Rebecca Motil
Thomas Repensek

Art and Design

Brian Crede Associates
Adele Scheff

Contents

Introduction   vii

Prediction   1

Answers and Explanations for the Predictor Tests   49
    Performance Analysis Charts   64

Instruction   69

Unit I: Writing Skills, Part I: Grammar   71
    Progress Chart   72

    Chapter 1   **Usage**   73
    Chapter 2   **Sentence Structure**   100
    Chapter 3   **Mechanics**   118
    Chapter 4   **Editing Paragraphs**   147

Unit II: Writing Skills, Part II: Essay-writing   169
    Progress Chart   170

    Chapter 1   **Daily Writing**   171
    Chapter 2   **The Writing Process**   175
    Chapter 3   **Reviewing the Writing Process**   192

Unit III: Reading Strategies   201
    Progress Chart   202

    Chapter 1   **A Strategy for Reading**   203
    Chapter 2   **Reading for Answers**   215
    Chapter 3   **The Three "Reading Tests"**   246

Unit IV: Social Studies   263
    Progress Chart   264

    Chapter 1   **Introduction to Social Studies**   265
    Chapter 2   **American History**   270
    Chapter 3   **Geography**   282
    Chapter 4   **Economics**   288
    Chapter 5   **Political Science**   298
    Chapter 6   **Behavioral Sciences**   305

Unit V: Science   313
        Progress Chart   314

        Chapter 1   **Introduction to Science**   315
        Chapter 2   **Biology**   322
        Chapter 3   **Earth Science**   334
        Chapter 4   **Chemistry**   347
        Chapter 5   **Physics**   356

Unit VI: Interpreting Literature and the Arts   369
        Progress Chart   370

        Chapter 1   **Introduction to Literature and Commentary on the Arts**   371
        Chapter 2   **Nonfiction**   375
        Chapter 3   **Fiction**   387
        Chapter 4   **Drama**   399
        Chapter 5   **Poetry**   411
        Chapter 6   **Commentary**   422

Unit VII: Mathematics   433
        Progress Charts   435

        Chapter 1   **Whole Numbers**   439
        Chapter 2   **Fractions**   461
        Chapter 3   **Decimals**   488
        Chapter 4   **Percents**   508
        Chapter 5   **Graphs**   523
        Chapter 6   **Algebra**   533
        Chapter 7   **Geometry**   553

Practice   579

Simulation   665

Answers and Explanations   A-1

Introduction

WHAT IS THE GED?

The initials GED stand for General Educational Development. You may also have heard the tests referred to as the High School Equivalency Tests. The GED diploma is widely regarded as the equivalent of a high school diploma.

The GED is a way for millions of adults in the United States and Canada to get diplomas or certificates without returning to high school. Each year about half a million people take advantage of the opportunity to take the GED Tests.

Who Recognizes the GED?

The GED is recognized by employers, unions, and state and federal civil services. Many vocational institutes, colleges, and universities accept students who have obtained a GED. All 50 states and parts of Canada use the GED Tests results to issue high school equivalency credentials. However, each state has its own standards for what constitutes a passing grade. For information on the requirements in your state, contact the High School Equivalency Program of the State Department of Education in your state capital.

What Is Tested on the GED Tests?

The material found on the GED is based on the subjects covered in most high schools around the country. Thus you will be learning about the subject areas that you would be most likely to study if you attended four years of high school. However, the focus of the GED is not on content, but on *skills*. You will not have to memorize specific dates, names, and places. For example, whether you recall the day on which a battle was fought or the title of a novel is less important than whether you can read and understand a passage on history or literature.

The Five GED Tests

The GED is actually five separate tests. With one exception, the tests are composed entirely of multiple-choice questions. The one exception is the 200-word essay that you will be required to write as part of the Writing Skills Test. The chart below describes the structure of the five tests:

Test #	Test Subject	Number of Items	Minutes Allowed

1	Writing Skills
	    Part I: Multiple Choice
	    Part II: Essay
		55
		1
			75
			45

2	Social Studies	64	85
3	Science	66	95
4	Interpreting Literature and the Arts	45	65
5	Mathematics	56	90

THE WRITING SKILLS TEST

The Writing Skills Test examines your knowledge of the conventions of written English and your ability to write.

What Kind of Questions Are on the Writing Skills Test?

The Writing Skills Test is composed of two parts. Part I tests your knowledge of the conventions of written English: usage, sentence structure, and mechanics (punctuation, capitalization, and spelling). Part II tests your ability to write an expository essay.

In Part I, you will read paragraphs made up of 10 to 12 sentences. Each sentence in each paragraph will be numbered. You will be asked to locate and correct the errors in certain sentences.

In Part II, you will be asked to write an essay that states your opinion or provides an explanation about a certain topic. You will write a 200-word essay in which you support your opinion or defend your explanation with specific details. There are no "correct answers" for this sort of test. Your essay will be judged not for the opinion or explanation you give, but rather on the overall effectiveness of your argument. Your writing will be rated on whether it is clear, well-organized, and generally free of errors in usage, sentence structure, and mechanics.

As with the other GED tests, all of the 55 questions in Part I of the Writing Skills Test are in multiple-choice format.

THE SOCIAL STUDIES TEST

The Social Studies Test examines your ability to understand, use, analyze, and evaluate social studies material: information from the fields of history, geography, economics, political science, and behavioral science.

What Kind of Questions Are on the Social Studies Test?

When you take the test, you will read passages and answer questions, some of which test your understanding: you will be required to restate information, summarize ideas, or identify implications of the information given in the passages you read. Other questions will test your ability to use, analyze, and evaluate what you understand. You may read a passage that defines social studies terms and then be asked to choose examples that demonstrate the meaning of those terms. Or you may be given a passage from, say, a newspaper editorial, and be asked to distinguish facts from opinions, to recognize a writer's assumption, to distinguish the author's conclusion from the supporting evidence, or identify a cause-and-effect relationship. Finally, you may read a passage that presents an argument about a social studies topic and then be required to decide how valid the argument is. You may be asked to decide whether the data presented proves what the author says it does. You may be asked to recognize the hidden values that are behind what the author writes.

About one third of the items are based on graphic material. The other two thirds are based on written material.

THE SCIENCE TEST

The 66 items on the Science Test examine your ability to understand, use, analyze, and evaluate information from the life and physical sciences: biology, earth science, chemistry, and physics.

What Kind of Questions Are on the Science Test?

As in the Social Studies Test, when you take the Science Test you will read passages and answer questions based on those passages. The questions will test your understanding and your ability to use, analyze, and evaluate what you understand. You may read a passage that describes a scientific phenomenon and then be asked to apply that information in a slightly different context. To do that, you have to imagine how another situation might work, based on what you have been told about the first situation. Some questions will test your ability to distinguish facts from opinions, to recognize assumptions, to tell the difference between a conclusion and its supporting statements, or to identify cause-and-effect relationships. A passage may describe a scientific experiment. You may be asked to evaluate whether the data provided supports a certain conclusion. About half the passages relate to biology; the others relate to the physical sciences: earth science, chemistry, and physics.

THE INTERPRETING LITERATURE AND THE ARTS TEST

The Interpreting Literature and the Arts Test examines your ability to understand and analyze popular and classical literature and commentary about literature and the arts.

What Kind of Questions Are on the Literature and the Arts Test?

Like the Social Studies and Science tests, the Interpreting Literature and the Arts Test will require you to read passages and answer questions that test your understanding and your ability to use and analyze what you understand. The passages you will read are all taken from actual published works. About half of the 45 questions will be based on popular literature—nonfiction, fiction, drama, and poetry (including song lyrics) recently written and widely enjoyed by today's readers. About one-fourth of the questions will be based on passages from classical literature—works that are considered to have earned a place in literary history. Finally, one-fourth of the questions will be based on commentary—writing about literature, theater, music, dance, film, and art.

THE MATHEMATICS TEST

The Mathematics Test examines your ability to use arithmetic, algebra, and geometry to solve the kind of math problems that you are likely to encounter in your daily life or at work.

What Kind of Questions Are on the Mathematics Test?

When you take the Mathematics Test, you will solve problems based on brief passages and graphic material. Solving some of the problems will require working through two or more steps. For example, you might be given information about two prospective jobs with different pay and different annual raises. You might also be told the cost of transportation to each job. Then you might be asked to calculate which job would net more money at the end of two years. To answer that question would require performing several different operations.

None of the questions will require that you use formulas you have memorized. If a question requires you to use a formula, it will be provided for you. About two-thirds of the problems are based on written passages. The other one-third is based on graphic material. You may be asked one or more questions about each of the pieces of graphic material. All of the items on the Mathematics Test are in multiple-choice format.

WHAT YOU WILL FIND IN THIS BOOK

This book gives you a four-step preparation for taking the GED Tests.

Step One: Prediction

In this first step, you will find the Predictor Tests. The tests are very much like the five actual GED Tests, but with the exception of Part II of the Writing Skills Test, the Predictor Tests are only about half as long as the GED Tests. Taking the Predictor Tests will give you an idea of what the real GED Tests will be like. By evaluating your performance on the Predictor Tests, you will get a sense of your strengths and weaknesses in the areas of writing, social studies, science, literature, and mathematics. This information will help you to plan your studies accordingly.

Step Two: Instruction

The instruction section is divided into seven units. The first two units, Writing Skills, Part I: Grammar, and Part II: Essay-writing, will help you learn grammar and the editing and essay-writing skills necessary for passing the Writing Test of the GED. The third unit, Reading Strategies, can help you develop your reading skills. This unit is a preparation for studying Units IV-VI and for taking the GED Tests successfully. Units IV-VI focus on Social Studies, Science, and Interpreting Literature and the Arts. Unit VII covers Mathematics.

Step Three: Practice

This section gives you valuable practice in answering the types of questions you will find on the actual GED Tests. The Practice Items section consists of GED-like questions grouped according to subject. This organization of the Practice Items section allows you to test your understanding of one branch of each subject at a time. Each group of Practice Items consists of the same number of items as are on the related GED Test. You can use your results to track your progress and to give you an idea of how prepared you are to take the real tests.

Step Four: Simulation

Finally, a simulated version of all five of the GED Tests is offered. They are as much like the real tests as possible. The number of questions, their level of difficulty, and the way they are organized are the same as you will find on the actual tests. You will have the same amount of time to complete each test as you will have when you take the GED.

Answers and Explanations

At the back of this book, you will find a section called Answers and Explanations. This section contains the answers to all the questions in the Previews, Lesson Exercises, Reviews, Chapter Quizzes, the Practice Items, and the Simulated Tests. The answer section is a valuable study tool: It tells you the right answer and explains why each answer is right. It shows solutions for mathematics problems. Entries in the answer section point out the writing, reading, or mathematics skill you need to answer an item successfully.

USING THIS BOOK

Whether you are working with an instructor or alone, you can use this book to prepare for the GED Tests in the way that works best for you.

Take a Glance at the Contents

Before doing anything else, look over the Contents and get a feel for this book. Leaf through the book to see what each section looks like.

Take the Predictor Tests

Your performance and score on the Predictor Tests will be very useful to you as you work with the rest of this book. Taking the tests will help you identify your particular strengths and weaknesses. This will help you plan your course of study.

Begin Your Instruction

After you have analyzed your strengths and weaknesses, you are ready to begin instruction. You can work through the instruction in many ways. You should complete Unit III, Reading Strategies, before you work on Units IV to VI. You can then apply the reading strategies to all the readings in the units that follow.

Your GED preparation will probably be most successful if you work on all five subjects of the tests at the same time. This way, you can make steady progress in each of the GED subjects throughout the period of your preparation.

At the beginning of each unit you will find a Progress Chart. As you complete an activity, such as a lesson exercise or a chapter quiz, you can record your performance on that chart. The chart allows you to see your progress from lesson to lesson. If you feel you are not making enough progress, you can vary your method of studying or ask your teacher for help.

Use the Practice Items

At certain points in your instruction, you have choices: you can proceed from one chapter directly to the next or you can go to the Practice section to work on GED-like items in the part of a subject you have just studied. Thus you can get practice on GED-like items frequently during the course of your instruction. Or, if you wish, you can wait until you've finished a whole unit—or all seven units—before you do the Practice Items.

Take the Simulated Tests

Finally, once you have completed the Instruction and Practice sections of the book, you should take the Simulated Tests. These tests will help you assess how ready you are to take the actual tests.

Try Your Best!

To attain a passing score on the GED Tests, you will probably need to have more than half of the items on each test correct. To give yourself a margin for passing, try to maintain a score of at least 80 percent correct as you work through this book. The Progress Charts and Performance Analysis Charts will help you compare your work with this 80 percent figure. If you maintain 80 percent scores, you are probably working at a level that will allow you to do well on the GED.

Prediction

Introduction

Imagine that you were going to take the GED Tests today. How do you think you would do? In which subjects and areas would you perform best, and which would give you the most trouble? The Predictor Tests that follow can help you answer those questions. They are called Predictor Tests because your test results can be used to predict where your strengths and weaknesses are in relation to the actual GED Tests.

You will find a Predictor Test for each of the five GED Tests: Writing Skills, Social Studies, Science, Interpreting Literature and the Arts, and Mathematics. The Predictor Tests are like the actual GED Tests in many ways. They will check your skills as you apply them to the kinds of passages you will find on the real tests. The questions are like those on the actual tests.

How to Take the Predictor Tests

The Predictor Tests will be most useful to you if you take them in a manner similar to that in which the actual tests are given. If possible, complete each test in one sitting with as little distraction as possible. It probably is best to take only one per day. The Writing Skills Test has two parts, and it might be best if you took only one part at a time.

So that you have an accurate record of your performance, write your answers neatly on a sheet of paper, or use an answer sheet provided by your teacher. For Part II of the Writing Skills Test, plan and write your essay on fresh sheets of paper.

As you take each test, don't be discouraged if you find you are having difficulty with some (or even many) of the questions. The purpose of these tests is to help you identify your strengths and weaknesses. So relax. You will have plenty of opportunities to correct any weaknesses and retest them.

You may want to time yourself to see how long you take to complete each test. With the exception of the Writing Skills Predictor Test, each Predictor Test is about half as long as the actual GED Test for that subject. Part II of the Writing Skills Predictor Test is the same length as the GED. If you complete each Predictor Test in half the time allotted for the corresponding real GED Test, you are right on target. You will be told how much time you should allow at the beginning of each test. You shouldn't worry too much if it takes you longer.

When you are done with each Predictor Test, check your answers by using the answer section that begins on page 49. Put a check by each item you answered correctly.

How to Use Your Score

On pages 64–67, you will find Performance Analysis Charts. Fill in the charts; they will help you find out which areas you are most comfortable with, and which give you the most trouble.

As you begin a chapter in the book, you may want to refer back to the appropriate Performance Analysis Chart to see how well you did in a specific area of a Predictor Test.

PREDICTOR TEST 1
Writing Skills, Part I

TIME: 38 minutes

Directions: The items in Part I of this test are based on a paragraph that contains numbered sentences. Some of the sentences may contain errors in sentence structure, usage, or mechanics. **A few sentences, however, may be correct as written.** Read each paragraph and then answer the nine to ten items that follow it. For each item, choose the answer that would result in the most effective writing of the sentence or sentences. The best answer must be consistent with the meaning and tone of the rest of the paragraph.

FOR EXAMPLE:

Sentence 1: **Although it may take only two hours to watch the average motion picture takes almost a year to make.**

What correction should be made to this sentence?

(1) replace it with they
(2) change take to have taken
(3) insert a comma after watch
(4) change almost to all most
(5) no change is necessary

The correct answer is **(3)**. In this example, a comma is needed after the clause Although it may take only two hours to watch.

Items 1 to 10 are based on the following paragraph.

(1) Now, as always, consumers must behave responsible in making their purchases. (2) There are many Consumer Commissions that check on products. (3) Some consumer groups are private. (4) Such as the one Ralph Nader formed. (5) Even with these groups, buyers must be watchful theirselves. (6) They cannot depend only on salesclerks, many stores are understaffed. (7) Buyers should examine each item carefully whenever they make a purchase. (8) They must make sure that the packages have not already been opened. (9) Consumers must also check the labels for warranties, warnings, and how to care for the product. (10) When buying a toy for young children, consumers should check it's construction to make certain that it is safe for their youngsters. (11) In order to feel secure about a purchase, consumers must buy with care.

1. Sentence 1: **Now, as always, consumers must behave responsible in making their purchases.**

    What correction should be made to this sentence?

    (1) change the spelling of *always* to *allways*
    (2) remove the comma after *always*
    (3) change *responsible* to *responsibly*
    (4) replace *their* with *there*
    (5) no correction is necessary

2. Sentence 2: **There are many Consumer Commissions that check on products.**

    What correction should be made to this sentence?

    (1) replace *there* with *they're*
    (2) change *are* to *is*
    (3) change the spelling of *Commissions* to *Comissions*
    (4) change *Consumer Commissions* to *consumer commissions*
    (5) insert a comma before *that*

3. Sentences 3 & 4: **Some consumer groups are private. Such as the one Ralph Nader formed.**

    Which of the following is the best way to write the underlined portion of these sentences? If you think the original is the best way, choose option (1).

    (1) private. Such as the one
    (2) private, such as the one
    (3) private; such as the one
    (4) private. For example, the one
    (5) private; for example, the one

4. Sentence 5: **Even with these groups, buyers must be watchful theirselves.**

    What correction should be made to this sentence?

    (1) change the spelling of *watchful* to *watchfull*
    (2) remove the comma after *groups*
    (3) change *watchful* to *watchfully*
    (4) replace *theirselves* with *themselves*
    (5) no correction is necessary

5. Sentence 6: **They cannot depend only on salesclerks, many stores are understaffed.**

    Which of the following is the best way to write the underlined portion of this sentence? If you think the original is the best way, choose option (1).

    (1) salesclerks, many stores
    (2) salesclerks many stores
    (3) salesclerks. Because many stores
    (4) salesclerks being that many stores
    (5) salesclerks because many stores

6. Sentence 7: **Buyers should examine each item carefully whenever they make a purchase.**

   If you rewrote sentence 6 beginning with

   Before making a purchase,

   the next words should be

   (1) buyers should examine
   (2) each item must be examined
   (3) whenever buyers examine
   (4) each item must examine
   (5) therefore, each item

7. Sentence 8: **They must make sure that the packages have not already been opened.**

   What correction should be made to this sentence?

   (1) change *sure* to *surely*
   (2) insert a comma after *that*
   (3) change the spelling of *already* to *all ready*
   (4) change *opened* to *open*
   (5) no correction is necessary

8. Sentence 9: **Consumers must also check the labels for warranties, warnings, and <u>how to care for the product.</u>**

   Which of the following is the best way to write the underlined portion of this sentence? If you think the original is the best way, choose option (1).

   (1) how to care for the product.
   (2) how the product must be cared for.
   (3) care instructions for the product.
   (4) there are ways of caring for the product.
   (5) instructing how to care for the product.

9. Sentence 10: **When buying a toy for young children, consumers should check it's construction to make certain that it is safe for their youngsters.**

   What correction should be made to this sentence?

   (1) change the comma after *children* to a semicolon
   (2) remove the comma after *children*
   (3) change *it's* to *its*
   (4) replace *their* with *there*
   (5) no correction is necessary

10. Sentence 11: **In order to feel secure about a purchase, consumers must buy with care.**

    If you rewrote sentence 11 beginning with

    Unless consumers buy with care,

    the next words should be

    (1) in order to feel secure
    (2) so that they will feel secure
    (3) they may feel secure
    (4) they may not feel secure
    (5) the purchase may not feel secure

6   Test 1: Writing Skills, Part I   PREDICTION

Items 11 to 19 are based on the following paragraph.

(1) The computer is an invention that affects my life in many ways. (2) Although we may not use computers at work, we find them in many other places. (3) For example, computers are used to record the prices of groceries at stores, to provide us with cash at banks, and they also process our bills. (4) Many new cars use computers to check they're engines and recommend any needed changes. (5) Our long-distance phone calls are handled by computers. (6) Many young children were used to working with computers in school. (7) Sometimes computers go down, but they usually work well. (8) Computers help us all by increasing the speed with which you can conduct business. (9) Computers are found throughout our lives. (10) We should learn more about them.

11. Sentence 1: **The computer is an invention that affects my life in many ways.**

What correction should be made to this sentence?

(1) replace *an* with *one*
(2) insert a comma before *that*
(3) change the spelling of *affects* to *effects*
(4) change *my life* to *our lives*
(5) no correction is necessary

12. Sentence 2: **Although we may not use computers at work, we find them in many other places.**

If you rewrote sentence 2 beginning with

We may not use computers

the next words should be

(1) at work, but we find
(2) at work, we find
(3) at work, and we find
(4) at work, however, we find
(5) at work, therefore, we find

13. Sentence 3: **For example, computers are used to record the prices of groceries at stores, to provide us with cash at banks, <u>and they also process our bills</u>.**

Which of the following is the best way to write the underlined portion of this sentence? If you think the original is the best way, choose option (1).

(1) and they also process our bills.
(2) and our bills are processed by them.
(3) and the processing of our bills.
(4) and billing us.
(5) and to process our bills.

14. Sentence 4: **Many new cars use computers to check they're engines and recommend any needed changes.**

What correction should be made to this sentence?

(1) replace *they're* with *there*
(2) replace *they're* with *their*
(3) insert a comma before *and*
(4) change the spelling of *recommend* to *reccomend*
(5) no correction is necessary

15. Sentence 5: **Our long-distance phone calls are handled by computers.**

    If you rewrote sentence 5 beginning with

    Computers

    the next words should be

    (1) are handled by our long-distance
    (2) handle our long-distance
    (3) handling our long-distance
    (4) phoning long-distance
    (5) long-distance phone calls

16. Sentence 6: **Many young children were used to working with computers in school.**

    What correction should be made to this sentence?

    (1) replace *were* with *are*
    (2) change *used* to *use*
    (3) insert a comma after *working*
    (4) insert a comma after *computers*
    (5) no correction is necessary

17. Sentence 7: **Sometimes computers <u>go down, but they usually work well</u>.**

    Which of the following is the best way to write the underlined portion of the sentence? If you think the original is the best way, choose option (1).

    (1) go down, but they usually work well.
    (2) go down but they usually work well.
    (3) go down but, they usually work well.
    (4) go down. But they usually work good.
    (5) go down, but, they usually work good.

18. Sentence 8: **Computers help us all by increasing the speed with which you can conduct business.**

    What correction should be made to this sentence?

    (1) insert a comma before *by*
    (2) insert a comma before *with*
    (3) replace *which* with *whom*
    (4) replace *you* with *we*
    (5) no correction is necessary

19. Sentences 9 & 10: **Computers are found throughout our lives. We should learn more about them.**

    The most effective combination of sentences 9 and 10 would include which of the following groups of words?

    (1) Computers are found throughout our lives, being that we should learn
    (2) Computers are found throughout our lives, but we should learn
    (3) Because computers are found throughout our lives, we should learn
    (4) Unless computers are found throughout our lives, we should learn
    (5) Computers are found throughout our lives, because we should learn

Items 20 to 28 are based on the following paragraph.

(1) Each one of you are facing important choices about your career. (2) While it may seem hard to decide. (3) There are some steps you can take to help you to choose. (4) First, make a list of your intrests, achievements, and talents. (5) If your talents lie in one field, you can explore the different careers within that field. (6) Career choices in the medical field, for example, can include jobs as Doctors, physical therapists, nurses, or assistants. (7) After reading about several careers, one should try to talk to people who work in those careers. (8) These talks with workers can help you learn more about their jobs. (9) You can discuss the pros and cons of a job and learn about the required training. (10) Once you have learned about several careers, you can decide on a career more easily.

20. Sentence 1: **Each one of you are facing important choices about your career.**

    What correction should be made to this sentence?

    (1) replace *are* with *is*
    (2) change *facing* to *faced*
    (3) change the spelling of *important* to *importent*
    (4) insert a comma after *choices*
    (5) no correction is necessary

21. Sentences 2 & 3: **While it may seem hard <u>to decide. There are</u> some steps you can take to help you to choose.**

    Which of the following is the best way to write the underlined portion of these sentences? If you think the original is the best way, choose option (1).

    (1) to decide. There are
    (2) to decide; there are
    (3) to decide, there are
    (4) to decide and there are
    (5) to decide so there are

22. Sentence 4: **First, make a list of your intrests, achievements, and talents.**

    What correction should be made to this sentence?

    (1) replace *your* with *you're*
    (2) change the spelling of *intrests* to *interests*
    (3) remove the comma after *intrests*
    (4) change the spelling of *achievements* to *acheivements*
    (5) no correction is necessary

23. Sentence 5: **If your talents lie in one <u>field, you can</u> explore the different careers within that field.**

    Which of the following is the best way to write the underlined portion of this sentence? If you think the original is the best way, choose option (1).

    (1) field, you can
    (2) field. You can
    (3) field; you can
    (4) field you can
    (5) field so that you can

24. Sentence 6: **Career choices in the medical field, for example, can include jobs as Doctors, physical therapists, nurses, or assistants.**

What correction should be made to this sentence?

(1) remove the comma after *example*
(2) change *Doctors* to *doctors*
(3) remove the comma after *Doctors*
(4) insert a comma after *physical*
(5) change the spelling of *assistants* to *assistance*

25. Sentence 7: **After reading about several careers, one should try to talk to people who work in those careers.**

What correction should be made to this sentence?

(1) change the spelling of *several* to *severel*
(2) replace the comma after *careers* with a period
(3) replace the comma after *careers* with a semicolon
(4) replace *one* with *you*
(5) change the spelling of *people* to *peeple*

26. Sentence 8: **These talks with workers can help you learn more about their jobs.**

If you rewrote sentence 7 beginning with

By talking with workers,

the next words should be

(1) you can learn
(2) more is learned
(3) jobs are learned
(4) helps you learn
(5) in order for you to learn

27. Sentence 9: **You can discuss the pros and cons of <u>a job and</u> learn about the required training.**

Which of the following is the best way to write the underlined portion of this sentence? If you think the original is the best way, choose option (1).

(1) a job and learn
(2) a job, and learn
(3) a job and, learn
(4) a job; and learn
(5) a job so that you learn

28. Sentence 10: **Once you have learned about several careers, you can decide on a career more easily.**

If you rewrote sentence 10 beginning with

Learning about several careers

the next words should be

(1) once you have decided
(2) their own jobs will be decided
(3) in order to decide
(4) and deciding about their own jobs
(5) will help you to decide

Answers are on pages 49–50

Writing Skills, Part II

TIME: 45 minutes

Directions: This is a test to see how well you can write. In this test, you are asked to write an essay in which you present your opinions about an issue. In preparing your essay, you should take the following steps.

Step 1. Read all of the information about the topic. Be sure that you understand the topic and that you write about only the assigned topic.

Step 2. Plan your essay before you write.

Step 3. Use scrap paper to make any notes.

Step 4. Write your essay on a separate sheet of paper.

Step 5. Read what you have written. Make sure that your writing is legible.

Step 6. Check your paragraphing, sentence structure, spelling, punctuation, capitalization, and usage; make any changes that will improve your essay.

TOPIC

> Many employers now offer alternatives to the traditional workweek, such as working part time, working at home, and working flexible hours.
>
> Decide which type of work schedule you would pick if you had the choice. Write a composition of about 200 words explaining why this option would be the best for you. Be specific, and use reasons or examples in your explanation.

When you take the GED test, you will have 45 minutes to write about the topic question you are assigned. Try to write the essay for this test within 45 minutes. Write legibly and use a ballpoint pen so that your writing will be easy to read. Any notes that you make on scrap paper will not be counted as part of your score.

After you complete this essay, you can judge its effectiveness by using the Essay Scoring Guide and Model Essays in the answer key to score your essay. They will be concerned with how clearly you make the main point of your essay, how thoroughly you support your ideas, and how clear and correct your writing is throughout the composition. You will receive no credit for writing about a question other than the one assigned.

Answers are on pages 51–55.

PREDICTOR TEST 2
Social Studies

TIME: 42½ minutes
Directions: Choose the one best answer to each question.

Items 1 to 3 are based on the following figure.

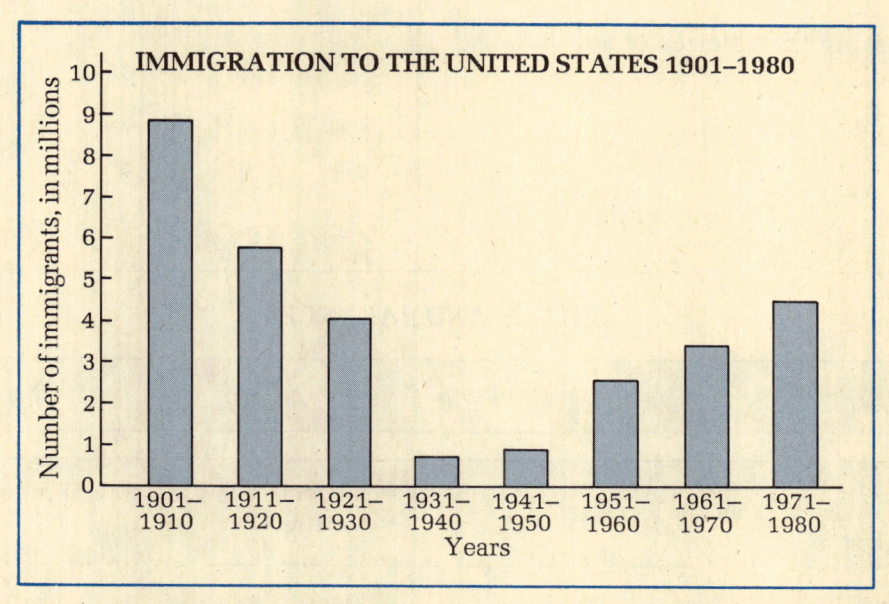

IMMIGRATION TO THE UNITED STATES 1901–1980

(Bar graph: Number of immigrants, in millions, by decade)
- 1901–1910: ~8.8
- 1911–1920: ~5.7
- 1921–1930: ~4.0
- 1931–1940: ~0.5
- 1941–1950: ~0.8
- 1951–1960: ~2.5
- 1961–1970: ~3.3
- 1971–1980: ~4.4

1. According to the graph, during which of the following periods was immigration lowest?

    (1) 1931–1940
    (2) 1941–1950
    (3) 1951–1960
    (4) 1961–1970
    (5) 1971–1980

2. For which of the following years would a federal government study show the greatest need for increased jobs and housing for immigrants?

    (1) 1921–1930
    (2) 1941–1950
    (3) 1951–1960
    (4) 1961–1970
    (5) 1971–1980

3. How would you describe the pattern of immigration levels between 1901 and 1980?

    (1) steady increase
    (2) steady decrease
    (3) increase then decrease
    (4) decrease then increase
    (5) no increase or decrease

11

4. Property taxes help to pay for services that benefit property owners. These taxes are the main source of income for local governments. They are also used by some state governments. Which of the following would most likely be paid for by a property tax?

   (1) building a new nuclear submarine
   (2) building a new house
   (3) increasing the number of FBI agents
   (4) building a new firehouse in a small town
   (5) increasing the salaries of soldiers

Item 5 is based on the following figure.

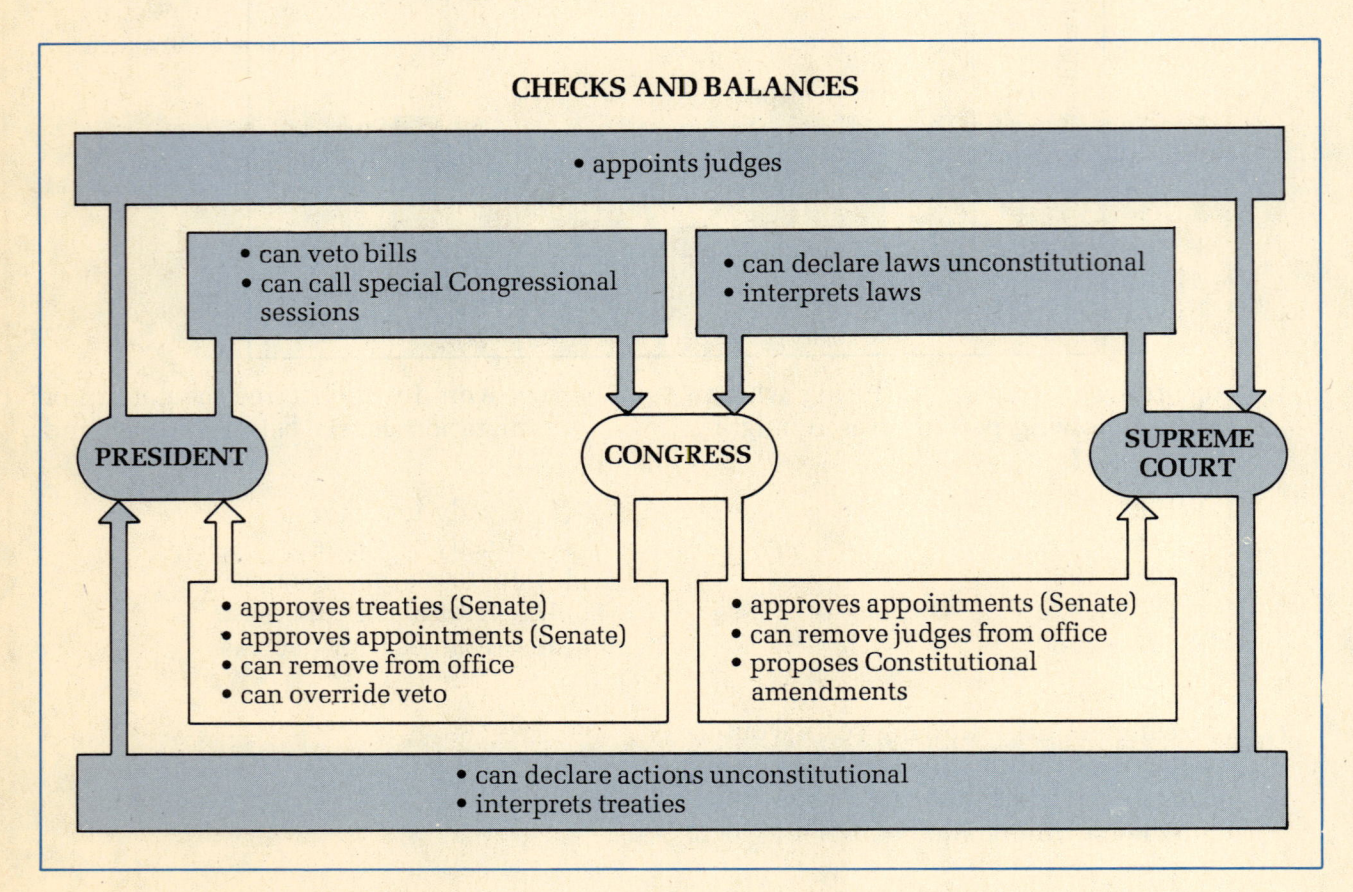

CHECKS AND BALANCES

- appoints judges

PRESIDENT
- can veto bills
- can call special Congressional sessions

CONGRESS

- can declare laws unconstitutional
- interprets laws

SUPREME COURT

- approves treaties (Senate)
- approves appointments (Senate)
- can remove from office
- can override veto

- approves appointments (Senate)
- can remove judges from office
- proposes Constitutional amendments

- can declare actions unconstitutional
- interprets treaties

5. President Reagan appointed Justice O'Connor, the first woman to sit on the Supreme Court. This appointment

   (1) was not legal for President Reagan to make
   (2) had to be approved by the Senate
   (3) had to be approved by the Supreme Court
   (4) did not have to be approved
   (5) should have been made by Congress

Items 6 to 10 are based on the following passage.

   Children, as well as adults, see a great deal of violence on television. Saturday morning cartoon programs show a violent act every two minutes. By high school graduation, an average youth has seen some 18,000 make-believe murders on television.

   Some television critics worry that watching so much violence has negative effects on children. Experiments show that children tend to be more aggressive and overactive after viewing violence on television. Unfortunately, there are no conclusive studies on the effects of television violence after weeks, months, and years of viewing.

   But even television critics agree that television is not all bad. Creative programs such as "Sesame Street" help children to develop basic skills. Many television programs, and even some commercials, allow young people to see different lifestyles and cultures. American children learn about life in faraway lands. Inner-city youths learn about the lives of farm children.

   Clearly, television is a powerful influence on children. Parents may need to judge it just as carefully as they judge teachers, playmates, and babysitters.

6. Which one of the following statements best summarizes the point of the passage?

   (1) Children watch too much television.
   (2) Television has too much violence.
   (3) Television teaches basic skills.
   (4) Television influences children.
   (5) Television violence causes crime.

7. A parent is looking over the Saturday morning TV program listings. Based on the above passage, which one of the following programs would he or she encourage the children to watch?

   (1) a science-fiction series showing space battles
   (2) a cartoon series based on martial arts
   (3) a rerun of a favorite monster movie
   (4) a film of young Americans visiting the Andes
   (5) a crime-fighter cartoon that has gun-fighting scenes

8. The passage says that critics think some programs and commercials can help children learn more about the world. Which of the following is the best example of the kind of program the critics meant?

   (1) a program about a science fair
   (2) a crime-fighting drama
   (3) a study of life in a village in the Alps
   (4) a drama based in a hospital
   (5) a local news broadcast

9. The author of the passage assumes, but does not state, which of the following ideas?

   (1) Some critics are fearful of TV's effects on children.
   (2) Most youngsters watch television.
   (3) Violent programs can affect children's behavior.
   (4) Parents judge teachers, playmates, and babysitters.
   (5) Television can expand children's horizons.

(Item 10 is on the following page.)

10. The following statements come from the passage. Which one provides evidence that television-viewing can affect children's behavior?

(1) Children, as well as adults, see a great deal of violence on television.
(2) By high school graduation, an average youth has seen some 18,000 make-believe murders on television.
(3) Experiments show that children tend to be more aggressive and overactive after viewing violence on television.
(4) Many television programs, and even some commercials, allow young people to see different lifestyles and cultures.
(5) Parents may need to judge it [television] just as carefully as they judge teachers, playmates, and babysitters.

---

11. The largest of the seven continents is Asia with an area of 44,400,000 square kilometers. The next largest is Africa, followed by North America and South America. Antarctica is smaller than South America, but larger than Europe. Europe's area is over 10,000,000 square kilometers, and Australia's area is 8,500,000 square kilometers.

The size of each continent's population is influenced by many factors. Two of the most important factors are how large the continent is and what its climate is like. Which continent could be expected to have the smallest population?

(1) Antarctica
(2) Australia
(3) Europe
(4) North America
(5) South America

12. In 1776, Adam Smith wrote a book called *The Wealth of Nations*. Smith believed that governments should not control economic development. He thought producers should produce whatever they wanted. The goods would then be sold at whatever price people were willing to pay. The free marketplace would control production and prices.

According to the passage, which one of the following statements expresses a belief held by Adam Smith?

(1) Governments should not control production and prices.
(2) Governments should pass laws that control prices.
(3) Producers should not be allowed to produce whatever they want.
(4) Producers should not try to make a profit.
(5) People who buy goods often pay too much for them.

Items 13 and 14 are based on the following table.

Population Changes in the Five Largest U.S. Cities					
	1900	1950	1960	1970	1980
Chicago	1,700,000	3,600,000	3,550,000	3,369,000	3,000,000
Houston	44,000	596,000	940,000	1,200,000	1,600,000
Los Angeles	102,000	1,970,000	2,480,000	2,800,000	2,966,000
New York	3,437,000	7,890,000	7,780,000	7,895,000	7,071,000
Philadelphia	1,290,000	2,070,000	2,000,000	1,950,000	1,688,000

Source: U.S. Bureau of the Census.

13. Which cities would city planners study to determine reasons for population increases since 1970?

(1) Chicago and Houston
(2) New York and Chicago
(3) Philadelphia and New York
(4) Houston and Los Angeles
(5) Philadelphia and Chicago

14. Based on the table, which area of the United States has shown a steady increase in population since the turn of the century?

(1) Northeast
(2) Southwest
(3) Southeast
(4) Midwest
(5) Northwest

Item 15 is based on the following cartoon.

(Copyright © 1981 by Newsday, Inc. Reprinted with permission of Newsday.)

15. Which one of the following statements best explains the message of the cartoon?

   (1) Cleaning ladies and sanitation engineers do the same jobs.
   (2) Employees with different jobs earn different salaries.
   (3) Men and women cannot perform the same tasks at work.
   (4) Men are often paid more than women for the same jobs.
   (5) Men and women have different titles for similar jobs.

Item 16 is based on the following quote.

"And so, my fellow Americans, ask not what your country can do for you—ask what you can do for your country. My fellow citizens of the world: Ask not what America will do for you, but what together we can do for the freedom of man."

John F. Kennedy

16. Which one of the following activities provides the best example of a response to the ideas expressed by John F. Kennedy?

   (1) joining an organization to encourage foreign travel
   (2) asking citizens of other countries to visit America
   (3) limiting the number of foreign embassies
   (4) joining a volunteer group to help needy citizens
   (5) signing a petition to limit foreign-aid programs

Items 17 to 21 are based on the following information.

Listed below are three types of political systems with brief descriptions of how power is distributed in them.

1. Monarchy: One person, the monarch, rules the country. The monarch usually inherits power and rules for life. In an *absolute* monarchy, the ruler has all of the power. In a *constitutional* monarchy, the ruler's power is limited by laws. In some countries, the monarch has no power at all. In these countries, the monarch is a symbol, rather than a real ruler.

2. Democracy: All qualified citizens have some say in how the country is run. In a *direct* democracy, the people vote on every law. In a *representative* democracy, citizens elect people to represent them. These representatives then vote on the laws.

3. Dictatorship: One person takes total control of a country. The dictator has power over all laws and economic matters. Dictators also try to control peoples' beliefs and values. People are usually not allowed to criticize the government.

17. A head of state wanted his policies to be carried on after his death. To assure that, he carefully directed his children's education. He was most likely head of what type of government?

    (1) absolute monarchy
    (2) constitutional monarchy
    (3) direct democracy
    (4) representative democracy
    (5) dictatorship

18. After the government of a certain country is overthrown, the leader of the revolution arrests the country's elected representatives and potential opposition leaders. He declares himself the sole head of the government. He then takes control of the nation's television stations and closes down its newspapers. Which of the following names the type of political system the leader has set up?

    (1) absolute monarchy
    (2) constitutional monarchy
    (3) direct democracy
    (4) representative democracy
    (5) dictatorship

19. The United States is an example of which type of political system?

    (1) absolute monarchy
    (2) constitutional monarchy
    (3) direct democracy
    (4) representative democracy
    (5) dictatorship

20. Under which system would the people be most responsible for the laws enacted?

    (1) absolute monarchy
    (2) constitutional monarchy
    (3) direct democracy
    (4) representative democracy
    (5) dictatorship

21. Great Britain has which of the following kinds of government?

    (1) absolute monarchy
    (2) constitutional monarchy
    (3) direct democracy
    (4) representative democracy
    (5) dictatorship

Item 22 is based on the following passage.

"Just because my grandfather was a carpenter and my father is a carpenter, it doesn't mean that I have to be a carpenter, even though I am the only son. I don't like to work with tools. I want to go to school to learn how to be an accountant. I know there are no accountants in my family, but I'm sure I can be one if I can find a way to afford college."

22. From what the speaker says, one of the most important values held by his family is probably

    (1) money
    (2) tradition
    (3) education
    (4) religion
    (5) status

Items 23 to 26 are based on the following table.

Employment Gains and Losses

Five industries with the largest number of employment gains and five with the largest number of losses since 1980

	Jobs (in thousands)
Gainers	
Communication equipment	119
Electronic components/accessories	119
Office and computing machines	102
Commercial printing	71
Miscellaneous plastics products	71
Losers	
Blast furnace and basic steel products	245
Construction and related machinery	145
Womens' and misses' outerwear	50
Plastics materials and synthetics	43
Footwear (except rubber)	42

Source: Bureau of Labor Statistics, U.S. Department of Labor.

23. Based on the information in the table, which one of the following statements is true?

    (1) Jobs that supply services rather than products are increasing.
    (2) Communications, electronics, and computer industries have provided the most new jobs since 1980.
    (3) It is easy to find a job making shoes.
    (4) More people would rather be construction workers than steelworkers.
    (5) The footwear industry has lost more jobs than the outerwear industry.

24. Based on the table, which one of the following people would be most likely to enroll in a program offering job retraining?

(1) a teacher
(2) a commercial printer
(3) a producer of computers
(4) a worker in a telephone manufacturing facility
(5) a worker in a shoe factory

25. Which one of the following statements CANNOT be justified from the information given in the table?

(1) Producers of office machines and computers have more new jobs available than producers of plastics materials and synthetics.
(2) Producers of communications equipment and electronic components have gained more than 200,000 new jobs.
(3) More shoes are imported than are produced in the United States.
(4) Shoe factories have lost fewer jobs than commercial printers have gained.
(5) Producers of plastics products have gained jobs while producers of plastics materials have lost jobs.

26. Which one of the following conclusions is best supported by the information in the table?

(1) The safest jobs are in the long-established skills areas.
(2) Most new jobs are being created by the newer technologies.
(3) It doesn't matter what you study in school if you want a secure job.
(4) Commercial printing has a doubtful future.
(5) Women's outerwear manufacturing has a bright future.

Item 27 is based on the following passage.

The First Amendment to the United States Constitution says:

"Congress shall make no law respecting an establishment of religion, or prohibiting the free exercise thereof; or abridging the freedom of speech, or of the press; or the right of the people to assemble, and to petition the government for a redress of grievances."

27. Which one of the following rights is not protected by the First Amendment?

(1) freedom of speech
(2) freedom of religion
(3) the right to a jury trial
(4) the right to protest to the government
(5) freedom of the press

28. Population density refers to the number of people living in a certain amount of space. Populations are more dense in cities than in rural areas. In the nineteenth century, where were populations densest in the United States?

(1) in deserts
(2) in mountainous areas
(3) near waterways
(4) in valleys
(5) in plains areas

Items 29 to 32 are based on the following passage.

Before the Civil War the Northern and Southern states were like two different societies. The Northern states had many large cities. Most of the country's industry was located in the North. Many people lived in cities and worked in factories.

The Southern states consisted mainly of small towns and farms. Southern cities were small. There were few factories in the South. Most Southerners lived on farms and plantations. The South's economy was based mainly on cotton.

In 1824, the federal government raised the tax on imported goods. Southerners felt that this tax law favored Northerners. The South depended on the North and foreign producers for manufactured goods, and on the North for shipping and receiving its own goods. In addition, Southerners had to go to Northern banks for loans. Because they depended on the North, many Southerners felt their states were like colonies of the North.

29. Which one of the following statements best explains how the South's lack of industry affected its economic status?

    (1) The North had more cities than the South.
    (2) The South had more cities than the North.
    (3) The South relied on cotton.
    (4) The South relied on the North for shipping, banking, and manufactured goods.
    (5) Southerners believed that taxes on imported goods were unfair to them.

30. Which one of the following statements best explains why Southerners believed that taxes on imported goods were unfair to them?

    (1) Southerners provided cotton for the North.
    (2) The South had to import more goods than the North.
    (3) Southerners went to Northern banks for loans.
    (4) Only Southerners had to pay the taxes.
    (5) The Southern states had few big cities.

31. Which one of the following statements best reflects the main emphasis of the passage?

    (1) Economic differences between the North and the South played no role in the Civil War.
    (2) Economic differences between the North and the South centered on the issue of bank loans.
    (3) The North and the South developed into different kinds of societies with different economies and different economic needs.
    (4) The South's lack of industry caused the Civil War.
    (5) The North and the South were more alike than they were different.

32. The passage states that many Southerners felt their states were like colonies of the North. Which of the following statements gives the most likely cause for that feeling?

    (1) The South was economically dependent on the North.
    (2) The South was settled by people from the North.
    (3) The South had no banks of its own.
    (4) The North and the South were like different societies.
    (5) The South had to pay more import taxes than the North.

Answers are on pages 56–57.

PREDICTOR TEST 3
Science

TIME: 47½ minutes
Directions: Choose the one best answer to each question.

Item 1 is based on the following passage.

A brewery worker lifts a 50-pound keg of beer onto a delivery truck. In doing so, the worker does 150 foot-pounds of work. Then the worker loads an identical keg onto a different truck. This time the worker does 200 foot-pounds of work.

1. Why does it take more work to lift the second keg?

   (1) The second truck is higher off the ground than the first.
   (2) The second keg contains more beer.
   (3) The man has gotten tired.
   (4) The first keg weighs less than the second.
   (5) Only the second lift requires energy.

2. Tides are the rise and fall of Earth's oceans, caused by the gravitational pull of the moon. The gravity of the planets affects Earth, too, but not as much as the moon's gravity. Larger bodies pull more strongly, but the planets' distances from Earth offset the effect of their sizes. Which of the following is true of the planets?

   (1) They are larger than the moon.
   (2) Some of them are larger than the moon; some are smaller.
   (3) They are smaller than the moon.
   (4) They are the same size as the moon.
   (5) Some of them are the same size as the moon.

Test 3: Science

Items 3 to 7 are based on the following passage.

Everywhere on Earth plants and animals are related to each other in food chains. Each organism's position in the chain is determined by two things: by what it eats and by what eats it.

Each organism in a food chain uses energy to sustain its life. It passes on *some* of that energy when it is eaten by the next link in the chain. At each step, less energy is available for use.

When a food chain is listed, arrows are used to show which way the energy passes. Here is an example: grain → chicken → human.

The following explains the links in a simple food chain.

1. Producer: Most of these are green plants. They convert energy from the sun directly into nourishment.

2. Primary Consumer: These are animals that eat vegetable matter. When you eat a salad, you are a primary consumer.

3. Secondary Consumer: Secondary consumers eat primary consumers. You do this when you eat hamburger, which is made from cattle that have eaten grass and grain.

4. Tertiary Consumer: These are meat-eaters that eat secondary consumers. For example, large fish that eat small fish that in turn eat shellfish are tertiary consumers. So are humans in those cultures that eat dog meat or lion meat.

5. Decomposer: These are usually bacteria and fungi. They bring about the decay of dead organisms and break down their waste products. The breakdown substances are reused by the producers.

3. Consider this food chain: leaf → insect → fish → bird → human. Which link has the least available energy?

   (1) bird
   (2) fish
   (3) human
   (4) insect
   (5) leaf

4. Consider this chain: lettuce → rabbit → human. The human is a

   (1) producer
   (2) primary consumer
   (3) secondary consumer
   (4) tertiary consumer
   (5) decomposer

5. Consider this chain: grass → insect → bird → snake → bacteria. The snake is a

   (1) producer
   (2) primary consumer
   (3) secondary consumer
   (4) tertiary consumer
   (5) decomposer

6. Which kind of food-chain link is not shown in this chain? pond weed → minnow → bass → otter

   (1) producer
   (2) primary consumer
   (3) secondary consumer
   (4) tertiary consumer
   (5) decomposer

7. Vegetarians claim that they make more efficient use of the world's food resources than do those who eat meat. Which of these statements from the passage might they use to justify this claim?

   (1) Each organism's position in the chain is determined by what it eats and by what eats it.
   (2) At each step, less energy is available for use.
   (3) Producers convert energy directly from the sun into nourishment.
   (4) Primary consumers eat vegetable matter.
   (5) The breakdown substances are reused by the producers.

Item 8 is based on the following diagram.

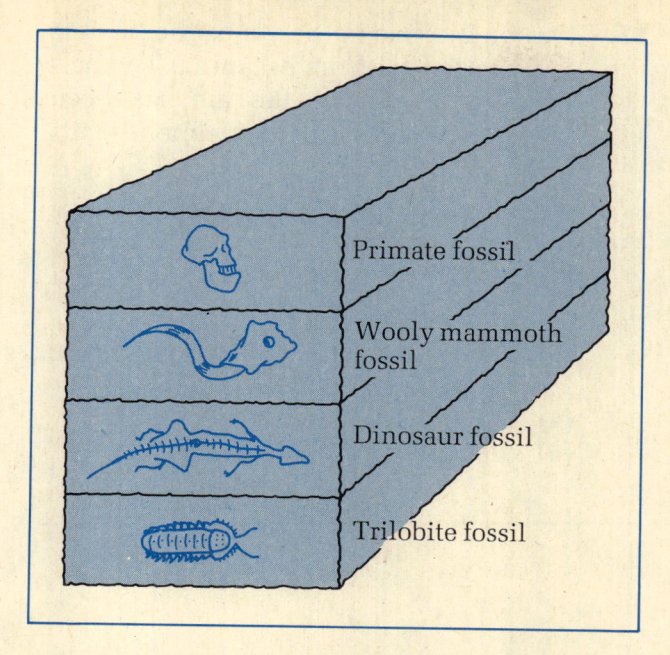

Primate fossil
Wooly mammoth fossil
Dinosaur fossil
Trilobite fossil

Younger rock layers and their fossils are usually found on top of older rock layers and their fossils. The diagram above shows a cross-section of rock from northern Canada.

8. The figure provides evidence to support which of the following conclusions?

   (1) The climate of northern Canada has remained essentially the same throughout Earth's history.
   (2) Northern Canada was once much drier than it is now.
   (3) Northern Canada has the kind of climate that allows many different animals to live together.
   (4) Northern Canada used to be much colder than it is now.
   (5) The climate of northern Canada was radically altered by a period of cooling and drying.

Item 9 is based on the following passage.

The parts of a rosebush perform different services. The flower attracts insects by its bright color and sweet smell. This is how the plant reproduces, because the insects carry pollen from one place to another. The broad, flat leaves use the sun's energy to produce food, and exchange oxygen for carbon dioxide. The roots have many long branches which take minerals and water from the soil. The minerals and water are conducted to the leaves by the tubelike stem.

9. What does this passage tell us about rosebushes?

   (1) Their color and scent are unimportant.
   (2) Each part serves a life-sustaining function.
   (3) The flower is the most important part.
   (4) The flower is necessary for nutrition.
   (5) Insects bring rosebushes food.

Items 10 to 12 are based on the following table.

Gases in the Atmosphere (by percentage weight)

Gas	Percent
Nitrogen	78
Oxygen	21
Argon	.9
Carbon dioxide	.03
Rare gases	.07

10. What percent of the atmosphere is made of the gas that sustains human and other animal life?

    (1) 78
    (2) 21
    (3) 99
    (4) .03
    (5) 21.03

11. Suppose that a burning candle is placed in a tightly closed container. The gas mixture in the container is different from the atmosphere's: it is 95% nitrogen. What will probably happen?

    (1) Oxygen concentration will increase.
    (2) Combustion will occur more easily.
    (3) The composition of the gases will not change any more.
    (4) Nitrogen will be consumed.
    (5) The candle will burn more slowly.

12. Carbon dioxide in the atmosphere tends to prevent heat from escaping. The percentage of CO_2 in the air has been changing. What might happen if its level reaches 5%?

    (1) Continental coastlines would be unaffected.
    (2) Areas now under water would become shores.
    (3) Life on Earth would be largely unchanged.
    (4) The polar icecaps would melt.
    (5) Glaciers would grow larger.

13. When blood pressure is measured, two values result. The first value represents the force with which the heart pumps blood. It is the higher of the two numbers. The second, lower value indicates the flexibility of the arteries. Pulse pressure is the difference between the two. Thus, a person whose blood pressure reads 120 over 80 has a pulse pressure of 40.

Suppose the person's blood pressure is measured again a week later. The lower number is still 80, but the pulse pressure is 50. What would the reason be?

(1) The heart is damaged.
(2) The heart is pumping harder.
(3) The first value is lower than it was the last time.
(4) One of the readings must be wrong.
(5) The arteries have become less elastic.

14. A mitochondrion is a cell's "powerhouse." There are many in cells that need the highest level of energy for body work. Which of these body cells would have the most mitochondria?

(1) a blood cell
(2) a bone cell
(3) a muscle cell
(4) a nerve cell
(5) a skin cell

Items 15 to 18 are based on the following passage.

What causes an object to have a certain color? Light from the sun or an ordinary light bulb is white light. White light includes all the colors of the visible spectrum. The color of an opaque object is the color light it reflects. When white light falls on an opaque object, no light passes through it. Any light that falls on the object is either absorbed or reflected. An apple looks red because red light is reflected while the other colors are absorbed. A white object, then, reflects all colors and absorbs none. A black object does just the opposite, so the color black is really an absence of color.

Transparent objects, like tinted glass, acquire color somewhat differently because light passes through them. Light that falls on a transparent object is either absorbed or transmitted. The color of the object is the color of the light it transmits. Blue glass, for example, transmits only blue light. Clear glass transmits all colors and absorbs no color.

15. Which of the following statements explains why bananas are yellow?

    (1) They absorb only yellow light.
    (2) They absorb all of the white light.
    (3) They reflect only yellow light.
    (4) They reflect all of the white light.
    (5) They transmit the yellow light.

16. In a dance concert, the only things on the stage that are blue are the dancers' shoes and gloves. In one scene the theater is dark. The audience should see hands and feet moving and nothing else. What color light should be directed at the stage?

    (1) white
    (2) black
    (3) red
    (4) blue
    (5) yellow

17. If only green light is shone on a red apple, the apple looks black. Based on the information provided, which of the following statements best explains why this is so?

    (1) The green light combines with red light to make black light.
    (2) The apple absorbs the green light and reflects no light.
    (3) The apple absorbs the green light and reflects black light.
    (4) The apple cannot absorb green light, so it reflects no light.
    (5) The apple reflects green light, which combines with black light.

18. A farmer notices that sunlight appears brighter in winter when his fields are snow-covered than in summer when the fields are lush and green. Based on the information provided, which of the following statements could explain his observation?

    (1) Warm air makes sunlight look dimmer in summer than in winter.
    (2) The field is closer to the sun in winter than in summer.
    (3) White snow reflects more light than green plants do.
    (4) Leaves on trees block the sunlight in summer.
    (5) Plants use up the sunlight in photosynthesis.

19. Pollution makes the water of many lakes and streams in America unsafe for drinking. Among the pollutants are particles of solid waste, which stay suspended in the water. Temperature changes will not purify water of solid wastes. What might a city do to purify its water of solid wastes?

   (1) Boil it.
   (2) Freeze it.
   (3) Let it settle.
   (4) Filter it.
   (5) Shake it.

20. The gene for brown eyes in humans is dominant, and the gene for blue eyes is recessive. A brown-eyed person has either two genes for brown eyes, or one for brown and one for blue. A blue-eyed person has only genes for blue eyes. Which of these couples will know the eye color of their children before birth?

   (1) Father and mother are both brown-eyed.
   (2) Father and mother are both blue-eyed.
   (3) The father has brown eyes; the mother, blue.
   (4) The mother has brown eyes; the father, blue.
   (5) The parents already have one blue-eyed child.

28 Test 3: Science

Items 21 to 25 are based on the following passage.

Most animal circulatory systems have three main parts: the heart, the blood vessels, and the blood.

The heart is a pump that forces blood through the body. Bird hearts and mammal hearts have four chambers. The left and the right auricles are above the left and the right ventricles. Each auricle sends blood to the ventricle on its side of the heart. The ventricles send it to all the body's organs and parts.

The right auricle receives blood from all over the body. This blood is low in oxygen and carries waste products from the cells, such as carbon dioxide. The right ventricle sends the blood to the lungs, where it exchanges the waste gases for fresh oxygen. Then the blood flows to the left auricle, which sends it to the left ventricle. From the left ventricle it passes into the aorta, the largest artery in the body. One of the heart's valves ensures that the blood entering the aorta does not return to the heart. From the aorta it flows through other arteries throughout the body.

Because it has this complete separation, the bird heart and the mammal heart does the best job of keeping blood clean. Other animals lack the advantage of a four-chambered heart. Fish have only a single pump, which takes blood to the gills to regain oxygen. Amphibians, such as frogs and salamanders, have three-chambered hearts: two auricles above a single ventricle. Reptile hearts, such as snakes' and lizards', almost have four chambers, but the wall between the ventricles is not complete.

21. What is an artery?

 (1) a blood vessel that takes blood away from the heart
 (2) a blood vessel that carries blood to the heart
 (3) a heart chamber below the auricles
 (4) a heart chamber above the ventricles
 (5) a valve under the left ventricle

22. A human heart suffers a break in the wall between its ventricles. What happens to the blood's oxygen concentration?

 (1) It increases in the aorta.
 (2) It increases in the left ventricle.
 (3) It decreases in the right ventricle.
 (4) It decreases in the left ventricle.
 (5) It remains the same throughout.

23. Select the most powerful pumping chamber of the heart.

 (1) aorta
 (2) left auricle
 (3) left ventricle
 (4) right auricle
 (5) right ventricle

24. A person has rheumatic fever as a child and suffers damaged heart valves. What problem is this person likely to have in later life?

 (1) The blood moves freely from the left ventricle to the aorta.
 (2) Blood moves in the wrong direction.
 (3) The heart lacks four full chambers.
 (4) The heart will not pump blood.
 (5) The lungs will not provide the blood with oxygen.

25. You are given a heart to study in biology lab. It is three-chambered. The best guess as to the animal it comes from is a

 (1) cat
 (2) fish
 (3) lizard
 (4) robin
 (5) toad

Item 26 is based on the following diagram.

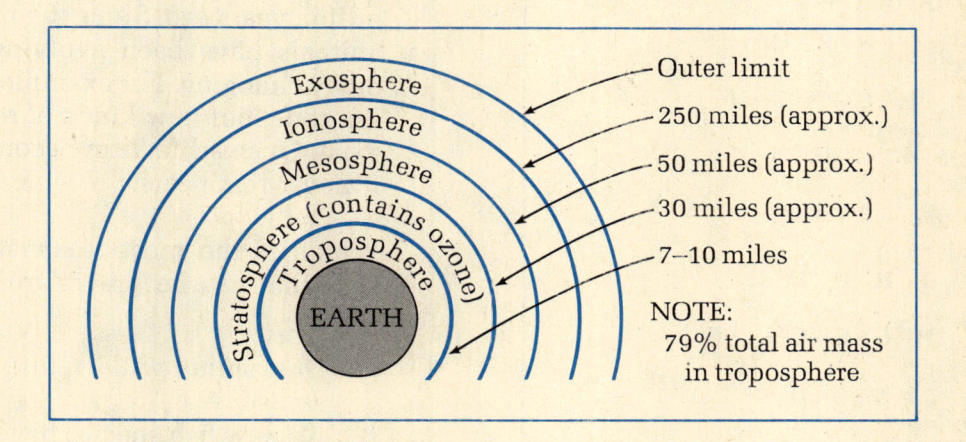

Outer limit
250 miles (approx.)
50 miles (approx.)
30 miles (approx.)
7–10 miles

NOTE: 79% total air mass in troposphere

Exosphere, Ionosphere, Mesosphere, Stratosphere (contains ozone), Troposphere, EARTH

26. Pollution of the atmosphere is a threat to life on Earth. Air pollution affects which layer of the atmosphere most?

(1) exosphere
(2) ionosphere
(3) mesosphere
(4) stratosphere
(5) troposphere

Item 27 is based on the following passage.

Heat is transferred in three different ways:

1. Conduction: Heat is transferred through solids by conduction. Molecules in the solid vibrate more and more. The result is the transfer of heat through the solid.

2. Convection: Heat is transferred through liquids and gases by convection. Molecules in the liquid or gas move long distances giving off energy that causes heat.

3. Radiation: Radiation transfers heat in waves or particles. It usually travels from a source in straight lines and strikes matter—any liquid, solid, or gas. The matter heats as a result.

27. A pot of water on a gas stove is boiling. How is heat transferred to make the water boil?

(1) by conduction only
(2) by convection only
(3) by radiation only
(4) by both conduction and convection
(5) by both radiation and conduction

Items 28 and 29 are based on the following diagram.

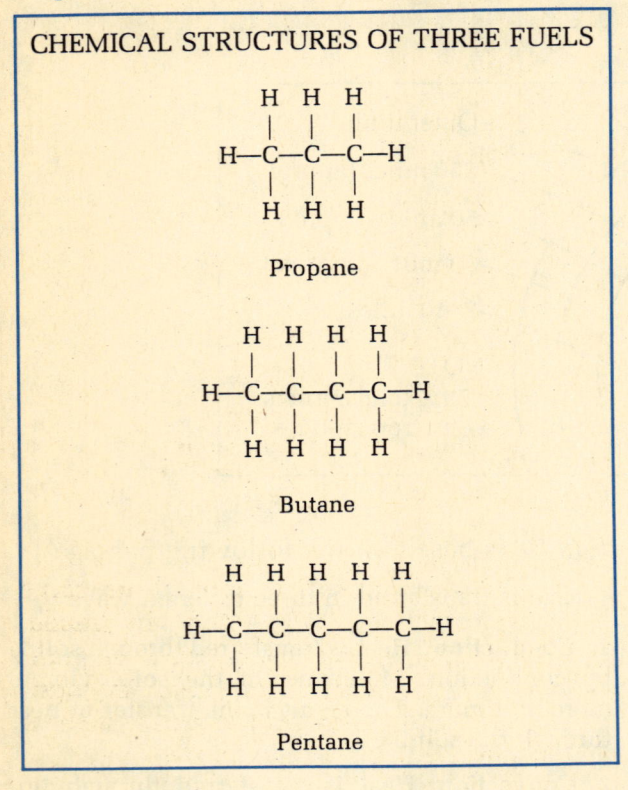

CHEMICAL STRUCTURES OF THREE FUELS

```
    H H H
    | | |
H—C—C—C—H
    | | |
    H H H
```
Propane

```
    H H H H
    | | | |
H—C—C—C—C—H
    | | | |
    H H H H
```
Butane

```
    H H H H H
    | | | | |
H—C—C—C—C—C—H
    | | | | |
    H H H H H
```
Pentane

28. C = 1 carbon atom. H₂ = 2 hydrogen atoms. Which fuel is represented by the formula C_4H_{10}?

(1) butane
(2) carbon
(3) hydrogen
(4) pentane
(5) propane

29. Each carbon atom weighs 12 units; each hydrogen atom, 1 unit. The weight of propane is 44. What is the weight of pentane?

(1) 14
(2) 17
(3) 58
(4) 72
(5) 204

30. Earth is about 5 billion years old. Fossil evidence shows that life started about 3 billion years ago. Since then, plants and animals have been evolving, continuously changing. For example, dinosaurs are gone, but new kinds of reptiles now exist. Once a life form becomes extinct, it never reappears.

Which is the most reasonable conclusion that can be drawn from this passage?

(1) Dinosaurs will return to Earth someday.
(2) No new fish species have developed since fish first appeared on Earth.
(3) Human evolution has stopped.
(4) Living organisms arose from a non-living source.
(5) Living organisms are a very recent occurrence on Earth.

31. Your body needs to maintain fluid balance. Improper fluid balance can affect your blood pressure. When you eat food or drink liquids, your body gains fluids. It makes fluids by chemical reactions. It releases fluids through sweat, urine, and feces. If your salt intake is high, your body may retain fluids. That can make your blood pressure rise. Sometimes reducing salt intake is enough to make high blood pressure return to normal.

Following a doctor's orders, several patients went on a strict salt-free diet. Later, the doctor read their blood pressures. Some patients had blood pressures that were still too high. The doctor told them to take medicine that would make them

(1) eat more salt
(2) eat less salt
(3) urinate more
(4) urinate less
(5) sweat less

Items 32 and 33 are based on the following chart.

Four Common Rock Textures		
Type of Texture	**Description**	**Examples**
Coarse-grained	Made up of visible grains or crystals	Granite Marble Sandstone
Fine-grained	Made up of microscopic grains or crystals	Limestone Basalt
Glassy	Containing no mineral crystals at all	Obsidian
Layered	Made up of mineral crystals all lined the same direction	Slate Schist Sandstone

Source: From Fariel et al., *Earth Science*. Menlo Park, Calif.: Addison-Wesley, 1984, page 86.

32. On a hike, you pick up a rock and can see mineral crystals in it. The rock's texture is not layered. It may be

(1) granite
(2) limestone
(3) basalt
(4) obsidian
(5) schist

33. Rocks are classified into three large groups by the ways they are made. There are igneous rocks (such as granite), sedimentary rocks (such as sandstone), and metamorphic rocks (such as slate).

Which of the following statements is supported by information from the chart?

(1) All igneous rocks have the same type of texture.
(2) Sandstone can be either igneous or sedimentary.
(3) Rocks of different textures may be sedimentary.
(4) No metamorphic rocks are layered.
(5) Granite is the only coarse-grained igneous rock.

Answers are on pages 58–59.

PREDICTOR TEST 4
Interpreting Literature and the Arts

TIME: 33 minutes
Directions: *Choose the one best answer to each question.*

Items 1 to 4 refer to the following passage.

HOW DOES SAM PROVE HIS FRIENDSHIP?

Sam . . . stood gazing for a moment, stock-still, gaping. A boat was sliding down the bank all by itself. With a shout Sam raced across the grass. The boat slipped into the
(5) water.

"Coming, Mr. Frodo! Coming!" called Sam, and flung himself from the bank, clutching at the departing boat. He missed it by a yard. With a cry and a splash he fell face downward
(10) into deep swift water. Gurgling he went under, and the River closed over his curly head.

An exclamation of dismay came from the empty boat. A paddle swirled and the boat came about. Frodo was just in time to grasp
(15) Sam by the hair as he came up, bubbling and struggling. Fear was staring in his round brown eyes.

"Up you come, Sam my lad!" said Frodo. "Now take my hand!"
(20) "Save me, Mr. Frodo!" gasped Sam. "I'm drownded. I can't see your hand."

"Here it is. Don't pinch, lad! I won't let you go. Tread water and don't flounder, or you'll upset the boat. There now, get hold of the side,
(25) and let me use the paddle!"

With a few strokes Frodo brought the boat back to the bank, and Sam was able to scramble out, wet as a water-rat. Frodo took off the Ring and stepped ashore again.

(30) "Of all the confounded nuisances, you are the worst, Sam!" he said.

"Oh, Mr. Frodo, that's hard!" said Sam shivering. "That's hard, trying to go without me and all. If I hadn't a guessed right, where
(35) would you be now?"

"Safely on my way."

"Safely!" said Sam. "All alone and without me to help you? I couldn't have a borne it, it'd have been the death of me."

(40) "It would be the death of you to come with me, Sam," said Frodo, "and I could not have borne that."

"Not as certain as being left behind," said Sam.

(45) "But I am going to Mordor."

"I know that well enough, Mr. Frodo. Of course you are. And I'm coming with you.". . .

"So all my plan is spoilt!" said Frodo. "It is no good trying to escape you. But I'm glad,
(50) Sam. I cannot tell you how glad. Come along! It is plain that we were meant to go together. We will go, and may the others find a safe road! Strider will look after them. I don't suppose we shall see them again."

(55) "Yet we may, Mr. Frodo. We may," said Sam.

From THE FELLOWSHIP OF THE RING by J.R.R. Tolkien. Copyright 1965 by J.R.R. Tolkien.
Reprinted by permission of Houghton Mifflin Company.

32

1. What is the "hard" thing to which Sam refers (lines 32–34)?

    (1) trying to swim
    (2) Frodo's wish to travel without him
    (3) the journey ahead of them
    (4) Frodo's angry speech at the shore
    (5) leaving Strider behind

2. Which of the following things would Sam be LEAST likely to do?

    (1) take care of a hurt animal
    (2) talk to a stranger
    (3) turn away from a neighbor in need
    (4) try to do something he knew was dangerous
    (5) ask for help when he needed it

3. Why does Sam prefer going with Frodo to staying with the others?

    (1) He knows they do not want to go to Mordor.
    (2) He is afraid of Strider.
    (3) He knows they will be safer without him.
    (4) He is loyal to Frodo.
    (5) He knows they do not want to travel by boat.

4. Why is Sam's final comment effective in holding the reader's interest?

    (1) It seems to hint at a later part of the story.
    (2) It has a humor that breaks the tension of the moment.
    (3) It reveals Sam's secret fears about the journey.
    (4) It is in direct contrast with what Sam told Frodo earlier in the passage.
    (5) It dramatizes the seriousness of the moment.

Items 5 to 8 refer to the following passage.

WHAT CAN BE DONE ABOUT UNEMPLOYMENT?

I remember the first time I looked for work. There were hundreds of classified ads in the paper under the Help Wanted heading and I figured it was going to be easy.
(5) Well, it didn't take me long to find out that the number of Help Wanted pages in the classified section of the newspaper has very little to do with getting a job.

First you count out all the ads looking for
(10) nuclear physicists, registered nurses, animal trainers and, if you don't know anything about computers, you count out the ads looking for computer programmers. I mention that because there seem to be a lot of ads for them
(15) these days. I don't know what they do but I assume it's a terrible job that doesn't pay much. If it wasn't, there wouldn't be so many ads for them under Help Wanted.

As soon as you get some experience looking
(20) in the classified section, you get discouraged. You begin to read the classifieds the way you read the phone book when you're looking for one number. You know all those hundreds of listings don't mean anything. You get to spot
(25) the ones looking for door-to-door salesmen to work on commission only. There's usually only one or two categories that mean anything to you and if anything is listed there, you're probably too late for it.

(30) Unemployment is as much of a mystery as cancer and almost as bad. I've never understood why there should be any real unemployment. Do we mean there isn't any work to be done anywhere in the country? Do we
(35) mean people have everything they want to eat? Everything they need by way of housing? All the clothes, cars and creature comforts they want? Of course not. Then why isn't there work for everyone?

(40) What we need is a President who can figure out a way to match up those ten million unemployed with the ten million Help Wanted ads. And when that's done, I hope everyone fires those miserable people in the personnel
(45) offices so they have to go out and look for work themselves.

From *Pieces of My Mind* by Andy Rooney. Copyright 1982, 1983, 1984 by Essay Productions, Inc. Reprinted with permission of Atheneum Publishers.

5. What does the author imagine about computer programmers?

   (1) There are a lot of them.
   (2) They don't know very much.
   (3) They are like nuclear physicists.
   (4) They are mysterious people.
   (5) They must not earn much money.

6. According to the author, why does unemployment continue?

   (1) Not enough careful thought has gone into a solution.
   (2) There are not enough jobs to go around.
   (3) Not enough people have the right kind of education.
   (4) Not enough people have the right kind of experience.
   (5) Newspapers don't run enough Help Wanted ads.

7. Which of the following changes in schools would the author probably recommend as the best way to help end unemployment?

   (1) Teach more computer courses.
   (2) Hire more teachers.
   (3) Withdraw federal aid.
   (4) Raise teachers' salaries.
   (5) Provide more student guidance.

8. The style of writing used in this passage would also be appropriate for

   (1) an editorial
   (2) a news report
   (3) a medical book
   (4) a dictionary entry
   (5) a science report

Items 9 to 11 refer to the following passage.

HOW HAS LORD GORING PLANNED FOR HIS FUTURE?

LORD CAVERSHAM: I wish you would go into Parliament.

LORD GORING: My dear father, only people who look dull ever get into the House of Com-
(5) mons, and only people who are dull ever succeed there.

LORD CAVERSHAM: Why don't you try to do something useful in life?

LORD GORING: I am far too young.

(10) LORD CAVERSHAM [*testily*]: I hate this affectation of youth, sir. It is a great deal too prevalent nowadays.

LORD GORING: Youth isn't an affectation. Youth is an art.

(15) LORD CAVERSHAM: Why don't you propose to that pretty Miss Chiltern?

LORD GORING: I am of a very nervous disposition, especially in the morning.

LORD CAVERSHAM: I don't suppose there is the
(20) smallest chance of her accepting you?

LORD GORING: I don't know how the betting stands today.

LORD CAVERSHAM: If she did accept you she would be the prettiest fool in England.

(25) LORD GORING: That is just what I should like to marry. A thoroughly sensible wife would reduce me to a condition of absolute idiocy in less than six months.

LORD CAVERSHAM: You don't deserve her, sir.

(30) LORD GORING: My dear father, if we men married the women we deserved, we should have a very bad time of it.

From *An Ideal Husband* by Oscar Wilde.

9. Lord Caversham is concerned because he thinks that his son

   (1) won't be able to find a job
   (2) is very nervous
   (3) is a gambler
   (4) won't amount to anything
   (5) will marry the wrong girl

10. From lines 25–28 it can be inferred that Lord Goring wants to marry a woman who is

    (1) deserving of him
    (2) thoroughly sensible
    (3) not too serious
    (4) talkative
    (5) intelligent

11. Which of the following best describes Lord Goring?

    (1) clever but evasive
    (2) ignorant and carefree
    (3) brave and adventurous
    (4) kindhearted but firm
    (5) open-minded and generous

WHAT HAS HAPPENED TO THE WALT DISNEY TRADITION?

When I was about five years old, my parents took me out late one afternoon. It was already dark. We walked several blocks, or maybe we took a bus—that part is fuzzy. Any-
(5) way, we entered a building that was also dark. It remained dark until the magic began.

Magic is what I associate with my first movie. Of course, what I saw that night was a delight conjured by Walt Disney. It hap-
(10) pened to be *Bambi*. My mother says that she used a package of tissues in that hour or so. I only remember staring at all those wonderful talking animals and wishing that I could live in such a world.

(15) Several weeks ago I turned on the "Disney Sunday Movie" and saw all people—not animated characters; just people. Now, it's not that I object to real people. It's just that the Disney gold came from something else. For
(20) example, I dimly remember a family I saw in a Disney movie years ago. I think there were two boys. But I can picture clearly the pair of raccoons that constantly visited the family's back door. One day they got inside the house
(25) and into everything—the dishes, the flour, the cereal. It was wonderful fun.

So, when I turned on that Sunday movie, I was disappointed. The title—"Help Wanted: Kids"—was promising; but neither the couple
(30) in need nor the horrible children available ever amounted to more than a poor try. Did this effort deserve the name "Disney"? Is the public so unimaginative today that it accepts this kind of movie over flights of fancy? Or
(35) has the Master's wand passed on to less able hands, to those who will allow *much* to replace *best*? Gain and art are, at best, uneasy companions.

I guess I'm lucky that I grew up with Don-
(40) ald and Jiminy and Sleepy and Doc. Oh, I'm sure that from time to time we'll be allowed another look at Cinderella's bird friends sewing her ball gown and Mickey's enchanted brooms carrying bucket after bucket of water.
(45) But I'm still looking for that new masterpiece from the old magic lantern.

12. The author's concern is that recent Disney movies lack

   (1) audience appeal
   (2) creativity
   (3) human characters
   (4) financial support
   (5) a true-to-life quality

13. Why did the author enjoy seeing *Bambi*?

   (1) She loved looking at a world in which animals talked.
   (2) She had been looking forward to seeing this Disney masterpiece.
   (3) She loved animal stories.
   (4) She and her mother cried at the end of the movie.
   (5) She was taken to the theater as a special treat for her fifth birthday.

14. How does the author use the word *wand* (line 35)?

   (1) to remind the reader of the magicians in several Disney movies
   (2) to show a contrast between fantasy movies and true-life adventures
   (3) to symbolize the popularity of Disney movies
   (4) to refer to plans for movies that went unfinished when Walt Disney died
   (5) to symbolize the art of creative moviemaking

15. The final paragraph indicates the author's belief that

  (1) animated characters are not believable
  (2) Walt Disney made many popular movies
  (3) memorable characters cannot be found in current Disney efforts
  (4) the Disney studio is unwilling to show the classic animated movies to current audiences
  (5) talking animals are the most memorable characters

16. What kind of people are most likely to identify with the author and her message?

  (1) Disney studio executives
  (2) people who work "behind the scenes" in the movie industry
  (3) children, for whom the classic movies are new
  (4) people who grew up with the classic Disney movies
  (5) students of moviemaking

Items 17 to 20 refer to the following passage.

WHY IS MR. ROCHESTER FEARFUL?

"Ah! Jane. But I want a wife."

"Do you, sir?"

"Yes: is it news to you?"

"Of course: you said nothing about it (5) before."

"Is it unwelcome news?"

"That depends on circumstances, sir—on your choice."

"Which you shall make for me, Jane. I will (10) abide by your decision."

"Choose then, sir—*her who loves you best.*"

"I will at least choose—*her I love best.* Jane, will you marry me?"

(15) "Yes, sir."

"A poor blind man, whom you will have to lead about by the hand?"

"Yes, sir."

"A crippled man, twenty years older than (20) you, whom you will have to wait on?"

"Yes, sir."

"Truly, Jane?"

"Most truly, sir."

"Oh! my darling! God bless you and reward (25) you!"

"Mr. Rochester, if ever I did a good deed in my life—if ever I thought a good thought—if ever I prayed a sincere and blameless prayer— if ever I wished a righteous wish,—I am re- (30) warded now. To be your wife is, for me, to be as happy as I can be on earth."

"Because you delight in sacrifice."

"Sacrifice! What do I sacrifice? Famine for food, expectation for content. To be privileged (35) to put my arms round what I value—to press my lips to what I love—to repose on what I trust: is that to make a sacrifice? If so, then certainly I delight in sacrifice."

"And to bear with my infirmities, Jane: to (40) overlook my deficiencies."

"Which are none, sir, to me. I love you better now, when I can really be useful to you, than I did in your state of proud independence, when you disdained every part but that (45) of the giver and protector."

"Hitherto I have hated to be helped—to be led: henceforth, I feel, I shall hate it no more. I did not like to put my hand into a hireling's, but it is pleasant to feel it circled by Jane's (50) little fingers. I preferred utter loneliness to the constant attendance of servants; but Jane's soft ministry will be a perpetual joy. Jane suits me: do I suit her?"

"To the finest fibre of my nature, sir."

(55) "The case being so, we have nothing in the world to wait for; we must be married instantly."

"He looked and spoke with eagerness: his old impetuosity was rising.

(60) "We must become one flesh without any delay, Jane: there is but the licence to get— then we marry."

From *Jane Eyre* by Charlotte Bronte. Reprinted from the Norton Edition with permission of W.W. Norton & Company, Inc.

17. Jane accepts Mr. Rochester's proposal because

   (1) she wants to see him get well
   (2) she loves him
   (3) she wants control of his business
   (4) she wants to do a good deed
   (5) she wants his money

18. Before the proposal, the relationship between Mr. Rochester and Jane was apparently that of

   (1) good neighbors
   (2) complete strangers
   (3) master and servant
   (4) patient and nurse
   (5) brother and sister

19. Which of the following best describes Jane's attitude toward Mr. Rochester's "infirmities"?

   (1) She thinks he uses them to get attention.
   (2) She fears they will cause his early death.
   (3) She forces herself not to think about them.
   (4) She is happy to know he needs her.
   (5) She is embarrassed by them.

20. The fact that some of Jane's responses are very brief indicates that she is

   (1) bashful
   (2) simple and direct
   (3) poorly educated
   (4) secretly dishonest
   (5) playful

Items 21 to 23 refer to the following song lyrics.

IS THE WORLD CHANGING FOR THE BETTER?

They paved paradise and put up a parking lot,
With a pink hotel, a boutique,
And a swinging hot spot.
(5) Don't it always seem to go
That you don't know what you've got till it's gone?
They paved paradise and put up a parking lot.

(10) They took all the trees and put them in a tree museum,
And they charged the people a dollar and a half
Just to see 'em.
(15) Don't it always seem to go
That you don't know what you've got till it's gone?
They paved paradise and put up a parking lot.

(20) Hey, farmer, farmer, put away the D.D.T. now.
Give me spots on my apples, but leave me the birds
And the bees. Please!
(25) Don't it always seem to go
That you don't know what you've got till it's gone?
They paved paradise and put up a parking lot.

BIG YELLOW TAXI, music and lyrics by Joni Mitchell.
Copyright 1970 & 1974 by Siquomb Publishing Corp.
Reprinted by permission of Warner Brothers Music.

21. What is *paradise* to the author?

(1) a place where trees are put in museums
(2) the unspoiled natural world
(3) farmland
(4) the afterlife
(5) a hotel with a parking lot and nightclub

22. What would the author prefer to have instead of D.D.T.?

(1) a boutique
(2) trees
(3) her music
(4) a room at a pink hotel
(5) spotted apples

23. Which of the following other topics probably would NOT be included in this song?

(1) chemical dumping
(2) protecting the whales
(3) enlarging wildlife preserves
(4) drug abuse
(5) oil spills

Answers are on pages 60–62.

PREDICTOR TEST 5
Mathematics

TIME: 45 minutes
Directions: Choose the one best answer to each question.

1. Sarah worked 10.75 hours overtime in one week. If she earns $9.00 per hour overtime, what was her overtime pay that week?

    (1) $ 6.00
    (2) $ 96.75
    (3) $145.13
    (4) $240.00
    (5) $336.75

2. Janet works part-time at a supermarket. Tuesday, she worked $2\frac{2}{3}$ hours. Thursday, she worked $3\frac{3}{4}$ hours. Saturday, she worked $6\frac{1}{2}$ hours. How many hours did she work altogether that week?

    (1) $11\frac{1}{12}$
    (2) $11\frac{1}{2}$
    (3) $12\frac{11}{12}$
    (4) $13\frac{3}{8}$
    (5) $14\frac{5}{12}$

3. Debbie sells and services computers. She earns a 30% commission on her sales and is paid a salary for her service work. If c = her annual sales and s = her monthly salary, which of the following expressions shows her annual income?

    (1) $s = .3c$
    (2) $.3(s + c)$
    (3) $.3(12s + c)$
    (4) $12s + .3c$
    (5) $12(s + .3c)$

Items 4 and 5 are based on the following information.

One feature of adjustable-rate mortgages (ARMs) is rates that are adjusted annually. The length of a loan varies from bank to bank. Most banks offer them for lengths of 15, 17, 20, or 25 years.

4. If a bank sets its ARM rate at 120% of the prime lending rate, and the ARM rate is 9%, what is the prime rate?

    (1) 7.5%
    (2) 10.8%
    (3) 11%
    (4) 13%
    (5) Not enough information is given.

5. If a $50,000 ARM loan is made at an average simple-interest rate of 10.5%, how much interest would be paid during the life of the loan?

    (1) $ 78,750
    (2) $ 89,250
    (3) $105,000
    (4) $525,000
    (5) Not enough information is given.

Test 5: Mathematics

Items 6 and 7 refer to the following figure.

Item 8 refers to the following figure.

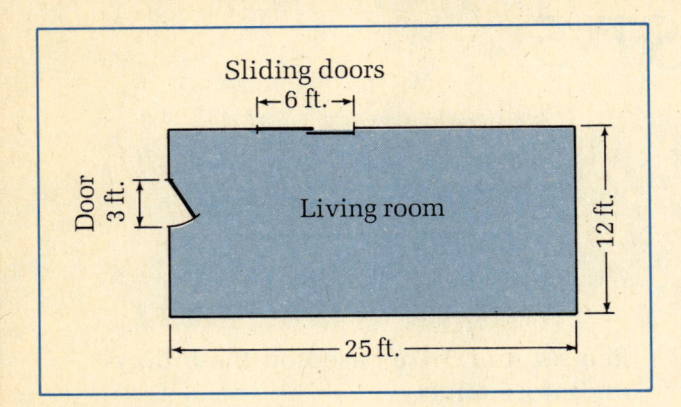

6. What is the minimum number of feet of baseboard needed for this room if none is needed for the doorways?

   (1) 37
   (2) 65
   (3) 68
   (4) 71
   (5) 74

7. If tiles are sold in boxes of 25 each, how many boxes of tiles would be needed to cover the floor in this room?

   (1) 12
   (2) 65
   (3) 74
   (4) 300
   (5) Not enough information is given.

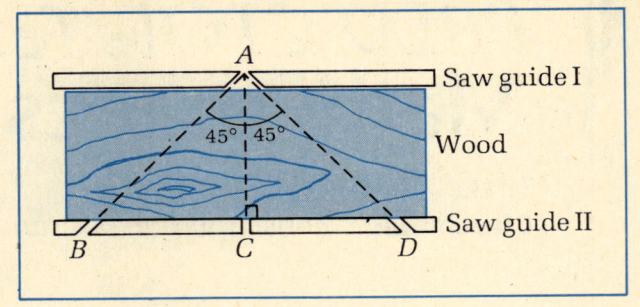

8. A carpenter wants to reuse a plank of wood. He wants to cut the end of the plank to be at a right angle to the length of the plank. Between which saw guides should he place his saw to cut the wood?

   (1) A and B
   (2) A and C
   (3) A and D
   (4) B and D
   (5) C and D

9. The cost of a quart of milk is $.60 plus 2% sales tax in state A, $.59 plus 5% sales tax in state B, $.57 plus 4% sales tax in state C, and $.55 plus 9% sales tax in state D. Which of the following sequences correctly shows the order of states listed from the most expensive to the least expensive total cost of a quart of milk?

   (1) A, B, C, D
   (2) B, A, D, C
   (3) D, B, C, A
   (4) C, D, A, B
   (5) Not enough information is given.

Item 10 refers to the following table.

County	Marriages	Divorces
Albany	293	172
Carbon	180	135
Converse	181	101
Natrona	801	698
Washakie	125	61

10. All the counties listed in the table had MORE marriages than divorces. In which county was the difference between the number of marriages and the number of divorces the smallest?

(1) Albany
(2) Carbon
(3) Converse
(4) Natrona
(5) Washakie

11. A mill produces bolts of a certain size. Quality-control standards allow the size of the bolts to vary, but none may be more than 15 ten-thousandths of an inch larger than the standard. Bolts that do not meet the standard are rejected. If b represents the size of the bolt being measured and s represents the desired size, which formula should be used to determine which bolts should be rejected?

(1) $b < s + .0015$
(2) $b > s + .0015$
(3) $b < s + .015$
(4) $b > s + .015$
(5) $b > .0015$

Item 12 refers to the following table.

Babies Born During One Week at Doctors Hospital

Day	Boys	Girls
Sunday	5	2
Monday	0	8
Tuesday	6	7
Wednesday	4	4
Thursday	8	1
Friday	2	0
Saturday	7	9

12. According to the table, what was the average number of babies born per day?

(1) 4
(2) 5
(3) 7
(4) 8
(5) 9

44 Test 5: Mathematics   PREDICTION

13. One share of Brite Lighting, Inc. stock sold on Monday for $13\frac{3}{8}$. Tuesday, it was down $\frac{1}{2}$. Wednesday, it was up $\frac{5}{8}$. Thursday, it was down $\frac{1}{4}$. What was the closing price of the stock on Thursday?

   (1) $12\frac{7}{8}$

   (2) $13\frac{1}{4}$

   (3) $13\frac{5}{8}$

   (4) $14\frac{1}{4}$

   (5) $14\frac{3}{4}$

Item 14 refers to the following figure.

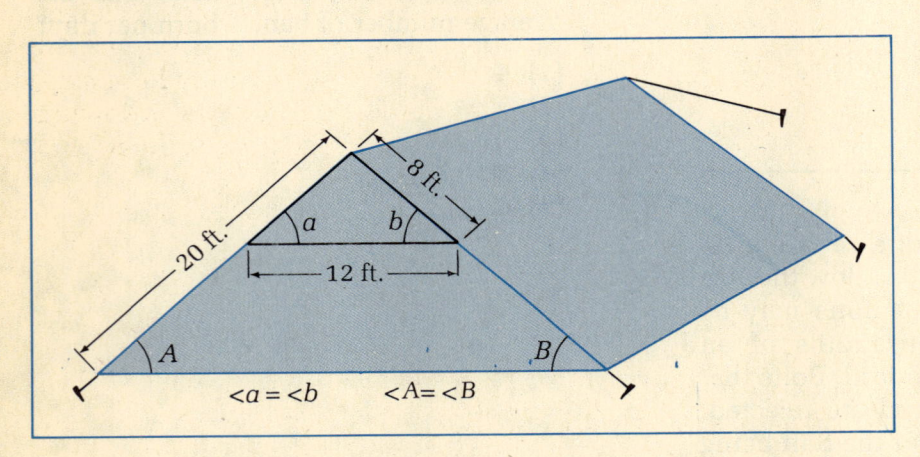

[Figure: tent diagram with 20 ft side, 8 ft side, 12 ft base of inner triangle, angles a, b at top and A, B at bottom; $\angle a = \angle b$, $\angle A = \angle B$]

14. How many feet wide is the base of the tent?

   (1) 13.3
   (2) 24
   (3) 28
   (4) 30
   (5) 40

15. The Nelsons are planning a two-week cross-country automobile trip. If they drive at an average speed of 53 miles per hour and drive 8 hours each day, how many miles will they travel altogether?

   (1) 112
   (2) 424
   (3) 848
   (4) 2968
   (5) 5936

16. Jeff and Sally are planning the spring planting for their farm. Crops will be planted on 360 acres and will include twice as many acres of soybeans as wheat and three times as many acres of corn as wheat. Which equation should be used to determine the correct acreage for each crop? (w = the number of acres of wheat to be planted.)

(1) $w - 5 = 360$
(2) $w + 5 = 360$
(3) $w + 2w + 3w = 360$
(4) $3w - (2w + w) = 360$
(5) $3w \times 2w \times w = 360$

17. In a recent gas-mileage test, the car that had the best gas mileage averaged 56 miles per gallon. That was 7 miles less than 5 times the mileage of the car that had the worst gas mileage. What was the mileage of the worst car?

(1) 3.5
(2) 5.6
(3) 9.2
(4) 11.2
(5) 12.6

18. In July 1986, scientists estimated that the world's population had reached 5×10^9 persons. Which of the following numbers does that equal?

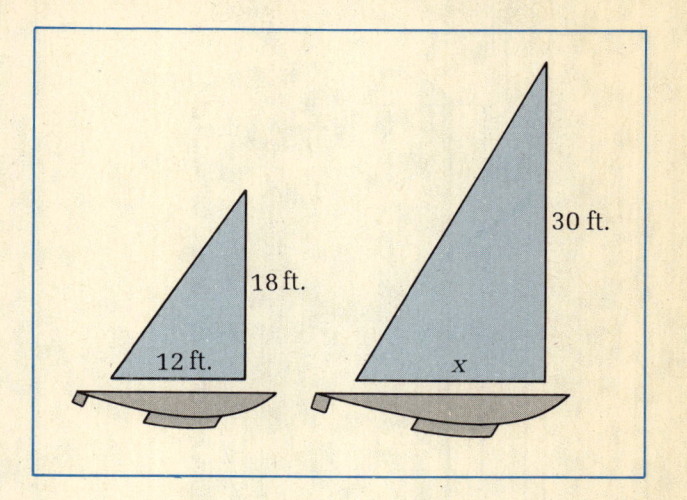

(1) 45
(2) 50
(3) 500,000,000
(4) 4,500,000,000
(5) 5,000,000,000

Item 19 refers to the following figure.

19. The height and the width of the smaller sail are 18 feet by 12 feet; the height and the width of the larger sail are 30 feet by x feet. If the two sails form similar triangles, which of the following proportions could be used to determine the length of x?

(1) 18:12 = x:30
(2) 18:12 = 30:x
(3) 18:30 = x:12
(4) 18:x = 12:30
(5) Not enough information is given.

20. Which of the following expressions equals $\dfrac{x^5}{x^2}$?

(1) x^{-1}
(2) x^3
(3) x^7
(4) x^{11}
(5) Not enough information is given.

Test 5: Mathematics

Item 21 refers to the following figure.

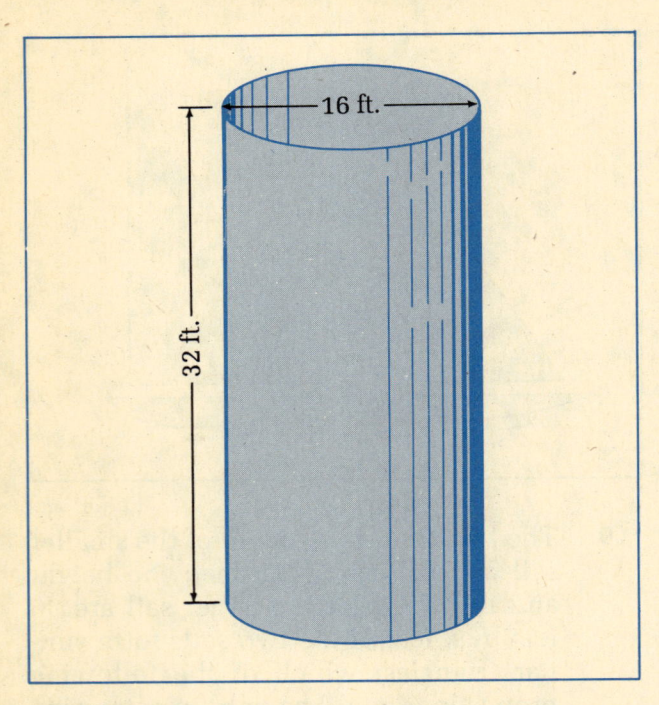

[figure: cylindrical storage tank, 16 ft diameter, 32 ft height]

21. Assume that one bushel equals 1.25 cubic feet. To the nearest whole bushel, how many bushels of grain can be stored in the storage tank?

(1) 161
(2) 1286
(3) 1608
(4) 5145
(6) 6431

22. Three friends recently had dinner together in a restaurant and decided to split the $32.40 check plus a 15% tip evenly among themselves. How much money was paid by each of the three friends?

(1) $10.80
(2) $12.42
(3) $15.80
(4) $26.40
(5) $37.26

Item 23 refers to the following figure.

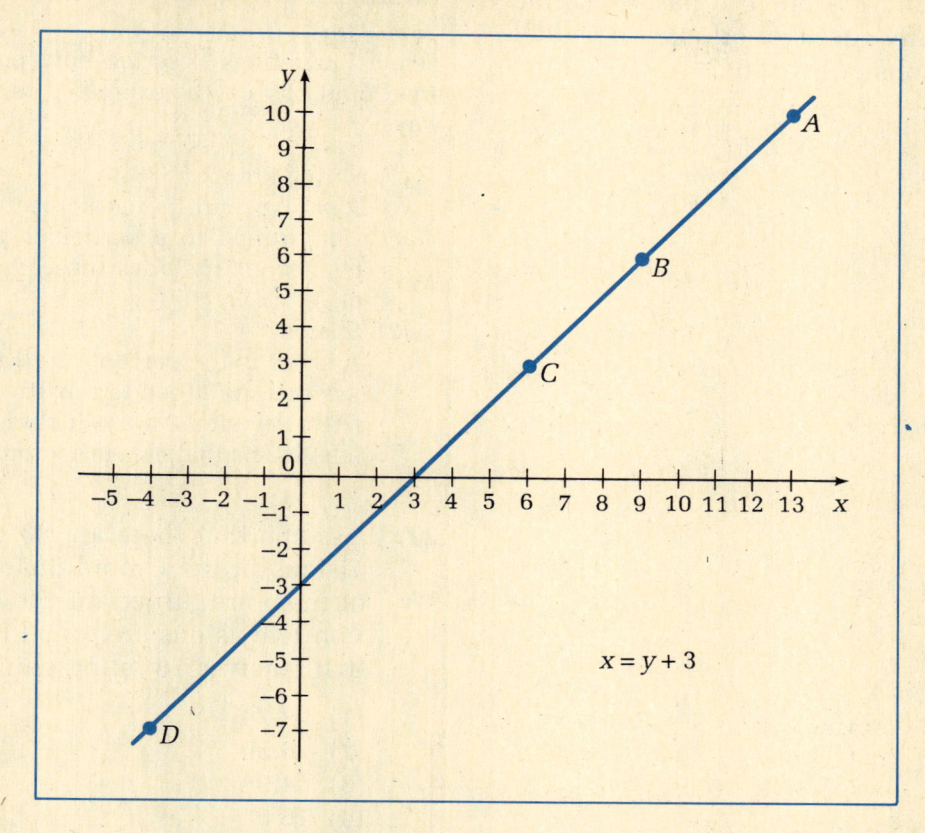

[Graph showing line $x = y + 3$ with points A at (9,10), B at (6,6), C at (6,3) approximately, and D at (-4,-7). Actually points on line: A near (9,10), B near (9,6), C near (6,3), D near (-4,-7).]

$x = y + 3$

23. What is the slope of the line on the graph?

(1) -1
(2) 1
(3) $.5$
(4) $-.5$
(5) 2

24. The ratio of hamburgers to hot dogs that were served at a school picnic was 7:4. If 245 hamburgers were served, how many hot dogs and hamburgers were served?

(1) 249
(2) 256
(3) 280
(4) 319
(5) 385

25. Amy types 70 words per minute. She has to type a 60-page report that contains, on the average, 275 words per page. Which of the following expressions shows the number of minutes that this should take her?

(1) $\dfrac{275 + 60}{70}$

(2) $\dfrac{275 \times 60}{70}$

(3) $\dfrac{275 + 70}{60}$

(4) $\dfrac{275 \times 70}{60}$

(5) $\dfrac{60 \times 70}{275}$

26. Fuel for a snowmobile is mixed at a ratio of 3 parts oil to 8 parts gasoline. How many quarts of oil must be added to 4 gallons of gasoline?

    (1) 1.5
    (2) 3
    (3) 6
    (4) 9
    (5) 12

Items 27 and 28 are based on the following information.

Television ratings describe how popular shows are. Popularity can be expressed in two different ways.

  (1) Rating Points
      A rating point is the percent of *all televisions* tuned to a particular program. (*All televisions* includes those that are turned off.)
  (2) Shares
      A share is the percent of *all televisions in use* that are tuned to a particular program. (*All televisions in use* includes ONLY those televisions that are turned on.)

27. Assume that there are 83 million televisions in the United States and that $\frac{1}{3}$ of them are turned on. How many million televisions are tuned to a program that receives 18 rating points?

    (1) 3.74
    (2) 6.50
    (3) 14.94
    (4) 16.61
    (5) 21.69

28. A televised sports event has a 20% share. During the sports event, 45% of the 83 million televisions were in use. How many televisions (in millions) were tuned to the event?

    (1) 7.47
    (2) 9.00
    (3) 16.60
    (4) 23.00
    (5) 37.35

Answers are on pages 62–63.

Answers to the Predictor Tests

Test 1 Writing Skills Part I

1. **(3)** *Usage/Adverb/Sentence Correction.* The adverb *responsibly* is needed to modify the verb phrase *must behave.*

2. **(4)** *Mechanics/Capitalization/Sentence Correction.* The words *consumer commissions* should not be capitalized since they refer to a general category and not a specific name.

3. **(2)** *Sentence Structure/Fragment/Sentence Revision.* The words *Such as the one Ralph Nader formed* are a fragment and must be joined to the previous sentence.

4. **(4)** *Usage/Pronoun Case/Sentence Correction.* There are no such words as *hisself* or *theirselves*; these reflexive pronouns are always written as *himself* and *themselves.*

5. **(5)** *Sentence Structure/Run-on/Sentence Revision.* A comma cannot join two independent sentences. Therefore, the second clause is made dependent on the first with the word *because.*

6. **(1)** *Sentence Structure/Dangling Modifier/Construction Shift.* A word must be placed next to a phrase modifying it. In this case, the word *buyers* must come immediately after the phrase *Before making a purchase.*

7. **(5)** *Usage/Mechanics/Sentence Correction.* The sentence is correct as is.

8. **(3)** *Sentence Structure/Parallelism/Sentence Revision.* A series of items must use parallel, or similar, structure. Because *warranties* and *warnings* are nouns, the third item must be a noun also. *Instructions* is a noun.

9. **(3)** *Mechanics/Spelling/Sentence Correction.* The possessive form of *its* never takes an apostrophe. An apostrophe with *it's* always means *it is.*

10. **(4)** *Sentence Structure/Coordination & Subordination/Construction Shift.* When *unless* is used in one clause, the other clause states the opposite possibility. In order to retain the meaning of the original sentence, *they may not feel secure* is needed.

11. **(4)** *Usage/Pronoun Shift/Sentence Correction.* Throughout the paragraph, *our* and *we* are used. The first sentence must also use the plural *our lives.*

12. **(1)** *Mechanics/Punctuation/Construction Shift.* The conjunction *but* is needed to retain the meaning of the original sentence. While *however* conveys the same meaning, the comma before *however* in choice (4) is not correct.

13. **(5)** *Sentence Structure/Parallelism/Sentence Revision.* Items written in a series require parallel structure. In this sentence, *to process our bills* is similar in structure to the two other phrases, *to record the prices* and *to provide us with cash.*

14. **(2)** *Mechanics/Spelling/Sentence Correction.* The possessive form *their* is needed before the word *engines.* The word *they're* means *they are.*

49

15. **(2)** *Sentence Structure/Active Voice/Construction Shift.* If the sentence is rewritten so that the word *computers* becomes the subject, the active verb *handle* is needed.

16. **(1)** *Usage/Tense Shift/Sentence Correction.* In order to maintain the same time sequence throughout the paragraph, the present verb *are* must be used.

17. **(1)** *Mechanics/Punctuation/Sentence Revision.* The original is correct. A comma is needed before the conjunction *but*, and the adverb *well* is needed to modify the verb *work*.

18. **(4)** *Usage/Pronoun Shift/Sentence Correction.* The paragraph has been written using the first person plural *we*. Therefore, the sentence is incorrect in shifting to the pronoun *you*.

19. **(3)** *Sentence Structure/Subordination/Construction Shift.* The best way of combining the two sentences is by making one sentence dependent on the other with the word *because*. The word *unless* would not provide the correct meaning.

20. **(1)** *Usage/Subject-Verb Agreement/Sentence Correction.* The subject *one* is singular and requires the singular verb *is*.

21. **(3)** *Sentence Structure/Fragment/Sentence Revision.* In order to avoid a fragment, the word group which begins with *while* must be joined to the main clause which begins with *there are*.

22. **(2)** *Mechanics/Spelling/Sentence Correction.* The word *interests* has three syllables.

23. **(1)** *Mechanics/Punctuation/Sentence Revision.* The original is correct. When a long, dependent word group introduces a sentence, it is set off with a comma.

24. **(2)** *Mechanics/Capitalization/Sentence Correction.* The term *doctors* is general and does not need to be capitalized.

25. **(4)** *Usage/Pronoun Shift/Sentence Correction.* The pronoun *you* should be used to refer to *the reader* and to maintain consistency throughout the paragraph.

26. **(1)** *Sentence Structure/Dangling Modifier/Construction Shift.* A noun, or pronoun, should be placed next to the phrase that modifies it. In this case *you* are the one who is talking with workers.

27. **(1)** *Mechanics/Punctuation/Sentence Revision.* When two verbs, *discuss* and *learn*, have the same subject, *you*, they should not be separated by a comma or other punctuation.

28. **(5)** *Sentence Structure/Subordination and Coordination/Construction Shift.* The phrase *learning about several careers* is the main subject of the sentence and requires the verb *will help* to follow it.

Test 1 Writing Skills Part II

Introduction to Holistic Scoring

The following GED Essay Scoring Guide provides a general description of the characteristics of GED essays that are scored by the Holistic Method.

GED ESSAY SCORING GUIDE

Papers will show *some or all* of the following characteristics

Upper-half papers make clear a definite purpose, pursued with varying degrees of effectiveness. They also have a structure that shows evidence of some deliberate planning. The writer's control of English usage ranges from fairly reliable at 4 to confident and accomplished at 6.

6 Papers scored as a 6 tend to offer sophisticated ideas within an organizational framework that is clear and appropriate for the topic. The supporting statements are particularly effective because of their substance, specificity, or illustrative quality. The writing is vivid and precise, though it may contain an occasional flaw.

5 Papers scored as a 5 are clearly organized with effective support for each of the writer's major points. The writing offers substantive ideas, though the paper may lack the flair or grace of a 6 paper. The surface features are consistently under control, despite an occasional lapse in usage.

4 Papers scored as a 4 show evidence of the writer's organizational plan. Support, though sufficient, tends to be less extensive or convincing than that found in papers scored as a 5 or 6. The writer generally observes the conventions of accepted English usage. Some errors are usually present, but they are not severe enough to interfere significantly with the writer's main purpose.

Lower-half papers either fail to convey a purpose sufficiently or lack one entirely. Consequently, their structure ranges from rudimentary at 3, to random at 2, to absent at 1. Control of the conventions of English usage tends to follow this same gradient.

3 Papers scored as a 3 usually show some evidence of planning or development. However, the organization is often limited to a simple listing or haphazard recitation of ideas about the topic, leaving an impression of insufficiency. The 3 papers often demonstrate repeated weaknesses in accepted English usage and are generally ineffective in accomplishing the writer's purpose.

2 Papers scored as a 2 are characterized by a marked lack of development or inadequate support for ideas. The level of thought apparent in the writing is frequently unsophisticated or superficial, often marked by a listing of unsupported generalizations. Instead of suggesting a clear purpose, these papers often present conflicting purposes. Errors in accepted English usage may seriously interfere with the overall effectiveness of these papers.

1 Papers scored as a 1 leave the impression that the writer has not only *not* accomplished a purpose, but has not made any purpose apparent. The dominant feature of these papers is the lack of control. The writer stumbles both in conveying a clear plan for the paper and in expressing ideas according to the conventions of accepted English usage.

0 The zero score is reserved for papers which are blank, illegible, or written on a topic other than the one assigned.

Copyright 1985, GED Testing Service, September, 1985

Source: *The 1988 Tests of General Educational Development: A Preview*, American Council on Education, 1985. Used with permission.

HOW TO SCORE YOUR ESSAY

The following six essays are designed to be used as models for the scoring of your essay. The essays are presented in order from the essay that deserves the lowest score (1) to the essay that deserves the highest score (6).

To score your essay, first compare your essay with the model essay that received a score of 1. If your essay is better than the 1 essay, compare it with the 2 essay and so on until you are able to decide where you essay fits when compared with the six model essays.

As you score your essay, read the character-trait analysis that follows each model essay. This analysis can help you to see how you might have improved your essay in order to have received a higher score.

Model Essay—Holistic Score 1

Exploring the options is a prewriting activity. These notes do not belong in the essay.

States the point of view. Undeveloped examples that do not support the point of view.

The point of view changes. Conclusion is vague.

    Many of these choice are hard to make. Because they all look good. Someone wants to go to work at different times. Someone else wants to go to work at other times. Its good that employers gives that choice to workers. That way workers can work parttime if they want. They can also work at home too. What if a person wanted to work at home and take care of these children? That be good. Everybody could get some thing from that way. Many people would like working better if then.

    I think I would work flexible hours. That way I could work whenever I want. I would like to work early in the morning and get out early in the afternoon. That way I'd be home when my children got home from school. That would be good for them. I could work at home too. That way I'd be there for them. That is how I would choose it.

Character-Trait Analysis

1. The organization is poor.
2. The first paragraph does not belong in the essay. It could be used as a prewriting activity to explore the options.
3. The essay does not address the topic immediately. The point of view is given in the middle of the essay; it should be stated immediately.
4. The examples do not support the point of view. Working early in the morning and getting out early in the afternoon does not tell us why the writer would like flexible hours; it simply lists one type of schedule.
5. If the essay were longer, there would be more opportunity to develop the examples.
6. There are many serious errors in accepted English usage.

Model Essay—Holistic Score 2

States the point of view

Unsupported opinions; needs specific examples

Restates the point of view

    Many alternatives to employers jobs is good. My favorite is working flexible hours. Reasons is for people to work at different times is so they can do things they like to do. I would go to afternoon baseball games if I could. Movies are cheeper in the afternoon to but if you work a regular job you cant go then. Early bird dinner specials costs less to if you can get there soon enough. It would be easier to look for another job if you didn't like your job. It would be easier to go shopping or even getting to work could be easier if the roads weren't crowded. Anyway, I would like to work at flexible hours for many reasons. I could do what I want and I could still work.

Character-Trait Analysis

1. The organization is better than model essay–1. However, it is organized for the writer, not for the reader. Paragraphing would help this essay.
2. The point of view is stated immediately.
3. The conclusion follows a listing of unsupported opinions. Specific examples for the writer's point of view such as *I would like to be able to try the early bird dinner specials that many restaurants offer. But because I work a regular work day, I get home too late to do so. If I worked flexible hours, I could leave early enough to try them.* would strengthen this essay.
4. The essay should be longer to allow more space for specific examples.
5. Errors in accepted English usage interfere with the writer's purpose.

6. Because of the consistent point of view, this essay is better than the 1 essay. However, it lacks the depth and the sophistication of higher-scoring essays.

Model Essay—Holistic Score 3

States the point of view

Haphazard listing of ideas about the topic

I would choose job sharing for my work schedule if I could because job sharing sounds like a good thing. It would let people share jobs. That way the employer can have a fresh person working all the time. That way he gets people who have lots of energy. It would make my job easier to do if I had someone else to do it with. I would like to share my job because of the extra time it would give me. The free time would let me do lots of things I don't have time to do now.

Restates the point of view

Sharing a job would give somebody else a job. Many people in todays world are out of jobs. Sharing would make two times as many jobs for the people out of work. Thats another good thing about sharing jobs. Besides giving people more free time. People spend too much time at work anyway. That is not good. It would be better if people did not have to work too much. Thats why I would choose job sharing if I could choose.

Character-Trait Analysis

1. The level of organization is similar to that of model essay–2. Better paragraphing might have brought the problems with the examples to the attention of the writer in time to correct them.
2. The supporting examples are too general. They are really a listing of ideas. *People spend too much time at work anyway.* does not tell the reader why the writer would choose job sharing. For writing to be effective, use specific examples, not unsupported opinions.
3. The essay contains many sentence fragments; *Besides giving people more free time.* is one example. There are other problems with accepted English usage that interfere with the essay's effectiveness.

Model Essay—Holistic Score 4

States the point of view and several reasons why the writer holds it

I would choose a traditional nine to five schedule if I had a choice about when I could work. I would select it so that I could have a steady income that I could count on. I do temporary work and can't count on where or when I will work or how much money I can make.

Elaborates on the first reason for the point of view with an abstract example

I would select it because I would like a regular job. I don't like working in a lot of different places, you meet a lot of people but you never get to know them. Working all day in one place lets you develop real friendships with people.

Elaborates on the second reason for the point of view with specific examples

The other reason is that it costs more to do freelance or temporary work than it does to work full-time. I have to pay for my own health insurance and I don't get paid if I get sick. I also can't count on working every day, so I don't know how much money I've made each week until the end of the week.

Suggests and overcomes counterevidence; restates the point of view; summarizes reasons

There are advantages to working freelance, like having time off whenever I want it, but I would select a traditional nine to five job because of the friends I could make, the benefits I would get, and the extra money that I would make.

Character-Trait Analysis

1. The level of organization in this essay is very good.

2. It addresses the topic immediately and explains the writer's reasons for choosing this option. The point of view is clear.
3. The supporting examples are better than those in model essay–3. Notice the use of specific examples in the third paragraph of this essay. But the examples are not as convincing as those used in model essays–5 and 6. Check those essays for the use of specific examples that better illustrate the writer's point of view.
4. The ideas and the vocabulary in this essay are more sophisticated than those in the 1 through the 3 essays, but this essay lacks the depth of the 5 and the 6 essays.

Model Essay—Holistic Score 5

States the point of view and two reasons why the writer holds it

If my employer offered alternatives to the traditional nine to five schedule, I would choose job sharing for two reasons. First, job sharing would make my job more secure. Second, job sharing would mean that I could work part-time.

Elaborates on the first reason for the point of view with a specific example

Job sharing could ensure that I could keep my present job. I work full-time processing mail orders for a sportswear company. However, business has been slow lately and the company has been looking for ways to cut back. If I shared my job with a coworker, the company would save money and we could both keep jobs that we enjoy.

Elaborates on the second reason for the point of view, but uses a more abstract example that has less impact

If I shared my job with a coworker, I would gain more time with my family, but I would also earn less money. I could not have a second car, and I would have to give up eating out and other luxuries. However, spending time with my family is more important to me than having these extras.

Summarizes the reasons; suggests and overcomes counterevidence; restates the point of view

For the above reasons, job sharing is the type of work schedule that I would choose. Job sharing would allow me to work part-time at my present job. The decrease in income would be more than offset by the increase in both job security and in the amount of time that I would have to spend with my family.

Character-Trait Analysis
1. Both the 4 and the 5 essays have a very good level of organization. This essay's style indicates that the writer has had more practice writing this type of essay. See below.
2. This essay is more interesting to read than the 4 because of the writer's command of the language and of a larger vocabulary.
3. The essay flows smoothly and has few problems with usage.
4. The examples used in this essay are good, but they are not as specific and vivid as those in the 6 essay. Therefore, this essay lacks the impact of the 6 essay.

Model Essay—Holistic Score 6

States the point of view and two reasons why the writer holds it

If I could choose my own schedule, I would like to do free-lance work at home. As a free-lancer, I could adjust my work schedule according to my own energy levels and my family's needs.

Elaborates on the first reason for the point of view with specific examples and contrasting details

My concentration is best early in the morning and late at night. At about 10 a.m., I often start to get drowsy. Most nine to five jobs have a short coffee break at this point but I would like a longer break. If I were working at home I could put my work away and go out for an hour or two. That way, I would get some exercise and a change of scene, rather than a rushed cup of coffee and a donut.

Elaborates on the second reason for the point of view with specific examples and contrasting details

Suggests and overcomes counterevidence; summarizes reasons; restates the point of view

      Having more time to spend with my preschooler would be another benefit of working at home. Whenever I chose, I could take a break and do something with my daughter. It would be wonderful to be able to put away a piece of frustrating work and make cookies with my child. I could enjoy having a relaxed lunch with her, rather than hurrying in the morning to make sandwiches for her to eat at daycare.

      To get work done at home would require added self-discipline on my part and extra cooperation from my little girl, but the benefits would be worth the effort. Overall, working at home would be the type of schedule best suited to my energy peaks and family life.

Character-Trait Analysis

1. The essay shows a high level of organizational ability and a solid command of the English language.

2. The writer has a smooth and confident writing style. This comes from practicing the writing process.

3. The examples that support the writer's point of view are very specific and personal. They have a vivid, illustrative quality. For example, it is very easy to picture the *rushed cup of coffee and a donut* described in paragraph two. It is easy to see why the writer would choose to work at home, which would allow her to *get some exercise and a change of scene.*

4. This essay is not perfect. There are minor errors, such as those in punctuation, but they are not enough to detract from the overall effectiveness of this essay.

Test 2 Social Studies

1. **(1)** *Comprehension/History.* In the graph, the shorter bars stand for the periods in which immigration was low. The shortest bar stands for the years 1931–1940, the decade with lowest immigration.

2. **(5)** *Application/History.* Because the level of immigration for 1971–1980 was about 4.5 million, the job and housing requirements would have been greatest.

3. **(4)** *Analysis/History.* Immigration was at a high point during the 1901–1910 period. It decreased to a low point during the 1930s and thereafter steadily increased.

4. **(4)** *Application/Economics.* Fire-fighting services are paid for by local governments and benefit property owners. Building a home is a private responsibility. The other choices include items that might be paid for by federal taxes. They do not benefit property owners more than non-property owners.

5. **(2)** *Application/Political Science.* Based on the chart, one of the functions of the Senate is to approve presidential appointments. Choices (1), (3), (4), and (5) are inaccurate.

6. **(4)** *Comprehension/Behavioral Science.* The main point of the passage is that television has a strong influence, both good and bad, on children. The passage indicates that television may show too much violence and may also teach basic skills, but neither of these statements is the main point.

7. **(4)** *Application/Behavioral Science.* Because the passage points out that television has an important influence on children, concerned parents are most likely to choose a program that is educational, entertaining, and relatively free from violence. In this case that would be choice (4).

8. **(3)** *Evaluation/Behavioral Science.* The critics meant programs and commercials that show different cultures. Choice (3) is such a program; the others are not.

9. **(2)** *Analysis/Behavioral Science.* While the other choices are stated or implied, choice (2) is the *assumption* made in the passage. The author says that children see a lot of violence on television and that television is a powerful influence on children. The author must assume that most children watch television.

10. **(3)** *Evaluation/Behavioral Science.* The only alternative that offers evidence is choice (3). Experiments show behavior changes. None of the other choices mention behavior changes.

11. **(1)** *Analysis/Geography.* Although Antarctica is not the smallest continent, its population is the smallest. Antarctica's climate is too severe to support a large population.

12. **(1)** *Comprehension/Economics.* The passage explains that Adam Smith believed that the free marketplace—rather than governments—should control production and prices.

13. **(4)** *Application/Geography.* Both Houston and Los Angeles have experienced population increases since 1970. In all other choices one or both of the cities have experienced a decrease in population during that time.

14. **(2)** *Analysis/Geography.* The table shows steady population growth since 1900 in Houston and Los Angeles, which are in the Southwest. Each city cited in other areas declined in population during at least two decades.

15. **(4)** *Comprehension/Behavioral Science.* The main point of the cartoon is that because of sex discrimination, women are paid less than men even when both do the same job. Employers sometimes give men and women with the same job different titles to hide this kind of discrimination.

16. **(4)** *Application/History.* Joining a volunteer group that helps other citizens is one way in which Americans can help their country. Other choices are not in the spirit of the quotation.

17. **(1)** *Evaluation/Political Science.* An absolute monarch's child inherits leadership and power. An absolute monarch would be the leader most likely to try to influence the future through one of his children.

18. **(5)** *Application/Political Science.* Because the revolutionary leader has suppressed all debate and dissent, taken control of the country's media, and has declared himself "sole head," he has established a dictatorship.

19. **(4)** *Application/Political Science.* In the United States, citizens choose people to represent them. Other choices are inaccurate.

20. **(3)** *Evaluation/Political Science.* In a direct democracy the people vote on every law. They would be directly responsible for the laws they enacted.

21. **(2)** *Application/Political Science.* Great Britain's monarch has power, but it is limited power.

22. **(2)** *Evaluation/Behavioral Science.* The speaker is arguing against the expectation that he carry on the family tradition by becoming a carpenter. He does not indicate anything about the family's value of money, religion, or status. Because there is no plan for his education, it must not be a very strong value.

23. **(2)** *Comprehension/Economics.* The table shows that the communication, electronic, and computer industries have provided the most new jobs since 1980.

24. **(5)** *Application/Economics.* Because the footwear industry has lost jobs, a worker in a shoe factory would be most likely to want job retraining. The other choices list jobs that are either not mentioned in the table or are in industries that have gained jobs.

25. **(3)** *Analysis/Economics.* The table does not provide the reasons industries have either gained or lost jobs.

26. **(2)** *Evaluation/Economics.* The only conclusion supported by the data in the table is that most new jobs are being created by the newer technologies: communications, electronics, and computers.

27. **(3)** *Comprehension/Political Science.* All of the rights listed are protected by the First Amendment, except the right to a jury trial. That right is not mentioned in the First Amendment.

28. **(3)** *Application/Geography.* In the United States through the last century, most transportation was by water. Towns and cities were built near waterways.

29. **(4)** *Comprehension/History.* The passage explains that the South's reliance on the North for shipping, banking, and manufacturing was caused by its own lack of these industries.

30. **(2)** *Analysis/History.* The passage states that the South lacked industry. It depended on the North and foreign producers for manufactured goods. The North did a lot of the manufacturing it needed for itself. The South would have to pay more import taxes than the North because it had to import more manufactured goods.

31. **(3)** *Comprehension/History.* The passage stresses the economic differences between the North and the South before the Civil War. These differences existed because the North and the South grew into two different kinds of societies. The North was more urban and industrial. The South was more rural and agricultural.

32. **(1)** *Analysis/History.* The South, primarily a producer of cotton, depended on the North for manufactured goods and services such as shipping and banking. Many Southerners felt that the North was prolonging this dependency, thus keeping the South economically weak.

Test 3 Science

1. **(1)** *Analysis/Physics.* Work = Force × Distance. Therefore, the first keg must have been lifted 3 feet and the second keg 4 feet (3 × 50 = 150; 4 × 50 = 200). If one is tired the work feels harder, but the same load moved over the same distance always equals the same work. Choices (2) and (4) are refuted by the word "identical." Every lift requires energy.

2. **(1)** *Comprehension/Physics.* The last sentence suggests that the planets are larger than the moon. It mentions the effect of the gravity of larger bodies. The word "but" indicates that the larger bodies referred to are the planets—all of them.

3. **(3)** *Comprehension/Biology.* Less energy is available at each successive link in the chain. Humans are the last link.

4. **(3)** *Application/Biology.* The human in this chain eats a primary consumer.

5. **(4)** *Application/Biology.* The snake eats the bird, which is a secondary consumer because it eats the insect.

6. **(5)** *Analysis/Biology.* The weed is a producer, the minnow a primary consumer, the bass a secondary consumer, and the otter a tertiary consumer. Only the decomposer is omitted.

7. **(2)** *Evaluation/Biology.* Suppose a human being needs 2000 calories per day, and could get it by eating three pounds of vegetable food. But suppose a person eats meat instead. Then suppose that the animal whose flesh the person eats has to eat six pounds of plant material in order to pass on 2000 calories. The person uses up six pounds of vegetable food instead of three.

8. **(5)** *Evaluation/Earth Science.* Coral and ocean animals and reptiles live in hot, wet climates. The presence of fossils of these organisms in older (bottom) layers of rock shows that northern Canada was probably first covered by water, and then had a tropical climate. Fossils of the wooly mammoth in a more recent (closer to the top) layer indicate a change in climate from hot to cold. The presence of these and later primate fossils indicates that the region must also have become drier.

9. **(2)** *Comprehension/Biology.* Each function mentioned is necessary to the survival of the plant.

10. **(2)** *Comprehension/Chemistry.* Only oxygen, 21% of the atmosphere, sustains animal life.

11. **(5)** *Application/Chemistry.* Ordinary combustion requires oxygen. The atmosphere in this container has at most 5% oxygen. Because this is less than one-fourth the amount in air, burning will be much slower.

12. **(4)** *Evaluation/Earth Science.* There would be more carbon dioxide if the level reached 5%. More heat would be retained on and near Earth. The large masses of ice at the poles would melt, raising the sea level all over the world. Land now exposed would be underwater.

13. **(2)** *Comprehension/Biology.* Because the second number hasn't changed, the first must have increased by 10 to make the difference 50. Therefore, the heart has to be pumping harder.

14. **(3)** *Application/Biology.* Muscle cells are used in all movement. Movement is associated with the expenditure of energy.

15. **(3)** *Comprehension/Physics.* An opaque yellow object reflects yellow light and absorbs all other color light.

16. **(4)** *Application/Physics.* Blue light is reflected only by blue objects. The shoes and gloves would reflect blue light. Because nothing else on the stage is blue, nothing else would reflect any light; nothing else could be seen.

17. **(2)** *Analysis/Physics.* Because a red apple absorbs all color light except red, it absorbs the

58

green light. In the absence of red light, there is no light for the apple to reflect, so the apple looks black.

18. **(3)** *Evaluation/Physics.* A white object reflects all color light, but a green object reflects only green light. Thus, there is more sunlight reflected by snow than by green plants. The additional reflected light would make sunlight appear brighter.

19. **(4)** *Application/Chemistry.* Only filtering will clean the water. Choices (1) and (2) are temperature changes; choices (3) and (5) will not work because suspended particles stay suspended.

20. **(2)** *Application/Biology.* Blue eyes is a recessive trait. So if both parents have blue eyes, they are both carrying genes for only blue eyes. They can have only blue-eyed children. The children of couples (1), (3), and (4) could have eyes of either color. A previous child's eye-color does not predict the eye-color of future brothers and sisters.

21. **(1)** *Comprehension/Biology.* The third paragraph says the aorta and other arteries take blood from the heart to the rest of the body.

22. **(4)** *Analysis/Biology.* High-oxygen left-side blood will mix with low-oxygen right-side blood. This will dilute left-side oxygen levels.

23. **(3)** *Analysis/Biology.* The left ventricle's role is to pump blood throughout the body. All other heart chambers pump over much shorter distances. The aorta is not a heart chamber.

24. **(2)** *Analysis/Biology.* Paragraph 3 mentions the importance of the valve that lets blood into the aorta and not back into the heart.

25. **(5)** *Evaluation/Biology.* A toad, like its close relative the frog, is an amphibian.

26. **(5)** *Analysis/Earth Science.* The troposphere contains 79% of the air molecules around Earth, as one of the labels on the diagram says. The item asks about *air* pollution. Air pollution affects the troposphere most because most of the air is in that layer.

27. **(4)** *Analysis/Physics.* The pot, a solid, heats by conduction; the water, a liquid, heats by convection. Choice (4) is the only alternative that mentions heat transference of both a solid and a liquid.

28. **(1)** *Application/Chemistry.* Count the atoms in the diagram. You will see that the butane molecule has 4 carbon atoms and 10 hydrogen atoms.

29. **(4)** *Analysis/Chemistry.* Pentane has 5 carbon atoms, each with a weight of 12, and 12 hydrogen atoms, each with a weight of 1. $(5 \times 12) + (1 \times 12) = 72$.

30. **(4)** *Evaluation/Earth Science.* Earth is older than the oldest evidence for life. Therefore, life may have developed from nonliving material. The other choices are contradicted by suggestions in the passage.

31. **(3)** *Analysis/Biology.* To lower blood pressure, body fluids must be released. Increasing urination releases more fluids. Choices (1), (4), and (5) would cause water retention. Choice (2) is incorrect because the patients are already on a salt-free diet.

32. **(1)** *Analysis/Earth Science.* According to the chart, crystals can be seen in coarse-grained rock, such as granite. Crystals cannot be seen in (2) limestone or (3) basalt without a microscope. There are no crystals in (4) obsidian. Choice (5) schist is layered.

33. **(3)** *Evaluation/Earth Science.* All sandstone is sedimentary, but some is coarse-grained and some is layered. Therefore, (3) is right and (2) is wrong. Choice (4) is wrong because slate is layered. The chart doesn't have information to support choices (1) or (5).

Test 4 Interpreting Literature and the Arts

1. **(2)** *Literal Comprehension, Specific/Fiction.* Sam defines the "hard" thing when he says, "That's hard, trying to go without me and all." The other choices indicate things that may have presented some difficulty for Sam, but seeing Frodo try to leave alone is the only thing Sam admits is hard.

2. **(3)** *Application/Fiction.* In this passage, Sam makes it clear that he will go with Frodo, even though Frodo warns him, "It would be the death of you to come with me . . ." (line 40). Sam is willing to risk all danger for the sake of his friend. Turning away from a neighbor in need—even if that neighbor, like Frodo, does not admit his need at first—would be completely out of character for Sam.

3. **(4)** *Inferential Comprehension, Global/Fiction.* Sam never says that he wants to leave the others. He says only, "I'm coming with you" (line 47), and he criticizes Frodo for trying to force him to do otherwise. He does not discuss the reasons for his loyalty, nor does the word "loyal" come up in his conversation. Instead, he states his decision to stay with Frodo as a fact, and he refuses to reconsider.

4. **(1)** *Analysis/Fiction.* Sam suggests to Frodo that they may see the other travelers again (line 55). This suggestion would make most readers wonder how events later in the plot might bring the travelers together. Most readers would want to read further to learn if Sam's suggestion turns out to be a prediction.

5. **(5)** *Literal Comprehension, Specific/Nonfiction.* Of computer programming, the author says, ". . . it's a terrible job that doesn't pay much" (lines 16–17). Earlier he says that there are many ads for computer programmers (lines 14–15). He also notes his ignorance of their work (line 15), but he does not classify such work as "mysterious." The only thing he says he "knows" about the career is that it must not pay a very good salary.

6. **(1)** *Inferential Comprehension, Global/Nonfiction.* The author raises the point in a series of questions (lines 33–39). The solution—a presidential plan (lines 40–44)—suggests that a proper solution will come about with proper planning. The implication is that unemployment has not been stopped because no one yet has given the problem the careful planning a solution would require. The author also implies that since he has given careful thought to the problem (lines 31–33), someone should be willing to give careful thought to a solution.

7. **(5)** *Application/Nonfiction.* Although teaching more computer courses (choice 1) would help to train more computer programmers, it would not help to put an end to unemployment in other fields. The author's solution to unemployment overall is a plan that would match people to job openings. Such a plan would require analyzing both the job and the person—the kind of analysis that is a regular part of school guidance programs.

8. **(1)** *Analysis/Nonfiction.* The passage is like an editorial. The author notes a few facts, but spends most of his writing expressing an opinion. The other choices emphasize facts rather than opinions.

9. **(4)** *Literal Comprehension, Global/Drama.* Lord Caversham urges his son to " . . . try to do something useful" (lines 7–8). His questions to Lord Goring about entering Parliament (lines 1–2) and marrying Miss Chiltern (lines 15–16) are ways of expressing his concern that his son will never settle down.

10. **(3)** *Inferential Comprehension, Specific/Drama.* Lord Goring responds to his father's comment that Miss Chiltern would be a fool to marry him by saying that he would like to marry someone like that (lines 25–26)—in other words, a fool. He then completely rejects the thought of having a "thoroughly sensible wife" (line 26). He is looking for a wife who, like himself, does not take life very seriously.

11. **(1)** *Analysis/Drama.* Lord Goring avoids giving direct answers. He tries to get around his father's probing questions by joking; in fact, every statement of his in this passage is either a joke or an attempt to change the subject. His jokes are clever, but they do not answer the questions asked of him. Even when Lord Caversham seems to pin him down with questions about marriage, Lord Goring makes fun of the issue.

12. **(2)** *Literal Comprehension, Global/Commentary.* The point of this passage is that newer Disney productions fail to capture the magic of the classic movies. The author considers a "Disney Summer Movie" episode and concludes, "...the Disney gold came from something else" (line 19). She asks if the current movies are acceptable only to an unimaginative public (lines 32–34). She looks for a "new masterpiece" that has the Disney magic (line 45)—and she has described that magic by discussing classic movies that have shown a lot of imagination, such as *Bambi* and *Cinderella*.

13. **(1)** *Literal Comprehension, Specific/Commentary.* The author describes the appeal of the movie by saying, "I only remember staring at all those wonderful talking animals and wishing that I could live in such a world: (lines 11–14).

14. **(5)** *Analysis/Commentary.* The "Master's wand" (line 35) is a metaphor, a figure of speech. It stands for all that made the name "Disney" special. The writer supports this metaphor by wondering if it has "...passed on to less able hands..." (lines 35–36), to people who seem to carry on the Disney tradition but who do not have the imaginative craftsmanship shown in earlier Disney movies.

15. **(3)** *Inferential Comprehension, Specific/Commentary.* In the final paragraph the author names classic Disney characters and concludes with a wish for "new masterpieces" like the movies in which they appeared. Such a wish implies that no such characters exist in recent productions.

16. **(4)** *Analysis/Commentary.* The author's work is not technical; as such, it probably would be of little interest to people studying about or involved in the movie industry. It also deals with concepts of little interest to children. The author's tone is basically nostalgic. By wishing for a return to standards of the past, she probably is appealing to others who also wish to recapture the magic of their own youth.

17. **(2)** *Literal Comprehension, Global/Fiction.* Jane states her motivation quite clearly. She tells Mr. Rochester, "To be your wife is, for me, to be as happy as I can be on earth" (lines 30–31). Twice she rephrases her wish when Mr. Rochester raises arguments (lines 37–38 and 41–45). She settles all arguments by stating that he "suits" her (line 54).

18. **(3)** *Inferential Comprehension, Specific/Fiction.* Mr. Rochester states that, before this moment, he hated to be helped (line 46), would not put his hand into a hireling's (line 48), and disliked the attention of servants (lines 50–51). He contrasts each of these with his feelings about Jane—an indication that he once considered her as part of that group.

19. **(4)** *Inferential Comprehension, Global/Fiction.* Mr. Rochester states concern about the effect of his physical condition on their relationship (lines 16–17 and 19–20). Jane, however, does not. Her responses throughout are immediate and sure. Specifically, she argues that to marry him would not be a sacrifice (lines 32–38). On the contrary, she says, she is happy to be of real use to him (lines 41–45).

20. **(2)** *Analysis/Fiction.* Brief responses could indicate any of the five choices. It is necessary to look at Jane's longer responses to understand her character. She speaks so plainly, openly, and seriously about her love that it would be hard to view her as bashful, playful, or dishonest. Her simple, direct approach comes not from a lack of education but from her fair, candid nature.

21. **(2)** *Inferential Comprehension, Global/Poetry.* The author defines *paradise* only by implying what it is not. It is not a place where land is paved over for parking lots, hotels, and such (lines 1–4). It is not a place where so many trees have been cut down that you must go to a museum to see a tree (lines 10–11). It is not a place where D.D.T. is used (line 20). In short, it is not a place that has been spoiled by people.

62 Answers to the Predictor Tests PREDICTION

22. **(5)** *Literal Comprehension, Specific/Poetry.* The author doesn't want to see birds and bees killed because farmers use D.D.T., an insecticide. She would rather have "spots on my apples" (line 22)—that is, fruit that doesn't look perfect—than risk killing animals such as birds and bees.

23. **(4)** *Application/Poetry.* In these verses the author talks about concern for nature. All of the choices except "drug abuse" continue the thought of protecting the natural environment.

Test 5   Mathematics

1. **(2)** *Arithmetic/Applications.*

   $10.75 \times 9 = 96.75$

2. **(3)** *Arithmetic/Applications.*

   $$2\tfrac{2}{3} = 2\tfrac{8}{12}$$
   $$3\tfrac{3}{4} = 3\tfrac{9}{12}$$
   $$+\ 6\tfrac{1}{2} = 6\tfrac{6}{12}$$
   $$11\tfrac{23}{12} = 12\tfrac{11}{12}$$

3. **(4)** *Algebra/Problem Solving.*

   Because the salary (s) is monthly, it must be multiplied by 12. The annual sales (c) must be multiplied by .3 (30%) in order to determine Debbie's commission.

4. **(1)** *Arithmetic/Applications.*

   $\frac{9}{1.20} = 7.5$

5. **(5)** *Arithmetic/Problem Solving.*

   The amount of time for the loan is not given.

6. **(2)** *Arithmetic/Problem Solving.*

   Find the perimeter of the room and subtract the width of the doorways.
   $$(2 \times 12) + (2 \times 25) = 74$$
   $$74 - 9 = 65$$

7. **(5)** *Arithmetic/Applications.*

   The size of each floor tile is not given.

8. **(2)** *Geometry/Applications.*

   A right angle is a 90° angle and is indicated by

   ⌐.

9. **(2)** *Arithmetic/Problem Solving.*

   B .59 + 5% = .6195, or .62 to the nearest cent
   A .60 + 2% = .6120, or .61 to the nearest cent
   D .55 + 9% = .5995, or .60 to the nearest cent
   C .57 + 4% = .5928, or .59 to the nearest cent

10. **(2)** *Arithmetic/Applications.*

    293 − 172 = 121 Albany County
    180 − 135 = 45 Carbon County
    181 − 101 = 80 Converse County
    801 − 698 = 103 Natrona County
    125 − 61 = 64 Washakie County

11. **(2)** *Algebra/Applications.*

    15 ten-thousandths = .0015. > means greater than. Any bolt (b) larger than the desired size (s) + .0015 should be rejected.

PREDICTOR TESTS

Answers to the Predictor Tests

12. (5) *Arithmetic/Problem Solving.*

Total babies born equals 63; $\frac{63}{7} = 9$

13. (2) *Arithmetic/Applications.*

$13\frac{3}{8} - \frac{1}{2} + \frac{5}{8} - \frac{1}{4} =$
$13\frac{3}{8} - \frac{4}{8} + \frac{5}{8} - \frac{2}{8} = 13\frac{2}{8} = 13\frac{1}{4}$

14. (4) *Geometry/Problem Solving.*

Use similar sides to set up a ratio. If b = the base of the house, then $8:12 = 20:b$.

15. (5) *Arithmetic/Applications.*

53 miles × 8 hours × 14 days = 5936

16. (3) *Algebra/Problem Solving.*

w = wheat acres
$2w$ = soybean acres
$3w$ = corn acres

The total of those three numbers equals the total acres to be planted = 360.

17. (5) *Algebra/Problem Solving.*

Let m = worst gas mileage.
$5m - 7 = 56$
$5m = 63$
$m = 12.6$

18. (5) *Arithmetic/Applications.*

10^9 = 10 × 10 × 10 × 10 × 10 × 10 × 10 × 10 × 10, or 1,000,000,000
5 × 1,000,0000,000 = 5,000,000,000

19. (2) *Geometry/Applications.*

To determine the correct proportion, compare the widths to the lengths.
$\frac{18}{12} = \frac{30}{x}$

20. (2) *Algebra/Applications.*

In x^5/x^2, x is the base in each term; 5 and 2 are the exponents. To divide, subtract exponents: $5 - 2 = 3$.

21. (4) *Arithmetic/Problem Solving.*

First find the volume of the storage tank:
8 × 8 × 3.14 × 32 = 6430.72 cubic feet
Then divide the volume by 1.25:
$\frac{6430.72}{1.25} = 5144.576$

The nearest whole number is 5145.

22. (2) *Arithmetic/Problem Solving.*

32.40 × 15% = 4.86
32.40 + 4.86 = 37.26
$\frac{37.26}{3} = 12.42$

23. (2) *Geometry/Problem Solving.*

Use the formula provided and any two points. For example, using points B (9,6) and C (6,3):
9 − 6 = 3
6 − 3 = 3
$\frac{3}{3} = 1$

24. (5) *Algebra/Problem Solving.*

$7x = 245$
$x = 35$
$4(x) = 4(35) = 140$ = number of hot dogs served
245 + 140 = 385 = total number of hot dogs and hamburgers served

25. (2) *Algebra/Applications.*

The number of words per page (275) times the number of pages (60) divided by the number of words typed per minute (70) gives the number of minutes required to finish the report.

26. (3) *Arithmetic/Problem Solving.*

4 gallons = 16 quarts; 3:8 = 6:16

27. (3) *Arithmetic/Problem Solving.*

83 × .18 = 14.94

28. (1) *Arithmetic/Problem Solving.*

83 × .45 = 37.35
37.35 × .2 = 7.47

Performance Analysis Charts for the Predictor Tests

Directions: Circle the number of each item that you got correct on each test. Count the number of items you got correct in each row; count the number of items you got correct in each column. Write the number correct per row and column as the numerator in the fraction in the appropriate "Total Correct" box. (The denominators represent the total number of items in the row or column.) Write the grand total correct over the denominator in the lower right corner of each chart. (For example, if you got 24 items correct in Writing Skills Part I, write 24 so that the fraction in the lower right corner of that chart reads 24/28.) Item numbers in color represent items based on graphic material.

TEST 1: WRITING SKILLS, Part I

Item Type	Usage (page 73)	Sentence Structure (page 100)	Mechanics (page 118)	TOTAL CORRECT
Construction Shift (page 149)		6, 10, 15, 19, 26, 28	12	/7
Sentence Correction (page 148)	1, 7, 11, 16, 18, 20, 25		2, 9, 14, 22, 24	/12
Sentence Revision (page 148)	4	3, 5, 8, 13, 21	17, 23, 27	/9
TOTAL CORRECT	/8	/11	/9	/28

WRITING SKILLS, Part II

Directions: After you have used the guidelines in the answer key to score your essay, make a record of your evaluation here.

Write the score for your essay in the box at the right. ☐

List some of the strong points of your essay.

List some of the weak points of your essay.

List improvements that you plan to make when you work on your next essay.

TEST 2: SOCIAL STUDIES

Item Type	History (page 270)	Geography (page 282)	Economics (page 288)	Political Science (page 298)	Behavioral Sciences (page 305)	TOTAL CORRECT
Comprehension (page 220)	1, 29, 31		12, 23	27	6, 15	/8
Application (page 224)	2, 16	13, 28	4, 24	5, 18, 19, 21	7	/11
Analysis (page 228)	3, 30, 32	11, 14	25		9	/7
Evaluation (page 232)			26	17, 20	8, 10, 22	/6
TOTAL CORRECT	/8	/4	/6	/7	/7	/32

Performance Analysis

TEST 3: SCIENCE

Item Type	Biology (page 322)	Earth Science (page 334)	Chemistry (page 347)	Physics (page 356)	TOTAL CORRECT
Comprehension (page 220)	3, 9, 13, 21		10	2, 15	/7
Application (page 224)	4, 5, 14, 20		11, 19, 28	16	/8
Analysis (page 228)	6, 22, 23, 24, 31	26, 32	29	1, 17, 27	/11
Evaluation (page 232)	7, 25	8, 12, 30, 33		18	/7
TOTAL CORRECT	/15	/6	/5	/7	/33

TEST 4: INTERPRETING LITERATURE AND THE ARTS

Item Type	Nonfiction (page 375)	Fiction (page 387)	Drama (page 399)	Poetry (page 411)	Commentary (page 422)	TOTAL CORRECT
Literal Comprehension Specific (page 220)	5	1		22	13	/4
Literal Comprehension Global (page 220)		17	9		12	/3
Inferential Comprehension Specific (page 220)		18	10		15	/3
Inferential Comprehension Global (page 220)	6	3, 19		21		/4
Application (page 224)	7	2		23		/3
Analysis (page 228)	8	4, 20	11		14, 16	/6
TOTAL CORRECT	/4	/8	/3	/3	/5	/23

68 Performance Analysis

PREDICTION

TEST 5: MATHEMATICS

Item Type	Arithmetic (page 439)	Algebra (page 533)	Geometry (page 553)	TOTAL CORRECT
Skills				
Applications	1, 2, 4, 7, 10, 13, 15, 18	11, 20, 25	8, 19	/13
Problem Solving	5, 6, 9, 12, 21, 22, 26, 27, 28	3, 16, 17, 24	14, 23	/15
TOTAL CORRECT	/17	/7	/4	/28

The page numbers in parentheses indicate where in this book you can find the beginning of specific instruction about the various skills and fields and about the types of questions you encountered in the Predictor Tests. In mathematics, however, the items in the chart are classified as Skills, Applications, or Problem Solving. In the chapters in Unit VII of this book, the three item types are covered in different levels:

Skills items are covered in Level 1;
Applications items are covered in Level 2;
Problem Solving items are covered in Level 3.

For example, the skills needed to solve Item 20 are covered in Level 2 of Chapter 6 in Unit VII. To locate in which chapter arithmetic items are addressed, reread the problem to see what kind of numbers (whole numbers, fractions, and so forth) are used and then go to the designated level of the appropriate chapter.

Instruction

Introduction

This section of the book contains seven units that can help you learn the things you need to know to pass the five GED tests.

Units I and II will help you learn grammar and develop the editing and essay-writing skills you need for success with the Writing Skills Test of the GED. Reading Strategies, the third unit, will help you develop your reading skills and prepare you for studying Units IV to VI—Social Studies, Science, and Interpreting Literature and the Arts. The final unit, Unit VII, is the Mathematics unit.

The units are divided into chapters, which are, in turn, further divided. There are many exercises, activities, reviews, and quizzes to give you several opportunities to apply and test your understanding of and skill with the materials you study. A Progress Chart at the beginning of each unit makes it easy for you to keep track of your work and record your performance on each lesson.

It would be best for you to prepare for all five of the GED tests at the same time. This way, you can make progress at building skills in every subject throughout your GED preparation.

Here is a suggested study pattern: Begin with Units I, II, III, and VII. When you finish Unit III, add Units IV, V, and VI to your study schedule. Continue progressing through Units I, II, and VII. The lessons are brief enough that you should be able to complete one lesson in each unit during one or two study sessions. Pace yourself so that you make progress in all of the subjects at a relatively even rate.

Unlike most of the items on the GED tests, many of the questions in the instruction units are *not* multiple-choice items. Multiple-choice questions are valid in a testing situation when everyone is at an equal advantage or disadvantage. While you are learning, however, it is to your advantage to be able to study, review, and think in order to formulate answers in your own words. Since your goal while learning is to add new information and skills to those you already have, the best procedure is to make new information your own and to develop skills by phrasing answers in your own words. In addition, the experience of writing is helpful in preparing you for the essay you will write on the actual GED.

There is an introduction at the beginning of each of the seven instructional units. The introductions suggest procedures for studying the units that should help you get the most out of each unit.

UNIT I

Writing Skills, Part I: Grammar

The lessons in this unit cover the conventions of written English and their application in editing. It is best to work through this unit in order. Chapters 1 to 3 are divided into Skills, which are, in turn, divided into lessons. Each Skill is a topic in usage, sentence structure, or mechanics. The lessons within each Skill explore various facets of the topic. The fourth chapter is divided into lessons that cover editing and the format of the items on the GED.

Each Skill in Chapters 1 to 3 begins with a Preview and ends with a Review. Previews and Reviews are made up of items that test how well you can apply your knowledge of the topic covered in the Skill. Previews allow you to test your present ability. If you get 80 percent of the examples in a Preview correct, you may not need to study the lessons in the Skill. To be sure, do the examples in the Review at the end of the Skill. If you get 80 percent correct again, you may feel comfortable in skipping the lessons in that Skill. If you get fewer than 80 percent of the examples in either the Preview or the Review correct, study all the lessons in the Skill.

Chapter 4 is not divided into Skills. The lessons in Chapter 4 will help you apply the knowledge you gain in Chapters 1 to 3 to editing in the format the GED uses.

You may want to work on Unit II at the same time you are working on this unit. Or, you may prefer to complete this unit before you go on to Unit II. Either way, you should start your work in this unit at the beginning of Chapter 1.

UNIT I PROGRESS CHART
Writing Skills, Part I

Use the following chart to keep track of your work. When you complete a lesson, circle the number of questions you answered correctly in the Lesson Exercise. When you complete a Skill Preview, a Skill Review, or a Chapter Quiz, also record your score below. The numbers in color represent scores at a level of 80% or better.

Lesson	Page		
		CHAPTER 1: Usage	
	73	Skill 1: SUBJECT-VERB AGREEMENT	
	73	Preview	1 2 3 4 5
1	73	The Basics of Subject-Verb Agreement	1 2 3 4 5 6 7 8 9 10
2	77	Interrupting Phrases	1 2 3 4 5
3	78	Inverted Sentence Structure	1 2 3 4 5
4	79	Expletives	1 2 3 4 5
5	80	Compound Subjects	1 2 3 4 5
	81	Skill 1 Review	1 2 3 4 5 6 7 8 9 10
	82	Skill 2: VERB TENSE	
	82	Preview	1 2 3 4 5
1	82	Verb Forms	1 2 3 4 5 6 7 8 9 10
2	87	Word Clues to Tense in Sentences	1 2 3 4 5
3	88	Word Clues to Tense in Paragraphs	
4	89	Using Tenses Consistently	1 2 3 4 5
	91	Skill 2 Review	1 2 3 4 5 6 7 8 9 10
	91	Skill 3: PRONOUN REFERENCE	
	91	Preview	1 2 3 4 5
1	92	Pronouns: Agreement with Antecedent	1 2 3 4 5
2	93	Avoiding Pronoun Shifts	1 2 3 4 5
3	94	Relative Pronouns	1 2 3 4 5
4	96	Avoiding Vague Pronoun References	1 2 3 4 5
5	97	Avoiding Ambiguous Pronoun References	1 2 3 4 5
	98	Skill 3 Review	1 2 3 4 5 6 7 8 9 10
	98	Quiz	1 2 3 4 5 6 7 8 9 10
			11 12 13 14 15 16 17 18 19 20
		CHAPTER 2: Sentence Structure	
	100	Skill 1: COMPLETE SENTENCES	
	100	Preview	1 2 3 4 5
1	100	Eliminating Sentence Fragments	1 2 3 4 5
2	101	Eliminating Run-on Sentences	1 2 3 4 5
3	102	Other Ways of Eliminating Run-on Sentences	1 2 3 4 5 6 7 8 9 10
	105	Skill 1 Review	1 2 3 4 5 6 7 8 9 10
	105	Skill 2: COORDINATION AND SUBORDINATION	
	105	Preview	1 2 3 4 5
1	106	Coordination	1 2 3 4 5
2	108	Subordination	1 2 3 4 5
3	109	Combining Sentences	1 2 3 4 5
	110	Skill 2 Review	1 2 3 4 5 6 7 8 9 10
	111	Skill 3: CLEAR SENTENCES	
	111	Preview	1 2 3 4 5
1	112	Clarity of Thought	1 2 3 4 5

Lesson	Page		
2	113	Proper Modification	1 2 3 4 5
3	114	Parallel Structure	1 2 3 4 5
	116	Skill 3 Review	1 2 3 4 5 6 7 8 9 10
	116	Quiz	1 2 3 4 5 6 7 8 9 10
			11 12 13 14 15 16 17 18 19 20
		CHAPTER 3: Mechanics	
	118	Skill 1: CAPITALIZATION	
	118	Preview	1 2 3 4 5
1	118	Proper Nouns and Proper Adjectives	1 2 3 4 5
2	119	Titles of People and Addresses	1 2 3 4 5
3	121	Times, Dates, Seasons, Special Events, and Historical Eras	1 2 3 4 5
	122	Skill 1 Review	1 2 3 4 5 6 7 8 9 10
	122	Skill 2: PUNCTUATION	
	122	Preview	1 2 3 4 5
1	123	Commas Between Items in a Series	1 2 3 4 5
2	124	Commas in Compound Sentences	1 2 3 4 5
3	125	Commas After Introductory Elements	1 2 3 4 5
4	126	Commas With Sentence Interrupters	1 2 3 4 5
5	128	Avoiding Overuse of Commas	1 2 3 4 5
	129	Skill 2 Review	1 2 3 4 5 6 7 8 9 10
	130	Skill 3: SPELLING	
	130	Preview	1 2 3 4 5
1	130	Basic Spelling Rules	1 2 3 4 5
2	132	Possessives	1 2 3 4 5
3	133	Contractions	1 2 3 4 5
4	135	Frequently Confused Words	1 2 3 4 5
	137	Spelling List	1 2 3 4 5 6 7 8 9 10
	144	Skill 3 Review	1 2 3 4 5 6 7 8 9 10
	145	Quiz	1 2 3 4 5 6 7 8 9 10
			11 12 13 14 15 16 17 18 19 20
		CHAPTER 4: Editing Paragraphs	
1	147	Three Types of Questions	1 2 3 4 5
2	151	The Editing Process	1 2 3 4 5
3	154	Editing for Correct Usage	1 2 3 4 5
4	156	Editing for Correct Sentence Structure	1 2 3 4 5
5	159	Editing for Mechanical Correctness	1 2 3 4 5
6	161	Editing Paragraphs	1 2 3 4 5
	164	Quiz	1 2 3 4 5 6 7 8 9 10
			11 12 13 14 15 16 17 18 19 20

Chapter 1: Usage

Objective

In this chapter, you will learn about

- Subject–verb agreement
- Verb tense
- Pronoun reference

Skill 1 Subject–Verb Agreement

Preview

Directions: Edit the following sentences to correct all errors in subject–verb agreement. Not all of the sentences have errors.

1. Americans buys $3 billion worth of pet food every year.
2. Lions spend an average of 21 hours a day resting or sleeping.
3. Across the plain races hundreds of zebras.
4. There is three different shapes of leaves on the sassafras tree.
5. Both cattle and horses craves salt.

Check your answers. Correct answers are on page A-3. If you have at least four answers correct, do the Skill 1 Review on page 81. If you have fewer than four answers correct, study Skill 1 beginning with Lesson 1.

Lesson 1 The Basics of Subject–Verb Agreement

The basic rule for subject–verb agreement is:

A singular subject must use a singular verb.
The banana plant <u>bears</u> fruit for only a single season.
A plural subject must use a plural verb.
Bananas <u>grow</u> on a plant stalk rather than on a tree.

To use this rule, you must be able to recognize the singular (one) and the plural (more than one) forms of subjects and verbs. This will enable you to determine whether or not a verb agrees with its subject.

Subject: The subject is always a noun or a pronoun. The usual way to change a noun from singular to plural is by adding -s or -es. Notice these singular nouns and their plural forms.

    radio—radios   feather—feathers   boy—boys
    box—boxes   glass—glasses   daisy—daisies

Some nouns have plural forms that are considered irregular; their plurals are not formed by adding -s or -es. Notice these singular nouns and their irregular plural forms.

    child—children   foot—feet
    mouse—mice   tooth—teeth

A dictionary can help you to determine the correct spelling of irregular plural nouns.

Verb: The verb shows what the subject is doing, what is happening to the subject, what the subject is, or what the subject is like.

If the subject of a sentence is *he, she, it,* or a singular noun, the verb must be singular. If the subject is *we, you, they,* or a plural noun, the verb must be plural. In many cases, a singular verb ends in -s or -es.

Singular		Plural	
subject	*verb*	*subject*	*verb*
daisy	grows	daisies	grow
he	walks	they	walk
child	guesses	children	guess
girl	was	girls	were
fox	does	foxes	do
mouse	has	mice	have

Note that the pronoun *you* always uses a plural verb.

    You <u>have</u> a warmer coat than mine.
    You <u>were</u> the best person for the job.

The pronoun *I* usually uses a plural verb.

    I <u>do</u> exercises for 15 minutes every day.
    I <u>walk</u> at least a mile each morning.

The forms of the verb *be* used with *I* are singular.

    I <u>am</u> not a very good singer.
    Last year I <u>was</u> the organizer of our block party.

The following sentences show how the verb form depends upon its subject.

The radio <u>was invented</u> by Guglielmo Marconi in 1895.
More radios <u>were sold</u> in the United States in 1971 than in any previous year.

Sometimes it is difficult to tell whether a subject is singular or plural. Follow these rules for subject–verb agreement.

Rule 1: The following *indefinite pronouns* are singular and take a singular verb.

anyone	everyone	someone	one
anybody	everybody	somebody	no one
anything	everything	something	each

No one <u>has left</u> work early today.
Someone <u>is</u> a victim of a violent crime every 28 seconds.

Rule 2: The following pronouns are plural and take a plural verb.

both   few   many   several

Both <u>were selected</u> to represent the department.
Many <u>were familiar</u> with the new procedure.

Rule 3: The following pronouns may be either singular or plural, depending on how they are used in a sentence.

some   most   part   any   all   none

In the following sentence, *most* refers to a portion of the meeting:

<u>Most</u> of the meeting <u>was</u> productive.

In this case, *most* is singular and takes a singular verb. In the following sentence, *most* is plural because it refers to more than one person:

<u>Most</u> of the committee members <u>were</u> present.

In this case, *most* takes a plural verb.

Rule 4: The following words can be either singular or plural. When they refer to a group of people or things that are together in one unit, they take a singular verb. When they refer to the individual members of a group, they take a plural verb.

audience	group	band
class	jury	orchestra
crowd	team	family

The audience is leaving. (acting as a unit)
The audience were clapping their approval of the performance. (acting as individuals within a group)

Rule 5: Although these subjects appear to be plural, they are singular in meaning and take a singular verb.

civics	physics	economics
mathematics	politics	athletics
measles	series	genetics
news	United States	mumps

Athletics has become a billion-dollar business.
The United States is the leading importer of coffee in the world.

Rule 6: The following have no singular form and are plural in meaning. They take a plural verb.

| pliers | shears | trousers |
| scissors | jeans | pants |

Are the scissors in the drawer?
My jeans are not dry yet.

NOTE: If the word *pair* precedes the noun, use the singular verb.

The pair of scissors is there in the drawer.

To help you edit sentences for subject–verb agreement, use this five-step agreement test. After reading a sentence,

Step 1. Find the subject by asking whom or what the sentence is about.
Step 2. Determine whether the subject is singular or plural.
Step 3. Locate the verb.
Step 4. Determine whether the verb is singular or plural.
Step 5. If the subject and the verb are both singular or both plural, they agree. If they do not agree, change the verb so that it agrees with the subject.

This example shows how the five-step method can be used to determine the agreement of a sentence.

Most nuts grows on trees.

Step 1. By asking what the sentence is about, you determine that the subject of the sentence is *nuts*.
Step 2. *Nuts*, which ends in *-s*, is plural.
Step 3. *Grows* is the verb of the sentence.
Step 4. Because *grows* ends in *-s*, it is singular.
Step 5. The plural subject and singular verb do not agree. The verb should be changed so that it agrees with the subject.

Most nuts grow on trees.

Lesson 1   Exercise

Directions: Use the five-step method to determine the agreement of the following sentences. Edit the sentences to correct all errors in subject–verb agreement. Not all of the sentences have errors.

1. Weather conditions changes rapidly in the summer months in the Midwest.
2. Both was eligible for the sweepstakes prize.
3. Effective speaking require practice and determination.
4. Everyone enjoys a vacation now and then.
5. You deserve a raise because of your outstanding work record.
6. The team are practicing on the field.
7. Somebody have the list of vacant apartments.
8. Listening skills needs to be taught in grade school.
9. Measles are a serious disease if not treated properly.
10. The pair of pants were torn near the seam.

Answers are on page A-3.

Lesson 2   Interrupting Phrases

A phrase is a group of words that has no subject or no verb. In each of these sentences, the subject and the verb are separated by a phrase that gives more information about the subject. These groups of words are called *interrupting phrases*. They break the normal sentence pattern of a subject followed by a verb.

The sentences below are incorrect. The edited versions, with changes made in handwriting, are correct.

The decision of the judges ~~were~~ *was* final.

Excessive salt intake, in addition to excessive fat intake, ~~have~~ *has* been the source of many health problems.

The singer, along with her equally talented pianist, ~~receive~~ *receives* great reviews at each concert.

The demand for teachers ~~are~~ *is* expected to increase well into the 1990s.

Notice that in two of the sentences, commas set off the interrupting words from the rest of the sentence. In the other two sentences there are no commas. Words that immediately follow the subject, whether set off by commas or not, do not change the number of the subject.

Before you use the five-step agreement test from Lesson 1, cross out all the interrupting phrases in a sentence. This will help you to locate the subject and the verb.

One ~~of the oldest living trees~~ *is* ~~are~~ the bristlecone pine.

When the interrupting phrase is crossed out, it is easier to see that the subject of the sentence is *one*. The verb must be changed to *is* so that it agrees with the singular subject.

Lesson 2   Exercise

Directions: *Edit the following sentences to correct all the errors in subject–verb agreement. First, cross out the interrupting phrases. Then, use the five-step agreement test described in Lesson 1. Not all of the sentences have errors.*

1. The greatest verified age of a human being are 113 years.
2. Clarity in writing and speaking are essential to success.
3. Horses, as well as zebras, sleep while standing up.
4. Mark Twain's stories of Mississippi River life has fascinated many people.
5. The rabbit, along with the antelope, see in a full circle without moving its head.

Answers are on page A-3.

Lesson 3   Inverted Sentence Structure

Most sentences follow the subject–verb sentence pattern. In some sentences, however, the subject comes after the verb. Such sentences have *inverted sentence structure*.

The sentences below, which have inverted structure, are incorrect as written. The edited versions, with changes made in handwriting, are correct.

Under several bridges ~~swim~~ *swims* the misguided whale.
~~Were~~ *Was* the sound of the sirens too harsh for you?

Sentences that ask questions often have inverted structure. An inverted sentence may also begin with a prepositional phrase such as *under several bridges*.

To find the subject of an inverted sentence, ask yourself whom or what the sentence is about. When you have located the subject, find the verb. Then put the sentence into subject–verb order.

Next to the honored guests <u>sits</u> the <u>mayor.</u>
The <u>mayor sits</u> next to the honored guests.

When the sentence is in subject–verb order, it is easier to make sure that the verb, *sits*, agrees with the subject, *mayor*, not with *guests*.

If a question has inverted sentence structure, put it in subject–verb order by rewording the sentence as a statement. Continue to cross out any phrases that separate the subject from the verb.

Do the <u>dresses</u> in your closet <u>fit</u> you well?

The <u>dresses</u> ~~in your closet~~ *do fit* you well.

Note that the verb, *do fit*, agrees with the subject, *dresses*.

Lesson 3   Exercise

Directions: *Edit the following sentences to correct all the errors in subject–verb agreement. Where necessary, put sentences in subject-verb order and cross out interrupting phrases. Not all of the sentences have errors.*

1. At the meeting was the president and his advisors.
2. At the foot of the cave was the hibernating bears.
3. Was the fireworks on the Fourth of July as spectacular as last year's?
4. For many reasons, we are unhappy with our new car.
5. Does the whales of the Pacific Ocean migrate every year?

Answers are on page A-3.

Lesson 4   Expletives

Read the following sentences. Observe that each begins with the word *here* or *there*. Notice how the sentences have been correctly edited.

Here ~~is~~ *are* the magazine articles you requested.

There ~~are~~ *is* no truth to the idea that all dinosaurs were huge.

There ~~is~~ *are* about 30,000 quills on a porcupine.

Here and *there* may seem to be the subjects of these sentences, because they come directly before the verb, but they are not. The subject of the first sentence, *articles*, needs the plural verb *are*. The subject of the second sentence, *truth*, needs the singular verb *is*. Be sure you understand why *quills*, the subject of the third sentence, requires the verb *are*.

The words *here* and *there* are called *expletives* when they begin a sentence such as those appearing above. *An expletive is never the subject of a sentence.* To determine subject–verb agreement in a sentence that begins with an expletive, use the five-step agreement test from Lesson 1. In addition to crossing out any interrupting phrases, cross out the expletive.

Here is a book about the forests of New England.

Lesson 4 Exercise

Directions: Edit the following sentences to correct all the errors in subject–verb agreement. Cross out interrupting phrases and expletives, where necessary. Not all of the sentences have errors.

1. There is approximately 2.5 million Americans audited by the IRS each year.
2. There is more than 2 billion pencils manufactured in the United States each year.
3. Here are the stack of new books from the library.
4. Here was the site of the last battle of the Civil War.
5. There are a type of shark that averages five inches in length when fully grown.

Answers are on page A-3.

Lesson 5 Compound Subjects

Frequently, a sentence will have more than one subject word. When this happens, the sentence has a *compound subject*. These compound subjects may be connected by a single connective word such as *and*, *or*, or *nor*. Notice how the sentence below has been correctly edited.

Lightning and thunder ~~is~~ *are* responsible for millions of dollars of property damage each year.

Whenever compound subjects are joined by *and*, a plural verb is used.
Compound subjects may also be connected by paired connective words such as *either . . . or*, *neither . . . nor*, *both . . . and*, or *not only . . . but also*. Look at the sentences below. Notice how they have been correctly edited.

Neither the pearl nor the amber ~~are~~ *is* a mineral.
Either Bob or his coworkers ~~was~~ *were* planning the company picnic.

In the first sentence, where both subject words, *pearl* and *amber*, are singular, a singular verb is used. In the second sentence, where one subject (*Bob*) is singular and one (*coworkers*) is plural, a plural verb is used.
To choose the correct verb form, follow these two rules.

Rule 1: When two subjects are joined by *or*, *nor*, *neither . . . nor*, *either . . . or*, or *not only . . . but also*, the verb agrees with the subject that is *closer* to the verb.

Neither the teachers nor the principal <u>approves</u> of the curriculum change.
Neither the principal nor the teachers <u>approve</u> of the curriculum change.

> **Rule 2:** Subjects joined by *and* or *both...and* usually take plural verbs. It does not matter if one subject is plural and one is singular. The connective *and* combines them to make a plural subject.
>
> Both the doctor and the nurses <u>were</u> in favor of joining the HMO.
> Both the nurses and the doctor <u>were</u> in favor of joining the HMO.
>
> NOTE: If the words of a compound subject refer to the same person, place, or thing, the verb is singular.
>
> My best friend and closest companion <u>is</u> visiting me for the weekend.

Lesson 5 Exercise

Directions: Edit the following sentences to correct all the errors in subject–verb agreement. Not all of the sentences have errors.

1. Sarah and Paul have been taking golf lessons.
2. Neither Neptune nor Uranus are visible without a telescope.
3. Either the zoo or the art museums was my choice for a day's vacation.
4. Not only a checking account but also a savings account were required for a free gift.
5. Both Prince Charles and Prince Andrew of England is married.

Answers are on page A-3.

Skill 1 Review

Directions: Edit the following sentences to correct all errors in subject–verb agreement. Not all of the sentences have errors.

1. There is more than 155 million telephones in the United States.
2. The various buttons on the telephone in my office produces different tones.
3. The orchestra give pop concerts every Saturday night.
4. This television station employ eleven announcers.
5. Parsley, a member of the herb family, were used by the ancient Romans.
6. Was Mark Twain's manuscripts the first to be typewritten?
7. At the bottom of the contract is the line for your signature.

8. Neither Alexander Graham Bell nor Thomas Edison were the first to design the telephone.
9. Peanuts provides more protein, minerals, and vitamins than beef liver.
10. The first railroad in the United States were the Baltimore and Ohio, which began to carry passengers in 1830.

Check your answers. Correct answers are on page A-3. If you have at least eight answers correct, go on to Skill 2. If you have fewer than eight answers correct, study Skill 1 beginning with Lesson 1.

Skill 2   Verb Tense

Preview

Directions: *Edit the following sentences to correct all errors in verb tense or form. Not all of the sentences have errors.*

1. He had knew about the early settlement of Louisiana by French colonists.
2. Tomorrow, we will learn about "the wizard of Menlo Park," Thomas A. Edison.
3. When we spoke about American Indian cultures, we mention differences in language.
4. In the last 20 years, many people learn to use computers.
5. After a meteor lands on Earth, it became a meteorite.

Check your answers. Correct answers are on page A-4. If you have at least four answers correct, do the Skill 2 Review on page 91. If you have fewer than four answers correct, study Skill 2 beginning with Lesson 1.

Lesson 1   Verb Forms

Categories of Verbs

To check to see that a verb has been used correctly, you need to identify the verb in a sentence. Verbs can be classified into two categories.

1. *Action verbs.* An action verb shows either physical or mental action.

   Some elevators <u>travel</u> as much as 1888 feet per minute.
   During the Middle Ages, people <u>thought</u> that taking a bath was a sin.

2. *Linking verbs.* A linking verb connects the subject of the sentence with a word or phrase that renames or describes the subject.

> *The United States is the world's largest producer of cheese.*
> *Brussels sprouts are more expensive than cabbage.*

The linking verbs in the two sentences above are forms of the verb *to be.* Other verbs that can be used as linking verbs include:

appear	feel	remain	smell	stay
become	look	seem	sound	taste

Verb Phrases

A verb may be a single word or a phrase. A *verb phrase* contains two or more verbs that act as a single verb.

> *Facial tissues originally were manufactured as gas-mask filters during World War I.*
> *A songbird's heart can beat more than a thousand times a minute.*
> *At one time, the legs of dancer Fred Astaire had been insured for $650,000.*

Verb phrases consist of one or more *helping verbs* followed by a *main verb.* In the first example sentence above, *were* is the helping verb. *Manufactured* is the main verb. In the second example sentence, the helping verb is *can* and the main verb is *beat.* The verb phrase in the third example sentence includes two helping verbs (*had been*) followed by the main verb (*insured*).

Forms of the verb *to be* (*am, are, was, were,* for example) are often used as helping verbs. Forms of the verb *to do* (*do, does, did*) and *to have* (*have, has, had*) are also common helping verbs. Other helping verbs include:

can	would	may
could	shall	might
will	should	must

Sometimes, a verb phrase is interrupted by a word such as *not, never, usually,* or *always.* These words are not part of the verb phrase.

> *A catfish does not have scales.*
> *Chicago is usually called the Windy City.*

Verb Tense

Locate the verb in each of the following sentences.

> *I hear a knock in the car's engine.*
> *I heard the same sound yesterday.*
> *You will hear it, too.*

Each sentence uses the same verb—*hear*—in a different tense. The *tense* of a verb shows the time of the action described. The first sentence describes something that is happening in the present; the second sentence describes something that happened in the past; the third sentence describes something that will happen in the future.

A verb in the present tense can also express something that is generally true or a current state of affairs.

A muffler lasts *about five years.* (general truth)
This car needs *new spark plugs.* (current state)

The three basic tenses of verbs are shown in the following chart.

Tense	Meaning	Form	Examples
Present	Something is happening now, or is true now, or is generally true.	Add -s or -es when used with singular nouns or with *he, she,* or *it.* No ending when used with plural nouns or with *I, you, we, they.*	The boy walks. He rushes. The boys walk. They rush.
Past	Something happened in the past.	Add -d or -ed to present tense.	The boy walks. The boy walked. They bake. They baked.
Future	Something will happen.	Add a helping verb, *will* or *shall,* to the present tense.	The boys will walk. I shall walk.

Principal Parts of Regular Verbs

The different tenses are formed from the principal parts of a verb. Every verb has three principal parts.

Present	**Past**	**Past Participle**
shout	shouted	shouted
smile	smiled	smiled
walk	walked	walked
look	looked	looked

These verbs are called *regular verbs.* This means that they form the past and the past-participle forms by adding -d or -ed to the present-tense form.

In a verb phrase with a form of the helping verb *have,* the main verb is always a past-participle form.

The referee <u>has shouted</u> several times.
Lee <u>has walked</u> more than five miles.
They <u>have looked</u> for a more convenient store.

Principal Parts of Irregular Verbs

Many verbs use endings other than -d or -ed to form the past and the past participle. These verbs are *irregular verbs*.

Incorrect: She <u>teared</u> up the old contract.
Correct: She <u>tore</u> up the old contract.

The following is a list of commonly used verbs that have irregular past and past-participle forms.

Irregular Verbs

Present	Past	Past Participle
am, is, are	was, were	been
become	became	become
begin	began	begun
bite	bit	bitten
blow	blew	blown
break	broke	broken
bring	brought	brought
build	built	built
burst	burst	burst
buy	bought	bought
choose	chose	chosen
come	came	come
dive	dived or dove	dived
do	did	done
drink	drank	drunk
draw	drew	drawn
drive	drove	driven
eat	ate	eaten
fall	fell	fallen
fly	flew	flown
forget	forgot	forgotten
freeze	froze	frozen
get	got	got or gotten
give	gave	given
go	went	gone
grow	grew	grown
hide	hid	hidden
know	knew	known
lay (put)	laid	laid
leave	left	left
lie (recline)	lay	lain
ride	rode	ridden

Chapter 1: Usage

Irregular Verbs

Present	Past	Past Participle
ring	rang	rung
rise	rose	risen
run	ran	run
say	said	said
see	saw	seen
set (put)	set	set
shake	shook	shaken
shrink	shrank or shrunk	shrunk or shrunken
sing	sang	sung
sit	sat	sat
speak	spoke	spoken
spend	spent	spent
spring	sprang or sprung	sprung
stand	stood	stood
steal	stole	stolen
swim	swam	swum
take	took	taken
teach	taught	taught
tear	tore	torn
think	thought	thought
throw	threw	thrown
wake	waked or woke	waked or woken
wear	wore	worn
write	wrote	written

UNIT I: WRITING SKILLS, PART 1: GRAMMAR   Skill 2: Lesson 2   **87**

Lesson 1   Exercise

Directions: *Complete the following sentences by adding the verb in the tense indicated in parentheses.*

1. Consumers _____ more money on motor vehicles than on furniture and household equipment. (*spend*, past tense)
2. The largest single cause of errors in business _____ illegible handwriting. (*be*, present tense)
3. The immigrants _____ ideas and customs from their native countries. (*bring*, past tense)
4. The average heart _____ four liters of blood per minute. (*pump*, present tense)
5. The Union Jack _____ the nickname of the British flag. (*be*, present tense)

Complete the following sentences by adding the past participle of the verb given in parentheses.

6. It had _____ 70 years to complete the Capitol building in Washington, D.C. (*take*)
7. By July 1969, the United States had _____ to withdraw troops from South Vietnam. (*begin*)
8. Farmers have _____ before Congress about the difficulties small farm owners face. (*speak*)
9. The water level of the Mississippi River has _____ this year. (*rise*)
10. Scientists have _____ conclusions about prehistoric animals by studying fossils. (*draw*)

Answers are on page A-4.

Lesson 2   Word Clues to Tense in Sentences

Sentences often contain words or phrases that answer the question *When?* These words or phrases tell us the time of an action. Here are some examples of such words and phrases.

Present	**Past**	**Future**
today	yesterday	tomorrow
now	recently	later
at the moment	last Saturday	next week

Some of the items in Part I of the GED Writing Skills Test require you to use these clues to determine the correct tense of a sentence. For example, read the following sentence.

Today, many people owned video cassette recorders.

Today tells you that the action is taking place in the present. However, *owned* expresses an action in the past. To edit the sentence, you need to change the verb to match the clue word given in the sentence.

Today, many people <u>own</u> video cassette recorders.

Also, look for words that give time references.

Eighteenth-century doctors prescribed onions as a cure for colds.

The words *eighteenth-century* tell you that the action took place in the past. Therefore, the use of the past-tense verb, *prescribed*, is correct.
Sometimes, a word that ordinarily indicates the present has a future sense.

Today, I will go to the store.

In this sentence, *today* means "later today," and a future-tense verb is needed. The sentence is correct as written.

Lesson 2 Exercise

Directions: *Edit the following sentences to correct all errors in verb tense. Not all of the sentences have errors.*

1. The first electric elevator is installed in New York City in 1889.
2. Next year, construction workers built a new amusement park on the island.
3. The past decade proved to be a critical one for our space program.
4. Recently, scientists study a supernova in the southern sky.
5. In 1916, a Model T Ford costs less than $400.

Answers are on page A-4.

Lesson 3 Word Clues to Tense in Paragraphs

Part I of the GED Writing Skills Test is made up of items based on paragraphs. As you read each of the paragraphs, you will need to determine whether the action described in the paragraph is present, past, or future.
Throughout a paragraph, tenses should be consistent. Notice the tenses of the verbs in this paragraph.

(1) The eruption of the volcano was a spectacular sight. **(2)** Lava and hot gases poured from the opening in the surface of the earth. **(3)** People see the orange and yellow cloud above the mountain. **(4)** Hundreds of newspaper photographers took pictures of the volcano in action, and all those who witness the eruption will form a permanent image of it in their minds.

This paragraph is about an event—the eruption of a volcano—that took place in the past. All of the actions described, therefore, should be expressed in the past tense. Sentence 3, however, is in the present tense. The second part of sentence 4, ". . . and everyone who witnesses the eruption will form a permanent image . . . ," uses the present tense and the future tense. It is difficult to follow the meaning of a paragraph when tenses are not used consistently.

Here is the edited paragraph. Notice that the past tense is used consistently throughout the paragraph.

The eruption of the volcano was a spectacular sight. Lava and hot gases poured from the opening in the surface of the earth. People saw the orange and yellow clouds above the mountain. Hundreds of newspaper photographers took pictures of the volcano in action, and all those who witnessed the eruption formed a permanent image of it in their minds.

Lesson 3 Exercise

Directions: *The writer of the following paragraph used a mixture of the present and the past tense. Rewrite the paragraph in the proper tense. Not all of the sentences will have to be changed.*

Hippopotamuses secrete a thick, reddish film. It resembled blood in color and texture, but it was not blood. In fact, it does not have any blood in it. The secretion kept the animals' hides from drying out. Hippos needed this protection when they are out of the water. When the animals are hot or in pain, the flow increases. The fluid also became a darker red.

Answers are on page A-4.

Lesson 4 Using Tenses Consistently

In Lesson 2, you saw how some words, such as *yesterday* and *tomorrow*, are clues that tell you what tense should be used in a sentence. Many sentences have more than one verb, as in the following example:

The sun <u>became</u> brighter as the fog <u>disappeared</u>.

The verb in the first part of the sentence, *became*, is in the past tense. It serves as a clue that can help you determine whether the verb in the second part of the sentence is in the correct tense. The verb, *disappeared*, in the second part is also in the past tense. Thus, the verb tenses used in this sentence are consistent.

Read the following sentences. Which one is correct?

1. *Suburban homes became expensive, and people move back to the cities.*
2. *The students left the dish out overnight, and the water evaporated.*

Sentence 2 describes a sequence of events that occurred in the past. Both verbs are in the past tense; sentence 2 is therefore correct. Sentence 1 is incorrect because it shifts from the past to the present tense. Here is the edited version of sentence 1:

Suburban homes became expensive, and people moved back to the cities.

To decide whether the tenses in a sentence are consistent, read the sentence for its meaning. Determine when the action is taking place and check whether the verbs express the time of the action. You may need to look at the paragraph in which the sentence is used to determine in which tense the action of the sentence should be expressed.

If a sentence expresses two actions that take place at different times, two different verb tenses may be needed.

Last week, economists predicted that prices of homes will increase sharply.

This sentence is correct. Although the prediction was made in the past, the prediction was made about an action in the future. Therefore, the use of the future tense in *will increase* is correct.

Lesson 4 Exercise

Directions: *Edit the following sentences for correct sequence of tenses. Choose the correct verb from the pair given in parentheses.*

1. There was a water shortage in the summer, and the city council (enact, enacted) strict conservation measures.
2. As oil prices fall, the nation (increased, increases) its consumption of gasoline.
3. Most people supported a change in tax laws, so Congress (passes, passed) new legislation.
4. We learned in biology class that enzymes (play, will play) an important part in digestion.
5. When the tide rises, ships (will be, were) able to enter the harbor.

Answers are on page A-4.

UNIT I: WRITING SKILLS, PART 1: GRAMMAR

Skill 2 Review

Directions: Edit the following sentences to correct all errors in verb usage. Not all of the sentences have errors.

1. Tea is the favorite drink of the early American colonists.
2. When scientists make new discoveries, they published papers about their findings.
3. A tidal wave broke the dam, and water floods the village.
4. A museum was builded inside the base of the Statue of Liberty.
5. When the water reached the boiling point, steam began to rise from the container.
6. The words "The reports of my death are greatly exaggerated" were wrote by Mark Twain.
7. Cowhands worn leather leggings over their trousers before riding their horses.
8. Tomorrow, the president discussed arms control agreements.
9. Passengers on the Concorde, a French aircraft, have rode faster than the speed of sound.
10. An ostrich can outrun a horse, but it could not fly.

Check your answers. Correct answers are on page A-4. If you have at least eight answers correct, go on to Skill 3. If you have fewer than eight answers correct, study Skill 2 beginning with Lesson 1.

Skill 3 Pronoun Reference

Preview

Directions: Edit the following sentences to correct all errors in pronoun reference. Not all of the sentences have errors.

1. Elizabeth Blackwell, who became the first American woman physician, had been rejected by many medical schools.
2. Tin or copper will turn to black powder when they are finely ground.
3. We must be aware of our skills, or you will not advance in our professions.
4. The giant squid continues to grow as long as they live.
5. Romans owned many chariots; they were banned from the streets of Rome during daylight hours.

Check your answers. Correct answers are on page A-4. If you have at least four answers correct, do the Skill 3 Review on page 98. If you have fewer than four answers correct, study Skill 3 beginning with Lesson 1.

Lesson 1 Pronouns: Agreement with Antecedent

Read the sentence below. To what do the words *his* and *he* refer?

> Paul Revere rode by horseback to tell his countrymen that he knew the British were advancing.

In this sentence the words *his* and *he* refer to the noun *Paul Revere*. A *pronoun* is a word that replaces or refers to a noun or another pronoun. The word that a pronoun replaces is called an *antecedent*. A pronoun must agree with its antecedent in number.

> **Rule 1:** A singular antecedent requires a singular pronoun.
>
> > Queen Elizabeth wore three different crowns on the day of her coronation.
>
> **Rule 2:** A plural antecedent requires a plural pronoun.
>
> > Many Indians, even though born in the United States, were not considered citizens until Congress granted them citizenship in 1924.
>
> **Rule 3:** When a pronoun is separated from its antecedent by a phrase, the pronoun should still agree with the antecedent.
>
> > The koala, one of the best-known marsupials, does not need water to supplement its food.
> > (The antecedent of *its* is *koala*, not *marsupials*.)
>
> **Rule 4:** A singular pronoun is used to refer to two or more singular antecedents that are joined by *or*.
>
> > A novel or a short story may bring fame to its author.
>
> **Rule 5:** A plural pronoun is used to refer to two or more antecedents that are joined by *and*.
>
> > July and August received their names from the Roman rulers Julius Caesar and Augustus Caesar.
>
> **Rule 6:** When two antecedents are joined by *neither . . . nor* or *either . . . or*, the pronoun agrees with the closer antecedent.
>
> > Neither the students nor the instructor is enjoying this class.
> > Neither Lincoln nor any other American presidents liked to wear their glasses in public.

The following chart lists singular and plural pronouns.

	Singular	Plural
Personal pronouns	I, you, he, she, it, me, him, her	we, you, they, us, them
Reflexive pronouns	myself, yourself, himself, herself, itself	ourselves, yourselves, themselves
Possessive pronouns	my, mine, your, yours, his, her, its	our, ours, your, yours, their, theirs
Demonstrative pronouns	this, that	these, those
Indefinite pronouns	anyone, anybody, everybody, no one, nobody, each, one, someone, somebody, either, neither, a person	others, few, both, several, many

Lesson 1 Exercise

Directions: Edit the following sentences to correct all the errors in pronoun–antecedent agreement. Not all of the sentences have errors.

1. Many mothers make clothing for her children.
2. A senator or a member of Congress must campaign for their election to office.
3. Everyone should be required to wear their seat belt.
4. A blacksmith tempers steel tools by plunging them into cold water while they are hot.
5. New Zealand and Australia sent its ambassadors to the United States.

Answers are on page A-4.

Lesson 2 Avoiding Pronoun Shifts

Although pronouns must agree in number with their antecedents, they must also agree in person. *Person* refers to the difference between the *person speaking* (first person), the *person spoken to* (second person), and the *person or thing being spoken about* (third person).

Read the following sentence.

We must be careful when lying in the sun because you might become sunburned.

This sentence sounds confusing because it has an error in pronoun usage. It shifts from the first person (*we*) to the second person (*you*). A correctly edited version is the following:

We must be careful when lying in the sun because we might become sunburned.

Be consistent when you use pronouns. Decide which person—first, second, or third—is appropriate to the sentence, and do not shift to another person.

The following chart gives examples of these three types of pronouns.

First-person pronouns	I, me, my, mine, we, us, ours; our
Second-person pronouns	you, your, yours
Third-person pronouns	he, him, his, she, her, hers, it, its, they, them, their, theirs

Lesson 2 Exercise

Directions: Edit the following sentences to correct all errors in pronoun shift. Not all of the sentences have errors.

1. Dreams are important to our emotional health as well as your physical health.
2. When you buy a car, you should test-drive it.
3. You should not take a driving test if they are not prepared for it.
4. When we fall in love, you might have a temporary change in personality.
5. A man who is afraid to try will not accomplish much until they change their thinking.
   Answers are on page A-4.

Lesson 3 Relative Pronouns

Read the following sentence. What does the word *which* refer to?

Kiev, which is the capital of the Ukraine, was rebuilt after World War II.

The word *which* refers to Kiev. *Which* is an example of a relative pronoun. *Kiev* is the antecedent of *which* in the sentence.

The following words are used as relative pronouns.

        which   that   who   whom

To choose the correct relative pronoun, remember the following rules:

Who and *whom* refer to people or animals.
Which refers to animals, places, or things.
That refers to people, animals, places, or things.

Computer games, <u>which</u> account for $35 million in sales per year, did not appear on the market until 1977.
People <u>who</u> experience shortness of breath may be under a lot of stress.
Puppies <u>that</u> eat nutritious food tend to be healthy in adult life.

The word *what* is sometimes incorrectly used as a relative pronoun. Notice how the following sentences have been edited.

The tree ~~what~~ *that* stands in our yard produces no fruit.

The gardener ~~what~~ *who* trimmed our hedges also weeded our flower bed.

To choose correctly between *who* and *whom*, substitute a personal pronoun for the relative pronoun in the sentence.

Marco Polo, (who, whom) was born in Venice, was the first European to visit ancient China.

To decide whether the correct relative pronoun is *who* or *whom*, think: *He was born in Venice*. If *I, we, he, she*, or *they* can be substituted for the relative pronoun, then the correct relative pronoun is *who*.

The explorer (who, whom) we studied was Marco Polo.

To decide whether the correct relative pronoun is *who* or *whom*, think: *We studied him*. If *us, me, him, her*, or *them* can be substituted for the relative pronoun, then the correct pronoun is *whom*.

Lesson 3 Exercise

Directions: Edit the following sentences to correct all the errors in relative-pronoun usage. Not all of the sentences have errors.

1. King James I of England was one of the first people which said that smoking was harmful.
2. The mountain range that extends from New Mexico to Alaska is the Rocky Mountains.

3. In *Macbeth*, the characters who I enjoyed most were Banquo and Macduff.
4. The cowbird is a bird what lays its eggs in the nests of other birds.
5. Venice, which includes more than 100 islands, often experiences severe floods.

Answers are on pages A-4–A-5.

Lesson 4 Avoiding Vague Pronoun References

A pronoun depends on other words for its meaning. If the antecedent of a pronoun is not clear, the meaning of the sentence in which the pronoun is used will be vague or confusing.

Read the following sentence.

You may want to study computer programming because they are always in demand.

The pronoun *they* does not have a clear antecedent. If the sentence is written as shown below, its meaning will be clear.

You may want to study computer programming because computer programmers are always in demand.

Notice that this sentence was made clear by replacing the pronoun *they* with a noun, *computer programmers*.

The example below also shows how you can rewrite a sentence by eliminating a pronoun that does not have a specific antecedent.

Unclear: *We were not given our pay increase, which is why morale is low.* (*Which* does not have a specific antecedent.)
Clear: *Morale is low because we were not given our pay increase.*

By rewording the unclear sentence, the pronoun *which* was eliminated.

Lesson 4 Exercise

Directions: *Edit the following sentences to correct all errors in vague pronoun reference.*

1. Although the movie won an award, they did not enjoy it as much as the movie reviewers did.
2. The government plans to increase the sales tax, which many people oppose.
3. The temperatures dropped steadily, which forced the cancellation of the outdoor barbecue.

4. In a recent news article, they said that more countries were asking for military aid.
5. Some people work more than eight hours a day, which is against many union rules.

Answers are on page A-5.

Lesson 5 Avoiding Ambiguous Pronoun References

In the last lesson, you studied examples of sentences that were unclear because they included pronouns that had no specific antecedents. Sometimes, a sentence is unclear because it includes a pronoun that can refer to more than one word in the sentence. In such sentences, the pronoun reference is *ambiguous.*

Read the following sentence.

The coaches told the players that they *were not prepared for today's game.*

In this sentence, *they* might refer to the coaches or to the players. Depending on the meaning that the writer intended, the sentence could be revised in two ways.

The coaches told the players, "We coaches are not prepared for today's game."

OR

The coaches told the players that they, the players, were not prepared for today's game.

A briefer version of the second rewording is possible, if it is clear from the context that the coaches are addressing the players:

The coaches said that the players were not prepared for today's game.

Lesson 5 Exercise

Directions: *Edit the following items to correct all errors in ambiguous pronoun reference.*

1. Shakespeare wrote many plays about English kings. They are very interesting.
2. Because of his controversial remarks, the president and the secretary of state held a news conference.
3. The teacher explained to the student that she needed to finish her project before the end of the semester.

4. One of the scouts told the scoutmaster that he was lost.
5. Some people read their horoscopes every day. They have a great deal of influence.

Answers are on page A-5.

Skill 3   Review

Directions: Edit the following sentences to correct all errors in pronoun usage. Not all of the sentences contain errors.

1. When quartz crystals were discovered, it was thought to be ice that would not melt.
2. My nephew, who I taught to ski, recently entered an amateur competition.
3. He dislikes eating in restaurants where he has to serve yourself.
4. Several of my friends have taught himself to use a word processor.
5. Tennessee and Missouri are the only states who are bordered by eight other states.
6. In many states, we need to take a vision test before you are issued a driver's license.
7. Neither the legislators nor the governor is satisfied with the proposed budget.
8. The boss informed the employee that she would no longer be working for the company.
9. Yesterday, I had a blood test and a booster shot. It made me feel weak.
10. Fish make sounds by grinding its teeth.

Check your answers. Correct answers are on page A-5. If you have at least eight answers correct, go on to the Chapter 1 Quiz. If you have fewer than eight answers correct, study Skill 3 beginning with Lesson 1.

Chapter 1   Quiz

Directions: Edit the following sentences to correct all errors in usage: subject–verb agreement, verb tense, and pronoun reference. No sentence has more than one error, although not all of the sentences have errors.

1. Several of our country's presidents has never held any other elective office.
2. We spend one-third of our life asleep, and you dream about one-fifth of that time.
3. Long ago, the Belgians really invents the French-fried potato.
4. Neither you nor I have tasted kiwi, an unusual but delicious fruit.
5. John Adams, whom was the first U.S. president to live in the White House, moved there in the year 1800.
6. At the crack of dawn was heard the crows of the rooster.
7. Generally, a person between the ages of five and fifteen are the healthiest.
8. People of ancient times washed himself with ashes and water.
9. The first aircraft carrier was build in 1918 by the British.
10. By next week, I probably am very good at hitting volleys.
11. There is seven red stripes in the United States flag.
12. All the gods of ancient Rome parallels those of Greece.
13. In 1491, James IV of Scotland signs a law that prohibited the playing of golf.
14. This morning I got out of bed and showered before the alarm rung.
15. Abraham Lincoln, who was the sixteenth president of the United States, was the first president to wear a beard.
16. If we were interested in studying mountains, you would study *orography*.
17. I dislike returning merchandise at that store because they give me a hard time.
18. George Custer had became a general by the age of 23.
19. Another interesting fact is that bird's-nest soup are really made from birds' nests.
20. Here are one of the newest electronic games on the market today.

Answers are on pages A-5–A-6.

Chapter 2 Sentence Structure

Objective

In this chapter, you will learn about
- Complete sentences
- Coordination and subordination
- Clear sentences

Skill 1 Complete Sentences

Preview

Directions: Edit the following items to correct all errors in complete sentence structure. Not all of the items have errors.

1. Napoleon who conquered Italy by the time he was 26.
2. David never went to camp he worked during the summer months.
3. Scientists can determine a person's age and race by examining a single strand of hair.
4. There are 20,000 television commercials made for children each year, 7,000 of them advertise sugared breakfast cereals.
5. Really holds less than a gallon.

Check your answers. Correct answers are on page A-6. If you have at least four answers correct, do the Skill 1 Review on page 105. If you have fewer than four answers correct, study Skill 1 beginning with Lesson 1.

Lesson 1 Eliminating Sentence Fragments

A sentence must express a clear, complete thought. The following sentence does not express a complete thought.

Voted in the election.

Who or what voted? This group of words is missing a subject.
To be complete, a sentence must meet three requirements.

1. A sentence must have a subject.
2. A sentence must have a verb.
3. A sentence must express a complete thought.

If a group of words fails one or more of these tests, it is called a *sentence fragment*. To correct a sentence fragment, identify the part that is missing; then add it to the fragment.

Mitch (subject) *voted in the election.*

Even when a group of words includes a subject and a verb, it may not express a complete thought.

Because computers have become a big industry.

Although this group of words has a subject (*computers*) and a verb (*have become*), the thought is not complete. *What* is happening because computers have become a big industry? To correct a sentence fragment of this type, words that complete the thought must be added.

Because computers have become a big industry, the number of job openings has increased.
OR
The number of job openings has increased because computers have become a big industry.

Lesson 1   Exercise

Directions: Edit the following items to correct all sentence-fragment errors. Not all of the items have errors.

1. Sweat through the pads of their feet.
2. The Fox River flowing into Green Bay, Wisconsin.
3. The first telephone operators were boys who worked standing up.
4. A snowstorm with low temperatures and severe winds.
5. When the hurricane reached land.

Answers are on page A-6.

Lesson 2   Eliminating Run-on Sentences

Run-on sentences are another type of error in sentence structure that you will find on the GED Writing Skills Test. Read the following example. Identify its subject, its verb, and its complete thought.

Water covers 70 percent of the Earth's surface only one percent is drinkable.

Is there more than one subject (*water, percent*)? Is there more than one verb (*covers, is*)? Is there more than one complete idea (the amount of surface area covered by water, the amount that is drinkable)? This "sentence" is actually two complete sentences that have been incorrectly written as one.

Water covers 70 percent of the Earth's surface. Only one percent is drinkable.

Two or more sentences that are joined together without punctuation or with incorrect punctuation form a *run-on sentence*. One way to correct a run-on sentence is to rewrite it as two separate sentences. When two complete thoughts are joined by a comma without any connecting word, a run-on sentence also results. This type of sentence is called a *comma splice*.

Incorrect: *Roman statues were made with removable heads, one head could be replaced by another.*
Correct: *Roman statues were made with removable heads. One head could be replaced by another.*

Lesson 2   Exercise

Directions: *Edit the following items to correct all run-on sentences.*

1. A crocodile cannot move its tongue its tongue is rooted to the base of its mouth.
2. Dry ice does not melt, it evaporates.
3. The first coin minted in the United States was a silver dollar it was issued on October 15, 1794.
4. The bark of a redwood tree is fireproof, a fire may take place inside the tree.
5. Cork comes from the bark of trees it takes more than ten years to produce one layer of cork.

Answers are on page A-6.

Lesson 3   Other Ways of Eliminating Run-on Sentences

A run-on sentence can be corrected in ways other than by dividing it into separate sentences.

Comma and Connecting Word

A comma and a connecting word (*and, but, or, nor, for, yet*) may be added after the first complete thought in a run-on sentence.

Incorrect: *A hard-boiled egg will spin a soft-boiled egg will not spin.*
Correct: *A hard-boiled egg will spin, but a soft-boiled egg will not spin.*

Semicolon

If the two ideas in a run-on sentence are closely related, a semicolon may be used at the end of the first complete sentence.

A hard-boiled egg will spin; a soft-boiled egg will not spin.

Sometimes a special kind of connecting word or phrase is used with a semicolon. The connecting word shows how the parts of the sentence are related.

A hard-boiled egg will spin; <u>however,</u> a soft-boiled egg will not spin.

Notice that a comma follows a connecting word that is used with a semicolon. The following connecting words and phrases often appear with semicolons when they join sentences.

as a result	in addition	nevertheless
besides	in fact	otherwise
consequently	instead	still
for example	likewise	therefore
furthermore	moreover	thus
however		

Compound Sentences

A sentence that expresses two complete thoughts joined with a comma and a connecting word such as *and* is called a *compound sentence*. A sentence in which two complete thoughts are connected by a semicolon is also a compound sentence. The following are both compound sentences.

Meteorologists prepare weather maps for a region, and these maps are used in forecasting weather.
Farmers need accurate weather forecasts; these predictions make it possible to protect crops.

A sentence containing a connecting word such as *and, or,* or *but* is not necessarily compound and may not require a comma.

> Weather satellites <u>photograph</u> the Earth and <u>measure</u> atmospheric temperatures.

In this sentence, *measure atmospheric temperatures* is not a complete thought. The sentence has one subject, *satellites*, and two verbs, *photograph* and *measure*. A comma after *Earth* in this sentence would be incorrect.

Use of a comma in a sentence such as the following is a common error.

> The weather service tracked the hurricane but could not predict its course.

Although this sentence contains a connecting word (*but*), it is not a compound sentence. The words *could not predict its course* do not express a complete thought.

Lesson 3 Exercise

Directions: *Edit the following items to correct all run-on sentences. Use any of the methods described in this lesson or in Lesson 2. Not all of the items have errors.*

1. An anteater is almost six feet long, its mouth is only an inch wide.
2. Great Britain has few natural resources therefore foreign trade is important to its economy.
3. The grand jury heard the evidence and issued an indictment against the commissioner.
4. The parachute was invented before the airplane, it was designed to help people jump from burning buildings.
5. More than 500 kinds of grass grow in Texas the largest city in Texas is Houston.
6. Thyme grows well in dry soil many gardeners grow this herb.
7. Tomato plants need sunlight, they can be grown in almost any soil.
8. The state of Arizona has never adopted daylight saving time, nor has Hawaii adopted it.
9. The invention of the steam engine made fast river travel possible it encouraged the expansion of railroads.
10. In 1953 the first color television broadcasts were made however few homes had color sets then.

Answers are on page A-6.

Skill 1 Review

Directions: Edit the following items to correct all errors in complete sentence structure. Not all of the items have errors.

1. The Soviet Union is the largest country in the world, Canada is the second largest.
2. Honey is the only food that does not spoil it has been found in the tombs of ancient Egyptians.
3. Ball lightning is often observed but has never been explained.
4. Professional tea tasters as well as wine tasters.
5. The A&P was the first established chain-store business it began in 1842.
6. The white shark is always hungry; therefore its appetite is never satisfied.
7. More Italians live in New York City than in Rome more Irish live in New York City than in Dublin.
8. More than one-third of the world's pineapples.
9. Theodore Roosevelt was the first president to ride in a car, Andrew Jackson was the first president to ride in a railroad train.
10. Type O is the most common blood type in the world, type AB is the rarest.

Check your answers. Correct answers are on page A-6. If you have at least eight answers correct, go on to Skill 2. If you have fewer than eight answers correct, study Skill 1 beginning with Lesson 1.

Skill 2 Coordination and Subordination

Preview

Directions: Edit the following sentences to correct all errors in coordination and subordination. Not all of the sentences have errors.

1. When you pay your full credit-card balance you may not have to pay interest.
2. Laser beams are being used in eye surgery although because they make the surgery safer.
3. Babe Ruth holds the record for hitting the most home runs in a 154-game season, next he hit a total of sixty.

4. **The first president to be born in the United States was Martin Van Buren, and he was born in 1782; on the other hand, the earlier presidents were born in the colonies, for the United States of America came into existence in 1776.**
5. **If you rent an apartment, it is a good idea to have renter's insurance.**

Check your answers. Correct answers are on pages A-6–A-7. If you have at least four answers correct, do the Skill 2 Review on page 110. If you have fewer than four answers correct, study Skill 2 beginning with Lesson 1.

Lesson 1 Coordination

A sentence that includes two or more complete ideas of equal importance is a compound sentence. The ideas in a compound sentence may be joined with a comma and a connecting word (*and, but, or, nor, for*). The ideas may also be joined with a semicolon and a special connecting word or phrase (such as *therefore* or *for example*). The words used to connect the complete ideas in a compound sentence are called *coordinators*.

Different coordinators express different relationships. Here is a list of the most commonly used coordinators, classified according to the relationship each expresses.

1. Coordinators that add one idea to another: *and, besides, furthermore, in addition, likewise, moreover.*
2. Coordinators that contrast one idea with another: *but, however, instead, nevertheless, on the contrary, on the other hand, still, yet.*
3. Coordinators that show time or order: *afterward, later, meanwhile, next, then.*
4. Coordinators that show a result or a conclusion: *accordingly, as a result, consequently, hence, so, therefore, thus.*
5. Coordinators that show a reason or an example: *for, for example, for instance, indeed, in fact, that is.*
6. Coordinators that express choice between ideas: *either . . . or, neither . . . nor, or, otherwise, nor.*

When joining ideas in a compound sentence, remember the following points.

1. The ideas in a compound sentence must be related in some way.

   Incorrect: *Yosemite National Park is located in California, and we took a vacation to Colorado.*
   Correct: *Yosemite National Park is located in California, and it contains high waterfalls and redwood trees.*

The unrelated ideas about Yosemite National Park and a vacation in Colorado do not belong in the same sentence.

2. The coordinator used should clearly express the relationship between ideas.

> Incorrect: *Depression is a common problem; however, it affects one person in five at some time.*
> Correct: *Depression is a common problem; in fact, it affects one person in five at some time.*

The ideas in this sentence are not in contrast to one another, so *however* is an incorrect choice of coordinator.

3. Sentences should not contain too many ideas.

> Incorrect: *The origin of ice hockey has been traced back to the time of the ancient Greeks; afterward, they passed it on to the Romans, and probably most of the American Indian tribes played it for hundreds of years; therefore, the game of ice hockey has a long history.*
> Correct: *The origin of ice hockey has been traced back to the time of the ancient Greeks; afterward, they passed it on to the Romans. Probably most of the American Indian tribes played it for hundreds of years. The game of ice hockey has a long history.*

Sentences that have too many ideas are difficult to understand. To correct this problem, divide this type of sentence into shorter sentences, as shown above.

Lesson 1 Exercise

Directions: Edit the following sentences to correct all errors in sentence coordination. Not all of the sentences have errors.

1. Amendments have been added to our Constitution; meanwhile, the income-tax amendment was added in 1913.

2. Calendar changes were made in the fourteenth century; as a result, Christmas was no longer celebrated on January 6.

3. The Klondike is a region of northwest Canada, and the United States and Canada have remained allies.

4. Cortez introduced horses to the American continent, but he brought them in his conquest of Mexico in 1519.

5. You might think that the cuttlefish is a fish, but it is actually a mollusk; in fact, it has sucker-bearing arms, and it ejects an inklike fluid; moreover, this fluid can be used in drawing.

Answers are on page A-7.

Lesson 2 Subordination

Sometimes a sentence contains two ideas, one of which is more important than the other. The more important idea is the *main idea*, and the idea that has less importance is the *subordinate idea*.

Although Bill Cosby was a high-school dropout, he eventually became a college graduate.

The main idea, *he eventually became a college graduate*, is complete. The subordinate idea, *Although Bill Cosby was a high-school dropout*, is a sentence fragment. The main idea may appear first or second, but it is always a complete thought.

Here is a list of the most common words that are used to connect ideas of unequal rank in a sentence. These words are called *subordinators*.

after	as though	since	whenever
although	because	so that	where
as	before	though	wherever
as if	even though	unless	while
as long as	if	until	
as soon as	in order that	when	

When joining ideas of unequal rank in a sentence, remember the following points.

1. Only one subordinator should be used at a time.

   Incorrect: *General Motors began to use robots since when manufacturing costs had to be reduced.*
   Correct: *General Motors began to use robots when manufacturing costs had to be reduced.*

2. The two sentence ideas must be related in some way.

   Incorrect: *Even though Florida is a popular vacation spot, I dislike rough boat rides.*
   Correct: *Even though Florida is a popular vacation spot, we decided it was not the place for us.*

3. A coordinator should not be used when ideas of unequal rank are joined by a subordinator.

   Incorrect: *Although victory looked doubtful, but the Dodgers eventually won the game.*
   Correct: *Although victory looked doubtful, the Dodgers eventually won the game.*

4. If the subordinate idea comes first in the sentence, it is followed by a comma.

Lesson 2 Exercise

Directions: Edit the following sentences to correct all subordination errors. Not all of the sentences have errors.

1. Although stress and anxiety are often associated with the fear of failure, but they can also occur as a result of success.
2. While Ms. Cintron was taking a course in word processing she continued to use her office typewriter.
3. The shortage of trained computer personnel is not limited to top-level jobs as the Japanese continue to compete for sales.
4. Since because running improves the efficiency of the lungs and strengthens the heart, doctors advise many patients to take part in this activity.
5. Unless we pay attention to the problem of adult illiteracy, our country will not maintain its position as a leading nation.
   Answers are on page A-7.

Lesson 3 Combining Sentences

Coordinators such as *and* and *but* are often useful in making sentences less repetitious. For example, read the following sentences.

> *Gloria belongs to the block association. Harry belongs to the block association.*

These sentences can be made smoother by *combining* them:

> *Gloria and Harry belong to the block association.*

The new sentence has two subjects, *Gloria* and *Harry*, joined by the coordinator *and*. Notice that when subjects are joined by *and*, a plural verb (*belong*) is needed.
How could the following sentences be combined?

> *Mr. Hamid is baking bread.*
> *Mr. Hamid is baking muffins.*

To avoid repeating the words *Mr. Hamid is baking*, use a coordinator:

> *Mr. Hamid is baking bread and muffins.*

Other coordinators can sometimes be used to combine sentences.

I saw that movie.
I did not like it.
Combined: *I saw that movie <u>but</u> did not like it.*
The sofa is old.
The sofa is comfortable.
Combined: *The sofa is old <u>but</u> comfortable.*

Notice that commas are not used in any of the sentences in this lesson. These are not compound sentences, and it would be incorrect to use a comma when combining sentences in any of these ways.

Lesson 3   Exercise

Directions: *Edit the following pairs of sentences to make them less repetitious. Combine sentences in any of the ways used in this lesson.*

1. Elise purchased a camera. Elise purchased two rolls of film.
2. Miss Levitt's apartment is small. Miss Levitt's apartment is cozy.
3. Terry Ohlsen enjoys baseball. Terry Ohlsen does not enjoy hockey.
4. The surgeon is examining the X-rays. The therapist is examining the X-rays.
5. The senator proposed a tax cut. The senator persuaded other senators to vote for it.

Answers are on page A-7.

Skill 2   Review

Directions: *Edit the following sentences to correct all errors in coordination and subordination. Not all of the sentences have errors.*

1. As long as you order from the catalog you will receive a 10-percent discount.
2. Marco Polo was an early Italian world traveler; nevertheless, he was probably the first westerner to visit China.
3. Because honey is somewhat more healthful than sugar, you may substitute it in many recipes.

4. The Dead Sea has no outlet, but the water is so salty that fish cannot live in it.
5. Depression affects your well-being, because it affects your ability to handle daily responsibilities.
6. Foxes do not hunt in bands, yet they prefer to hunt alone.
7. Alaska and Hawaii were granted statehood in 1959, but I am originally from Nebraska.
8. Since before the Salk and Sabin vaccines were developed, polio was a national health problem.
9. The Revolutionary War lasted about seven years, and it began soon after the Declaration of Independence was signed; however, the peace treaty was not signed until January 21, 1783.
10. Unless we explore safe, new energy sources, or our energy crisis will continue.

Check your answers. Correct answers are on page A-7. If you have at least eight answers correct, go on to Skill 3. If you have fewer than eight answers correct, study Skill 2 beginning with Lesson 1.

Skill 3 Clear Sentences

Preview

Directions: Edit the following sentences to correct all errors in clarity. Not all of the sentences have errors.

1. Turning the corner, the baseball stadium suddenly came into view.
2. He hopes that he can finish college in three more years and then to visit Europe.
3. Writing clear, concise sentences is essential to effective communication.
4. Mr. and Mrs. Bohl were surprised at the heat vacationing in Arizona.
5. She is tall, having a slim appearance, with brown eyes.

Check your answers. Correct answers are on page A-7. If you have at least four answers correct, do the Skill 3 Review on page 116. If you have fewer than four answers correct, study Skill 3 beginning with Lesson 1.

Lesson 1 Clarity of Thought

It is possible for a sentence to be grammatically correct but still not express a clear meaning. Is the meaning of the following sentence easily understood?

The supervisor was talking to Jim about his next project.

Who has the next project, the supervisor or Jim? From the sentence, it is impossible to tell.

When the meaning of a sentence is unclear, it usually has one or more of the following problems.

1. *Unclear references.* Pronouns should clearly refer to their antecedents. In fact, a sentence should make sense on the first reading. If it does not, you should reword the sentence so that its meaning is clear.

Unclear: *There is a town named Tidikelt in the Sahara Desert; once, it went ten years without rainfall.*
(Does *it* refer to the town of Tidikelt or the Sahara Desert?)
Clear: *The town of Tidikelt, located in the Sahara Desert, once went ten years without rainfall.*

There may be several ways to correct an unclear reference. Any way is satisfactory if the meaning is clear and the sentence is not awkward.

2. *Unclear word choice.* The words that are used in a sentence should express an idea in the simplest way possible. Difficult words in long, involved sentences do not help to make an idea clear. Clear and simple word choice will help to make the idea understandable.

Unclear: *It has come to my attention that the committee did not communicate to you about the planned excursion; consequently, you proceeded with an alternative plan in which you occupied yourself for that period of time.*
Clear: *I realize that we did not tell you about our plans; consequently, you had something else to do that day.*
Unclear: *The execution of a single stitch at an appropriate opportunity may eliminate the necessity for additional needlework in the future.*
Clear: *A stitch in time saves nine.*

3. *Unclear ideas caused by wordiness.* Using more words than you need to express an idea is called *wordiness*. Wordiness is often caused by unclear word choice, as you can see in the examples above. Sometimes, however, a short sentence can be wordy. Avoid unnecessary repetition by simply getting to the point.

Wordy: *In my opinion, I think Hawaii is the most beautiful state.* (If it is your opinion, it is what you think.)
Clear: *I think Hawaii is the most beautiful state.* OR
In my opinion, Hawaii is the most beautiful state.

Lesson 1   Exercise

Directions: Edit the following sentences to correct all errors in clarity. Not all of the sentences have errors.

1. I undertook an obligation of indebtedness because I purchased furniture on a system of deferred payments.
2. The accountant studied her client's latest tax return, and she found a costly error.
3. I am positively certain that I really saw a meteor fall.
4. A ruby is red in color, and it is usually round in shape.
5. Senator Brown conferred with the president after he visited the Middle East.

Answers are on page A-7.

Lesson 2   Proper Modification

When the parts of a sentence are not presented in a logical order, the meaning of the sentence becomes unclear. For example, read the following sentences.

1. *To increase your vocabulary, I advise you frequently to read.*
2. *We gazed at the cherry blossoms walking through the park.*

In both sentences, there is some confusion. In sentence 1, does the word *frequently* belong with *advise* or *read*? It is difficult to tell. Sentence 2 appears to be saying that cherry blossoms were walking through the park. This surely is not what the writer meant to say.

Here are the correctly edited versions of these sentences.

To increase your vocabulary, I advise you to read frequently.
Walking through the park, we gazed at the cherry blossoms.

A word or phrase that describes or explains another word in a sentence is said to *modify* that word. In the edited sentences above, *frequently* modifies (or describes) *read*, and *Walking through the park* modifies *we*. A sentence should be worded so that it is clear what word a modifier is describing.

There are two basic modification errors.

1. *Dangling modifiers.* A modifying word or group of words must clearly and logically modify a word in the sentence. If there is no word that can be modified logically, the modifier is said to be a *dangling modifier*. In other words, it cannot "attach" its meaning to another word to make a clear idea.

Thirsty after running two miles, a cool drink sounded good.

One way to correct this sentence is to add a word that the modifier can logically modify.

> *Thirsty after running two miles, I thought a cool drink sounded good.*

Another way is to change the wording of the group of words that acts as the modifier.

> *Because I was thirsty after running two miles, a cool drink sounded good.*

2. *Misplaced modifiers.* A word or phrase that acts as a modifier should be placed as close as possible to the word being described. A modifier is *misplaced* if it is too far from the word it modifies. A misplaced modifier may make the meaning of a sentence unclear.

> Incorrect: *Jan lent the bicycle to her cousin with new tires.*
> Correct: *Jan lent the bicycle with new tires to her cousin.*

The phrase *with new tires* modifies, or describes, the bicycle, not the cousin.

Lesson 2   Exercise

Directions: Edit the following sentences to correct all modification errors. Not all of the sentences have errors.

1. Walking through the White House, a feeling of awe might overtake you.
2. He bought a minivan from a friend with power steering.
3. Laughing quietly, Mrs. Perez closed the book and returned it to the shelf.
4. Sitting in the rocking chair, Whistler painted his mother.
5. Entering the theater, the curtain was just beginning to rise.

Answers are on page A-7.

Lesson 3   Parallel Structure

Read the following sentence, which mentions three activities that Luisa likes.

> Luisa likes to swim, to bowl, and to ride horses.

Notice that each activity is named with the word *to* and a verb: *to swim, to bowl, to ride.* The activities have similar roles in the sentence because all are things Luisa likes to do. When ideas have similar roles in a sentence, they should be worded with similar, or *parallel*, structures.

The following sentences do not have parallel structure. Decide what is incorrect about each one.

1. *To think, to create, and dreaming are the rights of every person.*
2. *Some people in our country are hungry, poor, and don't have jobs.*

In sentence 1, the similar items are not expressed in the same form. Two ideas begin with the word *to* (*to think, to create*), but the third idea (*dreaming*) ends in *-ing*. To give this sentence parallel structure, choose either form and use it for all related items.

To think, to create, and to dream are the rights of every person.
OR
Thinking, creating, and dreaming are the rights of every person.

In sentence 2, three ideas describe some people. The sentence would have parallel structure if *don't have jobs* was replaced by a descriptive word expressing the same idea:

Some people in our country are hungry, poor, and unemployed.

When you check a sentence for parallel structure

1. See if the sentence has a listing in it. The connecting words *and, or, nor,* or *but also* are used most often.
2. Check to make sure each item in the listing is written in the same form.
3. If there is an error in parallel structure, change the sentence so that each part of the listing is written in the same form.

Lesson 3   Exercise

Directions: Edit the following sentences to correct all errors in parallel structure. Not all of the sentences have errors.

1. His latest movie was exciting, informative, and had a lot of interest.
2. Her reputation was that of a dedicated, sincere, and knowledgeable person.
3. Remedies used in the fourteenth century to eliminate the Black Plague included killing all swallows, smoking tobacco, and wear packets of arsenic.
4. At the age of 35, Dr. Cott had acheived neither success nor to be famous.
5. Inventing wax paper, developing the electric light, and to design the motion picture camera were some of Thomas Edison's important contributions.

Answers are on page A-8.

Chapter 2: Sentence Structure

Skill 3   Review

Directions: Edit the following sentences to correct all errors in clarity. Not all of the sentences have errors.

1. The Yo-Yo was originally designed to be a weapon; it weighed four pounds and had a 20-foot cord developed in the sixteenth century.
2. During the Middle Ages, German men went to the barber to get a shave and taking a bath.
3. There is an old car in that shed; it needs a coat of paint.
4. You cannot sneeze and keep your eyes open at the same time.
5. During the peace demonstration, the building was surrounded on all sides.
6. Jack tried not only to follow the recipe but also to adjust it for ten servings.
7. Staring at the bulldozer, the last wall of the old building fell.
8. Doctors recommend plenty of sleep, an adequate diet, and to exercise regularly for their patients.
9. At the beginning of the trip, Vincent at first felt nervous.
10. I would rather read the newspaper than watching the news on television.

Check your answers. Correct answers are on page A-8. If you have at least eight answers correct, go on to the Chapter 2 Quiz. If you have fewer than eight answers correct, study Skill 3 beginning with Lesson 1.

Chapter 2   Quiz

Directions: Edit these sentences to correct all errors in sentence structure: incomplete or run-on sentences, improper coordination and subordination, and unclear sentences. No sentence has more than one error, although not all of the sentences have errors.

1. The white area on an archery target is worth one point the red area is worth seven points.
2. Although deaf, dumb, and blind, English, German, and French were the languages spoken by Helen Keller.

3. An American Olympic decathlon winner in 1976.
4. Willa showed the canary to her friend in the cage.
5. The George Washington Bridge joins New York and New Jersey, the Oakland Bay Bridge joins Oakland and San Francisco.
6. Excited by the applause, the performance of the actors became even better.
7. An island located off the coast of South America.
8. The members of the debating team were instructed to be organized, to be prepared, and speak clearly.
9. The Pacific is the largest, and the deepest ocean.
10. The Lincoln Memorial is the building pictured on the back of the five-dollar bill.
11. Millie wears glasses for reading she does not need them for traveling.
12. For that reason that is why I cannot attend the meeting.
13. After the Salk vaccine was successfully tested it was distributed nationally in 1955.
14. Excavating, ordering materials, and to make bids for contracts are part of a contractor's job.
15. Canberra is the capital of Australia; also, many people think that Sydney is.
16. John Kennedy was the first Catholic to become president he was also the youngest elected president.
17. Wiley Post made the first solo airplane flight around the world, but I do not like to fly.
18. Americans are becoming more informed about their health, which is wonderful.
19. Although while it is thought that most people have credit cards, fewer than three in ten actually own one.
20. By wearing the glass slipper, the prince was able to identify Cinderella.

Answers are on page A-8.

Chapter 3 Mechanics

Objective

In this chapter, you will learn about

- Capitalization
- Punctuation
- Spelling

Skill 1 Capitalization

Preview

Directions: Edit the following sentences to correct all errors in capitalization. Not all of the sentences have errors.

1. There are twelve players on a canadian football team.
2. The acme packing company provided uniforms for the first Green Bay Packers football team.
3. Weather forecasters are predicting a mild Winter this year.
4. In 1643, the Puritans enacted a law in England that made the singing of christmas carols a crime.
5. Queen Elizabeth I of England ended the war with France soon after she succeeded her half-sister to the throne.

Check your answers. Correct answers are on page A-8. If you have at least four answers correct, do the Skill 1 Review on page 122. If you have fewer than four answers correct, study Skill 1 beginning with Lesson 1.

Lesson 1 Proper Nouns and Proper Adjectives

A word is *capitalized* if it begins with a capital letter. The first word of a sentence should always be capitalized to show that it is the beginning of a sentence. In addition, certain kinds of adjectives should always be capitalized.

Rule 1: A *proper noun* names a specific person, place, or thing. A specific thing could be an organization, an institution, a language, a religion, a publication, a business, a vehicle, an award, or a building. A proper noun should always be capitalized.

Names of People	Names of Places	Names of Things
John Kennedy	Wisconsin	*Newsweek*
Barbara Walters	San Diego	Atlanta Braves
Bill Cosby	Mexico	*U.S.S. Titanic*
Jane Goodall	Lake Erie	Academy Award

Rule 2: An adjective is a word that describes a noun or a pronoun. When an adjective is formed from a proper noun, it is called a *proper adjective*. Proper adjectives should always be capitalized.

Proper Noun	Proper Adjective
America	American exports
Japan	Japanese cooking
New England	New England fisheries

NOTE: A proper adjective is always capitalized, but the noun that it modifies is not capitalized.

Lesson 1 Exercise

Directions: *Edit the following sentences to correct all capitalization errors. Not all of the sentences have errors.*

1. In Boston, the Red Sox play in fenway park.
2. The largest privately owned ranch in the United States is parker ranch in Hawaii.
3. In 1915, a british ship, the *lusitania*, was sunk by a german submarine.
4. We visited the Grand Canyon on our way to California.
5. The founder of the american red cross Society was Clara Barton.

Answers are on page A-9.

Lesson 2 Titles of People and Addresses

A person's name is always capitalized because it is a proper noun. In addition, titles of people are also capitalized.

Rule 1: The first letter of an abbreviation that stands for a title, such as *Mr., Mrs., Ms.,* or *Dr.,* is always capitalized.

    Mrs. Johnson   *Ms. Carlson*
    Dr. Palmer   *Mrs. Lee*

Rule 2: The title of a person, when it is used as part of a person's name, is always capitalized.

    President Johnson   *Reverend Williams*
    Senator Dole   *Sergeant Weston*

Titles that are *not* used as part of a person's name are not capitalized.

Lyndon Johnson became president of the United States in 1964.
The sergeant was assigned a new job.
Jake Garn, a senator from Utah, took part in a space shuttle flight.

Rule 3: Words such as *aunt, uncle, mother,* and *father* are capitalized only when they are used as part of a person's name.

We enjoyed seeing the pictures that Aunt Vera took in Arizona.

Titles indicating family relationships are not capitalized when they are not part of a person's name.

I spoke to my father about my plans. My uncle will stay with us for three weeks.

The names of streets and highways are capitalized. Abbreviations of streets and highways are also capitalized.

    Concord Street   *Prospect Ave.*
    Sunset Boulevard *Mason Rd.*

The words *north, south, east,* and *west* are also capitalized when they are used in addresses.

    South Elm Street   *North Lincoln Avenue*
    Sharon lives on South Michigan Avenue.

Lesson 2   Exercise

Directions: Edit the following sentences to correct all capitalization errors. Not all of the sentences have errors.

1. Many laws regulating big business were passed under president Theodore Roosevelt.

2. Many best-selling children's books have been written by dr. Seuss.
3. The president of the United States is elected to a four-year term.
4. My uncle and aunt had met Lieutenant Brown before.
5. Disneyland is located at 1313 Harbor boulevard in Anaheim, California.

Answers are on page A-9.

Lesson 3   Time, Dates, Seasons, Special Events, and Historical Eras

> **Rule 1:** The abbreviations A.M. and P.M. to show the time of day are always capitalized. The abbreviations B.C. and A.D. in reference to a specific date are also capitalized.
>
> *The memo stated that the meeting would begin at 9:30 A.M.*
> *Augustus ruled the Roman Empire from 27 B.C. to A.D. 14.*
>
> **Rule 2:** The days of the week, months of the year, and holidays are always capitalized.
>
> *In some states, Martin Luther King Day is celebrated on the third Monday in January.*
>
> **Rule 3:** The names of the seasons are not capitalized.
>
> *Heavy rains in the summer guaranteed a good fall harvest.*
>
> **Rule 4:** The names of historical events and special events are capitalized. The names of historical periods are also capitalized.
>
> *The Boston Tea Party was an act of protest by the colonists.*
> *We predicted the winner of the Kentucky Derby.*
> *The ideals of knighthood flourished during the Middle Ages.*

Lesson 3   Exercise

Directions: Edit the following sentences to correct all capitalization errors. Not all of the sentences have errors.

1. Sadie Hawkins Day falls on the first saturday after November 11.
2. The first official day of Summer is June 22.
3. The attack on Pearl Harbor occurred during world war II.
4. During the renaissance, great art and literature were developed in Europe.
5. The celebration of Easter occurs on the first Sunday after the first full moon on or after March 21.

Answers are on page A-9.

Chapter 3: Mechanics

Skill 1 Review

Directions: Edit the following sentences to correct all capitalization errors. Not all of the sentences have errors.

1. The famous carol "Silent Night" was written the day before christmas in 1818.
2. A popular soda was invented in 1886 in a drug store at 107 marietta street in Atlanta, georgia.
3. The first Steam Engine, built by John Fitch, was a toy train.
4. The average american spends about one year of his or her life talking on the telephone.
5. We decided to go to Texas during our Summer Vacation.
6. On october 31, the streets were crowded with children in halloween costumes.
7. During the civil war, general grant and general lee led the opposing armies.
8. We arrived at the observation deck of the world trade center at 4:00 p.m.
9. John Quincy Adams was the first president to live in the White House.
10. The stone age probably ended between 10,000 and 8,000 b.c.

Check your answers. Correct answers are on page A-9. If you have at least eight answers correct, go on to Skill 2. If you have fewer than eight answers correct, study Skill 1 beginning with Lesson 1.

Skill 2 Punctuation

Preview

Directions: Edit the following sentences to correct all errors in punctuation. Not all of the sentences have errors.

1. The three softest minerals are, talc, gypsum, and calcite.
2. It is a good idea to cover an air conditioner during the winter in order to prevent cold air from entering.
3. To celebrate the Fourth of July thousands of tourists visited the Statue of Liberty.
4. Many government buildings are protected by highly trained dependable guard dogs.

5. Bill Gore an Englishman, once yodeled continuously for five hours and three minutes.

Check your answers. Correct answers are on page A-9. If you have at least four answers correct, do the Skill 2 Review on page 129. If you have fewer than four answers correct, study Skill 2 beginning with Lesson 1.

Lesson 1 Commas Between Items in a Series

The word *series* means "a number of similar things arranged one after another." Many sentences include words or phrases in a series.

Rule 1: Commas are used to separate three or more items in a series.

The three primary colors are red, blue, and yellow.
The city of Houston is known for its busy port, impressive skyline, and modern freeways.

In the first example, single words—*red, blue,* and *yellow*—are listed in a series. In the second example, the items listed in a series are phrases—*busy port, impressive skyline,* and *modern freeways.* Notice that commas are used after all the items in a series except the last one.

Incorrect: *The "four C's" of the diamond business are cut, clarity, carat, and, color.*
Correct: *The "four C's" of the diamond business are cut, clarity, carat, and color.*

NOTE: Pairs of words are sometimes listed as items in a series. Each pair of words is considered to be one item.

Engineers inspect bridges and tunnels, roads and highways, and houses and office buildings.

Rule 2: Commas are not used when each of the items in a series are joined by a connecting word such as *and, or,* or *nor.*

Dogs can develop fears about thunderstorms or television or loud music.

Rule 3: When two or more adjectives modify the same noun, commas are used after each adjective.

Volunteer work can provide rewarding, valuable experience.
Large, colorful, striped fish swam in the tropical waters.

NOTE: If one of the adjectives in a series modifies another adjective in the series, the two adjectives are *not* separated by a comma.

> *A small, dark blue car blocked the driveway.*
>
> In the sentence above, *dark* is an adjective that modifies *blue*, another adjective.

Lesson 1 Exercise

Directions: Edit the following sentences to correct all punctuation errors. Not all of the sentences have errors.

1. Avoid buying toys that have sharp points, and unfinished surfaces.
2. The exhausted, courageous, and relieved, runner crossed the finish line.
3. The United States Postal Service maintains that neither snow nor sleet nor dark of night will stop mail delivery.
4. The words, *beginner, novice, intermediate,* and *expert,* are used to classify the abilities of cross-country skiers.
5. The three color words in the English language that have no rhyme are, *orange, silver,* and *purple.*

Answers are on page A-9.

Lesson 2 Commas in Compound Sentences

Two sentences that express related ideas can be joined to form a *compound sentence*.

> Sentence 1: *Many old Mexican cities were rebuilt by Spanish settlers.*
> Sentence 2: *The plaza is still the center of city life.*
> Compound Sentence: *Many old Mexican cities were rebuilt by Spanish settlers, and the plaza is still the center of life.*

In the example above, the word *and* is used to join the two separate sentences.

Words that join two sentences to form a compound sentence are called *coordinators*. *And, but, yet, or, nor,* and *for* can be used as coordinators.
When punctuating a compound sentence, a comma is needed before the coordinator.

> *The urban population of the United States has increased steadily, but many young people move to rural areas every year.*
> *Wires that carry electric current must be insulated, or serious accidents can occur.*

NOTE: If the two complete ideas that are expressed in a compound sentence are very short, you may omit the comma.

The train arrived and we boarded it.

Lesson 2   Exercise

Directions: Edit the following sentences to correct all punctuation errors. Not all of the sentences have errors.

1. The name *Chang* is the most common last name in the world but many people mistakenly think *Smith* is more common.
2. The most widespread disease in the world is tooth decay, for it affects more than 53 percent of the population of the United States.
3. The Mississippi River is the longest river in the United States and it is the nation's most important inland waterway.
4. Antibiotics are extremely helpful in fighting disease but some people develop a tolerance to them.
5. A new bus route was created and commuting time, for many people was reduced greatly.

Answers are on page A-9.

Lesson 3   Commas After Introductory Elements

The following sentences begin with a word or a group of words that introduce each sentence but are not part of the main idea. These words are called *introductory elements*.

Yes, Mount Everest is the highest point on Earth.
Since it was first conquered in 1953, more than 15 groups have successfully reached its summit.

Introductory elements are usually followed by a comma. The following rules illustrate the kinds of introductory elements that require a comma after them.

Rule 1: Words such as *yes*, *no*, *well*, *however*, *therefore*, and *besides* that appear at the beginning of a sentence are always followed by a comma.

No, I did not realize the marathon was held today.
However, I will be able to see the highlights on television tonight.

Rule 2: When a writer uses *direct address*, he or she addresses remarks directly to a person or to a group of people. Names or expressions used in direct address are always followed by a comma.

Joyce, I would like a copy of your report.
Ladies and gentlemen, the meeting is about to begin.

Rule 3: Many introductory phrases are followed by a comma.

Measuring only 19 inches wide, St. John's Lane in Rome is the narrowest street in the world.
Looking through old magazines, Tom found an article about the history of jazz.
Pedaling rapidly, the bicycle rider circled the park twice.

Rule 4: Some sentences express two ideas: a main idea and a subordinate idea. A subordinate idea is a sentence fragment—it does not express a complete thought. When a subordinate idea appears at the beginning of the sentence, it is followed by a comma.

After he left Scotland to make his fortune in the United States, Andrew Carnegie began working in a factory for $1.20 a week.
Since computers have few mechanical parts, they require little maintenance.

Lesson 3 Exercise

Directions: Edit the following sentences to correct all punctuation errors. Not all of the sentences have errors.

1. After years of training professional divers learn to land in water that is only 12 feet deep.
2. Nevertheless it is important to set goals for yourself throughout your life.
3. Covering eight acres of ground the Goodyear Airship hanger is the largest hanger in the world.
4. No, I did not know that astronauts must not be more than six feet tall.
5. Students and faculty I am proud to announce the winners of the scholarship contest.

Answers are on pages A-9—A-10.

Lesson 4 Commas with Sentence Interrupters

Sometimes, a group of words in a sentence explains or describes a noun in the sentence.

Loretta Lynn, a popular country and western singer, was a grandmother at the age of 29.

In the sentence above, the phrase *a popular country and western singer* describes Loretta Lynn, the subject of the sentence. The phrase is not essential to the meaning of the sentence, but it provides additional information about the subject. Phrases that "interrupt" a sentence in this way are set off from the rest of the sentence by commas.

Interrupting phrases can be long or short.

Brick, the oldest manufactured building material, was used by the Egyptians more than 7,000 years ago.
The longest river in the world, the Nile, empties into the Mediterranean Sea.

In the first sentence, the phrase *the oldest manufactured building material,* describes brick. In the second sentence, *the Nile* identifies the longest river in the world.

If a word or phrase that describes a noun in a sentence is essential to the meaning of the sentence, it is *not* set off by commas.

The album Can't Slow Down *won a Grammy Award in 1984.*
Your friend Michael called earlier today.

In the first sentence, the name of the album, *Can't Slow Down*, is needed to make the meaning of the sentence clear. Without it, you would not know which album won the Grammy Award. Similarly, the meaning of the second sentence would not be clear without the name *Michael*, which tells *which* friend called.

The main idea of a sentence may be also interrupted by an expression that simply adds a "pause" to the sentence.

Swimming, in my opinion, is a much more enjoyable exercise than jogging.

The words *in my opinion* do not add information to the main idea of the sentence.

Common expressions that are used as sentence interrupters are:

I believe	on the contrary	after all
I think	on the other hand	by the way
I hope	incidentally	of course
I know	in my opinion	for example
I am sure	nevertheless	however

The crowd, nevertheless, was calm and cooperative.
Ignition systems in cars, for example, are now electronic.

Like other interrupters that are not essential to the main idea of the sentence, these expressions are set off by commas from the rest of the sentence.

Lesson 4 Exercise

Directions: Edit the following sentences to correct all punctuation errors. Not all of the sentences have errors.

1. A caterpillar I believe has more than 2,000 muscles.
2. *E*, by the way is the most frequently used letter in the English alphabet.
3. The nursery rhyme, "Old King Cole," is based on a real king who ruled England about 2,000 years ago.
4. The right lung, however, takes in more air than the left.
5. Charles Dickens the British novelist never graduated from grade school.

Answers are on page A-10.

Lesson 5 Avoiding Overuse of Commas

In Lessons 1 through 4, the use of commas to punctuate elements in sentences was discussed. This lesson is about when *not* to use commas. The comma is the most frequently misused punctuation mark. Many writers make the mistake of using commas unnecessarily or incorrectly.

The chart below shows the mistakes that are most frequently made in using commas. Compare the italicized portions of the correct and incorrect sample sentence as you read each pair of sentences.

Rule	Incorrect	Correct
Do not use a comma between the subject and verb of a sentence.	One of the most popular movies ever *made, was Gone With the Wind.*	One of the most popular movies ever *made was Gone With the Wind.*
Do not use commas with compound subjects or with compound verbs.	A mile *on land, and* a mile on the ocean are not the same distance.	A mile *on land and* a mile on the ocean are not the same distance.
Do not use a comma between two complete sentences that are not joined by a coordinator.	Judy Garland's real name was *Frances Gumm, Natalie Wood's* was Natasha Gurdin.	Judy Garland's real name was *Frances Gumm, and Natalie Wood's* was Natasha Gurdin. (NOTE: If the two sentences are *not* joined, *Frances Gumm* should be followed by a period.)

Rule	Incorrect	Correct
Do not use a comma after a coordinator that joins two complete sentences.	The United Nations was formed in *1942 but,* its charter was not signed until 1945.	The United Nations was formed in *1942, but* its charter was not signed until 1945.
Do not use a comma before the first item in a series or before the last one.	A meal that is high in fat *includes, a hamburger, French fries, and, a milkshake.*	A meal that is high in fat *includes a hamburger, French fries, and a milkshake.*
Do not use a comma to separate an adjective from the noun it describes.	The new restaurant serves tasty, *inexpensive, food.*	The new restaurant serves tasty, *inexpensive food.*

Lesson 5 Exercise

Directions: *Edit the following sentences to correct all punctuation errors. Not all of the sentences have errors.*

1. Colorful flowers, and many kinds of vegetation, cover some deserts after a rainfall.
2. Decisions in a democracy are made according to majority rule, but, majority rule does not mean that the majority can do whatever it wants.
3. The six coins currently minted in the United States are, the penny, nickel, dime, quarter, 50-cent piece, and silver dollar.
4. London is known for its damp, foggy weather.
5. Before being named the Cleveland Indians, the team, was known as the Spiders.

Answers are on page A-10.

Skill 2 Review

Directions: *Edit the following sentences to correct all punctuation errors. Not all of the sentences have errors.*

1. If you need to reduce the amount of salt in your diet, you should not eat canned vegetables, or dill pickles, or olives.
2. The oldest stained-glass window in the world was made almost one thousand years ago and, it can be found in Bavaria, Germany.

3. There are, for example plants that consist of only one cell.

4. Never overload circuits, sockets, or extension cords.

5. Ellen please have your report ready by 10:00 A.M. today.

6. Many people change jobs because of a need to perform interesting, fulfilling, and challenging, work.

7. The monkey wrench named after Charles Moncke is a useful tool.

8. According to scientists, gold, exists on Mercury, Venus, and Mars.

9. Discovered in 1891 in Arizona Barringer Crater is the largest crater ever formed by a meteor that crashed into Earth.

10. Healthy snack foods include, carrots, cauliflower, cucumbers, green peppers and spinach.

Check your answers. Correct answers are on page A-10. If you have at least eight answers correct, go on to Skill 3. If you have fewer than eight answers correct, study Skill 2 beginning with Lesson 1.

Skill 3 Spelling

Preview

Directions: Edit the following sentences to correct all errors in spelling. Not all of the sentences have errors.

1. Eating too many carrots can make a persons' skin turn orange.
2. Delicate crystal can brake easily.
3. The swallow used small twigs to build it's nest.
4. Spinach is an excellent source of vitamins and minerals.
5. The Germans built many of they're castles along the Rhine River.

Check your answers. Correct answers are on page A-10. If you have at least four answers correct, do the Skill 3 Review on page 144. If you have fewer than four answers correct, study Skill 2 beginning with Lesson 1.

Lesson 1 Basic Spelling Rules

It is often difficult to figure out the spelling of a word in English by listening to the way it is pronounced. However, some basic spelling rules can be used when changing the form of a word, such as changing a singular noun to a plural noun or a present-tense verb to a past-tense verb.

Noun Forms

Rule 1: In general, plural nouns are formed by adding -s or -es to the singular form. The -es ending is used with nouns that end in -s, -x, -ch, or -sh:

  bench/benches   box/boxes   crash/crashes

Rule 2: Singular nouns that end in y preceded by a consonant form the plural by replacing the -y with i and adding -es:

  mystery/mysteries   party/parties

NOTE: Nouns that end in y preceded by a vowel usually form their plurals by the addition of s:

  key/keys   pulley/pulleys

Rule 3: Some nouns are the same in the singular and the plural form:

  sheep/sheep   deer/deer

Rule 4: Many singular nouns that end in -f are made plural by changing the f to v and adding -es:

  shelf/shelves   leaf/leaves

The plurals of many nouns ending in fe are formed by changing the -f to v and adding -s:

  knife/knives   life/lives

Verb Forms

Rule 5: To form the -ing form of a verb that ends in e, drop the final e:

  wave/waving   decide/deciding   precede/preceding

Rule 6: Many one-syllable verbs that end in a single consonant require a doubling of the consonant in the past tense and in the -ing form.

  wrap/wrapped/wrapping   plot/plotted/plotting
  pet/petted/petting   strum/strummed/strumming
  fit/fitted/fitting

Note that this rule applies to words that contain short vowel sounds, as illustrated in the above examples.

Lesson 1   Exercise

Directions: Edit the following sentences to correct all errors in spelling. Not all of the sentences have errors.

1. Recent discoverys in medicine have changed the way people live.

2. In many citys, trolleys used to run along main streets.

3. The train was delayed for several hours before arriving at the station.
4. The candidates runing for office appeared to have similar views.
5. Many families are prepareing their children for school by helping them learn to read.

Answers are on page A-10.

Lesson 2 Possessives

An *apostrophe* (') is used to show possession or ownership.

The world's first cat show was held in London in 1871.
The pioneers' courage enabled them to survive many hardships.

The underlined words in the above examples are *possessive nouns*. The possessive form of a noun shows that something belongs to something or to someone else.

> **Rule 1:** The possessive form of a singular noun is formed by adding an apostrophe and the letter s to the noun.
>
> | Singular Noun | Possessive Noun |
> |---|---|
> | explorer | explorer's trip |
> | Mark | Mark's car |
> | pilot | pilot's instructions |
>
> NOTE: If a singular noun ends in s, the possessive is formed in the same way—an apostrophe and the letter s are added to the noun.
>
> The audience admired the actress's performance.
>
> **Rule 2:** The possessive form of a plural noun ending in -s is made by adding only an apostrophe.
>
> | Plural Noun | Possessive Form |
> |---|---|
> | girls | girls' locker room |
> | cities | cities' mayors |
> | swimmers | swimmers' performance |
>
> **Rule 3:** The possessive form of a plural noun that does not end in s is formed by adding an apostrophe and the letter s.
>
> | Plural Noun | Possessive Form |
> |---|---|
> | children | children's game |
> | men | men's vote |

> Pronouns as well as nouns can show possession or ownership. Notice the spelling of the underlined pronoun in each pair of sentences below.
>
> *The record belongs to her. The record is* hers.
> *The next train will be our train. The next train will be* ours.
>
> **Rule 4:** Do not use an apostrophe with a possessive pronoun. The possessive pronouns *its* and *your*, for example, are frequently misspelled.
>
> Incorrect: *A kitten likes to wash it's fur.*
> Correct: *A kitten likes to wash* its *fur.*
> Incorrect: *I returned you're book to the library.*
> Correct: *I returned* your *book to the library.*

Lesson 2 Exercise

Directions: *Edit the following sentences to correct all errors in the spelling of possessive nouns and pronouns. Not all of the sentences have errors.*

1. One-fourth of Indias people live in cities.
2. The telephone companys employees attended a training course.
3. Earth's rotation on it's axis causes day and night.
4. The Dead Sea and the Caspian Sea have one thing in common—their surfaces are below sea level.
5. One of Texas' most popular tourist attractions is the Alamo.

Answers are on page A-10.

Lesson 3 Contractions

A *contraction* is a word that is formed by combining two words into one and omitting one or more letters.

Scientists did not *discover Pluto until 1930.*
Scientists didn't *discover Pluto until 1930.*

An apostrophe is used to replace the letter or letters that have been omitted in forming the contraction.

Here is a list of frequently used contractions and the words that form them.

I am	I'm
you are	you're
he is, he has	he's
she is, she has	she's
it is, it has	it's
we are	we're
they are	they're
I will	I'll
you will	you'll
he will	he'll
she will	she'll
we will	we'll
I have	I've
you have	you've
we have	we've
they have	they've
I would	I'd
is not	isn't
are not	aren't
was not	wasn't
were not	weren't
cannot	can't
could not	couldn't
should not	shouldn't
would not	wouldn't
who is	who's
let us	let's
of the clock	o'clock

Possessive pronouns such as *its*, *your*, and *their* are frequently confused with contractions.

Contraction: <u>It's</u> harder to breathe at high altitudes.
Possessive Pronoun: *The bird spread <u>its</u> wings.*
Contraction: *I think <u>you're</u> right.*
Possessive Pronoun: *I agree with <u>your</u> opinion.*
Contraction: <u>They're</u> *ready to leave now.*
Possessive Pronoun: *The students completed <u>their</u> work.*

NOTE: The apostrophe in a contraction always replaces the missing letter(s).

	Correct	**Incorrect**
do not	don't	do'nt

Lesson 3 Exercise

Directions: Edit the following sentences to correct all errors in the spelling of contractions. You may need to respell some words as contractions. Not all of the sentences have errors.

1. If your suffering from *islomania*, you have an irresistible attraction to islands.
2. Some of the company's employees think their overworked.
3. Do'nt believe that Swiss steak originated in Switzerland; it was invented in the United States.
4. Its true that Thomas Jefferson was the first president to serve spaghetti at a state dinner.
5. Wasn't Admiral Richard E. Byrd the first person to explore Antarctica by airplane?

Answers are on page A-10.

Lesson 4 Frequently Confused Words

Words that are pronounced the same way but that are spelled differently and have different meanings are called *homonyms*.

In writing, using the wrong homonym is considered a spelling error.

Incorrect: The <u>principle</u> cause of accidents is carelessness.
Correct: The <u>principal</u> cause of accidents is carelessness.

In this example, the writer wishes to say that the main cause of accidents is carelessness. The word *principal* means "main" or "major." (The head of a school is also called the *principal*.) The word *principle*, on the other hand, means "a basic law," as in a *scientific principle*.

The following pairs of words are homonyms that are frequently confused. Study the list carefully.

1.	already	previously
	all ready	(1) completely ready, (2) everyone ready
2.	altar	a table or stand in a church
	alter	to change
3.	altogether	completely or entirely
	all together	everyone or everything in the same place
4.	bored	not interested
	board	(1) a piece of wood, (2) a group of people who set policy
5.	brake	a device used to stop a machine
	break	to fracture

6.	Capitol	the name of a building in Washington, D.C.
	capital	the official seat of government in a state
7.	coarse	rough
	course	(1) part of a meal, (2) subject studied in school
8.	complement	something that completes something else
	compliment	a flattering remark
9.	dessert	the final course of a meal
	desert	(1) to leave, (2) a dry region
10.	herd	a group of cattle
	heard	the past tense of the verb *to hear*
11.	miner	a worker in a mine
	minor	of little importance
12.	passed	the past tense of the verb *to pass*
	past	(1) time that has gone by, (2) beyond in position
13.	peace	the opposite of war
	piece	a part of something
14.	plain	(1) clear, (2) ordinary, (3) flat land
	plane	(1) an airplane, (2) a tool
15.	principal	(1) head of a school, (2) main
	principle	a basic law or rule of action
16.	stationery	writing paper
	stationary	in a fixed position
17.	there	(1) in that place, (2) expletive, as in "There is no problem."
	their	a possessive pronoun
18.	to	indicates direction
	too	also; excessive
	two	the number 2
19.	waist	a part of the body
	waste	(1) to squander, (2) unused material
20.	whether	if, as in "I will check whether the mail arrived."
	weather	outdoor conditions

Lesson 4 Exercise

Directions: *Edit the following sentences to correct all homonym errors. Not all of the sentences have errors. Some sentences may have more than one error.*

1. We visited the capital building as part of our coarse in United States government.

UNIT I: WRITING SKILLS, PART 1: GRAMMAR Skill 3: Lesson 5 **137**

2. I asked for another piece of pie, since dessert is my favorite part of a meal.
3. The principal spoke too the students who had already completed their studies.
4. The plain past over the Rocky Mountains.
5. Receiving a miner compliment can altar the way you feel about yourself.

Answers are on pages A-10.

Lesson 5 Spelling List

To reduce the chances of making spelling errors, always refer to your dictionary when you are uncertain of the spelling of a word. When you have finished writing, check your work for errors in the use of homonyms, contractions, and the possessive forms of nouns and pronouns.

Study the following list of frequently misspelled words. These words, and forms of these words, should be reviewed as part of your preparation for the GED Writing Skills Test.

Master List of Frequently Misspelled Words

a lot	across	almost
ability	address	already
absence	addressed	although
absent	adequate	altogether
across	advantageous	always
abundance	advantage	amateur
accept	advertise	American
acceptable	advertisement	among
accident	advice	amount
accommodate	advisable	analysis
accompanied	advise	analyze
accomplish	advisor	angel
accumulation	aerial	angle
accuse	affect	annual
accustomed	affectionate	another
ache	again	answer
achieve	against	antiseptic
achievement	aggravate	anxious
acknowledge	aggressive	apologize
acquaintance	agree	apparatus
acquainted	aisle	apparent
acquire	all right	appear

Master List of Frequently Misspelled Words (*continued*)

appearance	benefit	clothes
appetite	benefited	clothing
application	between	coarse
apply	bicycle	coffee
appreciate	board	collect
appreciation	bored	college
approach	borrow	column
appropriate	bottle	comedy
approval	bottom	comfortable
approve	boundary	commitment
approximate	brake	committed
argue	breadth	committee
arguing	breath	communicate
argument	breathe	company
arouse	brilliant	comparative
arrange	building	compel
arrangement	bulletin	competent
article	bureau	competition
artificial	burial	compliment
ascend	buried	conceal
assistance	bury	conceit
assistant	bushes	conceivable
associate	business	conceive
association	cafeteria	concentration
attempt	calculator	conception
attendance	calendar	condition
attention	campaign	conference
audience	capital	confident
August	capitol	congratulate
author	captain	conquer
automobile	career	conscience
autumn	careful	conscientious
auxiliary	careless	conscious
available	carriage	consequence
avenue	carrying	consequently
awful	category	considerable
awkward	ceiling	consistency
bachelor	cemetery	consistent
balance	cereal	continual
balloon	certain	continuous
bargain	changeable	controlled
basic	characteristic	controversy
beautiful	charity	convenience
because	chief	convenient
become	choose	conversation
before	chose	corporal
beginning	cigarette	corroborate
being	circumstance	council
believe	citizen	counsel

Master List of Frequently Misspelled Words (*continued*)

counselor	disappoint	especially
courage	disappointment	essential
courageous	disapproval	evening
course	disapprove	evident
courteous	disastrous	exaggerate
courtesy	discipline	exaggeration
criticism	discover	examine
criticize	discriminate	exceed
crystal	disease	excellent
curiosity	dissatisfied	except
cylinder	dissection	exceptional
daily	dissipate	exercise
daughter	distance	exhausted
daybreak	distinction	exhaustion
death	division	exhilaration
deceive	doctor	existence
December	dollar	exorbitant
deception	doubt	expense
decide	dozen	experience
decision	earnest	experiment
decisive	easy	explanation
deed	ecstasy	extreme
definite	ecstatic	facility
delicious	education	factory
dependent	effect	familiar
deposit	efficiency	fascinate
derelict	efficient	fascinating
descend	eight	fatigue
descent	either	February
describe	eligibility	financial
description	eligible	financier
desert	eliminate	flourish
desirable	embarrass	forcibly
despair	embarrassment	forehead
desperate	emergency	foreign
dessert	emphasis	formal
destruction	emphasize	former
determine	enclosure	fortunate
develop	encouraging	fourteen
development	endeavor	fourth
device	engineer	frequent
dictator	English	friend
died	enormous	frightening
difference	enough	fundamental
different	entrance	further
dilemma	envelope	gallon
dinner	environment	garden
direction	equipment	gardener
disappear	equipped	general

Master List of Frequently Misspelled Words (*continued*)

genius	insistent	loaf
government	instead	loneliness
governor	instinct	loose
grammar	integrity	lose
grateful	intellectual	losing
great	intelligence	loyal
grievance	intercede	loyalty
grievous	interest	magazine
grocery	interfere	maintenance
guarantee	interference	maneuver
guess	interpreted	marriage
guidance	interrupt	married
half	invitation	marry
hammer	irrelevant	match
handkerchief	irresistible	material
happiness	irritable	mathematics
healthy	island	measure
heard	its	medicine
heavy	it's	million
height	itself	miniature
heroes	January	minimum
heroine	jealous	miracle
hideous	judgment	miscellaneous
himself	journal	mischief
hoarse	kindergarten	mischievous
holiday	kitchen	misspelled
hopeless	knew	mistake
hospital	knock	momentous
humorous	know	monkey
hurried	knowledge	monotonous
hurrying	labor	moral
ignorance	laboratory	morale
imaginary	laid	mortgage
imbecile	language	mountain
imitation	later	mournful
immediately	latter	muscle
immigrant	laugh	mysterious
incidental	leisure	mystery
increase	length	narrative
independence	lesson	natural
independent	library	necessary
indispensable	license	needle
inevitable	light	negligence
influence	lightning	neighbor
influential	likelihood	neither
initiate	likely	newspaper
innocence	literal	newsstand
inoculate	literature	nickel
inquiry	livelihood	niece

Master List of Frequently Misspelled Words (*continued*)

noticeable	permanence	prevalent
o'clock	permanent	primitive
obedient	perpendicular	principal
obstacle	perseverance	principle
occasion	persevere	privilege
occasional	persistent	probably
occur	persuade	procedure
occurred	personality	proceed
occurrence	personal	produce
ocean	personnel	professional
offer	persuade	professor
often	persuasion	profitable
omission	pertain	prominent
omit	picture	promise
once	piece	pronounce
operate	plain	pronunciation
opinion	playwright	propeller
opportune	pleasant	prophecy
opportunity	please	prophet
optimist	pleasure	prospect
optimistic	pocket	psychology
origin	poison	pursue
original	policeman	pursuit
oscillate	political	quality
ought	population	quantity
ounce	portrayal	quarreling
overcoat	positive	quart
paid	possess	quarter
pamphlet	possession	quiet
panicky	possessive	quite
parallel	possible	raise
parallelism	post office	realistic
particular	potatoes	realize
partner	practical	reason
pastime	prairie	rebellion
patience	precede	recede
peace	preceding	receipt
peaceable	precise	receive
pear	predictable	recipe
peculiar	prefer	recognize
pencil	preference	recommend
people	preferential	recuperate
perceive	preferred	referred
perception	prejudice	rehearsal
perfect	preparation	reign
perform	prepare	relevant
performance	prescription	relieve
perhaps	presence	remedy
period	president	renovate

Master List of Frequently Misspelled Words (*continued*)

repeat	solemn	tongue
repetition	sophomore	toward
representative	soul	tragedy
requirements	source	transferred
resemblance	souvenir	treasury
resistance	special	tremendous
resource	specified	tries
respectability	specimen	truly
responsibility	speech	twelfth
restaurant	stationary	twelve
rhythm	stationery	tyranny
rhythmical	statue	undoubtedly
ridiculous	stockings	United States
right	stomach	university
role	straight	unnecessary
roll	strength	unusual
roommate	strenuous	useful
sandwich	stretch	usual
Saturday	striking	vacuum
scarcely	studying	valley
scene	substantial	valuable
schedule	succeed	variety
science	successful	vegetable
scientific	sudden	vein
scissors	superintendent	vengeance
season	suppress	versatile
secretary	surely	vicinity
seige	surprise	vicious
seize	suspense	view
seminar	sweat	village
sense	sweet	villain
separate	syllable	visitor
service	symmetrical	voice
several	sympathy	volume
severely	synonym	waist
shepherd	technical	weak
sheriff	telegram	wear
shining	telephone	weather
shoulder	temperament	Wednesday
shriek	temperature	week
sight	tenant	weigh
signal	tendency	weird
significance	tenement	whether
significant	therefore	which
similar	thorough	while
similarity	through	whole
sincerely	title	wholly
site	together	whose
soldier	tomorrow	wretched

UNIT I: WRITING SKILLS, PART 1: GRAMMAR

Lesson 5 Exercise

Directions: In each group of words, one or more words are misspelled. Circle the misspelled words and write the correct spelling of each word in the exercise.

1. acomodate
   acheivement
   artificial
   batchelor
2. beleive
   calendar
   compell
   congradulate
3. confident
   corporel
   desireable
   different
4. doubt
   endevor
   exhorbitant
   facillity
5. Febuary
   guarrantee
   humerous
   instead
6. journel
   knew
   lightning
   maintainence
7. mispelled
   negligence
   occassional
   pamflet
8. pleasent
   quarter
   reciept
   resistence
9. supress
   sylable
   tenant
   truley
10. unecessary
    variaty
    weigh
    Wensday

Answers are on pages A-10–A-11.

Skill 3 Review

Directions: Edit these sentences to correct all spelling errors. No sentence has more than one error. Some sentences have no errors.

1. Would you beleive that Russian dressing was invented in the United States?
2. On June 6, 1933, a drive-in theater, the first of it's kind, opened in Camden, New Jersey.
3. John Jeffries was the first American to keep thorough records of whether conditions in our country.
4. Time-management courses teach you how not to waist your time.
5. The second New York World's Fair was held on the same site as the first fair.
6. Asking for someone's advise may be the first step toward forming a friendship.
7. People usualy forget a foreign language if they do not speak it for a long time.
8. Were'nt Lewis and Clark famous explorers of the western region of the United States?
9. He didn't mind keepping his promise.
10. A presidential proclamation stated that Thomas Jeffersons' birthday would be observed on April 13 every year.

Check your answers. Correct answers are on page A-11. If you have at least eight answers correct, go on to the Chapter 3 Quiz. If you have fewer than eight answers correct, study Skill 3 beginning with Lesson 1.

Chapter 3   Quiz

Directions: Edit these sentences to correct all errors in mechanics: capitalization, punctuation, and spelling. No sentence has more than one error. Some sentences have no errors.

1. The United States imports more oil then any other country.
2. In the Soviet Union, World War II is called the great patriotic war.
3. According to the U.S. Department of Agriculture the average American eats 1,425 pounds of food each year.
4. Soup is the last course in an authentic chinese meal.
5. The spice Caraway was first used in the country Turkey.
6. Walter Mondale was nominated for president in 1984.
7. Japan's largest auto makers are, Toyota, Nissan, Isuzu, Mitsubishi, Honda, and Mazda.
8. South Americas largest country is Brazil.
9. The world's tallest building the Sears Tower, is located in Chicago, Illinois.
10. There are, 42 gallons in a barrel of oil.
11. The United States air force academy is located in Colorado.
12. P.T. Barnum and his circus began they're first tour of the United States in 1835.
13. Pluto, Mickey Mouse's dog was first called *Rover*.
14. China has only one time zone but, the Soviet Union has eleven.
15. Julius Caesar was assassinated on March 15, 44 b.c.

16. The first dayly television newscast was broadcast on NBC on February 16, 1948.

17. Christopher Sholes patented a typewriter that only had capital letters.

18. The Secret Service was created by an act of Congress on june 23, 1860.

19. The Mason-Dixon Line was established to settle a border dispute between Maryland, and Pennsylvania.

20. You do'nt get rid of a bad temper by losing it.

Answers are on page A-11.

Chapter 4
Editing Paragraphs

> **Objective**
>
> In this chapter, you will learn about
>
> - The three types of questions on Part I of the GED Writing Skills Test:
>   Sentence-Correction Items
>   Sentence-Revision Items
>   Construction-Shift Items
> - The editing process, including the 5-R method of editing
> - Editing for correct usage
> - Editing for correct sentence structure
> - Editing for mechanical correctness
> - Editing paragraphs

Lesson 1 Three Types of Questions

Chapters 1 to 3 demonstrated how to recognize and correct errors in single sentences. However, we usually read or write groups of sentences. A group of sentences that is held together by a main idea is called a *paragraph*. In this chapter, you will learn how to recognize and correct errors in usage, mechanics, and sentence structure in sentences within paragraphs.

The skill of recognizing and correcting errors in written material is called *proofreading*. It is one of the skills you will need to use in order to successfully complete the GED Writing Skills Test. Altogether, this test will require that you do four basic tasks: read paragraphs, proofread sentences, evaluate suggested answers, and select answers that illustrate effective writing.

To help you to accomplish this, each sentence in a paragraph will be numbered. These numbers will correspond to the multiple-choice test items that follow each paragraph. For example, a test item might look like this:

(1) Medicines were not always as available as they are today. **(2)** Because of this, home remedies were developed by people which had to make do with what they had on hand. **(3)** For example, it was thought that lying down and putting a dime on your heart would cure a nosebleed. **(4)** Tying baked onions around your neck would help to cure a sore throat. **(5)** Medical science might laugh at these attempts; however, they clearly demonstrate imaginative thinking on the part of people who had a real need.

Sentence 2: **Because of this, home remedies were developed by people which had to make do with what they had on hand.**

What correction should be made to this sentence?

(1) remove the comma after *this*
(2) change the spelling of *remedies* to *remidies*
(3) change *were* to *are*
(4) insert a comma after *developed*
(5) replace *which* with *who*

Notice that the sentence to be corrected is repeated and is followed by five alternatives (or answers) that are presented in the order in which they occur in the sentence. These alternatives may suggest different kinds of changes in the sentence. The alternatives in this example cover spelling, punctuation, verb tense, and pronoun reference.

It is important to remember that *there is only one possible error in a given sentence*. Therefore, only one alternative can be correct in any given test item. In this example, the correct answer is alternative 5.

The Three Types of Test Items

There are three types of multiple-choice items on the Writing Skills Test. Together, they will test your knowledge of sentence structure, usage, and mechanics.

Sentence-correction items will be used in approximately 50 percent of the questions. They will test your knowledge of sentence structure, usage, spelling, punctuation, and capitalization. The sentence-correction items will repeat one of the sentences from the paragraph and then ask you to choose the correction that should be made.

Sentence 4: **For example, employees must communicate their ideas and share in the goals of the company.**

What correction should be made to this sentence?

(1) remove the comma after *example*
(2) change the spelling of *communicate* to *comunicate*
(3) replace *their* with *there*
(4) insert a comma after *ideas*
(5) no correction is necessary

Some sentences in this category may be correct as written. In several of the items, the fifth alternative will be *no correction is necessary*, and sometimes it will be the correct answer. In this example, alternative (5) is the correct choice.

Sentence-revision items will be used to test your skills in the areas of sentence structure, usage, and punctuation. A part of the sentence will be underlined and that part may or may not contain an error. Again, five alternatives will be listed. The first alternative will always be the same as the original sentence. The remaining alternatives will suggest possible ways to correct the sentence. Here is an example of a sentence-revision item.

Sentence 5: **<u>Once considered expensive toys personal</u> computers are now found in many households.**

Which of the following is the best way to write the underlined portion of this sentence? If you think the original is the best way, choose option (1).

(1) Once considered expensive toys personal
(2) Once considered expensive toys, personal
(3) Once considered, expensive toys, personal
(4) Once, considered expensive toys personal
(5) Once considered expensive, toys personal

The first four underlined words are an introductory element of the sentence. For this reason, a comma must be inserted after *toys*. The correct choice for this example is alternative (2).

Construction-shift items will also test your knowledge of sentence structure and punctuation. Unlike sentence-revision and sentence-correction items, construction-shift items do not contain errors. In these items you will need to strengthen a sentence that may be awkward or unclear. In each item, you will be given specific instructions as to how the sentence might be changed. Very often, the changes will involve combining two sentences or the combining of other elements of the sentence. Here is an example of this type of item.

Sentence 10: **My mother is staying home today. She is not feeling well.**

If you rewrote sentence 10 beginning with

My mother is not feeling well

the next word should be

(1) therefore
(2) because
(3) when
(4) if
(5) should

Carefully read the sentences for their meaning. The sentence that results from your change must have the same meaning as the original sentence or sentences and must be stated clearly. When you have identified the change, try each alternative to see which one improves the structure of the sentence. Then, check to see that your choice has not changed the meaning of the sentence. Alternative (1) is the correct choice. It shows the relationship between the two sentences that are now combined. If you need more information about combining, review Chapter 2.

Try the following exercise. If you have difficulty with it, you may need to review Chapters 1 to 3.

Lesson 1   Exercise

Directions: *Read the following sentences. They contain errors in sentence structure, usage, and mechanics. No sentence contains more than one error. Answer the questions that follow by circling the number of the* **one** *best answer for each question.*

1. Sentence 1: **Because every item in these stores were too expensive, we left without buying anything.**

    What correction should be made to this sentence?
    - (1) change *were* to *was*
    - (2) replace *too* with *to*
    - (3) remove the comma after *expensive*
    - (4) replace the comma after *expensive* with a semicolon
    - (5) no correction is necessary

2. Sentence 2: **Many people attended the <u>meeting some</u> had to leave early.**

    Which of the following is the best way to write the underlined portion of this sentence? If you think the original is the best way to write the sentence, choose option (1).
    - (1) meeting some
    - (2) meeting
    - (3) meeting, some
    - (4) Meeting. Some
    - (5) meeting and some

3. Sentence 3: **At last night's meeting, several opinions were expressed about the controversy of starting a union in the shop.**

    What correction should be made to this sentence?
    - (1) delete the apostrophe in *night's*
    - (2) insert a comma after *several*
    - (3) change the *were* to *are*
    - (4) change the spelling of *controversy* to *contraversy*
    - (5) no correction is necessary

4. Sentence 4: **Ms. Jones an exceptional worker, will receive an award and a bonus check at the April board meeting.**

    What correction should be made to this sentence?
    - (1) add a comma after *Jones*
    - (2) change the spelling of *exceptional* to *exceptonial*
    - (3) remove the comma after *worker*
    - (4) add a coma after *award*
    - (5) capitalize the words *board meeting*.

5. **Sentence 5: Women are now a significant part of our labor force; they still earn lower wages than men.**

If you rewrote sentence 5 beginning with
Women still earn lower wages than men
the next word(s) should be

(1) accordingly
(2) however
(3) likewise
(4) in fact
(5) for example

Answers are on page A-11.

Lesson 2 The Editing Process

Proofreading is a process of recognizing and correcting errors in written material. In addition, writing must also be checked for correct meaning and word choice. The process of applying all of these skills is called *editing*. To edit correctly, ask yourself the following questions about each sentence.

Is it correct? Apply your proofreading skills to look for capitalization, punctuation, grammar, and spelling errors.
Is it complete? Look for errors in sentence-structure. Every idea must be expressed in a well-written, complete sentence.
Is it clear? Check the word choice. The meaning of the sentence should be easy to understand.
Is it consistent? The sentence should be consistent in meaning and tone with the rest of the paragraph.

This lesson will introduce a process for using your proofreading and editing skills to identify and correct errors in paragraphs. It is called the 5-R method of editing.

The 5-R Method of Editing

In this method you will read, reflect, revise, reread, and record. To use this method, complete each step in this order.

Step 1. *Read.* Carefully read the paragraph for its meaning and writing style.
Step 2. *Reflect.* Read through the paragraph and underline errors that you recognize. Ask yourself: Is it correct? complete? clear? consistent?
Step 3. *Revise.* Read the first item and its alternatives. Decide which alternative identifies and corrects the error.

Step 4. *Reread.* Read the revised sentence with the selected correction. If you are satisfied with the answer, you are ready to go on to the next step. If you are not satisfied with the answer, go back to Step 3.
Step 5. *Record.* Mark the number of the alternative that you have chosen. Then, move on to the next item.

Use the following exercise to practice the 5-R method.

Lesson 2 Exercise

Directions: *Read the following paragraph. It contains errors in usage, sentence structure, and mechanics. No sentence contains more than one error. Use the 5-R method of editing to work through the first three items and to record your response at each step. Your final answer should be written on the line for Step 5.*

Items 1 to 5 are based on the following paragraph.

(1) When we think of people who have sleep disorders we usually think of people who have difficulty falling asleep. (2) This problem is called "insomnia." (3) There is, in fact, another kind of sleep disorder. (4) This kind causes uncontrollable attacks of sleep. (5) The attacks may happen anytime throughout the day. (6) In fact, its not unusual for a person suffering from this disorder to experience 15 to 20 attacks per day. (7) Each attack may last for as long as fifteen minutes, this disorder is called "narcolepsy." (8) Frequently, people have had attacks while driving cars, while using hazardous materials, or on the job. (9) For that reason, doctors feel it is a more dangerous disease then insomnia since it occurs without warning.

1. Sentence 1: **When we think of <u>people who have sleep disorders</u> we usually think of people who have difficulty falling asleep.**

   Which of the following is the best way to write the underlined portion of this sentence? If you think the original is the best way, choose option (1).

   (1) people who have sleep disorders
   (2) people, who have sleep disorders
   (3) people who have sleep disorders,
   (4) people, who have sleep disorders,
   (5) people, who have sleep disorders;

   Step 1. Read: _____
   Step 2. Reflect: _____
   Step 3. Revise: _____
   Step 4. Reread: _____
   Step 5. Record: _____

UNIT I: WRITING SKILLS, PART 1: GRAMMAR   Lesson 2   **153**

2. Sentence 3: **There is, in fact, another kind of sleep disorder.**

   What correction should be made to this sentence?

   (1) change *is* to *are*
   (2) remove the comma after *is*
   (3) remove the comma after *fact*
   (4) change the spelling of *another* to *anothur*
   (5) no correction is necessary

   Step 1. Read: _____
   Step 2. Reflect: _____
   Step 3. Revise: _____
   Step 4. Reread: _____
   Step 5. Record: _____

3. Sentence 6: **In fact, its not unusual for a person suffering from this disorder to experience fifteen to twenty attacks per day.**

   What correction should be made to this sentence?

   (1) remove the comma after *fact*
   (2) change *its* to *it's*
   (3) change the spelling of *unusual* to *unusuall*
   (4) replace *to experience* with *to have experienced*
   (5) insert a comma after *attacks*

   Step 1. Read: _____
   Step 2. Reflect: _____
   Step 3. Revise: _____
   Step 4. Reread: _____
   Step 5. Record: _____

Directions: For the next two items, do not write any response to the steps. Simply check each step after you have completed thinking about it. Circle the correct answer within the test item itself.

4. Sentence 7: **Each attack may last for as long as fifteen <u>minutes, this disorder</u> is called "narcolepsy."**

   Which of the following is the best way to write the underlined portion of this sentence? If you think the original is the best way, choose option (1).

   (1) minutes, this disorder
   (2) minutes this disorder
   (3) minutes. This disorder
   (4) minutes: this disorder
   (5) minutes: This disorder

154 Chapter 4: Editing Paragraphs

Step 1. _____
Step 2. _____
Step 3. _____
Step 4. _____
Step 5. _____

5. Sentence 8: Frequently, <u>people have had attacks</u> while driving cars, while using hazardous materials, or on the job.

   Which of the following is the best way to write the underlined portion of this sentence? If you think the original is the best way, choose option (1).

   (1) people have had attacks
   (2) people, having attacks
   (3) while driving cars, use
   (4) or while working on the job.
   (5) materials while on the job

   Step 1. _____
   Step 2. _____
   Step 3. _____
   Step 4. _____
   Step 5. _____

   Answers are on page A-11.

Lesson 3 Editing for Correct Usage

About 35 percent of the items on Part I of the GED Writing Skills Test will test your ability to recognize and correct errors in usage. To answer these questions effectively, you will need to organize your thinking in two ways.

First, follow the 5-R method of editing. Second, ask yourself these three questions.

1. *Do the subjects agree with the verbs?*

   Incorrect: One of the computers *were* on display.
   Correct: One of the computers *was* on display.

2. *Are the verbs in the correct tense?*

   Incorrect: The papers *had blew* all over the street.
   Correct: The papers *had blown* all over the street.

3. *Are the pronouns used correctly and clearly?*

   Incorrect: My sister gave Mary and *I* free concert tickets.
   Correct: My sister gave Mary and *me* free concert tickets.

As you read the following paragraph, apply the three usage questions listed above.

(1) A recent survey conducted by the Men's Clothing Retailers of America shown that most men buy clothes only to replace those that have worn out. (2) These men are more concerned with comfort than he are with fashion. (3) The survey also showed that 43 percent of the male shoppers uses the help of women when shopping.

You should have found one verb that did not agree with its subject (sentence 3), one verb that was not in the correct tense (sentence 1), and one pronoun that was not used correctly (sentence 2). If you had difficulty finding these errors, you may need to review Chapter 1 before doing the exercise for this lesson.

Lesson 3   Exercise

Directions: *Read the following paragraph. As you read, ask yourself the three basic questions that are used when editing for usage. No sentence contains more than one error. Use the 5-R method of editing as you work through each question.*

Items 1 to 5 are based on the following paragraph.

(1) John Naisbitt, in his book, *Megatrends*, says that people are becoming more concerned with our health. (2) There is several examples to prove this. (3) First, we are eating better and smarter. (4) We have reduced our fat intake. (5) We have decreased our intake of butter, milk, and cream. (6) Second, we are exercising more. (7) In 1960, only one-fourth of our population exercises regularly. (8) Today, that number had grown to almost one-half. (9) Third, we are smoking less. (10) Studies have showed that cigarette smoking is down by 28 percent. (11) Naisbitt concludes that because we want to stay healthy, you are willing to work at it.

1. Sentence 1: **John Naisbitt, in his book, *Megatrends*, says that people are becoming more concerned with our health.**

   What correction should be made to this sentence?

   (1)   remove the comma after *Naisbitt*
   (2)   change *says* to *said*
   (3)   change the spelling of *becoming* to *becomeing*
   (4)   change *our* to *their*
   (5)   no correction is necessary

2. Sentence 2: **There is several examples to prove this.**

   Which of the following is the best way to write the underlined portion of this sentence? If you think the original is the best way, choose option (1).

   (1)   There is several
   (2)   There are several

Chapter 4: Editing Paragraphs

(3) There are sevaral

(4) There is sevaral

(5) There is now several

3. **Sentences 4 and 5: We have reduced our fat intake. We have decreased our intake of butter, milk, and cream.**

   The most effective combination of sentences 4 and 5 would include which of the following groups of words?

   (1) fat intake by decreasing our intake

   (2) fat intake and we have decreased our intake

   (3) fat intake so we have decreased our intake

   (4) fat intake, intake of butter, milk, and cream.

   (5) fat intake to decrease our intake

4. Sentence 7: **In 1960, only one-fourth of our population exercises regularly.**

   What correction should be made to this sentence?

   (1) remove the comma after *1960*

   (2) insert a comma after *only*

   (3) change *our* to *are*

   (4) change *exercises* to *exercised*

   (5) change the spelling of *regularly* to *regulerly*

5. Sentence 10: **Studies have showed that cigarette smoking is down by 28 percent.**

   What correction should be made to this sentence?

   (1) change *Studies* to *Studys*

   (2) replace *showed* with *shown*

   (3) insert a comma after *that*

   (4) change *is* to *will be*

   (5) no correction is necessary

   Answers are on page A-11.

Lesson 4 Editing for Correct Sentence Structure

About 35 percent of the items in Part I of the GED Writing Skills Test will test your ability to recognize and correct errors in sentence structure. To answer these questions effectively, you will need to organize your thinking in two ways.

First, follow the 5-R method of editing. Second, ask yourself these three questions.

1. *Do all groups of words that have a subject and verb express a complete thought?*

    Incorrect: After we attend the baseball game.
    Correct: We will take the train home after we attend the baseball game.

2. *Are all compound sentences written in proper form?*

    Incorrect: Marty is on a *diet he* still eats ice cream.
    Correct: Marty is on a *diet, but he* still eats ice cream.

3. *Are the sentences clearly written and logically organized?*

    Incorrect: The police officer chased the woman down the street wearing a yellow dress.
    Correct: The woman in the yellow dress was chased down the street by a police officer.

As you read the following paragraph, apply the three sentence-structure questions that are listed above.

(1) Self-esteem is the attitude we develop about our sense of worth in society. **(2)** This attitude is influenced by the way we handle our successes and failures. **(3)** If we do not develop a balanced sense of our strengths and weaknesses, we can develop a negative view of our self-worth. **(4)** However, if we focus on our successes and learn from our mistakes. **(5)** We develop positive attitudes. **(6)** This style of thinking is called "positive thinking," it says, "It is O.K. to fail." **(7)** It also says, "I am important." **(8)** Using this kind of thinking, your self-esteem will increase.

You should have found one incomplete sentence (sentence 4), a run-on (sentence 6), and one sentence that was not written clearly (sentence 8). If you had difficulty finding these errors, you may need to review Chapter 2 before doing the exercise for this lesson.

Lesson 4 Exercise

Directions: Read the following paragraph. As you read, ask yourself the three basic questions that are used when editing for sentence structure. No sentence contains more than one error. Use the 5-R method of editing as you work through each question.

Items 1 to 5 are based on the following paragraph.

(1) Most people have used prescription drugs, too often, however, they are not told how to store these medicines properly. **(2)** Many medicines lose their effectiveness. **(3)** They need to be protected from heat and moisture. **(4)** Therefore, most prescription drugs should be stored at room temperature, out of direct sunlight, and use tightly fitting covers. **(5)** Some drugs require storage in a refrigerator this does not mean in the freezer compartment.

(6) Because many liquid medicines will separate into layers that cannot be remixed. **(7)** Stored in a medicine cabinet, you should not put drugs in a bathroom. **(8)** A bathroom changes in its humidity and temperature throughout the day. **(9)** These effects can lessen the strength of the drugs. **(10)** Following these guidelines will help to increase the effectiveness of the drugs prescribed for you.

1. Sentence 1: **Most people have used prescription drugs, too often, however, they are not told how to store these medicines properly.**

    What correction should be made to this sentence?

    (1) change the spelling of *prescription* to *perscription*
    (2) remove the comma after *drugs*
    (3) replace the comma after *drugs* with a period and capitalize *Too*
    (4) insert a semicolon after *often*
    (5) change the spelling of *medicines* to *medisines*

2. Sentences 2 and 3: **Many medicines lose their effectiveness. They need to be protected from heat and moisture.**

    The most effective combination of sentences 2 and 3 would include which of the following groups of words?

    (1) if they are not protected
    (2) so that they are not protected
    (3) although they are not protected
    (4) and they are not protected
    (5) therefore, they are not protected

3. Sentence 4: **Therefore, most prescription drugs should be stored at room temperature, out of direct sunlight, and use tightly fitting covers.**

    What correction should be made to this sentence?

    (1) remove the comma after *therefore*
    (2) change the spelling of *prescription* to *perscription*
    (3) insert a comma after *stored*
    (4) replace *use* with *with*
    (5) no correction is necessary

4. Sentence 5: **Some drugs require storage in a <u>refrigerator this does</u> not mean in the freezer compartment.**

    Which of the following is the best way to write the underlined portion of this sentence? If you think the original is the best way, choose option (1).

    (1) refrigerator this does
    (2) refrigerator, this does
    (3) refrigerator. This does
    (4) refrigerator; this does
    (5) refrigerator: this does

UNIT I: WRITING SKILLS, PART 1: GRAMMAR Lesson 5 **159**

5. Sentence 6: **Because many liquid medicines will separate into layers that cannot be remixed.**

   What correction should be made to this sentence?

   (1) remove the word *because* from the sentence
   (2) change the spelling of *medicines* to *medisines*
   (3) insert a comma after *medicines*
   (4) change the spelling of *separate* to *seperate*
   (5) no correction is necessary

   Answers are on pages A-11–A-12.

Lesson 5   Editing for Mechanical Correctness

About 30 percent of the items in Part I of the GED Writing Skills Test will test your ability to recognize and correct errors in mechanics. To answer these questions effectively, you will need to organize your thinking in two ways.

First, follow the 5-R method of editing. Second, ask yourself these three questions.

1. *Are all appropriate words capitalized correctly?*

   Incorrect: We tried sushi at the new japanese restaurant.
   Correct: We tried sushi at the new Japanese restaurant.

2. *Are all words and sentences punctuated correctly?*

   Incorrect: Janets parents will be here this Saturday.
   Correct: Janet's parents will be here this Saturday.

3. *Are all words spelled correctly?*

   Incorrect: The heighth of this year's corn crop is exceptional.
   Correct: The height of this year's corn crop is exceptional.

As you read the following paragraph, apply the three mechanics questions listed above.

(1) The first computer was huge, unreliable, and expensive. (2) It weighed 30 tons, and used 18,000 vacuum tubes. (3) One of these tubes failed every seven minuets. (4) This enormous machine cost $487,000. (5) For these reasons, only top Technical institutions could afford to have this kind of computer.

You should have found one punctuation error (sentence 2), one spelling error (sentence 3), and one capitalization error (sentence 5). If you had difficulty finding these errors, you may need to review Chapter 3 before doing the exercise for this lesson.

Lesson 5   Exercise

Directions: *Read the following paragraph. As you read, ask yourself the three basic questions that are used when editing for mechanical errors. No sentence contains more than one error. Use the 5-R method of editing as you work through each question.*

(1) Because our world is rapidly changing we must be able to adapt to change. (2) We need to become aware of the affects that these changes will have on our lives. (3) An important way, to develop awareness, is to develop a willingness to learn. (4) Those who refuse to learn, and change will find themselves outdated. (5) Those who adapt will grow to become productive members of society. (6) Ultimately, better informed citizens will help to strengthen america.

1. Sentence 1: **Because our world is rapidly changing we must be able to adapt to change.**

    What correction should be made to this sentence?
    - (1) change the spelling of *changing* to *changeing*
    - (2) insert a comma after *changing*
    - (3) change *we* to *you*
    - (4) replace *adapt* with *adopt*
    - (5) no correction is necessary

2. Sentence 2: **We need to become aware of the affects that these changes will have on our lives.**

    What correction should be made to this sentence?
    - (1) replace *affects* with *effects*
    - (2) change *these changes* to *this change*
    - (3) insert a comma after *changes*
    - (4) change *will have* to *have had*
    - (5) change the spelling of *lives* to *lifes*

3. Sentence 3: **An important <u>way, to develop awareness,</u> is to develop a willingness to learn.**

    Which of the following is the best way to write the underlined portion of this sentence? If you think the original is the best way, choose option (1).
    - (1) way, to develop awareness,
    - (2) way to develop awareness,
    - (3) way, to develop awareness;
    - (4) way to develop awareness;
    - (5) way to develop awareness

4. Sentence 4: **Those who refuse to learn, and change will find themselves outdated.**

   What correction should be made to this sentence?
   - (1) change *who* to *which*
   - (2) remove the comma after *learn*
   - (3) insert a comma after *change*
   - (4) change *will find* to *find*
   - (5) change the spelling of *themselves* to *themselfs*

5. Sentence 6: **Ultimately, better informed citizens will help to strengthen america.**

   What correction should be made to this sentence?
   - (1) remove the comma after *Ultimately*
   - (2) insert a comma after *informed*
   - (3) change the spelling of *citizens* to *citisens*
   - (4) insert a comma after *citizens*
   - (5) change the spelling of *america* to *America*

Answers are on page A-12.

Lesson 6 Editing Paragraphs

Lessons 1 to 5 showed you how to edit for correctness in three separate areas: usage, sentence structure, and mechanics. Like the GED Writing Skills Test, this lesson will show you how to edit paragraphs that combine all three content areas. You should continue to use the 5-R method of editing as you answer the items in these paragraphs. The following chart reviews the process.

5-R Step	That Means:
Read	Read the paragraph for meaning and for organization.
Reflect	Locate possible errors by asking the three groups of content questions.

        Usage
1. Do the subjects agree with the verbs?
2. Are the verbs in the correct tense?
3. Are the pronouns used correctly and clearly?

        Sentence Structure
1. Do all groups of words that have a subject and a verb express a complete thought?
2. Are all compound sentences written in proper form?

3. Are the sentences written in clear, logically organized, and consistent form?

Mechanics

1. Are all appropriate words capitalized correctly?
2. Are all words and sentences punctuated correctly?
3. Are all words spelled correctly?

Revise   Choose the correct alternative.

Reread   Check your selection.

Record   Mark your answer.

Keep these points in mind when answering the questions on the GED Writing Skills Test.

Four Points to Remember

1. You will not be told the kinds of errors that will appear in a paragraph.
2. The alternatives to an item will suggest possible errors.
3. There will be only one kind of error in each sentence.
4. Not all sentences have errors. In some items, your choice will show that the sentence is correct.

Lesson 6 Exercise

Directions: *Read the following paragraph and answer the items based on it.*

(1) One of the most enjoyable yet frustrating family experiences is the sunday drive. (2) To prepare for this, parents need to think of imaginative ideas to keep their children occupied. (3) When traveling for a long time it's a good idea to stop for rest. (4) The rest stop gives children a chance to refresh them. (5) Another idea is to pack a surprise box. (6) This could be a shoebox full of interesting items, these might include old keys, small mirrors, crayons, paper, small books, buttons, and string. (7) An additional travel aid is a food kit. (8) Taking along individual packages of cereal, pretzels, and raisins helps to keep hungry children busy. (9) Any of these ideas can be adapted to a parents budget.

1. Sentence 1: **One of the most enjoyable yet frustrating family experiences is the sunday drive.**

    What correction should be made to this sentence?

    (1) insert a comma after *enjoyable*
    (2) insert a comma after *frustrating*
    (3) change the spelling of *experiences* to *experences*
    (4) change the word *sunday* to *Sunday*
    (5) no correction is necessary

2. Sentence 3: **When traveling for a long <u>time it's</u> a good idea to stop for rest.**

   Which of the following is the best way to write the underlined portion of this sentence? If you think the original is the best way, choose option (1).
   - (1) time it's
   - (2) time, it's
   - (3) time its,
   - (4) time its
   - (5) time; it's

3. Sentence 4: **The rest stop gives children a chance to refresh them.**

   What correction should be made to this sentence?
   - (1) change *gives* to *give*
   - (2) insert a comma after *chance*
   - (3) change *refresh* to *refreshed*
   - (4) replace *them* with *themselves*
   - (5) no correction is necessary

4. Sentence 6: **This could be a shoebox full of interesting <u>items, these might</u> include old keys, small mirrors, crayons, paper, small books, buttons, and string.**

   Which of the following is the best way to write the underlined portion of this sentence? If you think the original is the best way, choose option (1).
   - (1) items, these might
   - (2) items these might
   - (3) items; these might
   - (4) items, these might,
   - (5) items; these might,

5. Sentence 9: **Any of these ideas can be <u>adapted to a parents budget.</u>**

   Which of the following is the best way to write the underlined portion of this sentence? If you think the original is the best way, choose option (1).
   - (1) adapted to a parents budget.
   - (2) adapted, to a parents budget.
   - (3) adapted to a parent's budget.
   - (4) adapted to a parents' budget.
   - (5) adapted, to a parent's budget.

   Answers are on page A-12.

Chapter 4 Quiz

1. What are the three types of items found on Part I of the GED Writing Skills Test?

   _____
   _____
   _____

2. The tasks that you complete when you use the 5-R method of editing are described below. Match the name of each step with its description.

   ____ 1. choosing the alternative   a. Reread
   ____ 2. checking your selection   b. Reflect
   ____ 3. marking your answer   c. Read
   ____ 4. locating an error   d. Record
   ____ 5. determining meaning and organization   e. Revise

3. Arrange the names of these steps in the order used in the 5-R method of editing.

   1. _____
   2. _____
   3. _____
   4. _____
   5. _____

Directions: *The following paragraph contains numbered sentences. These sentences may have errors in usage, sentence structure, or mechanics. Read each paragraph and then answer the items that are based on it. For each item, choose the answer that would result in the most effective writing of the sentence.*

Items 4 to 11 are based on the following paragraph.

(1) Many Americans are concerned about traveling in certain parts of the world because of terrorist activities. (2) There is however a much greater chance that an American would be faced with a legal problem abroad. (3) In the past, Americans are held or arrested for a variety of reasons. (4) These include not having a proper passport, taking unauthorized objects out of a country, and to possess alcohol in a country where it is illegal. (5) In addition, a person involved in a motor-vehicle accident is routinely held while the problem is investigated. (6) The U.S. Government is limited in the help that it can provide. (7) Consular officers are permitted to visit the detained person. (8) They may provide a list of local attorneys. (9) In general, however, the officers can offer help only as far as seeing that a person's rights is not violated under the local law.

4. Sentence 1: **Many Americans are concerned about traveling in certain <u>parts of the world because</u> of terrorist activities.**

   Which of the following is the best way to write the underlined portion of this sentence? If you think the original is the best way, choose option (1).
   - (1) parts of the world because
   - (2) parts of the world, because
   - (3) parts of the world. Because
   - (4) parts of the world; because
   - (5) parts of the world because,

5. Sentence 2: **<u>There is however</u> a much greater chance that an American would be faced with a legal problem abroad.**

   Which of the following is the best way to write the underlined portion of this sentence? If you think the original is the best way, choose option (1).
   - (1) There is however
   - (2) There is, however
   - (3) There is however,
   - (4) There is; however,
   - (5) There is, however,

6. Sentence 3: **In the past, Americans are held or arrested for a variety of reasons.**

   What correction should be made to this sentence?
   - (1) remove the comma after *past*
   - (2) change *Americans* to *americans*
   - (3) change *are held* to *have been held*
   - (4) insert a comma after *held*
   - (5) change the spelling of *variety* to *vareity*

7. Sentence 4: **These include not having a proper passport, taking unauthorized objects out of a <u>country, and to possess</u> alcohol in a country where it is illegal.**

   Which of the following is the best way to write the underlined portion of this sentence? If you think the original is the best way, choose option (1).
   - (1) country, and to possess
   - (2) country and to possess
   - (3) country, and possessing
   - (4) country, and possess
   - (5) country; and, possess

8. Sentence 5: **In addition, a person involved in a motor-vehicle accidant is routinely held while the problem is investigated.**

   What correction should be made to this sentence?
   - (1) remove the comma after *addition*
   - (2) change the spelling of *accidant* to *accident*
   - (3) insert a comma after *accidant*
   - (4) insert a comma after *held*
   - (5) no correction is necessary

9. Sentence 6: **The U.S. Government is limited in the help that it can provide.**
   What correction should be made to this sentence?
   (1) change *Government* to *government*
   (2) change *is* to *are*
   (3) insert a comma after *help*
   (4) replace *it* with *they*
   (5) no correction is necessary

10. Sentences 7 and 8: **Consular officers are permitted to visit the detained person. They may provide a list of local attorneys.**
    If you rewrote sentences 7 and 8 beginning with *Consular officers are permitted to assist a detained person* the next word should be
    (1) by
    (2) so
    (3) though
    (4) that
    (5) therefore

11. Sentence 9: **In general, however, the officers can offer help only as far as seeing that a person's rights is not violated under the local law.**
    What correction should be made to this sentence?
    (1) remove the comma after *general*
    (2) change the spelling of *offer* to *ofer*
    (3) change *person's* to *persons'*
    (4) change *is* to *are*
    (5) insert a comma after *violated*

Items 12 to 20 are based on the following paragraph.

    (1) Learning how to look for a job is a vital skill for anyone entering the world of work. **(2)** Many potential workers looked for jobs in the want ads, but did you know that less than 30 percent of job vacancies are advertised? **(3)** Some people use employment agencies, who charge a fee for their services. **(4)** The same services are offered, at no cost to employer or employee, by a state employment agency. **(5)** This agency offers occupational information, aptitude testing, and referral services. **(6)** About 50 percent of all applicants are placed in jobs. **(7)** The Civil Service Commission administers free tests required for government jobs, you may be placed on a long waiting list. **(8)** Networking is one of the best employment services that was available. **(9)** Networking makes use of personal contacts as an important part of the job search. **(10)** You make connections with people who can give job information, made introductions to other people, or even place people in jobs. **(11)** All of these methods requires planning and work. **(12)** However, you may ultimately reap the benefits of your time and effort by landing the "perfect" job!

12. Sentence 2: **Many potential workers looked for jobs in the want ads, but did you know that less than 30 percent of job vacancies are advertised?**

UNIT I: WRITING SKILLS, PART 1: GRAMMAR   Chapter 4 Quiz   **167**

What correction should be made to this sentence?

(1) replace *Many* with *All*
(2) change *looked* to *look*
(3) replace *less* with *fewer*
(4) change the spelling of *advertised* to *advertized*
(5) remove the question mark after *advertised*

13. Sentence 3: **Some people use employment <u>agencies, who charge</u> a fee for their services.**
    Which of the following is the best way to write the underlined portion of this sentence? If you think the original is the best way to write the sentence, choose option (1).

    (1) agencies, who charge
    (2) agencies who charge
    (3) agencies, whom charge
    (4) agencies, which charge
    (5) agencies, which charged

14. Sentence 4: **The same services are offered, at no cost to employer or employee, by a state employment agency.**
    If you rewrote sentence 4 beginning with
    State employment agencies offer the same services but
    the next word should be
    (1) doesn't
    (2) do'nt
    (3) don't
    (4) aren't
    (5) wasn't

15. Sentences 5 and 6: **This agency offers occupational information, aptitude testing, and referral services. About 50 percent of all applicants are placed in jobs.**
    If you were to combine sentences 5 and 6 beginning with
    It offers occupational information, aptitude testing, referral services,
    the next word should be

    (1) but
    (2) since
    (3) besides
    (4) and
    (5) because

16. Sentence 7: **The Civil Service Commission administers free tests required for <u>government jobs, you may</u> be placed on a long waiting list.**
    Which of the following is the best way to write the underlined portion of this sentence? If you think the original is the best way to write the sentence, choose option (1).

    (1) government jobs, you may
    (2) a government job, you might
    (3) government jobs. He may
    (4) government jobs you could
    (5) government jobs, but you may

17. Sentence 8: **Networking is one of the best employment services that was available.**

    What correction should be made to this sentence?

    (1) change *is* to *was*
    (2) insert *most* after *the*
    (3) change *was* to *is*
    (4) change the spelling of *available* to *availabel*
    (5) no correction necessary

18. Sentence 9: **Networking makes use of personal contacts as an important part of the job search.**

    What correction should be made to this sentence?

    (1) change *makes* to *is making*
    (2) change the spelling of *personal* to *personnel*
    (3) change *an* to *a*
    (4) replace *search* with *hunt*
    (5) no correction necessary

19. Sentence 10: **You make connections with people who can give job information, made introductions to other people, or even place people in jobs.**

    What correction should be made to this sentence?

    (1) replace *who* with *which*
    (2) replace *give* with *provide*
    (3) change *made* to *make*
    (4) remove the comma after *people*
    (5) change *place* to *placed*

20. Sentence 11: **All of these methods requires planning and work.**

    What correction should be made to this sentence?

    (1) replace *these* with *those*
    (2) change *requires* to *require*
    (3) change *requires* to *required*
    (4) insert a comma after *planning*
    (5) no correction is necessary

    Answers are on page A-12.

UNIT II

Writing Skills, Part II: Essay-writing

The purpose of this unit is to help you prepare for Part II of the Writing Skills Test. It is made up of chapters that are divided into lessons. It is important that you work through the unit in order.

The lessons at the beginning of the unit offer several suggestions about ways you can help yourself become more comfortable with writing. Other lessons explain and demonstrate a process approach to essay-writing. By doing all the activities in the lessons, you will get plenty of practice at developing compositions on topics like those assigned in GED testing centers.

For most of the activities in this unit, you will find no entries in the Answers and Explanations section. However, there are discussions, examples, and guidelines provided within the activities to assist your evaluation of your writing.

As you work through this unit, it will probably help to have the benefit of other people's reactions to your writing. A teacher or someone else may be able to help you to judge your essays and other writing better than you could by working alone.

As is stressed in this unit, the best way to develop skill at writing is to write. If you use the suggestions in this unit, you will develop your skills and write essays like the one you will be expected to write when you take the GED.

UNIT II PROGRESS CHART
Writing Skills, Part II

Use the following chart to keep track of your work. When you complete a lesson and its activity, check the box to show you have completed that lesson.

Lesson	Page		
		CHAPTER 1: Daily Writing	
1	171	Introduction to Personal Writing	☐
2	171	Developing a Personal Writing Plan	☐
3	173	Keeping a Journal	☐
		CHAPTER 2: The Writing Process	
1	175	Introduction to Writing as a Process	☐
2	176	Understanding Essay Topics	☐
3	178	Generating Ideas	☐
4	180	Organizing Ideas	☐
5	183	Writing an Essay	☐
6	185	Revising an Essay	☐
7	189	Editing an Essay	☐
		CHAPTER 3: Reviewing the Writing Process	
1	192	Practice the Process	☐
2	196	The Writing Process: A Summary	☐

Chapter 1

Daily Writing

Objective

In this chapter you will start to become familiar with various techniques and processes for writing. You will work on a series of writing exercises that are designed to help you

- Begin personal writing
- Develop a personal writing plan
- Keep a daily journal

Lesson 1 Introduction to Personal Writing

The best way to improve your writing is to practice writing every day. By making writing a habit that comes naturally and easily to you, you will find that your skills and your confidence develop quickly. You will also find that it is easier to think of ideas to write about and to put them on paper.

A good way to practice is to start with fastwriting. In fastwriting, the idea is to write as fast as possible and not to worry about correctness. *What you write is not important. What is important is that you are writing.* You can start by writing as little as five minutes each day. Fastwriting is a good warm-up for the writing activities in this chapter and for all your personal writing.

Lesson 1 Activity

Write for five minutes about your favorite possession or about any other topic that comes to mind. Use the fastwriting method. Write as fast as you can and do not stop to correct any mistakes that you might make. Don't pause to think of changes to make to your writing, just keep writing for five minutes.

Lesson 2 Developing a Personal Writing Plan

To develop the habit of daily writing, use fastwriting. As you become used to writing, gradually increase your writing time to ten minutes daily. Your choice of writing topics is unlimited: the more personal your topic is to you, the more enjoyable writing will become. The topics suggested in this lesson activity may help you to find your own favorite subjects.

Use a calendar to record your progress: each day, write down the number of words you have written, as well as the amount of time you spent writing. If you continue to write every day and to keep track of your progress, you will soon find that you are writing more each day. Look at the sample calendar in Figure 1.

Sunday	Monday	Tuesday	Wednesday	Thursday	Friday	Saturday
1	2	3	4	5	6	7
98 words 5 minutes	120 words 5 minutes	175 words 7 minutes	180 words 7 minutes	200 words 8 minutes	210 words 8 minutes	220 words 10 minutes
8	9	10	11	12	13	14

FIGURE 1

Lesson 2 Activity

Try at least ten minutes of fastwriting every day. The topics listed in this activity are examples of the sort of subjects you might be interested in writing about. Choose a different topic every day, or think of ones that concern you in a more personal way. You will probably do your best writing when you find a topic that interests you.

Suggested Topics

1. Sit in one place for about ten minutes and observe what's happening around you. Take notes on what you see and hear. Later, use your notes to refresh your memory, and write for ten minutes about your observations.
2. Write about your job, or about how conditions could be improved where you work.
3. Write about the person in your life who has had the most influence on you. Describe the person and explain how that person has influenced you.
4. Write as though you were writing a letter to someone you haven't seen in a long time. Write about recent events in your life.
5. Write about what the world would be like if there were no automobiles.

6. Write as though you were writing a letter to the president of a company whose product you have bought recently. Explain what you like or dislike about the product.

7. Write about a place or a time that means a lot to you.

Lesson 3 Keeping a Journal

Many people keep a journal, which is a daily written record of their experiences, thoughts, and feelings. A journal can be kept in a diary or in a notebook.

You may find that keeping a journal is a good way to practice your daily writing. It can become an interesting and important part of your life. It may also help you to reflect on how you feel about yourself, your work, or your relationships.

To keep a journal, set aside a regular time each day when you will have about ten or fifteen minutes to yourself. Try to make your journal writing a daily habit, as that is the best way to measure progress and to improve your writing skills. When you write in your journal, remember that you are writing for yourself alone. Your only concern is to put your thoughts, feelings, and experiences on paper. Read the following examples of journal entries.

EXAMPLE 1

"... I would like to have another job. I am fed up with loading these railroad cars with sugar. And I don't want to work the graveyard shift anymore. It's not much fun to go to bed when everybody else is just getting up. But I guess it's not all bad. I can go to afternoon ballgames. And it's easier to shop for things when the stores aren't crowded."

EXAMPLE 2

"... it would be nice if Jim talked more about himself to me. He seems so worried all the time. I'm sure I could help him to sort things out if he confided in me. But I guess I'm too nervous to ask him what's wrong. Tomorrow I will be sure to let him know how much I care about him."

EXAMPLE 3

"... I'm going to buy a pickup truck this fall (sooner if I have the money). That one at Pete's Garage would be great if it's still for sale. A pickup costs a lot less than a car—and lasts longer. It would be really good for my work and I could also use it to haul things around."

These entries show some of the types of writing you might find in a journal. Keep in mind that you should write about the things that interest *you*. Do not worry about correctness because no one should read your journal, except you or someone you wish to share it with.

Keeping a journal will help you to write more easily. It will help the writing process to become easier, just as driving a car or riding a bicycle becomes easier with practice.

Suggestions for Keeping a Journal

- Keep your journal in a special notebook or diary.
- Try writing in the same place and at the same time each day.
- Record the date of each journal entry.
- Write in your journal every day. Don't worry about grammar, spelling, or punctuation. Write quickly without being concerned about whether your writing is perfect.
- Use your journal as an opportunity to think about yourself, other people, and events in your life.

Lesson 3   Activity

Begin keeping a journal today. Find a comfortable place to write. Start by choosing a topic that interests you.

The following topics are suggestions to help you get started, but you may find that there are other, more personal subjects that you prefer to write about.

At first, write in your journal for at least ten minutes. As you become used to journal writing, try increasing your writing time. Try to get as many thoughts as possible on paper. Some journal topics that you may find interesting are

- Something that may be bothering you
- Recent events in your life
- Something you read about in a book, newspaper, or magazine
- Family members and how you get along with them
- Your work, or how it feels to be out of work
- Political events and how they affect your life
- Humorous experiences you have had
- How you might help a friend in need

Chapter 2

The Writing Process

> **Objective**
>
> In this chapter, you will begin to develop your writing skills by applying them to essay writing. You will read about and follow the process of writing an essay. You will also develop an essay using a five-step process that helps you
>
> - Generate ideas
> - Organize ideas for essays
> - Write essays
> - Revise essays
> - Edit essays

Lesson 1 Introduction to Writing as a Process

Now that you have practiced personal writing, the next step is to learn how to write for others, specifically for Part II of the Writing Skills Test. This chapter teaches a process approach to writing essays. With this process you generate and organize ideas, write an essay, and then revise and edit it. The result is an effective essay.

Writing essays can be as simple as personal writing if you follow this step-by-step process. The following list briefly explains each step in the process. The process works for any topic you write about.

The Five Steps in the Writing Process

1. **Generate ideas**
   - Use brainstorming or clustering to generate ideas about your essay topic.

2. **Organize ideas**
   - Select the most appropriate ideas to support your point of view or opinion.
   - Decide how to arrange your ideas for your audience (the reader).
   - Decide which examples best support your point of view.
   - Decide which examples to present first, second, and so on.

3. **Write essay**
   - Put your ideas in sentences and paragraphs following the organization you planned.

> **4. Revise essay**
> - Make sure that your point of view or opinion is stated clearly and that your examples support your point of view.
> - Add information needed for clarity.
> - Remove information that is not needed.
>
> **5. Edit essay**
> - Correct errors in usage, sentence structure, spelling, punctuation, and capitalization.

You may already use some or all of the steps in the writing process when you write an essay. Think about the procedures you now use. The following activity is made up of questions that will help you pinpoint how much of the writing process you already use. It will also help you identify which steps you should add to your method so that your essays become more effective.

Lesson 1 Activity

When you took the Predictor Test, you wrote an essay (see page 10). How many of the steps in the writing process did you use? Answer the following questions.

1. **Generating ideas.** Did you spend time thinking about ideas (brainstorming) to put in your essay? Did you write your ideas?
2. **Organizing ideas.** If you did Step 1, did you take time to plan what to write first, second, third, and so on? Did you make notes about your plan?
3. **Writing.** If you did Step 1 and Step 2, did you follow your plan when you wrote your essay?
4. **Revising.** After you wrote your essay, did you read it over to see how effectively you presented your ideas? Did you make any changes to increase your essay's effectiveness?
5. **Editing.** Did you correct all the errors you could find in your essay—errors in usage, sentence structure, spelling, punctuation, and capitalization?

Discussion

Every time you answered *yes* to one of the questions, you identified a step in the writing process that you already use. Whenever you answered *no*, you identified a step you should learn to use.

Lesson 2 Understanding Essay Topics

When you take the GED, you will write an essay approximately 200 words long. You will have 45 minutes to write it. Therefore, you will want to spend some of that time making sure you understand the topic and what its limits are.

This lesson will show you a method for reading topics carefully and beginning to develop your point of view about them. This will help you to write your best essay on the assigned topic in the time allowed.

When you are assigned a topic to write about, take time to be absolutely sure you understand the topic.

> **Steps in Reading a Topic Carefully and Developing Your Point of View**
>
> **Step 1.** Underline the important or key words in the topic.
> **Step 2.** Make sure you have noticed and understood all the topic's key ideas or concepts.
> **Step 3.** Decide on your own point of view and state it in one sentence.

The best way to learn to follow the steps is to put them into practice. Read the following topic and then follow the directions in the Activity for this lesson.

> **TOPIC**
>
> Drunk driving is a problem in our society. One judge makes first-offense drunk drivers place bumper stickers on their cars that will <u>identify them as convicted drunk drivers.</u> Some people feel this is an <u>unfair</u> and extreme punishment for a first offender.
>
> If you were a judge, would you be for or against this punishment? Give the reasons for your position and support your position with specific examples.

Lesson 2 Activity

1. In the topic, some of the key words are already underlined. Reread the topic and underline five additional key words. Do not read any further until you have underlined those five words.

Discussion

Words you might have underlined are: <u>drunk driving</u>, <u>first offense</u>, <u>bumper sticker</u>, <u>extreme punishment</u>, <u>for or against</u>. Those words are important because an essay on this topic has limits. It *must* be about whether you are **for or against bumper stickers** to **identify convicted, first-offense drunk drivers.** As you generate ideas, you must be aware that some people think the **punishment** is **extreme**.

One way to be sure that you have all the important concepts of the topic in mind is to turn it into a question. Use most or all of the underlined words in the question.

Is it an <u>extreme punishment</u> for <u>first-offense drunk drivers</u> to have to place <u>bumper stickers</u> on their cars that will <u>identify</u> them as having been convicted of drunk driving? As you work through this chapter you will do all five steps in the writing process to write an essay on this topic.

2. Complete the following **answer** to the question about the topic. "I believe that it is a fair punishment . . ." (Finish this sentence to indicate that you favor bumper stickers.)

Discussion

What you just wrote is the topic of the essay you will begin to plan in the next lesson.

Lesson 3 Generating Ideas

This lesson introduces the planning phases of writing an essay like the one you will be asked to write for the Writing Skills Test. It will show you two ways to generate ideas for your essay: brainstorming and clustering.

Information about writing suggests that many writers do not do well on essay tests because they do not make a plan before they start writing. Generally, the most successful way to approach a writing test is to spend some time generating ideas before you begin to write. People who spend time planning their essays can write longer, better organized, and more effective essays.

Brainstorming

Brainstorming is a strategy that will help you find out what you already know about the topic you are going to write about. When you brainstorm, you write down all the words that come to mind when you think about the topic. You may spend only three or four minutes brainstorming, but these few minutes can make a difference in your score on an essay exam. The topic for this chapter will be used to illustrate this strategy.

> **TOPIC**
>
> Drunk driving is a problem in our society. One judge makes first-offense drunk drivers place bumper stickers on their cars that will identify them as convicted drunk drivers. Some people feel that this is an unfair and extreme punishment for a first offender.
>
> If you were a judge, would you be for or against this punishment? Give the reasons for your position and support your position with specific examples.

One writer thought about the topic and decided to write from this point of view.

UNIT II: WRITING SKILLS, PART 2: ESSAY-WRITING Lesson 3 **179**

I believe it is an <u>extreme punishment</u> for <u>first-offense drunk drivers</u> to have to place <u>bumper stickers</u> on their cars that let <u>everyone know</u> that they have been <u>convicted</u> of drunk driving.

The writer then began to brainstorm and wrote down all the words that came to mind. The result looked like the following.

> *humiliated usually a fine family suffers*
> *unfair children service fits crime*
> *society doesn't gain rehabilitation demeaned*

Clustering

Clustering is another way to brainstorm. It makes the ideas you generate easier to see and to organize. When you cluster, you write your position or point of view about the topic in the center of a piece of paper and draw a circle around it. Next, you brainstorm supporting ideas and place the words on extensions around the circle.

Figure 2 shows a cluster made by the same writer whose brainstorming ideas you have read.

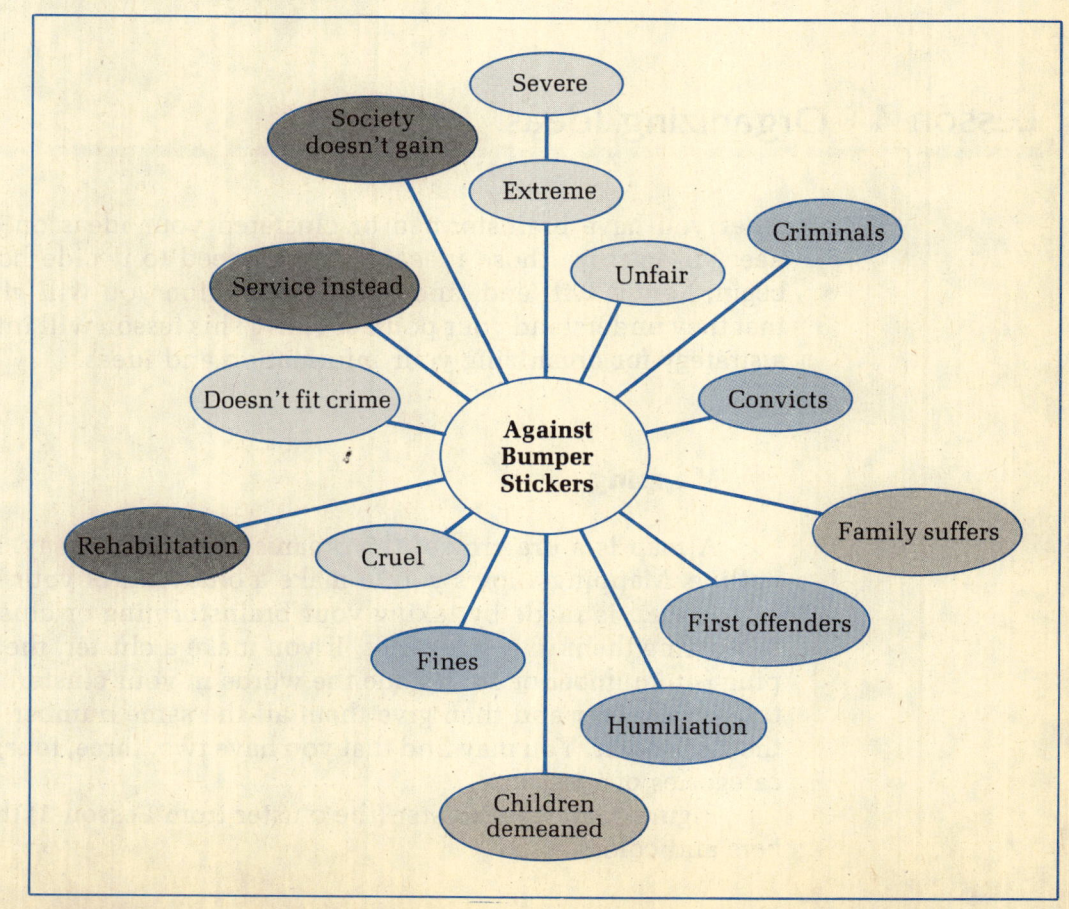

(Cluster diagram centered on "Against Bumper Stickers" with branches to: Severe, Society doesn't gain, Extreme, Criminals, Service instead, Unfair, Convicts, Doesn't fit crime, Family suffers, Rehabilitation, Cruel, First offenders, Fines, Humiliation, Children demeaned)

FIGURE 2

Lesson 3 Activity

This activity will help you begin planning for the essay you will write on the "bumper sticker" topic. Read the topic again on page 178. Your essay will take this point of view.

> "I believe that it is a <u>fair punishment</u> for <u>first-offense drunk drivers</u> to have to place <u>bumper stickers</u> on their cars that <u>let everyone know</u> that they have been <u>convicted</u> of drunk driving."

1. With the "For Bumper Stickers" point of view in mind, brainstorm. Write at least ten words or phrases that come to mind about the "For" point of view. (You may look at the example of the "Against" brainstorm on page 179.)
2. Again, with the "For Bumper Stickers" point of view in mind, brainstorm. This time, however, cluster your ideas. Start by writing "For Bumper Stickers" in the middle of a piece of paper. Draw a circle around that phrase. Continue by writing ideas on extensions from the circle. (You may look at the example of the "Against" cluster just before the Lesson Activity.) After you finish making your cluster, save it. You will need to use it as you work through the next lesson.

Lesson 4 Organizing Ideas

After you have brainstormed or clustered your ideas on a topic, you will need to organize those ideas. You will need to decide how the essay will begin, how it will end, and what information you will give the readers so that they understand your point of view. This lesson will introduce mapping, a strategy for organizing your information and ideas.

Mapping

A map is a drawing of the organization of an essay. It is similar to an outline. Mapping allows you to make a *blueprint* of your essay.

A map is made by taking your brainstorming or clustering words and organizing them into categories. If you make a cluster, the first step in mapping is to number or color-code the words in your cluster. Find all the ideas that go together and then give them all the same number, or color them all the same color. You may find that you have two, three, four, or more different categories of ideas.

Figure 3 shows a cluster (the cluster from Lesson 3) that has both numbers and colors.

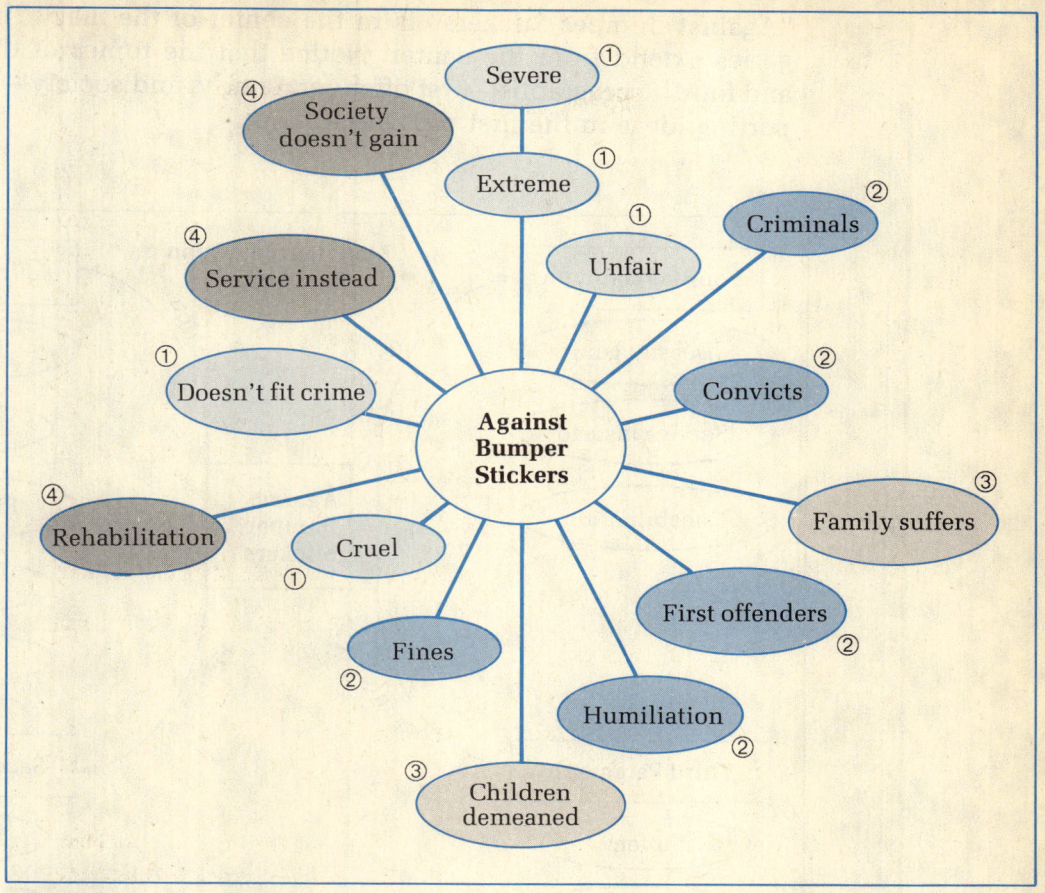

UNIT II: WRITING SKILLS, PART 2: ESSAY-WRITING   Lesson 4 **181**

(Cluster diagram centered on "Against Bumper Stickers" with surrounding bubbles:)

- Severe ①
- Society doesn't gain ④
- Extreme ①
- Criminals ②
- Service instead ④
- Unfair ①
- Doesn't fit crime ①
- Convicts ②
- Family suffers ③
- Rehabilitation ④
- Cruel ①
- First offenders ②
- Fines ②
- Humiliation ②
- Children demeaned ③

FIGURE 3

The following directions explain the next step, creating a map.

Creating a Map

1. **Gather all the words from your brainstorming or clustering activities.**

2. **Eliminate words that have similar meanings.**

3. **Arrange words in categories. Give the categories titles. The titles will suggest your main idea, and the words listed will be used as examples to support those ideas.**

4. **Decide which paragraph should come first. Label it. Because it is the introductory paragraph, remember to list the topics of the other paragraphs since the first paragraph will introduce them.**

5. **Decide which paragraph should be second, third, fourth, and so on. Label each one.**

   A map based on the cluster on page 179 might look like the one in Figure 4. Compare the cluster to the map. Notice that you do not have to use all the words in the cluster or the map. In this example, the point of view

"Against Bumper Stickers" is in the center of the map. The different categories extend from the center. Notice that the topics of the second, third, and fourth paragraphs—first offender, family, and society—are listed as supporting ideas in the first paragraph.

Map in preparation for an essay

Fourth Paragraph
- Doesn't gain
- Service instead
- Rehabilitation

First Paragraph
- Too Severe
- Unfair
- First offender
- Family
- Society

Third Paragraph
- Suffers
- Children demeaned

Second Paragraph
- Humiliated
- Usually a fine

Center: Against Bumper Stickers

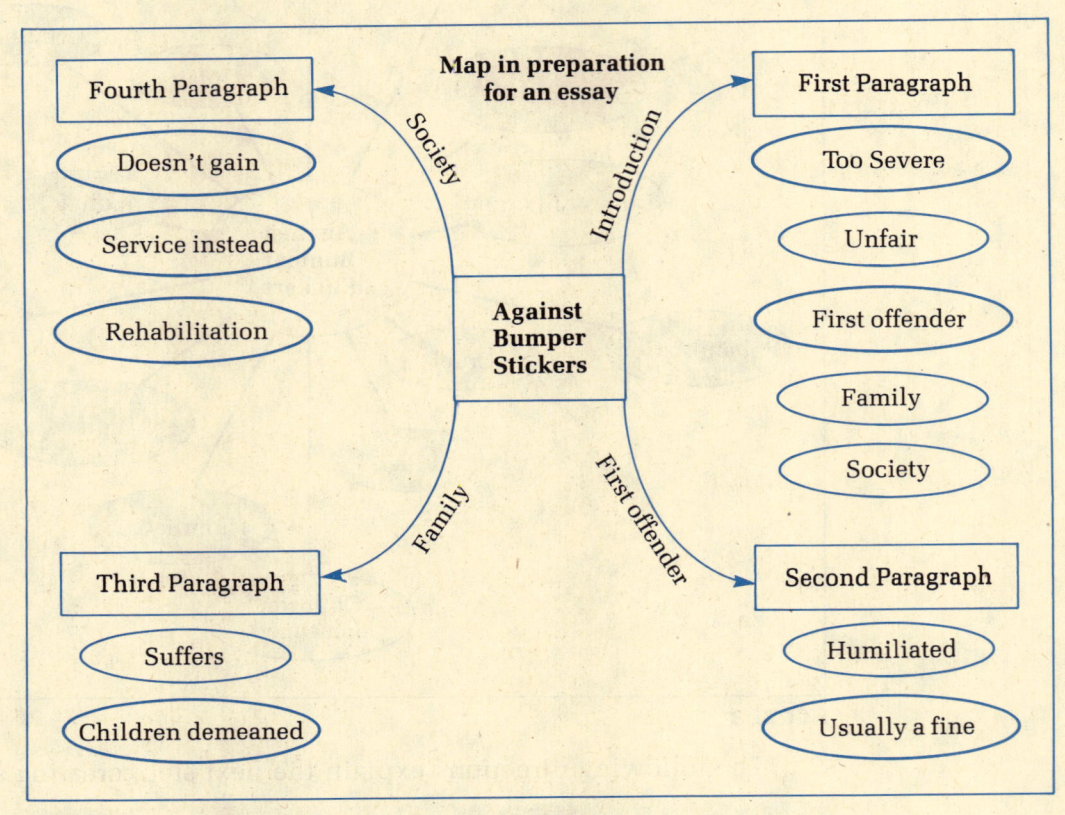

Arrows labeled: Society, Introduction, Family, First offender

FIGURE 4

As you become more experienced with making maps, you will be able to make them in one step: that is, you will be able to brainstorm and cluster ideas in your head, and then make the map in only a few minutes.

Lesson 4   Activity

To do this activity, you will need to use the cluster you made during the Lesson 3 Activity.

1. Color-code or number the ideas in your cluster. Use the same color or number for ideas that go together. How many different groups do you have?
2. Use your cluster to create a map. Remember that your point of view is "For Bumper Stickers." (You may look at the map in this lesson as an example.)

Discussion

Did you label which paragraph comes first, second, and so on? Did you remember to include later paragraph topics among the first paragraph's supporting ideas?

Lesson 5 Writing an Essay

In this lesson you will use your map from the activity in Lesson 4 to begin writing your essay. The opening of your essay should give the reader your point of view. The next paragraphs, following the plan of your map, will give the main reasons for your point of view. To explain your point of view effectively, you should use specific examples that support your opinion. The following are the steps to follow to write an essay.

Steps in Writing an Essay

1. In the opening paragraph, state your central point of view about the topic immediately. Then give your reasons for your point of view.
2. In the second, third, and following paragraphs, develop supporting examples to explain each of the reasons for your point of view.
3. In the final paragraph, restate and explain why you hold your central point of view.

The essay in the following example is based on the demonstration map in Lesson 4. The comments on the left indicate how it follows the map. After the essay, a discussion explains how the essay was written according to the steps outlined above on writing essays.

You may notice a few small errors in usage, sentence structure, or mechanics in this essay, but remember that this is a first draft. The writer is concentrating only on getting the ideas on paper in an organized manner. In Lessons 6 and 7, this essay will be revised and edited.

Sample Essay

Central point of view is stated: "too severe."
First reason for point of view: "unfair."
Second reason for point of view: "family."
Third reason for point of view: "society."
Makes suggestion: "better punishment."

The punishment the judge gives to drunk drivers is too severe and unfair for first offenders. It is too severe and unfair because it is harsher than many punishments given for worse crimes. The punishment can effect the family of the drunken driver in a bad way. Society does not really seem to benefit from this type of punishment. The judge should think of a better punishment.

The punishment for first offenders is too severe. It would tend to humiliate the person for the time he or she had to have it on thier car. Drunk drivers and criminals get off much easier.

Elaborates on first reason for point of view: "unfair."
Elaborates on second reason for point of view: "family."

Elaborates on third reason for point of view: "society." Offers specific suggestion: "rehabilitation program." Restates point of view and concludes.

The judge in this case should treat first offenders the way other judges do. They should be given fines and a chance to rehabilitate themselves.

The punishment is even more unfair to the first offender's family. They will have to be in the car when the bumper sticker is on it, they will have to be unnecessarily offended and humiliated by the sticker's prescence. The sticker harms the offender's children by holding them up to ridicule by their friends and neighbors.

In addition to being unfair to first offenders and their families, the use of the bumper sticker as a punishment does not benefit society. A better approach might be to place first offenders in rehabilitation programs where they could get help for their drinking problems. This kind of punishment might serve to help the offender and the family as well. The bumper sticker serves no good purpose for the offender. This punishment should be abandoned.

Discussion

Following the steps shown on page 183, the first paragraph begins by presenting the central point of view: *The punishment the judge gives to drunk drivers is too severe and unfair for first offenders.* It goes on to present the three most important reasons for this central point of view: (1) the punishment is unfair, (2) it affects the family, and (3) society does not benefit from it.

In the following paragraphs, the writer gives more details about each of the important supporting ideas. The second paragraph explains and gives evidence for the writer's feeling that punishment is unfair because it is too severe: (1) it is humiliating, (2) worse criminals get off easier, and (3) other judges treat drunk drivers differently. The third paragraph gives supporting evidence for the idea that the punishment affects innocent family members. The last paragraph supports the idea that society does not benefit from the punishment. It then restates the main idea, makes a suggestion for a better punishment (a rehabilitation program), and then concludes.

Lesson 5   Activity

Write an essay, approximately 200 words long, with the point of view that having convicted, first-offense drunk drivers place bumper stickers on their cars is a fair punishment.

Use the map you created in the Lesson 4 Activity to develop your essay. Review the steps on Writing an Essay (page 183) before you begin. Concentrate on getting your ideas on paper in an organized manner. Write your essay quickly. You can always change what you don't like about your essay when you revise it.

When you have finished, keep your essay. You will revise it when you do the Lesson 6 Activity.

Lesson 6 Revising an Essay

Revision is an important part of the writing process. It is the step you use to improve what you have written. This lesson presents guidelines for you to follow that will help you improve your essay.

An essay is written for other people to read. Keep your reader or audience in mind when you revise an essay. It is not enough that your ideas are clear to you. Your ideas must be organized and stated clearly enough for someone else to be able to follow and understand them. Think of the reader as someone you are talking to. You must explain your opinion or central point of view very clearly because the reader cannot ask any questions.

The following revision reminders give suggestions for some of the things to look for when you revise an essay. Good, clear organization is one of the most important keys to making your ideas clear to a reader. Several of the suggestions focus on organization.

Reminders for Revising Essays

Key Ideas
- Did you state the central idea of your essay in one sentence?
- Is the central idea or point of view stated clearly enough that any reader would be able to restate it?

Content
- Did you use specific examples that support your point of view?
- Are your examples explained clearly enough that your reader can see how they support your point of view?
- Did you consider the opinions of a person who does not agree with your point of view? If so, did you answer that person's argument?

Organization
- Did you state your point of view right away?
- Did you present two or three important supporting ideas?
- Would your reader be able to restate what the important supporting ideas are?
- Did you use words that show how your supporting ideas relate to the central idea and to each other?

Summary or Conclusion
- Does your summary or conclusion restate your point of view and supporting ideas?
- Does your summary or conclusion follow logically from what you said in your essay?

186 Chapter 2: The Writing Process INSTRUCTION

Demonstration

For this demonstration, the essay from Lesson 5 is printed again, paragraph by paragraph, just as it was written. It is shown with handwritten changes made during revision. Straight lines through words, or phrases, indicate material to be taken out. Arrows and ⌃ marks indicate words, or phrases, that are to be inserted. The *Discussion* section explains why the changes were made. The sentences from the original essay are numbered to make the discussion easier to follow. Study this demonstration very carefully. You soon will be revising your own essay.

Paragraph 1

(1) ~~The punishment the judge gives to~~ [Punishing convicted] drunk drivers [by having them place bumper stickers on their cars, which identify them as convicted felons,] is too severe and unfair for first offenders. (2) It is too severe and unfair because it is harsher than many punishments given for worse crimes. (3) ~~The~~ [In addition, this] punishment can effect the family of the drunken driver ~~in a bad way~~ [adversely]. (4) [Most important,] ~~S~~ociety does not really seem to benefit from this type of punishment. (5) ~~The judge~~ [Judges] should think of a ~~better~~ punishment [that would fit the crime and benefit society.]

Discussion

Revised Sentence 1: Punishing convicted drunk drivers by having them place bumper stickers on their cars, which identify them as convicted felons, is too severe and unfair for first offenders.—The reminders suggest that the central idea should be stated *right away* (see Organization), in *one* sentence, and *clearly* (see Key Ideas). The changes to sentence 1 make clear exactly what "The punishment" is.

Revised Sentence 3: In addition, this punishment can effect the family of the drunken driver adversely.—The original sentence 3 was changed to begin with *In addition*. That change makes it clear that the ideas before and after *In addition* are equally important. To make the meaning clearer, the words *in a bad way* become *adversely*.

Revised Sentence 4: Most important, society does not really seem to benefit from this type of punishment.—*Most important* was added to sentence 3 to show that the third reason is more important than the first two. Note that a slash was drawn through the capital *S* in *Society*. A slash through a capital letter is an editor's mark meaning that the letter is intended to be lower case.

Revised Sentence 5: Judges should think of a punishment that would fit the crime and benefit society.—In Sentence 5, *The judge* was changed to *Judges* so that it is clear that the writer's idea applies to all judges who try first-offense drunk-driving cases. The word *better* was replaced by *that would fit* to make the idea clearer.

With the changes, Paragraph 1 presents the central idea and introduces the three supporting ideas that the next three paragraphs discuss.

UNIT II: WRITING SKILLS, PART 2: ESSAY-WRITING   Lesson 2   187

Paragraph 2

(1) The punishment for first offenders is too severe. (2) ~~It would tend to~~ because it humiliate~~s~~ the person for the time he or she had to have it on thier car~~.~~ (3) ~~Drunk drivers get off much easier.~~ Additionally, it is unfair because other criminals, like robbers, don't have to wear labels that identify them as convicted criminals. (4) ~~The~~ Judge~~s~~ in ~~this~~ these case~~s~~ should treat first offenders the way ~~other judges do~~ they traditionally have been treated. (5) They should be given fines and a chance to rehabilitate themselves.

Discussion

Revised Sentence 1: The punishment for first offenders is too severe because it humiliates people who have bumper stickers on thier cars.—Sentences 1 and 2 are combined with *because* to show how the ideas relate to each other. The words *people who have* are added so that it is clear that the idea is about all people who have bumper stickers.

Revised Sentence 2: Additionally, it is unfair because other criminals, like robbers, don't have to wear labels that identify them as convicted criminals.—The words *Additionally, it is unfair* show that the second reason has to do with unfairness. (The first was about severity.) The other changes (beginning with *like robbers*) explain why the punishment is unfair by making the sentence more specific.

Revised Sentence 3: Judges in these cases should treat first offenders the way they have traditionally been treated.—These changes remind the reader that the recommendation applies to all *Judges* and all *cases*. The revision makes it clear that traditional treatment is recommended.

The changes in Paragraph 2 make it clearer how the ideas relate to each other. The changes also explain the logic of the writer's ideas, which makes the argument more convincing to a reader who has a different opinion.

Paragraph 3

(1) The punishment is even more unfair to the first offender's family. (2) Family members are forced to ride in a car with a ~~They will have to be in the car when the~~ bumper sticker~~ is on it~~, they also are ~~will have to be unnecessarily offended and~~ humiliated by the sticker's prescence. (3) The sticker harms the offender's children by holding them up to ridicule by their friends and neighbor.

Discussion

Paragraph 3 explains a second reason for the unfairness of bumper stickers.

188 Chapter 2: The Writing Process INSTRUCTION

Revised Sentence 1: The punishment is even more unfair to the first offender's family.—In Sentence 1, *offenders* was changed to *offender's* to show possession. (During revision, the writer concentrates on making ideas clearer. If a mechanical error is noticed, however, it should be corrected.)

Revised Sentence 2: Family members are forced to ride in a car with a bumper sticker.—Sentence 2 was changed so that it is clearer that *Family members* have no choice about being in the car. Also, the original Sentence 2 was a run-on sentence, so it was divided into two sentences.

Revised Sentence 3: They also are humiliated by the sticker's presence.—Since this is now a sentence of its own, the first word must be capitalized. The words *also are* replace the original wording to show how this idea related to the idea at the beginning of Paragraph 2: both the first offender and the family are humiliated.

Like the changes in Paragraph 2, these changes highlight the relationship between the writer's ideas, and they also make each idea clearer.

Paragraph 4

(1) In addition to being unfair to first offenders and their families, the use of the bumper sticker as a punishment does not benefit society. (2) A better approach might be to place the first offenders in rehabilitation programs where they could get help for their drinking problems. (3) This ~~kind of punishment~~ *type of sentence* might serve to help the offender ~~and the family as well~~ *s their families, and society*. (4) ~~The~~ *¶ In summary,* bumper sticker*s* serves no ~~good~~ purpose ~~for the offender~~ *beyond humiliating offenders and their families*. (5) The punishment should be abandoned *in favor of a positive rehabilitation program that could benefit the offender, family, and society.*

Discussion

Revised Sentence 3: This type of sentence might serve to help the offenders, their families, and society.—The word *punishment* was changed to *sentence* because rehabilitation is not punishment. The words *and society* were added to tie the sentence into the main concern of this paragraph—society. That addition made a small change in sentence structure necessary.

Revised Sentence 4: In summary, bumper stickers serve no purpose beyond humiliating offenders and their families.—Because Sentences 4 and 5 are the restatement and conclusion, the writer added the sign for a new paragraph (¶). The last two sentences became the fifth paragraph. The words *In summary* were added to indicate that what follows is the restatement and conclusion. (See Summary or Conclusion in the reminders on page 186.) The other words added to the sentence make the ideas clearer and more forceful by stating more precisely what purpose the writer thinks the punishment serves.

Revised Sentence 5: The punishment should be abandoned in favor of a positive rehabilitation program that could benefit the offender, family, and society.—Words were added to the last part of the sentence to make this more clearly a restatement of the writer's position.

read your essay. Ask yourself questions that will help you see how you can improve your essay. When you are satisfied that your ideas are organized, keep your revision. You will edit it in the Lesson 7 Activity.

Lesson 7   Editing an Essay

The last step in the writing process is editing. When you edit, you look mainly for errors in usage, sentence structure, and mechanics (punctuation, capitalization, and spelling). You may notice a sentence or part of a sentence that you want to revise one more time. It's all right to make last-minute revisions, but you should concentrate most of your attention on editing. The corrections you make when you edit an essay give it a polish that enhances its effectiveness. The more effective the essay you write for the GED is, the higher your Writing Skills Test score will be.

One excellent way to find errors in an essay is to read it aloud, or in a whisper. That way, you can hear your essay in the way that a reader might "hear" it. You may hear words that do not have the right endings. When you hear pauses in your reading, you may notice the need for a punctuation mark.

Try reading your essay at a normal reading speed. You may find that a normal speed helps you "hear" better. Some people prefer to read very slowly, word for word, when they edit. Try it both ways. Find out what works best for you.

Use the 5-R editing method used in Unit I of this book. With that method you can check for correctness in a systematic way.

Sometimes spelling errors are difficult to see, especially after you have reread your essay. One strategy you can use to find spelling errors is to read your essay backward, from the bottom of the page to the top. That way you have to concentrate on each word. Reading backward also helps you find words that you may have written twice in a row by mistake.

The following summarizes the strategies you can use.

1. Read your essay aloud or in a whisper.
2. Read at the speed—normal or slow—that works best for you.
3. Use the 5-R editing method.
4. Read your essay backward while you concentrate on spelling.

Demonstration

To demonstrate how an essay can be polished by editing, portions of the revised essay from Lesson 6 (pages 186–188) are discussed here.

Using the strategies listed above, the writer read the essay in a whisper, noticed some errors, and corrected them. Sentences or parts of sentences that contained errors are reprinted and identified by paragraph number.

Paragraph 1
Revised Sentence 2: In addition, this punishment can affect the family . . .

Paragraph 2
Revised Sentence 1: . . . people who have bumper stickers on their cars.

Paragraph 3
Revised Sentence 3: . . . by the sticker's presence.
Revised Sentence 4: . . . their friends and neighbors (last sentence)

After the editing and the last-minute revisions were completed, the essay was in its final form, as follows.

> Punishing convicted drunk drivers by having them place bumper stickers on their cars, which identify them as convicted felons, is too severe and unfair for first offenders. It is too severe and unfair because it is harsher than many punishments given for worse crimes. In addition, this punishment can affect the family of the drunken driver adversely. Most important, society does not really seem to benefit from this type of punishment. Judges should think of a punishment that would fit the crime and benefit society.
>
> The punishment for first offenders is too severe because it humiliates people who have bumper stickers on their cars. Additionally, it is unfair because other criminals, like robbers, don't have to wear labels that identify them as convicted criminals. Judges in these cases should treat first offenders the way they have traditionally been treated. They should be given fines and a chance to rehabilitate themselves.
>
> The punishment is even more unfair to the first offender's family. Family members are forced to ride in a car with a bumper sticker. They also are humiliated by the sticker's presence. The sticker harms the

offender's children by holding them up to ridicule by their friends and neighbors.

In addition to being unfair to first offenders and their families, the use of the bumper sticker as a punishment does not benefit society. A better approach might be to place first offenders in rehabilitation programs where they can get help for their drinking problems. This type of sentence would benefit the offenders, their families, and society.

In summary, bumper stickers serve no purpose beyond humiliating offenders and their families. The punishment should be abandoned in favor of a positive rehabilitation program that could benefit the offender, the family, and society.

This essay—a product of the five-step writing process that includes clustering, mapping, writing, revising, and editing—is an effective essay. You may have noticed, as you read the final, edited version that some of the essay could be improved further. The essay is not perfect. There is no such thing as a perfect essay. There are, however, effective and ineffective essays. The model is an effective essay: it makes its point, it is clear, its supporting ideas are sound and logical, and it has few mechanical errors.

The final version of this essay is more than 200 words long. If it had been written as part of The Writing Skills Test, its length would not influence a reader to give it a lower score. The reader would notice its effectiveness and score it accordingly. As you continue with your essay-writing practice, you will probably write essays that are either too short or too long at first. Don't be concerned. With practice, you will be able to write 200-word essays within 45 minutes. Concentrate on writing effectively.

By practicing the process (the next chapter helps you do that) you can learn to make the process work more quickly, more efficiently, and more automatically for you. After you do this lesson's Activity, think about the essay that you will have completed. Is it better than other essays you have written in the past? Is it better organized? Are your ideas clearer? Would what you feel about the topic be clear to a reader?

If your writing has improved, you are on your way to becoming a more proficient writer. Practice will make you better. Writing is not a magic act; it is a skill that most people can attain by practicing the writing process you have used in this chapter.

Lesson 7   Activity

Edit the essay that you revised in the Lesson 6 Activity. Follow the suggestions in Reminders for Revising Essays on page 185. When you have finished this activity, you will have developed an essay that uses every step in the writing process. You should then go to Chapter 3 to practice writing other essays.

Chapter 3 | Reviewing the Writing Process

Objective

In this chapter, you will

- Review the steps in the writing process
- Practice the writing process by developing several essays on your own

Lesson 1   Practice the Process

The only way to become comfortable with writing is to write. The more you write, whether for yourself (by keeping a journal), or for others (in notes, reports, letters, or essays), the easier it is. You may even find yourself enjoying writing. This lesson contains suggestions and tools to help you make writing a habit and to help you prepare for the GED.

One way to help yourself improve your writing is to stick with your journal or, if you have put it aside, to pick it up again.

To prepare yourself for the GED, however, you also need to practice writing essays. You can think of topics for essays on your own. Just as some people write letters to newspapers to express their opinions, so can you write an essay to argue your ideas. You can also write to a newspaper if you like.

What makes the GED essay special is that you will be *assigned* a topic. It's a good idea, therefore, to practice writing on assigned topics. When you practice writing, always use all five steps of the writing process.

In the next lesson in this chapter, you will find a summary of the activities you should do at each step in the writing process.

The summary of the process in Lesson 2 is there for you to use as a handy reference as you develop more essays. You may also find it helpful to reread Chapter 2.

So that you can practice writing on assigned topics, this lesson ends with a list of topics on which you can develop essays. They are topics you can assign yourself or have someone else assign to you.

When you take the GED, you probably won't know what topic you will be assigned until the last minute. You may wish to use this list in a way that allows you to write about a topic you haven't seen before. Following are a few suggestions for using the topic list.

Ways to Use the Topic List

1. Read all the topics in the list. Write first about the topics that interest you most. Save the topics that interest you least for later when your skill and confidence have reached higher levels.
2. Keep the topics a secret from yourself. Decide to write on Topic 1 first, Topic 2 second, and so on. Look at each topic only when you are ready to write an essay.
3. Have someone else assign topics from the list to you.

There's nothing wrong with writing on a topic more than once. You might take a new and better approach the second time. It would be a good way to measure your progress.

When you feel you have become comfortable enough with the writing process, begin to set time limits for yourself. Work toward completing essays in no more than 45 minutes.

The list of topics for you to use as assigned topics follows.

Topic List

Topic 1—A city recently proposed to ban the sale of markers and spray cans to most teenagers because it wanted to stop the spread of graffiti in that city. The city also proposed fining any store caught selling markers or spray cans to anyone under 18 years of age. In addition, the city proposed fining any teenager under 18 caught with spray cans or markers.

Are you for or against the city's proposals? Write an essay that presents your point of view. Use reasons and examples to support your opinions.

Topic 2—Many people in the United States are highly competitive. They are ready to accept any challenge, and they like any sport, game, or business that allows them the chance to prove that they can do better than someone else.

Do you view this competitive spirit as good or bad? In an essay, state your opinion and support it with specific reasons and examples.

Topic 3—Many people have a favorite object or possession that they would not want to lose.

Select a favorite object of your own and write an essay to explain why you would not want to lose it. Include reasons that support your explanation.

Topic 4—Many people feel that the death penalty should be used more often in the United States as a deterrent to crime. Others are opposed to it.

Write an essay that explains why you feel the death penalty should or should not be used to deter crime. Include examples or reasons that support your opinion.

Topic 5—A city council recently prohibited a group of musicians from giving a scheduled concert inside the city's boundaries.

Should local governments be permitted to decide which entertainers may perform in a city? State your view in an essay. Support your opinion with specific reasons and examples.

Topic 6—Some people say that a person's education takes place in school and ends when the person leaves school. Others believe that a person's education is a lifelong activity that doesn't depend on going to school.

Write an essay to present and support your opinion about where and when education occurs.

Topic 7—The role of dreams has been viewed in many different ways. They have been thought to be a way to communicate with people who are no longer in our lives, a means of looking into the future, or a way of working out the frustrations of our daily lives.

Write an essay to explain the role you think dreams play. Use examples and reasons to support your opinion.

Topic 8—The national speed limit is 55 miles per hour. It has proven to be effective in saving lives and conserving fuel. Many people use radar scanners that allow them to detect police speed traps. Some people feel such scanners should be outlawed.

Write an essay explaining your own opinion about this issue. Support your point of view with examples and reasons.

Topic 9—Some people have been looking at the possibility of rating records in a manner similar to the way movies are rated. They say that some of the lyrics in recorded music today could be harmful to younger children and that a rating system would help solve this problem.

Are you for or against the idea of a rating system for records? Write an essay to express your opinion. Support your essay with reasons and examples.

Topic 10—Living in a fast-paced society may have many advantages, but one disadvantage is that today's hectic pace makes life more stressful.

Write an essay that explains how you cope with stress, what you do to reduce stress, or how you deal with it when it becomes a problem. Support your explanation with specific details and examples.

Topic 11—In many states students have to take a driver's education course before they can receive a driver's license.

Write an essay to explain why you think this is or is not a good law. Support your opinion with reasons and examples.

Topic 12—Television has been a part of American life for about 50 years. It has become a principal source of information and entertainment for most people.

Write an essay to explain whether you think television has had a positive effect or a negative effect on American culture. Support your opinion with reasons and examples.

Topic 13—Unemployment has been a problem in our society for a long time.

Write an essay explaining what you would do for people who are unemployed if you had the power. Use examples and reasons that support your explanation.

Topic 14—Many states have lotteries, and some, such as New Jersey and Nevada, allow gambling. Lotteries and gambling both provide support for education through taxes. State-approved lotteries and gambling also allow many people to experience financial hardship.

Write an essay to explain whether or not you think the lotteries and legal gambling in some states are good for the residents. Support your opinion with reasons and examples.

Topic 15—If a friend who did not know the city or the town where you lived asked you for advice about where to go on a weekend, what would you suggest?

Write an essay that suggests weekend spots in your town or city. For each place that you suggest, give specific reasons for your choice.

Lesson 1 Activity

1. Continue or resume keeping your journal on a daily basis.
2. Whenever you see an opportunity, write something that you intend other people to read: notes, letters, reports, and so on.
3. Set a schedule that will allow you to develop essays on all 15 topics listed in this lesson before you take the GED.
4. Decide how you will use the Topic List to assign yourself topics.

Before you develop any more essays, look over Lesson 2.

Lesson 2 The Writing Process: A Summary

This lesson summarizes all the steps in the writing process. It presents in brief form everything you studied and practiced in Chapter 2. Read this lesson carefully to refresh your memory.

Use this lesson as a guide when you write essays. The charts will help you to remember what you should do at each step in the writing process.

After you have written a few essays using this lesson as a guide, you may find yourself relying on the guide less and less. If that happens, the writing process may be becoming second nature to you. When using the process is almost automatic, you are on your way to becoming an accomplished writer.

Before Beginning the Process

When you write an essay about an assigned topic, before you can begin Step 1 in the writing process, you must (1) be sure you understand the topic and (2) decide on the point of view you want to take in your essay. When an essay topic is assigned, read it through once or twice. Then follow the following steps.

Steps in Reading a Topic Carefully and Developing a Point of View

Step 1. Underline the important or key words in the topic.
Step 2. Make sure you have noticed and understood all the topic's key ideas or concepts.
Step 3. Decide on your own point of view and state it in one sentence.

Suggestions for Step 2: One way to do Step 2 is to write a question that uses most of the words you underlined in Step 1.

Suggestions for Step 3: To do Step 3, write your answer to the question you developed in Step 2. The sentence you write will state the point of view you will present in your essay.

You are now ready to begin the writing process.

The Five Steps in the Writing Process

Step 1. Generate Ideas

- Use brainstorming or clustering to generate ideas about your essay topic.

To brainstorm, write down all the words that come to mind as you think about your point of view on the topic.

Clustering is another form of brainstorming. To cluster, follow these steps:

1. Using a few words, write your point of view on the topic in the center of a piece of paper. Circle your point of view.

2. Write the words that come to mind on extensions from the point-of-view circle. Draw a circle.

When you are finished brainstorming or clustering, go to the next step.

Step 2. Organize Your Ideas

- Select the most appropriate ideas to support your point of view or opinion.
- Decide how to arrange your ideas for your audience.
- Decide which examples best support your point of view.
- Decide which examples to present first, second, and so on.

One method for organizing ideas is mapping. Before you begin to map, however, number or color-code the ideas in your cluster. Use the same number or color for all ideas that go together. The cluster in Figure 5 is both numbered and color-coded.

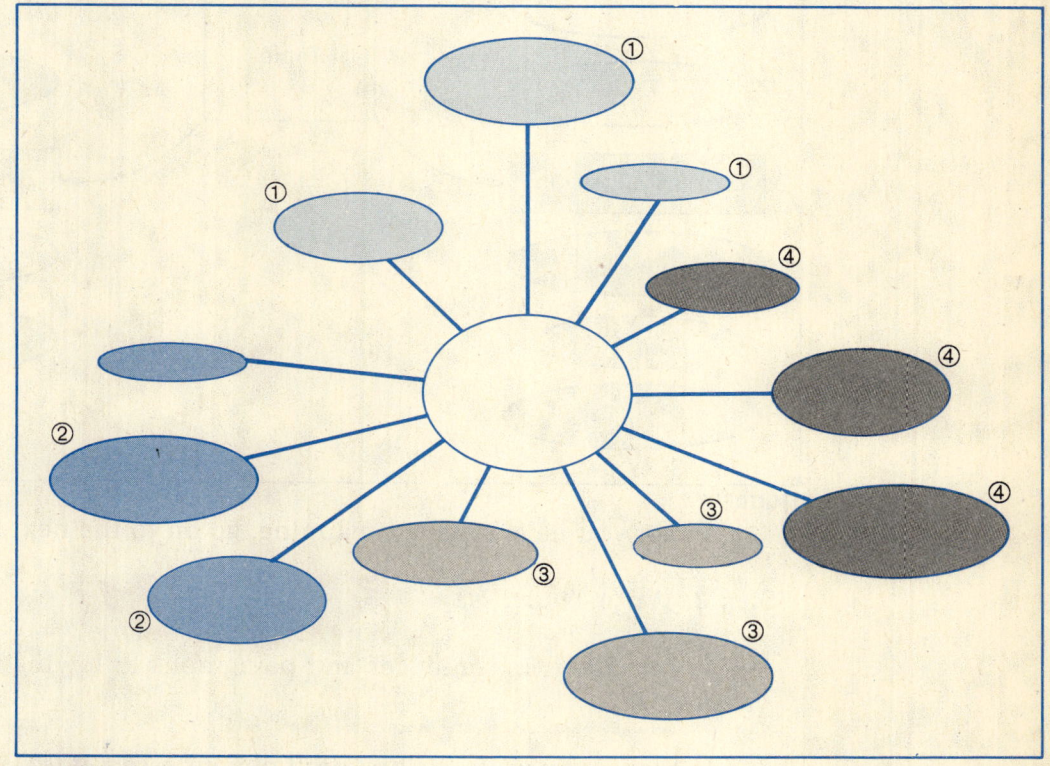

FIGURE 5

After you have grouped the ideas in your cluster, follow these instructions to create a map.

Creating a Map

1. Gather all the words from your brainstorming or clustering activities.
2. Eliminate words that have similar meanings.

3. Arrange words in categories. Title the categories. The titles will suggest your main ideas and the words listed will be used as examples to support those ideas.

4. Decide which paragraph should come first. Label it. Because it is the introductory paragraph, remember to list the topics of the other paragraphs, since the first paragraph will introduce them.

5. Decide which paragraph should be second, third, fourth, and so on. Label each one.

Figure 6 shows an example of a map.

Example of a map

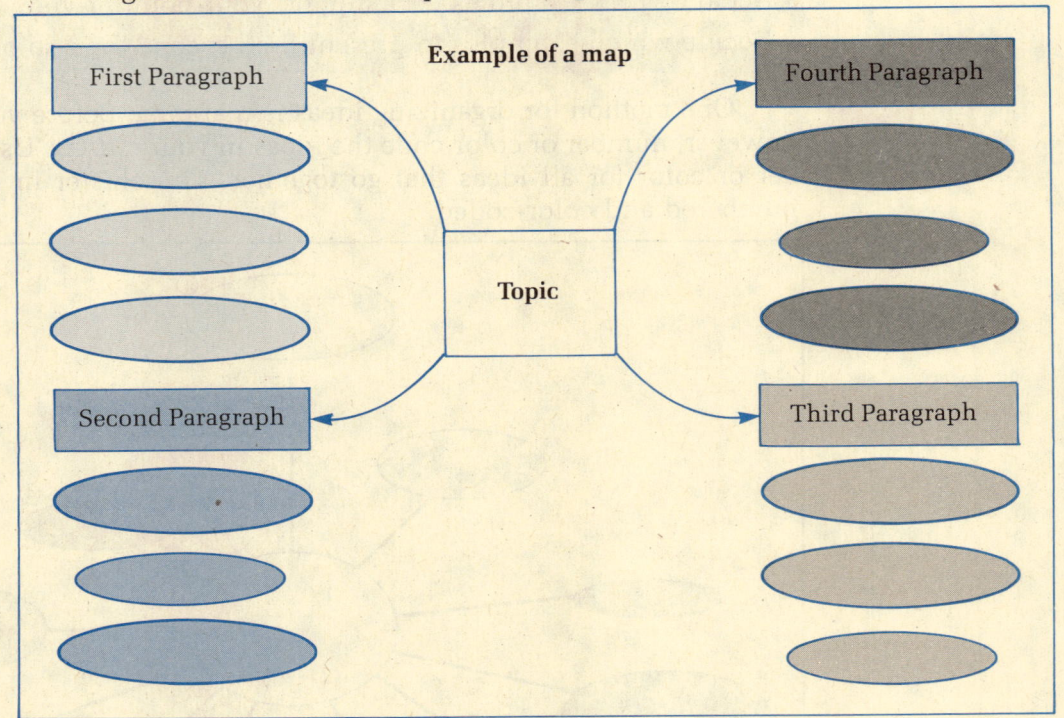

FIGURE 6

When you have finished mapping, go on to the next step.

Step 3. Write Your Essay

- Put your ideas in sentences and paragraphs following the organization you planned.

In Step 3 you write the first draft of your essay. It is not the final version. Concentrate on getting all your ideas written in sentences and paragraphs. Do not spend too much time changing things you write. Changes can be made in the next step.

When you write your essay, follow the instructions in this list.

Writing Your Essay

1. In the opening paragraph, state your central point of view about the topic immediately. Then give your reasons for your point of view.

2. In the second, third, and following paragraphs, develop supporting examples to explain each of the reasons for your point of view.
3. In the final paragraph, restate and explain why you hold your central point of view.

When you have finished writing, go to the next step.

Step 4. Revise Your Essay

- Make sure that your point of view or opinion is stated clearly and that your examples support your point of view.
- Add information needed for clarity.
- Remove information that is not needed.

Revision is a very important step in the writing process. A revised essay is nearly a completed essay.

To revise your essay, read it with your audience in mind. Make any changes that make your essay clear and effective.

Ask yourself the following questions. If you answer *no* to any of the questions, make changes.

Revising Your Essay

Key Ideas

- Did you state the central idea of your essay in one sentence?
- Is the central idea or point of view stated clearly enough that any reader would be able to restate it?

Content

- Did you use specific examples that support your point of view?
- Are your examples explained clearly enough that your reader can see how they support your point of view?
- Did you consider the opinions of a person who doesn't agree with your point of view? If so, did you answer that person's argument?

Organization

- Did you state your point of view right away?
- Did you present two or three important supporting ideas?
- Would your reader be able to restate what the important supporting ideas are?
- Did you use words that show how your supporting ideas relate to the central idea and to each other?

Summary or Conclusion

Does your summary or conclusion follow logically from what you said in your essay?

When you have finished revising, your essay is almost in its final version. To polish it, go to the next and last step.

> **Step 5. Edit Your Essay**
> - Correct errors in usage, sentence structure, spelling, punctuation, and capitalization.

Your essay should be close to completed by now. However, because you have been concentrating on organization, clarity, and effectiveness, you may have overlooked some mechanical issues. In this step, you correct any errors you discover.

Use the following suggestions to help you polish your essay.

Editing Your Essay

1. Read your essay aloud or in a whisper.
2. Read at the speed—normal or slow—that works best for you.
3. Use the 5-R editing method.
4. Read your essay backward while you concentrate on spelling.

When you have finished editing, your essay is in its final form.

Lesson 2 Activity

1. Continue making daily entries in your journal.
2. Without looking back at this lesson, write a brief summary of the major activities that belong in each of the five steps of the writing process. When you have finished, see how well you remembered by checking your summary against the summary in this lesson.
3. Write on all 15 of the topics provided in Lesson 1 of this chapter (pages 193–195). When you develop an essay, follow the writing process summary in this lesson. Refer to the sample of a developed essay in Chapter 2 (pages 190–191). If you practice writing essays and follow the guidelines outlined in this unit, you should get a good score on the Writing Skills Test.

UNIT III

Reading Strategies

In this unit, you will learn important strategies for reading. When you take the Social Studies, Science, and Interpreting Literature and the Arts tests, you will be asked to read passages related to those fields, and then answer questions based on those passages. The better you understand the passages you read, the better you will perform on the tests. The strategies you will study in this unit will help you to understand the passages you read better.

The questions that make up the three GED tests mentioned above ask you to demonstrate both that you understand what you read and that you can read critically. As you study the next three units in this book, you will need to apply the same kinds of thinking skills. This unit will help you in three important ways. First, it will help you improve your study skills. Second, it will show you ways to determine how a question based on a social studies or science passage, or a selection from literature, requires you to think. Third, it will show you strategies for answering questions effectively.

You should complete Unit III before going on to Units IV to VI, the Social Studies, Science, and Interpreting Literature and the Arts units.

UNIT III PROGRESS CHART
Reading Strategies

Use the following chart to keep track of your work. When you complete a lesson, circle the number of questions you answered correctly in the Lesson Exercise. When you complete a Chapter Quiz, also record your score below. The numbers in color represent scores at a level of 80% or better.

Lesson	Page		
		CHAPTER 1: A Strategy for Reading	
1	203	What Previewing Is	1 2 3
2	205	Previewing the Lessons in This Book	1 2 3
3	206	Previewing Test Items	1 2 3 4
4	209	Questioning As You Read Lessons	1 2 3
5	211	Questioning As You Read Test Items	1 2 3
	213	Quiz	1 2 3 4 5 6 7 8 9 10
		CHAPTER 2: Reading for Answers	
1	215	The Four Levels of Questions	1 2 3
2	218	Order for Reading	1 2 3 4
3	220	Comprehension Questions	1 2 3 4
4	224	Application Questions	1 2 3 4
5	228	Analysis Questions	1 2 3 4
6	232	Evaluation Questions	1 2 3 4
7	236	How to Answer Questions	1 2 3 4
8	241	Reviewing Answers	1 2 3
	243	Quiz	1 2 3 4 5 6 7 8 9 10
		CHAPTER 3: The Three "Reading Tests"	
1	246	Steps in Reading Items	1 2 3
2	248	The Social Studies and Science Tests	1 2 3 4 5 6 7
3	256	The Interpreting Literature and the Arts Test	1 2 3 4
	260	Quiz	1 2 3 4 5 6 7 8 9 10

Chapter 1

A Strategy for Reading

> **Objective**
>
> In this chapter you will read about and practice
> - Previewing material you are about to read
> - Questioning material before and during reading

Lesson 1 What Previewing Is

Why should you preview reading material?

When you preview, you quickly look over material you will later read carefully. **Previewing** helps you make a mental outline of how the writing is organized. This mental outline will make it easier for you to understand what you read later.

You preview many things you read. For example, the first time you picked up *TV Guide*, you probably previewed it.

- You noticed the picture of the actor or the actress on the cover.
- You skimmed the print on the cover and discovered that the magazine contained TV listings for a certain week.
- You flipped through the magazine to see how it was arranged.
- You saw that the names of shows appeared in lists.
- You noticed that shows were organized by day, time, and channel.
- You observed that some shows were described briefly.
- You found that some shows had special ads near their listings.
- You discovered that the magazine contained articles about the television industry and ads for products.

By previewing, you learned what you could expect to find in *TV Guide*. You also learned where you should look for particular things without reading through the entire magazine.

You can preview anything you plan to read: books, magazines, manuals, graphs, schedules, and other materials. Previewing can help you to find, understand, and think about ideas of special interest to you.

Directions for Previewing a Book

- Look at the cover and the title.
- Look over the table of contents.
- Glance at illustrations.
- Look at headings and words in italics or in dark print.
- Find out where sections begin and end.
- See if there is an index or glossary at the end of the book.

By spending a few minutes previewing a book, you will know what to expect when you read it. Preview this book.

1. Look at the front cover. Examine the title. What does the cover tell you about the book's contents?

2. What do you learn from the back cover?

3. Look at the table of contents on page v. Use it to see how this book is organized. You will notice that some headings are treated differently from others. How are the unit titles different from the chapter titles? You find out that units are made up of chapters.

4. Flip back and forth between the table of contents and the book pages to get a sense of where sections begin and end. Where are the Predictor Tests? Flip through them. Where are the instruction units located? the GED Practice Items? the unit on social studies? the Simulated Tests? Quickly flip through these pages. Where is the Answer Key? Glance through it.

Now that you have previewed this book, you have a mental map of where things are in it.

Lesson 1 Exercise

Use the table of contents of this book to answer the following.

1. Where are the Predictor Tests located in relation to the instruction units? Are they before or after them?

2. Suppose you wanted practice in answering only geography items. Would you turn to Social Studies Practice Items or Social Studies Simulated Test? Why?

3. Where are the answers to Simulated Tests located in relation to the answers for GED Practice Items? Are they before or after them?

Answers are on page A-13.

Lesson 2 Previewing the Lessons in This Book

What should you look at when you preview a lesson?

Now that you have found out about the overall organization of this book, preview a lesson to find how it is organized. Keep your place on this page as you follow these directions that tell you to look at other pages in the book.

Directions for Previewing a Lesson

1. Look at the table of contents to find where the first chapter of science instruction begins. What is the title of that chapter?

2. Now, turn to the beginning of Chapter 1 in the unit on science. Look at the chapter number and title. Are you on the correct page?

3. Notice that the very first thing in the chapter is the Objective. What does the Objective tell you?

4. After the Objective comes the title of Lesson 1. What is the general topic of the lesson?

5. Look at the question following the title. What clues does it provide about the content of Lesson 1?

6. Glance over the text. You will see that some words are in dark print: *science, phenomena, matter,* and others. What more do these words tell about the content of the lesson?

7. Glance over the list at the end of the lesson. There are words in dark print followed by brief phrases. You can guess that the phrases define the terms *biology, earth science,* and so on.

8. Look at the last element in the lesson: Lesson 1 Exercise. It is made up of numbered questions. You know you are looking at the part of the lesson that tests your understanding. There are two questions. One asks you to write out a short answer; the other question requires an answer for each of five parts.

9. After the exercise, a short note tells you where you can find the answers to the questions. That note lets you know that you will be able to check your answers yourself.

You now have a good idea of how the first science lesson is organized. Find out if other lessons are organized in the same way. Preview the lessons after Lesson 1. Do they have titles? questions after the titles? exercises? Are there other elements, such as illustration, in those lessons? So far your preview has suggested to you that the organization of lessons in this book follows a standard format.

Lesson 2 Exercise

Find Lesson 2 in Chapter 1 of Unit V (the science unit). Preview the lesson; then answer the following items.

1. The question following the title suggests that which of the following topics is probably covered in Lesson 2?

    (1) the history of science

    (2) one scientist's life

    (3) a modern-day invention

    (4) methods used by scientists

    (5) preservation of natural resources

2. In the lesson, what words are in dark print? Why are those words in dark print?

3. How many items are there in the Lesson 2 Exercise? How many of those items are multiple choice?

    Answers are on page A-13.

Lesson 3 Previewing Test Items

What should you look at when you preview a test item?

You have previewed this book as a whole as well as a couple of lessons within the book. Now it is time to focus on how to preview the type of test items you will find on the GED.

When you preview a test item or item set (material followed by more than one question), note where the directions are; the general form of the passage; titles, labels, captions, words in italics or dark print; how many items are based on the material; and the general form of the choices.

A sample item set follows. Preview it by following the directions that come after it.

Sample Item Set

Items 1 and 2 refer to the following passage.

An advertisement for a popular breakfast cereal states

A. composed of 100% whole grain wheat

B. a flavorful cereal your whole family will enjoy

C. no sugar added

D. the cereal you are wise to choose

1. Which of the above statements is most likely based on fact rather than on opinion?
   - (1) A only
   - (2) B only
   - (3) A and B only
   - (4) A and C only
   - (5) B and D only

2. Which of the above statements could not be proven in a chemical analysis of the cereal?
   - (1) A only
   - (2) B only
   - (3) A and B only
   - (4) A and C only
   - (5) B and D only

Directions for Previewing the Sample Item Set

1. Read the directions: "*Items 1 and 2 refer to the following passage.*" That line shows how many items are based on the advertisement.

2. Since the next line stands by itself, take a quick look at it. What is the topic of the passage? In what format is the topic presented: in a paragraph? in a list? in an illustration?

3. Notice that there is a list of four statements, lettered A, B, C, and D.

4. Glance at the two items that follow the advertisement. Notice that each choice refers to one or two statements from the advertisement.

You have finished previewing the item set. When you take the GED, you should always spend a few seconds previewing each test item or item set. That way, you will be prepared to read the passage in the most efficient way.

Lesson 3   Exercise

Preview the following portion of an item set. Answer the questions that follow it.

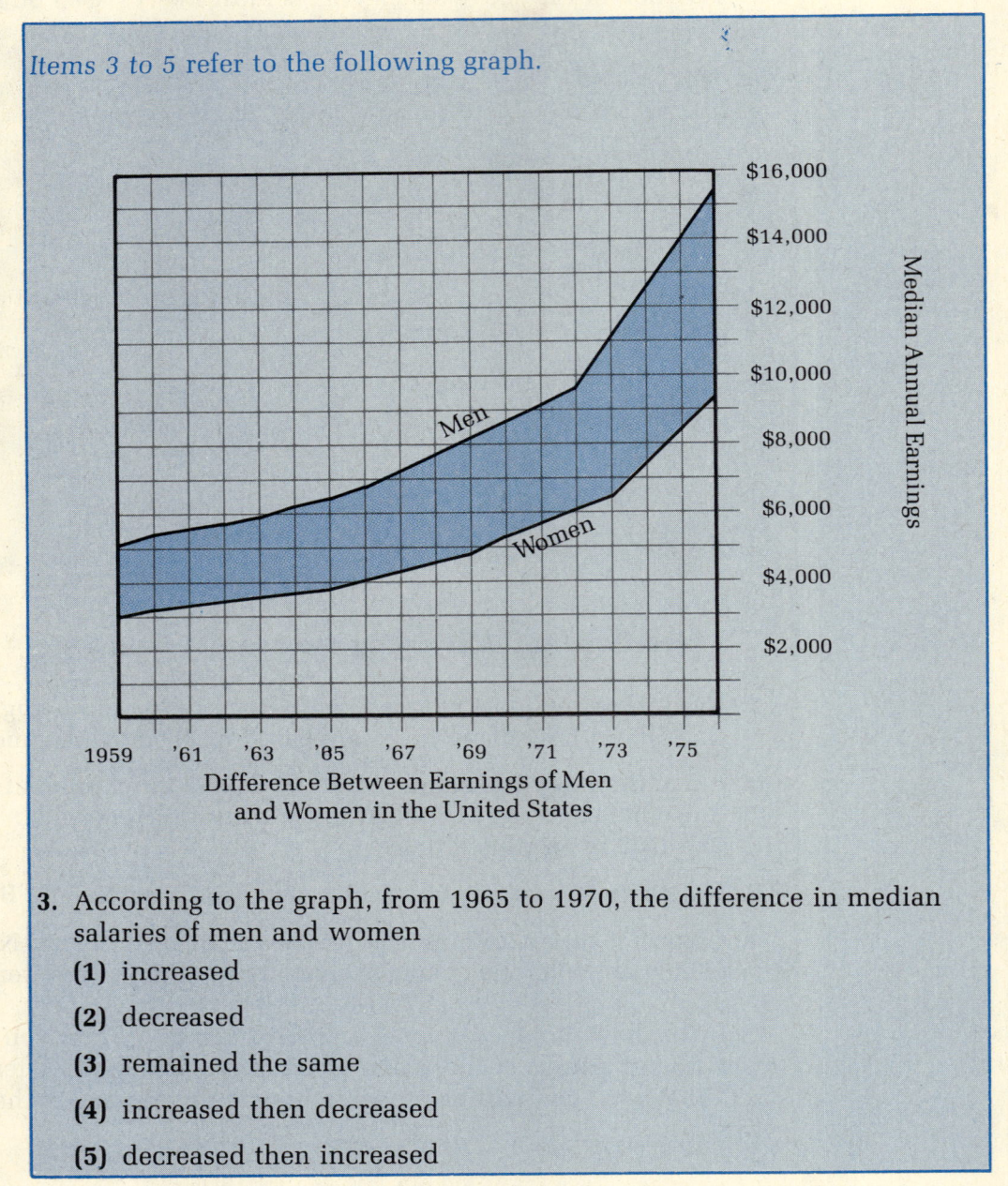

Items 3 to 5 refer to the following graph.

Difference Between Earnings of Men and Women in the United States

(Graph shows Median Annual Earnings from $2,000 to $16,000 on the vertical axis, and years from 1959 to '75 on the horizontal axis, with two curves labeled "Men" and "Women.")

3. According to the graph, from 1965 to 1970, the difference in median salaries of men and women
   - (1) increased
   - (2) decreased
   - (3) remained the same
   - (4) increased then decreased
   - (5) decreased then increased

---

1. How many items do the directions indicate make up the item set?
2. Based on the title, what do you think the topic of the graph is?
3. What do the numbers along the bottom of the graph refer to?
4. What do the numbers along the the right side of the graph refer to?

Answers are on page A-13.

Lesson 4 Questioning as You Read Lessons

How and why should you question as you read a lesson?

Active reading is the most effective reading. If you are interested in what you read, and if you think actively about it, you will get the most from it. **Questioning**—asking questions before and during reading—will help you read actively.

Questioning is the step that follows previewing in an effective reading strategy. Previewing shows how ideas are organized. Questioning helps you set a purpose for reading. When you actually read material, questioning helps you fulfill your purpose.

You probably already question as you read some material, especially material that interests you. After you preview the sports page of the newspaper, for example, you may look for an article about your favorite team. As you read each paragraph describing the team's latest game, you probably ask yourself what you will find out in the next paragraph. You may make predictions and read to test your predictions. You can apply questioning to anything you plan to read.

Steps in Questioning as You Read

1. Think more carefully about the title or headings you previewed. If there are no headings, think about other clues you found about the topic.

2. Ask yourself a question you think might be answered in the material.

3. Make a prediction about the answer.

4. Read to find out if your prediction is right.

To practice questioning, follow these directions as you read through Lesson 3 in the first chapter in the science unit (page 317).

1. Preview the lesson and the exercise questions that end it.

2. Begin your questioning by reading the exercise questions at the end of the lesson.

3. Carefully read the title of the lesson and the question below the title. Put the question into your own words.

4. Make a prediction about the answer to your question.

5. Keeping the question in mind, begin reading the passage.

6. The first sentence immediately suggests another question. The word in dark print, *experimentation*, might lead you to ask: What is experimentation? You will find the answer in the next sentence.

7. Now you can ask another question: What does experimentation have to do with scientific validity? As you continue reading, you learn that one scientist's findings are valid only if another scientist can get the same

210 Chapter 1: A Strategy for Reading

results. This answer generates another question: When first designing experiments, how can scientists increase their chances of getting valid results?

8. Continue reading to answer this question.

9. After you finish the first paragraph, read the second paragraph using the same questioning method.

    Did you find questioning helpful in understanding and remembering information? As you were reading the second paragraph, did you find that some of your predictions were wrong? Were some of your questions never answered at all? That is okay. Just making the predictions will help improve your comprehension, because it will help you to read actively. Now continue.

10. Read the first sentence of the third paragraph. You might ask yourself: How will the experiment be set up? You might answer: Maybe a group of mice will be put in the light and then put in the dark.

11. You know as soon as you read the second sentence in the paragraph that two groups of baby mice are used, so you change your prediction about how the experiment is set up: Maybe the lengths of the mice in both groups will be measured, some after being in the light and the others after being in the dark.

12. After you read a few more sentences, you learn that *every week the weight of each mouse is recorded in a table.* Again, your prediction was not quite correct: weight, not length, is measured. Furthermore, measurements are made once a week.

13. Since your original question about how the experiment was set up has been answered, ask a new question. You might ask: What were the results of the experiment? You might predict: Sunlight slows growth in baby mice.

14. After examining the table and finishing the paragraph, you realize that your prediction was incorrect. The final sentence tells you that *sunlight helps baby mice grow.*

If your predictions turn out to be wrong, it doesn't matter. The important thing is that you read actively. By asking questions, predicting answers, and reading to check your answers, you help yourself to understand and to remember material.

Lesson 4   Exercise

Items 1 to 3 are based on Lesson 4 of Chapter 1 in the unit on science (page 319). Preview the lesson to see how it is organized; then answer the following items as you apply the questioning process.

1. A question appears before the passage: "What is a *scientific fact*?" Reword the question. Begin your question with "How do you _____?"

2. Suppose someone predicts that a scientific fact is something scientists know will always be true. Read the first paragraph to test that prediction. Is the prediction right? Explain how the paragraph supports or does not support the prediction.

3. Read the second paragraph. Then, before you read the third paragraph, predict the answer to the following question: How might the use of instruments lead to changes in scientific knowledge? Check your prediction. What answer does the third paragraph give to the question?

Answers are on page A-13.

Lesson 5 Questioning as You Read Test Items

How and why should you question a test item as you read it?

Questioning is especially helpful when you are reading material on a test. Reading GED test items actively will improve the accuracy of your answers. After a quick preview, begin questioning.

Steps in Questioning as You Read a Test Item

1. Read and put into your own words the question or questions you will answer later.
2. Do not read through the five choices until later.
3. If there is a question before the passage, read and reword it.
4. Read the passage with your questions in mind and read to test predictions you make.
5. For passages longer than a couple of sentences, continue creating your own questions, making predictions, and reading to test your predictions.
6. When you finish the passage, reread the test question(s) following it.
7. Predict the answer(s), if possible, and search for your prediction(s) among the choices.

Turn to Items 21 to 23 on the Interpreting Literature and the Arts Predictor Test (page 40). Follow these directions.

1. Preview the passage and the questions that follow it. Notice that the directions tell you that the passage is a song. How many items are based on the song? Since you observe that there are three verses, you can predict that the author will present three ideas.

2. Read the three questions. You might reword them: How is *paradise* defined? What would the author consider a better alternative to DDT? What topic would the author NOT put into her song?

3. Read the question preceding the song. You might reword it: Is the world improving? You might already predict, based on the question about DDT, a harmful insecticide, that the author does not think so.

4. Read the first line of the song. Since you find the word *paradise*, you might think about your question: How is *paradise* defined?

5. You might predict that *paradise* means "heaven," or "a wonderful place where people end up after they die." Read the rest of the verse.

6. You discover, instead, that the author seems to be talking about a real place that has been replaced by a parking lot. From your own experience, you might ask: Has a field or wooded area been paved and made into a parking lot?

7. Read the second verse. You see that the paved spot had been a wooded area, in fact.

8. Read the first line of the third verse. Since you find the word, DDT, you might ask: What would the author consider a better alternative to DDT?

9. Finish the third verse. You discover that the author would rather have spots on her apples than kill the birds and the bees with DDT.

    You might want to take a minute or two to reread the song now, just to enjoy it. When you enjoy what you are reading, you tend to relax and understand it better. Keeping your anxiety down and your interest up will help your performance on the GED.

10. Reread the three items. You have already predicted answers to the first two questions. Simply read each choice until you find the one that is closest to your prediction. Choice (1) of Item 21, *a place where trees are put in museums*, does not match your prediction, "a wooded area." Choice (2), *the unspoiled natural world*, seems to be an appropriate answer. Skim the other alternatives just to make sure that they are not better matches for your prediction, but do not spend much time on them. After skimming the alternatives for Item 22, you select (5), *spotted apples*, because it matches your prediction.

11. Because Item 23 is worded *Which of the following other topics probably would* NOT *be included in this song?* you cannot make a precise prediction. You can probably make the general prediction that the song would only include examples related to environmental problems. Since you have read the question carefully, you know that you must look for topics that are NOT about damage to the environment. Choice (4), *drug abuse*, is the only alternative not related to environmental problems.

    Do you see how using the questioning process on test items helps you read the passage effectively and answer the items accurately?

Lesson 5 Exercise

Items 1 to 3 are based on Items 15 to 18 in the Science Predictor Test (page 26). Preview the passage that begins, "Items 15 to 18 are based on the following article," and continue previewing through Item 18.

1. Read the question asked in Item 15. Predict a possible answer based on what you already know about color and on any clues you picked up during your preview of the choices. What question will you ask yourself in order to test your prediction while you read?

2. The first sentence in the article is in the form of a general question you should ask yourself as you read the passage. Reword the question to make sure you understand it.

3. After reading the first paragraph in the article, read the first sentence of the second paragraph. Ask a question that you think will be answered in the rest of the paragraph. Begin your question with "How do _____?"

Answers are on page A-13.

Chapter 1 Quiz

1. Which of the following things would you do if you were previewing a book you had not yet read? (a) Look at the cover. (b) Look over the table of contents. (c) Carefully read the first chapter. (d) Flip through the book. (e) Read the glossary entries.

2. Write general instructions to explain how to preview a lesson in this book. List four or five steps.

3. Which of the following would you NOT do if you were previewing a test item set? (a) Read the passage. (b) See how many items are based on the passage. (c) Glance at the questions you will answer later. (d) Read the Answer Key entry.

Items 4 and 5 require you to flip between the table of contents (page v) and the text pages while previewing this book.

4. Name and describe the element that comes between the chapter title and first lesson of every chapter in this book.

5. Name the two elements that appear at the beginning of every lesson in Units III–VI of this book.

Items 6 and 7 are based on Lesson 1 of Chapter 1 in the Social Studies unit (page 265).

6. How many exercise items based on Lesson 1 should you preview?

7. Based on repeated words you note during a preview of the lesson, what topic do you think the lesson is about?
   - **(1)** social studies
   - **(2)** economics
   - **(3)** history
   - **(4)** religion
   - **(5)** geography

Item 8 is based on the set that includes items 3 to 7 on the Science Predictor Test (page 22).

8. In previewing this item set, what is the last thing you should look at?

9. Questions you ask as you read a lesson could be your rewordings of the ones that you find after the lesson title or in the lesson exercises. Where might other questions come from?

10. A good reason for you to reword the questions in test items is to
    - **(1)** help you understand the questions
    - **(2)** save time in reading the questions
    - **(3)** make sure you know the answers

Answers are on pages A-13.

Chapter 2

Reading for Answers

> **Objective**
>
> In this chapter, you will read about and practice answering the four kinds of questions on the GED:
>
> - Comprehension questions, which ask you to state the meaning of what is written
> - Application questions, which ask you to extend your understanding to a new situation
> - Analysis questions, which ask you to think about relationships between ideas
> - Evaluation questions, which ask you to judge the accuracy of ideas
>
> You will also read about and practice
>
> - Answering the various types of items on the GED: graphic items, narrative items, single items, item sets
> - The order for reading the parts of each type of item
> - Strategies for answering multiple-choice questions
> - Strategies for answering nonmultiple-choice questions
> - How to check and review answers

Lesson 1 The Four Levels of Questions

What are the four levels of questions on the GED? Why should you learn to identify them?

In Chapter 1 you learned about previewing and questioning, two steps that will help you do all kinds of reading. In this chapter you will learn more about how to read the kinds of items on the GED.

It is important to remember that all items on the GED require you to think about information you are given. This makes your job both easy and difficult:

- You will never have to come up with an answer based only on what you knew before walking into the testing room.
- You will never be asked simply to find facts given in the material. You will always be asked to show that you understand and can use the information presented.

In other words, you should read the test material actively. As you read, you will be constantly relating what you know from past experience to what you are learning. Having to think about what you are reading is worth the effort. When you read actively, reading becomes more interesting. Being interested in what you read boosts your understanding.

It should not be difficult to make a conscious effort to be interested in the material on the GED. The test is designed to present information relevant to your daily life. To answer the items, you will use the same skills you use in everyday decision-making.

Just as questions you face in real life vary in difficulty, so do the items on the GED. There are four levels of questions on the GED: comprehension, application, analysis, and evaluation.

Examples of the Four Question Types

Comprehension questions, those at the lowest level, require you to show that you understand what you read. For example, suppose you are presented with the following statement:

The snowman melted by noontime the day the weather changed.

A comprehension question might be: During what part of the day was the snowman melting? Your answer will show whether or not you understand the sentence.

Application questions require that you apply information you understand to a new situation. An application question based on the statement about the snowman might be: If there had been a snowball on the snowman's head, what would have happened to it by noontime?

Analysis questions require that you think about relationships between ideas, such as a cause-and-effect relationship. An analysis question might be: What caused the snowman to melt?

Evaluation questions require that you judge the accuracy of ideas based on the information you have been given. To evaluate ideas well, you must also be able to comprehend, apply, and analyze them. An evaluation question might be: Is it more likely that the event described took place in Florida or in Maine?

You should learn to identify questions at each of the four levels. Each type of question places a different kind of demand on your thinking. Once you recognize these demands, you will know how to answer the item successfully.

Questions on the Social Studies and Science tests are at all four levels. Questions on the Interpreting Literature and the Arts Test are at the comprehension, application, and analysis levels. The following chart shows how often you will be asked each type of question on each of the GED "reading" tests.

UNIT III: READING STRATEGIES   Lesson 1   **217**

	Social Studies	Science	Interpreting Literature and the Arts
Comprehension	20%	20%	60%
Application	30%	30%	15%
Analysis	30%	30%	25%
Evaluation	20%	20%	—

This book offers you three ways to learn about the four levels of questions.

1. The lessons in this chapter focus on the four levels.
2. All Lesson Exercises, Chapter Quizzes, Practice Items, and Simulated Tests in the book give you practice in answering the four levels of questions.
3. Each entry in the Answer Key is labeled by question level.

Lesson 1   Exercise

1. Based on the information in this lesson, which of the following statements is true?

    (1) The situations presented on the GED test are not usually realistic.

    (2) GED items often test your understanding of information.

    (3) Answers to GED items often can be taken word for word from the passages.

    (4) The GED will often ask for facts you should have memorized.

    (5) The GED only requires you to use what you know from your experience in life.

2. Match the name of the level of question with the phrase that best describes it.

    (1) Comprehension   (a) asks you to judge ideas

    (2) Application   (b) asks you to examine how ideas relate

    (3) Analysis   (c) asks you to use ideas in a new situation

    (4) Evaluation   (d) asks you to demonstrate that you understand what you read

3. How will learning about the four levels of questions improve your performance on the GED?

Answers are on page A-13.

Lesson 2 Order for Reading

What is the order of steps for reading the parts of a GED item?

Besides previewing and questioning, a third activity that will help you understand, think about, and remember what you read is **reconstructing,** or rebuilding, the main points into a new form. The *new form* may be an outline, a list, a diagram, a sketch, or any other quick summary of what you read. Reconstructing is particularly helpful in answering test items.

You probably already practice reconstructing after some of your reading. After you read *TV Guide*, you may draw stars next to the programs you want to remember to watch. After you read a magazine description of how to make chili, you might jot down the recipe as a list of steps in your own shorthand.

On the GED, you will find test items in several different formats.

- Graphics, (tables, charts, cartoons, maps, or diagrams) followed by one or more items
- A sentence or short passage followed by one item
- A longer passage followed by a set of items

Whatever the format, it helps to follow these steps in reading: (1) preview; (2) question while reading; (3) reconstruct; and (4) reread. (You may find that you can answer some items without reconstructing or rereading.)

Steps in Reading a GED Item

You have read a little about the general order for previewing and questioning items. Now, here are specific steps to follow while answering a typical GED item. This example is based on the passage before Item 4 on the Social Studies Predictor Test (page 12).

1. Previewing reveals the repeated words, *taxes* and *governments*. That repetition indicates that the passage is about government use of taxes. (If you were previewing a graphic item, you would scan all the major parts of the graphic, including captions and repeated words.)

2. Preview the item following the passage or graphic. In this case, read the question. Since it is worded *Which of the following would most likely . . .* , you will need to read all of the choices later. Which of the four levels of questions do you think this is? (If there is more than one question, read each question in the same manner and notice which one(s) you can predict an answer to without examining the choices.)

3. Think of a question to ask yourself as you read the passage. Based on the specific question you will need to answer, you might ask, What do property taxes pay for?

4. You might predict: Property taxes pay those who take care of government property, such as gardeners at City Hall.

5. Now read the passage. As you read the first sentence, you realize that the prediction is wrong. *Property* must mean private property, not government property.

6. After completing the passage, questioning as you read, reconstruct it. You might draw a quick sketch to show the relationships among taxes, government, and property owners. See Figure 1.

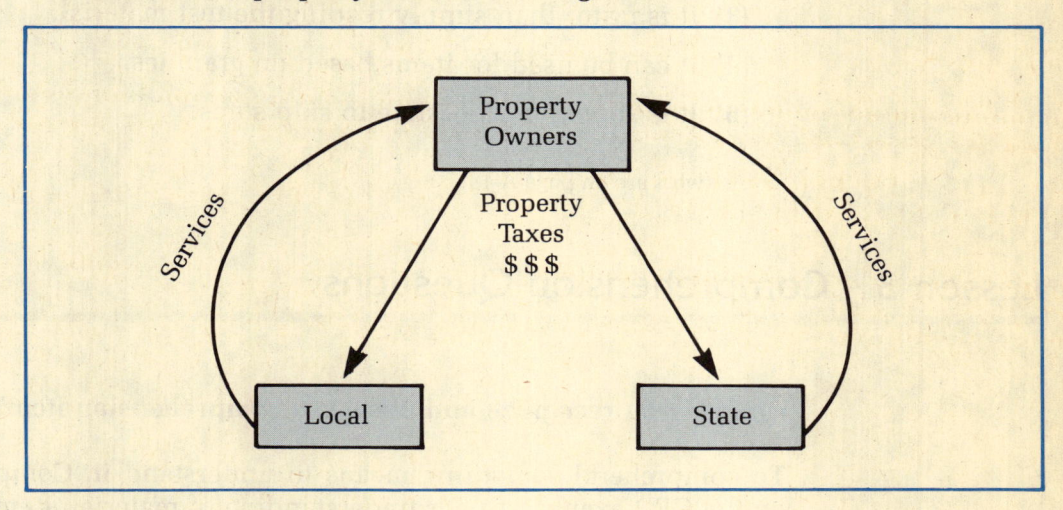

FIGURE 1

(If the item has a graphic instead of a passage, reverse the above process. Imagine that you are explaining, in words, the diagram or graph to someone else.)

7. If you have time, reread the passage or graphic for pleasure and to get a sense of the whole.

8. Reread the question, read the choices, and select the best answer. Repeat this process if there is more than one question.

You have learned about four general steps to follow in reading an item: preview, question while reading, reconstruct, and reread. You might want to change the order and the number of steps described above, depending on how difficult you find a particular reading.

Lesson 2 Exercise

1. The first step to take when reading a test item is called ____, which means ____.

2. Why might you want to read a question BEFORE you read the passage or graphic on which it is based?

3. Place the following in the order that is generally the best one to follow when reading a test item or item set: questioning while reading, rereading, previewing, reconstructing.

4. Which of the following is NOT true about following the suggested order of steps for reading the parts of test items?

   (1) It will help you understand the test material.

   (2) It will help you in selecting the right answer.

   (3) It is faster than simply reading the test material.

   (4) It can be used for items based on graphics.

   (5) It is sometimes possible to skip steps.

Answers are on page A-14.

Lesson 3   Comprehension Questions

How do you recognize and answer a comprehension item?

To comprehend something means to understand it. Comprehension items on the GED exam test your understanding of material. Items at the comprehension level usually ask you to:

1. Restate ideas
2. Summarize information
3. Identify implications (underlying meanings)

You will find comprehension items on the GED Social Studies, Science, and Interpreting Literature and the Arts tests.

Look at Item 1 on the Social Studies Predictor Test (page 11). You are asked: *According to the graph, during which of the following periods was immigration lowest?* You are asked to show that you understand the information on the graph, nothing more. The lowest bar on the graph is captioned "1931–1940." When you answer, you restate that portion of the information as follows: Immigration was lowest during the period between 1931 and 1940.

Item 9 on the Science Predictor Test (page 23) is another item at the comprehension level. You are asked to summarize the main idea. The question *What does this passage tell us about rosebushes?* makes clear what is being tested: your understanding of the passage, nothing more.

Item 21 on the Interpreting Literature and the Arts Predictor Test (page 40) is another example of a comprehension item. You are asked to show that you understand what the writer means by *paradise*, even though she does not come right out and explain it.

You will find four types of comprehension items on the Interpreting Literature and Arts Test. Each of the four types will be covered fully in

UNIT III: READING STRATEGIES   Lesson 3

Chapter 3. For now, it is enough for you to know that items may ask about: (a) a specific part of a passage; (b) ideas throughout the text; (c) ideas that are stated; or (d) ideas that are implied.

Identifying Comprehension Questions

Comprehension items may begin with the following phrases.

- In the passage, what does _____ mean?
- We can state from the information that _____.
- Based on the diagram, you can calculate that _____.
- Based on the map, which of the following is true?
- The cartoon reveals that _____.
- The writer draws the conclusion that _____.
- Which of the following best describes the author's opinion?
- The main point is that _____.
- Which of the following best describes the purpose of the article?
- The author uses the example to show that _____.

Here are some examples that will help you identify comprehension level questions.

Item 6 on the Social Studies Predictor Test (page 13) begins:

Which one of the following statements best summarizes the point of the passage?

The word *summarizes* should suggest to you that this is a comprehension item. You are asked to show that you understand the article by summarizing the main idea. To answer the item correctly, think about which alternative covers the whole passage, not just part of it.

In Item 10 on the Science Predictor Test (page 24), you are asked:

What percent of the atmosphere is made of the gas that sustains human and other animal life?

You are required to put the information from a chart into words. Notice, too, that you need to use your own general knowledge that oxygen is the gas that sustains humans and other animal life.

Item 18 of the Interpreting Literature and the Arts Predictor Test (page 39) begins:

Before the proposal, the relationship between Mr. Rochester and Jane was apparently that of . . .

A key word here is *apparently*. You are asked to show that you understand the *implications* of what you read. You must use the available information to "read between the lines."

Steps in Answering a Comprehension Question

Focus now on how to predict an answer before looking at alternatives; later you will read how to choose the best alternative.

Look again at Item 6 of the Social Studies Predictor Test (page 13).

1. Preview the passage. In which GED format is it organized? graphic? short passage followed by a single item? longer passage followed by two or more items?

2. Key words give you the general idea that the passage is about children's TV watching.

3. Read Item 6. The item is written at the comprehension level. It simply asks you to show that you understand what the passage is about.

4. You might reword the question for yourself: In a nutshell, what is the writer trying to say? Keep this general question in the back of your mind as you read.

5. Begin reading the passage, questioning as you read. Your preview has given you the main idea that the passage is about children's TV watching. You may well have heard discussions of the problems associated with children seeing violence on TV. The first question to consider as you read may be: How does TV violence affect children?

6. When you come to the line *Experiments show that children tend to be more aggressive and overactive after viewing violence on television*, you have the answer to your question.

7. The third paragraph begins, *But even television critics agree that television is not all bad*. You might ask yourself: What is good about television?

8. As you read the rest of the passage, you find the answer to your question: Some television programs are educational.

9. Take a moment to reconstruct the passage for yourself. You might draw or imagine a scale with "TV violence" on one side and "educational programs" on the other. The last line of the passage points out that parents need to judge the programs their children watch; you might include this information in your reconstruction by imagining a parent in judge's robes behind the scale.

10. Carefully reread the question asked in Item 6. Come up with your own answer. Be sure to give a *summary* of the information provided. You are asked to grasp the thought of the passage as a whole, *not* just to restate one of its parts. You are NOT asked to use the information in this particular item or to judge it in any way.

11. You might come up with the answer: In short, the writer is saying that TV can have both good and bad effects on children.

12. Look for the alternative that most closely matches your answer. You select (4) because the statement *Television influences children* includes both good and bad effects.

UNIT III: READING STRATEGIES   Lesson 3   **223**

This lesson has explored special demands that comprehension items place on your thinking about test material. Comprehension items require you to show that you understand material by restating part of it, summarizing it, or explaining what is implied.

Lesson 3   Exercise

1. Based on what you have read in this lesson, comprehension questions
   - (1) ask you to repeat the words found in part of a passage
   - (2) always require you to restate part of a passage
   - (3) sometimes ask you to summarize the main idea of a passage
   - (4) require more than simply understanding what material means
   - (5) will never be asked following a graphic

2. If you can identify an item as a comprehension question, it is helpful because
   - (1) the GED test will ask you to identify which items are comprehension questions
   - (2) most GED items on the Social Studies and Science tests are comprehension questions
   - (3) knowing that an item is a comprehension question helps you in thinking about the answer
   - (4) once you know an item is at the comprehension level, you have to comb the passage to find the exact words in the question
   - (5) comprehension questions require the highest level of thinking to answer

3. Which of the following activities might a comprehension item ask you to do? (More than one choice is correct.)
   - (a) repeat facts
   - (b) restate ideas
   - (c) summarize ideas
   - (d) figure out implications of ideas
   - (e) judge whether statements are true

Item 4 is based on Item 12 of the Interpreting Literature and the Arts Predictor Test (page 36).

4. Read the Predictor Test item and the passage on which it is based. Use the steps you have learned: preview, question while reading, reconstruct, reread. Then answer the questions on page 224.

A. Does Item 12 ask a comprehension question? How can you tell?

B. Put the incomplete statement in Item 12 into your own words.

C. Which alternative would you choose? Why?

Answers are on page A-14.

Lesson 4   Application Questions

How do you recognize application items? How is answering an application item different from answering a comprehension item?

To apply something means to use it. Application items on the GED test your ability to use information you are given in a new situation. Application is a higher level thinking skill than comprehension because you can apply information only if you understand it. Unlike comprehension questions, application items require you to go beyond the material given.

Differences Between Comprehension and Application Items

Item 2 on the Social Studies Predictor Test (page 11) asks:

For which of the following years would a federal government study show the greatest need for increased jobs and housing for immigrants?

You are required to show that you can make a prediction about a new situation based on the graph. The words *would show* indicate that you are being asked about a new situation. You cannot simply go back and read the graph for an answer to the question, as you often can with comprehension items. You should look for information that will help you link the graph and the new situation described in the question. Common sense tells you that the more immigrants there are, the more jobs and housing they will need. You then look at the graph to see when immigration was highest. You are using the graphic information to answer the question.

Item 14 on the Science Predictor Test (page 25) also requires the skills of application. After reading the short passage, you are asked to use what you have learned in a new situation.

Which of these body cells would have the most mitochondria?

The words *would have* help you identify the question as one requiring application skills. No body cells are named in the passage; a new situation is being described in the question. You will need to connect the ideas in the passage with the new situation. The passage makes a connection between mitochondria and energy. The question asks for a connection between body cells and mitochondria. You need to make the connection between body cells and energy. Ask yourself: Which body cells need the most energy? You can make some general predictions about the answer, but you are forced by the wording of the question to examine the specific alternatives. You can predict that one of the alternatives will be a type of body cell that needs a lot of energy. You then need to compare all alternatives and decide which type of cell needs the *most* energy.

You are not asked to produce a definition for *mitochondria* out of thin air. You have to use your general background knowledge to figure out that muscles use up a lot of energy. You do not have to know anything about mitochondria, however, before you read the passage.

Item 23 on the Interpreting Literature and the Arts Predictor Test (page 40) also uses application skills. You know from the wording of the question that the correct alternative is NOT one of the topics in the song. You must apply what you learn from the song to a new situation. Ask yourself: How can I use what I know about this song to decide what the writer would NOT put into other verses of the song?

Some Typical Application Questions

Application items may begin with the following phrases.

- From the definitions provided, choose the one that fits the example in the following passage.

- Based on the general ideas described, what would happen in the following case?

- What parallel could you draw to the situation described in the passage?

- Which of the following ideas is one that would NOT fit into the passage you just read?

- Based on the passage, the author would agree with which one of the following?

Take a closer look at how you decide that an item is written at the application level. Application questions are often easy to identify.

Item 7 of the Interpreting Literature and Arts Predictor Test (page 34) begins:

Which of the following changes in schools would the author probably recommend as the best way to help end unemployment?

The words *would the author probably recommend* help you identify the item as an application item. The author does not offer suggestions about education; you must use what is said to predict what he would say in a new situation.

The author suggests that unemployment would be reduced by a president who could match up the unemployed with the help wanted ads. The author is implying that unemployment is caused by a problem in matching people and job openings. You have some general knowledge of what guidance counselors do. Add this knowledge to your understanding of what the author believes about unemployment. Since guidance counselors provide vocational guidance, the author might well recommend providing more student guidance as a way to match more people with job openings. Notice that the wording of the question forces you to compare all alternatives before choosing the most likely.

While application questions require you to go beyond the material, you must accept and manipulate the ideas you are provided, even if you disagree with them. Application questions do not ask you to judge whether the author's ideas are good ones. You might think that hiring more teachers would be the best way to help end unemployment because it would provide better training for job hunters. There is nothing in the passage, however, that leads to that view. Read the question very carefully. Application questions require you to stay with the ideas you are presented and to predict how these ideas would transfer to a new situation.

Item 4 on the Science Predictor Test (page 22) is another example of an application item. The material you are presented includes a passage about food chains, a graphic example of a food chain, and a list of related definitions. The item then presents you with a new example of a food chain, which is not included in the earlier material. The appearance of the new material in the item signals that you are looking at an application item.

The passage describes the human who eats hamburger as a secondary consumer. The new graphic in the item shows a human eating a rabbit. You need to connect the ideas by applying the information from the passage to the item: Eating a rabbit that eats grass is like eating a cow that eats grain. In both cases the human is the secondary consumer.

Item 7 on the Social Studies Predictor Test (page 13) reads: *A parent is looking over the Saturday morning TV program listings. Based on the above passage, which one of the following programs would he or she encourage the children to watch?* The fact that you are being given a specific situation not mentioned in the passage indicates that this is an application item. You are asked to show that you understand the article and can apply what you have learned from it. You cannot read the article for the exact answer to the question, because the article does not mention Saturday morning listings. You can get an idea of the kind of program the writer feels will help children learn.

Item 2 on the Interpreting Literature and the Arts Predictor Test (page 33) asks: *Which of the following things would Sam be LEAST likely to do?* None of the actions listed in the item are mentioned in the passage; the item is an application item. To answer the item correctly, you must comprehend the passage and apply your comprehension. You need to understand what Sam does say and do in order to predict what actions would be "out of character" for him.

Steps in Answering an Application Question

Now that you know how to identify application questions, follow the process of reading an application item from beginning to end. How should

UNIT III: READING STRATEGIES Lesson 4 **227**

you read the passage to arrive at the correct answer for Item 19 of the Science Predictor Test (page 27)?

1. The item asks you: *What might a city do to purify its water of solid wastes?* Since the question is phrased hypothetically ("What *might* a city do . . ."), and the passage says nothing about cities, you can see that the item involves application.

2. Read the passage for information that will help you understand the properties of solid wastes in water. You might read the passage with the following question in mind: How do solid wastes act in water?

3. You might predict, on the basis of previous knowledge, that some kind of chemical treatment is necessary to purify solid wastes.

4. After reading the passage, notice that chemical treatment is not mentioned as a way of purifying solid wastes. In fact, the passage itself gives no direct answer to the question raised. Instead, you must use the information to help you to find the answer indirectly.

5. Examine the choices to see how the information in the passage can be applied to the new situation described in the question. The information in the passage enables you to rule out four choices.

6. The only remaining answer, and therefore the correct one, is *(4) Filter it.* You had to understand the information in the passage in order to rule out all the other choices.

In this lesson you have learned how to identify application questions. You have also learned how the demands on your thinking are different from those made by comprehension items. Application questions require not only that you comprehend, but also that you use the available information in a new setting.

Lesson 4   Exercise

1. Based on what you have read in this lesson, application questions
   (1) ask you to repeat the words found in part of a passage
   (2) ask you to restate the main idea of a passage
   (3) ask you to evaluate the accuracy of an idea
   (4) require more than simply understanding what material means
   (5) are never asked following a graphic

Items 2 and 3 are based on the following passage. Read the passage. Then label each question based on the passage as a comprehension question or an application question.

Erosion of the soil by water is rapid in places where the soil is not held in place by vegetation, where the slope is steep, or where hills have not been plowed according to their natural shape. Heavy rainfall is especially damaging, since the soil cannot absorb all the rain as it falls, whereas light showers cause little damage.

2. Based on the passage, erosion would probably be most severe in
   (1) a primary forest
   (2) a treeless area with above average rainfall
   (3) the arctic region
   (4) a steep mountain with terraced plots
   (5) a cultivated field plowed along natural contours

3. From the passage, you could describe erosion as
   (1) a useful way to move soil
   (2) inevitably rapid wherever there is rainfall
   (3) a process that hits some areas harder than others
   (4) a process whose activity cannot be predicted
   (5) something caused by anything falling from the sky

Item 4 is based on Item 24 of the Social Studies Predictor Test (page 19).

4. Read the item and the table on which it is based and answer the following questions.
   a. How can you tell Item 24 is an application item?
   b. What situation is mentioned in the item but not in the table?
   c. Which part of the table is relevant to the new situation?
   d. What background knowledge might you use to answer the item?
   e. After you apply the stated ideas to the new situation, which alternative would you choose? Why?

Answers are on page A-14.

Lesson 5 Analysis Questions

How do you recognize analysis items? How are analysis items different from comprehension and application items?

To analyze something means to look at the relationships between its parts. When laboratory technicians analyze blood samples, they look at the elements that make up the blood. Analysis items on the GED tests assess your ability to understand how separate ideas are organized or related to each other. Items at the analysis level often require you to:

- Tell the difference between facts and hypotheses
- Tell the difference between facts and opinions
- Recognize something that is assumed but not stated
- Tell the difference between a general conclusion and a supporting statement
- Identify causes and effects

Some Typical Analysis Questions

Look at an analysis question, Item 30 of the Social Studies Predictor Test (page 20).

Which one of the following statements best explains why Southerners believed that taxes on imported goods were unfair to them?

You are to figure out the cause of Southerners' feelings that they had been unfairly treated. This is not simply a comprehension question, because the passage does not tell you why Southerners felt this way. The passage does tell you that the South depended on the North and foreign producers for manufactured goods. You have to draw the connection between two ideas: (a) the South needed more manufactured goods than the North, and (b) the South had to pay more import taxes as a result.

Item 1 of the Science Predictor Test (page 21) is an analysis question that requires you to supply the cause for the effect described. Two similar incidents are described. You have to explain why the outcomes are different. Based on the information provided, you must assume that the two trucks have different heights. You may conclude that the height difference accounts for the difference in the amount of work.

Analysis questions on the Interpreting Literature and the Arts Test are different from those on the Social Studies and Science tests. (See Unit VI.) Analysis questions on the Interpreting Literature and the Arts Test usually ask you to look at *how* a writer achieves a certain effect. For example, Item 4 on the Interpreting Literature and the Arts Predictor Test (page 33) asks you to examine how a character's words hold the reader's interest. You need to comprehend not only the words but also the relationship between the writer's goal, the character's words, and the reader's interest.

Analysis items can often be identified by the following wordings.

- Which of the following is the central hypothesis of the study?
  (Alternatives may include the central hypothesis as well as facts from the passage.)
- Which of the following describes the author's opinion?
  (Alternatives may include the author's opinion as well as facts and other opinions from the passage.)
- Which of the following is a statement the author uses to support his or her conclusion?

It is important that you read questions that require analysis very carefully. All the alternatives may describe ideas in the passage, but you must figure out whether you are looking for facts, opinions, hypotheses, supporting statements, conclusions, causes, or effects. (Alternatives may include a statement that supports the conclusion as well as the conclusion itself, and statements that do not support it.)

Steps in Answering Analysis Questions

Consider in more detail how to answer an analysis item. Preview the following chart and the analysis item based upon it.

Population Changes in the Five Largest U.S. Cities

	1900	1950	1960	1970	1980
Chicago	1,700,000	3,600,000	3,550,000	3,369,000	3,000,000
Houston	44,000	596,000	940,000	1,200,000	1,600,000
Los Angeles	102,000	1,970,000	2,480,000	2,800,000	2,966,000
New York	3,437,000	7,890,000	7,780,000	7,895,000	7,071,000
Philadelphia	1,290,000	2,070,000	2,000,000	1,950,000	1,688,000

Source: U.S. Bureau of the Census.

Which of the following statements is the most likely explanation for the population changes in Los Angeles and Houston between 1970 and 1980?

(1) Those cities require fewer goods and services than previously.
(2) People in those cities are retiring at an older average age.
(3) There are more job opportunities opening up in those cities.
(4) In those cities, a higher percentage of women are working than ever before.
(5) There has been a general shift in population to the Northeast.

What steps should you take in approaching this item?

1. Read the question the item asks. You can tell that this is an analysis item because you are being asked to think about how ideas are related: What is the cause of the changes?
2. Examine the chart for information related to the question. The question is about the population changes in Los Angeles and Houston between 1970 and 1980. You should zero in on population figures for only those two cities and those two years.
3. What was the change? You have to comprehend the change and then analyze it. The populations of Los Angeles and Houston *rose*.
4. To analyze *why* the populations rose, you link your own background knowledge with the information provided about the population change.

What do you know about why people move to new areas? What do you know about Houston and Los Angeles?

5. Make a prediction about the cause for the rise in population. You might predict that people moved to Los Angeles and Houston because housing was less expensive there.

6. Examine the choices. You can see that the housing-cost prediction is not listed, so you need to consider each alternative. What other factors could draw people to an area?

7. You can eliminate choice (5) right away because you know that Los Angeles and Houston are not in the Northeast. Choices (2) and (4) would not cause a population rise or any change in population size. Choice (1) might be an *effect* of a *decline* in population.

8. You can link information in the chart with choice (3). The alternative talks about job opportunities. The chart shows more people in Los Angeles and Houston in 1980 than in 1970. The connection you draw is: People move to or stay where there are job opportunities. Of the choices given, choice (3) is the only one that could *cause* a population rise.

Analysis questions make demands on your thinking that are different from those made by comprehension or application questions. Analysis questions require you to explore how ideas are organized. When answering analysis questions, you need to think about relationships such as those between a cause and an effect, a fact and an opinion, an observation and a hypothesis, a supporting detail and a conclusion.

Lesson 5   Exercise

1. One example of the form an analysis question might take is: What is the cause for this effect? List two other forms an analysis item might take.

2. Test makers often arrange questions in order from less demanding to more demanding. Suppose you find three items based on one map: an analysis item, a comprehension item, and an application item. In which order would they probably appear?

Item 3 is based on the following passage.

Popular opinion holds that men have a better sense of direction than women. K. Bryant believes that people's levels of confidence affect their ability to sense direction. They were given sense-of-direction tests and personality tests. Men rated their sense-of-direction more highly than women did. They were also more confident than women and did better on the sense-of-direction tests. Some women scored as well as the top-scoring men on the sense of direction tests. Bryant noted that because women tend to be more anxious about getting lost, they may get less practice finding their way around new areas.

3. Which of the following is the central hypothesis of Bryant's study?

   (1) Men receive high scores on sense-of-direction tests more often than women.

   (2) Confidence results from having a good sense of direction.

   (3) Women get more practice than men at finding their way around.

   (4) Sense-of-direction ability is related to level of confidence.

   (5) Men are born with a better sense of direction than women.

4. How can you tell that Item 3 above is an analysis item?

Answers are on page A-14.

Lesson 6 Evaluation Questions

How do you recognize evaluation items? How is answering an evaluation item different from thinking about comprehension, application, and analysis items?

To evaluate something means to judge it. When a supervisor gives you a performance rating, he or she is evaluating, or judging, the quality of your work. The employer uses accepted criteria to make a judgment. The employer may evaluate your punctuality, your persistence, and your cooperation with coworkers.

Evaluation items on the GED test your ability to judge whether information or methods are accurate. You are often asked to use the criteria or "mental yardsticks" provided in a passage or graphic to measure the accuracy, clarity, relevance, validity, or effectiveness of various alternatives.

Evaluation is a higher level thinking skill than comprehension, application, or analysis. Evaluation requires that you step back from the material you are given and look at it in a variety of ways. Before you can evaluate, you must comprehend and analyze, and, sometimes, apply.

Examine these two questions to see why they require evaluation. This lesson will only consider social studies and science evaluation questions. The Interpreting Literature and the Arts Test does not have evaluation questions.

Some Examples of Evaluation Questions

Item 17 on the Science Predictor Test (page 26) presents a situation not mentioned in the passage: only green light is shown on an apple. You are asked to use the information from the passage to judge which of the alternatives "best explains" why the apple appears black. First you need to comprehend the information in the passage, apply it to a new situation, and analyze a cause-and-effect relationship. Then you must use what you learned from the passage to judge which is the most accurate explanation. Considering a piece of information in a variety of contexts is typical of evaluation.

Item 26 on the Social Studies Predictor Test (page 19) asks:

Which one of the following conclusions is best supported by the information in the table?

The phrase *best supported* is often found in evaluation items. You are required to judge which of several opinions is most valid based on what you have read.

An analysis item might ask you to distinguish a conclusion about the table from facts presented in the table. Item 26, however, requires you to analyze how each conclusion is related to the facts, and then to judge the quality of each conclusion. It is a good idea to try to come up with a conclusion of your own before you look at the alternatives, but you will need to examine each alternative carefully.

Be sure that you use the information in the table as your "yardstick." Do NOT use personal opinion as your "yardstick." The question does not ask which conclusion you agree with, or which conclusion you think is the most accurate statement. It asks which conclusion follows most clearly from the information in the table. Evaluation items may be worded in the following ways.

- Which of the following conclusions is best supported by the information provided in the passage (graph, diagram, chart, cartoon)?
- Which of these statements from the passage provides the best support for the following opinion?
- Which of the following hypotheses can most likely be made about the facts described in the passage?
- Which of the statements from the passage could not be proven?

Preparing to Answer Evaluation Questions

Look at these evaluation items to see what demands are placed on your thinking as you read to answer them.

Item 7 on the Science Predictor Test (page 22) follows a passage about food chains that does not specifically mention vegetarians. The item reads: *Vegetarians claim that they make more efficient use of the world's food resources than do those who eat meat. Which of these statements from the passage might they use to justify this claim?* The word *justify* indicates that you are being asked to make a judgment or evaluation.

Read the item carefully. You are not asked to identify which statements are true. You need to read the passage for information that will help you compare the efficiency of food use by vegetarians versus meat-eaters. Since efficiency has to do with not wasting energy, think about how much energy is passed on at each step of the food chain. Before you read the alternatives, imagine that you are a vegetarian. Can you find evidence in the passage that you would point to during an argument with a meat-eater?

Now look at the following item. This item refers to the following advertisement for a GED class.

> **A.** Ninety percent of those who took the class last year passed the GED.
>
> **B.** It is the best GED review class offered in this city.
>
> **C.** If you care about job advancement, you will take the class.
>
> **D.** The finest, most qualified teachers teach the class.
>
> Which of the above statements could NOT be proven by scientific methods?
>
> **(1)** A only
>
> **(2)** B only
>
> **(3)** B and C only
>
> **(4)** C and D only
>
> **(5)** B, C, and D

The key word *proven* suggests that this is an evaluation item. You are being asked to separate facts from values and opinions, which is an analytic task. You are required to make a judgment. The criterion to use in making your judgment is given: You are to determine which statements could not be proven. Only statement A could be proven.

A different evaluation question based on the same ad could present you with a different "yardstick": If you know that 95% of all the people in the country who took the GED test last year passed it, which statement would you leave out of the advertisement? Always keep the "yardstick" in mind as you read for information to help you answer the item.

Steps in Answering Evaluation Questions

Look at Item 10 on the Social Studies Predictor Test (page 14).

1. Preview the passage and the items based on it. Read the question asked in Item 10. You can tell that this is an evaluation item by the wording *Which . . . provides evidence that . . .*

2. Examine the passage for information relevant to the question. You are given a hypothesis: *. . . television-viewing can affect children's behavior.* Then you are given several statements from the passage and asked to judge which one supports the hypothesis. Your "yardstick" is the question: Does this statement support the hypothesis? As you read the passage, keep your "yardstick" in mind.

3. Ask: What is the connection between the question and the passage? Which of the statements discusses TV changing the way children act by reference to evidence?

4. Make a prediction about the answer to the question, but read each alternative carefully. Is there more than one alternative that shows that TV has an impact on children's behavior?

5. All of the alternatives contain facts or opinions from the passage, but only choice (3) supports the hypothesis by evidence that television viewing affects children's behavior.

In this lesson you have read about how to identify evaluation questions. You now know how the demands on your thinking are different from those made by lower-level questions (comprehension, application, and analysis). Once you recognize an evaluation item, you need to: (1) figure out what "yardstick" you are told to use in measuring ideas; (2) read the passage for information that will help you make your judgment; (3) make a prediction; and (4) read all of the alternatives carefully to see which one "measures up best" to the requirements of the question. When answering evaluation items, you need to judge how appropriate or accurate information is by reference to a standard.

Lesson 6   Exercise

1. Which of the following is NOT an example of what an evaluation question would ask you to do?
   (1) identify how values affect decisions discussed in a passage
   (2) identify what is wrong with the logic of an argument
   (3) express your own opinion of the writer's opinion
   (4) pick out the conclusion that is best supported by the reading
   (5) decide which statements in a passage cannot be proven

2. Evaluations you make about information you read on the tests will usually require you to judge
   (1) accuracy, clarity, and relevance
   (2) truthfulness, wisdom, and earnestness
   (3) originality, creativity, and humor
   (4) power, force, and spirit
   (5) imagination, sympathy, and empathy

3. Match the following questions with the appropriate labels.

   (1) Comprehension   (a) Which of the following is an opinion the writer has about the situations described?
   (2) Application   (b) The situations described in the passage would be similar to ____? (Alternatives are all new situations.)
   (3) Analysis   (c) Which of the following hypotheses best explains the findings described?
   (4) Evaluation   (d) An appropriate title for the story might be . . .

Item 4 is based on the first graph on the Social Studies Predictor Test (page 11) and the item below.

> Which of the following statements is best supported by the data in the graph?
>
> (1) Poor weather conditions during 1931–40 slowed immigration.
>
> (2) The number of people leaving Asia declined between 1901 and 1920.
>
> (3) The greatest need for more jobs and housing for immigrants was between 1951 and 1960.
>
> (4) The number of immigrants competing for jobs in the U.S. has been growing in recent decades.
>
> (5) We need to limit immigration in order to protect the jobs of U.S. citizens.

4. Read the item and the graph on which it is based. Answer the following questions.

   a. How can you tell the item is an evaluation item?

   b. Which of the statements is contradicted by information in the graph?

   c. Which alternative would you select? Why?

Answers are on page A-14.

Lesson 7   How to Answer Questions

How do you answer a question that is not multiple choice? How do you choose between alternatives in a multiple-choice question?

In Lessons 3, 4, 5, and 6 of this chapter you have concentrated on four levels of questions. You will meet these four types of questions in the lesson exercises in this book, on the GED tests, and in other situations where you face questions.

You have read about how to look for information that will help you answer questions at each level. What do you do once you have the necessary information? In this lesson you will read about what to do when it is time to write out or choose an answer.

Non-multiple-Choice Items

You will find only one non-multiple-choice item on the GED: Part II of the Writing Skills Test, which is where you write an essay. Material that you will use to prepare for the test, however, contains non-multiple-choice questions. Such non-multiple-choice items can take several forms: short answer, fill-in-the-blank, labeling, matching, and true-false.

The Lesson 1 Exercise in social studies in Unit IV, Chapter 5 (page 299) contains two examples of non-multiple-choice item forms.

1. The first item tells you to label a statement true or false. What else does the item require you to do?

2. The second item requires you to read a short explanation of an event and answer a question about it. This is one example of a short-answer item form.

Steps in Answering Non-multiple-Choice Items

Look at the first science item in the Lesson 1 Exercise in Chapter 1 (page 316).

1. Read the lesson and exercise following the steps you have learned: preview, question while reading, reconstruct, reread.

2. Read Item 1 carefully. No matter how well you read the passage, if you misread the question, you will get the wrong answer. Try rewording it: What is another word for *facts and events*?

3. Ask yourself what form the question takes. Do you have to fill in a blank? draw a sketch? write a short answer? You see that you need to write one word.

4. Ask yourself what level of question you are being asked. The key word *mean* indicates that this is a comprehension question.

5. Since you are answering a comprehension question, you know that you need to think about what the material means, no more. Without looking back at the passage, can you remember what word was used to mean "facts and events?"

6. You may remember the word *phenomena*. If you do, skim the passage until you find it. See if you can replace *phenomena* with *facts and events* and get the same meaning.

7. Even if the word *phenomena* does not pop into your mind as you read the question, think for a second about which part of the passage you need to skim. Often you can remember where the answer is, even if you cannot remember what it is. You will not need to reread the entire passage.

8. As you skim, either the boldface word *phenomena* or the words *facts and events* in the question should catch your eye.

9. After you decide that the answer is *phenomena*, check it by putting it back into the question. In other words, say to yourself: *Phenomena* is the word in the passage that is used to mean "facts and events." You have answered the original question correctly.

Multiple-Choice Items

All but one of the GED test items are multiple choice. Sometimes you can predict an answer before you look at the alternatives; in other cases, the wording of the question requires you to compare alternatives. Sometimes the item begins with a question; at other times the item starts with part of a statement that is completed by one of the alternatives you choose. Sometimes the alternatives are complete sentences. Other times the alternatives are phrases, single words, or numbers.

The Interpreting Literature and the Arts Predictor Test (page 32) provides examples of several multiple-choice item forms.

1. Item 1 begins with a question; the alternatives are phrases. The item is worded so that you can predict the answer before looking at the alternatives.

2. Item 2 also requires you to select a phrase that answers a complete question. Notice the importance, once again, of reading the item carefully: *Which of the following things would Sam be* LEAST *likely to do?* This is not a trick question, but it does need to be read carefully. That is, you must be sure to remember to choose an action that would be *uncharacteristic* of Sam.

There are no trick questions on the GED; choosing the correct answer is a matter of close reading. Being on the alert for items that contain words such as NOT and LEAST is part of such careful reading. Careful reading of items is every bit as important as careful reading of the passage or graphic.

3. Items 3 and 4 are complete questions for which you must choose full-sentence answers. It probably took you longer to read these items and the alternatives than it took to read Item 1 and Item 2.

    Expect to spend a little longer on items that are longer or written at higher questioning levels, but do not spend too long on any one item. All items contribute equally to your final score, whether they take a short or a long time to complete. You will have a limited amount of time on the test, so budget it. You can always return to a more difficult item later if you have time left over.

4. Item 12 is the first part of a statement that must be completed by an alternative. Try to predict how the statement will end before you look at your choices. If you have no idea how the statement should end, it may help to try completing the sentence with each alternative, in turn. Some-

times you know more than you think you do. You may be surprised to find that when you try completing the sentence with alternative (2), the completed statement makes sense: *The author's concern is that recent Disney movies lack creativity.*

Narrowing the Choices in a Multiple-Choice Item

Whenever you answer a multiple-choice item, you have to narrow your choices to one—the correct answer. Your job is easier if you can predict the answer before you look at the choices. When you predict, you narrow down your choices. You can quickly skim the alternatives until you find what you are looking for. Afterward, it is a good idea to read all the alternatives just to make sure that none makes more sense than the one you predicted.

Sometimes, however, you will find it difficult to choose between two choices. You may even find it hard to choose among three or four. In such cases: (1) reread the relevant part(s) of the material; (2) reword and try out each of the alternatives; (3) eliminate alternatives; (4) guess, if necessary. There is no penalty for guessing, and you may guess correctly.

Item 16 on the Social Studies Predictor test (page 16) is a challenging item for a couple of reasons. To start with, the question itself is not simple to read. Also, as you may have found when you took the test, it is not easy to narrow down the possibilities. A good strategy to follow in answering this item successfully would be:

1. Attack the item by using your skills at previewing, questioning, and identifying thinking levels. Notice that you are asked to read a quote by John F. Kennedy and to apply what you learn.

2. Pay careful attention to the wording of the question. Reword it for yourself: What action could I take that would be in keeping with JFK's ideas?

3. You will not be able to predict the exact situation that the writer of the test came up with, but you can make a general prediction: An action by which I do something for my country or cooperate with other countries to promote freedom would be in the spirit of JFK's ideas.

4. Look at each alternative, narrowing down the possibilities as you go. You can eliminate (1) right away, because it is clear that encouraging foreign travel will not in itself help the United States or promote freedom. At first, you might think (2) is a possible answer, since tourists from other countries bring money into this country. Inviting foreign tourists to visit the U.S. might help the American economy. You might eliminate (3); if we limit foreign embassies, we will cut down on working with other nations to promote freedom. When you get to (4), you decide that volunteering to help the needy would be one way to improve our country. You eliminate (5), because limiting foreign aid might work against world freedom.

Two possible answers remain: (2) and (4). You predict that (4) is the better answer. At this point, reread Kennedy's words. Ask yourself: Was he talking about something like inviting foreign visitors or something more like helping needy Americans? The better answer would seem to be (4). While the money brought in by foreign visitors might help the United States, helping the needy seems a more direct way of serving the country and working for the *freedom of man*.

Steps in Answering a Multiple-Choice Item

In summary, when you answer a multiple-choice item:

1. Read the question *carefully* and reword it.
2. Predict an answer, if you can.
3. Read the choices and eliminate those you know are wrong.
4. Try to predict which of the remaining choices is best. (Try to narrow down the field to no more than two choices.)
5. Reread the passage for evidence to support your prediction; also read to check that no other choice is better.
6. Mark your answer.

Taking a systematic approach toward multiple-choice items on the GED and other tests will help you narrow down your choices to the correct answer.

Lesson 7   Exercise

Items 1 to 4 are based on the following diagrams and the multiple-choice question about them.

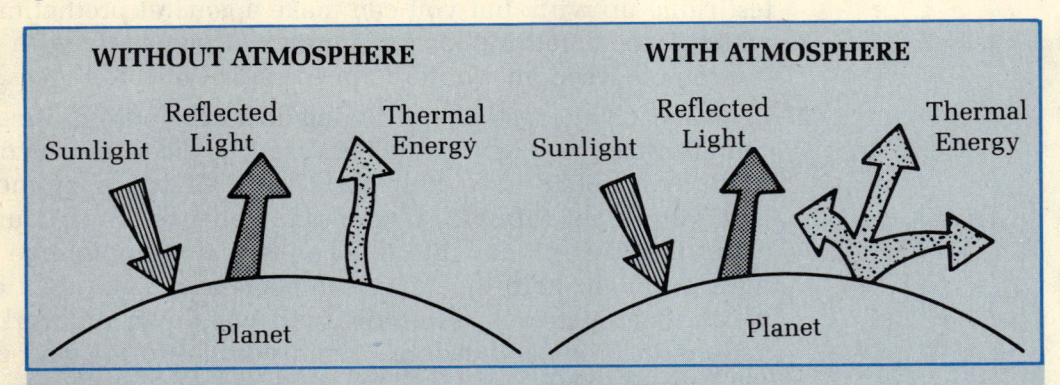

WITHOUT ATMOSPHERE

Sunlight   Reflected Light   Thermal Energy

Planet

WITH ATMOSPHERE

Sunlight   Reflected Light   Thermal Energy

Planet

Which of the following conclusions is best supported by the information shown in the diagrams?

(1) The atmosphere affects reflection of light from the planet.

(2) Without an atmosphere, Earth would retain more thermal energy.

> **(3)** The atmosphere influences the amount of sunlight hitting Earth.
>
> **(4)** The atmosphere keeps some thermal energy near Earth.
>
> **(5)** There is no thermal energy near the sun.

1. Explain the differences between the diagrams.

2. Which of the choices could you eliminate because they contradict what the diagrams show? Why?

3. There is no evidence in the diagrams that does or does not support alternative ____.

4. In order to answer the question correctly, you must use your background knowledge that Earth is a ____. Why?

Answers are on pages A-14–A-15.

Lesson 8 Reviewing Answers

Why should you review your answers?

How do you review non-multiple-choice and multiple-choice items? Lesson 7 discusses how to answer a question. In Lesson 8 you will see how to use your answers for additional learning. You have answered questions in several parts of this book: Predictor Tests, Lesson Exercises, and Chapter Quizzes. Such questions are designed not only to measure what you know, but also to help you assess which areas you need to study.

Non-multiple-Choice Items

A non-multiple-choice question often offers you more opportunities for learning than does a multiple-choice question on the same material. While you will get credit for a good guess on a multiple-choice item, you really have to know what you are talking about to produce a good written answer. Take advantage of the learning opportunities non-multiple-choice items present. As you write out an answer:

1. Think about what you do and do not know.
2. Read the Answers and Explanations as soon as you complete a set of questions to get quick feedback.
3. Compare your answer with the book's, not just to see if your answer is right, but to learn what material you should review.
4. Later, use the questions and answers for a general review. For example, suppose that you had some difficulty doing Item 2 of the Lesson 7 Exercise (page 241). At such a time, ask yourself: Where am I getting stuck? Maybe

you will realize you had trouble explaining how you arrived at the answer to the first question.

Read the Answers and Explanations to see how it answers what you could not. You may feel you need a more complete review of the system for narrowing down possibilities on multiple-choice items. If so, reread the relevant section of the lesson.

When you need to do a general review later—for example, when preparing for a Chapter Quiz—look over your answers to past exercises. As you read, mentally improve your answers. You will jog your memory about important points in each lesson.

Multiple-Choice Items

You have practiced deciding which of several alternatives in a multiple-choice item is best. After you have made your decision, it is a good idea to check your answer. Do not forget to use what you know about the four questioning levels to predict the level of each item. The answer's label can be particularly helpful when you have answered an item incorrectly. For instance, suppose you answered Item 11 of the Social Studies Predictor Test (page 14) incorrectly. You read the question: *Which continent could be expected to have the smallest population?* You decide that this is a comprehension question requiring that you understand the material but not go beyond it. You predict that the answer to the question is *Europe*, since the passage said Europe was smaller than Antarctica. Then you notice that the answer is labeled as an analysis item. You realize that you have not read the question carefully enough. It asks about population size, not land size.

Since analysis items require you to look at the relationships between ideas, you see that you will have to put pieces of information together for yourself. You will not find a direct reference to the size of populations of the continents. You have to think about the effect that the size and climate of a given continent will have on its population size. As the explanation points out, you can expect that Antarctica will have the smallest population because its climate is very severe and its size is relatively small.

Notice that the Answers and Explanations have been helpful in three ways.

- It showed you a better way to think about answering the item.
- It explained the correct answer.
- If you did not already know that Antarctica has a severe climate, the explanation gave you some information to add to your store of background knowledge.

In this lesson, you learned why it is important to review your answers. You also saw how the Answers and Explanations in this book can help you assess your own performance. When you get such feedback, you find out whether or not you should change your way of thinking. In addition, seeing your performance improve gives your confidence a boost.

Lesson 8 Exercise

1. Suppose that you find the following item in a science lesson exercise:

   The process by which plants use sunlight, water, and carbon dioxide to make food is called ____.

   The complete answer entry for this item would consist of

   (1) the level of the question and a sketch of the process

   (2) a sketch of the process and a one-word answer

   (3) a one-word answer and a brief explanation of the answer

   (4) the level, sketch, and one-word answer

   (5) the level, one-word answer, and explanation of the answer

2. Look at the answers for the Social Studies Predictor Test (pages 56–57). What level of thinking skill is required for Items 8, 10, 20, 22, and 26?

3. If, when you took the Predictor Tests, you incorrectly answered many of the items mentioned in the second question of this exercise, what lesson in this chapter might help you improve your skill with that kind of item?

Answers are on page A-15.

Chapter 2 Quiz

1. Preview the next chapter (Chapter 3). How is the organization of the chapter similar to that of previous chapters?

2. For practice at rewording questions, ask the following question using your own words: How did this invention change the South?

3. Label the following statements true or false.

   a. No GED item will depend entirely on your background knowledge.

   b. Twenty percent of the social studies items will be comprehension items.

   c. Twenty percent of the literature items will be comprehension items.

   d. All items you answer in this book are comprehension items.

4. Suppose you preview a passage about the parts of the brain. (a) What do you do just before you reconstruct the passage? (b) Explain how you could reconstruct a passage about where various parts of the brain are located? (c) Explain why you would reconstruct such a passage.

5. Read the following social studies comprehension item. Then answer questions a and b.

Country	Population Density per Square Mile	Average Income Per Person	Life Expectancy at Birth M/F	Persons Per Hospital Bed
Japan	793	$4478	71/76	96
Mexico	85	$1130	63/67	604
United States	60	$6995	69/76	152

The table shows that

(1) Mexicans have a higher income per person than U.S. citizens.
(2) The population of the United States is less dense that that of Japan.
(3) Japanese males have a shorter life expectancy than American males.
(4) Mexico has ninety-six persons per hospital bed.
(5) Few U.S. citizens earn more than $6995 per year.

a. Which answer would you select?
b. Why?

6. Read the following science application item. Then answer questions a and b.

Like most liquids, glass flows when heated, but it is a very viscous fluid; it resists flow. It acts differently from most substances when it solidifies, however. Instead of forming a crystalline structure, hardened glass is amorphous, or without form. Liquid maple syrup is

(1) glass
(2) solidified
(3) crystalline
(4) viscous
(5) nonresistant

a. Which answer would you select?
b. In this science item, you must use information you read about ____ and apply it to ____.

7. How does an answer entry for a nonmultiple-choice item differ from the entry for a multiple-choice item?

8. Explain how the following item is different from most items on the GED.

> Explain the differences between stars and planets in a few sentences.

9. Write the answer entry that you might find for the following item.

> We work all our lives as productive members of society. We give a great deal to this country. Then, all of a sudden, we get to a certain age and we are treated as if we do not fully belong any longer. In this society, our needs are increasingly ignored.
>
> Which of the following people is probably the speaker?
>
> (1) an immigrant to the U.S. in the 1890s
> (2) a black American in the 1950s
> (3) an Asian American in the 1960s
> (4) an elderly American in the 1970s
> (5) an American woman in the 1980s

10. For practice in checking your answers as soon as you finish a set of questions, check your answers to this quiz. How many did you get right? If you got any wrong, find the lesson you should review.

Answers are on page A-15.

Chapter 3 | The Three "Reading Tests"

> **Objective**
>
> In this chapter you will
>
> - Review the steps in reading an item
> - Go over skills useful in reading graphs, maps, diagrams, and cartoons
> - Read about a new item format you will meet on the GED
> - Discover how to handle the types of questions on the Interpreting Literature and the Arts Test

Lesson 1 Steps in Reading Items

What are the steps in reading test items?

Review what you have learned about a strategy for reading test items. For any material on the GED—short passage, long passage, or graphic—you can take the following steps: (1) preview; (2) question while reading; (3) reconstruct; (4) choose your alternative; (5) review your choice.

Preview

Begin by scanning the passage and the related items. Often there will be directions stating which items go with a passage. For instance, a line reading "*Items 1 to 5 are based on the following passage*" might precede a passage. Such a line would let you know that you should preview the passage, plus Items 1 through 5.

When you preview, remember to use visual clues about the organization of the material. The visual clues provided by graphs, charts, diagrams, maps, and cartoons will be discussed further in the next lesson. Examples of visual clues you might find in the Interpreting Literature and the Arts Test are indentations before paragraphs in a story excerpt, breaks between sections of a poem, and markings that introduce dialogue in a play.

Notice the general form of the item(s) following a passage. Are the alternatives numbers? words? sentences? Are key words repeated throughout the alternatives? If there is a set of items, are the alternatives the same in all items?

Question

Look more closely at the question the item asks. Reword it for yourself to make sure you know what it means. Note the level of the question.

For **comprehension** questions, the answers to these questions are often in or implied by the material itself. However, the answer choices will be in words that are different from those used in the passage.

For **application** questions, the answers to these questions will not be found directly in the material. It is by understanding and applying the information in the material to a new situation that you can answer application items.

For **analysis** questions, you must relate or distinguish between several ideas in the passage or graphic to find the answers. On the Interpreting Literature and the Arts Test, analysis questions focus on how the writer produces certain effects or on the elements of style and structure in an excerpt.

For **evaluation** questions, again, you will not find the answers to these questions in the material. Instead, you need to absorb the material and to identify the criteria you must use to judge a statement.

Once you identify the type of question you have been asked, you will have a better idea of how to look for the answer. You can read to find the answer to many comprehension questions. The three other types of questions require finding and using information. You do independent thinking to arrive at the answer.

As you read the material, keep the question in mind. Make up your own questions based on clues you picked up during the preview plus new information you read. Read to the end of the passage or graphic while asking questions, predicting answers, and reading to test predictions.

Reconstruct

Summarize the material in another form for yourself. Do this in your head or on paper. Make a sketch, connect labels with arrows, or use some other way to remind yourself about how key ideas are related.

Choose Your Alternative

If possible, predict the answer before examining each alternative. Narrow down your possibilities. Reread the appropriate part of the material if you feel the need to in order to eliminate alternatives. Remember, however, that you will probably not find the answer word for word in the material.

Review Your Choice

Make sure you noticed all the words in the question, such as NOT and EXCEPT, that would affect your answer. Change your answer only if you find a specific reason to change it. Your first answer is usually your best; hasty changes waste time, increase anxiety, and often result in errors.

Lesson 1 Exercise

Items 1 to 7 are based on the passage preceding Item 31 on the Science Predictor Test (page 30). Preview the relevant material and then answer the following questions.

1. How many items are based on the passage?
2. What is the general topic of the passage? How do you know?
3. How many paragraphs does the passage contain?
4. Read the first sentence in the passage. Based on that sentence, write a question beginning "Why . . . ?" that could be used to guide your reading.
5. Reword the paragraph beginning "Following a doctor's orders . . ."
6. Which is the highest of the four levels of thinking required to complete the statement at the end of the second paragraph?
7. Which is the best alternative in Item 31? How did you eliminate each of the other alternatives?

Answers are on page A-15.

Lesson 2 The Social Studies and Science Tests

What is special about reading graphic material such as charts and graphs?

There are two features of the Social Studies and Science tests that deserve special attention. First, you will find that information in those tests is often presented in graphic form, including:

—tables   —pictographs
—line graphs   —diagrams
—bar graphs   —cartoons
—circle graphs —maps

Second, there is a special kind of item set on the Social Studies and Science tests. It consists of information followed by several application items. The alternatives for each item in the set are the same.

In Lesson 1 of this chapter you reviewed the general steps to take when reading any item. In this lesson, you will learn about reading graphic items and the special kind of item set.

Information in Graphic Form

Tables

A **table** is a chart in which numbers or words are arranged into columns and rows. When organized in a table, information is often easier to find, understand, and compare.

1. PREVIEW. As you preview a table, notice the title of the table and the headings of columns.

U.S. Total Gas Supply and Demand (thousands of 42-gallon barrels)

Year	Gasoline Production	Total Demand	Year	Gasoline Production	Total Demand
1950	1,024,181	1,019,011	1974	2,371,004	2,436,681
1960	1,522,497	1,525,126	1975	2,420,962	2,479,857
1965	1,733,258	1,756,419	1976	2,549,627	2,597,305
1970	2,135,838	2,165,598	1977	2,565,950	2,625,080
1971	2,231,157	2,246,025	1978	2,612,670	2,702,095
1972	2,352,310	2,384,734	1979	2,494,655	2,566,128

A glance at the title tells you that the table has something to do with gas in the United States. A quick look at the column headings tells you that the numbers are organized by year, gasoline produced, and gasoline demanded. Notice that the table is cut into two halves to save space; there are really only three headings, not six.

2. QUESTION. As you examine the table more closely, do not try to remember specific numbers. Rather, ask yourself questions about how the numbers are organized. What years are covered? What does the phrase below the title tell you?

Pay close attention to the words in a graphic. Because there are so few words in a graphic, each word is very important. The words tell you what the figures mean. Notice that the numbers tell you how many thousands of 42-gallon barrels of gasoline are involved. Be careful *not* to assume that 1950 production was 1,024,181 gallons.

Try to get a sense of the table as a whole. Look for trends—patterns over time. To do this, find the heading that says "Production" and run your eyes down the numbers for the years 1950–1979. Do you notice a general rise or fall? Look for a trend in the figures showing total demand. As time passes,

250 Chapter 3: The Three "Reading Tests" INSTRUCTION

does demand rise or fall? Now run your eyes across the rows. Which figure is usually lower, year after year—production or demand?

3. RECONSTRUCT. Put the information into another form for yourself. The new form could be as simple as a few sentences telling what you have noticed, or a line graph like the one in the next section.

Line Graphs and Bar Graphs

A **line graph** is a useful way to show trends that occur over time. The chart in Figure 1 includes three types of graphs. Focus on the line graph in the lower left-hand corner.

TRENDS IN AGRICULTURE IN THE UNITED STATES

FARM POPULATION (As percent of total population)

Year	Percent
1940	23.2
1950	15.3
1960	8.7
1966	5.9

FARM POPULATION (in millions)

Year	Millions
1940	30.5
1950	23.1
1960	15.5
1966	11.5

FARM OUTPUT PER MAN-HOUR (Index 1960 = 100)

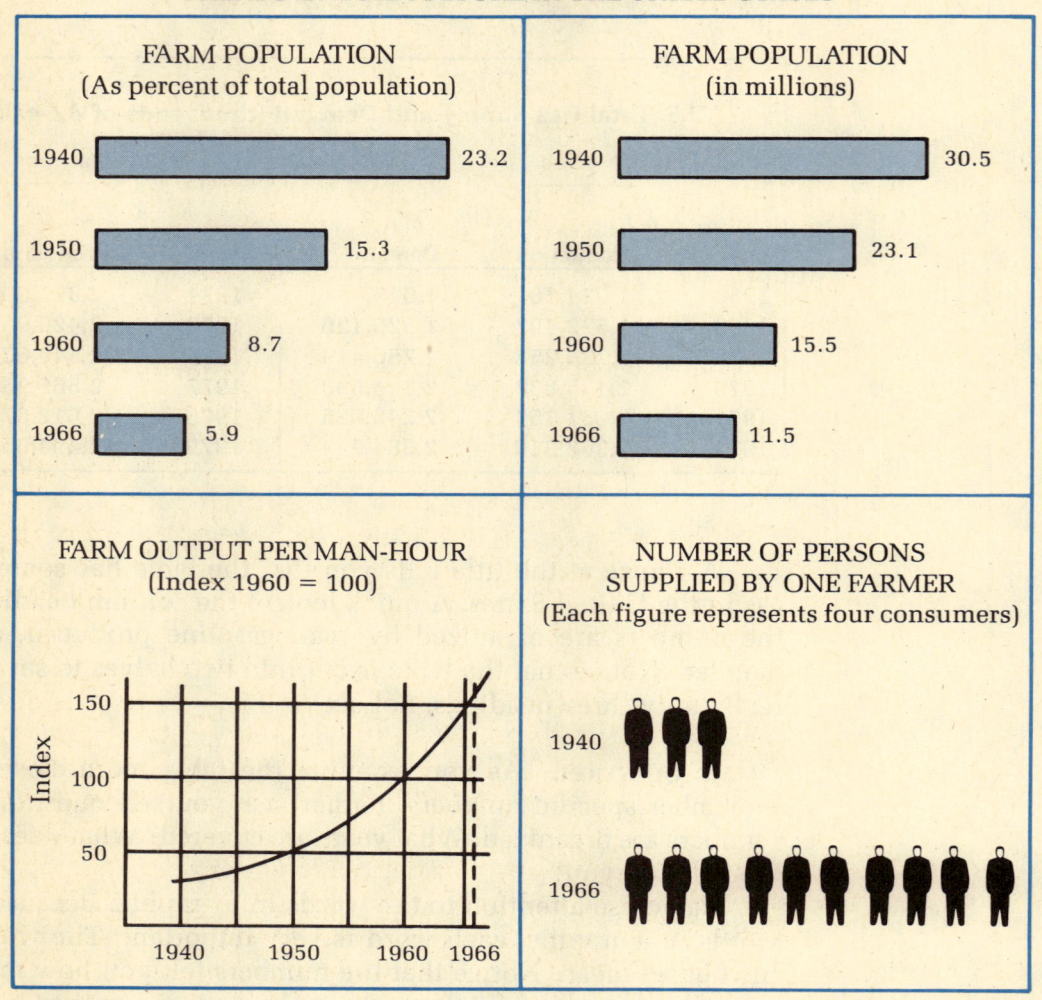

NUMBER OF PERSONS SUPPLIED BY ONE FARMER (Each figure represents four consumers)

FIGURE 1

1. PREVIEW. As you preview the line graph, first notice the title. The graphs shows something about farm output. The vertical part of the graph is labeled "Index." The horizontal part of the graph is labeled in years. An index is an artificial number that is made up for the purpose of making

UNIT III: READING STRATEGIES   Lesson 2   **251**

comparisons. You are never told how large the output really is, but you can compare the relative output of one year with that of another.

2. QUESTION. What does the graph show? Pay close attention to any words you see. The phrase under the title, *Index 1960 = 100,* means that everything on the graph is given in comparison to 1960. Nothing is given in exact amounts; the relative output for each year is compared with that in 1970. The curve goes up more sharply with passing time. What does this tell you?

3. RECONSTRUCT. How would you explain the important points in the graph to someone who could not see it?

A **bar graph** is another efficient way to organize information visually. A bar graph contains bars of varying lengths that stand for amounts. Longer bars represent greater amounts. A bar graph is an especially good way of showing that a particular amount has increased, decreased, or stayed the same over time. Sometimes bars run across the page and sometimes up and down. Look at the two bar graphs in Figure 1.

1. PREVIEW. The bars in each are arranged horizontally. The titles of the bar graphs show that they are about farm population.

2. QUESTION. What seems to be happening to farm populations as time passes?

It is important to pay attention to every word in a graph. The shades of meaning among words are sometimes very close. For example, the two graphs look very similar. They even have the same title in capital letters at the top: "FARM POPULATION." Still, each of the graphs reports something different. The clue to the difference between the two graphs is in the small print below the title. The graph on the left measures the farm population *as a percent of total population.* The word *percent* should tell you that those numbers on the right—23.2, 15.3, 8.7, 5.9—report percents of the total population living on a farm in different years.

The graph on the right measures the farm population *in millions.* The numbers—30.5, 23.1, 15.5, 11.5—tell you how many millions of people lived on a farm. The two graphs report different information. Suppose an item asked you how many millions of people lived on farms in 1960. If you were not looking carefully, you might notice only the words *FARM POPULATION* on the left-hand graph. If so, you would answer *8.7,* when the correct answer would actually be found in the right hand graph: *15.5.*

Do the four graphs refer to farming in a particular state? a particular nation? the entire world? The title at the very top—"TRENDS IN AGRICULTURE IN THE UNITED STATES"—tells you that all figures have to do with the U.S.

It is important to read the words carefully and look at the entire picture before making assumptions about any one part of a graph.

3. RECONSTRUCT. Summarize the information in the two bar graphs. You could say: Between 1940 and 1966 the farm population decreased by nearly 20 million. In 1940 the farm population was nearly 25% of the U.S. population, but by 1966 it had dropped to below 6%.

Circle Graphs and Pictographs

In a **circle graph,** the circle represents the whole of something. Pie-shaped pieces represent the parts of the whole. The larger a "slice" is, the greater is its portion of the whole. A circle graph is an efficient way to display the various sizes of the parts that make up something.

1. **PREVIEW.** As you preview the circle graph in Figure 2, notice its title. What does the circle represent as a whole? What do the "slices" represent?

DISSOLVED SOLIDS IN SEAWATER

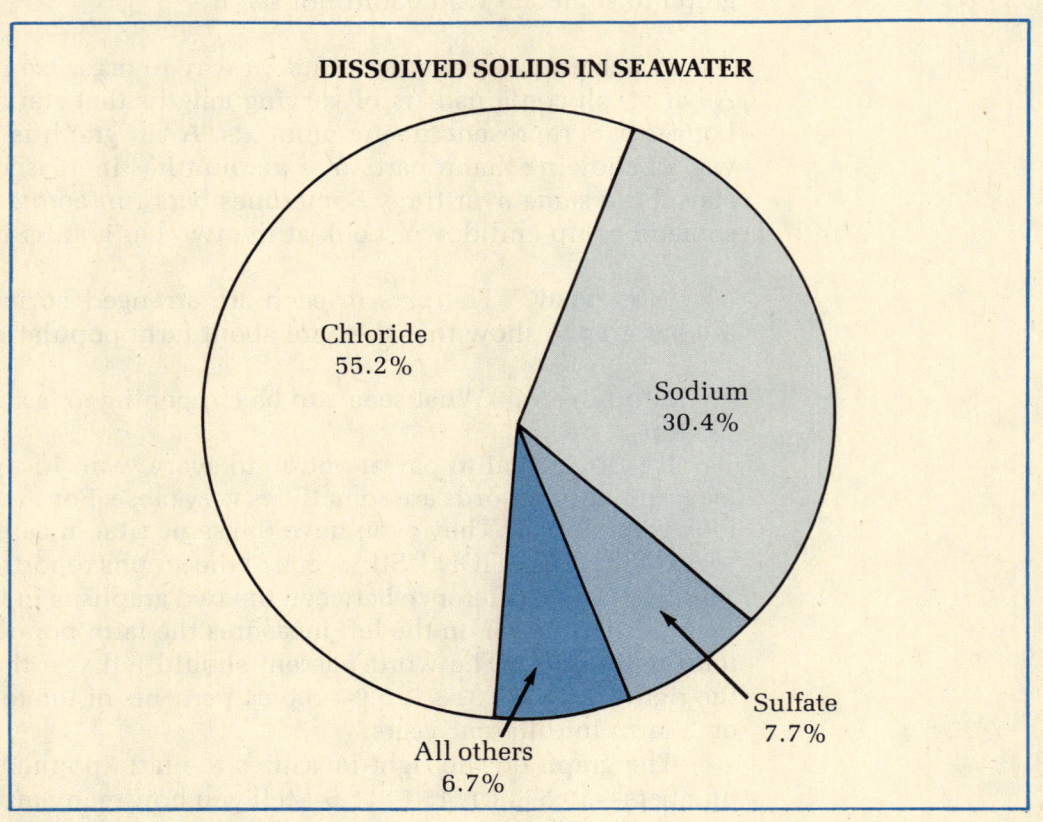

- Chloride 55.2%
- Sodium 30.4%
- Sulfate 7.7%
- All others 6.7%

FIGURE 2

2. **QUESTION.** Ask yourself what solids are dissolved in seawater. Which of these makes up the biggest percentage of dissolved solids? What are the other dissolved solids in descending order? What is the total of all the percentages provided? Seeing the size of a "slice" helps you to understand how large the percentage for a particular solid is.

3. **RECONSTRUCT.** You could write a sentence or two to explain what the circle graph reports.

A **pictograph** uses repeated symbols to show amounts of something. The symbols are simple pictures that show what is being measured. Look at the pictograph on agricultural trends in Figure 1 (page 250).

1. PREVIEW. Look briefly at the form of the pictograph. Notice that there are two rows of people-symbols. Each row is labeled with a year.

2. QUESTION. What does the pictograph show overall? What does each figure represent? How many people are represented by each figure? What does the top row show? What does the bottom row show? Has the number of people that each farmer supplies gone up or down between 1940 and 1966? Why do you suppose this is? Do you think this trend has worked in the farmer's favor or not?

3. RECONSTRUCT. Summarize the pictograph in words. Could you summarize it by sketching another kind of graph?

Diagrams and Maps

Diagrams are simple pictures, usually showing the parts of a thing or process. They are especially useful for showing how something changes over time or in different situations.

Look back at the diagram on page 249. In previewing, questioning, and reconstructing the diagram in Chapter 2, you observed differences between the left and right halves of the diagram. You had to pay attention to differences between titles as well as between pictures. Suppose the information presented in the diagram had been presented in a short passage instead. Would you have found it as easy to understand and remember?

Like other graphics, **maps** require careful reading because every word and symbol can affect your total understanding. Two maps are shown in Figure 3.

AFRICA IN 1914　　　　　　　　**AFRICA IN THE 1970s**

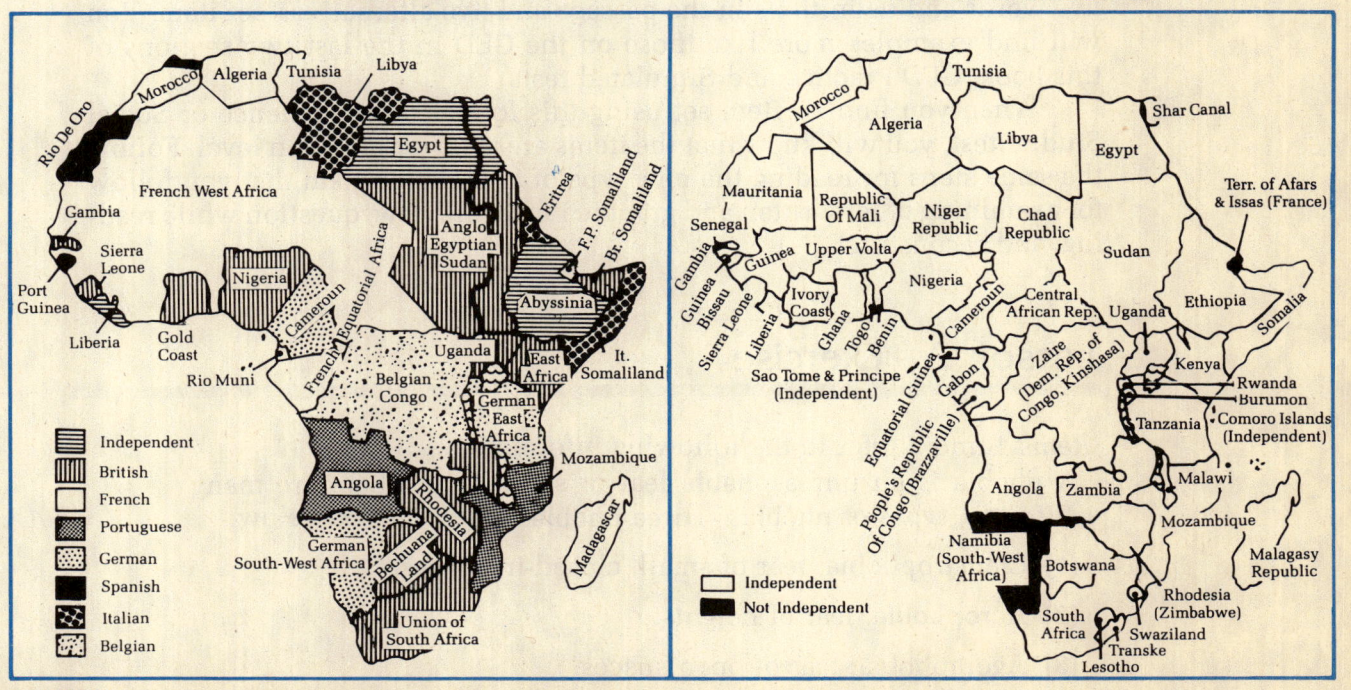

FIGURE 3

1. PREVIEW. Preview the two maps briefly. What continent is shown in each?

2. QUESTION. How are the titles different? The little shaded squares in the left-hand corner of each map are known as **keys.** The key to a map unlocks the information by telling you what the different symbols stand for. What do the keys tell you about the two maps? Which countries were colonies in 1914? Which ones were still not independent in 1970? Look carefully at the names of countries on both maps. Are they the same? Look at the white square in both keys. Does it have the same meaning? Careful reading of words and symbols on maps is important.

3. RECONSTRUCT. In your own words, what happened to Africa between 1914 and 1970? What do you know now that you did not know before looking at the maps?

A Special Kind of Item Set

Take a look at the special kind of item set you will find on the Social Studies and Science tests. Look ahead to the beginning of the exercise at the end of this lesson. The reading passage for Items 1 and 2 describes what phobias are. In a numbered list, three different types of phobias are defined.

The two items that follow are application items. You will read descriptions of two people's phobias and choose the name that describes each. Notice that the three alternatives are numbered the same as the definitions in the passage. Notice also that both Items 1 and 2 have the same alternatives. It is possible that the same alternative is correct for more than one item in a set like this.

On the GED you will see item sets similar to this one. They will have five words and definitions in the passage and five alternatives per item. You will find examples more like those on the GED in the last two sections of this book, GED Practice and Simulated tests.

When you find an item set using this format on the Science or Social Studies test, you will know that the items are at the application level. Follow the same steps for reading the new type of application item that you follow for examining other written and graphic items: preview, question while reading, and reconstruct.

Lesson 2   Exercise

Items 1 and 2 refer to the following information.

A phobia is an unreasonable fear of something. There are many different types of phobias. Three phobias are described below.

(1) Claustrophobia: fear of small, closed-in spaces.

(2) Acrophobia: fear of heights.

(3) Agoraphobia: fear of open spaces.

1. "Luis is not afraid of many things," Joan told her friend. "I know that his favorite sport is hang gliding, and he even won a medal for bravery when he was in the Army. There is one funny thing I have noticed about Luis, though. He never rides in an elevator if he can avoid it. He always takes the stairs!" The name for Luis's phobia is

   (1) claustrophobia
   (2) acrophobia
   (3) agoraphobia

2. Jenny has to climb onto a chair to get things from the top shelf of her closet. When she climbs up, her heart pounds very quickly and she has to take a deep breath or two to calm down. The name for her condition is:

   (1) claustrophobia
   (2) acrophobia
   (3) agoraphobia

Items 3 to 7 are based on the following chart.

Countries of Central America	Population	Gross Domestic Product	Per Capita Annual Income	Exports	Cultivable Land	Illiteracy	Life Expectancy
Guatemala	7.2 million, 62% rural	$6.6 billion	$900	Coffee, cotton, sugar, nickel	10 mil. acres	50%	57
Costa Rica	2.2 million, 56% rural	$3.7 billion	$1,600	Coffee, bananas, meat	7.7 mil. acres	10%	70
El Salvador	4.7 million, 56% rural	$3.5 billion	$750	Coffee, cotton, sugar, meat	3.9 mil. acres	59%	63

3. Preview the chart. If you had to write a title for the chart stating its topic, what would the title be?

4. Examine the column under the heading "Population." What two kinds of information can you find in this section of the graph?

5. According to the chart, which Central American country has a per capita annual income of less than $800?

6. True or False: 59% of the people in El Salvador are able to read and write.

7. In which of the countries shown is the average person probably the most well-off in terms of income and health?

Answers are on pages A-15—A-16.

Lesson 3 The Interpreting Literature and the Arts Test

How are literature items different from other test items?

Comprehension Items

Comprehension items make up 60 percent of the Interpreting Literature and the Arts Test. Those comprehension items come in four types. Knowing how to identify each of these types will help you to read to answer them. Take a look at examples of each type.

The Four Types of Comprehension Questions

Preview the passage that goes with Items 12 to 16 on the Interpreting Literature and the Arts Predictor Test (page 36). Notice that a question comes before this and every other excerpt on the Interpreting Literature and the Arts Test. Preview Items 12 to 16. Then read the passage while questioning. Look more closely at Item 13.

You can tell that Item 13 is a comprehension question because it asks you to show that you understand what the author is saying. Does the author tell you directly why she enjoyed Bambi, or does she only imply the reason? Do you have to look for the answer in a specific part of the passage, or are the relevant ideas found throughout the writing?

Item 13 is know as a **Literal Comprehension, Specific** item. This means two things: (1) The answer can be found stated directly, or literally, in the passage: you do not have to read between the lines to find hints about the answer; (2) The answer can be found in a specific part of the passage: you do not have to consider the entire text. The author tells you outright in lines 11 to 14: *I only remember staring at all those wonderful talking animals and wishing that I could live in such a world.* In other words, she loved looking at a world in which animals talked.

Item 12, on the other hand, is a **Literal Comprehension, Global** item. As with Item 13, you do not need to infer the answer; the ideas relevant to the answer are stated, or literal. Unlike Item 13, Item 12 requires you to consider the ideas in the passage as a whole: you must have a global understanding of the ideas. Item 12 asks about *the author's concern*. Words such as *concern, hope,* and *opinion* are often clues that an item questions a global, overall meaning. For such an item, you usually need to look at several sentences. For Item 12, you need to examine several paragraphs. The writer talks about the *magic* (lines 6 and 7) and *wonderful fun* (line 26) of old Disney movies. In line 31 she refers to the *poor try* by new Disney films compared with the *flights of fancy* (line 34) provided by old Disney movies. The author tells you in several places of her concern that recent Disney films lack creativity.

Item 15 is an **Inferential Comprehension, Specific** item. You need to figure out, or infer, what the author is saying. You need to look in a specific place in the passage for clues to the author's meaning. In fact, Item 15 tells you exactly where to look for the answer: the last paragraph. In the item, the word *indicates* is a clue that you have to read between the lines, or infer. By naming old Disney characters, the author indicates, or implies, her belief that memorable characters cannot be found in current Disney efforts.

For an example of the fourth type of comprehension item, review Item 21 (page 40) and the lyrics on which it is based. Item 21 is an **Inferential Comprehension, Global** item. You are required to show that you comprehend the author's use of the word *paradise*. To do so, you need to look at the entire song. If you look only at the first verse, you might mistakenly think paradise is a hotel with a parking lot and a nightclub, choice (5). If you rely on your own background knowledge instead of the song, you might mistakenly decide on choice (4). If you consider that each of the three verses talks about the destruction of the environment, you can correctly infer that *paradise* refers to the unspoiled natural world.

Identifying Types of Comprehension Items

Sometimes the way a question is asked can suggest how and where you should read to find the answer. Some examples of each of the four types of comprehension items follow.

- Literal/Specific
  What does the following word (phrase) mean in the passage?
  In line 15 (paragraph 2) what opinion does the author express?
- Literal/Global
  According to the excerpt (passage, poem), how is _____ explained?
  In paragraphs 2 and 3, the author mentions _____ to show _____.
- Inferential/Specific
  The author includes line 14 to show that _____.
  In line 6, the author reveals (indicates, implies) that _____.
- Inferential/Global
  What is the main idea of the passage? The author uses the phrase _____, to refer to _____ (when the author does not define the phrase whose meaning is based on the whole passage).

You will read more about these comprehension items in Unit VI.

Application and Analysis Items

On the Interpreting Literature and the Arts Test, the application and analysis items are somewhat different from those on the Social Studies and Science tests. These types of items will also be discussed in detail in Unit

VI. Briefly, these items require you to do something most science and social studies items do not require you to do: you must think about the author's point of view and how he or she uses words to convey it to you.

Application items often require you to apply the author's or a character's point of view to a new situation. Such items may begin with phrases like:

The author would be likely (LEAST likely) to enjoy which of the following types of _____ (books, movies, art, music, dance, plays)? In which of the following topics is the author likely to be interested? Which of the following would _____ (a character) be most likely (unlikely) to do?

Item 2 of the Interpreting Literature and the Arts Predictor Test (page 33) is an example of an application item. You are asked to guess how one of the characters in the passage would be LEAST likely to act in a new situation. You have to apply what you know about Sam to predict that he would not turn away from a neighbor in need.

Analysis items often ask you to examine how a writer uses words to get a point of view across. Analysis items may have the following wording:

Why is the author's first sentence (last sentence) effective?
The writing style used in this passage could be described as _____.

Item 4 of the Interpreting Literature and the Arts Predictor Test (page 33) is an analysis item. You are asked to think about the relationship between the writer's words and the reader's interest. Of course, the passage itself does not explain why Sam's final comment keeps your interest. You need to analyze the way the writer uses words to capture or hold your interest.

Analysis items may ask about other aspects of the writer's technique. You may be asked to:

- Choose the best description of a character or scene
- Show that you understand why a figure of speech is effective
- Show which words help create a certain effect
- Indicate what effect certain words create

Items on the Interpreting Literature and the Arts Test are different from social studies and science items because of the kind of writing literature is. The purpose of social studies and science passages is to convey information. Literature and writing about the arts does convey information and ideas. However, literature is also written to be enjoyed for itself. Questions, therefore, ask you to explore how authors get meanings across and what their meanings are. Note that there are no evaluation questions on the Interpreting Literature and the Arts Test. You will read more about this test in Unit VI.

Lesson 3 Exercise

Directions: Read the following passage and answer the four comprehension items that follow it. Explain what evidence you used to decide on each answer.

WHAT DO THESE TWO MEN DISAGREE ABOUT?

"Where's my story?" I asked.

"It's in galleys," he said.

"What's that?" I asked; I did not know what galleys were.

"It's set in type," he said. "We're publishing it."

(5) "How much money will I get?" I asked, excited.

"We can't pay for manuscript," he said.

"But you sell your papers for money," I said with logic.

"Yes, but we're young in business," he explained.

"But you're asking me to give you my story, but you don't give your papers
(10) away," I said.

He laughed.

"Look, you're just starting. This story will put your name before our readers. Now, that's something," he said.

"But if the story is good enough to sell to your readers, then you ought to give
(15) me some of the money you get from it," I insisted.

He laughed again and I sensed that I was amusing him.

"I'm going to offer you something more valuable than money," he said. "I'll give you a chance to learn to write."

From *Black Boy*, Richard Wright, copyright 1937, 1942, 1944, 1945, by Richard Wright. Reprinted by permission of Harper & Row, Publishers, Inc.

1. The word *galleys* (lines 2 and 3) means
   - (1) long wooden ships
   - (2) published newspaper stories
   - (3) handwritten manuscripts
   - (4) typesetters who work in publishing
   - (5) stories ready to be printed

2. The narrator in the passage wants to be paid for his work because
   - (1) his earlier stories are already well-known
   - (2) the publisher will make money from the story
   - (3) he worked on the story for a long time
   - (4) he can get money from another publisher
   - (5) he doesn't need to learn how to write

3. At the time of the passage, the narrator had probably
   - (1) already become popular as a writer
   - (2) never had a story published before
   - (3) had a few stories published
   - (4) had several stories published
   - (5) been paid well for stories before

4. The man laughs at the narrator because he is amused by the narrator's
   - (1) inexperience
   - (2) bad writing
   - (3) jokes
   - (4) lack of money
   - (5) clever arguments

Answers are on page A-16.

Chapter 3   Quiz

Items 1 to 5 are based on the following graph.

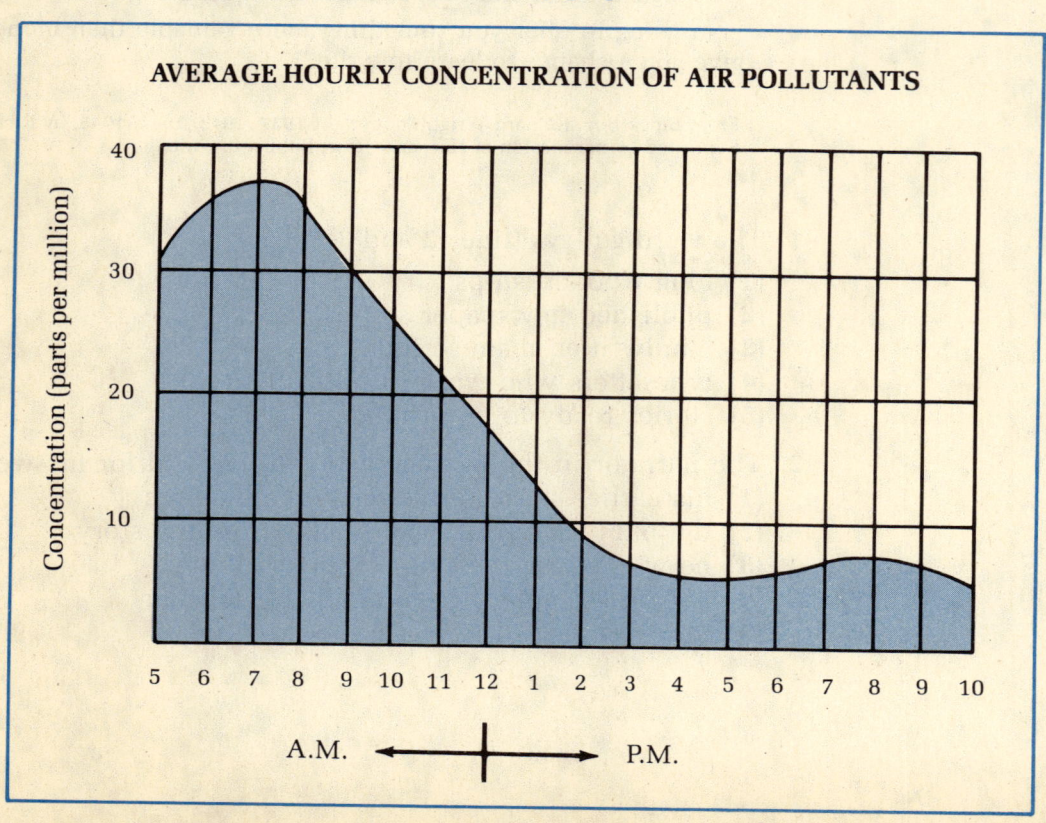

AVERAGE HOURLY CONCENTRATION OF AIR POLLUTANTS

UNIT III: READING STRATEGIES   Chapter 3 Quiz   **261**

1. Preview the graph. The topic of the graph is ____.

2. A question that could be asked based on the title and labels is: What changes ____?

3. What does the label on the left side of the graph tell you about how pollutants are measured?

4. What does the label at the bottom of the graph tell you about the time period that is shown?

5. What does a rise in the line on the graph show? a fall? a level portion?

Item 6 is based on the following passage.

Archaeologists study human cultures of the past by looking at artifacts. Some archaeologists study ancient cultures and civilizations; others study more recent times.

Anthropologists study human cultures that currently exist. They often go to live in different societies to observe them firsthand.

Sociologists study modern society. Many sociologists collect and analyze data about contemporary ways of life in their own cultures.

6. To reconstruct the information in the passage, draw lines to connect each career to the Period(s) Studied and Place(s) Studied.

Career	Period(s) Studied	Place(s) Studied
Archaeologist	Present	Own society
Anthropologist	Past	Other societies
Sociologist		

Items 7 to 9 are based on the following passage.

WHY ARE ALICIA AND BILL DIVIDING UP BELONGINGS?

ALICIA: (*Distributing the tags among the furniture*) Let's see—this sofa is yours—Bill—(*A Bill tag*). This chair's mine—Alicia—(*An Alicia tag*). You did say I could have it, didn't you?

BILL: Help yourself.

(5) ALICIA: This table is yours—Bill—this small sofa is mine—Alicia—that chair is yours—Bill. Oh, I've already tagged that—this chair is mine—Alicia's—somehow it's more feminine. That pretty well divides up the furniture...Now the paintings. (*She goes to an interesting painting—is about to tag it with her name*) I would like to have this one, if you don't mind, Bill.

(10) BILL: Suits me.

ALICIA: Now, Bill, you're sure?—I mean, that you don't want it? Of course, I love it, but then, you love it too.

BILL: No, sweetie, you saw it first—I remember very clearly. Paris, '53. What was the name of that restaurant? Chez something.

(15)   ALICIA: Nico.

BILL: Chez Nico. Too much to eat, too much to drink, too much for this painting.

From "Amicable Parting," by George S. Kaufman and Leureen McGrath. Copyright 1957 by George S. Kaufman and Leureen McGrath. Reprinted by permission from the Dramatists Play Service, Inc.

7. Preview the passage. Why are the speakers' names in capital letters? What do the italicized words tell you?

8. Answer the comprehension item that follows. Which of the four types of comprehension items is it? How do you know?
   Alicia and Bill are
   (1) about to be married
   (2) happily married
   (3) unhappily married
   (4) recently separated
   (5) separated for a long time

9. If a question asks you to explain why Alicia's opening line is effective in capturing your interest, you must
   (1) comprehend, only
   (2) apply, only
   (3) analyze, only
   (4) comprehend and apply
   (5) comprehend and analyze

---

10. What are the advantages of trying to predict an answer before looking at the alternatives?

    Answers are on page A-16.

UNIT IV

Social Studies

In this unit you will study the five areas of social studies that are covered on the Social Studies Test. In the lessons, you will get practice in applying your reading skills to social studies materials.

The first chapter in the Social Studies unit explains what social studies is. Each of the five chapters that follow cover one of the content areas of social studies that appear on the GED Test: history, geography, economics, politicial science, and behavioral sciences.

The six chapters in Unit IV are divided into lessons. Each lesson ends with an exercise that is made up of questions that require you to think the way you will have to when you take the GED. Each chapter ends with a quiz that draws on the material presented in the chapter.

This unit will help you develop a manner of thinking that will improve your ability to understand and interpret social studies materials. Your increased ability should help you perform better on the Social Studies Test. Use the chart on the next page to record your progress as you work through the unit.

Unit III shows you important reading strategies that you can use when you read social studies passages. If you have not yet done so, you should complete Unit III before working on this unit.

UNIT IV PROGRESS CHART
Social Studies

Use the following chart to keep track of your work. When you complete a lesson, circle the number of questions you answered correctly in the Lesson Exercise. When you complete a Chapter Quiz, also record your score below. The numbers in color represent scores at a level of 80% or better.

Lesson	Page		
		CHAPTER 1: Introduction to Social Studies	
1	265	An Overview of the Social Studies	1 2 3 4 5
2	266	Organizing Information	1 2 3 4 5
	268	Quiz	1 2 3 4 5 6 7 8 9 10
		CHAPTER 2: American History	
1	270	Exploration and Settlement	1 2 3
2	271	National Unity	1 2 3
3	273	Regional Differences	1 2 3
4	274	Industrial Growth	1 2 3 4
5	275	Reform Movements	1 2 3 4
6	276	International Affairs	1 2 3
7	278	International Relations Between the Superpowers	1 2 3
8	279	The Present	1 2 3 4
	280	Quiz	1 2 3 4 5 6 7 8 9 10
		CHAPTER 3: Geography	
1	282	The Study of Geography	1 2 3 4
2	284	Climates: How and Why They Differ	1 2 3 4
3	285	Natural Resources and the Environment	1 2 3 4
	287	Quiz	1 2 3 4 5 6 7 8 9 10
		CHAPTER 4: Economics	
1	288	Types of Economic Systems	1 2 3 4
2	289	Consumer Influence	1 2 3
3	290	Structure of Business	1 2 3 4 5
4	292	Government Revenues and Expenditures	1 2 3
5	293	Business Cycles and Government Regulation	1 2 3 4
6	294	International Economics	1 2 3
	296	Quiz	1 2 3 4 5 6 7 8 9 10

Lesson	Page		
		CHAPTER 5: Political Science	
1	298	Foundations of Government	1 2 3
2	299	Writing the Constitution	1 2 3
3	300	The Development of Federalism	1 2 3 4
4	302	The Election Process	1 2 3
	303	Quiz	1 2 3 4 5 6 7 8 9 10
		CHAPTER 6: Behavioral Sciences	
1	305	Behavioral Sciences: Aims and Methods	1 2 3 4
2	306	Principles of Learning	1 2 3 4
3	307	What Sociologists Study	1 2 3 4
4	309	Types of Group Behavior	1 2 3 4
5	310	Anthropology: Branches and Concepts	1 2 3 4
	311	Quiz	1 2 3 4 5 6 7 8 9 10

Chapter 1

Introduction to Social Studies

> **Objective**
>
> In this chapter, you will read and answer questions about
> - The different fields of social studies
> - Ways to display data

Lesson 1 An Overview of the Social Studies

What fields does social studies include and how are they related?

The term *social studies* refers to the fields of history, geography, economics, political science, and behavioral science. Each of these fields has the same basic goal—understanding certain aspects of the relationship between people and society. However, each field has a different focus and asks different questions about the world in which we live.

History is concerned with people, ideas, and events in the past. The events may relate to politics, science, art, religion, or economics. The events studied may be ancient or recent. Historians want to know what happened, how it happened, and why it happened. A knowledge of history may provide insight for a better understanding of current problems and conflicts.

Geography has two main branches. Physical geography is the study of the physical structure of Earth. Cultural geography looks at the interrelationships between this physical structure and human groups. Its concerns therefore include the ways in which people use the land and the ways in which the Earth influences their lives.

Economics focuses on the production, distribution, and consumption of a country's goods and services. Economic factors have an important influence on how people in a society live.

Political science studies and compares different types of governments. Political scientists try to understand decision making in politics and how individuals and groups obtain and use political power.

Behavioral science includes three important areas. Psychology is the study of the mind. Sociology is concerned with human relationships in a group or society. Anthropology attempts to understand people by examining cultures and the history of the culture.

Often, the various social studies cannot be considered separately. For example, studying the Prohibition era is not just history. It may also be important to know about the economic, sociological, and political issues involved in that era.

Lesson 1 Exercise

Items 1 and 2 are based on the following questions:
- **(1)** What compromises were made in drawing up the U.S. Constitution?
- **(2)** What is the longest river in North America?
- **(3)** How many automobiles were imported by the United States in 1982? How many U.S.-made cars were sold abroad that year?
- **(4)** What are the essentials of a well-balanced diet?
- **(5)** How do people learn?

1. Which one of the above questions would NOT be a concern of social studies?
2. Name the branch of social studies that most applies to each of the four questions that *are* concerns of social studies.
3. Explain the meaning of the following statement: Historians are interested in the past because they are interested in the future.
4. Which branch of behavioral science would describe family relations in primitive societies in the world today?

Answers are on page A-17.

Lesson 2 Organizing Information

What different types of graphs do social scientists use to present information?

Social scientists gather a great deal of facts and figures about people's activities. By organizing these data in different ways, they may observe certain patterns and relationships that will lead to useful conclusions.

Statistics are numerical data that represent information about a given subject. There are many ways to display statistics, and these can be used in all areas of the social sciences. Graphs are a convenient way of organizing data. An economist could use a line graph, like the one at the bottom of the next page, to show the change in oil production over time. A sociologist might present statistics in a bar graph. The bar graph on page 268 shows the average income for groups with different educational backgrounds.

A circle graph is an easy way to show the parts, or percentages, into which a total amount is divided. The full circle represents 100%, a half circle is 50%, and so on. Circle graphs are useful for showing percentages; for example, how much each of the various types of taxes contributes to total government income, or the percentage of the population of a large city that each of its ethnic groups represents. (See Figure 1.)

There are other visual means to present information. A time line is an effective method of illustrating time spans between events. Maps are used to show distances, strategic locations, boundaries, physical features, resources, climate, and so on. Charts and tables are also important means for organizing and displaying information.

Photographs can be used to present visual data. Cartoons may be used to express political or personal opinions.

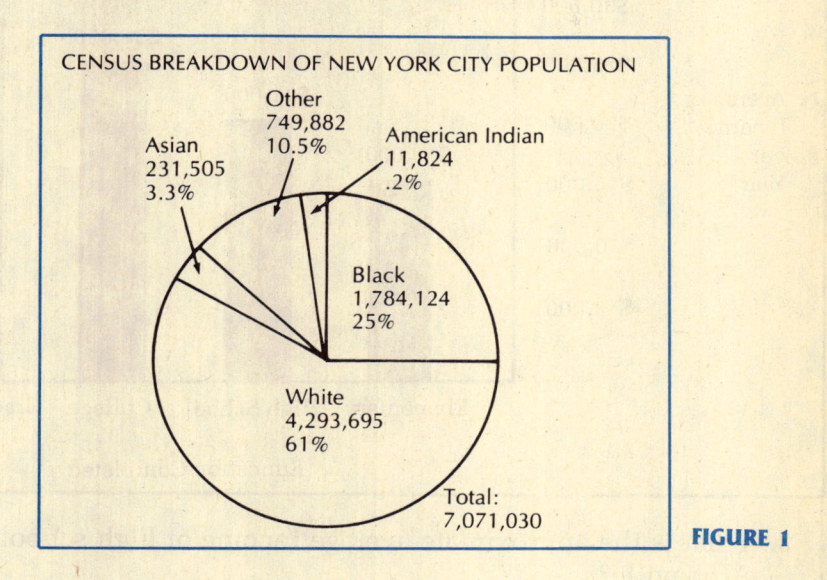

CENSUS BREAKDOWN OF NEW YORK CITY POPULATION

- Other: 749,882 — 10.5%
- Asian: 231,505 — 3.3%
- American Indian: 11,824 — .2%
- Black: 1,784,124 — 25%
- White: 4,293,695 — 61%
- Total: 7,071,030

FIGURE 1

Lesson 2 Exercise

Items 1 and 2 are based on the following graph.

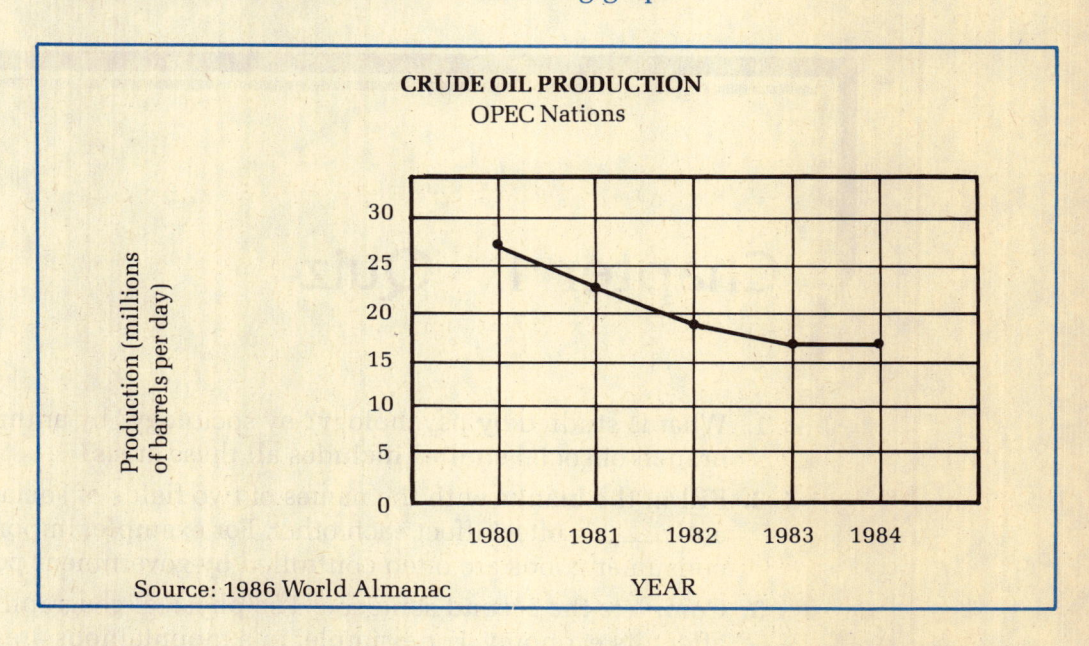

CRUDE OIL PRODUCTION
OPEC Nations

(Production in millions of barrels per day, 1980–1984)

Source: 1986 World Almanac

1. According to the line graph, what was the approximate OPEC crude oil production in 1981?
2. Based on the graph, what happened to oil production between 1980 and 1984?

268   Chapter 1: Introduction to Social Studies   INSTRUCTION

Items 3 and 4 are based on the following graph.

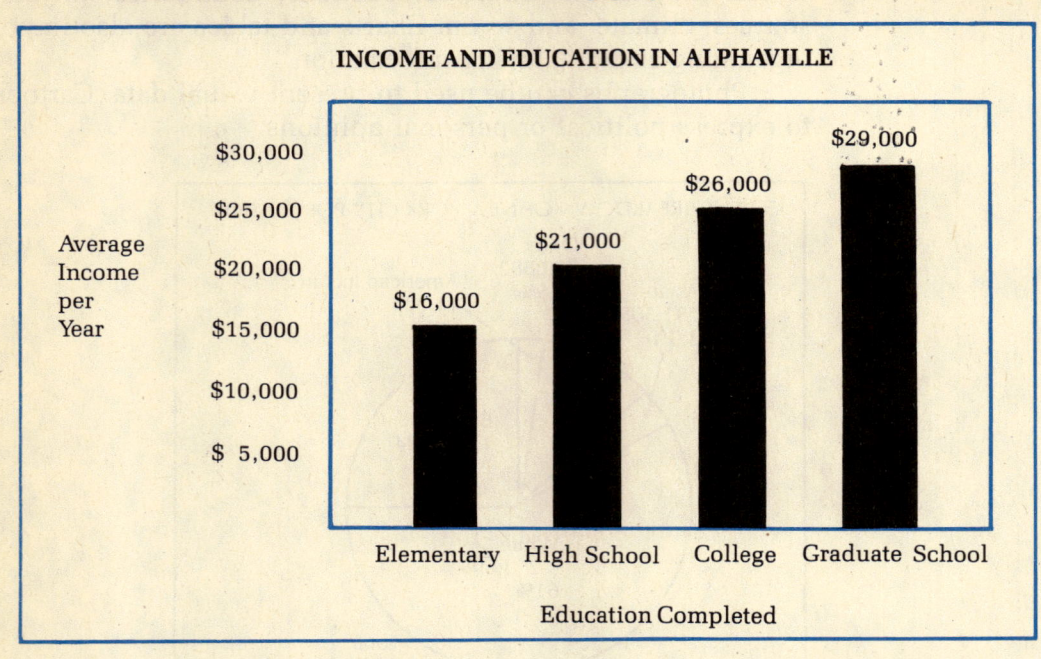

INCOME AND EDUCATION IN ALPHAVILLE

Average Income per Year

Education Completed	Income
Elementary	$16,000
High School	$21,000
College	$26,000
Graduate School	$29,000

3. What is the approximate average income of high school graduates in Alphaville?
4. What can you determine about the relationship between amount of education and average income?

Answers are on page A-17.

Chapter 1   Quiz

1. What is studied by psychology? by sociology? by anthropology? What branch of social studies includes all these areas?
2. Fill in the blanks with the names of two fields of social studies: _____ and _____ often affect each other. For example, imports and exports of consumer goods are often controlled by government policy.
3. Complete the second sentence: The physical geography of a country can affect its economy. For example, in a mountainous area with low annual rainfall, farming is _____.
4. A report on the Indian population of Guatemala from 1500 to the present time might involve which branches of social studies?

UNIT IV: SOCIAL STUDIES   Chapter 1 Quiz   **269**

5. Give the name of the branch or branches of social science that would apply to each of the following topics.
   (a) The Nineteenth Amendment—women's right to vote—changed the balance of power in the Congress.
   (b) Childhood experiences often affect the way we treat our own children.
   (c) Vocational training programs help lower the unemployment rate.

Items 6 and 7 are based on the following graph.

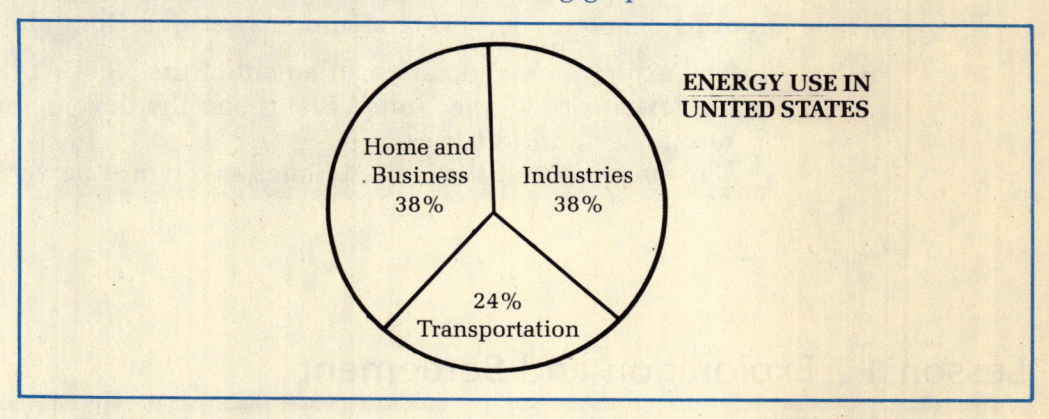

ENERGY USE IN UNITED STATES

Home and Business 38%
Industries 38%
24% Transportation

6. How does this circle graph help you compare the percentage of energy used by three different groups?
7. Can this graph be used to determine which sector wastes energy most? Explain your answer.

Items 8 to 10 are based on the following time line.

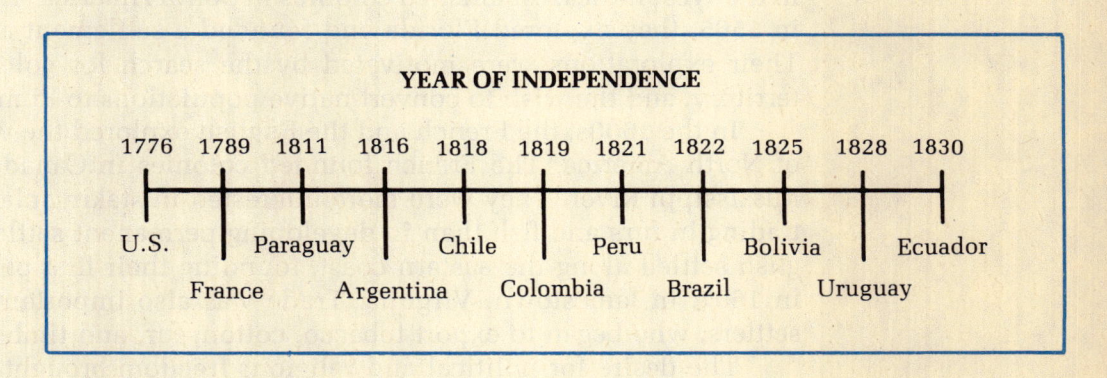

YEAR OF INDEPENDENCE

1776 1789 1811 1816 1818 1819 1821 1822 1825 1828 1830

U.S.   Paraguay   Chile   Peru   Bolivia   Ecuador
     France   Argentina   Colombia   Brazil   Uruguay

8. What time span does this time line cover?
9. For which of the following topics might this time line be useful?
   (1) the establishment of nations in South America
   (2) the French monarchy in the seventeenth century
   (3) changes in South America in the twelfth century
10. Use the time line to support this statement: The American and French revolutions had a great effect on South America.

Answers are on page A-17.

Chapter 2

American History

> **Objective**
>
> In this chapter, you will read and answer questions about
>
> - The exploration and early settlement of the New World
> - The expansion of the United States and the development of its resources and industries
> - The emergence of the United States as a world power

Lesson 1 Exploration and Settlement

How did a desire for freedom influence daily life and government in early America?

From the fifteenth through the seventeenth centuries, European nations explored and settled large parts of the **New World.** The Spaniards, landing first in the West Indies, established colonies in South America and Mexico. Later, in 1565, they explored Florida and founded a settlement at St. Augustine. Their explorations were motivated by the search for gold, the desire for territory, and the wish to convert native populations to Roman Catholicism.

In the 1600s, the French and the English explored the wilderness lands of North America. The French founded colonies in Canada and along the Mississippi River. They were more interested in staking claims to land and trading in furs and fish than in developing permanent settlements. The English settled along the eastern coast, founding their first permanent colony in 1607, in Jamestown, Virginia. Trade was also important to the English settlers, who began to export tobacco, cotton, fur, and timber.

The desire for political and religious freedom brought many colonists to the New World. Puritans, Catholics, Quakers, and Pilgrims sought the right to worship without government interference. The Pilgrims who came to America on the *Mayflower* drafted an agreement, the **Mayflower Compact,** committing these settlers of the Plymouth Colony in Massachusetts to self-government and majority rule. Thus, the compact outlined the first form of democracy in America. By the 1700s, **town meetings** were conducted throughout the New England colonies. People voted, created their own laws, and sent representatives to colonial assemblies. By the eighteenth century, **individualism,** the belief in the dignity and worth of each person, had a firm religious and political base in the British colonies.

Colonial economies experienced rapid growth as settlers worked to establish their own farms and businesses. Differing geographical and economic conditions led to three distinctive groups of colonies. The **New England colonies**—Massachusetts, New Hampshire, Rhode Island, and Connecticut—which had poor soil, developed fishing, trading, and shipbuilding industries. The **Middle colonies**—New York, New Jersey, Pennsylvania, and Delaware—grew large quantities of grain on family-size farms. The **Southern colonies**—Maryland, Virginia, North Carolina, South Carolina, and Georgia—had a climate and soil that favored the development of large plantations, on which tobacco, indigo, and rice were grown.

Lesson 1 Exercise

1. Which statement is NOT true of the exploration and settlement of the New World?
   - (1) The Spaniards settled the area around St. Augustine after they established themselves in Mexico and South America.
   - (2) The wildlife in the vast forests of the North provided French colonists with a prosperous industry.
   - (3) The fertile, level coastal regions offered the English a major resource for producing income.
   - (4) The Puritans, Quakers, and Pilgrims came to the New World primarily to achieve economic freedom.
   - (5) English colonists in the New World were more willing to farm the land than were French settlers.
2. What agreement was outlined in the Mayflower Compact?
3. Give three examples of individualism that are valued in the United States today.

Answers are on page A-17.

Lesson 2 National Unity

What led the states to adopt a central government in 1790?

During the first half of the eighteenth century, England pursued a policy of **salutary neglect** and did not attempt to exercise much economic or political control over its North American colonies. In 1763, however, as a result of enormous debts arising from the French and Indian War, England decided to levy taxes on the prospering colonies. The **Stamp Act** of 1763 was a tax on newspapers and legal documents. Following colonial protests, this tax was repealed. In 1767, England imposed new taxes on tea, glass, paint, and paper. Angry colonists threw all the tea from English cargo ships into Boston Harbor. In response to the **Boston Tea Party,** England closed the port of Boston and severely limited self-government in Massachusetts.

The colonists protested to England and began to organize a militia to protect themselves. Fighting broke out in 1775, marking the beginning of the **Revolutionary War.** The colonists issued the **Declaration of Independence** in 1776, in which the basic principles of the United States government were set forth. George Washington led the American army. Seven years later, with the signing of the **Treaty of Paris,** the colonies had won their freedom from England.

After the Revolutionary War, the colonies became independent states, joined together in a association under the **Articles of Confederation,** which were ratified in 1781. The Articles established a weak central government with a Congress that could declare war but was not allowed to recruit an army. There were no central courts. States taxed each other's goods and used different currencies.

Shays' Rebellion, an uprising of debtor farmers in Massachusetts, showed the states how inadequate the Articles of Confederation were. The central government did not have the authority to put down the rebellion. Recognizing the Articles' many weaknesses, deligates from the various states met in Philadelphia and eventually drafted the **Constitution,** which was adopted in 1790.

The Constitution was a result of a series of compromises. Among the most important were those concerning representation in the legislature and the method of electing the president. the debate over ratification divided the nation into **Federalists,** who supported the Constitution, and **anti-Federalists,** who feared a strong central government might abuse its power, the liberties of the people and the states. The promise of a **Bill of Rights** led the anti-Federalists to accept the new government.

Lesson 2   Exercise

1. How did England's participation in the French and Indian War lead to the Boston Tea Party?
2. Before the Constitution, each state could tax goods from the other states. Its goods would in turn be taxed differently by every other state, too. How could this situation lead to friction in the new nation?
3. Before the Constitution, there were two plans for Congress: either there would be one house with the same number of representatives for every state, large and small alike, or there would be a single house with a different number of representatives for each state, according to population. Explain how either plan would have been unfair to some states.

Answers are on pages A-17–A-18.

Lesson 3 Regional Differences

How did the territorial and economic growth of the country lead to the War Between the States?

During the first half of the nineteenth century, through wars, treaties, and purchases, the United States acquired more and more land west of the original 13 colonies. In 1803, President Jefferson bought territory from the French, the **Louisiana Purchase,** which nearly doubled the size of the United States. Protected from Europe by an ocean, American leaders continued to encourage **territorial expansion** and adopted a policy of **neutrality** toward foreign powers. In 1823, President James Madison restated this policy of noninterference in the **Monroe Doctrine** to warn European nations against intervening in the Western Hemisphere. By the 1840s, people began to believe in **manifest destiny,** the idea that the United States was destined to expand from ocean to ocean.

As the country grew and prospered, regional differences became more pronounced. The Northeast developed an industrial and trading economy, while the South became more dependent on exporting cash crops to Europe. In the West, cheap land encouraged smaller family farms, which sent foodstuffs to Northeastern cities.

Regional differences led to **sectionalism,** with Americans looking at issues increasingly in terms of what would benefit their region. Northerners favored tariffs on imported goods to protect their industries. Southerners, who imported more goods, opposed tariffs. Northerners favored the National Bank, which gave them a stable currency and investment funds. Westerners and Southerners favored state banks, which would give them easier credit. Westerners wanted federal funds for the construction of roads and canals, so they could get their produce to market. Southerners favored the extension of slavery to new territories, something Northerners and Westerners both opposed.

With the 1828 election of Andrew Jackson, sectional issues dominated national politics. A Westerner, Jackson antagonized Southerners by enforcing tariffs and alienated Northerners by dismantling the National Bank.

Sectional disputes further intensified when the Supreme Court, in the **Dred Scott** case, invalidated compromises over the issues of extending slavery into new territories. The gap between the industrial North and agricultural South widened as both sought to control the central government. When Abraham Lincoln was elected president in 1860, the South felt that its interests were no longer represented by the federal government and **seceded** from the Union. Under the leadership of Jefferson Davis, 11 states formed the **Confederate States of America.** Four slaveholding border states and 19 free states remained in the Union.

The **Civil War** began in 1861 when Confederate soldiers fired on federal troops at Fort Sumter in South Carolina. The Union had a decided advantage over the **Confederacy,** with twice the population of the South and three quarters of the nation's wealth. In addition, it had more factories and railroads. By 1865, the Confederacy was defeated. Southern General Robert E. Lee formally surrendered to Union general Ulysses S. Grant at Appomattox, Virginia, and the nation began the hard task of recovery.

Lesson 3 Exercise

1. Within many states today, cities, suburbs, and farmlands compete for federal aid. Which of the following terms best applies to this current situation?

    (1) manifest destiny
    (2) neutrality
    (3) sectionalism
    (4) secession
    (5) territorial expansion

2. Fill in the blanks: Natural resources can influence the development of a region. The South had better cropland and a mild climate, so its economy was _____. The North developed an economy based on _____, making use of water power from its rivers and the natural harbors along its coast.

3. Why did the South secede from the Union?

Answers are on page A-18.

Lesson 4 Industrial Growth

What were the effects of industrial growth on farms and cities?

In the South, during the Civil War and **Reconstruction,** blacks were given constitutional guarantees of freedom and protection through the **Emancipation Proclamation** and the **Civil War amendments** to the Constitution. Then Southern states passed **Jim Crow laws,** which legalized segregation, and other laws that denied blacks the right to vote. Most blacks became **sharecroppers,** who farmed other people's land in exchange for a portion of their crops.

Unlike Southern sharecroppers, Western and Midwestern farmers benefited from the industrial revolution. As agriculture became more mechanized, they were freed from backbreaking labor. However, they felt they were denied their fair share of the nation's wealth. Farmers often went into debt to purchase new equipment. Railroads charged them exorbitant rates to transport produce to markets, and middlemen siphoned off much of their profits. Farmers therefore demanded government regulation of railroad rates and cheap money to ease their debts. They joined the **Grange,** a movement pressing their demands for reform, and also formed the backbone of the **Greenback** and **Populist parties.**

In 1880, only one quarter of the population of the United States lived in cities, but by 1910, that figure had almost doubled. Rapid technological advances of the **industrial revolution** fostered the development and expansion of industries. Between 1880 and 1910, **immigrants** as well as farmers flocked to American cities to take jobs in the factories. They received low wages and worked under hazardous conditions. To help workers, the Knights of Labor and other unions were started. Samuel Gompers founded the **American Federation of Labor** in 1886.

At the same time, industrial leaders, such as Andrew Carnegie and Cornelius Vanderbilt, created trusts to consolidate their control over steel and railroad companies. They virtually eliminated competition so that they could set high prices and control the market for their products. They became active in state and national politics in order to impede attempts to regulate their industries.

Lesson 4   Exercise

1. Define the following:
   (a) Jim Crow laws
   (b) sharecropper
   (c) the Grange
   (d) industrial revolution
   (e) the American Federation of Labor

2. What were conditions like for blacks in the rural South after the Civil War?

3. What caused the United States to become a more urban nation between 1880 and 1910?

4. Today, migrant workers from Mexico sometimes work in the United States under poor conditions for low pay. With what group mentioned in the lesson can Mexican migrant workers be compared?

Answers are on page A-18.

Lesson 5   Reform Movements

How did reforms improve the life of Americans in the first half of the twentieth century?

From the turn of the century until the First World War, members of the **Progressive Movement** sponsored legislation to improve the quality of American life. Reformers enacted **pure food and drugs laws** to protect consumers. They supported women's efforts to gain the right to vote, which was finally granted in the **Nineteenth Amendment.** Through their efforts, children were guaranteed schooling under **compulsory education laws.** With the passage of **antitrust laws** to eliminate **monopolies** and other unfair trade practices and the creation of the **Federal Reserve System,** government took on a greater role in regulating the economy.

After World War I, Americans grew tired of reforms and wanted a **Return to Normalcy,** an era in which government would play a less important role in people's lives. The economy boomed, and Americans devoted themselves to the making and spending of money. Sports and film stars attracted national attention. Jazz music gained popularity. Then in 1929, the **stock market crash** brought national prosperity and good times to a sudden and violent end. Stock prices fell rapidly, thousands of people lost their investments, and businesses and banks closed. The nation was soon in the grip of the **Great Depression,** with millions of people unemployed.

President Franklin Roosevelt proposed a **New Deal** to combat the effects of the depression. He proposed legislation to offer relief to the unemployed, to prevent economic abuses, and to reconstruct the economy. The **Social Security Act Commission** was set up to regulate the stock market. The **Works Progress Administration** gave jobs to the unemployed. The **Tennessee Valley Authority** put people to work building a series of dams that provided electricity to one of the most depressed rural areas in the nation. These and other measures helped to restore the American economy.

Lesson 5   Exercise

1. Match the reform on the left with the legislation on the right:
   - (1) sets standards for food and medicine
   - (2) gives women the vote
   - (3) government takes larger part in regulating economy
   - (4) guarantees education for children
   - (5) guards against unfair trade practices

   - (a) Nineteenth Amendment
   - (b) compulsory education laws
   - (c) pure food and drug laws
   - (d) antitrust laws
   - (e) Federal Reserve System

2. The New Deal was created to provide immediate assistance to those in need and to prevent a future economic collapse. Label each of the following "assist" or "prevent."

   (a) Social Security Act
   (b) Securities and Exchange Commission
   (c) Works Progress Administration
   (d) Tennessee Valley Authority

   Answers are on page A-18.

Lesson 6   International Affairs

What was American foreign policy during the first half of this century?

From the 1890s to the 1940s, American foreign policy alternated between **isolationism,** or retreat from international concerns, and **internationalism,** or active involvement in world affairs. In the late 1890s, the United States adopted an activist foreign policy toward the Caribbean and the Pacific. It began to pursue a policy of **imperialism,** the political and economic control of other territories for purposes of prestige, power, and wealth.

In 1898 the United States went to war to free Cuba from Spanish rule to protect American trading interests. As a result of the Spanish-American War, the United States gained control of Puerto Rico, Guam, and the Philippines. Cuba was liberated but soon became an American protectorate. At the same time, the United States annexed the Hawaiian Islands. In 1903, the American government gained control of a ten mile strip of land across which the Panama Canal was built.

In 1914 **World War I** broke out in Europe. The United States maintained a policy of neutrality until 1917, when Germany resumed submarine warfare and sank unarmed American merchant ships. The United States joined the **Allied Powers**—Great Britain, France, and Russia, among others—in fighting the **Central Powers**—Germany, the Austro-Hungarian Empire, and their allies. When Germany accepted defeat in 1918, both sides signed an **armistice.** During the treaty-making at Versailles, President Woodrow Wilson's idealist **Fourteen Points** to foster world trade and fair territorial settlements were ignored by the European powers.

Disillusioned with the peace-making process, Americans returned to an isolationist policy and rejected United States membership in the **League of Nations,** an international organization intended to settle international disputes peaceably. With the rise of militaristic governments in Germany, Italy, and Japan, the postwar territorial settlements did not last long. In the 1930s, the **Axis** powers sought to absorb neighboring countries, and Western leaders' efforts to appease their desires failed.

World War II erupted when German troops threatened Poland's independence. The United States supported the **Allies,** including France, Great Britain, and the Soviet Union, against the Axis powers but remained neutral. In 1941, when the Japanese bombed Pearl Harbor in Hawaii, the United States entered the war. American forces fought the war in both Europe and the Pacific. The war ended in 1945 with the surrender of German troops and the use of nuclear weapons against Japan.

Lesson 6   Exercise

1. Match the term on the left with the meaning of the policy on the right:
   - (1) isolationism
   - (2) internationalism
   - (3) imperialism
   - (a) active involvement in world affairs
   - (b) political and economic control of other territories

2. What event caused the United States to enter World War I?

3. How might American isolationism have contributed to the outbreak of World War II?

Answers are on page A-18.

Lesson 7   International Relations Between the Superpowers

How did the United States react to Soviet expansion after World War II?

Since World War II, relations between the Soviet Union and the United States have dominated world affairs. The two nations, along with their allies, kept their wartime pledge to create an international organization, the **United Nations,** to replace the disbanded League of Nations. However, in the late 1940s, the Soviet Union gained control of the governments of Poland, Bulgaria, East Germany, Rumania, and Czechoslovakia. The United States responded with the **containment doctrine,** to block further Soviet expansion, and with the **Truman Doctrine,** to provide military and economic aid to countries threatened by Communism. In 1947, the American government offered the **Marshall Plan** to all European nations requiring assistance to rebuild their economies after World War II. In 1949, the United States and its Western allies formed the **North Atlantic Treaty Organization (NATO)** to provide for a common military defense against the Soviet Union and its allies.

The relationship between the two superpowers, particularly during the late 1940s and early 1950s, has been characterized as a **cold war,** a state of tension and hostility short of war. The superpowers have also experienced periods of **detente,** or a relaxation of tensions. During such periods, summit conferences, cultural exchanges, and agreements such as the **Limited Nuclear Test Ban Treaty,** the **Helsinki Accords,** and the **Strategic Arms Limitations Treaties** have taken place.

Recognizing Soviet threats to the **Third World**—the underdeveloped nations of Asia, Africa, and Latin America—the United States undertook policies of military alliances and economic and technical aid to contain communism. In Asia, relations between the superpowers were severly strained when Communist forces won the civil war in China in 1949. The United States refused to recognize the existence of the mainland (Communist) Chinese government until 1979. In 1950, the United States fought the **Korean War** to prevent the further expansion of Communism. Then it fought Communist forces in Southeast Asia for more than ten years, withdrawing its forces from the **Vietnam War** in 1975. In Latin America, since the 1960s, the United States has been unable to oust a Communist regime in Cuba. [Efforts to remove leftist governments from Chile and Guatemala were more successful.] In the Middle East, American recognition and support of Israel has antagonized Arab nations and jeopardized the flow of oil. However, superpower competition for influence in the Middle East continues.

Lesson 7   Exercise

1. What is the purpose of the North Atlantic Treaty Organization?
2. What was the purpose of the containment doctrine?
3. Fill in the blanks with *cooperation* or *confrontation*: Relations during the cold war involved superpower _____ while relations during periods of detente show superpower _____.

Answers are on page A-18.

Lesson 8 The Present

What sorts of issues has the United States faced in the last 40 years?

Since World War II, the United States government has been confronted with a variety of problems and challenges. Slowly, the nation moved toward becoming an integrated society. President Truman desegregated the armed services by executive order, and in 1954, the Supreme Court declared segregation unconstitutional in **Brown v. the Board of Education of Topeka.** During the 1960s, Dr. Martin Luther King, Jr., helped make Americans aware of continuing racial injustices. Congress responded by passing the **Civil Rights Act of 1964,** barring discrimination in housing.

President Kennedy was concerned with the needs of the poor, but important domestic poverty legislation was only passed after he was assassinated. Under President Johnson, Congress enacted the **War on Poverty** to provide job training and rebuild inner cities. It also passed **Great Society** legislation such as Medicare, insuring the health of the elderly, to improve the quality of American life.

Abuse of power became a major problem during Richard Nixon's presidency. Nixon and his advisors withheld and covered up information concerning a burglary at Democratic National Headquarters in the **Watergate** building complex during the 1972 presidential campaign. The president and his aides had also used government agencies, such as the FBI and the IRS, for political purposes. When Congress took steps to impeach him, President Nixon resigned from office.

When the Soviet Union launched **Sputnik** in 1957, President Eisenhower played an active role in establishing the **National Aeronautics and Space Administration (NASA)** and getting the **National Defense Education Act** passed, to train more scientists and engineers. President Kennedy vowed to get a man on the moon by the end of the 1960s. In 1969, President Nixon congratulated Neil Armstrong when he became the first man to walk on the moon. With the explosion of the space shuttle **Challenger,** American space programs underwent review.

Through the efforts of Rachel Carson and others, Americans became aware of the need to clean up and preserve their environment. During the Nixon administration, Congress established the **Environmental Protection Agency** and passed legislation to provide clean air and water.

The economy has been a constant source of worry to American presidents. Under President Johnson, **inflation** increased at an alarming rate. Presidents Nixon, Ford, and Carter found it difficult to control inflation, especially because Arab oil policies raised the price of energy, thereby affecting the costs of manufacturing and transporting goods. Under President Reagan, inflation was finally halted. The mounting budget deficit remained an unsolved problem.

Lesson 8 Exercise

1. What was the first piece of legislation promoting integration in the United States after World War II?
2. In the debate over ratification of the Constitution, the anti-Federalists feared that a strong central government could abuse its power. What incident in the 1970s made many concerned about central government's abuse of power?
3. In the early years of the nation, Americans explored their continent. How do their efforts compare with those of America's astronauts?

Answers are on page A-18.

Chapter 2 Quiz

1. A philosopher said, "England is the paradise of individuality . . ." Would the Pilgrims agree? Explain your answer.
2. Explain the difference between the Federalists and the anti-Federalists.
3. How did the Constitution help to strengthen the United States government without creating a tyrannical state?
4. Tell whether the following is TRUE or FALSE and explain your answer: The real cause of the Civil War was sectionalism, not slavery.

Items 5 to 7 are based on the following passage.

In the early 1900s, a journalist named Ida Tarbell became interested in the growth and practices of monopolies. Ida Tarbell's articles took on such massive corporations as the Standard Oil Trust Company. She described the methods that these monopolies would use to drive rival companies out of business. For example, she described how big companies would make deals with railroad companies. According to the terms of these deals, the railroad companies would charge the big companies lower rates to transport goods. Smaller companies who competed with the big companies would be charged the regular rate, which was much higher.

Soon, the public began to take a special interest in Ida Tarbell's articles. Before long, politicians were taking steps to regulate monopolies.

5. Which of the following best states the main idea of the passage?
    (1) Monopolies are businesses that have exclusive control over a certain market.
    (2) Ida Tarbell wrote articles about the Standard Oil Trust Company.
    (3) The writings of Ida Tarbell helped bring about the regulation of monopolies.
    (4) Ida Tarbell was interested in monopolies.
    (5) Monopolies tried to drive smaller companies out of business.

6. Which of the following conclusions is supported by the information in the passage?
    (1) Politicians were not aware of the abuses of monopolies until Ida Tarbell began to write articles about monopolies.
    (2) The Standard Oil Trust Company was a monopoly.
    (3) A corporation could not be a monopoly.
    (4) Ida Tarbell's articles led to laws making it illegal to form monopolies.
    (5) Railroad companies formed their own monopoly.

7. Which of the following laws would have helped prevent the abuses that were pointed out by Ida Tarbell?
    (1) A law that required monopolies to have their products inspected
    (2) A law that required big corporations to share their profits among their stockholders
    (3) A law that required monopolies also to manufacture nonessential goods
    (4) A law that made it illegal for railroad companies to charge different rates for different companies
    (5) A law that made it illegal for railroads to transport goods manufactured by small companies

8. During the Depression, unemployment made it difficult for many people to purchase necessities such as food, clothing, and housing. Then, in the early 1930s, great dust storms ruined many farms in the Great Plains and farm families had to abandon the land and move elsewhere to find work. How did this situation make matters worse?

9. Why did the United States fight the Spanish-American War?

10. Why was additional civil rights legislation needed in the 1960s?

Answers are on page A-19.

Chapter 3

Geography

Objective

In this chapter, you will read and answer questions about

- The two areas of geography
- The basic tools of geographers
- How climates and natural resources affect our lives

Lesson 1 The Study of Geography

What are two major areas of the study of geography?

Geography studies both our planet and the people who live on it. There are two main branches of geography—physical geography and cultural geography.

Physical geography focuses on the Earth itself, that is, on the physical environment. Changes in the Earth's **crust**, or surface, have created the mountains, plateaus, and other **landforms** we see today. Factors such as weather, earthquakes, and volcanic eruptions continue to alter these landforms. Also included in physical geography are soils, vegetation, climate, and resources—in short, antying that pertains to our land, water, or atmosphere.

Cultural geography studies how human groups have lived and changedc in relation to the physical environment. Cultural geographers have defined various useful concepts to aid them in this study. One such concept is **population density,** or the average number of people living within a given amount of space such as a square mile. **Urban areas,** or cities, are more densely populated than **rural areas. Migration** is another important concept, since it refers to the movement of groups of people out of (**emigration**) or into (**immigration**) different regions.

Other areas of cultural geography include the development of political systems (for example, how physical factors such as mountains and rivers help set the boundaries of nations), the development of economic systems (for example, how the amount of rainfall in an area helps determine its economy), and the geography of natural resources (for example, how the presence or absence of resources affects population distribution).

Lesson 1   Exercise

1. Which term does NOT belong?
   (1) vegetation
   (2) urban areas
   (3) landforms
   (4) mountains
   (5) climates

2. In order to learn how population decline in the northeastern United States relates to population growth in the Southwest, a researcher would have to study patterns of emigration and immigration, that is, _____ patterns.

Items 3 and 4 are based on the following graph.

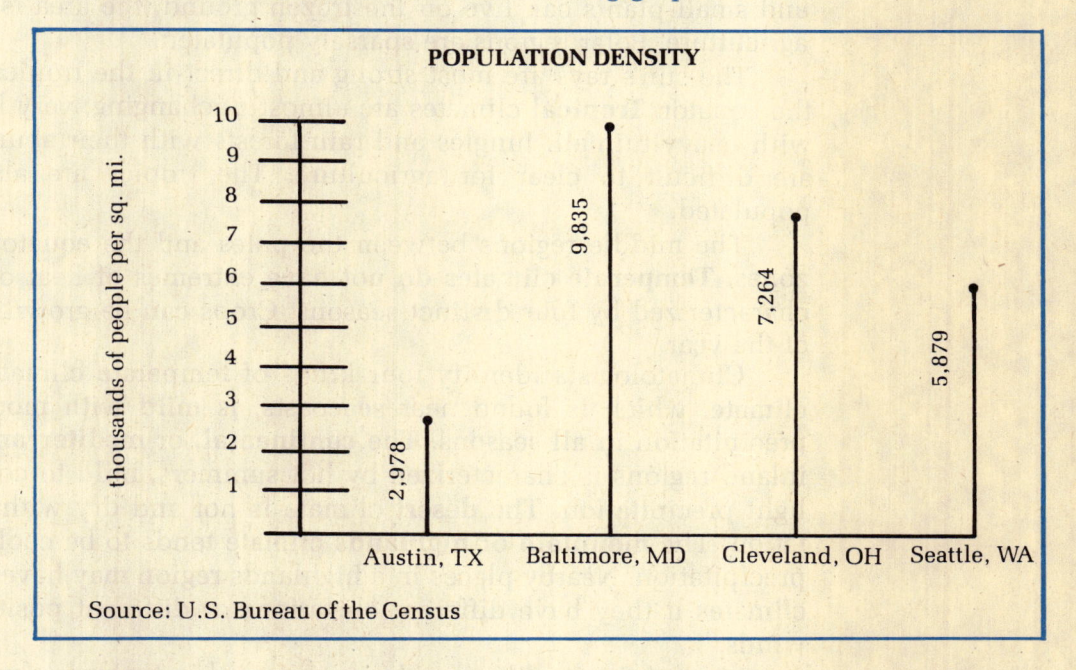

POPULATION DENSITY

(thousands of people per sq. mi.)

- Austin, TX: 2,978
- Baltimore, MD: 9,835
- Cleveland, OH: 7,264
- Seattle, WA: 5,879

Source: U.S. Bureau of the Census

3. Which city probably would be best able to handle a sudden growth in population? Which city probably would be least able to absorb a population increase?

4. Tell whether the following is TRUE or FALSE and explain your answer: Since the population densities of Cleveland and Seattle are the most similar, we can assume that the ethnic make-up of the populations is similar.

Answers are on page A-19.

Lesson 2 Climates: How and Why They Differ

What are the types of temperate climates?

Wherever people live, **climate** has an important effect on the way of life. It influences the clothing worn, food grown, housing constructed, and transportation used. Climate refers to average weather conditions over a long period of time, taking into account temperatures, winds, and amounts of **precipitation** (rain, sleet, snow). **Weather** is the atmospheric conditions during a short period; weather may change from day to day.

To a large extent, climate depends on the amount of the sun's heat that reaches a place. Because Earth is tilted as it revolves, the strength of the rays varies in different parts of the Earth. The rays are least strong on the polar regions, that is, the areas around the North and South poles. **Polar** climates are cold with light precipitation, usually in the form of snow. As only mosses and small plants can live on the frozen ground, the area is unsuitable for agriculture. Polar regions are sparsely populated.

The sun's rays are most strong and direct in the tropics, the area near the equator. **Tropical** climates are almost unchanging, very hot and humid, with heavy rainfall. Jungles and rain forests with their abundant plant life are difficult to clear for agriculture. The tropics are also not heavily populated.

The middle regions between the poles and the equator are temperate zones. **Temperate** climates do not have extremes of heat or cold, and are characterized by four distinct seasons. Crops can be grown for a good part of the year.

Climatologists identify four kinds of temperate climates. The **marine** climate, which is found near seacoasts, is mild with moderate to heavy precipitation in all seasons. The **continental,** or **mediterranean,** climate of inland regions is characterized by hot summers, mild to cold winters, and light precipitation. The **desert** climate is hot and dry with scarce precipitation. The **mountain** or **highlands** climate tends to be cool with moderate precipitation. Nearby places in a highlands region may have rather different climates if they have different elevations or different positions relative to winds.

Most of the world's population is found in temperate zones, where the climate is favorable for mental and physical activity, and the natural resources for agriculture and industry are accessible.

Lesson 2 Exercise

1. The Barnett family has decided to move to a new state because the climate is said to be more healthful there. On the day they arrive to look for a new home, the weather is cold and rainy. The Barnetts decide not to make the move. Why was this an unfair and uninformed decision?
2. On what factors does climate depend? In what way do climates differ most?

Item 3 is based on the following map.

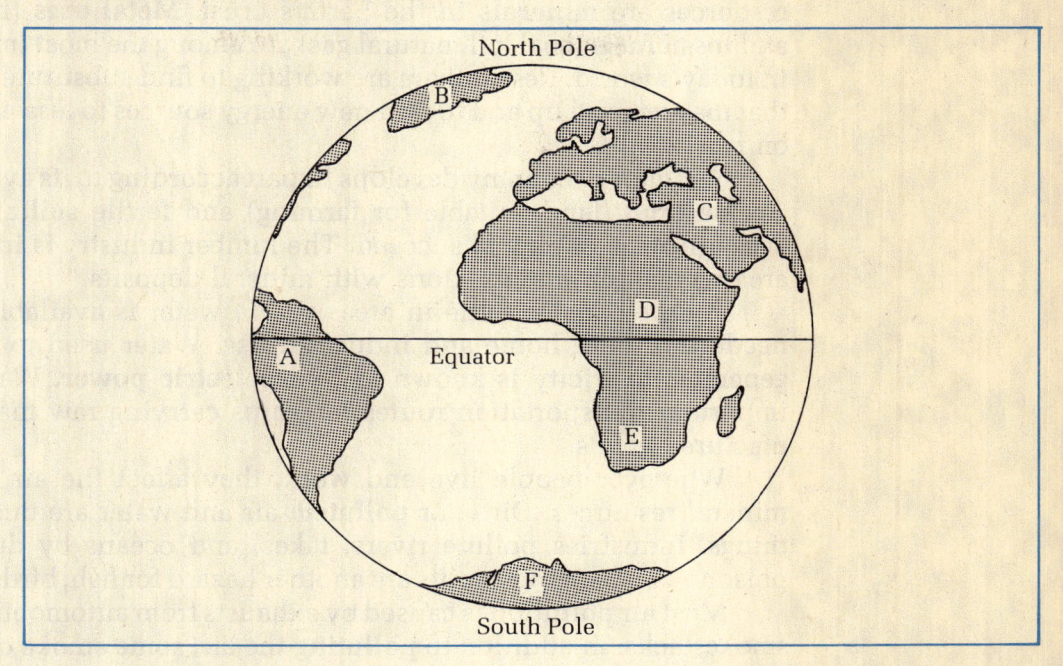

[Globe diagram showing regions labeled A through F, with North Pole, Equator, and South Pole marked. B is near the North Pole; A is in South America near the Equator; C is in the Middle East/North Africa area; D is in central Africa; E is in southern Africa; F is near the South Pole.]

3. A portion of the globe is shown above. Give the letter or letters of regions that are most likely to have a
   (a) polar climate
   (b) tropical climate
   (c) temperate climate

4. Read the description of the two Canadian cities given below. Then identify the type of temperate climate each one has.
   (a) Winnipeg, Manitoba, is located far inland. Hot summers give way to very cold winters.
   (b) Vancouver, British Columbia, is at Canada's western edge, close to the Pacific Ocean. The weather is mild, with frequent heavy rainfall.

Answers are on page A-19.

Lesson 3 Natural Resources and the Environment

What are the basic types of resources?

Any material supplied by the Earth that people can put to use is called a **natural resource. Renewable** resources are those that can be replaced in the foreseeable future. For example, forests can be replanted after trees are cut, and the water supply is replenished by rain. Examples of **nonrenewable** resources are **minerals** in the Earth's crust. **Metal ores** (iron, gold, silver) and **fossil fuels** (coal, oil, natural gas) are among the most important minerals in today's world. Researchers are working to find substitutes for some metals that may be used up and to find new energy sources to lessen our dependence on fossil fuels.

A region's economy develops in part according to its available resources. **Arable land** (land suitable for farming) and fertile **soil** are needed for an agricultural economy to succeed. The lumber industry is important in forest areas, as is mining in regions with mineral deposits.

People usually settle in areas where water is available. Fresh water is needed for both home and industrial use. Water used to turn wheels and generate electricity is known as **hydroelectric power.** Waterways serve as important transportation routes for ships carrying raw materials and manufactured goods.

Wherever people live and work, they affect the air, water, soil, and mineral resources. Dirty, or **polluted,** air and water are unsafe for all living things. Industries pollute rivers, lakes, and oceans by dumping **toxic,** or poisonous, wastes. Oil spills are another hazard for fish, birds, and vegetation.

Most air pollution is caused by exhausts from automobiles and industrial smokestacks. In addition to polluting the air, some smoke can combine with moisture in the air to form acids. These acids return in rain to pollute the land as well as bodies of water. Air pollution is dangerous to health and may cause severe respiratory problems.

Local health departments and a federal government agency, the EPA (Environmental Protection Agency), monitor air and water and track down polluters. The government also protects the environment by banning the use of cancer-causing chemical pesticides such as DDT and regulating vehicle exhausts. Pollution remains one of the world's most serious problems. Our industrialized society must learn to take responsibility for the environment.

Lesson 3 Exercise

1. Which of the following is *not* a renewable resource?
   - (1) water
   - (2) trees
   - (3) copper
   - (4) wind
   - (5) sunshine

2. The waters in and around the Pacific Northwest contain many salmon. Discuss two ways in which careful maintenance of this resource might affect the economy of the region.

3. In regard to the conservation of our natural resources, what is the advantage of hydroelectric power compared to electricity generated by burning fossil fuels?

4. Which one of the following statements is implied in the lesson?
   - (1) Water supply does not influence where people live.
   - (2) Natural methods of crop protection are preferable to the use of chemical pesticides.
   - (3) Industry can be trusted to act in environmentally safe ways.
   - (4) The government has little interest in protecting the environment.

Answers are on page A-19.

Chapter 3 Quiz

1. Would cultural geography or physical geography be used in the following situations?
   (a) studying the influx of Asians to the U.S. in the last 10 years
   (b) comparing soil from the Rocky Mountains and the Ural Mountains
   (c) studying the ethnic groups in Morocco

2. Which would be likely to have the denser population: a region in which the land is used for agriculture or a region near a seaport?

3. Explain the difference between dry weather and a dry climate.

4. Explain how climate can affect physical activity and work habits.

5. Tell whether the following is TRUE or FALSE: The land areas around the equator have four distinct seasons. Explain your answer.

Items 6 to 8 are based on the following map.

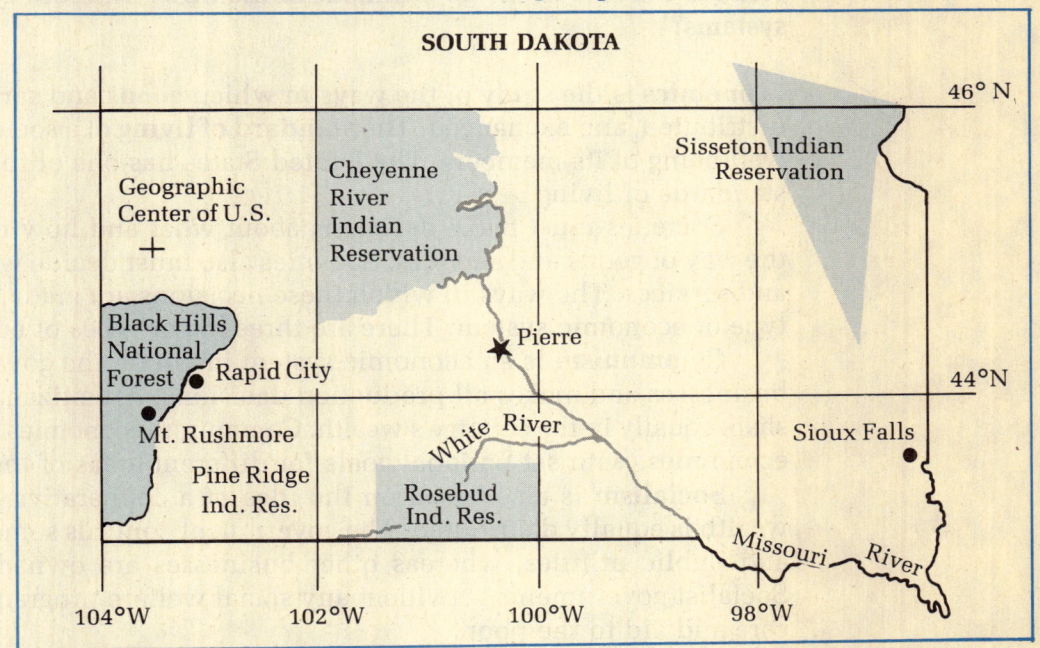

SOUTH DAKOTA

6. Which city is closest to 44° north latitude, 100° west longitude?

7. Explain why a researcher might choose South Dakota to study relationships between Indians and other residents of the state.

8. Tell whether the following is TRUE or FALSE. The map shows that Indians made up the majority of the population in South Dakota.

---

9. Explain why it is crucial that we find substitutes for our nonrenewable resources.

10. How does water pollution by industries affect the environment?
    Answers are on pages A-19–A-20.

Chapter 4

Economics

> **Objective**
>
> In this chapter, you will read and answer questions about
>
> - Major kinds of economic systems
> - The relationships between consumers, businesses, and the government in economics
> - International trade

Lesson 1   Types of Economic Systems

What is the role of the government in the three different types of economic systems?

Economics is the study of the ways in which **goods** and **services** are created, distributed, and exchanged. The **standard of living** of a society is the material well-being of its members. The United States has one of the world's highest standards of living.

Societies must make decisions about what and how much to create in the way of goods and services. Societies also must decide who gets the goods and services. The ways in which these decisions are made depend upon the type of economic system. There are three major types of economic systems:

Communism is an economic system in which the government owns all businesses and makes all production decisions. All citizens are supposed to share equally in the country's wealth. Communist economies are often **planned economies,** with set national goals for different areas of the economy.

Socialism is also based on the idea of a cooperative society in which wealth is equally distributed. The government controls some basic industries and public utilities, whereas other businesses are owned by individuals. Socialist governments provide many social welfare programs such as health care and aid to the poor.

Capitalism is an economic system in which individuals control the means of production, distribution, and exchange. The government usually does not interfere in business. Capitalism is a **free-enterprise system** because, with the exception of some limitations imposed by the government, citizens may engage in whatever business they choose and may produce and charge what they want.

Most modern countries have **mixed economies** that emphasize one system but use elements of others. For example, the United States has a capitalist system. However, because of the complex nature of our society, the government needs to exercise some control over business and industry. There are also government-owned and operated enterprises in the United States, including the Postal Service, the public schools, some railroad lines, and social welfare projects such as public housing developments.

Lesson 1 Exercise

1. In which type of system—capitalist, communist, or socialist—would you expect to find wealth most unevenly distributed?
2. In which of the following economic systems would the government most likely set wages for the workers?
    - **(1)** capitalist
    - **(2)** socialist
    - **(3)** communist
    - **(4)** mixed
3. Even though the United States has a free enterprise system, the government regulates the quality of certain goods—such as food and medical products—that are produced. Explain why these controls are important.
4. In which type of economic system—capitalist, communist, or socialist—would you assume the profit motive operates most strongly?

Answers are on page A-20.

Lesson 2 Consumer Influence

What is the relationship between the price of and the demand for a product?

An individual who buys or uses goods and services for personal wants is a **consumer.** Consumers buy more of some products than others. The ways in which consumers spend their money influence producers' decisions about which goods to make or which services to provide.

Businesses must always consider supply and demand. **Supply** is the amount of available goods and services. **Demand** is how many people want to buy the product or service. Goods and services can be sold at different prices. Usually, prices affect demand. An increase in price results in a decrease in demand. A lower price means a greater demand. However, this relationship is not always true.

The demand for some goods and services is not greatly affected by price. For example, the demand for milk or bread does not change much even if prices go higher. The demand for these products is said to be **inelastic.** In contrast, the demand for video recorders or computers is greatly increased when the price drops. The demand for these products is **elastic.**

Businesses study the changes in supply and demand for their goods and services to determine an **equilibrium point**—the price at which consumers will buy exactly the amount supplied by the producer. When there is overproduction, a **surplus** is created and prices fall. When there is underproduction, a **shortage** occurs and prices rise.

Because of the importance of consumers, businesses try to gain favor for their goods and services through advertising. **Consumer protection groups** check the safety and reliability of products and services and the accuracy of the claims in advertisements.

Lesson 2   Exercise

1. As the prices of hand calculators have decreased, more and more people have bought them. Is the demand for hand calculators elastic or inelastic?
2. Suppose the price of beef increases from $3.49 a pound to $4.29 a pound. During the same time, the price of other meat products, such as pork and poultry, does not change. What will probably happen next?
   (1) The demand for beef will increase.
   (2) There will be a shortage of beef.
   (3) The demand for meat products other than beef will increase.
   (4) The demand for meat products other than beef will decrease.
   (5) There will be a surplus of meat products other than beef.
3. Suppose the price of steel increases. As a result, automobile makers must pay more for the steel they need. Why might an automobile maker consider making certain features optional rather than standard instead of raising the prices of its cars?

Answers are on page A-20.

Lesson 3   Structure of Business

What three elements are needed for the operation of any business?

To create goods or services, a business needs three things—natural resources, labor, and capital. These things are known as **factors of production.**

Natural resources are materials that can be found in nature. Metal ores, water, wood, and land are examples of natural resources.

Labor is the human activity that is required to produce goods or services. Labor can be classified into two types. **Blue-collar** workers are **manual laborers** such as construction workers, electricians, or factory employees. **White-collar** workers are employed at "desk jobs" in offices. Examples include lawyers, bankers, and journalists.

Capital is wealth used to produce more wealth. Machinery, tools, and equipment are examples of capital. Money also is capital if it is producing more wealth, as in interest-paying savings accounts. Money can be used to buy other capital or to buy natural resources or labor.

Business is any activity in which goods and services are **exchanged for profit.** Businesses are organized in different ways. A **sole proprietorship** is a business owned by one person. Today, sole proprietorships make up over 75 percent of U.S. businesses. About 8 percent of U.S. businesses are **partnerships,** in which two or more people are owners and operators.

A **corporation** is a business that is **licensed,** or **chartered,** by state or local governments. Corporations are owned by people who buy shares, or **stock,** in the business. **Stockholders** receive **dividends,** or **earnings** from the business, based on the number of shares they own. Stockholders elect a **board of directors** to make decisions for the business. About 17 percent of U.S. businesses are corporations. A **conglomerate** is a corporation that owns or controls companies in many fields.

Lesson 3 Exercise

1. Match the term on the left with the explanation on the right.
   - **(1)** sole proprietorship
   - **(2)** partnership
   - **(3)** corporation
   - **(4)** conglomerate

   - **(a)** owns or controls companies in many fields
   - **(b)** business owned by one person
   - **(c)** business owned by stockholders
   - **(d)** business owned by two or more people

2. In which type of society would you find production requiring a greater amount of manual labor: a highly industrialized society or a society that it not yet industrialized?

3. Which of the following is an example of capital?
   - **(1)** money kept in a checking account to pay household bills
   - **(2)** the ovens used by a bakery to bake bread and cakes
   - **(3)** an automobile used for family transportation
   - **(4)** middle-level management
   - **(5)** natural resources that are owned but not yet developed

4. How do stockholders in a corporation benefit from the corporation's success?

Answers are on page A-20.

Lesson 4   Government Revenues and Expenditures

What are the two main sources of government revenues?

The U.S. government raises and spends billions of dollars each year. To pay for its activities, the government accumulates **revenue** (income), mainly through a variety of taxes.

The **personal income tax** brings in the most money. The second largest amount of revenue comes from social insurance taxes such as that for **Social Security** (a proportional tax taken out of payroll). Substantial amounts of revenue also come from **corporate income taxes, excise taxes** (taxes on non-essential items), **customs duties** and **tariffs** (charges levied on imported items), **state income taxes, school** and **property taxes, highway tolls, fines, licensing fees,** and **sales taxes.**

In recent years, government expenditures have been greater than revenues; this results in a **budget deficit.** The accumulated total of these deficits is called the **federal debt.** To get the money it needs, the government **borrows** money through the sale of **bonds.** The largest government expenditures are for payments made directly to Americans in the form of **Social Security** and **Medicare** benefits, **federal retirement pensions, unemployment compensation,** and social welfare programs. **Defense** is the second largest spending category. **Interest** on the federal debt is the third largest cost and will continue to be a major expense for many years. Economists and government officials propose different ways to reduce the debt: reducing government spending, raising taxes, or a combination of both of these approaches.

The government also spends money on public health programs, job training, research, veterans' benefits, and payments to state and local governments to operate publicly funded programs.

Lesson 4   Exercise

1. Match the tax on the left with the source(s) of revenue on the right to which that tax specifically applies.
    - **(1)** income tax
    - **(2)** excise tax
    - **(3)** tariff
    - **(4)** sales tax
    - **(a)** Japanese automobile
    - **(b)** cigarettes made in United States
    - **(c)** savings account interest
    - **(d)** gasoline for car

2. Suppose a state is prevented by law from spending more money than it receives. If there is no money in the current budget for new schools, what are some of the ways in which the state can finance their construction?

3. Suppose you heard someone say, "People shouldn't be concerned with the size of the federal debt. As long as the government has the ability to

borrow money, it will always be able to finance its operations." Bearing in the mind the interest on the federal debt, is this argument valid or not?

Answers are on page A-20.

Lesson 5 Business Cycles and Government Regulation

What methods does the government use to fight inflation?

Most countries experience periodic changes in the economy. The movement from one level of economic activity to another and back again is known as the **business cycle.** When the economy moves down from **prosperity** to **recession**, production decreases and unemployment increases. A very bad recession, such as the one the United States experienced in the 1930s, is called a **depression.**

Another condition that has an adverse effect on the economy is **inflation.** Inflation is a general rise in prices. People can buy less with the same amount of money. The real value of the dollar declines.

During periods of recession or depression, the government tries to stimulate the economy with public works projects and low-cost business loans. The government can also influence business cycles through **monetary policy.** The **Federal Reserve System** (or the Fed), consisting of 12 regional Federal Reserve Banks, is a regulatory agency with the power to supervise the country's banks and adjust the money supply. The Fed can lower the amount of cash reserves banks must keep, making more money available for loans. Raising the reserve limit decreases the amount of available money.

The Fed can also adjust interest rates. Higher rates mean fewer loans to people and businesses, who then have less to spend. In this way, the Fed can shrink the money supply to combat inflation.

The government makes decisions affecting the economy by studying various statistics. The **Consumer Price Index** (CPI) is a way of measuring the dollar's value. The CPI is the average price of essential goods and services, such as food, housing, and transportation.

Another important economic statistic is the **Gross National Product** (GNP). The GNP is the value of everything produced in one year. It is reported in terms of **constant dollars** to compensate for inflation. Constant dollars are calculated using a **base year.**

Lesson 5 Exercise

1. State whether the following is TRUE or FALSE and explain your answer: During a recessionary period, the Federal Reserve Bank might consider lowering interest rates to stimulate the economy.

2. Name two important economic measurements and tell what each measures.

Item 3 is based on the following graph.

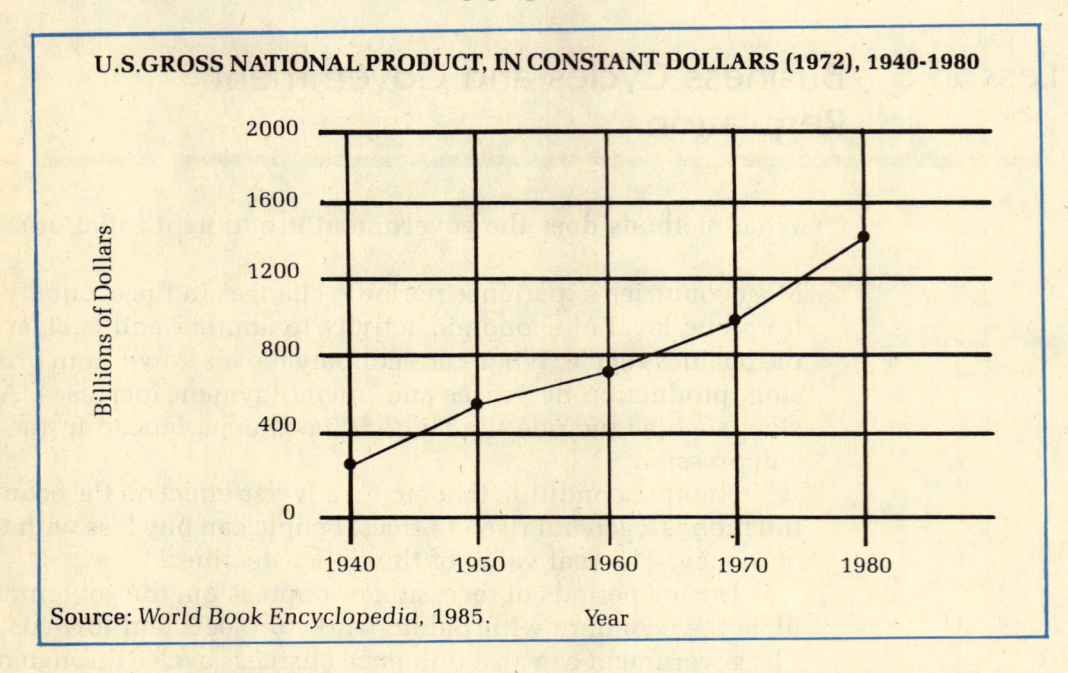

U.S. GROSS NATIONAL PRODUCT, IN CONSTANT DOLLARS (1972), 1940-1980

[Graph showing Billions of Dollars (y-axis, 0 to 2000) vs. Year (x-axis, 1940 to 1980). Data points approximately: 1940: 200, 1950: 500, 1960: 700, 1970: 1000, 1980: 1400]

Source: *World Book Encyclopedia*, 1985.

3. Which one of the following conclusions is supported by the graph?
   (1) The U.S. Gross National Product can never decrease.
   (2) The U.S. Gross National Product showed a fairly steady increase from 1940 to 1980.
   (3) The U.S. Gross National Product in the year 2000 will be about $2,000 billion.
   (4) The U.S. Gross National Product is not affected by inflation.
   (5) The U.S. Gross National Product has doubled its rate of increase every ten years from 1940 to 1980.

4. How are people who have set aside money in savings accounts hurt economically during an inflationary period?

   Answers are on pages A-20—A-21.

Lesson 6 International Economics

Why are protected markets created?

Most Americans wear clothes, drive automobiles, consume food, or use radios or TVs that were manufactured in other countries. As the leading trade nation, the United States **imports** and **exports** billions of dollars of goods annually.

The combination of imports and exports makes up a country's **balance of trade.** A country has a **favorable balance** of trade when it exports more than it imports. If a country imports more than it exports, then it has an **unfavorable balance** of trade.

Imports mean a greater variety of goods and allow consumers to purchase some products at lower prices. However, some U.S. industries complain that they cannot compete with foreign manufacturers that are able to produce goods more cheaply than U.S. companies.

The United States exports many goods that other countries do not make or cannot produce as cheaply. Many of this country's industries—especially agriculture—depend on exports for a large share of their profits. Although exports increase sales and provide employment for U.S. workers, heavy exports of some goods can sometimes keep prices high at home.

Countries trade with one another for their mutual economic benefit. However, most countries find it necessary to regulate foreign trade to protect their economies. If the United States imposed no limits on imports of certain products, many American businesses would be forced to close. Special taxes, or **tariffs,** are therefore sometimes imposed on certain foreign goods to make them more expensive.

When tariffs are used to make foreign goods more expensive than similar items made at home, then a **protected market** is created. If restrictions that trading partners impose on one another become too severe, however, both countries can suffer economically.

Sometimes, countries prohibit their usual trade with each other because of a political conflict. A ban imposed on trade because of foreign policy is called an **embargo.**

Lesson 6 Exercise

1. Which of the following would NOT affect U.S. trade with other countries?
   - (1) A California company decides to open a plant in Wyoming.
   - (2) A tariff is imposed on all imported television sets.
   - (3) The price of automobiles manufactured in the United States rises as a result of increased labor costs.
   - (4) The United States prohibits the export of grain to the Soviet Union.
   - (5) Domestic oil production increases sharply.
2. Why do most countries regulate foreign trade?
3. Suppose Country A exports a product in great quantities to Country B. Businesses in Country B make the same product less cheaply, and their sales begin to suffer. What would the government of Country B be likely to do to help its business?

Answers are on page A-21.

Chapter 4   Quiz

1. A company that manufactures color film is producing more film than it can sell. What can the company do to help its product reach an equilibrium point?
2. Name two major ways that the federal government can reduce the size of its debt.
3. Identify which of the following methods the government might use to stimulate the economy during a depression or a recession.
   - (a) increase personal income taxes
   - (b) provide low-cost loans to businesses
   - (c) finance public works projects
   - (d) lower the amount of cash reserves banks must keep
   - (e) raise interest rates
4. Which one of the following groups of people would be most hurt economically during an inflationary period?
   - (1) people who work in education, medicine, and other service industries
   - (2) people who work for manufacturing companies
   - (3) retired people, living on fixed incomes
   - (4) people with investments in stocks and bonds
   - (5) people who have mortgages on their homes
5. Would consumers or manufacturers be more likely to favor protected markets? Explain your answer.
6. The U.S. government guarantees that, by means of government subsidies if necessary, farmers will receive no less than a certain amount of money for each bushel of wheat grown. Suppose a worldwide wheat shortage occurs. What effect would this have on government payments to farmers?
7. Explain the major characteristics of these economic systems: capitalism, communism, and socialism.
8. Sometimes, several hospitals within a metropolitan area decide to purchase medical equipment together. The participating hospitals share the expense and use of the equipment. What is the major reason that hospitals do this?
   - (1) to reduce their capital expenditures
   - (2) to reduce labor costs
   - (3) to increase the number of patients they can treat
   - (4) to increase their tax deductions

Items 9 and 10 are based on the following graph.

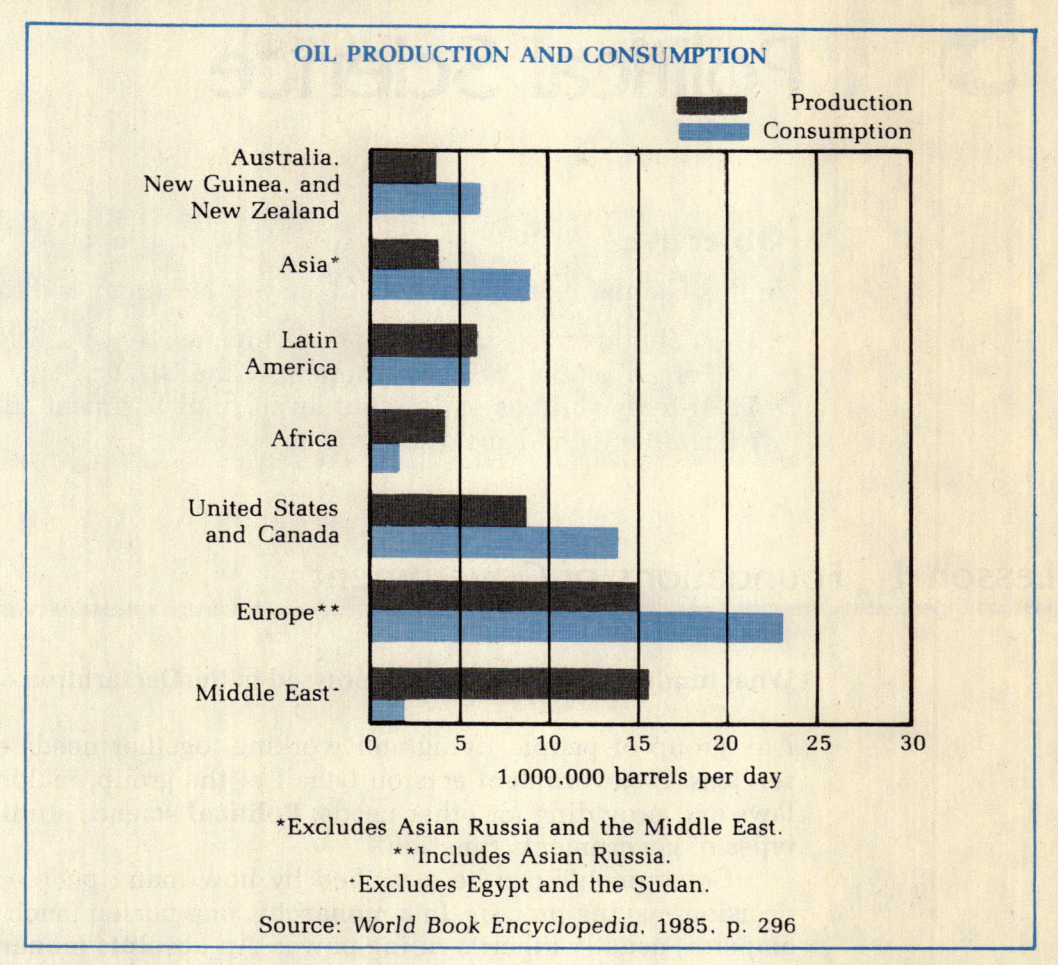

OIL PRODUCTION AND CONSUMPTION

■ Production
■ Consumption

Regions (bar chart, 1,000,000 barrels per day, scale 0–30):
- Australia, New Guinea, and New Zealand
- Asia*
- Latin America
- Africa
- United States and Canada
- Europe**
- Middle East·

*Excludes Asian Russia and the Middle East.
**Includes Asian Russia.
·Excludes Egypt and the Sudan.

Source: *World Book Encyclopedia*, 1985, p. 296

9. Which of the regions shown on the graph must import oil to meet their needs?

10. Is this a valid or an invalid conclusion based on the information in the graph: Because the Middle East produces so much more petroleum than it consumes, petroleum will always be a major source of income for the Middle East?

Answers are on page A-21.

Chapter 5

Political Science

Objective

In this chapter, you will read and answer questions about

- The nature of various types of governments
- The organization of the government of the United States
- The responsibilities of different levels of government and of divisions within the federal government

Lesson 1 Foundations of Government

What fundamental ideals are expressed in the Declaration of Independence?

Any group of people living and working together needs certain laws and services. A **government** acts on behalf of the group, making and enforcing laws and providing for other needs. **Political science** studies how different types of governments function.

Governments can be classified by how many people take part in the decision-making process. In a **monarchy,** one person (such as a queen or an emperor) usually inherits ruling power. An **absolute monarch** has complete authority to govern. A **constitutional monarch** has limited power and must work with other government officials. In a **dictatorship** or **totalitarian government,** one person or a small group has total power and exerts extensive control over people's lives. Dictators often rise to power during times of national unrest.

In an **oligarchy,** a small governing class rules. In a **democracy,** all of the people take part in governing the country. Ancient Greece was an example of a **direct democracy** because all the citizens met to make decisions. The United States is a **representative democracy** in which the people elect representatives, such as the members of Congress, to carry out the work of the government.

When the 13 colonies decided to free themselves from British rule, the writers of the **Declaration of Independence** expressed a political philosophy of individualism that is still basic to American government today. This philosophy emphasizes the equality of all people and the right to "life, liberty, and the pursuit of happiness." The United States government exists to protect these rights, and the power of the government comes from the consent of the people. If the government ignores the people's will, the people have the right to elect new officials.

Lesson 1 Exercise

1. Match the type of government on the left with the description on the right:
   - (1) monarchy
   - (2) dictatorship
   - (3) oligarchy
   - (4) democracy

   - (a) All the people take part in governing, either directly or through elected representatives.
   - (b) A single person inherits the authority to rule.
   - (c) A small class of people rule.
   - (d) A person or group has complete control of government.

2. In 1689, the English Parliament had William and Mary agree to certain conditions before they could be crowned king and queen. These conditions were set forth in a Bill of Rights. Among other provisions, the rulers of England were forbidden to proclaim or suspend any law without Parliament's consent. What type of government was established?

3. President X has been the leader of Country A for six years. X's leadership was strong for the first two years but has not been effective for the last four years. What is likely to happen if Country A is a representative democracy?
   - (1) The military will overthrow the leader and take control of the government.
   - (2) The citizens will elect a new leader as soon as the system permits.
   - (3) Leader X will try to regain control by jailing his opponents.
   - (4) Leader X will resign from office after choosing his successor.

   Answers are on page A-21.

Lesson 2 Writing the Constitution

At the Constitutional Convention, what compromise was made regarding representation?

Five years after the Declaration of Independence was written, the first national constitution governing the United States was approved, or **ratified,** by all of the states. This document was known as the **Articles of Confederation.**

The Articles created a central government with very limited powers. It could not make laws without unanimous state agreement, nor could it settle conflicts between states. There was no president or national court system. It soon became clear that these weaknesses had to be corrected.

In 1787, delegates from all the states met at the **Constitutional Convention** to develop a new system of government. A debate about the nature of representation of individuals and of states was settled by the **Great Compromise.** Under the terms of this compromise, a two-part or **bicameral congress** consisting of a **House of Representatives** (representation determined by state population) and a **Senate** (two representatives for each state) was created. The new **U.S. Constitution** also provided for shared power and responsibilities in three ways: (1) a **separation of powers** that defines three branches of government with distinct powers; (2) a system of **checks and balances** that allows each branch to oversee the other two (see chart below); (3) a **federal system** that divides governing power between the **federal government** and state governments.

The three branches of the federal government are the **executive branch,** whose main power resides in the presidency; the **legislative branch,** which includes the two houses of Congress; and the **judicial branch,** which includes the Supreme Court and lower federal courts.

Lesson 2   Exercise

Item 1 is based on the following chart.

Federal Government: Checks and Balances

Legislative	Executive	Judicial
Initiates laws	Suggests laws	Interprets laws
May override executive veto	May veto laws	May declare laws unconstitutional
Can impeach presidents and approves Supreme Court justices	Appoints Supreme Court justices	

1. Fill in the blanks: In 1974 the House of Representatives' Judiciary Committee voted to recommend three articles of impeachment against Richard Nixon. By this action, the _____ branch of government was checking the _____ branch of government.

2. Name two ways by which the Articles of Confederation limited the power of the central government.
3. How does the bicameral congress insure representation that is more fair than would be provided in a system having a single house?

Lesson 3   The Development of Federalism

How does the federal system provide for the sharing of power between the states and the federal government?

After much debate between **Federalists** (those who favored the ratification of the Constitution) and **anti-Federalists** (those against ratification), the Constitution was finally approved by the required number of states in 1788. Because the anti-Federalists were concerned that the Constitution did not provide strong enough guarantees of state power or of individual liberties, the Federalists promised to pass a Bill of Rights during the first Congress.

The first ten amendments to the Constitution are called the **Bill of Rights.** They guarantee civil liberties such as freedom of speech, press, and religion and the right to a speedy trial by an impartial jury. They also guarantee that no one may be deprived of life, liberty, or property without due process of law. The Bill of Rights limits the power of the federal government with respect to individual rights. Thus far, there have been a total of 26 amendments to the Constitution. These amendments were passed following one of the two methods outlined in the Constitution. An amendment must be proposed by two-thirds of both houses of Congress or by two-thirds of the state legislatures. Approval by three-fourths of the state legislatures is needed for amendment ratification.

The federal system was a logical compromise that allows the national government and the states to share power. Powers given specifically to the national government, such as establishing post offices and coining money, are **delegated powers.** Other powers—those not specifically granted to the national government and not denied to the states—are called **reserved powers** of the states. Examples would include the administration of education and the regulation of police forces. **Concurrent powers,** such as tax collection, are shared by both the national and state governments.

Because powers are divided in various ways, no group or part of government can become too powerful. The principles of the Constitution encourage national, state, and local governments to work together to serve the American people.

Lesson 3   Exercise

1. Match the power on the left with the examples on the right.
    - (1) delegated power
    - (2) reserved power
    - (3) concurrent power

    - (a) education, police, marriage laws
    - (b) taxation, courts, highway-construction
    - (c) defense, post office, trade among states

2. What are the two requirements that a Constitutional amendment must meet before it is considered the law of the land?

3. Each state in the United States has the right to regulate commerce within its borders. This is an example of
    - (1) a delegated power
    - (2) a reserved power
    - (3) an inherent power
    - (4) a concurrent power
    - (5) anti-Federalism

Answers are on page A-22.

Lesson 4 The Election Process

How does the method for electing the president differ from the way in which members of Congress are elected?

Elections and voting are the foundations of American democracy. On the federal level, voters elect the president and members of Congress. At the state and local levels, voters cast ballots for governors, mayors, state legislators, and city or town council representatives. Voters also have opportunities to express their opinions on laws and amendments. Any citizen eighteen years of age or older may **register** to vote.

The United States has a **two-party** system: the two major **political parties** are the **Democrats** and the **Republicans**. Today, Democrats usually favor a strong federal government involved in economic and social issues. Republicans usually want less federal involvement and greater state responsibility. Citizens can become affiliated with a party simply by registering with it when they register to vote. The parties **nominate** candidates for various public offices.

In most states, **primary elections** are held to choose presidential candidates. At these preliminary elections, voters from each major political party select delegates who will decide on the party's candidate for president. These delegates generally pledge to vote for a particular candidate at the party's national convention.

Presidential elections are held every four years. Citizens do not elect the president or vice-president directly; they choose **electors** to the **electoral college.** Each state has a number of electors equal to the total number of its senators and representatives. In most states, the electors are usually pledged to vote for the candidate who won the popular vote in their state. To be elected, a presidential candidate needs a **majority** of electoral votes. If no candidate receives a majority, the president is chosen by the House of Representatives (this happened in 1800 and 1824) and the vice-president is chosen by the Senate.

The House of Representatives has 435 members. This total is divided or **apportioned** among the states according to population. Representatives serve two-year **terms.** There are 100 senators, two from each state. Senators are elected for six years, with a third of the Senate being elected every two years. Both senators and representatives are elected by direct popular vote.

Lesson 4 Exercise

1. In what ways do primary elections illustrate a representative democracy at work?
2. If no presidential candidate wins a majority of the electoral votes, then
    (1)   the current president stays in office
    (2)   the House of Representatives selects the new president

- (3) the Senate selects the new president
- (4) a new election is held
- (5) new electors for the electoral college are selected

3. The United States holds a census, or a population count, every 10 years. How could results of a census affect the way the representatives are apportioned among the states?

Answers are on page A-22.

Chapter 5 Quiz

1. The requirements for passage of a constitutional amendment are purposely strict for this reason:
   - (1) the Constitution was nearly perfect when it was first written
   - (2) if it were easy to pass amendments, the Constitution would be less effective as a stable foundation of law and government
   - (3) a two-thirds vote of both houses of Congress is required for proposing an amendment
   - (4) ratification by three-fourths of the state legislatures is required for passing an amendment
   - (5) the Federalists and anti-Federalists disagreed about the amount of power that should be given to the national government

2. Fill in the blanks:

   A form of government in which one person or a small group of people has total authority is called _____.

3. Explain why a representative democracy is a more workable form of government for the United States than a direct democracy.

4. Based on information in the text, compare the political philosophies of the Democratic and Republican parties to those of the Federalists and anti-Federalists.

5. The framers of the Constitution intended the House of Representatives to be responsive to popular demands. The Senate, on the other hand, was intended to concern itself more with long-term national interests. How is this difference reflected in the way in which representation is determined? How is it reflected by the difference in terms of office?

6. In the 1984 presidential election, Ronald Reagan received 97% of the votes in the electoral college. Can you conclude from this fact that 97% of voters voted for Reagan?

7. The Equal Rights Amendment (ERA), a proposed amendment to the Constitution that would have guaranteed equal treatment of men and women under the law, was voted on but not ratified. What does this imply about the voting of the state legislatures on this proposed amendment?

8. Article I of the Constitution gives Congress the power to regulate commerce with foreign nations and among the individual states. This would be an example of
   (1) a delegated power
   (2) a concurrent power
   (3) a reserved power

9. For the following powers, write L for legislative power, E for executive power, or J for judicial power.
   (a) Interprets laws _____
   (b) May veto laws _____
   (c) Initiates laws _____
   (d) Can override executive veto _____
   (e) Suggests laws _____
   (f) May declare laws unconstitutional _____
   (g) Appoints Supreme Court justices _____
   (h) Approves Supreme Court justices
   (i) Can impeach president _____

10. In 1954, the Supreme Court ruled in *Brown v. Board of Education* that segregation in public school systems denied Americans equal protection under the law. How did this decision limit the power of the states to administer education?

Answers are on page A-22.

Chapter 6

Behavioral Sciences

Objective

In this chapter, you will read and answer questions about
- The types of behavioral science
- Methods of gathering data in social studies
- The development of behavioral science

Lesson 1 Behavioral Science: Aims and Methods

What are the three main behavioral sciences and how do they differ?

To a scientist, the term **behavior** means any activity that can be observed in a person or other living thing. Some behavior, such as jumping or writing, can be observed directly. Remembering and dreaming are examples of behaviors that can only be studied using special methods and instruments, since they cannot be observed directly.

There are three main fields of behavioral science. **Psychology** focuses on individual behavior. **Sociology** emphasizes group relationships and ways in which individual behavior is influenced by the social environment. **Anthropology** investigates behavior in different cultures.

A scientific **theory** is a generalization, based on data, to explain what has been observed in the past and, thus, to predict what will happen in the future. Some methods of gathering data are especially useful for behavioral scientists. **Surveys** measure people's attitudes and opinions about various subjects. Most surveys are conducted using written **questionnaires.** The **interview method** uses a series of planned questions asked by a trained interviewer. The interviewer records answers, as well as gestures, expressions, and other behavior of the person being interviewed. **Controlled experiments** are used primarily for studying small but similar groups. The groups differ in one important feature, called a **variable.** The variable may be age, sex, level of education, economic background, and so forth. The scientist observes each group to see if the variable produces a significant difference in behavior. For a **case study,** the researcher gathers detailed information from many sources about one individual or group. During a **field study,** people are observed in their everyday environment. The researcher is a **participant observer** if he or she actually joins the activities of the group being studied.

Each of the above methods has advantages and disadvantages which must be recognized when scientists draw conclusions.

Lesson 1 Exercise

1. Complete each of the following sentences.
   (a) Psychology, sociology, and anthropology are all _____ sciences.
   (b) Any activity of a living thing that can be observed is called _____.
   (c) The science of _____ studies the behavior of the individual, without a regard for the individual's culture. _____ studies the behavior of people in groups. _____ studies and compares the behavior of people in different cultures.

2. Which branch of behavioral science might best deal with each of the following questions?
   (a) Why do people remember some things and forget others?
   (b) How did the religious ceremonies of the Incas compare with those of the Mayas?
   (c) Does economic class influence the age at which individuals marry?
   (d) Does the order in which a child is born into a family influence the child's personality?

3. A psychologist is helping a space agency select two future astronauts from a group of five finalists. For each finalist, the psychologist checks school and work records, gathers information about family background and home life, and questions close associates, such as teachers, friends, coworkers, and relatives. What is this method of data collection called?

4. A sociologist studies two groups of students to determine if family size has any effect on school performance. The variable that was different between the groups was probably _____.

Answers are on page A-22.

Lesson 2 Principles of Learning

How may an individual be taught certain behavior through operant conditioning?

Because it is so important, learning is among the most widely studied topics in psychology. **Learning** is a lasting change in behavior that is the result of practice or other experience. Learning may involve facts or skills. Behavior that is automatic and does not require learning, such as blinking, is called a **reflex**. An event that causes certain behavior is called a **stimulus**.

The Russian scientist **Ivan Pavlov** (1849–1936) developed the concept of **classical conditioning**: the individual learns that the appearance of one thing is followed by another. Pavlov observed that a dog salivates when given food. The dog was conditioned to associate food with the sound of a bell. Eventually the dog salivated when the bell was rung, even though no food was given. Psychologists now use **counter-conditioning** to help people get rid of certain undesirable behaviors such as eating or drinking alcohol to excess. The behavior to be avoided is associated with something unpleasant.

Behavior is also learned through **operant conditioning.** A dog that learns to obey a command may be rewarded with a biscuit—that is **positive reinforcement.** When a child learns not to touch a flame to avoid being burned, the child has learned through **negative reinforcement. Punishment** is something unpleasant applied after undesirable behavior. For example, people who park in restricted areas are punished with tickets (fines).

The psychologist **B. F. Skinner** (1904–   ) is known for his studies of conditions that affect the learning of behavior. Skinner emphasizes strengthening desirable behavior through rewards rather than weakening undesirable behavior through punishment.

Lesson 2   Exercise

1. Someone who is not at all hungry sees a picture of a big, juicy hamburger and his mouth waters.
   - **(a)** This is an example of what type of learned behavior?
   - **(b)** If this person is overweight, what method might be used to help him break the habit of overeating?

2. All of the following are examples of positive reinforcement EXCEPT
   - **(1)** a bird is given some seeds each time it performs a trick correctly
   - **(2)** a child is spanked for breaking a dish
   - **(3)** a teacher says "good work" to students who pass a test
   - **(4)** a town gives awards for careful driving

3. Tell whether the following statement is TRUE or FALSE: All behavior must be learned. Explain your answer.

4. Based on information given in the lesson, what type of conditioning most resembles the method of B.F. Skinner?

Answers are on page A-23.

Lesson 3   What Sociologists Study

What are some of the things sociologists try to discover about a society?

Sociologists study the attitudes, behavior, and types of relationships within a society. A **society** is a group of people who have common traditions and institutions and who share basic values. Sociologists want to know about the **social structure** or organization of the society. For example, are there different classes within the society? What kinds of groups does the society consist of, and how are these organized?

Sociologists are concerned with **function** as well as structure: What purposes does the group serve? What part do individual members play in the group? **Patterns** of behavior are also important. **Social interaction** describes the way group members respond to one another and to other groups. In most societies, there are certain **standards of behavior,** or **norms,** that are passed from one generation to the next. **Socialization** is the general process through which individuals learn to conform to these norms. There are many sources, or **agents,** of socialization. **Deviant** behavior is behavior that does not follow the norms of the society.

Sociologists also study social roles and statuses. A **social role** is the expected behavior of an individual within a group. Each individual has various roles—for example, husband, father, friend, employee, citizen. When an individual's roles are associated with conflicting expectations, **role conflict** occurs. **Status** is the "importance" or "rank" of the person. Status may be based on such factors as wealth, occupation, and education.

All societies include various **social institutions** to meet fundamental needs. The family, government, religion, education, and the economy are examples of important social institutions. A society's **culture** includes its social institutions as well as its arts, customs, languages, and even the goods it produces. Sociologists study the interaction of different elements of culture. For example, religion may deeply influence certain laws of the society. Sociologists also look for **changes** in the society's organizations and patterns of behavior and examine the reasons for these changes.

Lesson 3 Exercise

1. Each of the following is a source of socialization EXCEPT
    (1) family
    (2) heredity
    (3) school
    (4) television

2. What word or phrase completes each of the following sentences?
    (a) The way group members respond to one another is called _____.
    (b) _____ is the position a person occupies within a group.
    (c) Government and the family are examples of _____.
    (d) Behavior that is unacceptable to the society is called _____.

3. List three qualities our society expects of people in their role as parents.

4. For each of the following behaviors, describe a situation in which the behavior would be considered the norm and a situation in which the behavior would be considered deviant.
    (a) applauding
    (b) laughing
    (c) wearing a coat

Answers are on page A-23.

Lesson 4   Types of Group Behavior

What different types of interaction can take place in groups?

Most people spend a great deal of time in groups. A **group** is considered to be two or more people who **interact** with one another. Different kinds of interaction can occur. When individuals oppose one another in striving toward the same goal, the individuals are in **competition.** If you run in a marathon, you are competing against the other runners to win. Competition may turn into **conflict,** the deliberate attempt to oppose or harm others. When people work together to achieve a goal that will benefit them all, the people are **cooperating.** Members of a relay race team cooperate. **Accommodation** is a type of interaction that falls between cooperation and conflict—you give something and get something in return. When distinct groups blend into one unified group, **assimilation** has occurred. Immigrants who have come to America are gradually assimilated into the society.

Groups that remain together for a long time, such as families or teams, are **recurrent groups.** Groups in which we participate only once, such as a crowd at a rock concert, are **transitory groups.**

Groups may also be classified according to the type of communication that occurs. **Primary groups** relate to the individual's whole personality; there is continual contact of a very intense, close nature. The individual cannot easily be replaced. Families and close friends represent primary relationships. **Secondary groups** relate to only part of the individual's personality; contact is limited and depends on the individual's function. Employers or people who perform services for you usually represent secondary relationships.

Lesson 4   Exercise

1. Identify the type of group behavior illustrated by each situation.
   - (a) Six people try out for the lead role in a play.
   - (b) One person writes the music for a song and another writes the lyrics.
   - (c) Labor gives up some of its demands and management agrees to a higher wage.
2. What is the main difference between recurrent and transitory groups? Give two examples of each.
3. For the following groups, if the group is primary, write *P*; if it is secondary, write *S*.
   - (a) brothers and sisters _____
   - (b) members of a GED class _____
   - (c) a gang _____
   - (d) a neighborhood softball team _____

Answers are on page A-23.

Lesson 5 Anthropology: Branches and Concepts

What are the differences between the two main areas of anthropology?

Anthropology is the study of the physical and cultural characteristics of humans. A society usually has a **dominant** or prevailing **culture**—that is, traditions, beliefs, and norms that are widely accepted—as well as a number of somewhat distinct **subcultures. Countercultures** are subcultures that conflict strongly with the dominant culture. Most anthropological research is comparative and cross-cultural—that is, studies focus on the similarities and differences of various groups.

Anthropology may be divided into two fundamental areas. **Physical anthropology,** also called **bioanthropology,** is the study of human physical characteristics. Physical anthropologists study brain size, posture, skin color, facial features, blood types, and even susceptibility to certain diseases (called **hereditary diseases**). They use fossil remains from prehistoric times to trace the development of these characteristics and investigate the ways in which humans have adapted to their environment.

Cultural anthropology studies the origins and development of different cultures. A cultural anthropologist would study how certain traditions developed within a culture; for example, when did the custom of afternoon tea begin in England? Why was it started? What was its original significance? How has it changed? Anthropologists must be objective in their work and careful to avoid **ethnocentrism,** or the belief that their own culture is better than other cultures.

Anthropologists are interested in the smaller, organized groups that form a society. Often, the **family** is the basic group. Other basic groups include the **tribe** (people who work together to maintain their way of life and provide basic needs) and the **clan** (people who believe that they share a common ancestor). The rituals, or ceremonies, of a society are also revealing, as are its taboos, or forbidden behaviors. Aspects of different cultures spread from one place to another by a process called **cultural diffusion.**

Lesson 5 Exercise

1. Fill in the blanks.

    A _____ anthropologist would be interested in the tools of an ancient civilization. A _____ anthropologist would study human remains from long ago to understand people living today.

2. Complete each of the following sentences.

    (a) Aspects of different cultures spread from place to place by _____.

    (b) A group of people who believe they share a common ancestor is called a _____.

    (c) The belief that one's own culture is superior to any other culture is called _____.

3. Explain why the residents of San Francisco's Chinatown can be said to form a subculture.
4. Which of the following are examples of rituals in our society?
    (a) Thanksgiving dinner
    (b) Dental checkup
    (c) Senior prom
    (d) Political nominating convention
    (e) Eating a balanced breakfast
    (f) Laughing at a good joke

    Answers are on page A-23.

Chapter 6 Quiz

1. A child psychologist is studying behavior in three groups of four year olds. One group is in group day care settings. Another group is cared for by individual babysitters. The third group stays at home with a parent. What kind of experiment is the psychologist performing? Name one characteristic besides age that should be similar among all three groups to assure that the results of the study are reliable.

2. Fill in the blanks:
   Both positive reinforcement and negative reinforcement are types of _____. An example of _____ reinforcement would be a bonus for one month of perfect attendance. An example of _____ reinforcement would be a stern warning from a supervisor in the case of repeated lateness.

3. Anita's coworkers are planning to take a long lunch because their boss is out of the office. As a friend, Anita would like to join them. As an employee, she does not feel right about taking a longer lunch. How would a sociologist describe Anita's problem?

4. Tell whether the following is TRUE or FALSE and explain your answer: Deviant behavior is the result of proper socialization.

5. Assimilation often causes conflicts between immigrants and their American-born children. Explain why this occurs.

6. Which of the following does not belong?
    (1) tribe
    (2) clan
    (3) rituals
    (4) case study
    (5) taboos

Items 7 and 8 are based on the following graph.

PERCENT OF PERSONS BELOW POVERTY LEVEL

Percent of Population

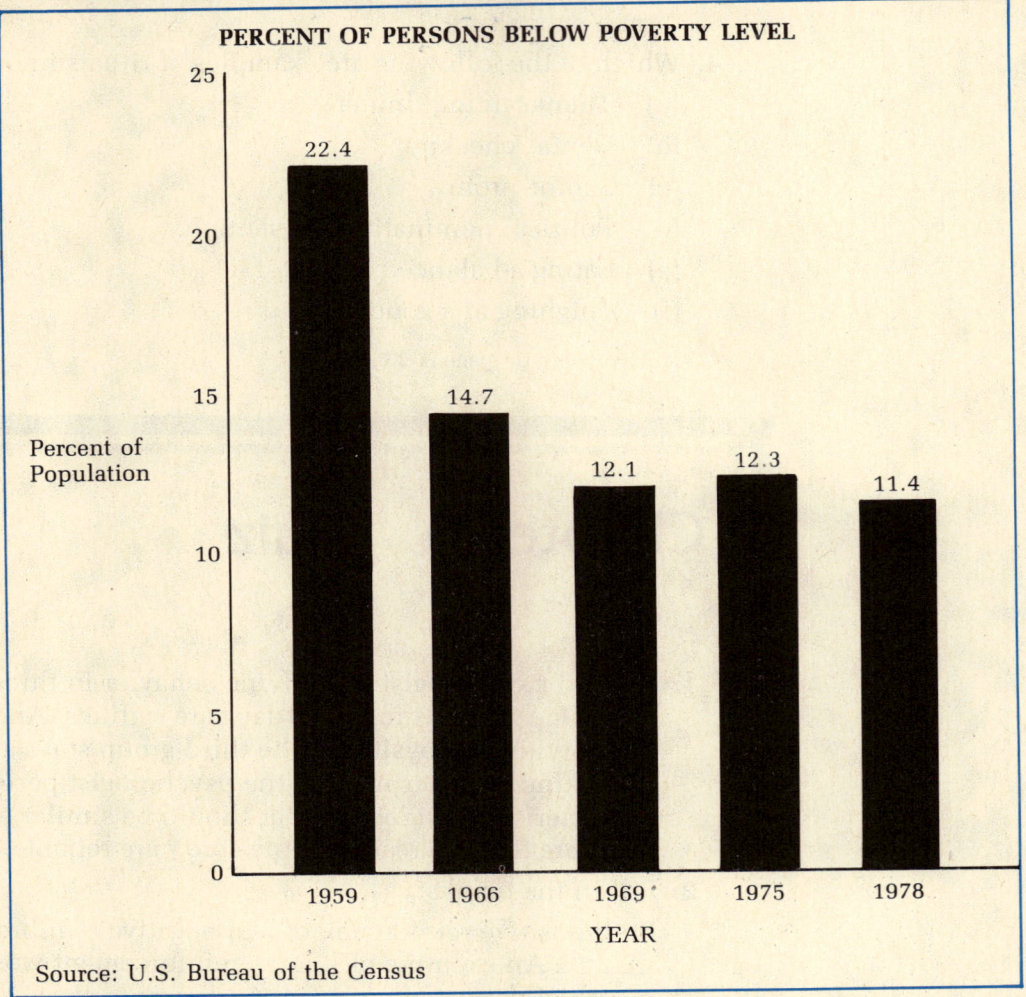

Year	Percent
1959	22.4
1966	14.7
1969	12.1
1975	12.3
1978	11.4

Source: U.S. Bureau of the Census

7. Tell whether the following is TRUE or FALSE: On the basis of the data in the graph, projections can be made for 1981 and 1984. Explain your answer.

8. Why might a sociologist who was working on a study of the morale of the population between the late fifties and late sixties be interested in the data in the graph?

---

9. Some programs that have been developed to help people quit smoking have participants sit in a windowless room and smoke cigarettes until they begin to feel ill. This technique is an example of
   (1) positive reinforcement
   (2) counter-conditioning
   (3) negative reinforcment
   (4) accomodation
   (5) reflex behavior

10. In two or three sentences, tell how cultural diffusion has affected urban areas in the United States.

Answers are on page A-23.

UNIT V

Science

In this unit you will study the four areas of science that are covered on the Science Test. The lessons will give you practice at applying your reading skills to science materials.

The Science unit begins with a chapter explaining what science is. Four other chapters each cover one of the content areas of science that appear on the GED Test: biology, earth science, chemistry, and physics.

The five chapters in Unit V are divided into lessons. Each of the lessons ends with an exercise. The exercise is made up of questions that require you to think the way you will have to when you take the GED. Each chapter ends with a quiz that draws on the material presented in the chapter.

This unit will help you develop a manner of thinking that will improve your ability to understand and interpret science materials. Your increased ability should help you perform better on the Science Test. Use the chart on the next page to record your progress as you work through the unit.

Unit III teaches important reading strategies that you can use when you read science passages. If you have not yet done so, you should complete Unit III before working on this unit.

UNIT V PROGRESS CHART
Science

Use the following chart to keep track of your work. When you complete a lesson, circle the number of questions you answered correctly in the Lesson Exercise. When you complete a Chapter Quiz, also record your score below. The numbers in color represent scores at a level of 80% or better.

Lesson	Page	CHAPTER 1: Introduction to Science	
1	315	What Science Studies	1 2
2	316	The Scientific Method	1 2 3
3	317	Scientific Validity	1 2 3 4
4	319	Scientific Fact	1 2 3 4
	320	Quiz	1 2 3 4 5 6 7 8 9 10

Lesson	Page	CHAPTER 2: Biology	
1	322	Life: Its Characteristics and Study	1 2 3 4
2	323	The Unity and Diversity of Life	1 2 3
3	324	How the Cell Stays Alive	1 2 3 4 5
4	326	Reproduction	1 2 3 4 5
5	328	The Theory of Natural Selection	1 2 3 4 5
6	329	Ecosystems and Their Parts	1 2 3 4 5
	331	Quiz	1 2 3 4 5 6 7 8 9 10

Lesson	Page	CHAPTER 3: Earth Science	
1	334	The Scope of Earth Science	1 2 3 4 5
2	335	The Earth's Structure	1 2 3
3	336	Plate Tectonics and the Rock Cycle	1 2 3 4 5
4	338	The Biosphere	1 2 3 4
5	340	Weather and Climate	1 2 3 4
6	341	The Solar System	1 2 3 4
	343	Quiz	1 2 3 4 5 6 7 8 9 10

Lesson	Page	CHAPTER 4: Chemistry	
1	347	The Structure of Matter	1 2 3
2	349	Chemical Reactions and Equations	1 2 3
3	350	Energy Changes During a Chemical Reaction	1 2 3 4 5
4	351	Acids, Bases, and Salts	1 2 3
	353	Quiz	1 2 3 4 5 6 7 8 9 10

Lesson	Page	CHAPTER 5: Physics	
1	356	Physical Properties of Matter	1 2 3 4 5
2	358	Machines, Work, and Energy	1 2 3 4 5
3	360	The Laws of Motion	1 2 3 4 5
4	362	The Nature of Waves	1 2 3 4
5	364	Electricity and Magnetism	1 2 3 4
	366	Quiz	1 2 3 4 5 6 7 8 9 10

Chapter 1

Introduction to Science

Objective
In this chapter, you will read and answer questions about
- What scientists study
- The scientific method
- Scientific validity
- Scientific fact

Lesson 1 What Science Studies

What is science, and what do scientists do?

Science can be defined as the body of knowledge about all natural **phenomena** and the process by which this knowledge is obtained. "All natural phenomena" means any fact, situation, or event that may be perceived by the senses and that can be scientifically described. Science is all our collected knowledge about the earth and the universe.

Scientists study the nature and the behavior of **matter, energy,** and **life.** They deal with objects that are smaller than one quintillionth of an inch and objects that are as large as 600 quadrillion miles. They examine events that take a quadrillionth of a second to happen and others that have been going on for 15 billion years.

This chapter introduces some ideas that are common to all four of the major branches of science.

The Four Branches of Science

Biology—the study of the structure and function of living things

Earth Science—the study of the surface, interior, and atmosphere of our planet, as well as the earth's place in the universe

Chemistry—the study of the composition, properties, and changes of matter

Physics—the study of the laws of motion and how matter and energy are related.

These four branches of science are not isolated from one another. The subject matter of one branch often overlaps the subject matter of the others.

Lesson 1 Exercise

1. Which word in the passage is used to mean "facts or events perceived by the senses"?
2. Which branch(es) of science studies each of the following?
   - **(a)** the formation of mountains
   - **(b)** the behavior of light
   - **(c)** how family traits are passed on
   - **(d)** the production of plastic
   - **(e)** the conversion of food to nutrients and energy

Answers are on page A-24.

Lesson 2 The Scientific Method

How do scientists acquire knowledge of natural phenomena?

Until about 200 years ago, people who studied the natural world were called "natural philosophers." They described and classified objects and events and also tried to explain their observations. However, they did not have a generally accepted method for proving that their explanations were correct.

Modern scientists follow what is known as scientific method. The scientific method is the way by which scientists gather information and answer questions about nature.

The first step in the scientific method is usually observation. An observation can be made directly by the senses or with the assistance of an instrument such as a telescope.

Observations lead scientists to ask questions about what has been seen. The scientist attempts to answer the questions by forming a **hypothesis.** For example, a scientist observes that light rays from the sun usually travel through space in straight lines. The scientist also observes that the rays bend slightly as they pass a large object such as a planet. On the basis of these observations, the scientist hypothesizes that light rays are affected by gravity.

Once a hypothesis has been formed, it must be tested. First, a **prediction** is made that something will occur. For example, the scientist predicts that if light rays are affected by gravity, then rays from the stars will bend a certain amount as they pass the sun.

An **experiment** is then performed. The angle at which light rays arrive on Earth from distant stars is measured. If the rays are found to arrive at the predicted angle, this finding is **evidence** in favor of the hypothesis. If enough evidence is collected to support the hypothesis, it will be concluded that the hypothesis is **valid,** or true.

Mathematics is an important tool in all scientific work. **Statistics** is a branch of mathematics that scientists use to study things and events that are both similar and numerous. For example, a fish may lay 10,000 eggs at one time. Perhaps 100, or 1 percent of them, will develop into baby fish, and the rest will die. It is not possible to predict what will happen to any particular egg. However, the chance that any egg has of survival can be predicted: the **probability** that any egg will survive is 1 percent.

Lesson 2 Exercise

1. A biologist who studies the migration of birds finds that an average of 150 birds in 1000 fail to reach their final destination. The biologist concludes that each bird has an 85 percent chance of arriving safely. How did the biologist arrive at this conclusion? Is the conclusion valid?

2. For the following statement, identify which part is the prediction and which is the hypothesis: If there is a tenth planet in the solar system, then the orbits of some of the other planets will be affected by it.

3. Suppose that you observe that a certain kind of plant grows well all year but produces flowers only during late spring and early summer. What hypothesis can you make about the effect of sunlight on this plant's ability to flower?

Answers are on page A-24.

Lesson 3 Scientific Validity

How can scientists be sure of the validity of their work?

Scientists determine the validity of one another's work through **experimentation**. Experimentation is the scientific testing of a hypothesis. In order for a hypothesis to be accepted as proved, several scientists, each experimenting separately, must achieve the same results in an experiment that is **repeatable.**

When designing an experiment, a scientist must be able to identify the **variable** and the **controls.** The variable is the condition or the factor being tested. The controls are the conditions that remain unchanged during the experiment. Scientists always make sure that they are testing only one variable at a time. Otherwise, they could not be certain that the results are caused by any particular factor. For instance, if they want to know how a substance reacts when its temperature is raised, they do not allow any other of the conditions, such as pressure, to change.

Suppose that the purpose of an experiment is to learn whether sunlight affects the growth of baby mice. Two groups of baby mice, all the same age, are used. Both groups receive the same food, are kept in cages of the same size, and are handled in the same way. To test the variable, one group is kept in the dark, and the other group is kept in the light. Every week the weight of each mouse is recorded in a table, as in Figure 1. After eight weeks, the results are examined. The average weight gain of each group is compared. The scientists conclude that sunlight helps baby mice grow.

		Week								Total Gain
		1	2	3	4	5	6	7	8	
Six Mice in Sunlight (Each letter identifies one mouse.)	A	12	18	17	20	12	16	14	15	124
	B	14	20	16	22	19	15	17	12	135
	C	18	21	19	17	20	15	22	24	156
	D	11	16	9	14	20	13	17	14	114
	E	22	30	22	18	18	22	20	16	168
	F	16	21	19	22	14	18	17	17	144
Six Mice in Dark (Each pair of letters identifies one mouse.)	Aa	11	10	9	13	13	9	11	14	90
	Bb	13	17	18	19	13	15	14	14	123
	Cc	11	14	8	14	18	14	16	14	109
	Dd	9	9	10	7	8	11	12	12	78
	Ee	12	12	10	13	15	11	15	13	101
	Ff	11	9	12	8	12	13	9	10	84

FIGURE 1

Lesson 3   Exercise

1. Explain what scientists mean by each of these words:
   (a) repeatability   (b) variable   (c) controls

2. To test a hypothesis, an astronomer experiments and finds that light bends as it passes the sun. Three other astronomers repeat the experiment and find that light does not bend as it passes the sun. What conclusion should be drawn about the hypothesis? Why?

3. A restaurant chef served the first-batch results of a new stew recipe to his fellow workers. "Not bad," they said, "but not up to your usual standards." Trying again, he lowered the oven temperature 25° and added more tarragon. His fellow workers all agreed that the stew was delicious. Why was the chef's procedure NOT a scientific experiment?

4. Imagine that you have ten houseplants of the same kind. Someone tells you that their leaves will grow larger if you put wet tea leaves on the soil once a week. How could you test this hypothesis scientifically?

Answers are on page A-24.

UNIT V: SCIENCE

Lesson 4 Scientific Fact

You may have heard someone say, "It's a scientific fact that . . ." What is a scientific fact?

To answer this question, think about the following example. For hundreds of years, it has been considered a scientific fact that any two objects dropped from the same height at the same time will land at the same time. Differences in size and mass have been thought not to matter. But recent observations indicate that this "fact" may not be entirely true. Close to the ground, the two objects may fall at slightly different rates.

In a certain sense, scientific knowledge is temporary. When scientists say that something is true, they mean that it is supported by all the experiments and observations made so far. New evidence may turn up that will change their minds. It has happened many times, often with the aid of new or improved instruments.

Consider a more familiar example. Until a few hundred years ago, no one doubted that Earth was the center of the universe. People thought that the sun, the moon, the planets, and the stars revolved around Earth, which stood still. As time passed, improved instruments and methods of observation helped scientists find out more about the structure and behavior of our solar system and other bodies in space. Telescopes allowed scientists to see parts of the universe that could not be seen with the naked eye. It became apparent that Earth is not at the center of the universe.

Who knows what scientific "fact" will be overturned tomorrow?

Lesson 4 Exercise

Item 1 is based on the following maps.

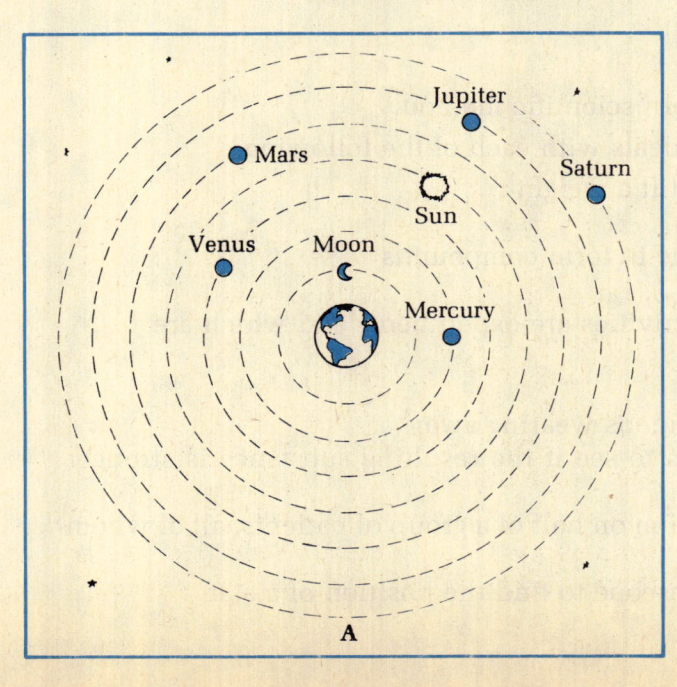

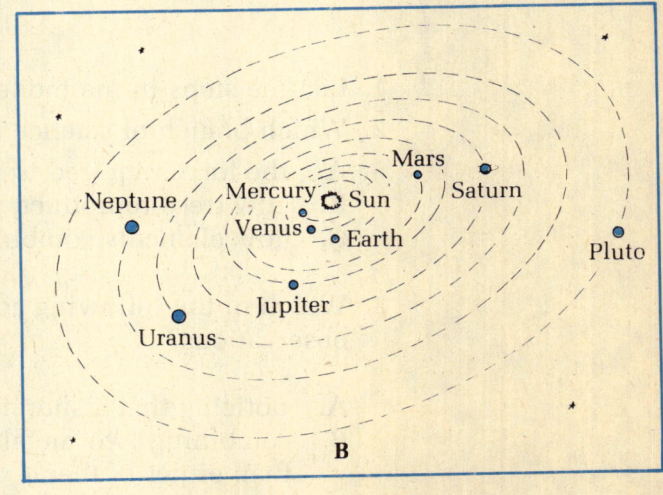

Chapter 1: Introduction to Science

1. Which part of the map shows the ancient view of the position of Earth in space? Which part is based on current knowledge?
2. Which of the following are scientific facts?
    (1) There are no living things on other planets in our galaxy.
    (2) All rivers flow in the same direction.
    (3) Light and heat from the sun support life on Earth.
    (4) Without the force of gravity, objects would fly off Earth into space.
3. The identification of scientific facts depends LEAST on which of the following?
    (1) new evidence
    (2) observation
    (3) prediction
    (4) experimentation
    (5) repeatability
4. How does the use of instruments such as telescopes affect the gathering of scientific information?

Answers are on page A-24.

Chapter 1 Quiz

1. List the steps in the modern scientific method.
2. Which branch of science deals with each of the following?
    A. the force required to lift a weight
    B. how trees reproduce
    C. how elements combine to form compounds
3. Which of the following activities are experiments and which are observations?

    A. noticing that a shoreline is wearing away
    B. combining two metals to see if the resulting substance is stronger than either of them
    C. testing a new medication on half of a group of patients, all of whom have the same illness
    D. looking through a telescope to find the position of a star

4. Which concept about scientific facts is illustrated by the passage that follows?

The following explanation for the origin of the oceans has long been accepted: "Steam escaping from the hot interior of Earth fell back down as rain." Recently, a scientist suggested a different theory. It is based on evidence that comets made of ice are constantly falling into the atmosphere, where they melt.

Items 5 to 10 are based on the following table and passage.

AVERAGE YIELD PER ACRE (in bushels)

		Soil Type 1	Soil Type 2	Soil Type 3	Soil Type 4
Test Group (fertilized)	Wheat	98	101	100	99
	Corn	85	87	90	88
	Alfalfa	102	78	60	130
	Oats	77	80	79	78
Control Group (not fertilized)	Wheat	120	118	121	119
	Corn	90	89	86	89
	Alfalfa	103	77	62	129
	Oats	94	93	96	95

The agriculture department tested a new chemical fertilizer on four kinds of grain. The fertilizer was tried on fields of equal size that had four different kinds of soil. The previous yield of each soil was known. This chart shows the results of the tests. (NOTE: You may want to graph the data in the chart to help find the answers to the questions.)

5. Which crops were affected most by the application of the fertilizer?
6. For which crop do the data indicate that the soil differences matter but that the fertilizer does not?
7. What was the effect of the fertilizer and soil types on the corn crop?
8. Do you predict that the agriculture department will recommend wide use of this fertilizer?
9. On the basis of the data, what conclusion can you reach about the effect of the fertilizer on the crops tested?
10. In order for the results of this experiment to be accepted as proved, what must other experimenters be able to do?

Answers are on page A-24.

Chapter 2 Biology

Objective

In this chapter, you will read and answer questions about

- life and its characteristics
- the diversity and unity of life
- the life of the cell
- the evolution of life on earth
- plants and animals
- ecosystems

Lesson 1 Life: Its Characteristics and Study

What is biology?

A **biologist** is a scientist who asks questions such as: How do living things stay alive? How do plants make their own food? Why is there such a variety of living things? Why do we need both a woman and a man to make a new person? How have living things changed since the beginning of the world? The list could go on and on, because **biology** is the study of life and all it involves.

Biologists define living things as those that exhibit all the characteristics of life. The first characteristic of life is the ability to grow. The second is the ability to **reproduce,** or make others of the same kind. The third is the use of energy: plants get energy from the sun, while animals use food as their energy source. All living things are also able to move themselves in some way. Animals can move from place to place. Plants can turn toward the light. Finally, all living things can respond to their environment. When it is cold, you put on a sweater. When the days grow shorter each fall, many trees lose their leaves, going into a resting period until spring.

You might be wondering how the study of biology applies to your life. In medicine, biology provides knowledge about how the human body works. In agriculture, an understanding of plant life has led to improved crops. Biologists were among the first scientists to point out that pollution harms many forms of life, which led to clean-up efforts in many parts of the world. They are also leaders in saving endangered animals. These are a few of the more important applications of biology. As you read the chapter, try to think of others.

Lesson 1 Exercise

1. On a distant planet, a scientist discovers objects that move about and use energy. Could the scientist conclude that the objects are alive?
2. Explain why your pencil is not alive.
3. Name at least one application of biology in your life.
4. How can a knowledge of biology help save an endangered animal?

Answers are on pages A-24—A-25.

Lesson 2 The Unity and Diversity of Life

What is the evidence that the unity of life is a basic biological principle?

A palm tree, an elephant, and a worm are alike in many ways despite their differences. All carry on their life functions in similar ways. Thus the unity of all life is as much a basic biological principle as is life's diversity and variety.

All living things share a common structure—the **cell.** The cell is the basic unit of life. Nearly all functions necessary to life begin at the cellular level, including energy production, reactions to the environment, and reproduction. These functions are carried out within tiny **organelles** in the cell. See Figure 1.

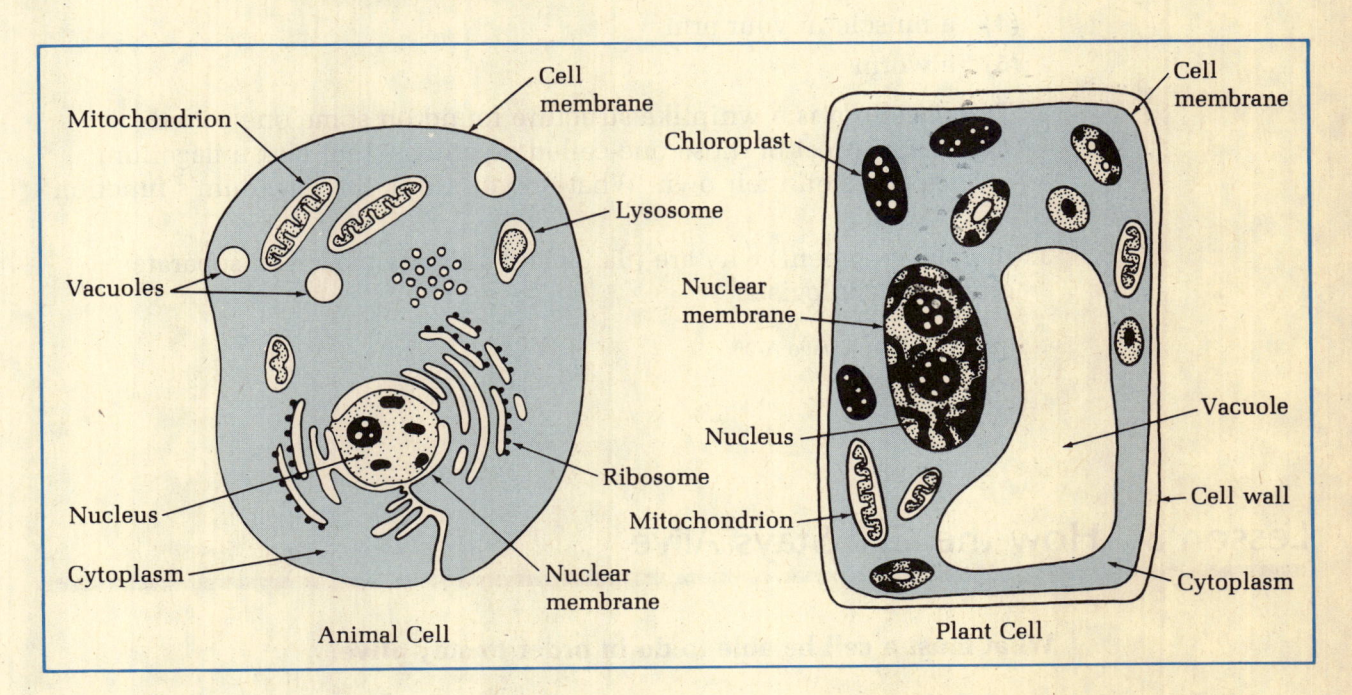

As you can see in Figure 1, plant and animal cells have several organelles in common. They also have certain basic differences. All cells have a **membrane** that separates one cell from another. Most cells also have a center body called the **nucleus.** The nucleus controls all life activities. Plant cells also have a cell wall. The **chloroplasts** in a plant cell make food for the plant. Moreover, plant cells tend to have one very large **vacuole**, while animal cells often have many small vacuoles. Vacuoles store food and water for the cell. Both plant and animal cells have **ribosomes,** which make **protein,** an important biological chemical. Animal cells also contain **lysosomes**, only found in plant cells, that are involved in the breakdown of food substances.

Some cells are organized into a group that performs a particular function. This kind of cell group is called a **tissue**. The outer layer of the skin is one such tissue. The muscles are another kind of tissue. Groups of different tissues that work together to carry out a certain function are known as **organs.** The heart is an organ. Organs may be part of an **organ system,** such as the circulatory system, which includes the heart and the blood vessels. All these systems working together make an **organism,** an independent living thing. You are an organism, as is a frog, a tree, or an amoeba.

Lesson 2 Exercise

1. Which of the following is an example of an organism?
    - **(1)** a heart cell
    - **(2)** a frog's heart
    - **(3)** a worm's reproductive system
    - **(4)** a muscle in your arm
    - **(5)** a worm

2. The flagellum is a whiplike structure found on some one-celled organisms. Most of those one-celled organisms that lack a flagellum cannot move on their own. What do you think the flagellum's function is?

3. In your judgment, why are plants and animals placed in separate groups by biologists?

Answers are on page A-25.

Lesson 3 How the Cell Stays Alive

What must a cell be able to do in order to stay alive?

To stay alive, a cell must be able to perform the basic functions necessary for life. These include the following functions.

1. *Absorption:* The cell can take in the materials necessary to life such as food and water.
2. *Digestion:* A cell can break down food into smaller, usable forms.
3. *Synthesis:* A cell is able to make food into the substances required for growth.
4. *Cellular Respiration:* A cell can release energy for its use from foods.
5. *Excretion:* A cell is able to rid itself of its waste materials.
6. *Response:* A cell can adjust to changes in its surroundings.
7. *Reproduction:* A cell can make more of its own kind.

    The path a given food might take through a cell is as follows. Raw materials are absorbed through the cell membrane. Once the raw materials are in the cell, they must be digested into a form the cell can use, such as the simple sugar called glucose. The glucose is then broken down into simpler parts. The energy in the food is captured by cellular respiration, which takes takes place mainly in an organelle called the **mitochondrion.** Most cells need oxygen for cellular respiration to take place. Cells use the energy for growth, maintenance, and repair.

    You might wonder where the energy in food comes from. All food energy comes orginally from the energy of sunlight, which is captured by green plants during a process called **photosynthesis.** During photosynthesis, plants make glucose by combining parts of two molecules, carbon dioxide and water, in the presence of sunlight. Carbon dioxide and water molecules contain oxygen. Some of the oxygen is used in making glucose. The rest is given off by the plant. The energy stored as food in glucose molecules may later be used by the green plant cell. An animal cell may use the food if the plant is eaten by an animal.

    Cells are able to synthesize the **biological molecules** they need. You have already learned that cells can make protein. Cells can also make **carbohydrates** in the form of starch or sugar. Plants make sugar and store it as sugar or starch for energy, while animals make and store a simple sugar for energy. In addition, both plants and animals make **lipids** or fats, and **nucleic acids,** two other important biological molecules.

    The waste products of cellular respiration and synthesis may be harmful to the cell. That is why a cell must be able to excrete waste products through its cell membrane.

Lesson 3 Exercise

1. Explain why a cell must be capable of absorption in order to stay alive.
2. Which two life functions is the cell membrane involved in?
3. Why is photosynthesis important to the functioning of an animal cell?
4. In which organelle is energy released from foods for use by the cell?
    - (1) cell wall
    - (2) cell membrane
    - (3) chloroplast
    - (4) mitochondrion
    - (5) ribosome

5. One gram of a simple lipid (fat) stores twice as much energy as one gram of carbohydrate. Use this information to explain why the body tends to store extra food as body fat.

Answers are on page A-25.

Lesson 4 Reproduction

What is the difference between mitosis and sexual reproduction?

A cell can live its whole life and never reproduce. But if no cells in an organism reproduced, the organism could neither survive nor reproduce itself. This is why cellular reproduction is so important to the life of an organism.

The simplest type of reproduction is when one cell divides into two cells. This splitting in two is called mitosis. During mitosis the nucleus divides into two parts. The chromosomes in the nucleus duplicate themselves so that each new cell contains an equal number of chromosomes. The chromosomes are important because they carry the cell's genes. The genes determine the traits of the cell or organism. Thus if you have brown hair and a short nose, it is because your chromosomes carry genes for these traits.

As mitosis in a plant cell is completed, a cell wall forms between the two nuclei. In an animal cell, the cell pinches in from each side until the division between the two daughter cells is complete.

Mitosis allows cells to produce new cells just like themselves. New cells are needed to take over the work of dead or dying cells.

Sexual reproduction occurs in a different way. In sexual reproduction, two cells or two parents are involved. The offspring gets half its chromosomes from one parent and half from the other, so it is not exactly like either one. Because of this, the offspring's traits are a combination of its parents' traits. See Figure 2.

Chromosomes

Male—sperm or pollen   Female—egg

Fertilization

Fertilized egg

The fertilized egg contains chromosomes from both parents.

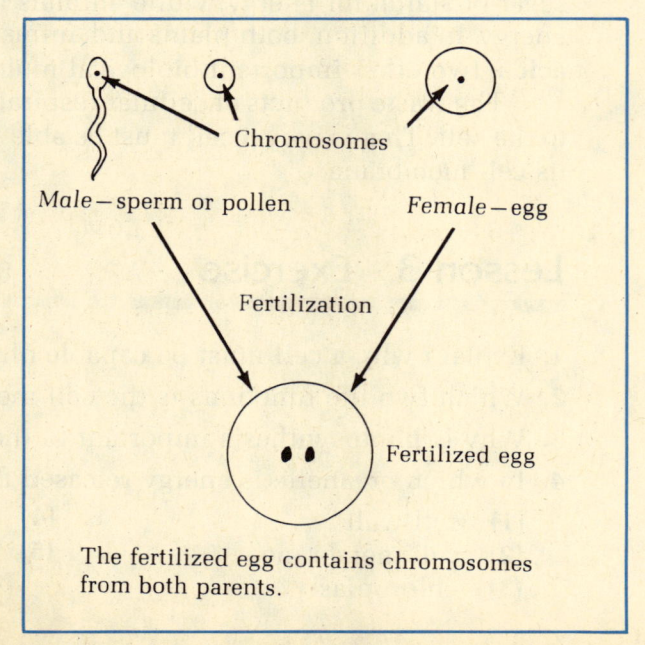

FIGURE 2

The advantage of sexual reproduction over mitosis in creating new organisms is that the characteristics of two different parents are brought together in the same cell. This means that each offspring will be different. If you have brothers or sisters, they probably don't look and act exactly as you do. These differences help a species to survive. Sexual reproduction also helps to account for the fact that life on Earth occurs in such a variety of forms.

Lesson 4   Exercise

1. A blueprint is to a house as genes are to a _____.

Items 2 to 5 refer to the following table and passage.

Traits	Father	Mother	Daughter
Eye Color	brown	brown	blue
Hair Color	brown	blond	brown
Skin Color	light	light	light

The color of a child's hair is determined by a pair of genes, one from each parent. If the child's hair is brown, it is the result of the combination of one gene for hair color from the father and one from the mother. However, both genes do not have to be for brown hair to produce a brown-haired child. This is because brown hair is a *dominant* trait. For example, if the gene from just one parent was for brown hair while the gene from the other parent was for light-colored hair, the child's hair would be brown. It would also be brown if the genes from both parents are for brown hair. The trait for light-colored hair is then said to be *recessive*.

Many traits are known to be either dominant or recessive. Dark hair color and brown eye color are dominant traits. Light hair color and blue eye color are recessive traits. Skin color is neither dominant nor recessive. Genes for skin color produce a blend when mixed.

2. Which trait does the daughter share with both parents?
   Which trait does she share with only one?
   Does she have any traits that neither parent has?
3. Which of the daughter's traits is dominant? Which is recessive?
4. How is it possible that two people with brown eyes can have a blue-eyed child?
5. Is it possible for two parents with light-colored hair to have a dark-haired child? Explain your answer.

Answers are on page A-25.

Lesson 5 The Theory of Natural Selection

How does natural selection cause species to change over time?

Over millions of years, the first cells slowly changed. They **evolved** to find food, to survive dangers, and to reproduce according to the conditions in which they lived. Scientists believe that all life on Earth, from moss to elephants, came from these first cells. How this could have happened is explained by the **theory of natural selection.**

The theory of natural selection was first put forth in a book by Charles Darwin, a nineteenth-century naturalist. According to Darwin's theory, an organism whose traits best suit life in its particular environment has a better chance of surviving than an organism whose traits are less well suited. In this sense, the best-suited organisms are "naturally selected" to survive and reproduce successfully. This principle is sometimes called "survival of the fittest."

Darwin noticed that within a **species**, or group of animals that can interbreed, offspring are often born with differences. Some of these differences may aid in survival, and some may not. For example, suppose a small fish is born with the ability to swim faster than its brothers and sisters. Because of this ability, the fish is more likely to escape being eaten and to survive for a longer time. The longer it survives, the more time it has to reproduce, and the better the chance that its valuable swimming ability will be passed on to the next generation. Other fish may pass on other favorable characteristics to their offspring. Over many generations, a group of favorable variations will collect in the offspring. A new species may result.

Biologists have modified Darwin's theory somewhat. For example, it is believed today that variations within a species happen because of the gene recombinations that take place during sexual reproduction and because of sudden changes in a gene itself, called **mutations.** Although many mutations are harmful, once in a while a mutation occurs that helps a species fit better into its environment. In general, though, biologists believe Darwin's explanation of evolution to be correct because it best fits the facts as we know them.

Lesson 5 Exercise

1. Through genetic variation, a plant-eating animal grows to be much taller than others of its species. How might this difference help it to survive?
2. Suppose that an animal with a favorable variation fails to mate and produce offspring. What happens to the genetic variation that produced its favorable chacteristic?
3. How might natural selection make it necessary for farmers to keep changing the pesticides they use to control insects?
4. A plant-eating animal on a desert island survives by learning to hold its breath and dive for underwater plants. According to the theory of

natural selection, will this behavior be passed along genetically to its offspring?

5. Farmers often mate animals with traits that are desirable to the farmer. Plants are also bred for certain characteristics such as a short time to maturity or a more abundant crop. What is the difference between such selective breeding and natural selection?

Answers are on page A-25.

Lesson 6 Ecosystems and Their Parts

How does an ecosystem work?

No living thing exists by itself. Animals depend on plants for food energy and oxygen. Plants in turn depend on animals for the nutrients in their wastes. All depend on the nonliving environment to supply them with the minerals, gases, energy, and water necessary for life. Taken together, all the organisms and their nonliving environment form an **ecosystem**. The study of how living things relate to each other and their environment is called **ecology**.

An ecosystem may be all the contents of a field, a forest, a cave, or an aquarium. Each organism within the ecosystem fills a particular **niche**. A niche is the role the organism plays in the ecosystem.

There are three major roles a living thing may take. The first is to be a **producer**. Producers make food and oxygen for themselves. All green plants fall into this category, from algae to trees. Producers provide the food base that all life in the ecosystem depends on.

The second role is to be a **consumer**. Animals are the consumers in an ecosystem because they obtain their nutrients and energy from other life forms. Those that feed directly on plants are **primary consumers**. Examples are horses, cattle, some fish, and many insects. **Secondary consumers** feed on other animals. Examples include weasels, cats, some fish, and hawks.

The third role is to be a **decomposer**. Decomposers such as bacteria and fungi break down dead plant and animal matter for their nutrients. In the process, they release some nutrients into the environment to the benefit of plants and other organisms. They also help dispose of plant and animal remains, mixing them with the soil. Without decomposers the world would be covered with wastes.

An ecosystem is constantly facing change. For example, algae may grow well one year because extra nutrients are available. As a result, more of the animals that feed on the algae will live long enough to reproduce. In a short while there may be many more animals. If left unchecked, the animals would overrun the pond. Yet this rarely happens. Over time, the size of a **population**, that is, the number of one kind of organism in a certain area, remains the same. How does this happen? The population is controlled by competition among organisms for food and other resources. It is also controlled by such factors as the death and birth rate. The size of the population is also influenced by factors in the physical environment such as temperature and rainfall.

Lesson 6   Exercise

Items 1 to 4 refer to the following illustration.

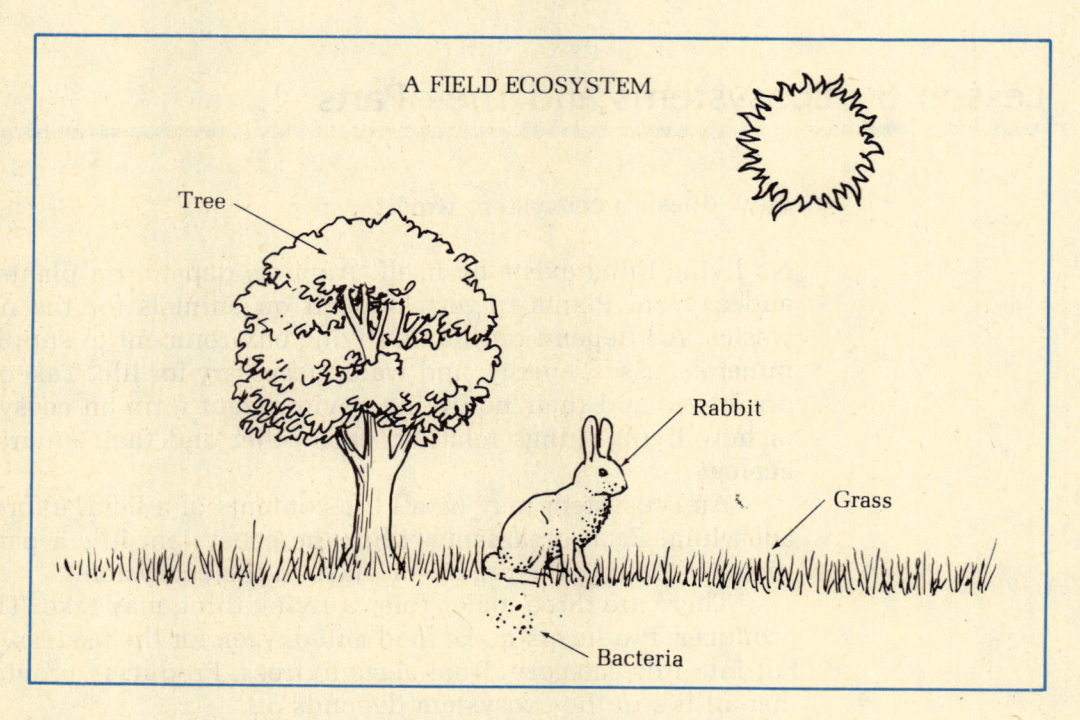

A FIELD ECOSYSTEM

- Tree
- Rabbit
- Grass
- Bacteria

1. What role does the grass play in the field ecosystem?
2. What would happen if all the bacteria suddenly died?
3. A fox catches the rabbit and eats it. The fox's role in this particular ecosystem is that of a _____.
4. Do you think consumers are an essential part of this ecosystem? Explain your answer.

---

5. When the mouse population in a given area is large, the animals that feed on mice find them easier to catch. Which population control factor is operating in this situation?
   (1) competition
   (2) death rate
   (3) rainfall
   (4) rate of reproduction
   (5) temperature

Answers are on pages A-25—A-26.

Chapter 2   Quiz

Items 1 and 2 are based on the following passage.

Pea plants produce seeds that are either round or wrinkled. The type of seed produced is governed by a pair of genes, one from each parent plant. Each gene can be for either round or wrinkled seeds. The round-seed trait is dominant over the wrinkled-seed trait; that is, if both or even one of the two genes is for round seeds, the plant will produce round seeds. Only if both genes are for wrinkled seeds will the plant produce wrinkled seeds.

1. A pea plant that produces round seeds is crossed with a pea plant that produces wrinkled seeds. Will every offspring of this cross produce round seeds? Why or why not?

2. Two pea plants that produce round seeds are crossed. There are four offspring, and all produce round seeds. Which of the following can you conclude about the parent plants?

    (1) Each has two genes for round seeds.
    (2) One has two genes for round seeds.
    (3) They can never have offspring with wrinkled seeds.
    (4) Each has at least one gene for round seeds.
    (5) Their next offspring must have wrinkled seeds.

Items 3 and 4 are based on the following information.

Animal behaviors are either inherited or learned. Inherited behavior is passed on through the genes and is practiced by every member of a species. Learned behaviors are of several types. *Trial and error learning* involves doing a task over and over until it is done correctly. In *conditioning*, an organism learns to link two different events that always occur in sequence. Whenever the first event occurs, the organism produces a response geared to the expected second event. The most complex learned behavior, however, is *reasoning*, which involves understanding relationships between several different ideas or events.

3. Which of the following is an example of a conditioned behavior?

    (1) A rat placed repeatedly in a maze learns to turn left instead of right in order to find a food pellet.
    (2) Fish learn to associate tapping on their tank with the arrival of food and swim to the surface whenever the tank is tapped.
    (3) Male bowerbirds attract a mate by performing an elaborate courtship dance.
    (4) A person learns to play a piece of classical music on the clarinet.
    (5) A student calculates the answer to a multiplication problem.

4. Some learned behaviors may help an organism to survive in its environment. One early theory claimed that learned behaviors play a role in evolution. According to this theory, short-necked animals might have evolved into giraffes by learning to stretch their necks to reach the leaves of trees. The results of this behavior might then have been passed on to future generations until eventually giraffes evolved. Based on the passage, what is the likelihood that learned behaviors can have such results?

Items 5 to 8 are based on the following information.

An animal that feeds on other animals is called a *predator*. The animals it feeds on are called its *prey*. Foxes and rabbits often live in a predator/prey relationship. A scientist who studied the fox and rabbit populations in a certain area drew the following graph of the size of each population over time.

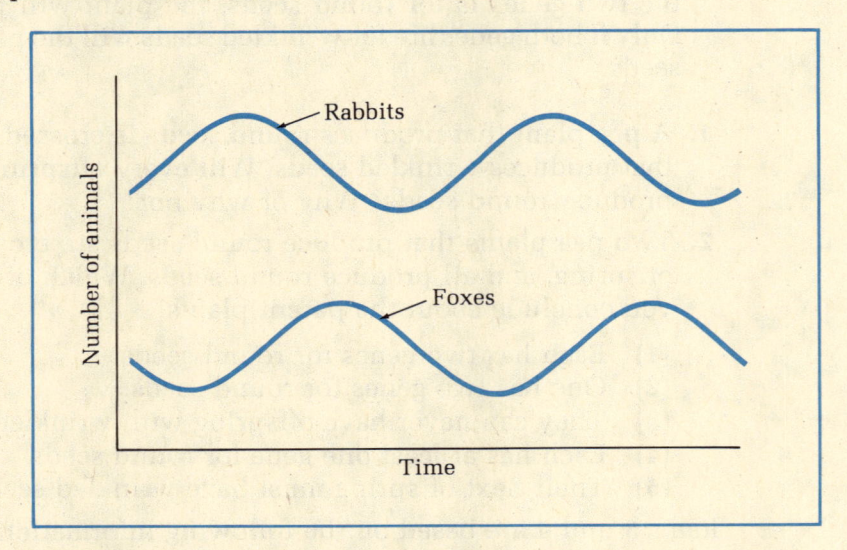

5. What happens to the size of the fox population as the rabbit population increases? Why does the rabbit population later decrease, and what then happens to the foxes?

6. Assuming the graph depicts a typical predator/prey relationship, which of the following conclusions can be drawn about populations of prey and predator animals?

(1) Each population increases and decreases independently of the other.
(2) Each population increases and decreases at the same time as the other.
(3) The size of each population constantly controls the size of the other.
(4) When the prey population is small, humans must remove some of the predator animals or the prey will become extinct.
(5) When the prey population is large, humans must import more predator animals or the prey will become too numerous.

7. Can you assume that the time period shown on the graph is short or relatively long? Explain your answer.
8. Based on the graph, which of the following might happen to the number of lions in a certain area when the zebras on which the lions feed begin declining in number?

    (1) The number of lions would soon start increasing.
    (2) The number of lions would immediately start increasing.
    (3) The number of lions would remain about the same.
    (4) The number of lions would immediately start decreasing.
    (5) The number of lions would soon start decreasing.

9. A certain species of poisonous toad lives in tropical South America. It competes for space and food with many nonpoisonous species, but all the toad populations are kept generally in balance by animals that feed on poisonous and nonpoisonous toads alike.

    A proposal is made to import some of the poisonous toads to Florida to control insects. Backers of the plan claim that the toads will flourish in the warm, moist climate. Also, experiments have shown that the animals that feed on Florida's nonpoisonous toads will avoid the South American ones because of their poison. A certain scientist opposes the plan to import the toads because she believes they might endanger the native toad species. Which of the following is most likely the reason for her opposition?

    (1) The native toads will interbreed with the imported ones to create a new species.
    (2) The native toads will be eaten by the imported ones.
    (3) The imported toads will be free of predators in Florida, and this advantage will enable them to win food and living space away from the native species.
    (4) The native toads will be poisoned by the imported ones.

10. Plants that can scatter their seeds over a wide area increase their seeds' chances of finding a favorable place in which to grow. Based on this information, what advantage does a maple tree gain from having "wing" structures on its seeds?

Answers are on page A-26.

Chapter 3

Earth Science

Objective

In this chapter, you will read and answer questions about

- the structure of the earth
- the rock cycle
- plate tectonics
- the biosphere and the water cycle
- the weather and climate
- the universe and the solar system

Lesson 1 The Scope of Earth Science

What are the four areas of earth science?

Earth science is the study of the land, water, and air. Earth science explains why mountains rise and then crumble away. It tells how bodies of water appear and disappear. It describes the movements of air and water vapor that make up the weather. Earth science is also concerned with the make-up of other planets and stars. In short, earth science is the study of the **universe** and its parts.

Earth science can be divided into four areas. Earth scientists called **geologists** study the surface and inner structures of the earth. **Meteorologists** study Earth's atmosphere. **Oceanographers** explore the oceans that cover most of the earth's surface. **Astronomers** study the universe, looking as far as stars that are billions of light-years away and as close as Earth's nearest neighbor in space, the moon.

Knowledge of earth science benefits us in many ways. For instance, geologists use earth science to locate oil, minerals, and water. Geologists also study earthquakes and other natural disasters in order to predict them and thus lessen the damage to life and property. Engineers use earth science to select safe, suitable places on which to build bridges, roads, and buildings.

Meteorologists use their knowledge of conditions in the atmosphere to make weather predictions. You use these predictions for something as simple as carrying an umbrella when rain is on the way. Or you could save your life someday by knowing in advance that heavy storms and flooding are predicted for your area.

Astronomers add to our knowledge about other planets and stars. This helps us to understand our own planet better. Studying the sun and other stars has added to our knowledge of **nuclear energy** used to produce electricity.

Lesson 1   Exercise

1. The television weather reporter predicts a cool, sunny day for tomorrow. This prediction is based on knowledge of what area of earth science?
2. You work for an oil company. Your task is to hire an earth scientist to help find new oil deposits. Which specific type of earth scientist will you choose?
3. Instruments carried by orbiting satellites can map the temperature and movement of ocean water. What specific type of earth scientist would be most interested in this information?
4. Which type of earth scientist discovered that there are mountains on the planet Venus?
5. Name at least one way in which earth science benefits you personally.

Answers are on page A-26.

Lesson 2   The Earth's Structure

What is the basic structure of the earth?

Seen from outer space, the earth looks like a bluish sphere spinning like a top. The sphere **rotates** from west to east as it **revolves** around the sun. The earth's rotation causes a slight bulge at the **equator,** the imaginary line that circles the middle of the earth. The two points farthest from the equator are called the **North** and **South Poles.** The **axis** is the imaginary line around which the Earth rotates. See Figure 1.

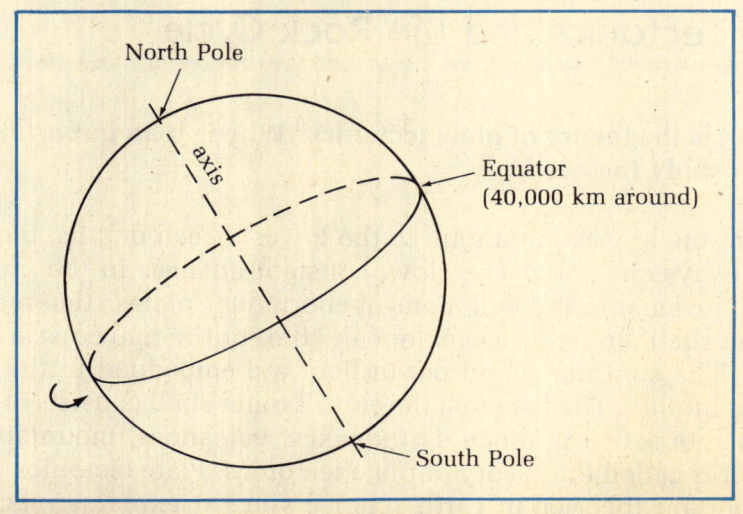

FIGURE 1

As you traveled closer to Earth, you would see seven large landforms known as the **continents.** North America is one such continent. The continents make up the **continental crust.** Underneath the ocean is found the **ocean crust.** Although the crust appears deep to us, compared to the size of the earth it is only as deep as a peach skin is to a peach.

Beneath the crust is the **mantle.** The mantle is believed to be a layer of solid rock under pressure. Hot temperatures cause the rock to flow much like a fluid. The **core** of the earth is thought to be made mostly of molten iron and nickel.

The rotation of the iron core as the earth spins gives the earth a **magnetic field,** as if the earth were a giant magnet. A magnetic field is the area around a magnet that is subject to its force. Like other magnets, the earth has a north and south magnetic pole. These poles are not in the same place as the geographic poles, although they are close to them. For example, the magnetic north pole is near Hudson Bay in Canada. A compass needle will point north to this pole, not to the geographic North Pole in the Arctic Ocean. The earth's magnetic north and south poles reverse about every five hundred thousand years. The next time the poles reverse, a south-seeking compass needle will point north, and vice versa.

Lesson 2   Exercise

1. Explain the difference between the earth's rotation and its revolution.
2. When a sailing ship leaves port, the decks of the ship disappear over the horizon before the top of the sails. What about Earth's structure explains this phenomenon?
3. A compass needle points exactly straight ahead of you. Will the direction to the geographic South Pole be exactly straight behind you?

Answers are on pages A-26–A-27.

Lesson 3   Plate Tectonics and the Rock Cycle

What is the theory of plate tectonics? Why is it an important theory to those who study the earth?

From the highest mountain to the lowest ocean depths, the face of the earth is always changing. The slow, constant changes in the crust are caused by the movements and collisions of enormous "plates" that make up the earth's outer shell. Both the ocean floor and the continental crust are split into plates.

The continents and ocean floor are embedded in the plates and share their motion. The idea that the earth's outer shell consists of individual plates that interact to produce earthquakes, volcanoes, mountains, and the crust itself is called the theory of plate tectonics. Plate tectonics is one of the most important theories in earth science since it explains many of the changes that occur on the earth's surface.

Most geological activity happens along plate boundaries. In one such instance, along the west coast of South America, the eastern edge of one plate is plunging slowly under the South American Plate. The less dense continental crust "floats" up, while the more dense oceanic crust sinks into the mantle. Deep beneath the surface of the earth, high temperatures and pressures melt the oceanic crust material and turn it into **magma**, hot molten rock. This magma then erupts at the surface as **lava**, forming the Andes Mountains in South America. The same forces also produce many earthquakes in the Andes.

In some places two plates are moving away from each other. As the plates separate, a gap forms. This gap is filled by hot rock moving up from the mantle. The rock cools to form new crust. This is how the Atlantic Ocean was formed over the past 200 million years.

In other places two plates are sliding past each other. This is happening at the San Andreas fault in California. A **fault** is a break in the crust. At the San Andreas fault, the Pacific Plate is moving toward the northwest, past the North American Plate. The rocks along the fault bend as the movement puts pressure on them. After a time, the stress becomes too great and the rocks snap, creating an earthquake as vibrations shake the surrounding area.

The earth's face is also affected by the rock cycle. In the earliest stage of the cycle, **igneous rock** is created when magma cools into a solid. This may happen deep inside the earth or on the surface. When rocks are deposited on the surface, they undergo **weathering**. Wind, rain, running water, and other forces gradually break the rock into little pieces. As these pieces, called sediment, build up, their weight cements the bottom pieces into **sedimentary rock.** Either igneous or sedimentary rock may be bent and folded deep within the earth as part of the earth's natural movements. As rock is subjected to great heat and pressure, it changes into the hardest type of rock, **metamorphic rock.** Metamorphic rock may eventually melt into magma, completing the rock cycle.

Lesson 3 Exercise

1. What are three ways the earth's plates interact with each other?
2. Obsidian forms when lava cools very quickly. Obsidian is a(n) _____ rock.
3. Most movement along a fault is slow. Yet one day a cliff near your home is suddenly raised eight feet. What probably happened?

Item 4 is based on the following figure.

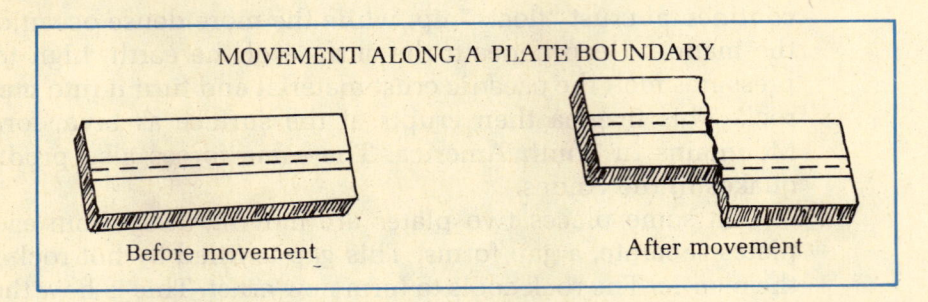

MOVEMENT ALONG A PLATE BOUNDARY

Before movement   After movement

4. Which kind of plate movement do these pictures illustrate?
5. New York and London are located on different plates. How could you prove that these two cities are moving in relation to each other *without* keeping a record over many years of the distance between the two?

   (1) Prove that the plates on which they rest are moving in relation to each other.
   (2) Show that the two plates are composed of different types of rock.
   (3) Show that the two plates are composed of the same types of rock.
   (4) Prove that one of the cities lie along a plate boundary.

Answers are on page A-27.

Lesson 4   The Biosphere

What is the biosphere?

The **biosphere** is a general term for all the parts of the earth that support life. The biosphere includes the various land surfaces, the bodies of water, and the atmosphere.

Of these different parts of the biosphere, the bodies of water support the most life. The largest bodies of water are the oceans, which together cover more than two-thirds of the earth's surface. Water also passes through the other parts of the biosphere by means of the **water cycle**. In this process, water evaporates into the air and then returns to the Earth as rain or snow. It collects on the land in lakes and other bodies of fresh water and then flows through rivers to the sea. Where rainfall is plentiful, a variety of plants and animals flourish. Where rainfall is scarce, the land becomes a **desert** and fewer life forms are found. Another function of running water on the land is to wear away or erode rock, turning it into particles that may become soil. See Figure 2.

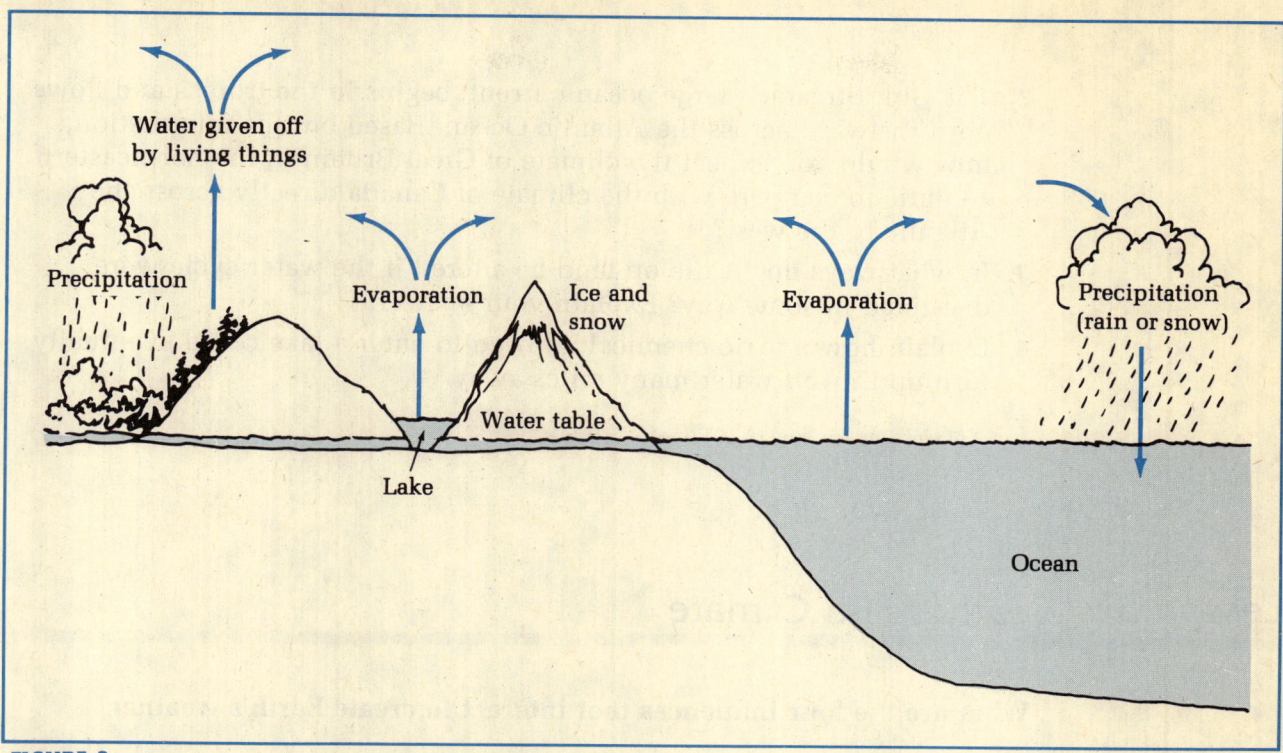

FIGURE 2

The biosphere is "powered" by solar energy. The sun's light is used by plants in photosynthesis to create the food on which all life depends. The sun's heat makes life possible by allowing water to exist as a liquid. This heat varies in intensity between the equator and the poles, creating wind and water currents. These currents in turn move heat energy around the earth to produce different climates, each of which supports a different mix of living organisms.

Landforms such as mountains and valleys also affect the kinds of life found on earth. The tops of some mountains are so cold that only a few hardy organisms can survive on them. A nearby valley, on the other hand, may contain enough water in a lake or a river to support a large population of living creatures. In fact, in mountainous areas it is not uncommon to find very different plant and animal communities only a few miles apart.

Lesson 4 Exercise

1. The water cycle is set in motion by solar energy. At which of the following points in the cycle does this most likely occur?

   (1) Water falls to Earth as rain or snow.
   (2) Water collects on the land in lakes.
   (3) Water flows through rivers to the oceans.
   (4) Water evaporates from the oceans into the atmosphere.

2. The Gulf Stream, a large ocean current, begins in the tropics and flows northeastward across the Atlantic Ocean. Based on this information, how would you expect the climate of Great Britain in the northeastern Atlantic to compare with the climate of Canada directly across the Atlantic to the west?
3. In what ways might life on land be altered if the water cycle were disrupted in some way? Explain your answer.
4. Explain how a toxic chemical allowed to enter a lake could eventually turn up in well water many miles away.

Answers are on page A-27.

Lesson 5 Weather and Climate

What are the four influences that interact to create Earth's weather?

In the 1930s, a long dry spell hit much of the Great Plains. Rain failed to fall for year after year. Wheat died in the fields, and farm animals went hungry. The bare ground was swept by winds that carried away millions of tons of topsoil, giving the area the name of "Dust Bowl." Many farm families left, unable to make a living under these conditions.

Weather and **climate** have a great effect on our lives. Weather is the state of the atmosphere at a particular place for a short time. Climate is a summary of weather conditions over a long period of time. Both are expressed in terms of temperature, moisture in the air, pressure, and wind. In the case of the Dust Bowl, the area's normal climate, a mix of dry and wet conditions, was disrupted for several years by an unusually long period of dry weather. This weather was caused by a stalled high-pressure system that brought prolonged clear skies. At the same time, it blocked the moist air from the Gulf of Mexico that normally brings rain to the Great Plains.

The weather cycle is a complex system in which the atmosphere, the sun, the oceans, and the land each have an influence. The sun warms the earth, which then warms the atmosphere. But different parts of the earth's surface heat absorb heat at different rates. Land warms up faster and cools down faster than the oceans. In addition, the equator receives more than twice as much sunlight as the poles do. These differences cause the winds, which are air currents flowing between areas of unequal temperature and air pressure. Warm air rises and expands. Cool, dense air sinks and flows under the warm air. Air currents are also affected by the earth's rotation, which pushes winds to the east in the Northern Hemisphere and to the west in the Southern Hemisphere. The result is a system of swirling rivers of air that carry moisture and heat around the earth and create different weather patterns in different areas.

UNIT V: SCIENCE

Lesson 5 Exercise

1. Why are coastal regions typically more moderate in temperature than inland areas that experience extremes of heat and cold?
2. On a hot day at the beach, why is there often a breeze off the ocean?
3. When airplanes fly over the desert on a sunny day, the ride is often "bumpy." What might be the reason for this problem?
4. Large high- and low-pressure systems regularly cross the United States from west to east, bringing changing weather to different regions as they pass. Which of the following is the probable cause of this west-to-east movement?
   (1) warming of the atmosphere
   (2) warming of the land
   (3) warming of the ocean
   (4) the sun
   (5) the earth's rotation

Answers are on page A-27.

Lesson 6 The Solar System

What is the solar system, and why is it important to us on Earth?

Our planet, Earth, is one of nine planets that orbit the sun, a star. This group of planets and their moons is known as the **solar system**. See Figure 3.

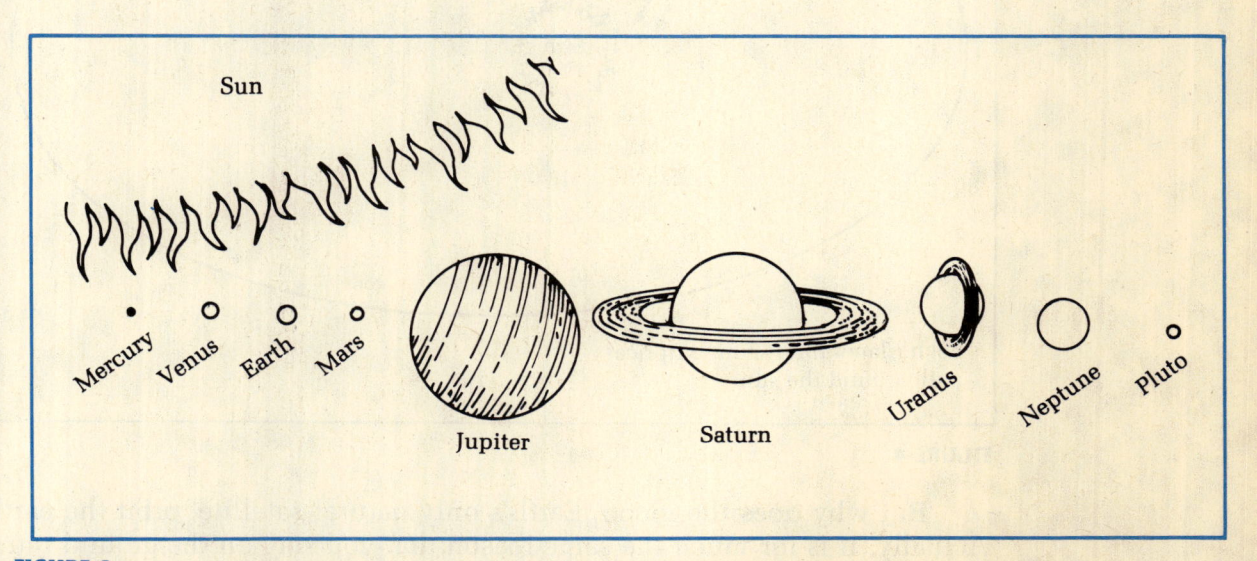

FIGURE 3

The solar system is part of a **galaxy.** Our sun is only one of the billions of stars that make up the Milky Way galaxy. Many other galaxies exist, forming the universe.

Although the sun is only one of trillions of stars, it is the source of all our energy, from fossil fuel to food. The sun's energy is generated by a reaction called **nuclear fusion.** Deep inside the sun, hydrogen gas is being changed into helium, another, heavier gas. The conversion of just a pinhead's worth of hydrogen to helium gives off more energy than burning many tons of coal.

Have you ever wondered why the planets orbit the sun instead of wandering through space? The reason is a combination of two basic laws of nature. The first law is that a moving object will continue moving unless some outside force acts on it. Since the planets are moving, they would move forever in a straight line until some outside force acted on them. The second law is the law of gravity, which states that every body in the universe attracts every other body. On Earth, gravity keeps things on the ground unless some other force pulls or pushes against them. In space, the sun's gravity pulls the planets toward it. This is the outside force that prevents the planet from continuing forever in a straight line. Because of gravity, each planet orbits the sun in an elliptical, or oval, path. See Figure 4.

Each planet follows an elliptical path around the sun.

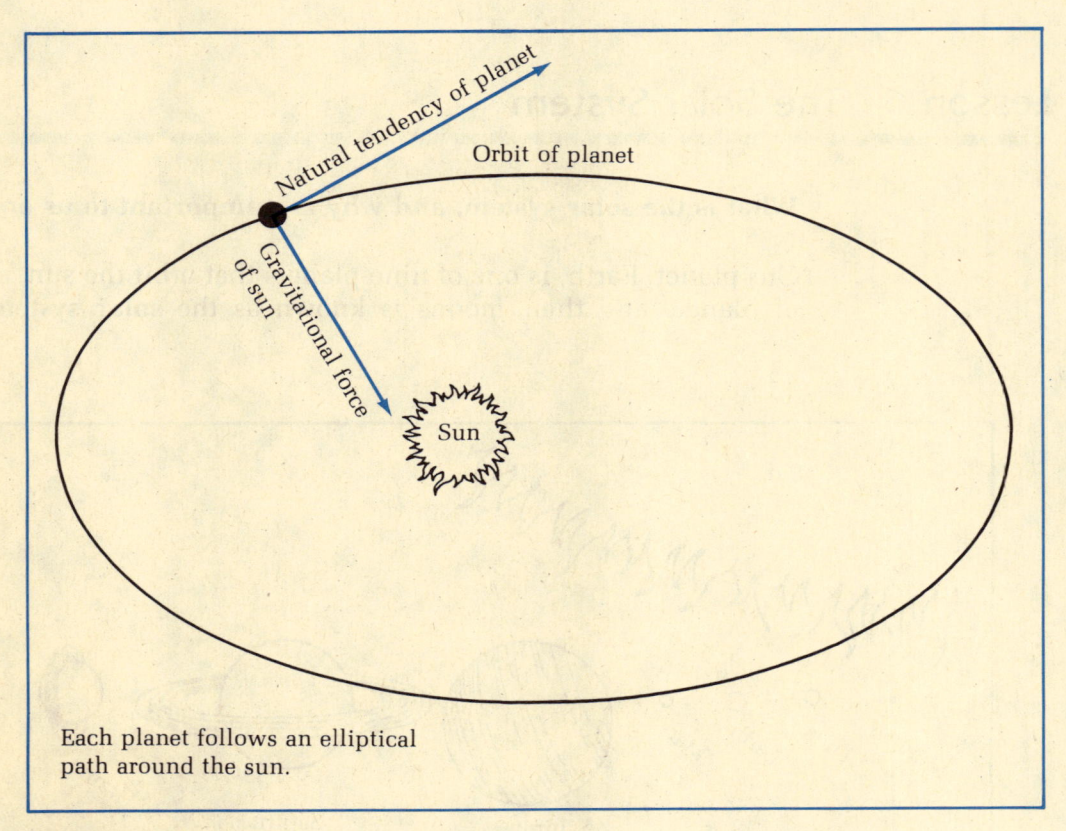

FIGURE 4

But why does the moon, Earth's only natural satellite, orbit the earth? Actually, it is for much the same reason that you stay on the ground rather than flying off into space. The moon is small enough and close enough to our planet for Earth's gravity to be the strongest influence on it, overcoming the sun's gravitational pull.

Lesson 6 Exercise

1. A galaxy is a group of

    (1) moons
    (2) planets
    (3) satellites
    (4) stars
    (5) universes

2. What would happen to Earth's orbit if the sun were suddenly removed from space?

3. It takes Earth about 365 days, or one year, to complete one revolution around the sun. Mars is about 50 million miles farther than Earth from the sun. Is the Martian year longer or shorter than our year?

4. When any portion of the ocean faces the moon, a high tide occurs in that area as water is pulled toward the moon. This is evidence of what law?

Answers are on page A-27.

Chapter 3   Quiz

Item 1 is based on the following information.

Rocks and minerals that are exposed at Earth's surface undergo weathering. In this process, wind, water, and other forces gradually break the rock into tiny pieces. Weathering can be physical or chemical. In physical weathering, the rock is broken up into pieces but remains otherwise unchanged. In chemical weathering, the rock is broken up and also changed into other substances.

1. Which of the following is an example of chemical weathering?

    (1) a fox burrowing in rocky ground and letting in water
    (2) repeated freezing and thawing of ice that breaks apart a road surface
    (3) rusting of automobile parts caused by water on the roads
    (4) tree roots extending into cracks in rocks and breaking the rocks apart
    (5) wind-blown sand scouring out a hole in the side of a cliff

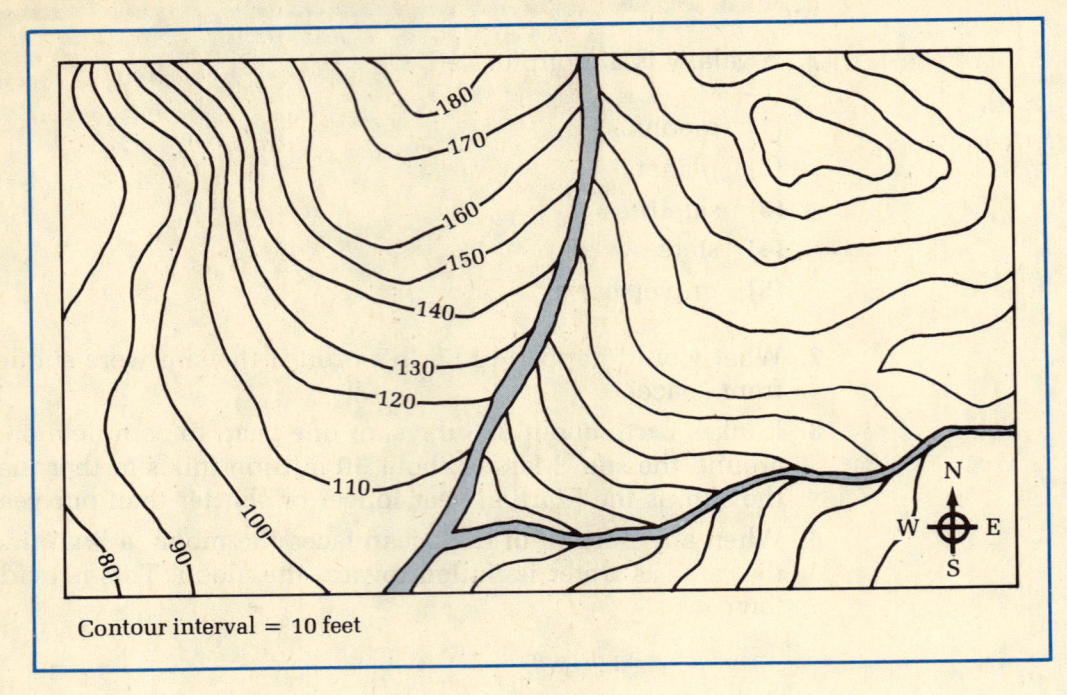

Items 2 and 3 are based on the following contour map.

Contour interval = 10 feet

2. If you walked north along the river at the center of the map, would you be walking upstream or downstream?

3. If the above map is a typical one, which of the following statements is most likely true of all contour maps?

   (1) The highest elevations are always at the top.
   (2) Contour lines of one elevation never cross those of another.
   (3) Contour lines drawn across a stream form "V's" that always point downstream.
   (4) Contour lines can never form closed circles.
   (5) Contour lines are far apart where the land is very steep.

Items 4 and 5 are based on the following information.

Some mountain ranges create a weather effect called a "rain shadow." This effect occurs when moist air flowing across the range is forced upward by the mountains. When the air rises, it cools, and the moisture in it condenses and falls as rain or snow. As a result, the air that reaches the far side of the range is dry. Consequently, a desert may form on the far side of the mountain range.

4. When a mountain range creates a rain shadow, where would you expect to find an area of heavy rainfall?

5. The mountains of California create a rain shadow when moist air moves inland from the Pacific Ocean. If you were seeking the driest possible climate, which of the following areas might you choose?

   (1) the edge of the Pacific Ocean
   (2) a valley between the ocean and the mountains
   (3) a plain just west of the mountains
   (4) the slopes of the mountains
   (5) a basin just east of the mountains

Item 6 is based on the following information.

The source of the sun's energy is a process called nuclear fusion. This process involves the conversion of hydrogen, a gas readily available in water, into helium, another gas. The conversion of just a tiny amount of hydrogen into helium produces more energy than burning many tons of oil. Today many scientists are seeking a way to make nuclear fusion a practical energy source on Earth.

6. Based on the passage, which of the following would be true of nuclear fusion as an energy source on Earth?

   A. Hydrogen fuel for the process would be easier to locate than today's oil and gas.
   B. Hydrogen fuel for the process would be less likely to run out than today's oil and gas.
   C. Hydrogen fuel for the process would be harder to locate than today's oil and gas.
   D. Hydrogen fuel for the process would be more likely to run out than today's oil and gas.

   (1) A only
   (2) B only
   (3) A and B only
   (4) A and D only
   (5) B and C only

Items 7 and 8 are based on the following information.

According to the theory of plate tectonics, Earth's crust is divided into huge plates that move and collide to create mountains, volcanoes, and earthquakes. In some places, molten rock moving up from below is pushing plates apart from each other. In other places, plates are grinding past each other, causing repeated earthquakes. In still other places, plates are colliding, raising mountain chains at the point of collision.

7. Deep in the interior of Asia, the Himalaya Mountains extend all along the boundary between India and the land mass to the north. In terms of plate tectonics, what might be happening to the Earth's crust in this area?

8. Scientists believe that at one time millions of years ago all the continents were joined together in a single supercontinent called Pangaea. Which of the following pieces of evidence most supports that belief?

   (1) Mountain chains are found on every continent.
   (2) Rock formations at the edges of many continents match those at the edges of other continents.
   (3) Birds on Pacific Islands resemble those in southern Asia.
   (4) Fossils of sea animals have been found on many mountaintops.
   (5) Plant fossils have been found in Antarctica.

Items 9 and 10 are based on the following information.

Many earth scientists believe that the Hawaiian Islands were created by a so-called "hot spot" beneath Earth's crust. According to these scientists, this spot is a point where molten rock from deep within the Earth rises close to the surface and repeatedly breaks through to create volcanoes. These volcanoes have formed the Hawaiian Islands. While this has been happening, however, the Pacific plate above the hot spot has been moving gradually toward the northwest. As it does so, it carries the islands with it. As each island moves off the hot spot, its volcanoes stop erupting, and the sea starts eroding the island away. The result is the geography of the islands as it appears today: the large and volcanically active island of Hawaii at the southeast end of the chain, and a string of successively smaller islands with inactive volcanoes leading away toward the northwest.

9. A new, active volcano has been found under the sea off the coast of the island of Hawaii. Based on the passage, where in relation to the island would you expect this volcano to be located?

10. Based on the passage, which of the following can you assume is true about the "hot spot"?

    (1) It is moving slowly to the southeast.
    (2) It remains in one place.
    (3) It is moving slowly to the northwest.
    (4) It moves in the same direction as the plate above it.
    (5) It moves in a direction opposite to that of the plate above it.

Answers are on pages A-27–A-28.

Chapter 4

Chemistry

Objective

In this chapter, you will read and answer questions about

- The structure of matter
- Chemical bonding
- Chemical reactions and equations
- Energy changes in chemical reactions
- Acids, bases, and salts

Lesson 1 The Structure of Matter

What is the difference between an atom, an element, and a compound?

An **atom** is a curious thing. A trillion atoms could fit into the period at the end of the sentence, yet each atom contains even smaller particles called **subatomic particles.** Atoms themselves are the basic building blocks of **matter,** which is any substance in the universe that has a given amount of material, or **mass,** and occupies space, or **volume.**

The center of an atom is called the **nucleus.** It contains **protons,** positively-charged subatomic particles, and **neutrons,** which have no electric charge.

Whirling around the nucleus at speeds of about 13,000 kilometers per hour are clouds of negatively-charged **electrons.** Electrons are arranged in energy levels. An **energy level** is where an electron is most likely to be. Each energy level can only hold a certain number of electrons. See Figure 1.

The number of protons in the nucleus of an atom determines what **element** it is. An element is a substance that cannot be broken down into further substances through ordinary means. Hydrogen and gold are examples of common elements. Hydrogen has one proton in its nucleus, and gold has 79. An element typically has distinctive physical and **chemical properties,** or characteristics. These might include the ability to combine with other elements or to conduct electricity, a shiny appearance, a particular boiling point and melting point, and so on.

Atoms combine to form new substances in a process called **chemical bonding.** Sometimes atoms of the same element bond together. Other times, atoms of different elements bond together, forming a **compound.** Any time atoms bond together, they form **molecules.** A molecule is an electrically neutral group of atoms that act as a unit. In a compound, the molecule is the smallest unit that still has all the compound's properties. For example,

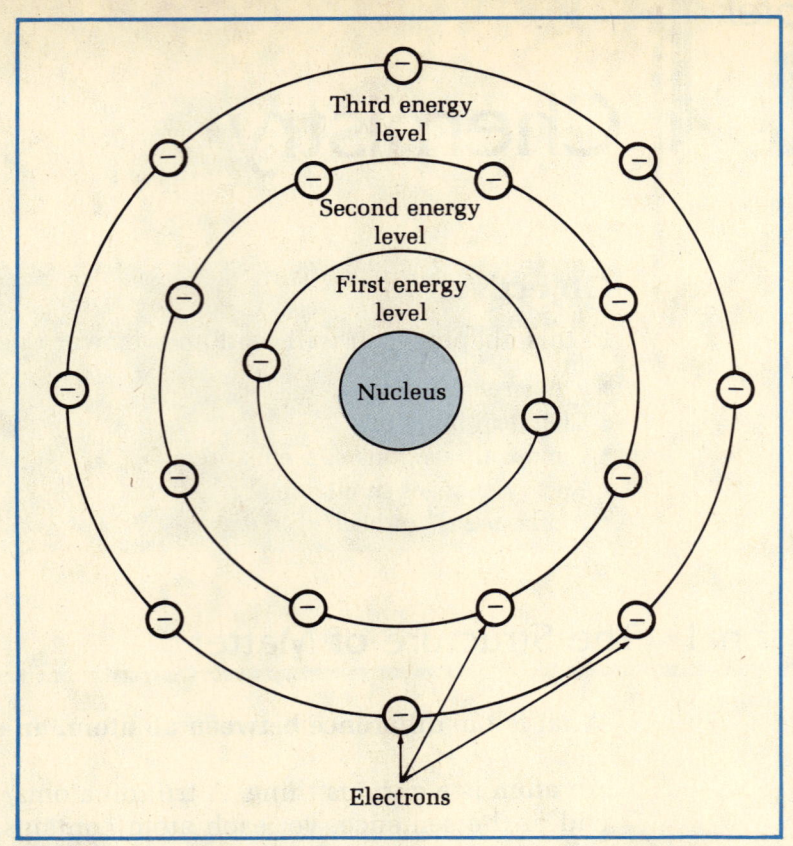

FIGURE 1

table salt (sodium chloride) is a common compound. It consists of molecules in which atoms of the elements sodium and chlorine are chemically bonded. Each molecule of sodium chloride has all the properties of table salt. However, if the atoms of sodium and chlorine are separated, they have quite different properties: Sodium is a soft metal, and chlorine is a poisonous gas.

Chemical bonds form between atoms' electrons. Atoms will bond with each other if the bonding results in a "complete" outer energy level for each atom. A level is complete when it contains a certain number of electrons. For most levels, this number is eight; for the innermost level, however, the number is two. To achieve a complete outer energy level, two types of bonds are used. In one type, electrons are passed from one atom to another. In the other, electrons are shared between two atoms.

Lesson 1   Exercise

1. Two hydrogen atoms often bond together to share electrons. Do the two atoms form a hydrogen molecule?
2. If a piece of pure gold were broken into atoms, would the atoms still be gold? Explain your answer.
3. The element fluorine has seven electrons in its outer energy level. Would you predict fluorine to easily form chemical bonds? Why or why not?

Answers are on page A-28.

Lesson 2   Chemical Reactions and Equations

How does a chemical equation express a chemical reaction?

When you set a lit match to a piece of wood and start a fire, you cause a **chemical reaction.** A chemical reaction is any action in which the chemical properties of a substance disappear as new substances form. When wood burns, the hydrogen in the wood combines with oxygen in the air to form water. The carbon in the wood combines with oxygen to form carbon monoxide and carbon dioxide.

To show exactly what takes place during a chemical reaction, chemists write **chemical equations.** A chemical equation represents the changes in bonding and energy that take place in a reaction.

A word equation could be used to describe the chemical reaction in which hydrogen gas reacts with oxygen gas to produce water:

hydrogen gas + oxygen gas → water

The arrow is read as "produces" or "yields." All substances to the left of the arrow are called **reactants.** All substances to the right of the arrow are called **products.**

For accuracy, a chemist uses formula equations. The symbol for hydrogen is H. However, the formula for hydrogen is H_2 because hydrogen gas is a two-atom molecule. The same is true for oxygen. Thus the formula equation for the reaction described above would read:

$$H_2 + O_2 \rightarrow H_2O$$

During a chemical reaction atoms are rearranged to form new substances, but they do not disappear. This is the important **law of conservation of matter: Matter cannot be created or destroyed.** This law is why a chemist would rewrite the equation so that the atoms are balanced on each side like this:

$$2H_2 + O_2 \rightarrow 2H_2O$$

The numbers written in front of formulas to balance the equation are called **coefficients.** The smaller, "dropped" numbers, which represent the number of atoms in that molecule, are called **subscripts.** If you add the number of atoms on the left and those on the right, you will find that now these numbers equal each other, making it a true equation.

Lesson 2   Exercise

1. Why is a balanced equation necessary to represent a chemical reaction correctly?
2. What is the difference between the symbol for oxygen and the formula for oxygen gas?
3. Hydrogen peroxide, a widely used antiseptic and bleach, decomposes into water and oxygen gas. The unbalanced equation for this reaction is $H_2O_2 \rightarrow H_2O + O_2$. Rewrite the equation so that it is balanced.

Answers are on page A-28.

Lesson 3   Energy Changes During a Chemical Reaction

Why do chemical reactions take place?

In 1937 hundreds of people watched in horror as a dirigible called the *Hindenberg* exploded in midair over New Jersey. The cause was a chemical reaction: The hydrogen gas that held the dirigible aloft combined with oxygen to form water. The reaction gave off a tremendous amount of energy. The equation for what happened is written like this:

$$2H_2 + O_2 \rightarrow 2H_2O + \text{energy}$$

When a chemical reaction occurs, there is always a change in energy. The energy may be in the form of heat, light, or electric energy. When energy is given off, it is called an **exothermic reaction.** The *Hindenberg* explosion is an example of a reaction that gives off heat and light. A reaction that absorbs energy is called an **endothermic reaction.** Baking bread is an example of a reaction that absorbs heat.

All matter has energy stored in it. Some is stored in the form of chemical bonds. Some, called **kinetic energy,** is stored in the motion of the atoms. One of the reasons chemical reactions take place is the tendency of matter to go from a state of higher to lower energy. This energy is not destroyed, however; it is given off to the environment.

Chemical reactions also take place because of the tendency toward **entropy.** Entropy is a measure of the disorder or randomness of a system. **The law of entropy states that in nature, systems tend to go from a state of order to states of increasing disorder.** Thus an endothermic reaction may take place because it leads to increased disorder of the molecules or atoms involved even though energy has increased.

To understand entropy, imagine two gases in separate containers. A valve connecting the containers is opened. Since the temperature stays the same throughout the process, no heat energy will be lost or gained. Yet the gases will become evenly mixed. The entropy in the system increases spontaneously.

Lesson 3   Exercise

1. The first law of thermodynamics states that the total amount of energy in the universe is constant and that energy cannot be created or destroyed. How then would you explain the fact that chemical reactions give off and absorb energy?

2. When you eat the carbohydrates in a potato, your body breaks down or digests the bonds between the sugars in carbohydrates and burns the sugars for fuel. Is digestion an example of an exothermic or endothermic reaction? Explain your answer.

3. Photosynthesis is a natural chemical reaction in plants in which energy from the sun is used to combine carbon dioxide and water, producing sugar and oxygen. Is photosynthesis an exothermic or endothermic reaction? Explain your answer.

4. Which of the following examples offers evidence for the law of entropy?

   A. When water evaporates, water molecules absorb enough heat to change from a liquid to a gas and move off to become part of the gases that make up the air.//
   B. Sugar is dissolved in water by heating the water and gradually stirring in more and more sugar. As the water cools, sugar crystals—ordered, repeating patterns of sugar molecules—are seen to form.//
   C. When bubble bath soap is poured into a tub of water, it tends to spread throughout the tub.

   (1) A only
   (2) B only
   (3) C only
   (4) A and C only
   (5) B and C only

5. This is an endothermic reaction: $2H_2O \rightarrow 2H_2 + O_2$. Write the word "energy" on the side of the equation where it belongs.

   Answers are on page A-28.

Lesson 4   Acids, Bases, and Salts

What is the difference between an acid, a base, and a salt?

Would you drink acid? If your answer is no, you may be surprised to find that you eat and drink acids every day. Acids are found in oranges, lemons, grapes, apples, milk, tea, pickles, and vinegar. Most shampoo is also slightly acidic. Of course, some acids are strong and can burn holes in skin or clothes.

What do the acetic acid found in vinegar and the boric acid used to wash out eyes have in common? All **acids** are compounds that contain hydrogen. Acids tend to taste sour. They also turn litmus paper, a specially treated type of paper used as an indicator, from blue to red.

Bases are a group of compounds that act quite differently from acids. Lye, ammonia, soap, sea water, and eggs are common bases. Bases are compounds that contain hydroxide, an oxygen-hydrogen compound. Bases tend to taste bitter and feel slippery. They turn red litmus paper blue.

Chemists use the pH scale to indicate the strength of acids and bases. See Figure 2. The middle of the scale, 7, is the neutral point. A substance with a pH of 7 is neither an acid nor a base. The pH scale is often used in industry and farming. Certain crops, for instance, grow better in basic soil, while others do better in acidic or neutral soils.

The chemical reaction between an acid and a base is called **neutralization.** In every such reaction, one of the products is water. The other product is a **salt** formed from part of the acid and part of the base. This salt may be sodium chloride (ordinary table salt), sodium sulfate, potassium chloride, or

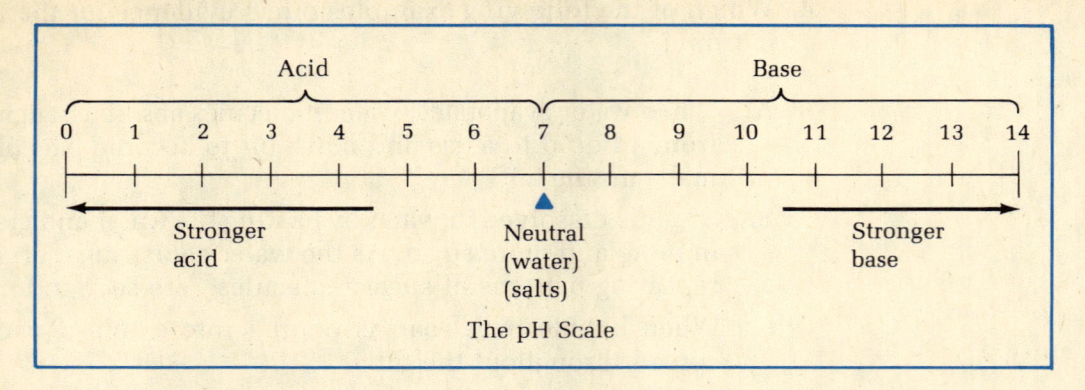

```
          Acid                                Base
   ┌──────────────────┐              ┌──────────────────┐
 0   1   2   3   4   5   6   7   8   9   10   11   12   13   14
 ├───┼───┼───┼───┼───┼───┼───┼───┼───┼────┼────┼────┼────┤
◄─────────────                ▲                ─────────────►
   Stronger                Neutral                  Stronger
    acid                   (water)                   base
                           (salts)
                        The pH Scale
```

FIGURE 2

any of the many other salts. The acid and base usually must first be dissolved in water for the reaction to take place. The water pulls the acid and base into **solution,** a mixture of particles, so that their parts are free to interact and thus to form the salt and water.

Lesson 4   Exercise

1. Milk of magnesia has a pH of about 10.5. Is it an acid or a base?
2. The pH of a lemon is around 2, while the pH of an apple is around 3. Use this information to explain why a lemon tastes more sour than an apple.
3. Some acids are strong enough to damage pipes if put down a drain. What chemical reaction could make a strong acid safe to discard?

Answers are on page A-28.

Chapter 4   Quiz

1. In a famous experiment, a chemist burned a clear diamond in pure oxygen. The product of the reaction was carbon dioxide. The chemist compared the mass of the carbon dioxide with the mass of the diamond and concluded that the diamond was made of pure carbon. Was the mass of the carbon dioxide less than or greater than the mass of the diamond? Explain your answer.

Items 2 to 4 are based on the following information.

Petroleum is broken down into usable products by a process called refining. Crude petroleum is a mixture of hydrocarbons, which are compounds of hydrogen and carbon. The hydrocarbons are not all alike: Different types have different numbers of carbon atoms per molecule. The refining process is illustrated in the diagram below. The petroleum is first heated until it vaporizes. The vapors are then piped into the bottom of a *fractionating tower*. As the vapors rise, they cool and condense. Each type of hydrocarbon condenses at a different temperature at a different level of the tower. As the hydrocarbons condense, they collect in "trays" and are drawn off. In this way, petroleum is broken down into separate products.

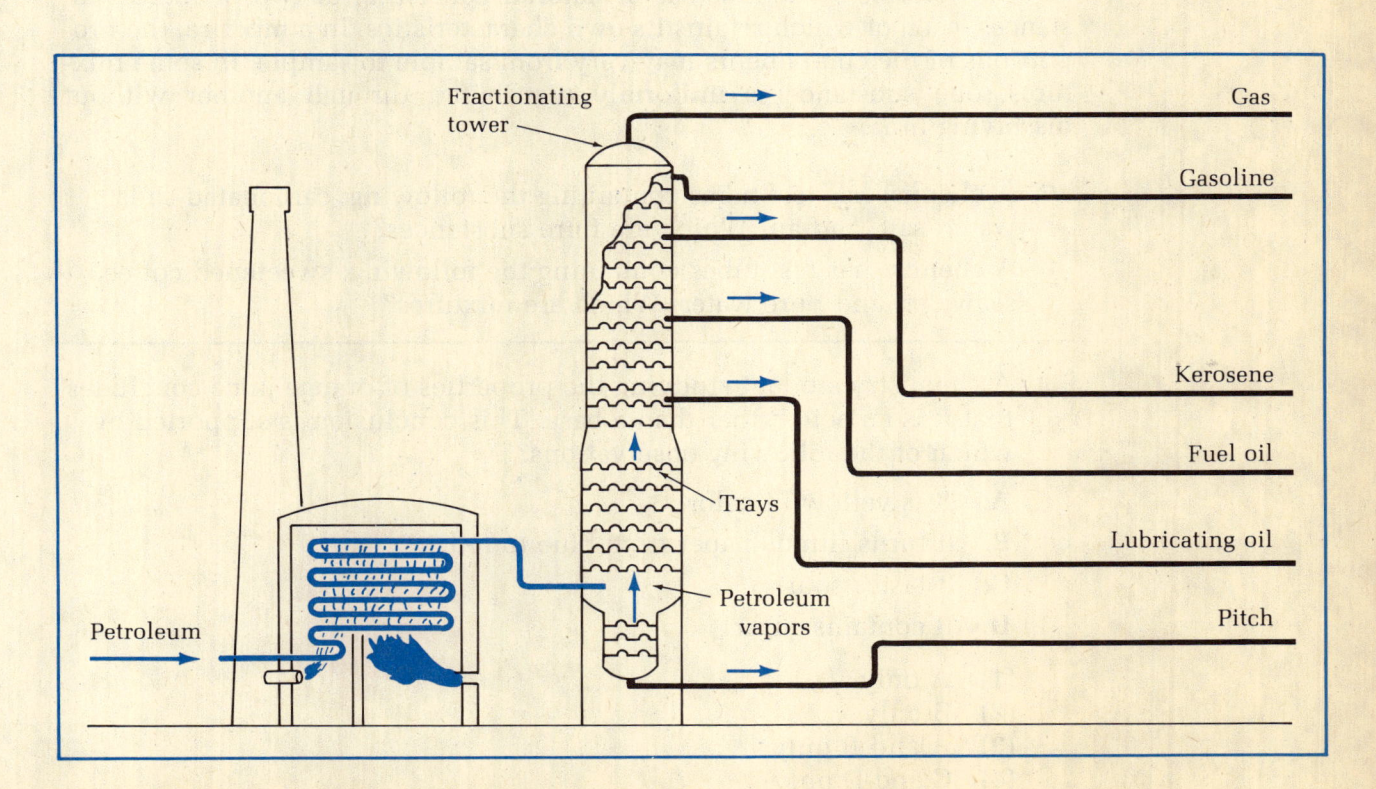

2. Where inside the fractionating tower are temperatures likely to be lowest? Explain your answer.
3. Which has a higher condensation temperature, kerosene or fuel oil? Explain your answer.
4. Would you expect the hydrocarbons in each product of the refining process to have the same or different numbers of carbon atoms per molecule?

---

5. Is the burning of natural gas an exothermic reaction or an endothermic reaction? Explain your answer.
6. An atom that forms a chemical bond is said to be seeking the stable electron structure of a noble gas. In other words, it gains or loses electrons until it achieves a "complete" outer energy level like that of a noble gas. At that point it becomes stable and does not form any further chemical compounds.

    Neon is a noble gas. Would you expect it to form compounds easily with other elements? Why or why not?

Items 7 and 8 are based on the following information.

Chemists define a *pure substance* as a material with a definite chemical composition. Any sample of a pure substance will always have the same composition and characteristics as any other sample. Pure substances include elements and compounds.

A *mixture*, by contrast, is a material consisting of two or more substances, each of which retains its own characteristics. In a mixture, the proportions of the components may vary from sample to sample. In some mixtures, one substance is uniformly distributed through another without dissolving in it.

7. A chemist has test tubes containing the following: carbonated soda water, salt, and air. Which are pure substances?
8. A chemist has test tubes containing the following: sweetened coffee, seawater, and pure water. Which are mixtures?

---

9. A chemistry student studying the properties of orange juice concludes that it is an acid rather than a base. This conclusion is supported by which of the following observations?

    A. It is yellow in color.
    B. It turns litmus paper from blue to red.
    C. It tastes sour.
    D. It contains sugar.

    (1) A only
    (2) B only
    (3) A and B only
    (4) C and D only
    (5) B and C only

10. In chemistry, the law of entropy states that the universe is moving toward increasing disorder. Evidence for this law is offered by which of the following examples?

   A. During chemical bonding, an electron will always enter the lowest energy level available.

   B. Water will change from a liquid to a solid when the temperature falls below freezing.

   C. Marbles dropped on the floor will scatter in many directions.

   (1) A only
   (2) B only
   (3) C only
   (4) A and B only
   (5) B and C only

Answers are on pages A-28—A-29.

Chapter 5

Physics

Objective

In this chapter, you will read and answer questions about

- The physical properties of matter
- Motion and the laws of motion
- Forces, work, and energy
- Simple machines
- The nature of waves
- Electricity and magnetism

Lesson 1 Physical Properties of Matter

What is the difference between a physical and a chemical change in matter?

On a sunny day in early spring, it is possible to see a water puddle move through the three states of matter: **solid, liquid,** and **gas.** If the night was cold enough, water begins the day as ice, a solid. As the day warms, the ice melts into liquid water. Some of the liquid molecules will absorb enough heat energy to escape the liquid form, evaporating into the air as a gas.

The atoms in a solid are close together, as shown in Figure 1. A solid is more **dense** than a liquid or gas, which means it has more mass per unit volume. Thus a solid has a definite shape and a fixed volume. Solids do not need a container.

The atoms in a liquid, as shown in Figure 2, are close together but are not held in a fixed position. They are able to slip and slide over each other, which is why you can pour a liquid. A liquid has a definite volume, but it takes on the shape of its container.

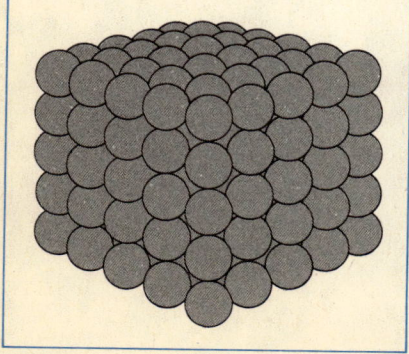

FIGURE 1

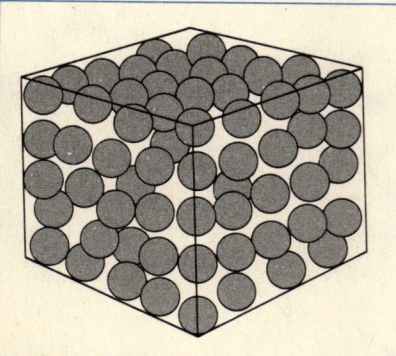

FIGURE 2

FIGURE 3

The atoms in a gas move about freely and are quite far apart, as shown in Figure 3. Under ordinary temperatures and pressures, the particles are about 1000 percent farther apart than those in the solid state. A gas tends to fill whatever container it occupies because it has no definite shape or volume. For example, if you pumped air into a volley ball, it would completely fill the ball. If you pumped a liquid in, it would settle into a puddle at the bottom.

Changes between solid, liquid, and gas states are examples of **physical changes.** A physical change is any change in which the physical properties of a substance change but its chemical makeup stays the same. Some physical properties are color, odor, density, boiling and melting point, solubility in water, and hardness. Melting ice, breaking up rock, and carving wood are examples of physical changes.

Lesson 1 Exercise

Items 1 to 4 are based on the following information.

- *Boyle's Law* states that for a fixed mass of gas at a constant temperature, the volume of the gas varies in inverse proportion to the pressure on the gas. In other words, the volume of a gas will decrease when the pressure on it increases, and vice versa.
- *Charles's Law* states that when the pressure is constant, the volume of a gas varies directly with the temperature. In other words, the volume of a gas will increase as the temperature increases, and it will decrease as the temperature decreases.
- *The Pressure versus Temperature Law* states that the pressure of a given mass of gas varies directly with the temperature. In other words, an increase in temperature will cause an increase in the pressure of a gas if the volume stays the same.

1. If you double the pressure on a gas, the volume decreases by half if the temperature stays the same. This is a proof of _____ Law.
2. According to Charles's Law, if you heat a gas, its volume will _____ at constant pressures.
3. A balloon is blown up at room temperature and then placed in a freezer. What will happen to the size of the balloon?
4. Why is the air pressure in your tires greater in the summer than in the winter?

5. Which of the following is *not* a physical change?

   (1) Nitrogen gas becomes a liquid at very cold temperatures.
   (2) Dust mixes with the gases in the air.
   (3) Soil is dissolved in the water of a river.
   (4) Wood is burned to generate heat.
   (5) Boiling water evaporates into the air.

   Answers are on page A-29.

Lesson 2 Machines, Work, and Energy

How do machines make work easier?

Imagine placing your hands palm to palm and pushing. One hand would be exerting a **force** on the other at the same time that the other hand pushes back. A force is a push or pull on an object.

Some forces that commonly act on us are **friction** and **gravity**. Friction is a force that opposes the motion of an object. Friction is the force that slows us down as we move through air or water. Gravity is the force of attraction between two objects. The gravitational pull of the earth causes dropped objects to fall and keeps us and everything around us on the ground.

A force can cause an object to accelerate, that is, change its velocity. You can find the force on a object by this equation:

$$\text{force} = \text{mass of an object} \times \text{acceleration}$$

Machines make **work** easier by affecting the force used to move an object. To a physicist, work is done only when enough force is applied to an object to move it. Thus, when you use a screwdriver to lift off a paint can lid, you are using a machine to do work, since in physics, a machine is anything that moves an object through a distance.

As you pry the lid off, you are using a machine called a **first-class lever**. A **lever** consists of a bar that turns around a fixed point known as a **fulcrum**. In this case the fulcrum is the lip of the paint can. You apply force or effort downward on the screwdriver handle. The lid provides an opposing force called the **resistance**. The lever makes the work easier because it increases the amount of force that you are applying. A nutcracker is an example of a **second-class lever**. A tennis player hitting a ball is using a **third-class lever**. See Figure 4.

Another simple machine is the **pulley,** a belt, chain, or rope wrapped around a wheel. A pulley makes work easier by changing the direction of the force being applied.

Still another machine is a **wheel and axle.** In this machine the radius of the wheel (distance from the center to the edge) is greater than the radius of the attached axle. As a result, a force that turns the wheel (the longer radius) is increased as it moves the axle (the shorter radius).

Machines are helpful because they reduce the amount of energy required to do a job. **Energy** is the ability to do work. **Potential energy** is stored energy that can do work in the future. Gasoline has the potential energy needed to drive a car. **Kinetic energy** is the energy of motion. The kinetic energy you generate when you swing a hammer creates the force you use to pound a nail into a board.

Many machines change potential energy to kinetic energy. When you wind a wristwatch, you work to tighten the spring, giving it potential energy. As the spring unwinds, the potential energy changes to kinetic energy, turning the watch's wheels to keep time.

UNIT V: SCIENCE   Lesson 2   **359**

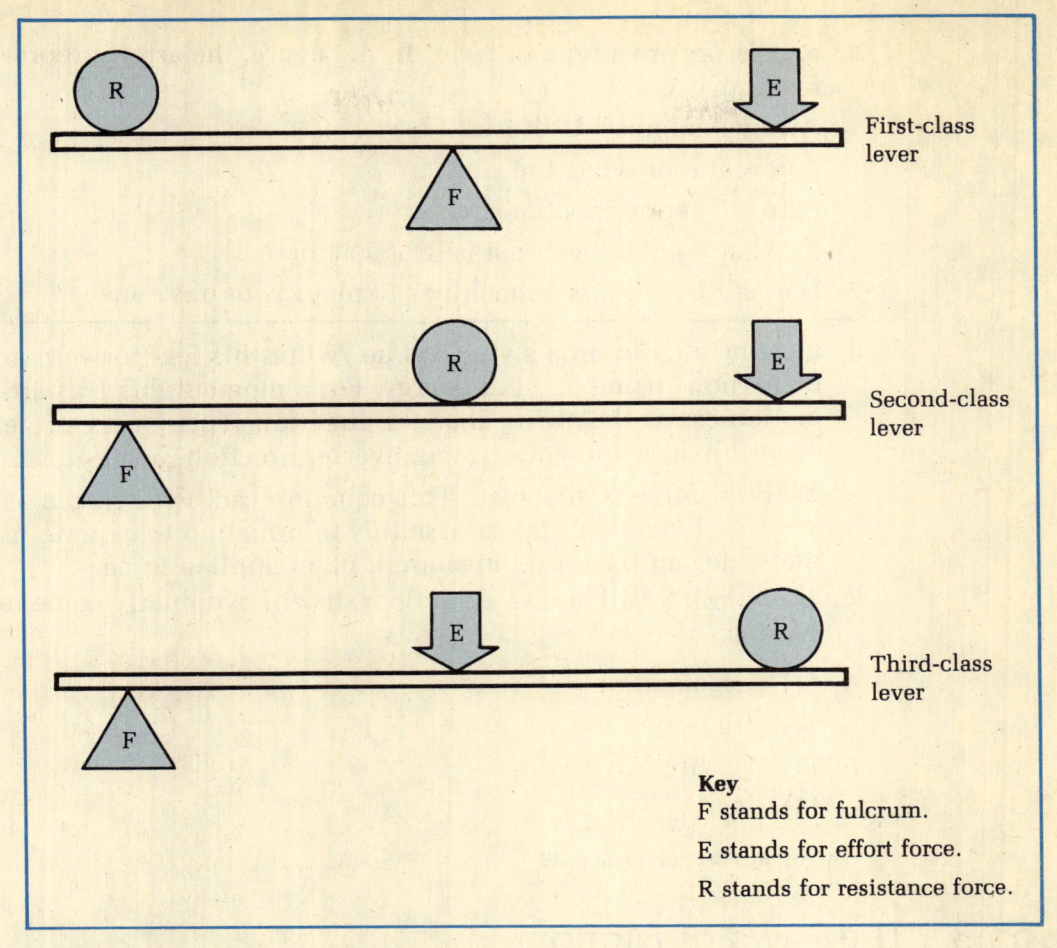

First-class lever

Second-class lever

Third-class lever

Key
F stands for fulcrum.
E stands for effort force.
R stands for resistance force.

FIGURE 4

Lesson 2   Exercise

Items 1 and 2 are based on the following figure.

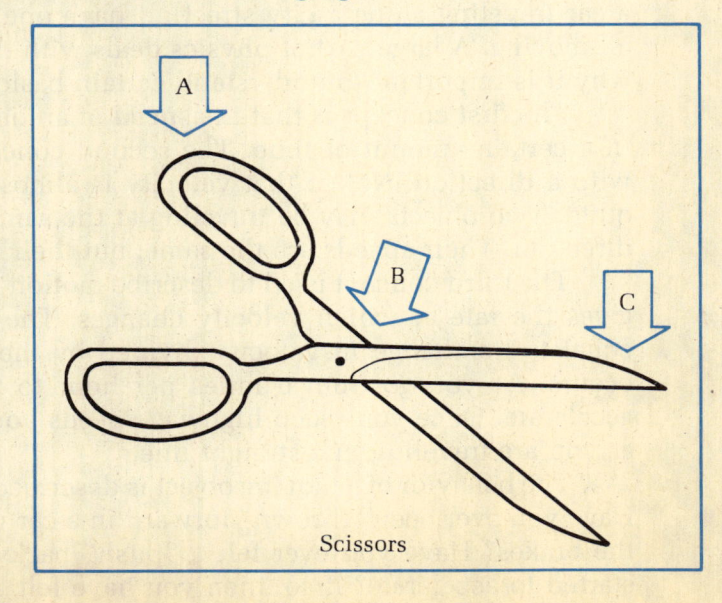

Scissors

1. a. Scissors are a type of lever. In the figure, the arrows represent effort, resistance, and fulcrum.

    Arrow A represents the _____.

    Arrow B represents the _____.

    Arrow C represents the _____.

    b. What type of lever is a pair of scissors?

2. Is a pair of scissors a machine? Explain your answer.

3. Imagine a child on a swing. As he swings his legs forward and raises them, he is using _____ energy. For a moment, his legs are held motionless as the swing changes direction. This is _____ energy. He drops his legs and goes in the reverse direction, using _____ energy.

4. Work = force × distance. This equation can be rewritten as follows: work ÷ force = distance. Use this information to explain how a wheel and axle can increase the amount of an applied force.

5. If you roll a ball across a flat floor, it will eventually come to a stop because of

    (1) deceleration

    (2) friction

    (3) gravity

    (4) work

    Answers are on page A-29.

Lesson 3   The Laws of Motion

What natural laws govern the behavior of a moving object?

The Earth revolving around the sun, a basketball falling through a hoop, and a car traveling along a city street all have one thing in common: They are all moving. A large part of physics deals with the study of motion, which is why it is important to understand certain basic concepts of motion.

    The first concept is that the **speed** of an object is the distance it travels in a certain amount of time. The second concept is that **velocity** is speed with a direction. Notice that velocity is almost the same as speed but not quite. Two objects may be traveling at the same speed but not in the same direction. Their speeds are the same, but their velocities are different.

    The third concept used to describe motion is **acceleration.** Acceleration gives the rate at which velocity changes. The acceleration of an object is equal to its change in velocity divided by the time in which this change occurs. As you go from 0 miles per hour to 55 mph on a highway, you accelerate. Once you reach highway speeds you are no longer accelerating, as you are traveling in a straight line.

    The behavior of a moving object is described by the three laws of motion. Have you ever been "thrown" forward in a car when the driver slammed on the brakes? Have you ever felt a "push" backward in a car that suddenly started to accelerate? If so, then you have felt the effects of the first law of motion, sometimes called the law of inertia: **Every object at rest will remain at rest, and every object in motion will stay in motion with constant speed in a straight line unless some force acts on the object to change that motion.** This and the other two laws of motion were first stated by Isaac Newton, a seventeenth-century scientist.

According to Newton's first law, you really are not thrown forward when a car stops quickly. What happens results from the fact that you are moving along with the car. When the brakes are applied, they stop the car's motion, but not yours. You keep moving until a seatbelt or the car's dashboard stops you. The opposite situation occurs when a car you are in begins to move.

The second law of motion states that **the acceleration of an object is directly proportional to the net force on the object and inversely proportional to the mass of the object. The acceleration is in the same direction as the net external force.** This law can be expressed as follows:

$$\text{acceleration} = \frac{\text{force}}{\text{mass}}$$

The second law of motion explains why a car can start and stop more easily than a truck. The truck has a larger mass, and so for the same amount of force, it accelerates less than a car. The third law, sometimes called the action-reaction law, states that **for every action there is an equal reaction force in the opposite direction.** For example, imagine a roller skater who exerts force on a basketball by throwing it forward. This skater will then roll backward because of the force created in the opposite direction from the throw.

Lesson 3 Exercise

1. A squid draws water into its body opening and then forces the water out at high speed, sending itself traveling in the opposite direction. The motion of a squid is an example of which law of motion?

Item 2 is based on the following diagram.

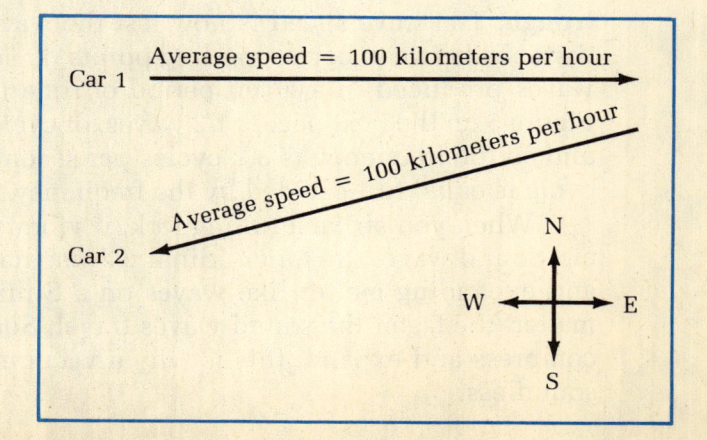

362 Chapter 5: Physics

2. Of the following statements about car 1 and car 2, which must be true?
   - A. Their speeds are the same.
   - B. Their speeds are different.
   - C. Their velocities are the same.
   - D. Their velocities are different.

   (1) A and C only
   (2) B and C only
   (3) A and D only
   (4) A only
   (5) D only

3. To make a car faster, an engineer designs a smaller and lighter body but keeps the power of the engine the same. This engineer is making use of which law of motion?

4. Use the third law of motion to analyze what happens when you walk across a floor.

5. The planets travel in curved orbits around the sun. Use the first law of motion to prove that there must be an outside force (the sun's gravity) acting on the planets.

Answers are on pages A-29—A-30.

Lesson 4   The Nature of Waves

What is a wave?

Imagine holding one end of a rope while the other end is attached to a fence. If you snap the rope once, a wave travels from one end to the other. What this wave and all others have in common is that they are the transmission of a disturbance that repeats its form across space and during time. See Figure 5.

The "hill" portion of a wave is called a **crest**. The "valley" is called a **trough**. The **wave speed** is how fast the wave travels. The **wavelength** is the distance between corresponding points on successive waves. The number of waves produced in a given period of time is the **frequency** of the wave. In Figure 5 on the next page, 1 1/2 waves, or cycles, are completed in one second, and so the frequency is 3/2 cycles per second. Since the time length of each cycle is equal to 1 divided by the frequency, the time length is 2/3 seconds.

When you strike a tuning fork, it vibrates, creating sound waves in the air. Sound waves are longitudinal waves; that is, they travel by compressing and expanding matter like waves on a Slinky toy. Usually, the denser the matter, the faster the sound waves travel. Sound waves must have matter to compress and expand; this is why a vacuum such as that of outer space is soundless.

```
                    ←——————— Wavelength ———————→
                         (one complete cycle)
                           Wave crest
```

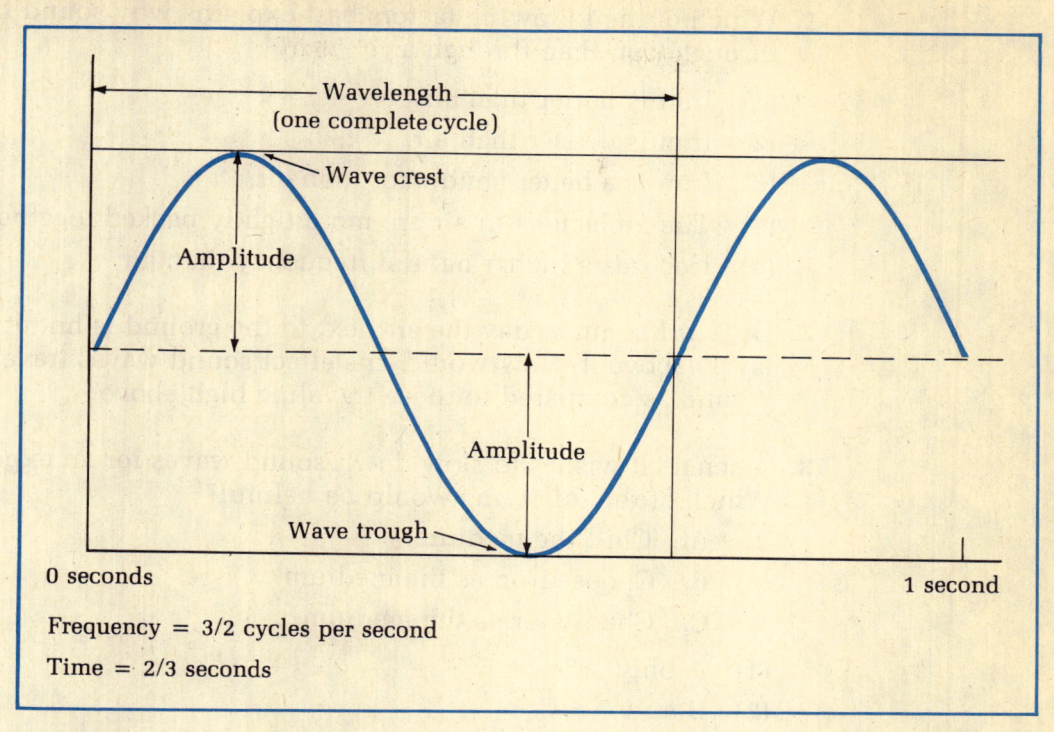

FIGURE 5

Frequency = 3/2 cycles per second
Time = 2/3 seconds

Unlike sound, light can travel through a vacuum. Light waves consist of alternating electric and magnetic forces that do not need a medium in which to travel. Light rays travel outward in all directions from their source. Besides traveling in a vacuum, light can travel through gases, liquids, and some solids.

In a sound wave, the higher the frequency, the higher the pitch of the sound. Also, the greater the amplitude, the louder the sound. In light waves, frequency determines color; for example, red light has slightly higher frequency than violet. A bright light has a large amplitude, and a dim light has a small amplitude.

Lesson 4 Exercise

Items 1 to 4 refer to the following passage.

The speed of sound depends on the type of medium through which it is traveling. For sound to travel at all, molecules of matter must be present. It follows that, in general, the more dense the medium, the faster sound will travel through it. Thus sound travels through iron nearly 15 times as fast as through air.

The temperature of the medium also influences the speed of sound traveling through it. As the temperature increases, sound waves travel faster. In solids and liquids, the increase is small, but for gases, the increase is large and must be included in any calculations.

1. Which of the following factors best explains why sound travels faster through iron than through air?

    (1) Iron is hotter than air.
    (2) Iron is denser than air.
    (3) Iron is a better conductor than air.
    (4) The molecules in air are more tightly packed together.
    (5) Iron has a higher natural frequency than air.

2. On a hot summer day the air next to the ground is hotter than the layers above it. How would this affect sound waves traveling near the ground as compared to those traveling high above?

3. A scientist wishes to slow down sound waves for an experiment. Which of the following would be helpful?

    A. Chill the medium.
    B. Choose iron as the medium.
    C. Choose air as the medium.

    (1) A only
    (2) B only
    (3) C only
    (4) A and C only
    (5) A and B only

4. When a solid is heated, its density decreases. Both the higher temperature and the lower density affect the speed of sound traveling through the solid. If the sound travels more slowly after the heating than before, which factor must have a greater effect?

    Answers are on page A-30.

Lesson 5   Electricity and Magnetism

How are electricity and magnetism related?

In 1819, Hans Oersted, a Danish physicist, discovered that when he put a compass close to a wire attached to the terminals of a battery, the compass needle pointed to a position perpendicular to the wire. When he reversed the current, the needle spun around to point in exactly the opposite direction. When he disconnected the battery, the compass pointed in a third direction, in line with the earth's magnetic field. It was clear that **electric current**—electrons flowing through wire—could cause a magnetic field.

   Later scientists realized that every electron in every substance exerts a magnetic pull. This pull is caused by the rotation of electrons as they orbit the nucleus. In most substances the electrons spin in many directions at random. As a result, their individual magnetic fields cancel each other out, giving a zero net magnetism.

In some substances, however, the electrons in the outermost energy level rotate in the same direction. Iron, for example, has four such electrons per atom. Their magnetism can combine to create a magnetic field so that iron can act as a magnet.

Engineers use what is known about electricity and magnetism to design machines such as **electric motors.** An electric motor converts electrical energy into kinetic energy. A simple electric motor (Figure 6) consists of a loop of wire placed within the field of a magnet. When an electric current flows through the wire, the resulting magnetic field comes into contact with the one already in place. The two produce a force that causes the loop to turn. This motion can be used to operate a stereo turntable or a sewing machine.

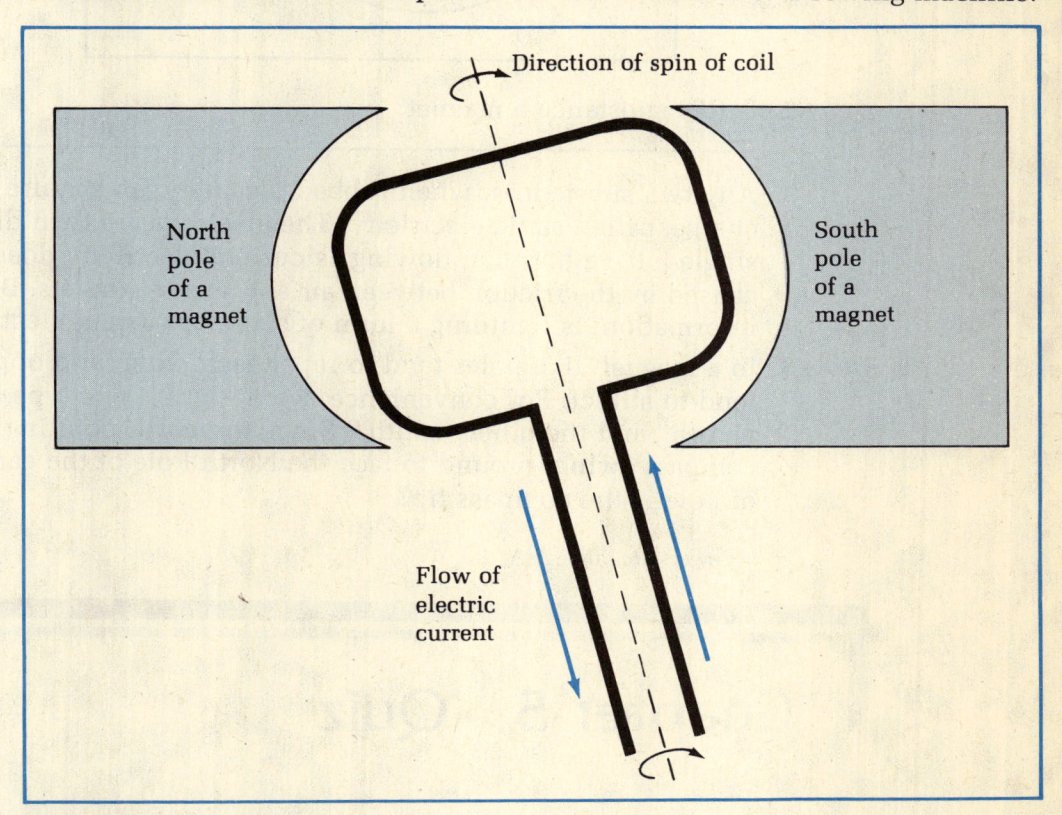

FIGURE 6

A similar machine is used to produce electricity. In this case, a changing magnetic field creates an electric current. For example, a hydroelectric **generator** uses water power to turn large coils of wire that cut through a magnetic field. The current generated is carried by cables for use as electrical energy.

Lesson 5 Exercise

1. Explain the difference between an electric motor and an electric generator.

Item 2 refers to the following diagram.

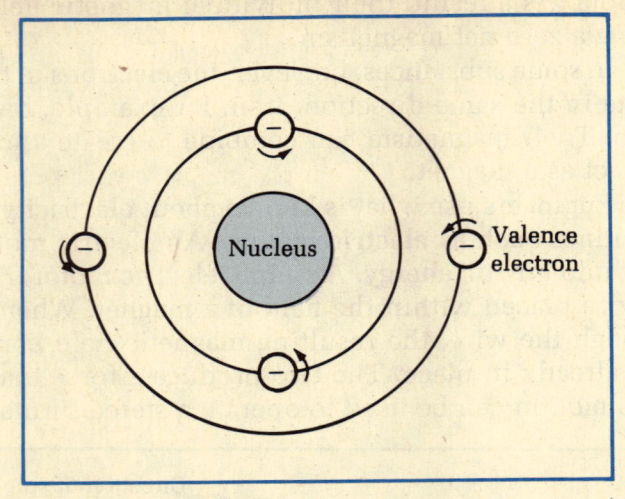

2. Is this substance a magnet?

3. Any two substances, when rubbed together, can acquire an electric charge, called static electricity. The electrons are then discharged in a single jolt, rather than flowing as current electricity does. Lightning is caused by the friction between air and water droplets. Based on this information, is lightning a form of static or current electricity?

4. In a magnet, like poles tend to repel each other, and opposite poles tend to attract. For convenience, we designate one type of poles "north" and the other "south." Since the north-pointing tip of a compass swings around to face the North Pole of the earth, what kind of pole is the compass tip?

Answers are on page A-30.

Chapter 5   Quiz

1. A solid is denser than a gas because it generally has

   (1) more atoms per given amount of volume.
   (2) fewer atoms per given amount of volume.
   (3) atoms that are at a higher temperature.
   (4) atoms that are at a lower temperature.
   (5) atoms that are under more pressure.

2. Electromagnetic rays, such as light, originate when electrons are accelerated. Is an electron moving at a constant velocity in an unchanging direction producing electromagnetic radiation?

Items 3 and 4 are based on the following passage and figure.

Light in which all the waves match crest to crest and trough to trough is said to be "in phase" or "coherent." A laser is an example of coherent light. Ordinary light is "out of phase" or "incoherent." It is a mixture of light waves of many different colors, which appear white when viewed all together.

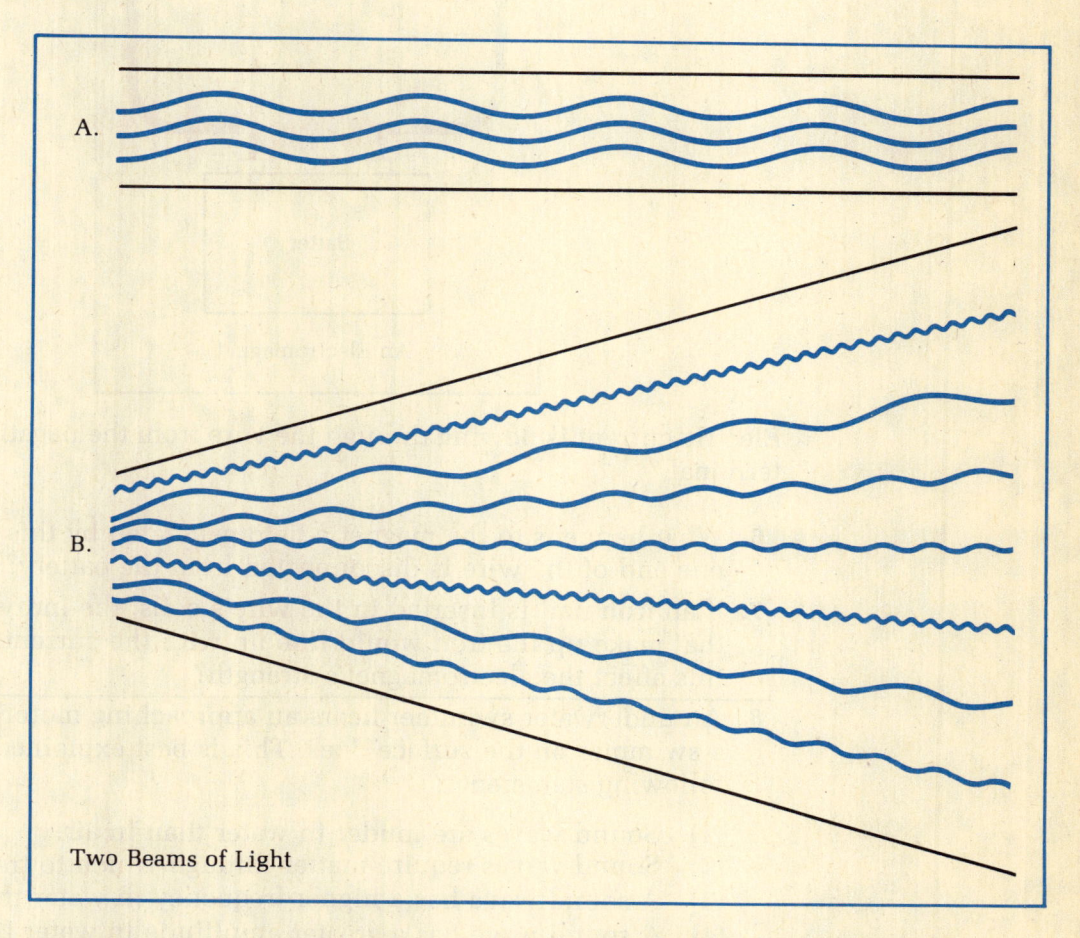

Two Beams of Light

3. In the figure, which drawing represents a laser? Which represents ordinary white light?
4. Which of the following facts regarding the difference between coherent and incoherent light can be inferred from the diagram?

   (1) Coherent light travels at a greater speed than incoherent light.
   (2) Coherent light is brighter than incoherent light.
   (3) Coherent light is more colorful than incoherent light.
   (4) Coherent light shoots straight out, while incoherent light tends to spread out.
   (5) Coherent light has a greater amplitude than incoherent light.

5. A woman is holding a 5-pound weight in each hand. Her arms are straight out from her sides and motionless. Is she doing work?

Items 6 and 7 refer to the following diagram.

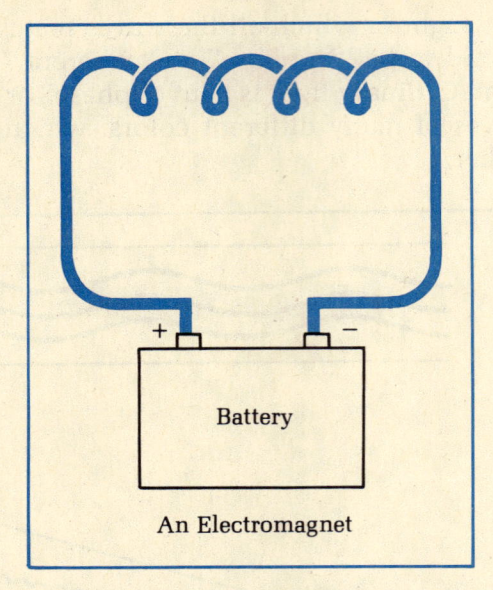

An Electromagnet

Electric current is flowing through the wire from the negative to the positive terminal.

6. What happens to the magnetic field generated by this electromagnet if one end of the wire is disconnected from the battery?

7. If an iron nail is inserted in the wire's coils, the individual magnets that make up the iron would line up with the current. How would this affect the electromagnet's strength?

8. An underwater swimmer hears an approaching motorboat sooner than a swimmer on the surface does. This is best explained by which of the following statements?

  (1) Sound waves are louder in water than in air.
  (2) Sound waves require matter through which to travel.
  (3) A sound wave has a higher frequency in water than in air.
  (4) A sound wave has a greater amplitude in water than in air.
  (5) Water is denser than air.

9. A student drops a rock and a feather out a second-floor window at the same time. The rock hits the ground first. The student concludes that the pull of gravity is not the same for objects with different shapes. Does the experiment support this conclusion? Explain your answer.

10. A sailor crossing a lake on a sailboat does not worry about becoming stuck in the middle if the wind suddenly stops. The sailor reasons that based on the first law of motion, once the sailboat is moving, it will keep going even with no wind pushing it. Is this reasoning correct? Explain your answer.

Answers are on page A-30.

UNIT VI

Interpreting Literature and the Arts

In Unit VI you will study the five types of literature that appear on the Interpreting Literature and the Arts Test. This unit will show you how to apply your reading skills to specific types of literature.

The Interpreting Literature and the Arts unit begins with a chapter that explains what literature is. Each of the other chapters covers one of the forms of literature that you will find on the GED Test: nonfiction, fiction, drama, poetry, and commentary on the arts.

Each chapter follows the same format. The first lesson in a chapter defines the type of literature to be studied, and provides two examples of that type of literature. The four lessons that follow help you see how to apply the reading skills that are covered in Unit III to the type of literature. Lessons 2 and 3 discuss identifying and answering comprehension questions based on passages. Lessons 4 and 5 cover using the critical reading skills of application and analysis to interpret passages.

As you work through this unit, the lessons will help you develop a manner of thinking that will improve your ability to understand and interpret literature. As a result of your increased ability, you should be able to perform better on the Interpreting Literature and the Arts Test.

Unit III teaches important reading strategies that you can use when you interpret literature or commentary passages. If you have not yet done so, you should complete Unit III before working on this unit.

UNIT VI PROGRESS CHART
Interpreting Literature and the Arts

Use the following chart to keep track of your work. When you complete a lesson, circle the number of questions you answered correctly in the Lesson Exercise. When you complete a Chapter Quiz, also record your score below. The numbers in color represent scores at a level of 80% or better.

Lesson	Page		
		CHAPTER 1: Introduction to Literature and Commentary on the Arts	
1	371	What Literature Is	1 2 3
2	372	What Commentary on the Arts Is	1 2 3
	373	Quiz	1 2 3 4 5
		CHAPTER 2: Nonfiction	
1	375	What Nonfiction Is	1 2 3
2	378	Understanding Nonfiction on a Literal Level	1 2 3 4 5
3	379	Understanding Nonfiction on an Inferential Level	1 2 3
4	381	Applying Ideas in Nonfiction	1 2 3
5	383	Analyzing Nonfiction	1 2 3
	384	Quiz	1 2 3 4 5 6 7 8 9 10
		CHAPTER 3: Fiction	
1	387	What Fiction Is	1 2 3
2	389	Understanding Fiction on a Literal Level	1 2 3 4 5
3	391	Understanding Fiction on an Inferential Level	1 2 3 4
4	393	Applying Ideas in Fiction	1 2 3
5	394	Analyzing Fiction	1 2 3 4
	396	Quiz	1 2 3 4 5 6 7 8 9 10

Lesson	Page		
		CHAPTER 4: Drama	
1	399	What Drama Is	1 2 3
2	402	Understanding Drama on a Literal Level	1 2 3
3	403	Understanding Drama on an Inferential Level	1 2 3 4 5
4	404	Applying Ideas in Drama	1 2 3 4
5	406	Analyzing Drama	1 2 3 4
	407	Quiz	1 2 3 4 5 6 7 8 9 10
		CHAPTER 5: Poetry	
1	411	What Poetry Is	1 2 3
2	413	Understanding Poetry on a Literal Level	1 2 3 4
3	415	Understanding Poetry on an Inferential Level	1 2 3 4
4	417	Applying Ideas in Poetry	1 2 3
5	418	Analyzing Poetry	1 2 3 4
	420	Quiz	1 2 3 4 5 6 7 8 9 10
		CHAPTER 6: Commentary	
1	422	What Commentary Is	1 2 3
2	425	Understanding Commentary on a Literal Level	1 2 3 4
3	427	Understanding Commentary on an Inferential Level	1 2 3 4
4	428	Applying Ideas in Commentary	1 2 3
5	430	Analyzing Commentary	1 2 3
	431	Quiz	1 2 3 4 5 6 7 8 9 10

Chapter 1

Introduction to Literature and Commentary on the Arts

> **Objective**
>
> In this chapter, you will read and answer questions about
> - What literature is and how it is different from other forms of writing
> - What commentary on the arts is

Lesson 1 What Literature Is

What are the chief characteristics of literature?

Each day you come across different kinds of writing. Much of that writing is very specific and very practical in nature—price lists in catalogs, operating instructions for machinery, recipes, supermarket advertisements, and train timetables, to name a few. Some writing is less practical and more general in interest. News stories, sports reports, and fashion features are examples of general-interest writing.

Literature, on the other hand, deals with subjects of permanent or universal interest—that is, authors of literature write about topics or ideas that are common to all people. They try to communicate their thoughts in fresh, interesting, and memorable ways. *Literature,* therefore, can be defined as "any writing that is both excellent in quality and lasting in value." When you not only understand the ideas that an author is trying to express but also take pleasure in the ways that those ideas are being expressed, you are responding to the two chief characteristics of literature.

Literature often is divided into two main categories: nonfiction and imaginative literature. **Nonfiction** usually deals with real people and actual events. *The Autobiography of Malcolm X* is an example of nonfiction; it tells the actual events of the man's life. **Imaginative literature** deals with people and events that authors create. The play *Raisin in the Sun* is an example of imaginative literature; the story and characters were made up in the mind of the author. There are three main types, or **genres,** of imaginative literature: **fiction, drama,** and **poetry.** In the GED you will read and answer questions about nonfiction, fiction, drama, and poetry. In Chapters 2–5, you will learn more about each of these genres. You also will learn about the kinds of questions you will be expected to answer about each genre when you take the GED.

When you read a passage, think carefully about its purpose. Is it meant only to provide specific, practical information (like a set of instructions)? Is it meant to provide general information that soon may be forgotten (like a news article)? If the answer to either question is *yes*, then the passage is probably not literature. If, however, the writing is meant to express an important idea and to give you, the reader, pleasure in reading, the passage can be considered literature.

Lesson 1   Exercise

1. State whether the following is TRUE or FALSE and explain your answer: Any piece of writing that is easy to understand is literature.
2. Name three genres of literature.
3. An article in a magazine discusses how to judge a child-care facility. Should you consider the writing in such an article to be literature? Why or why not?

Answers are on page A-31.

Lesson 2   What Commentary on the Arts Is

What are the main purposes of commentary?

Have you ever recommended a TV show to a friend? Have you ever talked about why you liked or disliked a new song? If so, you already know something about **commentary.** Basically, commentary is opinion-giving. The author presents his or her opinion about the topic and then defends that opinion.

On the GED, "commentary" is opinion-giving specifically about literature and the arts. Such writing expresses an author's feelings about literature, music, theater, film, television, dance, or one of the visual arts (for example, painting, drawing, or sculpture). Authors of commentary—often called **critics** or **reviewers**—are usually experts in their field. Because they are very familiar with the form of art about which they are writing, they can offer educated opinions and defend their views well.

Commentary on literature and the arts takes two major forms. A **review** focuses on one art form in limited performance, such as a new movie (which probably will run for only a few weeks) or a recent concert (which probably had only one performance). A review might begin like this:

> In *Sign of the Falcon,* which opened today at the Strand Theater, director Rhanna Jackson has proven once again why she is so worthy of her many Academy Awards. . . .

An **essay** deals with broader subjects that have a more enduring influence, such as a comparison of two kinds of painting styles or an explanation of the popularity of a certain kind of music. An essay might begin like this:

Will the art world ever see a return to the Romantic style of painting championed by Delacroix and Goya? I think not. Let me explain. . . .

Both reviews and essays may serve some or all of these purposes: (1) They may *summarize*, or provide information about a work of art; (2) They may *analyze*, or show how a work of art achieves a particular effect; and (3) They may *evaluate*, or make judgments about the value of a work of art.

When you take the GED, you will read and answer questions about reviews and essays. Therefore, you must be prepared to think about what makes good commentary—even when you may not agree with the opinion being offered. In Chapter 6, you will learn more about what authors of commentary look for when they form their opinions. You also will learn to judge how effectively they present and defend those opinions.

Lesson 2   Exercise

1. Which two of the following might be considered commentary?
   - an article that praises an exhibition of photographs by Ansel Adams
   - an interview with a friend of Ansel Adams
   - a story about a magazine photographer in Vietnam
   - an essay that explains why black-and-white photographs can be powerful

2. Give two examples of topics that would be suitable for a review.

3. Can two critics with different opinions about the same subject write equally good commentary? Explain your answer.

Answers are on page A-31.

Chapter 1   Quiz

1. Which of the following could NOT be considered literature?
   - (1) a play about a couple's failing marriage
   - (2) directions to a popular art museum
   - (3) a short story about an author's humorous relatives
   - (4) the lyrics to your favorite song
   - (5) a biography of Martin Luther King, Jr.

2. Think of two television shows that you enjoy. How might one or both of them be included in an essay about trends in television viewing?

Items 3 to 5 are based on the following passage.

WHAT IS "DEMOCRACY"?

We received a letter from the Writers' War Board the other day asking for a statement on "The Meaning of Democracy." It presumably is our duty to comply with such a request, and it is certainly our pleasure.

(5) Surely the Board knows what democracy is. It is the line that forms on the right. It is the don't in don't shove. It is the hole in the stuffed shirt through which the sawdust slowly trickles; it is the dent in the high hat. Democracy is the recurrent suspicion that more than half of the people are right more than half of the time. It is the feeling of privacy in the voting booths, the feeling of communion in the libraries, the feeling
(10) of vitality everywhere. Democracy is a letter to the editor. Democracy is the score at the beginning of the ninth. It is an idea which hasn't been disproved yet, a song the words of which have not gone bad. It's the mustard on the hot dog and the cream in the rationed coffee. Democracy is a request from a War Board, in the middle of a morning in the middle
(15) of a war, wanting to know what democracy is.

From "Democracy" by E. B. White. Copyright 1943 by E. B. White. Reprinted with permission of *The New Yorker*.

3. According to the definitions in Chapter 1, does this passage come from a work of literature or from a piece of commentary? Explain your answer.

4. In part, the author explains what *democracy* is by
    (1) quoting definitions from a variety of dictionaries
    (2) explaining what democracy is *not*
    (3) telling what great leaders have said about democracy
    (4) giving examples of democracy in action
    (5) comparing democracy to other forms of government

5. This passage was written during a time of war. Do you think that the author would be willing to fight in the war? Why or why not?

Answers are on page A-31.

Chapter 2

Nonfiction

Objective

In this chapter, you will learn about one of the four types of literature discussed in Chapter 1. In your study of the type of literature known as **nonfiction,** you will

- Read and answer questions about what nonfiction literature is and what distinguishes it from other forms of literature
- Read two excerpts from works of nonfiction—one called a social commentary, the other an eyewitness account
- Read and write about the elements of nonfiction

Lesson 1 What Nonfiction Is

How is nonfiction distinguished from other types of literature?

Nonfiction literature is about actual people, events, or situations. One nonfiction author may write about a current social or political problem to convince others of his or her opinion. Other nonfiction authors describe events in their own lives or the lives of others. By sharing these events with their readers, these authors hope to give an understanding of problems that are common to everybody, such as getting along with family members or friends, finding a job, or adjusting to life in a new city.

As you learned in Chapter 1, not all nonfiction writing is considered literature. A news report about a fire or an accident, a description of a ballgame, or a guarantee that comes in the box with a new appliance may interest readers when they are first read, but they are not saved and read repeatedly once they have served their purpose. The authors of this kind of nonfiction are interested in conveying information that is of immediate interest or of practical value. The authors of nonfiction literature, however, are concerned with communicating information about human events of lasting interest. The nonfiction writer of literature will also be concerned with the choice of words and the beauty of the expression when the words are arranged in sentences. If a work of nonfiction focuses on a subject or an idea that is of universal interest and that will continue to attract readers in the future, it is considered literature.

Many types of nonfiction may be considered literature. Some examples of nonfiction literature include the following:

375

Biographies   A biography is an account of a person's life.

Autobiographies   An autobiography is an account written about one's own life.

Articles and essays   An article or an essay is a short piece about a specific topic, which may appear in a magazine or in a collection of short pieces.

Diaries   A diary is a daily record of a writer's experiences, observations, or feelings.

Travel books   A travel book is an account of a person's experiences in a particular part of the world.

The following two passages from works of nonfiction will be used as references throughout the chapter. Before you read each passage, read the purpose question. After you finish reading the passage, read the purpose question again. Use the information that was communicated in the nonfiction passage to try to answer the purpose question in your own words. Always try to answer the purpose question before going on to answer any questions about the passage—whether in this book or on the GED test, where purpose questions will also appear.

Passage A

HOW CAN A CHILD'S ENVIRONMENT AT HOME CONFLICT WITH THE ENVIRONMENT AT SCHOOL?

More often than not, families and schools, like divorced parents, hold different sets of expectations and goals, different views of one child, and of childhood.

(5) When kids are young, families are the world they live in. Our power as parents is largely unshared. We are their environment, their standard, their reality, their value-tenders and the people who interpret the outside to them.

If families work right, they are the place in which love is uncon-
(10) ditional. If they work right, there is an assumption of love, even under discipline or anger. Good families don't flunk their children.

But on the first day of school—nursery school, first grade, seventh grade, college—we give our children over to a system that doesn't love them. Give them over to be judged, to see if they can "measure up" to another standard. They enter a world in which they
(15) are only rewarded for how they perform.

I don't mean to present the schools as cold, and teachers as uncaring. But parents see kids as special individuals; the school inevitably sees them as part of a group. School is the essential but scary halfway house between the home and the world.

(20) I suppose we also give up our own teaching monopoly when we send them to school. There is nothing new in that. Since the beginning schools have been the melting pots of a complex society. They taught immigrant children English and order; taught country people

urban skills; taught everyone the "American" ways. We can only (25) guess at how those lessons were at odds with family tutoring.

Even today the hottest issues at school are not about new math or phonetics, but about conflicting values. A parent may encourage questioning, while the school has a bias toward passivity. A parent may believe literally in the Bible, while the children are told that (30) Jonah and the Whale is a story. A parent may praise order, while a school allows chaos. If sex education is the flash point, it is no surprise.

I don't know a single parent who has not been aghast at some attitude or information lugged home with the school books. I don't (35) know a teacher who hasn't felt that same flash of horror at some family opinion. We compete (as much as we cooperate) for influence, for space in the children's heads.

Eventually, I suppose it's the kids who make a kind of truce, even an uneasy one, by becoming their own people.

From "Seventh Grade Isn't Seventh Heaven" by Ellen Goodman. Copyright 1981 The Boston Globe Newspaper/Washington Post Writer's Group. Reprinted with permission.

Passage B

HOW DOES THE AUTHOR COME TO REALIZE THE SANCTITY OF A HUMAN LIFE?

It was about forty yards to the gallows. I watched the bare brown back of the prisoner marching in front of me. He walked clumsily with his bound arms, but quite steadily, with that bobbing gait of the Indian who never straightens his knees. At each step his muscles slid (5) neatly into place, the lock of hair on his scalp danced up and down, his feet printed themselves on the wet gravel. And once, in spite of the men who gripped him by each shoulder, he stepped slightly aside to avoid a puddle on the path.

It is curious, but till that moment I had never realised what it (10) means to destroy a healthy, conscious man. When I saw the prisoner step aside to avoid the puddle, I saw the mystery, the unspeakable wrongness, of cutting a life short when it is in full tide. This man was not dying, he was alive just as we were alive. All the organs of his body were working—bowels digesting food, skin renewing itself, nails (15) growing, tissues forming—all toiling away in solemn foolery. His nails would still be growing when he stood on the drop, when he was falling through the air with a tenth of a second to live. His eyes saw the yellow gravel and the grey walls, and his brain still remembered, foresaw, reasoned—reasoned even about puddles. He and we were a (20) party of men walking together, seeing, hearing, feeling, understanding the same world; and in two minutes, with a sudden snap, one of us would be gone—one mind less, one world less.

From "A Hanging" by George Orwell. Copyright 1968 by Sonia Brownell Orwell. Reprinted with permission of Harcourt Brace Jovanovich.

Lesson 1 Exercise

1. State whether or not Passages A and B are concerned with ideas of permanent or universal interest. What are those ideas, if any? Give examples.
2. Explain why Passage B is nonfiction.
3. In what way does the author of Passage A view parents and schools as competitors?

Answers are on page A-31.

Lesson 2 Comprehending Nonfiction on a Literal Level

How can you often find the main idea of a nonfiction work?

Topic and Main Idea

Every work of nonfiction has a topic. The **topic** is the subject matter of the piece of nonfiction writing. The life of Theodore Roosevelt, the history of rock music, and the participation of the Soviet Union in World War II are all possible topics. To determine the topic of a nonfiction work, you should ask yourself, "What is this work about?"

The topic of a work of nonfiction is not the same as the main idea of that work. The **main idea** is the particular point that the author wants to make about the topic. For example, three authors might write about the same topic, the country Greece, but their articles might have three different main ideas. One might argue that Greece was the birthplace of a great civilization. The second author might make the point that Greece is an ideal choice for vacationers. The third might discuss the military importance of Greece as an ally of the United States and Western Europe. To determine the main idea of a nonfiction work, you should ask yourself, "What point is the author trying to make?"

Figuring out the topic of an essay, article, or newspaper column is easier than figuring out the main idea. You need only look at the title or glance through the opening paragraph to learn what the topic is. A quick look at Passage A, for example, tells you that the topic is the role of families and schools in the lives of children.

Figuring out the main idea of a nonfiction work may be more difficult. Often, an author will state the main idea of an article or an essay directly. To find the main idea, read the work carefully to find a sentence or a passage that expresses the author's purpose or main point. The author of Passage B reveals the main idea in lines 10–12. In these lines, the author expresses his feeling about the "unspeakable wrongness" of destroying a human life.

Supporting Details

Authors make the main idea in a work of nonfiction convincing and effective by supplying **supporting details.** The main idea may be supported through examples, statistical proof or factual evidence, or strong reasons. Supporting details are important because they illustrate and prove an author's ideas—both the main idea of the work and the idea of each paragraph. In the paragraph in Passage A that begins on line 26, the author presents a number of supporting details to illustrate her point that the "hottest issues at school" are about conflicting values. When she writes that "A parent may encourage questioning, while the school has a bias toward passivity" and "A parent may believe literally in the Bible, while the children are told that Jonah and the Whale is a story," she uses examples as supporting details.

Lesson 2   Exercise

1. State whether the following is TRUE or FALSE and explain your answer: The topic of Passage A is the American educational system.
2. In Passage B, what does the word "gait" (line 3) refer to?
3. Using the information in Passage A, explain how parents and schools view children differently.
4. What evidence does the author of Passage B present to show that the prisoner is capable of reasoning?
5. According to the author of Passage A, schools have been the "melting pots of a complex society." List three supporting details that the author mentions to illustrate this idea.

Answers are on pages A-31–A-32.

Lesson 3   Comprehending Nonfiction on an Inferential Level

How can you know an author's purpose or figure out the meaning of a particular word or expression when neither is explained directly?

Point of View

The **point of view** of a piece of writing is the "voice" that the author uses to write about a subject. In literature, there are two major points of view. If the author addresses his or her readers by using "I," the author is using what is called the **first-person** point of view.

The other major point of view in literature is called the **third-person** point of view. In a work written from the third-person point of view, the person recounting the events is speaking of someone else, "he" or "she," rather than "I." The third-person point of view puts a distance between the author and the subject. The first-person point of view, on the other hand, allows the author to address both the subject and the reader on a personal level.

The author of Passage A uses the first-person point of view to share her opinions about the conflicting roles of the family and the school. The author makes it clear that she is presenting her own evaluation of this conflict that comes out of her personal experience, with all its thoughts and feelings.

Passage B is also written from the first-person point of view. The author's choice of this point of view permits him to share his feelings as well as his ideas about events he is witnessing. In lines 9–10, for example, when the author says, "It is curious, but till that moment I had never realised what it means to destroy a healthy, conscious man," he is telling the reader how he felt as he watched the prisoner walk in front of him. In Passage B, the reactions and reflections of the author form the main idea of the piece. The point of view is, therefore, important in the communication of his ideas.

Making Inferences and Using Context Clues

Most of the ideas in a nonfiction piece can be understood literally. The main idea is often stated directly so that readers immediately understand it. However, authors do not always state ideas or conclusions directly. Many times, they say things in a way that implies a meaning, expecting the readers to understand it based on their experience. It is important to read a passage carefully so that you can make an inference about what an author is trying to say. Making an **inference** means drawing a conclusion about the author's meaning by using information in the piece.

Sometimes, you can use the **context** of a word—the sentence in which the word appears or the sentences just before or after it—to help you to understand how a particular word or expression is used. In Passage A, the author states, "If families work right, they are the place in which love is unconditional" (line 8). If you are not sure of the meaning of *unconditional*, the next sentence in the passage will help you understand what the author means. Families love their children even when they are angry with them or need to discipline them. The love that families have for a child is unconditional because the child does not have to earn that love. It is given to the child automatically, and it is not withdrawn even though the child may misbehave.

In Passage B, the meaning of the expression "solemn foolery" (line 15) may not be clear at first. The expression can be appreciated only by looking at the context in which it is used. The work that our bodies do to keep us alive is solemn, or serious. The continued functioning of the prisoner's body seems like "foolery" at the same time, however, since the prisoner is only moments away from death.

Implied Main Idea

You may also need to use inferential skills to help you figure out the main idea of a passage. The authors of Passages A and B state their main ideas directly. Some authors, however, imply, or indirectly express, their main idea. To understand a main idea that is implied, you need to find all the facts and supporting details of a passage. Then you need to figure out how they work together to communicate the main idea.

The author of Passage A tells us the main idea in the first sentence of the passage: ". . . families and schools . . . hold different sets of expectations and goals, different views of one child and of childhood." The author of Passage B expresses the main idea in lines 11–12, where he expresses his feelings about the "unspeakable wrongness" of "cutting a life short when it is in full tide."

Lesson 3   Exercise

1. Quote at least two expressions that the author of Passage B uses to imply that he does not view the prisoner as any different from the rest of the men.
2. State whether the following is TRUE or FALSE and explain your answer: The author of Passage A believes that schools help children to grow up.
3. Based on your reading of Passage B, which of the following inferences can you make? Explain your answer.

   (1)   The prisoner has been unjustly found guilty.

   (2)   The prisoner feared his death.

   (3)   The author is an observant person.

   (4)   The author is a prison guard.

Answers are on page A-32.

Lesson 4   Applying Ideas in Nonfiction

How can you predict an author's belief about a subject by understanding the author's belief about another subject?

Applying Main Ideas and Details

Nonfiction literature communicates facts and opinions. On the GED test, there will be questions asking you to apply those facts and opinions from one setting or situation to a new one.

For example, information about one cause-effect relationship can be applied to other cause-effect relationships. Suppose you read an article explaining how pocket calculators have made slide rules obsolete. Reading such an article may make you realize the effect that other inventions have had in the past or might have in the future. You may speculate that word processors will one day make typewriters a thing of the past. This thought may, in turn, lead you to wonder about the future of companies that manufacture typewriters—or about the general economic consequences of technological change. In other words, what you learned from the original article is not limited to the content of that article. You can apply that knowledge in a number of ways.

Application of knowledge is not limited to cause-effect relationships. You can also apply ideas about values and behavior to new settings. In

Passage A, for example, the author concludes that children eventually resolve conflicting values at home and at school. In other words, they learn to develop their own thoughts and ideas by juggling all the ideas they have learned at home and in school. This principle of resolving values that may be in conflict with each other can be found in other situations. Elected representatives, for example, sometimes shape their own positions by juggling a variety of demands among their constituents.

Applying the Author's Attitude

If you understand an author's beliefs, or attitudes, about a particular subject, you can sometimes predict how the author will feel about a different subject. The key to applying the author's beliefs is understanding the principle behind his or her beliefs about the subject at hand. In Passage B, the author makes clear his belief in the essential value of an individual's life. Although we know nothing about the prisoner, you can see the author's conviction that the prisoner's right to life is a basic human right. You can apply this attitude of the author to the existence of the caste system in India and assume that he would oppose its practice of treating some people as not deserving of basic human rights.

Lesson 4   Exercise

1. Based on the ideas the author of Passage A expresses, which of the following events would be most likely to create a conflict between a school and the parents of a student? Explain your answer.

    (1) a French teacher choosing a new textbook

    (2) a school making the lunch period ten minutes longer

    (3) a history teacher telling a class that it is sometimes right to disobey the law

    (4) a music teacher adding an extra song to the assembly program

2. With which of the following statements regarding capital punishment would the author of Passage B most likely agree? Explain your answer.

    (1) Capital punishment is sometimes necessary.

    (2) Capital punishment is never justified.

    (3) Capital punishment is the best way to deter crime.

    (4) Capital punishment should be used only in extreme circumstances.

3. The poet John Donne wrote, "Any man's death diminishes me [makes me smaller], because I am involved in Mankind." Explain in your own words why you think the author of Passage B would agree or disagree with this statement.

Answers are on page A-32.

Lesson 5   Analyzing Nonfiction

What are the techniques authors use to express their ideas and address their readers?

Purpose

If you pull apart the methods an author uses to express his or her ideas, you are **analyzing** the writing. To help you analyze nonfiction, ask yourself: What is the purpose of the writing? Ask this question about the purpose of the overall passage or of any part of the passage, such as a paragraph or a sentence. These are some basic purposes:

- to *explain* or provide information about a subject
- to *convince* the reader of the truth of a given idea or opinion
- to *persuade* the reader to take some form of action
- to *describe* physical details or create an impression of a subject
- to *recount* an event, or a series of events, in a way that resembles the telling of a story

In any given piece of nonfiction, a writer might use one or several of these approaches.

The author of Passage A seeks to *convince* her readers of a particular point: the conflict between the environment at home and the environment at school. Some of the supporting details used by the author are facts that explain her subject. In general, however, the author's purpose is to share a personal opinion rather than to present facts.

Style

Authors of nonfiction literature are concerned with how they express their ideas. The words they choose and the sentences they create determine the style. The style can be single-syllable words in short sentences. The style may consist, on the other hand, of long sentences with much description.

The style that authors choose depends on their purpose and on what they want to say about a subject. The elements of style include the author's sentence structure, use of descriptive words, and use of comparisons and other literary techniques to communicate ideas more vividly.

In Passage A, when the author writes, "Good families don't flunk their children" (line 10), she has intentionally used a word, *flunk*, that is normally associated with school. Families do not flunk their children in the sense that they do not judge them on the basis of their performance and then decide whether they are worthy children. The author's deliberate use of the word *flunk* in this context helps her achieve a major purpose of her essay: to show the contrast between the child's environment at home and at school.

Tone

The author's feeling about the subject of her or his writing is called the **tone.** The tone of a nonfiction work helps convey the author's purpose and beliefs. An author may choose a light-hearted or a serious tone, a detached or a more personal tone, depending upon his or her purpose. Some authors use an informal tone in addressing their readers, others use a formal tone. Authors frequently use what is called an **ironic** tone—they use words that express an unexpected meaning in order to emphasize a contradiction. The sentence "I worked hard to meet the demands of a job that required less effort than ever," for example, illustrates an ironic tone. Authors will choose a particular tone based on their belief about the most effective way to communicate their ideas or to capture the interest of their readers.

Lesson 5 Exercise

1. Which of the five purposes listed on page 383 does the author of Passage B use? What is the author's primary purpose?
2. Which passage is more informal in style and tone: Passage A or Passage B? Explain your answer.
3. State whether the following is TRUE or FALSE and explain your answer: An author who uses an informal tone does not consider his or her subject as especially serious.

Answers are on page A-32.

Chapter 2   Quiz

Items 1 to 4 are based on the following passage.

WHY IS LANGUAGE IMPORTANT?

It begins to look, more and more disturbingly, as if the gift of language is the single human trait that marks us all genetically, setting us apart from all the rest of life. Language is, like nest-building or hive-making, the universal and biologically specific activity of human
(5) beings. We engage in it communally, compulsively, and automatically. We cannot be human without it; if we were to be separated from it our minds would die, as surely as bees lost from the hive.

From *The Lives of a Cell* by Lewis Thomas. Copyright 1974 by Lewis Thomas. Reprinted with permission of the author and the Viking Press.

UNIT IV: INTERPRETING LITERATURE AND THE ARTS   Chapter 2 Quiz   **385**

1. According to the passage, the ability to use language
   - (1) is one of many characteristics that set humans apart from other forms of life
   - (2) varies from one culture to another
   - (3) is the only characteristic that sets humans apart from other forms of life
   - (4) is learned with great difficulty
   - (5) is a gift that most humans do not fully appreciate

2. Based on the expression "more and more disturbingly" (line 1), which of the following beliefs about humanity do you think the author holds?
   - (1) Human beings have made little progress since the beginning of civilization.
   - (2) The differences between human life and other forms of life are not that varied.
   - (3) Human life is sacred, despite all the shortcomings of humanity.
   - (4) The progress of humanity depends on understanding differences among cultures.
   - (5) Humanity is incapable of solving problems rationally.

3. Does the author use a first-person point of view or a third-person point of view? Give proof from the passage for your answer.

4. Which word best describes the tone of the author?
   - (1) ironic
   - (2) comic
   - (3) serious
   - (4) compassionate
   - (5) detached

Items 5 to 10 are based on the following passage.

WHY DID THE AUTHOR ENJOY SPENDING TIME IN THE STORE?

Until I was thirteen and left Arkansas for good, the Store was my favorite place to be. Alone and empty in the mornings, it looked like an unopened present from a stranger. Opening the front doors was pulling the ribbon off the unexpected gift. The light would come in softly
(5) (we faced north), easing itself over the shelves of mackerel, salmon, tobacco, thread. It fell flat on the big vat of lard and by noontime during the summer the grease had softened to a thick soup. Whenever I walked into the Store in the afternoon, I sensed that it was tired. I alone could hear the slow pulse of its job half done. But just before
(10) bedtime, after numerous people had walked in and out, had argued over their bills, or joked about their neighbors, or just dropped in "to

give Sister Henderson a 'Hi y'all,'" the promise of magic mornings returned to the Store and spread itself over the family in washed life waves.

From *I Know Why the Caged Bird Sings* by Maya Angelou. Copyright 1969 by Maya Angelou. Reprinted with permission of the author and Random House, Inc.

5. Did the author ever return to Arkansas to live?
6. What inference can you make about who owned the store and why the author spent so much time there?
7. The author of the passage twice compares the store to a gift in order to
   (1) show how beautiful it was
   (2) show how exciting and magical it was to a child
   (3) show that it was almost Christmastime
   (4) show that she was never sure what was inside it
   (5) show that it was managed for the family by a friend

8. State whether the following is TRUE or FALSE and explain your answer: The author would probably develop a strong attachment to a house in which she or her family lived for a long time.
9. Find two sentences in which the author indicates that she thinks of the store as a living thing.
10. Look at the list of items mentioned in lines 5 and 6 that were found in the store. What kind of store can you assume it was?

Answers are on pages A-32—A-33.

Chapter 3 Fiction

Objective

In this chapter, you will learn more about the ways in which literature can inform and entertain an audience. In your study of the type of literature known as **fiction,** you will

- Read and answer questions about what fiction is
- Study the basic elements of all fiction literature, including plot, character, setting, atmosphere, point of view, and theme
- Read two excerpts from works of fiction that deal with human relationships—one a story about a boy's relationship with his father, the other a story about a girl's relationship with older people
- Read and write about the elements of fiction

Lesson 1 What Fiction Is

In what ways is fiction different from nonfiction?

Kinds of Fiction

Fiction is one type of **imaginative literature**—that is, the people and events of which it tells come from the writer's imagination. Fiction sometimes may include factual information, but its main focus is on imagination rather than fact.

Although fiction does not focus on actual people or actual events, the characters and experiences that appear in it usually seem very true to life. On the other hand, magical beings, animals that can think and talk, and events on other planets can appear in fiction. Both realistic stories and fantasy stories are examples of fiction.

Novels and **short stories** are the two best-known kinds of fiction. Novels are longer than short stories, but length is not the only difference. A novel usually tells a complicated story that involves many characters; a short story is simpler and may concentrate on only one character.

The following two passages from works of fiction will be used as references throughout this chapter. As you read, use the purpose question that begins each passage to help you focus on important ideas.

Passage A

DOES THE BOY HAVE A TRADITIONAL FATHER-SON RELATIONSHIP?

Father was in the army all through the war—the first war, I mean—so, up to the age of five, I never saw much of him, and what I saw did not worry me. Sometimes I woke and there was a big figure in khaki peering down at me in the candlelight. Sometimes in the early morn-
(5) ing I heard the slamming of the front door and the clatter of nailed boots down the cobbles of the lane. These were Father's entrances and exits. Like Santa Claus he came and went mysteriously.

In fact, I rather liked his visits, though it was an uncomfortable squeeze between Mother and him when I got into the big bed in the
(10) early morning. He smoked, which gave him a pleasant musty smell, and shaved, an operation of astounding interest. Each time he left a trail of souvenirs—model tanks and Gurkha knives with handles made of bullet cases, and German helmets and cap badges and button-sticks, and all sorts of military equipment—carefully stowed away
(15) in a long box on top of the wardrobe, in case they ever came in handy. There was a bit of the magpie about Father; he expected everything to come in handy. When his back was turned, Mother let me get a chair and rummage through his treasures. She didn't seem to think so highly of them as he did.

From "My Oedipus Complex" by Frank O'Connor. Copyright 1930, 1952 by Frank O'Connor. Reprinted with permission of *The New Yorker*.

Passage B

HOW DOES MARIAN FEEL ABOUT NURSING HOMES?

It was mid-morning—a very cold, bright day. Holding a potted plant before her, a girl of fourteen jumped off a bus in front of the Old Ladies' Home, on the outskirts of town. She wore a red coat, and her straight yellow hair was hanging down loose from the pointed white
(5) cap all the little girls were wearing that year. She stopped for a moment beside one of the prickly dark shrubs with which the city had beautified the Home, and then proceeded slowly toward the building, which was of whitewashed brick and reflected the winter sunlight like a block of ice. As she walked vaguely up the steps she shifted the
(10) small pot from hand to hand; then she had to set it down and remove her mittens before she could open the heavy door.

"I'm a Campfire Girl . . . I have to pay a visit to some old lady," she told the nurse at the desk. This was a woman in a white uniform who looked as if she were cold; she had close-cut hair which stood
(15) up on the very top of her head exactly like a sea wave. Marian, the little girl, did not tell her that the visit would give her a minimum of only three points in her score.

"Acquainted with any of our residents?" asked the nurse. She lifted an eyebrow and spoke like a man.

(20) "With any old ladies? No—but—that is, any of them will do," Marian stammered. With her free hand she pushed her hair behind her ears, as she did when it was time to study Science.

The nurse shrugged and rose. "You have a nice *multiflora cineraria* there," she remarked as she walked ahead down the hall of
(25) closed doors to pick out an old lady.

There was loose, bulging linoleum on the floor. Marian felt as if she were walking on the waves, but the nurse paid no attention to it. There was a smell in the hall like the interior of a clock. Everything was silent until, behind one of the doors, an old lady of some kind
(30) cleared her throat like a sheep bleating. This decided the nurse. Stopping in her tracks, she first extended her arm, bent her elbow, and leaned forward from the hips—all to examine the watch strapped to her wrist; then she gave a loud double-rap on the door.

"There are two in each room," the nurse remarked over her
(35) shoulder.

"Two what?" asked Marian without thinking. The sound like a sheep's bleating almost made her turn around and run back.

From "A Visit of Charity" by Eudora Welty. Copyright by Eudora Welty. Reprinted with permission of Harcourt Brace Jovanovich.

Lesson 1   Exercise

1. State whether the following is TRUE or FALSE and explain your answer: Passage A makes references to factual information.
2. Name two of the characters in Passage B.
3. Are Passages A and B examples of realistic fiction or fantasy fiction? Explain your answer.

Answers are on page A-33.

Lesson 2   Comprehending Fiction on a Literal Level

What are some of the elements that an author includes in a story?

Plot

To understand a work of fiction, you first must have a clear idea of the sequence of events that make up the story. The way an author of fiction organizes this sequence of events is known as the **plot** of the story. For example, an important part of the plot of Passage A is that the boy's father is not always at home; instead, he comes and goes on occasional visits. A plot may be a complex series of major and minor events and involve a great many characters. On the other hand, a simple plot, involving only one character and one major action, can be equally effective if told well.

Narrator

The plot of a story is always told by a **narrator,** the author's "voice." As in nonfiction, that "voice" may speak either from a first-person or a third-person point of view. In Passage B, for example, a third-person point of view is used; the author is not obviously present in the story. However, the author may choose to appear as a first-person narrator. When that narrator is a **participant,** "I" is an active character in the story. When that narrator is an **observer,** "I" tells about the events but is not actively involved in the story.

Setting

Setting is the location and time period in which a story takes place. For example, the author of Passage A makes it clear that this story is set during World War I ("the first war"). The wartime setting is important here because it provides the explanation for the father's absence and for the collection of "treasures" that the boy finds so fascinating. Some stories are completely dominated by their settings; for example, the setting would be a basic part of a story that takes place on a drifting lifeboat or in an enchanted forest. In other stories, setting is not an essential element.

Characters

A **character** is any person who takes part in the plot of a story. As noted above, even the author can be a character in a story. In a work of fiction—and especially in a novel—the author may provide a great deal of description about some characters. Generally, the characters about whom the author gives the most information are the most important, or **major,** characters in the story.

The plot of a story moves forward as characters interact with each other. That interaction may take the form of **physical action** (for example, a slap across the face, laughter, running from the scene), or it may be revealed through **dialogue** (what the characters say to each other). Over the length of a story, both forms are generally used.

Lesson 2   Exercise

1. In Passage B, to what does the term *multiflora cineraria* refer?
2. In Passage A, how do the narrator's parents disagree about the value of Father's souvenirs?
3. Complete this sentence: Passage B is set during the _____.
   • spring   • summer   • fall   • winter
4. In which passage does the narrator use a first-person point of view?
5. Summarize the plot of Passage B.

Answers are on page A-33.

Lesson 3 Comprehending Fiction on an Inferential Level

What methods might an author use in a story to reveal information without giving that information outright?

Implied and Psychological Settings

In some works of fiction, the location and time period are stated either unclearly or not at all. In cases of **implied setting,** realize that the author is focusing on characters and plot. You will, however, be able to make assumptions about the setting if you pay close attention to details. For example, if a character in a story talked about Harry Truman as the current president, you could assume that the story was set in America in the late 1940s or early 1950s.

Sometimes stated, but usually implied, the **psychological setting** of a work of fiction indicates the way the characters in a story think. Certain events in the plot may have their basis in the way that the characters think. Again, careful reading of details can provide clues about the psychological setting. In Passage B, for example, the author mentions that the nurse takes no notice of the bulging linoleum. She also is described as looking cold and talking like a man. A reader might question the amount of compassion she has for her patients. In addition, the author describes a smell like the interior of a clock—a smell associated more with machines than with people. These details might lead the reader to assume that the psychological setting at the Old Ladies' Home is one in which it is common to deny some people basic human respect. It would not be surprising, then, if the reader were to learn that the patients are being ignored or even mistreated.

Characterization

Authors sometimes make direct comments or observations about their characters. More often, they ask the reader to make observations by offering details that suggest certain physical characteristics or qualities of character. Clues about **characterization** can come from what a character says and does. Read these lines about Marian in Passage B (lines 20–22):

> "With any old ladies? No—but—that is, any of them will do," Marian stammered. With her free hand she pushed her hair behind her ears, as she did when it was time to study Science.

Stammering is often considered a sign of nervousness. In Marian's case, it is one indication that she is uneasy about her visit. Also, Marian is said to push her hair behind her ears, as she does when she studies Science. Visiting a nursing home and studying Science are very different activities. Seeing that Marian has the same reaction in both situations, the reader can infer that perhaps she views her visit as some kind of scientific experiment, not as an act of kindness. Such an attitude would characterize her as insensitive.

Theme and Conflict

Most works of fiction contain the author's insights about people and about life. These insights make up the main idea, or **theme,** of a story. A theme is rarely stated directly. To figure out the theme of a story, ask yourself, "What is the point or lesson of this story?" Look carefully at the details—especially the details about the plot and the major characters—and consider what the author might be trying to show about human behavior.

A major clue about the theme can come from determining the **conflict,** or struggle in a story. A conflict is usually a psychological struggle, though it may be demonstrated in a physical struggle. The struggle may be internal, occurring within a character. It may be external, occurring between one character and another, between a character and his or her society, or between a character and a force of nature.

For example, think about the situation of the narrator in Passage A. The boy, who considers his father an interesting diversion but of little real importance to his life, would face an internal conflict if the father later came home to stay. He would have to reconcile his earlier opinion of the man with the fact of the man's new importance in his life. That conflict might even be expressed externally, as through an argument with the father. Watching the boy work through his feelings, the reader probably would find that the theme of the story says something about family relationships.

Figurative Language

Sometimes an author offers descriptions or observations by making comparisons. Through the use of **figures of speech,** or **figurative language,** the author creates mental images. The words are not to be taken literally; rather, the meaning is implied.

Similes and **metaphors** are the most common kinds of figurative language. Both compare things that are not apparently alike. A simile uses *like* or *as* to make comparisons. In Passage A, for example, the narrator refers to his father's mysterious comings and goings as "like Santa Claus." The comparison helps to reveal the child's almost fairy-tale-like view of his father. A metaphor does not use *like* or *as*. An author who writes "The moon was a silver medallion" would be basing that metaphor on the fact that both objects shine.

Lesson 3   Exercise

1. In Passage A, the narrator says, "There was a bit of the magpie about Father; he expected everything to come in handy" (lines 16–17). A magpie is a kind of bird. What can you assume about its habits?

2. In Passage B, the Old Ladies' Home is described as reflecting the winter sunlight "like a block of ice." What might the reader infer from the comparison?

3. Assume that Passage B comes from the early part of the story. What theme might be expected to arise from the rest of the story? Explain your answer.

4. Which of the following examples of figurative language would present a positive mental image? Which would present a negative mental image?
   - "The wind howled like a hungry wolf."
   - "The sun was a golden ship, sailing through a cloudy sea."
   - "You didn't donate to the Clothing Drive? What a Scrooge you are!"

Answers are on page A-33.

Lesson 4   Applying Ideas in Fiction

What kinds of information about a character might help you to predict his or her reactions to events outside the story?

Applying Themes and Details

If a story is well told, it is possible for the reader to imagine certain qualities of characters in other settings. For example, suppose you read a novel about a woman who fought hard for the civil rights of blacks in America in the late 1950s and early 1960s. Now imagine that same character in present-day South Africa. You could predict that she probably would be working hard to abolish apartheid, the legal system that separates the races in that country. Similarly, in Passage A, you could imagine how an attitude like the narrator's at home might be demonstrated by a schoolchild in class. The narrator of Passage A is close to his mother and becomes somewhat irritated when someone else (his father) intrudes. That feeling is rather similar to that of a schoolchild who feels possessive of his or her teacher and irritated when others (classmates) make demands on the teacher's attention.

Furthermore, once you understand the theme of a story, it is possible to transfer the insights you gain about human behavior and experience to new situations. For example, if the theme in the novel about the civil-rights worker were "one person can make a difference," you could apply that theme to a story about keeping a marriage alive, or repealing mandatory retirement, or even saving a disease-plagued alien civilization.

Applying the Author's Attitude

In a work of fiction, you can determine the attitude of the author by remembering not only the theme of the story but also the characters and events that the author has emphasized. For example, suppose that many events in a plot revealed the author's love for wild animals. Now imagine that this author is a senator who is faced with a law that denies protection to an endangered species. You could assume that the author would campaign for the rejection of such a law.

It is true that you may not gain much factual knowledge from a given work of fiction. The knowledge you can gain about human nature and human relationships, however, can be applied elsewhere. It can increase your understanding of yourself, of the people around you, and of the world.

Lesson 4 Exercise

1. If the father in Passage A were later killed in the war, do you think that boy would mourn for him? Explain your answer.
2. State whether the following is TRUE or FALSE and explain your answer: The author of Passage B probably would approve of community programs such as Meals on Wheels and federal programs such as Medicare.
3. Think about the character of Marian in Passage B. If an adult who thought like Marian were choosing a career, which career goal would seem more attractive—helping other people or helping oneself to get ahead?

Answers are on page A-33.

Lesson 5 Analyzing Fiction

How can an author's style, purpose, and use of irony affect the reader?

Style

Authors of fiction can approach a subject in any number of ways and can use a variety of techniques to tell a story effectively. Every story has a distinctive **style**—that is, the way in which a story is written reflects the author's personality. Style is an author's characteristic way of writing, and several elements help make an author's style distinctive.

Some authors are known for their ability to describe. Choosing vivid words and appealing to the reader's senses make descriptive writing memorable. Passages A and B contain a great deal of description; note these examples:

> Each time he left a trail of souvenirs—model tanks and Gurkha knives with handles made of bullet cases, and German helmets and cap badges and button-sticks, and all sorts of military equipment—carefully stowed away in a long box on top of the wardrobe, in case they ever came in handy.

[Passage A, lines 11–16]

This decided the nurse. Stopping in her tracks, she first extended her arm, bent her elbow, and leaned forward from the hips—all to examine the watch strapped to her wrist; then she gave a loud double-rap on the door.

[Passage B, lines 30–33]

The example from Passage A uses nouns to describe. The list of items that the father has collected is not intended primarily to make the reader remember the individual items; rather, the author wants the reader to be affected by the overall impression—by the number and variety of the father's "treasures." That impression could encourage the reader to like the father. The example from Passage B uses verbs to describe. Focusing on the nurse's odd actions (using so many actions just to check her watch), the description leads the reader to feel uneasy about the woman and even mistrustful of her.

Many authors are known for either the simplicity or complexity of their writing. Both kinds of writing can be used effectively. Writing that contains many long, complicated sentences may result in a slower, more thoughtful reading. On the other hand, writing that contains sentences that are relatively brief produce a very matter-of-fact effect.

Some authors are known for their wordplay. They may give new meanings to old words or include very clever conversation in their works. They also may make heavy use of figurative language. Such authors seem to love language itself, not just the art of storytelling, and they are appealing to readers who share that love of language.

Purpose and Audience

An author who writes many books usually has different reasons for writing each one. The **purpose,** or intent, often changes from story to story. Similarly, the author's expectations about his or her **audience,** or probable readers, may change. In both cases, the author's style will reflect the author's purpose and will attempt to reach a given audience. For example, an author whose style is marked by vivid description and figurative language may be writing both to tell a story and to impress the reader with the beauty of the writing itself. Likewise, an author who uses simple sentence structure and little description probably wants to create an impression of sparseness, perhaps to stress a feeling of isolation or emptiness in the characters in the story.

Irony

Sometimes one purpose in an author's work is to surprise the reader. In **irony,** the author presents information about characters or plot that goes against what the audience has come to believe. By using irony, the author can twist the reader's expectations and create a surprise. Read this example:

"I admit it!" gasped the detective. "I—yes, I—murdered Major Hawthorne!"

In the investigation of a murder, the detective would be the least likely suspect. Therefore, a murder mystery would have an ironic turn of plot if it were discovered that the detective was the actual murderer. Sometimes the surprise can be humorous; at other times, it can be tragic. By including irony in a work of fiction, however, an author makes the reader stop and think again about what the story is intended to show.

Lesson 5 Exercise

1. What kinds of details does the author of Passage A include to help his audience understand the way a five-year-old thinks?
2. Does the atmosphere suggested in Passage B indicate a pleasant experience ahead for Marian? Explain your answer.
3. State whether the following is TRUE or FALSE and explain your answer: Because the major character in Passage A is very young, the passage is probably intended to be read by children.
4. Imagine a story about an adult who is afraid of the dark. Which of the following plot events would be ironic for such a character?
   - The adult is caught in a blackout.
   - The adult overcomes his or her fear through the help of a friend.

Answers are on pages A-33—A-34.

Chapter 3   Quiz

Items 1 to 10 are based on the following passage.

WHAT IS THE TOPIC OF THIS COUPLE'S DISCUSSION?

The woman brought two glasses of beer and two felt pads. She put the felt pads and the beer glasses on the table and looked at the man and the girl. The girl was looking off at the line of hills. They were white in the sun and the country was brown and dry.

(5) "They look like white elephants," she said.
"I've never seen one," the man drank his beer.
"No, you wouldn't have."
"I might have," the man said. "Just because you say I wouldn't have doesn't prove anything."

(10) The girl looked at the bead curtain. "They've painted something on it," she said. "What does it say?"
"Anis del Toro. It's a drink."
"Could we try it?"

(15) The man called "Listen" through the curtain. The woman came out from the bar.

"Four reales."

"We want two Anis del Toro."

"With water?"

"Do you want it with water?"

(20) "I don't know," the girl said. "Is it good with water?"

"It's all right."

"You want them water?" asked the woman.

"Yes, with water."

"It tastes like licorice," the girl said and put the glass down.

(25) "That's the way with everything."

"Yes," said the girl. "Everything tastes of licorice. Especially all the things you've waited so long for. . . ."

"Oh, cut it out."

"You started it," the girl said. "I was being amused. I was having (30) a fine time."

"Well, let's try to have a fine time."

"All right. I was trying. I said the mountains looked like white elephants. Wasn't that bright?"

"That was bright."

(35) "I wanted to try this new drink. That's all we do, isn't it—look at things and try new drinks?"

"I guess so."

The girl looked across at the hills.

From "Hills Like White Elephants" by Ernest Hemingway. Copyright 1955 by Ernest Hemingway. Reprinted with permission of Charles Scribner's Sons, Inc.

1. What is "Anis del Toro"?
   (1) the name of the town
   (2) the name of a drink
   (3) the man's secret identity
   (4) the name of the bar
   (5) the name of the nearby mountains
2. State whether the following is TRUE or FALSE and explain your answer: There are indications in this passage that the girl and the man have known each other for some time.
3. The author states that the hills "were white in the sun and the country was brown and dry" (lines 3–4). How does this early description help to introduce the two major characters?
4. Do the characters in this passage interact primarily through physical action or through dialogue?

5. The girl uses a simile to compare the hills to white elephants. Is this figure of speech intended to produce a positive mental image or a negative mental image? Explain your answer.

6. When the girl says, "Everything tastes of licorice" (line 26), she means that this trip
   (1) will provide her with many sweet memories
   (2) has been too exotic for her to appreciate fully
   (3) makes her feel like a child
   (4) has been full of happy surprises
   (5) is proving to be a disappointment

7. State whether the following is TRUE or FALSE and explain your answer: From questions such as "Wasn't that bright?" it seems that the girl needs to know that the man approves of her.

8. Is the narrator of this story a first-person participant, a first-person observer, or a third-person?

9. Note the couple's discussion of their search for "a fine time" and the activities that make up a large part of that search (lines 31–36). Which of the following activities would the couple be most likely to pursue in their search for a "fine time"?
   (1) a reunion with old friends
   (2) attending a lecture at a museum
   (3) a visit to a new nightclub
   (4) a visit to the couple's parents
   (5) listening to classical music

10. Briefly describe the kind of audience for whom you think this story is intended.

Answers are on page A-34.

Chapter 4: Drama

Objective

In this chapter, you will

- Read and answer questions about what drama is and what makes it different from other forms of literature
- Read two excerpts from works of drama
- Read and write about the techniques that playwrights use to communicate their ideas

Lesson 1 What Drama Is

What is drama?

Elements of Drama

Drama shares some common elements with other forms of literature. Like fiction, drama tells a story and contains plot, character, setting, and theme. Like all literature, drama uses figurative language. But unlike other forms of literature, drama is written to be performed. A **play** is a work of drama. Authors of plays, known as **playwrights,** create stories and characters with the intention of having them presented on a stage before an audience. Other types of plays may be intended for television (**teleplay**) or film (**screenplay**).

Because drama is written to be performed, it has a different appearance on the page than other kinds of literature. For example, read the following passage from a play:

(*The scene opens with* SUSAN *reading on a couch in the living room. Her daughter,* KATHY, *enters.*)

KATHY: Mom, where's my new shirt?

SUSAN (*looking up*): I have no idea, dear.

(5) KATHY (*getting irritated*): But I left it on the kitchen table.

SUSAN (*looking down at book*): Then I probably moved it.

KATHY (*getting angry*): Why don't you leave my stuff alone? (*Stamps out of the room.*)

399

This play excerpt consists of three basic parts common to all drama:

- **stage directions**: These appear in italics, or parentheses, or both. Stage directions are important because they give you information about the setting and about the actions of the characters.
- **character names**: These often appear in capital letters or boldface type to the left of the page. The character names always let you know who is speaking.
- **dialogue**: This is found after the character's name.

It is important to imagine the stage, setting, and action of the play while you read. The better you are able to see and hear a play in your head, the better you will be able to understand that play.

The following passages from plays will be used as references throughout this chapter. Before you read, use the purpose question that begins each passage to help you focus on important ideas.

Passage A

HOW DO THE CHARACTERS DIFFER IN THEIR THOUGHTS ABOUT LIFE?

WALTER: I want so many things that they are driving me kind of crazy. Mama—look at me.

MAMA: I'm looking at you. You are a good-looking boy. You got a job, a nice wife, a fine boy and—

(5) WALTER: A job. (*Looks at her.*) Mama, a job? I open and close car doors all day long. I drive a man around in his limousine and say, "Yes, sir," "No, sir," "Very good, sir," "Shall I take the drive, sir?" Mama, that ain't no kind of job—that ain't nothing at all. (*Very quietly.*) Mama, I don't know if I can make you understand.

(10) (*Crosses D.R.C. to* MAMA *on sofa.*)

MAMA: Understand what, baby?

WALTER: (*Quietly.*) Sometimes it's like I can see the future stretched out in front of me—just plain as day. The future, Mama. Hanging over there at the edge of my days. Just waiting for me—a big, looming blank
(15) space—full of *nothing*. Just waiting for me. But it don't have to be. (*Big pause.* WALTER *waits—crosses to* MAMA.) Mama—sometimes when I'm downtown driving that man around and I pass them cool, quiet-looking restaurants where them white boys are sitting back and talking 'bout things—(*He kneels L. end of sofa near* MAMA *on the sofa.*) Sitting there
(20) turning deals worth millions of dollars—sometimes I see guys don't look much older than me—

MAMA: Son—how come you talk so much 'bout money?

WALTER: (*With immense passion.*) Because it is life, Mama!

MAMA: (*Quietly.*) Oh—(*Very quietly.*) So now money is life. Once upon
(25) a time freedom used to be life—now it's money.

WALTER: No—it was always money, Mama. We just didn't know about it.

MAMA: No—something has changed. (*She looks at him.*) You something new, boy. In my time we was worried about not being lynched and getting to the North if we could and how to stay alive and still have a
(30) pinch of dignity too—Now here come you and Beneatha—talking about things we ain't never even thought about hardly, me and your daddy. You ain't satisfied or proud of nothing we done. I mean that you had a home; that we kept you out of trouble till you was grown; that you don't have to ride to work on the back of nobody's street car—You my
(35) children—but how different we done become.

From *A Raisin in the Sun* by Lorraine Hansberry. Copyright 1959 by Robert Nemiroff as Executor of the Estate of Lorraine Hansberry. Reprinted with permission of Random House, Inc.

Passage B

HOW DO NAMES INFLUENCE US?

JACK: Charming day it has been, Miss Fairfax.

GWENDOLEN: Pray don't talk to me about the weather, Mr. Worthing. Whenever people talk to me about the weather, I always feel quite certain that they mean something else. And that makes me so nervous.

(5) JACK: I do mean something else.

GWENDOLEN: I thought so. In fact, I am never wrong.

JACK: And I would like to be allowed to take advantage of Lady Bracknell's temporary absence. . . .

GWENDOLEN: I would certainly advise you to do so. Mamma has a way of
(10) coming back suddenly into a room that I have often had to speak to her about.

JACK (*nervously*): Miss Fairfax, ever since I met you I have admired you more than any girl . . . I have ever met since . . . I met you.

GWENDOLEN: Yes, I am quite aware of the fact. And I often wish that in
(15) public, at any rate, you had been more demonstrative. For me you have always had an irresistible fascination. Even before I met you I was far from indifferent to you. (JACK *looks at her in amazement.*) We live, as I hope you know, Mr. Worthing, in an age of ideals. The fact is constantly mentioned in the more expensive monthly magazines, and has
(20) reached the provincial pulpits I am told: and my ideal has always been to love someone of the name of Ernest. There is something in that name that inspires absolute confidence. The moment Algernon first mentioned to me that he had a friend called Ernest, I knew I was destined to love you.

(25) JACK: You really love me, Gwendolen?

GWENDOLEN: Passionately!

JACK: Darling! You don't know how happy you've made me.

GWENDOLEN: My own Ernest!

JACK: But you don't really mean to say that you couldn't love me if my
(30) name wasn't Ernest?

GWENDOLEN: But your name is Ernest.

JACK: Yes, I know it is. But supposing it was something else? Do you mean to say you couldn't love me then?

(35) GWENDOLEN (*glibly*): Ah! that is clearly a metaphysical speculation, and like most metaphysical speculations has very little reference at all to the actual facts of real life, as we know them.

From *The Importance of Being Earnest* by Oscar Wilde.

Lesson 1 Exercise

1. How is drama different from other forms of literature?
2. How can you tell that Passages A and B are not examples of fiction?
3. Which passage contains more stage directions: Passage A or Passage B?

Answers are on page A-34.

Lesson 2 Comprehending Drama on a Literal Level

How do stage directions add life to a play?

Most fiction contains a mixture of description and dialogue. Drama, on the other hand, consists mainly of dialogue that is interrupted occasionally with stage directions. To find out the basic facts about the events, people, and setting of a play, it is important to be sure to read both the dialogue and stage directions.

Fiction writers can spend pages describing the events and explaining the conflicts in their plots. Playwrights, however, must use dialogue and stage directions to convey plot details. The conversation between two characters in the first scene of a play might give information about action that took place before the play began. That same conversation might introduce you to the basic situation or main conflict of the play.

Look again at Passage A. Many background facts are presented in this conversation. For example, you learn that Walter is married. The dialogue also shows that the characters' different feelings about the importance of money will probably result in an important conflict in the play.

Playwrights also use dialogue and stage directions to convey basic information about characters. By paying close attention to the dialogue and stage directions, you can often determine how old characters are, what they look like, how they are related, and what they do for a living.

Finally, dialogue and stage directions can help you to grasp the setting of a play. Sometimes playwrights will state the setting directly in their stage directions. At other times, a conversation between characters will reveal the time period and location of a play. To read a play successfully you should try to imagine how the dialogue would sound being spoken, and try to picture the stage directions being performed.

Lesson 2   Exercise

1. According to Passage A, what does Walter do for a living?
2. Based on the evidence in Passage B, what is the relationship between Lady Bracknell and Gwendolen?
3. In Passage B the male character is named Jack, but what does Gwendolen think his name is?

Answers are on pages A-34—A-35.

Lesson 3   Comprehending Drama on an Inferential Level

In what ways are inferential skills helpful when reading plays?

Fiction writers can describe their characters' looks and thoughts, the scenery, things that happened before the opening of their story, and so on. But playwrights cannot do such things. Because their dramas take place on a stage that is supposed to represent the real world, they must rely on other devices to make their audience understand what is happening in the story.

Playwrights sometimes convey plot details and setting directly either through stage directions or dialogue. However, such information is more often implied indirectly. Imagine, for instance, a situation in a play in which two people are having a chat in an apartment. If the playwright wants the audience to know that the scene takes place in New York City, one character might look out a window and point out how beautiful the Empire State Building looks in the sunset. It would not be realistic to have a character say: "We are in New York City," because both characters always know that and would not be likely in real life to say something they both know. Instead, the playwright has told the audience where the scene takes place in such a way that the information seems to come naturally. The playwright has implied the information without stating it directly.

Motivation

Because many plays rely heavily on inference, inferential skills are essential in helping you to understand the characters in a play and their actions. To figure out what characters are like, you must pay attention not only to what they say and do, but to what other characters say about them. You also should read the stage directions for information that will help you to make conclusions about the feelings and motives of these characters.

When you read a play, you do not have the advantage either of seeing a character's facial expressions or hearing the rhythms or tones of that character's voice. It is therefore even more important when reading a play instead of seeing it on stage, to be able to make logical guesses, or inferences, from the dialogue and stage directions. Look at line 24 in Passage A. Since the stage directions tell you that Mama is speaking "very quietly," you might infer that she is very upset at what Walter has said. If, instead, you were told that she was laughing as she spoke, you might infer that she was amused by Walter. You can see from this how important inference can be to understanding a character's deeper feelings.

Mood

Inferential skills are also important in helping you to determine the mood of a work of drama. Playwrights, unlike authors of fiction, cannot use long descriptive passages to set the mood of a piece. In a play, mood can be shown by events, by the development of the characters, and even by the way the scenery is designed. For example, a play that focuses on the birth of a much-wanted child would probably set a warm, happy tone. The stage directions might call for brightly colored costumes and pleasant, natural lighting. In contrast, a play about a murder would probably require a sinister mood, which might be conveyed by dark costumes and gloomy lighting. In either case, you can infer the mood of the play by paying careful attention to such details. Remember, too, that the playwright has a good reason for adding even the smallest detail, so you should ignore none of these elements, no matter how trivial or unimportant they may seem at first.

Lesson 3 Exercise

1. State whether the following is TRUE or FALSE and explain your answer: Passage A takes place in a living room.
2. State whether the following is TRUE or FALSE and explain your answer: Jack's use of a fake name, in Passage B, suggests that he dislikes Gwendolen.
3. Based on information in Passage A, would you infer that Walter is black or white? Give two reasons for your answer.
4. What two remarks can you find in Passage B that suggest Gwendolen is either a thoughtful or a shallow person?
5. Based on the conversation in Passage A, tell in two or three sentences what the playwright is implying about parents and children.

Answers are on page A-35.

Lesson 4 Applying Ideas in Drama

How can the action in a play be applied to other situations?

Like fiction writers, playwrights write about people and the experiences people have. In their plays, they show how people behave in certain situations. They also illustrate some of the basic characteristics and conflicts of life. When you read a play you gain insights about the author's view of human experiences. Such knowledge about people and life can be applied to different situations.

Applying Main Ideas and Details

In Passage A, you learned something about the kind of people Walter and his mother are. Walter feels that money is the most important thing in life. In contrast, Mama realizes that material goods are not the essence of life (lines 24–25).

Try to picture this conflict in a different situation. How would wealthy parents react if their child decided to join the Peace Corps instead of working in the family business? How might their views differ from their child's view on what is important in life?

Passage A also gives you information about human experience that you can apply to different situations. For instance, Mama's speech suggests that people who have struggled through persecution often look at life differently. Do you think similar conflicts occurred between American-born children and their refugee parents? What else do you learn about relationships between family members in this passage? If you understand, after reading the passage, that family members often see the world in different ways and come into conflict, then you have applied the knowledge you gained in the passage.

Applying the Author's Attitude

The author's attitude about the subject of the play usually is represented in the dialogue. For example, toward the end of Passage B (lines 32–33), Jack becomes uneasy about Gwendolen's strong feelings about the name Ernest. Because he is using a false name, Jack realizes that trouble will develop soon. The author shows that problems develop when people misrepresent themselves or deceive others in business matters, social situations, and the like. Knowing that this is the playwright's attitude, you can imagine what the playwright might think about other situations. For example, the author would probably disapprove of people who pretended to be rich in order to be accepted.

Lesson 4   Exercise

1. Would Walter's mother be happy or unhappy if he took a job that he didn't like but that paid him much more money?
2. In two or three sentences, describe how Gwendolen might feel if she were asked to change her name.

3. Imagine that Mama has been offered a beautiful new home, but that it is 2000 miles away from her family. Do you think she would move? Explain your answer.

4. Tell whether the following is TRUE or FALSE and explain your answer: Gwendolen would be more likely to buy a coat with a designer label than a warmer, more useful coat.

Answers are on page A-35.

Lesson 5   Analyzing Drama

What are the important techniques used by playwrights?

Playwrights use a variety of techniques to help them shape their ideas about people and life into a drama. They depend on both dialogue and gestures to convey meaning. They also depend on such techniques as setting and figurative language to tell their stories.

Dialogue

Playwrights do not have the opportunity to describe the action and people in as much detail as a novelist does. As a result, they must depend on dialogue to reveal events that happened before the play began or to explain the basic situation of the play. Before the twentieth century, for example, authors often would open their plays with a conversation between two servants. From this conversation readers or theatergoers would learn not only about past events and present conflicts, but also something about the characters in the play.

The kind of words playwrights use in the dialogue of their plays also reveals something about what each character is like. For example, if a character said, "I made a speech in class today and I was very good," it shows self-confidence. Rough language might indicate that a character has a mean or violent nature, whereas difficult, complicated words could suggest that a character is well-educated or a show-off (or both).

Gestures

When you read a play you must look closely at the stage directions to figure out the gestures and actions of the characters. These gestures and actions are important, since they often reveal more about a character's feelings or personality. For instance, in a direction such as, *The bride and groom come down the aisle, radiant, but trying to be very dignified*, we see that they are happy but are trying to act the way they think a mature married couple should. Playwrights, moreover, can use their characters' exits from and entrances onto the stage to move along the plot and to create suspense.

Setting and Figurative Language

Like fiction writers, playwrights sometimes use setting to emphasize the theme or meaning of their works. In Arthur Miller's *Death of a Salesman*, the setting represents, or symbolizes, one of the play's main ideas. In this instance, the skyscrapers that surround and tower over Willy Loman's house illustrate the pressures that society places on this man.

Figurative language is as important to playwrights as it is to all writers of literature. In plays, however, figurative language must be spoken by characters in the dialogue. As a result, playwrights must be careful to use comparisons and other figures of speech that are believable for the character who speaks them.

Many of the techniques found in works of drama are similar to those used in other types of literature. However, since some of the techniques playwrights use are designed for performance, it is important that you try to imagine the characters moving on a stage while you read. Picturing the movements and facial expressions of the characters can add to the enjoyment and understanding of a play.

Lesson 5 Exercise

1. In Passage A, why are Mama's words about freedom and life (lines 24–25) so important to the scene?
2. In two or three sentences, tell how the author uses the dialogue in the last eight lines of Passage B to show that there will be an important conflict in the play.
3. State whether the following is TRUE or FALSE and explain your answer: Walter's movements in Passage B suggest that he is agitated.
4. "The future, Mama. Hanging over there at the edge of my days. Just waiting for me—a big looming blank space—full of *nothing*." (Passage A, lines 13–15) What is the purpose of the author's use of figurative language in these lines?

Answers are on page A-35.

Chapter 4   Quiz

Items 1 to 5 are based on the following passage.

WHY DOESN'T JOHNNY WANT TO WORK?

JULIA: Johnny, I've known quite a few men who don't work—and of all the footling, unhappy existences—it's conceivable that you could stand it—it's unthinkable you could!

JOHNNY: I might do it differently.

(5) JULIA: Differently!

JOHNNY (*a moment, then*): Julia, do you love me? (*She looks at him swiftly, then looks away.*)

JULIA (*slowly*): You—you have a great time standing me against a wall and throwing knives around me, don't you? (*In an instant he has taken (10) her in his arms.*)

JOHNNY: Oh, sweet—

JULIA (*against his shoulder*): What do you do things like that for? What's the matter with you, anyway?

JOHNNY (*he stands off and looks at her*): Haven't you the remotest idea (15) of what I'm after? (*She looks at him, startled.*) I'm after—all that's in me, all I am. I want to get it out—where I can look at it, know it. That takes time. Can't you understand that?

JULIA: But you haven't an idea yet of how exciting *business* can be—you're just beginning! Oh, Johnny, see it through! You'll love it. I know you (20) will. There's no such thrill in the world as making money. It's the most—what are you staring at?

JOHNNY: Your face.

JULIA (*she turns away*): Oh—you won't listen to me—you won't hear me—

From HOLIDAY by Philip Barry. Copyright 1955, 1956 (in renewal) by Ellen S. Barry. Reprinted with permission of Samuel French, Inc.

1. Complete this sentence: Julia wants Johnny to pursue a career in _____.
2. In your own words, tell what the passage implies about what Johnny wants to do.
3. Why is Julia's line "What are you staring at?" (line 21) so startling?
    (1) It shows Johnny's approval of Julia.
    (2) It reflects his wish to be left alone by everyone—including Julia.
    (3) It indicates Johnny's sudden realization that he doesn't really know Julia.
    (4) It reveals that Johnny is feeling very pleased with his mastery of the conversation.
    (5) It indicates Johnny's realization that he agrees with Julia.
4. State whether the following is TRUE or FALSE and explain your answer: Julia is finding it difficult to understand Johnny's position.
5. Which of the following statements best describes Johnny's feelings toward Julia as illustrated by the dialogue?
    (1) He loves Julia.
    (2) He is happy with Julia.
    (3) He is worried about Julia.
    (4) He is disappointed with Julia.
    (5) He is furious at Julia.

Items 6 to 10 are based on the following passage.

WHAT PLAN DO NORA AND LAURIE DEVISE?

LAURIE: So? What are you going to do?

NORA: I don't know. Leave me alone. Don't just sit there watching me.

LAURIE: It's my room as much as yours. I don't have to leave if I don't want to.

(5) NORA: Do you have to stare at me? Can't I have any privacy?

LAURIE: I'm staring into space. I can't help it if your body interferes. (*There is a pause.*) I bet you're worried?

NORA: How would you feel if your entire life depended on what your Uncle Jack decided? . . . Oh, God, I wish Daddy were alive.

(10) LAURIE: He would have said "No." He was really *strict*.

NORA: Not with me. I mean, he was strict but he was fair. If he said "No," he always gave you a good reason. He always talked things out . . . I wish I could call him somewhere now and ask him what to do. One three-minute call to heaven is all I ask.

(15) LAURIE: Ask Mom. She talks to him every night.

NORA: Who told you that?

LAURIE: She did. Every night before she goes to bed. She puts his picture on her pillow and talks to him. Then she pulls the blanket halfway up the picture and goes to sleep.

(20) NORA: Oh, God, he was so handsome. Always dressed so dapper, his shoes always shined. I always thought he should have been a movie star . . . like Gary Cooper . . . only very short. Mostly I remember his pockets.

LAURIE: His pockets?

(25) NORA: When I was six or seven he always brought me home a little surprise. Like a Hershey or a top. He'd tell me to go get it in his coat pocket. So I'd run to the closet and put my hand in and it felt as big as a tent. I wanted to crawl in there and go to sleep. And there were all these terrific things in there, like Juicy Fruit gum or Spearmint Life
(30) Savers and bits of cellophane and crumbled pieces of tobacco and movie stubs and nickels and pennies and rubber bands and paper clips and his gray suede gloves that he wore in the wintertime.

LAURIE: With the stitched lines down the fingers. I remember.

NORA: Then I found his coat in Mom's closet and I put my hand in the
(35) pocket. And everything was gone. It was emptied and dry-cleaned and it felt cold . . . And that's when I knew he was really dead. (*She thinks for a moment.*) Oh, God, I wish we had our own place to live. I hate being a boarder. Listen, let's make a pact . . . The first one who makes

(40) enough money promises not to spend any on herself, but saves it all to get a house for you and me and Mom. That means every penny we get from now on, we save for the house. We can't buy *anything*. No lipstick or magazines or nail polish or bubble gum. *Nothing* . . . Is it a pact?

LAURIE: (*Thinks*) What about movies?

(45) NORA: Movies too.

LAURIE: Starting when?

NORA: Starting today. Starting right now.

LAURIE: Can we start Sunday? I wanted to see *The Thin Man*.

NORA: Who's in it?

(50) LAURIE: William Powell and Myrna Loy.

NORA: Okay. Starting Sunday . . . I'll go with you Saturday.

From *Brighton Beach Memoirs* by Neil Simon. Copyright 1984 by Neil Simon. Reprinted with permission of Random House, Inc.

6. How are Nora and Laurie related?
7. Do lines 3–7 imply any conflict between Nora and Laurie? Explain your answer.
8. If Laurie and Nora did not share a room, do you think they would have agreed to their pact as quickly?
9. Are both of Nora and Laurie's parents alive?
10. Suppose Nora could discuss her problems with both of her parents. Would she be less upset?

Answers are on pages A-35–A-36.

Chapter 5 Poetry

> **Objective**
>
> In this chapter, you will learn about an unusual form of imaginative literature. In your study of the genre known as **poetry,** you will
>
> - Read and answer questions about what poetry is
> - Study some of the techniques that poets use to evoke feelings and to communicate ideas
> - Read two poems about remembering—one dealing with family relationships, the other dealing with nature
> - Read and write about the elements of poetry

Lesson 1 What Poetry Is

What makes poetry special?

A poem can create a mood, tell a story, concentrate on the characteristics of a person, or examine the meaning of an important idea. Like fiction and drama, **poetry** is imaginative literature; its essence comes from the author's mind. It concentrates more on ideas and feelings than on factual information.

Poetry has a unique **form.** A poem usually consists of **lines** that begin in definite places (for example, every fourth line indented, or only the last two lines indented). Its look on a page is quite different from that of a work of drama or other works of prose (nonpoetry), which usually appears as a series of paragraphs. Furthermore, many poems **rhyme,** or have similar sounds (especially at the ends of lines), as well as a regular **rhythm.** You may know children's poems or song lyrics with these characteristics.

However, there is more to poetry than rhyme and rhythm. Some poems do not rhyme. Some poems do not have a regular rhythm. A major characteristic of all poetry is its use of **compact language.** Unlike authors of other kinds of literature, poets express themselves in an extremely limited space. As a result, poets choose words very carefully and often use figurative language to bring other levels of meaning into their work. They also can use the sound, rhythm, and connotations of words to convey meaning. The poet Amy Lowell once said, "Concentration is the very essence of poetry." Because poetry is "concentrated," you should ask yourself questions as you read and be prepared to read every poem at least twice to be sure that you understand the poet's meaning. You may find that the poem has several meanings, some of which become apparent only after you have worked with the various poetic characteristics.

The following two poems will be used as references throughout this chapter. Before you read, use the purpose question that begins each poem to help you to focus on important ideas.

Poem A

HOW DOES THE POET FEEL TOWARD HIS FATHER?

    The whiskey on your breath
    Could make a small boy dizzy;
    But I hung on like death:
    Such waltzing was not easy.

(5) We romped until the pans
    Slid from the kitchen shelf;
    My mother's countenance
    Could not unfrown itself.

    The hand that held my wrist
(10) Was battered on one knuckle;
    At every step you missed
    My right ear scraped a buckle.

    You beat time on my head
    With a palm caked hard by dirt,
(15) Then waltzed me off to bed
    Still clinging to your shirt.

"My Papa's Waltz" by Theodore Roethke. Copyright 1942 by Hearst Magazines Inc. Reprinted with permission of Doubleday & Company, Inc.

Poem B

WHAT DOES THE POET WANT TO REMEMBER ABOUT SUMMER?

    Lyric night of the lingering Indian Summer,
    Shadowy fields that are scentless but full of singing,
    Never a bird, but the passionless chant of insects,
        Ceaseless, insistent.

(5) The grasshopper's horn, and far-off, high in the maples,
    The wheel of a locust leisurely grinding in the silence
    Under a moon warning and worn, broken,
        Tired with summer.

    Let me remember you, voices of little insects,
(10) Weeds in the moonlight, fields that are tangled with asters,
    Let me remember, soon will the winter be on us,
        Snow-hushed and heavy.

Over my soul murmur your mute benediction,
While I gaze, O fields that rest after harvest,
(15) As those who part look long in the eyes they lean to,
Lest they forget them.

"Indian Summer" by Sara Teasdale. From *Collected Poems* (New York: Macmillan Publishing Company, 1920, renewed 1948 by Mamie T. Wheless).

Lesson 1   Exercise

1. Why is poetry classified as imaginative literature?
2. Is each of the following statements TRUE or FALSE? Explain your answers.
   - A poem cannot contain characters and action.
   - The lines of a poem can be of different lengths.
   - A poem can rhyme.
3. Poem A and Poem B are each 16 lines long. Which poem do you think concentrates more on ideas and feelings than on factual information? Explain your answer.

   Answers are on page A-36.

Lesson 2   Comprehending Poetry on a Literal Level

What should you look for to find the literal meaning of a poem?

Kinds of Poems

There are two basic kinds of poems. **Narrative poems** tell a story. They have characters, setting, and plot. **Lyric poems** concentrate on the poet's thoughts and emotions. Poem B is a lyric poem. At first glance, Poem A may seem to be a narrative poem, but its major focus is on the poet's thoughts rather than on his telling of events in a plot, so Poem A is also a lyric poem.

Title

When you are considering the literal meaning of a poem, look first for its **title**, if one is given. The title can provide you with useful information. For example, the title of Poem A is "My Papa's Waltz." Even before you begin to read the poem, you know that its subject is probably the poet's father and that dancing will somehow be part of the description. The title of Poem B—"Indian Summer"—establishes the time of year about which the poet will speak.

As you read a poem, repeat the title after each verse. Even when the poem uses figurative language that may make the subject less clear, the title can help you to grasp its meaning.

Stated Main Idea (Theme)

Occasionally a poet will state the **main idea,** or **theme,** of a poem directly. In such cases, you should be able to locate a line or phrase in the poem that sums up the poet's thoughts and feelings about the subject. The main idea of Poem B, for example, is expressed twice, in lines 9 and 11: "Let me remember. . . ." The poet wishes to hold in her memory all the things that make Indian summer such a special time. She wants you, the reader, to know that this wish runs deep within her.

Literal Reading of Details

By asking yourself the meanings of words and phrases in a poem, and then looking up any words that are unfamiliar, you can determine the basic situation of that poem.

Look at lines 1–8 of Poem A. Notice the details that describe the vigorousness of the dance. The dancing made pans fall from the kitchen shelf (lines 5–6) and made the mother frown deeply (lines 7–8). It was a "hard" kind of dancing—"not easy" (line 4).

Poem A also provides many vivid details about the father himself. In lines 9–16, the poet states that the father had a "battered . . . knuckle" (line 10) and "a palm caked hard by dirt" (line 14). From these literal details you can determine that the poem is set in the poet's childhood home and that its major focus is on the poet's vivid memories of his father's rather rough dance. There are other levels of meaning to this poem. However, by making that first determination about setting, based on the literal meanings of words, you are well on your way to discovering the richness of meaning in the poem.

The author of Poem B talks of her love for warm weather as she spends an evening outdoors during Indian summer (the warmer days that suddenly may appear in late fall or early winter). She lists the things about the last taste of summer that she wants to remember during the winter ahead. Most of this poem is devoted to her list of vivid memories.

Lesson 2   Exercise

1. In Poem A, what could make the boy dizzy?
2. State whether the following is TRUE or FALSE and explain your answer: The waltz in Poem A concludes when the mother angrily interrupts the dancers.

3. Name the four words that the author of Poem B uses to describe the moon (lines 7–8).
4. What is the source of the singing that is heard by the author of Poem B?

Answers are on page A-36.

Lesson 3   Comprehending Poetry on an Inferential Level

How can unstated information add another level of meaning to a poem?

Implied Main Idea (Theme)

Although some poems contain a clear statement of theme, many poems suggest their themes indirectly. Therefore, you often must rely heavily upon your inferential skills when you read poetry. When the theme is not stated directly, you must look at other aspects of the poem and draw conclusions about the important ideas.

Be careful not to confuse the theme of a poem with the subject of the poem or with the mood of the poem. The **subject** of a poem is its topic. In Poem A, for example, the subject is the poet's boyhood memory of waltzing with his father. The **theme** is an idea or insight that arises from that situation—in this case, perhaps an implied statement about the quality of the father-son relationship. The feelings and mental images expressed in the poem function as examples of the theme. The **mood** of a poem is the emotion or emotions that dominate it. For example, a poem full of images of spring would perhaps make use of words that create a mood of hope and happiness. An understanding of the subject and mood of a poem will help you to understand the theme.

Point of View

The **point of view** of a poem can add to its overall meaning. If a poet wants to emphasize the personal nature of a poem or wants to seem to take the reader into his or her confidence, he or she would be likely to use the word *I* to express the ideas in the poem. This way of expressing ideas is known as a *first-person point of view*. On the other hand, if the poet wants to take a more impersonal, less emotional approach to a subject or wants to create a feeling of distance, he or she probably would choose a *third-person point of view*.

The "I" of a poem may not always be the poet. Poets sometimes write as if they were other people. In such cases, they create a **speaker** to voice the views set forth in the poem. A speaker may be the "I" of the poem, but that speaker may not express the same views that the poet holds. Nevertheless, the use of a first-person point of view will maintain a closeness between the speaker (and, through that speaker, the poet) and the reader.

Figurative Language

One of the ways in which poetry differs most from other genres is in its reliance upon **figures of speech,** or **figurative language,** to express an author's thoughts. Figurative language is language that is used to express additional or special meaning—meaning that is more than just the "dictionary definition" of the words. Figurative language can express a great deal of meaning in the space of only a few words—that is, it is compact language. As such, it is ideal for poetry. In Chapter 3 you were introduced to **similes** and **metaphors,** the two most common kinds of figurative language.

As you may remember, a *simile* compares two unlike things by saying that one is *as* or *like* the other. "The clouds looked like sheep" is an example of a simile. In Poem B, the poet implies a comparison between a harvested field and a loved one. The poem concludes with a simile that compares the poet's gaze upon a harvested field with the way that a person gazes at a loved one who is going away: "I gaze, . . . As those who part look long in the eyes they lean to" (lines 14–15).

A *metaphor* compares two unlike things by saying that one *is* the other. For example, when the author of Poem B speaks of "The wheel of the locust leisurely grinding in the silence" (line 6), she is comparing the noise that a locust makes to the slow grinding of a wheel.

Another type of figurative language, found often in poetry, is **personification.** Personification occurs when a nonhuman object or creature is described as if it were human. In Poem B, for example, the author says that the moon is "Tired with summer" (line 8). She also asks the natural creatures and objects in that Indian summer evening to bless her (line 13).

Another kind of figurative language that is very important to poetry is **symbolism.** A symbol is an object that represents a larger idea. For example, in Poem B the "weeds in the moonlight" and the "fields that are tangled with asters" (line 10) symbolize life that has been lived to its fullest. The poet associates this quality with the rapidly departing Indian summer.

Lesson 3 Exercise

1. Quote two details from Poem A that suggest that the child may not be enjoying his father's "waltz."
2. Name the one simile that appears in Poem A. Restate the thought of that simile in your own words.
3. Give an example of personification that the author of Poem B uses to describe the fields upon which she is gazing.
4. Which two of the following words best describe how the speaker in Poem B feels about the close of summer? Explain your answer.
    - bitter   • sad   • relieved   • worried   • nostalgic   • amused

Answers are on page A-36.

Lesson 4 Applying Ideas in Poetry

How might a poem suggest an author's reaction to a given real-life situation?

Applying Themes and Details

You can apply what you learn from poetry about human nature and human experience to a variety of other situations.

The key to applying poetic themes and details is first to determine the ideas that a poet is expressing and then to consider those ideas at work in a new setting. For example, in Poem A you can conclude from a number of details that the father works hard (as evidenced by his battered knuckle and his dirt-encrusted hands) and "plays" hard (as evidenced by his rough dance and his implied drinking habits). "Translating" those conclusions into other areas of the man's life, you would have reason to conclude that he might express his emotions freely and perhaps even violently during moments of great joy or sorrow or stress. Similarly, if the theme of Poem A is that some family relationships are not as society expects them to be, you might see that theme at work in families from many backgrounds, not just the family background that is implied here.

Applying the Author's Attitude

In poetry, you can determine the attitude of the author by remembering the theme of the poem. Both literal and implied details (especially details expressed in figurative language) help to reveal the author's attitude, as well. For example, Poem B reveals the poet's love for natural detail. You might imagine that, if given a choice, she would prefer a bouquet of real flowers to a bouquet of plastic flowers. You might even conclude that she would prefer to have flowers growing in her garden than to have either kind of bouquet.

Lesson 4 Exercise

1. Do you think that the father in Poem A would make a good business executive? Why or why not?
2. The attitude of the author of Poem B toward the natural things of summer is similar to which of the following?
   - the attitude of some students toward their teacher's authority
   - the attitude of some parents toward their children's growing up
   - the attitude of some artists toward the source of their inspiration

3. Suppose that the author of Poem B were thinking about her own death instead of the coming winter. Based on information in the poem, do you think that she would be afraid to die? Explain your answer.

Answers are on pages A-36–A-37.

Lesson 5 Analyzing Poetry

What are some stylistic techniques that a poet might use to create a given mood?

Effects of Stylistic and Structural Techniques

A poet arranges the lines of a poem to create a given effect. For example, the lines can be arranged into **stanzas,** or groups, like verses of a song. The break between stanzas may indicate a shift in the poet's thoughts or some shift of focus in the poet's description. Poem A and Poem B both are arranged in stanzas. When the lines of a poem aren't broken up into stanzas, the poet probably intends for the poem to be considered as one continuous thought.

Furthermore, the lines themselves can vary in length to achieve an effect. Poem A, for example, has rather short lines. One effect of such a short line could be to imitate the breathless talk of a boy who has just participated in the kind of activity described in the poem. Notice also the very short fourth line of each stanza in Poem B. The length of that line catches the reader's attention and emphasizes the important ideas in the poem—the fullness of life in the scene (line 4), the soon departure of summer (line 8) and soon coming of winter (line 12), and the poet's own desire to remember that Indian summer evening (line 16).

Rhyme Scheme

The **rhyme scheme,** or pattern of similar sounds in a poem, also can help to achieve an overall effect. Although some rhymes take place within lines, most rhyming words appear at the ends of lines. In the second stanza of Poem A, for example, *shelf* (line 6) rhymes with *itself* (line 8). Sometimes, too, rhymes are not exact, as in *pans* (line 5) and *countenance* (line 7).

The rhyme scheme of a poem can be described with letters. For example, in the stanza from Poem A that was just discussed, the sound of the last word in the first line (*pans*) would be labeled with the letter *A*. Any end-of-line word that rhymes with it (*countenance*) would also be labeled with an *A*. The first different end-of-line sound (*shelf*) would be labeled with the letter *B*. Any end-of-line sound that rhymed with it (*itself*) would also be labeled with a *B*. When the letters are listed in the order of the lines in which they appear, the rhyme scheme becomes apparent: *A B A B*. The first end-of-line sound that did not rhyme with either *A* or *B* would be labeled with a *C*, then with a *D*, and so on.

Rhyme has two major functions in a poem. It can appeal to the reader purely on the basis of its excellence of expression. It also can help to show the division of a poet's thought: when the rhyme scheme changes (as from *A B A B* to *C D C D*), there often is a change of thought, too. For example, compare the first and second stanzas in Poem A. In the first stanza, the poet concentrates on the way he felt about *waltzing*. In the second stanza, the thought changes. The poet expands the view and lets the reader know how the *waltzing* affected his house and someone else who lived there (his mother).

Devices of Sound

You have already seen how poets can create mental images through similes, metaphors, and other figures of speech. Poets also can create images and moods through nonrhyming patterns of sound—both the kinds of sounds and the frequency with which those sounds are used.

Repetition is one way in which poets use sound to create a given effect. One common kind of repetition of sound is **alliteration.** Alliteration is the repeating of the same consonant sounds used to begin words. In Poem B, the author uses the beginning "W" sound to describe the moon as "warning" and "worn" (line 7). Such repetition helps the reader to develop a feeling for the mood that the poet is expressing. Notice also the frequency with which the beginning "L" sound appears in the final two lines of the poem ("look long . . . lean . . . Lest") and imitates the poet's own desire to linger over the scene.

Assonance is the repetition of vowel sounds in words. In the second stanza of Poem A, the short "I" sound appears four times ("until," "Slid," "kitchen," and "itself"). Assonance, too, can have a variety of effects. Perhaps in this case the shortness of the sound imitates the mother's shortness of patience, which is mentioned in the same stanza. The "OW" sound in "countenance" and "unfrown" may express the same idea. To make the sound, the reader's mouth moves in a slight frown, which also imitates the mother's reaction to the "waltzing." In Poem A, alliteration and assonance work together to give the poem a sing-song quality that reminds the reader of childhood poetry.

Another sound device, which may or may not be repeated, is **onomatopoeia**—the use of words whose pronunciation reflects their meaning. In Poem A, the pronunciation of *scraped* (line 12) suggests its meaning. Similarly, in Poem B, the word *murmur* (line 13) is an example of onomatopoeia. In both cases, the reader is encouraged to give special thought to the word and how its meaning adds to the imagery of the poem.

Lesson 5 Exercise

1. The lines in Poem B are rather long. What emotions of the poet might be reflected by the length of the lines?
2. Letter the rhyme scheme of the third and fourth stanzas of Poem A. (REMEMBER: *A B A B* and *C D C D* have been used for the first and second stanzas.)

3. Which poem makes greater use of alliteration? Explain your answer.
4. In the third stanza of Poem B, do the words *you* (line 9), *moonlight* (line 10), and *soon* (line 11) illustrate alliteration, assonance, or onomatopoeia? Explain your answer.

Answers are on page A-37.

Chapter 5   Quiz

Items 1 to 10 are based on the following poems.

Poem 1

WHY ARE DREAMS TO BE TREASURED?

    Hold fast to dreams
    For if dreams die
    Life is a broken-winged bird
    That cannot fly.

(5) Hold fast to dreams
    For when dreams go
    Life is a barren field
    Frozen with snow.

"Dreams" by Langston Hughes. Copyright 1932, 1960 by Langston Hughes. Reprinted with permission of Harold Ober Associates.

Poem 2

WHY IS THE SPIDER'S PATIENCE TO BE ADMIRED?

    A noiseless patient spider
    I mark'd where on a promontory it stood isolated,
    Mark'd how to explore the vacant vast surrounding,
    It launch'd forth filament, filament, filament, out of itself,
(5) Ever unreeling them, ever tirelessly speeding them.

    And you O my soul where you stand
    Surrounded, detached, in measureless oceans of space,
    Ceaselessly musing, venturing, throwing, seeking the spheres to connect them,
(10) Till the bridge you will need to be form'd, till the ductile armor hold,
    Till the gossamer thread you fling catch somewhere, O my soul.

"A Noiseless Patient Spider," by Walt Whitman.

1. Which of the following words best identifies the emotion that dominates Poem 1?
   - (1) loneliness
   - (2) despair
   - (3) contentment
   - (4) urgency
   - (5) anticipation

2. State whether the following is TRUE or FALSE and explain your answer: Both Poem 1 and Poem 2 depend heavily upon the use of simile to express the poet's ideas.

3. Is Poem 2 a narrative poem or a lyric poem? Explain your answer.

4. Name the sight that inspires the author of Poem 2.

5. What does the author of Poem 1 suggest by comparing a life without dreams to a "broken-winged bird" and a "barren field"?
   - (1) People must dream if they are to grow.
   - (2) People who dream are closer to nature.
   - (3) People should not spend so much time dreaming.
   - (4) The ability to dream is what separates people from animals.
   - (5) Most people have lost the ability to dream.

6. In Poem 2, why do you think the word *filament* is repeated?

7. State whether the following is TRUE or FALSE and explain your answer: In Poem 2, the "bridge" (line 10), the "ductile armor" (line 10) and the "gossamer thread" (line 11) all refer to the same idea.

8. In Poem 2, the work of the spider symbolizes
   - (1) the importance of perseverance
   - (2) each person's search for meaning in life
   - (3) the hopelessness of all human endeavor
   - (4) the satisfaction that beauty can bring to the human soul
   - (5) the selfish ambitions that people try to hide

9. Name one example of alliteration that appears in Poem 1 and one that appears in Poem 2.

10. Based on what he says in his poem, how might you expect the author of Poem 2 to feel about organized religion?

Answers are on page A-37.

Chapter 6 Commentary

> **Objective**
>
> In this chapter, you will learn about the ways in which people have expressed their feelings about literature and other forms of art in writing. In your study of **commentary,** you will
>
> - Read and answer questions about the functions of commentary and the different forms that commentary can take
> - Study the various techniques that writers of commentary use to organize and express their ideas
> - Read two examples of commentary—one an essay, the other a review
> - Read and write about the effectiveness of commentaries

Lesson 1 What Commentary Is

What is appropriate subject matter for commentary?

Nonfiction literature focuses on actual people and events. Imaginative literature—fiction, drama, or poetry—usually focuses on people and events that writers create. **Commentary,** on the other hand, is writing *about* literature and other kinds of creative works. In the past few chapters you have been reading about the **literary arts** (novels, poems, scripts of plays, and so on). However, there are other kinds of creative work—in particular, **visual arts** (such as painting, drawing, and sculpture) and **performing arts** (such as music, dance, films, plays in performance, and television). These three kinds of creative work are known together as "the arts," and all three are worthwhile subjects for commentary.

Why is commentary valuable? As you examine the passages in this chapter, you will discover that commentary serves three main purposes: (1) It *summarizes* or provides information about art; (2) it *analyzes* or shows how art achieves a particular effect; and (3) it *evaluates*, or makes judgments about the value of art.

Whatever its purpose, commentary generally takes one of two forms. A **review** focuses on the author's opinion of a particular work of art, often in limited performance—for example, a concert, an exhibition of photographs, or a dance recital. An **essay** focuses on broader issues regarding art—for example, the analysis of a trend in music or a contrast between two styles of painting.

The following two passages from commentaries will be used as references throughout this chapter. Before you read, use the purpose question that begins each passage to help you to focus on important ideas.

Passage A

WHAT IS THE DIFFERENCE BETWEEN A CHRISTIE BOOK AND A CHRISTIE MOVIE?

In its short essay on Agatha Christie, the *Columbia Encyclopedia* states that after the publication of *The Mysterious Affair at Styles* in 1920, Miss Christie went on to write a number of other books featuring Hercule Poirot, the Belgian detective. Among those books was
(5) *The Murder of Roger Ackroyd,* "famous for its unexpected ending." Miss Christie, who later became Dame Agatha, wrote many, many books, most of them immensely popular and famous for their unexpected endings.

These books encouraged dozens of imitators, some almost as suc-
(10) cessful as Dame Agatha. The imitators eventually inspired Edmund Wilson's classic essay, "Who Cares Who Killed Roger Ackroyd?"

As someone who has as much difficulty plowing through the Christie prose as through Noam Chomsky's, I suppose I agree with Mr. Wilson. However, I agree only up to the point at which the Chris-
(15) tie whodunit becomes a movie. Then I'm likely to get hooked, and stay hooked, right up to the necessary scene in which everyone is called into the drawing room to hear several thousand words of explanations that nearly always leave me wondering. It makes no difference how humorously elegant the circumstances, how foolish the
(20) characters or how unbelievable the plot, I continue to watch. When one reads a Christie, one has to work. The film's images, though, are poured into the brain, as effortlessly as weak tea into a cup crack'd, immediately to dribble away.

My weakness has to do with having spent a large part of my
(25) youth watching films in which continuing characters such as Charlie Chan, Philo Vance, Bulldog Drummond and Sherlock Holmes solved all sorts of bloodless, humdrum slayings. Many of these took place in drawing rooms where, occasionally, real eyes would peer out of the eyes of the portraits over the mantelpiece. They were not great films,
(30) but in my day 10-year-olds would rather turn to salt in their seats than walk out of any movie in the middle.

From "Whodunits—The Fine Art of Doing Them Well" by Vincent Canby. Copyright 1982 by The New York Times Company. Reprinted by permission.

Passage B

IS *UP 'TIL NOW* AN ENJOYABLE BOOK?

. . . When [Eugene] McCarthy stood up to challenge President Johnson—no one else was willing to—he set in motion a series of changes in American politics that are still very much with us. . . .

(5) But what is striking about Mr. McCarthy's memoir, *Up 'Til Now*, is that he thinks that a great many of the changes that have taken place since 1968 are just plain bad for the country. Gene McCarthy . . . takes swipes here at some of the very sorts of people who followed his lead in the 60's. . . . He attacks Common Cause, Congressional reformers, and members of Congress whose attendance records
(10) are too *high*—they must not be doing much real work if they show up for all those meaningless votes, he says. He also attacks Federal campaign finance laws and the new Democratic convention rules. . . .

In keeping with his dislike of the way politicians do things these days, Mr. McCarthy has not written one of those thick, boring, tell-all
(15) memoirs. In fact, if there is a disappointment in *Up 'Til Now*, it is that one wishes he had told more. He gives his version of some old feuds, most of which he wants to settle in a friendly way. But, alas, there is no real forgiveness for Robert F. Kennedy, who, in Mr. McCarthy's view, jumped into the 1968 Presidential race only after the
(20) McCarthy forces paved the way. Mr. McCarthy tells of the nasty things Kennedy and his people said about him and concludes that Kennedy "divided the antiwar forces and introduced the element of power politics."

There are many who will disagree with this and other judgments
(25) in what is frequently a provocative book. . . . But as a meditation on American politics, *Up 'Til Now* certainly proves that Mr. McCarthy is still the poetic Isaiah whose plain literacy puts many other politicians to shame.

And like many conservative critics of modern issues, Mr. Mc-
(30) Carthy can seem downright radical in his analysis of our current failures. He uses these words to describe American society: overfed, overtransported, overfueled, overheated, overcooked, overlighted, overdrugged, overadvertised, overbureaucratized, overincorporated, overdefensed.

(35) . . . [This] means that Mr. McCarthy gives everyone something to disagree with. That is probably why he did not make it to the very top in American politics. But he has always been willing to stand up alone in the hope that, once in a while, something good might happen. Still, as Mr. McCarthy . . . would remind us, don't expect too
(40) much.

From a review of *Up 'Til Now* by E. J. Donne, Jr. Copyright 1987 by The New York Times Company. Reprinted by permission.

Lesson 1 Exercise

1. Which passage is a review? What specific work of art does it review?
2. Which two art forms are compared in Passage A?
3. Which category of the arts is not discussed in either passage?
   - literary arts • visual arts • performing arts

Answers are on page A-37.

Lesson 2 Comprehending Commentary on a Literal Level

Do authors of commentary usually state and support their opinion in an obvious way?

Stated Main Idea

In commentary, it is very important to have a clear understanding of the opinion of the author, who usually is referred to as a **critic** or a **reviewer**. Most critics state their opinions rather early in their writing; then they devote most of their writing to explaining their reasons for holding these opinions.

In commentary, the main idea usually is stated in one of two ways:

- It appears as a conclusion that is drawn from several broad statements, or generalizations.
- It appears as a contrast to the ideas that are expressed in the first paragraph or two of the writing.

Illustrating the first kind of statement, an opera critic might write:

> Fans of *Aida* have come to expect lavish sets. They look forward to great spectacle on stage. Certainly, they were not disappointed last night at Wilson Hall, where the stage property—which glittered—overshadowed the music—which did not.

Look at Passage B for an example of the second kind of statement. In the first paragraph, the critic presents Eugene McCarthy as he is best known—as the liberal reformer who challenged President Johnson in the 1960s. In the second paragraph, however, the critic states that what makes McCarthy's book notable is that it shows how the onetime reformer has changed. Speaking of that change, the critic states, ". . . he takes swipes here at some of the very sorts of people who followed his lead in the 60's" (lines 7–8). By expressing his main idea through a contrast, the critic mirrors the contrast between the somewhat idealized view of the McCarthy of the 60s and the more critical McCarthy who appears in *Up 'Til Now*.

Supporting Details

You probably have had the experience of comparing your opinion about a movie, a book, or a TV show with a friend's and finding that you strongly disagree. Similarly, you often may find that you disagree with the opinion that a critic expresses in a passage of commentary. Is such commentary ineffective?

Generally, the effectiveness of commentary is not based on how many people agree with the opinion. Rather, commentary is considered effective if the critic can present a good defense of his or her opinion. A "good defense" is based on giving factual details that support the opinion. Those factual details can take many forms. Here are just a few.

- Quotations from people who are known to be experts about the subject and who agree with the critic's opinion
- Comparison or contrast with similar works on which judgment has already been passed
- Quotations from the work (or its script, in the case of some of the performing arts) that seem to support the opinion
- A series of statements about what the work is *not*, after which the only statement that seems to say what the work *is* is the critic's own opinion

In a review, the critic often supports his or her opinion by referring to the plot or other details. In Passage B, remember the critic's view: that *Up 'Til Now* is surprising because it shows McCarthy taking a stand against some of the leaders or movements that arose from the stands he used to take. Notice how much time he spends giving examples of the movements or practices that McCarthy now stands against.

In an essay, which often is longer than a review, the critic may use several kinds of support. In Passage A, he compares an Agatha Christie-style novel, on which "one has to work" (line 21), to an Agatha Christie-style movie, in which "images . . . are poured into the brain, as effortlessly as weak tea" (lines 21–22). He gives examples of characters who appear in the kinds of "whodunit" movies he enjoys (lines 25–26). He also names turns of plot that are characteristic—even if "unbelievable" (line 20)—in such films.

Lesson 2 Exercise

1. In Passage A, with whom does the critic compare Agatha Christie's writing style to emphasize its difficulty?
2. Look again at Passage B. Name two examples of people or movements that the critic uses to illustrate McCarthy's apparent change of attitudes.
3. According to the author of Passage B, what is the one disappointing aspect of *Up 'Til Now*?
4. What are the main elements of the kinds of movies on which the author of Passage A is "likely to get hooked, and stay hooked" (lines 15 and 16)?

Answers are on pages A-37–A-38.

Lesson 3 Comprehending Commentary on an Inferential Level

How can bias and objectivity add to the meaning in a commentary?

Although most commentary contains a stated main idea, occasionally the critic's main point must be inferred. If you understand the ways in which a particular passage may be colored by the critic's personal tastes, you can begin to make assumptions about the important ideas that the passage expresses.

Bias

All writers possess certain **biases,** or opinions, that form the background of thought against which a writer considers a subject. Since one of the purposes for commentary is to offer opinions about art, the biases of critics are usually more obvious than those of other writers. Furthermore, most critics have a background of special training and a lot of experience in evaluating the arts. They already have general opinions about what they like or dislike in art. Those opinions help to form biases that will color their evaluation of the subject at hand.

By reading a passage of commentary carefully, you often can infer some of the critic's biases. In Passage A, for example, the critic discusses the difficulty he has "plowing through the Christie prose" (lines 12–13). He then says that Agatha Christie's writing style makes him want to agree with Edmund Wilson, who wrote an essay entitled "Who Cares Who Killed Roger Ackroyd?" The title makes the essay sound less than complimentary about Christie's writing. You can assume that the critic does not enjoy reading novels that require the reader to do a lot of thinking. Notice, however, that he doesn't say that such novels have no value. Rather, his use of "I" throughout indicates that his view is a matter of personal taste.

Objectivity

As mentioned, effective commentary depends upon factual support of the critic's opinion. The more that a passage of commentary is based upon recognized standards for quality in the arts, and the less it is based on the critic's personal opinion, the more objective it is considered to be.

Based on that definition, Passage A is not very objective. In fact, referring to what makes for quality in films, the critic says of the kind of "whodunit" under consideration, "They were not great films" (line 29). The explanations they offer usually leave him "wondering" (line 16), the circumstances are often "humorously elegant" (line 19) and the characters "foolish" (line 19). The stories are sometimes "unbelievable" (line 20). Nevertheless, he concludes, "I continue to watch" (line 20). In this passage, even though the critic freely admits his lack of objectivity, he still has a point to make about the popularity of that kind of movie. In fact, his lack of objectivity is part of the point of the passage—namely, that such films are memorable not because they meet recognized standards for quality, but because they appeal to the personal tastes of their audiences.

When you read commentary, look for signs of objectivity and bias. Be careful not to accept a commentary merely because the critic has been objective, nor reject it merely because the critic reveals same personal bias. Rather, judge its effectiveness by the way in which the critic defends his or her opinion.

Lesson 3 Exercise

1. In your own words, state the main idea of Passage A.
2. In the last paragraph of Passage A, the critic suggests a source for his bias toward the Christie-style movie "whodunit." What is that source?
3. With what bias about most books of memoirs does the author of Passage B approach *Up 'Til Now*?
4. The author of Passage B refers to McCarthy as "the poetic Isaiah whose plain literacy puts many other politicians to shame." Which of the following assumptions can you make about Isaiah—a prophet in the Bible—from this comparison?

   • Isaiah was a quiet man who loved poetry more than politics.

   • Isaiah did not care what people thought about him.

   • Isaiah preached in an eloquent but easy-to-understand manner.

   Answers are on page A-38.

Lesson 4 Applying Ideas in Commentary

How can ideas in a passage about the arts be applied to situations that are outside the arts?

Applying Main Ideas and Details

In the previous chapters you have learned that you can judge the effectiveness of a piece of literature, in part, by trying to apply the ideas in a passage to new situations. If an applied idea makes sense in a new situation—or if you can find a good reason for why it does not make sense—then the original passage is probably effective.

The same test can be used for commentary. For example, suppose you read an essay about the work of a famous eighteenth-century writer. According to the essay, this writer was not popular or successful during his lifetime because his style was nontraditional, or too different from accepted styles. After reading this piece of commentary, you probably would have a better understanding of why many brilliant nontraditional artists (not just writers, but composers, painters, and so on) were ignored by their generation. From the comparison, you might conclude that popularity is not always the best gauge of an artist's talent.

Similarly, think again about the main idea of Passage B. The critic states that the most surprising and memorable quality of Up 'Til Now is McCarthy's condemnation, or speaking against, many who claim to follow the ideas that made McCarthy famous during the 60s. The surprise that McCarthy-era politicians would feel might be similar to what would be felt by followers of a religious leader if that leader were to condemn their practices. It also would be similar to what would be felt by scientists today if a scientist of an earlier generation were to condemn the uses to which they have put his or her original discovery.

Applying the Author's Attitude

To determine a critic's attitude, you should determine the critic's biases as well as his or her opinion.

Think again about the bias expressed in Passage A. Imagine that a teacher with that bias were developing a series of courses for a night school. Which learning tool would that teacher be more likely to recommend—readings from a college textbook and additional printed materials, or a set of videocassettes that taught the same skills by dramatizing real-life situations? Remember that part of the bias of the author of Passage A is his dislike of "plowing through" difficult reading, especially as opposed to his love of the same story when presented on screen. The author is not against reading, but he does have an understanding of the difficulties that some reading presents. It would not be unreasonable to assume that a teacher with a similar understanding would promote the use of videocassettes as a teaching tool.

Lesson 4 Exercise

1. If the author of Passage B were speaking to a group of business students, which of the following pieces of advice would he be more likely to give? Explain your answer.
    - "The best way to become a success is to point out the differences between yourself and those who went before you."
    - "If you want to be successful, you have to learn to make some compromises."
2. Complete this sentence: The author of Passage A probably gets along well with children because _____.
3. Would the authors of Passages A and B probably enjoy the same types of television shows? Why or why not?

Answers are on page A-38.

Lesson 5 Analyzing Commentary

What techniques do authors of commentary use to present their ideas?

Structure of the Argument

The form that a piece of commentary takes depends both on how the author wishes to approach the subject and on what the author has to say about the subject. Commentary can summarize, analyze, and evaluate. In any given piece of commentary, an author may emphasize some of these purposes more than others. Reviews generally summarize and evaluate more than they analyze. Summary usually appears in the early part of a piece of commentary.

Most commentary contains an *opinion, support* of that opinion, and a *conclusion*. The conclusion usually comes in the form of a generalization or restatement of the original point of the passage. For example, in Passage A the critic's opinion about "whodunit" movies is that he is "likely to get hooked, and stay hooked" when watching one (line 14). At the end of the passage, he points out that, even as a child, he "would rather turn to salt" than fail to watch such a movie all the way through. The conclusion emphasizes the author's opinion.

Tone and Diction

The tone of a piece of writing shows the attitude of the critic toward his or her subject and audience. Some commentaries may be **formal** in tone, sounding somewhat separated from the audience. Others may be **informal,** sounding more personal. Some commentaries may be very serious; others may be playful.

The tone of a review reflects the author's **diction,** or word choice. Consider this critic's comment:

> Sitting through a three-hour movie about a chess tournament was not nearly as exciting as watching paint dry.

The critics tone is sarcastic. The critic's point is made through a carefully chosen comparison. Most people would agree that watching paint dry is not exciting. If a movie has even less to offer than that, then it must be very poor. The diction in the comment emphasizes the critic's opinion.

Lesson 5 Exercise

1. Which two of the following words best describe the tone of Passage A?
   - sarcastic • informal • nostalgic • bitter • serious
2. How does the way in which the author of Passage B conclude his commentary emphasize the opinion he expresses about the "contemporary" McCarthy (as opposed to the McCarthy of the 1960s)?
3. The author of Passage B gives 11 words that McCarthy uses to describe contemporary American society (lines 28–30). What effect do you think this list of words is intended to have upon the reader?

Answers are on pages A-38—A-39.

Chapter 6   Quiz

Items 1 to 5 are based on the following passage.

WHY IS "THE GOOD WAR" AN INTERESTING BOOK?

Solemn-minded historians speak ill of oral history [history told as stories by those who were involved in the events], at least when it's published in book form. For them, oral history is self-serving and therefore suspect. It isn't history, it's the material of history; it must
(5) be analyzed and interpreted. And yet in the hands of a master interviewer and editor, oral history acquires a weight and perspective of its own. Studs Terkel knows very well that his books have less to do with "hard fact and precise statistic" than with memory, attitude and aspiration.

(10)   It's this distinction that makes "The Good War" so interesting. (The title comes with quotation marks: they imply that Terkel reserves judgment as to how "good" World War II really was.) Terkel's book contains well over a hundred interviews with men and women of every social condition. It differs from the hundreds of personal ac-
(15) counts we have of that war, even from other collections of personal accounts, because he has invited his witnesses to speculate on the value of their experience, the value of the war itself.

From "What Did You Do in the War?" by Peter S. Prescott. Appeared in *Newsweek* 10/15/84, p. 84. Copyright by Newsweek Incorporated. All rights reserved. Reprinted by permission.

1. According to the passage, why did Studs Terkel put quotation marks around the title "*The Good War*"?

2. State whether the following is TRUE and FALSE and explain your answer: The critic suggests that professional historians would have a negative opinion about "*The Good War*."

3. By establishing the value of oral history in the first paragraph, the critic is able to

    (1) prove that all oral history is worth recording and publishing
    (2) demonstrate that historians are usually wrong
    (3) stress the value of a particular work of oral history
    (4) suggest that other kinds of history are untrustworthy
    (5) demonstrate the importance of professional historians

4. According to this critic, what makes "*The Good War*" different from the many other books like it?

5. Is this passage of commentary an example of a review or of an essay? Explain your answer.

Items 6 to 10 are based on the following passage.

IS THE SEAGRAM BUILDING BEAUTIFUL?

When the bronze-and-glass Seagram Building opened in Manhattan in 1958, it was a revelation. No one had ever seen a skyscraper like it. Slim and elegant, it was raised above street level on a block-long pink-granite podium and surrounded by a glorious, wide-open
(5) plaza. Inside, its floors were covered with granite and marble, its elevators with woven stainless steel and copper. Overnight, its distinguished creator, the expatriate German designer Mies van der Rohe, became the hero of 20th-century architecture. Some of the original tenants still remember the excitement. "I couldn't believe I was going
(10) to work here," recalls one. Another, a lawyer, remembers hailing taxis to drive by it at night, when the lights gleamed like beacons through the darkly tinted amber glass.

Three decades later, a different view holds. The man called "Mies" (his real surname, "van der Rohe" was borrowed from his
(15) mother) is no longer a god but a devil, a dour, dictatorial man whose sharply angled buildings and blunt dogmas—"Less is more," "Build, don't talk," "I don't want to be interesting, I want to be good"—persuaded too many imitators that architecture could be approached like engineering. Most large cities are filled with sad imitations of the Sea-
(20) gram Building. It is no longer a beloved icon, either for architects or for the younger people who currently work in it. They concede its perfection. But they often call it severe and inhuman.

From "Modern Master Builder" by Douglas Davis. Appeared in *Newsweek*, 2/17/86 p. 67. Copyright 1986 by Newsweek Incorporated. All rights reserved. Reprinted by permission.

6. What is the main idea of this passage?
  (1) Buildings with dark-glass exteriors are ugly.
  (2) The Seagram Building shows the genius of Mies van der Rohe.
  (3) The Seagram Building is an inspiration to architects everywhere.
  (4) The Seagram Building is an eyesore.
  (5) Tastes in art change with the passing of time.

7. One of the critic's points is that the Seagram Building was once considered to be beautiful. How does the critic's inclusion of people's early recollections of the building strengthen this point?

8. State whether the following is TRUE or FALSE and explain your answer: The critic gives his own opinion of the Seagram Building at the end of the passage.

9. If this critic were part of a committee supervising the building of a memorial, he probably would recommend that the memorial
  (1) not reflect any one contemporary kind of design
  (2) be located in a busy part of town
  (3) be made of bronze and glass
  (4) include the most recent statue by a popular sculptor
  (5) be designed by an engineer

10. Briefly describe the tone of this passage.

Answers are on page A-39.

UNIT VII

Mathematics

This unit is made up of seven chapters that can help you learn the things you need to know to pass the Mathematics Test.

The chapters (except Chapter 5) are divided into levels, which are, in turn, divided into individual lessons. You can think of the levels in each chapter as levels of difficulty. In each chapter, the lessons in Level 1 cover the basics. For example, in Level 1 in Chapter 1, the lessons cover how to calculate with whole numbers. In Chapter 2, Level 1 lessons cover calculating with fractions. In Chapter 6, the Level 1 lessons cover the basics of algebra.

The lessons in each Level 2 are at the middle level of difficulty. To do the lessons in Level 2, you must already know how to do the kinds of problems covered in Level 1. In Level 2 you solve GED-like problems by applying the skills covered in Level 1. The lessons in each Level 3 are at the highest level of difficulty. Level 3 lessons present complex problems similar to many of the problems you will find on the GED.

Two Methods for Using This Unit

There are two methods for working through the math instruction.

Method 1. Work through the instruction section in order. Start with Level 1 in Chapter 1 and go straight through to the end of Level 3 in Chapter 7. As you work through the chapters, you will frequently tackle complex (Level 3) problems. This will give you practice with rather complex problems similar to those on the GED rather early in and frequently during your period of instruction.

Method 2. Work through all the lessons in every Level 1. Then do the lessons in every Level 2. Finally, do the lessons in every Level 3. (Chapter 5 has no levels; it can be done when you are working through the Level 3's.) This way you can become comfortable with the basics of arithmetic, algebra, and geometry before you begin working with more complex problems.

Previews and Reviews. Level 1 always begins with a Preview; each level ends with a Review. Previews and Reviews are made up of the kinds of problems covered in the level they begin and end. Previews allow you to test your present skill at the material covered in the level. If you get 80 percent of the problems in a Preview correct, you may not have to work through that level. To be sure, try to solve the problems in the Review at the end of the level. If you get 80 percent correct again, you may feel comfortable in skipping the level. However, if you get fewer than 80 percent correct in either the Preview or Review, you should study all the lessons in the level.

Decide whether you want to use Method 1 or Method 2 to work through the instruction. You may want to talk it over with a teacher. Then go to Level 1 in Chapter 1 and begin.

The Progress Chart on the next pages will make it easy for you to keep track of your work and record your performance on each lesson. There are many exercises and quizzes throughout the unit, so you will have several opportunities to apply and test your understanding of the material you study. At the end of all the instruction is a test on all the material covered in the instruction. You will be able to record your score on a Performance Analysis Chart.

UNIT VII PROGRESS CHART
Mathematics

Use the following chart to keep track of your work. When you complete a lesson, circle the number of questions you answered correctly in the Lesson Exercise. When you complete a Chapter Quiz, also record your score below. The numbers in color represent scores at a level of 80% or better.

Lesson	Page		
		CHAPTER 1: Whole Numbers	
		Level 1: WHOLE-NUMBER SKILLS	
	439	Preview	1 2 3 4 5
1	440	Addition of Whole Numbers	1 2 3 4 5
2	440	Subtraction of Whole Numbers	1 2 3 4 5
3	441	Multiplication of Whole Numbers	1 2 3 4 5 6 7 8 9 10
4	442	Division of Whole Numbers	1 2 3 4 5
	443	Level 1 Review	1 2 3 4 5 6 7 8 9 10
		Level 2: WHOLE-NUMBER APPLICATIONS	
1	444	Rounding	1 2 3 4 5 6 7 8 9 10 11 12
2	444	Distance and Cost Formulas	1 2 3 4 5
3	445	Powers and Roots	1 2 3 4 5 6 7 8 9 10
4	447	Perimeter and Area of Polygons	1 2 3 4 5
5	449	Volume	1 2 3 4 5
6	450	Mean and Median	1 2 3 4 5
	451	Level 2 Review	1 2 3 4 5 6 7 8 9 10
		Level 3: WHOLE-NUMBER PROBLEM SOLVING	
1	452	Multistep Problems	1 2 3 4 5
2	454	Estimating	1 2 3 4 5
3	454	Item Sets	1 2 3 4 5
4	456	Setup Answers	1 2 3 4 5
	456	Level 3 Review	1 2 3 4 5 6 7 8 9 10
	459	Quiz	1 2 3 4 5 6 7 8 9 10 11 12 13 14 15 16 17 18 19 20
		CHAPTER 2: Fractions	
		Level 1: FRACTION SKILLS	
	461	Preview	1 2 3 4 5
1	461	Reducing Fractions	1 2 3 4 5
2	462	Raising Fractions to Higher Terms	1 2 3 4 5 6 7 8 9 10
3	463	Mixed Numbers	1 2 3 4 5 6 7 8 9 10
4	465	Finding Common Denominators and the LCD	1 2 3 4 5 6 7 8 9 10
5	466	Adding Fractions and Mixed Numbers	1 2 3 4 5 6 7 8 9 10
6	467	Subtracting Fractions and Mixed Numbers	1 2 3 4 5 6 7 8 9 10
7	469	Multiplying Fractions and Mixed Numbers	1 2 3 4 5 6 7 8 9 10

Lesson	Page		
8	470	Dividing Fractions and Mixed Numbers	1 2 3 4 5 6 7 8 9 10
	472	Level 1 Review	1 2 3 4 5 6 7 8 9 10
		Level 2: FRACTION APPLICATIONS	
1	472	Standard Units of Measure	1 2 3 4 5 6 7 8 9 10
2	473	Comparing and Ordering Fractions	1 2 3 4 5 6 7 8 9 10
3	474	Tables	1 2 3 4 5
4	475	Ratio	1 2 3 4 5
5	477	Probability	1 2 3 4 5
	478	Level 2 Review	1 2 3 4 5 6 7 8 9 10
		Level 3: FRACTION PROBLEM SOLVING	
1	479	Setup Problems	1 2 3 4 5
2	481	Mixed Units with Perimeter, Area, and Volume	1 2 3 4 5
3	482	Extraneous Information	1 2 3 4 5
	483	Level 3 Review	1 2 3 4 5 6 7 8 9 10
	485	Quiz	1 2 3 4 5 6 7 8 9 10 11 12 13 14 15 16 17 18 19 20
		CHAPTER 3: Decimals	
		Level 1: DECIMAL SKILLS	
	488	Preview	1 2 3 4 5
1	489	Reading and Writing Decimals	1 2 3 4 5 6 7 8 9 10
2	490	Adding and Subtracting Decimals	1 2 3 4 5 6 7 8 9 10
3	491	Multiplying and Dividing Decimals	1 2 3 4 5 6 7 8 9 10
4	493	Interchanging Decimals and Fractions	1 2 3 4 5 6 7 8 9 10
	494	Level 1 Review	1 2 3 4 5 6 7 8 9 10
		Level 2: DECIMAL APPLICATIONS	
1	495	Rounding Decimals	1 2 3 4 5 6 7 8 9 10
2	495	Decimal Word Problems	1 2 3 4 5
3	496	Metric Measurement	1 2 3 4 5

Lesson	Page		
4	498	Circumference and Area of Circles	**1 2 3** 4 5
5	499	Volume of a Cylinder	**1 2 3** 4 5
6	500	Comparing and Ordering Decimals	**1 2 3** 4 5
	500	Level 2 Review	**1 2 3 4 5 6 7** 8 9 10
		Level 3: DECIMAL PROBLEM SOLVING	
1	501	Sketching Travel Problems	**1 2 3** 4 5
2	503	Insufficient Data	**1 2 3** 4 5
	504	Level 3 Review	**1 2 3 4 5 6 7** 8 9 10
	506	Quiz	**1 2 3 4 5 6 7 8 9 10 11 12 13 14** 15 16 17 18 19 20

CHAPTER 4: Percents

Lesson	Page		
		Level 1: Percent Skills	
	508	Preview	**1 2 3** 4 5
1	508	Interchanging Percents and Decimals	**1 2 3 4 5 6 7** 8 9 10
2	510	Interchanging Percents and Fractions	**1 2 3 4 5 6 7** 8 9 10
3	511	Common Equivalent Fractions, Decimals, and Percents	**1 2 3 4 5 6 7** 8 9 10
4	511	Finding a Percent of a Number	**1 2 3** 4 5
5	512	Finding What Percent One Number Is of Another	**1 2 3** 4 5
6	513	Finding a Number When a Percent of It Is Given	**1 2 3** 4 5
	515	Level 1 Review	**1 2 3 4 5 6 7** 8 9 10
		Level 2: PERCENT APPLICATIONS	
1	514	Word Problems Involving Percent	**1 2 3 4 5 6 7** 8 9 10
2	516	Interest	**1 2 3** 4 5
	516	Level 2 Review	**1 2 3 4 5 6 7** 8 9 10
		Level 3: PERCENT PROBLEM SOLVING	
1	517	Multistep Percent Problems	**1 2 3** 4 5
2	519	Percent Increase and Percent Decrease	**1 2 3** 4 5
	520	Level 3 Review	**1 2 3 4 5 6 7** 8 9 10
	521	Quiz	**1 2 3 4 5 6 7 8 9 10 11 12 13 14** 15 16 17 18 19 20

CHAPTER 5: Graphs

Lesson	Page		
	523	Preview	**1 2 3** 4 5
1	523	Pictographs	**1 2 3** 4 5
2	525	Circle Graphs	**1 2 3** 4 5
3	527	Bar Graphs	**1 2 3** 4 5
4	528	Line Graphs	**1 2 3** 4 5
	530	Quiz	**1 2 3 4 5 6 7 8 9 10 11 12 13 14** 15 16 17 18 19 20

CHAPTER 6: Algebra

Lesson	Page		
		Level 1: ALGEBRA SKILLS	
	533	Preview	**1 2 3** 4 5
1	534	The Number Line	**1 2 3** 4 5
2	535	Adding and Subtracting Signed Numbers	**1 2 3 4 5 6 7** 8 9 10
3	536	Multiplying and Dividing Signed Numbers	**1 2 3 4 5 6 7** 8 9 10
4	538	Adding and Subtracting Monomials	**1 2 3 4 5 6 7** 8 9 10
5	539	Multiplying and Dividing Monomials	**1 2 3 4 5 6 7** 8 9 10
	540	Level 1 Review	**1 2 3 4 5 6 7** 8 9 10
		Level 2: ALGEBRA APPLICATIONS	
1	540	Solving Equations	**1 2 3 4 5 6 7** 8 9 10
2	542	Multistep Equations	**1 2 3** 4 5
3	543	Inequalities	**1 2 3** 4 5
4	544	Writing Algebraic Expressions and Equations	**1 2 3** 4 5
5	545	Multiplying Binomials	**1 2 3** 4 5 6
	546	Level 2 Review	**1 2 3 4 5 6 7** 8 9 10
		Level 3: ALGEBRA WORD PROBLEMS	
1	547	Proportion	**1 2 3** 4 5
2	548	Algebra Setup Problems	**1 2 3** 4 5
	549	Level 3 Review	**1 2 3 4 5 6 7** 8 9 10
	551	Quiz	**1 2 3 4 5 6 7 8 9 10 11 12 13 14** 15 16 17 18 19 20

CHAPTER 7: Geometry

Lesson	Page		
		Level 1: GEOMETRY SKILLS	
	553	Preview	**1 2 3** 4 5
1	554	Angles	**1 2 3 4 5 6 7** 8 9 10
2	555	Naming Angles and Pairs of Angles	**1 2 3** 4 5
3	557	Triangles	**1 2 3** 4 5
	559	Level 1 Review	**1 2 3 4 5 6 7** 8 9 10
		Level 2: GEOMETRY APPLICATIONS	
1	560	Congruent and Similar Triangles	**1 2 3** 4 5
2	564	Pythagorean Relationship	**1 2 3** 4 5
3	565	Coordinate Geometry	**1 2 3 4 5 6 7** 8 9 10
4	567	Finding Distance Between Points	**1 2 3** 4 5
	569	Level 2 Review	**1 2 3 4 5 6 7** 8 9 10
		Level 3: GEOMETRY WORD PROBLEMS	
1	571	Slope	**1 2 3** 4 5
2	573	Graphs of Linear Equations	**1 2 3** 4 5
	575	Level 3 Review	**1 2 3 4 5 6 7** 8 9 10
	576	Quiz	**1 2 3 4 5 6 7 8 9 10 11 12 13 14** 15 16 17 18 19 20

Table of Measures
U.S. Customary System

Length
12 inches (in.) = 1 foot (ft.)
3 feet = 1 yard (yd.)
$16\frac{1}{2}$ feet = 1 rod (rd.)
$5\frac{1}{2}$ yards = 1 rod
5280 feet = 1 mile (mi.)
1760 yards = 1 mile

Weight
16 ounces (oz.) = 1 pound (lb.)
2000 pounds = 1 short ton (sh. tn.)
2240 pounds = 1 long ton (l. tn.)

Liquid
8 fluid ounces (fl. oz.) = 1 cup (c.)
2 cups = 1 pint (pt.)
2 pints = 1 quart (qt.)
4 quarts = 1 gallon

Time
60 seconds (sec.) = 1 minute (min.)
60 minutes = 1 hour (hr.)
24 hours = 1 day (da.)
365 days = 1 year (yr.)

Area
144 square inches = 1 square foot
(sq. in. or in.^{2}) (sq. ft. or ft.^{2})
9 square feet = 1 square yard (sq. yd. or yd.^{2})
$30\frac{1}{2}$ square yards = 1 square rod (sq. rd. or rd.^{2})
43,560 square feet = 1 acre (ac. or A)
4840 square yards = 1 acre
160 square rods = 1 acre
640 acres = 1 square mile (sq. mi. or mi.^{2})

Volume
1728 cubic inches = 1 cubic foot
(cu. in. or in.^{3}) (cu. ft. or ft.^{3})
27 cubic feet = 1 cubic yard (cu. yd. or yd.^{3})

Dry
2 pints (pt.) = 1 quart (qt.)
8 quarts = 1 peck (pk.)
4 pecks = 1 bushel (bu.)

Abbreviations for Units of Measurement
U.S. Customary System

Length
inch(es) = in.
foot, feet = ft.
yard(s) = yd.
rod(s) = rd.
mile(s)* = mi.
*statute mile

Area
square inch = (in.^{2}) or sq. in.
square foot = (ft.^{2}) or sq. ft.
square yard = (yd.^{2}) or sq. yd.
square rod = (rd.^{2}) or sq. rd.
acre = ac. or A

Volume
cubic inch = (in.^{3}) or cu. in.
cubic foot = ft.^{3}) or cu. ft.
cubic yard = (yd.^{3}) or cu. yd.

Weight
ounce = oz.
pound = lb.
short ton = sh. tn.
long ton = l. tn.

Liquid
pint = pt.
quart = qt.
gallon = gal.

Dry
pint = pt.
quart = qt.
peck = pk.
bushel = bu.

Time
second = sec.
minute = min.
hour = hr.
day = da.
week = wk.
month = mo.
year = yr.

Metric System

Length
10 millimeters (mm) = 1 centimeter (cm)
10 centimeters = 1 decimeter (dm)
1000 meters = 1 kilometer (km)

Weight (or Mass)
10 milligrams (mg) = 1 centigram (cg)
10 centigrams = 1 decigram (dg)
1000 grams = 1 kilogram (kg)

Capacity
10 milliliters (ml) = 1 centiliter (cl)
10 centiliters = 1 deciliter (dl)
1000 liters = 1 kiloliter (kl)

Formulas

Description	Formula
AREA (A) of a:	
square	$A = s^2$; where s = side
rectangle	$A = lw$; where l = length, w = width
parallelogram	$A = bh$; where b = base, h = height
triangle	$A = \frac{1}{2}bh$; where b = base, h = height
circle	$A = \pi r^2$; where π = 3.14, r = radius
PERIMETER (P) of a:	
square	$P = 4s$; where s = side
rectangle	$P = 2l + 2w$; where l = length, w = width
triangle	$P = a + b + c$; where a, b, and c are the sides
circumference (C) of a circle	$C = \pi d$; where π = 3.14, d = diameter
VOLUME (V) of a:	
cube	$V = s^3$; where s = side
rectangular container	$V = lwh$; where l = length, w = width, h = height
cylinder	$V = \pi r^2 h$; where π = 3.14, r = radius, h = height
Pythagorean relationship	$c^2 = a^2 + b^2$; where c = hypotenuse, a and b are legs of right triangle
distance (d) between two points in a plane	$d = \sqrt{(x_2 - x_1)^2 + (y_2 - y_1)^2}$; where (x_1, y_1) and (x_2, y_2) are two points in a plane
slope of a line (m)	$m = \frac{y_2 - y_1}{x_2 - x_1}$; where (x_1, y_1) and (x_2, y_2) are two points in a plane
mean	mean $= \frac{x_1 + x_2 + \ldots + x_n}{n}$; where the x's are the values for which a mean is desired, and n = number of values in the series
median	median = the point in an ordered set of numbers at which half of the numbers are above and half of the numbers are below this value
simple interest (i)	$i = prt$; where p = principal, r = rate, t = time
distance (d) as function of rate and time	$d = rt$; where r = rate, t = time
total cost (c)	$c = nr$; where n = number of units, r = cost per unit

Chapter 1

Whole Numbers

Objective

In this chapter, you will learn to

- Add, subtract, multiply, and divide whole numbers
- Round whole numbers
- Use distance and cost formulas
- Work with powers and roots of whole numbers
- Find the perimeter and the area of plane figures; find the volume of solid figures
- Find the mean and the median of a set of numbers
- Solve multistep problems
- Estimate the best solution to a problem
- Solve the problems in item sets
- Set up solutions to multistep problems

Level 1 Whole-Number Skills

Preview

Directions: *Solve each problem.*

1. Find the sum of 217, 1281, 323, and 89.
2. Find the difference between 2196 and 328.
3. Multiply 206 by 38.
4. Divide 588 by 28.
5. Divide 1462 by 34.

Check your answers. Correct answers are on page A-40. If you have at least four answers correct, do the Level 1 Review on page 443. If you have fewer than four answers correct, study Level 1 beginning with Lesson 1.

Lesson 1 Addition of Whole Numbers

Whole numbers are numbers that are written in one or more digits from 0 through 9. A digit's value depends on its position in a number. Each position has a place value: units, tens, hundreds, and so on.

Addition problems require you to find the sum, or total, of two or more numbers. List the numbers in order of decreasing value. Line the numbers up so that digits are directly under other digits that have the same place value.

Example: Find the sum of 810, 16, and 9404.

Step 1. Set the problem up: place the largest number, 9404, at the top of the list. Be sure that digits that have the same place value are in line.

Step 2. Add. First, add the digits in the ones column (4 + 0 + 6). The sum is 10. Write the 0 (10) in the ones place in the answer. Carry the 1 (10) to the top of the tens column. Then, add the tens, hundreds, and thousands columns in order. The answer is 10,230.

ten-thousands	thousands	hundreds	tens	ones
	1		1	
	9	4	0	4
		8	1	0
+			1	6
1	0,	2	3	0

Lesson 1 Exercise

Directions: *Find each sum.*

1. 328 + 16 + 1029
2. 28 + 149 + 1632
3. 1619 + 8 + 419
4. 16,725 + 309 + 4692
5. 76 + 830 + 5901 + 18,263

Answers are on page A-40.

Lesson 2 Subtraction of Whole Numbers

When you subtract, you find the difference between two numbers. Place the larger number on top, and keep numbers that have the same place value correctly aligned.

Example: Subtract 265 from 1284.

Step 1. Set the problem up with the larger number, 1284, on top. Be sure that digits that have the same place value (ones, tens, and so on) are in line.

Step 2. Subtract. First borrow one 10 from the tens column. That makes the value in the ones column of the top number (now 14) greater than the value of the ones column in the bottom number (5). Then, subtract each column in order, beginning with the ones column, then the tens column, and so on. The answer is 1019.

thousands	hundreds	tens	ones
		7	14
1	2	8̸	4̸
−	2	6	5
1	0	1	9

Step 3. Check. Add the subtraction answer, 1019, to the bottom number of the subtraction problem, 265. Compare the sum, 1284, to the top number in the subtraction problem. They are the same.

```
  1 0 1 9
+   2 6 5
  1 2 8 4
```

Lesson 2   Exercise

Directions: *Solve each problem.*

1. 1059 − 328
2. 216 − 98
3. Subtract 426 from 1005.
4. 13,328 − 8,379
5. Find the difference between 37 and 219.

Answers are on page A-40.

Lesson 3   Multiplication of Whole Numbers

When you multiply, you find the product of two numbers. Multiplication is a shortcut for the repeated addition of a number. Place the larger number on top, and keep numbers that have the same place value aligned.

In multiplication, as in addition, it is sometimes necessary to carry. Writing the carry numbers in the appropriate columns will help you obtain the correct answer.

Example: Multiply 123 by 42.

Step 1. Set the problem up with the larger number, 123, on top, and the smaller number, 42, on the bottom. Be sure the digits are aligned by place value.

Step 2. Multiply the top number by the digit in the ones place of the bottom number (2). Start with the ones column: 2 × 3 = 6, then 2 × 2 = 4, and 2 × 1 = 2.

Step 3. Multiply the top number by the digit in the tens place of the bottom number (4). Since 4 × 3 = 12, write 2 in the tens column and carry 1. Continue: 4 × 2 = 8. Add the carried 1: 8 + 1 = 9. Continue: 4 × 1 = 4.

thousands	hundreds	tens	ones
		1	
	1	2	3
×		4	2
	2	4	6
4	9	2	
5	1	6	6

Step 4. Add the products of the two multiplication operations to find the answer.

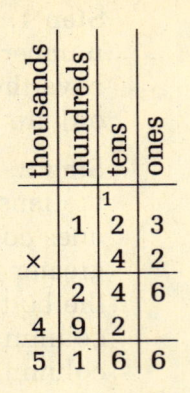

Sometimes you must multiply by zero. Remember that the product of any number and zero is zero.

You know that × indicates multiplication. For example, 3 × 5 tells you to multiply. Two other symbols also indicate multiplication: a dot, 3 · 5, and parentheses, (3)(5).

Lesson 3   Exercise

Directions: *Find each product.*

1. 234 × 12
2. 53 × 4
3. 321 × 44
4. 205 × 37
5. 140 × 2
6. 532 · 108
7. (79)(604)
8. (45)(397)
9. Multiply 3028 by 16.
10. Multiply 163 by 129.

Answers are on page A-40.

Lesson 4   Division of Whole Numbers

Division requires you to find how many groups of one number are in another number. For example, 10 has 2 groups of 5, or 10 ÷ 5 = 2. Division is simply the opposite of multiplication: 2 × 5 = 10. The division sign, ÷, is always read as *divided by*. Therefore, 10 ÷ 5 means *10 divided by 5*. The ⟌ is also used to mean division. You must remember to change the order of numbers when you change the ÷ sign to the ⟌ sign: 10 ÷ 2 becomes 2⟌10.

Example: Divide 484 by 20.

Step 1. Set the problem up.

Step 2. Divide. How many groups of 20 are in 48? Think: 2 × 20 = 40. Write the 2 in the tens place and the 40 under the 48. Subtract: 48 − 40 = 8.

Step 3. Bring down the next number, 4. How many groups of 20 are in 84? Think: 4 × 20 = 80. Write the 4 in the ones place and the 80 under the 84. Subtract: 84 − 80 = 4. You cannot divide 4 by 20, and there are no more numbers to bring down. The answer is 24 with a remainder of 4.

Step 4. Check. Multiply 24 by 20. Then add the remainder to that product: 24 × 20 = 480, and 480 + 4 = 484. The answer is correct.

```
        2 4
2 0 ) 4 8 4
    − 4 0
        8 4
      − 8 0
          4


      2 4
    × 2 0
    4 8 0
  +     4
    4 8 4
```

Lesson 4   Exercise

Directions: *Solve each problem.*

1. 40)1440
2. 1556 ÷ 27
3. 7084 ÷ 34
4. Divide 19,584 by 204.
5. Divide 5096 by 196.

Answers are on page A-40.

Level 1   Review

Directions: *Solve each problem.*

1. Add $550, $300, $75, and $35.
2. Find the sum of 328,509 and 213,694.
3. Find the difference between $40 and $28.
4. Subtract 82,478 from 92,984.
5. Multiply 16 by 54.
6. Find 5684 divided by 28.
7. (3062)(208)
8. 2250 ÷ 50
9. $140 − $65
10. 603)31,356

Check your answers. Correct answers are on page A-40. If you have at least eight answers correct, go to Level 2. If you have fewer than eight answers correct, go back to Lesson 1 and study Level 1.

Chapter 1: Whole Numbers INSTRUCTION

Level 2 Whole-Number Applications

Lesson 1 Rounding

Rounding is used to estimate. You can use rounding to answer the questions *about how many?* or *about how much?*

To round a number, find the digit in the place you want to round to. If the digit to the right of this place is less than 5, leave the digit in the place you are rounding to as it is. If the digit to the right is 5 or more, add 1 to the digit you are rounding to. Change the digit(s) to the right of the number you are rounding to zero.

Example: Round 12,634 to the nearest ten.

Step 1. Find the digit in the place you are rounding to. In this example it is the 3 in the tens place.   1 2 , 6 <u>3</u> 4

Step 2. Examine the digit to the right of the 3. Since 4 is less than 5, leave the 3 as it is.   1 2 , 6 3 <u>4</u>

Step 3. Change the digit to the right of the 3 to 0. The answer is 12,630.   1 2 , 6 3 <u>0</u>

Lesson 1 Exercise

Directions: *Round each number to the nearest ten.*

1. 263   2. 1849   3. 13,255   4. 116,886   5. 47,908

Directions: *Round each number to the nearest thousand.*

6. 1499   7. 9862   8. 13,281   9. 110,523   10. 116,949

Answers are on page A-40.

Lesson 2 Distance and Cost Formulas

Distance Formula

To calculate a distance traveled, multiply the rate (speed) by the amount of time traveled.

distance = rate × time
$d = rt$

In a formula, when two letters are written together, such as *rt*, it means that the values for those letters are to be multiplied.

Example 1: John drove 55 miles per hour for 6 hours. How many miles did he travel?

Step 1. Substitute the numbers for the rate and time in the formula.

Step 2. Multiply. John traveled 330 miles.

$$d = rt$$
$$= 55 \times 6$$
$$= 330 \text{ miles}$$

Cost Formula

To calculate the total cost, multiply the number of units by the rate (cost per unit).

total cost = number of units × rate

$$c = nr$$

Example 2: A six-pack of soda costs $2. What will be the total cost of 4 six-packs?

Step 1. Substitute the values for the number of units and rate in the formula.

Step 2. Multiply. The total cost is $8.

$$c = nr$$
$$= 4 \times 2$$
$$= \$8$$

Lesson 2   Exercise

Directions: *Use the distance or cost formula to solve each problem.*

1. A plane travels 600 miles per hour for 8 hours. What distance in miles has it traveled?
2. Stephen jogs 6 miles per hour for 15 hours each week. What is the total number of miles he jogs each week?
3. If cherries cost $2 per pound, how much will 28 pounds cost?
4. A pair of socks costs $3. How much will a dozen pairs cost?
5. How much will 14 gallons of gas cost at $1 per gallon?

Answers are on pages A-40–A-41.

Lesson 3   Powers and Roots

Powers

When a number is to be multiplied by itself one or more times, there is a shorthand way to show that. Here are some examples.

$$3^2 = 3 \times 3 = 9$$
$$2^3 = 2 \times 2 \times 2 = 8$$
$$6^4 = 6 \times 6 \times 6 \times 6 = 1296$$

In the expression 2^3, the 3 is the *exponent*. The expression 2^3 is read as *two to the third power* or *two cubed*. When a number is raised to the second power, it is squared. So, 3^2 may be read as *three to the second power* or *three squared*.

Example 1: Find the value of 4^3.

Step 1. Write 4^3 as a product. Since the exponent is 3, use 4 three times in the multiplication.

$$4^3 = 4 \times 4 \times 4 = 64$$

Step 2. Multiply. Four cubed is 64.

Below are some commonly used squares. Memorizing these will help you solve problems involving these squares more quickly.

$1^2 = 1$	$4^2 = 16$	$7^2 = 49$	$10^2 = 100$
$2^2 = 4$	$5^2 = 25$	$8^2 = 64$	$11^2 = 121$
$3^2 = 9$	$6^2 = 36$	$9^2 = 81$	$12^2 = 144$

Roots

You know that 5 squared is 25. Another way to say this is to say that 5 is the *square root* of 25. When you find the square root of a number, you find the number that is multiplied by itself to give you the original number. The sign for a square root is $\sqrt{}$.

Example 2: Find the value of $\sqrt{49}$.

Step 1. Ask: What number times itself equals 49?

Step 2. Since 7 times 7 is 49, the square root of 49 is 7.

$$49 = 7 \times 7$$
$$\sqrt{49} = 7$$

It will be easier to work with roots if you memorize this table of square roots for some common numbers.

$\sqrt{1} = 1$	$\sqrt{16} = 4$	$\sqrt{49} = 7$	$\sqrt{100} = 10$
$\sqrt{4} = 2$	$\sqrt{25} = 5$	$\sqrt{64} = 8$	$\sqrt{121} = 11$
$\sqrt{9} = 3$	$\sqrt{36} = 6$	$\sqrt{81} = 9$	$\sqrt{144} = 12$

Lesson 3 Exercise

Directions: *Find the value of each expression.*

1. 8^2
2. 15^2
3. 7^3
4. 10^3
5. 3^4
6. $\sqrt{36}$
7. $\sqrt{81}$
8. $\sqrt{225}$
9. $\sqrt{400}$
10. $\sqrt{625}$

Answers are on page A-41.

Lesson 4 Perimeter and Area of Polygons

Perimeter

Perimeter is the measurement of the distance around a plane (flat) figure. You use different formulas to find the perimeter of different plane figures.

- rectangle: $P = 2l + 2w$ (where l is the length and w is the width)
- square: $P = 4s$ (where s is the length of each side)
- triangle: $P = a + b + c$ (where a, b, and c are the sides)

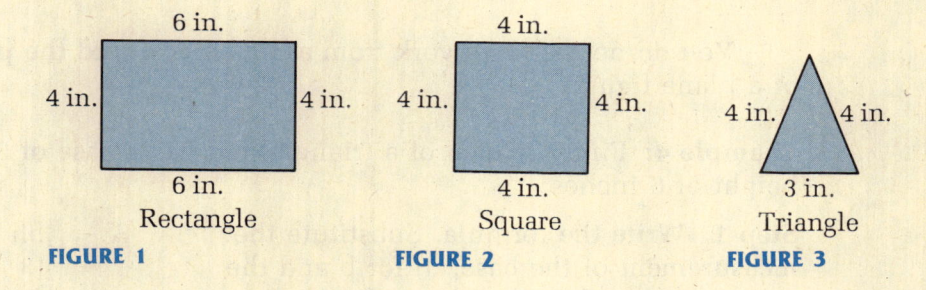

```
       6 in.                  4 in.
   ┌─────────┐            ┌─────────┐              △
4 in.        4 in.    4 in.         4 in.      4 in. / \ 4 in.
   └─────────┘            └─────────┘            /_____\
       6 in.                  4 in.               3 in.
     Rectangle                Square             Triangle
     FIGURE 1                FIGURE 2            FIGURE 3
```

Example 1: Find the perimeter of the rectangle in Figure 1.

Step 1. Set the problem up. Substitute the measurement of the length, 6, for l and the measurement of the width, 4, for w.

$P = 2l + 2w$
$\quad = (2 \times 6) + (2 \times 4)$
$\quad = (12) + (8)$
$\quad = 20$ inches

Step 2. Multiply, then add. The perimeter of the rectangle is 20 inches.

Example 2: Find the perimeter of the triangle in Figure 3.

Step 1. Set the problem up. Substitute the measurements of the sides, 3, 4, and 4, for a, b, and c.

$P = a + b + c$
$\quad = 3 + 4 + 4$
$\quad = 11$ inches

Step 2. Add. The perimeter of the triangle is 11 inches.

Area

Area is the measurement of the space within a plane figure. Area is expressed in *square* units, such as square inches, square feet, and square yards. The area is the total number of square units that make up the surface of the plane figure.

These are the formulas for finding the area of different plane figures.

- square: $A = s^2$ (where s is the length of each side)
- rectangle: $A = lw$ (where l is the length and w is the width)
- triangle: $A = \frac{1}{2}bh$ (where b is the base and h is the height)

Example 3: Find the area of the square in Figure 2.

Step 1. Substitute the length of a side, 4, in the formula.

Step 2. Multiply. The area of the square is 16 square inches.

$$A = s^2$$
$$= 4^2$$
$$= 4 \times 4$$
$$= 16 \text{ square inches}$$

You do not need to work from a drawing to find the perimeter or area of a plane figure.

Example 4: Find the area of a triangle that has a base of 3 inches and a height of 6 inches.

Step 1. Write the formula. Substitute the measurement of the base, 3, for b and the measurement of the height, 6, for h.

Step 2. Perform the operations. Remember that $\frac{1}{2}(18)$ means $\frac{1}{2} \times 18$, or $18 \div 2$. The area of the triangle is 9 square inches.

$$A = \tfrac{1}{2}bh$$
$$= \tfrac{1}{2}(3 \times 6)$$
$$= \tfrac{1}{2}(18)$$
$$= 9 \text{ square inches}$$

Lesson 4   Exercise

Directions: *Use the formulas for finding perimeter and area to solve each problem.*

1. David wants to fence his square backyard. If each side of the yard measures 45 feet, how many feet of fencing will he need?
2. Jonathan has to frame a rectangular picture. If the picture is 36 inches by 12 inches, how many inches of framing will he need?
3. Find the perimeter of a triangular highway sign whose sides measure 5 feet, 6 feet, and 5 feet.
4. Cindy's rectangular living room measures 16 feet by 12 feet. What is the area of the room?
5. Pietro wants to cover a triangular plot of ground with sod. If the base is 20 feet and the height is 18 feet, how many square feet of sod does Pietro need?

Answers are on page A-41.

Lesson 5 Volume

Volume is the measurement of space inside a solid (three-dimensional) figure. Volume is expressed in *cubic* units, such as cubic inches, cubic feet, cubic yards, and so forth. The volume is the total number of cubic units that make up the space of the solid. For example, refrigerator sizes are usually expressed in terms of cubic feet. Use the following formulas to find the volume.

- rectangular container: $V = lwh$ (where l is the length, w is the width, and h is the height)
- cube: $V = s^3$ (where s is the measure of a side)

Example: Find the volume of the rectangular container in Figure 4.

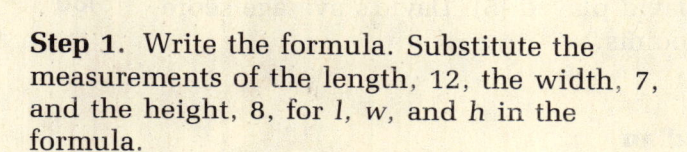

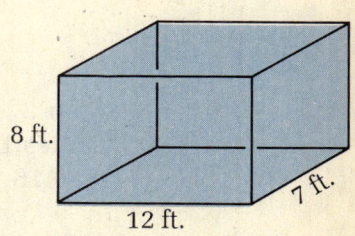

Step 1. Write the formula. Substitute the measurements of the length, 12, the width, 7, and the height, 8, for l, w, and h in the formula.

FIGURE 4 (8 ft., 12 ft., 7 ft.)

Step 2. Multiply. The volume of the rectangular container is 672 cubic feet.

$$V = lwh$$
$$= (12)(7)(8)$$
$$= 672 \text{ cubic feet}$$

Lesson 5 Exercise

Directions: Find the volume of the following rectangular containers.

1. 5 in., 20 in., 7 in.
2. 7 yd., 14 yd., 10 yd.

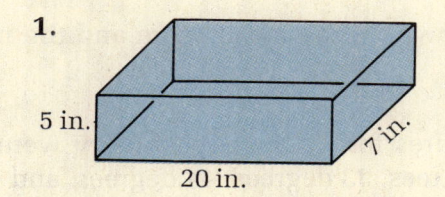

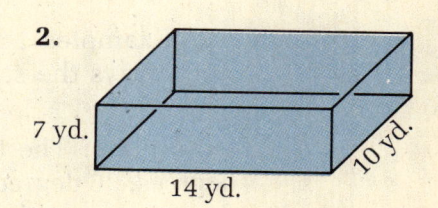

Directions: Find the volume of the following cubes.

3. $s = 6$ in.
4. $s = 10$ ft.
5. $s = 8$ yd.

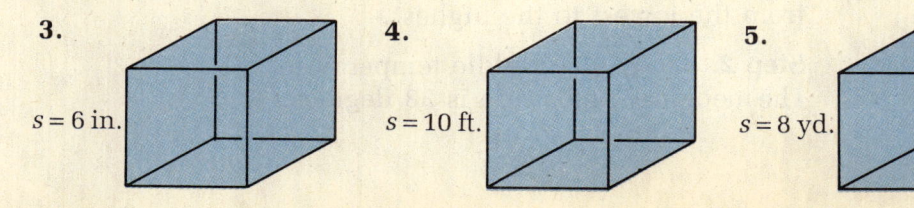

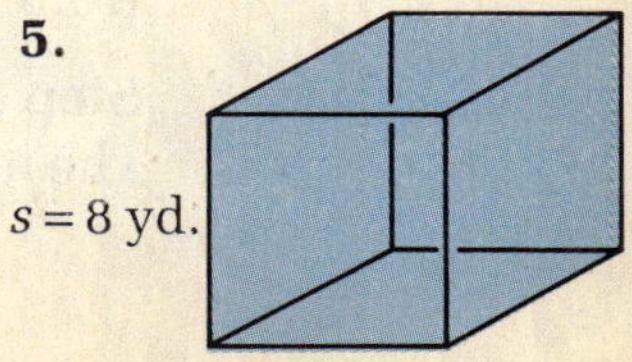

Answers are on page A-41.

# Lesson 6 Mean and Median

Mean

To find the average, or *mean*, of a group of numbers, divide the sum by however many numbers are being added.

Example 1: David scored 11 points, 19 points, 15 points, 14 points, and 21 points in each of 5 basketball games. What was the average number of points that he scored?

Step 1. Add to find the total points David scored in the five games (80).

```
   11
   19
   15
   14
 + 21
   80 points
```

Step 2. Divide the total, 80, by the number of games David played (5). David's average score was 16 points.

```
   16
 5)80
```

Median

The *median* is the middle value in a series of numbers arranged from the lowest to the highest.

Example 2: Find the median of David's basketball scores.

Step 1. Write David's scores in order from the lowest to the highest.   11 14 <u>15</u> 19 21

Step 2. Locate the middle score. The median score is 15.

Examples 1 and 2 show that the mean score and the median score are not always the same.

Example 3: The temperatures for 7 days in February were 27 degrees, 32 degrees, 26 degrees, 36 degrees, 33 degrees, 44 degrees, and 40 degrees. Find the median of these temperatures.

Step 1. Write the temperatures in order from the lowest to the highest.   26 27 32 <u>33</u> 36 40 44

Step 2. Locate the middle temperature. The median temperature is 33 degrees.

Lesson 6 Exercise

Directions: *Solve each problem.*

1. Lauren received the following scores on a series of quizzes in her math class: 75, 85, 65, 90, and 80. What was her average quiz score?
2. Suzanne earned money by baby-sitting. In January, she earned $58; in February, $62; in March, $63; and in April, $33. What were her mean monthly earnings?
3. Arlene has been dieting for the past 3 months. The first month, she lost 9 pounds; the second month, 10 pounds; and the third month, 8 pounds. What was her average monthly weight loss?
4. Seven students received the following scores on a test: 68, 92, 84, 86, 78, 81, and 90. What was the median score?
5. The members of the Johnson family have the following heights: 6 feet 1 inch; 5 feet 6 inches; 5 feet 9 inches; 5 feet 4 inches; and 5 feet 1 inch. What is the median height of the Johnson family?

Answers are on page A-41.

Level 2 Review

Directions: *Solve each problem.*

1. Danny earned $12,485 last year. Round his earnings to (a) the nearest hundred dollars and (b) the nearest thousand dollars.
2. Sal rode his bicycle at an average speed of 12 miles per hour for 8 hours. What is the total distance in miles that he rode?
3. What is the value of 3^4?
4. What is the value of $\sqrt{121}$?
5. Alice wants to put a lace border on a rectangular tablecloth that is 72 inches by 42 inches. How many inches of lace does she need for the border?
6. Debby's bedroom is 15 feet by 12 feet. How many square feet of carpeting does she need to cover her bedroom floor?
7. How many cubic inches of water will an aquarium 24 inches by 12 inches by 12 inches hold?
8. A box is in the shape of a cube with sides 4 feet long. What is the volume of the box?

Items 9 and 10 are based on the following table.

Jackson Family Food Expenses for Five Weeks

Week 1	$ 75
Week 2	85
Week 3	110
Week 4	80
Week 5	80

9. What is the mean amount of money the Jackson family spends for food per week?

10. What is the median amount of money the Jackson family spends for food each week?

Check your answers. Correct answers are on page A-41. If you have at least eight answers correct, go to Level 3. If you have fewer than eight answers correct, go back to Lesson 1 and study Level 2 again.

Level 3   Whole-Number Problem Solving

Lesson 1   Multistep Problems

Multistep problems require you to use more than one operation to solve the problem. You must decide what is being asked, identify the relevant information, and use the appropriate operations.

Example 1: Mary bought a record for $7 and a cassette for $8. She handed the cashier $20. How much change did she receive?

Step 1. Add to find the total cost of her purchases.

Step 2. Subtract to find the difference between this cost and the amount she gave the cashier.

```
$  7  record
+  8  cassette
$15   total cost

$20   amount tendered
− 15  total cost
$  5  Mary's change
```

Multistep area problems require you to find the area of more complicated figures. These are often made up of two simple figures.

Example 2: Find the area of the shaded portion on Figure 5.

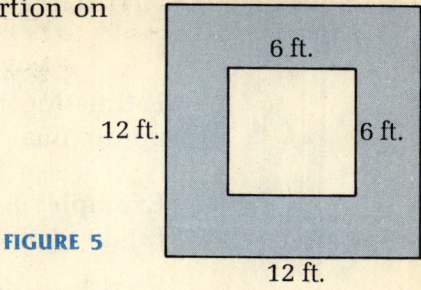

FIGURE 5

12 ft. 6 ft. 6 ft. 12 ft.

Step 1. Use the formula for the area of a square to find the area of the larger square.

$A = s^2$
$= 12 \times 12$
$= 144$ square feet

Step 2. Now find the area of the smaller square.

$A = s^2$
$= 6 \times 6$
$= 36$ square feet

Step 3. To find the area of the shaded part of the figure, find the difference between the areas of the two squares.

144 square feet
− 36 square feet
108 square feet

Lesson 1 Exercise

Directions: *Solve each problem.*

1. Dale bought items that cost $18, $9, and $7. How much change did he receive when he gave the cashier $50?
2. Darlene earns $16,500 per year. Her employer deducts $2,100 per year for taxes and Social Security. What is her net monthly income?
3. A school spent $480 on a dance. If 300 people paid $4 each to attend, how much money was earned?

Directions: *Find the area of the shaded part of each figure.*

4. 13 yd. 12 yd. 4 yd. 28 yd.

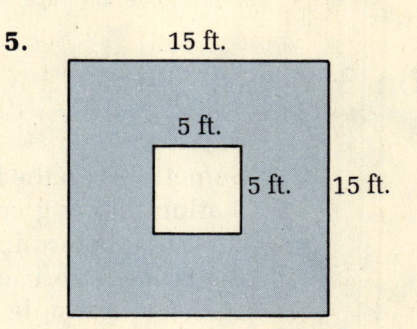

5. 15 ft. 5 ft. 5 ft. 15 ft.

Answers are on page A-41.

Lesson 2 Estimating

Estimating is an operation that can be used when a question asks for an approximate answer. Rounding is often used to make calculations simpler.

Example: 813 × 492 is approximately equal to (1) 30,000 (2) 40,000 (3) 300,000 or (4) 400,000.

Step 1. Instead of multiplying 813 by 492 to find an exact answer, first round 813 and 492 to the nearest hundred.

813 rounds to 800
492 rounds to 500

Step 2. Now multiply the rounded numbers. The correct answer is choice (4).

```
    800
  × 500
400,000
```

Lesson 2 Exercise

Directions: *Estimate to solve each problem.*

1. Bud has a board that is 12 feet long. Approximately how many shelves that are each 2 feet 9 inches long can be cut from that board?
2. A plane can carry 398 passengers. About how many passengers can 22 planes carry altogether?
3. If a pair of gerbils produces 18 offspring in one year, approximately how many offspring will 286 pairs of gerbils produce in one year?
4. On the New York Stock Exchange, 87,340 shares of a certain stock were traded by 982 brokers. Approximately how many shares did each broker trade?
5. Assemblyperson Guerro's district contains 33 electoral precincts. There are 985 voters in each electoral precinct. Approximately how many voters does Assemblyperson Guerro represent?

Answers are on page A-42.

Lesson 3 Item Sets

Sometimes on the Mathematics Test several questions will be based on information that is given in a paragraph. Read the paragraph and each question carefully, determine what information is given and what you must find, select the strategy to use, and solve the problem.

The example is based on the following paragraph.

The four members of the Alvarez family are taking a trip to Boston. They could take a plane, which would cost $158 round trip for each of the two adults and $98 for each of the two children. They could rent a car instead. The car rental would cost $43 per day including unlimited mileage. They plan to leave on Friday morning and return Monday night. The car gets 20 miles to a gallon of gas; gas costs $1 per gallon. The distance from New York to Boston is 200 miles.

Example: How much would the trip cost if the Alvarezes rented a car?

Step 1. The paragraph gives the cost per day to rent a car. You must determine how many days the family will be gone. Multiply this result by the rental cost per day.

Friday to Monday = 4 days

$$\begin{array}{r}\$\ 43 \text{ rental per day} \\ \times\ \ \ \ 4 \text{ days} \\ \hline \$172 \text{ car rental}\end{array}$$

Step 2. To find the cost of gas for the round trip: (a) add the distances to and from Boston; (b) divide the result by miles per gallon; (c) multiply the result by cost per gallon.

a. 200 + 200 = 400 miles

b. $20 \overline{)400}$ = 20 gallons of gas

c. 20 gals × $1 = $20

Step 3. Add the rental cost to the cost for gas

$$\begin{array}{r}\$172 \text{ car rental} \\ +\ \ \ 20 \text{ cost of gas} \\ \hline \$192 \text{ total cost}\end{array}$$

Lesson 3 Exercise

Items 1 to 5 are based on the following paragraph.

Steve has to decide whether to continue his present part-time job or to participate in the work-study program at his community college. At his current job, he earns $8 per hour and works 30 hours per week. He spends $2 daily, Monday through Friday, on transportation from his job to college. If he participates in the work-study program, he will be paid $4 per hour for 40 hours per week and receive free tuition benefits. Since his work-study job would be at the college, he would not have to pay for transportation. In either case, he plans to take a total of 30 credits per year at $40 per credit. Either way, he would work and go to school 50 weeks per year.

1. How much more would Steve earn per hour at his part-time job than in the work-study program.
2. What is the difference between the two weekly wages?
3. If tuition benefits were counted as income, what would Steve's annual income from the work-study program be?
4. With his part-time job, how much money does Steve spend on transportation per year?
5. Considering tuition and transportation, would Steve's net income per year be higher from his part-time job or from the work-study program?

Answers are on page A-42.

Lesson 4 Setup Answers

Some of the items on the GED Test require you only to set up the problem without actually solving it.

Example: John and Lisa earn $255 and $325 per week. Write the expression that would yield their combined annual income.

Step 1. You would use addition to find the combined weekly income.   255 + 325

Step 2. To find the combined annual income, you would multiply by 52, the number of weeks in a year.   52(255 + 325)

Lesson 4 Exercise

Directions: *Set up the solutions to the following problems.*

1. Eric earns $145 and $85 weekly at his two part-time jobs. What is his annual income?
2. The high temperatures for 7 days in May were 76 degrees, 67 degrees, 65 degrees, 74 degrees, 77 degrees, 75 degrees, and 70 degrees. What was the average high temperature for the seven days?
3. Mr. and Mrs. Akbar took out a loan for a new car that costs $8600. They agreed to pay the loan by making 48 payments of $252 each. How much more than the price of the car did the loan cost the Akbars?
4. George earns $18,542 per year. His employer withholds $3286 for taxes and Social Security. How much is George's net weekly income?
5. The measurement of each window in Joanne's house is 2 yards by 3 yards. At $4 per square yard, how much will fabric cost to make window shades for 12 windows?

Answers are on page A-42.

Level 3 Review

Directions: *Solve each problem.*

1. The town of Elmsville spends $550,000 on fire and police protection, $270,000 on administration, $400,000 on flood control, and $1,500,000 on building and roads. How much more is spent on building and roads than on the other categories combined?

UNIT VII: MATHEMATICS   Level 3 Review   **457**

2. A student organization collected $1575 during a fund-raising drive. Expenses amounted to $250. If the net amount is divided equally among 5 charitable organizations, how much will each organization receive?

3. Marco had $648 in his checking account. He wrote checks for $75, $35, $28, $155, and $262. What is his new balance?

Items 4 to 6 are based on the following table.

Personal Energy Cost of Various Activities	
Average Calories Used per Hour	**Activities**
330	Playing volleyball Playing doubles tennis
390	Ice-skating Roller-skating
460	Walking at 5 miles per hour Playing singles tennis
520	Jogging at 5 miles per hour Playing basketball
630	Cycling at 13 miles per hour

4. In an average week, Jan plays singles tennis for 2 hours, ice-skates for 3 hours, and jogs at 5 miles per hour for 4 hours. How many calories does she use doing these activities?

5. How many more calories does Mark use walking 5 miles per hour for 3 hours, than he does jogging at 5 miles per hour for 2 hours?

6. Bob uses up 3340 calories per day cycling and playing basketball. He cycles at 13 miles per hour for 2 hours. How many hours of basketball does he play each day?

Directions: *Refer to the formulas on page 438 to solve each problem.*

7. Find the area in square centimeters of the shaded part of the figure.

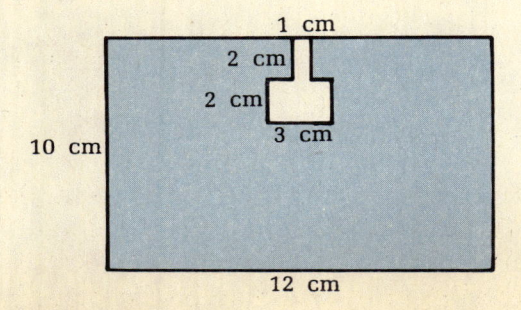

8. John is using tiles that measure 12 inches by 12 inches. What is the smallest number of tiles he needs to cover the floor of the shown room?

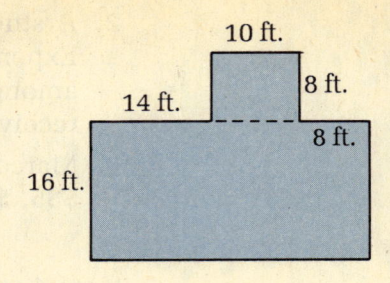

10 ft.
8 ft.
14 ft.
8 ft.
16 ft.

Directions: *Set up, but do not solve, each problem.*

9. Resa works part-time at two different jobs. In one week, she worked 15 hours at $4 per hour at one job and 20 hours at $5 per hour at the other job. How much did she earn during that week?

10. A teacher has 2 classes of 25 pupils each, 3 classes of 28 pupils each, and 1 class of 30 pupils. How many pupils does the teacher have altogether?

Check your answers. Correct answers are on page A-42. If you have at least eight answers correct, go to the Chapter Quiz. If you have fewer than eight answers correct, go back to Lesson 1 and study Level 3 again.

Chapter 1 Quiz

1. The Ching family traveled 385 kilometers on the first day of their trip, 255 kilometers on the second day, 305 kilometers on the third day, and 628 kilometers on the fourth day. What is the total number of kilometers that they traveled?

2. Jamal's restaurant check came to $28. If he gives the waitress $40, how much change should she bring him?

3. Ray calls an average of 15 people per hour in his telephone sales job. How many people does he call during a 40-hour workweek?

4. A local fast-foods restaurant serves 6000 hamburgers per week. It is open 75 hours per week. On the average, how many hamburgers does it serve per hour?

5. On a recent trip, the Ramirez family traveled at approximately 53 miles per hour. Rounded to the nearest 10 miles, how far did they travel after 42 hours?

6. If one gallon of orange juice costs $3, how much do 8 quarts cost? Remember that 1 gallon equals 4 quarts.

7. What is the value of 5^3?

8. What is the square root of 81?

Directions: *Refer to the formulas on page 438 for items 9 to 15.*

9. What is the perimeter of the rectangle in this figure?

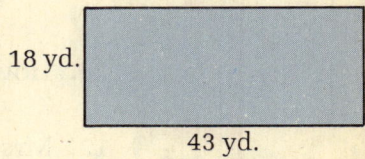

   18 yd.
   43 yd.

10. What is the area of this square?

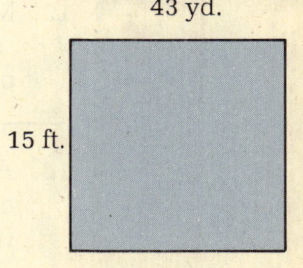

    15 ft.

11. How many cubic feet of sand does this sandbox hold?

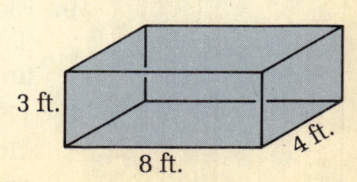

    3 ft.
    8 ft.
    4 ft.

12. Paul wants to plant a border of flowers around his patio. What is the area of the patio without the border?

13. If the border is 2 feet wide, what is the area of the border?

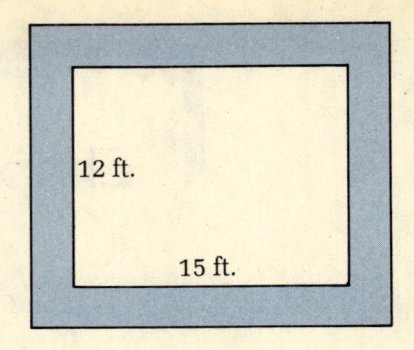

12 ft.

15 ft.

14. What is the area of this room?

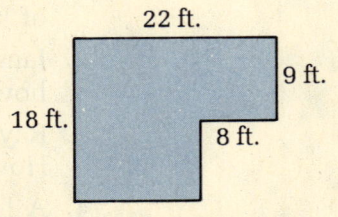

22 ft.

9 ft.

18 ft.

8 ft.

15. How much is a lot that measures 60 feet by 100 feet worth if the land is valued at $8 per square foot?

Items 16 and 17 are based on the table at the right.

Energy Needs Through Life

Daily Calorie Requirements

Age	Males	Females
11–14	1700	2200
15–18	2800	2100
19–22	2900	2100
23–50	2700	2000
51–75	2050	1800

16. How many more calories do 22-year-old men need daily than 20-year-old women?

17. Mrs. Schmidt is 44 years old. Her husband is 43 years old. They have a 17-year-old daughter and a 13-year-old son. What is the mean calorie requirement per member of the Schmidt family?

18. A family bought a color television for $450. They paid $50 in cash and paid the balance in 10 equal monthly installments with no finance charge. What was the amount of each monthly installment?

19. Elaine mailed 4 books to her nephew. Each book weighed 2 pounds. If books cost $4 per pound to mail, how much postage did she have to pay in all?

20. The Johnson family spends $125 per week on food and $350 per month on rent. Write the expression that shows how much they spend annually on food and rent. Do not solve the problem.

Answers are on pages A-42–A-43.

Chapter 2 Fractions

Objective

In this chapter, you will learn to

- Reduce fractions to lowest terms; raise fractions to higher terms
- Change improper fractions to whole or mixed numbers
- Change mixed numbers to improper fractions
- Find lowest common denominators
- Add and subtract fractions that have like and unlike denominators
- Multiply and divide using fractions and mixed numbers
- Solve problems involving standard units of measurement, comparing and ordering fractions, tables, ratios, and probability
- Work with problems that feature setup answers; mixed units with perimeter, area, and volume; and extraneous information

Level 1 Fraction Skills

Preview

Directions: *Express answers in lowest terms. Change improper fractions to whole or mixed numbers.*

1. Add $\frac{1}{4}$, $\frac{4}{5}$, and $\frac{7}{10}$.
2. Subtract $\frac{3}{5}$ from $\frac{14}{15}$.
3. Multiply $2\frac{5}{8}$ by $\frac{5}{9}$.
4. Divide $\frac{6}{11}$ by $\frac{21}{22}$.
5. Divide $4\frac{1}{5}$ by $1\frac{13}{15}$.

Check your answers. Correct answers are on page A-43. If you have at least four answers correct, do the Level 1 Review on page 472. If you have fewer than four answers correct, study Level 1 beginning with Lesson 1.

Lesson 1 Reducing Fractions

Fractions are used to show parts of a whole.

$$\frac{\text{part shaded}}{\text{total number of parts}} = \frac{3}{4} \begin{array}{l}\text{numerator}\\ \text{denominator}\end{array}$$

461

To reduce a fraction, divide both the numerator and the denominator by the same number. This number has to divide into both the numerator and the denominator evenly. Reducing changes the numbers in a fraction, but the value of the fraction stays the same. A fraction has been reduced to its *lowest terms* or *simplest form* when no number, other than 1, can be divided into its numerator and its denominator evenly.

Sometimes you may not divide by the largest number possible when you reduce a fraction. If you do not, you will have to reduce the fraction at least once again to express it in lowest terms.

Example: Reduce $\frac{16}{24}$ to lowest terms.

Step 1. Divide both 16 and 24 by one number that divides into each of them evenly. **4** divides into 16 and 24 evenly.

$$\frac{16 \div 4}{24 \div 4} = \frac{4}{6}$$

Step 2. Check to see whether any number, other than 1, divides into both 4 and 6 evenly. **2** divides into both numbers evenly.

$$\frac{4 \div 2}{6 \div 2} = \frac{2}{3}$$

Step 3. Check to see whether any number, other than 1, divides into both 2 and 3 evenly. Since none does, $\frac{2}{3}$ represents $\frac{16}{24}$ in lowest terms.

$$\frac{2 \div ?}{3 \div ?}$$

$$\frac{16}{24} = \frac{2}{3}$$

It is possible to reduce $\frac{16}{24}$ by dividing once by 8.

Lesson 1   Exercise

Directions: *Reduce each fraction to lowest terms.*

1. $\frac{5}{20}$ 2. $\frac{6}{9}$ 3. $\frac{4}{24}$ 4. $\frac{56}{63}$ 5. $\frac{15}{21}$

Answers are on page A-43.

Lesson 2   Raising Fractions to Higher Terms

When you raise a fraction to higher terms, you increase the numbers in both the numerator and the denominator, but the value of the fraction stays the same. When two or more fractions have the same value, they are called *equivalent fractions*.

Usually you know what higher denominator you want in an equivalent fraction. In such cases, to raise a fraction to higher terms, divide the larger denominator by the denominator of the original fraction. Then multiply the numerator of the original fraction by the answer from your division.

Example: Raise the fraction $\frac{1}{2}$ to a fraction that has a denominator of 16.

Step 1. Write an equation showing $\frac{1}{2}$ (the original fraction) equal to a fraction with an unknown numerator and a denominator of 16.

$$\frac{1}{2} = \frac{?}{16}$$

Step 2. Divide 16 (the larger denominator) by 2 (the original denominator). The answer is 8.

$$2\overline{)16}^{\,8}$$

Step 3. Multiply the numerator in $\frac{1}{2}$ by 8. $\frac{1}{2}$ raised to sixteenths is $\frac{8}{16}$. $\frac{1}{2}$ and $\frac{8}{16}$ are equivalent fractions.

$$\frac{1 \times 8}{2 \times 8} = \frac{8}{16}$$

Lesson 2 Exercise

Directions: Raise each fraction to higher terms by finding the missing numerator.

1. $\frac{1}{4} = \frac{?}{12}$
2. $\frac{1}{2} = \frac{?}{20}$
3. $\frac{2}{5} = \frac{?}{15}$
4. $\frac{5}{8} = \frac{?}{32}$
5. $\frac{5}{6} = \frac{?}{36}$
6. $\frac{7}{9} = \frac{?}{27}$
7. $\frac{2}{3} = \frac{?}{24}$
8. $\frac{5}{6} = \frac{?}{30}$
9. $\frac{3}{7} = \frac{?}{35}$
10. $\frac{5}{12} = \frac{?}{60}$

Answers are on page A-43.

Lesson 3 Mixed Numbers

Changing Improper Fractions to Whole or Mixed Numbers

An *improper fraction* is a fraction in which the numerator is equal to or greater than the denominator. A *mixed number* is a number that consists of a whole number plus a fraction.

To change an improper fraction to a whole or a mixed number, divide the numerator by the denominator and write the answer as a whole number.

Example 1: Change $\frac{21}{7}$ to a whole or a mixed number.

Step 1. $\frac{21}{7}$ is an improper fraction. To express its value in simpler terms, divide the numerator, 21, by the denominator, 7.

$$\frac{21}{7} = ?$$

Step 2. Write 3, the answer to the division, as a whole number. Since 7 divides into 21 evenly, there is no remainder. The final answer is 3.

$$7\overline{)21}^{\,3}$$

$$\frac{21}{7} = 3$$

When you divide, if there is a remainder, write it as the numerator of a fraction with the denominator from the original improper fraction. Reduce that fraction to simplest terms.

Example 2: Change $\frac{15}{6}$ to a whole or a mixed number.

Step 1. Divide 15 by 6. Write 2 as a whole number. There is a remainder of 3. Write 3 over the denominator, 6. This gives you the mixed number $2\frac{3}{6}$.

$$\frac{15}{6} = ?$$

$$\begin{array}{r} 2\frac{3}{6} \\ 6\overline{)15} \\ \underline{12} \\ 3 \end{array}$$

Step 2. The fraction $\frac{3}{6}$ can be reduced by dividing the numerator and the denominator by 3. The fraction becomes $\frac{1}{2}$. The final answer in simplest form is $2\frac{1}{2}$.

$$\frac{3 \div 3}{6 \div 3} = \frac{1}{2}$$

$$\frac{15}{6} = 2\frac{1}{2}$$

Changing Mixed Numbers to Improper Fractions

To be able to solve some fraction problems, you must be able to change mixed numbers to improper fractions. To do that, multiply the whole number by the denominator. Add the result to the numerator.

Example 3: Change $5\frac{7}{8}$ to an improper fraction.

Step 1. Multiply the whole number, 5, by the denominator, 8. The product is 40.

$$5\frac{7}{8} = ?$$

$$5 \times 8 = 40$$

Step 2. Add 40 to 7, the numerator. The sum is 47.

$$40 + 7 = 47$$

Step 3. The new numerator of the improper fraction is 47. Keep the denominator from the mixed number (8). The mixed number $5\frac{7}{8}$ is equal to $\frac{47}{8}$.

$$5\frac{7}{8} = \frac{47}{8}$$

Lesson 3   Exercise

Directions: Change each improper fraction to a whole or a mixed number in simplest form.

1. $\frac{7}{7}$ 2. $\frac{28}{4}$ 3. $\frac{22}{10}$ 4. $\frac{66}{9}$ 5. $\frac{54}{8}$

Directions: Change each mixed number to an improper fraction.

6. $1\frac{1}{2}$ 7. $2\frac{5}{6}$ 8. $8\frac{3}{7}$ 9. $4\frac{2}{5}$ 10. $5\frac{11}{12}$

Answers are on page A-43.

UNIT VII: MATHEMATICS

Lesson 4   Finding Common Denominators and the LCD

Common denominators are found by using multiples. A *multiple* of a number is the product of that number multiplied by any other number. For example, the product of 3 and another number is a multiple of 3: $3 \times 1 = 3$, $3 \times 2 = 6$, and $3 \times 3 = 9$. The products—3, 6, and 9—are multiples of 3.

A **common multiple** is a multiple of several numbers: 36 is a common multiple of 3, 4, 6, 9, 12, and 18. All of those numbers divide into 36 evenly.

A **common denominator** is a multiple of all the denominators in a given group of fractions. A *least common denominator* (LCD) is the smallest common multiple of several denominators.

To change a group of fractions that have unlike denominators to fractions that have a common denominator, you first find the LCD. Then raise each fraction to higher terms using the LCD as the denominator for each equivalent fraction.

Example: Write equivalent fractions for $\frac{3}{4}$ and $\frac{1}{6}$ that have the same denominator. Be sure that the denominator is the LCD.

Step 1. List the multiples of both denominators and determine the LCD. The LCD for 4 and 6 is 12.

Multiples of 4:
  4, 8, 12, 16 . . .
Multiples of 6:
  6, 12, 18, 24 . . .

Step 2. Raise $\frac{3}{4}$ to an equivalent fraction that has a denominator of 12. Multiply the original numerator and denominator by 3.

$\frac{3 \times 3}{4 \times 3} = \frac{9}{12}$

Step 3. Now raise $\frac{1}{6}$ to an equivalent fraction that has a denominator of 12. Multiply the original numerator and denominator by 2.

$\frac{1 \times 2}{6 \times 2} = \frac{2}{12}$

Lesson 4   Exercise

Directions: *Find the LCD for each group of fractions. Then change each fraction in a group to an equivalent fraction that has the LCD as its denominator.*

1. $\frac{1}{3}$ and $\frac{2}{9}$
2. $\frac{2}{5}$ and $\frac{3}{8}$
3. $\frac{3}{4}$ and $\frac{5}{6}$
4. $\frac{1}{4}$ and $\frac{7}{10}$
5. $\frac{2}{3}$ and $\frac{5}{8}$
6. $\frac{2}{3}$, $\frac{9}{10}$, and $\frac{11}{15}$
7. $\frac{1}{3}$, $\frac{5}{6}$, and $\frac{7}{8}$
8. $\frac{1}{2}$, $\frac{3}{8}$, and $\frac{2}{5}$
9. $\frac{1}{4}$, $\frac{4}{5}$, and $\frac{5}{6}$
10. $\frac{5}{6}$, $\frac{5}{7}$, and $\frac{5}{8}$

Answers are on pages A-43–A-44.

Chapter 2: Fractions INSTRUCTION

Lesson 5 Adding Fractions and Mixed Numbers

Adding Fractions and Mixed Numbers That Have Like Denominators

To add fractions that have like denominators, add the numerators. Write the sum of the numerators over the common denominator. If the result is an improper fraction, change it to a whole or a mixed number. Remember to reduce fractions.

Example 1: Add $\frac{5}{8}$ and $\frac{7}{8}$.

Step 1. Add the numerators: $5 + 7 = 12$. Then write the total over the common denominator, 8.

$$\begin{array}{r} \frac{5}{8} \\ + \frac{7}{8} \\ \hline \frac{12}{8} = 1\frac{4}{8} = 1\frac{1}{2} \end{array}$$

Step 2. Change $\frac{12}{8}$ to a mixed number by dividing 12 by 8. You get $1\frac{4}{8}$.

Step 3. Reduce $\frac{4}{8}$ by dividing the numerator and the denominator by 4. The final answer is $1\frac{1}{2}$.

When adding mixed numbers, add the whole numbers separately. Then combine the fraction total with the whole-number total to get the final answer.

Adding Fractions and Mixed Numbers That Have Unlike Denominators

To add fractions or mixed numbers that have unlike denominators, first find the LCD. Change all fractions to equivalent fractions with the same LCD. Then follow the procedure for adding fractions that have like denominators.

Example 2: Find the sum of $3\frac{3}{4}$, $2\frac{1}{2}$, and $1\frac{2}{5}$.

Step 1. Find the LCD for $\frac{3}{4}$, $\frac{1}{2}$, and $\frac{2}{5}$. The lowest number that 4, 2, and 5 all divide into evenly is 20. Change each fraction to an equivalent fraction that has a denominator of 20.

$$\begin{array}{r} 3\frac{3}{4} = 3\frac{15}{20} \\ 2\frac{1}{2} = 2\frac{10}{20} \\ + 1\frac{2}{5} = 1\frac{8}{20} \\ \hline 6\frac{33}{20} = 7\frac{13}{20} \end{array}$$

Step 2. Add the new numerators and put the sum over the common denominator, 20.

Step 3. Add the whole numbers.

Step 4. Simplify the mixed number: $6\frac{33}{20} = 7\frac{13}{20}$.

UNIT VII: MATHEMATICS

Lesson 5 Exercise

Directions: Find each sum. Express the answers in simplest form.

1. $\frac{3}{5} + \frac{1}{5}$
2. $\frac{7}{12} + \frac{11}{12}$
3. $6\frac{3}{8} + 7\frac{3}{8}$
4. $4\frac{7}{10} + 3\frac{3}{10}$
5. $\frac{1}{2} + \frac{3}{8}$
6. $\frac{2}{3} + \frac{3}{4}$
7. $\frac{1}{2} + \frac{1}{4} + \frac{5}{6}$
8. $4\frac{1}{6} + 8\frac{3}{8}$
9. $7\frac{2}{3} + 6\frac{1}{2}$
10. $3\frac{4}{5} + \frac{13}{15}$

Answers are on page A-44.

Lesson 6 Subtracting Fractions and Mixed Numbers

Subtracting Fractions and Mixed Numbers That Have Like Denominators

To subtract fractions that have like denominators, subtract the numerator in the bottom fraction from the numerator in the top fraction. Write the difference over the common denominator. Then, if necessary, reduce the answer to lowest terms. When subtracting mixed numbers, subtract the fractions and the whole numbers separately.

Example 1: Find $7\frac{9}{10} - 3\frac{1}{10}$.

Step 1. Subtract the fractions by subtracting the numerators. Write 8 over the common denominator, 10.

$$\begin{array}{r} 7\frac{9}{10} \\ - 3\frac{1}{10} \\ \hline 4\frac{8}{10} = 4\frac{4}{5} \end{array}$$

Step 2. Subtract the whole numbers.

Step 3. Combine the whole number and the fraction to get $4\frac{8}{10}$. Reduce $\frac{8}{10}$ to get the final answer, $4\frac{4}{5}$.

Subtracting Fractions and Mixed Numbers That Have Unlike Denominators

To subtract fractions or mixed numbers that have unlike denominators, first find the LCD. Then change both fractions to equivalent fractions that have the same LCD. Then follow the procedure for subtracting fractions or mixed numbers that have like denominators.

Example 2: Subtract $2\frac{1}{9}$ from $10\frac{5}{6}$.

Step 1. Set up the problem with the larger number on top. Find the LCD for $\frac{1}{9}$ and $\frac{5}{6}$. It is 18. Raise each fraction to an equivalent fraction that has a denominator of 18.

$$10\frac{5}{6} = 10\frac{15}{18}$$
$$-\ 2\frac{1}{9} =\ \ 2\frac{2}{18}$$
$$\overline{\ \ \ \ \ \ \ \ \ \ \ \ \ \ 8\frac{13}{18}}$$

Step 2. Subtract the numerators. Write 13 over the common denominator, 18.

Step 3. Subtract the whole numbers. Then combine the whole number and fraction difference. Check to see if the fraction can be reduced. The final answer is $8\frac{13}{18}$.

Borrowing From a Whole Number

When a fraction or a mixed number is subtracted from a whole number, it is necessary to borrow 1 from the whole number. Rewrite the 1 as an improper fraction with the same denominator as the other fraction.

Example 3: Subtract $2\frac{3}{5}$ from 9.

Step 1. Set up the problem with the larger number on top. Borrow 1 from 9 and write it as an improper fraction, $\frac{5}{5}$.

$$9 = 8\frac{5}{5}$$
$$-\ 2\frac{3}{5} =\ 2\frac{3}{5}$$
$$\overline{\ \ \ \ \ \ \ \ \ \ \ 6\frac{2}{5}}$$

Step 2. Subtract $\frac{3}{5}$ from $\frac{5}{5}$.

Step 3. Subtract 2 from 8. The final answer is $6\frac{2}{5}$.

You must also borrow 1 when the numerator in the top fraction is less than the one in the bottom fraction. Write the borrowed 1 as an improper fraction with the same denominator as the other fraction. Then add it to the original top fraction. The fraction on top is then large enough to do the subtraction.

Example 4: Find $3\frac{1}{8} - 2\frac{7}{8}$.

Step 1. You cannot subtract $\frac{7}{8}$ from $\frac{1}{8}$, so you borrow 1 from 3. Write it as $\frac{8}{8}$. Add $\frac{8}{8}$ to $\frac{1}{8}$.

$$3\frac{1}{8} = 2\frac{1}{8} + \frac{8}{8} = 2\frac{9}{8}$$
$$-\ 2\frac{7}{8}\ \ \ \ \ \ \ \ \ \ \ \ \ \ \ \ \ \ = 2\frac{7}{8}$$
$$\overline{\ \frac{2}{8} = \frac{1}{4}}$$

Step 2. Subtract $\frac{7}{8}$ from $\frac{9}{8}$.

Step 3. Subtract 2 from 2. The result is 0, so there is no whole number in the answer.

Step 4. Reduce $\frac{2}{8}$ to lowest terms. The final answer is $\frac{1}{4}$.

When subtracting fractions that have unlike denominators, first change them to fractions that have the same LCD. Then borrow from the whole number if necessary.

UNIT VII: MATHEMATICS   Level 1: Lesson 7   **469**

Lesson 6   Exercise

Directions: Subtract. Express each answer in lowest terms.

1. $\frac{8}{9} - \frac{7}{9}$
2. $\frac{7}{16} - \frac{3}{16}$
3. $9\frac{3}{4} - 3\frac{1}{4}$
4. $\frac{2}{3} - \frac{1}{6}$
5. $6\frac{4}{5} - 2\frac{1}{2}$
6. $7\frac{2}{5} - 5$
7. $11 - 2\frac{5}{6}$
8. $8\frac{2}{5} - 1\frac{4}{5}$
9. $12\frac{2}{3} - 6\frac{3}{4}$
10. $13\frac{1}{8} - 4\frac{7}{12}$

Answers are on page A-44.

Lesson 7   Multiplying Fractions and Mixed Numbers

Multipying Fractions by Fractions

To multiply fractions, you find the product of the numerators and write it over the product of the denominators. Then reduce the answer to lowest terms.

Sometimes you can divide a numerator and a denominator by the same number before you multiply. This is called **canceling**. It is similar to reducing fractions. If all numbers that can be canceled are canceled, the answer will come out in lowest terms.

Example 1: Find $\frac{3}{4} \times \frac{8}{9}$.

Step 1. Set up the problem. Divide 3 and 9 by 3.

$$\frac{\overset{1}{\cancel{3}}}{4} \times \frac{8}{\underset{3}{\cancel{9}}} =$$

Step 2. Divide 4 and 8 by 4.

Step 3. Multiply the new numerators and multiply the new denominators. The final answer is $\frac{2}{3}$, which is in lowest terms.

$$\frac{\overset{1}{\cancel{3}}}{\underset{1}{\cancel{4}}} \times \frac{\overset{2}{\cancel{8}}}{\underset{3}{\cancel{9}}} = \frac{2}{3}$$

Multiplying Fractions by Whole Numbers and Mixed Numbers

To multiply a fraction by a whole number, change the whole number to a fraction. Write the whole number as the numerator and use 1 as the denominator.

Example 2: Multiply $\frac{7}{9}$ by 6.

Step 1. Write 6 as a fraction. Use 6 as the numerator and 1 as the denominator.

$6 = \frac{6}{1}$

Step 2. Set up the problem. To cancel 6 and 9, divide by 3.

$\frac{7}{\cancel{9}_{3}} \times \frac{\cancel{6}^{2}}{1} = \frac{14}{3} = 4\frac{2}{3}$

Step 3. Multiply the numerators. Multiply the denominators.

Step 4. Change the improper fraction to a mixed number: $\frac{14}{3} = 4\frac{2}{3}$.

To multiply a fraction by a mixed number, change the mixed number to an improper fraction.

Example 3: Find $\frac{3}{5} \times 7\frac{1}{2}$.

Step 1. Write the mixed number as an improper fraction.

$7\frac{1}{2} = \frac{15}{2}$

Step 2. Set up the problem. Cancel the 5 and 15 by dividing by 5.

$\frac{3}{\cancel{5}_{1}} \times \frac{\cancel{15}^{3}}{2} = \frac{9}{2}$

Step 3. Multiply the numerators and multiply the denominators.

Step 4. Write the improper fraction as a mixed number.

$\frac{9}{2} = 4\frac{1}{2}$

Lesson 7 Exercise

Directions: *Multiply. Express each answer in lowest terms.*

1. $\frac{3}{4} \times \frac{1}{4}$
2. $\frac{5}{6} \times \frac{3}{8}$
3. $\frac{2}{3} \times \frac{5}{9} \times \frac{3}{8}$
4. $\frac{3}{4} \times 8$
5. $2\frac{1}{2} \times \frac{4}{5}$
6. $2\frac{1}{4} \times 3\frac{1}{3}$
7. $1\frac{2}{3} \times 9$
8. $1\frac{1}{6} \times \frac{3}{7} \times 4\frac{2}{3}$
9. $3\frac{1}{5} \times 6 \times 1\frac{1}{4}$
10. $1\frac{1}{11} \times \frac{11}{12}$

Answers are on page A-44.

Lesson 8 Dividing Fractions and Mixed Numbers

Dividing by Fractions

To divide a fraction by a fraction, invert the fraction to the right of the division sign. To *invert* means to reverse the numbers of the fraction by placing the numerator on the bottom and the denominator on the top. For example, when you invert $\frac{2}{3}$, you have $\frac{3}{2}$. After you invert the fraction to the right of the division sign, change the sign to a multiplication sign and multiply.

Example 1: Divide $\frac{2}{3}$ by $\frac{1}{6}$.

Step 1. Set up the problem. Invert the fraction to the right of the division sign: $\frac{1}{6}$ becomes $\frac{6}{1}$. Change the division sign to a multiplication sign.

$$\frac{2}{3} \div \frac{1}{6} =$$
$$\frac{2}{3} \times \frac{6}{1} =$$

Step 2. Cancel. Divide 3 and 6 by 3.

Step 3. Multiply the numerators. Multiply the denominators.

$$\frac{2}{{}_1 3} \times \frac{{}^2 6}{1} = \frac{4}{1} = 4$$

Step 4: Change the improper fraction to a whole number.

Dividing With Whole Numbers and Mixed Numbers

To divide with whole or mixed numbers, change every whole or mixed number to an improper fraction. Then divide as in Example 1.

Example 2: Find $\frac{7}{8} \div 3$.

Step 1. Change 3 to the improper fraction $\frac{3}{1}$.

$$\frac{7}{8} \div 3 =$$

Step 2. Invert $\frac{3}{1}$ to $\frac{1}{3}$. Change the division sign to a multiplication sign.

$$\frac{7}{8} \div \frac{3}{1} =$$

Step 3. Multiply.

$$\frac{7}{8} \times \frac{1}{3} = \frac{7}{24}$$

Example 3: Divide $1\frac{1}{3}$ by $2\frac{2}{9}$.

Step 1. Change $1\frac{1}{3}$ and $2\frac{2}{9}$ to improper fractions.

$$1\frac{1}{3} \div 2\frac{2}{9} =$$

Step 2. Invert $\frac{20}{9}$ to $\frac{9}{20}$ and change the division sign to a multiplication sign.

$$\frac{4}{3} \div \frac{20}{9} =$$

Step 3. Cancel. Then multiply.

$$\frac{{}^1 4}{{}_1 3} \times \frac{{}^3 9}{20{}_5} = \frac{3}{5}$$

Lesson 8   Exercise

Directions: *Divide. Express each answer in simplest form.*

1. $\frac{1}{3} \div \frac{3}{4}$
2. $\frac{4}{5} \div \frac{7}{10}$
3. $8 \div \frac{1}{2}$
4. $\frac{5}{6} \div 10$

5. $1\frac{2}{3} \div 3$
6. $\frac{3}{5} \div 5\frac{1}{4}$
7. $5\frac{1}{3} \div 4$
8. $5 \div 4\frac{1}{6}$

9. $3\frac{1}{2} \div 4\frac{5}{8}$
10. $2\frac{2}{3} \div 1\frac{1}{5}$

Answers are on page A-44.

472   Chapter 2: Fractions   INSTRUCTION

Level 1   Review

Directions: *Solve each problem. Express each answer in simplest form.*

1. Reduce $\frac{21}{36}$ to lowest terms.
2. Change $7\frac{3}{4}$ to an improper fraction.
3. $\frac{2}{3} + \frac{5}{8}$ 4. $5\frac{7}{12} + 3\frac{1}{6} + 7\frac{2}{3}$ 5. $5\frac{6}{7} - 2\frac{2}{5}$ 6. $9\frac{2}{3} - 4\frac{7}{9}$
7. $\frac{4}{5} \times 2\frac{1}{2}$ 8. $4\frac{3}{8} \times \frac{4}{7} \times 3$ 9. $5 \div \frac{10}{11}$ 10. $\frac{11}{12} \div 2\frac{4}{9}$

Check your answers. Correct answers are on page A-45. If you have at least eight answers correct, go to Level 2. If you have fewer than eight answers correct, go back to Lesson 1 and study Level 1.

Level 2   Fraction Applications

Lesson 1   Standard Units of Measure

This lesson will cover the U.S. Customary System of commonly used units of measure. Use the Table of Measures at the start of this unit for reference.

When working with units of measure, you often have to use fractions, particularly when changing from one unit of measure to another. Use these steps to help you make such changes.

- Find how many of the smaller units equal one larger unit. For example, 3 feet (the smaller unit) equals 1 yard (the larger unit).
- To change from a larger unit to a smaller unit, multiply.
- To change from a smaller unit to a larger unit, divide.

Example 1: Change $\frac{2}{3}$ yard to feet.

Step 1. Refer to the Table of Measures. See that 3 feet equals 1 yard.

Step 2. Multiply to change from a larger unit (yards) to a smaller unit (feet).

$\qquad$ 3 feet = 1 yard

$\qquad$ $\frac{2}{3} \times \frac{3}{1} = \frac{6}{3} = \frac{2}{1} = 2$ feet

Example 2: Express 40 ounces as pounds.

Step 1. Refer to the Table of Measures. Find that 16 ounces equals 1 pound.

Step 2. Divide to change from a smaller unit (ounces) to a larger unit (pounds).

$\qquad$ 16 ounces = 1 pound

$\qquad$ $2\frac{8}{16} = 2\frac{1}{2}$ pounds

$\qquad$ $16 \overline{)40}$
$\qquad\quad\;\;\underline{32}$
$\qquad\quad\;\;\;\;8$

UNIT VII: MATHEMATICS   Level 2: Lesson 2   **473**

Sometimes when you are changing from a smaller unit to a larger unit, the remainder, after dividing, can be expressed as the smaller unit instead of as a fraction of the larger unit.

Example 3: Change 80 minutes to hours and minutes.

Step 1. Refer to the Table of Measures. See that 60 minutes equals 1 hour.

60 minutes = 1 hour

Step 2. Divide 80 minutes by the number of minutes in 1 hour, 60. Instead of writing the remainder as a fraction, $\frac{20}{60}$ or $\frac{1}{3}$, express the remainder as a number of minutes, 20.

$$\begin{array}{r} 1 \text{ hour } 20 \text{ minutes} \\ 60\overline{)80} \\ \underline{60} \\ 20 \end{array}$$

Lesson 1   Exercise

Directions: Find the quantity in the new unit that is equivalent to the quantity in the old unit. Refer to the Table of Measures at the start of this unit.

1. 12 ft. = _____ in.
2. 24 oz. = _____ lb.
3. 10 qt. = _____ gal.
4. 45 min. = _____ hr.
5. $\frac{1}{4}$ yr. = _____ mo.
6. $1\frac{1}{2}$ pt. = _____ fl. oz.
7. 80 hr. = _____ da.
8. $\frac{5}{6}$ min. = _____ sec.
9. $2\frac{1}{2}$ mi. = _____ ft.
10. 400 square rods = _____ acres

Answers are on page A-45.

Lesson 2   Comparing and Ordering Fractions

To compare the size of two fractions

- Find the least common denominator for the fractions
- Change both fractions to equivalent fractions that have the same denominator
- Compare the numerators to find which fraction is the larger and which is the smaller

Example 1: Which is larger, $\frac{7}{15}$ or $\frac{5}{9}$?

Step 1. The LCD for 15 and 9 is 45.

Step 2. Raise the fractions to equivalent fractions with 45, the LCD, as their denominator.

$$\frac{7 \times 3}{15 \times 3} = \frac{21}{45}$$

$$\frac{5 \times 5}{9 \times 5} = \frac{25}{45}$$

Step 3. The larger fraction is $\frac{25}{45}$ because its numerator is larger. Thus, $\frac{5}{9}$ is larger than $\frac{7}{15}$.

Example 2: Arrange in order from the smallest to the largest, $\frac{2}{3}$, $\frac{3}{8}$, and $\frac{5}{6}$.

Step 1. The LCD for 3, 8, and 6 is 24.

Step 2. Raise each fraction to an equivalent fraction with 24 as the denominator.

Step 3. Arrange the equivalent fractions in order from the smallest to the largest: $\frac{9}{24}$, $\frac{16}{24}$, and $\frac{20}{24}$. Therefore, the original fractions are, from smallest to largest, $\frac{3}{8}$, $\frac{2}{3}$, and $\frac{5}{6}$.

$$\frac{2 \times 8}{3 \times 8} = \frac{16}{24}$$

$$\frac{3 \times 3}{8 \times 3} = \frac{9}{24}$$

$$\frac{5 \times 4}{6 \times 4} = \frac{20}{24}$$

Lesson 2 Exercise

Directions: Name the smaller fraction in each pair.

1. $\frac{7}{8}$ or $\frac{5}{12}$
2. $\frac{3}{5}$ or $\frac{3}{4}$
3. $\frac{9}{10}$ or $\frac{13}{15}$
4. $\frac{2}{3}$ or $\frac{5}{7}$

Directions: Name the larger fraction in each pair.

5. $\frac{2}{11}$ or $\frac{1}{6}$
6. $\frac{1}{3}$ or $\frac{3}{7}$
7. $\frac{1}{2}$ or $\frac{6}{13}$
8. $\frac{5}{8}$ or $\frac{7}{12}$

Directions: Arrange each set of fractions in order from the smallest to the largest.

9. $\frac{5}{7}$, $\frac{3}{14}$, $\frac{1}{4}$, $\frac{15}{28}$
10. $\frac{4}{9}$, $\frac{2}{3}$, $\frac{1}{2}$, $\frac{1}{6}$

Answers are on page A-45.

Lesson 3 Tables

Comparing data in tables sometimes involves using fractions.
The following table shows the batters' number of hits and times at bat.

Home-Team Batting Record		
Name	Hits	Times at Bat
Alberto	24	60
Elizabeth	35	70
John	30	54
Roger	27	63
Sam	12	48
Victoria	9	24
Vincent	22	55
William	32	72
Zachary	9	36

UNIT VII: MATHEMATICS   Level 2: Lesson 4   **475**

Example: In what fraction of his times at bat did Alberto get a hit?

Step 1. Read the table. How many hits did Alberto get? Use 24 as the numerator. How many times did Alberto bat? Use 60 as the denominator.

$$\frac{24 \text{ hits}}{60 \text{ times at bat}}$$

Step 2. Simplify the fraction. Alberto got a hit $\frac{2}{5}$ of his times at bat.

$$\frac{24 \div 12}{60 \div 12} = \frac{2 \text{ hits}}{5 \text{ times at bat}}$$

Lesson 3   Exercise

Directions: *Use the table in Lesson 3 to answer the following questions.*

1. What fractions show each of the other players' hits in relation to times at bat?
2. Which player's fraction equals Alberto's? Which equals Zachary's?
3. Who had more hits per time at bat, Victoria or Zachary?
4. List the following players in order—Elizabeth, Roger, Sam, and Victoria—according to hits per times at bat, from best to worst.
5. List these players in order—John, Vincent, and William—according to hits per times at bat, from worst to best.

Answers are on page A-45.

Lesson 4   Ratio

A **ratio** is used to compare two numbers. A ratio can be written in several ways: as a fraction ($\frac{3}{5}$), using the word *to* (3 to 5), or using a colon (3:5).

When written as a fraction, the number being compared is the numerator and the number it is being compared to is the denominator.

Example 1: Gary used 5 gallons of gas to drive 75 miles. What is the ratio of miles to gallons for Gary's trip?

Step 1. You are comparing miles driven to gallons of gas used. Write a fraction that has 75 as the numerator and 5 as the denominator.

$$\frac{75 \text{ mi.}}{5 \text{ gal.}} = \frac{75 \div 5}{5 \div 5} = \frac{15 \text{ mi.}}{1 \text{ gal.}}$$

Step 2. Reduce the fraction to lowest terms. You do not simplify $\frac{15}{1}$ because you are showing the relationship between the two numbers. The answer can also be written as 15 to 1 or 15:1.

$\frac{15}{1}$ or 15 to 1 or 15:1

What was actually found in Example 1 was the number of miles Gary drove on one gallon of gas, or the miles per gallon.

Sometimes problems do not provide all the numbers you need to write a ratio, but other numbers are given that help you obtain those not provided.

Example 2: Irene budgets her monthly income as follows: $565 for rent and utilities; $250 for food and household expenses; $60 for transportation; $75 for entertainment; $50 for miscellaneous expenses; and $250 for her savings. What is the ratio of Irene's savings to her total monthly income?

Step 1. Add to find Irene's total monthly income.

$$\begin{array}{r} \$565 \\ 250 \\ 250 \\ 75 \\ 60 \\ +\ 50 \\ \hline \$1250 \text{ income} \end{array}$$

Step 2. Compare Irene's savings to her total income. Write a ratio using her savings, $250, as the numerator and her total monthly income, $1250, as the denominator.

Step 3. Simplify the ratio. Irene saves $1 for every $5 she earns: $\frac{1}{5}$, 1 to 5, or 1:5.

$$\frac{250 \div 250}{1250 \div 250} = \frac{1 \text{ savings}}{5 \text{ income}}$$

Lesson 4 Exercise

Directions: *Write a ratio to solve each problem.*

1. The gas tank in David's pickup truck holds 22 gallons. The gas tank in his wife's car holds 10 gallons. What is the ratio of the smaller gas tank to the larger gas tank?

2. Last year, Josh ran 6 miles per hour in the marathon. This year, he ran 10 miles per hour. What is the ratio of Josh's running speed this year to his running speed last year?

3. Michele burns 3000 calories on days on which she goes to the gym. On days on which she does not go to the gym, she burns 2000 calories. What is the ratio of calories Michele burns on days when she does not go to the gym to calories she burns on gym days?

4. Oliver prepared a growing mixture that contained 2 parts topsoil, 1 part peat moss, and 1 part vermiculite. What is the ratio of topsoil to the total mixture?

5. Nancy answered 100 questions on a test. She had 20 incorrect answers. What is the ratio of her correct answers to the number of questions on the test?

Answers are on page A-46.

Lesson 5   Probability

Probability is the chance that a given event will occur. For example, when you flip a coin, two kinds of events are possible: (1) heads will show, or (2) tails will show.

Probability can be expressed in fractions. The probability that heads will show when a coin is flipped is written as:

$$\frac{1}{2} \frac{\text{the number of heads on a coin (one kind of event)}}{\text{the number of sides on a coin (all possible events)}}$$

The probability of heads in a coin flip is $\frac{1}{2}$. That means that if a coin is flipped, there is one chance in two that heads will show.

To show probability as a fraction, write the number of possibilities that one kind of event will occur as the numerator. Write the number of all possible events as the denominator.

Probability problems often involve picking an object from a group of similar objects without looking.

Example 1: There are 8 black checkers and 12 red checkers in a box. Bob picks a checker from the box without looking. What is the probability that it is a black checker?

Step 1. There are 8 chances of picking a black checker. Write 8 as the numerator.

$$\frac{8}{8 + 12} \frac{\text{one kind of event}}{\text{all possible events}}$$

Step 2. Find the number of possible events: 8 black checkers + 12 red checkers = 20 checkers. Write 8 + 12 as the denominator. Add the terms in the denominator: 8 + 12 = 20.

$$\frac{8}{20} = \frac{2}{5}$$

Step 3. Reduce the fraction to lowest terms. There are 2 chances in 5 of picking a black checker.

Example 2: A bag contains 6 marbles. There are 3 red marbles, 2 yellow marbles, and 1 green marble in the bag. A red marble is picked from the bag and not replaced. What is the probability that the next marble, picked without looking, will be yellow?

Step 1. There are 2 yellow marbles in the bag. Write 2 as the numerator.

$$\frac{2}{6 - 1} \frac{\text{yellow marbles}}{\text{total marbles}}$$

Step 2. How many marbles in all are left in the bag? 6 marbles − 1 red marble = 5 marbles. Use 5 as the denominator. There are 2 chances in 5 of picking a yellow marble.

$$\frac{2}{5}$$

Lesson 5 Exercise

Directions: Find each probability. All picks are made without looking.

1. A purse contains two pennies, a dime, and a nickel. What is the probability that the first coin taken from the purse will be the dime?
2. What is the probability of picking a pair of brown socks from a drawer that contains 2 pairs of black socks, 3 pairs of brown socks, and 4 pairs of white socks?
3. A carton contains 15 cans of tomato soup and 20 cans of chicken soup. What is the probability that the first can taken from the carton will be a can of tomato soup?
4. There were 5 red lollipops, 3 purple lollipops, and 2 green lollipops in a bag. Karen chose a purple lollipop. What is the probability the next person will pick a green lollipop?
5. In a bag of 20 apples, 3 are bruised. What is the probability of picking an apple that is not bruised from the bag?

Answers are on page A-46.

Level 2 Review

Directions: Solve each problem.

1. A velour fabric costs $3 per yard. How many yards can you purchase for $18?
2. Change $6\frac{1}{2}$ gallons to pints.
3. Change 24 ounces to pounds. Express your answer as a mixed number.
4. How many feet of fence are needed to build a square enclosure around a tree when one side of the enclosure measures $5\frac{1}{4}$ feet?
5. A garden club has set aside 4 planting beds for experimental crops. Each bed measures $7\frac{1}{3}$ feet by $3\frac{1}{2}$. What is the total area of the 4 planting beds?
6. Arrange the following fractions in order from the smallest to the largest: $\frac{2}{3}, \frac{5}{8}, \frac{1}{6},$ and $\frac{1}{2}$.
7. Carla answered 75 questions correct on a 100-question exam. What is the ratio of her incorrect answers to the total number of questions on the exam?
8. There are 15 white buttons and 13 black buttons in a box. What is the probability of choosing a white button from the box on the first pick without looking?

Items 9 and 10 are based on the following table.

Heights of Marching Band Members

Height	Number of Members	Height	Number of Members
5 ft. 1 in.	2	5 ft. 8 in.	10
5 ft. 2 in.	2	5 ft. 9 in.	8
5 ft. 3 in.	5	5 ft. 10 in.	8
5 ft. 4 in.	6	5 ft. 11 in.	6
5 ft. 5 in.	8	6 ft.	4
5 ft. 6 in.	8	6 ft. 1 in.	0
5 ft. 7 in.	12	6 ft. 2 in.	1

9. What part of the total number of members are those whose heights are 6 feet and above?

10. Of those members whose heights are less than 6 feet, what part are those whose heights are 5 feet 4 inches or less?

Check your answers. Correct answers are on page A-46. If you have at least eight answers correct, go to Level 3. If you have fewer than eight answers correct, go back to Lesson 1 and study Level 2 again.

Level 3   Fractions Problem Solving

Lesson 1   Setup Problems

Some fraction problems on the GED test may give you a choice of *setup* answers. As with other problems, you must choose the correct answer from among five alternatives. The correct answer, however, is not the solution to the problem. It may be an expression or a formula you would use to find the solution.

Example: Which of the following expressions shows how you would find the rate if the distance is 230 miles and the time is 5 hours and 20 minutes?

(1) $230 \times \frac{16}{3}$ (2) $\frac{230}{3}$ (3) $230 \div \frac{3}{16}$ (4) $230 \times \frac{3}{16}$ (5) 230×16

480 Chapter 2: Fractions   INSTRUCTION

Step 1. The distance formula is $d = rt$. You are asked how you would find the rate. Use this version of the formula: $r = d/t$.

$d = rt$

$r = d/t$

Step 2. Change 5 hours 20 minutes to a mixed number and then to an improper fraction.

$5\frac{20}{60} = 5\frac{1}{3}$

$5\frac{1}{3} = \frac{16}{3}$

Step 3. Substitute the numbers in the formula. Choice (4) is correct.

$r = 230 \div \frac{16}{3}$

$= 230 \times \frac{3}{16}$

Lesson 1 Exercise

Directions: *Pick the setup that you think shows the correct way to solve each problem.*

1. Change the total of 60 ounces, 3 quarts, 24 ounces, and 12 ounces to quarts.

    (1) $(60 + 24 + 12)/32 \times 3$

    (2) $\dfrac{60 + 24 + 12 \times 3}{32}$

    (3) $3\dfrac{(60 + 24 + 12)}{32}$

    (4) $\dfrac{60 + 24 + 12}{32} + 3$

    (5) $\dfrac{60 + 24 + 12 + 3}{32}$

2. Change 120 hours and 2880 minutes to weeks.

    (1) $(120 + 2880)/7$

    (2) $\left(\dfrac{120}{24} + \dfrac{2880}{1440}\right)/7$

    (3) $\left(\dfrac{120 + 2880}{24 + 1440}\right)7$

    (4) $7\left(\dfrac{120}{24}\right)\left(\dfrac{2880}{1440}\right)$

    (5) $\left(\dfrac{24}{120}\right)\left(\dfrac{1440}{2880}\right)\left(\dfrac{7}{1}\right)$

3. A roulette wheel is numbered 1 to 36, 0, and 00. How would you find the probability of a spin resulting in an even number? (0 and 00 are not considered even.)

    (1) $\dfrac{(36 + 1 + 1) + 18}{36}$

    (2) $(36 + 2)18$

    (3) $\dfrac{18}{36 + 1 + 1}$

    (4) $\dfrac{(36 - 18) + 2}{36}$

    (5) $\dfrac{36 + 2}{18}$

4. A plumber needed 8 pipes that each measures $2\frac{1}{2}$ feet. If the pipes cost $4 per yard, how would he find the total cost?

(1) $\dfrac{8 \times 2\frac{1}{2}}{4 \times 3}$

(2) $\dfrac{8 \times 2\frac{1}{2}}{3} \times 4$

(3) $3 \times 8 \times 2\frac{1}{2} \times 4$

(4) $\dfrac{4 \times 3}{8 \times 2\frac{1}{2}}$

(5) $\dfrac{2\frac{1}{2}}{8} + \dfrac{3}{4}$

5. A contractor must give an estimate for a new patio. The concrete slab he must pour measures $\frac{1}{6}$ yard by $3\frac{1}{3}$ yards by 6 yards. Concrete costs the contractor $18 per cubic yard. There is a delivery charge of $25. How would he estimate the total cost?

(1) $\$18(\frac{1}{6} + 3\frac{1}{3} + 6) + \$25$

(2) $(\frac{1}{6} \times 3\frac{1}{3} \times 6)(\$18 + \$25)$

(3) $\$18(\frac{1}{6} \times 3\frac{1}{3} \times 6) + \$25$

(4) $(\$25 - \$18)(\frac{1}{6} \times 3\frac{1}{3} \times 6)$

(5) $\$25(\frac{1}{6} + 3\frac{1}{3} + 6) + \$18$

Answers are on page A-46.

Lesson 2   Mixed Units with Perimeter, Area, and Volume

When you solve perimeter, area, or volume problems, make sure that every dimension is in the same unit of measure.

Example: Find the area, in square feet, of the rectangle below.

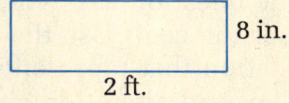

8 in.
2 ft.

Step 1. Change 8 inches to feet.   8 in. = $\frac{2}{3}$ ft.

Step 2. Use the formula $A = lw$. Multiply. $A = lw$

Step 3. Change the improper fraction to a mixed number.
$= 2 \times \frac{2}{3}$
$= \frac{4}{3} = 1\frac{1}{3}$ sq. ft.

Lesson 2   Exercise

Directions: *Solve each problem. Refer to page 000 for the perimeter, area, and volume formulas.*

1. Find the area in square yards of this rectangle.

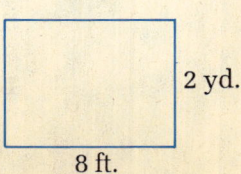

2 yd.
8 ft.

482   Chapter 2: Fractions   INSTRUCTION

2. What is the area, in square inches, of a square that has a side of $\frac{1}{4}$ foot?

3. Find the perimeter in feet of this triangle.

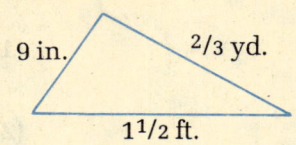

   9 in.   2/3 yd.
   1 1/2 ft.

4. What is the area, in square inches, of a triangle that has a height of $\frac{1}{2}$ foot and a base of 11 inches?

5. Find the volume, in cubic feet, of this rectangular container.

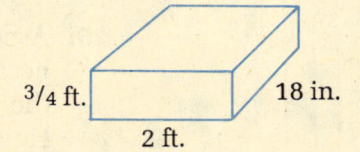

   3/4 ft.   18 in.
   2 ft.

Answers are on pages A-46—A-47.

Lesson 3   Extraneous Information

Some problems contain extraneous information—facts that you do not need to solve the problem.
 Concentrate on the information that is necessary to solve the problem, and ignore anything extraneous.

Example: Daryl bought a coat on sale. The original price was $150. The sale price was $\frac{1}{5}$ off the original price. He paid a sales tax of $10 and he paid $15 for alterations. What was the sale price of the coat?

Step 1. The question asks you to find the sale price of the coat. Use the original price and the fraction that represents the discount. The sales tax and alteration charge are extraneous information. Multiply to find the discount.

$150 \times \frac{1}{5}$

$\frac{150}{1} \times \frac{1}{5} = \frac{150}{5} = \$30$

Step 2. Subtract to find the sale price.

$150
− 30
$120

Lesson 3   Exercise

Directions: *Solve each problem. Identify the extraneous information.*

1. Nick used $3\frac{1}{2}$ of 5 boxes of vinyl tiles. There are 20 tiles in each box. The boxes cost $15 each. Find the number of tiles that Nick had left.

2. Diane built a large storage shed. She purchased $1\frac{1}{2}$ pounds of 2-inch nails and $\frac{3}{4}$ pound of 3-inch nails at an average price of $1 per pound. She used $\frac{5}{8}$ pound of 2-inch nails and $\frac{1}{2}$ pound of 3-inch nails. How many pounds of 2-inch nails did Diane have left?

3. Chuck takes care of a total of 150 trees and plants every day at five office buildings. He spends $\frac{3}{4}$ hour at the first building, 50 minutes at the second, $2\frac{1}{2}$ hours at the third, $1\frac{1}{2}$ hours at the fourth, and 1 hour 10 minutes at the fifth. It takes him an average of 15 minutes to travel from one building to another. How much time in hours does Chuck spend every day taking care of trees and plants?

4. Sylvia saved $5 on her grocery bill by using coupons. At a special window, she was also given a refund of $1 for returning 20 deposit bottles. The bill came to $55 before the coupons were subtracted. What fraction represents the coupon savings in relation to the original bill?

5. Conrad uses $1\frac{1}{4}$ cups of detergent to wash his clothes. He also uses 1 capful of water conditioner and $\frac{1}{2}$ cup of bleach. If he does 3 loads of laundry per week, how many cups of detergent does he use in 4 weeks?

Answers are on page A-47.

Level 3 Review

Directions: *Solve each problem.*

1. If health insurance benefits for an employee cost $42 per month and if the employee pays $\frac{2}{7}$ of the cost, which of the following expressions shows how much the employer pays?

    (1) $42 + (42 \times \frac{2}{7})$

    (2) $(42 \times \frac{2}{7}) - 42$

    (3) $42 - (42 \times \frac{2}{7})$

    (4) $(42 \times \frac{2}{7}) + 42$

    (5) $\frac{7}{2} \times 42$

2. If Mark's salary is $2000 per month and he takes home $1500 after taxes, which of the following expressions shows the ratio of taxes Mark pays in relation to his salary before taxes?

    (1) $\frac{2000 + 1500}{3500}$

    (2) $\frac{2000 - 1500}{3500}$

    (3) $\frac{2000 + 1500}{2000}$

    (4) $\frac{2000 - 1500}{2000}$

    (5) $\frac{1500}{2000}$

484 Chapter 2: Fractions

3. Which of the following expressions tells how to find the total number of quarts you would get from $1\frac{1}{2}$ gallons 14 pints?

   (1) $\dfrac{1\frac{1}{2}}{(4)} + 2(14)$

   (2) $(1\frac{1}{2} \times 4) + \dfrac{14}{2}$

   (3) $\dfrac{(1\frac{1}{2} + 14)}{4}$

   (4) $2(1\frac{1}{2} + 14)$

   (5) $(1\frac{1}{2} \times 2) + \dfrac{14}{2}$

4. Which of the following expressions tells you how to find the perimeter of the triangle in inches?

   (1) $12(3\frac{1}{2})^3$

   (2) $(3\frac{1}{2} \times 3\frac{1}{2} \times 3\frac{1}{2})12$

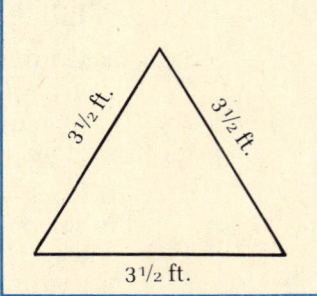

   (3) $3\frac{1}{2} + 3\frac{1}{2} + 3\frac{1}{2}$

   (4) $(3\frac{1}{2} + 3\frac{1}{2} + 3\frac{1}{2})/12$

   (5) $3\frac{1}{2} \times 3\frac{1}{2}$

   (Triangle with sides $3\frac{1}{2}$ ft., $3\frac{1}{2}$ ft., and $3\frac{1}{2}$ ft.)

5. One rectangle measures $2\frac{2}{3}$ yards by 3 feet. Another rectangle measures 4 feet by $\frac{2}{3}$ yard. What is the ratio of the area of the smaller rectangle in square feet to the area of the larger rectangle in square feet?

6. Find the area in square inches of a rectangle $1\frac{1}{2}$ feet long and 9 inches wide.

Items 7 to 10 are based on the following information.

An electronics firm uses $8\frac{3}{4}$ feet of wire for each coil that it manufactures. The wire costs 10 cents per foot and comes from 140-foot spools. All other materials that are used in the coils cost $11\frac{1}{2}$ cents per coil. Coil winders earn $15 per hour and produce 5 coils per hour. The ratio of coils made to rejects is 35:1.

7. In a 35-hour week, how many bad coils would 2 coil winders produce, on the average?

8. If the firm makes 200 coils, how many spools of wire will be used?

9. How much wire does each coil winder use in one hour?

10. What information in the paragraph had nothing to do with solving items 7, 8, and 9?

Check your answers. Correct answers are on page A-47. If you have at least eight answers correct, go to the Chapter Quiz. If you have fewer than eight answers correct, go back to Lesson 1 and study Level 3 again.

UNIT VII: MATHEMATICS   Chapter 2 Quiz   **485**

Chapter 2 Quiz

1. Patrick needed an extension cord to reach $1\frac{1}{2}$ rods from an indoor socket to a piece of electrical equipment at the back of his yard. Cord A was 290 inches. Cord B was $8\frac{1}{4}$ yards. Cord C was $28\frac{1}{2}$ feet. Which cord (a) reached the distance with length to spare? (b) was too short? (c) just reached the distance exactly? (Refer to the Table of Measures at the start of this unit.)

2. There are approximately 6,500,000 cubic miles of ice in the world. Antarctica has $\frac{9}{10}$ of all the ice. About how many cubic miles of ice are in Antarctica?

3. The gas tank in Rachel's car holds 20 gallons. Before she started on a trip, she saw that the meter on the dashboard showed the tank to be $\frac{1}{4}$ full. She usually gets $16\frac{1}{2}$ miles per gallon. If she does not refill her tank, how far can she drive before she runs out of gas?

4. Felix spends at least 30 hours per month doing volunteer work at the local hospital. He helped at the hospital for $7\frac{1}{2}$ hours the first week, $6\frac{3}{4}$ hours the second week, and $9\frac{1}{4}$ hours the third week. How much more time must he help for the rest of the month to reach his goal of 30 hours? Express your answer in hours and minutes.

5. Glenn has paid $\frac{5}{6}$ of his tuition loan. If the amount he borrowed was $3000, how much does he still owe?

6. Arrange in order from smallest to largest: $\frac{5}{12}, \frac{1}{4}, \frac{2}{3}, \frac{7}{9}$.

7. There are 25 fiction books and 30 nonfiction books on a shelf. What is the probability of picking a fiction book from the shelf?

Items 8 to 10 are based on the following recipe. (Refer to the Table of Measures at the start of this unit.)

Three-Grain Fruit Bread

(makes 4 loaves)
Ingredients (a partial list)

$8\frac{1}{2}$ cups all-purpose flour
$2\frac{1}{4}$ cups uncooked oatmeal
$1\frac{3}{4}$ cups uncooked whole-wheat cereal
$1\frac{2}{3}$ cups cornmeal
$\frac{1}{3}$ cup skim milk powder
3 cups fruit juice
1 cup yogurt

8. The first five ingredients are equal to (a) how many cups? (b) how many pints? (c) how many quarts?

486 Chapter 2: Fractions INSTRUCTION

9. What is the ratio of dry ingredients (first five) to liquid ingredients (last two)?
10. Express the total quantity of dry ingredients as quarts and ounces.

Items 11 to 14 are based on the following information.

Tim and Nancy purchased supplies to remodel their home. They bought four lengths of pipe measuring $2\frac{3}{4}$ feet, $4\frac{1}{3}$ feet, $5\frac{3}{8}$ feet, and $2\frac{7}{8}$ feet. They also purchased $4\frac{1}{2}$ yards of self-adhesive caulking at 18 cents per yard, $7\frac{1}{3}$ feet of hollow tubing at $10\frac{1}{2}$ cents per foot, and four $6\frac{1}{2}$-foot-by-4-inch boards.

11. If they used $\frac{5}{6}$ of the hollow tubing, how many feet did they have left?
12. What is the total area, in feet, of the boards?
13. What was the cost per foot of the self-adhesive caulking?
14. How many yards of plumbing pipe did they purchase?

Directions: *Refer to the formulas at the start of this unit to solve items 15 and 16.*

15. Find the area of a triangle that has a base of $1\frac{1}{3}$ feet and a height of $\frac{1}{2}$ foot.
16. What is the volume, in cubic yards, of this rectangular container?

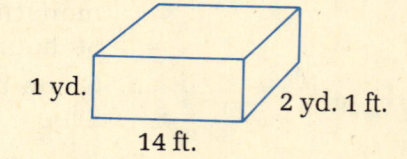

1 yd. 2 yd. 1 ft. 14 ft.

Items 17 to 20 are based on the following paragraph and chart.

Adam was eating 300 calories more than he needed each day. He figured that this was causing a weight gain of $\frac{3}{35}$ pound per day. He wanted to lose weight by exercising more without changing his diet. He made the following chart to help himself.

Calorie-Burning Chart

Activity	Calories Burned per Minute	Activity	Calories Burned per Minute
Bicycling	$5\frac{2}{3}$	Reading	$1\frac{1}{2}$
Driving	$2\frac{1}{4}$	Watching television	$1\frac{1}{2}$
Gardening	$3\frac{3}{4}$		
Jogging	$6\frac{1}{12}$	Office work	$2\frac{1}{4}$

17. How many calories would Adam burn per activity if he did each for one hour?

18. If Adam jogged for 45 minutes and worked in the garden for 30 minutes, how many more calories would he burn than he would if he watched television for the same amount of time?

19. If Adam spent $1\frac{1}{2}$ hours per day bicycling to and from work instead of driving and working in the office during that period of time, how many more calories per day would he burn?

20. How many pounds would Adam gain in a year if he did not change his eating habits or exercise?

Answers are on pages A-47—A-48.

Chapter 3 Decimals

Objective

In this chapter, you will learn to

- Read and write decimals
- Add, subtract, multiply, and divide decimals
- Interchange decimals and fractions
- Round off decimals
- Solve word problems that involve decimals
- Use decimals in metric measurement
- Find circumference and area of circles, and volume of cylinders
- Compare and order decimals
- Solve distance problems that involve decimals
- Identify decimal problems that have insufficient data for solution

Level 1 Decimal Skills

Preview

1. Write seven ten-thousandths as a decimal.
2. What is the sum of .431, .73, and .6?
3. What is the difference between .79 and .124?
4. What is the product of 2.5 and .43?
5. What is 1.261 divided by 9.7?

Check your answers. Correct answers are on page A-49. If you have at least four answers correct, do the Level 1 Review on page 494. If you have fewer than four answers correct, study Level 1 beginning with Lesson 1.

Lesson 1 Reading and Writing Decimals

A **decimal** is a fraction whose denominator is not written but is indicated by the position of the decimal point. Like a fraction, a decimal can express a value less than 1. Unlike fractions, the denominators of decimals are limited to 10 or to powers of ten such as 100; 1000; 10,000; and so forth. The place-value table summarizes the names of the decimal places as well as those of whole numbers.

Decimal Place Values

thousands	hundreds	tens	units or ones	• decimal point	tenths	hundredths	thousandths	ten-thousandths	hundred-thousandths	millionths	How Read
				.	4						four tenths
				.	0	4					four hundredths
			4	.	0	0	4				four and four thousandths
		4	4	.	0	0	4	4			forty-four and forty-four ten-thousandths
				.	0	0	4	0	4		four hundred four hundred-thousandths
	4	0	4	.	0	0	0	0	0	4	four hundred four and four millionths
		4	0	.	4	0					forty and forty hundredths or as forty and four tenths

Decimal parts of a number are written to the right of the decimal point. The last digit to the right of the decimal point determines the place value. The decimal .04 is the same as the fraction $\frac{4}{100}$; .004 represents $\frac{4}{1000}$.

Zeros at the beginning of a decimal serve as place holders. With no zeros in .04 and .004, these decimals would have the same value. Zeros at the end of a decimal have no value. For example, the decimals .4 and .40 have the same value.

Mixed numbers include a whole number followed by a decimal; the decimal point separates them and is read as *and*. The temperature 98.6 degrees is read *98 and six tenths degrees*.

When there is no whole number to the left of the decimal point, a zero is sometimes added for clarity; both 0.4 and .4 are correct.

To write a decimal, put the last digit of the numerator in the place that is named by the denominator. Then fill any empty places between the numerator and the decimal point with zeros.

In Fractions	In Words	In Digits
$\frac{9}{100}$	nine hundredths	.09
$\frac{13}{1000}$	thirteen thousandths	.013
$\frac{6}{10,000}$	six ten-thousandths	.0006
$\frac{6}{10}$	six tenths	.6

Lesson 1 Exercise

Directions: *Match the number in the left-hand column with the words in the right-hand column that have the same meaning.*

1. 0.0075
2. 0.75
3. 100.01
4. 100.001
5. 0.075

a. seventy-five thousandths
b. one hundred and one thousandth
c. seventy-five ten-thousandths
d. one hundred and one hundredth
e. seventy-five hundredths

Directions: *Write each number as a decimal.*

6. seven and thirteen thousandths
7. twenty-seven ten-thousandths
8. ten and two hundred three millionths
9. thirteen hundredths
10. three hundred and seven tenths

Answers are on page A-49.

Lesson 2 Adding and Subtracting Decimals

To add and subtract decimals, be sure that the decimal points are lined up. When all the numbers do not have the same number of digits after the decimal point, it is a good idea to add zeros so that all the numbers in the column have the same number of decimal places. Then indicate where the decimal point will be placed in the answer, and add or subtract as you would for whole numbers.

Example 1: Find the sum of .35, .7, and .984.

Step 1. Set up the problem. Write the numbers in a column; line up the decimal points. Add zeros to .35 and .7 to even up the columns. Indicate where the decimal point will be in the answer.

Step 2. Add the digits in each column; carry as needed.

units or ones	decimal point	tenths	hundredths	thousandths
²	.	¹3	5	0
	.	7	0	0
+	.	9	8	4
2	.	0	3	4

When adding or subtracting whole numbers and decimals, write a decimal point after each whole number to ensure correct alignment of digits.

Example 2: Subtract 0.46 from 12.

Step 1. Set up the problem. Write a decimal point after 12. Write 0.46 under it; line up the decimal points. Add two zeros to the right of the decimal point after 12. Indicate where the decimal point will be in the answer.

Step 2. Subtract; borrow as needed.

tens	units or ones	decimal point	tenths	hundredths
1	¹2	.	⁹0̸	¹0
−	0	.	4	6
1	1	.	5	4

Lesson 2 Exercise

Directions: *Add or subtract.*

1. .19 + .8 + .326
2. $.73 + $.26 + $.11
3. .059 + .07 + .0694
4. 12 + .073 + .38
5. 39.6 + .8 + .007
6. .7 − .006
7. 30 − .8
8. 39.1 − .2
9. $86.30 − $23
10. 5.004 − 1.999

Answers are on page A-49.

Lesson 3 Multiplying and Dividing Decimals

Multiplying Decimals

Multiplying decimals is like multiplying whole numbers. The key is to position the decimal point correctly in the answer. To do this, count the number of decimal places in the two numbers that have been multiplied. The answer of the multiplication problem should have the same number of decimal places as the total in the two multiplied numbers. Then if the decimal in the answer ends in one or more zeros. It is good practice to eliminate them.

Sometimes an answer has too few digits to allow you to position the decimal point. When that happens, add just enough zeros directly after the decimal point so that the answer has the right number of decimal places.

Example 1: Find the product of .075 and .2.

Step 1. Set up the problem and multiply.

Step 2. Total the number of decimal places in the numbers that have been multiplied. Position the decimal point so that the answer has the same number of places: four. Add one zero and then place the decimal point. Drop the zero at the end.

```
   .075
 ×  .2
 .0150
```

Dividing Decimals by Whole Numbers

Division of a decimal by a whole number is similar to division of a whole number. The key is to place the decimal point in the answer above the decimal point in the number into which you have divided.

If there are not enough digits in the answer, add zeros immediately after the decimal point so that the answer will have the correct place value.

Example 2: Divide .728 by 8.

Step 1. Set up the problem and divide.

Step 2. Place a decimal point in the answer above the decimal point in .728. Add a zero after the decimal point in the answer so that the 9 and the 1 will have the correct place value.

```
    .091
8).728
    72
     8
     8
```

Dividing by Decimals

To divide by a decimal, it is necessary to change the divisor (the decimal that you are dividing by) to a whole number. To do this, move the decimal point all the way to the right in the divisor. Then move the decimal point in the dividend (the number that is being divided) the same number of places to the right.

Example 3: Divide 7.38 by .9.

Step 1. Set up the problem. Change .9 to a whole number by moving the decimal point one place to the right. Also, move the decimal point in 7.38 one place to the right. It becomes 73.8. Divide.

.9.)7.3.8

Step 2. Place the decimal point in the answer above the decimal point in the dividend.

```
    8.2
9)73.8
   72
    1 8
    1 8
```

Step 3. To check the problem, multiply the answer by the original divisor. The result should be the original dividend.

```
  8.2
× .9
 7.38
```

If necessary, add zeros to the dividend to fill any empty places.

Lesson 3 Exercise

Directions: *Multiply or divide.*

1. 9.6 × 23
2. (.72)(.3)
3. (.705)(5)
4. .884 × 1.029
5. $\frac{75.4}{5}$
6. $\frac{71.68}{14}$
7. $\frac{.00806}{13}$
8. $\frac{.9}{6}$
9. $\frac{198}{.18}$
10. $\frac{.615}{.5}$

Answers are on pages A-48–A-49.

Lesson 4 Interchanging Decimals and Fractions

Changing Decimals to Fractions

When you change a decimal to a fraction, you write the number in a different but equivalent form. The digits in the decimal become the numerator. The denominator is the place name. To simplify the fraction, reduce it to lowest terms.

Example 1: Change .075 to a fraction.

Step 1. Write 75 as the numerator. Because .075 has three places in it, the denominator is thousandths, or 1000. $.75 = \frac{75}{1000}$

Step 2. Reduce the fraction to lowest terms. $\frac{75 \div 25}{1000 \div 25} = \frac{3}{40}$

Changing Fractions to Decimals

To change a fraction to a decimal, divide its numerator by its denominator.

Example 2: Change $\frac{3}{4}$ to a decimal.

Step 1. Divide 3 by 4. Place a decimal point and two zeros after the 3 in the dividend. Divide.

```
  .75
4)3.00
  2 8
    20
    20
```

Step 2. Place the decimal point in the answer above the decimal point in the dividend.

Answers do not always come out even. When they don't, carry the division to two places. Then make the remainder a fraction and round the decimal.

Example 3: Change $\frac{5}{9}$ to a decimal.

Step 1. Divide 5 by 9. Place a decimal point and two zeros after the 5. Divide.

Step 2. Place the decimal point in the answer above the decimal point in 5.00. The remainder is 5. Since $\frac{5}{9}$ is more than half, the answer is rounded to .56.

$$\begin{array}{r} .55\frac{5}{9} \text{ or } .56 \\ 9\overline{)5.00} \\ \underline{4\ 5} \\ 50 \\ \underline{45} \\ 5 \end{array}$$

Lesson 4   Exercise

Directions: *Write each decimal as a fraction or a mixed number reduced to lowest terms.*

1. .9   2. 18.375   3. 7.08   4. 6.4   5. .85

Directions: *Write each fraction as a decimal.*

6. $\frac{7}{8}$ 7. $\frac{4}{9}$ 8. $\frac{8}{10}$ 9. $\frac{7}{15}$ 10. $\frac{9}{20}$

Answers are on page A-50.

Level 1   Review

Directions: *Solve each problem.*

1. Which of the following number names mean the same as 9.76?
   (1) nine hundred seventy-six
   (2) ninety-seven and six tenths
   (3) nine and seventy-six tenths
   (4) nine and seventy-six hundredths
   (5) nine and seventy-six thousandths
2. Write seventy-two and sixteen thousandths as a decimal.
3. Write .625 as a fraction reduced to lowest terms.
4. Write 7.96 as a mixed number reduced to lowest terms.
5. Write $\frac{4}{25}$ as a decimal.

Directions: *Perform each operation indicated.*

6. .938 + 9.79 + 9   7. 6 − .4192   8. 97.5 × .56
9. .0437 ÷ 19   10. .4984 ÷ .89

Check your answers. Correct answers are on page A-50. If you have at least eight answers correct, go to Level 2. If you have fewer than eight answers correct, go back to Lesson 1 and study Level 1.

Level 2 Decimal Applications

Lesson 1 Rounding Decimals

Some decimals are hard to work with because they have several places. Rounding them to just a few places makes them easier to work with. To do this, follow the same procedure as for rounding whole numbers.

Example 1: Round 12.764 to the nearest tenth.

Step 1. Circle the digit in the tenths place, 7. 12.⑦64

Step 2. Because the next digit to the right, 6, is greater than 5, add 1 to the 7. Drop the last two digits, 6 and 4. 12.8

Example 2: Round 1.714 to the nearest hundredth.

Step 1. Circle the digit in the hundredths place, 1. 1.7①4

Step 2. Because the next digit to the right, 4, is less than 5, leave the 1 alone and drop the 4. 1.71

Lesson 1 Exercise

Directions: Round each number to the nearest tenth.

1. .949   2. .371   3. 1.535   4. 10.061   5. 78.394

Directions: Round each number to the nearest hundredth.

6. 5.8562   7. .7644   8. 23.7131   9. .5959   10. 8.1106

Answers are on page A-50.

Lesson 2 Decimal Word Problems

Decimal skills are often required to solve word problems that involve money and measurement. Word problems require you to think about what the problem is asking, to decide which operation to use, and to set up the problem correctly.

Example: Cerra Machine Design, Inc., used 22 ounces of copper to manufacture 8 rotors. How much copper was needed for each rotor?

Step 1. Decide the operation that is required: division.

Step 2. Set up the problem.

Step 3. Divide. Carry the division to two decimal places.

```
   2.75
8)22.00
  16
   6 0
   5 6
     40
     40
      0
```

Lesson 2   Exercise

Directions: Determine which operation to use. Then solve each problem.

1. Julia Piagga earns $10.80 per hour. How much does she earn in a 7.25-hour workday?
2. George Thompson paid $72.89 for 3.7 meters of gold tape. How much did the tape cost per meter?
3. The premium for Potaboc City's liability insurance cost $119,583.54 the year before last, $142,568.45 last year, and $186,294.36 this year. What was the three-year cost of liability insurance for the city?
4. At the end of the week a tank held 374.2 liters of fuel oil. If it held 976.9 liters at the beginning of the week, how much fuel oil was burned that week?
5. A truck rental firm charges $.89 per mile. What would be the charge for 195 miles?

Answers are on page A-50.

Lesson 3   Metric Measurement

Metric measurement is standard in most parts of the world; its use is increasing in the United States. One reason is its simplicity: there are only three basic units of measurement.

1. The basic unit of length is the **meter**. A meter is a little longer than a yard.
2. The basic unit of weight is the **gram**. A gram is about the weight of a paper clip.
3. The basic unit of volume is the **liter**. A liter is a little larger than a quart.

UNIT VII: MATHEMATICS

To make larger and smaller units than the basic units, the metric system uses prefixes. These prefixes indicate powers of 10 (10, 100, 1000) or decimals (.1, .01, .001). The following prefixes are the most commonly used.

Prefix	Meaning
kilo (k)	1000
deci (d)	.1
centi (c)	.01
milli (m)	.001

The most commonly used units of measurement and their abbreviations can be found in the Table of Measures at the start of this unit.

To change a larger unit to a smaller unit, multiply by the number of smaller units in the larger unit.

Example 1: Change 2.7 kilograms to grams.

Step 1. Multiply 2.7 by the number of grams in a kilogram, 1000.

Step 2. Drop the zero to the right of the decimal point.

```
      2.7 kg
  × 1000 g per kg
   2700.0 g
      or
    2700 g
```

To change a smaller unit to a larger unit, divide by the number of smaller units in the larger unit.

Example 2: Change 137 centimeters to meters.

Step 1. Set up the division problem to divide 137 cm by 100 cm per m.

Step 2. Carry out the division to two decimal places.

```
           1.37 m
     100)137.00 cm
         100
          37 0
          30 0
           7 00
           7 00
```

Lesson 3   Exercise

Directions: *Solve each problem.*

1. Change 17.21 meters to millimeters.
2. Change 3764 centimeters to meters.
3. Change .7 liter to centiliters.
4. Change 17 centigrams to grams.
5. Change 1.85 kilograms to grams.

Answers are on page A-50.

Lesson 4 Circumference and Area of Circles

A circle differs in two important ways from the straight-sided figures we have worked with. Its side is curved, and every point of its side is the same distance from the center. Figure 1 illustrates some parts of a circle. The **diameter** is

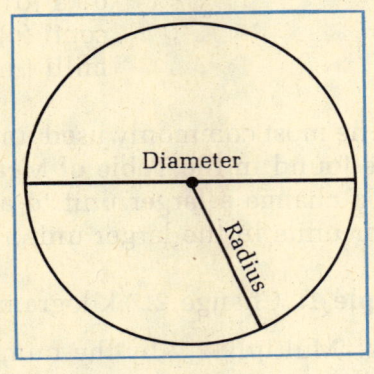

FIGURE 1

a line from the edge of a circle, through the center, to the other edge. The **radius** is a line from the center to the edge. The diameter is 2 times the length of the radius: $d = 2r$. The radius is half the length of the diameter: $r = \frac{d}{2}$.

The **circumference** is the measure of the perimeter of a circle. The ratio of the circumference of a circle to its diameter is called π (pronounced "pie"). π is usually rounded to 3.14.

To find the circumference of a circle, multiply the diameter by 3.14: $C = \pi d$.

Example 1: Find the circumference of a circle that has a radius of 2 feet.

Step 1. Find the diameter of the circle. Use the formula $d = 2r$.

$d = 2r$
$= 2 \times 2$
$= 4$ feet

Step 2. Find the circumference by using the formula $C = \pi d$.

$C = \pi d$
$= (3.14)(4)$
$= 12.56$ feet

The area of a circle is equal to π multiplied by the radius squared. Remember that area is expressed in square units.

Example 2: Find the area of a circle that has a radius of 3 meters.

Step 1. Set up the problem. Use the formula $A = \pi r^2$.

$A = \pi r^2$
$= (31.4)(3 \times 3)$
$= (3.14)(9)$
$= 28.26$ square meters

Step 2. Multiply 3.14 by r^2.

Lesson 4   Exercise

Directions: *Items 1 to 3 are about a circle that has a diameter of 6 inches.*

1. What is its radius?
2. What is its circumference?
3. What is its area?

Directions: *Items 4 and 5 are about a circle that has a radius of 10 inches.*

4. What is its circumference?
5. What is its area?

Answers are on page A-50.

Lesson 5   Volume of a Cylinder

A cylinder is a three-dimensional figure that has straight sides and whose top and bottom are circles of equal radius. A soda can is an example of a cylinder. To find the volume of a cylinder, use the formula $V = \pi r^2 h$, where r is the radius of an end (top or bottom) of the cylinder and h is the height.

Example: Find the volume of a can 5 inches high whose end has a radius of 1.5 inches.

Step 1. Set the problem up. Use the formula $V = \pi r^2 h$.

Step 2. Multiply. Be sure to place the decimal point correctly.

$V = \pi r^2 h$
$= (3.14)(1.5 \times 1.5)(5)$
$= (3.14)(2.25)(5)$
$= 35.325$ cubic inches

Lesson 5   Exercise

Directions: *Find the volume of each cylinder.*

1. a 6-inch high cylinder whose end has a 6-inch radius
2. a 12-foot high cylinder whose end has a 4-foot diameter
3. a 7.5-meter high cylinder whose end has a 10-meter radius
4. a 1-yard high cylinder whose end has a .5-yard radius
5. a 20-centimeter high cylinder whose end has an 8-centimeter radius

Answers are on page A-50.

Lesson 6 Comparing and Ordering Decimals

To determine which of two decimals is larger, first add zeros so that both decimals have the same number of places. Then compare the digits of the decimals, beginning with the tenths place.

Example 1: Which is larger, .706 or .7?

Step 1. Add zeros to make the number of decimal places the same.

.7 = .700
.706 = .706

Step 2. The digits in the tenths places of the two decimals are equal (7). The digits in the hundredths places are equal (0). In the thousandths places, 6 is the larger digit. So .706 is larger than .700.

Follow the same procedure to order three or more decimals.

Example 2: Arrange .401, .4, and .41 in order from the smallest to the largest.

Step 1. Add zeros so that all the decimals have the same number of decimal places.

.401 = .401
.4 = .400
.41 = .410

Step 2. Compare the decimals to determine .400 is less than .401 and .401 is less than .410.

.4, .401, .41

Lesson 6 Exercise

Directions: Find the larger decimal in each set.

1. .51, .501   2. .901, .9001   3. .4, .04

Directions: Arrange each set of decimals in order from the largest to the smallest.

4. .79, .7901, .7091, .791   5. .631, .6301, .6031, .63

Answers are on page A-50.

Level 2 Review

Directions: Solve each problem.

1. Round 3.14156 to the nearest thousandth.

UNIT VII: MATHEMATICS

2. A plant is 1.7 inches tall. Forty days ago, the plant was .3 inch tall. How many inches did the plant grow?
3. A graphic artist charges $22.50 per hour. What does the artist charge for a 9.5-hour job?
4. Divide 108 by .12.
5. How many meters are there in 7.7 kilometers?
6. Arrange the following decimals in order from the largest to the smallest: .68, .068, .681, .6.

Directions: *Refer to the formulas on page 438 to solve each problem.*

7. A triangle has a base of 19.4 feet and a height of 3.6 feet. What is the area rounded to the nearest tenth?
8. To the nearest square inch, what is the area of a circle that has a 9-inch radius?
9. What is the volume of a 10-inch tall cylinder that has a 10-inch diameter?
10. 60 feet of plumbing pipe cost $132.00. What was the cost per foot?

Check your answers. Correct answers are on page A-51. If you have at least eight answers correct, go to Level 3. If you have fewer than eight answers correct, go back to Lesson 1 and study Level 2 again.

Level 3   Problem Solving That Involves Decimals

Lesson 1   Sketching Travel Problems

The formula $d = rt$ is used to solve distance problems. However, if the problem involves the movement of more than one person or vehicle, it usually helps to make a sketch of their different movements. A simple way to do this is to sketch the face of a compass—north at the top, south at the bottom, east to the right, and west to the left. Place the starting point in the middle. Then use arrows to show the movements that are described in the problem. The sketch will help you decide whether to use addition or subtraction to solve the problem.

Example 1: Two planes leave Cleveland at the same time and travel in opposite directions. One flight travels east at 400 miles per hour, and the other flight travels west at 450 miles per hour. How far apart are the planes in a half hour?

Step 1. Draw a picture, as in Figure 2, showing the different movements.

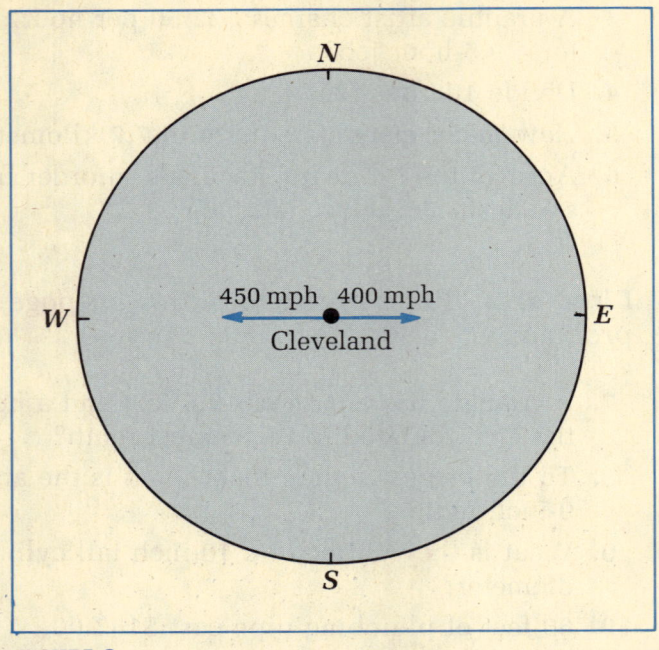

FIGURE 2

Step 2. There are two planes. Use the distance formula to calculate the distance traveled for each plane.

$d = rt$
$= (400)(.5)$ Plane A
$= 200$ miles

Step 3. The distance between two planes that traveled in opposite directions equals the sum of the distances that each traveled.

$d = rt$
$= (450)(.5)$ Plane B
$= 225$ miles

$200 + 225 = 425$ miles

Lesson 1 Exercise

Directions: *Sketch a picture to help solve each problem.*

1. Cyrus and Martin left Metropolis on the interstate highway at the same time. Cyrus drove west at an average speed of 50 miles per hour. Martin went east at an average speed of 45 miles per hour. How far apart were they in 3.4 hours?

2. The winning car in a road race traveled at an average speed of 72.65 miles per hour. The average speed of the second-place car was 70.89 miles per hour. How far ahead was the winning car at the end of the 3.5 hour race?

3. Gilberta and Alonzo jog for an hour every morning along Flemen River. If Gilberta runs north at 7.1 miles per hour and Alonzo runs south at 6.92 miles per hour, how far apart are they in 15 minutes?

4. One day, Gilberta and Alonzo took canoe trips on the Flemen River. She canoed upstream at 3.5 miles per hour. He canoed downstream at 8.53 miles per hour. How far apart were they in 1.5 hours?

5. Two trucks left Tuzbuz Trucking at 9:00 A.M. One truck traveled west at 54 miles per hour for 15 minutes and then returned east at 47 miles per hour. The other truck traveled east at 51 miles per hour. How far apart were they at 9:30 A.M.?

Answers are on page A-51.

Lesson 2   Insufficient Data

The GED test has questions for which one possible answer is "insufficient data is given to solve the problem." This means that a fact or a number is missing from the information you are given. The problem cannot be solved.

The example is based on the following information.

Edna and Roger are planning to carpet 3 rooms of their apartment. The living room measures 16.5 feet by 18 feet. The dining room is 11 feet by 9.5 feet. One wall of the bedroom is 10.5 feet long. The carpeting they want costs $11.50 per square yard.

Example: How much will the three rooms of carpeting cost?
(1) $4513.00
(2) $3295.50
(3) $2296.50
(4) $1539.00
(5) Insufficient data is given to solve the problem.

Read the question carefully. You must find the area of each of the three rooms, then multiply to find the cost. Only one measurement is given for the bedroom; therefore, you cannot find the area and the problem cannot be solved. Choice (5) is correct.

Lesson 2   Exercise

Directions: *If there is enough information, solve the problem. If there is insufficient data, identify the missing piece of information.*

1. Olga's children saved part of their lunch money to buy her a present. Juan saved $.25 per day. Sean and Ivan each saved $.20 per day. How much did they save altogether for the present?

2. To the nearest tenth, what is the area of a circle that has a diameter of 6.3 inches?

3. Feng Construction Company ordered 5 truckloads of concrete conduit at $9.50 per foot. How many feet of conduit did the company order?

4. Kwame Appliances ordered 120 televisions at $140 each and 40 stereos at $65 each. Shipping costs were $1.30 per pound. What was the total cost of the order?

5. Elena bought a 250-milliliter bottle of cough syrup for $3.99. Sales tax was $.24. She also bought 3 boxes of tissues at $1.19 each. Sales tax on each box was $.07. How much change did she receive from a ten-dollar bill?

Answers are on page A-51

Level 3 Review

Directions: *Items 1 to 4 refer to the following table.*

U.S. Energy Use					
Year	BTUs in Quadrillions	Population in Millions	Year	BTUs in Quadrillions	Population in Millions
1976	74.4	218	1980	76.0	228
1977	76.3	220	1981	74.0	230
1978	78.1	223	1982	70.8	232
1979	78.9	225	1983	70.5	235

1. To the nearest ten-thousandth, how much did energy use per million people decrease from 1982 to 1983?

2. To the nearest ten-thousandth, what was the difference in energy use per million people between 1976 and 1981?

3. In 1979, the population of the State of New York was approximately 18 million people. To the nearest ten-thousandth, what was New York's energy use in 1979?

4. To the nearest ten-thousandth, what is the difference between the year with the highest energy use per million people and the year with the lowest energy use per million people?

Directions: *Solve each problem.*

5. Wynne and John jog in different directions from their home. If Wynne jogs north at 6.7 miles per hour and John jogs south at 5.9 miles per hour, how far apart are they in .25 hour?

6. One day Wynne and John jog around a track in the same direction. Wynne runs at 6.9 miles per hour and John runs at 6.1 miles per hour. How far ahead is Wynne in 1.25 hours?

UNIT VII: MATHEMATICS Level 3 Review

Directions: *If there is enough information, solve the problem. If there is insufficient data, identify the missing information.*

7. Patrick excavated a hole in his backyard for a swimming pool. The hole was 30 feet long, 8 yards wide, and an average of 1.5 yards deep. Patrick must pay a contractor $50 to load the dirt and $3.25 per cubic yard to haul it away. What was the total price Patrick paid to dispose of the dirt?
   (1) $120.00
   (2) $170.00
   (3) $420.00
   (4) $1270.00
   (5) Insufficient data is given to solve the problem.

8. Marcia needs 2.5 yards of material for each of 3 blouses. She also needs 3.75 yards of denim at $4.50 per yard to make 3 skirts. What is the total cost of the material?
   (1) $8.44
   (2) $16.88
   (3) $25.32
   (4) $33.76
   (5) Insufficient data is given to solve the problem.

9. Marcus Swenson bought 15 pigs that had an average weight of 102.6 pounds. They gained an average of 9.6 pounds per week for 14 weeks. The pigs were sold for $.57 per pound. To the nearest dollar, what was the average price per pig?

10. Maria Delgada's annual income is $24,000. Monthly household expenses include $450 rent, $75 for utilities, and $225 for groceries. What decimal shows the amount of her monthly income that is left after these expenses?
    (1) .375
    (2) .45
    (3) .625
    (4) .75
    (5) Insufficient data is given to solve the problem.

Check your answers. Correct answers are on page A-51. If you have at least eight answers correct, go to the Chapter Quiz. If you have fewer than eight answers correct, go back to Lesson 1 and study Level 3 again.

Chapter 3   Quiz

Directions: *Find the value of each expression.*

1. 114.682 + 70.53
2. 60.01 − 8.951

Directions: *Items 3 and 4 refer to the following table.*

Women's Olympic Downhill Skiing		
Year	Skier	Time
1960	Biebl	1 min. 37.60 sec.
1964	Hass	1 min. 55.39 sec.
1968	Pall	1 min. 40.87 sec.
1972	Nadig	1 min. 36.68 sec.
1976	Mittermaier	1 min. 46.16 sec.
1980	Moser	1 min. 37.52 sec.
1984	Figini	1 min. 13.36 sec.

3. Arrange the winning speeds under 1 minute 40 seconds in order from the slowest to the fastest.
4. Arrange the years according to the winning speeds in order from the fastest to the slowest.

Directions: *Solve each problem.*

5. Lee, George, Karen, and Jim shared the cost of a party for Marie. They spent $125.35 for food, $56.76 for beverages, $14.60 for a cake, $9.85 for invitations and postage, and $20 each for a present. What was each person's share of the cost?
6. Coaxial cable costs $3.65 per foot. To the nearest cent, how much does 3.9 yards cost?
7. Isaac spends an average of 3.4 hours of each 8-hour workday contacting clients by telephone. Half of the remaining time he spends on paperwork. Write a ratio that shows the amount of time he spends on paperwork to his workday.
8. Larry worked an average of 7.25 hours per day at $22.40 per hour in a 5-day work week. His weekly paycheck showed $242 in deductions. What was his take-home pay for the week?
9. Casey spent $13\frac{3}{4}$ hours over two days writing a 33-page term paper. Express the average number of pages she wrote per hour as a decimal.

Directions: *Refer to the formulas at the start of this unit to solve each problem. Use 3.14 for π if necessary.*

10. Jon and Ingrid mixed 10 hundred-pound sacks of cement, 5 fifty-pound sacks of sand, and 10 seventy-five-pound sacks of gravel to make a concrete patio. What decimal shows the amount of gravel in the concrete mixture?

11. A rectangular room measures 14.25 feet by 12.75 feet. At $9.50 per square yard, what is the cost of carpeting for the room to the nearest cent?

12. Oil tank A is a cylinder 6.2 feet high with an end that has a radius of 5 feet. Oil tank B is 6.9 feet high with an end that has a radius of 4.5 feet. Which tank holds more?

13. A rectangle has a length of 19.6 inches and a width of 6.6 inches. Express the area of the rectangle as a mixed number fraction in lowest terms.

14. A cube-shaped aquarium has a side of .5 meters. It contains 20 tropical fish. How many cubic centimeters of water are there per tropical fish?

15. Find the circumference of a circle that has a radius of .4 yards.

Directions: *Items 16 to 18 are based on the following information.*

Sound travels through different materials at different speeds. Sound travels through steel at approximately 16,400 feet per second. It travels through air at approximately 1087 feet per second. By comparison, light travels at 186,000 miles per second.

16. How many more feet will sound travel through a block of steel in 1 thousandth of a second than it will travel through air?

17. How many inches will sound travel through air in .03 second?

18. How many miles farther does light travel in .00001 second than in .000001 second?

Directions: *Solve each problem.*

19. Clark and Lois left Metropolis in separate cars at 8:30 A.M. Clark drove west at 53 miles per hour for 1.5 hours, turned around, and then drove east at 52 miles per hour. Lois drove east at 49 miles per hour. How far apart were they at 10:30 A.M.?

20. The 4:40 P.M. train for Boston left New York at 4:50 P.M., the same time as the 4:35 P.M. train from New York to Washington. The train to Boston traveled at an average speed of 85 miles per hour. The train to Washington traveled at $\frac{3}{4}$ of that speed. How far apart were they at 5:20 P.M.?

Answers are on pages A-51–A-52.

Chapter 4 Percents

Objective

In this chapter, you will learn to:
- Interchange percents, decimals, and fractions
- Find a percent of a number
- Find what percent one number is of another
- Find a number when a percent of it is given
- Apply percent skills to word problems
- Use percent skills to compute interest
- Solve multistep problems that involve percents
- Find percent of increase and decrease

Level 1 Percent Skills

Preview

Directions: *Solve each problem.*

1. Change .137 to a percent.
2. Change $\frac{17}{20}$ to a percent.
3. What number is 37.5% of 104?
4. Rounded to the nearest percent, what percent of 153 is 68?
5. $16\frac{2}{3}$% of what number is 37?

Check your answers. Correct answers are on page A-52. If you have at least four answers correct, do the Level 1 Review on pages 513-514. If you have fewer than four answers correct, study Level 1 beginning with Lesson 1.

Lesson 1 Interchanging Percents and Decimals

Fractions, decimals, and percents are all ways of telling how a part relates to the whole. For example, $\frac{17}{100}$, .17, and 17% all mean 17 parts out of 100. When you solve a problem that involves a percent, change the percent to a decimal or a fraction.

Changing Percents to Decimals

The denominator of a percent is always understood to be 100. The number before the percent sign is the numerator.

To change a percent to a decimal, write the numerator as a decimal to the hundredths place by moving the decimal point two places to the **left** and removing the percent sign.

Example 1: Change 10% to a decimal.

Step 1. Write the decimal point that is under-   10% = 10.%
stood to follow the number in the percent.

Step 2. Move the decimal point two places to   10.% = .10. or .1
the left and remove the percent sign. Drop
the trailing zero.

Example 2: Change $7\frac{1}{2}$% to a decimal.

Step 1. Change the fraction in the percent to $7\frac{1}{2}$% = 7.5%
a decimal.

Step 2. Move the decimal point two places to   7.5% = .7.5
the left and remove the percent sign.

Step 3. Place a zero in the tenths place to   .075
maintain place value.

Changing Decimals to Percents

To change a decimal to a percent, move the decimal point two places to the **right** and add a percent sign.

Example 3: Change .7 to a percent.

Step 1. Move the decimal point two places to   .7 = .7.%
the right and add a percent sign.

Step 2. Write a zero in the ones place to   70%
maintain place value.

Lesson 1   Exercise

Directions: Change each percent to a decimal.

1. 29%   2. 3%   3. $1\frac{7}{10}$%   4. .07%   5. 3.09%

Directions: Change each decimal to a percent.

6. 7.13   7. .0396   8. .8   9. 30.001   10. .05

Answers are on page A-52.

Lesson 2 Interchanging Percents and Fractions

Changing Percents to Fractions

A percent is a fraction whose denominator is understood to be 100. To change a percent to a fraction, remove the percent sign, write the number in the percent as the numerator, and use 100 as the denominator.

If a percent includes a decimal, add one zero to the denominator of the fraction for each place in the decimal. Then, remove the decimal point.

Example 1: Change 1.25% to a fraction.

Step 1. Remove the percent sign. Write 1.25 as the numerator and 100 as the denominator. $1.25\% = \frac{1.25}{100}$

Step 2. Add the same number of zeros to the denominator as there are decimal places in the numerator. Drop the decimal point. $\frac{1.25}{100} = \frac{125}{10,000}$

Step 3. Reduce to lowest terms. $\frac{125}{10,000} = \frac{125 \div 125}{10,000 \div 125} = \frac{1}{80}$

When a percent contains a fraction, first change the fraction to a decimal.

Changing Fractions to Percents

To change a common fraction to a percent, multiply the fraction by 100, and divide the numerator by the denominator. Add a percent sign. Sometimes the denominator will not evenly divide the numerator. Then the percent can be written with either a fraction or a decimal. Choose whichever is easier to work with.

Example 2: Change $\frac{5}{6}$ to a percent.

Step 1. Multiply the fraction by 100. $\frac{5}{6} \times \frac{100}{1} = \frac{500}{6}$

Step 2. Divide the numerator by the denominator. Write the remainder as a fraction or a decimal. Add the percent sign. $\frac{500}{6} = 83\frac{1}{3}\%$, or 83.33%

Lesson 2 Exercise

Directions: *Change each percent to a fraction in simplest terms.*

1. 96%   2. $37\frac{1}{2}\%$ 3. 62.5%   4. $56\frac{1}{4}\%$ 5. 18.75%

Directions: *Change each fraction to a percent.*

6. $\frac{3}{15}$ 7. $\frac{1}{8}$ 8. $\frac{15}{16}$ 9. $\frac{11}{40}$ 10. $\frac{4}{5}$

Answers are on pages A-52–A-53.

Lesson 3 Common Equivalent Fractions, Decimals, and Percents

Interchanging fractions, decimals, and percents takes time. You may save time on the GED by memorizing the equivalents in the table below.

Equivalent Fractions, Decimals, and Percents						
Fraction	Decimal	Percent	Fraction	Decimal	Percent
$\frac{1}{2}$	.5	50%	$\frac{9}{10}$	.9	90%
$\frac{1}{4}$	.25	25%	$\frac{1}{8}$	.125	$12\frac{1}{2}$%, or 12.5%
$\frac{3}{4}$	.75	75%	$\frac{3}{8}$	.375	$37\frac{1}{2}$%, or 37.5%
$\frac{1}{5}$	.2	20%	$\frac{7}{8}$	.875	$87\frac{1}{2}$%, or 87.5%
$\frac{4}{5}$	.8	80%	$\frac{1}{3}$	.333	$33\frac{1}{3}$%, or 33.3%
$\frac{1}{10}$	.1	10%	$\frac{2}{3}$	.667	$66\frac{2}{3}$%, or 66.7%
$\frac{3}{10}$	.3	30%	$\frac{1}{6}$	.167	$16\frac{2}{3}$%, or 16.7%

Lesson 3 Exercise

Directions: Test yourself to see if you know the decimal and the percent equivalents of these fractions.

1. $\frac{3}{10}$ 2. $\frac{4}{5}$ 3. $\frac{5}{6}$ 4. $\frac{5}{8}$ 5. $\frac{1}{2}$
6. $\frac{3}{4}$ 7. $\frac{1}{3}$ 8. $\frac{2}{5}$ 9. $\frac{1}{6}$ 10. $\frac{7}{8}$

Answers are on page A-53.

Lesson 4 Finding a Percent of a Number

The *percent formula* is used to find the percent of a number.

percentage = rate × base

p = rb

The percentage, p, and the base, b, are numbers; the rate, r, is a percent.
You can use either the fraction or decimal form of the percent for the multiplication. You will find approximately the same answer either way.

Example 1: What is $83\frac{1}{3}$% of 702?

Step 1. Set up the problem. Use the percent formula.

Step 2. Change $83\frac{1}{3}$% to $\frac{5}{6}$.

Step 3. Multiply.

$p = rb$
$= 83\frac{1}{3}\% \times 702$
$= \frac{5}{6} \times 702$
$= 585$

Example 2: What is 70% of 900?

Step 1. Set up the problem. Use the percent formula.
Step 2. Change 70% to .7.
Step 3. Multiply.

$$p = rb$$
$$= 70\% \times 900$$
$$= .7 \times 900$$
$$= 630$$

Lesson 4   Exercise

Directions: *Find the percent of each number.*

1. $16\frac{2}{3}\%$ of 102
2. $87\frac{1}{2}\%$ of 776
3. 90% of 81
4. 10% of 79
5. $66\frac{2}{3}\%$ of 351

Answers are on page A-53.

Lesson 5   Finding What Percent One Number Is of Another

To find the percent that one number is of another, use a variation of the percent formula to divide the first number by the second number.

rate = percentage ÷ base

$r = p \div b$

If the division results in a remainder, write the remainder as either a fraction or a decimal, whichever is easier.

Example: 45 is what percent of 24?

Step 1. Set up the problem. Use the formula $r = p \div b$.
Step 2. Divide. Change the result to a percent.

$$r = p \div b$$
$$= 45 \div 24$$
$$= 1.875$$
$$= 187.5\%, \text{ or } 187\frac{1}{2}\%$$

Lesson 5   Exercise

Directions: *Solve each problem.*

1. What percent of 65 is 52?
2. What percent of 102 is 85?
3. 98 is what percent of 112?
4. 55 is what percent of 275?
5. 234.9 is what percent of 87?

Answers are on page A-53.

Lesson 6   Finding a Number When a Percent of It Is Given

When you are given the percentage and the rate and are asked to find the base, use another variation of the percent formula.

$$\text{base} = \text{percentage} \div \text{rate}$$
$$b = p \div r$$

Example 1: 783 is 87% of what number?

Step 1. Set up the problem. Use the formula $b = p \div r$.

Step 2. Change 87% to a decimal. Divide.

$$\begin{aligned} b &= p \div r \\ &= 783 \div 87\% \\ &= 783 \div .87 \\ &= 900 \end{aligned}$$

Example 2: 87.5% of what number is 147?

Step 1. Set up the problem. Use the formula $b = p \div r$.

Step 2. Change 87.5% to a decimal. Divide.

$$\begin{aligned} b &= p \div r \\ &= 147 \div 87.5\% \\ &= 147 \div \tfrac{7}{8} \\ &= 168 \end{aligned}$$

Lesson 6   Exercise

Directions: *Solve each problem.*

1. 1195 is 62.5% of what number?
2. 259 is $87\tfrac{1}{2}$% of what number?
3. 200 is $166\tfrac{2}{3}$% of what number?
4. 19% of what number is 285?
5. 37% of what number is 3737?

Answers are on page A-53.

Level 1   Review

Directions: *Solve each problem.*

1. Change 3.4% to a decimal.
2. Write seventeen and five hundredths as a percent.
3. Change 3.75% to a fraction expressed in simplest terms.
4. Write $\tfrac{11}{40}$ as a percent.

Directions: Use the formula $p = rb$, $r = p \div b$, or $b = p \div r$ to solve each problem. Round to the nearest percent or whole number if necessary.

5. 115% of 360 is what number?
6. 3.78% of 1500 is what number?
7. What percent of 128 is 18?
8. 600 is what percent of 96?
9. 176 is 160% of what number?
10. $1\frac{3}{4}$% of what number is 7?

Check your answers. Correct answers are on page A-53. If you have at least eight answers correct, go to Level 2. If you have fewer than eight answers correct, go back to Lesson 1 and study Level 1.

Level 2 Percent Applications

Lesson 1 Word Problems Involving Percent

When you are given a word problem using percents, read the problem carefully. Decide what you are asked to find, select the facts that you need to work with, and decide what version of the percent formula to use.

When the problem is to find the percent of a number, use the formula $p = rb$.

Example 1: Sheila is buying a reduction valve that costs $39.75. Her professional discount is 8%. How much is the discount?

Step 1. Set up the problem. $\quad p = rb$
Step 2. Change 8% to a decimal. Multiply. $\quad = 8\% \times \$39.75$
$\quad = .08 \times 39.75$
$\quad = \$3.18$

Some percent word problems ask you to find what percent one number is of another. Remember to use the formula $r = p \div b$. Then change the result to a percent.

Example 2: The net profit last year at Baffle Industries was $385,000. The year before last, it was $350,000. What percent of the previous year's profit was last year's profit?

Step 1. Set up the problem. Use the formula $r = p \div b$. $\quad r = p \div b$
$\quad = \$385,000 \div \$350,000$
Step 2. Divide. $\quad = 1.1$
Step 3. Change the decimal to a percent. $\quad = 110\%$

Some word problems on the GED test will give you the percentage and the rate and ask you to find the base. Remember to use the formula $b = p \div r$, and change the percent to either a fraction or a decimal.

Example 3: It rained 12 days during Norma Nelson's vacation; this was 80% of her vacation time. How long was her vacation?

Step 1. Set up the problem. Use the formula $b = p \div r$.

Step 2. Change 80% to a decimal. Divide. Norma's vacation lasted 15 days.

$$b = p \div r$$
$$= 12 \div 80\%$$
$$= 12 \div .8$$
$$= 15 \text{ days}$$

Lesson 1 Exercise

Directions: *Use the percent formula to solve problems 1 to 4.*

1. If 12% of Neri Productions' output of 9850 widgets was defective, how many defective widgets were produced?
2. An automobile costs $5999. The state sales tax rate is 8%. What sales tax is paid on the price of the automobile?
3. Gilberta Sutton's daily diet provides only 70% of the 2400 calories she used to get. How many calories per day does her current diet supply?
4. Gotham City's 1970 population of 3,005,000 had increased 12% by 1980. How many more people lived there in 1980 than in 1970?

Directions: *Use the formula $r = p \div b$ to solve problems 5 to 7.*

5. Mary Grant received patents on 9 of her 15 inventions. What percent of her inventions were patented?
6. Leo increased the number of cattle on his farm from 52 to 65. What percent of the size of his former herd is the size of his current herd?
7. Rathmullan Associated bought property for $297,000 and sold it for $341,550. What percent of the original price was the sale price?

Directions: *Use the formula $b = p \div r$ to solve problems 8 to 10.*

8. The bank requires a 10% down payment for a 30-year mortgage on a home. Ayesha Jones made the minimum down payment of $12,150. What was the price of her home?
9. After processing 35 applications, Martha Pearl learned that this was only $83\frac{1}{3}\%$ of the number that was received that day. What was the total number that was received?
10. Although Alex Stakhanov completed 81 assemblies, his total was only 90% of that of the best worker. What was the best worker's output?

Answers are on page A-53.

Lesson 2 Interest

Interest is a fee paid for the use of money. Banks, for example, pay interest for the money that they borrow and charge interest for the money that they lend.

To find interest, multiply the principal, the money borrowed or lent, by the rate of interest by the length of time. This can be expressed in a formula.

$$\text{interest} = \text{principal} \times \text{rate} \times \text{time}$$
$$i = prt$$

Example 1: Find the interest for 3 years on a $20,000 note at 10% interest.

Step 1. Set up the problem. Use the formula $i = prt$.

Step 2. Change 10% to a decimal. Multiply.

$i = prt$
$= \$20{,}000 \times 10\% \times 3$
$= 20{,}000 \times .1 \times 3$
$= \$6000$

Example 2: Find the interest that is due on a 6-month $4000 loan at 11% annual interest.

Step 1. Set up the problem.

Step 2. Change 11% to a fraction. Write 6 months as a fraction. Multiply.

$i = prt$
$= \$4000 \times 11\% \times 6 \text{ mo.}$
$= 4000 \times \frac{11}{100} \times \frac{1}{2}$
$= \$220$

Lesson 2 Exercise

Directions: *Find the interest on each loan.*

1. a $5000 loan at 9% annual interest for 2 years
2. a $1750 loan at 12% annual interest for 1 year
3. a $200 loan at 11% annual interest for 9 months
4. a $750 loan at 18% annual interest for 30 months
5. a $2000 loan at $7\frac{1}{2}$% annual interest for 2 years

Answers are on page A-53.

Level 2 Review

1. Of all Nori Sloth convertibles that were sold last year, 75% cost less than $10,000. Of the 25,000 sold, how many cost less than $10,000?
2. In an election, one candidate received 26,000,000 of the 61,600,000 total votes. To the nearest percent, what percent of the vote did the candidate receive?

3. If the 156 million automobiles that were registered in the United States were 38% of the world total, how many automobiles were registered in the world?
4. Mutual Conglomerate's FastMeal Division accounts for $37\frac{1}{2}$% of sales. If the total annual sales last year were $88,000,000, how much of that came from FastMeal?
5. If 38,500,000 of 175,000,000 registered motor vehicles are trucks, what percent of the registered motor vehicles are trucks?
6. The price of a theater ticket is $40. This is about $266\frac{2}{3}$% higher than the price of a ticket in 1967. To the nearest dollar, what was the price of a theater ticket in 1967?
7. If 54% of the 160 million people who were eligible voted in a presidential election, how many people voted in the election?
8. The national debt decreased from $83,000,000 in 1800 to $65,000,000 in 1860. To the nearest percent, what percent of the 1860 debt was the 1800 debt?
9. If the interest rate on a credit card is 18%, what will the interest charge be on $250 for 6 months?
10. What is the interest charge on a 2-year loan of $4500 at $7\frac{1}{2}$% interest?

Check your answers. Correct answers are on page A-54. If you have at least eight answers correct, go to Level 3. If you have fewer than eight answers correct, go back to Lesson 1 and study Level 2 again.

Level 3 Problem Solving That Involves Percents

Lesson 1 Multistep Percent Problems

To solve word problems, first read the problem carefully. Determine what the problem is asking you to find. Then decide which facts to use and which calculations to perform.

Some problems will give a percentage and a base. You will be asked to find a new percentage and a rate.

Example 1: If 19 of every 25 new customers who were attracted to Julia's Grazing Grotto by a radio advertisement came back a second time, what percent did not come back?

Step 1. Subtract to find the number of customers that did not return. $25 - 19 = 6$

Step 2. Use the formula $r = p \div b$. Divide to find the percent of customers that did not return.

$r = p \div b$
$= 6 \div 25$
$= .24$

Step 3. Change the result to a percent. $= 24\%$

Sometimes a problem will give a percentage and a rate. You will be asked to find the base and a new percentage.

Example 2: When General Hospital has pledges of $1,400,000, it will have reached 80% of its goal. How much more is needed?

Step 1. Use the formula $b = p \div r$ to find the hospital's goal. Change 80% to a decimal.

$b = p \div r$
$= \$1,400,000 \div 80\%$
$= 1,400,000 \div .8$
$= \$1,750,000$

Step 2. Subtract the amount already raised from the goal.

$\$1,750,000$
$- 1,400,000$
$\$350,000$

Lesson 1   Exercise

Directions: *Solve each problem.*

1. Shelley budgets $50 per week for expenses. One week she spent $10 for carfare and $23 for meals. What percent of her weekly budget was left?
2. By waiting for a sale and using her employee discount, Marcia Stein bought an outboard motor for $220, which is 55% of its original price. How much less than the original price did she pay?
3. To be listed on the ballot, the Neighborhood Coalition needs 20% of the total number of voters to sign a petition. They have 135 signatures, which is 18% of the total number of voters. How many more signatures do they need?
4. At Art Warehouse, the auctioneer's fee is $2\frac{1}{2}\%$ of the selling price of art objects. If the auctioneer's share of the sale of a painting was $68.75, how much did the seller receive?
5. At her doctor's suggestion, Georgia lost 18 pounds, which is 12% of her former weight. What does she weigh now?

Answers are on page A-54.

Lesson 2 Percent Increase and Percent Decrease

Percent increase and **percent decrease** are used in science and business to reflect change. For example, you can find how much a temperature or a price goes up or down in relation to the original number.
  Percent increase and percent decrease problems are multistep problems. You first subtract to find the **actual** increase or decrease. Then use the formula $r = p \div b$ to find what percent the increase or decrease is of the original number.

Example 1: After 6 months of advertising, Julia's average daily number of customers rose from 275 to 330. What percent increase was this?

Step 1. Subtract to find the actual increase. $330 - 275 = 55$

Step 2. Use the formula $r = p \div b$ to find the percent increase of the original amount.

$r = p \div b$
$= 55 \div 275$
$= .2$
$= 20\%$

Remember, be sure to read word problems carefully. Sometimes it is not readily apparent what you are being asked to find.

Example 2: The Goal Line Shop advertises a $13.99 football on sale for $9.99. To the nearest percent, what is the discount rate?

Step 1. What is the problem asking you to find? When working with money, *discount rate* is another way of saying percent decrease. Subtract to find the actual decrease.

$13.99
$- 9.99$
$4.00

Step 2. Use the formula $r = p \div b$ to find the percent decrease of the original amount.

$r = p \div b$
$= \$4.00 \div \$13.99$
$= .2859$
$= .29$
$= 29\%$

Lesson 2 Exercise

Directions: *Find each percent increase or percent decrease.*

1. The average daily number of customers at Potobac Shopping Mall rose from 15,280 to 17,572. What percent increase in customers is this?
2. Sales of crops on Sam's farm dropped from $71,326 to $66,298. To the nearest percent, what percent decrease was this?
3. The population of Palmetto rose from 2,590,000 in 1970 to 3,120,000 in 1980. To the nearest percent, by what percent did the population increase?

4. The regular price of a scarf is $15.00. The sale price is $9.00. What is the discount rate?
5. The Sound Store purchased speakers for $46 per pair. The speakers were sold for $115 per pair. By what percent did the Sound Store mark up the speakers?

Answers are on page A-54.

Level 3 Review

Directions: *Items 1 to 5 refer to the following table.*

| Agricultural Exports in Millions of Dollars |||||||
Year	Wheat and Wheat Products	Feed Grains	Fodders and Feeds	Cotton	Rice
1965	1214	1162	278	495	244
1970	1144	1099	496	377	314
1975	5292	5492	987	991	858
1980	6660	9759	1126	2864	1288

1. In which year were dollars from wheat and wheat product exports lowest in relation to total exports? What percent of all exports did wheat and wheat products constitute that year?
2. What percent of all export income did rice bring in during the year its income was proportionally highest?
3. To the nearest percent, what was the rate of increase or decrease for each export from 1965 to 1970?
4. To the nearest percent, what percent of all 1980 exports was feed-grain exports?
5. Which export, cotton or rice, had the greater percent increase from 1970 to 1975?

Directions: *Solve each problem.*

6. The population of Apple City fell from 7,900,000 in 1970 to 7,070,000 in 1980. To the nearest tenth, by what percent did the population decrease?
7. Sheila Swenson went on a 1500-calorie-per-day diet to lose weight. This was $66\frac{2}{3}\%$ of her former daily caloric intake. How many fewer calories per day did she take in on her diet?
8. Billy Joe Wheatfield and a friend paid $9000 for a fishing boat. His partner put up $3600. What percent of the price did Billy Joe pay?

9. Of the people who took the test for a driver's license, 75% passed. If 312 people failed, how many people took the test?

Directions: *Item 10 is based on this table.*

Sanda Carter's Credit Card Costs		
Credit Card	Annual Fee	Monthly Interest Rate
CreditCharge	$65	16.9%
SavingCard Gold	60	18%
PrestigePlatinum	50	21.9%
ColossalCard	55	20%

10. Sanda Carter maintains an average balance of $150 on each of her credit cards. Which of her cards costs her the least per year?

Check your answers. Correct answers are on pages A-54–A-55. If you have at least eight answers correct, go to the Chapter 4 Quiz. If you have fewer than eight answers correct, go back to Lesson 1 and study Level 3 again.

Chapter 4 Quiz

Directions: *Solve each problem.*

1. Change .0075 to a percent.
2. Change $31\frac{1}{4}$% to a fraction written in lowest terms.
3. Find 21.8% of 146.
4. Radio advertising attracted $5\frac{1}{2}$% of the first 600 customers of InstaBell Answering Service. How many of the 600 were not attracted by this advertising?
5. What is the total charge for a $78.70 coat if the sales tax is $7\frac{1}{2}$%?
6. To the nearest percent, 51 is what percent of 357?
7. The 300 miles from Chicago that Fatima Faad has already driven is about $28\frac{3}{8}$% of the distance to Denver. To the nearest mile, how many more miles does she have to drive to reach Denver?
8. Mark Claret has a $2500 municipal bond that earns $7\frac{1}{2}$% annual interest. How much interest does it earn in 18 months?

9. Kareen Beekman buys onions at a cost of $15 per hundred-pound sack. He sells them for $.39 per pound. To the nearest percent, what percent of the selling price is his cost?

10. If 51 of the 340 runners in the United Charities Marathon were first-time runners, what percent had run before?

11. 3819 candidates for election were endorsed by the Good Government Coalition. This was 57% of all candidates. How many candidates ran?

12. A recent survey showed that 36% of the states in the United States require blood tests for couples planning to marry. How many states do not require blood tests?

13. The sales tax on a $17,500 sports car is $1443.75. What is the sales tax rate?

14. Arnoldo Lorca is buying new kitchen appliances. Which of the following payment plans costs the fewest dollars?
    (1) $130 per month for 18 months with a 2% manufacturer's rebate
    (2) $1000 down and $100 per month for one year
    (3) $23 per week for 104 weeks
    (4) $105 per month for 24 months with a $12\frac{1}{2}$% manufacturer's rebate
    (5) $500 down and $87.50 per month for 24 months

15. If 17.9% of the spectators at the Behemoths game did not pay, how many of the 29,000 spectators did pay?

Directions: *Items 16 to 20 are based on the following table.*

Group	Apple City – Average Tax Deductions, 1983				
	Adjusted Gross Income	Medical Expenses	Other Taxes	Charitable Contributions	Interest
A	$10,000–12,000	$2153	$1201	$747	$2441
B	12,001–14,000	1870	1197	732	2697
C	14,001–16,000	1482	1331	772	2672
D	16,001–18,000	1416	1539	732	2883
E	18,001–20,000	1544	1791	734	3016

16. For which group was interest the highest percent of the deductions?

17. For which group were other taxes the lowest percent of the deductions?

18. For which group was the combination of medical expenses and other taxes the lowest percent of the deductions?

19. For which group was the combination of other taxes and charitable contributions the highest percent of the deductions?

20. The average income of people in Group D was $17,000, and the average income for the people in Group E was $19,000. For which group were the total deductions a higher percent of their income?

Answers are on pages A-55–A-56.

Chapter 5: Graphs

Objective

In this chapter, you will learn to

- Read and interpret pictographs
- Read and interpret circle graphs
- Read and interpret bar graphs
- Read and interpret line graphs

Preview

1. Look at the pictograph in Figure 1 on page 524. How much milk was sold in Pennsylvania in one year?

2. Based on the circle graph in Figure 3 on page 526, how much more of each dollar is invested in real estate than in all the other categories combined?

3. Look at the bar graph in Figure 4 on page 527. What was the percent increase in the number of subscribers between 1970 and 1982?

4. Look at the line graph in Figure 5 on page 528. How much did net farming income increase between 1983 and 1984?

5. Use the information in the line graph in Figure 5 on page 528 to find the yearly average of net income from farming for the years 1975 to 1984.

Check your answers. Correct answers are on page A-56. If you have at least four answers correct, do the Chapter 5 Quiz on pages 530–532. If you have fewer than four answers correct, study this chapter beginning with Lesson 1.

Lesson 1 Pictographs

A **graph** is a diagram that shows the relationship among several items. Graphs are often used to present information in newspapers and magazines and on computer screens.

A **pictograph** uses pictorial symbols to present data. The key explains what each symbol stands for. To understand a pictograph, read the title, the key, and the labels for the columns and the rows of information.

524 Chapter 5: Graphs INSTRUCTION

The title of the pictograph in Figure 1 is *Quantity of Milk Sold in One Year*. The column on the left lists state names. The key tells that each symbol stands for 1 billion pounds of milk.

QUANTITY OF MILK SOLD IN ONE YEAR

State

California: 14 milk cartons

Wisconsin: 14 milk cartons (row 1), 7 milk cartons (row 2)

Minnesota: 9 milk cartons

New York: 11 milk cartons

Pennsylvania: 9 milk cartons

LEGEND: 🥛 = 1,000,000,000 pounds of whole milk

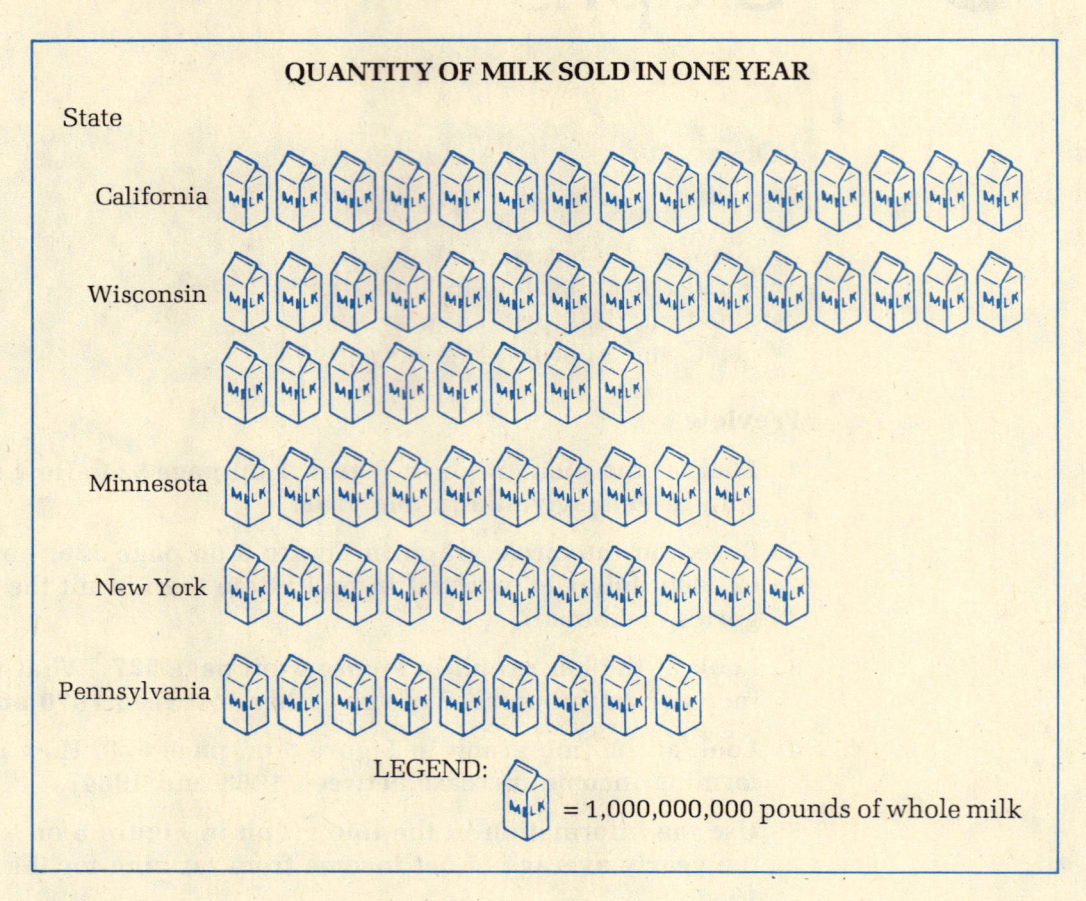

FIGURE 1

Example 1: How much milk was sold in New York in one year?

Step 1. Locate the row labeled New York.
Count the number of symbols (11).

Step 2. Each symbol represents 1,000,000,000 pounds of milk. Multiply 1,000,000,000 by 11 to find the answer.

```
     1,000,000,000
   ×            11
  11,000,000,000 lb of
                 milk
```

Example 2: If the milk was sold for $.14 per pound, what was the cash value of the milk that was sold in Pennsylvania in one year?

Step 1. Multiply the number of symbols for milk by their value.

Step 2. Multiply the amount of milk by the cost.

```
     1,000,000,000
   ×             9
     9,000,000,000
   ×           .14
       360 000 000 00
       900 000 000 0
   $1,260,000,000.00
```

Lesson 1 Exercise

Directions: Items 1 to 5 are based on the pictograph in Figure 2.

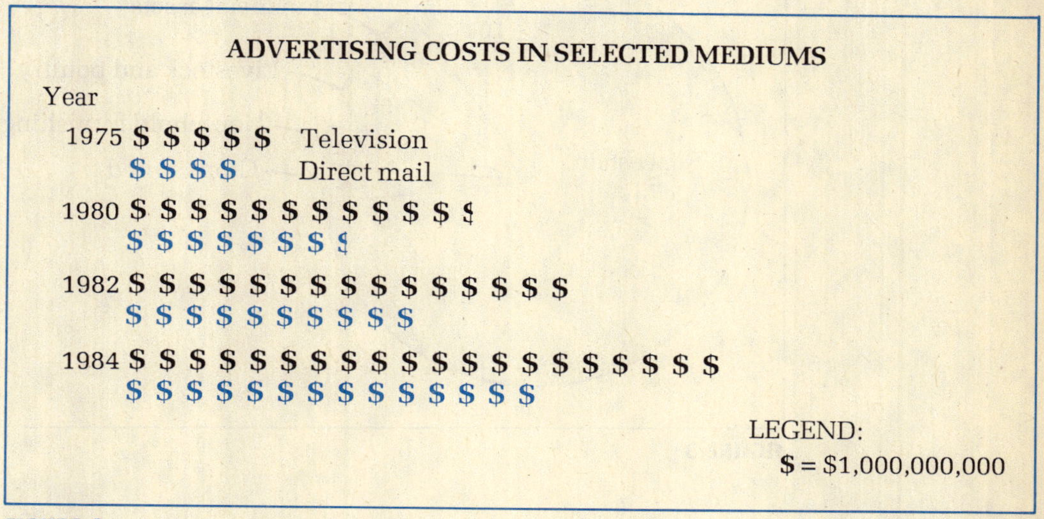

```
                ADVERTISING COSTS IN SELECTED MEDIUMS
    Year
    1975  $ $ $ $ $       Television
          $ $ $ $         Direct mail
    1980  $ $ $ $ $ $ $ $ $
          $ $ $ $ $ $ $
    1982  $ $ $ $ $ $ $ $ $ $ $
          $ $ $ $ $ $ $ $
    1984  $ $ $ $ $ $ $ $ $ $ $ $ $ $ $
          $ $ $ $ $ $ $ $ $ $ $ $

                                          LEGEND:
                                          $ = $1,000,000,000
```

FIGURE 2

1. How much does one dollar sign stand for?
2. What was the total amount spent on both types of advertising in 1975? In 1982?
3. In 1984, direct-mail advertising costs were what percent of the combined advertising costs for that year?
4. How much more was spent on television advertising in 1982 than in 1975?
5. What was the dollar increase in direct-mail advertising between 1980 and 1984?

Answers are on page A-56.

Lesson 2 Circle Graphs

A circle graph shows the parts that make up a whole. A circle is divided into pie-shaped pieces that stand for percents or for parts of a dollar. The pieces of a circle graph add up to 100%.

To understand a circle graph, read the title of the graph and the labels for each part carefully.

The following example is based on the circle graph in Figure 3. The graph shows how each dollar that is invested in the farming sector is used. It shows how many cents out of each dollar are invested in various assets.

DOLLAR INVESTMENT IN THE FARMING SECTOR

- Machinery and vehicles: 10¢
- Financial assets: 6¢
- Livestock and poultry: 5¢
- Household furnishings and equipment: 3¢
- Crops stored: 3¢
- Real estate: 73¢

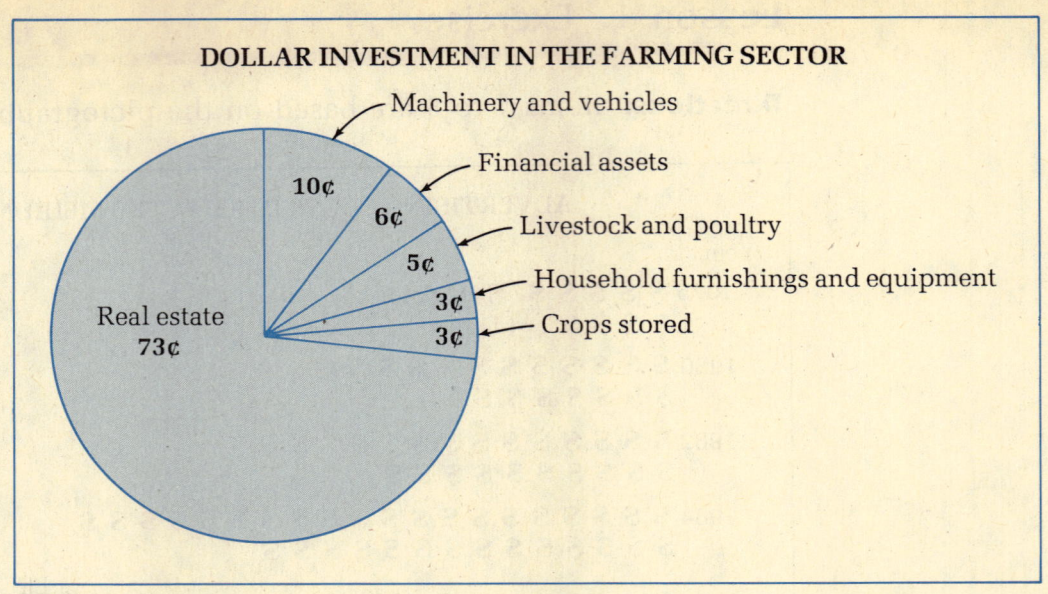

FIGURE 3

Example: What percent of the dollar is invested in crops stored?

Step 1. Find the amount spent on crops stored. It is $.03.

$.03

Step 2. Change $.03 to a percent. Since the graph represents $1.00, or 100 cents, multiply by 100.

```
  100
× .03
─────
3.00%, or 3%
```

Lesson 2   Exercise

Directions: *Items 1 to 5 refer to the circle graph in Figure 3.*

1. What percent of the dollar is invested in financial assets and in real estate combined?
2. What category has twice as much of each dollar invested as is invested in livestock and poultry?
3. What percent of the dollar is NOT invested in livestock and poultry or in crops stored?
4. What fraction of each dollar is invested in machinery and vehicles and in household furnishings and equipment combined?
5. If the total investment in livestock and poultry is approximately $49 billion, what is the total dollar investment in the farming sector?

Answers are on pages A-55–A-56.

UNIT VII: MATHEMATICS   Lesson 3   **527**

Lesson 3   Bar Graphs

A **bar graph** uses rectangles to compare quantities. The length of each rectangle is proportional to the size of the quantity it represents. Rectangles may run vertically or horizontally. To find the amount each rectangle stands for, use the *scale* on the side or the bottom of the bar graph. Read the title of the graph and the labels on each scale carefully.

The bar graph in Figure 4 shows how many cable-television subscribers there were in selected years. The scale at the left of the graph shows the number of subscribers in millions. The scale across the bottom shows the years.

CABLE-TELEVISION SUBSCRIBERS

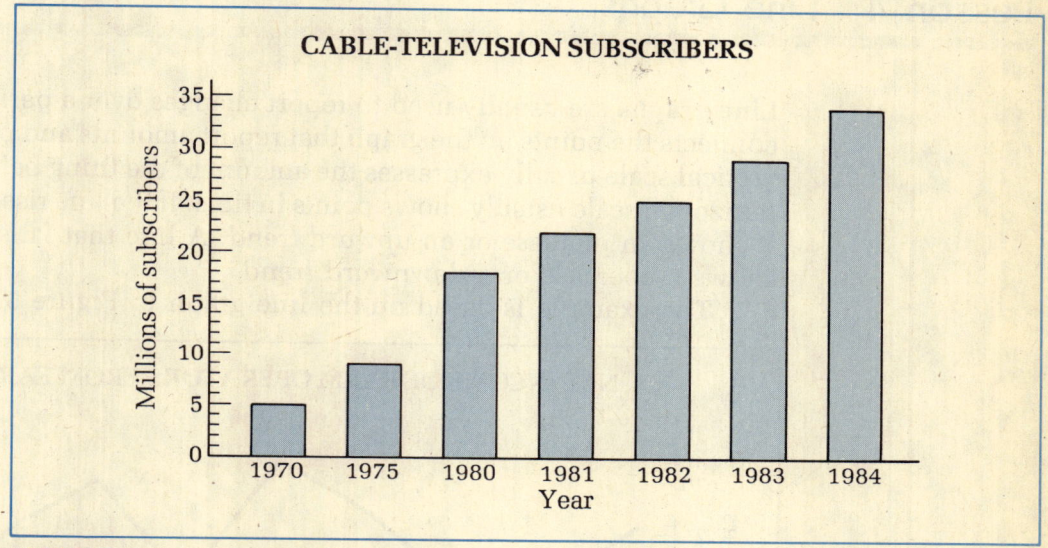

FIGURE 4

Example: How many cable-television subscribers were there in 1975?

Step 1. Find the year on the scale at the bottom of the graph. Follow the rectangle above *1975* to the top.

Step 2. Look directly to the left at the vertical scale. Each line stands for 1 million subscribers. The rectangle above *1975* ends one line below *10 million*. There were 9 million subscribers.

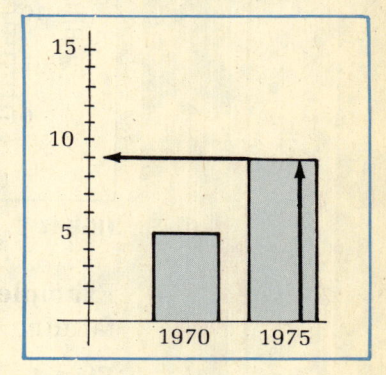

Lesson 3   Exercise

Directions: *Items 1 to 5 are based on the bar graph in Figure 4.*

1. How many cable-television subscribers were there in 1970?
2. In which year was the number of subscribers 22 million?

3. Between which two years was there an increase of 5 million subscribers?
4. The number of cable-television subscribers in 1970 was what fraction of the number of subscribers in 1982?
5. What was the percent increase in the number of subscribers between 1970 and 1984?

Answers are on page A-57.

Lesson 4   Line Graphs

Line graphs are usually used to report changes over a period of time. A line connects the points on the graph that report amounts and points in time. The vertical scale usually expresses the amount of the thing being measured. The horizontal scale usually shows points in time. If the line rises from left to right, it shows an increase or an *upward trend*. A line that falls from left to right shows a decrease or a *downward trend*.

The example is based on the line graph in Figure 5.

NET INCOME OF FARM OPERATORS FROM FARMING

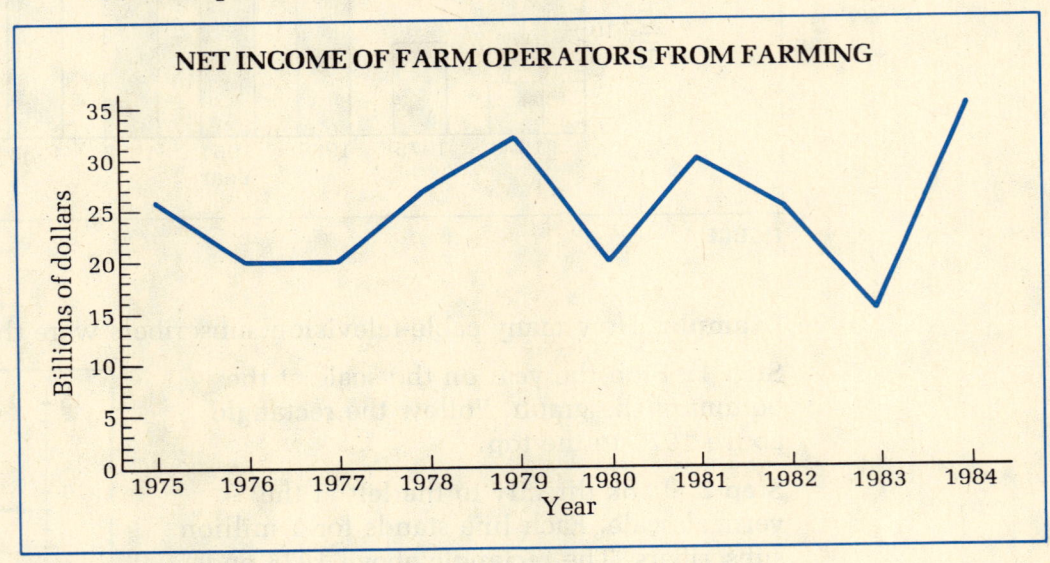

(Billions of dollars, Year 1975–1984)

FIGURE 5

Example: What was the net income from farming in 1978?

Step 1. Find the year on the horizontal scale at the bottom of the graph. Then follow the line marked 1978 straight up to the point at the top.

Step 2. Look straight across to the vertical scale. You should be two lines above the $25 billion mark. The net income from farming in 1978 was $27 billion.

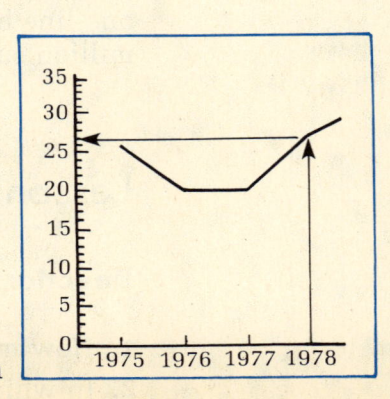

Lesson 4 Exercise

The line graph in Figure 6 shows a comparison between the number of gas wells and the number of oil wells that were drilled between 1974 and 1984. Notice that there are two lines: one shows the number of oil wells that were drilled; the other shows the number of gas wells that were drilled.

GAS WELLS AND OIL WELLS DRILLED, 1974–1984

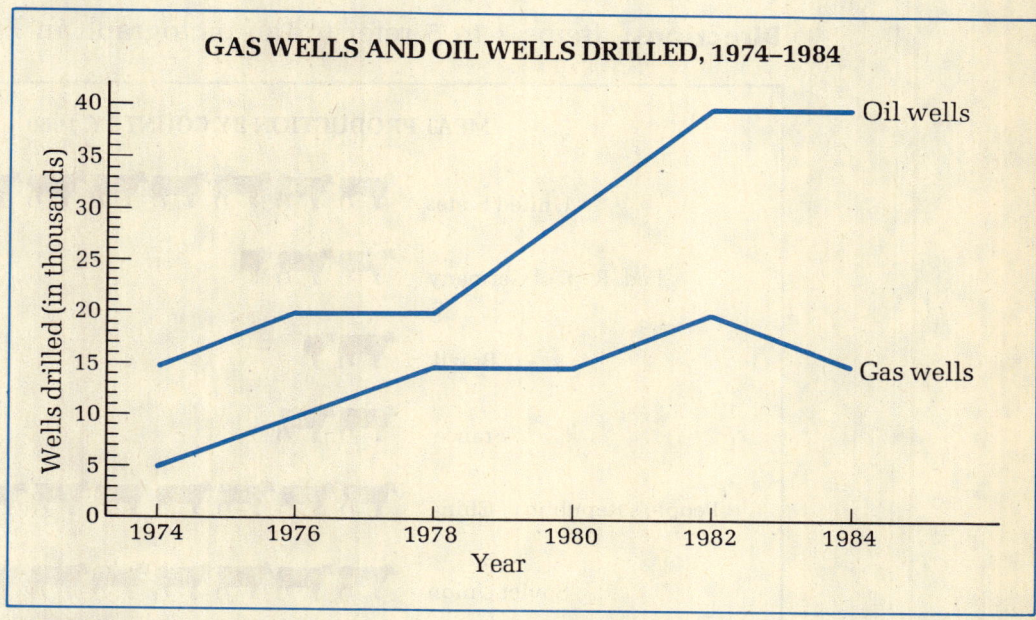

FIGURE 6

Directions: Items 1 to 5 are based on the line graph in Figure 6.

1. How many oil wells were drilled in 1980?
2. How many gas wells were drilled in 1974?
3. How many gas wells and oil wells combined were drilled in 1984?
4. Between which years did the number of gas wells drilled show a downward trend?
5. In which year was the gap between the number of gas wells and the number of oil wells that were drilled the smallest?

Answers are on page A-57.

Chapter 5 Quiz

Directions: *Items 1 to 5 refer to the pictograph in Figure 7.*

MEAT PRODUCTION BY COUNTRY, 1980

United States	🐄🐄🐄🐄🐄🐄🐄🐄🐄
Fed. Rep. of Germany	🐄🐄🐄
Brazil	🐄🐄
France	🐄🐄
People's Republic of China	🐄🐄🐄🐄🐄🐄🐄🐄🐄
Soviet Union	🐄🐄🐄🐄🐄🐄

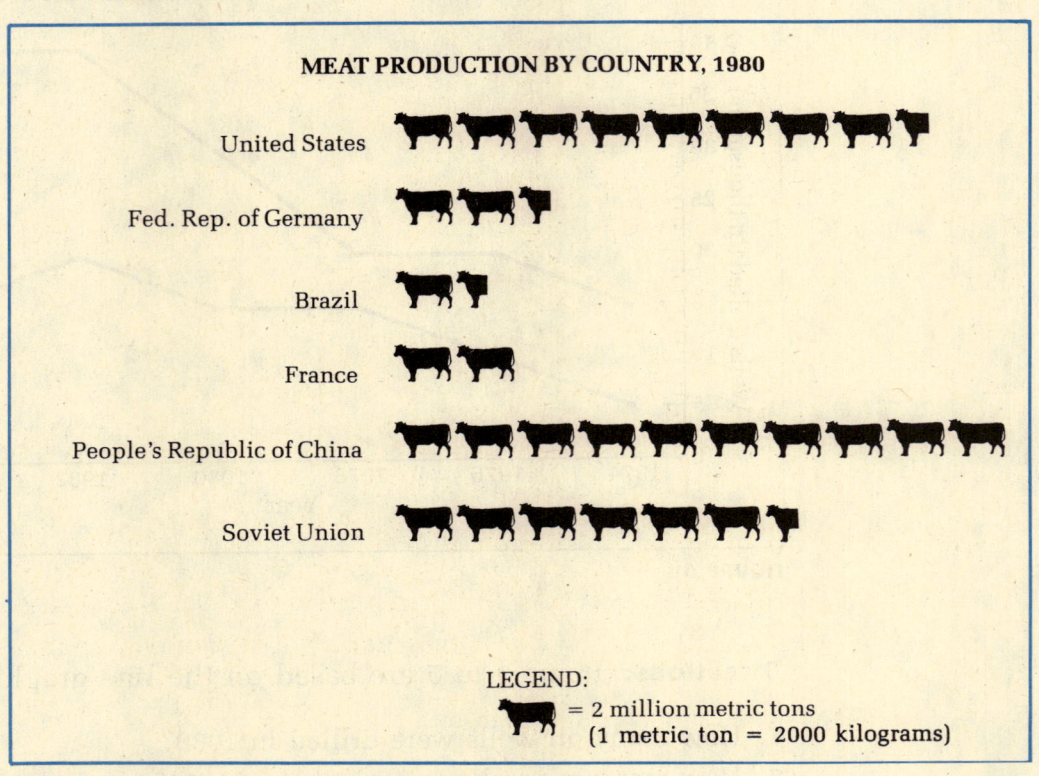

LEGEND:
🐄 = 2 million metric tons
(1 metric ton = 2000 kilograms)

FIGURE 7

1. How much meat was produced in the United States in 1980?
2. Meat production in the People's Republic of China is how many times that of the Federal Republic of Germany?
3. Meat production in Brazil is what fraction of the meat production in France?
4. The combined meat production of the United States and the Soviet Union is what percent of the meat production of the People's Republic of China?
5. The population of the United States in 1980 was approximately 226,500,000 people. To the nearest kilogram, how many kilograms of meat did the United States produce per person in 1980?

UNIT VII: MATHEMATICS   Chapter 5 Quiz **531**

Directions: Items 6 to 10 refer to the circle graphs in Figure 8.

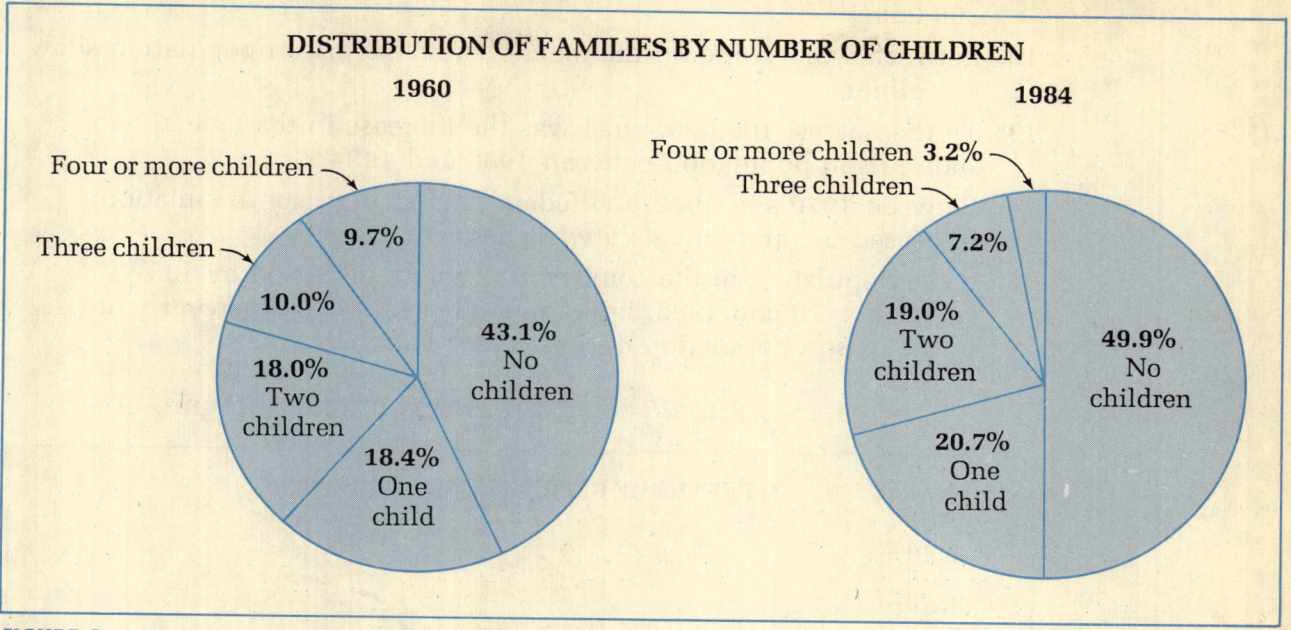

DISTRIBUTION OF FAMILIES BY NUMBER OF CHILDREN

1960

- Four or more children — 9.7%
- Three children — 10.0%
- 18.0% Two children
- 18.4% One child
- 43.1% No children

1984

- Four or more children 3.2%
- Three children 7.2%
- 19.0% Two children
- 20.7% One child
- 49.9% No children

FIGURE 8

6. What percent of the families in 1960 had one or more children?
7. What category showed the greatest change between 1960 and 1984?
8. What category showed the least change between 1960 and 1984?
9. By how many percentage points did the number of families having three or more children decrease from 1960 to 1984?
10. The 1984 United States population included approximately 62 million families. How many families in 1984 had no children?

Directions: Items 11 to 15 refer to the bar graph in Figure 9.

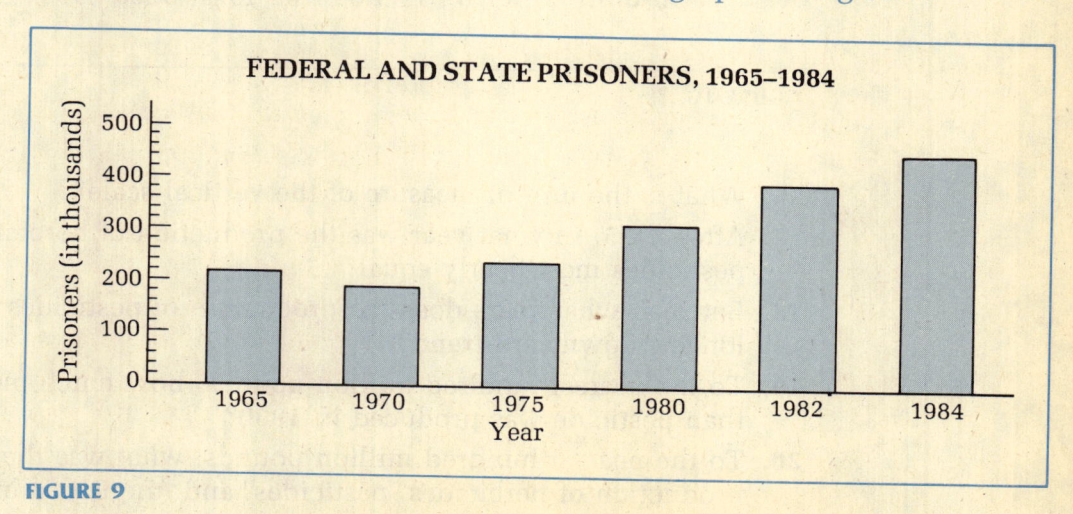

FEDERAL AND STATE PRISONERS, 1965–1984

Prisoners (in thousands) vs. Year (1965, 1970, 1975, 1980, 1982, 1984)

FIGURE 9

11. In what year did the federal and state prison population first exceed 300,000?
12. Between what years did the federal and state prison population show a decline?
13. To the nearest 100,000, what was the increase in the federal and state prison population between 1980 and 1984?
14. Between 1970 and 1982, the federal and state prison population increased by approximately what percent?
15. If the population of the country as a whole increased by 13% between 1970 and 1982, how much greater was the percent increase in the prison population during those years?

Directions: Items 16 to 20 refer to the line graph in Figure 10.

PESTICIDE PRODUCTION, 1970–1983

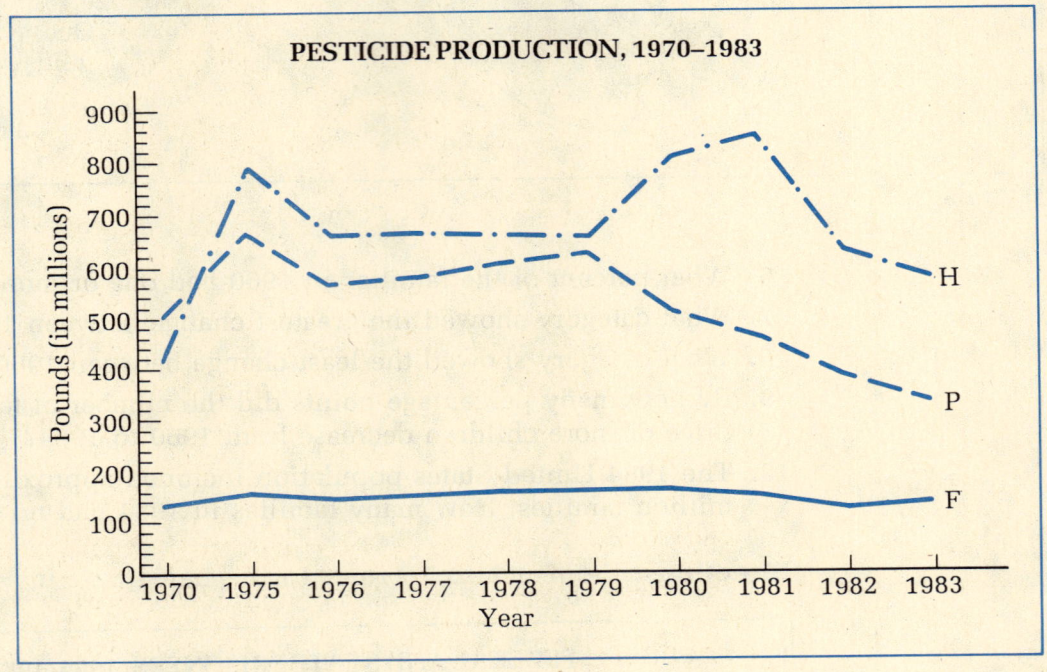

(Line graph showing Pounds (in millions) on vertical axis from 0 to 900, and Year on horizontal axis: 1970, 1975, 1976, 1977, 1978, 1979, 1980, 1981, 1982, 1983. Three lines labeled H, P, and F.)

FIGURE 10

16. What is the unit of measure of the vertical scale?
17. After 1975, in what year was the production of herbicides and pesticides most nearly equal?
18. Between what years does the production of pesticides show the longest downward trend?
19. To the nearest hundred million pounds, how much more herbicide than pesticide was produced in 1980?
20. To the nearest hundred million pounds, what was the combined production of herbicides, pesticides, and fungicides in 1982?

Check your answers. Correct answers are on page A-57. If you have at least sixteen answers correct, go to the next chapter. If not, study Chapter 5 again.

Chapter 6 Algebra

Objective

In this chapter, you will learn to

- Use a number line
- Add, subtract, multiply, and divide signed numbers
- Add, subtract, multiply, and divide monomials
- Solve one-step equations
- Solve multistep equations
- Solve inequalities
- Translate words into algebraic expressions and equations
- Multiply binomials
- Solve proportions
- Solve algebra setup problems

Level 1 Algebra Skills

Preview

Directions: *Item 1 is based on the following number line.*

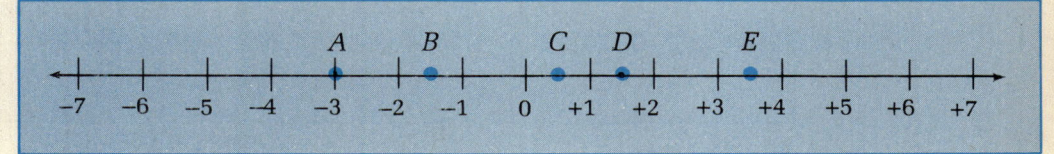

1. Which point represents $\frac{+3}{2}$?

Directions: *Solve each problem.*

2. $(^+8) + (^-4) - (^-10) + (^+3)$
3. $^-6 \cdot \frac{3}{8}$
4. $(^-4c^2a) + (18c^2a)$
5. $\frac{^+20a^5}{^-2a^3}$

Check your answers. Correct answers are on page A-57. If you have at least four answers correct, do the Level 1 Review on page 540. If you have fewer than four answers correct, study Level 1 beginning with Lesson 1.

Lesson 1 The Number Line

Look at the number line in Figure 1.

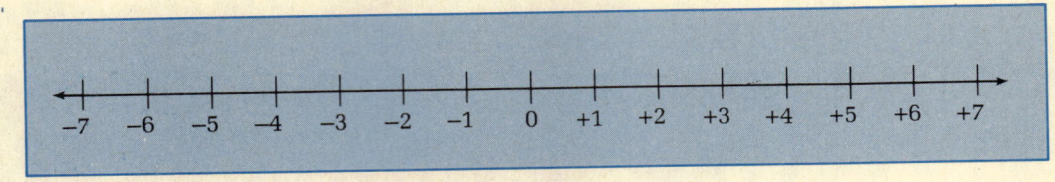

FIGURE 1

Notice that there are numbers on both sides of zero. The numbers to the right of zero have a plus sign and are called **positive numbers**. The numbers to the left of the zero have a minus sign and are called **negative numbers**. Both positive and negative numbers are called signed numbers. If a number has no sign, it is positive. The arrows at the end of the number line mean that the numbers go on with no end.

The value of a point on a number line is determined by its position on the line in relation to zero.

Example 1: What is the value of point A on the number line in Figure 2?

Step 1. Find the point on the number line labeled A.

Step 2. Find the value of the same point. It is three spaces to the left of zero. The value of point A is ⁻3 (negative 3).

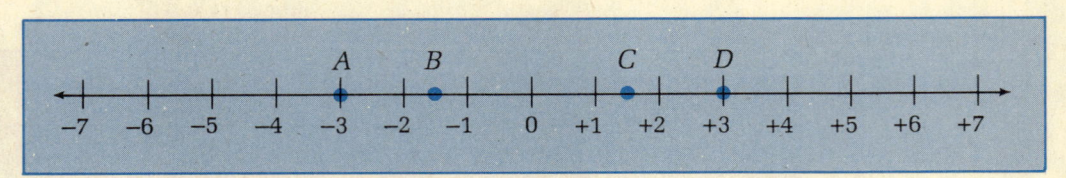

FIGURE 2

Points on a number line can fall between whole numbers to express fraction or decimal values.

Example 2: What are the values of point B and point C on the number line in Figure 2?

Step 1. Find the points labeled B and C.

Step 2. Find the value of the same points. Point B is halfway between ⁻1 and ⁻2; its value is ⁻1$\frac{1}{2}$, or ⁻1.5. Point C is halfway between ⁺1 and ⁺2; its value is ⁺1$\frac{1}{2}$, or ⁺1.5.

Lesson 1 Exercise

Directions: Choose the correct letter on the number line for each corresponding value below.

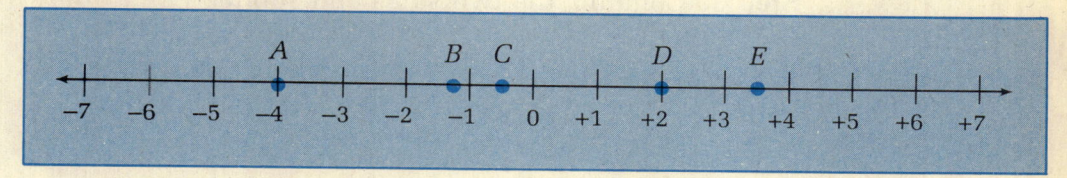

```
         A          B  C        D     E
<—+—+—+—●—+—+—●—●—+—+—●—+—●—+—+—+—>
 −7 −6 −5 −4 −3 −2 −1  0 +1 +2 +3 +4 +5 +6 +7
```

1. $^+2$ 2. $^-4$ 3. $^+3.5$ 4. $\dfrac{^-7}{6}$ 5. $^-.5$

Answers are on page A-57.

Lesson 2 Adding and Subtracting Signed Numbers

Adding Signed Numbers

To add signed numbers when the signs are alike, add the numerical values and use the same sign for the sum.

Example 1: Add $(^+9) + (^+4)$.

Step 1. Add the numerical values of the two numbers.

$$9 + 4 = 13$$
$$(^+9) + (^+4) = {^+13}$$

Step 2. Because both numbers are positive, use the + sign for the sum.

To add two numbers with different signs, subtract the smaller numerical value from the larger numerical value. Use the sign of the larger numerical value for the sum.

Example 2: Add $(^-20) + (^+13)$.

Step 1. Because the signs are different, subtract the smaller numerical value from the larger one.

$$20 - 13 = 7$$
$$(^-20) + (^+13) = {^-7}$$

Step 2. Use the sign of the larger numerical value for the sum. (Because 20 is larger than 13, use the minus sign.)

Sometimes you must add a group of signed numbers, some positive and some negative. To add more than two signed numbers, first find the sum of the positive numbers. Then find the sum of the negative numbers. Finally, add these two sums as you would for numbers with different signs.

Example 3: Add $(^+5) + (^-2) + (^+8) + (^-7) + (^+3)$.

Step 1. Find the sum of the positive numbers. $(^+5) + (^+8) + (^+3) = {^+16}$

Step 2. Find the sum of the negative numbers. $(^-2) + (^-7) = {^-9}$

Step 3. Combine the two sums and subtract the numerical values. $(^+16) + (^-9) = {^+7}$

Step 4. Use the sign of the larger numerical value in the final sum.

Subtracting Signed Numbers

To subtract signed numbers you must first change the sign of the *number being subtracted* to the opposite sign. Next, change the operation from subtraction to addition. Then follow the rules for adding signed numbers.

Example 4: Find $(^+5) - (^-8)$.

Step 1. Change the sign of the number being subtracted. $(^-8)$ is changed to $(^+8)$

Step 2. Add. Change the "subtract" symbol $(-)$ to an "add" symbol $(+)$. $(^+5) + (^+8) = {^+13}$

Lesson 2   Exercise

Directions: *Solve each problem.*

1. $(^+4) + (^+8)$
2. $(^-10) + (^-20)$
3. $(^+14) + (^-16)$
4. $(^-9) + (^+13)$
5. $(^+4) + (^-2) + (^+6)$
6. $(^-15) + (^+3) + (^-6) + (^+7)$
7. $(^+4) - (^-8)$
8. $(^-9) - (^+6)$
9. $(^-13) - (^+3) + (^-16)$
10. $(^+3) - (^-2) - (^-20)$

Answers are on page A-58.

Lesson 3   Multiplying and Dividing Signed Numbers

Multiplying Signed Numbers

To multiply two signed numbers, multiply the numerical values. Then if the signs are alike, the answer is positive.

Example 1: Find $(^-12)(^-2)$.

Step 1. Multiply the numerical values.

Step 2. Because the signs are alike, the answer is positive.

$12 \times 2 = 24$
$(^-12) \times (^-2) = {^+24}$

If the signs are different, the answer is negative.

Example 2: Find $(^+4) \cdot (^-3)$.

Step 1. Multiply the numerical values.

Step 2. Because the signs are different, the answer is negative.

$4 \times 3 = 12$
$(^+4) \times (^-3) = {^-12}$

Dividing Signed Numbers

When dividing signed numbers, follow the same rule as for multiplication to determine whether the answer is positive or negative.

Example 3: Find $(^-84) \div (^+7)$.

Step 1. Divide the numerical values.

Step 2. Because the signs are different, the answer is negative.

$84 \div 7 = 12$
$(^-84) \div (^+7) = {^-12}$

In algebra, when a number or a numerical phrase is written as a fraction, it means to divide the numerator by the denominator.

Sometimes you must multiply or divide more than two signed numbers. Count the number of minus signs in the original numbers. If there is an even number of minus signs or no minus signs, the answer will be positive; an odd number of minus signs means the answer will be negative.

Example 4: Find $(^-3)(^-1)(^+5)(^-2)$.

Step 1. Multiply the numerical values.

Step 2. There are 3 minus signs, an odd number, so the answer is negative.

$3 \times 1 \times 5 \times 2 = 30$
$(^-3)(^-1)(^+5)(^-2) = {^-30}$

Lesson 3 Exercise

Directions: *Solve each problem.*

1. $(^+3)(^-9)$
2. $^-5(^-5)$
3. $^+7 \cdot {^+9}$
4. $(^+50) \div (^-5)$
5. $(17)(^-8)$
6. $\dfrac{(104)}{(^-13)}$
7. $\dfrac{40}{^+10}$
8. $\dfrac{(^-6)(^-3)}{10}$
9. $(^-2)(4)(^-5)(^-3)$
10. $\dfrac{(6)(^+1)(^-2)(^-3)}{2}$

Answers are on page A-58.

Lesson 4 Adding and Subtracting Monomials

A **monomial** is an algebraic expression that consists of only one term. A **term** is a number, letter, or a group of numbers and letters not separated by plus or minus signs. Each of the following expressions is a term.

$4, a, 6b, 10ab, 7x^2, 16a^2b^3$

In $7x^2$, x is the **base**, 7 is the **coefficient**, and 2 is the **exponent**. **Like terms** have the same base and the same exponent.

Adding Monomials

To add monomials with like terms, add only the coefficients. The rules for signed numbers apply in the addition of monomials.

Example 1: $14y^2 + 3y^2$.

Step 1. The monomials are like terms. Add the coefficients.

$14 + 3 = 17$
$14y^2 + 3y^2 = 17y^2$

Step 2. The answer is the sum of the coefficients together with the original base.

Subtracting Monomials

When subtracting monomials with like terms, use the same rules that you would for subtracting signed numbers.

Example 2: Simplify $(7x^2y) - (2x^2y) + (^-3x^2y)$.

Step 1. Change the sign of the coefficient of the term to be subtracted and add all the coefficients.

$7 + (^-2) + (^-3) = 2$

Step 2. The answer is the sum of the coefficients together with the original base and exponents.

$2x^2y$

Whenever a coefficient is 1, it is not written; only the base is written.

Lesson 4 Exercise

Directions: *Solve each problem.*

1. $19x + 7x$
2. $(4b^2) + (13b^2)$
3. $(2abc) + (abc)$
4. $(13n^2) - (4n^2)$

5. $(^-8s^3) - (^+4s^3)$
6. $(^+13b^2c^2) - (^-13b^2c^2)$
7. $(^-9.5a) + (10.2a) - (a)$
8. $(8st) - (^+3st) + (^-14st)$
9. $c - (^-4c) - 4c$
10. $(10p^2q^2) + (p^2q^2) - (^-9p^2q^2)$

Answers are on page A-58.

Lesson 5 Multiplying and Dividing Monomials

Multiplying Monomials

There are two simple steps to follow when multiplying monomials.

- Multiply the coefficients. (Use the rules for signed numbers to determine whether the answer will be positive or negative.)
- Add the exponents of the bases.

Example 1: Find $(^-6x^2)(^-3x^3)$.

Step 1. Multiply the coefficients. Because the signs of the original monomials are the same, the answer is positive. $^-6 \cdot ^-3 = ^+18$

Step 2. Add the exponents. $x^2 \cdot x^3 = x^{2+3} = x^5$

Step 3. The answer is the product of both the coefficients and the base. $18x^5$

When an exponent is not written, it is 1.

Dividing Monomials

The rules for the division of monomials are similar to those for multiplication. In division, divide the coefficients and *subtract* the exponents.

Example 2: Find $\frac{18s^5t^2}{^-6s^2}$.

Step 1. Divide the coefficients. $18 \div (^-6) = ^-3$

Step 2. Subtract the exponents. $s^5t^2 \div s^2 = s^3t^2$

Step 3. The answer includes both the coefficient and the base. $^-3s^3t^2$

Lesson 5 Exercise

Directions: *Simplify each expression.*

1. $2t^3 \cdot 2t^2$
2. $(3ab)(5ab^2)$
3. $(^-3x)(4xy)(^-3y)$
4. $\frac{y^4}{y^2}$

Chapter 6: Algebra

5. $\dfrac{-6s^6}{2s^2}$ 6. $(32x^5) \div (-8x^3)$ 7. $\dfrac{2a \cdot 2b}{4ab}$ 8. $\dfrac{6(3x^6y^4z^6)}{3(4x^4y^4z^3)}$

9. $(4 \cdot 5a^2b^3)(2 \cdot 7b^2c)$ 10. $\dfrac{20x^2}{-2x^3}$

Answers are on page A-58.

Level 1   Review

Directions: Solve each problem.

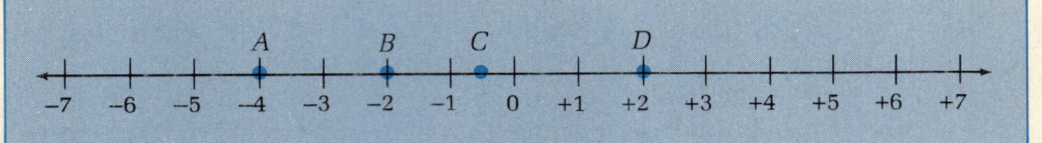

Number line with points A at −4, B at −2, C at 0, and D at +2.

1. In the number line above, which point represents $\dfrac{-4}{2}$?
2. Find the sum of $(-4) + (+3) + (-2) + (-1)$.
3. Simplify $-(-5) + (-3) - (-4) + (+2)$.
4. Subtract $(+5)$ from (-13).
5. Simplify $(8m^2n) + (m^2n) + (-6m^2n)$.
6. Simplify $(9x^2y)(2xy^2)$.
7. $(-6)(+5)(-2) =$ 8. $\dfrac{54}{-9} =$ 9. $(-9abc) - (-7abc) =$ 10. $\dfrac{-6s^4t^3}{24st^2} =$

Check your answers. Correct answers are on page A-58. If you have at least eight answers correct, go to Level 2. If you have fewer than eight answers correct, go back to Lesson 1 and study Level 1.

Level 2   Algebra Applications

Lesson 1   Solving Equations

An **equation** is a number sentence that states that two amounts are equal. In solving equations, the sides of the equation must be kept balanced; when you perform an operation on one side of the equation, you must do exactly the same thing to the other side.

One-step equations use **inverse operations** (opposite operations) to find the unknown.

- The inverse of addition is subtraction.
- The inverse of subtraction is addition.
- The inverse of multiplication is division.
- The inverse of division is multiplication.

To solve an equation, use inverse operations to get the unknown alone on one side of the equation. The other side of the equation will be the value of the unknown.

Example 1: What is the value of x in 25x = 100?

Step 1. In this example, x is multiplied by 25. To get x by itself, use the inverse of multiplication, division. Divide each side of the equation by 25.

$$\frac{25x}{25} = \frac{100}{25}$$

Step 2. x is now by itself. The solution is 4. To prove your answer, substitute 4 for x in the original equation. If the sides of the equation equal each other, the solution is correct.

$$x = 4$$
$$25 \cdot 4 = 100$$

Some solutions require addition.

Example 2: Find the value of c in the equation c − 8 = 10.

Step 1. Add 8 to each side.
Step 2. Prove your answer.

$$\begin{array}{r} c - 8 = 10 \\ + 8 \quad + 8 \\ \hline c = 18 \end{array}$$
$$18 - 8 = 10$$

When a fraction is in an equation, multiply by its reciprocal. The reciprocal of any fraction is the fraction inverted: $\frac{1}{2}$ and $\frac{2}{1}$ are reciprocal; 6 and $\frac{1}{6}$ are reciprocal.

Example 3: Solve $\frac{1}{2}p = 36$.

Step 1. Set up the problem. Multiply each side by 2.
Step 2. Prove your answer.

$$\frac{1}{2}p = 36$$
$$\frac{2}{1} \times \frac{1}{2}p = 36 \times \frac{2}{1}$$
$$p = 72$$
$$\frac{1}{2} \times 72 = 36$$

Lesson 1 Exercise

Directions: *Solve each equation. Prove your answers.*

1. 9x = 72
2. g + 20 = 64
3. c − 14 = 39
4. $\frac{b}{5} = 30$
5. 32 = y + 7
6. $\frac{1}{2}x = 6$
7. 42 = x − 1
8. b + 16 = 40
9. $\frac{1}{4}k = 24$
10. x − 18 = 108

Answers are on pages A-57–A-58.

Lesson 2 Multistep Equations

You may be asked to solve equations that involve using more than one step. If the unknown appears in two terms on the same side of the equation, use the rules for the addition and subtraction of monomials to combine the terms.

Example 1: Solve for x in $4x + 2x - 6 = 18$.

Step 1. Add the like monomials on the left side of the equation.

Step 2. Using the rules for inverse operations, add 6 to both sides.

Step 3. Now divide each side by 6 to get the variable by itself.

Step 4. Prove your answer.

$$4x + 2x - 6 = 18$$
$$6x - 6 = 18$$
$$\underline{+ 6 \quad\quad + 6}$$
$$6x = 24$$
$$\frac{6x}{6} = \frac{24}{6}$$
$$x = 4$$

$$4(4) + 2(4) - 6 = 18$$
$$16 + 8 - 6 = 18$$
$$18 = 18$$

Some equations have the unknown on both sides of the equation. The first step to solve this kind of equation is to use inverse operations to eliminate the unknown from one side of the equation. Work with the unknown having the smaller coefficient.

Example 2: Solve $3n - 4 = 2n + 5$.

Step 1. Subtract 2n from both sides of the equation. This results in an equation with the unknown on only one side.

Step 2. Then use inverse operations and proceed as before.

Step 3. Prove your answer.

$$3n - 4 = 2n + 5$$
$$\underline{-2n \quad\quad -2n}$$
$$n - 4 = 5$$
$$\underline{+ 4 \quad\quad + 4}$$
$$n = 9$$

$$(3 \cdot 9) - 4 = (2 \cdot 9) + 5$$
$$27 - 4 = 18 + 5$$
$$23 = 23$$

Sometimes you must eliminate parentheses in an equation before you can solve for an unknown. To do this, multiply each term inside the parentheses by the term outside the parentheses. For example, $4(3 - x) = 4 \cdot 3 - 4 \cdot x = 12 - 4x$.

Remember the order of these steps to solve equations.

- Eliminate any parentheses.
- Combine separated unknowns.
- Use inverse operations to get the variable by itself.

UNIT VII: MATHEMATICS

Lesson 2 Exercise

Directions: *Solve each equation.*

1. $3n + 5n = 40$
2. $8t + 12 = 2t - 6$
3. $2(y + 10) = 38$
4. $3x - 4 - x = 16$
5. $9s - 27 = 3s + 27$

Answers are on page A-59.

Lesson 3 Inequalities

Inequalities show two quantities that are not equal. Four symbols are used in writing inequalities.

- $<$ means *is less than.* $5 < 6$ means 5 is less than 6.
- $>$ means *is greater than.* $8 > 6$ means 8 is greater than 6.
- $\leq$ means *is less than or equal to.* $x \leq 3$ means that x represents numbers that are less than or equal to 3.
- $\geq$ means *is greater than or equal to.* $x \geq 3$ means that x represents numbers that are greater than or equal to 3.

Use inverse operations to solve for the unknown in inequalities.

Example: Solve the inequality $n - 2 < 5$.

Step 1. As in an equation, you must get the unknown by itself on one side of the inequality. Add 2 to both sides.

$$\begin{array}{r} n - 2 < 5 \\ +2 +2 \\ \hline n < 7 \end{array}$$

Step 2. Solutions to this inequality include all numbers less than 7. Substitute any of these numbers to prove your solution.

$6 - 2 < 5$
$5 - 2 < 5$
$4 - 2 < 5$

Lesson 3 Exercise

Directions: *Solve each inequality.*

1. $4y - 10 \geq 14$
2. $5t + 2 > 12$
3. $9v - 2 \leq 25$

Directions: *Solve the inequality to answer each question.*

4. In the inequality $13d - 4 > 22$, can d be 1?
5. In the inequality $5m + 3 \geq 33$, can m be 6?

Answers are on page A-59.

Lesson 4 Writing Algebraic Expressions and Equations

Sometimes you can write an algebraic expression to help you solve a problem. To do that, you translate words into algebraic expressions. Look for key words to help determine what operation to use.

addition	division
$x + 6$ can be expressed as:	$b \div 5$ can be expressed as:
x increased by 6	*b divided by 5*
the sum of x and 6	*the quotient of b divided by 5*
6 more than x	*one-fifth of b*

subtraction	multiplication
$n - 8$ can be expressed as:	$2a$ can be expressed as:
n decreased by 8	*2 times a*
n diminished by 8	*twice a*
8 subtracted from n	*a multiplied by 2*
8 less than n	*the product of 2 and a*

Example 1: Write an algebraic expression for the phrase four times the sum of six and a number.

Step 1. You are given two values, 4 and 6, and an unknown quantity, a number. Let n stand for the unknown quantity.

    a number = n

Step 2. What must be done to n? It must be added to 6. Write this part of the expression.

    the sum of 6 and a number = $6 + n$

Step 3. Because the sum of $6 + n$ is multiplied, place $6 + n$ in parentheses and finish writing the expression.

    four times the sum of 6 and a number = $4(6 + n)$

Writing equations is the same as writing two algebraic expressions separated by an equal sign. The word *is* or *equals* tells you where to place the equal sign. You can then solve the equation using the same rules you learned previously.

Example 2: Write an equation for seven more than twice a number equals 23. Then solve the equation.

Step 1. Write the expression on the left side of the equation. Place the equal sign. Then finish the equation.

$$7 + 2n = 23$$
$$-7 -7$$
$$\frac{2n}{2} = \frac{16}{2}$$

Step 2. Use the rules for inverse operations to solve for n.

$$n = 8$$

UNIT VII: MATHEMATICS Level 2: Lesson 5 **545**

Example 3: Write an equation for eight times a number equals three less than five times the number. Find the number.

Step 1. Write the two algebraic expressions and place the equal sign.

Step 2. Use inverse operations to find the number.

$$\begin{aligned} 8n &= 5n - 3 \\ -5n & \quad -5n \\ \frac{3n}{3} &= \frac{-3}{3} \\ n &= {}^-1 \end{aligned}$$

Lesson 4   Exercise

Directions: *Write an equation for each of the following verbal expressions. Use n for the unknown. Then solve each problem.*

1. Three times a number added to five times the number equals 24.
2. A number is eleven more than five-sixths of the number.
3. The product of eight and a number, decreased by the number, is equal to three more than the number.
4. Six times a number increased by eleven is the same as three times the number decreased by four.
5. Twelve is the result of a number divided by eight.

Answers are on page A-59.

Lesson 5   Multiplying Binomials

A binomial is an algebraic expression that has two terms, such as $5x + 8$, $c - 6$, and $t^2 + 2$. To multiply binomials, each term in one binomial is multiplied by each term in the other binomial.

Example 1: Find $(3x - 8)(2x + 2)$.

Step 1. Set up the problem. Use the rules for the multiplication of signed numbers to multiply each term in the top expression by $^+2$: $^+2 \cdot {}^-8 = {}^-16$; $^+2 \cdot 3x = 6x$.

Step 2. Now multiply each term in the top expression by $2x$: $2x \cdot {}^-8 = {}^-16x$; $2x \cdot 3x = 6x^2$.

Step 3. Add each column.

$$\begin{array}{r} 3x - 8 \\ \times \quad 2x + 2 \\ \hline 6x - 16 \\ 6x^2 - 16x \quad\quad \\ \hline 6x^2 - 10x - 16 \end{array}$$

Example 2: Find $(c - 6)(c + 6)$.

Step 1. Set up the problem. Multiply both terms on top by $^+6$: $^+6 \cdot {}^-6 = {}^-36$; $^+6 \cdot c = {}^+6c$.

Step 2. Now multiply both terms on top by c: $c \cdot {}^-6 = {}^-6c$; $c \cdot c = c^2$.

$$\begin{array}{r} c - 6 \\ \times c + 6 \\ \hline + 6c - 36 \\ c^2 - 6c \\ \hline c^2 - 36 \end{array}$$

Step 3. Add each column. Notice that ^+6c and ^-6c in the middle column cancel out, leaving $c^2 - 36$.

Lesson 5 Exercise

Directions: *Refer to the examples in this lesson as you multiply to solve each problem.*

1. $\;3t + 4$
   $\times\;\;\;t - 6$

2. $\;x - 6$
   $\times\;\;x + 6$

3. $\;2b - 3$
   $\times\;\;3b - 4$

4. $\;c + 3$
   $\times\;\;c - 3$

5. $\;4a + 6$
   $\times\;\;2a - 3$

Answers are on page A-59.

Level 2 Review

Directions: *Solve each problem.*

1. $\dfrac{w}{8} = 16$

2. $3n - \tfrac{1}{2}n = 10$

3. $3x - 24 = x + 2\tfrac{1}{2}$

4. $\tfrac{2}{3}b + 62 = 4(b + 3)$

5. $8d + 4 \geq 20$

6. $12y - 12 < 12$

7. Use n for the unknown to write an algebraic expression: The difference between a number and 14, all divided by 7.

8. Use x for the unknown to write and solve this equation: The product of 10 and a number all reduced by 3 is 29 more than twice the number.

9. Multiply $4b - 3$ and $2b + 4$.

10. Multiply $x - 9$ and $x + 9$.

Check your answers. Correct answers are on page A-59. If you have at least eight answers correct, go to Level 3. If you have fewer than eight answers correct, go back to Lesson 1 and study Level 2 again.

UNIT VII: MATHEMATICS

Level 3 Algebra Word Problems

Lesson 1 Proportion

A **proportion** is an expression that shows that two ratios are equal. Setting up a proportion finds an equivalent ratio for larger or smaller amounts. For example, proportions can help you find how much to increase or decrease recipe ingredients or the height of an object in relation to another object.

In a proportion the cross products are equal. This means that the top of one side times the bottom of the other side is equal to the bottom of the first side times the top of the other side.

$$\frac{a}{b} = \frac{c}{d} \qquad ad = bc$$

The cross products of a proportion can be written as an equation.

Example 1: Show that $\frac{4}{10} = \frac{6}{15}$ is a proportion.

Step 1. Identify the numbers to be multiplied.

$$\frac{4}{10} = \frac{6}{15}$$

Step 2. Write the cross products as an equation. Multiply $4 \times 15 = 60$ and $6 \times 10 = 60$. The two ratios form a proportion.

$$4 \times 15 = 6 \times 10$$
$$60 = 60$$

In many proportion problems, one of the four numbers is unknown. Write an equation of the cross products to solve these problems.

Example 2: A recipe for pancakes requires 2 cups of flour for 6 servings. If you want to make only 4 servings, how much flour should you use?

Step 1. Write the proportion. The parts of the proportion must correspond to each other. On the left, put the ratio of the recipe: 2 cups of flour to 6 servings. Put the ratio for the number of servings you want on the right: x cups of flour to 4 servings.

$$\frac{2}{6} = \frac{x}{4}$$
$$2 \times 4 = 6x$$
$$8 = 6x$$

Step 2. Write the two cross products as an equation.

$$\frac{8}{6} = \frac{6x}{6}$$
$$1\frac{2}{6} = x$$
$$1\frac{1}{3} = x$$

Step 3. Divide both sides of the equation by 6 to find x. Simplify the fraction.

Lesson 1 Exercise

Directions: Use proportions to solve the following problems.

1. If a car uses 8 gallons of gas for a 120-mile trip, how many gallons of gas will it use to travel 195 miles?

548 Chapter 6: Algebra   INSTRUCTION

2. If $\frac{1}{2}$ inch represents a distance of 20 miles on a map, how many miles would 3 inches represent?

3. If you use $1\frac{1}{2}$ cups of water to cook $\frac{2}{3}$ cups of cereal, how much water would you need to cook 2 cups of cereal?

4. The ratio of women to men in an office is 4 : 7. If there are 33 people in the office, how many are women?

5. The ratio of votes for the two candidates in the primary election was 2 : 5 for Candidate A as compared to Candidate B. If Candidate A received 3000 votes, how many people voted altogether?

Answers are on page A-60.

Lesson 2   Algebra Setup Problems

In some GED questions, instead of being asked to solve the problems, you will need to use your skills in writing equations and reading algebra word problems to find the expression that correctly shows how the problem *may* be solved.

Example: Marie had a certain amount of money on Friday. On Saturday, she spent $9 for a movie, snacks, and gas. If she used $\frac{1}{3}$ of the remaining money to repay a loan, which expression shows the amount of money she repaid on the loan?

(1) $(x + 9)\frac{1}{3}$ (2) $x - (9 \div 3)$ (3) $(x - 9) \div 3$
(4) $3(x - 9)$ (5) $\frac{x}{3} - 9$

The best way to solve problems of this type is to write an expression that will lead to the solution.

Reading this problem carefully, you will see that you must subtract what Marie spent from what she started with. Then divide the remainder by 3. The correct answer is (3).

$$\underbrace{(x}_{\text{started with}} - \underbrace{9)}_{\text{spent}} \div 3$$
$$\text{repaid}$$

Lesson 2   Exercise

Directions: *Choose the expression that shows the procedure for solving each problem.*

1. Angela and Burt won a cash prize. They gave part of the prize money to their mother and divided the rest of the money between themselves. If each of them received $225 from what was left, which expression shows the amount of the original cash prize?

(1) $225 + 2x$ (2) $2(225 + x)$ (3) $2(225) + x$
(4) $\frac{x}{2} + 225$ (5) $225 + .5x$

UNIT VII: MATHEMATICS

2. Carl weighs 65 pounds more than his wife, Cindy. Their son, Todd, weighs 115 pounds. Which of the following expressions shows the average weight of Carl, Cindy, and Todd?
   - (1) (2x + 180)
   - (2) $\frac{2}{3}$x + 180
   - (3) (2x + 180) ÷ 3
   - (4) 2x + 65
   - (5) 3(2x + 180)

3. Leon spends $\frac{1}{3}$ of his monthly budget on rent. He also spends $45 per month for utilities and $130 per month for food. Which expression shows the amount of money Leon has left after he pays his rent, utilities, and food?
   - (1) $\frac{1}{3}$x(x − 175)
   - (2) $\frac{2}{3}$x − 175
   - (3) $\frac{2}{3}$(x − 175)
   - (4) 175 − $\frac{2}{3}$x
   - (5) $\frac{3}{2}$x − 175

4. An amateur team gave a dinner to raise money. Tickets were $5 each. After subtracting expenses of $118, enough tickets were sold to raise $357. How many tickets were sold?
   - (1) 357 − 118 = x
   - (2) 5x − 118 = 357
   - (3) 357 − $\frac{x}{5}$ = 118
   - (4) $\frac{x}{5}$ − 118 = 357
   - (5) 357 − 5x = 118

5. It will cost $375 to charter a bus for a team trip. The team already has $265. How much will each of the 15 team members have to pay to make up the difference?
   - (1) $\frac{375}{15}$ = 265x
   - (2) 15x − 265 = 375
   - (3) 265 + 15x = 375
   - (4) 265 − 5x = 375
   - (5) $\frac{x}{15}$ + 265 = 375

Answers are on page A-60.

Level 3 Review

1. If one number is three more than another and the smaller is increased by 18, the resulting number is four times the larger. Find the numbers.

2. Sam, Jim, and Al studied for a math test. Sam studied three hours more than Jim, and Al studied twice as long as Sam. Altogether, they studied 13 hours. How long did Al study?

3. Barbara is three times as old as Lisa. The difference between their ages is 24 years. Find their ages.

Directions: *Items 4 to 6 are based on the following table.*

Calorie Content of Sandwich Foods

Food	Serving Size	Calories
Breads		
rye bread	1 slice	65
white bread	1 slice	65
hard roll	1 roll	105
Fillings		
roast beef	1 slice	85
boiled ham	1 slice	135
turkey	1 slice	115
Swiss cheese	1 slice	75
Dressings		
mustard	1 tablespoon	27
mayonnaise	1 tablespoon	105

4. A turkey sandwich made with 2 slices of white bread and 1 serving of mayonnaise totals 580 calories. How many slices of turkey were used?

5. A sandwich made on a hard roll contained 2 servings of mayonnaise, 2 slices of Swiss cheese, and 2 slices of meat. It totaled 735 calories. What meat was used?

6. What one meat can be used to make a 470-calorie sandwich using 2 slices of rye bread and 4 slices of meat?

7. Stan bought 16 tickets to a concert. This was 5 less than 3 times the number Betty sold. Choose the equation that shows how many tickets Betty sold.
    (1) $3x - 5 = 16$
    (2) $(5)(16) = 3x$
    (3) $3x = 16 - 5$
    (4) $3x + 5 = 16$
    (5) $5 - 3x = 16$

8. Jerry lives 2.4 miles more than 4 times as far from work as Lou. Lou lives 8 miles from work. Choose the equation that shows how far from work Jerry lives.
    (1) $2.4 + (4 \cdot 8) = x$
    (2) $2.4 + 8 = 4x$
    (3) $4x + 2.4 = 8$
    (4) $\frac{1}{2}x = 2.4$
    (5) $2.4 - (4 \cdot 8) = x$

9. A juice drink is priced at 2 quarts for $.96. What is the price per fluid ounce?

10. On the average, 9 tomato plants produce 70 tomatoes. How many tomatoes will 630 plants produce?

Check your answers. Correct answers are on page A-60. If you have at least eight answers correct, do the Chapter 6 Quiz. If you have fewer than eight answers correct, go back to Lesson 1 and study Level 3 again.

Chapter 6 Quiz

Directions: *Item 1 is based on the following number line.*

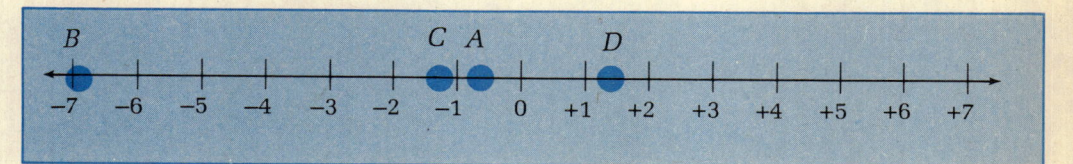

```
  B              C A      D
<-+--+--+--+--+--●●--+--●--+--+--+--+--+->
 -7 -6 -5 -4 -3 -2 -1  0 +1 +2 +3 +4 +5 +6 +7
```

1. Which letter represents $\frac{-7}{6}$?
2. $(^+14) - (^-4) + (^-8) - (^+2) =$
3. $\left(\frac{^+1}{3}\right)(^-18)(^+4)(^-3) =$
4. Simplify $\frac{72}{-6}$.
5. Simplify $(^-10m^2n^2)(^+4mn)(^-3m^3n^2)$.
6. Solve for b: $46 - 3b = 7b + 6$.
7. Solve for x: $8x + 5 = 3(x - 5)$.
8. Solve for n: $12n + 3 \geq 2n + 23$.
9. Solve for w: $\frac{2}{3}w + 14 < 26$.
10. Write an algebraic expression: Eight less than one-half a number.
11. Five times a number decreased by sixteen is two more than three times the number. Find the number.
12. One-half of a number subtracted from three times the number increased by six equals sixteen. Find the number.
13. Multiply $4c - 8$ by $2c + 6$.
14. Multiply $(k - 11)$ by $(k + 11)$.
15. On Saturday, Hal and Phil helped Chris to paint his house. Hal worked three hours more than Phil. Chris worked two hours more than Hal. Altogether, they worked 17 hours. How long did each one work?
16. Linda's household budget is $480 per month. For every $3 she spends on rent, she spends $1 for entertainment and $2 for food. How much does she spend for rent?

Directions: *Item 17 is based on the following chart.*

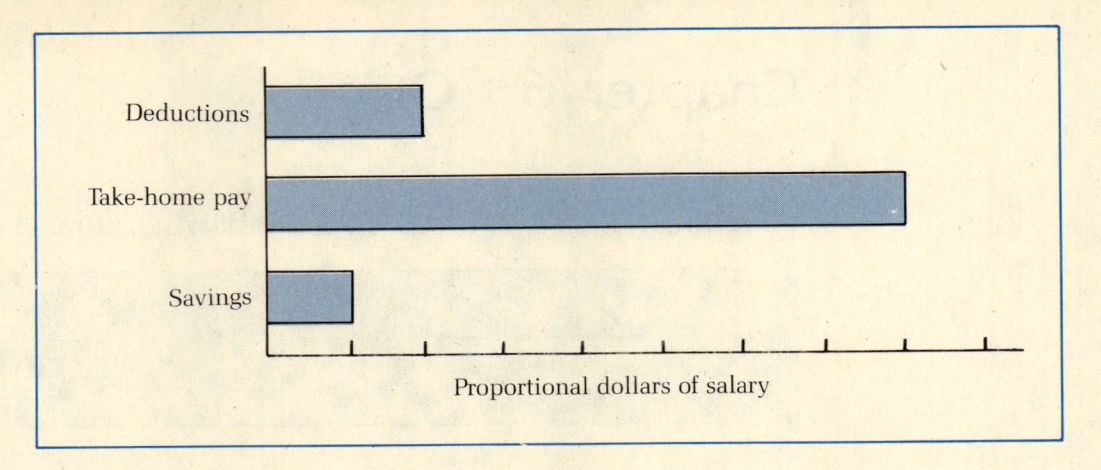

Deductions
Take-home pay
Savings

Proportional dollars of salary

17. The chart shows how Mr. Walker's monthly take-home pay compares to his deductions and savings. If his gross salary is $990, how much money does he take home each month?

18. A blueprint is drawn to a scale of 2 inches : 2.5 feet. If a wall measures 25 feet, what is its length on the blueprint?

19. Which of the following expressions shows the total number of employees of two companies if one company has 30 more than three times as many employees as the other company?
    (1) 3x(x + 30)
    (2) 3x + 30
    (3) 4x + 30
    (4) 4x − 30
    (5) 2x + 30

20. In a miniature golf game, Suzanne had 3 more strokes than Gail. Ann scored twice as many strokes as Suzanne. Which expression shows the total number of strokes the three women scored?
    (1) 3x + 9
    (2) 4x + 9
    (3) 4x + 6
    (4) 2x + 6
    (5) 3x + 6

Answers are on pages A-60–A-61.

Chapter 7 Geometry

Objective

In this chapter, you will learn to

- Recognize types of angles
- Learn the properties of pairs of angles
- Learn the relationships between parallel lines and transversals
- Recognize types of triangles
- Find the degrees of certain angles in triangles
- Recognize congruent triangles
- Recognize similar triangles
- Use the Pythagorean relationship
- Plot points on a graph
- Find where lines intersect and the distance between points
- Calculate slope
- Identify graphs of linear equations

Level 1 Geometry Skills

Preview

Item 1 is based on Figure 1.

1. a. What kind of angle is shown?
   b. How many degrees are there in the angle?

   FIGURE 1

Item 2 is based on Figure 2.

2. In the drawing, if ∠a = 110°, how large is ∠b?

   FIGURE 2

Item 3 is based on Figure 3.

3. Name all the angles that are equal to ∠c in the drawing.

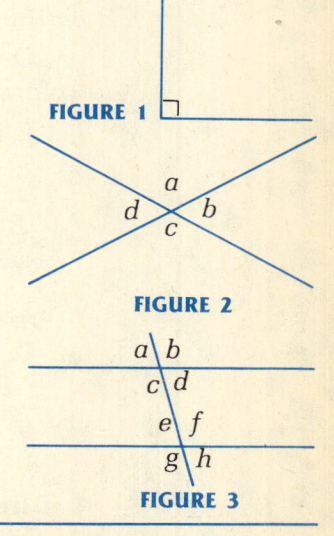

   FIGURE 3

4. If the vertex angle of an isosceles triangle is 76°, how many degrees are there in each base angle?

554 Chapter 7: Geometry INSTRUCTION

Item 5 is based on Figure 4.

5. If ∠a = 45° and ∠b = 85°, what is the measure of ∠c?

FIGURE 4

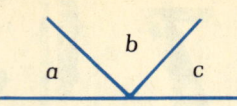

Check your answers. Correct answers are on page 000. If you have at least four answers correct, do the Level 1 Review on page 000. If you have fewer than four answers correct, study Level 1 beginning with Lesson 1.

Lesson 1 Angles

An **angle** is formed by two lines that extend from a single point. The point is called the **vertex**. The symbol for angle is ∠. The distance that the lines are "open" from the vertex is measured in degrees. The symbol for degree is °. One full revolution, or circle, is 360°. A partial revolution makes an angle.
Figure 5 shows the five types of angles.

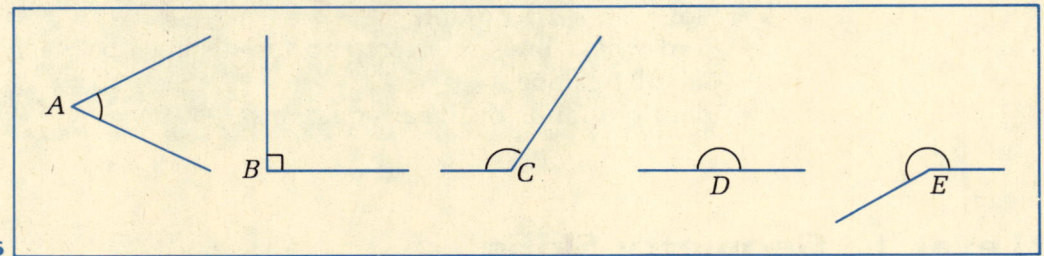

FIGURE 5

∠A is an **acute** angle. Acute angles measure less than 90°.
∠B is a **right** angle. A right angle measures exactly 90°.
∠C is an **obtuse** angle. Obtuse angles measure more than 90°, but less than 180°.
∠D is a **straight** angle. A straight angle measures exactly 180°. Straight angles form straight lines.
∠E is a **reflex** angle. Reflex angles measure more than 180°.

Lesson 1 Exercise

Directions: *Name the type of angle pictured.*

1.   2.   3.   4.   5.

Directions: *Name the type of angle described.*

6. 130°   7. 60°   8. 180°   9. 90°   10. 250°

Answers are on page A-61.

Lesson 2 Naming Angles and Pairs of Angles

Naming Angles

Angles are usually named by three capital letters. The letter that names the vertex is the middle letter of the three.

Example 1: Name the three angles that measure 180° or less in Figure 6.

The straight angle is ∠AOB.
The acute angle is ∠AOC.
The obtuse angle is ∠COB.

FIGURE 6

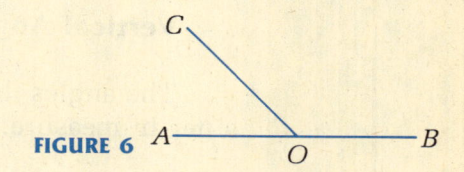

Complementary Angles

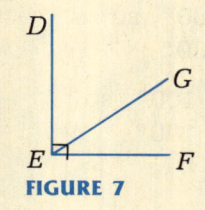

Two angles that form a right angle—90°—are called **complementary angles**. In Figure 7, ∠DEF is a right angle. The two smaller angles that make up the right angle, ∠DEG and ∠GEF, are complementary angles. If you know the measure of one of the complementary angles, you can find the measure of the other.

FIGURE 7

Example 2: In Figure 7, ∠GEF = 40°. How many degrees is ∠DEG?

Step 1. You know that ∠DEF is a right angle measuring 90° and that ∠GEF is one of two complementary angles.

∠DEF = 90°
∠GEF = 40°
∠DEG = 50°

Step 2. Subtract 40° from 90° to find the measure of ∠DEG, the other of the two complementary angles.

Supplementary Angles

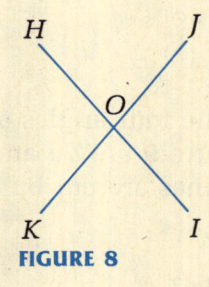

Supplementary angles are a pair of angles that, together, form one straight (180°) angle. In Figure 8 there are two straight angles; ∠HOI and ∠JOK. Each of them is made up of supplementary angles.

FIGURE 8

Example 3: Name the four pairs of supplementary angles in Figure 8.

Step 1. Consider ∠HOI. On the right side of ∠HOI there are two supplementary angles.

∠HOJ + ∠JOI

Step 2. On the left side of ∠HOI there is another pair of supplementary angles.

∠HOK + ∠KOI

Step 3. Find the two pairs of supplementary angles that make up ∠JOK.

∠JOI + ∠IOK
∠KOH + ∠HOJ

If you know the measure of one in a pair of supplementary angles, you can subtract to find the measure of the other.

Example 4: In Figure 8, if ∠HOJ is 80°, what is the measure of ∠JOI?

Step 1. You know that ∠HOI = 180° and that ∠HOJ = 80°.

∠HOI = 180°
∠HOJ = 80°
∠JOI = 100°

Step 2. Subtract to find ∠JOI.

Vertical Angles

The angles that are opposite to each other in Figure 8 are equal to each other in measure. They are called **vertical angles**.

Example 5: If ∠HOJ is 80° and ∠JOI is 100°, what are the measures of ∠KOI and ∠HOK?

Step 1. ∠HOJ and ∠KOI are vertical angles: their measures are the same.

∠HOJ = 80°, so
∠KOI = 80°

Step 2. Find the angle opposite ∠HOK. It is ∠JOI, which measures 100°.

∠JOI = 100°, so
∠HOK = 100°

Corresponding Angles

Lines AB and CD in Figure 9 are **parallel**. This means that they are the same distance apart no matter how long they extend. Lines AB and CD are cut by a **transversal**, line EF. The resulting angles have special relationships.

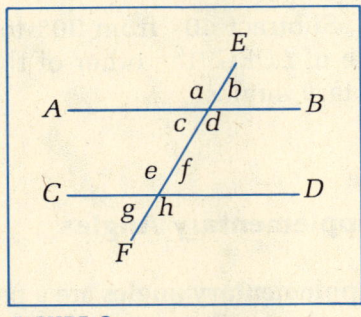

FIGURE 9

The four angles at the top of Figure 9 **correspond** to the four angles at the bottom of the figure. The corresponding angles in Figure 9 are ∠a and ∠e, ∠b and ∠f, ∠c and ∠g, and ∠d and ∠h. When parallel lines are cut by a transversal, the corresponding angles are equal.

Example 6: If ∠a measures 110°, what is the measure of ∠e?

Because ∠a and ∠e are corresponding angles, the measure of ∠e is equal to the measure of ∠a.

∠a = ∠e
∠a = 110°, so
∠e = 110°

Example 7: If ∠a measures 110°, what is the measure of ∠h?

∠h corresponds to ∠d, and ∠d is vertical to ∠a. Therefore, ∠d = ∠a because they are vertical angles, and ∠h = ∠d because they are corresponding angles.

∠h = ∠d = ∠a
∠a = 110°, so
∠d = 110°, so
∠h = 110°

Lesson 2   Exercise

Item 1 refers to Figure E-1.

1. Name each type of angle.
   (a) ∠d   (b) ∠a   (c) ∠c

FIGURE E-1

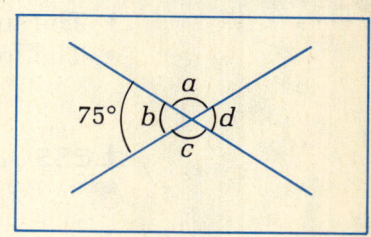

Items 2 to 5 refer to Figure E-2.
Lines WX and YZ are parallel.

2. Which angle corresponds to ∠b?
3. Name all the angles that are equal to ∠d.
4. If ∠e measures 115°, what is the measure of ∠f?
5. If ∠h = 115°, what is the measure of ∠b?

FIGURE E-2

Answers are on pages A-61–A-62.

Lesson 3   Triangles

A **triangle** is a three-sided plane (two-dimensional) figure. The three angles inside the triangle total 180°.

The triangles that are shown in Figure 10 are described in terms of their sides and their angles.

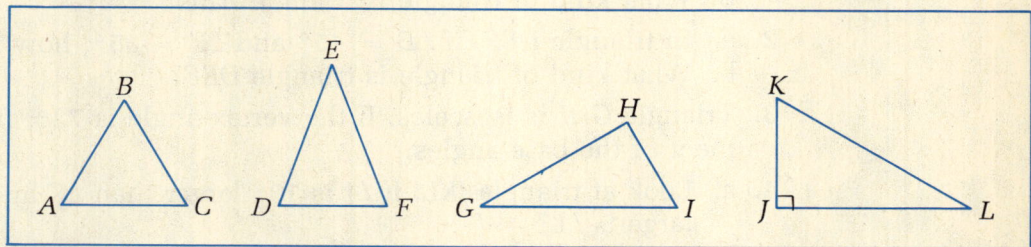

FIGURE 10

Triangle ABC has three equal sides and is called an **equilateral** triangle. It can also be described as **equiangular** because the three angles are equal. Because the angles are equal and the total number of degrees is 180, each angle measures $\frac{180°}{3}$, or 60°.

Triangle *DEF* has two equal sides, *DE* and *FE*. It is called an **isosceles** triangle. The angles that are opposite the equal sides are also equal. Therefore, ∠*D* = ∠*F*. Angle *E* is called the **vertex angle**. The other two angles are called **base** angles.

Triangle *GHI* is called a **scalene** triangle. It has no equal sides or angles.

Triangle *JKL* has a right (90°) angle and is called a **right** triangle. The side that is opposite the right angle, *KL*, is called the **hypotenuse**. The other two sides, *JK* and *JL*, are called **legs**.

These facts are true of all triangles:

- The sum of any two sides of a triangle is always larger than the third side.
- The longest side of a triangle is opposite the largest angle.

Lesson 3 Exercise

Items 1 to 5 refer to Figure E-3.

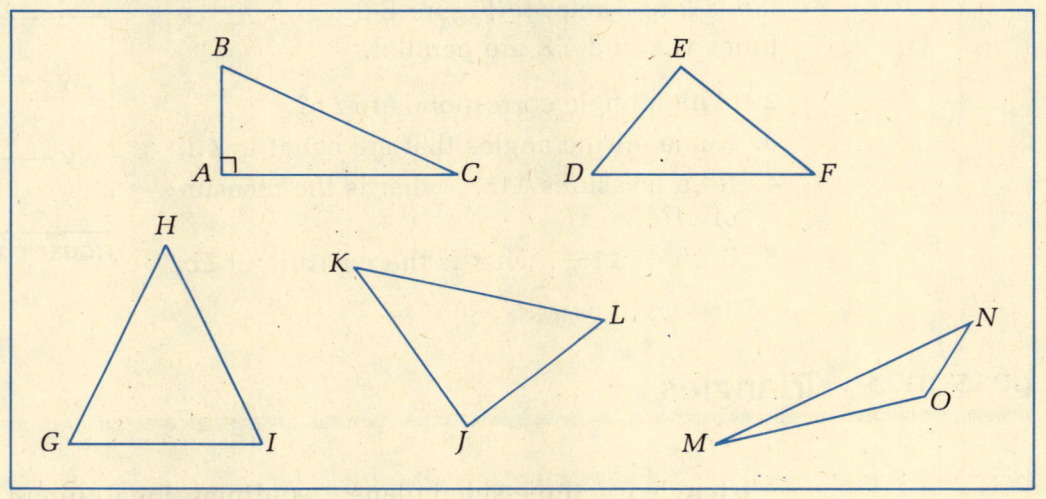

FIGURE E-3

1. a. In triangle *ABC*, if ∠*C* = 40°, what does ∠*B* measure?
   b. What kind of triangle is triangle *ABC*?
2. a. In triangle *DEF*, if ∠*D* = 45° and ∠*F* = 35°, how large is ∠*E*?
   b. What kind of triangle is triangle *DEF*?
3. Triangle *GHI* is isosceles. If the vertex angle is 72°, find the measurement of the base angles.
4. a. Look at triangle *JKL*. If ∠*J* is 10° larger than ∠*K* and ∠*K* is 55°, how large is ∠*L*?
   b. What kind of triangle is triangle *JKL*?
5. a. In triangle *MNO*, ∠*O* is 120°, and ∠*M* is 26°. What is the size of ∠*N*?
   b. What kind of triangle is triangle *MNO*?

Answers are on page A-61.

Level 1 Review

Item 1 is based on Figure 11.

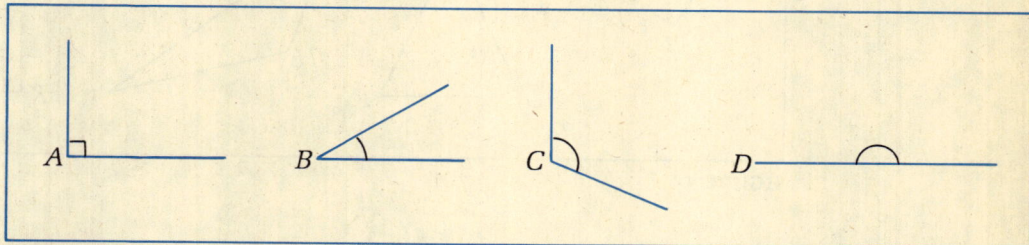

FIGURE 11

1. Name the types of angles.

2. What is the measurement of the complement of a 50° angle?
3. Two angles that total 180° are called _____ angles.

Item 4 is based on Figure 12.

4. If ∠k is 85°, how large is ∠m?

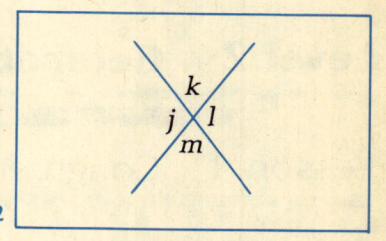

FIGURE 12

Item 5 is based on Figure 13.

5. Lines WX and YZ are parallel. List all the angles that equal ∠a.

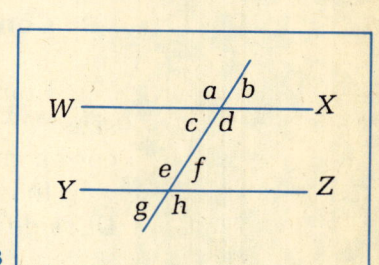

FIGURE 13

6. The three angles in a triangle total how many degrees?

Items 7 to 10 are based on Figure 14.

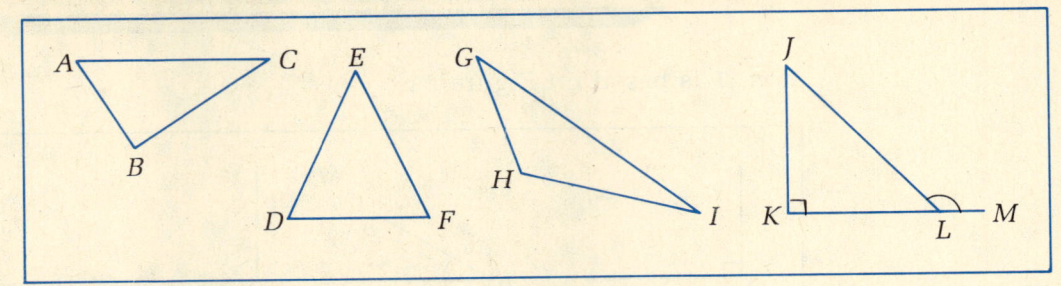

FIGURE 14

7. In triangle ABC, ∠A = 32° and ∠B = 73°. What is the size of ∠C?
8. In isosceles triangle DEF, if base ∠D = 64°, what is the size of ∠E?
9. In triangle GHI, if ∠G is 4° more than ∠I and ∠I = 23°, how large is ∠H?
10. In triangle JKL, JK = KL. Find the size of ∠JLM.

Check your answers. Correct answers are on page A-61. If you have at least eight answers correct, go to Level 2. If you have fewer than eight answers correct, go back to Lesson 1 and study Level 1.

Level 2 Geometry Applications

Lesson 1 Congruent and Similar Triangles

Congruence

Congruent triangles are triangles that have the same shape and the same size. When two triangles are **congruent**, the corresponding sides and the corresponding angles of the two triangles are equal.

In Figure 15, triangle ABC is congruent to triangle DEF. Side AB = side DE; side BC = side EF; side AC = side DF. Also ∠A = ∠D; ∠B = ∠E; ∠C = ∠F.

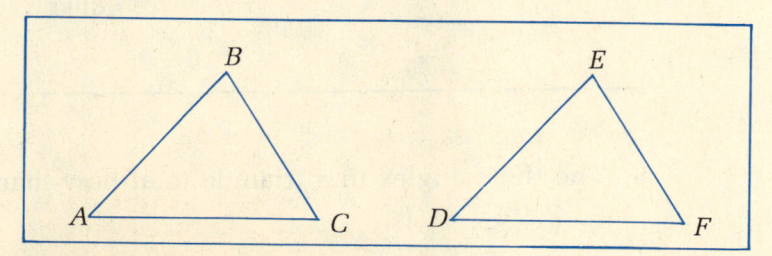

FIGURE 15

Example 1: In Figure 15, $AB = 8$ cm, $BC = 7$ cm, and $AC = 9$ cm. What are the lengths of the shortest and longest sides of triangle DEF?

Step 1. The shortest side of triangle DEF corresponds to the shortest side of triangle ABC, side BC. That side is EF.

$EF = BC = 7$ cm

Step 2. The longest side of triangle DEF corresponds to the longest side of triangle ABC, side AC. That side is DF.

$DF = AC = 9$ cm

Example 2: In Figure 15, $\angle A = 45°$ and $\angle B = 60°$. Find the size of $\angle F$.

Step 1. Find the size of $\angle C$, which corresponds to $\angle F$.

$\angle C = 180° - (\angle A + \angle B)$
$= 180° - (45° + 60°)$
$= 180° - 105° = 75°$

Step 2. Use the definition of congruent triangles to find the size of $\angle F$.

$\angle F = \angle C$
$\angle F = 75°$

Similarity

Similar triangles are triangles that have corresponding angles equal and corresponding sides proportional.

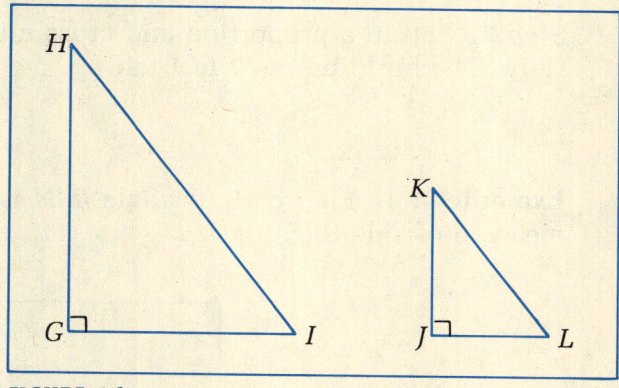

FIGURE 16

In the triangles in Figure 16, both angles G and J are right angles. $\angle H$ corresponds to $\angle K$, and $\angle I$ corresponds to $\angle L$.

- GH is twice as long as JK.
- HI is twice as long as KL.
- GI is twice as long as JL.

Therefore, corresponding sides are proportional at a ratio of 2:1, and triangles GHI and JKL are similar.

If you know that the angles of one triangle are equal to the corresponding angles of another triangle, you can conclude that the triangles are similar. Then you can also conclude that the corresponding sides are in proportion.

562   Chapter 7: Geometry   INSTRUCTION

Example 3: Figure 17 illustrates this problem: If a building casts a shadow 48 feet long and, at the same time, a flagpole that is 18 feet high casts a 12-foot shadow, how tall is the building?

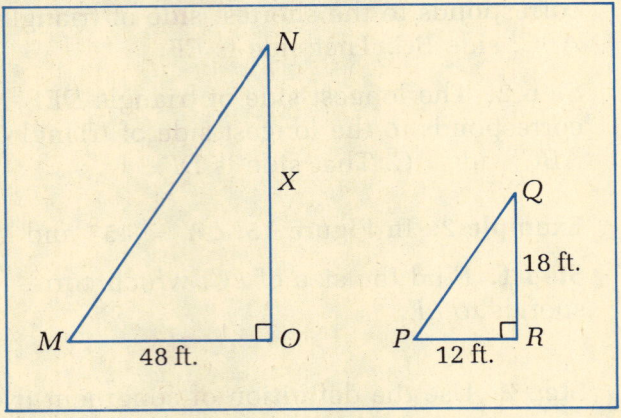

FIGURE 17

Step 1. Determine which sides of the triangles correspond. The length of the building shadow corresponds to the length of the flagpole shadow. The building height corresponds to the flagpole height.

$$\frac{\text{flagpole height}}{\text{flagpole shadow}} \diagdown\diagup \frac{\text{building height}}{\text{building shadow}}$$

Step 2. Set up a proportion and cross multiply. The building is 72 feet tall.

$$\frac{18}{12} = \frac{x}{48}$$

$$\frac{12x}{12} = \frac{864}{12}$$

$$x = 72$$

Example 4: In Figure 18, triangle *JMN* is similar to triangle *JKL*. Find the measure of side *KL*.

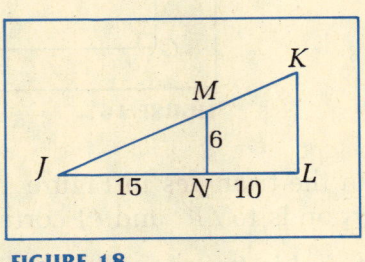

FIGURE 18

Step 1. Determine the corresponding sides and set up the proportion.

$$\frac{MN}{JN} = \frac{KL}{JL}$$

Step 2. Cross multiply to solve for x.

$$\frac{6}{15} = \frac{x}{25}$$

$$\frac{15x}{15} = \frac{150}{15}$$

$$x = 10$$

UNIT VII: MATHEMATICS Level 2: Lesson 1 **563**

Lesson 1 Exercise

Directions: *Solve each problem.*

Item 1 refers to Figure E-4.

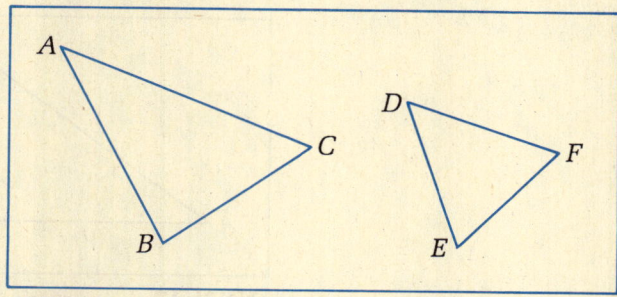

FIGURE E-4

1. If ∠A = ∠D, and ∠B = ∠E, are the triangles similar? Why?

2. A lamp post that is 10 feet high casts a 12-foot shadow. At the same time, a fence casts an 8-foot shadow. How tall is the fence?

3. A man who is 6 feet tall casts a 24-foot shadow. A tree casts a shadow of 72 feet. How tall is the tree?

Item 4 refers to Figure E-5.

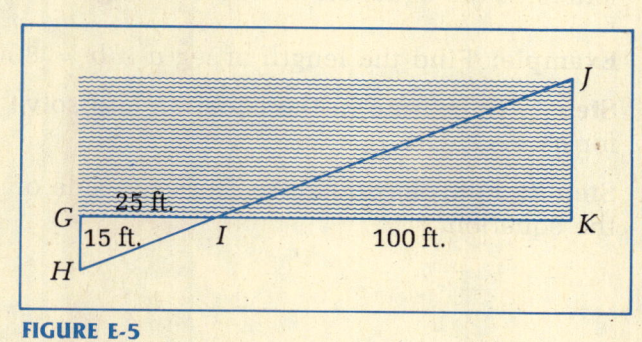

FIGURE E-5

4. Find the distance across the river at JK.

Item 5 refers to Figure E-6.

5. AD = 4 feet, DC = 8 feet, and AB = 6 feet. Find DE.

FIGURE E-6

Answers are on pages A-61.

Lesson 2 Pythagorean Relationship

A Greek mathematician named Pythagoras (who lived in about 550 B.C.) discovered a special relationship among the sides of a right triangle.

Look at the triangle in Figure 19.

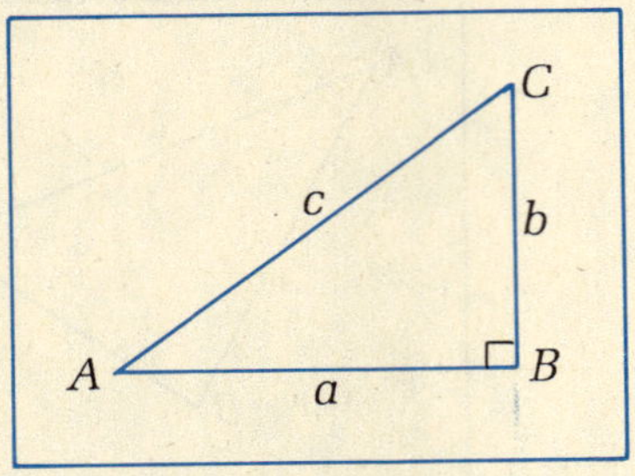

FIGURE 19

Side *AC* is the hypotenuse. Sides *AB* and *BC* are the legs. The relationship among the sides may be expressed in this way:

For any right triangle, the square of the hypotenuse (the side opposite the right angle) is equal to the sum of the squares of the other two sides.

The Pythagorean relationship may be written as

$c^2 = a^2 + b^2$.

To solve problems that concern right triangles, substitute values for the letters in the equation to find the lengths of the sides of the triangle.

Example: Find the length of leg *a* if $b = 8$ and $c = 17$.

Step 1. Substitute in the equation and solve for a^2.

Step 2. Find the square root of each side of the equation.

$$c^2 = a^2 + b^2$$
$$17^2 = a^2 + 8^2$$
$$289 = a^2 + 64$$
$$-64 \quad\quad -64$$
$$\sqrt{225} = \sqrt{a^2}$$
$$15 = a$$

Lesson 2 Exercise

Directions: *Use the Pythagorean relationship to solve each problem.*

1. Find the hypotenuse of a right triangle if the legs are 9 inches and 12 inches long.
2. In the formula $c^2 = a^2 + b^2$, find *b* when $a = 8$ feet and the hypotenuse equals 10 feet.

UNIT VII: MATHEMATICS   Level 2: Lesson 3   **565**

3. If a painter leaned the top of a 50-foot ladder against a building at a height of 40 feet, how far from the building is the base of the ladder?
4. The Millers drove 20 miles north and 15 miles west. How far were they from their starting point?
5. A guy wire was stretched from a tower that was 16 feet high to a point on the ground that was 12 feet from the tower. How long is the wire?

Answers are on pages A-61—A-62.

Lesson 3   Coordinate Geometry

Rectangular Coordinates

Look at Figure 20. It is a special kind of graph called a **rectangular coordinate system**. It uses principles from both algebra and geometry.

- Numbers to the *right* of zero on the x-axis are positive.
- Numbers to the *left* of zero on the x-axis are negative.
- Numbers *above* zero on the y-axis are positive.
- Numbers *below* zero on the y-axis are negative.

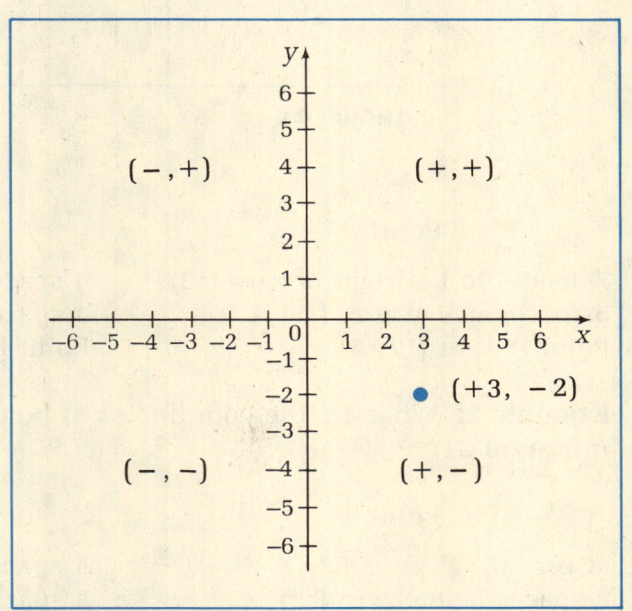

FIGURE 20

Plotting Points

Look at Figure 20 again. The position of any point on the graph can be labeled by two numbers that are called **coordinates**. The coordinates are placed inside parentheses.

The *first* coordinate tells how far to the *left* or to the *right* of zero the point is placed. The *second* coordinate tells how far *above* or *below* zero the point is placed. For example, the point (⁺3,⁻2) is 3 spaces to the right of 0 and 2 spaces below 0, as shown in Figure 20.

Example 1: What are the coordinates of point *A* and point *B* in the graph in Figure 21?

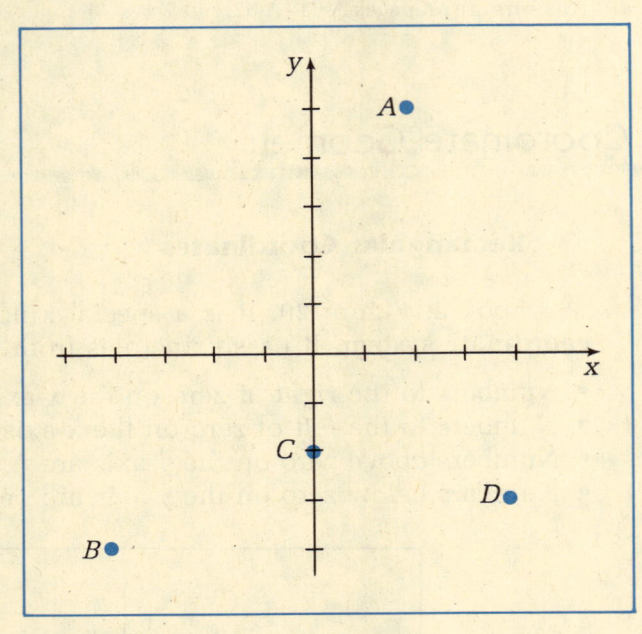

FIGURE 21

      Point A   **Point B**

2 spaces to the *right* of zero (⁺2)   4 spaces to the *left* of zero (⁻4)
5 spaces *above* zero (⁺5)   4 spaces *below* zero (⁻4)
Point *A* is at (⁺2,⁺5).   Point *B* is at (⁻4,⁻4).

Example 2: What are the coordinates of point *C* and point *D* in the graph in Figure 21?

      Point C   **Point D**

at zero (0)   4 spaces to the *right* of zero (⁺4)
2 spaces *below* zero (⁻2)   3 spaces *below* zero (⁻3)
Point *C* is at (0,⁻2).   Point *D* is at (⁺4,⁻3).

UNIT VII: MATHEMATICS   Level 2: Lesson 4   **567**

Lesson 3

Directions: Find the coordinates of each point on the graph in Figure E-7.

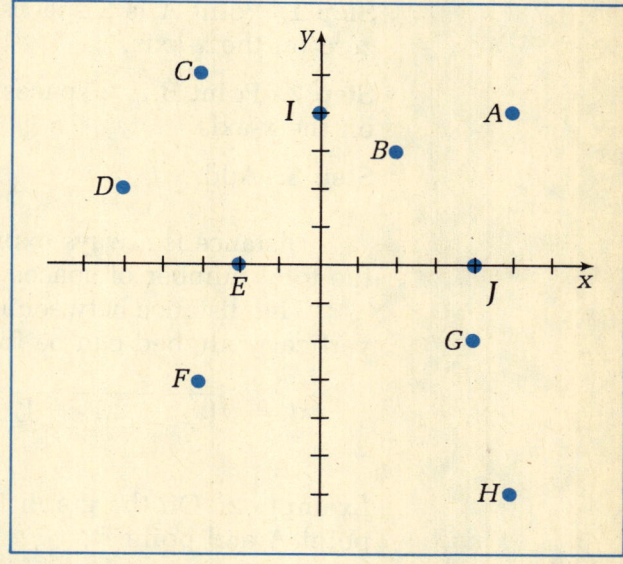

1. A   2. B
3. C   4. D
5. E   6. F
7. G   8. H
9. I   10. J

FIGURE E-7

Answers are on page A-62.

Lesson 4 Finding the Distance Between Points

Look at the graph in Figure 22. Line BD and line AC cross, or intersect, at the point (0, -2).

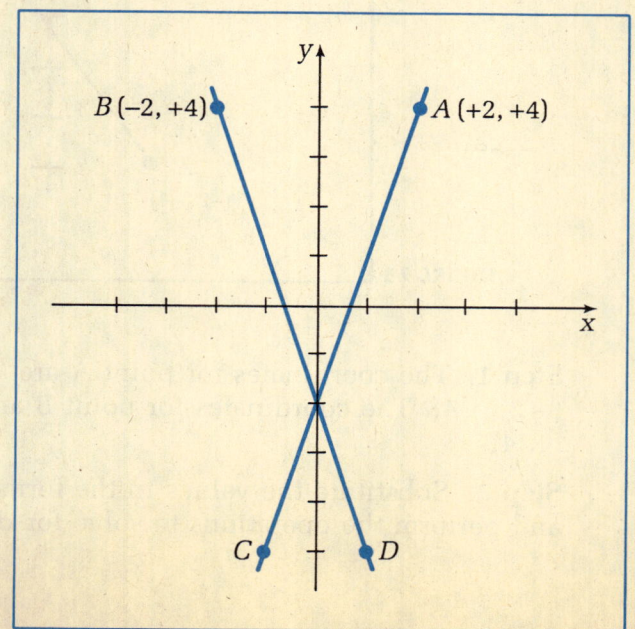

FIGURE 22

Chapter 7: Geometry

The *distance* between two points on a graph is the number of spaces between them.

Example 1: What is the distance from point A to point B on the graph in Figure 22?

Step 1. Point A is 2 spaces to the *right* of zero on the x-axis.

Step 2. Point B is 2 spaces to the *left* of zero on the x-axis.

Step 3. Add.

$$\begin{array}{l} \text{point } A = 2 \text{ spaces right} \\ \text{point } B = \underline{2 \text{ spaces left}} \\ \phantom{\text{point } B = }4 \text{ spaces} \end{array}$$

Distance is always expressed as a positive number because it is simply the total number of spaces from one point to another.

The distance between two points in a plane that are not horizontally or vertically aligned can be found by using the formula

$$d = \sqrt{(x_2 - x_1)^2 + (y_2 - y_1)^2}.$$

Example 2: On the graph in Figure 23, what is the distance between point A and point B?

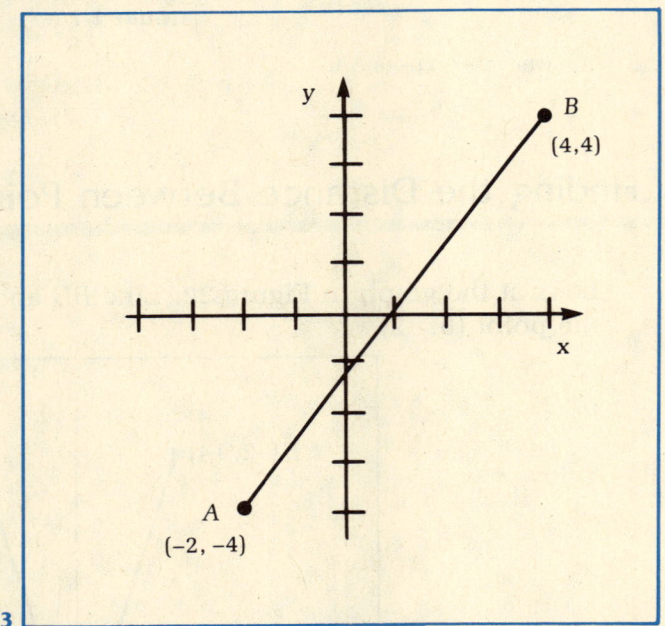

FIGURE 23

(Graph showing point B at (4,4) and point A at (−2, −4))

Step 1. The coordinates for point A are (−2, −4). The coordinates for point B are (4, 4).

Step 2. Substitute the values in the formula and perform the operations to solve for d.

$$d = \sqrt{(x_2 - x_1)^2 + (y_2 - y_1)^2}$$
$$d = \sqrt{(4 - (-2))^2 + (4 - (-4))^2}$$
$$d = \sqrt{(6)^2 + (8)^2}$$
$$d = \sqrt{36 + 64}$$
$$d = \sqrt{100}$$
$$d = 10$$

Lesson 4 Exercise

Directions: Items 1 to 5 refer to Figure E-8.

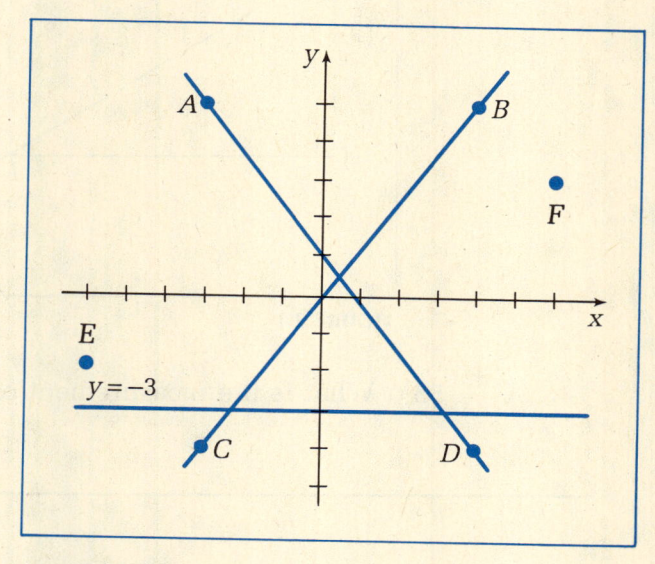

FIGURE E-8

1. What is the distance from point A to point B?
2. What is the distance from point C to point D?
3. What is the distance from point B to point D?
4. What is the perpendicular distance from point A to line $y = {}^-3$?
5. What is the distance from point E to point F?

Answers are on page A-62.

Level 2 Review

1. In triangles ABC and DEF, ∠B and ∠E are right angles. Side AB = 4 inches and side DE = 8 inches. If ∠A = 35° and ∠F = 55°, are the triangles similar?
2. A building that is 60 feet tall casts a 20-foot shadow. At the same time, a streetlight casts a 5-foot shadow. How tall is the streetlight?
3. In right triangle LMN, the hypotenuse, LM, is 17 inches long. Side LN is 8 inches long. Find the length of side MN.

Item 4 is based on Figure 24.

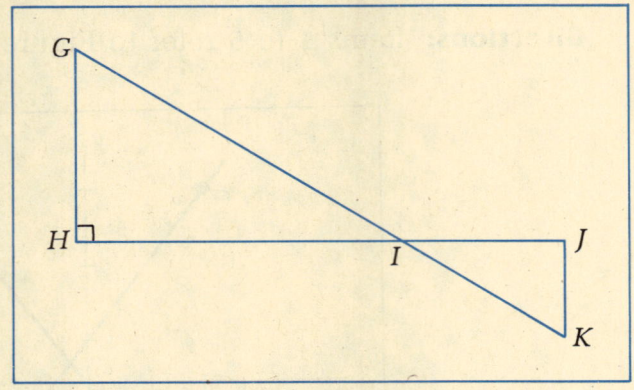

FIGURE 24

4. ∠G = 55°. What is the measurement of ∠JIK?

5. Bob's nature club hiked 12 miles north on Saturday and continued 5 miles west on Sunday. What is the shortest distance they can hike on Monday to reach their starting place?

Items 6 to 8 are based on Figure 25.

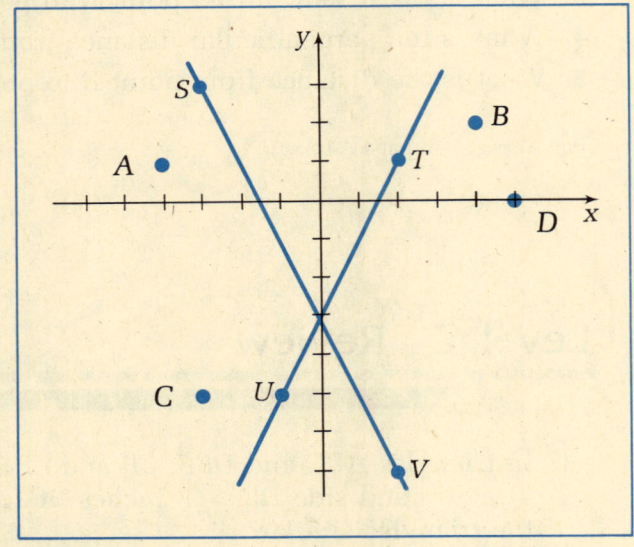

FIGURE 25

6. Give the coordinates for points A to D.
7. What is the distance between point T and point V?
8. At what point does line SV intersect line TU?

Items 9 and 10 are based on Figure 26.

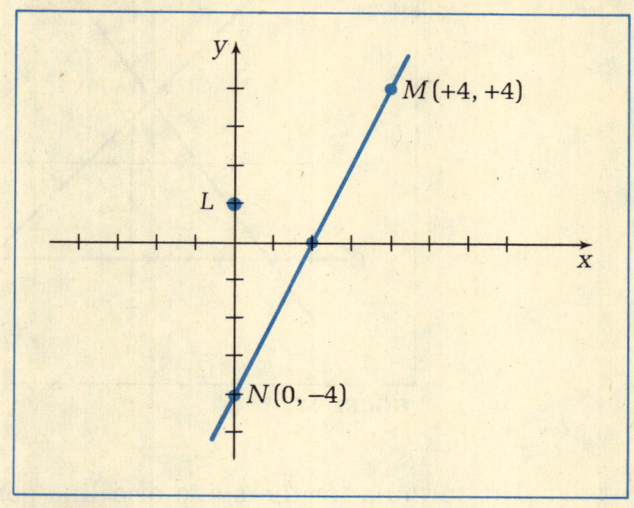

FIGURE 26

9. What is the distance between point L and point M?
10. Give the coordinates of the point at which line MN intersects the x-axis.

Check your answers. Correct answers are on page A-62. If you have at least eight answers correct, go to Level 3. If you have fewer than eight answers correct, go back to Lesson 1 and study Level 2 again.

Level 3   Word Problems

Lesson 1   Slope

On the GED, you may be asked to find the slope of a line on a graph. The **slope** of a line is the measure of its angle of inclination.

Study the graph in Figure 27.

- Line A goes uphill from left to right and has a positive slope.
- Line B goes downhill from left to right and has a negative slope.
- Line C goes straight across with no slant and has a zero slope (0).

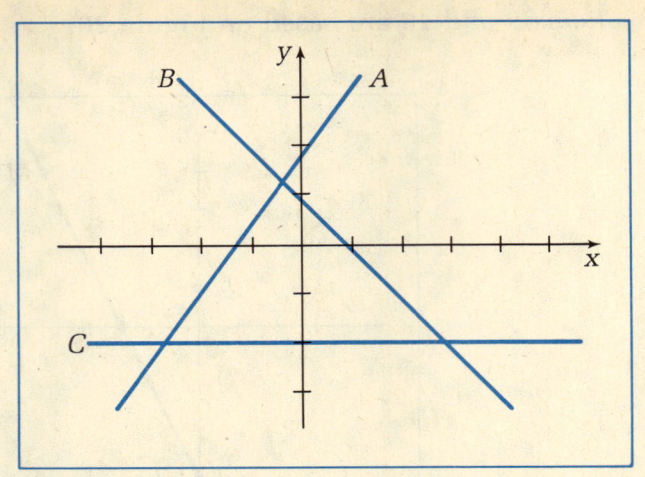

FIGURE 27

The formula for the slope of a line containing the points (x_1, y_1) and (x_2, y_2) is

$$m = \frac{y_2 - y_1}{x_2 - x_1}.$$

The letter m is often used for slope.
 A picture of a graph is not needed in order to find the slope of a line. Just substitute the coordinates in the formula.

Example: What is the slope of the line containing the points $(^+2, ^+2)$ and $(^+3, ^+4)$?

Step 1. The coordinates for (x_2, y_2) are $(^+3, ^+4)$; for (x_1, y_1) they are $(^+2, ^+2)$.

$$m = \frac{y_2 - y_1}{x_2 - x_1}$$

Step 2. Substitute the values in the formula and perform the operations to solve for m.

$$m = \frac{^+4 - ^+2}{^+3 - ^+2}$$

$$m = \frac{2}{1} = 2$$

Lesson 1

Directions: Find the slope of the line containing the points with these coordinates.

1. (5,3) and (0,1)
2. (2,2) and (3,-2)
3. (-2,-2) and (4,2)
4. (-3,2) and (2,-5)
5. (4,0) and (3,4)

Answers are on page A-62.

UNIT VII: MATHEMATICS   Level 3: Lesson 2   **573**

Lesson 2 Graphs of Linear Equations

On the GED, you may also be asked to choose which of the lines on a graph represents a given equation. One way to do this is to choose three values for one of the unknowns. Then set up a table of sample values to find the values of the other unknown.

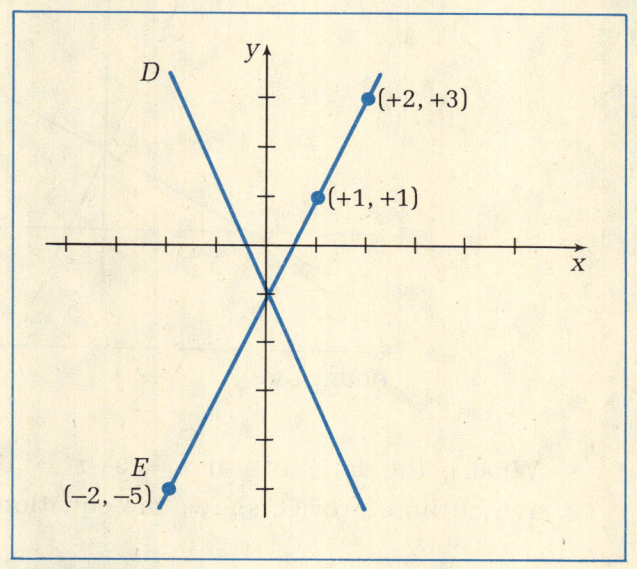

FIGURE 28

Example: On the graph in Figure 28, which line represents the equation $y = 2x - 1$?

Step 1. Choose three values for x. The values should be low numbers to make the problem-solving easy.

Step 2. Set up the table of sample values. Solve for y for each value of x.

x	y = 2x − 1
+2	+3
+1	+1
−2	−5

Step 3. Write each set of coordinates. $(^+2, ^+3)$ $(^+1, ^+1)$ $(^-2, ^-5)$

Step 4. Locate the coordinates on the graph. Which line runs through all these points?
Line E represents the equation $y = 2x - 1$.

Lesson 2   Exercise

Directions: Use the equation $y = ^-2x + 3$ and the graph in Figure E-9 to answer items 1 and 2.

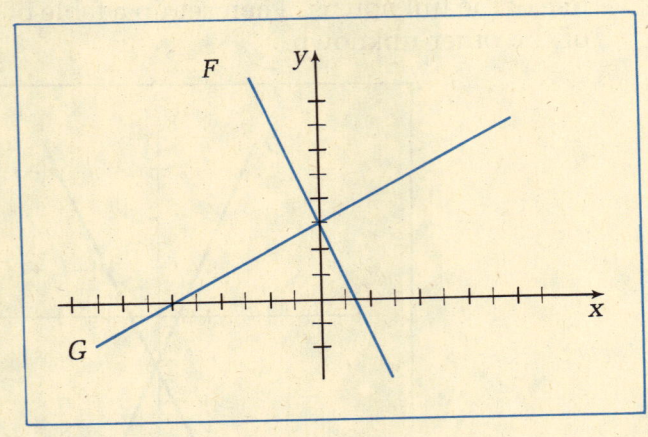

FIGURE E-9

1. What is the value of y if x = 3? x = 1? x = 2?
2. Which line, F or G, shows the equation $y = ^-2x + 3$?

Directions: Use the equation $y = \frac{1}{2}x - 2$ and the graph in Figure E-10 to answer items 3 and 4.

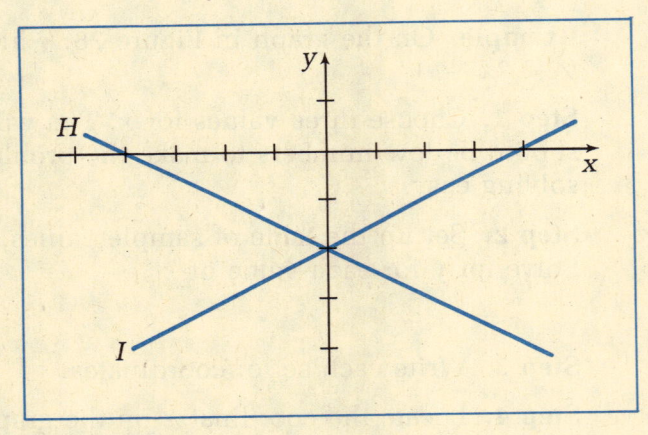

FIGURE E-10

3. What is the value of y if x = 4? x = 2? x = $^-$4?
4. Which line, H or I, shows the equation $y = \frac{1}{2}x - 2$?
5. What are the coordinates of the point where lines H and I intersect?

Answers are on page A-62.

Level 3 Review

1. Find the slope of a line containing the points (⁻2,⁻6) and (5,1).
2. Find the slope of a line containing the points (⁻3,7) and (3,⁻5).

Items 3 to 9 are based on Figure 29.

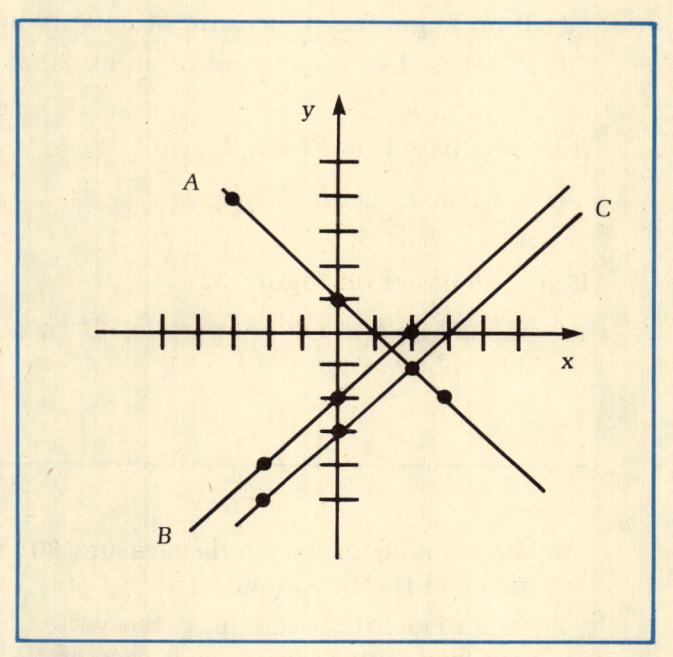

FIGURE 29

3. Which line shows the equation y = x − 2?
4. Which line shows the equation y = −x + 1?
5. Which line shows the equation y = x − 3?
6. What is the slope of line A?
7. What is the slope of line C?
8. Which line contains the point (⁻2, 3)?
9. Which line contains the point (⁻1, ⁻4)?

10. The top of a ramp rests on a platform 6 feet above the ground. The lower end of the ramp is at ground level, 18 feet from the platform. What is the slope of the ramp?

Check your answers. Correct answers are on page A-63. If you have at least eight problems correct, go to the Chapter Quiz. If you have fewer than eight problems correct, go back to Lesson 1 and study Level 3 again.

Chapter 7   Quiz

1. What kind of angle measures less than 90°?
2. If an angle has a measure of 340°, what kind of angle is it?
3. What is the supplement of an angle of 79°?

Item 4 is based on Figure 30.

4. How large is ∠BAC?

FIGURE 30

Item 5 is based on Figure 31.

5. Lines MN and OP are parallel. If ∠a = 115°, how large is ∠f?

FIGURE 31

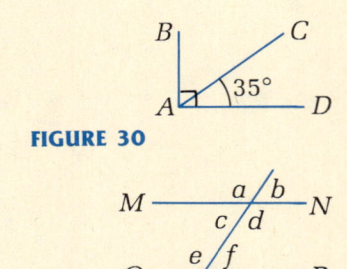

6. Two angles of a triangle measure 80° and 55°. Find the measurement of the third angle.
7. In an isosceles triangle, if the vertex angle measures 110°, find the number of degrees in each base angle.

Item 8 is based on Figure 32.

8. If ∠B = ∠E, prove that the triangles are similar.

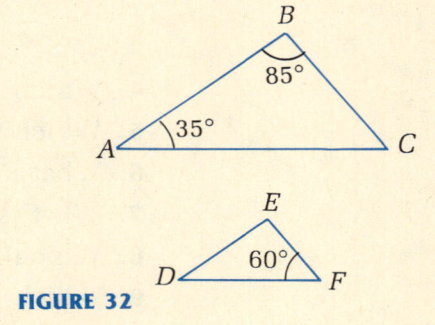

FIGURE 32

Item 9 is based on Figure 33.

9. A radio tower is 3 miles north of city hall. The Bradys' farm is 4 miles east of city hall. What is the shortest distance between the farm and the radio tower?

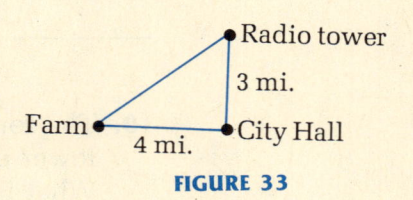

FIGURE 33

UNIT VII: MATHEMATICS   Chapter 7 Quiz   **577**

Item 10 is based on Figure 34.

10. Tell which point on the graph has the coordinates (⁺2,⁻3).

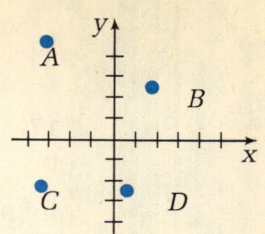

FIGURE 34

Item 11 is based on Figure 35.

11. What is the distance from point *A* to point *B*?

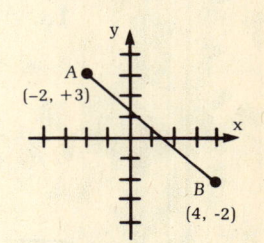

FIGURE 35

Item 12 is based on Figure 36.

12. Which two letters on the graph name the line that has zero slope?

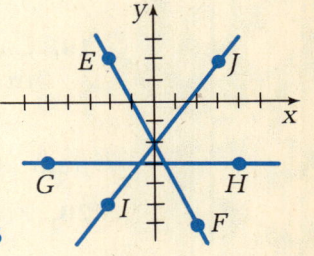

FIGURE 36

---

13. Find the slope of a line that contains the points (⁻3,2) and (2,⁻5).

14. A man who is 6 feet tall casts a 2-foot shadow at the same time that a building casts an 18-foot shadow. How tall is the building?

Items 15 to 17 are based on the graph in Figure 37.

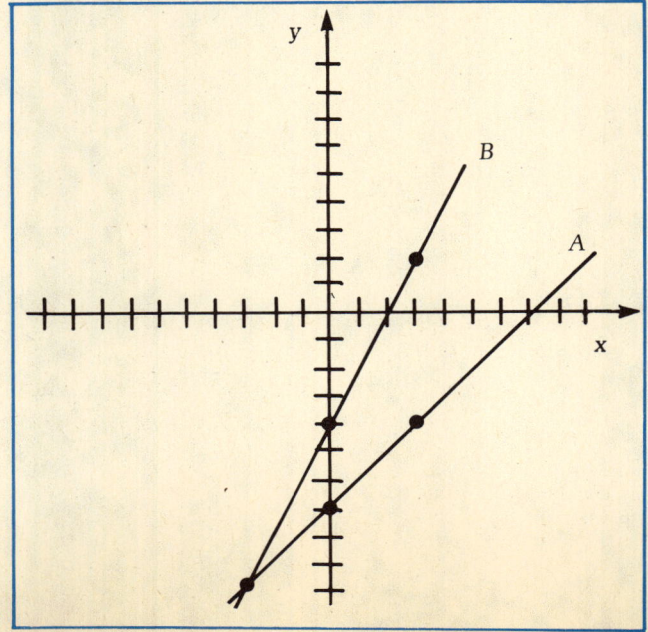

FIGURE 37

15. Which line shows the equation y = x − 7?

16. Which line shows the equation y = 2x − 4?

17. Which line contains the point (6, ⁻1)?

Item 18 is based on Figure 38.

18. What is the slope of ramp *AB*?

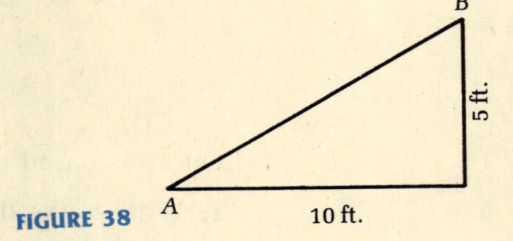

FIGURE 38

---

19. Gary bicycled 10 miles west and 24 miles south. How far was he from his starting point?

Item 20 is based on Figure 39.

20. Find the length of the diagonal line, *LK*.

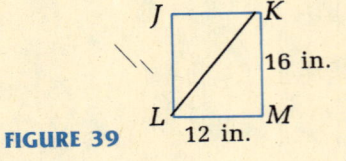

FIGURE 39

Answers are on page A-63.

Practice

Introduction

This GED Practice section provides you with valuable experience in answering GED-type questions, or *items*.

All of the Practice Items are like those on the actual GED Tests. They are all multiple choice—except for those in Part II of the Writing Skills section. There are as many Practice Items for each subject as there are on the related GED Test. The items are as challenging as actual test items.

Although this Practice section is similar to the real GED Tests in many ways, there is one major difference. The arrangement of the Social Studies, Science, Interpreting Literature and the Arts, and Mathematics Practice Items allows you to focus on one content area at a time. For example, in the Science Practice Items, biology items are grouped together, earth science items are grouped together, and so on. The actual GED Tests for all subjects present items related to various subject areas in mixed order.

Using the Practice to Best Advantage

You can use the Practice in any of the following ways:

- You may use the Practice Items while you are studying the units in this book. Whenever you finish a segment of instruction, practice with the related group of Practice Items. You can use sections of the Practice Items when you finish each of the following sections of instruction:

Unit I	Unit V, Chapters 2, 3, 4, & 5
Unit II	Unit VI, Chapters 2, 3, 4, 5 & 6
Unit IV, Chapters 2, 3, 4, 5, & 6	Unit VII, Chapters 1-5, 6 & 7

- For Units IV to VII, you may save the Practice until you've completed an entire unit. Then, work through the Practice doing one group of items at a time. Review the chapters for the areas in which you have difficulty.

- You may use each set of Practice Items as a practice test for a subject. To do this, complete a set of items (such as all the Science Practice Items) in one sitting and time yourself. Since each set of Practice Items is as long as the actual test, you should allow yourself the amount of time that the real test allows you. (The chart on page vii shows the time allowed for each test.)

Using the Answers and Explanations

Compare your answers to those in the answer section beginning on page A-64. Whether you get an item correct or not, read the explanations of the correct answer. This will reinforce your knowledge of the subjects and develop your test-taking skill. For Part II of the Writing Skills Test, follow the directions in the answer section for scoring your essay.

How to Use Your Score

After you score your work, fill in the Performance Analysis Charts that follow the Practice Items. The charts will help you determine the areas you are strongest in and direct you to parts of the book where you can review.

PRACTICE ITEMS 1
Writing Skills, Part I: Grammar

Directions: *The items in Part I of this test are based on paragraphs that contain numbered sentences. Some of the sentences may contain errors in sentence structure, usage, or mechanics.* **A few sentences, however, may be correct as written.** *Read each paragraph and then answer the items that follow it. For each item, choose the answer that would result in the most effective writing of the sentence or sentences. The best answer must be consistent with the meaning and tone of the rest of the paragraph.*

Items 1 to 9 are based on the following paragraph.

(1) Suppose you, like so many others, have desided to buy a computer. (2) There is several questions to ask yourself before you go to the computer store. (3) How much money do you intend to spend? (4) How will you use the computer? (5) Perhaps you plan to type Technical papers on your machine. (6) In this case, a printer, as well. (7) Maybe you want a computer for playing games and to draw pictures. (8) In that case, you chose a computer with a color screen. (9) Perhaps you are looking for a computer, with teaching programs for your family. (10) If you plan to move the computer often, you ask about portables. (11) You considered these points about your needs, and were ready to ask a computer dealer for help in finding it.

1. Sentence 1: **Suppose you, like so many others, have desided to buy a computer.**

   What correction should be made to this sentence?

   (1) remove the comma after *others*
   (2) change *have* to *has*
   (3) change the spelling of *desided* to *decided*
   (4) replace *buy* with *by*
   (5) change *computer* to *Computer*

2. Sentence 2: **There is several questions to ask yourself before you go to the computer store.**

   What correction should be made to this sentence?

   (1) change *is* to *are*
   (2) change the spelling of *several* to *sevarel*
   (3) insert a comma after *questions*
   (4) replace *yourself* with *oneself*
   (5) change *computer store* to *Computer Store*

3. Sentence 5: **Perhaps you plan to type Technical papers on your machine.**

   What correction should be made to this sentence?

   (1) insert a comma after *Perhaps*
   (2) change *plan* to *plans*
   (3) change *Technical* to *technical*
   (4) replace *your* with *you're*
   (5) no correction is necessary

581

4. Sentence 6: **In this <u>case, a</u> printer, as well.**

   Which of the following is the best way to write the underlined portion of the sentence? If you think the original is the best way, choose option (1).

   (1) case, a
   (2) case. A
   (3) case, one will have to buy a
   (4) case, you will have to buy a
   (5) case, buying a

5. Sentence 7: **Maybe you want a <u>computer for playing games and to draw pictures.</u>**

   Which of the following is the best way to write the underlined portion of the sentence? If you think the original is the best way, choose option (1).

   (1) computer for playing games and to draw pictures.
   (2) computer, for playing ames and to draw pictures.
   (3) computer to play games and for drawing pictures.
   (4) computer. For playing games and drawing pictures.
   (5) computer for playing games and drawing pictures.

6. Sentence 8: **In that case, you chose a computer with a color screen.**

   What correction should be made to this sentence?

   (1) change *chose* to *would choose*
   (2) change *chose* to *choose*
   (3) insert a comma after *computer*
   (4) replace *color screen* with *Color Screen*
   (5) no correction is necessary

7. Sentence 9: **Perhaps you are looking for a <u>computer, with</u> teaching programs for your family.**

   Which of the following is the best way to write the underlined portion of the sentence? If you think the original is the best way, choose option (1).

   (1) computer, with
   (2) computer with
   (3) computer. With
   (4) computer and with
   (5) computer; with

8. Sentence 10: **If you plan to move the computer <u>often, you ask</u> about portables.**

   Which of the following is the best way to write the underlined portion of the sentence? If you think the original is the best way, choose option (1).

   (1) often, you ask
   (2) often you ask
   (3) often, you should ask
   (4) often, one asks
   (5) often. You ask

9. Sentence 11: **You considered these points about your needs, and were ready to ask a computer dealer for help in finding it.**

   If you rewrote sentence 11 beginning with

   You will be ready to ask a computer dealer for help in finding

   the next word should be

   (1) needs
   (2) the
   (3) it
   (4) computer
   (5) one

PRACTICE ITEMS

Test 1: Writing Skills, Part I: Grammar 583

Items 10 to 19 are based on the following paragraph.

(1) Someday accompanying your application for a job, you may be writing a business letter. (2) Without knowing exactly who will receive and read your letter. (3) You probably understand how important it is to write a neat, clear letter you may not realize how important it is to choose an appropriate greeting. (4) When in doubt, research shows, when you do choose a greeting, you should avoid the phrases *Dear Sirs* and *Gentlemen*. (5) A study using 75 letters of application for a university job were done. (6) Of the 28 applicants who used masculine greetings, none were chosen as a finalist for the job. (7) Every one of the 11 finalists for the position was from the group that found a way to avoid masculine greetings. (8) Each of the finalists uses a neutral greeting, such as *Dear Committee Members* or *To Whom It May Concern*. (9) Why should the form of the greeting make such a difference? (10) Masculine greetings are read by female employers, at times, and they may be annoyed by them. (11) In any case, you should find a neutral greeting because of you want to make a good first impression.

10. Sentence 1: **Someday accompanying your application for a job, you may be writing a business letter.**

If you rewrote sentence 1 beginning with

Someday you may be writing a business letter

the next words should be

(1) for a job
(2) to a job
(3) for application
(4) to accompany
(5) that accompanied

11. Sentence 2: **Without knowing exactly who will receive and read your letter.**

What correction should be made to this sentence?

(1) replace *Without knowing* with *You may not know*
(2) change the spelling of *receive* to *recieve*
(3) insert a comma after *receive*
(4) replace *your* with *you're*
(5) no correction is necessary

12. Sentence 3: **You probably understand how important it is to write a neat, clear letter you may not realize how important it is to choose an appropriate greeting.**

What correction should be made to this sentence?

(1) change the spelling of *probably* to *probally*
(2) change *understand* to *understands*
(3) insert a comma after *letter*
(4) replace *letter you* with *letter. You*
(5) replace *it is to choose* with *is your choice of*

13. Sentence 4: **When in doubt, research shows, when you do choose a greeting, you should avoid the phrases Dear Sirs and Gentlemen.**

If you rewrote sentence 4 beginning with

Research shows that

the next word should be

(1) when
(2) unless
(3) however
(4) because
(5) since

14. Sentence 5: **A study using 75 letters of application for a university job were done.**

    What correction should be made to this sentence?

    (1) change *using* to *uses*
    (2) insert a comma after *job*
    (3) change *were* to *was*
    (4) change the spelling of *application* to *apliccation*
    (5) no correction is necessary

15. Sentence 6: **Of the 28 applicants who used masculine greetings, none were chosen as a finalist for the job.**

    Which of the following is the best way to write the underlined portion of this sentence? If you think the original is the best way, choose option (1).

    (1) greetings, none were chosen
    (2) greetings none were chosen
    (3) greetings. None were chosen
    (4) greetings, none was chosen
    (5) greetings: none was chosen

16. Sentence 8: **Each of the finalists uses a neutral greeting, such as *Dear Committee Members* or *To Whom It May Concern*.**

    What correction should be made to this sentence?

    (1) replace *Each* with *All*
    (2) insert a comma after *finalists*
    (3) change *uses* to *used*
    (4) change the spelling of *committee* to *comittee*
    (5) change *Members* to *members*

17. Sentence 9: **Why should the form of the greeting make such a difference?**

    What correction should be made to this sentence?

    (1) replace *should* with *had*
    (2) insert a comma after *greeting*
    (3) change *make* to *makes*
    (4) change the spelling of *difference* to *diffarence*
    (5) no correction is necessary

18. Sentence 10: **Masculine greetings are read by female employers, at times, and they may be annoyed by them.**

    If you rewrote sentence 10 beginning with

    Perhaps masculine greetings

    the next word should be

    (1) annoy
    (2) at
    (3) read
    (4) to
    (5) they

19. Sentence 11: **In any case, you should find a neutral greeting because of you want to make a good first impression.**

    Which of the following is the best way to write the underlined portion of this sentence? If you think the original is the best way, choose option (1).

    (1) greeting because of you want
    (2) greeting because of one wants
    (3) greeting. Because of you want
    (4) greeting because you want
    (5) greeting. Because you want

Items 20 to 28 are based on the following paragraph.

(1) If you buy a computer, you may want to join a club known as a user Group. (2) All members of the group use the same type of computer. (3) There are several advantages, to being part of a user group. (4) You can borrow programs from other members. (5) You may be able to copy a program you have borrowed and keep the copy for yourself. (6) If you are having a problem with your machine, you may find an other member who has already solved that very problem. (7) Others will trade notes with you about new software additions on the market, often there is a user group newsletter. (8) In the newsletter, one will find useful information about special software deals and computer shows, among other items of interest. (9) To locate the user group that is nearest for your type of computer, check with your local computer dealer. (10) The dealer will either direct you to a nearby group or provide you with the phone number of a national user group manager. (11) The dues you pay are usually well worth the money you save, the knowledge you gain, and making friends.

20. Sentence 1: **If you buy a computer, you may want to join a club known as a user Group.**

What correction should be made to this sentence?

(1) replace *If* with *Since*
(2) replace *buy* with *by*
(3) remove the comma after *computer*
(4) change *join* to *have joined*
(5) change *Group* to *group*

21. Sentence 3: **There are several advantages, to being part of a user group.**

What correction should be made to this sentence?

(1) change the spelling of *There* to *They're*
(2) change *are* to *is*
(3) change the spelling of *advantages* to *advantiges*
(4) delete the comma after *advantages*
(5) no correction is necessary

22. Sentence 5: **You may be able to copy a program you have borrowed and keep the copy for yourself.**

If you rewrote sentence 5 beginning with

Having borrowed a program,

the next word should be

(1) you
(2) yourself
(3) one
(4) copy
(5) copying

23. Sentence 6: **If you are having a problem with your machine, you may find an other member who has already solved that very problem.**

What correction should be made to this sentence?

(1) change the spelling of *an other* to *another*
(2) insert a comma after *member*
(3) change *who* to *which*
(4) change *has* to *have*
(5) change the spelling of *already* to *all ready*

24. Sentence 7: **Others will trade notes with you about new software additions on the <u>market, often</u> there is a user group newsletter.**

Which of the following is the best way to write the underlined portion of the sentence? If you think the original is the best way, choose option (1).

(1) market, often
(2) market often
(3) market so often
(4) because often
(5) market. Often

25. **Sentence 8: In the newsletter, <u>one will find useful information</u> about special software deals and computer shows, among other items of interest.**

    Which of the following is the best way to write the underlined portion of the sentence? If you think the original is the best way, choose option (1).

    (1) one will find useful information
    (2) one will find information that is useful
    (3) one found useful information
    (4) you will find useful information
    (5) you will find information which is useful

26. **Sentence 9: To locate the <u>user group that is nearest</u> for your type of computer, check with your local computer dealer.**

    Which of the following is the best way to write the underlined portion of this sentence? If you think the original is the best way, choose option (1).

    (1) user group that is nearest
    (2) user group, that is nearest
    (3) user group who is nearest
    (4) user group, which is nearest
    (5) nearest user group

27. **Sentence 10: The dealer will either direct you to a nearby group or provide you with the phone number of a national user group manager.**

    What correction should be made to this sentence?

    (1)
    (2) change *provide* to *provides*
    (3) change the spelling of *either* to *ether*
    (4) change *national* to *National*
    (5) no correction is necessary

28. **Sentence 11: The dues you pay are usually well worth the money you save, the knowledge you gain, and making friends.**

    What correction should be made to this sentence?

    (1) change *you pay* to *one pays*
    (2) change the spelling of *knowledge* to *knowlege*
    (3) insert a comma after *pay*
    (4) remove the comma after *gain*
    (5) change *making friends* to *the friends you make*

Items 29 to 37 are based on the following paragraphs.

(1) It pays to do some research before buying a new car. (2) One one hand, car prices are offen inflated by expensive options. (3) Sometimes dealers add such extras as cassette players or floor mats, although these items cost fairly little to install, the dealers may charge car buyers an exorbitant amount. (4) It certainly make sense to wait and put in a radio or car alarm later if you will save thousands of dollars by doing so. (5) On the other hand, a relatively low car price at the cost of safety. (6) Find out how the car you are considering does on crash tests. (7) In these tests, dummies were fastened into the two front seats. (8) It is driven at 35 miles per hour into wall. (9) Their condition is examined. (10) A prediction is made about whether actual passengers would have been severely injured, or killed. (11) It is likely that you will often travel at 35 miles per hour or more therefore you probably do not want a car that fails the test. (12) Learn all you can about the various American and foreign cars on the market so that you can exercise good judgment in how you spend your money.

29. **Sentence 2: On one hand, car prices are offen inflated by expensive options.**

    What correction should be made to this sentence?

    (1) remove the comma after *hand*
    (2) change *are* to *is*
    (3) change the spelling of *offen* to *often*
    (4) insert a comma after *inflated*
    (5) change *options* to *Options*

30. Sentence 3: **Sometimes dealers add such extras as cassette players or floor mats, although these items cost** fairly little to install, the dealers may charge car buyers an exorbitant amount.

Which of the following is the best way to write the underlined portion of the sentence? If you think the original is the best way, choose option (1).

(1) mats, although these items cost
(2) mats. Although these items cost
(3) mats, although these items cost
(4) mats although these items, cost
(5) mats, because these items cost

31. Sentence 4: **It certainly make sense to wait and put** in a radio or a car alarm later if you will save thousands of dollars by doing so.

Which of the following is the best way to write the underlined portion of the sentence? If you think the original is the best way, choose option (1).

(1) make sense to wait and put
(2) make sense waiting and putting
(3) make sense to wait, and put
(4) makes sense to wait and put
(5) make sense to wait. And put

32. Sentence 5: **On the other hand, a relatively low car price at the cost of safety.**

What correction should be made to this sentence?

(1) replace *On the other hand* with *However*
(2) remove the comma after *hand*
(3) insert *may come* after *price*
(4) replace *at the cost of* with *costing*
(5) replace *hand, a* with *hand. A*

33. Sentence 7: **In these tests, dummies were fastened into the two front seats.**

What correction should be made to this sentence?

(1) remove the comma after *tests*
(2) change *dummies* to *Dummies*
(3) change *were* to *are*
(4) insert a comma after *two*
(5) no correction is necessary

34. Sentences 8 and 9: **It is driven at 35 miles per hour into a wall. Their condition is examined.**

The most effective combination of sentences 8 and 9 would include which of the following groups of words?

(1) After the dummies' condition
(2) After the car is driven
(3) After their condition
(4) After driving them
(5) After they drive

35. Sentence 10: **A prediction is made about whether actual passengers would have been severely injured, or killed.**

Which of the following is the best way to write the underlined portion of the sentence? If you think the original is the best way, choose option (1).

(1) been severely injured, or killed.
(2) been severely injured or killed.
(3) severely been injured, or killed.
(4) been injured, severely, or killed.
(5) severe injuries, or death.

36. Sentence 11: **It is likely that you will often travel at 35 miles per hour or <u>more therefore you probably do not want</u>** a car that fails the test.

Which of the following is the best way to write the underlined portion of the sentence? If you think the original is the best way, choose option (1).

(1) more therefore you probably do not want
(2) more, therefore you probably did not want
(3) more therefore you probably did not want
(4) more. Therefore, you probably do not want
(5) more and therefore, you probably did not want

37. Sentence 12: **Learn all you can about the various American and foreign cars on the market so that you can exercise good judgment in how you spend your money.**

What correction should be made to this sentence?

(1) change *American* to *american*
(2) change *foreign* to *Foreign*
(3) change the spelling of *exercise* to *exercize*
(4) change *spend* to *spends*
(5) no correction is necessary

Items 38 to 47 are based on the following paragraph.

(1) Many jobs involving more writing than they appear to at first glance. (2) For example, the position of national park ranger. (3) Many people look into ranger jobs because they want to work outdoors. (4) They learn that they must first take a test given by the U.S. park service. (5) Many applicants take the test and the finalists are the applicants with excellent scores. (6) The fortunate few which are chosen as rangers soon discover how much paperwork they must do. (7) You must keep records of guests' names, payments, campsite numbers and departure dates. (8) Dayly schedules of activities need to be posted. (9) Displays in the park museums change, and they must relabel them. (10) Job duties also include writing comments for slide shows typing list of park rules, and even filling out police reports. (11) Of course, park rangers do get to work outdoors, but they usually spend some time each day at their desks.

38. Sentence 1: **Many jobs involving more writing than they appear to at first glance.**

What correction should be made to this sentence?

(1) insert *are* after *jobs*
(2) change *involving* to *involve*
(3) insert a comma after *writing*
(4) replace *than* with *then*
(5) change the spelling of *appear* to *appeer*

39. Sentence 2: **For example, the position of national park ranger.**

Which of the following is the best way to write the underlined portion of this sentence? If you think the original is the best way, choose option (1).

(1) For example, the
(2) For example; the
(3) For example the
(4) One good example, is the
(5) One good example is the

PRACTICE ITEMS
Test 1: Writing Skills, Part I: Grammar

40. Sentence 4: **They learn that they must first take a test given by the U.S. park service.**

What correction should be made to this sentence?

(1) change *learn* to *learns*
(2) insert a comma after *test*
(3) change *U.S.* to *u.s.*
(4) change *park service* to *Park Service*
(5) no correction is necessary

41. Sentence 5: **Many applicants take the test and the finalists are the applicants with excellent scores.**

If you rewrote sentence 5 beginning with

Since many applicants take the test

the next word should be

(1) applicants
(2) therefore
(3) so
(4) only
(5) many

42. Sentence 6: **The fortunate few which are chosen as rangers soon discover how much paperwork they must do.**

What correction should be made to this sentence?

(1) change the spelling of *fortunate* to *fortunat*
(2) replace *which* with *who*
(3) change *are* to *is*
(4) insert a comma after *rangers*
(5) replace *they* with *one*

43. Sentence 7: <u>**You must keep**</u> **records of guests' names, payments, campsite numbers, and departure dates.**

Which of the following is the best way to write the underlined portion of this sentence? If you think the original is the best way, choose option (1).

(1) You must keep
(2) You must have kept
(3) He must be keeping
(4) She must keep
(5) A ranger must keep

44. Sentence 8: **Dayly schedules of activities need to posted.**

What correction should be made to this sentence?

(1) change the spelling of *Dayly* to *Daily*
(2) change the spelling of *schedules* to *scheduals*
(3) insert a comma after *activities*
(4) change *need* to *needs*
(5) no correction is necessary

45. Sentence 9: **Displays in the park museums change, and they must relabel them.**

If you rewrote sentence 9 beginning with

Rangers must relabel changing

the next word should be

(1) park
(2) museums
(3) displays
(4) in
(5) and

46. Sentence 10: **Job duties also include writing comments for slide <u>shows typing lists</u> of park rules, and even filling out police reports.**

Which of the following is the best way to write the underlined portion of this sentence? If you think the original is the best way, choose option (1).

(1) shows typing lists
(2) shows. Typing lists
(3) shows and typing lists
(4) shows, typing lists
(5) shows, typed lists

47. Sentence 11: **Of course, park rangers do get to work <u>outdoors, but</u> they usually spend some time each day at their desks.**

Which of the following is the best way to write the underlined portion of this sentence? If you think the original is the best way, choose option (1).

(1) outdoors, but
(2) outdoors. But
(3) outdoors but
(4) outdoors but,
(5) outdoors so

Items 48 to 55 are based on the following paragraph.

(1) If you have not visited your public library recently, you may be surprised to find a computer where a magazine rack had been. (2) Computers has arrived at even the smallest town libraries. (3) Some people used these computers to play video games. (4) There are programs that teach about the machine, itself, and are taken advantage of by others. (5) Some libraries have learning programs. (6) These programs range from lessons about shapes for preschoolers to practice tests for adults taking the ged. (7) Visitors are not the only ones using the library's computers. (8) If you ask for help in finding a book, the librarian done a computer search. (9) In a few minutes, the computer tells which library in the area has the book you want. (10) When you hand your old library card to the librarian you may be in for another surprise. (11) Many libraries have replaced paper cards with plastic ones that are read by computers. (12) Computers have truly changed the appearances and how most libraries are used.

48. Sentence 2: **Computers <u>has arrived</u> at even the smallest town libraries.**

Which of the following is the best way to write the underlined portion of this sentence? If you think the original is the best way, choose option (1).

(1) has arrived
(2) have arrived
(3) has arriven
(4) have arriven
(5) have arrove

49. Sentence 3: **Some people used these computers to play video games.**

What correction should be made to this sentence?

(1) change *used* to *use*
(2) insert a comma after *computers*
(3) change *play* to *plays*
(4) change *video* to *Video*
(5) no correction is necessary

PRACTICE ITEMS Test 1: Writing Skills, Part I: Grammar **591**

50. Sentence 4: **There are programs that teach about the machine, itself, and are taken advantage of by others.**

If you rewrote sentence 4 beginning with

Others take advantage of programs

the next word should be

(1) by
(2) the
(3) there
(4) that
(5) about

51. Sentence 6: **These programs range from lessons about shapes for preschoolers to practice tests for adults taking the ged.**

What correction should be made to this sentence?

(1) change *range* to *ranges*
(2) change the spelling of *lessons* to *lessens*
(3) insert a comma after *shapes*
(4) change *tests* to *test's*
(5) change *ged* to *GED*

52. Sentence 7: **Visitors are not the only ones using the library's computers.**

What correction should be made to this sentence?

(1) change the spelling of *Visitors* to *Visiters*
(2) change *are* to *is*
(3) change *ones using* to *ones. Using*
(4) change *library's* to *libraries*
(5) no correction is necessary

53. Sentence 8: **If you ask for help in finding a book, the <u>librarian done</u> a computer search.**

Which of the following is the best way to write the underlined portion of this sentence? If you think the original is the best way, choose option (1).

(1) librarian done
(2) librarian has done
(3) librarian did
(4) librarian may do
(5) librarian is doing

54. Sentence 10: **When you hand your old library card to the librarian you may be in for another surprise.**

What correction should be made to this sentence?

(1) replace *When* with *Unless*
(2) replace *you hand* with *one hands*
(3) insert a comma after *card*
(4) insert a comma after *librarian*
(5) change the spelling of *surprise* to *surprize*

55. Sentence 12: **Computers have truly changed the appearances and <u>how most libraries are used.</u>**

Which of the following is the best way to write the underlined portion of the sentence? If you think the original is the best way, choose option (1).

(1) how most libraries are used.
(2) how most libraries is used.
(3) manners in which most libraries are used.
(4) uses of most libraries.
(5) what most libraries are used for.

Answers are on pages A-64—A-65.

PRACTICE ITEMS 1: WRITING SKILLS, Part I
Performance Analysis Chart

Directions: Circle the number of each item that you got correct on the Practice Items. Count how many items you got correct in each row; count how many items you got correct in each column. Write the amount correct per row and column as the numerator in the fraction in the appropriate "Total Correct" box. (The denominators represent the total number of items in the row or column.) Write the grand total correct over the denominator **55** at the lower right corner of the chart. (For example, if you got 50 items correct, write 50 so that the fraction reads 50/55.)

Item Type	Usage (page 73)	Sentence Structure (page 100)	Mechanics (page 118)	TOTAL CORRECT
Construction Shift (page 149)	9, 18, 34, 45	10, 22, 50	13, 41	/9
Sentence Correction (page 148)	2, 6, 14, 16, 27, 33, 42, 49	11, 12, 28, 32, 38, 52	1, 3, 17, 20, 21, 23, 29, 37, 40, 44, 51, 54	/26
Sentence Revision (page 148)	8, 15, 25, 26, 31, 43, 48, 53	4, 5, 19, 24, 30, 36, 39, 55	7, 35, 46, 47	/20
TOTAL CORRECT	/20	/17	/18	/55

The page numbers in parentheses indicate where in this book you can find the beginning of specific instruction about the areas of grammar and about the types of questions you encountered in the Practice Items.

PRACTICE ITEMS 1
Writing Skills, Part II: Essay-writing

Directions: This is a test to see how well you can write. In this test, you are asked to write an essay in which you present your opinions about an issue. In preparing your essay, you should take the following steps.

Step 1. Read all of the information about the topic. Be sure that you understand the topic and that you write about only the assigned topic.

Step 2. Plan your essay before you write.

Step 3. Use scrap paper to make any notes.

Step 4. Write your essay on a separate sheet of paper.

Step 5. Read what you have written. Make sure that your writing is legible.

Step 6. Check your paragraphing, sentence structure, spelling, punctuation, capitalization, and usage; make any changes that will improve your essay.

TOPIC

> In many jobs, when employees reach a certain age, they must retire. Some people are against having a mandatory retirement age, and others feel that there are reasons to support a required retirement age.
>
> Decide whether you agree or disagree that people should be required to retire from their jobs when they reach a certain age. Write an essay, approximately 200 words long, that presents your opinion about this issue. Be specific, and use examples to support your point of view.

When you take the GED test, you will have 45 minutes to write about the topic question you are assigned. Try to write the essay for this test within 45 minutes. Write legibly and use a ballpoint pen so that your writing will be easy to read. Any notes that you make on scrap paper will not be counted as part of your score.

After you complete this essay, you can judge its effectiveness by using the Essay Scoring Guide and Model Essays in the answer key to score your essay. They will be concerned with how clearly you make the main point of your essay, how thoroughly you support your ideas, and how clear and correct your writing is throughout the composition. You will receive no credit for writing about a question other than the one assigned.

Answers are on pages A-66–A-67.

594 Performance Analysis

WRITING SKILLS, Part II

Directions: After you have used the guidelines in the answer key to score your essay, make a record of your evaluation here.

Write the score for your essay in the box at the right.

List some of the strong points of your essay.

List some of the weak points of your essay.

List improvements that you plan to make when you work on your next essay.

PRACTICE ITEMS 2
Social Studies

Directions: *Choose the one best answer to each question.*

History

Items 1 to 3 are based on the following passage.

In 1777, the Second Continental Congress submitted the Articles of Confederation to the states for ratification. They went into effect in 1781. Under the Articles, a unicameral congress had the power to make war and peace, but it lacked the power to tax, to raise a national army, or to regulate international trade. Each state was equally represented in Congress. There was no provision for a federal judiciary, and the executive consisted of a committee of states, representing all thirteen former colonies.

1. The system of government under the Articles of Confederation resembled that which was to follow under the Constitution in that

   (1) the executive appointed heads of government departments
   (2) the national court could strike down legislative acts
   (3) the legislature was divided into two houses
   (4) the states were represented in the national government
   (5) the national government could impose tariffs on foreign goods

2. Which of the following statements best characterizes government under the Articles of Confederation?

   (1) The national government delegated a certain amount of power to the states.
   (2) The power of the national government was limited and decentralized.
   (3) The executive was given more extensive powers than the legislature.
   (4) The government was based on the principle of no taxation without representation.
   (5) The national government was granted direct authority over citizens.

3. In view of the kind of government established by the Articles of Confederation, which of the following likely occurred?

   (1) The government had problems raising funds to pay Revolutionary War troops who were owed money.
   (2) Southern trade with the British West Indies flourished because of congressional subsidies.
   (3) The new government put down a rebellion of Massachusetts farmers who wanted to halt foreclosure of mortgages.
   (4) Congress placed a tariff on imported goods to help new industries in the Northern states.
   (5) Property qualifications for voting were dropped.

595

Item 4 is based on the following cartoon.

4. Which of the following statements best summarizes the cartoonist's attitude toward President Andrew Jackson?

    (1) Andrew Jackson was being admired for rising above his somewhat uncouth frontier background.
    (2) The president was being criticized for abusing the power of his office.
    (3) Jackson was being praised for remaining aloof from government controversies and disputes.
    (4) The president was being presented as a loyal supporter of the British monarchy.
    (5) President Jackson was being accused of taking on regal airs and ignoring the common folk who elected him.

Item 5 is based on the following passage.

When the leaders of the major powers met at Yalta in 1945, although the Cold War had not yet started, there was already considerable distrust among them. In discussing the organization of the United Nations, they reached a compromise concerning the U.N. Security Council. Any permanent member of the Security Council would have the right to veto a decision that did not meet with its approval. (The major powers were to be the permanent members of the Security Council; other members were to serve on a rotating basis.)

5. Which of the following statements best explains why the veto was acceptable to the major powers.

    (1) The leaders believed in the principle of majority rule.
    (2) The uncertainties of postwar cooperation made it necessary for each of the great powers to protect its own interests.
    (3) The major powers were suspicious of the small powers.
    (4) The strongest nations were the best guardians of world peace.
    (5) The great powers thought it would be easy for them to agree on important issues.

Items 6 to 8 are based on the following passage.

After the Civil War there emerged two views concerning the conditions under which Southern states would be readmitted to the Union. Under the president's Ten Percent Plan, all Confederates, other than high military and civil officers, could be pardoned by taking an oath of loyalty to the Constitution and swearing to accept the abolition of slavery. If they did so, all property they had possessed, other than slaves, would be restored to them. After 10 percent of the 1860 voters in a state had sworn allegiance, these voters could write a new state constitution and send members to Congress.

Congressional proposals were more severe and called for more changes. The First Reconstruction Act divided the South into five military districts governed by generals. Constitutional conventions were to be held in each state. For purposes of electing delegates to these conventions and of holding subsequent elections, all adult males were to be given suffrage, with the exception of Confederates who had held public office before the war. The state governments that would be elected under the new constitutions had to ratify the recently proposed Fourteenth Amendment, which extended citizenship to blacks and granted them equal protection under the law. Only then would military rule be ended and the states readmitted.

Reconstruction initially proceeded under the Ten Percent Plan. But by 1867 congressional Reconstruction held sway.

6. Which of the following provisions were common to both presidential and congressional plans for Reconstruction?

   (1) military control of the South until new state constitutions had been written
   (2) prohibition of slavery and restrictions on certain high-ranking Confederates
   (3) citizenship and voting rights for blacks
   (4) restoration of property to Southerners and federal assumption of Southern debts incurred during the war
   (5) assistance for freed slaves and prohibition of sharecropping

7. Which of the following was the most likely effect of the Ten Percent Plan on freed blacks?

   (1) their admission into the electorate in large numbers
   (2) their return to former conditions of servitude
   (3) the passage of state laws restricting their rights
   (4) the election of black legislators on state and federal levels of government
   (5) a vast improvement in their standard of living

8. Based on the passage, the congressional plan for Reconstruction was most supportive of the needs of

   (1) Southern planters
   (2) Southern poor whites
   (3) Northern businessmen
   (4) freed blacks
   (5) former Confederate officers

Item 9 is based on the following cartoon.

McCutcheon in the Chicago Tribune

9. Which of the following conclusions is best supported by the information suggested by this early World War I cartoon?

   (1) European nations depended on American trade for their survival.
   (2) The American government's position of neutrality was not anchored in public support.
   (3) The U.S. government insisted that the warring nations transport American purchases in their own ships.
   (4) Great Britain respected American neutrality.
   (5) American neutrality policy was almost certainly doomed to failure.

Items 10 to 12 are based on the following passage.

Farmers, many of whom had heavy debts, wanted higher prices for their crops and a reduction of mortgage payments on their lands. Businesses wanted high tariffs to protect their products from foreign competition, a steady supply of labor, and a sound currency to support continued investment. Most middle-class Americans wanted the value of their savings, insurance, and investments to be secure. Workers, who were generally on fixed wages, wanted their wages to have the purchasing power to supply them with life's necessities.

Against this background, the 1896 presidential campaign between Democrat William Jennings Bryan and Republican William McKinley was fought over the issue of the free and limited coinage of silver. Free silver would have had an inflationary effect on the economy: With more money in circulation, the real value of the dollar would go down and prices would rise. The anti-silverite candidate, McKinley, won the election. However, the advocates of free silver found their problems eased by the discovery of gold in Alaska and elsewhere and its introduction into the U.S. economy.

10. Which of the following statements best summarizes the purpose of the passage?

    (1) to explain the effect of unlimited coinage of silver
    (2) to discuss the reasons for farmers' dissastisfaction
    (3) to analyze late nineteenth-century economic conditions in the United States
    (4) to show how the discovery of gold fields affected American politics
    (5) to present the main issue of the 1896 presidential campaign in terms of the needs of the electorate

11. Which of the following groups was most likely to support the free-silver policy of the Democratic Party in 1896?

    (1) workers on fixed wages
    (2) middle-class Americans concerned about their savings
    (3) industrialists needing investors
    (4) consumers seeking low-priced commodities
    (5) farmers faced with high mortgage rates

12. Which of the following statements best describes the impact of the discovery of gold on the American economy?

    (1) It increased the money supply.
    (2) It reduced the cost of living.
    (3) It upset the balance of trade.
    (4) It benefited people living on fixed incomes.
    (5) It threw the country into a depression.

Item 13 is based on the following information.

In 1774, Parliament passed the Coercive Acts, closing the port of Boston. The acts also permitted the royal governor of Massachusetts to appoint members to local councils and juries and to control the agendas of town meetings. The colonists perceived these acts as denying them certain freedoms to govern themselves—freedoms they had enjoyed for more than a hundred years. In response, they organized a meeting of delegates to seek ways to protect their traditional rights as Englishmen. The meeting became known as the First Continental Congress. The Congress issued a Declaration of Resolves, which was sent to George III.

13. Based on the passage, which of the following would most likely be found in the Declaration of Resolves?

    (1) assertions of independence from Britain
    (2) demands for the restoration of colonial self-government
    (3) arguments that the British Empire be dissolved
    (4) discussion of how colonial rights should differ from the rights of Englishmen
    (5) recognition of the need for colonial contributions to the cost of defending the British Empire.

Items 14 and 15 are based on the following cartoon.

14. Which of the following statements best describes the message conveyed by the cartoon?

(1) Eastern and Western leaders are racing to see who will be first to control the spread of nuclear weapons, and Third World countries will judge who the winner is.
(2) Nuclear weapons are like a genie in a bottle.
(3) Leaders of the Soviet Union and the United States are forcing nuclear weapons on reluctant Third World countries.
(4) Leaders of the East and West are trying to limit the nuclear arms race while Third World nations are seeking to develop their own nuclear weapons.
(5) The superpowers and the Third World nations are working together to "bottle up" nuclear arms.

15. Which of the following statements is best supported by the cartoon?

(1) Cooperation between the superpowers could successfully end the arms race.
(2) The major problem of arms control is the spread of nuclear weapons.
(3) The nuclear arms race has shifted the balance of power to the Third World.
(4) Nuclear warfare is probably inevitable.
(5) No Third World nation as yet has nuclear arms.

Items 16 to 17 are based on the following passage.

In 1895, Cuban rebels rose up against their Spanish colonial rulers. A sensationalist press and the blowing up of the U.S. battleship *Maine* in the Havana harbor stirred Americans to demand that the government declare war against Spain. For several years, President McKinley withstood the war fever, but in 1898, he finally asked Congress for a declaration of war. The Teller Amendment was attached to that declaration. It pledged the United States to support not only freedom from Spain but an independent government in Cuba. The United States easily won the the Spanish-American War, and Cuba was freed of Spanish control.

In 1902, the Platt Amendment was passed by Congress as part of an army appropriation bill. Under strong pressure from the United States, the Cubans included its content in their new constitution. The measure limited Cuba's right to conduct international relations, to borrow money, or to yield territory to foreign powers. It empowered the United States to intervene in Cuba for the protection of "life, property, and individual liberty." And it allowed the United States to lease a naval base at strategically important Guantanamo Bay.

16. Based on the passage, which of the following statements best describes the relationship between the Teller and Platt amendments?

(1) The Platt Amendment implements the provisions of the Teller Amendment.
(2) The two amendments have little in common.
(3) The provisions of the Platt Amendment contradict those of the Teller Amendment.
(4) The two amendments together formed the basis for early twentieth-century U.S. foreign policy regarding the Western Hemisphere.
(5) Both amendments changed provisions of the U.S. Constitution.

17. Which of the following conclusions is best supported by the passage?

(1) Between 1895 and 1902, imperialists were becoming less powerful in the U.S. government.
(2) In 1902, a goal of U.S. foreign policy was to make Cuba and the Caribbean an American sphere of influence.
(3) In 1902, a major concern of U.S. foreign policy was improving relations with Latin American governments.
(4) By late 1898, the Spanish-American War had become unpopular in the United States.
(5) From 1898 to 1902, the influence of American business interests in Cuba declined.

Geography

Items 18 to 19 are based on the following map.

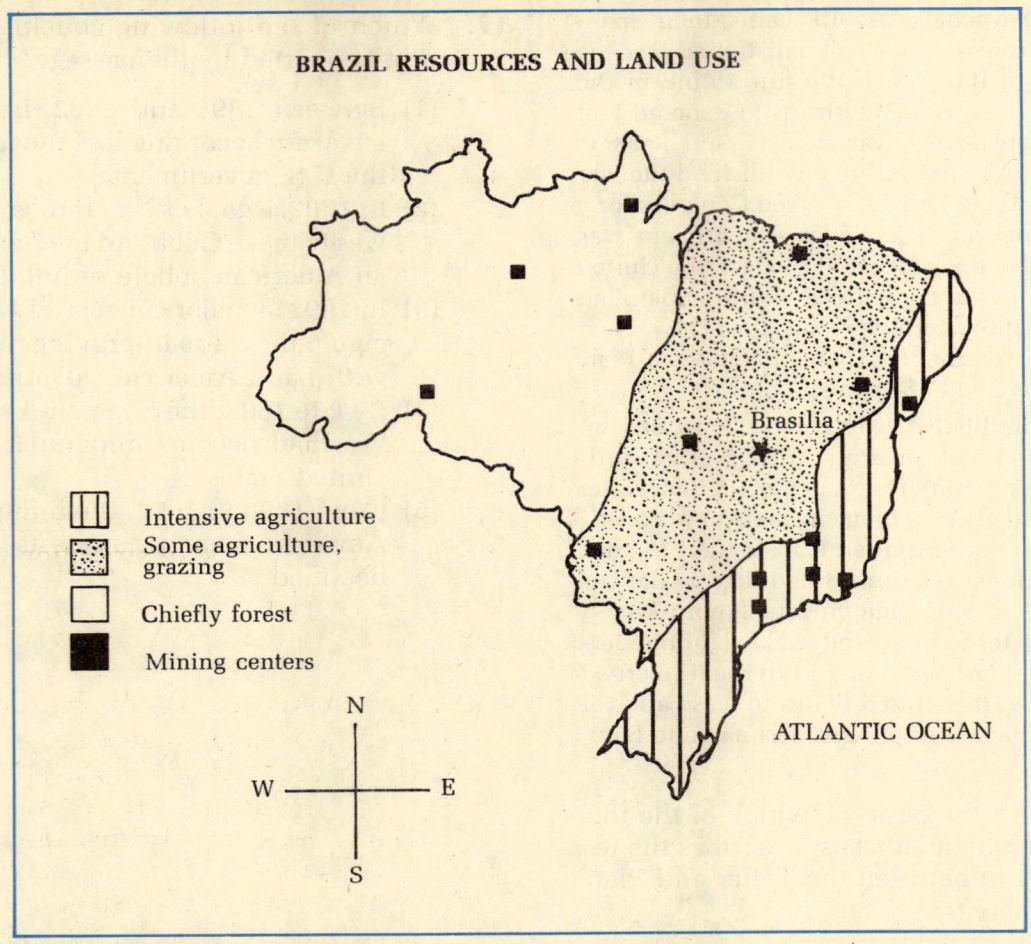

BRAZIL RESOURCES AND LAND USE

- Intensive agriculture
- Some agriculture, grazing
- Chiefly forest
- Mining centers

Brasilia

ATLANTIC OCEAN

18. Based on the data in the map, which part of Brazil would likely have the lowest population density?

    (1) the northwest
    (2) the northeast
    (3) the Atlantic coast
    (4) the southeast
    (5) the center

19. Which of the following statements about Brazil is supported by the map?

    (1) Brazil mainly exports agricultural products.
    (2) One of the chief obstacles to Brazil's growth is its lack of resources.
    (3) Much of Brazil's land remains underused.
    (4) Brazil's resources are inadequate in view of the size of its population.
    (5) Farmers and mining companies must often compete for the same land.

20. *Head-link cities* link a country to the rest of the world. Which of the following statements do NOT describe the activities of a head-link city?

    (1) The city of Lagos served to give British colonists access to the interior of Nigeria.
    (2) Australia's agricultural products are shipped out of Sydney, destined in particular for Western Europe.
    (3) Much of the oil used by Dutch industries passes through the port of Rotterdam.
    (4) Many American goods are exported through New York.
    (5) The major link for transportation of goods between the Eastern states and the Midwest is provided by Chicago.

Items 21 to 23 are based on the following passage.

In the hydrologic cycle, water is evaporated from the ocean and land surfaces. It condenses into the water droplets of clouds, falls to the earth as precipitation, and is once again evaporated.

By subtracting the amount of evaporation in an area from the amount of precipitation, we can figure out the amount of surface water—that is, the area's water supply. There are significant differences between regions. In the United States, for example, if a north-south line is run through Kansas City, we find great differences between areas east and west of that line. East of the line, precipitation exceeds evaporation. West of the line, in contrast, with the exception of the Pacific Northwest and northern California, evaporation exceeds precipitation.

Nowhere is water supply guaranteed. Any area can be hit by a period of drought—that is, by extreme lack of precipitation. The northeast suffered from severe drought in the early sixties, as did states from Michigan to California in the late seventies.

Patterns of human use of water do not always correspond to patterns of water distribution. That is, areas that require a lot of water are not always those that have an ample supply. Sometimes human activities are limited by water supply. Moreover, the demand for water by agriculture, industry, and people in general is growing. As this occurs, development of certain areas may be limited by lack of water, and numerous other areas may face frequent shortages. We will have to continue to find ways to overcome, or accommodate ourselves to, the problems of water supply and distribution.

21. Based on the passage, which of the following statements best summarizes the reason for the water distribution problem?

(1) The possibility of droughts means that an area's water supply is never guaranteed.
(2) Areas that don't have extensive water supplies are often heavy users of water.
(3) Agriculture, industry, and individuals are consuming too much water.
(4) The hydrologic cycle distributes water unevenly.
(5) Much of the Earth's surface is covered by oceans, and water from oceans is not readily usable.

22. One likely result of the different patterns exhibited by Eastern and Western states is

(1) the greater possibility of droughts in the Eastern states
(2) a greater abundance of rivers and streams in the Western states
(3) the concentration of agriculture in the Western states
(4) the concentration of industry in the Eastern states
(5) the extensive use of irrigation for farming in the Western states

23. Which of the following statements about water supply and distribution is NOT supported by the passage?

(1) There are sources of water other than the hydrologic cycle.
(2) Water supply patterns can vary over time as well as across space.
(3) Humans contribute to water supply and distribution problems.
(4) Technology has helped people deal with water supply and distribution problems to some extent.
(5) Problems of water supply can be expected to become more severe in the future.

Test 2: Social Studies

Item 24 is based on the following map.

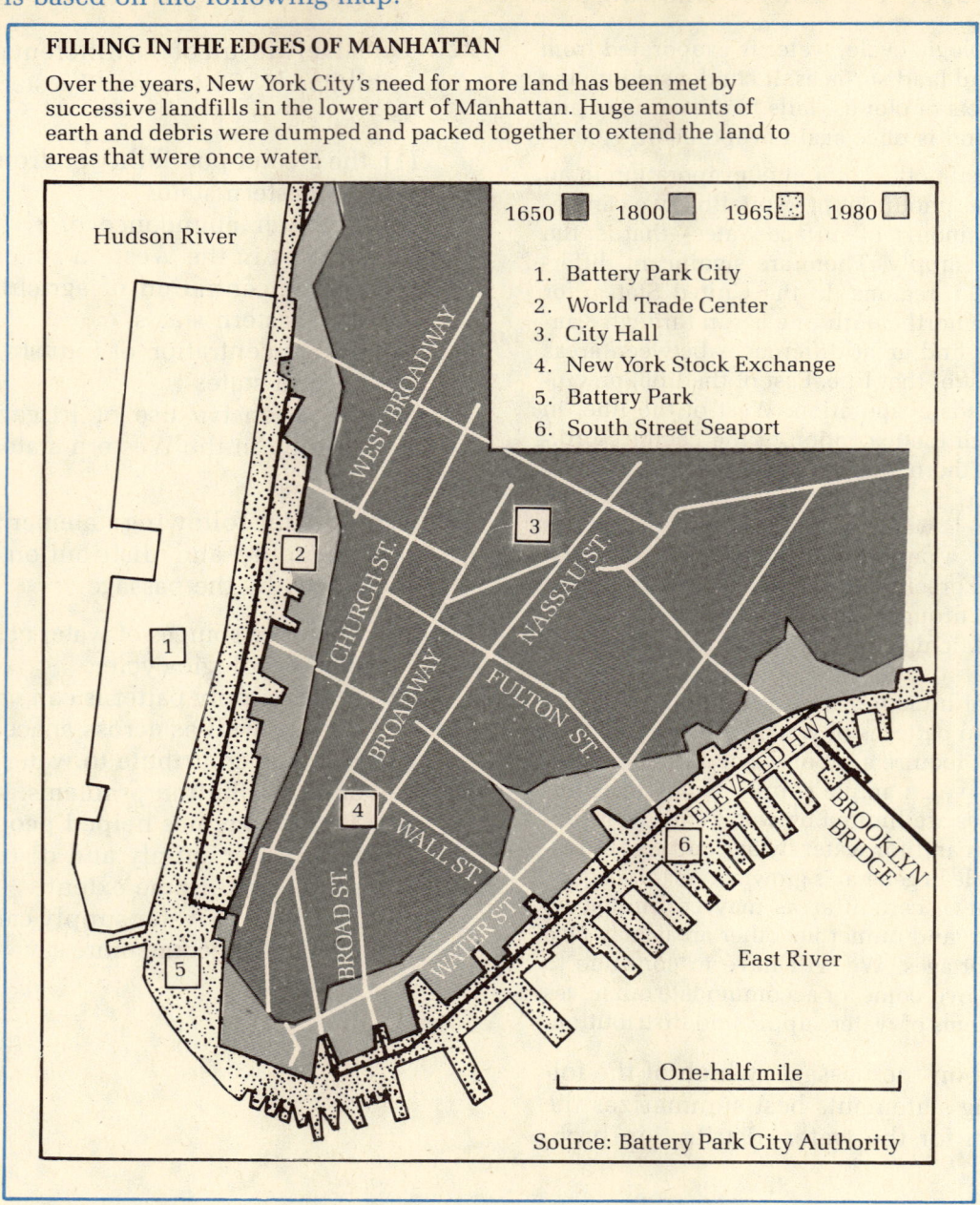

FILLING IN THE EDGES OF MANHATTAN

Over the years, New York City's need for more land has been met by successive landfills in the lower part of Manhattan. Huge amounts of earth and debris were dumped and packed together to extend the land to areas that were once water.

1650 1800 1965 1980

1. Battery Park City
2. World Trade Center
3. City Hall
4. New York Stock Exchange
5. Battery Park
6. South Street Seaport

Hudson River

East River

One-half mile

Source: Battery Park City Authority

24. A visitor to New York in 1850 would NOT have found

  (1) a view of the East River from Water Street.
  (2) the entire present-day length of Fulton Street.
  (3) the site of The New York Stock Exchange.
  (4) West Street.
  (5) the corner of Broad and Water Streets.

Item 25 is based on the following information.

In South America, as elsewhere in the Third World, geographical factors have often hindered, or complicated, development. The Andean mountain system, for example, splits the countries through which it runs into several regions apiece. Most rivers in South America are short; the Amazon River, the major exception, flows largely through sparsely inhabited jungle.

25. The problem presented in the passage is best described as one of

  (1) insufficient natural resources
  (2) geographic isolation
  (3) low population densities
  (4) lack of navigable rivers
  (5) extreme climatic conditions

Economics

Items 26 to 29 are based on the following information.

Competition among firms in the marketplace is the basic element underlying a capitalist economy. However, there are a number of situations in which firms or other entities are able to limit competition. Listed below are five such situations.

  monopoly—firm is the only supplier of a product for which there is no substitute

  oligopoly—a small number of firms dominate the market for a product

  cartel—firms or other entities act together to regulate production and prices of their products, in order to eliminate competition and/or raise prices

  trust—firms formally merge by means of a common board of trustees, which manages the member companies in such a way as to eliminate competition

  corner—firms or individuals gain virtually complete control of a commodity, so that buyers may be forced to pay exorbitant prices

Each of the following descriptions exemplifies one of the five situations listed above. The categories may be used more than once, but no question has more than one best answer.

26. In its infancy the U.S. automobile industry comprised more than 80 firms. Over the years, mergers and failures greatly reduced the field. By the early 1960's, three firms accounted for about 90 percent of total sales. This situation involves a(n)

  (1) monopoly   (4) trust
  (2) oligopoly (5) corner
  (3) cartel

27. In 1973 a group of major oil-producing nations were able, in large part by deliberately restricting output, to quadruple the price per barrel commanded by oil, all within the short space of six months. This situation involves a(n)

  (1) monopoly   (4) trust
  (2) oligopoly (5) corner
  (3) cartel

28. In the 1880s John D. Rockefeller combined various oil companies under the control of one large company he created for this purpose. This situation involves a(n)

  (1) monopoly   (4) trust
  (2) oligopoly (5) corner
  (3) cartel

29. If numerous electric companies serviced an area, the result would be inefficiency and higher, not lower, costs. Thus, state and local governments allow service to be handled by a single firm, although under the supervision of a public utility commission. This situation involves a(n)

  (1) monopoly   (4) trust
  (2) oligopoly (5) corner
  (3) cartel

Items 30 to 31 are based on the following graph.

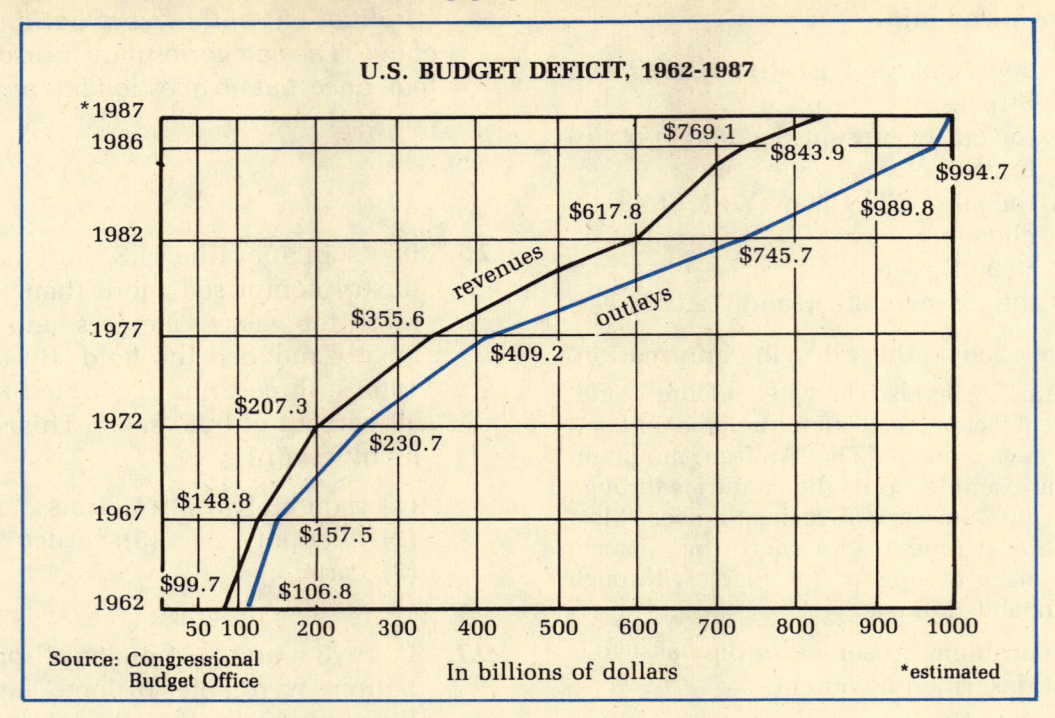

U.S. BUDGET DEFICIT, 1962-1987

[Graph showing revenues and outlays in billions of dollars from 1962 to 1987:
- 1962: $99.7 (revenues), $106.8 (outlays)
- 1967: $148.8, $157.5
- 1972: $207.3, $230.7
- 1977: $355.6, $409.2
- 1982: $617.8, $745.7
- 1986: $769.1, $989.8
- 1987: $843.9, $994.7]

Source: Congressional Budget Office
In billions of dollars
*estimated

30. Based on the graph, which of the following statements is true?

    (1) Revenues and outlays remain fairly constant over the period shown.
    (2) Revenues and outlays fluctuate up and down over the years in ways that are difficult to predict.
    (3) Revenues exceed outlays in each of the years shown.
    (4) Outlays exceed revenues in each of the years shown.
    (5) Prior to 1962, no data are available concerning the U.S. budget.

31. The largest deficits shown in this graph would be associated with which of the following U.S. presidents?
    (1) Kennedy
    (2) Johnson
    (3) Nixon
    (4) Carter
    (5) Reagan

Items 32 to 35 are based on the following passage.

Dramatic changes have been taking place in industry in the United States over the last few decades—changes that have great significance for the nation's work force. Manufacturing industries (that is, industries that produce goods) have run into troubling times. Industries that produce services, on the other hand, have undergone an explosive growth. And service industries are expected to account for nine out of every ten new jobs created between now and the end of the century.

There are several factors contributing to this shift from a manufacturing to a service economy. A very important factor is that U.S. companies in all industries—including manufacturing industries—are taking advantage of technological advances that allow them to work more efficiently. This technology often requires service workers, such as computers programmers. A number of developments that are social, rather than strictly economic, also contribute. For example, the growing number of old people in America means there is a growing need for service workers in the health care field.

But, as already suggested, there is another factor behind the shift: The manufacturing sector has failed to expand. The main reason for this lack of expansion is that U.S. manufacturing companies, once dominant, have in recent decades had trouble competing with their foreign counterparts. They have lost a good part of their markets to Japanese and Western European companies in particular. Unless U.S. manufacturing companies make the kinds of decisions that will restore their competitiveness, the U.S. manufacturing sector can be expected to remain weak.

32. Based on the passage, those entering the labor force could be advised to consider all the following careers except

 (1) computer programmer
 (2) social worker
 (3) textile worker
 (4) car mechanic
 (5) hair stylist

33. Based on the passage, which of the following could best be cited as a small example of why the manufacturing sector has no longer been expanding rapidly?

 (1) An English vistor to the United States buys a raincoat in New York City but selects one made in England.
 (2) A restaurant owner in Detroit buys all vegetables for her menu from a store in Canada.
 (3) An American manufacturing company decides to build its new plant in Taiwan instead of in the United States.
 (4) A family in St. Louis, Missouri, buys an automobile made in West Germany as the family vehicle.
 (5) An established New York manufacturer of men's hats ceases production because the market for hats has shrunk.

34. Which of the following conclusions can be drawn from the manufacturing industry's increasing use of new technologies?

 (1) The need for manufacturing workers will probably increase again.
 (2) The U.S. manufacturing industries will regain their competitiveness.
 (3) The kinds of goods produced by manufacturing industries will change.
 (4) The manufacturing sector will begin to grow faster than the service sector.
 (5) The manufacturing sector will produce more goods with fewer workers.

35. On the basis of the passage, it can be concluded that the number and kinds of jobs available for U.S. workers in the years to come will be affected by all of the following EXCEPT

 (1) developments in the economies of other countries
 (2) developments in American society
 (3) technological changes
 (4) government legislation regulating business
 (5) the kinds of decisions made by U.S. businesses

Items 36 to 37 are based on the following graph.

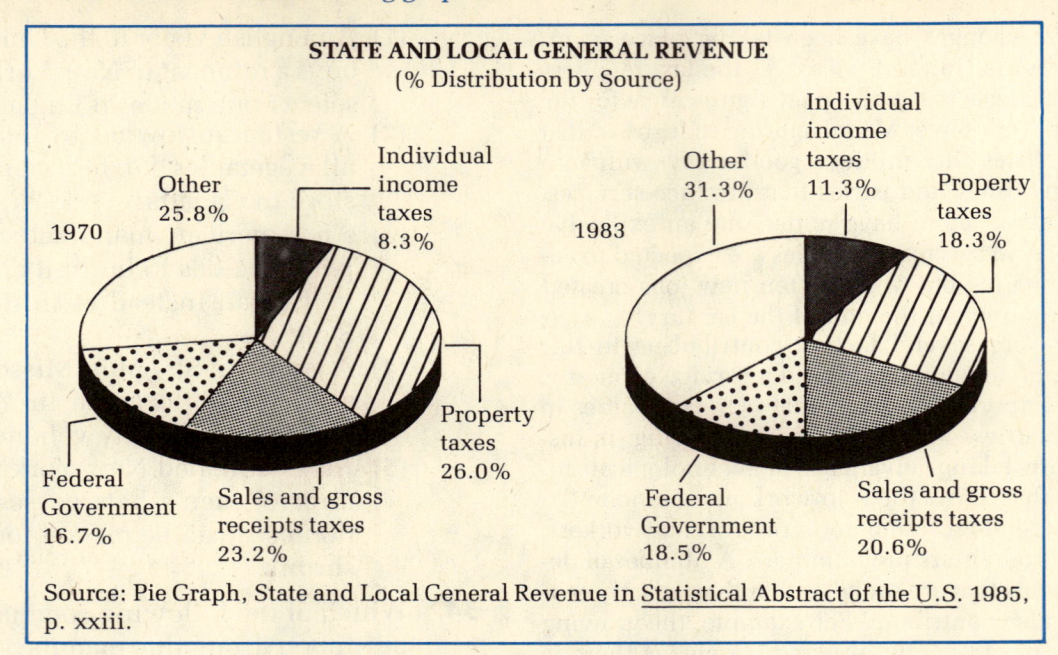

STATE AND LOCAL GENERAL REVENUE
(% Distribution by Source)

1970
- Other 25.8%
- Individual income taxes 8.3%
- Property taxes 26.0%
- Sales and gross receipts taxes 23.2%
- Federal Government 16.7%

1983
- Other 31.3%
- Individual income taxes 11.3%
- Property taxes 18.3%
- Sales and gross receipts taxes 20.6%
- Federal Government 18.5%

Source: Pie Graph, State and Local General Revenue in Statistical Abstract of the U.S. 1985, p. xxiii.

36. The source of state and local general revenues that showed the greatest decline between 1970 and 1983 was

    (1) federal government outlays
    (2) property taxes
    (3) sales and gross receipts taxes
    (4) individual income taxes
    (5) other sources

37. Which of the following factors might partially explain why one source of state and local revenues exhibited a greater decline than any other betwen 1970 and 1983?

    (1) rising unemployment rates
    (2) reduced use of state and local highways
    (3) fewer housing starts and more abandoned buildings
    (4) less consumer spending
    (5) mandated cuts in the federal budget

Political Science

Items 38 to 39 are based on the following passage.

When Congress sends the president a bill, or proposed law, that displeases him, he has two alternatives to signing it. First, he may veto the bill,—that is, return it to Congress with a message explaining his objections. Congress will often try to write bills in a way that will be acceptable to the president, since overriding a veto requires a two-thirds vote of both houses. Alternatively, instead of vetoing a bill, the president may let it sit on his desk and do nothing with it. If Congress adjourns within ten days, the bill will not become a law. This is called a pocket veto.

Often Congress will attach riders, or extraneous provisions, to bills the president thinks are important. The president, unlike many state governors, does not have an item veto, the power to strike out those parts of a bill he does not like. He must accept or reject the entire measure, for he lacks the power to edit what Congress has written.

38. Which of the following statements is implied in the passage?

(1) Presidents are more powerful than state governors.
(2) Bills become law when the president signs them.
(3) Presidents propose laws.
(4) Bills automatically become laws once they reach the president.
(5) Presidents have unlimited veto power.

39. Which of the following statements is supported by information in the passage?

(1) Presidents have often used their veto power to judge acts of Congress unconstitutional.
(2) Pocket vetoes are frequently overridden by a two-thirds vote of Congress.
(3) Presidents play a more important role in the legislative process than Congress does.
(4) Lack of an item veto has not prevented presidents from exerting influence on the legislative process.
(5) Riders may force presidents to sign bills they might otherwise veto.

Item 40 is based on the following information.

Ranked in order of importance, education, income, and age are the most influential factors in determining whether people will vote in elections. The more education people have, the more likely they are to vote. Those with higher incomes and higher status careers are more inclined to vote than those with lower incomes or lower status jobs. Older people (with the exception of the aged and infirm) are more apt to vote than younger people. Racial minorities turn out in lower numbers at the polls than whites do.

40. Which of the following statements is best supported by the passage?

(1) Those who most need help from government are most likely to vote.
(2) Nonvoting is a random behavior.
(3) Voting is unrelated to sociological factors such as class and wealth.
(4) Dynamic leadership would get nonvoters to vote.
(5) A significant portion of the population is underrepresented in the U.S. government.

Items 41 and 42 are based on the following passage.

The Supreme Court exercises judicial review; that is, it determines whether acts of the Congress are constitutional. This raises the question of how the Constitution should be interpreted. Thoughout American history to the present, there have been two basic views. Strict constructionists hold that the Constitution should be interpreted narrowly according to the intent of its framers and literally according to the words the framers used. This view has been used to justify the status quo. Loose constructionists claim that the document should be interpreted broadly according to the general purposes of the framers and that its words should be understood within a modern context. This view has adapted the Constitution to shifting national needs.

41. Which of the following statements is NOT an implication of the strict constructionist perspective?

(1) The Constitution's words have the same meaning for all time.
(2) The Court should follow the dictates of public opinion.
(3) The intent of the framers can be readily discovered.
(4) The framers intended their words to be taken at face value.
(5) The needs and interests of the nation are unchanging.

42. Which of the following excerpts from judicial opinions is most in keeping with the loose constructionist view?

(1) "The Constitution speaks not only in the same words but with the same meaning and intent with which it spoke when it came from the hands of the Framers."—Chief Justice Taney

(2) "[T]he judicial branch has only one duty—to lay the article of the Constitution which is invoked beside the statute which is challenged and to decide whether the latter squares with the former."—Justice Roberts

(3) "A Constitution that is viewed as only what the judges say it is is no longer a constitution in the true sense."—Attorney General Meese

(4) "However, the Constitution does not vest in this Court the authority to strike down laws because they do not meet our standards of desirable social policy, 'wisdom,' or 'common sense.'"—Chief Justice Burger

(5) "We must never forget that it is a constitution we are expounding . . . [a] constitution intended to endure for ages to come, and consequently to be adapted to the various crises of human affairs."—Chief Justice Marshall

Items 43 to 44 are based on the following passage.

According to the Constitution, when government officials are formally accused of having committed "high crimes and misdemeanors," they are impeached before the House of Representatives. Then they are tried in the Senate, a procedure which determines their guilt or innocence. An important test of the proper use of this congressional power came with the proceedings against President Andrew Johnson in 1868. Johnson was impeached by an opposition House, on the grounds that he had violated the Tenure of Office Act. But the reasons for his impeachment were in fact largely political, and he was acquitted of the charges. To the present, a total of 65 people have appeared in impeachment proceedings before the House of Representatives. Of these, only 14 have been impeached and five convicted. When officials are found guilty, they are removed from office.

43. Which of the following statements is supported by the passage?

(1) A finding of guilt in the congressional procedure requires even stronger evidence than is required for a finding of guilt in a criminal case.

(2) Impeachment is similar to an indictment because it determines whether or not there is probable cause for a trial.

(3) After the House of Representatives impeaches a government official, that person is removed from office.

(4) Removal from office is an option that may be exercised when a government official is found guilty of "high crimes and misdemeanors."

(5) Congress has made frequent use of its power to impeach and try government officials.

44. Which of the following statements best describes the purpose of the impeachment process?

(1) to rid the government of incompetent officials

(2) to remove members of the opposition party from government

(3) to deny seats to unqualified members of Congress

(4) to make government officials loyal to Congress

(5) to find a remedy for officials who abuse their power

Items 45 and 46 are based on the following graph.

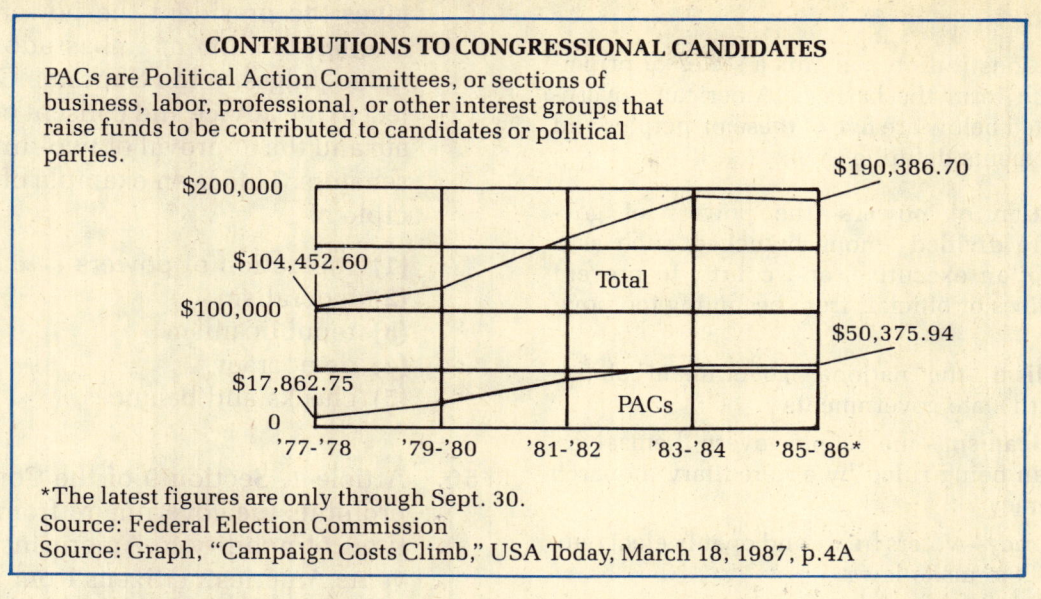

CONTRIBUTIONS TO CONGRESSIONAL CANDIDATES

PACs are Political Action Committees, or sections of business, labor, professional, or other interest groups that raise funds to be contributed to candidates or political parties.

```
$200,000                                          $190,386.70
         $104,452.60
$100,000              Total
                                                  $50,375.94
         $17,862.75
       0              PACs
         '77-'78  '79-'80  '81-'82  '83-'84  '85-'86*
```

*The latest figures are only through Sept. 30.
Source: Federal Election Commission
Source: Graph, "Campaign Costs Climb," USA Today, March 18, 1987, p.4A

45. Which of the following statements about campaign contributions between 1977–1978 and 1985–1986 is not supported by the graph?

(1) Contributions to congressional campaigns increased significantly.
(2) PAC contributions more than doubled.
(3) Average PAC contributions provided about a fourth of the money raised by candidates during the last year shown on the graph.
(4) The sharpest increases of both PAC and non-PAC contributions occurred between 1979 and 1984.
(5) Contributions from other sources increased at a faster rate than contributions from PACs.

46. Which of the following statements is best supported by the data in the graph?

(1) PACs are the main source of campaign contributions.
(2) PACs are exerting too much influence on votes in Congress.
(3) Congressional campaigns are becoming so expensive that only the rich can afford to run for office.
(4) Campaign law limits on PAC contributions need to be rewritten.
(5) PACs are playing a greater role in the financing of political campaigns.

47. In many states, there are a number of mechanisms by which voters can play an active role in the legislative process at the state and local levels. One such mechanism is the referendum. The referendum enables voters to accept or reject proposed legislation. Which of the following actions offers the best example of participation in a referendum?

(1) circulating a petition to put an amendment to the state's constitution extending the debt limit on the ballot
(2) pressing a lever in a voting booth to indicate support of a measure requiring the fluoridation of water.
(3) signing a petition to remove a local judge from office
(4) selecting one of two nominees to run as the party's candidate
(5) writing a letter to a senator asking for a change in the speed limit on federal highways

Items 48 to 51 are based on the following information.

The U.S. Constitution contains a series of principles which form the basis of American government. Listed below are five of these principles and brief statements defining them.

separation of powers—the powers of governmnt are divided among branches, such as a legislature, an executive, and courts, to prevent public offices or officials from becoming too powerful

federalism—the national government shares power with state governments

republicanism—the people govern themselves, rather than being ruled by a hereditary monarch or aristocracy

democracy—voters freely and openly elect public officials to make laws

checks and balances—each of the three branches of the government can limit and/or offset the actions of the others, so that no one branch becomes too powerful and each can share in some activities of the others

Each of the following specific provisions of the U.S. Constitution illustrates one of the basic principles described. Choose the principle that is most likely to apply in each example. The principles may be used more than once in the set of items, but no one question has more than one best answer.

48. Article 1, Section 6 of the Constitution prohibits senators and representatives from holding any other public office in the government while they are serving in Congress and prevents people who are holding other public offices from serving in Congress at the same time. This is an example of the principle of

(1) separation of powers
(2) federalism
(3) republicanism
(4) democracy
(5) checks and balances

49. Article 2, Section 2 of the Constitution gives the president the power to make treaties, to appoint ambassadors, and to name judges to the Supreme Court subject to the advice and consent of the Senate and the approval of two-thirds of the senators. This is an example of the principle of

(1) separation of powers
(2) federalism
(3) republicanism
(4) democracy
(5) checks and balances

50. Article 1, Section 9 of the Constitution prohibits the government from granting titles of nobility to Americans and prevents American citizens from accepting aristocratic titles from foreign governments without the consent of Congress. This is an example of the principle of

(1) separation of powers
(2) federalism
(3) republicanism
(4) democracy
(5) checks and balances

51. Article 5 of the Constitution specifies that constitutional amendments must be proposed by two-thirds of both houses of Congress or two-thirds of the state legislatures and must be ratified by three-quarters of state legislatures or of special state conventions called for the purpose of ratification. This is an example of the principle of

(1) separation of powers
(2) federalism
(3) republicanism
(4) democracy
(5) checks and balances

Behavioral Science

Items 52 to 53 are based on the following passage.

Research on newborns shows that they have very different temperaments. Infants differ from one another in many ways, including the length of their attention span, their level of activity, how responsive they are to new stimuli, and how adaptable they are. Follow-up research has shown that these differences remain throughout childhood.

Other research suggests that temperament is not the only major factor influencing a child's development. From infancy on, the way the parents respond to their child's temperament can also be very important. Consider a child who feels uncomfortable in new situations. Parents' understanding of this fact and supportiveness of the child in such situations can help her or him become well adjusted and happy. If, on the other hand, parents fail to understand and put pressure on her or him, she or he might, as a result, withdraw further.

52. A parenting manual influenced by the research cited might advise parents of infants to

   (1) try to know and understand their infant as an individual
   (2) establish and maintain regular routines for their infant
   (3) let instinct guide them in providing care for their infants
   (4) be well-informed about current research in child development
   (5) provide their infant with plenty of stimulation

53. People have often debated whether heredity (nature) or family situation and other environmental factors (nurture) primarily influence human development. Which of the following claims is best supported by the research cited in the passage?

   (1) Nature is the primary influence on human development.
   (2) Nurture is the primary influence on human development.
   (3) Nature and nurture, acting together, are both primary influences on development.
   (4) The relative importance of nature and nurture will depend on the particular society.
   (5) Neither nature nor nurture can be considered a primary influence on development; other factors are more important.

Item 54 is based on the following information.

There are several basic research methods in behavioral science, including field studies, experiments, and surveys. In a survey, for example, people are asked about their opinions or behavior. Each method produces a different kind of data. Therefore, the method used in a study will depend on the hypotheses to be tested.

54. Which of the following hypotheses could best be tested using a survey?

   (1) People unconsciously react toward strangers in different ways, depending on the strangers' appearance.
   (2) People pride themselves on being independent, but often their actions are governed by a desire to conform to their peers.
   (3) Over the past one hundred years, the crime rate in the United States has risen dramatically.
   (4) Most Americans believe that stronger gun control legislation is needed.
   (5) There is little real possibility of a nuclear war.

Items 55 to 58 are based on the following graph.

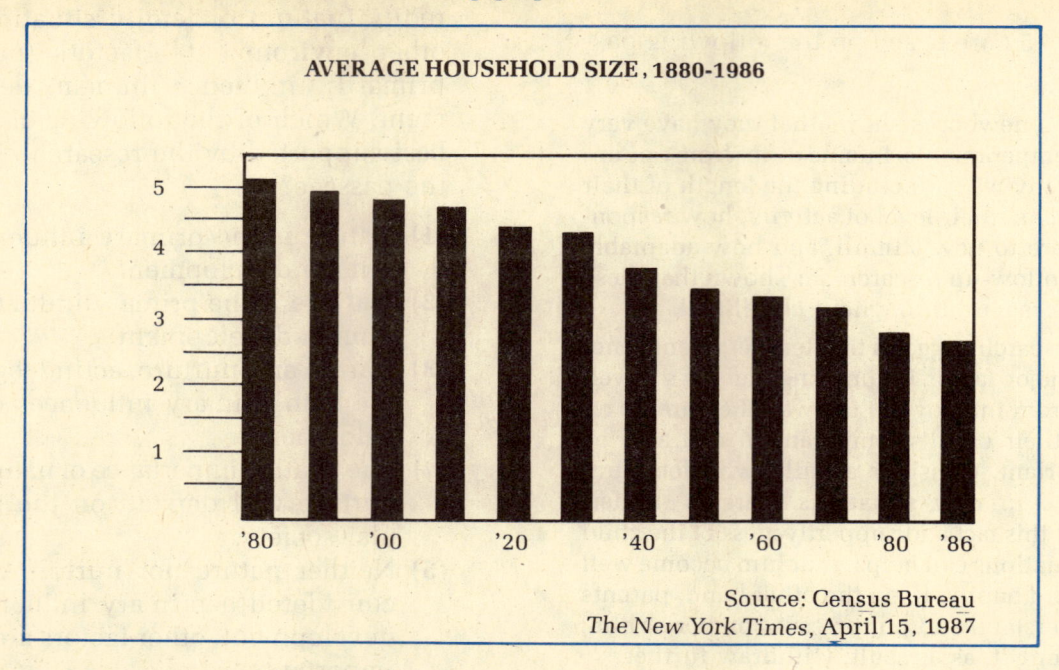

AVERAGE HOUSEHOLD SIZE, 1880-1986

Source: Census Bureau
The New York Times, April 15, 1987

The Census Bureau defines a household as all the people who live together in a house or apartment, whether or not they are related by blood or marriage.

55. Which of the following statements is best supported by the information in the graph?

(1) The trend toward a decrease in average household size has reversed itself in recent years.
(2) The trend toward a decrease in average household size appears to be continuing.
(3) Household size remains stable during periods of economic depression, when available income is smaller.
(4) The increase in the population of the United States has led to a decrease in average household size.
(5) One-person households, although common today, were virtually nonexistent in nineteenth-century America.

56. The decrease in household size over the last 100 years is a product of many demographic causes. Which of the following is NOT a cause?

(1) Families are having fewer children.
(2) The percentage of the population over age 65 has increased.
(3) Immigration to the United States has steadily decreased.
(4) The number of single-parent households has increased.
(5) More adults are choosing to live alone.

57. On the basis of the data in the figure, what advice might a market researcher offer a client?

(1) Use more TV advertising to market your product.
(2) Adapt your packaging to attract younger buyers.
(3) Target your products to a middle-class audience.
(4) Assign sales people to market your product house-to-house.
(5) Package your products for home consumption in smaller units.

58. The data in the figure ultimately reflect the personal decisions of many individuals regarding the life-style they prefer, etc. Each decision involves judgments and values as well as assessments of economic and social conditions. An emphasis on which of the following values would likely contribute to the trend shown in the graph?

    (1) loyalty to friends and family
    (2) personal and collective security
    (3) personal rights and freedom
    (4) cooperation with others
    (5) fear of loneliness and isolation

Items 59 to 62 are based on the following article.

An increasing amount of sociological, psychological, and political research into how citizens decide to cast their ballots is confirming what astute politicians already knew: personality matters. In recent elections in particular, traditional concerns such as a candidate's stand on the issues, party affiliation, voting record, and philosophy have often seemed less important than questions about what kind of person the candidate is.

Many psychologists think the phenomenon is on the rise because of television. The camera brings viewers so close to politicians that they react on a personal and emotional level, rather than analyze the issues involved.

The University of Michigan's Institute for Social Research has documented the declining importance of party affiliation over the past three decades. Its surveys show that the proportion of people voting a straight ticket has dropped from nearly two-thirds in 1960 to only a third today.

In 1980 the Institute asked voters to name the principal character traits of each of the six leading presidential contenders, and then to explain how they felt about each contender. These character judgments proved much more reliable than party affiliation or issues in predicting who a voter would support.

Adapted from "Winning Hearts Not Minds," *Discover*, Nov. 1984.

59. Based on the article, which response to a televised debate among presidential candidates best illustrates the impact of television on voter behavior? I won't vote for a candidate who

    (1) has little experience in foreign affairs
    (2) has taken stands against the working man
    (3) isn't a member of my party
    (4) doesn't come across as a strong leader
    (5) wants to spend so much money on defense

60. Which of the following is the conclusion of the research discussed in the article?

    (1) Television has had a major impact on the way people vote.
    (2) In recent elections, party affiliation has become less important to voters.
    (3) Politicians base their campaigns on their knowledge of what really matters to voters.
    (4) In recent elections, voters have been focusing increasingly on candidates' personalities.
    (5) Character judgments individual voters made proved to be better indicators of how they would vote than either issues or party affiliation.

61. Which of the following statements is best supported by research presented in the article?

    (1) Voters are no longer interested in candidates' voting records and stands on issues.
    (2) Television is responsible for voters' focusing on personality rather than issues.
    (3) Voters are better able to get an accurate sense of candidates' personalities than of their stands on issues.
    (4) The proportion of voters voting on straight party lines has declined.
    (5) The proportion of eligible voters who actually vote has been declining in recent elections.

62. Based on the article, it can be argued that a potential threat to democracy in America lies in

   (1) declining voter turnout
   (2) excessive media influence
   (3) failure of voters to sufficiently inform themselves about the candidates
   (4) the failure of the two-party system
   (5) the increasing role of money in determining the outcomes of elections

Item 63 is based on the following passage.

Propaganda is the deliberate dissemination of the message of an interest group. Propagandists seek to shape public opinion by focusing the public's attention on one view or choice to the exclusion of all others. Messages are designed to appeal to the audience's values and attitudes and thus to influence opinion in the desired direction.

63. Which of the following statements is supported by ideas in the passage?

   (1) Propaganda messages are untrue.
   (2) Advertising is a form of propaganda.
   (3) Debate and discussion are tools of the propagandist.
   (4) The opinions of experts are not used by propagandists.
   (5) Propaganda has no place in a democratic society.

64. The table shows the results of a poll that asked children how they felt about working mothers. Which of the following statements accurately describes a finding of the poll?

   (1) A majority of children whose mothers work full time would prefer that they stay home.
   (2) Teenagers, more than younger children, wish their mothers would stay home.
   (3) Children whose mothers work tend to prefer that they work, and children whose mothers don't, tend to prefer that they don't.
   (4) Children whose mothers work part time are decidedly more satisfied than children whose mothers work full time.
   (5) Children whose mothers don't work wish that they would.

Answers are on pages A-68—A-72.

Item 64 is based on the following table.

Perceptions Regarding Attributes if Children Whose Mothers Work Compared with Those Who Don't

Children whose mothers work:	Total %	Age 8–12 %	Age 13–17 %	Mother works: Full Time %	Part Time %	Not at All %
Do better in school	7	10	5	9	7	5
Do worse in school	26	22	29	22	21	36
About the same	62	62	62	66	67	51
Get into more trouble	40	36	43	34	38	51
Get into less trouble	7	9	4	6	6	7
Same amount of trouble	48	47	49	54	51	35
Are more independent	47	30	63	49	51	42
Are less independent	7	8	7	6	7	9
About the same	38	50	27	37	38	40

PRACTICE ITEMS 2: SOCIAL STUDIES
Performance Analysis Chart

Directions: Circle the number of each item that you got correct on the Practice Items. Count how many items you got correct in each row; count how many items you got correct in each column. Write the number correct per row and column as the numerator in the fraction in the appropriate "Total Correct" box. (The denominators represent the total number of items in the row or column.) Write the grand total correct over the denominator **64** at the lower right corner of the chart. (For example, if you got 57 items correct, write 57 so that the fraction reads 57/64.) Item numbers in color represent items based on graphic material.

Item Type	History (page 270)	Geography (page 282)	Economics (page 288)	Political Science (page 298)	Behavioral Sciences (page 305)	TOTAL CORRECT
Comprehension (page 220)	1, 2, 4, 6, 10, 14	21, 24, 25	30, 31, 36	38, 41, 44, 45	64	/17
Application (page 224)		20	26, 27, 28, 29, 32	47, 48, 49, 50, 51	52, 57, 59	/14
Analysis (page 228)	3, 5, 7, 11, 12, 13, 16	18, 22	33, 37		56, 58, 60, 63	/15
Evaluation (page 232)	8, 9, 15, 17	19, 23	34, 35	39, 40, 42, 43, 46	53, 54, 55, 61, 62	/18
TOTAL CORRECT	/17	/8	/12	/14	/13	/64

The page numbers in parentheses indicate where in this book you can find the beginning of specific instruction about the various fields of social studies and about the types of questions you encountered in the Practice Items.

PRACTICE ITEMS 3
Science

Directions: *Choose the one best answer to each question.*

Biology

Items 1 to 5 are based on the following passage.

Normal blood contains trillions of small, round cells called red blood corpuscles. These corpuscles carry oxygen from the lungs to your body. They are able to do this because they are spotted with molecules of a chemical called hemoglobin. Hemoglobin forms a loose bond with oxygen where oxygen is plentiful, and releases oxygen where there is little available.

In people with a condition called sickle-cell anemia, the hemoglobin is slightly different. Molecules of sickle-cell hemoglobin do not remain separate when they lose their oxygen as normal hemoglobin molecules do. Instead, they stick to one another, forming long, stiff rods or spirals. The rods push the red blood cell into a shape similar to a crescent moon, or sickle.

Sickle-shaped cells tend to clog the tiny blood vessels called capillaries. The body reacts to the blockage by trying to destroy the clogged cells. Soon, more red corpuscles are being destroyed than are being made by the body. The number of red blood cells in the blood drops. The sufferer becomes anemic, often feeling great pain. The condition may cause death.

Scientists first suspected that sickle-cell anemia was hereditary when they found that in the United States it tended to strike people whose ancestors came from Africa. Later research showed that the sickle-cell trait was common in central Africa, southern Italy and Sicily, Greece, Turkey, and parts of India. An experiment by Dr. James V. Neel added to the evidence that sickle-cell anemia was passed down through families. He found that both parents of patients with the disease always had some sickle cells in their blood, even though the parents did not have the disease. Later, scientists proved that the parents were carriers of the sickle-cell trait. Each parent had one gene for normal hemoglobin and one gene for sickle-cell hemoglobin. In patients with the disease, each parent had passed on his or her gene for sickle cell.

1. At which body site would you expect to find the most hemoglobin bound to oxygen?

    (1) capillaries
    (2) heart
    (3) lungs
    (4) muscles
    (5) nose

2. A carrier of the sickle-cell trait who does not suffer from the disease marries a person with two genes for normal hemoglobin. What are the chances that at least one of their children will have sickle-cell anemia?

    (1) 0
    (2) 1 in 2
    (3) 1 in 4
    (4) 1 in 6
    (5) 1 in 8

3. Before Dr. Neel's experiment, scientists believed that sickle-cell anemia was caused by a single dominant gene. According to this idea, a child could inherit the gene from either parent. A child with even one sickle-cell gene would always get the disease. What did Dr. Neel find that DISPROVED this belief?

(1) A parent of an anemia patient did not have the disease.
(2) Both parents of an anemia patient always had some sickle cells in their blood.
(3) All the children of parents with signs of sickle cell developed anemia.
(4) In cases where only one parent showed the sickle-cell trait, some offspring still developed anemia.
(5) In cases where only one parent showed the sickle-cell trait, some offspring did not develop anemia.

4. A person who suffers from sickle-cell anemia marries a person with two genes for normal hemoglobin. Which of the following predictions can you make about their children?

(1) All will be carriers of the sickle-cell trait.
(2) None will be carriers of the sickle-cell trait.
(3) At least one will not be a carrier of the sickle-cell trait.
(4) All will suffer from sickle-cell anemia.
(5) At least one will suffer from sickle-cell anemia.

5. Scientists believe that the sickle-cell trait evolved as a defense against the protozoan parasite that causes malaria. Which of the following statements best supports this theory?

(1) Malaria is most common in the same areas where the sickle-cell trait is common.
(2) Malaria is least common in the same areas where the sickle-cell trait is common.
(3) The malarial parasite rarely can establish itself in persons with the sickle-cell trait.
(4) The malarial parasite easily establishes itself in persons without the sickle-cell trait.
(5) The malarial parasite establishes itself more easily in persons with the sickle-cell trait than in those without it.

6. Activity is a characteristic of life. Every living organism has the ability to react to the environment. The reactions are called behavior. Animal behavior may be either learned or inherited. A learned behavior is an activity that comes from experience. An inherited behavior is passed on through the genes. Which of the following is an inherited behavior?

(1) the ability to speak English
(2) the ability to blink
(3) the ability to write
(4) the ability to make friends
(5) the ability to raise children

7. A homeowner is trying to grow a lawn, but her front yard and backyard are both on the side of a hill and erosion is a problem. The woman seeds both yards with Kentucky bluegrass, which grows well in the area. Then she rakes the front yard in order to cover the seed. Before she has time to rake the back yard, it suddenly rains very heavily. Two weeks later the back yard is green with seedlings, while the front yard has only a few blades of grass. Which of the following factors is probably responsible for the difference in the growth of the grass?

   (1) the amount of rain
   (2) the type of soil
   (3) the type of seed
   (4) the amount of sunlight
   (5) rate of erosion

Item 8 is based on the following figure.

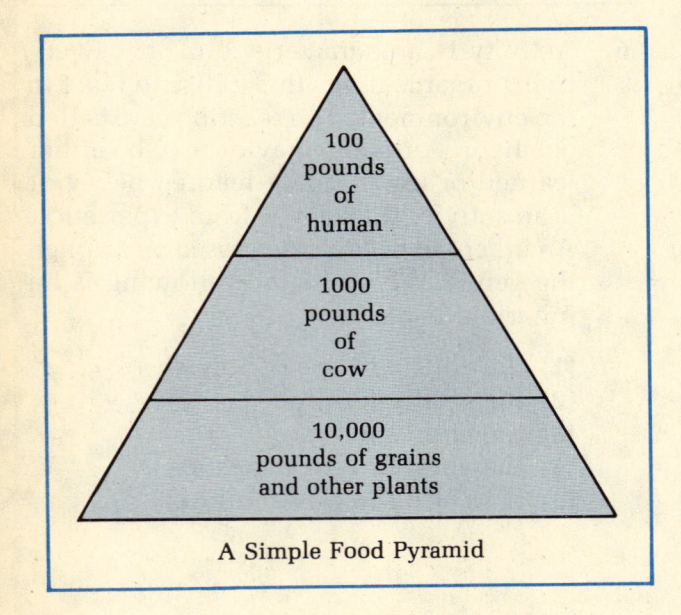

```
        100
       pounds
         of
       human
      1000
     pounds
       of
       cow
   10,000
  pounds of grains
  and other plants
```
A Simple Food Pyramid

8. A large amount of useful energy is lost with each step up a food pyramid. Thus 10,000 pounds of grains and other plants produces only 1,000 pounds of cow, and so on. Based on this information, which of the following would be the most efficient way for a country with a limited amount of farmland to feed a large number of people?

   (1) Produce food grains and livestock in the proportions depicted by the figure.
   (2) Produce exactly equal amounts of food grains and livestock.
   (3) Concentrate on raising livestock.
   (4) Concentrate on growing food grains.
   (5) Stop growing food grains.

9. The results of an experiment using marigolds are as follows:

   A. A marigold plant that is not given water droops and wilts.
   B. A marigold plant kept in the shade doesn't grow as well as one in the sun.
   C. A marigold plant in which the new growth is pinched back on top grows more side branches and flowers, for a more bushy look.

   You wish to grow bushy-looking marigolds in a window box. Which of the following will yield the best results?

   (1) infrequent watering, little sunlight, pinching back new growth on top
   (2) frequent watering, little sunlight, pinching back new growth on top
   (3) frequent watering, plentiful sunlight, not pinching back new growth on top
   (4) frequent watering, plentiful sunlight, pinching back new growth on top
   (5) infrequent watering, plentiful sunlight, pinching back new growth on top

Items 10 to 14 refer to the following passage.

Plants, like animals, begin life as zygotes, the fusion of egg and sperm. In flowering plants, the egg is called a stigma, and the sperm is a pollen grain. The pollen is usually transferred to the stigma by the wind or by insects in a process called pollination. After pollination, the fertilized egg cell divides again and again, slowly becoming an embryo. At this point the embryo is made up of seed leaves and a stem. Both the embryo and the food supply that surrounds it are enclosed in a hard seed covering. Together, these make up the plant's seed.

When conditions—such as light, temperature, and moisture—are right for growing, the seed germinates. The cells in the embryo that make up the roots absorb water rapidly until they burst out of the seed coat. The roots grow down toward water and nutrients. The rest of the plant arches until it points toward the sun. The seed leaves begin to make food for the plant. After the first leaves mature, the seed leaves usually wither and fall off.

Many flowering plants reproduce asexually or vegetatively as well. Some send out runners on which a small, new plant forms. Plants that can reproduce in this way include strawberries and spider plants. Plants such as the African violet, coleus, and geranium can reproduce through cuttings placed in water. The cuttings grow roots and eventually new leaves.

10. The juicy white fruit of an apple surrounds the tiny embryo of the apple plant. What function does the fruit serve?

    (1) protection
    (2) water absorption
    (3) pollination
    (4) food supply
    (5) seed covering

11. Some people are allergic to the pollen grains of certain plants. Their allergies flare up at a certain time of the year. This is probably the time when plants to which they are allergic are

    (1) reproducing
    (2) germinating
    (3) growing
    (4) dividing to become embryos
    (5) maturing

12. For a plant species, what is the advantage of producing small, light grains of pollen?

    (1) The pollen grains tend to fertilize the plant's own stigma, ensuring reproduction.
    (2) The pollen grains are more easily transferred from plant to plant, ensuring genetic variation.
    (3) The pollen grains require little energy to produce, so the plant can make more of them.
    (4) The pollen grains are easily hidden within the flower, so they are not disturbed by animals.
    (5) The pollen grains are able to be transported long distances, so the plants spread across an ever-widening territory.

13. Which of the following statements about the offspring of vegetative reproduction is the most accurate?

    (1) The offspring have few commercial uses.
    (2) The offspring require fewer nutrients than plants grown from seeds.
    (3) The offspring are genetically identical to the parent plant.
    (4) The offspring become seeds before growing into mature plants.
    (5) The offspring will not grow into flowering plants.

14. A biochemist has discovered that water hyacinths will absorb and store dangerous chemicals found in water, including mercury and lead. One of the advantages of using hyacinths is that they reproduce very quickly. Through vegetative reproduction, one plant can make up to 65,000 new plants in a year. When one plant has absorbed all the chemicals it can, it is removed, and new ones quickly take its place. Which of the following is not a possible use of the biochemist's discovery?

(1) beautify polluted water
(2) clean up waterways to make them suitable for boating
(3) purify drinking water
(4) purify fishing ponds
(5) decrease the amount of harmful chemicals in the environment

Items 15 to 16 are based on the following passage.

In times of severe cold, animals may hibernate for days or weeks at a time. Their body temperature drops, and they breathe only a few times a minute. A hibernating animal uses the fat stored in its body for nourishment.

In times of extreme heat, other animals estivate. Just as with hibernating animals, the body functions of estivating animals slow down almost to a stop. To an observer, the animal appears to be either in a deep sleep or dead.

15. Which of the following facts about hibernation probably does not increase the animal's chances for survival?

(1) The animal's temperature drops.
(2) The animal breathes only a few times a minute.
(3) The animal exists on body fat.
(4) The animal cannot move around.
(5) The animal stays underground for weeks at a time.

16. Which of the following is an accurate generalization about hibernation and estivation?

(1) Both help protect the animal from predators.
(2) Both use more energy than when the animal is awake.
(3) Both are a response to winter.
(4) Both are a response to summer.
(5) Both are a response to extreme temperature changes.

Item 17 refers to the following figure.

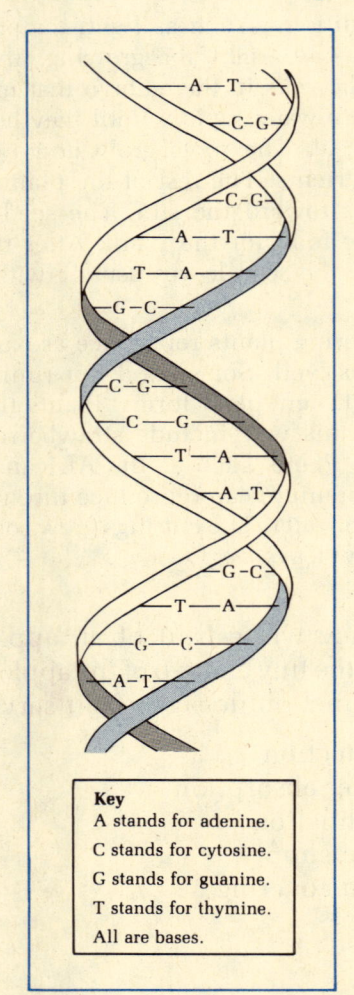

Key
A stands for adenine.
C stands for cytosine.
G stands for guanine.
T stands for thymine.
All are bases.

The structure of a DNA molecule is a double helix made up of two strands. The paired bases on the inside hold the strands together.

PRACTICE ITEMS

17. Suppose you have one half of a DNA molecule; that is, one strand and the bases attached to it. What is the only fact you need to know to predict which bases go where on the other strand?

(1) the sequence of the bases on the first strand
(2) the sequence of the bases in a normal DNA molecule
(3) the molecular structure of the bases
(4) the chemical composition of the bases
(5) the force that holds the bases together

---

18. Animals tend to adapt to the environment around them. On land, the only way for an animal to obtain food is to move about, so land animals are generally mobile. In the sea, by contrast, certain animals attach themselves as young adults to a rock or the ocean floor. They rarely, if ever, move about. These include sponges, corals, and oysters. Why is this adaptation successful in a marine environment?

A. Marine animals conserve energy by remaining still.
B. Marine animals make food from the sunlight that filters down through the water.
C. Adult marine animals no longer require food.
D. Marine animals are nourished by elements in the ocean floor.
E. Marine animals can wait for edible plants and small animals to be brought to them by the motion of the water.

(1) A and C only
(2) B only
(3) C only
(4) D only
(5) A and E only

Items 19 and 20 are based on the following chart.

FUNCTIONS, SOURCES, AND DEFICIENCY SYMPTOMS OF VITAMINS

Vitamins	Sources	Essential for
vitamin A	fish liver oils liver and kidney green and yellow vegetables yellow fruit tomatoes butter egg yolk	growth health of the eyes structure and functions of the cells of the skin and mucous membranes
vitamin B_1 (thiamin)	meat soybeans milk whole grain legumes	growth carbohydrate metabolism functioning of the heart, nerves, and muscles
vitamin B_2 or G (riboflavin)	meat and fowl soybeans milk green vegetables eggs yeast	growth health of the skin and mouth carbohydrate metabolism functioning of the eyes
vitamin B_3 (niacin)	meat, fowl, and fish peanut butter potatoes whole grain tomatoes leafy vegetables	growth carbohydrate metabolism functioning of the stomach and intestines functioning of the nervous system
vitamin B_{12}	green vegetables liver	preventing pernicious anemia
vitamin C (ascorbic acid)	citrus fruit other fruit tomatoes leafy vegetables	growth maintaining strength of the blood vessels development of teeth gum health
vitamin D	fish-liver oil liver fortified milk eggs irradiated foods	growth regulating calcium and phosphorus metabolism building and maintaining bones, teeth
vitamin E	wheat germ oil leafy vegetables milk and butter	normal reproduction
vitamin K	green vegetables soybean oil tomatoes	normal clotting of the blood normal liver functions

19. Based on the information in this chart, which of the following statements is correct?

   (1) All vitamins can be found in fish-liver oil.
   (2) Meat is necessary for proper vitamin intake.
   (3) Fruits contain all necessary vitamins.
   (4) A vegetarian diet would provide all necessary vitamins.
   (5) Vitamin B_2 is the most important vitamin.

20. The following symptoms might be caused by a deficiency of which vitamin?
   retarded growth
   night blindness
   susceptibility to infections
   changes in skin and membranes

   (1) vitamin A
   (2) vitamin B_2
   (3) vitamin C
   (4) vitamin D
   (5) vitamin K

Items 21 to 23 refer to the following graph.

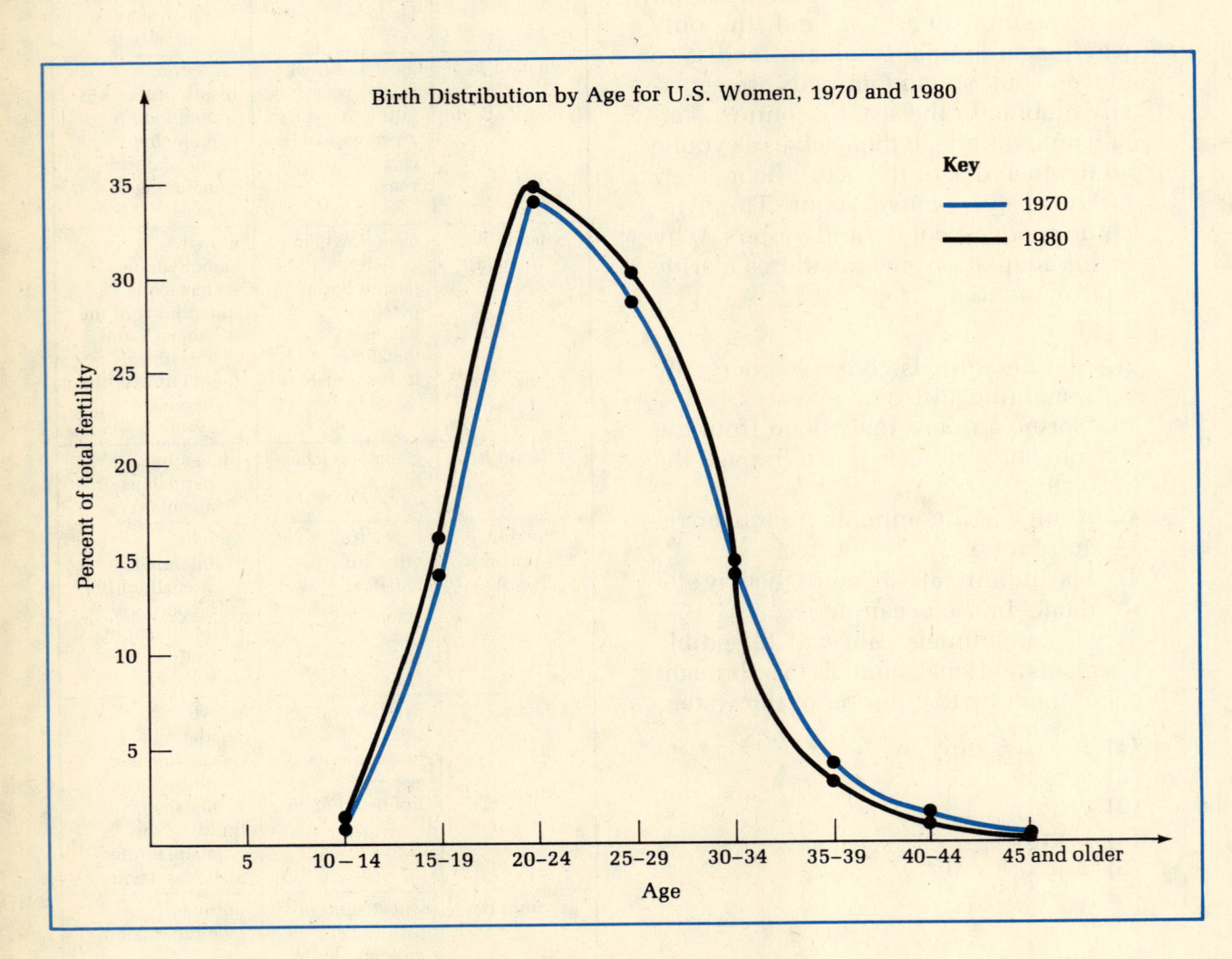

Birth Distribution by Age for U.S. Women, 1970 and 1980

21. The largest share of births each year in the United States are to women between the ages of

(1) 10 and 14
(2) 15 and 19
(3) 20 and 24
(4) 25 and 29
(5) 30 and 34

22. Young women give birth to more males than females. In higher age groups, the percentage of males born declines. This information and the graph will support which of the following conclusions?

(1) Male babies are tougher than female babies.
(2) The actual number of boys born to women in their later teens was greater in 1970 than in 1980.
(3) In both years shown, the actual number of boys born to women in their later teens was greater than the number of boys born to women in their early 30s.
(4) Natural selection favors young boys over young girls.
(5) The number of girls born in the United States increased from 1970 to 1980.

23. Which of the following conclusions can be drawn from the graph?

(1) The fertility rate is rising because more women are living longer lives.
(2) The fertility rate of the U.S. population is dropping.
(3) During the 1970s, the average American woman was between 20 and 24 years old.
(4) The number of births to American women aged 20 to 24 was the same in 1980 as it was in 1970.
(5) The age group of American women with the largest share of births was about the same in 1980 as it was in 1970.

Items 24 to 28 refer to the following passage.

People have different nutritional needs based on age, sex, body size, activity level, and special conditions such as pregnancy or illness. The proper balance of nutrients supplies your body with energy, promotes growth and repair of body tissues, and regulates body processes. Poor food choices can increase your chances of getting such diseases as cancer, heart disease, and diabetes. But how do you judge which foods and how much of them you should eat?

One way is to follow the U.S. Department of Agriculture's (U.S.D.A.) seven dietary guidelines for Americans. These are:

1. Eat a variety of foods. Your body needs amino acids from proteins, essential fatty acids from vegetable oils and animal fats, and vitamins and minerals. Your diet should also include energy sources such as carbohydrates, fats, and proteins.

2. Maintain your ideal weight. Being too fat or too thin are both associated with increased health risks. A good way to maintain a healthy weight is not to eat past the point where you are full, and to exercise several times a week.

3. Avoid too much fat, saturated fat, and cholesterol. The U.S.D.A. advises choosing lean meat, fish, poultry, and dry beans and peas as protein sources. Limit the amount of butter, cream, eggs, and fats you eat.

4. Eat foods with adequate starch and fiber. Complex carbohydrate foods such as grains, legumes, fruits, and vegetables contain many essential nutrients, and ounce for ounce, contain half the calories fats do.

5. and 6. Avoid too much sugar and sodium. Sugar increases tooth decay. Excess sodium—found in table salt, baking soda and powder, soft drinks, and many processed foods—can raise your blood pressure, which in turn affects the health of your heart.

7. If you drink alcohol, do so in moderation. Alcoholic beverages are high in calories and low in nutrition. Heavy drinking can damage the liver and cause neurological disorders. Pregnant women should never drink more than two ounces of alcohol in a day.

24. Which of the following snack foods best meets the dietary guidelines?

(1) air-popped popcorn
(2) ice cream
(3) potato chips
(4) cake
(5) cookies

25. Which of the following dairy foods best meets the dietary guidelines?

(1) four ounces of ice cream (3 grams protein, 9 grams fat, .035 grams sodium)
(2) one ounce of American cheese (6 grams protein, 7 grams fat, .390 grams sodium)
(3) six ounces of fruited yogurt (7 grams protein, 5 grams fat, .095 grams sodium)
(4) six ounces of plain yogurt (7 grams protein, 3 grams fat, .125 grams sodium)
(5) six ounces of whole milk (6 grams protein, 6 grams fat, .125 grams sodium)

26. Which of the following breakfast cereals best meets the dietary guidelines?

(1) a cereal containing 2 grams of protein, 12 grams of complex carbohydrates, and 14 grams of sugar per serving
(2) a cereal containing 4 grams of protein, 17 grams of complex carbohydrates, and 1 gram of sugar per serving
(3) a cereal containing 2 grams of protein, 23 grams of complex carbohydrates, and 12 grams of sugar per serving
(4) a cereal containing 2 grams of protein, 12 grams of complex carbohydrates, and 5 grams of sugar per serving
(5) a cereal containing 4 grams of protein, 8 grams of complex carbohydrates, and 9 grams of sugar per serving

27. A study of a large group of vegetarians who drink no alcohol or coffee and do not smoke found that they live at least seven years longer than the general American population. The group tended to have low rates of heart disease, diabetes, and cancers of the lungs and colon. From which of the following guidelines does their diet differ?

(1) Eat a variety of foods.
(2) Avoid too much fat, saturated fat, and cholesterol.
(3) Eat foods with adequate starch and fiber.
(4) Avoid too much sugar.
(5) If you drink alcohol, do so in moderation.

28. An overweight friend announces that he is on a new "miracle" diet. He tells you that the diet calls for avoiding vegetables, fruits, breads, and other starches, since these are fattening. The diet replaces these with meat and other protein sources. Would you advise your friend to continue this diet; and on which guideline(s) are you basing your judgment?

(1) No, because he is violating guidelines 1 and 4
(2) No, because he is violating guideline 2
(3) No, because he is violating guidelines 5 and 6
(4) Yes, because he is following guideline 5
(5) Yes, because he is following guidelines 2 and 4

29. Foxes that live in the Arctic region are predators that feed principally on lemmings, a type of small rodent. From time to time, usually when food supplies have been reduced by overgrazing, the lemming population declines. When this happens, the foxes go hungry, and their numbers diminish. Eventually, however, with the lemmings no longer numerous, the plants that make up their food supply can once again grow abundantly. Then the lemmings, no longer threatened by many foxes, can again increase their numbers. Eventually the foxes, with more lemmings to feed on, also increase in number and the cycle begins again. If the relationship between foxes and lemmings is a typical one, which of the following conclusions can be drawn about predator/prey relationships in the wild?

(1) Predators safeguard their food supply by limiting the number of prey they eat.
(2) Predators will eventually eliminate any given population of prey.
(3) Populations of predators and prey tend to evolve in a way that keeps the numbers of each type of animal in balance.
(4) As the number of prey animals decreases, predators become more numerous.
(5) As the number of prey animals increases, predators become less numerous.

30. The placenta is the organ of exchange between an embryo and its mother. Nutrients and oxygen from the mother's blood diffuse across the placenta into the embryo's blood. In turn, carbon dioxide and other wastes from the embryo diffuse into the mother's blood.

Which of the following statements explains how drugs in the mother's blood can harm her baby?

(1) Drugs deplete the oxygen in the mother's blood, and thus the baby's.
(2) Drugs deplete the nutrients in the mother's blood, and thus her baby's.
(3) Drugs cross from the mother's blood to the baby's blood through the placenta, affecting the baby directly.
(4) Drugs slow down the diffusion of carbon dioxide from the baby's blood into the mother's blood, so that the baby's blood contains too much CO_2.
(5) Drugs affect the rate at which the mother removes wastes from the baby, so that the baby is poisoned.

31. Scientists rely on a variety of clues in determining evolutionary history. They look at similarities and differences in modern-day organisms, as well as the fossil record. A similarity at the cellular level often indicates that two quite different organisms shared a common ancestor.

Which of the following is the best indication that mosses and trees may have evolved from a common green algal ancestor?

(1) All three live in forests.
(2) All three require water to live.
(3) All three are eaten by animals.
(4) All three possess chlorophylls a and b, and store food as starch.
(5) All three are land dwellers.

Earth Science

32. A solar eclipse occurs when the moon passes directly between the sun and Earth. The moon casts a shadow over a small area on the daylight side of Earth, and for a short time this small area cannot see the sun.

Which of the following statements about a solar eclipse is true?

(1) A solar eclipse affects only the part of Earth that is already in darkness.
(2) A solar eclipse affects all parts of Earth equally.
(3) During a solar eclipse, Earth is between the sun and the moon.
(4) A solar eclipse affects only a small part of Earth.
(5) A solar eclipse affects areas that are on opposite sides of Earth.

Items 33 to 36 are based on the following maps and information.

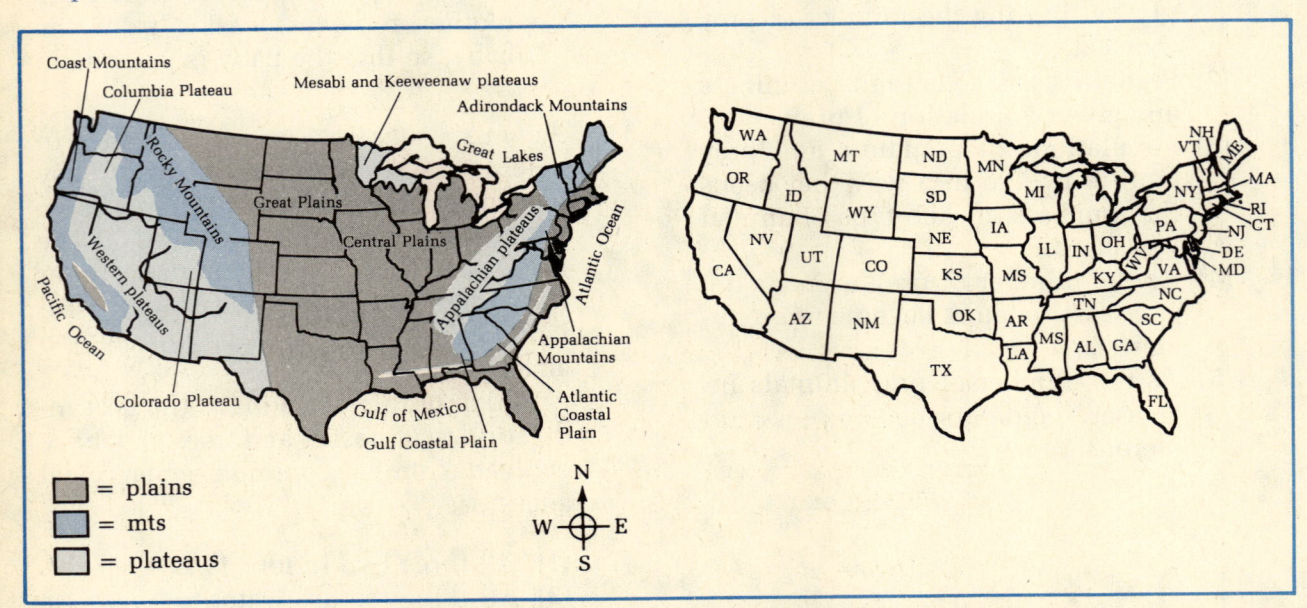

The shape of Earth's surface is called its topography. Earth's topography consists of three main landscape types: plains, mountains, and plateaus.

Plains are flat areas that are not very high above sea level. Plains in the interior of continents are somewhat higher than coastal plains. Mountains have elevations of 600 or more meters above sea level. Plateaus also have elevations of 600 or more meters, but they are not considered mountains because their surfaces are fairly flat.

The map above left shows the topography of the United States. The map above right is given to help you identify the states.

PRACTICE ITEMS Earth Science Items **629**

33. Two states that have similar landscape types are

    (1) California and Texas
    (2) Maine and Florida
    (3) Oregon and Indiana
    (4) Florida and Delaware
    (5) Idaho and Texas

34. A person is warned by a doctor not to live at any elevation higher than 600 meters. Which of the following locations would most likely be suitable as a place for this person to live?

    (1) Denver, Colorado
    (2) Phoenix, Arizona
    (3) Reno, Nevada
    (4) Boise, Idaho
    (5) Baton Rouge, Louisiana

35. Water flowing off the western slopes of the Appalachian Mountains would most likely eventually flow into which of the following?

    (1) the Atlantic Ocean
    (2) the Great Lakes and the Gulf of Mexico
    (3) the Great Lakes only
    (4) the Pacific Ocean
    (5) the Western plateaus

36. The Midwestern states and the Atlantic coast states are noted for farming. According to the information provided, which of the following statements would best explain this fact?

    (1) High elevations are best suited to farming.
    (2) The best soils are found in areas that are mountainous.
    (3) The largest areas of rich soil are usually found in plains regions.
    (4) Many people in the coastal and Midwestern states are interested in farming.
    (5) There is a lot of open land in the coastal and Midwestern states.

Item 37 is based on the following information and chart.

The color of a star can help scientists determine its temperature. The following chart shows the average temperatures of different-colored stars.

Color	Temperature (°C)	Example
Blue or blue-white	35,000	Oridani
White	10,000	Sirius
Yellow	6,000	Sun
Red-orange	5,000	Centauri B
Red	3,000	Proxima

37. Based on the chart, which of the following statements is true?

    (1) The brighter a star is, the hotter its temperature.
    (2) The more closely a star resembles the sun, the hotter its temperature.
    (3) The more red in color a star is, the cooler its temperature.
    (4) The more white in color a star is, the cooler its temperature.
    (5) The nearer to the sun a star is located, the hotter its temperature.

Items 38 to 42 are based on the following passage.

Distances on Earth can be measured in meters or kilometers (1 kilometer = 1000 meters). In space, however, distances are often too great to be measured in kilometers. As a result, scientists use a unit of distance called the light-year to measure distances in space.

A light-year is the distance light travels in one year. Light travels at a speed of approximately 300,000 kilometers per second. This is more than seven times the distance around the Earth. In one year, light travels about 9.5 trillion kilometers, so one light-year is equal to about 9.5 trillion kilometers.

The nearest star system to ours is a little more than 4 light-years away. Some distant star systems are more than 12 billion light-years away. Although it may seem hard to imagine, the light from those star systems must have begun its journey toward Earth long before our planet was even formed.

38. According to the article, which of the following quantities would be measured in light-years?

    (1) distance around Earth
    (2) distance between two continents
    (3) distance between two star systems
    (4) time needed to travel around Earth
    (5) time needed to travel between two star systems

39. According to the information provided, light from the star system closest to Earth would

    (1) take less time to reach us than light from the sun
    (2) take about the same time to reach us as light from the sun
    (3) take twice as long to reach us as light from the sun
    (4) take about one year to reach us
    (5) take more than four years to reach us

40. When you look into the night sky and see a star that is 1000 light-years away, which of the following are you actually seeing?

    (1) the star as it appears at the moment you see it
    (2) the star as it appeared one year ago
    (3) the star as it appeared 1000 years ago
    (4) a star that no longer exists
    (5) one of the most distant stars in the universe

41. It can be inferred from the passage that the age of Earth is

    (1) about the same as the age of the nearest star
    (2) much less than the age of the nearest star
    (3) about 12 billion years
    (4) considerably less than 12 billion years
    (5) considerably more than 12 billion years

42. Two galaxies are four light-years apart. Which of the following statements about the galaxies must be true?

    (1) It would take a space vehicle four years to travel between the two galaxies.
    (2) Light from the farthest galaxy would take four years to reach Earth.
    (3) It would require a trip of 1.2 million kilometers to travel from Earth to either galaxy.
    (4) It would require a trip of 38 trillion kilometers to travel between the two galaxies.
    (5) Light from the brighter galaxy would have to travel 4.5 trillion kilometers to reach the other galaxy.

43. Locations on Earth's surface are described in terms of imaginary lines called parallels of longitude and latitude. Parallels of longitude extend from pole to pole at varying distances east or west of an imaginary line running through Greenwich, England. Parallels of latitude extend around Earth at varying distances north or south of the equator. Any point on Earth's surface is said to be located at a certain number of degrees "north latitude" (if the point is north of the equator) or "south latitude" (if the point is south of the equator).

    Which of the following cities has a location described as "south latitude"?

    (1) Paris, France
    (2) Moscow, Soviet Union
    (3) Sydney, Australia
    (4) Los Angeles, California
    (5) Toronto, Canada

PRACTICE ITEMS

Chemistry Items **631**

44. Earth scientists disagree about just how much petroleum is left on Earth. Some say that given our present rate of use, we have only enough petroleum to last until the year 2020. Others claim that we have enough to last until the year 2330. All agree, however, that eventually the world will experience a serious petroleum shortage.

Based on the passage, which of the following represents an opinion rather than a statement of fact?

(1) There is only a limited amount of petroleum on Earth.
(2) Much of the petroleum on Earth has already been used up.
(3) Earth scientists are concerned about the world's petroleum supply.
(4) By the year 2021, the world's petroleum supply will be gone.
(5) Earth scientists' estimates of how long our petroleum will last vary by 300 years.

Chemistry

Item 45 refers to the following figure, in which cysteine and glycine, two amino acids, combine to form a dipeptide, one of the peptide linkages in protein.

$$HS-\underset{\underset{\underset{H}{\overset{H}{\diagdown}N\diagup}}{\overset{H}{\mid}}}{C}-\underset{\overset{H}{\mid}}{C}-\underset{\overset{\diagup}{OH}}{\overset{\overset{O}{\parallel}}{C}} \;+\; \underset{\underset{\underset{H}{\overset{H}{\diagdown}N\diagup}}{\mid}}{\underset{\overset{O}{\diagdown}}{C}}-\underset{\overset{H}{\mid}}{C}-H \;\longrightarrow\; HS-\underset{\overset{H}{\mid}}{C}-\underset{\overset{H}{\mid}}{\overset{\overset{O}{\parallel}}{C}}-\underset{\overset{H}{\mid}}{N}-\underset{\overset{H}{\mid}}{C}-\underset{\overset{\diagup}{OH}}{\overset{\overset{O}{\parallel}}{C}} \;+\; H_2O$$

    Cysteine   Glycine   Dipeptide   Water

45. If the above reaction is a typical one, which of the following can be assumed?

    (1) A peptide linkage cannot be broken.
    (2) All dipeptides have the same molecular weight.
    (3) All dipeptides have the same amino acid sequence.
    (4) Every amino acid has the same number of atoms, although they are arranged in different configurations.
    (5) Water is produced every time a peptide linkage is formed.

46. Proteins are arranged in complex shapes that are related to their functions. The action of enzymes, for example, depends on their having binding sites that attract and match sites on certain other molecules. Enzymes increase the rate of specific chemical reactions in the cell. So when an enzyme binds to the molecule for which it is designed, it speeds up the particular reaction in which that molecule is involved.

    Which of the following conclusions about enzymes can be drawn from the passage?

    (1) Most enzymes can bind to several different molecules.
    (2) Changing an enzyme's shape will change its function.
    (3) Changing an enzyme's shape will not change its function.
    (4) The effect of the enzyme depends on the temperature at which the reaction takes place.
    (5) Too many enzymes can slow down a reaction.

47. A balanced chemical equation is one in which the number of atoms on the left side equals the number of atoms on the right side. Which of the following is a balanced equation?

    (1) $Na + HOH \longrightarrow NaOH + H_2$
    (2) $Na + 2HOH \longrightarrow NaOH + H_2$
    (3) $2Na + 3HOH \longrightarrow 2NaOH + H_2$
    (4) $2Na + 2HOH \longrightarrow 2NaOH + H_2$
    (5) $3Na + 3HOH \longrightarrow 3NaOH + H_2$

48. The basic particles of an atom are protons, neutrons, and electrons. Each proton has a charge of +1. Each electron has a charge of −1. Neutrons have no electric charge.

    An atom with 10 protons, 8 neutrons, and 10 electrons loses 2 electrons. The electron charge of the atom is now equal to which of the following?

    (1) −8
    (2) −2
    (3) 0
    (4) +2
    (5) +10

Items 49 and 50 are based on the following graph.

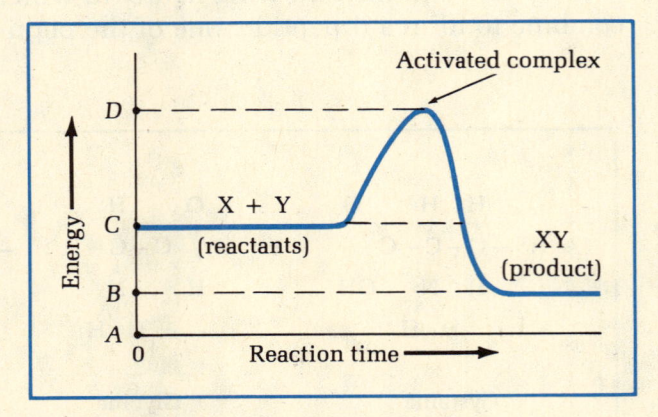

A certain amount of energy is necessary for a chemical reaction to occur. Once this energy is reached, the reactants form a temporary, high-energy arrangement called an activated complex. The products then form from the activated complex. The graph above shows the energy changes during the burning of graphite, a form of pure carbon.

49. When graphite is burned, the two reactants first form an activated complex; then, after burning, the CO₂ (carbon dioxide) is produced. Based on this information and on the graph, which of the following statements must be true?

(1) The reaction uses more energy than it gives off.
(2) There is more energy in the CO₂ than there was in the graphite and oxygen.
(3) There is the same amount of energy in the CO₂ as there was in the graphite and oxygen.
(4) Energy is absorbed in the creation of CO₂.
(5) There is less energy in the CO₂ than there was in the graphite and oxygen.

50. Which of the following statements best accounts for the change in energy level from point D in the activated complex to point B in the product CO₂?

(1) Energy is absorbed during the reaction by the activated complex.
(2) Energy is gained by CO₂.
(3) Energy is given off as heat and light.
(4) Energy is regained by the reactants.
(5) Energy is lost in forming the activated complex.

51. The boiling point of a substance is the temperature at which it changes from a liquid into a gas. The boiling point of water is 100°C. The boiling point of benzene is 80°C. The boiling point of chloroform is 60°C.

A chemist has a mixture of water, benzene, and chloroform. The chemist heats the mixture to a temperature of 85°C. The benzene and chloroform boil off, leaving the water. Which of the following conclusions does this experiment support?

(1) A chemist can take advantage of different boiling temperatures to separate substances in a compound.
(2) A chemist can take advantage of different boiling temperatures to separate substances in a mixture.
(3) Benzene and chloroform cannot be separated.
(4) A chemical reaction can be used to separate substances with different boiling temperatures.
(5) Substances with different boiling temperatures will not react with each other.

52. Baking powder contains the compound sodium bicarbonate. When baking powder is added to bread dough, the sodium bicarbonate reacts with acid to produce a gas, carbon dioxide. It is the carbon dioxide that causes bread to rise as it is being baked.

According to the passage, which of the following statements must be true?

(1) Bread dough contains at least one substance that is acidic.
(2) Bread dough contains oxygen.
(3) Bread dough cannot absorb carbon dioxide.
(4) Bread contains a mixture of gases.
(5) Bread rises more quickly when salt is present.

Items 53 to 56 are based on the following passage.

Carbon-14 is a radioactive form of the element carbon. When an element is radioactive, its atoms undergo spontaneous decay at a fixed rate. This fixed rate is called the half-life. The half-life of an element is the amount of time it will take for half of the atoms of that element to decay.

The half-life of carbon-14 is 5730 years. This means that after 5730 years, a 10-gram sample of carbon-14 will contain 5 grams of carbon-14 and 5 grams of a nonradioactive substance. In another 5730 years, the 5 grams will be reduced to 2.5 grams, and so on. Scientists can use the radioactive properties of carbon-14 to date the remains of ancient organisms. Every organism contains a certain amount of carbon-14 when it is alive. Once the organism dies, however, the carbon-14 begins to decay. By comparing the amount of carbon-14 present in the remains of an organism with the amount of carbon-14 known to have been present in the living organism, scientists can determine the approximate age of the remains.

53. According to the passage, carbon-14 is useful in dating the remains of ancient organisms mainly because it

(1) decays at a fixed rate
(2) is a form of the element carbon
(3) is present in dead organisms
(4) has a mass number of 14
(5) is present in only a few organisms

54. The skeleton of an ancient reptile contains one-fourth the amount of carbon-14 known to have been present in the living reptile. The approximate age of the reptile skeleton is

(1) 14 years
(2) 1432.5 years
(3) 5730 years
(4) 11,460 years
(5) 22,920 years

55. A radioactive form of the element iodine has a half-life of 8 days. A 40-gram sample of this radioactive iodine is placed in a test tube. How much of the iodine will remain after 32 days?

(1) 0 grams
(2) 2.5 grams
(3) 5 grams
(4) 20 grams
(5) 32 grams

56. Which of the following statements about carbon-14 can be inferred from the article?

(1) Scientists know how much carbon-14 was present in ancient organisms when they were alive.
(2) Scientists do not know why living organisms contain carbon-14.
(3) The half-life of carbon-14 varies from one organism to another.
(4) Organisms alive today do not contain carbon-14.
(5) Scientists are presently doing research to learn more about carbon-14.

Physics

Item 57 is based on the following information.

The velocity of an object is equal to the distances traveled per unit of time. This can be represented by the equation

$$velocity = distance/time$$

57. A car travels 150 miles in 3 hours. Which of the following measurements represents the velocity of the car?

(1) 5 miles/hour
(2) 30 miles/hour
(3) 50 miles/hour
(4) 150 miles/hour
(5) 450 miles/hour

Items 58 to 61 are based on the following information.

What makes popcorn pop? At first glance, a kernel of popcorn looks just like a grain of ordinary corn. But a kernel of popcorn has two special features: a thick outer coat and a tiny bit of water inside the kernel.

When popcorn is heated, the water changes into steam. As the steam gets hotter and expands, pressure builds up inside the kernel. The kernel's thick outer coat keeps the steam inside until just the right moment. Then, all of a sudden, the coat gives way to the pressure and the kernel pops open. The white "fluff" that you see is the white pulp of the kernel that has reacted to the heat and sudden explosion.

58. According to the passage, which of the following events takes place before popcorn pops?

   (1) White pulp in the kernel changes into steam.
   (2) Water in the kernel combines with oxygen in the air.
   (3) Air in the kernel suddenly expands.
   (4) Water in the kernel changes into steam.
   (5) Oxygen in the kernel explodes.

59. Which of the following actions would make popcorn pop faster?

   (1) Add water to the popcorn.
   (2) Leave the popcorn uncovered.
   (3) Grease the pot containing the popcorn.
   (4) Add salt to the popcorn.
   (5) Raise the temperature of the popcorn.

60. A teacher wishes to use popcorn to demonstrate a scientific rule. Which of the following rules could be demonstrated?

   (1) As pressure increases, volume decreases.
   (2) As volume decreases, pressure decreases.
   (3) As temperature increases, pressure decreases.
   (4) As temperature increases, pressure increases.
   (5) As temperature increases, volume decreases.

61. An uncovered jar of popcorn has been left on a shelf for several months. When the popcorn is heated, it does not pop. Which of the following statements best explains why this has happened?

   (1) Insects have eaten away the hearts of the kernels.
   (2) Exposure to air has dried out the kernels.
   (3) Oxygen from the air has reacted chemically with the white pulp in the kernels.
   (4) Moisture from the air has made the kernels soggy.
   (5) The kernels have germinated into seedlings.

62. An iron bar may be magnetized by stroking it with a magnet. The magnets cause the tiny magnetic domains in the bar to line up in the same direction. In other words, all the north poles face in one direction, and the south poles face in the opposite direction. In unmagnetized iron, the north and south poles are arranged randomly.

If a magnetized iron bar is heated to the point that its molecules are rearranged, which of the following statements will be true when it cools?

   (1) The north and south poles will have switched positions.
   (2) The position of the magnetic domains will be unchanged.
   (3) The magnetic domains will rotate to face perpendicular to their former position.
   (4) The bar will no longer be a magnet.
   (5) The bar's magnetic field will be greater than Earth's magnetic field.

Item 63 is based on the following diagram.

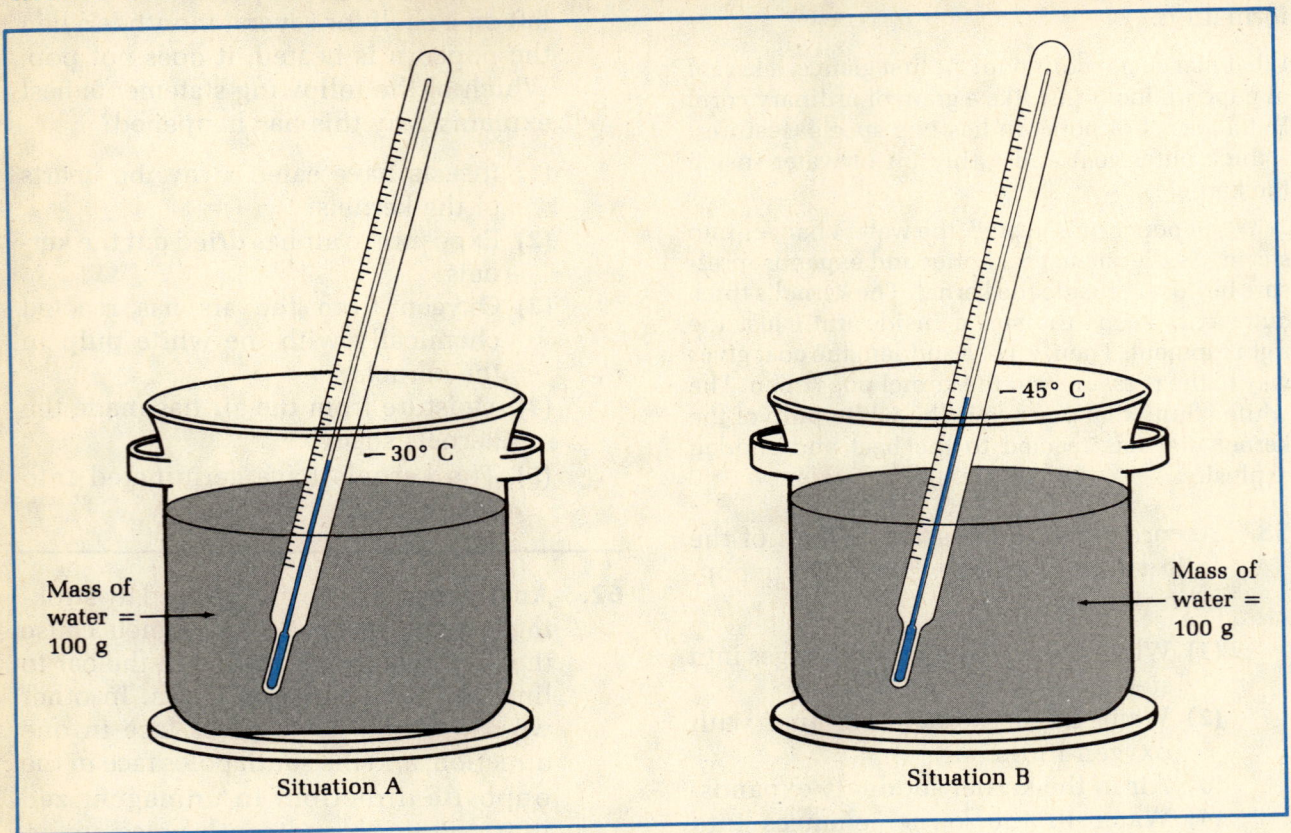

Situation A: Mass of water = 100 g, thermometer reads 30° C

Situation B: Mass of water = 100 g, thermometer reads 45° C

One calorie is the amount of heat needed to raise one gram of water 1°C.

63. Based on the diagram, which of the following represents the change in calories from **A** to **B**?

(1) −1500 calories
(2) −75 calories
(3) +15 calories
(4) +100 calories
(5) +1500 calories

Items 64 to 66 are based on the following graph.

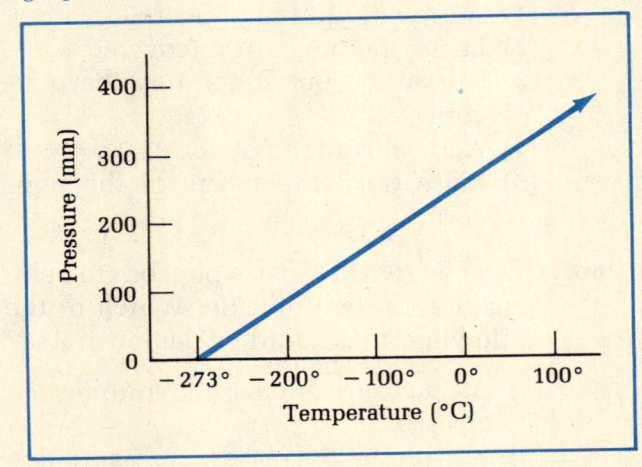

[Graph: Pressure (mm) vs. Temperature (°C), showing linear relationship from −273° at 0 mm rising through positive values]

This graph represents the relationship between temperature and pressure for a gas kept at constant volume inside a sealed container.

64. According to the graph, which of the following statements describes how pressure changes with temperature?

(1) Pressure steadily decreases as temperature increases.
(2) Pressure steadily increases as temperature increases.
(3) Pressure remains constant as temperature increases or decreases.
(4) Pressure sometimes increases and sometimes decreases as temperature increases.
(5) Pressure remains constant at low temperatures but increases sharply at high temperatures.

65. The information provided by the graph can explain which of the following events?

(1) A tire goes flat when punctured by a nail.
(2) A balloon expands as it is filled with air.
(3) A can of aerosol spray explodes when thrown into a fire.
(4) A carbonated beverage goes flat when exposed to air.
(5) An inflatable toy shrinks as air escapes through a leak.

66. Which of the following would you expect to happen if the sealed container were opened and the heated gas suddenly increased in volume?

(1) The pressure of the gas would stay the same.
(2) The pressure of the gas would increase.
(3) The temperature and pressure of the gas would both stay the same.
(4) The temperature and pressure of the gas would both increase.
(5) The pressure of the gas would decrease.

Answers are on pages A-73—A-75.

PRACTICE ITEMS 3: SCIENCE
Performance Analysis Chart

Directions: Circle the number of each item that you got correct on the Practice Items. Count how many items you got correct in each row; count how many items you got correct in each column. Write the number correct per row and column as the numerator in the fraction in the appropriate "Total Correct" box. (The denominators represent the total number of items in the row or column.) Write the grand total correct over the denominator **66** at the lower right corner of the chart. (For example, if you got 60 items correct, write 60 so that the fraction reads 60/66.) Item numbers in color represent items based on graphic material.

Item Type	Biology (page 322)	Earth Science (page 334)	Chemistry (page 347)	Physics (page 356)	TOTAL CORRECT
Comprehension (page 220)	2, 7, 9, 10, 21, 30	32, 33, 38, 39	53	58, 63, 64	/14
Application (page 224)	6, 8, 24, 25, 26, 31	34, 43	47, 48, 49, 54, 55	57, 62, 65	/16
Analysis (page 228)	1, 4, 11, 12, 13, 15, 17, 18, 19, 27	35, 40, 41, 44	45, 50, 52, 56	59, 61, 66	/21
Evaluation (page 232)	3, 5, 14, 16, 20, 22, 23, 28, 29	36, 37, 42	46, 51	60	/15
TOTAL CORRECT	/31	/13	/12	/10	/66

The page numbers in parentheses indicate where in this book you can find the beginning of specific instruction about the various fields of science and about the types of questions you encountered in the Practice Items.

PRACTICE ITEMS 4
Interpreting Literature and the Arts

Directions: *Choose the one best answer to each question.*

Nonfiction

Items 1 to 4 are based on the following passage.

WHAT DO INTELLIGENCE TESTS PROVE?

What is intelligence, anyway? When I was in the army I received a kind of aptitude test that all soldiers took and, against a normal of 100, scored 160. No one at the base had ever seen
(5) a figure like that and for two hours they made a big fuss over me. (It didn't mean anything. The next day I was still a buck private with KP as my highest duty.)

All my life I've been registering scores like
(10) that, so that I have the complacent feeling that I'm highly intelligent, and I expect other people to think so, too. Actually, though, don't such scores simply mean that I am very good at answering the type of academic questions
(15) that are considered worthy of answers by the people who make up the intelligence tests—people with intellectual bents similar to mine?

For instance, I had an auto-repair man once, who, on these intelligence tests, could not pos-
(20) sibly have scored more than 80, by my estimate. I always took it for granted that I was far more intelligent than he was. Yet, when anything went wrong with my car I hastened to him with it, watched him anxiously as he
(25) explored its vitals, and listened to his pronouncements as though they were divine oracles—and he always fixed my car.

Well, then, suppose my auto-repair man devised questions for an intelligence test. Or sup-
(30) pose a carpenter did, or a farmer, or, indeed, almost anyone but an academician. By every one of those tests, I'd prove myself a moron. And I'd be a moron, too. In a world where I could not use my academic training and my
(35) verbal talents but had to do something intricate or hard, working with my hands, I would do poorly. My intelligence, then, is not absolute but is a function of the society I live in and of the fact that a small subsection of that
(40) society has managed to foist itself on the rest as an arbiter of such matters.

From Isaac Asimov, "What Is Intelligence, Anyway?" *Psychology Today,* 1975.

1. Which of the following best states the author's view concerning intelligence tests?

   (1) No one is better at them than he is.
   (2) They only test a certain kind of intelligence.
   (3) The information they provide is totally inaccurate.
   (4) People who do well on them are usually very successful.
   (5) Farmers usually do better on them than carpenters.

2. Which of the following words is the best synonym for *aptitude* (line 2)?

   (1) mathematical
   (2) military
   (3) difficult
   (4) intelligence
   (5) general

639

3. If the author were to suggest an aptitude test for a plumber, whom would he probably recommend to write it?

   (1) other plumbers
   (2) the people who make up other intelligence tests
   (3) himself
   (4) companies that manufacture plumbing supplies
   (5) the military

4. The author's writing style can best be described as

   (1) formal
   (2) impartial
   (3) full of double meanings
   (4) academic
   (5) conversational

Items 5 to 8 are based on the following passage.

WHAT IS IT LIKE TO BE A NONCOMFORMIST?

What I must do is all that concerns me, not what the people think. This rule, equally arduous in actual and in intellectual life, may serve for the whole distinction between great-
(5) ness and meanness. It is harder because you will always find those who think they know what is your duty better than you know it. It is easy in the world to live after the world's opinion; it is easy in solitude to live after your
(10) own; but the great man is he who in the midst of the crowd keeps with perfect sweetness the independence of solitude.

For noncomformity the world whips you with its displeasure.
(15) The other terror that scares us from self-trust is our consistency; a reverence for our past act or word because the eyes of others have no other data for computing our orbit than our past acts, and we are loath to dis-
(20) appoint them.

But why should you keep your head over your shoulder? Why drag about this corpse of your memory, lest you contradict some what you have stated in this or that public place?
(25) Suppose you should contradict yourself; what then? It seems to be a rule of wisdom never to rely on your memory alone, scarcely even in acts of pure memory, but to bring the past for judgment into the thousand-eyed present, and
(30) live ever in a new day.

From Ralph Waldo Emerson, *Self-Reliance*.

5. Which of the following best sums up the main idea of the essay?

   (1) You should behave like everyone else.
   (2) Knowing your own mind is the first step to trusting yourself.
   (3) Your decisions should be guided by your trust in yourself.
   (4) Your present actions should be consistent with your past actions.
   (5) Living alone is the best way to live.

6. By referring to memory as a "corpse," (line 22) the author is implying that

   (1) he is losing his memory
   (2) the dead have no memory
   (3) we should remember and honor the dead
   (4) we should not dwell on past events
   (5) monuments are not always appropriate

7. What two things does the author say are impediments to our own self-reliance?

   (1) love of solitude and the desire to be consistent
   (2) the opinions of others and desire to be consistent
   (3) the forgetfulness of human nature and the opinions of others
   (4) the inability to compute data and the tendency to contradict yourself
   (5) the fear of living alone and the forgetfulness of human nature

8. For which of the following would this essay be appropriate?

   I. a high school workshop on drug and alcohol abuse
   II. seminar for young artists
   III. a training session for nurses

   (1) I only
   (2) II only
   (3) I and II
   (4) I and III
   (5) II and III

Items 9 to 12 are based on the following passage.

WHAT ARE THE BENEFITS OF SYNTHETIC FOOD?

Let us imagine the day when a country's economy is based on the manufacture of synthetic food instead of on traditional methods of food production. A few huge factories sited in dif-
(5) ferent parts of the country where coal and petroleum are to be found prepare all the food required by the population. Altogether, these factories occupy barely a few hundred square miles. Agriculture, with its need for a vast la-
(10) bor force and its limited capacity for progress, has been abolished, with the exception perhaps of market gardens and horticulture.

There is no longer any need for the vast industry which formerly provided agriculture
(15) with its equipment—tractors, machines, tools. Nor for the metal used in making them, nor for the fuel used to power them. Nor for chemical fertilizers, pesticides, etc. A large proportion of the population previously engaged in
(20) these industries and in agriculutre itself is thus freed for more productive work. Only a minute part of this manpower is needed for the production of synthetic food.

The old food industry gives way to an en-
(25) tirely new industry, infinitely more compact. No more bad years, poor harvests, unproductive land. No more calamitous losses due to climate, natural catastrophes, parasites, plant diseases, all of which today still take their toll
(30) on a considerable part of every harvest.

All the conditions are to hand for the transformation of villages into towns and towns into garden cities. Food products, ready to eat, packaged or tinned like the products on sale
(35) today, but with the fundamental difference that they contain the normal amount of vitamins and have the highest nutritive value, have only to be heated.

The appearance of these dishes leaves noth-
(40) ing to be desired. With a standard composition (proteins, carbohydrates, fats, salts, vitamins) adapted to each age need, these foods are the best source of health and energy the human system can have, infinitely better, at all events,
(45) than the best natural products.

No more obesity, no more fatty degeneration of the heart, liver and other complaints of the kind. At the least sign of physical abnormality, special diets can be composed with more or less of one or another ingredient.
(50)
Vast tracts of land previously reserved for crop growing give way progressively to forests and parks. The silting and drying up of rivers is stopped and the abundance of food products
(55) leads to the solution of the world shortage of drinking water which at present is steadily worsening.

The society of the future gains on all fronts: economic, social and also moral, as the slaugh-
(60) ter of animals, a cruel vestige of the past, is progressively done away with.

From Alexander Nesmeyanov and Vassily Belikov (*Unesco Courier*, March 1969).

9. What does the author mean by "synthetic" food?

   (1) 100% natural foods
   (2) food grown on experimental farms
   (3) foods cultivated from the ocean
   (4) food manufactured from chemicals
   (5) food high in nutrition

10. Based on the excerpt, which of the following might also be a result of synthetic food production?

    (1) increased silting of rivers
    (2) loss of flavor in food
    (3) increased pollution from factories
    (4) increased malnutrition
    (5) loss of all market gardens

11. The writer might use the same reasoning to argue for

(1) no preservatives or additives in food
(2) plastic clothing and accessories
(3) hand-made furniture
(4) increased agricultural production
(5) communal living, eating, and working

12. Which of the following best describes the tone of the passage?

(1) bored
(2) optimistic
(3) resigned
(4) ironic
(5) pessimistic

Fiction

Items 13 to 16 are based on the following passage.

DO CHEE AND OLD MAN FAT AGREE ABOUT WORKING THE LAND?

Chee rode the first part of the fifteen miles to Red Sands expectantly. The sight of sandstone buttes near Cottonwood Spring reddening in the morning sun brought a song almost to his
(5) lips. He twirled his reins in salute to the small boy herding sheep toward many-colored Butterfly Mountain, watched with pleasure the feathers of smoke rising against tree-darkened western mesas from the hogans sheltered there.
(10) But as he approached the familiar settlement sprawled in mushroom growth along the highway, he began to feel as though a scene from a bad dream was becoming real.

Several cars were parked around the trading
(15) store, which was built like two log hogans side by side, with red gas pumps in front and a sign across the tar-paper roofs: *Red Sands Trading Post—Groceries—Cold Drinks—Sandwiches—Indian Curios*. Back of the trading post
(20) an unpainted frame house and outbuildings squatted on the drab, treeless land. Chee and the Little One's mother had lived there when they stayed with his wife's people. That was according to custom—living with one's wife's
(25) people—but Chee had never been convinced that it was custom alone which prompted Old Man Fat and his wife to insist that their daughter bring her husband to live at the trading post.

(30) Beside the post was a large hogan of logs, with brightly painted pseudo-Navajo designs on the roof—a hogan with smoke-smudged windows and a garnish blue door which faced north to the highway. Old Man Fat had offered
(35) Chee a hogan like this one. The trader would build it if he and his wife would live there and Chee would work at his forge, making silver jewelry where tourists could watch him. But Chee had asked instead for a piece of land
(40) for a cornfield and help in building a hogan far back from the highway and a corral for the sheep he had brought to this marriage . . . .

Chee's lips tightened as he began to look around for Old Man Fat. Finally, he saw him
(45) passing among the tourists collecting coins.

Then the Little One saw Chee. The uncertainty left her face, and she darted through the crowd as her father swung down from his horse. Chee lifted her in his arms, hugging her tight.
(50) While he listened to her breathless chatter, he watched Old Man Fat bearing down on them, scowling.

As his father-in-law walked heavily across the graveled lot, Chee was reminded of a state-
(55) ment his mother sometimes made: "When you see a fat Navajo, you see one who hasn't worked for what he has."

From Juanita Platero and Siyowin Miller from "Chee's Daughter," *Common Ground*, Vol. 8, Winter 1948 (American Council for Nationalities Service).

13. Chee and Old Man Fat are

(1) Chinese
(2) brothers
(3) Navajo
(4) tourists
(5) ranchers

14. What do lines 43–45 show about Chee's feelings toward Old Man Fat?

(1) Chee respects him.
(2) Chee was happy to see him.
(3) Chee worked for Old Man Fat.
(4) Chee did not see him often.
(5) Chee did not really like Old Man Fat.

15. Why is the phrase "familiar settlement sprawled in mushroom growth along the highway" (line 10) effective in conveying Chee's feelings about Red Sands?

(1) It emphasizes Chee's love of nature.
(2) It suggests that Red Sands is like a beautiful plant.
(3) It makes Red Sands seem like an ugly thing.
(4) It captures the sensations of a bad dream.
(5) It distances the reader by describing Red Sands in an unusual way.

16. Which statement might reflect the author's attitude toward the American farm crisis of the 1980s?

(1) The farmers should sell their land.
(2) The farmers should be respected and helped.
(3) Farmers should be given job training for factory jobs.
(4) Large corporations should buy the farmland.
(5) Farmers should handle the crisis without any outside help.

Items 17 to 20 are based on the following passage.

WHAT ARE THE PLANS FOR THE SOCIALIST REVOLUTION?

Stavrogin stood still, looking intently into Peter's mad eyes.

"Listen, first we'll start unrest," Verkhov-
(5) ensky said in a terrible hurry, tugging constantly at Stavrogin's left sleeve. "As I told you, we are penetrating deep into the masses themselves. Do you know that, even now, we are terribly strong? We have people other than
(10) those who cut throats, set places on fire, go in for classical assassinations, and go around biting people. Those people only get in the way. Without discipline, what they do can have no sense for me. In reality, I'm a crook and not a socialist, ha-ha-ha! I have them all at hand
(15) already: we have the teacher who makes the children entrusted to his care laugh at their God and at their families; we have the lawyer defending the well-educated murderer because he has reached a higher stage of devel-
(20) opment than his victims and couldn't get hold of their money without killing them; the schoolboys who, to experience a strong sensation, kill a peasant, are also with us; the juries who acquit criminals are all working for
(25) us; the prosecutor torn by his anguished fear of not being liberal enough does us a service. Ah, we have so many high government officials with us, and so many literary figures who don't even know it themselves! On the other
(30) hand, the obedience of schoolboys and little fools has reached the high-water mark; the educators' gall bladders have ruptured and everywhere people's vanity and appetites have reached unheard-of proportions. Have you any
(35) idea how much we can do with ready-made ideas alone?"

From Fyodor Dostoyevsky, *The Possessed* (New York: New American Library, 1962).

17. What does Verkhovensky mean by "ready-made ideas" (line 35)?

    (1) ideas denied by the masses
    (2) propaganda published by the government
    (3) attitudes held by the general population
    (4) doctrines held by an industrialist society
    (5) beliefs held by an industrialist society

18. The teachers, schoolboys, lawyers, and juries all "work for" the revolution because they

    (1) are all socialists
    (2) are members of the working class
    (3) do not "get in the way" of the Socialist party
    (4) contribute to the breakdown of society
    (5) perpetuate political corruption

19. The author's attitude toward the revolutionaries may best be described as

    (1) sympathetic and encouraging
    (2) ironic and reproachful
    (3) fearful and hesitant
    (4) apathetic and uninvolved
    (5) confused and questioning

20. In lines 16–17, the phrase "laugh at their God and at their families" means

    (1) celebrate religious holidays together
    (2) enjoy reading the Bible
    (3) attend group worship services
    (4) reject religious beliefs and family principles
    (5) laugh at religious paintings

Items 21 to 24 are based on the following passage.

WHAT DID GRANDFATHER SAY AS HE DIED?

I am not ashamed of my grandparents for having been slaves. I am only ashamed of myself for having at one time been ashamed. About eighty-five years ago they were told that they
(5) were free, united with others of our country in everything pertaining to the common good, and, in everything social, separate like the fingers of the hand. And they believed it. They exulted in it. They stayed in their place, worked
(10) hard, and brought up my father to do the same. But my grandfather is the one. He was an odd old guy, my grandfather, and I am told I take after him. It was he who caused the trouble. On his death-bed he called my father to him
(15) and said, "Son, after I'm gone I want you to keep up the good fight. I never told you, but our life is a war and I have been a traitor all my born days, a spy in the enemy's country ever since I give up my gun back in the Re-
(20) construction. Live with your head in the lion's mouth. I want you to overcome 'em with yeses, undermine 'em with grins, agree 'em to death and destruction, let 'em swoller you till they vomit or bust wide open." They thought the
(25) old man had gone out of his mind. He had been the meekest of men. The younger children were rushed from the room, the shades drawn and the flame of the lamp turned so low that it sputtered on the wick like the old man's
(30) breathing. "Learn it to the younguns," he whispered fiercely; then he died.

But my folks were more alarmed over his last words than over his dying. It was as though he had not died at all, his words caused so
(35) much anxiety. I was warned emphatically to forget what he had said and, indeed, this is the first time it has been mentioned outside the family circle. It had a tremendous effect upon me, however. I could never be sure of
(40) what he meant. Grandfather had been a quiet old man who never made any trouble, yet on his deathbed he had called himself a traitor and a spy, and he had spoken of his meekness as a dangerous activity. It became a constant
(45) puzzle which lay unanswered in the back of my mind.

PRACTICE ITEMS

21. What does Grandfather mean when he says, "Live with your head in the lion's mouth" (line 20)?

    (1) retreat from the enemy
    (2) become a spy and a traitor
    (3) overcome the enemy through violence
    (4) place yourself in constant danger
    (5) live in the wild

22. Grandfather called himself a "traitor and a spy" (lines 17–18) because he

    (1) fought in the Civil War
    (2) did not stay in his place and work hard
    (3) was ashamed of being a slave
    (4) caused trouble for the family by going insane
    (5) did not stand up against the white man's oppression

23. If Grandfather were alive today, he most likely would

    (1) support the unions
    (2) join the military
    (3) work in a service job
    (4) become a secret agent
    (5) dodge the draft and move to Canada

24. Why might the author have situated Grandfather on his death bed?

    (1) to describe the poverty and despair of the family
    (2) to show that the family was not alarmed over his dying
    (3) to cause the narrator to feel guilty and uncomfortable
    (4) to represent the social weakness of slaves
    (5) to emphasize the importance of Grandfather's last words

Drama

Items 25 to 27 are based on the following passage.

DOES CALIGULA WANT TO BE A GOD ON EARTH?

CALIGULA: What's the use of the amazing power that's mine, if I can't have the sun set in the east, if I can't reduce the sum of suffering and make an end of death? No, Caesonia, it's
(5) all one whether I sleep or keep awake, if I've no power to tamper with the scheme of things.

CAESONIA: But that's madness, sheer madness. It's wanting to be a god on earth.

CALIGULA: So you, too, think I'm mad. And
(10) yet—what is a god that I should wish to be his equal? No, it's something higher, far above the gods, that I'm aiming at, longing for with all my heart and soul. I am taking over a kingdom where the impossible is king.

(15) CAESONIA: You can't prevent the sky from being the sky, or a fresh young face from aging, or a man's heart from growing cold.

CALIGULA (*with rising excitement*): I want...I want to drown the sky in the sea, to infuse
(20) ugliness with beauty, to wring a laugh from pain.

CAESONIA (*facing him with an imploring gesture*): There's good and bad, high and low, justice and injustice. And I swear to you
(25) these things will never change.

CALIGULA (*in the same tone*): And I'm resolved to change them...I shall make this age of ours a kingly gift—the gift of equality. And when all is leveled out, when the im-
(30) possible has come to earth and the moon is in my hands—then, perhaps, I shall be transfigured and the world renewed; then men will die no more and at last be happy.

From Albert Camus/Justin O'Brien, *Caligula* (New York: International Creative Management, 1961).

25. What does Caligula desire?

   (1) to beautify the earth as an artist
   (2) to end equality and be king of a large empire
   (3) to be a spokesman for minorities and equal rights
   (4) to enjoy life more and dream for the impossible
   (5) to eliminate all differences and rule over nature itself

26. Which of the following most likely describes the author's purpose for including the phrase "or a man's heart from growing cold" in Caesonia's speech (line 17)?

   (1) to imply that the world is a cold place in which to live
   (2) to emphasize Caligula's desire to overcome death
   (3) to give the reader a sense of the numerous tasks Caligula faces
   (4) to reveal Caesonia's cynical nature
   (5) to hint at Caesonia's underlying beliefs about Caligula's character

27. What do the stage directions (line 22) reveal about Caesonia's feelings?

   (1) They show that she agrees with Caligula.
   (2) They show that she is laughing at Caligula.
   (3) They illustrate her anger.
   (4) They show that she is begging Caligula to give up his ideas.
   (5) They illustrate her love for Caligula in the way she looks at him.

Items 28 to 30 are based on the following passage.

WHAT DILEMMA DOES KEN FACE AS A PARALYZED INVALID?

KEN: I am serious you know...about deciding to die.

DR. SCOTT: You will get over the feeling.

KEN: How do you know?

(5) DR. SCOTT: But if we acted on your decision now, there wouldn't be an opportunity for you to accept it.

KEN: I grant you, I may become lethargic and quiescent. Happy when a nurse comes to
(10) put in a new catheter, or give me an enema, or to turn me over. These could become the high spots of my day. I might even learn to do wonderful things, like turn the pages of a book with some miracle of modern science,
(15) or to type letters with flicking my eyelids. And you would look at me and say "Wasn't it worth waiting?" and I would say: "Yes" and be proud of my achievements. Really proud. I grant you all that, but it doesn't alter the
(20) validity of my present position.

DR. SCOTT: But if you became happy?

KEN: But I don't want to become happy by becoming the computer section of a complex machine. And morally, you must
(25) accept my decision.

DR. SCOTT: Not according to my morals.

KEN: And why are yours better than mine?

From Brian Clark, *Whose Life Is It Anyway?* (Chicago: Dramatic Publishing Company, 1978).

PRACTICE ITEMS

28. What does Ken mean by "becoming the computer section of a complex machine" (lines 23–24)?

(1) becoming the victim of himself
(2) being the "guinea pig" of medical research
(3) being the thinking part of his life-support systems
(4) "selling out" to the establishment
(5) training to be a computer analyst

29. Which of the following best expresses Ken's attitude toward moral standards?

(1) Individual moral rights are to be respected by all.
(2) Morality should have no place in life-and-death decisions.
(3) There is one "universal" morality.
(4) A good, moral life leads to happiness.
(5) Upstanding morals lead to high achievement.

30. The exchange of dialogue in this passage suggests that

(1) Dr. Scott will discharge Ken
(2) Ken will recover
(3) Dr. Scott and Ken will become friends
(4) Ken will learn to type
(5) the conflict between Ken and Dr. Scott will continue

Poetry

Items 31 to 33 are based on the following poem.

WHAT KIND OF LIFE HAS MOTHER HAD?

Mother to Son

Well, Son, I'll tell you:
Life for me ain't been no crystal stair.
It's had tacks in it,
And splinters,
(5) And boards torn up,
And places with no carpet on the floor,
Bare.
But all the time
I'se been aclimbin' on
(10) And reachin' landin's,
And turning corners,
And sometimes goin' in the dark
Where there ain't been no light.
So boy, don't you turn back.
(15) Don't you set down on the steps
'Cause you finds it's kinder hard.
Don't you fall now
For I'se still goin', Honey,
I'se still climbin'
(20) And life for me ain't been no crystal stair.

From Langston Hughes, "Mother to Son" (New York: Alfred A. Knopf, 1926, 1954).

31. According to the poem, what does the mother conclude about her life?

(1) She is going to keep trying no matter how difficult it is.
(2) She is going to turn over her struggle to her son.
(3) Her life is too difficult to try to continue.
(4) She is going to make more money from now on.
(5) She has achieved everything she wanted to.

648   Test 4: Interpreting Literature and the Arts   PRACTICE

32. Based on the mother's statement to her son, you can infer that the son

  (1) was determined never to be a quitter
  (2) was a failure in his career
  (3) was tempted to quit and needed encouragement
  (4) had never known defeat
  (5) had acquired great wealth

33. Which of the following best describes the tone of this poem?

  (1) angry
  (2) bitter
  (3) encouraging
  (4) happy
  (5) depressed

Items 34 to 36 are based on the following poem.

HOW DO WORDS AFFECT THE PERSON IN THIS POEM?

> He ate and drank the precious words.
> His spirit grew robust;
> He knew no more that he was poor,
> Nor that his frame was dust.
> (5) He danced along the dingy days,
> And this bequest of wings
> Was but a book. What liberty
> A loosened spirit brings!

From Emily Dickinson, The Poems of Emily Dickinson (Cambridge, Mass.: The Belknap Press of Harvard University Press, 1951).

34. The poem tells us that the person is

  (1) eating
  (2) drinking
  (3) growing
  (4) flying
  (5) reading

35. What does the first line of the poem imply?

  (1) The man was poor and hungry.
  (2) The man had just learned to read.
  (3) The words were difficult to swallow.
  (4) The words were like food to a hungry man.
  (5) The man was reading at the table.

36. The tone of this poem is

  (1) literary
  (2) joyous
  (3) somber
  (4) funny
  (5) educational

Commentary

Items 37 to 41 are based on the following passage.

WHAT ARE THE EFFECTS OF TELEVISION ON CHILDREN?

Concern about the effects of television on children has centered almost exclusively upon the *contents* of the programs children watch. Social scientists and researchers devise ex-
(5) periments . . . to determine whether watching violent programs make children behave more aggressively, or conversely, whether watching exemplary programs encourages "prosocial" behavior in children. Studies are conducted
(10) to discover whether television commercials make children greedy and materialistic or, as some have suggested, generous and spiritual. Investigators seek to discover whether stereotypes on television affect children's ways of
(15) thinking, causing them to become prejudiced, or open-minded, or whatever . . . .

Preschool children are the single largest television audience in America, spending a greater number of total hours and a greater
(20) proportion of their waking day watching television than any other age group. According to one survey made in 1970, children in the 2–5 age group spend an average of 30.4 hours each week watching television, while children

(25) in the 6–11 group spend 25.5 hours watching. The weekly average for adult viewers in 1971 was 23.3 hours. Another survey made in 1971 documented a weekly viewing time of 34.56 hours for preschool boys and 32.44 hours for
(30) preschool girls. Still other surveys suggest figures up to 54 hours a week for preschool viewers. Even the most conservative estimates indicate that preschool children in America are spending more than a third of their waking
(35) hours watching television.

What are the effects upon the vulnerable and developing human organism of spending such a significant proportion of each day engaging in this particular experience? How does
(40) the television experience affect a child's language development, for instance? How does it influence his developing imagination, his creativity? How does the availability of television affect the ways parents bring up their
(45) children? Are new child-rearing strategies being adopted and old ones discarded because the television set is available to parents for relief? Is the child's perception of reality subtly altered by steady exposure to television unreal-
(50) ities? How does watching television for several hours each day affect the child's abilities to form human relationships? What happens to family life as a result of family members' involvement with television?

(55) Though there may never be clear-cut and final answers to these questions, the very fact that they are rarely raised, that the experience . . . is rarely considered, signals the distorted view American parents take of the role of tele-
(60) vision in their children's lives.

From Marie Winn, *The Plug-In Drug: Television, Children and the Family* (New York: Bantam Books, 1977).

37. According to the excerpt, the older television watchers are, the

  (1) more television they watch
  (2) more susceptible they are to television's influence
  (3) less they watch television
  (4) less they are affected by television
  (5) more thay are able to distinguish between good and bad programming

38. How might "exemplary programs" encourage "prosocial behavior in children" (line 8)?

  (1) by providing good role models for children to follow
  (2) by discouraging children to follow social norms
  (3) by instructing children how to fight authority
  (4) by showing common social experiences
  (5) by showing the problems of underprivileged children

39. Which of the following questions about reading behavior would the author of this passage be most interested in?

  (1) What type of book do people most like to read?
  (2) What age groups are most likely to read westerns?
  (3) How do ghost stories affect people's beliefs in the supernatural?
  (4) Do people who read a lot have greater imaginations than people who seldom read?
  (5) Do people prefer to spend time reading books or watching movies?

40. Which of the following techniques can be found in the passage?
  I. statistics
  II. quotations from authorities
  III. ironic examples
  IV. figurative language

  (1) I only
  (2) II only
  (3) I and II
  (4) II and III
  (5) I, III, and IV

41. The tone used in the excerpt would be *least* effective in which of the following?

  (1) news report
  (2) political speech
  (3) magazine article
  (4) personal letter
  (5) sociology textbook

Items 42 to 45 are based on the following passage.

WHAT DID MARTHA GRAHAM CONTRIBUTE TO DANCE?

Martha Graham, like the Colorado River, seems too small to have changed the face of the world. On stage, magnified by the passion of her dancing, Graham was a figure as monumental as
(5) the tragic heroines she portrayed; in her living room, surrounded by art objects gathered during a lifetime of traveling, she is a tiny, fine-boned woman with a rich, seductive voice and dark eyes deep enough to hold the answers to
(10) all the questions in the universe.

The Colorado River required eons in which to carve out the Grand Canyon; Graham has needed only fifty-nine years since making her first independent work of choreography to re-
(15) shape the art of dance. At ninety-one, she ranks with Picasso, Stravinsky, and Joyce as an artist who formed the taste, the vision, and the style of the twentieth century—who changed the way we see the world. She not only altered
(20) the subject matter of dance, she devised and codified a technique that has become as widely recognized and used as the academic technique of ballet. She has commissioned major composers and sculptors to provide music and
(25) decor for her works; she has invented a complete dance-theater that, for all its opulence, admits no extraneous elements. Moreover, she has created an image of modern dance that still holds the popular imagination. . . .

(30) "Life today is nervous, sharp, zigzag," she asserted in 1929. "It often stops in midair. That is what I aim for in my dances." Graham was a rebel then: modern dance was an angry, young art; ballet was the aging, effete enemy—an ad-
(35) versary to be raged against. The real problem with ballet, the choreographer said recently, was that "back then, it was pretty terrible ballet; it was facetious. I had to find something to dance about, and the about was myself and
(40) the world around me."

That need set Graham—and a few of her contemporaries—apart and led to the development of modern dance as a major art form. It is an art invented in the United States and
(45) exported to the world—a distinction shared only with jazz.

From Joseph H. Mazo, *Horizon*, October 1985.

42. According to the excerpt, Graham was innovative because she

    (1) utilized movements from ballet in modern dance
    (2) expressed the attitudes of her time in unique movement
    (3) was the first woman choreographer
    (4) used fluid movements which were often compared to rivers
    (5) was the peer of Stravinsky and Picasso

43. The description of Graham's choreography as admitting "no extraneous elements" for all its "opulence" (line 27) suggest that the dance is

    (1) very elaborate
    (2) minimal
    (3) flamboyant
    (4) stiff
    (5) controlled

44. Based on the excerpt's description of Graham's style, which of the following types of music would be most appropriate to accompany her choreography?

    (1) soft rock
    (2) medieval chants
    (3) jazz
    (4) military march
    (5) heavy metal

45. Why is the writer's opening image of the Colorado River effective in conveying Martha Graham's accomplishments?

    (1) It evokes the fluid movement of Graham's choreography.
    (2) It introduces a dramatic situation at the beginning of the text.
    (3) It emphasizes the power and impact of Graham on the dance world.
    (4) It introduces a note of humor and irony.
    (5) It provides a scene of "nature" to reflect Graham's "organic" dance philosophy.

Answers are on pages A-76–A-77.

PRACTICE ITEMS 4: INTERPRETING LITERATURE AND THE ARTS
Performance Analysis Chart

Directions: Circle the number of each item that you got correct on the Practice Items. Count how many items you got correct in each row; count how many items you got correct in each column. Write the number correct per row and column as the numerator in the fraction in the appropriate "Total Correct" box. (The denominators represent the total number of items in the row or column.) Write the grand total correct over the denominator **45** at the lower right corner of the chart. (For example, if you got 40 items correct, write 40 so that the fraction reads 40/45.)

Item Type	Nonfiction (page 375)	Fiction (page 387)	Drama (page 399)	Poetry (page 411)	Commentary (page 422)	TOTAL CORRECT
Literal Comprehension Specific (page 220)	9	20, 21	28			/4
Literal Comprehension Global (page 220)	1, 5, 7	13, 18	25	31, 34	37, 42	/10
Inferential Comprehension Specific (page 220)	2, 6	14, 17	27	35	38, 43	/8
Inferential Comprehension Global (page 220)	10	19, 22	29, 30	32		/6
Application (page 224)	3, 8, 11	16, 23			39, 44	/7
Analysis (page 228)	4, 12	15, 24	26	33, 36	40, 41, 45	/10
TOTAL CORRECT	/12	/12	/6	/6	/9	/45

The page numbers in parentheses indicate where in this book you can find the beginning of specific instruction about the various types of literature and commentary and about the types of questions you encountered on the Practice Items.

PRACTICE ITEMS 5
Mathematics

Directions: *Choose the one best answer to each question.*

Arithmetic Items

1. Ronald sleeps 7 hours 45 minutes per night. How much sleep does he get in a week?

    (1) 45 hours 45 minutes
    (2) 49 hours 15 minutes
    (3) 49 hours 25 minutes
    (4) 54 hours 15 minutes
    (5) 54 hours 25 minutes

2. Annette earned $12,766 last year. What was her weekly salary?

    (1) $ 245.50
    (2) $ 255.32
    (3) $ 425.53
    (4) $1063.83
    (5) $1276.60

3. A box of Krunch-o-Wheats weighs 1 pound 9 ounces. How much does a case containing 24 boxes weigh?

    (1) 13 pounds 8 ounces
    (2) 19 pounds 8 ounces
    (3) 24 pounds 8 ounces
    (4) 28 pounds 8 ounces
    (5) 36 pounds 8 ounces

4. A grocery store offered eggs on sale for $.79 per dozen, and an additional $.30 saving by use of a coupon from its advertisement. Which of the following expressions would show the cost per egg, including the use of the coupon?

    (1) .79 − .30/12
    (2) (.79 − .30)/12
    (3) (.79 + .30)/12
    (4) .79/12 − .30
    (5) .79/12

5. Michael rode his bike at 12 miles per hour for 1 hour 45 minutes. How many miles did he ride?

    (1) 9
    (2) 12
    (3) 17.4
    (4) 21
    (5) 24

6. To reach work, Deborah rides the subway, which travels at 35 miles per hour. She rides for 30 minutes and then walks at 4 miles per hour for 25 minutes. Which of the following expressions would show the distance Deborah travels to work?

    (1) $(35 \times 4) \times 30$
    (2) $\frac{35}{2} + 4$
    (3) $\left(35 \times \frac{1}{2}\right) + \left(4 \times \frac{5}{12}\right)$
    (4) $(35 + 4)(30 + 25)$
    (5) $(35 \times 30) + (4 \times 25)$

PRACTICE ITEMS

Items 7 to 10 are based on the following information.

Competitive interest rates are being offered for some new-model cars in order to increase sales. The Sleuth sells for $7985; list price for the Blair is $8888; the Simplex is priced at $11,896. Dealer A is offering financing for the Blair at 6% interest for 4 years or, with a $1000 rebate, at 11% interest for 3 years; dealer A is also offering the Sleuth at 9.5% interest for 3 years. Dealer B is offering the Simplex at 7.7% interest for 3 years and the Sleuth at 8% interest for 4 years. Dealer C is offering the Blair at 8% interest for 3 years.

7. Ed bought a new Simplex with dealer financing. How much interest did he pay?

   (1) $ 916.00
   (2) $ 1,544.04
   (3) $ 2,747.98
   (4) $12,812.00
   (5) $14,643.98

8. If Wanda buys a new Blair from dealer A, which financing option would cost her less, and by how much?

   (1) rebate with 11% interest for 3 years, by $530.08
   (2) 8% interest for 4 years, by $530.08
   (3) rebate with 11% interest for 3 years, by $469.92
   (4) 6% interest for 4 years, $469.92
   (5) Insufficient data is given to solve the problem.

9. If Nancy will pay $2275.73 interest over 3 years, which car did she buy and from which dealer?

   (1) the Blair from dealer C
   (2) the Sleuth from dealer A
   (3) the Sleuth from dealer B
   (4) the Blair from dealer A
   (5) Insufficient data is given to solve the problem.

Arithmetic Items **653**

10. Irving is buying a Sleuth from dealer B. If he finances the purchase price, what will be his total cost?

    (1) $ 9,901.40
    (2) $10,140.95
    (3) $10,260.73
    (4) $10,540.20
    (5) $11,019.30

Items 11 and 12 are based on the following figure.

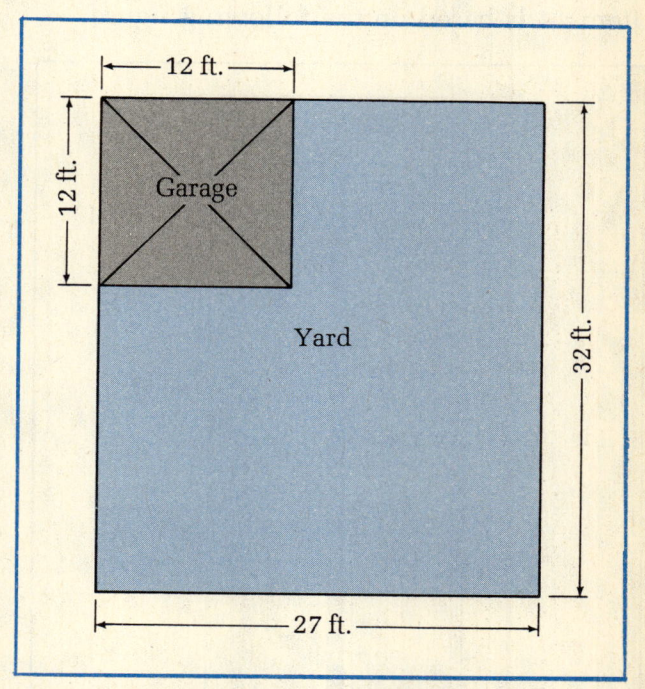

11. How many feet of fencing will be needed to enclose this yard?

    (1) 24
    (2) 47
    (3) 70
    (4) 94
    (5) 118

12. If a garden is planted behind the garage, what will its area be in square feet?

    (1) 180
    (2) 240
    (3) 300
    (4) 480
    (5) Insufficient data is given to solve the problem.

13. Pam's round wading pool has a diameter of 6 feet. Her parents want to build a round cover that has a 6-inch overlap. What would be the approximate area of the cover in square feet?

    (1) 21.89
    (2) 28.26
    (3) 38.47
    (4) 113.04
    (5) 132.67

Item 14 is based on the following figure.

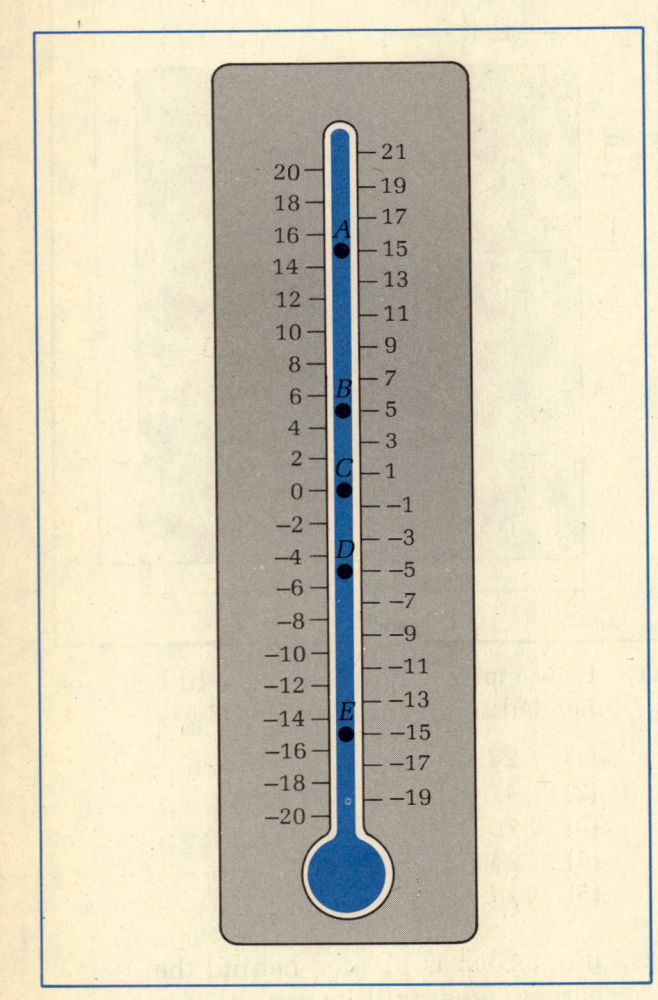

14. If the temperature was −10° and it warmed up 5°, to which point on the thermometer would the mercury rise?

    (1) 5
    (2) −15
    (3) 0
    (4) −5
    (5) 10

Item 15 is based on the following figure.

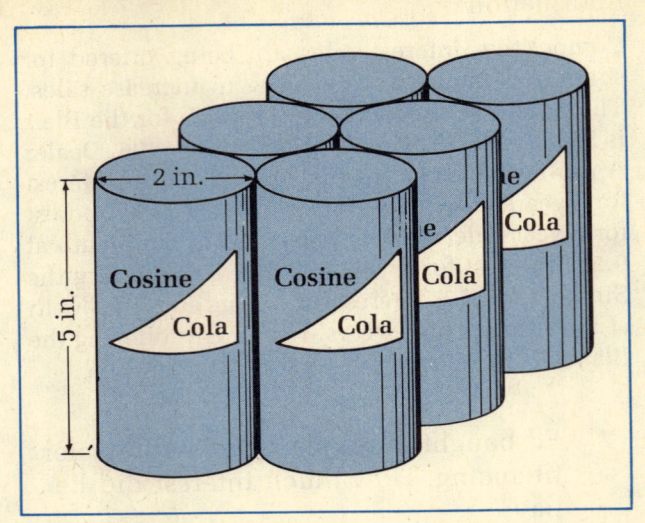

15. In cubic inches, what is the volume of a six-pack of Cosine Cola?

    (1) 15.7
    (2) 62.8
    (3) 94.2
    (4) 188.4
    (5) 376.8

16. At the end of a trading day, the prices of these five stocks changed in the following ways.

    | Stock A | $+\frac{1}{4}$ |
    | Stock B | $-\frac{1}{2}$ |
    | Stock C | $-\frac{1}{8}$ |
    | Stock D | $+\frac{7}{8}$ |
    | Stock E | $+\frac{3}{4}$ |

    Which of the following sequences correctly lists the changes in stock prices from the greatest to the least?

    (1) A, B, C, D, E
    (2) B, C, A, E, D
    (3) C, B, A, D, E
    (4) D, E, B, A, C
    (5) E, B, D, C, A

17. Which of the following candy purchases wold cost the LEAST: 9 pieces of bubble gum at $.05 each, 13 jelly beans at $.03 each, one candy bar at $.40, or 7 sour balls at $.06 each?

   (1) bubble gum
   (2) jelly beans
   (3) candy bar
   (4) sour balls
   (5) Insufficient data is given to solve the problem.

Item 18 is based on the following graph.

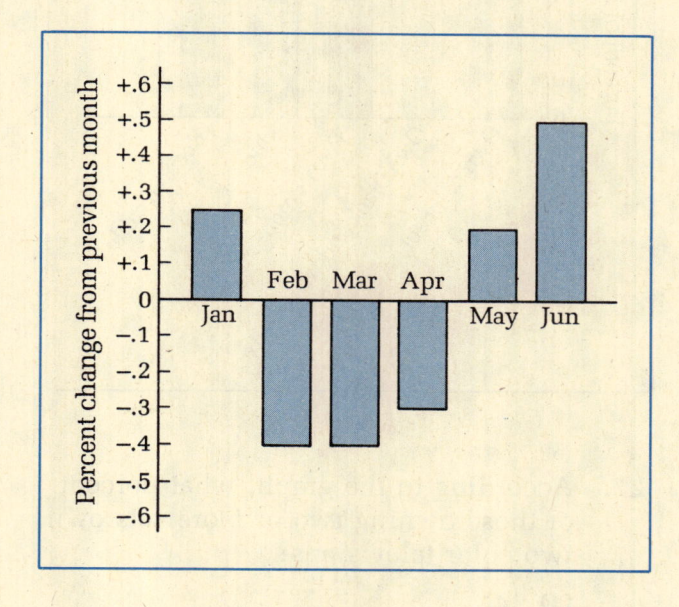

18. According to the graph, which month showed the greatest percent change in the Consumer Price Index?

   (1) January
   (2) February
   (3) April
   (4) May
   (5) June

19. When home computers first hit the market, a computer with 4 kilobytes of memory cost $500 and up. Today, a 64-kilobyte computer can be purchased for less than $150. How can the memory of the new computers be expressed in terms of the old memory?

   (1) 4^1
   (2) 4^2
   (3) 4^3
   (4) 4^4
   (5) 4^5

20. Light travels at a speed of 1.86×10^5 miles per second. How many miles can light travel in a minute?

   (1) 111.6
   (2) 558
   (3) 111,600
   (4) 558,000
   (5) 11,160,000

21. Riverville has a total of 6780 households. According to the recent census, 7973 boys and 8638 girls live in the town. What is the average number of children per household?

   (1) 1.18
   (2) 1.27
   (3) 2.08
   (4) 2.45
   (5) 3.45

22. Helen received a catalog in the mail stating that she would win a prize if she were one of the first 400 persons to send an order to the company. The same catalog and offer was sent to 15,000,000 persons. If ¼ of the people who received the catalog, including Helen, send an order, what will be her chance of winning a prize?

   (1) $\frac{1}{400}$
   (2) $\frac{1}{9,375}$
   (3) $\frac{1}{37,500}$
   (4) $\frac{1}{3,750,000}$
   (5) $\frac{1}{15,000,000}$

Test 5: Mathematics

23. Nora borrowed $50,000 at 6% simple interest for one year. How much interest will she pay if she repays the loan in 6 months?

    (1) $1500
    (2) $1800
    (3) $3000
    (4) $5000
    (5) $6000

24. Marcus walks at an average speed of 4 mph for 2 hours every day. What are the total number of miles Marcus walks in one week?

    (1) 14
    (2) 20
    (3) 28
    (4) 40
    (5) 56

25. A triangular lot measures 75 meters by 100 meters by 125 meters. What is the perimeter of the lot in meters?

    (1) 30
    (2) 150
    (3) 232.5
    (4) 300
    (5) 3000

26. What is the area in inches of a triangle that has a base of 28 inches and a height of 18.5 inches?

    (1) 172.6
    (2) 189
    (3) 259
    (4) 518
    (5) 1036

Items 27 and 28 are based on the following graph.

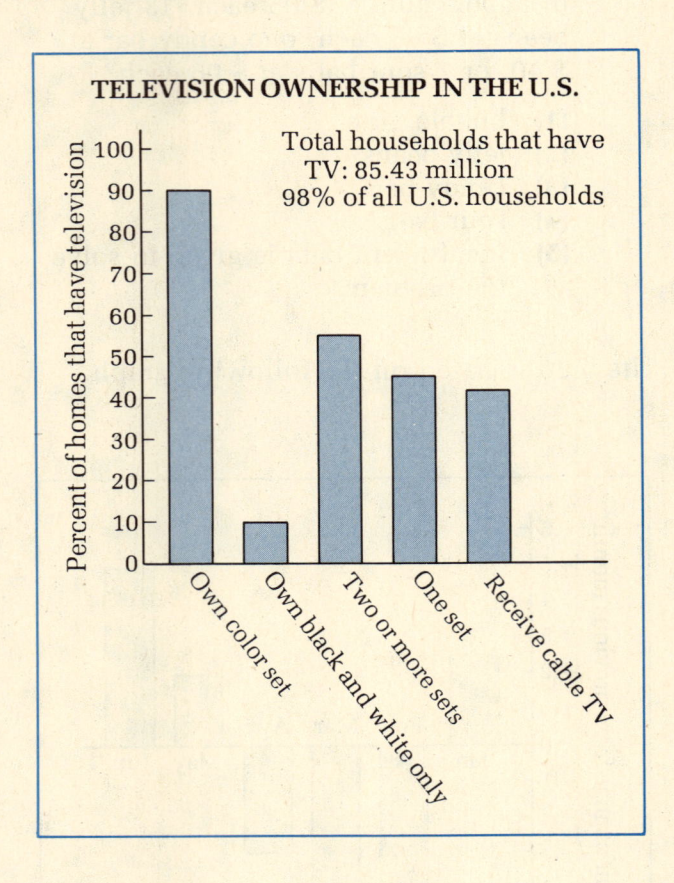

TELEVISION OWNERSHIP IN THE U.S.

Total households that have TV: 85.43 million
98% of all U.S. households

(Bar graph: Own color set ≈ 90%; Own black and white only ≈ 10%; Two or more sets ≈ 55%; One set ≈ 45%; Receive cable TV ≈ 42%)

27. According to the graph, what percent of those owning two or more sets own two color televisions?

    (1) 45
    (2) 55
    (3) 51
    (4) 90
    (5) Insufficient data is given to solve the problem.

28. Approximately how many million homes have only one television set?

    (1) 8.54
    (2) 38.44
    (3) 42.72
    (4) 46.99
    (5) Insufficient data is given to solve the problem.

PRACTICE ITEMS　　　　　　　　　　　　　　　　　　　　　　　　Algebra Items

Algebra Items

29. For every $25 that the Shipleys spend for clothing, they spend $45 for entertainment. If the Shipleys spent $4000 for clothing in one year, how much did they spend for entertainment?

    (1) $3600
    (2) $4800
    (3) $5000
    (4) $7200
    (5) $8000

30. A movie theater sells adults' tickets for $4.00 and children's tickets for $2.50. If a = the adults' tickets and c = the children's tickets that are sold for a show, which of the following expressions would give the amount of money the theater received?

    (1) $4a + 2.5c$
    (2) $4a - 2.5c$
    (3) $\frac{a}{4} + \frac{c}{2.5}$
    (4) $(a + 4)(c + 2.5)$
    (5) $ac(4 + 2.5)$

31. Marcia has $200-deductible automobile insurance. Her insurance company will pay 80% of the amount that she is charged for repairs that exceed $200. If r = the cost of car repairs, which of the following expressions would give the amount of money that the insurance company should pay her?

    (1) $.8(r + 200)$
    (2) $.8(r - 200)$
    (3) $.8r - 200$
    (4) $.8r + 200$
    (5) Insufficient data is given to solve the problem.

32. At a furniture-store sale, a couch can be purchased for half price when a dinette set is purchased at regular price. Which of the following expressions would show the total cost of a dinette set and a couch, if s = the price of the dinette set and c = the regular price of the couch?

    (1) $2(s + c)$
    (2) $s + 2c$
    (3) $\frac{(s + c)}{2}$
    (4) $\frac{s + 2}{c}$
    (5) $s + \frac{c}{2}$

33. Albert has candy to share with his friends. He will divide the candy equally among his friends and himself. If f = the number of friends and p = the number of pieces of candy, which of the following expressions would show the number of pieces each one would receive?

    (1) $\frac{p}{f}$
    (2) $\frac{p}{f - 1}$
    (3) $\frac{(f + 1)}{p}$
    (4) $\frac{p + 1}{f}$
    (5) $\frac{p}{(f + 1)}$

34. Paula plans to donate 6% of her annual income in equal amounts to her five favorite charities. If a = her annual income, which of the following expressions would show the amount each charity would receive from Paula?

    (1) $\frac{a}{.6}$　　　　(4) $\frac{.06a}{5}$
    (2) $\frac{a}{5}$　　　　(5) $\frac{5a}{.6}$
    (3) $\frac{.6a}{a}$

35. Angie exercises for one hour every day. She does aerobics for twice as long as she warms up and cools down for ⅝ the amount of time she warms up. If w = the warm-up time, which equation should be used to determine how long her warm-up is?

   (1) $2.625w = 60$
   (2) $2w + \dfrac{w}{8} = 60$
   (3) $\dfrac{10w}{8} = 60$
   (4) $w + 2w + \dfrac{5w}{8} = 60$
   (5) $60 - 2w + \dfrac{5w}{8} = 60$

36. Ted has $37 to spend on gifts for his two nephews and three nieces. He intends to spend an equal amount on each gift. The store charges 6% sales tax. If g = the gift cost before sales tax is added, which of the following equations should be used to determine the amount Ted should spend on each gift?

   (1) $5g - .06(5g) = 37$
   (2) $5g + .06(5g) = 37$
   (3) $5g - .06 = 37$
   (4) $5 \times .06g = 37$
   (5) Insufficient data is given to solve the problem.

37. The ratio of rye grass seed to bluegrass seed in a bag of grass seed is 9:4. If the bag contains 24 pounds of bluegrass seed, how many pounds does the bag weigh?

   (1) 6
   (2) 10.7
   (3) 30
   (4) 54
   (5) 78

38. Natalie paid one long-distance telephone company $.50 more than ⅓ the cost for a similar call through another company's system. If the less expensive company charged $3.95 for the call, what did the other company charge?

   (1) $ 1.15
   (2) $ 3.45
   (3) $10.35
   (4) $11.85
   (5) $13.35

39. As a clothing salesclerk, Beth earns $200 per week plus an 18% commission on her sales. What were her sales the week she earned $483.68?

   (1) $1576
   (2) $1800
   (3) $2687
   (4) $3798
   (5) Insufficient data is given to solve the problem.

40. As a heating company estimator, Juan estimates whether houses can efficiently use the Enermizer II furnace. To estimate, Juan uses the expression, $1500 > f > 950$, in which f = the square footage of a house. According to the expression, which of the following houses can use the Enermizer II?

HOUSE	DIMENSIONS IN FEET
A	30 × 40
B	35 × 15
C	40 × 42
D	45 × 32
E	37 × 37

   (1) A only
   (2) B only
   (3) A and E
   (4) A, D, and E
   (5) B and C

PRACTICE ITEMS

Algebra Items

41. Phonograph records are produced in two speeds, 33 and 45 revolutions per minute (RPM). If a song requires 297 revolutions to be played at 33 RPM, how many revolutions would it take at 45 RPM?

    (1) 217
    (2) 342
    (3) 330
    (4) 405
    (5) 660

42. For their daughter's wedding, the Morgansterns plan to spend f for flowers, the same amount for the wedding gown, and 4 times the amount spent on flowers for food. Which of the following expressions would show how much they plan to spend?

    (1) $f + f + 4f$
    (2) $f + 2f + 4f$
    (3) $f + 4f + 4f$
    (4) $\frac{f}{4}$
    (5) $\frac{f}{6}$

43. Which of the following expressions is equal to $x^2 + x - 42$?

    (1) $(x - 6)(x + 7)$
    (2) $(x + 6)(x - 7)$
    (3) $(x - 6)(x - 7)$
    (4) $(x + 6)(x + 7)$
    (5) Insufficient data is given to solve the problem.

44. Which of the following expressions is equal to $(y + 9)(y - 5)$?

    (1) $45y^2$
    (2) $y^2 - 4y + 45$
    (3) $y^2 + 4y - 45$
    (4) $y^2 + 4y + 45$
    (5) $y^2 + 4y - 45$

45. If $p^2 - p - 12 = 0$, what does p equal?

    (1) 4 only
    (2) $^-3$ only
    (3) 3 and 4
    (4) 3 and $^-4$
    (5) $^-3$ and 4

46. Which of the following expressions is equal to $\frac{3x^2}{x^{-1}}$?

    (1) $3x^1$
    (2) x^3
    (3) $2x^2$
    (4) $3x^3$
    (5) $4x^3$

660 Test 5: Mathematics

Geometry Items

Item 47 is based on the following figure.

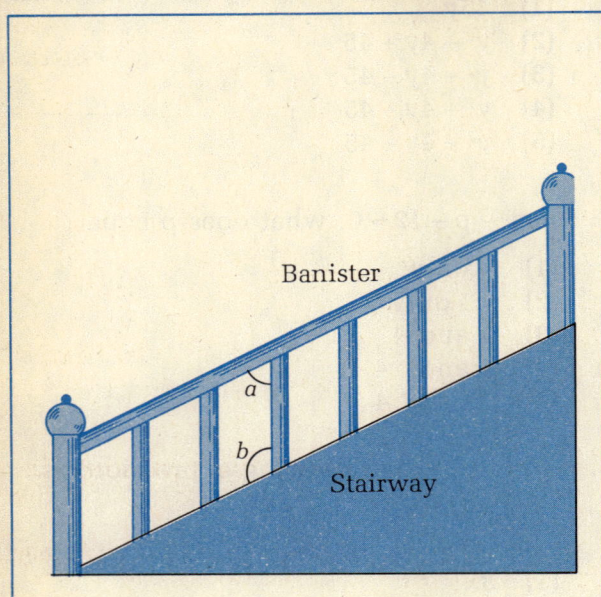

47. If the banister is parallel to the stairway and if angle a = 54°, then what must be the measure of angle b?

   (1) 36°
   (2) 54°
   (3) 90°
   (4) 126°
   (5) 180°

Item 48 is based on the following figure.

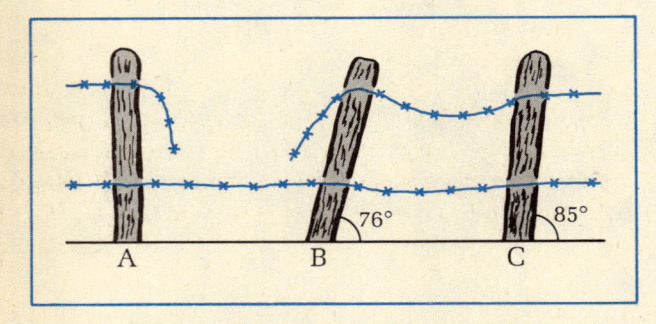

48. Which of the following should Kevin do to make fence-post B perpendicular to the ground again?

   (1) Increase its angle by 14°.
   (2) Increase its angle by 104°.
   (3) Decrease its angle by 31°.
   (4) Make it parallel to fence-post C.
   (5) Make it the hypotenuse of fence-post A.

Item 49 is based on the following figure.

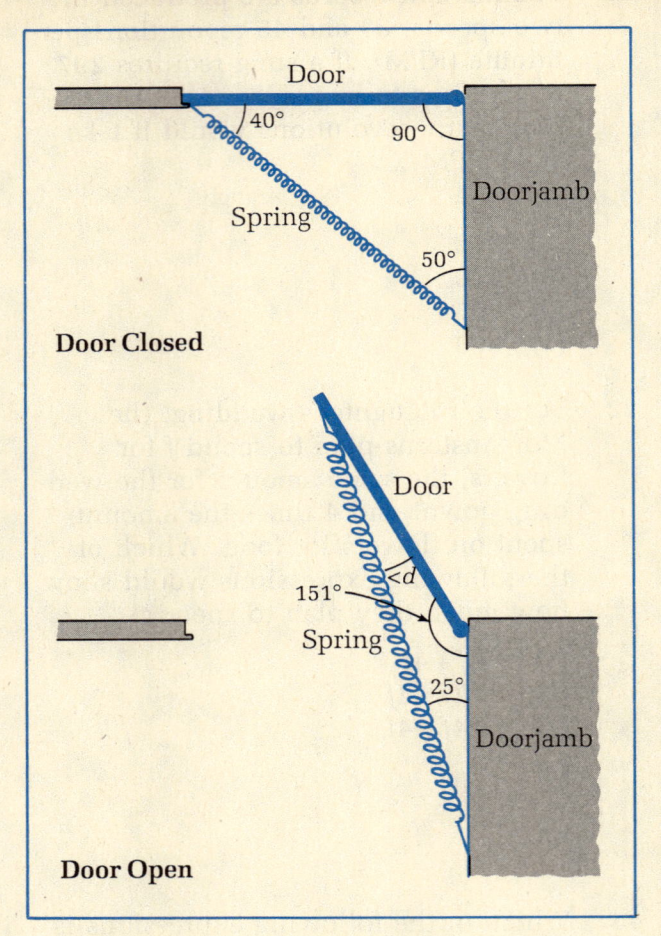

49. When the door is open, angle d would measure how many degrees?

   (1) 4°
   (2) 10°
   (3) 14°
   (4) 20°
   (5) 25°

PRACTICE ITEMS   Geometry Items   **661**

Items 50 to 52 are based on the following figure.

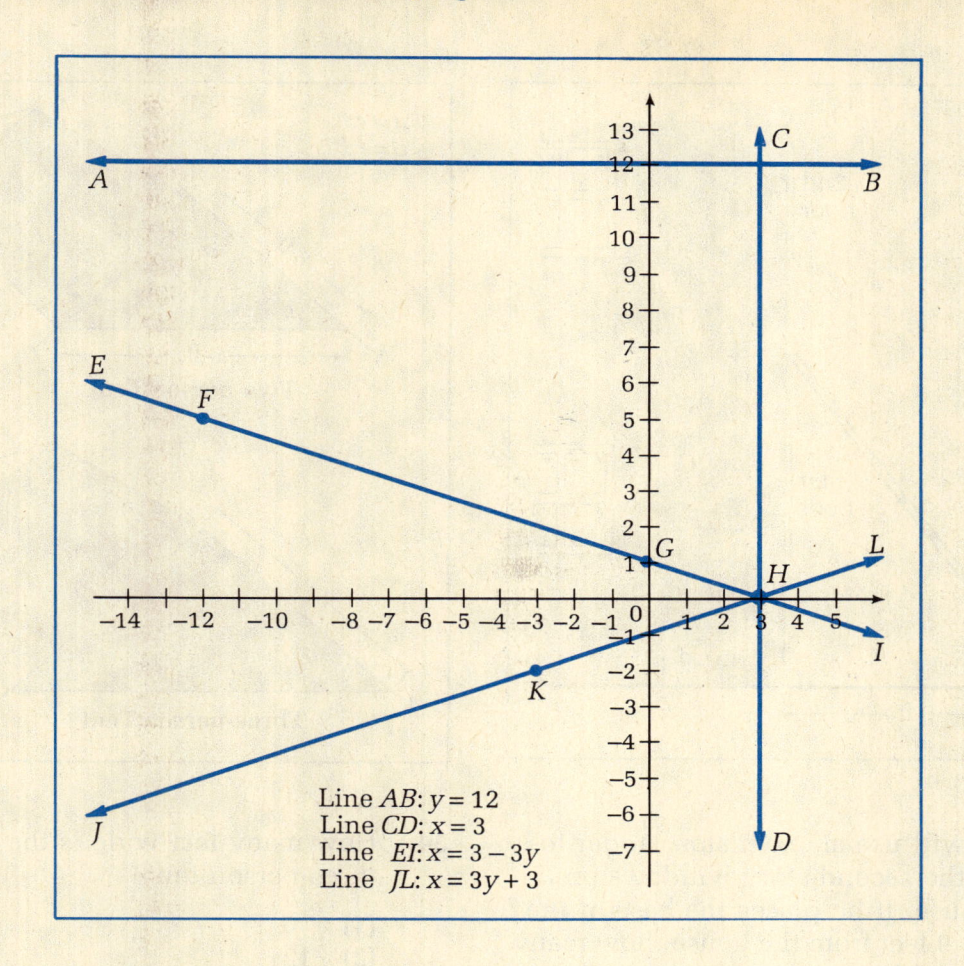

Line AB: $y = 12$
Line CD: $x = 3$
Line EI: $x = 3 - 3y$
Line JL: $x = 3y + 3$

50. Which line has a negative slope?

    (1) AB
    (2) CD
    (3) EI
    (4) JL
    (5) Insufficient data is given to solve the problem.

51. Use the formula midpoint equals $((x_1 + x_2)/2, (y_1 + y_2)/2)$ to find the midpoint of segment KH.

    (1) $(-1, 0)$
    (2) $(0, -1)$
    (3) $(0, 1)$
    (4) $(1, 0)$
    (5) $(-1, 1)$

52. What is the distance between points H and F?

    (1) $\sqrt{-25}$
    (2) $\sqrt{106}$
    (3) $\sqrt{148}$
    (4) $\sqrt{200}$
    (5) $\sqrt{250}$

Test 5: Mathematics

Item 53 is based on the following figure.

Item 54 is based on the following figure.

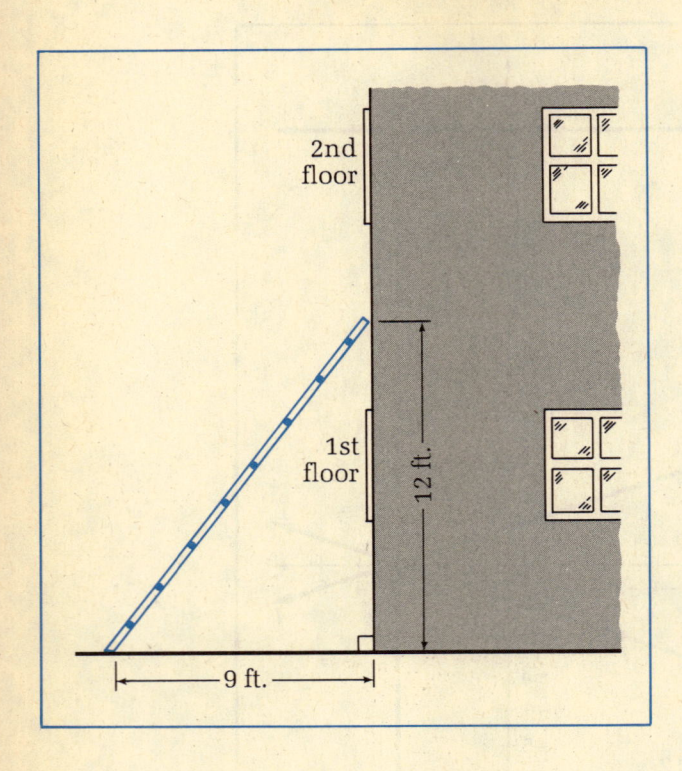

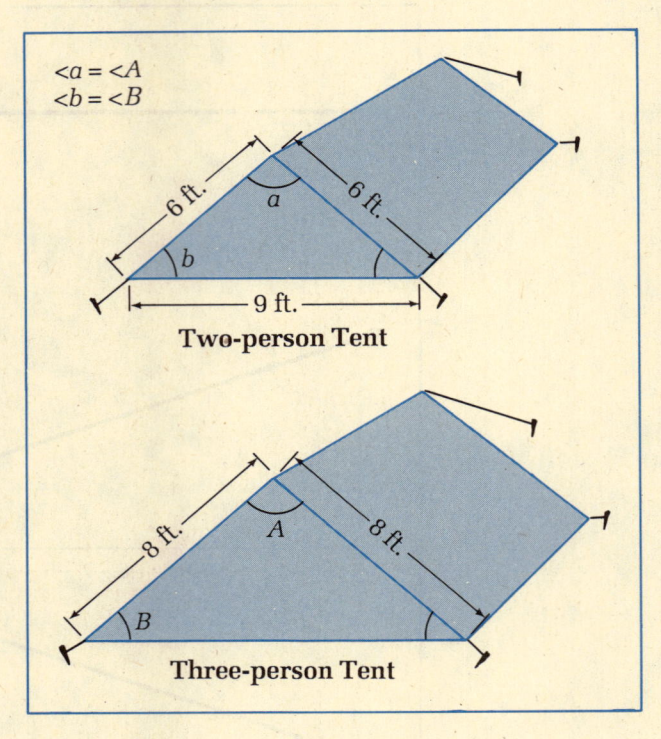

$\angle a = \angle A$
$\angle b = \angle B$

Two-person Tent

Three-person Tent

53. Merv will use an extension ladder to wash the second-story windows on his house. If he places the base of the ladder 9 feet from the house, how many feet should he extend his ladder?

   (1)   9
   (2)   12
   (3)   15
   (4)   21
   (5)   108

54. How many feet wide is the base of the three-person tent?

   (1)   6
   (2)   12
   (3)   13.5
   (4)   15.5
   (5)   18.75

PRACTICE ITEMS   Geometry Items   **663**

Item 55 is based on the following figure.

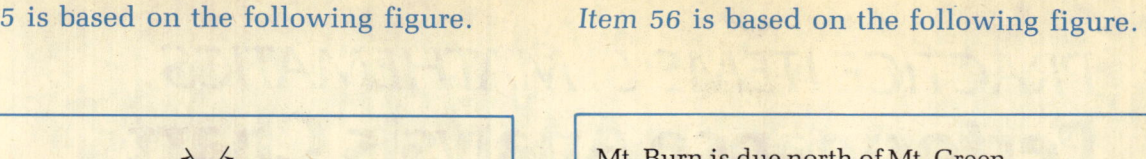

Item 56 is based on the following figure.

Mt. Burn is due north of Mt. Green.
Mt. Blue is due west of Mt. Green.

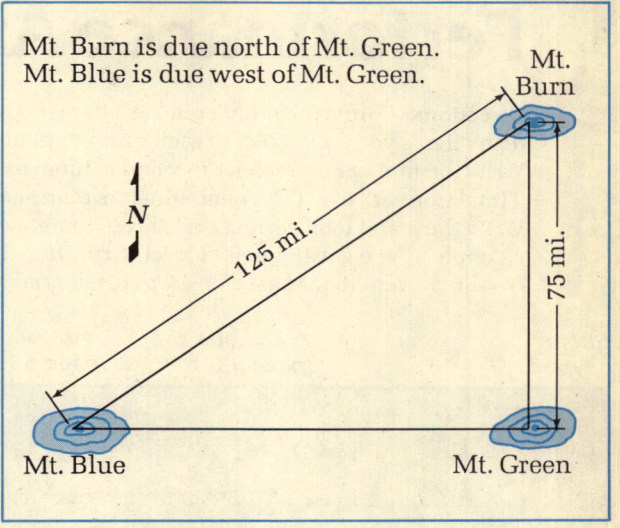

56. What is the distance in miles from Mt. Green to Mt. Blue?

    (1) 100
    (2) 145
    (3) 200
    (4) 275
    (5) Insufficient data is given to solve the problem.

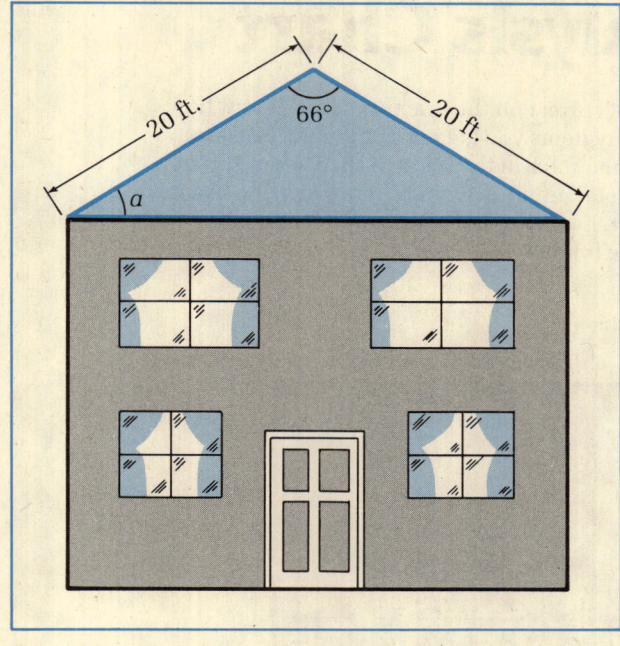

55. What is the measurement in degrees of angle a?

    (1) 12
    (2) 33
    (3) 46
    (4) 57
    (5) 66

Answers are on pages A-78–A-80.

PRACTICE ITEMS 5: MATHEMATICS
Performance Analysis Chart

Directions: Circle the number of each item that you got correct on the Practice Items. Count how many items you got correct in each row; count how many items you got correct in each column. Write the number correct per row and column as the numerator in the fraction in the appropriate "Total Correct" box. (The denominators represent the total number of items in the row or column.) Write the grand total correct over the denominator **56** at the lower right corner of the chart. (For example, if you got 48 items correct, write 48 so that the fraction reads 48/56.) Item numbers in color represent items based on graphic material.

Item Type	Arithmetic (page 439)	Algebra (page 533)	Geometry (page 553)	TOTAL CORRECT
Skills	2	14, 46	47, 49, 55	/6
Applications	7, 9, 19, 24, 25, 26	43, 44, 45	48, 50, 51, 52	/13
Problem Solving	1, 3, 4, 5, 6, 8, 10, 11, 12, 13, 15, 16, 17, 18, 20, 21, 22, 23, 27, 28	29, 30, 31, 32, 33, 34, 35, 36, 37, 38, 39, 40, 41, 42	53, 54, 56	/37
TOTAL CORRECT	/27	/19	/10	/56

The page numbers in parentheses indicate where in this book you can find the beginning of specific instruction about the various areas of mathematics you encountered on the Practice Items.

On the chart, items are classified as Skills, Applications, or Problem Solving. In the chapters in this book, the three problem types are covered in different levels:

Skills items are covered in Level 1;
Applications items are covered in Level 2;
Problem Solving items are covered in Level 3.

For example, the skills needed to solve Item 53 are covered in Level 3 of Chapter 7. To locate in which chapter arithmetic items are addressed, reread the problem to see what kind of numbers (whole numbers, fractions, and so forth) are used and then go to the designated level of the appropriate chapter.

Simulation

Introduction

By this time, you are probably asking yourself, "Am I ready to take the GED Tests?" The Simulated Tests will help you answer that question.

In this section there are Simulated Tests for each of the five GED subject areas. The tests are as much like the real tests as possible. The items are like those on the GED—in quantity and difficulty. The time limits and the mixed order of the test items are like those in the real tests. By taking the five Simulated Tests, you will get a better idea about just how ready you are to take the actual GED Tests.

Using the Simulated Tests to Best Advantage

You should take each Simulated Test under the same conditions as there will be when you take the actual test.

- When you take each real GED Test, you will be given a time limit. Adhere to that same time limit, as indicated, for each Simulated Test.
- Work without interruptions. Do not talk to anyone or consult any books. If you have a question, ask your instructor.
- If you are not sure of an answer, guess. On the real GED, guessing a correct answer will better your score. Guessing a wrong answer will not affect your score any more than not answering.
- When you take the Writing Skills Simulated Test, begin with Part I. If 75 minutes elapse before you finish Part I, proceed to Part II. If you finish Part II before 120 minutes have elapsed, you can go back to finish the items in Part I.

Try to relax as you take each Simulated Test.

Using the Answers and Explanations

Use the Answers and Explanations (beginning on page A-81) to check your answers. Mark each correct answer. Regardless of whether you correctly answered an item or not, read the explanation of the correct answer. This will reinforce your testing skills and your understanding of the material.

How to Use Your Scores

Determine if you did 80 percent work or better on each test. If you got 80 percent or more correct, you are most likely working at a level that would allow you to do well on the actual GED Test for that subject. If your score was below the 80 percent mark, the Skills Chart at the end of the test will help you identify your stronger and weaker areas.

SIMULATED TEST 1
Writing Skills, Part I: Grammar

TIME: 75 minutes

Directions: *The items in Part I of this test are based on paragraphs that contain numbered sentences. Some of the sentences may contain errors in sentence structure, usage, or mechanics. A few sentences, however, may be correct as written. Read each paragraph and then answer the eight to ten items that follow it. For each item, choose the answer that would result in the most effective writing of the sentence or sentences. The best answer must be consistent with the meaning and tone of the rest of the paragraph.*

FOR EXAMPLE:

Sentence 1: **Although it may take only two hours to watch the average motion picture takes almost a year to make.**

What correction should be made to this sentence?

(1) replace <u>it</u> with <u>they</u>
(2) change <u>take</u> to <u>have taken</u>
(3) insert a comma after <u>watch</u>
(4) change <u>almost</u> to <u>all most</u>
(5) no change is necessary

The correct answer is **(3)**. In this example, a comma is needed after the clause <u>Although it may take only two hours to watch</u>.

667

Items 1 to 9 are based on the following paragraph.

(1) Payment by credit card became a popular substitute for payment with cash or check. (2) It is important to think carefully about your choice and how you use credit cards. (3) Before one applies for a card, find out each company's finance charge. (4) This charge, a portion of the unpaid balance, added to your bill each month. (5) You will be considering different cards. (6) Think about how widely it is accepted. (7) Not every type of credit card is accepted by every store. (8) Some companies give a donation to a certain organization, such as the Sierra club, if you buy their card. (9) Other companies give you credit toward buying spesified items every time you use your card. (10) Once you do choose a card put the account number and emergency phone number in a safe place. (11) The card may be lost or stolen, report the loss immediately. (12) Finally, each time you are tempted to pay with plastic, remember that the convenience does have its cost.

1. Sentence 1: **Payment by credit card became a popular substitute for payment with cash or check.**

   Which of the following is the best way to write the underlined portion of this sentence? If you think the original is the best way, choose option (1).

   (1) credit card became
   (2) Credit Card became
   (3) credit card, became
   (4) credit card become
   (5) credit card has become

2. Sentence 2: **It is important to think carefully about your choice and how you use credit cards.**

   What correction should be made to this sentence?

   (1) change the spelling of carefully to carefuly
   (2) insert a comma after choice
   (3) replace and with or
   (4) replace how you use with use of
   (5) no correction is necessary

3. Sentence 3: **Before one applies for a card, find out each company's finance charge.**

   What correction should be made to this sentence?

   (1) replace one applies with you apply
   (2) change applies to applied
   (3) remove the comma after card
   (4) change company's to Company's
   (5) change the spelling of company's to companies

4. Sentence 4: **This charge, a portion of the unpaid balance, added to your bill each month.**

   Which of the following is the best way to write the underlined portion of this sentence? If you think the original is the best way, choose option (1).

   (1) balance, added
   (2) balance added
   (3) balance, adding
   (4) balance, is added
   (5) balance is added

GO ON TO THE NEXT PAGE

5. Sentences 5 and 6: **You will be considering different cards. Think about how widely it is accepted.**

    The most effective combination of sentences 5 and 6 would include which of the following groups of words?

    (1) When considering different ones
    (2) When considering how widely
    (3) and thinking about it
    (4) think about how widely it
    (5) about how widely each card

6. Sentence 8: **Some companies give a donation to a certain organization, such as the Sierra club, if you buy their card.**

    What correction should be made to this sentence?

    (1) remove the comma after organization
    (2) change Sierra to sierra
    (3) change club to Club
    (4) replace if with even if
    (5) no correction is necessary

7. Sentence 9: **Other companies give you credit toward buying spesified items every time you use your card.**

    What correction should be made to this sentence?

    (1) change give to gave
    (2) change the spelling of spesified to specified
    (3) insert a comma after items
    (4) change use to used
    (5) replace your card with it

8. Sentence 10: **Once you do choose a card put the account number and emergency phone number in a safe place.**

    Which of the following is the best way to write the underlined portion of this sentence? If you think the original is the best way, choose option (1).

    (1) do choose a card put
    (2) did choose a card put
    (3) do choose a card, put
    (4) do choose a card; put
    (5) do choose a card. Put

9. Sentence 11: **The card may be lost or stolen, report the loss immediately.**

    Which of the following is the best way to write the underlined portion of this sentence? If you think the original is the best way, choose option (1).

    (1) The card may be lost
    (2) The card may be losed
    (3) When the card may be lost
    (4) The card being lost
    (5) If the card is lost

GO ON TO THE NEXT PAGE

Items 10 to 19 are based on the following paragraph.

(1) Although it may be inconvenient to write a thank-you note after a job interview, the effort is worth the bother. (2) Many employers say that they are impressed by applicants which take the time to write a note of thanks. (3) These applicants are demonstrating that they have an important job skill, the ability to treat others with consideration. (4) The note that is clear and concise as well as effectively written shows that the writer has good communication skills. (5) By arriving in the mail soon after your meeting, the interviewer is prompted to think about you again. (6) The more he or she think about you, the better your chances. (7) The note can be used such that you emphasize, correct, or add to what you have already said. (8) You can ask questions in the letter to get information you still need. (9) Having been told that the job starts right after Memorial Day, for example, perhaps one sees a July starting date listed. (10) Clear up confusion by asking for the correct date in your thank-you note. (11) You received added attention along with your answer. (12) Take a moment to write a thank-you note shortly after you leave a job interview, the effort may get you the job.

10. Sentence 1: **Although it may be inconvenient to write a thank-you note after a job interview, the effort is worth the bother.**

    If you rewrote sentence 1 beginning with

    It may be inconvenient to write a thank-you note after a job interview,

    the next word should be

    (1) but
    (2) and
    (3) or
    (4) for
    (5) because

11. Sentence 2: **Many employers say that they are impressed by applicants which take the time to write a note of thanks.**

    What correction should be made to this sentence?

    (1) insert a comma after applicants
    (2) replace which with who
    (3) change take to taken
    (4) change the spelling of write to right
    (5) no correction is necessary

12. Sentence 3: **These applicants are demonstrating that they have an important job skill, the ability to treat others with consideration.**

    What correction should be made to this sentence?

    (1) change are to is
    (2) remove the comma after skill
    (3) change the spelling of ability to abilaty
    (4) change others to other's
    (5) no correction is necessary

13. Sentence 4: **The note that is clear and concise as well as effectively written shows that the writer has good communication skills.**

    If you rewrote sentence 4 beginning with

    The note that is clear, concise,

    the next word should be

    (1) as
    (2) in
    (3) or
    (4) but
    (5) and

GO ON TO THE NEXT PAGE

14. Sentence 5: **By arriving in the mail soon after your <u>meeting, the interviewer is prompted</u> to think about you again.**

    Which of the following is the best way to write the underlined portion of this sentence? If you think the original is the best way, choose option (1).

    (1) meeting, the interviewer is prompted
    (2) meeting the interviewer is prompted
    (3) meeting, the interviewer, is prompted
    (4) meeting; the thank-you note prompts
    (5) meeting, thoughts about you are prompted

15. Sentence 6: **The more <u>he or she think about you,</u> the better your chances.**

    Which of the following is the best way to write the underlined portion of this sentence? If you think the original is the best way, choose option (1).

    (1) he or she think about you
    (2) he, or she think about you
    (3) he or she thinks about you
    (4) they think about you
    (5) they thought about you

16. Sentence 7: **The note can be used such that you emphasize, correct, or add to what you have already said.**

    What correction should be made to this sentence?

    (1) replace <u>such that you</u> with <u>to</u>
    (2) change the spelling of <u>emphasize</u> to <u>emphisize</u>
    (3) remove the comma after <u>emphasize</u>
    (4) change <u>add</u> to <u>adding</u>
    (5) replace <u>you have</u> with <u>one has</u>

17. Sentence 9: **Having been told that the job starts right after Memorial Day, for example, perhaps one sees a July starting date listed.**

    What correction should be made to this sentence?

    (1) change <u>Day</u> to <u>day</u>
    (2) remove the comma after <u>example</u>
    (3) change the spelling of <u>perhaps</u> to <u>purhaps</u>
    (4) replace <u>one sees</u> with <u>you see</u>
    (5) change <u>July</u> to <u>july</u>

18. Sentence 11: **You received added attention along with your answer.**

    What correction should be made to this sentence?

    (1) change the spelling of <u>received</u> to <u>recieved</u>
    (2) change <u>received</u> to <u>will receive</u>
    (3) insert a comma after <u>attention</u>
    (4) change <u>your</u> to <u>you're</u>
    (5) change the spelling of <u>answer</u> to <u>anser</u>

19. Sentence 12: **Take a moment to write a thank-you note shortly after you leave a job interview, the effort may get you the job.**

    What correction should be made to this sentence?

    (1) insert a comma after <u>note</u>
    (2) change <u>leave</u> to <u>left</u>
    (3) replace <u>interview, the</u> with <u>interview. The</u>
    (4) replace <u>the</u> with <u>so this</u>
    (5) no correction is necessary

GO ON TO THE NEXT PAGE

672 Test 1: Writing Skills SIMULATION

Items 20 to 28 are based on the following paragraph.

(1) The Internal Revenue Service, like other agencies handling a lot of information, uses computers widely. (2) It all starts with the income tax return you are supposed to put in the mail by the deadline in April its destination depends on your location. (3) For instance, if you live in New York city, you send your return to Holtsville, New York. (4) Workers at the Internal Revenue Servise Center type information from your return into a computer, which checks your additon and subtraction. (5) The computer then searches a data base, a computerized library, for storing large amounts of information. (6) There were many kinds of information in the data base about each American citizen. (7) For example, your bank sends information to the IRS about interest you make on your savings account. (8) Your employer sends salary information, and information about your car registration is sent by the Department of Motor Vehicles. (9) The computer looks through the data base. (10) It searches for information that should be reported on your tax forms. (11) If you have reported your earnings correctly, either your payment check or a refund check.

20. Sentence 1: **The Internal Revenue Service, like other agencies handling a lot of information, uses computers widely.**

    What correction should be made to this sentence?

    (1) change the spelling of Service to Servise
    (2) change Service to service
    (3) change the spelling of a lot to alot
    (4) change uses to use
    (5) no correction is necessary

21. Sentence 2: **It all starts with the income tax return you are supposed to put in the mail by the deadline in April its destination depends on your location.**

    What correction should be made to this sentence?

    (1) change starts to start
    (2) change April to april
    (3) insert a comma after April
    (4) change April its to April. Its
    (5) change its to it's

22. Sentence 3: **For instance, if you live in New York city, you send your return to Holtsville, New York.**

    What correction should be made to this sentence?

    (1) remove the comma after instance
    (2) replace you live with one lives
    (3) change city to City
    (4) change send to sent
    (5) replace your return with them

23. Sentence 4: **Workers at the Internal Revenue Servise Center type information from your return into a computer, which checks your addition and subtraction.**

    What correction should be made to this sentence?

    (1) change the spelling of Servise to Service
    (2) change Center to center
    (3) remove the comma after computer
    (4) replace which with who
    (5) change checks to checked

GO ON TO THE NEXT PAGE

24. Sentence 5: **The computer then searches a data base, a computerized library, for storing large amounts of information.**

    What correction should be made to this sentence?

    (1) change <u>searches</u> to <u>searched</u>
    (2) remove the comma after <u>library</u>
    (3) replace <u>data base, a</u> with <u>data base. A</u>
    (4) change the spelling of <u>amounts</u> to <u>amountes</u>
    (5) no correction is necessary

25. Sentence 6: <u>**There were many kinds of information**</u> **in the data base about each American citizen.**

    Which of the following is the best way to write the underlined portion of this sentence? If you think the original is the best way, choose option (1).

    (1) There were many kinds of information
    (2) Many kinds of information were
    (3) There was many kinds of information
    (4) There are many kinds of information
    (5) There were many kinds; of information

26. Sentence 8: **Your employer sends salary information, and <u>information about your car registration is sent by the Department of Motor Vehicles</u>.**

    Which of the following is the best way to write the underlined portion of this sentence? If you think the original is the best way, choose option (1).

    (1) information about your car registration is sent by the Department of Motor Vehicles.
    (2) the Department of Motor Vehicles sends car registration information.
    (3) information about your car registration, by the Department of Motor Vehicles.
    (4) They know about your car registration from the Department of Motor Vehicles.
    (5) it is sent by the Department of Motor Vehicles, about your car.

27. Sentences 9 and 10: **The computer looks through the data base. It searches for information that should be reported on your tax forms.**

    The most effective combination of sentences 9 and 10 would include which of the following groups of words?

    (1) It looks through the data base
    (2) The computer searches the data base
    (3) and it searches for information
    (4) or it searches for information
    (5) The information should be reported

28. Sentence 11: **If you have reported your earnings correctly, either your payment check <u>or a refund check</u>.**

    Which of the following is the best way to write the underlined portion of this sentence? If you think the original is the best way, choose option (1).

    (1) or a refund check.
    (2) nor a refund check.
    (3) or a check is refunded.
    (4) or a refund check is processed.
    (5) or a refund check are processed.

GO ON TO THE NEXT PAGE

Items 29 to 37 are based on the following paragraph.

(1) More people than ever are interested in higher education. (2) There has been a fortunate result. (3) The number of people taking the GED Tests in order to become eligible for it has risen. (4) An unfortunate result, has been the increase in diploma mills offering worthless degrees. (5) The American Council on Education reporting that there are now several hundred of these phony schools in existence. (6) Many advertised in well-known magazines and newspapers. (7) You can avoid wasting time, energy, and spending money on a useless degree. (8) Watch out for any school whose address changes frequently. (9) Beware if catalogs don't mention facilities such as libraries and laboratories. (10) Catalogs should describe degree requirements, they shouldn't stress the appearance of diplomas. (11) Neither you nor anyone else need to remain in doubt about the quality of a program. (12) To find out whether a school has official accreditation, write to the American Council on Education, One Dupont Circle, N.W., Washington, D.C. 20036.

29. Sentences 2 and 3: **There has been a fortunate result. The number of people taking the GED Tests in order to become eligible for it has risen.**

The most effective combination of sentences 2 and 3 would include which of the following groups of words?

(1) There has been a fortunate result that
(2) There has been, fortunately, a rise
(3) A fortunate result will be the rise
(4) so that they obtain eligiblity for it
(5) to become eligible for further education

30. Sentence 4: **An unfortunate result, has been the increase in diploma mills offering worthless degrees.**

What correction should be made to this sentence?

(1) remove the comma after result
(2) change has to have
(3) change the spelling of increase to increse
(4) insert a comma after mills
(5) replace offering with who offer

31. Sentence 5: **The American Council on Education reporting that there are now several hundred of these phony schools in existence.**

What correction should be made to this sentence?

(1) change American to american
(2) replace reporting with reports
(3) replace there with they're
(4) change are to is
(5) change the spelling of existence to existance

32. Sentence 6: **Many advertised in well-known magazines and newspapers.**

Which of the following is the best way to write the underlined portion of this sentence? If you think the original is the best way, choose option (1).

(1) advertised in well-known magazines
(2) advertised in magazines that are well-known
(3) advertising in well-known magazines
(4) advertise in well-known magazines
(5) advertises in well-known magazines

GO ON TO THE NEXT PAGE

33. Sentence 7: **You can avoid <u>wasting time, energy, and spending money</u> on a useless degree.**

    Which of the following is the best way to write the underlined portion of this sentence? If you think the original is the best way, choose option (1).

    (1) wasting time, energy, and spending money
    (2) wasting time, wasting energy, and money spent
    (3) wasting time, energy, and money
    (4) wasting time, spending energy and money
    (5) wasted time, wasted energy, and spending money

34. Sentence 9: **Beware if catalogs do'nt mention facilities such as libraries and laboratories.**

    What correction should be made to this sentence?

    (1) replace <u>do'nt</u> with <u>don't</u>
    (2) change <u>mention</u> to <u>mentioned</u>
    (3) change the spelling of <u>facilities</u> to <u>fasilities</u>
    (4) insert a comma after <u>facilities</u>
    (5) change the spelling of <u>laboratories</u> to <u>labratories</u>

35. Sentence 10: **Catalogs should describe degree <u>requirements, they</u> shouldn't stress the appearance of diplomas.**

    Which of the following is the best way to write the underlined portion of this sentence? If you think the original is the best way, choose option (1).

    (1) requirements, they
    (2) requirements they
    (3) requirements; they
    (4) requirements, so they
    (5) requirements, because they

36. Sentence 11: **Neither you nor anyone else need to remain in doubt about the quality of a program.**

    What correction should be made to this sentence?

    (1) insert a comma after <u>you</u>
    (2) replace <u>nor</u> with <u>or</u>
    (3) change <u>need</u> to <u>needs</u>
    (4) change the spelling of <u>doubt</u> to <u>doute</u>
    (5) no correction is necessary

37. Sentence 12: **To find out whether a school has official accreditation, write to the American Council on Education, One Dupont Circle, N.W., Washington, D.C. 20036.**

    What correction should be made to this sentence?

    (1) remove the comma after <u>accreditation</u>
    (2) change the spelling of <u>Council</u> to <u>Counsel</u>
    (3) change <u>Circle</u> to <u>circle</u>
    (4) replace <u>write</u> with <u>a letter should be written</u>
    (5) no correction is necessary

GO ON TO THE NEXT PAGE

Items 38 to 47 are based on the following paragraph.

(1) Job hunting is something what you will probably do more than once. (2) Either because they choose to change jobs, or because it is necessary, many workers change jobs. (3) Since most of today's new jobs are created in the service industries many job hunters will find service job openings. (4) Service jobs included a wide range of positions, from nursing aides to stockbrokers. (5) Although it may be fairly easy to get a service job, it is often difficult to find career ladders within service jobs. (6) Career ladders are steps for working up to higher wages. (7) Some service jobs, such as industry positions for Nurses and cafeteria workers, pay fairly well from the start. (8) The problem with these jobs, however, are that they are disappearing. (9) Because of financial problems many American companies are having, not only factory workers but also the employees are losing their jobs who serve them. (10) Many job hunters are attenting to get jobs in the growing field of technology. (11) You may be among those who are taking classes to prepare for the level of reading and writing skills such jobs demand. (12) Time spent in such classes is time well spent; even if this is one's first job hunt, it probably will not be your last.

38. Sentence 1: **Job hunting is something what you will probably do more than once.**

    What correction should be made to this sentence?

    (1) replace what with that
    (2) change do to done
    (3) insert a comma after do
    (4) replace than with then
    (5) change the spelling of once to ones

39. Sentence 2: **Either because they choose to change jobs, or because it is necessary, many workers change jobs.**

    If you rewrote sentence 2 beginning with

    Many workers change jobs, either by

    the next word should be

    (1) their
    (2) choosing
    (3) choice
    (4) changing
    (5) necessary

40. Sentence 3: **Since most of today's new jobs are created in the service industries many job hunters will find service job openings.**

    Which of the following is the best way to write the underlined portion of this sentence? If you think the original is the best way, choose option (1).

    (1) industries many job hunters will find
    (2) industries. Many job hunters will find
    (3) industries; many job hunters will find
    (4) industries, many job hunters will find
    (5) industries many job hunters found

41. Sentence 4: **Service jobs included a wide range of positions, from nursing aides to stockbrokers.**

    Which of the following is the best way to write the underlined portion of this sentence? If you think the original is the best way, choose option (1).

    (1) included a wide range of positions, from
    (2) included a wide range of positions from
    (3) including a wide range of positions, from
    (4) included a wide range of positions; from
    (5) include a wide range of positions, from

GO ON TO THE NEXT PAGE

42. Sentences 5 and 6: **Although it may be fairly easy to get a service job, it is often difficult to find career ladders within service jobs. Career ladders are steps for working up to higher wages.**

    The most effective combination of sentences 3 and 4 would include which of the following groups of words?

    (1) service jobs, steps
    (2) career ladders, steps
    (3) difficulty in finding steps
    (4) find career ladders that are steps
    (5) and career ladders are steps

43. Sentence 7: **Some service jobs, such as industry positions for Nurses and cafeteria workers, pay fairly well from the start.**

    What correction should be made to this sentence?

    (1) remove the comma after jobs
    (2) change Nurses to nurses
    (3) change the spelling of cafeteria to cafateria
    (4) change pay to pays
    (5) no correction is necessary

44. Sentence 8: **The problem with these jobs, however, are that they are disappearing.**

    What correction should be made to this sentence?

    (1) remove the comma after jobs
    (2) change are that to is that
    (3) replace that with because
    (4) change are disappearing to had disappeared
    (5) change the spelling of disappearing to disapearring

45. Sentence 9: **Because of financial problems many American companies are having, not only factory workers but also the employees are losing their jobs who serve them.**

    Which of the following is the best way to write the underlined portion of this sentence? If you think the original is the best way, choose opition (1).

    (1) employees are losing their jobs who serve them.
    (2) employees are losing their jobs, who serve them.
    (3) employees are losing their jobs who serve the factory workers.
    (4) employees are losing their jobs that serve them.
    (5) employees who serve them are losing their jobs.

46. Sentence 10: **Many job hunters are attenting to get jobs in the growing field of technology.**

    What correction should be made to this sentence?

    (1) change are to is
    (2) change the spelling of attenting to attempting
    (3) insert a comma after jobs
    (4) change technology to Technology
    (5) no correction is necessary

47. Sentence 12: **Time spent in such classes is time well spent; even if this is one's first job hunt, it will probably not be your last.**

    Which of the following is the best way to write the underlined portion of this sentence? If you think the original is the best way, choose option (1).

    (1) spent; even if this is one's
    (2) spent even if this is one's
    (3) spent, even if this is one's
    (4) spent. Even is this is one's
    (5) spent; even if this is your

    GO ON TO THE NEXT PAGE

Items 48 to 55 are based on the following paragraph.

(1) Computers are increasingly being used in the practice of medicine. (2) When doctors and computers work together, they are less likely to forget important details. (3) To prepare for a patient's visit physicians can have computers retrieve patient records from a data base, or information storehouse. (4) Mr. Jones, for example, may have an appointment with dr. Smith for a routine blood pressure check. (5) Dr. Smith can get a computer report of relevant information about Mr. Jones, such as medications he takes and his recent blood pressure readings. (6) Another patient may make an unscheduled visit to see the doctor because a problem that has just developed. (7) The computer can scan thousands of patients' records for information about people with similar symptoms. (8) No longer does doctors have to look through pages and pages of records for the information they need. (9) No longer did they need to rely on their own experience with a limited number of patients when making a decision about treatment. (10) Doctors can use computers to provide improved health care in many ways, and just one of these is putting medical records into data bases.

48. Sentence 2: **When doctors and computers work together, they are less likely to forget important details.**

    Which of the following is the best way to write the underlined portion of this sentence? If you think the original is the best way, choose option (1).

    (1) work together, they are
    (2) works together, they are
    (3) work together, they is
    (4) work together they are
    (5) work together, doctors are

49. Sentence 3: **To prepare for a patient's visit physicians can have computers retrieve patient records from a data base, or information storehouse.**

    What correction should be made to this sentence?

    (1) replace patient's with patience
    (2) insert a comma after visit
    (3) replace can have with had
    (4) replace computers with them
    (5) change retrieve to retrieving

50. Sentence 4: **Mr. Jones, for example, may have an appointment with dr. Smith for a routine blood pressure check.**

    What correction should be made to this sentence?

    (1) remove the comma after Jones
    (2) remove may
    (3) replace may have with had
    (4) change dr. to Dr.
    (5) insert a comma after Smith

51. Sentence 6: **Another patient may make an unscheduled visit to see the doctor because a problem that has just developed.**

    Which of the following is the best way to write the underlined portion of this sentence? If you think the original is the best way, choose option (1).

    (1) doctor because a problem that
    (2) doctor, because a problem that
    (3) doctor because of a problem that
    (4) doctor, because of a problem that
    (5) doctor, about a problem that

GO ON TO THE NEXT PAGE

52. Sentence 7: **The computer can scan thousands of patients' records for information about people with similar symptoms.**

   What correction should be made to this sentence?

   (1) change patients' to patient's
   (2) replace records for with records; for
   (3) replace information about with information. There are
   (4) change the spelling of similar to similer
   (5) no correction is necessary

53. Sentence 8: **No longer does doctors have to look through pages and pages of records for the information they need.**

   What correction should be made to this sentence?

   (1) change does to do
   (2) change doctors to Doctors
   (3) replace through with threw
   (4) change they need to one needs
   (5) no correction is necessary

54. Sentence 9: **No longer did they need to rely on their own experience with a limited number of patients when making a decision about treatment.**

   Which of the following is the best way to write the underlined portion of this sentence? If you think the original is the best way, choose option (1).

   (1) did they need to
   (2) does they need to
   (3) do they need to
   (4) do they need, to
   (5) does one need to

55. Sentence 10: **Doctors can use computers to provide improved health care in many ways, and just one of these is putting medical records into data bases.**

   If you rewrote sentence 10 beginning with Putting medical records into data bases is just one of

   the next word should be

   (1) many
   (2) these
   (3) computers
   (4) doctors
   (5) records

   Answers are on pages A-81–A-82.

GO ON TO THE NEXT PAGE

SIMULATED TEST 1
Writing Skills, Part II: Essay-writing

TIME: 45 minutes

Directions: This is a test to see how well you can write. In this test, you are asked to write an essay in which you present your opinions about an issue. In preparing your essay, you should take the following steps.

Step 1. Read all the information about the topic. Be sure that you understand the topic and that you write about only the assigned topic.
Step 2. Plan your essay before you write.
Step 3. Use scrap paper to make any notes.
Step 4. Write your essay on a separate sheet of paper.
Step 5. Read what you have written. Make sure that your writing is legible.
Step 6. Check your paragraphing, sentence structure, spelling, punctuation, capitalization, and usage; make any changes that will improve your essay.

TOPIC

> Technology has been responsible for many changes in how we live our lives, including changes in how we spend our free time. Think about how you spend your free time.
>
> Write an essay, approximately 200 words long, explaining how technology has affected the way you spend your free time. Be specific and use examples to support your explanation.

When you take the GED test, you will have 45 minutes to write about the topic question you are assigned. Try to write the essay for this unit test within 45 minutes. Write legibly and use a ballpoint pen so that your writing will be easy to read. Any notes that you make on scrap paper will not be counted as part of your score.

After you complete this essay, you can judge its effectiveness by using the Essay Scoring Guide and Model Essays in the answer key to score your essay. They will be concerned with how clearly you make the main point of your essay, how thoroughly you support your ideas, and how clear and correct your writing is throughout the composition. You will receive no credit for writing about a question other than the one assigned.

Answers are on pages A-83–A-84.

SIMULATED TEST 2
Social Studies

TIME: 85 minutes
Directions: Choose the one best answer for each question.

<u>Items 1 and 2</u> are based on the following passage.

The impact of the Western frontier on American life has been subject to considerable debate among historians. Frederick Jackson Turner claimed that nineteenth-century westerners contributed qualities such as nationalism, resourcefulness, and individualism to American society. Turner argued that the westerner had to think and act in innovative, radically different ways, in order to meet the new and challenging conditions of the frontier. Many modern historians disagree with these claims, maintaining that the West was essentially conservative and simply sought to achieve the eastern goals of prosperity and success through access to open lands.

1. Which of the following developments associated with the West best supports Turner's thesis?

   (1) community barn-raising and land-clearing enterprises
   (2) disputes between farmers and cattlemen over land enclosure
   (3) the Midwest inventions of barbed wire, the steel plow, and the reaper
   (4) the rise of the Grange and other farm organizations
   (5) the national government's great giveaways of land to railroads

2. Which of the following statements is the least likely explanation of why westerners were more nationalistic than easterners?

   (1) As recent arrivals on an ever-moving frontier, westerners lacked their own local traditions and therefore tended to give their loyalty to Washington.
   (2) People in the West needed U.S. government sponsored improvements in transportation for access to eastern markets.
   (3) Westerners were dependent on the national government for protection from Indians.
   (4) Westerners distrusted the eastern establishment and its control of the financial and political centers of power.
   (5) From their interior position, westerners were insulated from and resented European ideas and influences.

GO ON TO THE NEXT PAGE

Item 3 is based on the following graph.

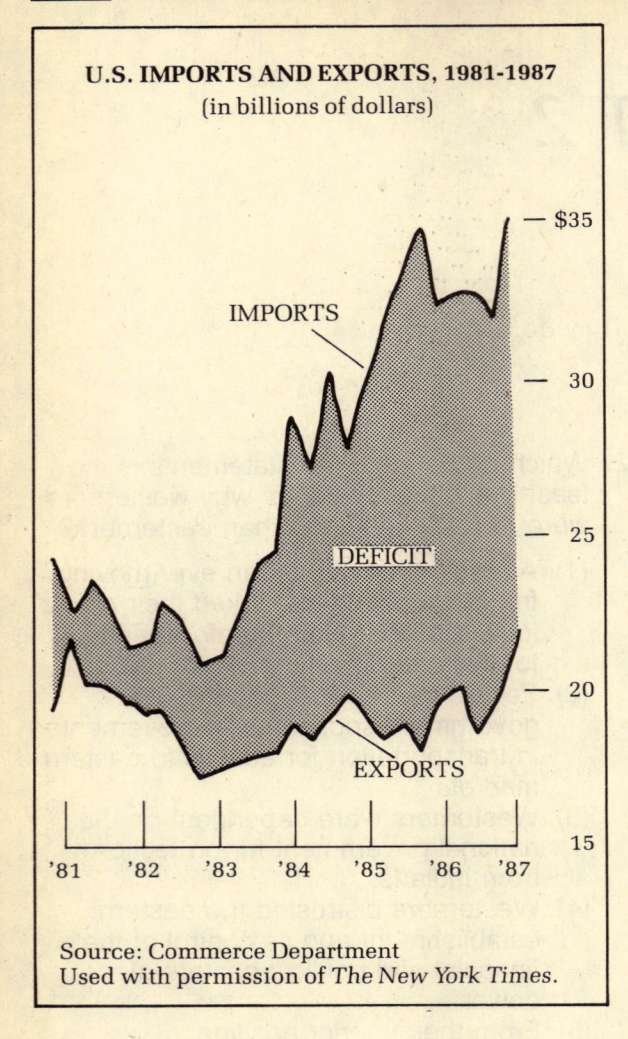

U.S. IMPORTS AND EXPORTS, 1981-1987
(in billions of dollars)

[Graph showing IMPORTS and EXPORTS lines from '81 to '87, with the area between labeled DEFICIT. Y-axis ranges from 15 to $35.]

Source: Commerce Department
Used with permission of *The New York Times*.

3. Which of the following generalizations is supported by information provided in the graph?
   (1) Imports tend to increase when exports decrease.
   (2) A trade deficit exists when imports increase.
   (3) A trade deficit exists when imports decrease.
   (4) A trade deficit decreases when the gap between imports and exports narrows.
   (5) A trade deficit occurs if there is a difference in value between exports and imports.

Item 4 is based on the following passage.

Ethnocentrism is the tendency of people to view their culture as superior to other cultures. Often ethnocentrism simply reflects people's positive feelings about their own culture. It can, however, be the basis for an aggressive and militaristic national policy toward other nations or cultures.

4. In which of the following American policies did ethnocentrism play a central role?
   (1) Good Neighbor Policy—a policy of nonintervention in Latin America, based on the view that Latin Americans should settle their own affairs
   (2) Open Door Policy—a policy according to which all nations would be assured equal trading rights in China, based on the view that open trade would bring greater profits to all
   (3) Manifest Destiny—a policy of westward expansion, based on the view that the United States had a mandate to carry its civilizing influence across the continent
   (4) Truman Doctrine—a commitment to lend economic and military assistance to countries threatened by totalitarian regimes, based on the idea that such aid could help these countries preserve their freedom
   (5) Monroe Doctrine—a policy to keep out of European affairs and to keep Europeans out of the affairs of North and South America, based on the desire to keep Europe from further colonization of the Americas

GO ON TO THE NEXT PAGE

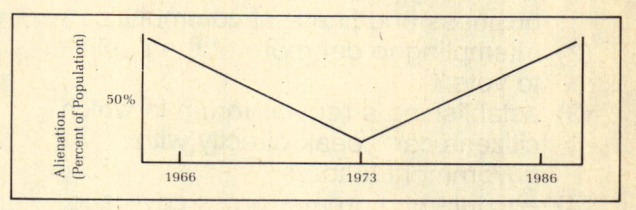

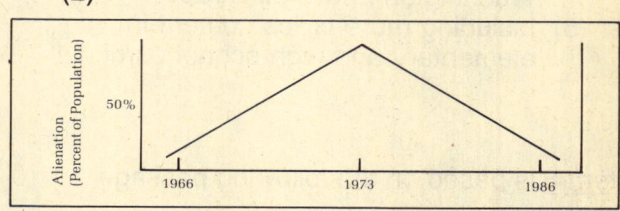

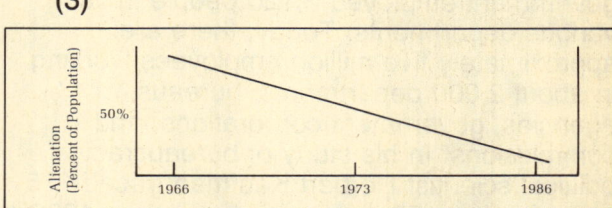

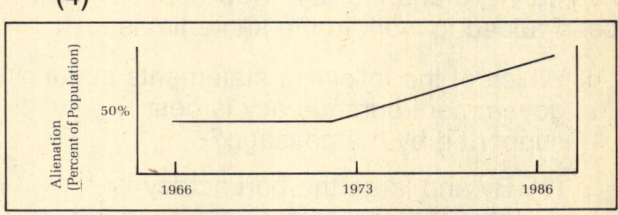

Items 5 to 7 are based on the following passage.

Pollsters have been assessing Americans' feelings about public issues for some time. For example, the Harris Survey has been measuring the sense of "alienation," or powerlessness, since the 1960s. The pollsters define this indicator as the feeling that there are two systems of justice—one for those who are insiders in Washington, Wall Street, and corporate America, and another for ordinary citizens.

The results of these polls are troubling. In 1966, 29 percent of Americans felt alienated. From 1966 through 1972, the percentage of people who had this feeling rose steadily. In 1973, in the wake of the Watergate disclosures, a solid majority had a sense of powerlessness. In the years since, the alienation index has only once dropped below 50 percent of those polled and has reached as high as 65 percent.

Some analysts believe that the strong feeling of alienation indicates the remoteness indivduals feel from the decision-making processes in the major institutions that affect their lives.

5. Which of the following statements best summarizes the main idea of the passage?

   (1) Pollsters have traced changes in the feeling of alienation among Americans over a period of several decades.
   (2) Watergate was a key event in that it solidified high levels of alienation.
   (3) "Alienation" refers to the feeling that the ordinary citizen is powerless and receives different treatment from those who are in power.
   (4) In recent decades, the feeling of alienation has become widespread among Americans.
   (5) Alienation may, in the final analysis, be related to a feeling of remoteness from decision-making processes.

6. Which of the following figures most accurately represents information discussed in the passage?

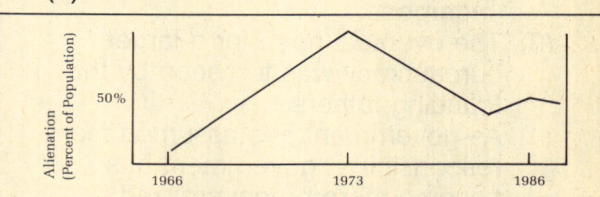

GO ON TO THE NEXT PAGE

7. Which of the following steps would be most likely to contribute to the resolution of the problem discussed in the passage?

    (1) establishing a high-level commission to investigate wrong doing in the business and financial communities
    (2) attempting to get more of the public to vote
    (3) establishing a regular forum in which citizens can speak directly with government leaders
    (4) encouraging greater press coverage of inside events concerning Washington and Wall Street
    (5) Including more civics content in elementary and high school curricula

Item 8 is based on the following passage.

During Jefferson's administration the government employed 2,120 people in its various departments. Today, there are approximately five million employees working in about 2,000 departments, bureaus, agencies, government corporations, and commissions. In his study of bureaucracy, political scientist Herbert Kaufman traced 175 agencies for a 50-year period ending in 1973. He found that all but 27 of these agencies had survived and that 246 new agencies had been added to work in the same fields.

8. Which of the following statements about government bureaucracy is best supported by the passage?

    (1) By and large the bureacracy is efficiently organized and operated.
    (2) The bureaucracy is in no way affected by political shifts the nation undergoes.
    (3) The eventual need for a larger bureaucracy was foreseen by the founding fathers.
    (4) As government has assumed more responsibility, government has become more bureaucratized.
    (5) Division of labor and specialization of function are methods government bureaucrats tend to ignore.

Item 9 is based on the following cartoon.

9. Which of the following statements is the cartoonist most likely making concerning the Marshall Plan, by which the U.S. government proposed to help revive the economies of European countries following World War II?

    (1) U.S. public opinion was sharply divided between isolationists and those who proposed to help Europe.
    (2) The United States was not really in a position to help Europe following the war.
    (3) Even with U.S. aid, the European economies were too weak to thrive.
    (4) Contrary to what some Americans believed, U.S. aid to Europe was crucial to the health of the United States as well as Europe.
    (5) Aid to Europe was a bad idea, since Europe could easily bail itself out and since America only stood to lose money in the process.

GO ON TO THE NEXT PAGE

Items 10 to 12 are based on the following passage.

The Electoral College system is the result of a compromise worked out at the Constitutional Convention. Many delegates felt a matter as important as the election of the president should be put in the hands of Congress. However, there was also fear that this would result in congressional domination of the president. Thus, the Electoral College system was devised. Under this system, states are granted a number of electors proportionate to their representation in Congress, adjusted every ten years to take population shifts into account. Initially, electors were often chosen by state legislatures. Today, of course, they are chosen by the voters and are pledged to support a certain candidate. A candidate either wins all the state's electoral votes or none. When the Electoral College meets, if no candidate receives a majority of the electoral vote, the election is thrown into the House of Representatives.

10. Which of the following statements is supported by the passage?

    (1) Small states often have a more important role than big states in the election of a president.
    (2) Voting in the Electoral College is weighted in favor of the thirteen original states.
    (3) Well-populated states have more influence than sparsely populated states in the Electoral College.
    (4) Agricultural states are more important than industrial states in presidential elections.
    (5) Each of the 50 states is given equal weight in the Electoral College.

11. Which of the following offers the best summary description of the Electoral College system?

    (1) secret balloting
    (2) popular voting
    (3) convention balloting
    (4) primary elections
    (5) indirect election

12. Based on the passage, which of the following statements is most likely one of the reasons for the existence of the Electoral College?

    (1) In early presidential elections, a property qualification reduced the number of eligible voters.
    (2) The framers feared too much democracy.
    (3) The president and Congress were to be elected at the same time.
    (4) A two-party system was not anticipated when the Constitution was written.
    (5) State legislatures were empowered to elect senators.

Item 13 is based on the following passage.

In today's world, innovation—finding different and better ways to do things—may be necessary in order to compete successfully and to generate sales in new markets. The United States leads the world in innovations, but it seems to be losing ground to Japan and to West Germany. One indicator of the problem is the number of patents applied for. In 1971 there were 56,000 applications for U.S. patents; in 1983 there were only 33,000, and an increasingly larger share of the applications were made by foreign interests.

13. Based on the passage, the United States may lose some of its share of world markets unless it takes which of the following steps?

    (1) denies foreign interests the right to secure U.S. patents
    (2) expands sales and promotion efforts to new markets
    (3) invests more money in research and development
    (4) innovates in areas where competing nations are not active
    (5) models its economic system more closely on those of West Germany and Japan

GO ON TO THE NEXT PAGE

Items 14 and 15 are based on the following map.

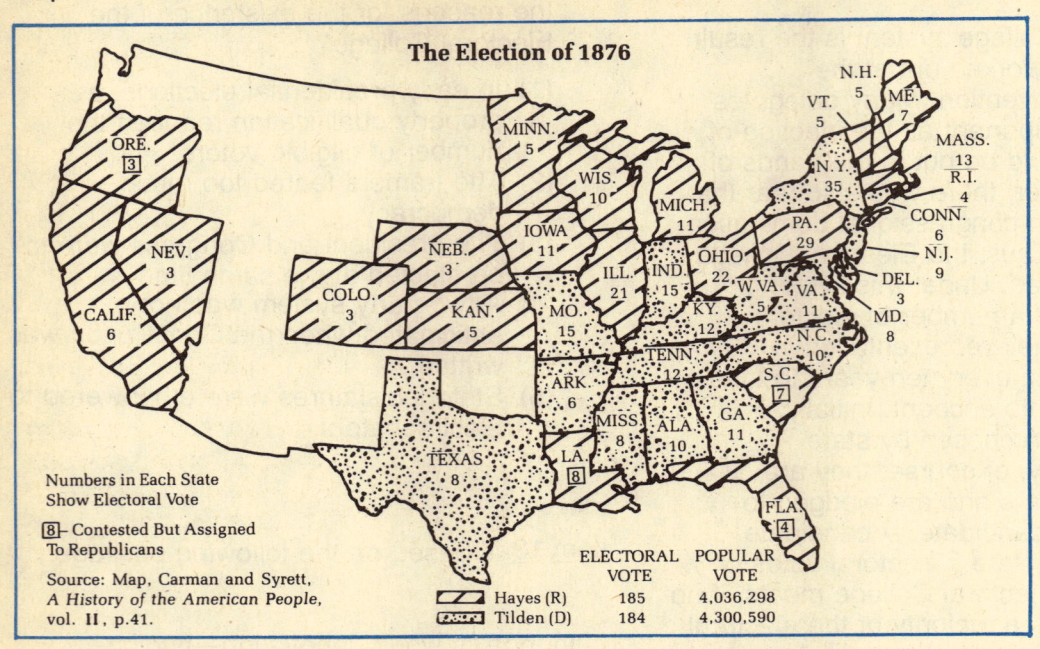

The Election of 1876

Numbers in Each State Show Electoral Vote
⬜8⬜ — Contested But Assigned To Republicans
Source: Map, Carman and Syrett, *A History of the American People,* vol. II, p.41.

	ELECTORAL VOTE	POPULAR VOTE
Hayes (R)	185	4,036,298
Tilden (D)	184	4,300,590

14. Which of the following statements is supported by the information presented in the map?

    (1) Third-party candidates played a role in the election of 1876.
    (2) The popular vote and the electoral vote were both won by the same candidate.
    (3) Tilden's support was based mainly in Northern states.
    (4) Hayes won the popular vote by only a narrow margin.
    (5) There were some states that both Tilden and Hayes claimed to have won.

15. Which of the following statements best explains the election results displayed on the map?

    (1) Although the election was close, the outcome was clear.
    (2) Hayes won solely because he was assigned all the contested states.
    (3) The balance of power in the election was held by U.S. territories.
    (4) The American electorate perceived definite differences between the two candidates for president.
    (5) Tilden captured mainly those states that were less populated and therefore had fewer electoral votes.

GO ON TO THE NEXT PAGE

Items 16 to 20 are based on the following information.

As the world population continues to grow, its demands for food, materials, and space put a greater and greater strain on the environment. Humans have therefore been forced to find ways to turn unproductive land into land that can be put to use to satisfy our needs. This often involves large and dramatic alterations of the landscape. Listed below are five ways in which humans commonly alter the environment to make it more productive.

(1) terracing—cuts "steps" into steep slopes of land to create flat surfaces that can be cultivated
(2) irrigation—provides water for agricultural use through dams and canals
(3) clearance—removes natural vegetation to provide areas for crops, livestock, and dwellings
(4) reclamation—drains swamps and other wet areas for agricultural use; also restores areas that have been spoiled by industrial and other human activities
(5) landfill—extends coastline and riverbanks by dumping large amounts of waste and soil, thereby creating new land

Each of the following descriptions exemplifies one of the types of alterations of the landscape listed above. The categories may be used more than once, but no question has more than one best answer.

16. When the first European settlers arrived in North America, they found huge forests covering the land. The settlers made this land fit for large-scale cultivation through

   (1) terracing
   (2) irrigation
   (3) clearance
   (4) reclamation
   (5) landfill

17. The island of Manhattan in New York City is in great demand as an area for business and residence. Because space is so limited, the city has increased the land available for construction through

   (1) terracing
   (2) irrigation
   (3) clearance
   (4) reclamation
   (5) landfill

18. There is a great demand for rice in Southeast Asia. Rice can only grow in swampy lands, but because most of Southeast Asia is mountainous, the water usually drains away into the rivers before it can be used to grow rice. The farmers of Southeast Asia have solved this problem through

   (1) terracing
   (2) irrigation
   (3) clearance
   (4) reclamation
   (5) landfill

19. The Nile River in Africa tends to flood seasonally. Farmers in the river valley take advantage of this by planting in the rich sediments left behind when the flood recedes. But during the rest of the year the river does not provide enough water to sustain crops. This problem has been solved through

   (1) terracing
   (2) irrigation
   (3) clearance
   (4) reclamation
   (5) landfill

20. In various parts of the world forests have been destroyed by the practice of slash-and-burn agriculture. In many such areas, reforestation efforts are currently underway. These are attempts to alter the environment through

   (1) terracing
   (2) irrigation
   (3) clearance
   (4) reclamation
   (5) landfill

GO ON TO THE NEXT PAGE

Items 21 and 22 are based on the following graph.

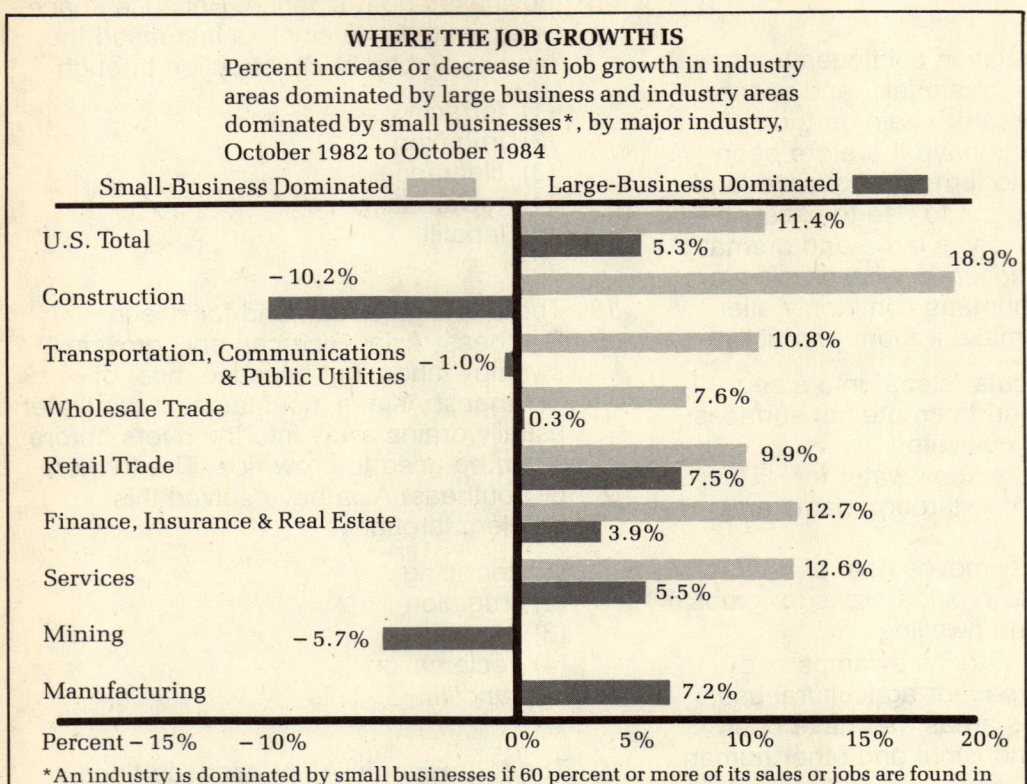

WHERE THE JOB GROWTH IS
Percent increase or decrease in job growth in industry areas dominated by large business and industry areas dominated by small businesses*, by major industry, October 1982 to October 1984

Small-Business Dominated   Large-Business Dominated

Industry	Small-Business	Large-Business
U.S. Total	11.4%	5.3%
Construction	−10.2%	18.9%
Transportation, Communications & Public Utilities	−1.0%	10.8%
Wholesale Trade	7.6%	0.3%
Retail Trade	9.9%	7.5%
Finance, Insurance & Real Estate	12.7%	3.9%
Services	12.6%	5.5%
Mining	−5.7%	—
Manufacturing	—	7.2%

Percent −15%   −10%   0%   5%   10%   15%   20%

*An industry is dominated by small businesses if 60 percent or more of its sales or jobs are found in businesses that employ fewer than 500 workers. Most major industries are partly dominated by large firms and partly dominated by small firms. In construction, for example, small firms do most of the home-building; large firms build most offices, roads, bridges, and so forth. The proportion of small businesses is so tiny in the mining and manufacturing industries, however, that those industries are considered to be totally dominated by large businesses.
Source: U.S. Small Business Administration, Office of Advocacy

21. Which of the following industries showed amounts of job growth for its large- and small-business-dominated areas that were most like the corresponding figures for the United States as a whole?

   (1) wholesale trade
   (2) retail trade
   (3) finance, insurance, and real estate
   (4) services
   (5) manufacturing

22. Which of the following statements is supported by the information presented?

   (1) No major industry with a small business component deviated from the overall job-growth pattern of greater increases in areas dominated by small business.
   (2) Total job growth was sufficient to accommodate the vast majority of new entrants into the labor force.
   (3) Small businesses created more jobs than large businesses.
   (4) Large construction firms lost business to smaller competitors.
   (5) Overall, the construction industry experienced an increase in the number of jobs.

GO ON TO THE NEXT PAGE

Items 23 to 25 are based on the following passage.

Recent years have witnessed major breakthroughs in testing and monitoring technology. There is concern, however, that these developments may have undesirable repercussions in the workplace, particularly in view of growing employer willingness to test and monitor employees. Thus, for example, Professor Alan F. Westin has stated: "Issues of employee privacy are becoming more and more important to 100 million workers in the late 1980s. These range from increased use of drug, psychological, and "honesty" tests for job applicants to the use of machine monitoring of employees using office systems technology. . . ." (*Columbia University Record* 12, February 27, 1987, p. 6.)

23. Which of the following statements best describes the purpose of the passage?

    (1) to discuss some recent breakthroughs in testing and monitoring technology
    (2) to advocate the use of modern technology in the workplace
    (3) to show the necessity to screen job applicants
    (4) to show why privacy in the workplace has become an important concern
    (5) to reveal the intrusion of government in people's lives

24. Which of the following may prove to be the least likely response to these threats to privacy?

    (1) making the public more aware of the dangers of testing and monitoring
    (2) negotiating by unions to get employers to minimize their use of testing and monitoring
    (3) writing limits on testing and monitoring into employee contracts
    (4) banning testing and monitoring technology
    (5) passing laws to restrict the use of testing and monitoring

25. Which of the following amendments to the U.S. Constitution may have been violated by use of these tests and monitoring devices?

    (1) First Amendment guarantees of free speech, a free press, freedom of assembly, and freedom to petition
    (2) Fourth Amendment protection from unauthorized searches and Fifth Amendment protection from self-incrimination
    (3) Sixth Amendment rights to be informed of charges against one and Seventh Amendment guarantees of jury trials
    (4) Eighth Amendment bans on cruel and unusual punishment and Ninth Amendment powers reserved to the people
    (5) Thirteenth Amendment bans on involuntary servitude and Fourteenth Amendment definitions of citizenship

Item 26 is based on the following passage.

Much economic competition in the United States is based on price. But companies also engage in nonprice competition. Such competition, for example, involves attracting customers by running advertising campaigns people will remember. Advertisements attempt to associate the product with an image that people find desirable. Advertising is by no means the only way of achieving this association. Packaging and labeling are equally crucial to establishing the right "image." They should also differentiate the product from its competitors, making it stand out in people's minds.

26. Which of the following would be the best title for this passage?

    (1) Pricing Your Competitors Out of the Market
    (2) How to Run Your Business
    (3) Some Psychological Tools of Competition
    (4) Developing Effective Advertisements
    (5) Differentiate and Succeed

GO ON TO THE NEXT PAGE

27. During the first quarter of the twentieth century, reporters revealed that some of the nation's largest businesses had engaged in corrupt practices and had made shady deals with one another at the expense of the public. Reformers set out to get the government to remedy the situation. Which of the following actions probably occurred as a result?

    (1) Congress legalized union organization and collective bargaining.
    (2) For a more flexible currency, the government abandoned the gold standard.
    (3) Businesses were given subsidies to make their goods more competitive with goods manufactured abroad.
    (4) Tariffs on imports were raised to new heights.
    (5) To prevent monopolies and foster competition, antitrust laws were passed.

Item 28 is based on the following passage.

The Arctic Ocean separates the Soviet Union from North America. Both the Soviet Union and the United States view the Arctic as vital to their national security. The Soviet Union has many military bases on its northern edge, along the Arctic coast. The United States has bases in Alaska. Its allies have bases in Canada, Iceland, and Norway. Beneath the polar ice cap, nuclear submarines constantly patrol icy waters.

28. The passage implies that both the United States and the Soviet Union believe the Arctic Ocean is vital to national security because

    (1) numerous military bases are located there
    (2) it is the only place where nuclear submarines can be used
    (3) the Arctic contains a number of scarce resources
    (4) both the United States and the Soviet Union border on the Arctic Ocean
    (5) the Arctic Ocean has many important transportation routes

Item 29 is based on the following passage.

Japan's economic success has been attributed to a number of factors. One often-mentioned factor is the "team spirit" of Japanese workers. Another is Japan's willingness to abandon previously successful areas, such as textiles, in which developing nations now produce and sell goods more cheaply. At the same time, Japan has made sizeable investments in areas such as computers that are becoming increasingly important in today's world. Moreover, by saving an average of about 20 percent of their income, Japanese households have provided the capital needed for investments.

29. Based on the passage, which of the following is a factor that has contributed to Japan's economic growth?

    (1) the failure of other nations to compete successfully with Japan in any area that it enters
    (2) the free-spending habits of Japan's citizens, which have greatly stimulated the demand for goods
    (3) the ability to import and master the technology of other nations
    (4) the growth of trade unions and their assumption of a major role in the decision-making process
    (5) the ability to base investment decisions on accurate assessments of the changing global economy

GO ON TO THE NEXT PAGE

Items 30 to 31 are based on the following cartoon.

THE LEAKY CONNECTION

According to this cartoonist, the farmer's profits were siphoned off into the pockets of middlemen through the leaks in the joints of the monopoly pipeline.

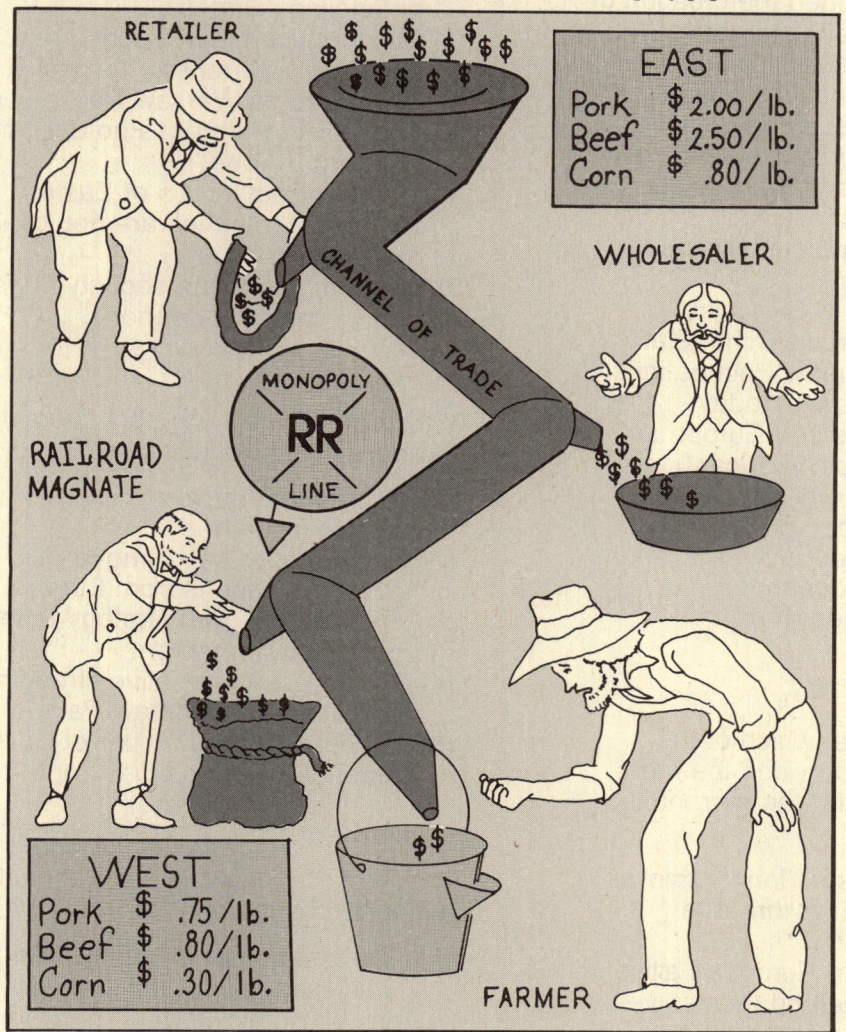

RETAILER

EAST
Pork $ 2.00/lb.
Beef $ 2.50/lb.
Corn $ .80/lb.

WHOLESALER

CHANNEL OF TRADE

MONOPOLY RR LINE

RAILROAD MAGNATE

WEST
Pork $ .75/lb.
Beef $ .80/lb.
Corn $ .30/lb.

FARMER

Source: Carman and Syrett, *A History of the American People*, 2nd ed., II (New York: Alfred A. Knopf, 1957), p. 266.

30. Which of the following statements is best supported by the cartoon?

   (1) Farmers are suffering because harvests are poor due to drought.
   (2) High mortgage rates on farmland are absorbing the farmers' profits.
   (3) Agricultural surpluses are driving down farm prices.
   (4) Farmers are not to blame if consumers pay high prices for food.
   (5) Farmers are victims of inflationary fiscal policies.

31. Based on the cartoon, which of the following policies would prove most beneficial to farmers?

   (1) price supports for their crops
   (2) antitrust and railroad regulatory legislation
   (3) lower mortgage interest rates
   (4) lower tariff rates to open foreign markets
   (5) technological improvements to get crops to market before they spoil

GO ON TO THE NEXT PAGE

Items 32 to 35 are based on the following passage.

In the past, American foreign policy expert George Kennan recommended the creation of a nuclear-free zone in Europe, in which East and West would remove atomic weapons stockpiles; however, his idea was rejected. It was feared that America's European NATO allies would think the United States was deserting them. The troops of the Soviet Union and its Warsaw Pact allies outnumbered their Western counterparts. They could easily overwhelm the NATO forces of Western Europe. U.S. nuclear weapons were therefore crucial. The relative strength of NATO and Warsaw Pact nations remains more or less the same today; however, the United States and Europe are now considering removal of American intermediate-range nuclear missiles from European soil. The American government would still be able to deliver nuclear weapons to Soviet and Eastern European targets if Western European countries were endangered.

32. Based on the passage, which of the following statements provides the most probable explanation for the current U.S. position?

    (1) The United States no longer thinks the Soviet Union is a threat to European security.
    (2) America's Western European allies are now able to defend themselves from the Soviet Union and the Eastern bloc.
    (3) Europeans resent the presence of intermediate-range missiles on their soil.
    (4) The U.S. has the long-range capacity to defend Europe from Soviet or Warsaw Pact threats to the peace.
    (5) Americans do not see how European security is related to the United States' national interests.

33. Based on the passage, which of the following statements represents the strategic hypothesis underlying the U.S. commitment to NATO?

    (1) The United States should avoid entangling alliances.
    (2) Western European troops are a sufficient deterrent to the Soviet Union and its Warsaw Pact allies.
    (3) The Soviet Union has no designs on Western Europe.
    (4) Warsaw Pact troops of Eastern European countries are not loyal to their Soviet allies.
    (5) Western European security depends on U.S. nuclear weapons.

34. Which of the following best characterizes the purpose of the passage?

    (1) to urge that nuclear weapons not remain in Europe
    (2) to trace efforts to remove U.S. nuclear weapons from Europe
    (3) to analyze Soviet strategy toward nuclear disarmament
    (4) To discuss the relative strength of NATO versus Warsaw Pact forces
    (5) to compare the number of Soviet and American missiles in Europe

35. Which of the following statements is supported by information in the passage?

    (1) The creation of a nuclear-free zone would reduce but not eliminate the risk of atomic warfare in that zone.
    (2) The creation of a nuclear-free zone in Europe would lead to the creation of similar zones elsewhere.
    (3) Nuclear-free zones require a reduction in the number of troops.
    (4) Peaceful uses of atomic energy, such as the operation of nuclear reactors to generate electricity, are prohibited in nuclear-free zones.
    (5) The removal of American nuclear weapons from Europe would make Europe a nuclear-free zone.

GO ON TO THE NEXT PAGE

Items 36 to 38 are based on the following passage.

In 1933, when President Franklin D. Roosevelt took office, the nation was in the throes of a severe economic depression. After the stock market crashed in 1929, corporations began to face bankruptcy since they could no longer sell their output, no matter how much they lowered their prices, nor could they raise money for new production. Twelve million Americans lost their jobs, and more than one million homeless people took to the road. Tens of thousands of mortgages were foreclosed; many savings accounts and the banks that had held them were wiped out. National income was more than halved.

To meet these difficulties, the Roosevelt administration proposed a New Deal, an unprecedented series of programs with three main goals: relief, recovery, and reform. "Relief" meant helping individuals in need, while "recovery" entailed aiding farmers, businesspeople, and workers in order to lift the nation out of the depression. Finally, "reform" meant government action to eliminate abuses in the economy and, through a range of new programs, to prevent future depressions. In short, the New Deal attempted to get the economy going again. Government officials promised to take steps to solve the nation's ills.

36. Which of the following statements is best supported by the passage?

   (1) New Deal legislation introduced the idea of government's responsibility for the nation's economic health.
   (2) The New Deal was consistent with the idea of rugged individualism and self-help.
   (3) New Deal programs brought the nation to recovery.
   (4) The New Deal was destructive to the private sector of the American economy.
   (5) New Deal reforms failed to survive the 1930s.

37. Based on the passage, which of the following statements best explains what caused the Great Depression of the 1930s?

   (1) Businesses raised their prices so high that people could not afford to buy their products, and, to make up their losses, corporations raised their prices even higher.
   (2) Labor unions demanded wages that were so high that companies could not afford to pay them, so businesses fired some of their workers, resulting in massive unemployment.
   (3) Businesses, lacking capital from a collapsed stock market, laid off workers to lower costs, but these workers then lacked purchasing power, so business output went unsold, leading to further layoffs.
   (4) Banks attempted to force businesses and individuals to whom they loaned money to accept unfavorable terms, but this move eventually backfired, resulting in numerous bank failures and a contraction of the economy.
   (5) Millions of Americans lost their jobs, and more than a million homeless people took to the road.

38. Which of the following government programs is the best example of a New Deal relief measure?

   (1) the Glass-Steagall Act, which separated commercial and investment banking and set up federal insurance to guarantee bank deposits up to a maximum amount
   (2) the Agricultural Adjustment Act, which subsidized farmers to withdraw acreage from production so that crop prices would be raised
   (3) the Revenue Act, which raised income taxes for corporations and individuals in the upper brackets to a historic level
   (4) the Works Progress Administration, which employed Americans from many walks of life in cultural and construction projects
   (5) the Wagner Act, which guaranteed collective bargaining and set up a National Labor Relations Board to supervise disputed union elections

GO ON TO THE NEXT PAGE

Items 39 to 41 are based on the following graph.

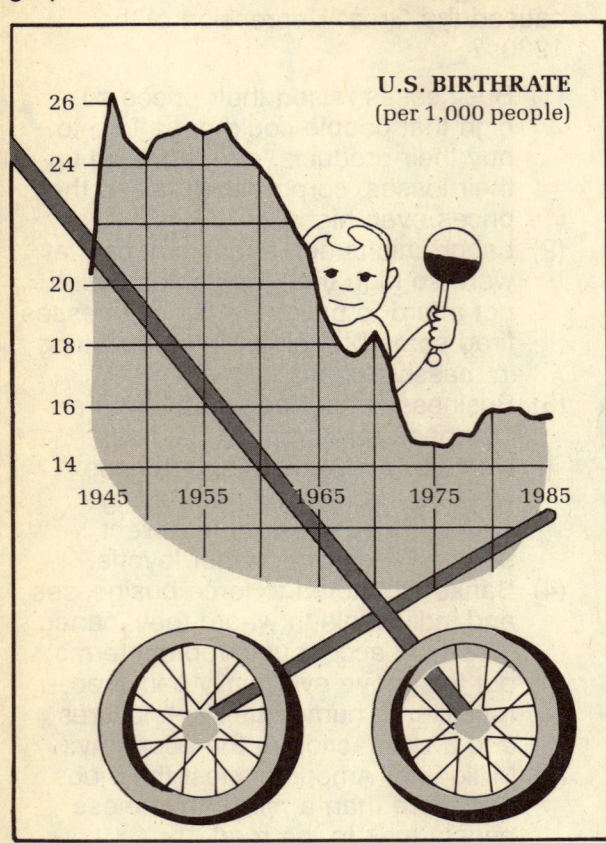

U.S. BIRTHRATE
(per 1,000 people)

Source: *Time*, February 23, 1987, page 29. Used with permission.

39. Which of the following accurately describes information given in the graph?

    (1) The period shown in the graph was marked by a continual decline in the birthrate.
    (2) The steepest five-year decline came between 1960 and 1965.
    (3) The birthrate reached a low point in 1975 but by 1980 had returned to the 1970 level.
    (4) The birthrate in 1980 was less than half the birthrate in 1945.
    (5) The birthrate in 1960 was actually slightly higher than that in 1950.

40. Children born within the same group of years are called a *cohort*. The life experiences of a cohort are influenced, among other things, by the sheer numbers of individuals in the cohort. Based on the figure, which of the following is most likely to be experienced by the cohort born between 1965 and 1980?

    (1) Competition for places in colleges and universities will be intense.
    (2) The kinds of jobs worked will in many cases be radically different from those worked by previous cohorts.
    (3) Jobs will be relatively plentiful.
    (4) Housing shortages will worsen.
    (5) The crime rate will soar.

41. Which of the following inferences follows logically from the data presented in the figure?

    (1) Falling birthrates over the past two decades mean that the United States is in a process of decline and will cease to be a world power.
    (2) Low birthrates over the past decades mean that there will be low birthrates in the decades to come.
    (3) High birthrates over the past two decades mean that the United States is a major contributor to the world population explosion.
    (4) Rising birthrates in the past few years suggest that the goal of zero population growth will not be reached soon.
    (5) Low birthrates over the last two decades are a result of the increasing percentage of the population that is over 65 years of age.

GO ON TO THE NEXT PAGE

SIMULATED TESTS   Test 2: Social Studies

Items 42 to 44 are based on the following graphs.

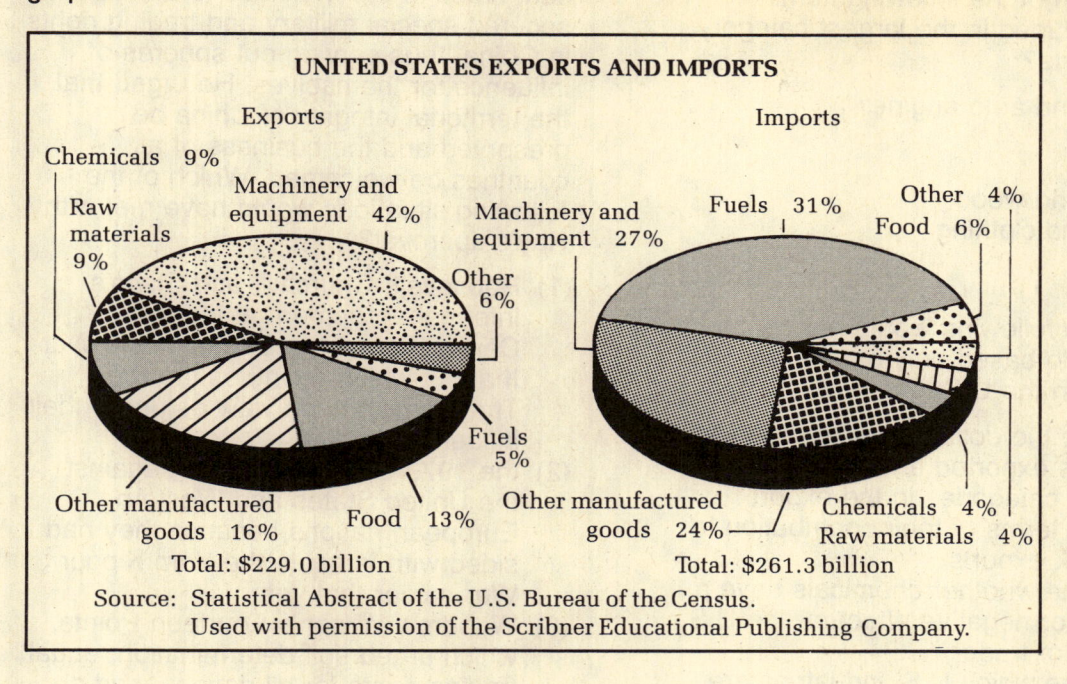

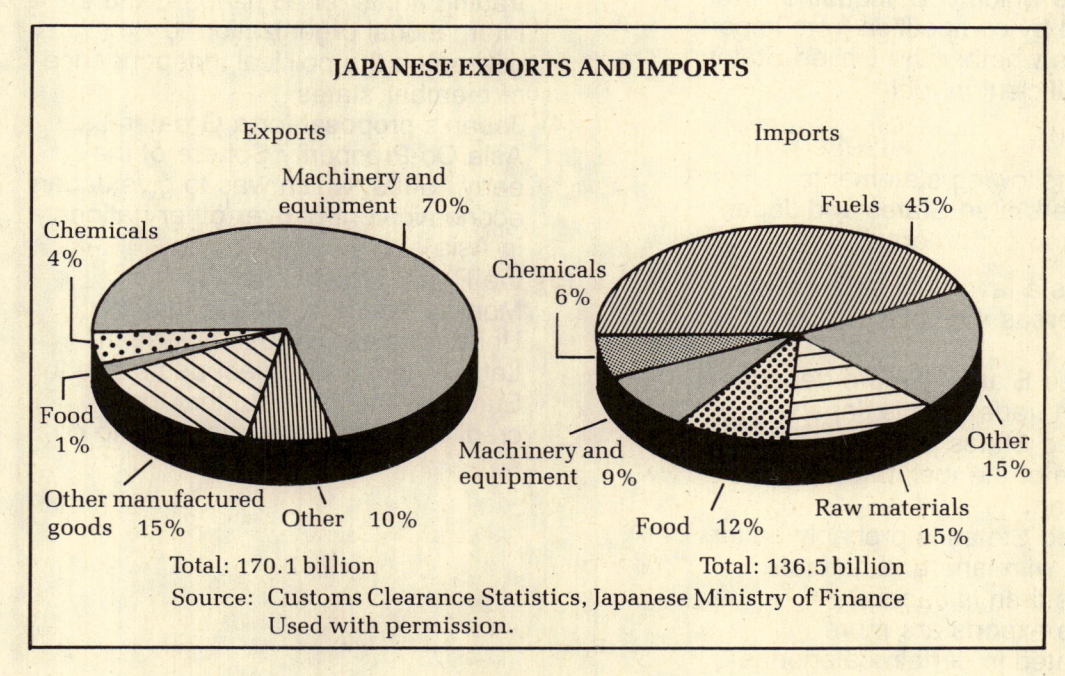

UNITED STATES EXPORTS AND IMPORTS

Exports:
- Chemicals 9%
- Raw materials 9%
- Machinery and equipment 42%
- Other 6%
- Fuels 5%
- Food 13%
- Other manufactured goods 16%

Total: $229.0 billion

Imports:
- Machinery and equipment 27%
- Fuels 31%
- Other 4%
- Food 6%
- Chemicals 4%
- Raw materials 4%
- Other manufactured goods 24%

Total: $261.3 billion

Source: Statistical Abstract of the U.S. Bureau of the Census. Used with permission of the Scribner Educational Publishing Company.

JAPANESE EXPORTS AND IMPORTS

Exports:
- Chemicals 4%
- Machinery and equipment 70%
- Food 1%
- Other manufactured goods 15%
- Other 10%

Total: 170.1 billion

Imports:
- Chemicals 6%
- Fuels 45%
- Machinery and equipment 9%
- Food 12%
- Raw materials 15%
- Other 15%

Total: 136.5 billion

Source: Customs Clearance Statistics, Japanese Ministry of Finance. Used with permission.

GO ON TO THE NEXT PAGE

42. Based on information provided in the graphs, which of the following items would be included in the largest category of U.S. exports?

    (1) aircraft and auto engines
    (2) cattle
    (3) coal
    (4) lumber and wood
    (5) shoes and clothing

43. Which of the following would not be possible to do based only on the information in the U.S. graphs?

    (1) calculate the dollar value of raw materials exported and imported
    (2) rank the categories in the export graph in terms of their contribution to total U.S. exports
    (3) determine whether chemicals have a positive or negative effect on the U.S. balance of trade
    (4) determine which U.S. industries are most hurt by competition from imports
    (5) determine whether the United States is self-sufficient in fuel

44. Which of the following statements comparing the United States and Japan is not supported by the graphs?

    (1) Japan has a favorable balance of trade whereas the United States does not.
    (2) The United States is more dependent on foreign trade than is Japan.
    (3) The United States produces a greater proportion of the fuel it needs than does Japan.
    (4) The United States is probably better endowed with land and natural resources than is Japan.
    (5) Japanese exports are more concentrated in certain categories than are U.S. exports.

45. In 1899, Secretary of State John Hay sent notes to the five nations that had secured special military and trading rights in China, thus carving out spheres of influence for themselves. He urged that the territorial integrity of China be preserved and the business of all countries be welcomed. Which of the following situations would have met with Hay's approval?

    (1) Roosevelt, Churchill, and Stalin's informal agreement at the Yalta Conference at the End of World War II about which countries the Big Three would each view as under their influence.
    (2) the 1973 OPEC oil boycott against the United States and Western European nations because they had sided with Israel in the Yom Kippur War earlier that year
    (3) Woodrow Wilson's Fourteen Points, which urged self-determination, equal trading rights for all nations, and an international organization to guarantee the political independence of member states
    (4) Japan's proposal for a Greater East Asia Co-Prosperity Sphere of the early 1940s, which was to give Japan economic control over other nations in Asia
    (5) the Roosevelt Corollary to the Monroe Doctrine, stating that the United States would intervene in Latin America to collect debts due to European nations, but that the creditors themselves were not to do so

GO ON TO THE NEXT PAGE

Items 46 and 47 are based on the following passage.

In 1940, before the United States entered World War II, President Roosevelt traded 50 aged U.S. destroyers for bases owned by the British in a simple exchange of notes with British government officials. Fearful of the delay that Senate approval of a treaty might have involved, President Roosevelt in effect found a quick way to help an embattled ally fighting for its survival. The agreement he made is considered a legitimate exercise of presidential power. The Constitution vests the president with primary responsibility for the conduct of foreign affairs even though Congress must fund foreign policy activities and assent to formal treaties.

46. Which of the following statements best describes the basis of the president's authority to arrange such a deal with Britain?

   (1) The president is empowered to enter into executive agreements with other nations.
   (2) The Constitution charges the president with responsibility to negotiate treaties subject to senatorial approval.
   (3) The president is empowered to see that the laws are faithfully executed.
   (4) The president may ask Congress to declare war against an enemy of the United States.
   (5) Acts of the federal government are considered the supreme law of the land.

47. In which of the following situations did a president use his power in a manner similar to Roosevelt in the destroyer-base deal?

   (1) President Carter's invitation to the leaders of Egypt and Israel to negotiate a peace treaty at Camp David
   (2) President Nixon's negotiations to limit antiballistic missiles, which resulted in the SALT I Treaty
   (3) President Theodore Roosevelt's informal Gentlemen's Agreement with Japanese leaders to limit immigration to the United States
   (4) President Reagan's meeting with the leader of the Soviet Union to discuss arms control proposals
   (5) President Lyndon Johnson's use of marines to help set up a government in the Dominican Republic friendly to the United States

Item 48 is based on the following passage.

In all societies people exchange goods and services. In simple societies, however, exchanges are not economic transactions, but reciprocal gift-giving. A gift requires a return gift. Social events of almost every kind—from marriage to the planting of a garden—initiate gift-giving between families, clans, villages, or other social groups. A group often gains in status by returning a gift of greater value than one recieved.

48. Which of the following statements is best supported by the information in the passage?

   (1) Calculations of profit and loss are basic to gift exchange.
   (2) A primary purpose of exchange is to establish or maintain relationships among groups.
   (3) Calculation of the value of gifts is forbidden in gift exchange.
   (4) Only a few members of society are allowed to participate in gift exchange.
   (5) The main purpose of gift exchange is to give people the opportunity to show off.

GO ON TO THE NEXT PAGE

Item 49 is based on the following map and information.

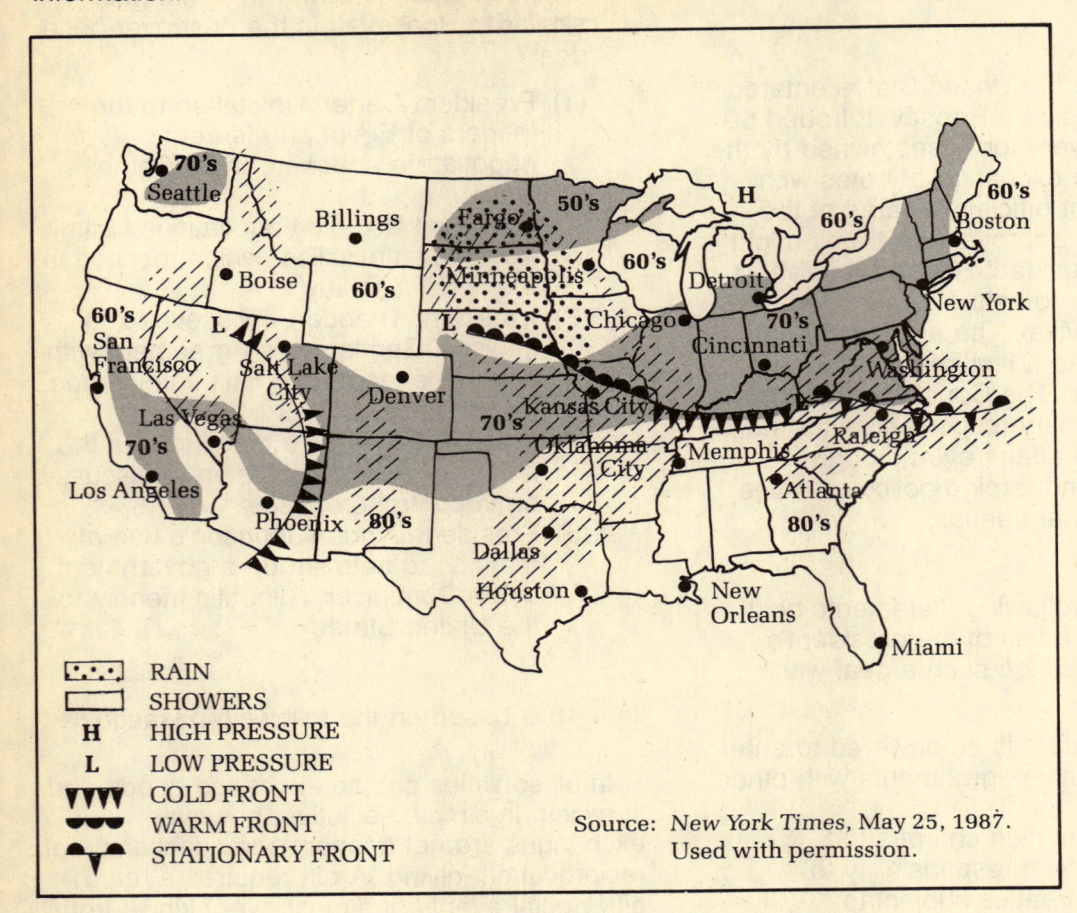

[Weather map of the continental United States showing temperatures and precipitation on May 25, 1987, with legend indicating RAIN, SHOWERS, H HIGH PRESSURE, L LOW PRESSURE, COLD FRONT, WARM FRONT, STATIONARY FRONT. Source: *New York Times*, May 25, 1987. Used with permission.]

The map shows temperatures and precipitation in the continental United States on May 25, 1987. Shaded and clear areas indicate regions having the same temperature.

49. Based on the map, which of the following cities had the most favorable weather conditions on May 25, 1987?

    (1) Fargo
    (2) Cincinnati
    (3) Las Vegas
    (4) Atlanta
    (5) Salt Lake City

GO ON TO THE NEXT PAGE

Items 50 to 54 are based on the following passage.

Most people obey the basic rules of their communities not only because they will be punished if they do not, but also because they believe the rules to be legitimate. People may believe rules are legitimate for a number of reasons. The following are principal types of reasons for which people believe rules are legitimate.

(1) **tradition**—belief that rules are legitimate because they have been passed down from generation to generation
(2) **emotion**—belief that rules are legitimate simply because the individual has a strong feeling that the rules and the overall model of society must be right
(3) **charisma**—belief that rules are legitimate based on faith in the leader who has established them
(4) **value principles**—belief that rules are legitimate because they are based on fundamental ethical or religious principles
(5) **lawfulness**—belief that rules are legitimate because they have been established through a legal process that is legitimate

Each of the following situations exemplifies one of the five bases for legitimacy of rules listed above. The types may be used more than once, but no question has more than one best answer.

50. A group adopts a constitution which sets forth a simple majority vote of the community as necessary for enacting a law. A law popular with only a small majority is nevertheless obeyed. In this example, the basis for belief in the legitimacy of the law is probably

    (1) tradition
    (2) emotion
    (3) charisma
    (4) value principles
    (5) lawfulness

51. A country has been governed by a single leader during the entire twenty years of its independence. Opposition politicians, who were already frustrated by the leader's popularity, now strenuously object to a new law that limits opposition parties. Nonetheless, much of the public supports the law. In this example, the basis for the public's belief in the legitimacy of the law is probably

    (1) tradition
    (2) emotion
    (3) charisma
    (4) value principles
    (5) lawfulness

52. A group passes a resolution urging its members to refuse to comply with a new law requiring registration for the draft. They argue that participation in the military runs counter to the group's belief in nonviolence. The members of the group overwhelmingly obey the resolution. The basis for their belief in its legitimacy is probably

    (1) tradition
    (2) emotion
    (3) charisma
    (4) value principles
    (5) lawfulness

53. When a monarch dies, his oldest son, who is next in line of succession, is proclaimed king. The public mourns the king and prepares for his son's coronation. The basis for their belief in the proclamation's legitimacy is probably

    (1) tradition
    (2) emotion
    (3) charisma
    (4) value principles
    (5) lawfulness

GO ON TO THE NEXT PAGE

54. A community is formed around a leader who preaches that the world as we know it is about to end. A skilled orator with a magnetic personality, he promises a new and better world to people who abide by his prophecy and by the rules of his community. The basis for members' belief in the legitimacy of the rules of the community is probably

   (1) tradition
   (2) emotion
   (3) charisma
   (4) value principles
   (5) lawfulness

55. During the 1830s, South Carolina Senator John C. Calhoun proposed the controversial doctrine of nullification. He argued that a state had the power to declare an act of Congress null and void. South Carolina put this doctrine into effect when it passed an ordinance annulling the Tariffs of 1828 and 1832 and prohibiting the collection of duties in South Carolina ports. However, the threat of President Andrew Jackson's Force Bill was sufficient to get the ordinance rescinded. Which of the following examples most closely carries out Calhoun's concept of nullification?

   (1) the Senate's rejection of the treaty establishing the League of Nations
   (2) President Truman's veto of the Taft-Hartley Act, which restricted and regulated unions
   (3) Soviet use of its veto power when the UN Security Council resolved to send a mediator to settle the Indian-Pakistani dispute over Kashmir
   (4) the Supreme Court's finding in the Dred Scott case that the Missouri Compromise of 1820 was unconstitutional
   (5) Southern state conventions repealing the U.S. Constitution and declaring their secession from the Union

Item 56 is based on the following cartoon.

"These weren't damaged in the riots — they went to pieces years before."

56. This 1967 cartoon was drawn in the aftermath of riots in Detroit, Newark, and other American cities during the administration of President Lyndon Johnson. Based on the cartoon, what was the main cause of the riots?

   (1) Opposition to the Vietnam War led to riots and demonstrations as youths protested being drafted to fight in Southeast Asia.
   (2) In spite of the civil rights movement, many American blacks felt that little had been done to improve the quality of their lives.
   (3) American blacks protested their exclusion from the political process.
   (4) Racism on the part of blacks and whites had taken a violent turn.
   (5) Slum clearance programs sparked opposition from those who would be displaced by urban renewal.

GO ON TO THE NEXT PAGE

Item 57 is based on the following graphs.

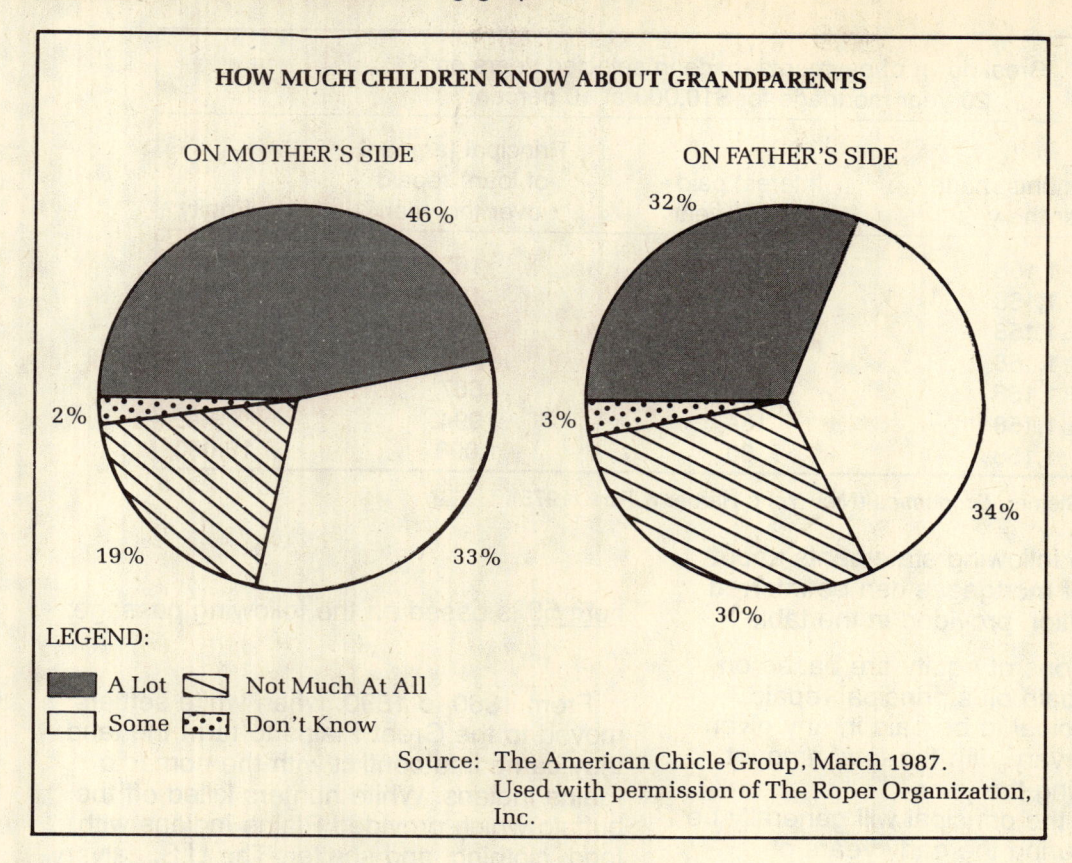

HOW MUCH CHILDREN KNOW ABOUT GRANDPARENTS

ON MOTHER'S SIDE
- 46%
- 2%
- 19%
- 33%

ON FATHER'S SIDE
- 32%
- 3%
- 30%
- 34%

LEGEND:
- ■ A Lot
- ▨ Not Much At All
- □ Some
- ⋯ Don't Know

Source: The American Chicle Group, March 1987. Used with permission of The Roper Organization, Inc.

57. Which of the following statements might explain the pattern shown in the two graphs?

   (1) Children tend to be closer to, and talk more with, their mother than their father.
   (2) Children more often live closer to their father's parents than their mother's parents.
   (3) Children today generally know little about grandparents on either side of the family.
   (4) Children tend to know more about their mother's parents than about their father's.
   (5) Children today only rarely see their grandparents.

GO ON TO THE NEXT PAGE

Item 58 is based on the following table.

	Breakdown of payments made in selected years on a 20-year mortgage for $10,000 at 10 percent			
Year	Payments made over the year	Interest paid over the year	Principal (amount of loan) repaid over the year	Equity
1	1,158	993	165	165
2	1,158	975	183	349
5	1,158	912	246	1,020
10	1,158	753	405	2,698
15	1,158	491	667	5,458
19	1,158	164	994	8,902
20	1,158	60	1,098	10,000

Source: Lipsey and Steiner, *Economics* (New York: Harper & Row, 1975).

58. Which of the following statements about repayment of mortgages can be inferred from information provided in the table?

    (1) Calculations of equity are based on interest paid plus principal repaid.
    (2) The principal to be paid in any given year will vary with the total amount paid during the year.
    (3) Much of the principal will generally be repaid during the early years of repayment.
    (4) Total interest payments can approach but cannot exceed total principal payments.
    (5) The interest to be paid in any given year will vary with the amount of the loan still outstanding.

Item 59 is based on the following passage.

From 1860 to 1890, when white settlers moved to the Great Plains to farm the land, they came into conflict with the nomadic Plains Indians. White hunters killed off the buffalo which provided Plains Indians with food, clothing, and shelter. The U.S. calvary destroyed the Indians' ability to defend their territory and then forced the survivors to move to reservations where they were expected to become farmers.

59. Which of the following statements is supported by the passage?

    (1) White settlers initially tried to coexist with the Indians.
    (2) Whites failed to understand or respect Indian culture.
    (3) The Great Plains was the area in which there was most conflict between Native Americans and white settlers.
    (4) Settlers destroyed the ecology of the Great Plains.
    (5) The Native Americans eventually abandoned their culture and way of life.

GO ON TO THE NEXT PAGE

Items 60 and 61 are based on the following graph.

GROWING ENTITLEMENT SPENDING

Benefits paid in four federal entitlement programs, in billions of dollars by fiscal year

(Figures for 1986 through 1991 are estimates from President Reagan's budget proposal)

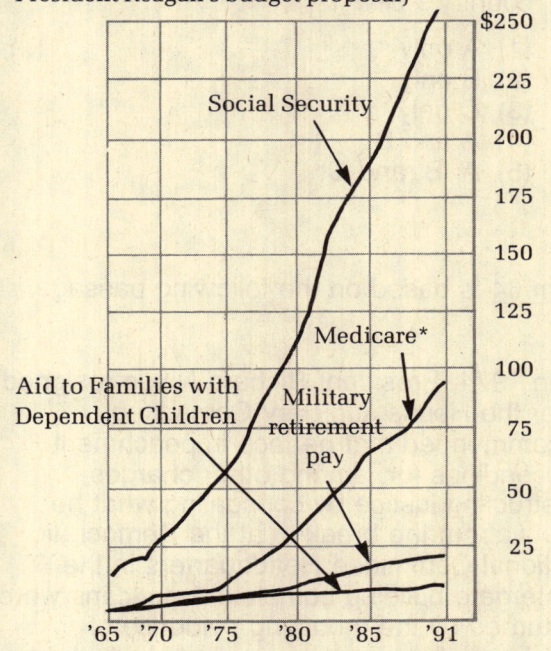

*Medicare payments (health care for retired people) began in 1966
Source: From Burns, Peltason, and Cronin, *Government By the People* (Englewood Cliffs: Prentice-Hall, Inc., 1987), page 549. Used with permission.

60. Which of the following conclusions is supported by the information presented in the graph?

    (1) The birth rate is soaring.
    (2) The unemployment rate is shrinking.
    (3) The American population is aging.
    (4) Enrollment in the armed services is declining.
    (5) Hospital costs are being brought under control.

61. Which of the following statements is best supported by the information in the graph?

    (1) Private charities are assuming more responsiblity for the nation's needy, reducing federal expenditures.
    (2) Until the Great Depression, the federal goverenment did little to aid the needy.
    (3) Most federal entitlement programs are administered by state and local governments.
    (4) The elderly probably have more interest group support pressuring Congress than do the young and the poor.
    (5) Poverty programs perpetuate poverty and create a culture of poverty.

GO ON TO THE NEXT PAGE

Items 62 and 63 are based on the following passage.

Gross national product (GNP) is essentially the market value of all goods and services produced by a nation during a specified period of time (for example, a year). The goods and services produced fall into two basic categories. Consumer goods and services—for example, televisions and haircuts—are used by individuals or households to meet their needs and wants. Capital (or "investment") goods and services are used in, or necessary to, the production of other goods. Machines, roads, and even maintenance work on office computers are examples of capital goods and services.

Both consumer goods/services and capital goods/services may be public as well as private. That is, the government purchases both consumer goods and services—for example, the services of public school teachers—and capital goods and services—for example, roads, dams, and sewage treatment plants.

By adding all public and private expenditures on both capital and consumer goods and services, we can obtain the GNP. Trends in the GNP are important data for economists and policymakers alike.

62. Which of the following is an example of a public consumer good/service?

   (1) a car
   (2) a factory building
   (3) a highway system
   (4) firefighters' services
   (5) income tax preparers' services

63. Data that economists and policymakers might want to obtain about a country include (A) the overall level of activity of the economy, (B) the level of expenditures on various kinds of goods and services, and (C) the extent to which goods and services are equally distributed among the population. What could they learn about by looking at the country's GNP?

   (1) A only
   (2) B only
   (3) C only
   (4) A and B
   (5) A, B, and C

Item 64 is based on the following passage.

In 1974, President Richard Nixon resigned after the House Judiciary Committee recommended that he face impeachment proceedings for, among other charges, obstructing justice by concealing what he knew about the break-in at the Democratic National Committee Headquarters in the Watergate building complex. Americans were disturbed by the mounting evidence of presidential wrongdoing, and public faith in the national government was badly shaken. Moreover, the incident did not end with the resignation, as Nixon still faced the possibility of indictment for his activities. Then, two months after being sworn in as president, Gerald Ford decided to pardon Nixon.

64. Based on the passage, which of the following statements best explains President Ford's decision?

   (1) his belief that Nixon was innocent
   (2) Nixon's request for clemency
   (3) pressure from leading Republicans
   (4) the need to give the nation a chance to recover
   (5) a lack of evidence concerning Nixon's role in Watergate

Answers are on pages A-85—A-89.

SIMULATED TEST 3
Science

TIME: 90 minutes
Directions: Choose the one best answer to each question.

Items 1 to 5 refer to the following passage.

Living matter may be classified into different levels according to its complexity of organization. Each level contains all lower levels within it and is in turn a part of all higher levels. The lowest level consists of subatomic particles such as electrons, protons, and neutrons. These make up atoms, which in turn form more complex combinations called chemical compounds. Chemical compounds are not living themselves; in fact, many of the common compounds in the human body are found in both living and nonliving matter. Water is an example of such a compound.

In living matter, chemical compounds often combine to form microscopic bodies called organelles. These organelles are contained within the cells and carry out each cell's life processes. The cell is the lowest level of matter considered to be alive since cells can exist independently of other cells and are capable of reproducing themselves.

Many cells function on their own. Unicellular organisms such as bacteria make up the majority of life on Earth. Other cells combine to form multicellular organisms. Multicellular organisms such as the human body include several levels of organization. The first is the tissue, a group of cells that are similar in structure and function. An example of a tissue is the nerves. Different tissues may join and work together, forming an organ such as the stomach. Groups of organs and tissues may, in turn, be united in an organ system. For example, the nervous system, which coordinates all body activities, consists of the brain, the spinal cord, and the nerves. For each of the following items, choose the correct level of organization based on the information in the passage. A level may be used more than once.

1. An amoeba is a one-celled protozoan able to move, feed, and reproduce itself. The amoeba is a(n)

   (1) chemical compound
   (2) organelle
   (3) organism
   (4) tissue
   (5) organ system

2. The heart is made up of muscle tissues, nerve tissue, and tissues that hold the various parts together. The heart is a(n)

   (1) organelle
   (2) cell
   (3) organ
   (4) organ system
   (5) organism

3. The chromosomes are microscopic bodies that contain the chemical codes that control life processes in the cell. The chromosomes are

   (1) subatomic particles
   (2) atoms
   (3) tissues
   (4) organelles
   (5) organs

4. Table salt is a combination of atoms necessary for life, although it is not alive itself. Table salt is a(n)

   (1) subatomic particle
   (2) chemical compound
   (3) organelle
   (4) cell
   (5) organism

GO ON TO THE NEXT PAGE

705

5. A dog is a combination of many cells working together and forming an independent being. A dog is a(n)

   (1) tissue
   (2) organ
   (3) organ system
   (4) unicellular organism
   (5) multicellular organism

Items 6 and 7 refer to the following passage.

An important part of the water cycle is the release of water into the atmosphere by plants and animals. This process is called transpiration. Both plants and animals use some of the water they take in for their life processes and then transpire the rest.

In plants, transpiration takes place through tiny pores in the leaves. Animals transpire in different ways. People give off water through pores in the skin. Dogs and other mammals release moisture by panting. The moisture carries heat away from the body and thus also acts as a cooling-off mechanism.

6. Why do desert plants, such as cactuses, have few or no leaves?

   (1) to increase the rate of transpiration
   (2) to decrease the rate of transpiration
   (3) to increase the rate at which photosynthesis takes place
   (4) to decrease the rate at which photosynthesis takes place
   (5) to discourage animals from eating them

7. Which of the following would most increase the relative humidity (amount of moisture in the air) in a room?
   A. Increase the number of animals.
   B. Decrease the number of animals.
   C. Increase the number of leafy plants.
   D. Decrease the number of leafy plants.

   (1) A only
   (2) A and D only
   (3) A and C only
   (4) C only
   (5) B and C only

Item 8 refers to the following diagram.

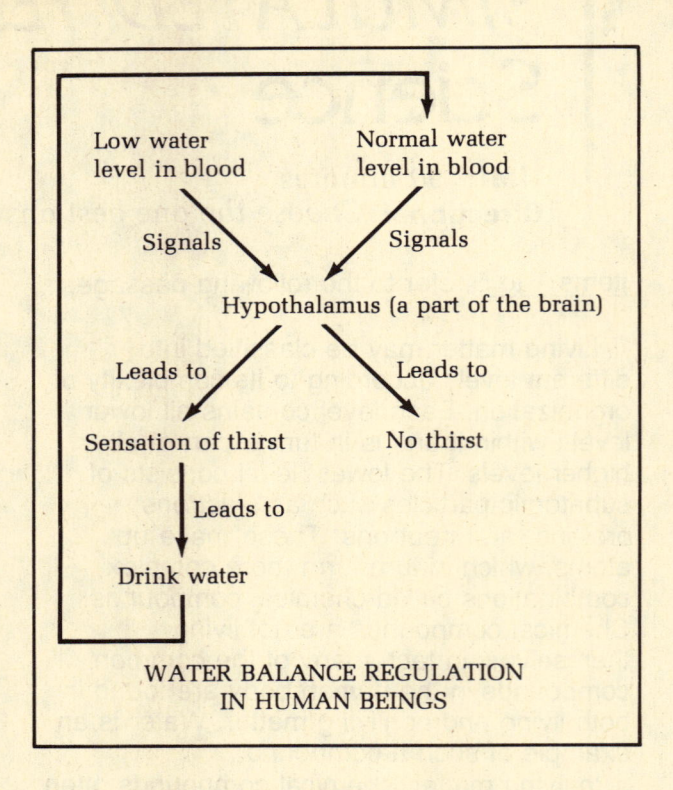

```
Low water                Normal water
level in blood           level in blood
        \               /
       Signals        Signals
          \           /
         Hypothalamus (a part of the brain)
         /                \
      Leads to          Leads to
        /                    \
  Sensation of thirst      No thirst
        |
     Leads to
        |
   Drink water
```

WATER BALANCE REGULATION
IN HUMAN BEINGS

8. A stimulus is an internal or external change in the environment. What is the direct stimulus for the thirst you feel on a hot day?

   (1) low water level in blood
   (2) the hypothalamus
   (3) sensation of thirst
   (4) a drink of water
   (5) the sun

9. The region of the atmosphere in which we live is called the troposphere. The troposphere extends an average of 12 kilometers above Earth's surface. As altitude increases in the troposphere, the air becomes colder and less dense. Based on this information, a person climbing Snowcap Mountain (elevation = 4.1 km) in July should be equipped with which of the following?

   (1) sunscreen and extra oxygen
   (2) protection against snow and rain
   (3) raingear and extra oxygen
   (4) extra food and sunscreen
   (5) warm clothing and extra oxygen

GO ON TO THE NEXT PAGE

Items 10 to 13 are based on the following diagram.

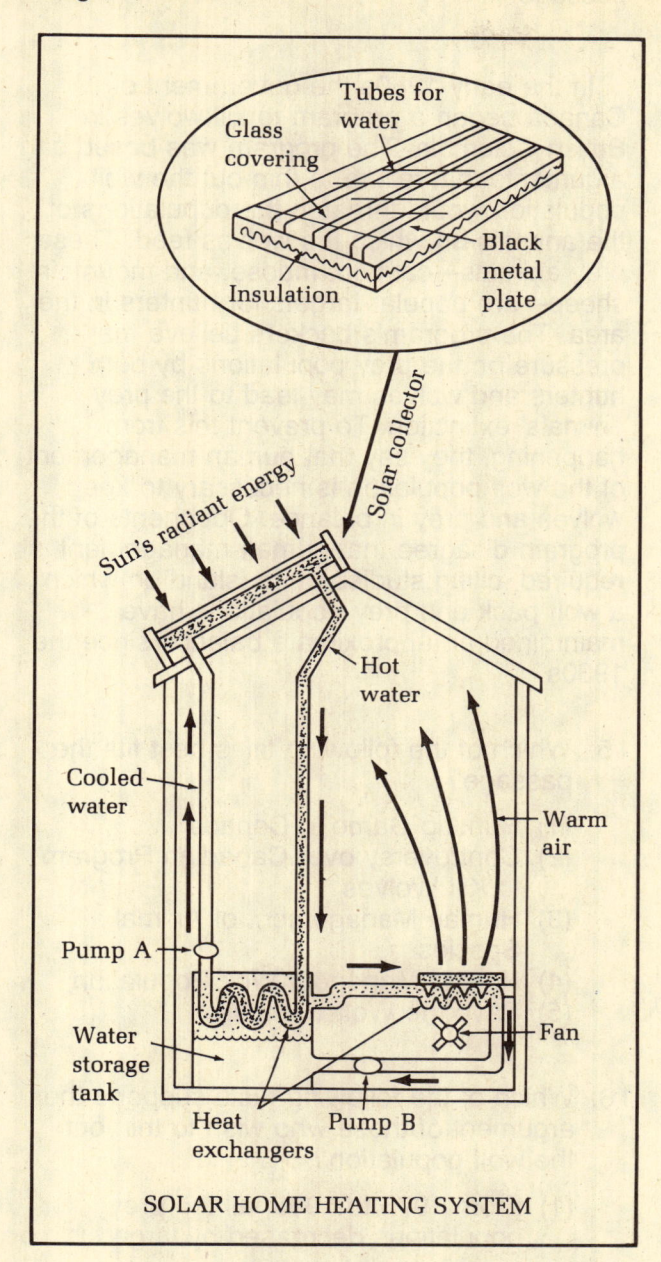

SOLAR HOME HEATING SYSTEM

10. Which of the following statements best summarizes the process of solar heating shown in the diagram?

    (1) Heat from the sun is circulated through the house by a pump and pipes and then moved to a storage tank.
    (2) Water heated by the sun is stored in a tank and then warm air is blown through the house.
    (3) Water heated by the sun in a solar collector is transferred to a storage tank and then moved through pipes to heat the house.
    (4) Water is pumped from a storage tank into a solar collector and then is moved back into the storage tank.
    (5) A fan circulates warm air through the house after water has been heated by the sun.

11. A camper wishes to use solar energy to heat some water. For the best results, which of the following set-ups should be used?

    (1) a black metal pot wrapped in a towel and covered with a piece of clear plastic food wrap
    (2) a shiny aluminum pot covered with a piece of black cardboard
    (3) a white pot wrapped in a towel and covered with a piece of clear plastic food wrap
    (4) an all-glass pot surrounded by newspaper and covered with a shiny metal cover
    (5) a black metal pot left uncovered and wrapped in aluminum foil

12. A homeowner whose home has a solar heating system notices that the water level in the system's solar collector is low, although the water level in the storage tank is normal. Which of the following is probably the cause of the problem.

    (1) a leak in the storage tank
    (2) a malfunction of the fan
    (3) a malfunction of pump A
    (4) a malfunction of pump B
    (5) a malfunction of a heat exchanger

GO ON TO THE NEXT PAGE

13. In an old-fashioned hot-water heating system, water heated in a boiler is moved through pipes to heat the house. Which of the following statements correctly compares a hot-water heating system to a solar heating system?

    (1) A solar heating system and a hot-water heating system are exactly alike.
    (2) The sun is to a solar heating system as a boiler is to a hot-water heating system.
    (3) A heat exchanger is to a solar heating system as a boiler is to a hot-water heating system.
    (4) The function of a heat exchanger is the same for both systems.
    (5) A solar collector is to a solar heating system as a boiler is to a hot-water heating system.

14. Leaves that turn yellow or orange in autumn have actually contained that color throughout the summer. However, in summer you cannot see the yellow or orange because the green pigment in chlorophyll hides it. Chlorophyll absorbs sunlight, providing the energy leaves need to produce sugar during photosynthesis. In autumn, the chlorophyll decays. When this happens, the yellow or orange color becomes visible, changing entire forests into beautiful displays of "fall foliage."
    Which of the following is true regarding a tree with orange or yellow leaves in the fall?

    (1) The tree is not carrying on photosynthesis at this time.
    (2) The leaves are absorbing sunlight to use as energy in the spring.
    (3) The tree is preparing for an active period of growth.
    (4) The leaves appeared orange and yellow in the summer as well.
    (5) The leaves formed new pigments as the chlorophyll decayed.

Items 15 and 16 are based on the following passage.

In the early 1980s the government of Canada began a program to kill wolves in British Columbia. The program was based on arguments that failure to thin out the wolf population would threaten the populations of the animals on which the wolves feed. These prey animals—caribou, moose, and mountain sheep—are popular targets for hunters in the area. The program's backers believe that pressure on the prey populations by both hunters and wolves may lead to the prey animals' extinction. To prevent this from happening, they say that human management of the wolf population is necessary to keep wolves and prey in balance. Opponents of the program disagree that human management is required, citing studies of an island on which a wolf pack and prey populations have maintained an approximate balance since the 1930s.

15. Which of the following titles best fits the passage?

    (1) Hunting Game in Canada
    (2) Controversy over Canadian Program to Kill Wolves
    (3) Human Management of Animal Species
    (4) How to Manage a Wolf Population
    (5) Save the Wolf Campaign

16. Which of the following facts supports the argument of those who wish to thin out the wolf population?

    (1) From 1975 to 1985, all the prey populations decreased by large numbers.
    (2) Hunting accounts for more animal kills than the wolves do.
    (3) If left to themselves, prey and predator populations tend to achieve a rough balance.
    (4) Canada has more wolves than any other country.
    (5) The prey populations have declined because of severe weather conditions.

GO ON TO THE NEXT PAGE

SIMULATION

Items 17 to 21 refer to the following passage.

There are several theories to explain how organisms evolve, or change and develop over time. One theory of evolution was first proposed almost 200 years ago by a French naturalist named Lamarck. Lamarck thought that if a body part were used frequently over several generations, it would grow larger and stronger with each generation. Unused body parts would tend to wither away. In this way, a species could acquire useful traits such as large eyes or a keen sense of smell. However, Lamarck's theory depended on the belief that a trait acquired in one generation, such as stronger legs due to frequent running, could be inherited by the next generation.

Some years later the English naturalist Charles Darwin put forth another theory. From extensive observations, Darwin concluded that most species would multiply extremely rapidly if not kept in check by natural conditions or predators. Darwin also noticed that the size of the population of a given species tends to remain the same over long periods of time. From these two observations, Darwin concluded that not all members of a species survive to reproduce. Each individual must struggle to exist.

Darwin also observed that individuals of the same species have a wide variety of different traits. Based on this fact, he suggested that certain traits might make some individuals more successful than others in the struggle for existence. Individuals with these "favorable" traits would be more likely to survive and reproduce, thus passing the traits on to the next generation. Darwin's ideas were called the theory of natural selection. However, the theory was incomplete because Darwin could not explain the mechanism by which traits are inherited. In his day, the fact that genes contain hereditary information was not generally understood.

Scientists today generally support the theory of natural selection, but they believe that it operates on the genetic variations that appear among members of a species population. In each generation, different combinations of genes from parents produce new traits in the offspring. By natural selection, organisms with favorable traits are more likely than others to survive and reproduce, and thus these traits are spread throughout the species population.

Test 3: Science

17. According to Darwin, an elephant with a favorable trait would

(1) be less likely to survive and reproduce
(2) be able to acquire other favorable traits such as a longer trunk
(3) lose against other elephants in the struggle for existence
(4) be more likely to survive and reproduce, passing the trait on to offspring
(5) be able to pass on acquired traits to offspring

18. Which of the following concepts is the main difference between Darwin's theory and the modern theory of evolution?

(1) natural selection
(2) inheritance of acquired traits
(3) not all individuals survive to reproduce
(4) individuals with favorable traits produce relatively more offspring
(5) natural selection acts on genetic variations

19. Which of the following statements best explains why Lamarck's theory of evolution is believed to be incorrect?

(1) Natural selection operates through the struggle for existence.
(2) Individuals vary within a species.
(3) Not all members of a species reproduce.
(4) A given species will reproduce at a rapid rate if unchecked.
(5) Acquired traits are not recorded in the genes and thus cannot be inherited.

20. Which of the following most determines the speed at which a species evolves?

(1) the rate at which the species reproduces
(2) the number of other animals that feed on the species
(3) the size of the species population
(4) the surrounding environment
(5) the average number of offspring produced by the species

GO ON TO THE NEXT PAGE

21. Which of the following examples might Lamarck have used to support his theory of evolution?

    (1) When we exercise, we grow bigger, stronger muscles.
    (2) A pair of mice can produce up to thirty offspring in a year.
    (3) A corn plant naturally grows toward the sun.
    (4) Brown-eyed parents may produce a blue-eyed child.
    (5) Not all sperm live to fertilize an egg.

---

22. A type of magnet called an electromagnet can be made by wrapping coils of wire around a piece of iron and then passing an electric current through the wire. The electromagnet acts as a magnet only while the current is running. Its magnetism disappears as soon as the current is turned off, but it returns when the current is turned back on.

    A manufacturer of heavy machinery equips a machine with a powerful electromagnet. For which of the following tasks would the machine be most effective?

    (1) welding together pieces of metal
    (2) picking up pieces of scrap metal and then depositing them in a refuse container
    (3) transporting heavy objects long distances
    (4) making magnets out of iron
    (5) increasing the ability of a wire to conduct electric current

23. In general, a mammal's life span is related to its body size. Small mammals live only two or three years, while an elephant may live for 60 years.

    Which of the following mammals most likely has the shortest life expectancy?

    (1) goat
    (2) horse
    (3) rabbit
    (4) rat
    (5) whale

24. A National Academy of Sciences report on passive cigarette smoking states that the risk of lung cancer is about 30 percent higher for a nonsmoking spouse of a smoker than for a nonsmoking spouse of a nonsmoker. It also states that respiratory infections such as pneumonia and bronchitis occur more often in children of smokers than in children of nonsmokers.

    Which of the following generalizations can be made about inhaling the cigarette smoke of others?

    (1) A smoker is harming his or her own health.
    (2) Inhaling the smoke of others has no effect on a nonsmoker.
    (3) Inhaling the smoke of others is a health hazard to a nonsmoker.
    (4) Smokers contract more respiratory infections than nonsmokers.
    (5) Children of smokers are more likely to try cigarettes themselves.

25. Recent experiments conducted on laboratory animals have shown that exposure to large amounts of ozone gas may cause cancer. Ozone, which pollutes the atmosphere when hydrocarbons from fossil fuels combine with nitrogen oxide, has already been known to cause headaches and breathing difficulties.

    Based on the information provided, which of the following statements represents a hypothesis rather than a fact or an opinion?

    (1) The link between ozone and cancer is pure speculation.
    (2) Hydrocarbons from fossil fuels cause air pollution.
    (3) Ozone can cause headaches and breathing difficulties.
    (4) Exposure to large amounts of ozone can cause cancer.
    (5) There is no conclusive evidence that ozone causes cancer.

GO ON TO THE NEXT PAGE

SIMULATED TESTS   Test 3: Science   **711**

Items 26 and 27 are based on the following portion of the Periodic Table of the Elements.

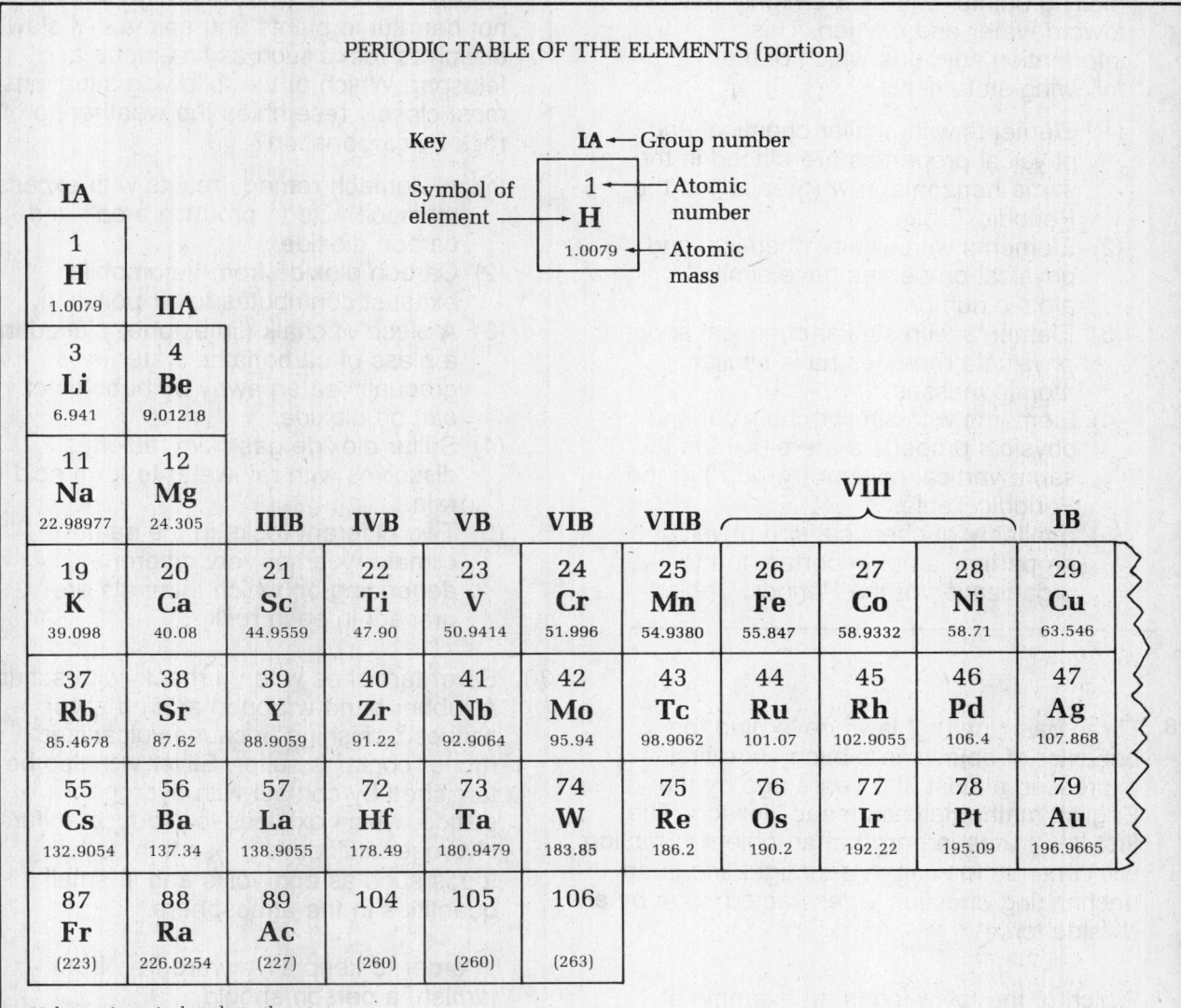

PERIODIC TABLE OF THE ELEMENTS (portion)

Key:
- Symbol of element → H
- Group number: IA
- Atomic number: 1
- Atomic mass: 1.0079

IA	IIA	IIIB	IVB	VB	VIB	VIIB	VIII			IB
1 H 1.0079										
3 Li 6.941	4 Be 9.01218									
11 Na 22.98977	12 Mg 24.305									
19 K 39.098	20 Ca 40.08	21 Sc 44.9559	22 Ti 47.90	23 V 50.9414	24 Cr 51.996	25 Mn 54.9380	26 Fe 55.847	27 Co 58.9332	28 Ni 58.71	29 Cu 63.546
37 Rb 85.4678	38 Sr 87.62	39 Y 88.9059	40 Zr 91.22	41 Nb 92.9064	42 Mo 95.94	43 Tc 98.9062	44 Ru 101.07	45 Rh 102.9055	46 Pd 106.4	47 Ag 107.868
55 Cs 132.9054	56 Ba 137.34	57 La 138.9055	72 Hf 178.49	73 Ta 180.9479	74 W 183.85	75 Re 186.2	76 Os 190.2	77 Ir 192.22	78 Pt 195.09	79 Au 196.9665
87 Fr (223)	88 Ra 226.0254	89 Ac (227)	104 (260)	105 (260)	106 (263)					

Values given in brackets denote the mass number of the isotope of the longest known half-life.

The Periodic Table shows the symbol for each element, the atomic number, and the atomic mass. Atomic number and atomic mass increase as one moves from left to right and from top to bottom across the table. All of the elements in this portion of the table have metallic properties.

26. A manufacturer of electronics equipment needs a fairly heavy substance with metallic properties to use in making a part for an audio receiver. Which of the following would be the least likely substance to use?

   (1) tungsten (W)
   (2) sodium (Na)
   (3) platinum (Pt)
   (4) copper (Cu)
   (5) nickel (Ni)

GO ON TO THE NEXT PAGE

27. Lithium (Li), Sodium (Na), potassium (K), rubidium (Rb), cesium (Cs), and francium (Fr) are all soft, silvery metals with low melting points, and all are highly reactive toward water and oxygen. This information supports which of the following statements?

   (1) Elements with similar chemical and physical properties are placed in the same horizontal row ("period") in the Periodic Table.
   (2) Elements with similar chemical and physical properties have similar atomic numbers.
   (3) Elements with similar chemical and physical properties have similar atomic masses.
   (4) Elements with similar chemical and physical properties are placed in the same vertical column ("group") in the Periodic Table.
   (5) Similarity of chemical and physical properties is not important in the organization of the Periodic Table.

28. Three basic natural laws governing the behavior of objects in motion were first expressed almost 300 years ago by the English mathematician Isaac Newton. The first law states in part that an object in motion will continue moving in a straight line in an unchanging direction unless acted upon by an outside force.

   Which of the following is an example of the law of motion described above?

   (1) An automobile starts up from a complete stop.
   (2) A stone dropped from a high tower speeds up as it falls to the ground.
   (3) A golf ball flies through the air after being hit by a golf club.
   (4) An arrow shot straight up into the air stops rising and falls back to the ground.
   (5) A gun recoils backward after shooting a bullet.

29. Weathering of rock can take place by carbonation. Carbonation occurs when carbon dioxide in the air dissolves in rain, forming carbonic acid. Although this acid is not harmful to plants and animals, it slowly dissolves rocks such as limestone and feldspar. Which of the following situations most closely resembles the weathering of rock by carbonation?

   (1) A stomach remedy reacts with excess stomach acid to produce a salt and carbon dioxide.
   (2) Carbon dioxide from automobile exhaust contributes to air pollution.
   (3) A piece of chalk (limestone) placed in a glass of carbonated water is gradually eaten away by bubbles of carbon dioxide.
   (4) Sulfur dioxide gas from factories dissolves with rainwater to form acid rain.
   (5) Two different rocks in the same climate weather very differently depending on which minerals are present in each rock.

30. Silver tarnishes when it reacts with sulfur. A rubber band wrapped around silver causes tarnishing because vulcanized rubber contains sulfer. Silver will also be tarnished by contact with hydrogen sulfide, which oxidizes to produce sulfur. Hydrogen sulfide is present in certain foods such as egg yolks and in small quantities in the atmosphere.

   In order to keep silverware free from tarnish, a person should

   (1) clean it with a sulfur-containing compound and then store it in an air-tight container
   (2) leave it untouched for several hours after use and then clean it and store it in an open container
   (3) expose it to hydrogen and oxygen and then store it in an open container
   (4) clean it immediately after use and then store it in rubber casing
   (5) clean it immediately after use and then store it in an air-tight container

GO ON TO THE NEXT PAGE

Items 31 to 34 are based on the following passage.

What is heat? Until a few hundred years ago, scientists believed that heat was a mysterious fluid called caloric. Caloric was thought to be invisible, weightless, and capable of flowing from hotter objects to colder ones.

The scientists who finally challenged this idea were an American known as Count Rumford and an Englishman named James Prescott Joule. Rumford, working in 1798, and Joule, working about 40 years later, performed experiments that showed that objects in motion produce heat. You can see for yourself that this is true by rubbing your hands briskly together several times and noticing how quickly they become warm.

Because Rumford and Joule observed that energy of motion was converted into heat, they concluded correctly that heat must also be a form of energy. Thus the transfer of heat from one object to another is not the flow of a mysterious fluid, but a transfer of energy.

Heat will always move from a hotter substance to a colder substance. When hot and cold water are mixed together, the hot water will give up heat to the cold water. This happens because the molecules of hotter substances have more energy than the molecules of colder substances. As the two substances come in contact with each other, the hotter molecules collide with the colder molecules, transferring some of their energy in the process. Thus a mixture of hot and cold water in equal amounts will come to a temperature that is just about in between the original temperatures of the hot and cold water.

31. Which of the following statements is not true of heat?

    (1) It can be produced by motion.
    (2) It is invisible.
    (3) It is a fluid.
    (4) It flows from hotter objects to colder objects.
    (5) It is a form of energy.

32. A recipe calls for one cup of milk at 70°C. A cook using the recipe has a cup of hot milk at 100°C and a cup of cold milk at 10°C. How should the hot milk and the cold milk be mixed in order to satisfy the recipe?

    (1) 1/2 cup hot milk and 1/2 cup cold milk
    (2) 1/4 cup hot milk and 3/4 cup cold milk
    (3) 1/4 cup cold milk and 3/4 cup hot milk
    (4) 1/3 cup hot milk and 2/3 cup cold milk
    (5) 1/3 cup cold milk and 2/3 cup hot milk

33. An athlete sliding too quickly down a rope experiences a rope burn. Which of the following statements explains why this happens?

    (1) Heat in the rope is converted into energy.
    (2) Some of the energy of the slide is converted into heat.
    (3) Energy in the rope is converted into heat.
    (4) The motion of the rope produces heat.
    (5) Molecules in the rope transfer energy to molecules in athlete's hand.

34. Which of the following conclusions is supported by the passage?

    (1) Molecules in hot water have twice as much energy as molecules in cold water.
    (2) The amount of energy transferred in a molecular collision is always the same.
    (3) The properties of heat are similar to those of a liquid.
    (4) Energy can change from one form to another.
    (5) A transfer of energy always involves a transfer of a fluid.

GO ON TO THE NEXT PAGE

Item 35 is based on the following diagram.

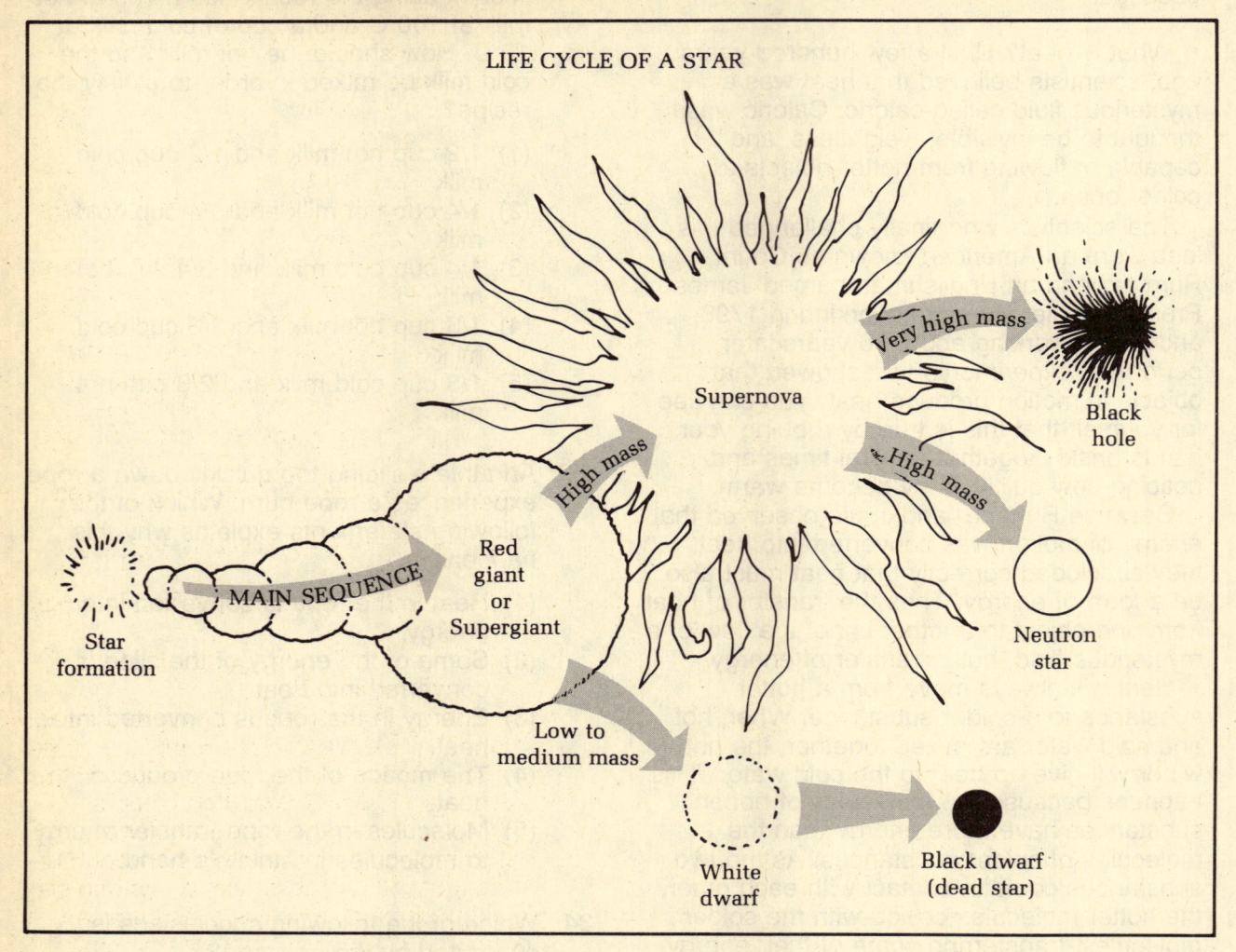

LIFE CYCLE OF A STAR

- Star formation → MAIN SEQUENCE → Red giant or Supergiant
- High mass → Supernova
  - Very high mass → Black hole
  - High mass → Neutron star
- Low to medium mass → White dwarf → Black dwarf (dead star)

35. Which of the following conclusions can be supported by the diagram?

   (1) No two stars begin life on the same path.
   (2) The greater the mass of a star, the longer it will live.
   (3) The ultimate fate of a star is determined by its mass.
   (4) The greater the mass of a star, the farther it must travel in its lifetime.
   (5) Of the three possible end stages of a star's life, the neutron star has the most energy.

36. An object's momentum (mv) is equal to the product of its mass multiplied by its velocity. An object's momentum will increase if which of the following events occur?

   (1) its mass doubles while its velocity is cut in half
   (2) its velocity doubles while its mass is cut in half
   (3) its mass increases by 50 percent while its velocity decreases by 75 percent
   (4) its mass triples while its velocity is cut in half
   (5) its mass is reduced by 1/4 while its velocity remains constant

GO ON TO THE NEXT PAGE

SIMULATED TESTS

Test 3: Science   **715**

Items 37 to 41 are based on the following diagram.

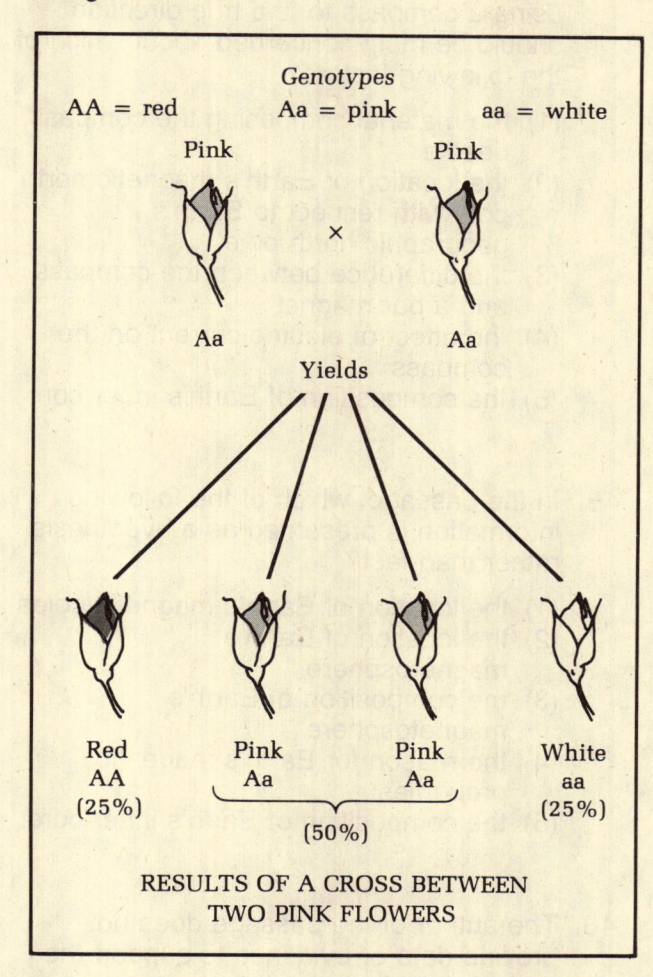

Genotypes
AA = red   Aa = pink   aa = white

Pink (Aa) × Pink (Aa)

Yields

Red AA (25%)   Pink Aa, Pink Aa (50%)   White aa (25%)

RESULTS OF A CROSS BETWEEN TWO PINK FLOWERS

37. Four pairs of the same type of pink flower are crossed. Sixteen new flowers result. How many of these new flowers are likely to be red?

    (1) one
    (2) two
    (3) four
    (4) eight
    (5) sixteen

38. If a red flower and a white flower were crossed, what would be the likely percentage(s) of each color offspring?

    (1) 25% red, 50% pink, 25% white
    (2) 50% red, 50% white
    (3) 75% red, 25% white
    (4) 100% pink
    (5) 100% red

39. A pink flower is crossed with a red flower. Of the resulting offspring, half are red and half are pink. Which of the following represents the genotypes of the offspring?

    (1) AA, Aa, Aa, aa   (4) AA, AA, AA, Aa
    (2) AA, AA, Aa, Aa   (5) Aa, Aa, aa, aa
    (3) AA, AA, aa, aa

40. A dominant gene is one that expresses itself regardless of its partner. In other words, even if it is paired with a gene for another variation, it will determine the trait. For the flowers shown in the diagram, neither the red gene nor the white gene is dominant. Which of the following provides evidence for this?

    (1) A flower with one red gene and one white gene is pink.
    (2) Two red flowers will produce a red flower.
    (3) Two white flowers will produce a white flower.
    (4) Two red flowers will produce a white flower.
    (5) Two white flowers will produce a red flower.

41. Skin color is inherited in a way similar to that in the diagram. For example, a dark-skinned father and a light-skinned mother will have a child whose skin color is between those of the parents. Two parents whose skin color is between dark and light will produce children whose skin color may be dark, light, or in between. A student argues that if one parent has light-colored skin and one parent has dark-colored skin, none of the children can have light-colored skin because the gene for dark-colored skin is dominant. What is incorrect about this argument?

    (1) The gene for medium-colored skin is dominant over the gene for dark-colored skin.
    (2) A dominant gene will determine a trait only part of the time.
    (3) The gene for light-colored skin is dominant, just like the gene for white color in flowers.
    (4) A gene for dark-colored skin could mutate into one for light-colored skin.
    (5) Neither the gene for light-colored skin nor the gene for dark-colored skin is dominant; just as in flowers, neither the gene for white color nor the gene for red color is dominant.

GO ON TO THE NEXT PAGE

Items 42 to 46 are based on the following passage.

If you suspend an iron bar magnet horizontally from a string, one end of the magnet will always point north. This happens because a magnetic field surrounds Earth.

The region that is subject to Earth's magnetic field is called the magnetosphere. The magnetosphere, which extends beyond Earth's atmosphere, is made up of charged particles blown out from the sun by the solar wind.

The magnetic forces that surround Earth are strongest near the poles. Earth's magnetic poles, however, do not coincide exactly with Earth's geographic poles. The north magnetic pole is located in northeastern Canada, about 1600 kilometers from the geographic North Pole. The south magnetic pole is located south of Australia, near the Antarctic Circle.

Scientists do not know exactly why Earth behaves like a magnet. For many years it was believed that Earth's magnetism was due to the presence of dense iron in the planet's inner core. In recent years, however, that idea has been challenged. Many scientists now believe that Earth's magnetism is caused by giant belts of electric current in the atmosphere and in Earth's crust.

42. The best title for this passage would be which of the following?

    (1) How to Use a Magnet
    (2) The Mysterious Solar Wind
    (3) Magnetic Properties of Earth
    (4) Iron and Magnetism
    (5) Why Is Earth a Magnet?

43. The passage suggests that a relationship exists between which of the following two factors?

    (1) magnetic properties and electricity
    (2) composition of Earth's inner core and electricity
    (3) location of Earth's magnetic poles and composition of Earth's inner core
    (4) the solar wind and the properties of magnets
    (5) location of the magnetosphere and composition of Earth's crust

44. A compass consists of a magnetized needle that is free to move. A person using a compass to find true direction should be most concerned about which of the following factors?

    (1) the material composing the compass needle
    (2) the location of Earth's magnetic north pole with respect to Earth's geographic north pole
    (3) the difference between the compass and a bar magnet
    (4) the effect of electric current on the compass
    (5) the composition of Earth's inner core

45. In the passage, which of the following information is presented as a hypothesis rather than fact?

    (1) the location of Earth's magnetic poles
    (2) the location of Earth's magnetosphere
    (3) the composition of Earth's magnetosphere
    (4) the reason for Earth's magentic properties
    (5) the composition of Earth's inner core.

46. The author of the passage does not provide data or evidence to support the assertion that

    (1) the magnetic north pole is not located at the geographic north pole
    (2) a magnetic field surrounds Earth
    (3) Earth exerts magnetic forces on magnets
    (4) Earth's magnetism is caused by bands of electric current in the atmosphere
    (5) the magnetic south pole is not located at the geographic south pole

GO ON TO THE NEXT PAGE

Items 47 to 50 are based on the following information.

Five types of chemical reactions are described below.

1. **synthesis:** a reaction in which two substances combine to form a new substance (A + B = C)
2. **decomposition:** a reaction in which a compound is broken down into two or more simpler substances (C = A + B)
3. **single replacement:** a reaction in which one element is replaced by another in a compound (AX + C = CX + A)
4. **double replacement:** a reaction in which the elements of the reacting compounds change places (AB + XY = AY + XB)
5. **no reaction:** the substance or substances involved remain chemically unchanged

Each of the following items describes an example of one of the five types of reactions listed above. For each item, choose the reaction type that best describes the procedure. Any type may be used more than once.

47. When hydrochloric acid (HCl) is mixed with sodium hydroxide (NaOH), table salt (sodium chloride, NaCl) and water (H_2O or HOH) are formed. This procedure is an example of

    (1) synthesis
    (2) decomposition
    (3) single replacement
    (4) double replacement
    (5) no reaction

48. Passing an electric current through water (H_2O) results in the release of oxygen gas (O_2) and hydrogen gas (H_2). This procedure is an example of

    (1) synthesis
    (2) decomposition
    (3) single replacement
    (4) double replacement
    (5) no reaction

49. Sulfuric acid (H_2SO_4) is poured onto a piece of zinc (Zn). Hydrogen gas (H_2) is released into the air as a salt called zinc sulfate ($ZnSO_4$) forms. This procedure is an example of

    (1) synthesis
    (2) decomposition
    (3) single replacement
    (4) double replacement
    (5) no reaction

50. One metal can replace another metal in a compound provided that the replacing metal is more active than the metal being replaced. Four metals in order of decreasing activity are lithium (Li), postassium (K), sodium (Na), and magnesium (Mg). Suppose that sodium (Na) is mixed in solution with lithium chloride (LiCl). The result would be an example of

    (1) synthesis
    (2) decomposition
    (3) single replacement
    (4) double replacement
    (5) no reaction

---

51. A magazine article on beef contains the following statements:
    A. Beef is a good source of protein, thiamin, riboflavin, niacin, vitamin B-12, iron, and zinc.
    B. Many consumers believe that beef contains high levels of fat and cholesterol.
    C. Meat labeled "lean" or "low-fat" has no more than 10 percent fat.
    D. Beef tastes better than other sources of protein.

    Which of the above statements is most likely based on opinion rather than on facts?

    (1) A and B only
    (2) B only
    (3) B and D only
    (4) A and C only
    (5) C and D only

GO ON TO THE NEXT PAGE

Item 52 is based on the following diagram and information.

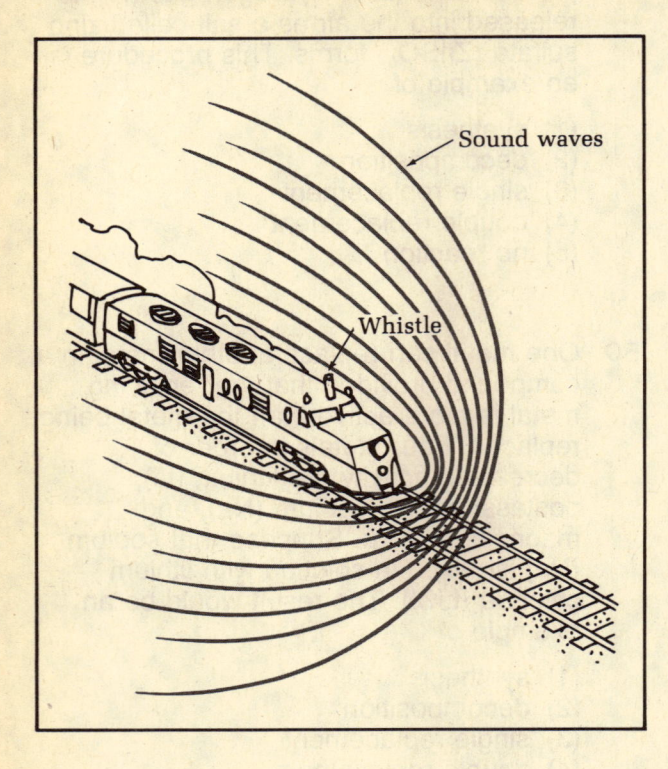

The diagram illustrates a phenomenon of sound waves called the Doppler Effect. When a moving object such as the train emits a sound such as a whistle, the sound waves spread out in all directions. However, the forward motion of the train compresses the sound waves ahead of the train. The more compressed the sound waves are, the higher the pitch of the sound. As a result, if you were standing ahead of the train, you would hear the whistle as a very high-pitched sound.

52. What change would you hear in the sound of the whistle as the train passed by where you were standing?

   (1) The pitch would sound higher because you would be hearing sound waves that were more compressed.
   (2) The pitch would sound higher because you would be hearing sound waves that were less compressed.
   (3) The pitch would sound the same.
   (4) The pitch would sound lower because you would be hearing sound waves that were more compressed.
   (5) The pitch would sound lower because you would be hearing sound waves that were less compressed.

53. Your immune system protects you by differentiating between your cells and foreign substances. Each cell has a unique chemical marker made up of a pattern of molecules at its surface. Because your particular gene combination is unique, the marks on your body cells differ from those on foreign substances. If the immune system detects a foreign mark, it will attack the substance.

   Which of the following substances in your body is *not* likely to trigger an attack by your immune system?

   (1) your red blood cells
   (2) staphylococcal bacteria
   (3) house dust
   (4) pollen grain
   (5) polio virus

GO ON TO THE NEXT PAGE

SIMULATED TESTS

Items 54 to 58 are based on the following information.

All living organisms need energy to carry out life processes. Organisms use the chemical energy that is stored in food, usually in the form of carbohydrates. This energy is released by chemical changes similar to burning a fuel. However, living things are unable to use this energy directly. Instead, the energy is stored as chemical energy to be used when necessary. The breakdown of food and the release of energy take place in individual cells through a process called cellular respiration. Most cellular respiration takes place in an organelle called the mitochondrion.

During cellular respiration, the energy released by the breakdown of food molecules is used to convert adenosine diphosphate (ADP) into adenosine triphosphate (ATP). ATP is a compound in a higher energy state than ADP. The high-energy ATP is then sent to whatever part of the cell needs energy. At that point, the ATP is converted back into ADP, releasing the stored energy to be used for cell activities. The leftover ADP may be reused by the cell. The energy from one molecule of glucose, a simple sugar, can be used to make as many as 36 molecules of ATP from ADP.

In most organisms, cellular respiration requires free oxygen. This is called aerobic respiration. In aerobic respiration, glucose is completely broken down into carbon dioxide and water. This is the kind of respiration that takes place in the cells of humans and other animals. Some one-celled organisms, such as yeast and bacteria, carry on anaerobic respiration, or respiration without oxygen. In this type of respiration the glucose molecule is only partly broken down.

Test 3: Science **719**

54. Three molecules of ATP are formed for every atom of oxygen used up during aerobic respiration. How many oxygen atoms are needed to use completely the energy in one molecule of glucose?

    (1) 1
    (2) 3
    (3) 12
    (4) 18
    (5) 36

55. During periods of intense activity, your muscle cells may use oxygen faster than your body can supply it. In such cases, the muscles can continue working for a short while without oxygen. Which of the following processes is (are) occurring in the muscle cells at such a time?
    A. conversion of ADP into ATP and back into ADP
    B. anaerobic respiration
    C. aerobic respiration

    (1) A only
    (2) B only
    (3) C only
    (4) A and B only
    (5) A and C only

56. Aerobic respiration of glucose is about 18 times more efficient than anaerobic respiration of glucose. Which of the following best explains the greater yield of energy through aerobic respiration?

    (1) The presence of oxygen allows the glucose to be completely broken down during aerobic respiration.
    (2) The ADP molecule cannot be reused following anaerobic respiration as it can after aerobic respiration.
    (3) Energy is released more quickly during aerobic respiration than during anaerobic respiration.
    (4) The glucose used in aerobic respiration comes from different carbohydrates than that used in anaerobic respiration.
    (5) Individual cells are more efficient at aerobic respiration than at anaerobic respiration.

GO ON TO THE NEXT PAGE

57. Biology is concerned with the study of life. Chemistry is the study of what matter is made of and how atoms change and combine. Earth science is the study of the earth, planets, stars, and the forces that act upon them. Physics is the study of different forms of energy and matter. Which branches of science might be concerned with the material in the passage?

    (1) chemistry and physics only
    (2) chemistry and earth science only
    (3) biology and physics only
    (4) biology, earth science, and chemistry only
    (5) biology, chemistry, and physics only

58. Scientists believe that the first living organisms evolved in an atmosphere without oxygen. Which of the following conclusions follows from this belief?

    (1) Aerobic respiration evolved earlier than anaerobic respiration.
    (2) Anaerobic respiration evolved earlier than aerobic respiration.
    (3) Anaerobic respiration is a favorable genetic trait.
    (4) Aerobic respiration is more efficient than anaerobic respiration.
    (5) Organisms that depend on aerobic respiration will quickly die in an atmosphere without oxygen.

Item 59 is based on the following graph.

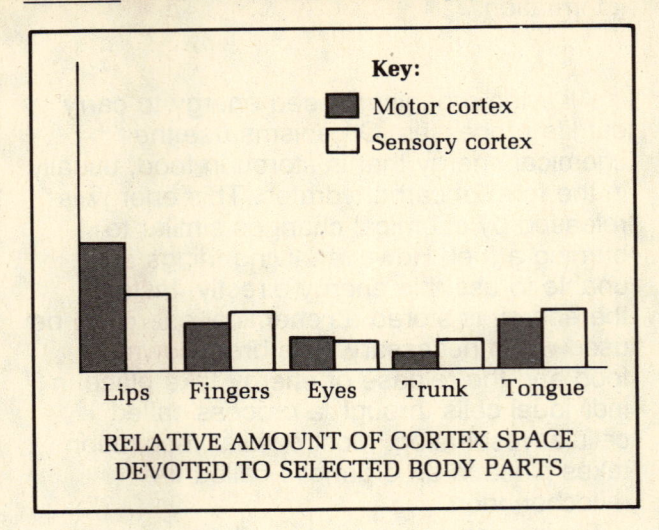

RELATIVE AMOUNT OF CORTEX SPACE DEVOTED TO SELECTED BODY PARTS

The sensory cortex is the part of the brain that receives signals from the skin, bones, joints, and muscles. The motor cortex moves the muscles.

59. Which of the following conclusions can be drawn from the graph?

    (1) The two cortexes make up the largest part of the brain.
    (2) The motor cortex is located opposite the sensory cortex in the brain.
    (3) The sensory cortex and the motor cortex do not receive signals from the same body parts.
    (4) The motor cortex is larger than the sensory cortex.
    (5) The amount of cortex space devoted to a body part is related to how the part is used, not to the size of the part.

GO ON TO THE NEXT PAGE

SIMULATED TESTS   Test 3: Science   **721**

Items 60 and 61 are based on the following diagrams.

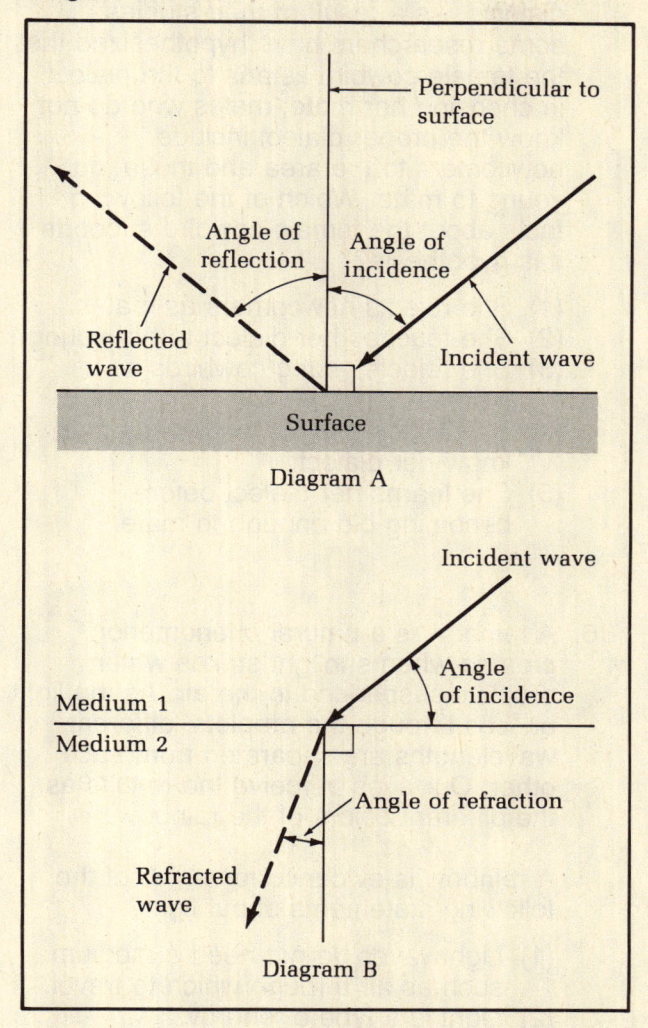

Diagram A
- Perpendicular to surface
- Angle of reflection
- Angle of incidence
- Reflected wave
- Incident wave
- Surface

Diagram B
- Incident wave
- Angle of incidence
- Medium 1
- Medium 2
- Angle of refraction
- Refracted wave

Reflection occurs when a wave strikes a surface and bounces back. The angle of incidence is equal to the angle of reflection (see Diagram A). Refraction is the bending of a wave as it strikes the boundary between two different mediums at an angle and passes from one medium into another (see Diagram B).

60. Sunlight striking a mirrored surface at an angle of incidence of 50° would be reflected back in which of the following ways?

    (1) equally in all directions
    (2) perpendicular to the mirror
    (3) directly back along the line of incidence
    (4) along a line 100° away from the line of incidence
    (5) along a line 25° away from the line of incidence

61. A straw placed in a glass of water looks bent. Which of the following statements could explain why this happens?

    (1) Light is refracted as it passes from the air to the water.
    (2) Light is reflected from the surface of the glass.
    (3) The curved surface of the glass distorts the light as it hits the straw.
    (4) Water molecules surrounding the straw are bent as light passes through them.
    (5) Water reflects light, while glass refracts light.

62. Coal and other industrial fuels contain sulfur impurities. When these fuels are burned, sulfur released into the air combines with oxygen and water to form acids. These acids eventually mix with rainwater to form acidic rain. Not all scientists agree that acid rain is harmful to the environment. Yet surely when rainwater becomes as acidic as vinegar, plants and animals will suffer.
    Which of the following statements represents the author's opinion?

    (1) Scientists disagree about the effects of acid rain.
    (2) Acid rain is caused by the careless burning of fuels by industry.
    (3) Acid rain can have approximately the same acidity as vinegar.
    (4) Industrial use of coal and other fuels pollutes the atmosphere.
    (5) Acid rain poses a threat to living things.

GO ON TO THE NEXT PAGE

Item 63 is based on the following information.

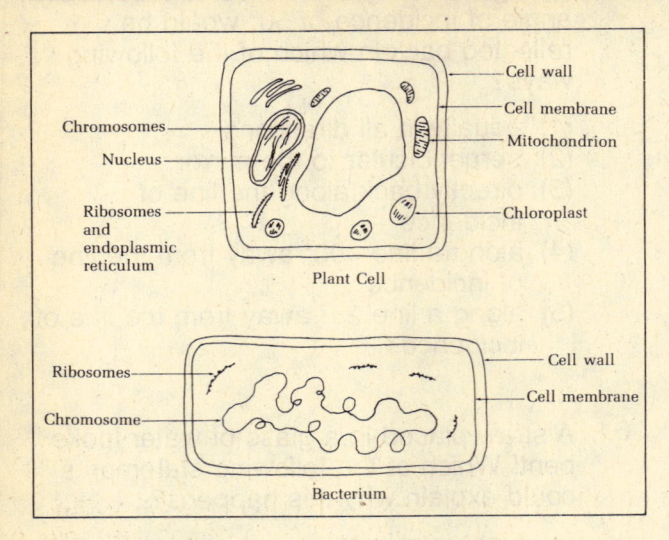

[Diagram of a Plant Cell labeled with: Chromosomes, Nucleus, Ribosomes and endoplasmic reticulum, Cell wall, Cell membrane, Mitochondrion, Chloroplast]

[Diagram of a Bacterium labeled with: Ribosomes, Chromosome, Cell wall, Cell membrane]

63. You are told that a particular cell that you are studying is either a bacterium or a plant cell. Which of the following observations would immediately tell you that the cell is a bacterium?

   (1) The cell has no nucleus.
   (2) The cell has a cell wall.
   (3) The cell has a cell membrane.
   (4) The cell has a chromosome.
   (5) The cell contains chloroplasts.

64. The molecular formula for a compound tells how many of each type of atom are present in each molecule of the compound. For example, the molecular formula for methane, CH_4, indicates that one molecule of methane contains one carbon atom and four hydrogen atoms. The molecular formula for ethanol, C_2H_6O, could be used to determine each of the following except

   (1) the ratio of carbon atoms to hydrogen atoms in each molecule
   (2) the elements present in the ethanol
   (3) the arrangement of the atoms in each molecule
   (4) the ratio of carbon atoms to oxygen atoms in each molecule
   (5) the number of hydrogen atoms in one million molecules of ethanol

65. Scientists have proof that groups of songbirds have their own particular dialects. As a result of their studies, some researchers have hypothesized that the female cowbird listens to the dialect in choosing her mate; males who do not know the proper dialect include newcomers to the area and those too young to mate. Which of the following facts about the female cowbird supports this hypothesis?

   (1) She rejects newcomers as mates.
   (2) She teaches her dialect to her young.
   (3) She rejects young cowbirds as mates.
   (4) She mates only with cowbirds that know her dialect.
   (5) She learns her dialect before becoming old enough to mate.

66. A rainbow is a natural phenomenon created when sunlight strikes water droplets suspended in the air. As the light passes through the droplets, different wavelengths are separated from each other. Our eyes perceive the results as the different colors of the rainbow.

   A rainbow is evidence for which of the following statements about light?

   (1) Lightwaves do not need a medium such as air through which to travel.
   (2) Light is a type of energy.
   (3) White light actually contains light of many different colors.
   (4) Some types of light, such as infrared, are not visible under ordinary circumstances.
   (5) Light may bend when passing through water.

Answers are on pages A-90–A-93.

SIMULATED TEST 4
Interpreting Literature and the Arts

TIME: 65 minutes
Directions: *Choose the one best answer for each question.*

Items 1 to 4 are based on the following passage.

WHY ARE THE EVERTONS MOVING TO MEXICO?

"Let's stop and ask the way," says Sara, "while there is still daylight." And, as they take a diagonal course across a cleared space of land, she and her
(5) husband notice how the flat, pale rays from the west have lengthened the shadows of a row of tattered cornstalks, stunned survivors or the autumn harvest.
But the owner of this field, the crooked
(10) fig tree, and the bent plowshare dulled by weeds and weather is nowhere in sight.
Richard points to a drifting haze. "There's some smoke from a cooking fire." But it turns out to be only a spiral of dust
(15) whirling behind an empty dam.
"We won't get to Ibarra before dark," says Sara. "Do you think we'll recognize the house?"
"Yes," he says, and without speaking
(20) they separately recall a faded photograph of a wide, low structure with a long veranda in front. On the veranda is a hammock woven of white string, and in the hammock is Richard's grandmother,
(25) dressed in eyelet embroidery and holding a fluted fan. Beyond is a tennis court and a rose garden.
Five days ago the Evertons left San Francisco and their house with a narrow
(30) view of the bay in order to extend the family's Mexican history and patch the present onto the past. To find out if there was still copper underground and how much of the rest of it was true, the width
(35) of sky, the depth of stars, the air like new wine, the harsh noons and long, slow dusks. To weave chance and hope into a fabric that would clothe them as long as they lived.
(40) Even their closest friends have failed to understand. "Call us when you get there," they said. "Send a telegram." But Ibarra lacks these services. "How close is the airport?" and to avoid having to answer,
(45) the Evertons promised to send maps. "What will you do for light?" they were asked. And, "How long since someone lived in the house?" But this question collapsed of its own weight before a reply
(50) could be composed.
Every day for a month Richard has reminded Sara, "We mustn't expect too much." And each time his wife has answered, "No." But the Evertons expect
(55) too much. They have experienced the terrible persuasion of a great-aunt's recollections and adopted them as their own. They have not considered that memories are like corks left out of bottles.
(60) They swell. They no longer fit.

From Harriet Doerr, *Stones for Ibarra* (New York: Viking Penguin, 1984), pages 2–3.

GO ON TO THE NEXT PAGE

723

1. Which of the following best describes the Evertons?

    (1) spontaneous thrill-seekers
    (2) pessimistic wanderers
    (3) brave adventurers
    (4) antisocial recluses
    (5) idealistic dreamers

2. Which of the following best describes Ibarra?

    (1) It is a medium-sized town.
    (2) It is a popular vacation spot with tourists.
    (3) It lacks many modern conveniences.
    (4) It resembles San Francisco in the style of its buildings.
    (5) It is an abandoned industrial site.

3. When the author states that the Evertons "have not considered that memories are like corks left out of bottles" (lines 58–59), she means that the Evertons

    (1) do not know that the weather in Mexico can be very hot and dry
    (2) have not considered that the great-aunt's memories may not be accurate
    (3) may not remember the directions to Ibarra
    (4) have not considered that the Mexicans may not like them
    (5) have not considered that their new life in Mexico will not have the luxuries of home

4. What is the author's purpose in using the present tense in telling of the Evertons' move?

    (1) It allows the author to predict events later in the story.
    (2) It emphasizes the Evertons' simple life in Mexico.
    (3) It brings the action closer to the reader.
    (4) It conveys the detached attitude of the author.
    (5) It emphasizes the Evertons' spontaneous decision to move.

Items 5 to 7 are based on the following poem.

WHAT IS THE SUBJECT OF THIS POEM?

Fog

The fog comes
on little cat feet
It sits looking
over harbour and city
(5) on silent haunches
and then moves on.

Carl Sandburg, "Fog," in *Chicago Poems* (New York: Holt, Rinehart and Winston, 1916).

5. Which of the following statements best summarizes the poet's description of fog?

    (1) The fog blows swiftly over the city and the harbor.
    (2) The harbor and the city have been covered with fog for days.
    (3) The fog is black.
    (4) One can see the shapes in the fog.
    (5) The fog approaches slowly and quietly and leaves the same way.

6. The "little cat feet" (line 2) is best interpreted as

    (1) the feet of pedestrians walking in the haze
    (2) animals scurrying for shelter from the weather
    (3) wisps of mist leading the fog into the city
    (4) black soot carried in the fog
    (5) short gusts of wind that accompany the fog

7. Why is the image of a cat effective in a description of fog?

    (1) Fog tickles like a cat's whiskers.
    (2) Fog looks like a slinking cat.
    (3) Fog is as cool as a cat's nose.
    (4) Fog moves in a catlike way.
    (5) Fog feels as soft as a cat's fur.

GO ON TO THE NEXT PAGE

Items 8 to 10 are based on the following passage.

WHAT IS ILLINGWORTH'S ADVICE TO GERALD?

GERALD (*Laughing*): I might be able to learn how to tie a tie, Lord Illingworth, but I should never be able to talk as you do. I don't know how to talk.

(5) ILLINGWORTH: Oh! Talk to every woman as if you loved her, and to every man as if he bored you, and at the end of your first season you will have the reputation of possessing the most perfect social tact.

(10) GERALD: But it is very difficult to get into society, isn't it?

ILLINGWORTH: To get into the best society, now-a-days, one has either to feed people, amuse people, or shock
(15) people—that is all.

GERALD: I suppose society is wonderfully delightful!

ILLINGWORTH: To be in it is merely a bore. But to be out of it is simply a tragedy.
(20) Society is a necessary thing. No man has any real success in this world unless he has got women to back him, and women rule society. If you have not got women on your side you are quite
(25) over. You might as well be a barrister, or a stockbroker, or a journalist at once.

From Oscar Wilde, *A Woman of No Importance*.

8. The conversation between Gerald and Illingworth is about

    (1) how to change society
    (2) how to establish a successful career
    (3) how to dress appropriately for social occasions
    (4) how to become part of society
    (5) how to entertain people

9. The author's tone in this passage can best be described as

    (1) harshly critical
    (2) serious
    (3) mocking
    (4) sympathetic
    (5) neutral

10. The definition of *society* that most closely fits the way it is used in the excerpt is

    (1) a group of people concerned with fashion and manners
    (2) a charitable organization
    (3) a club that meets occasionally for social purposes
    (4) the world as a whole
    (5) an organization of people that belong to the same profession

Items 11 to 15 are based on the following passage.

ACCORDING TO JOYCE CAROL OATES, WHAT FUNCTION DOES BOXING SERVE?

Not all boxing fans are hard-drinking, cigar chewing, heavyset guys yelling themselves hoarse in a crowded arena. Picture instead a soft-spoken, frail-looking
(5) woman with the dignity of a Princeton professor, which is what she is. You might not think that one of our most prolific novelists would have the time to develop a passion for pugilism. But Joyce Carol
(10) Oates is as hooked on boxing as Marianne Moore was on the Brooklyn Dodgers.

Boxing, Oates argues, is "a celebration of the lost religion of masculinity, all the
(15) more trenchant for its being lost." The 48-year-old novelist writes about the sport as a way of honoring her working-class background. She comes, she says, from "a world in which a man who wouldn't
(20) fight another man would be characterized as a coward. In other classes, he would simply get a lawyer."

. . . The book is part prose poem, part history lesson. Oates rapidly sketches
(25) boxing's past, starting with its Greco-Roman origins as gladiatorial homicide, and works on up to the present, pausing over the introduction of the referee in the late 19th century. The "third man in the
(30) ring," she notes, is what "makes boxing possible." Otherwise, "the spectacle of two men fighting each other unsupervised in an elevated ring would seem hellish, if not obscene—life rather than art."

GO ON TO THE NEXT PAGE

(35) Considered as theater, Oates writes, a boxing match is a "dialogue of split-second reflexes," whose "text is improvised in action." Considered as a political parable, it is "a striking, if
(40) unintended, image of the political impotence of most men," who can't hit "the legitimate objects of their anger."
. . . Oates acknowledges that she started "On Boxing" with a feminist
(45) preconception. "I was interested in the sociology of masculine violence, and then I got more sympathetic with it, and saw it as really inevitable and quite natural." To those who favor abolishing the sport, she
(50) would point out that some fighters feel in more danger on the streets than in the ring. Boxing is their ticket out of the ghetto, a way to discipline aggression for the sake of somethng large—and
(55) potentially lucrative. . . . As for the fight fan's point of view, Oates gives the floor to Emily Dickinson, whose view of great poetry applies at ringside: "You know it's great when it takes the top of your head
(60) off."

From "The Novelist at Ringside" (a review of Joyce Carol Oates' *On Boxing*), *Newsweek*, March 9, 1987, page 68.

11. What is the topic of the book that Joyce Carol Oates had written?

   (1) masculinity
   (2) sociology
   (3) the nature of art
   (4) boxing
   (5) political parables

12. In lines 39–42, Oates implies that she originally viewed her subjects

   (1) negatively
   (2) enthusiastically
   (3) with envy
   (4) as actors in a play
   (5) as skilled artists

13. Joyce Carol Oates impresses the reader with the importance of boxing by

   (1) comparing it to various forms of art
   (2) criticizing boxing fans
   (3) emphasizing the role of the referee
   (4) mentioning its history
   (5) describing the reflexes of boxers

14. Calling boxing "gladiatorial homicide" (line 26) is a reference to

   (1) the popularity of professional boxers today
   (2) the lack of safety precautions for boxers
   (3) the commitment of professional boxers to their sport
   (4) the historical origins of boxing
   (5) the carnival atmosphere at many boxing matches

15. With which of the following statements would Joyce Carol Oates probably agree?

   (1) Children should not be disciplined when they misbehave.
   (2) All violent sports should be banned.
   (3) Funding for school athletic programs should be reduced.
   (4) Human beings are not aggressive by nature.
   (5) Participation in school sports is a healthy expression of competitive instinct.

GO ON TO THE NEXT PAGE

Items 16 to 18 are based on the following poem.

WHY DOES THE POET THINK GOD MIGHT BE LONELY?

The Preacher Ruminates Behind the Sermon

    I think it must be lonely to be God.
    Nobody loves a master. No. Despite
    The bright hosannas, bright dear-Lords, and bright
(5)   Determined reverence of Sunday eyes.

    Picture Jehovah striding through the hall
    Of His importance, creatures running out
(10) From servant-corner to acclaim, to shout
    Appreciation of His merit's glare.

    But who walks with Him?—dares to take His arm,
(15) To slap Him on the shoulder, tweak His ear,
    Buy Him a Coca-Cola or a beer,
    Pooh-pooh His politics, call Him a fool?

    Perhaps—who knows?—He tires of
(20) looking down.
    Those eyes are never lifted. Never straight.
    Perhaps sometimes He tires of being great
(25) In solitude. Without a hand to hold.

Gwendolyn Brooks, "The Preacher Ruminates Behind the Sermon," in *Black Voices: Poetry* (New York: Abraham Chapman, 1968), page 462.

16. Which of the following questions does the poem address?

  (1) Who can understand what God is like?
  (2) Who dares to question the ways of God?
  (3) Why does God allow people to suffer?
  (4) Does God really care about the details of our daily lives?
  (5) Does God ever feel lonesome?

17. By referring to "bright hosannas, bright dear-Lords, and bright/Determined reverence" (lines 3–5), the poet implies that

  (1) God does not notice the praise that comes from His worshippers
  (2) God deserves the best that His worshippers can offer
  (3) a lot of religious devotion is forced, not sincere
  (4) worship is most meaningful to elderly people
  (5) everyone worships God in his or her own way

18. Based on the poem, of which of the following churches would the poet most likely approve?

  (1) one that has elaborate, dignified worship services
  (2) one that is actively involved in social programs within the community
  (3) one that is actively involved in community politics
  (4) one that makes its members feel that they are friends of God
  (5) one that supports a great number of missionaries

Items 19 to 22 are based on the following passage.

WHAT HAPPENED WHEN CHARLEY LOCKJAW DIED?

    Charles Lockjaw died last summer on the reservation. He was very old—a hundred years, he had claimed. He still wore his hair in braids, as only the older
(5) men do in his tribe, and the braids were thin and white. His fierce old face was like a withered apple. He was bent and frail and trembling, and his voice was like a wailing of the wind across the prairie
(10) grass. . .
    Old Charley died in his sleep in the canvas-covered tepee where he lived in warm weather. In the winter he was crowded with the younger ones among his
(15) descendants in a two-room log cabin, but in the summer they pitched the tepee. Sometimes they left him alone there, and

GO ON TO THE NEXT PAGE

sometimes his great-grandchildren scrambled in with him like a bunch of (20) puppies.

His death was no surprise to anyone. What startled the Indian agent and some of Charley's own people, and the white ranchers when they heard about it, was (25) the fact that some of the young men of the tribe sacrificed a horse on his grave. Charley wasn't buried on holy ground; he never went near the mission. He was buried in a grove of cottonwoods down by (30) the creek that is named for a dead chief. His lame great-grandson, Joe Walking Wolf, and three other young Indians took this horse out there and shot it. It was a fine sorrel gelding, only seven years old, (35) broke fairly gentle and nothing wrong with it. Young Joe had been offered eighty dollars for that horse.

The mission priest was disturbed about the killing of the horse, justifiably (40) suspecting some dark pagan significance, and he tried to find out the reason the young men killed it. He urged Joe's mother, Mary, to find out, but she never did—or if she did, she never told. Joe only (45) said, with a shrug, "It was my horse."

The white ranchers chuckled indulgently, a little shocked about the horse but never too much upset about anything Indians did. The rancher who (50) told the story oftenest and with most interest was the one who had made the eighty-dollar offer to Joe Walking Wolf. Joe had said to him, "Ain't my horse." But Joe was the one who shot it on old (55) Charley's grave, and it didn't belong to anyone else.

But the Indian agent guessed what had been going on. He knew more about Indians than the Federal Government (60) required him to know. The horse was not government property nor the tribe's common property; everybody knew it belonged to Joe. The agent did not investigate, figuring it was none of his (65) business.

That was last summer, when old Charley died and the young men took the horse out to where he was buried.

From Dorothy Johnson, "Scars of Honor" from *Argosy* (McIntosh and Otis, Inc., 1950).

19. What reason did Joe give to the white rancher for refusing to sell Charley's horse?

   (1) He planned to donate it to the mission in memory of his great-grandfather.
   (2) He wanted more money than the rancher was willing to pay.
   (3) He thought that the horse was part of the tribe's common property.
   (4) He would never let a white man ride the horse.
   (5) He said that the horse was not his to sell.

20. Based on the passage, one can assume that the death of the horse

   (1) had a ritual significance for the younger Indians
   (2) must have been an accident
   (3) had some dark, pagan significance
   (4) earned Joe Walking Wolf eighty dollars
   (5) represented a form of revenge for the young men

21. The mission priest's reaction to the event is somewhat similar to a tourist's reaction to

   (1) ethnic dances
   (2) a bullfight
   (3) a safari
   (4) a local festival
   (5) native handicrafts

22. The reader becomes aware of the irony in the great-grandson's name when it is revealed that the young man

   (1) is a half-breed
   (2) is lame
   (3) is illegitimate
   (4) loves to race horses
   (5) loves to hunt wolves

GO ON TO THE NEXT PAGE

Items 23 to 26 are based on the following passage.

WHAT DID THE SPEAKER DO WHILE IN PRISON?

Estebita made our nights pleasanter by telling us in amazing detail about movies he'd seen. He was very frail, but his voice was extremely powerful, so even from
(5) behind the steel plates of his cell he could be heard by everyone. The place, all closed with metal doors, had good acoustics.
Estebita gave such richness to his
(10) stories, so many details, that even today I confuse them with movies I've actually seen.
My will to survive grew stronger; my determination became as steely as my
(15) cell walls.
In spite of my weakness, I would lie on the floor and move my body to help my circulation. I did yoga exercises in meditation and concentration. I knew
(20) darkness could damage my vision. There were small holes in the iron sheet over the window. In the afternoon when the sheet had cooled, I would use first one eye and then the other, and look through
(25) the holes toward the blue sky and the green hills. I did these visual exercises daily, and believe I owe my sight to them.
There were men whose vision was permanently affected by those years in
(30) darkness.
I would put my ear against the metal plate to try to hear whether the guards were walking by. The only opening at the door was at the bottom, where there was
(35) about a half-inch space between the floor and the bars. If you squeezed against the floor a yard from the door, you might see a little piece of the hallway. (It was while lying face down on the floor, to take
(40) advantage of the ghastly waxen light that filtered into the hallway under the main gate, that I wrote the first notes about my ordeal.) The guards constantly walked by on tiptoe, sliding along the walls, so they
(45) could overhear our conversations. Sometimes Political Police officers did the same thing. We used a slang which was a crazy mixture of English, French, and Spanish and words we invented ourselves
(50) so they couldn't understand us.
We never knew who might be walking the hallways.

From Armando Valladares, *Against All Hope: The Prison Memoirs of Armando Valldares*, translated by Andrew Hurley (New York: Alfred A. Knopf, Inc., 1986)

23. That the prison had good "acoustics" (lines 7–8) means that

   (1) the building was heavily guarded and locked
   (2) the light in the halls was very bright
   (3) the men entertained themselves
   (4) the food was good
   (5) sound traveled well in the building

24. Which of the following titles best expresses the main idea of this passage?

   (1) The Determination to Live
   (2) How Political Prisoners are Tortured
   (3) Spanish Prisons
   (4) Defeated by the Enemy
   (5) Estebita the Storyteller

25. If the speaker were stranded on a desert island, he would most likely

   (1) do exercises in meditation and concentration
   (2) give up hope of being rescued
   (3) not want to return to civilization
   (4) figure out how to find food and shelter
   (5) lead a carefree life in the sun

26. The speaker helps the reader to imagine what prison life was like by

   (1) repeating Estebita's stories
   (2) explaining the political background of his imprisonment
   (3) providing many descriptive details about his life in prison
   (4) including lengthy passages of dialogue
   (5) expressing his anger and frustration in short speeches to the other prisoners

GO ON TO THE NEXT PAGE

Items 27 to 29 are based on the following passage.

WHAT CAUSES THE ARGUMENT BETWEEN RAMIREZ AND THE SOCIAL WORKER?

SOCIAL WORKER: What is the name of your father?
CANDIDO: I got two fathers.
SOCIAL WORKER: What are you trying to do, kid me? (5)
RAMIREZ (*repressing his anger*): All right, I explain to you. Fernandez is the name of the uncle which is dead. He lives with the family Gomez upstairs. I give him a job in my restaurant because they have many mouths to feed. I am one of the fathers. I am Ramirez. With so many answers I should get a refrigerator! (10)
SOCIAL WORKER: I don't understand it.
RAMIREZ (*letting it out*): Ha! You do not understand many things, Mr. Palm-Beach-Suit. (15)
SOCIAL WORKER: Don't you go insulting me. I work for the city. You ought to be glad we have free schools. (20)
RAMIREZ: We are glad, very glad. Every night we give thanks to you, Mr. Palm-Beach-Suit. Also to God and the Santos.
SOCIAL WORKER: I'll have to report this to the Attendance Officer. Send the boy to school. That's the law. Remember, I can make trouble for you. (25)
RAMIREZ: Ha! Trouble we got, we do not need any more. If the law say the boy must go to the school, he go to the school. (*The Social Worker hands Ramirez a dollar bill in payment for the coffee.*) (30)
SOCIAL WORKER: See that he does. I'll be back . . . (*Ramirez brings the change.*) You people always give us a hard time. (35)
RAMIREZ: (*throwing the dollar bill back on the counter*) I got no change. It's on the house . . .

From Walt Anderson, *Me, Candido*

27. How does Ramirez feel toward the social worker?

    (1) He is jealous of the social worker's job.
    (2) He admires the social worker's expensive suit.
    (3) He appreciates what the social worker is trying to do for his family.
    (4) He thinks that the social worker is wealthy.
    (5) He resents the social worker's attitude.

28. In what sense is Ramirez the "father" of Candido?

    (1) He is Candido's biological father.
    (2) He once was married to Candido's mother.
    (3) He helps to take care of Candido.
    (4) He has been paying for Candido's education.
    (5) He listens to Candido as if he were a priest.

29. Which of the following responses would the social worker be most likely to give if he were asked about solving the money problems of the Gomez family?

    (1) "Of course they have money problems. They're probably too lazy to get jobs."
    (2) "Here is twenty dollars. I hope it will help."
    (3) "Why haven't they asked the community charities for assistance?"
    (4) "I don't want to hear about their problems. I have problems of my own."
    (5) "I'll help them to register for food stamps."

GO ON TO THE NEXT PAGE

Items 30 to 33 are based on the following passage.

ARE THE RICH ALWAYS HAPPY?

"It is only on the surface that the rich seem to be happy," said Elena Ivanovna. "Every man has his sorrow. Here my husband and I do not live poorly, we have
(5) means, but are we happy? I am young, but I have had four children; my children are always being ill. I am ill, too, and constantly being doctored."

"And what is your illness?" asked
(10) Rodion.

"A woman's complaint. I get no sleep; a continual headache gives me no peace. Here I am sitting and talking, but my head is bad, I am weak all over, and I should
(15) prefer the hardest labor to such a condition. My soul, too, is troubled; I am in continual fear for my children, my husband. Every family has its own trouble of some sort; we have ours. I am not of
(20) noble birth. My grandfather was a simple peasant, my father was a tradesman in Moscow; he was a plain, uneducated man too, while my husband's parents were wealthy and distinguished. They did not
(25) want him to marry me, but he disobeyed them, quarreled with them, and they have not forgiven us to this day. That worries my husband; it troubles him and keeps him in constant agitation; he loves his
(30) mother, loves her dearly. So I am uneasy, too, my soul is in pain."

Peasants, men and women, were now standing around Rodion's hut and listening. Kozov came up, too, and stood
(35) twitching his long, narrow beard. The Lytchkovs, father and son, drew near.

"And say what you like, one cannot be happy and satisfied if one does not feel in one's proper place," Elena Ivanovna went
(40) on. "Each of you has his strip of land, each of you works and knows what he is working for; my husband builds bridges—in short, everyone has his place, while I, I simply walk about. I have not my bit to
(45) work. I don't work, and feel as though I were an outsider. I am saying all this that you may not judge from outward appearances; if a man is expensively dressed and has means it does not prove
(50) that he is satisfied with his life."

She got up to go away and took her daughter by the hand.

From Anton Chekov, "The New Villa" from *The Witch and Other Stories* (David Garnett and Chatto and Windus, Ltd. Publishers, 1946).

30. According to Elena a person might feel "in one's proper place" (line 39) by

   (1) staying in the social class into which one is born
   (2) having a good education
   (3) marrying into a respectable family
   (4) working hard at one's personal goals
   (5) being in good health

31. What is Elena's attitude toward wealth?

   (1) She despises wealth and would prefer to be poor.
   (2) She is very happy being wealthy and not having to work.
   (3) She is embarrassed by her wealth and resents the peasants for making her feel uncomfortable.
   (4) She resents her husband for coming from a wealthy family.
   (5) She would gladly trade her wealth for good health and a purpose in life.

32. What is Elena's "illness" (line 11)?

   (1) loss of both vision and hearing
   (2) headaches and asthma
   (3) tuberculosis
   (4) sleeplessness and a stomach ulcer
   (5) weakness, headaches, and sleeplessness

33. The gathering of peasants around Rodion's hut (line 32–34) lets the reader know that

   (1) Elena is about to leave her husband and children
   (2) Elena is moving her listeners to anger, not sympathy
   (3) they agree with the husband's parents' opinion of Elena
   (4) Elena's words are a lesson for everyone
   (5) only poor people have problems

GO ON TO THE NEXT PAGE

Items 34 to 37 are based on the following passage.

WHAT DOES DR. KING HOPE FOR?

I say to you today, my friends, that in spite of the difficulties and frustrations of the moment, I still have a dream. It is a dream deeply rooted in the American
(5) dream....
 I have a dream today.
 I have a dream that one day every valley shall be exalted, every hill and mountain shall be made low, the rough
(10) places will be made plains, and the crooked places will be made straight, and the glory of the Lord shall be revealed, and all flesh shall see it together.
 This is our hope. This is the faith with
(15) which I return to the South. With this faith we will be able to hew out of the mountains of despair a stone of hope. With this faith we will be able to transform the jangling discords of our nation into a
(20) beautiful symphony of brotherhood. With this faith we will be able to work together, to pray together, to struggle together, to go to jail together, to stand up for freedom together, knowing that we will be free one
(25) day.
 This will be the day when all of God's children will be able to sing with new meaning, "My country, 'tis of thee, sweet land of liberty, of thee I sing. Land where
(30) my fathers died, land of the Pilgrim's pride, from every mountainside, let freedom ring."
 When we let freedom ring, when we let it ring from every village and every
(35) hamlet, from every state and every city, we will be able to speed up that day when all of God's children, black men and white men, Jews and Gentiles, Protestants and Catholics, will be able to join hands and
(40) sing in the words of that old Negro spiritual, "Free at last! Free at last! Thank God almighty, we are free at last!"

Martin Luther King, Jr., "I Have a Dream," presented on August 28, 1963. Copyright c 1963 by Martin Luther King, Jr.

34. What is the topic of Dr. King's speech?
 (1) the value of dreams
 (2) the American dream
 (3) better educational opportunities for children
 (4) equality for all people
 (5) compassion for the needy

35. The repetition of "I have a dream" has which of the following effects?
 (1) It contrasts with the later repetition of "let freedom ring."
 (2) It reveals Dr. King's strong beliefs about the topic.
 (3) It is a reference to all of the great dreamers throughout history.
 (4) It is a plea for Dr. King's listeners to solve their problems peacefully.
 (5) It emphasizes that Dr. King's hopes will not be realized in the lifetime of his listeners.

36. Which of the following does Dr. King NOT state to be a result of his faith (lines 14–25)?
 (1) the freedom to pray together
 (2) the right to vote in all elections
 (3) the desire to work together
 (4) the possibility of going to jail
 (5) the ability to give people a new sense of hope

37. The quotation from the Bible (lines 7–13), a patriotic song (lines 28–32), and a Negro spiritual (lines 41–42) are intended
 (1) to show that Dr. King worships America
 (2) to recall the religious beliefs of colonial America
 (3) to make Dr. King's listeners understand that only God can bring about the changes that must occur in America
 (4) to inspire the listeners to worship Dr. King
 (5) to make Dr. King's listeners feel as strongly about political change as they do about their religious heritage

GO ON TO THE NEXT PAGE

Items 38 to 42 are based on the following passage.

HOW DID THE BEATLES' MUSIC SET A STANDARD?

Recently, I watched a television documentary on the Beatles—those mop-haired boys from Liverpool who changed pop music, moving their songs forward on
(5) a rock beat but giving the music strange harmonies and haunting melodies. Song after song catches the emotions and the imagination through a mixture of lyric lines and poetry. I wondered what was different
(10) about them and if the Beatles really sounded as different to our generation as heavy metal does to today's youngsters.

The difference seems to be that the Beatles and their imitators were
(15) concerned with music. Heavy metal—with its synthesizers; electronic guitars; electronic drums; and amplifiers, mixers, tweeters, woofers, and whatever other paraphernalia go into making the total
(20) effect—is about sound, not music. Perhaps that's an artificial distinction, since music was historically defined by its uses: *musica divina* or *musica sacra* was church music; *musica vulgaris* was
(25) secular and had no sound restrictions.

Whatever the definitions, there is something profoundly disturbing about heavy metal, just as there was something tremendously engaging about the Beatles
(30) and the music of the sixties. The group expressed and reflected the spirit of their time, but most of all, they were good.

When they played on Ed Sullivan's famous variety show on February 9, 1964,
(35) to an audience of seventy million—60 percent of all American television viewers—the Beatles had stolen most of the hearts of American pop fans. Even if the critics were almost forced not to like
(40) them, the public did. They had a natural grace and charm, and they were obviously enjoying themselves and hoping that the fun would last. . . .

The new recording technologies were
(45) increasingly used by the Beatles, but they were enhancers rather than an end in themselves. When one listens to heavy metal and searches for something at its core, all one hears is the throb of the
(50) technology hyping the beat. And in most pop rock, synthesized handclaps and artificial impulses (providing the acoustic equivalent of the zaps of an electric game gallery) take the place of melody and
(55) harmony. The quest seems to be anarchist: today technology, tomorrow nothing but a barren landscape.

Perhaps we will find some undiscovered riches in today's pop just as
(60) we have in the pop classics of the past. But for the moment, I'm content to listen to my old Beatles records and happily remember those wonderful songs.

From Peter J. Rosenwald, "Strawberry Fields Forever". (Tuscaloosa, AL: *Horizon*, March 1985).

GO ON TO THE NEXT PAGE

38. According to the critic, what is the main difference between the Beatles' music and heavy metal?

    (1) One appeals to the older generation; the other appeals to the younger generation.
    (2) One is concerned with music; the other is concerned with sound and technology.
    (3) One is accepted by most music critics; the other is not.
    (4) One is concerned with melody; the other is concerned with harmony.
    (5) One reflects the spirit of its time; the other makes predictions about the future.

39. By stating "today technology, tomorrow nothing but a barren landscape" (lines 56–57), the critic predicts that

    (1) computers, not people, soon will be writing the most popular music
    (2) society will lose its interest in all forms of music
    (3) melody and harmony will be lost to electronic sounds
    (4) advances in technology will lead to better music
    (5) advances in technology will kill composers' interest in attempting new musical styles

40. The critic offers his praise by

    (1) calling the Beatles "mop-haired boys" (lines 2–3)
    (2) referring to the "strange harmonies and haunting meoldies" of the Beatles' music (lines 5–6)
    (3) comparing his generation's reaction to the Beatles' music to this generation's reaction to heavy metal (lines 10–12)
    (4) comparing the Beatles' music to church music (line 21–25)
    (5) referring to the Beatles' "natural grace and charm" (lines 40–41)

41. Which of the following techniques does the critic use to support his views?

    I. examples
    II. quotations from musical authorities
    III. historical references
    IV. disproving opposing opinions

    (1) I and III
    (2) I and IV
    (3) II and III
    (4) I, II, and IV
    (5) II, III, and IV

42. This critic might be expected to compare the changes in musical styles to the

    (1) growth in popularity of personal computers
    (2) development of modern dance from classical ballet
    (3) movement from rhymed poetry to unrhymed poetry
    (4) political upheavals in third-world countries
    (5) increased use of special effects in movies

GO ON TO THE NEXT PAGE

Items 43 to 45 are based on the following passage.

WHAT IS THE PROBLEM FACED BY AFRICA'S RHINO POPULATION?

Wars, drought, a human population explosion and simple greed have all conspired against Africa's animals. The black rhino, a lumbering prehistoric tank
(5) that has survived for more than 70 million years, is already extinct in most parts of the continent. "No elephant is safe in Africa," says professional big-game hunter Robin Hurt in Tanzania. "Now if there are
(10) any survivors, they are cowering, frightened, in the deepest forest." Pessimists predict that wild Africa will soon become little more than a string of glorified safari parks as the true
(15) wilderness shrivels and the animals die out. The process is already under way in some of the continent's most popular game-viewing regions. "A few decades ago Africa was a sea of wild animals
(20) surrounding a few islands of humans," says Hurt. "Today the reverse is true." Poaching is one of the biggest threats— and it has decimated Africa's rhino poulation. As late as 1970, a healthy
(25) population of 65,000 was scattered throughout east, central and southern Africa. Today 4,500 rhinos are left, living in tiny groups that could die out unless they are immediately protected.
(30) It is a cruel trick of nature that rhinos are easy targets for poachers. Despite a keen sense of smell, they have poor eyesight, and many are so docile that a poacher adept at imitating animal sounds
(35) can call a rhino to its death. They are also creatures of habit and must drink daily. Often a poacher can stake out a watering hole to find ready prey. The prize is the rhino's horn. Prices have soared from $17
(40) per pound whlolesale in the early 1970s to $300 per pound in the main markets in North Yemen, where rhino horn is used to make dagger handles, and in Asia, where it is used to make traditional medicines.
(45) The trade is illegal almost everywhere, but the laws are rarely enforced, and traders continue to sell as much as the poachers can provide.

From "Africa: The Last Safari?" *Newsweek*, August 18, 1986, pages 40–41.

43. What is the main reason that poachers hunt rhinos?

    (1) Tourists come to Africa to hunt wild game.
    (2) Museums often ask for a variety of African animals for their natural-history displays.
    (3) Local farmers want revenge for the damage that rhinos do to crops.
    (4) Local craftspeople want to use rhinoceros hide to make souvenirs for tourists.
    (5) High prices are paid for rhinoceros horn.

44. According to the passage, what is the probable future of African wildlife?

    (1) Animals bred in zoos will gradually repopulate the African plains.
    (2) Most animals will escape from wildlife parks.
    (3) Wildlife population will continue to decline.
    (4) Only the elephants will survive.
    (5) Pollution will destroy most African wildlife.

45. Which of the following techniques can be found in the passage?

    I. statistics
    II. quotations from authorities
    III. dramatic dialogue
    IV. figurative language

    (1) I and IV
    (2) III and IV
    (3) I, II, and III
    (4) I, II, and IV
    (5) II, III, and IV

Answers are on pages A-94–A-96.

SIMULATED TEST 5
Mathematics

TIME: 90 minutes

Directions: *Choose the one best answer to each question.*

Item 1 is based on the following figure.

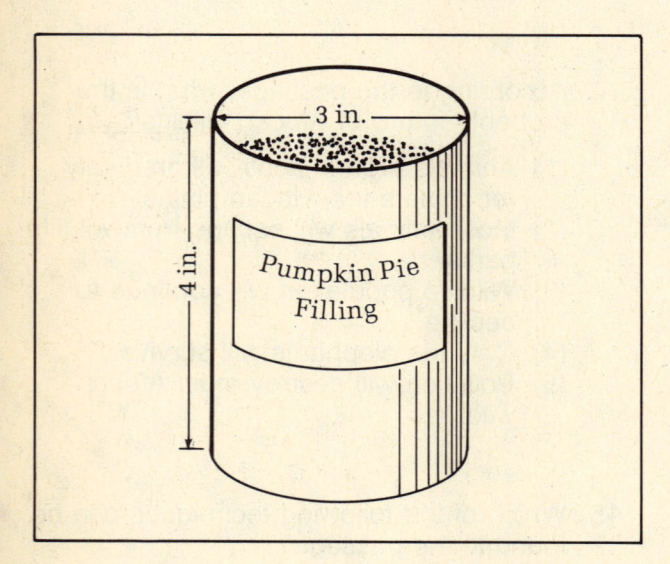

1. What is the volume in cubic inches of the can of pumpkin-pie filling?

   (1) 12
   (2) 13.04
   (3) 18.84
   (4) 28.26
   (5) 37.68

2. The ride from Newark to Philadelphia on a Metroliner train takes 55 minutes. If the train's average speed is 87.8 miles per hour, what is the approximate distance in miles between the two cities?

   (1) 32.8
   (2) 48.3
   (3) 65.9
   (4) 80.5
   (5) 87.8

3. What is the average number of miles per gallon (MPG) of the Wabash family's vehicles?

VEHICLE	MPG
Station wagon	15.6
Sedan	22.4
Pickup truck	19.3
Recreation vehicle	8.1
Motorcycle	39.8

   (1) 15.65
   (2) 16.35
   (3) 21.04
   (4) 105.2
   (5) Insufficient data is given to solve the problem.

GO ON TO THE NEXT PAGE

4. Harvey is a leasing agent for a building that is 6 tenants more than 65% occupied. Which of the following expressions would indicate the number of tenants in the building if u = the total number of units in the building?

   (1) $.65(6) + u$
   (2) $.65(u + 6)$
   (3) $.65(u - 6)$
   (4) $.65u - 6$
   (5) $.65u + 6$

5. The Donovans are moving into a new house that measures 1500 square feet. That is 75 square feet more than 3 times the size of the apartment they shared when they were first married. How many square feet did their apartment measure?

   (1)   250
   (2)   475
   (3)   500
   (4)   525
   (5)   1425

Item 6 is based on the following figure.

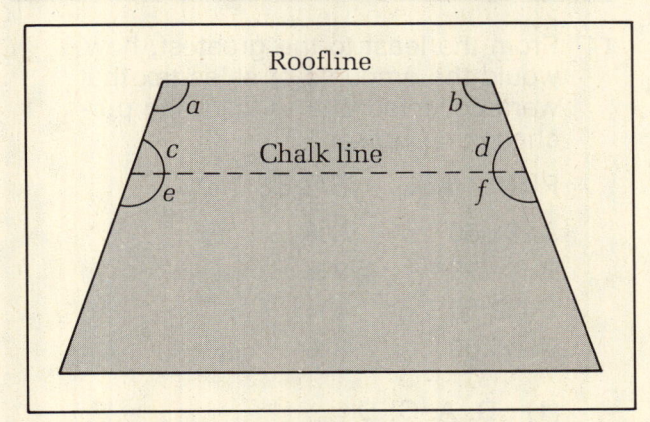

6. Which one of the following pairs of angles are supplementary if the chalk line is parallel to the roofline?

   (1)   a and b   (4)   b and e
   (2)   a and c   (5)   b and f
   (3)   a and f

Items 7 and 8 are based on the following figure.

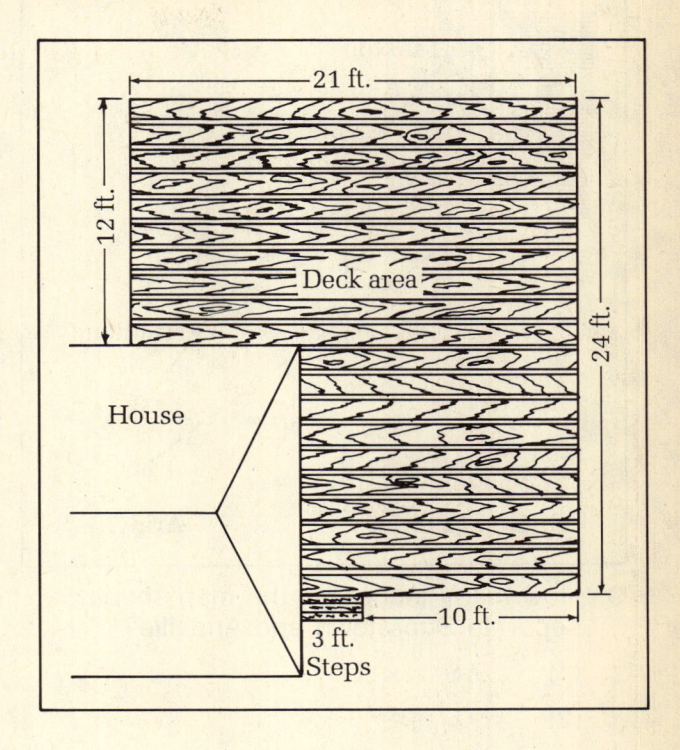

7. Except for where the steps are, a railing will be put around the open edges of the deck. How many feet of railing will be needed?

   (1)   66
   (2)   67
   (3)   70
   (4)   90
   (5)   252

8. How many square feet of wood will be needed for the floor of the deck?

   (1)   120
   (2)   156
   (3)   252
   (4)   372
   (5)   408

GO ON TO THE NEXT PAGE

Item 9 is based on the following figure.

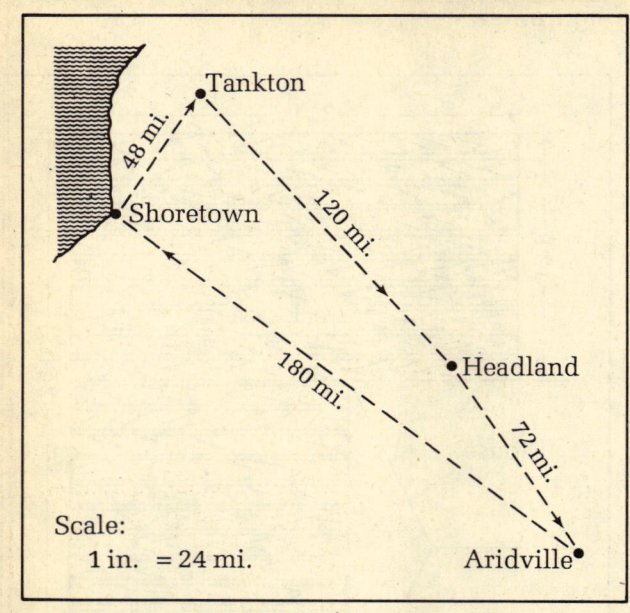

Scale: 1 in. = 24 mi.

9. How many inches on the map should separate Shoretown and Aridville?

   (1) 7.5
   (2) 9.5
   (3) 18.0
   (4) 75.0
   (5) 180.0

Items 10 to 13 are based on the following information.

Bank credit cards are a convenient and a popular method of payment. Annual interest rates for purchases that have been made with bank credit cards vary, however. In Tompkinsville, bank A charges 10% interest, bank B 15% interest, bank C 16% interest, and bank D 18% interest. In addition, each bank charges a $25 annual fee for its card.

10. Bud charged a $588 couch on his card from bank B. If he pays for the couch in a year, how much interest will he pay?

    (1) $ 49.98
    (2) $ 70.56
    (3) $ 88.20
    (4) $499.80
    (5) $676.20

11. Maria charged the following amounts on her card from bank D: $29.50, $84.75, $15.68, and $88.44. If she plans to pay her balance in 3 months, what is the total she must pay?

    (1) $ 9.83   (4) $228.20
    (2) $ 39.31   (5) $257.68
    (3) $218.37

12. One year, Herb was charged $689 in interest and annual fees for his card from bank A. What did his purchases total?

    (1) $6640   (4) $6890
    (2) $6865   (5) $6915
    (3) $6875

13. Robin paid $84 in interest to bank C. What was the amount she had charged if she repaid the loan in 9 months?

    (1) $112
    (2) $525
    (3) $700
    (4) $763
    (5) Insufficient data is given to solve the problem.

14. From the least to the greatest, how would the amounts of sales tax that were collected on the following purchases be ranked?

PURCHASE	SALES TAX
A $1.50	6%
B $ .78	8%
C $2.50	4%
D $5.00	3%

    (1) B, A, C, D
    (2) C, D, A, B
    (3) D, C, A, B
    (4) D, C, B, A
    (5) Insufficient data is given to solve the problem.

GO ON TO THE NEXT PAGE

SIMULATED TESTS

Items 15 to 17 are based on the following figure.

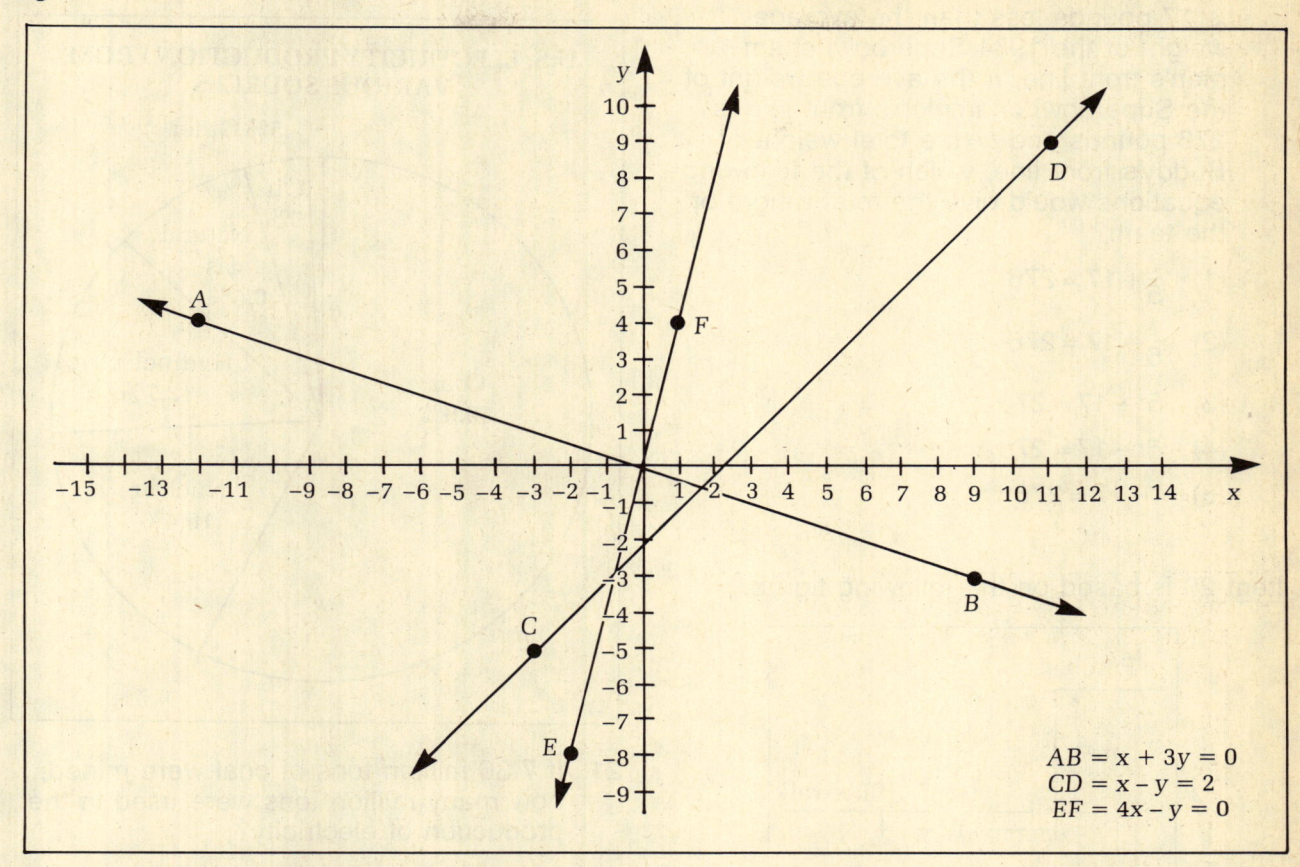

$AB = x + 3y = 0$
$CD = x - y = 2$
$EF = 4x - y = 0$

15. What is the slope of line EF?
    (1) $\frac{1}{4}$
    (2) $\frac{1}{2}$
    (3) 2
    (4) 4
    (5) 8

16. Use the formula midpoint equals $\left(\frac{(x_1 + x_2)}{2}, \frac{(y_1 + y_2)}{2}\right)$ to find the midpoint of segment CD.
    (1) (2,4)
    (2) (3,3)
    (3) (4,2)
    (4) (8,4)
    (5) (7,7)

17. What is the distance from (0, 0) to point B?
    (1) $\sqrt{16}$
    (2) $\sqrt{64}$
    (3) $\sqrt{81}$
    (4) $\sqrt{90}$
    (5) Insufficient data is given to solve the problem.

18. Which of the following expressions equals $(z + 7)(z - 1)$?
    (1) $z^2 - 6z - 6$
    (2) $z^2 - 6z - 7$
    (3) $z^2 + 6z - 7$
    (4) $z^2 + 7z + 7$
    (5) $z^2 + 7z + 7$

GO ON TO THE NEXT PAGE

19. The average weight of the 5 front linemen of Buddy's Corner Bar football team is 17 pounds less than the average weight of the 1984 Superbowl champion's front line. If the average weight of the Superbowl champion's front line is 276 pounds and $t=$ the total weight of Buddy's front line, which of the following equations would give the total weight of the team?

   (1) $\frac{t}{5} + 17 = 276$
   (2) $\frac{t}{5} - 17 = 276$
   (3) $5t + 17 = 276$
   (4) $5t - 17 = 276$
   (5) $t - 17 = 276$

Item 20 is based on the following figure.

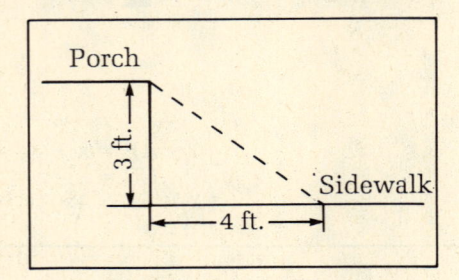

20. If a stairway is to be built from the porch to the sidewalk, how many feet long will it be?

   (1) 5
   (2) 6
   (3) 7
   (4) 8
   (5) 12

Items 21 to 23 are based on the following graph.

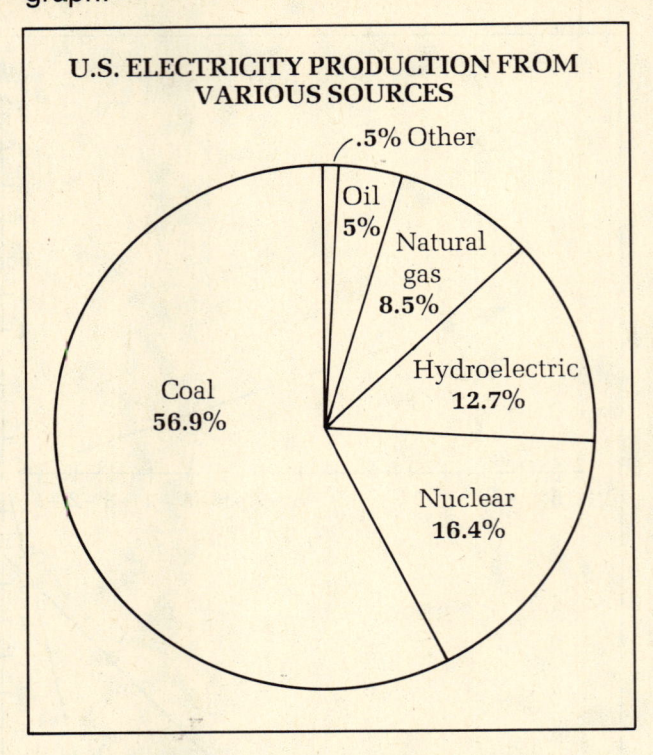

U.S. ELECTRICITY PRODUCTION FROM VARIOUS SOURCES

- .5% Other
- Oil 5%
- Natural gas 8.5%
- Hydroelectric 12.7%
- Nuclear 16.4%
- Coal 56.9%

21. If 7.36 million tons of coal were mined, how many million tons were used in the production of electricity?

   (1) 1.67
   (2) 3.07
   (3) 4.19
   (4) 7.73
   (5) Insufficient data is given to solve the problem.

22. If 2,310,000 million kilowatt hours of electricity were produced, how many million kilowatt hours were produced by hydroelectric power?

   (1) 293,370
   (2) 378,840
   (3) 623,700
   (4) 3,788,400
   (5) Insufficient data is given to solve the problem.

GO ON TO THE NEXT PAGE

23. What is the ratio of the amount of energy produced by other methods to the amount produced by oil?

    (1) 1:1
    (2) 1:2
    (3) 1:10
    (4) 1:200
    (5) Insufficient data is given to solve the problem.

Items 24 and 25 are based on the following figure.

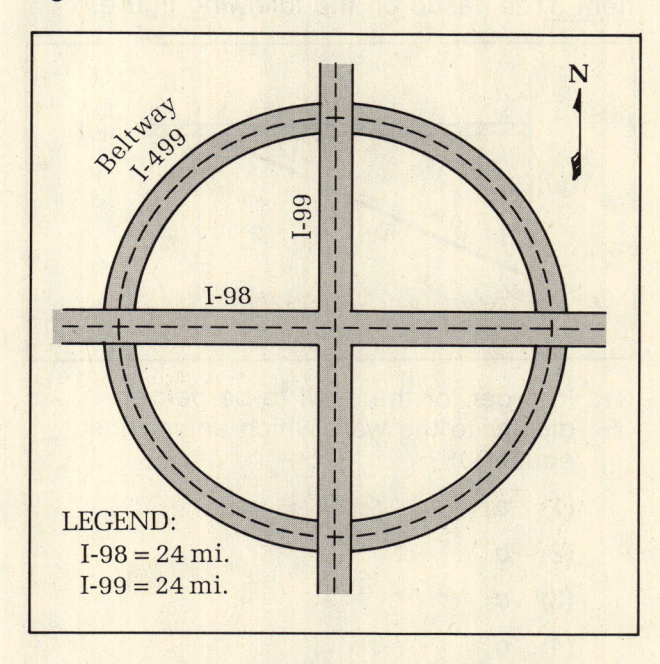

LEGEND:
I-98 = 24 mi.
I-99 = 24 mi.

24. How many miles long is the beltway?

    (1) 37.68
    (2) 75.36
    (3) 87.24
    (4) 113.04
    (5) 150.72

25. Three-fourths of a city's area is inside the beltway. What is the city's area in square miles?

    (1) 339.12
    (2) 452.16
    (3) 565.20
    (4) 602.88
    (5) Insufficient data is given to solve the problem.

26. If $s^2 - 9s + 18 = 0$, what does s equal?

    (1) 3 only
    (2) 6 only
    (3) 9 only
    (4) 3 or 6
    (5) 2 or 9

27. Anita mailed 10 packages, each costing p in postage. She paid with a $20 bill and received $1.46 change. Which equation should be used to determine the cost of one package?

    (1) $10p = 1.46$
    (2) $10 - 20p = 1.46$
    (3) $10p - 20 = 1.46$
    (4) $20p - 10 = 1.46$
    (5) $20 - 10p = 1.46$

GO ON TO THE NEXT PAGE

Item 28 is based on the following figure.

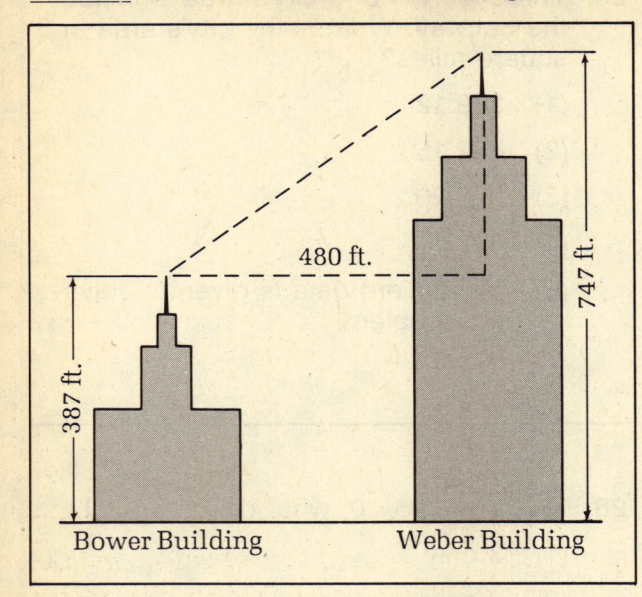

28. What is the distance in feet from the top of the Bower Building to the top of the Weber Building?
    (1) 360
    (2) 600
    (3) 840
    (4) 1094
    (5) 1227

Item 29 is based on the following figures.

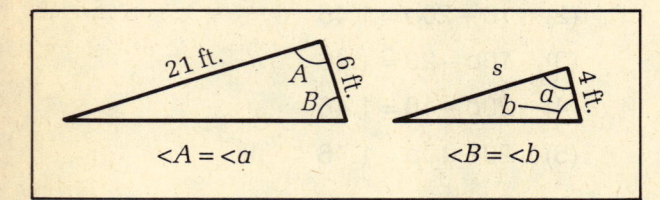

29. How many feet long is side S?
    (1) 14
    (2) 15
    (3) 17
    (4) 21
    (5) 24

30. Carla's computer can do as many calculations in 1 second as it would take her 3 hours to do without it. Which of the following expressions is the ratio of the computer's calculating speed to her speed?
    (1) 1:3
    (2) 1:60
    (3) 1:360
    (4) 1:3,600
    (5) 1:10,800

Item 31 is based on the following figure.

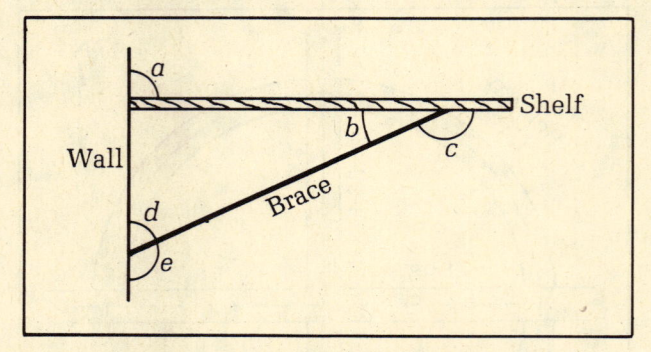

31. In order for the shelf to be perpendicular to the wall, which angle must equal 90°?
    (1) a
    (2) b
    (3) c
    (4) d
    (5) e

32. Twice the time it takes Joe to ride his bicycle to work is still 5 minutes faster than the time it takes him to walk. If it takes him 45 minutes to walk to work, how many minutes does it take him to ride?
    (1) 20
    (2) 25
    (3) 30
    (4) 40
    (5) 50

GO ON TO THE NEXT PAGE

33. Paul spends $25 less than 3/7 of his salary on rent. If s = his salary, which of the following expressions shows his rent?

   (1) $\frac{3s}{7} - 25$

   (2) $\frac{3s}{7} + 25$

   (3) $\frac{7s}{3} - 25$

   (4) $\frac{7s}{3} + 25$

   (5) Insufficient data is given to solve the problem.

34. Mercury's orbit is 36 million miles from the sun. Pluto's orbit is 3.6 billion miles from the sun. What is the distance in miles from Mercury's orbit to Pluto's orbit?

   (1) 3.240×10^6
   (2) 3.240×10^8
   (3) 3.564×10^7
   (4) 3.636×10^9
   (5) 3.963×10^{10}

35. What should David's checking-account balance be if his starting balance was $1215.00?

CHECK NUMBER	DEPOSITS	WITH-DRAWALS
256		$ 46.88
257		$ 99.24
	$106.07	
258		$ 5.77
	$789.50	
259		$977.01

   (1) $ 175.90
   (2) $ 895.57
   (3) $ 981.67
   (4) $1128.90
   (5) $2110.57

Items 36 and 37 refer to the following figure.

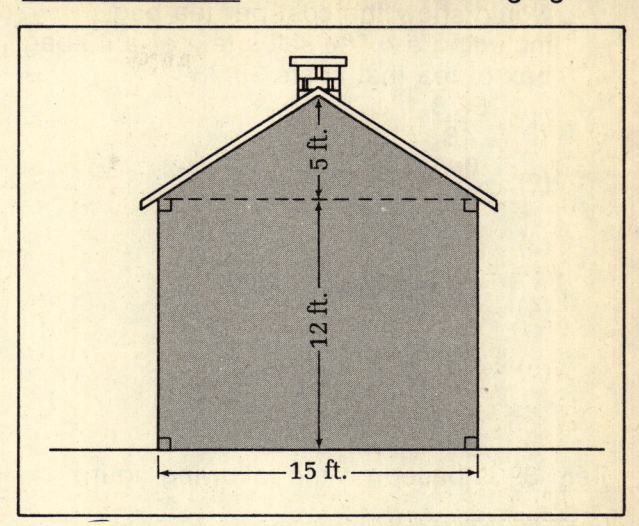

36. How many square feet of siding will be needed to cover this side of the house?

   (1) 37.5
   (2) 142.5
   (3) 180.0
   (4) 217.5
   (5) 255.0

37. If covering the house with aluminum siding would cost $1.75 per square foot and painting it would cost $.75 per square yard, how much more per square yard would it cost to have the house covered with aluminum siding?

   (1) $ 1.00
   (2) $ 4.00
   (3) $ 5.25
   (4) $15.00
   (5) $15.75

GO ON TO THE NEXT PAGE

38. Which of the following expressions would show the cost per tea bag, including a 4.5% sales tax, of a 48-bag box of tea that costs $5.78?

    (1) $\frac{5.78}{48}$

    (2) $\frac{.045(5.78)}{48}$

    (3) $\frac{.45(5.78)}{48}$

    (4) $\frac{1.045(5.78)}{48}$

    (5) $\frac{1.45(5.78)}{48}$

Item 39 is based on the following figure.

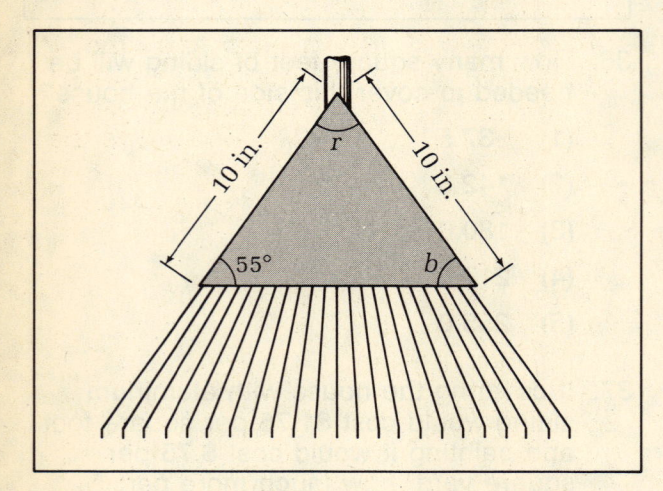

39. In the above drawing of a rake, what is the measure in degrees of angle r?

    (1) 55
    (2) 70
    (3) 90
    (4) 110
    (5) Insufficient data is given to solve the problem.

40. A new model car weighs 1750 pounds. If a truck transports 7 of these cars, how much weight will it be carrying?

    (1) 6 tons 125 pounds
    (2) 6 tons 250 pounds
    (3) 8 tons 50 pounds
    (4) 12 tons 250 pounds
    (5) 14 tons 50 pounds

41. What does $\frac{32a^8b^7c^6}{8a^2b^7c^3}$ equal?

    (1) $4a^4c^3$
    (2) $4a^6c^3$
    (3) $4a^{10}b^{14}c^9$
    (4) $8a^4c^2$
    (5) $16a^6c^3$

42. Orange-juice concentrate is mixed at a ratio of one part concentrate to 3 parts water. How many ounces of water should be used for an 18-ounce can of orange juice?

    (1) 6   (4) 54
    (2) 36   (5) 72
    (3) 48

43. A box that has the measurements 4 feet × 4 feet × 8 feet could hold how many cubic feet?

    (1) 2^3 (4) 2^7
    (2) 2^4 (5) 2^9
    (3) 2^5

44. Geraldine drives a truck for m hours per week. If her average speed is 50 miles per hour, which of the following expressions would give the number of miles she drives in a week?

    (1) $\frac{m}{50}$

    (2) $\frac{50}{m}$

    (3) $50m$

    (4) $\frac{50m}{5}$

    (5) $\frac{50m}{7}$

GO ON TO THE NEXT PAGE

SIMULATED TESTS Test 5: Mathematics **745**

45. Jeremy runs for 45 minutes at 11 miles per hour 5 days per week. How many miles does he run in a week?

    (1) 41.25
    (2) 45.25
    (3) 49.5
    (4) 55.00
    (5) 82.5

46. Jack's computer screen can display 80 characters per line and a maximum of 23 lines. What is the total number of characters it can display?

    (1) 1600
    (2) 1760
    (3) 1840
    (4) 2400
    (5) 2560

47. Which of the following expressions equals $c^2 - 2c - 24$?

    (1) $(c-2)(c-12)$
    (2) $(c+2)(c-12)$
    (3) $(c+3)(c-8)$
    (4) $(c+4)(c-6)$
    (5) $(c-4)(c+6)$

Item 48 is based on the following figure.

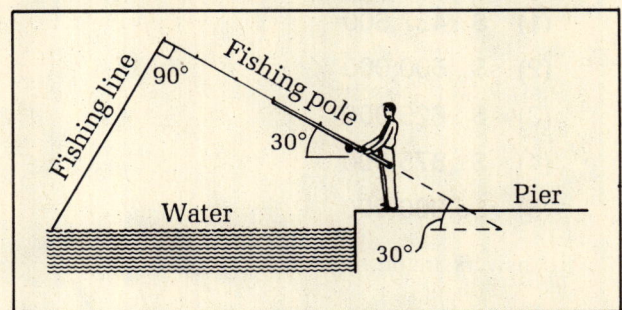

48. At what angle in degrees is the fishing line entering the water?

    (1) 30
    (2) 45
    (3) 60
    (4) 90
    (5) Insufficient data is given to solve the problem.

49. Each traffic light at a busy intersection is equipped with a sensor to measure traffic flow. When the traffic flow from any direction is greater than 347 vehicles per hour, the light pattern changes. If t = the traffic flow, which of the following expressions would be used to determine when to change the light pattern?

    (1) $t > 347$
    (2) $t < 347$
    (3) $2t > 347$
    (4) $2t < 347$
    (5) $\frac{t}{2} < 347$

50. An exhibition hall hosted 75 concerts and 49 exhibitions one year. If c = the total attendance at concerts and e = the total attendance at exhibitions, which of the following expressions would give the average attendance per event?

    (1) $\frac{c}{75} + \frac{e}{49}$
    (2) $\frac{(c+75)}{(e+49)}$
    (3) $\frac{(75+49)}{(c+e)}$
    (4) $\frac{(c+e)}{(75+49)}$
    (5) Insufficient data is given to solve the problem.

51. Cara quit her job for a better one. If that year she earned q at the first job and b at the second job, which of the following expressions would give her average weekly salary?

    (1) $\frac{(q+b)}{52}$
    (2) $\frac{(q-b)}{52}$
    (3) $\frac{52}{(q+b)}$
    (4) $\frac{52}{(q-b)}$
    (5) $52(q+b)$

GO ON TO THE NEXT PAGE

52. At a recent farm-association dinner, a drawing for 10 door prizes was held. Winners had to be present for the drawing, which was the last item of business. A total of 643 people attended the meeting, but some left early. What were the chances that someone who stayed would win a prize?

   (1) $\frac{10}{643}$
   (2) $\frac{2}{177}$
   (3) $\frac{10}{585}$
   (4) $\frac{58}{643}$
   (5) Insufficient data is given to solve the problem.

53. During a flu epidemic, 4 employers reported that the following fractions of their employees were unable to work because of illness.

COMPANY	TOTAL EMPLOYEES WHO WERE ILL
A	$\frac{125}{500}$
B	$\frac{300}{1250}$
C	$\frac{219}{876}$
D	$\frac{8}{32}$

   What was the total number of work days lost?

   (1) 652
   (2) 2658
   (3) 3260
   (4) 20
   (5) Insufficient data is given to solve the problem.

54. The lid of a 1-gallon can of paint has a radius of 3 inches. What is its area in square inches?

   (1) 9.42
   (2) 18.84
   (3) 28.26
   (4) 37.68
   (5) 113.04

55. Laura works for 7 hours 15 minutes per day. If she works for 22 days during one month, for how many hours will she have worked?

   (1) 154 hours 30 minutes
   (2) 157 hours 30 minutes
   (3) 158 hours 30 minutes
   (4) 159 hours 30 minutes
   (5) 181 hours 30 minutes

56. A well-known singer was offered $15,000,000 to appear in 3 television commercials for a soft-drink company. If each commercial requires 8 hours of the singer's time to produce, how much will the singer make per hour?

   (1) $ 487,500
   (2) $ 600,000
   (3) $ 625,000
   (4) $1,875,000
   (5) $5,000,000

Answers are on pages A-97–A-99.

Performance Analysis Charts for the Simulated Test

Directions: Circle the number of each item that you got correct on each test. Count the number of items you got correct in each row; count the number of items you got correct in each column. Write the number correct per row and column as the numerator in the fraction in the appropriate "Total Correct" box. (The denominators represent the total number of items in the row or column.) Write the grand total correct over the denominator in the lower right corner of each chart. (For example, if you got 49 items correct in Writing Skills Part I, write 49 so that the fraction in the lower right corner of that chart reads 49/55.) Item numbers in color represent items based on graphic material.

SIMULATED TEST 1: WRITING SKILLS, Part I

Item Type	Usage (page 73)	Sentence Structure (page 100)	Mechanics (page 118)	TOTAL CORRECT
Construction Shift (page 149)	5, 29, 39	10, 27, 42, 55	13	/8
Sentence Correction (page 148)	3, 11, 17, 18, 20, 36, 44, 53	2, 16, 19, 21, 31, 38, 52	6, 7, 12, 22, 23, 24, 30, 34, 37, 43, 46, 49, 50	/28
Sentence Revision (page 148)	1, 15, 25, 32, 41, 47, 48, 54	4, 9, 14, 26, 28, 33, 35, 45, 51	8, 40	/19
TOTAL CORRECT	/19	/20	/16	/55

WRITING SKILLS, Part II

Directions: After you have used the guidelines in the answer key to score your essay, make a record of your evaluation here.

Write the score for your essay in the box at the right.
List some of the strong points of your essay.

List some of the weak points of your essay.

List improvements that you plan to make when you work on your next essay.

SIMULATED TEST 2: SOCIAL STUDIES

Item Type	History (page 270)	Geography (page 282)	Economics (page 288)	Political Science (page 298)	Behavioral Sciences (page 305)	TOTAL CORRECT
Comprehension (page 220)	14	28, 49	21, 26, 29, 42	10, 11, 23, 34	5, 6, 39	/14
Application (page 224)	31, 38, 45, 47, 55	16, 17, 18, 19, 20	13, 62, 63		4, 7, 50, 51, 52, 53, 54	/20
Analysis (page 228)	2, 15, 27, 37, 46, 56, 64		3, 58	12, 24, 32, 33, 60	57	/15
Evaluation (page 232)	1, 9, 30, 36, 59		22, 43, 44	8, 25, 35, 61	40, 41, 48	/15
TOTAL CORRECT	/18	/7	/12	/13	/14	/64

SIMULATED TEST 3: SCIENCE

Item Type	Biology (page 322)	Earth Science (page 334)	Chemistry (page 347)	Physics (page 356)	TOTAL CORRECT
Comprehension (page 220)	15, 17, 18, 23, 37, 39, 53	10, 29, 42, 43		31, 60	/13
Application (page 224)	1, 2, 3, 4, 5, 8, 38, 54, 57	9, 11	26, 30, 47, 48, 49, 50	22, 28, 32	/20
Analysis (page 228)	6, 14, 19, 20, 51, 55, 56, 59, 63	12, 25, 44, 45	62, 64	33, 36, 52, 61	/19
Evaluation (page 232)	7, 16, 21, 24, 40, 41, 58, 65	13, 35, 46	27	34, 66	/14
TOTAL CORRECT	/33	/13	/9	/11	/66

SIMULATED TEST 4: INTERPRETING LITERATURE AND THE ARTS

Item Type	Nonfiction (page 375)	Fiction (page 387)	Drama (page 399)	Poetry (page 411)	Commentary (page 422)	TOTAL CORRECT
Literal Comprehension Specific (page 220)	23, 36, 43	2, 19, 32			14	/7
Literal Comprehension Global (page 220)	34		8	5, 16	11, 38	/6
Inferential Comprehension Specific (page 220)		3, 30	28	6, 17	12, 39	/7
Inferential Comprehension Global (page 220)	24, 44	1, 20, 31	10, 27			/7
Application (page 224)	25	21	29	18	15, 42	/6
Analysis (page 228)	26, 35, 37, 45	4, 22, 33	9	7	13, 40, 41	/12
TOTAL CORRECT	/11	/12	/6	/6	/10	/45

Performance Analysis

SIMULATED TEST 5: MATHEMATICS

Item Type	Arithmetic (page 439)	Algebra (page 535)	Geometry (page 555)	TOTAL CORRECT
Skills	46	41	6, 31, 39, 48	/6
Applications	1, 7, 9, 10, 24, 54	18, 26, 47	15, 16, 17	/12
Problem Solving	2, 3, 8, 11, 12, 13, 14, 21, 22, 23, 25, 30, 34, 35, 36, 37, 38, 40, 43, 45, 52, 53, 55, 56	4, 5, 19, 27, 32, 33, 42, 44, 49, 50, 51	20, 28, 29	/38
TOTAL CORRECT	/31	/15	/10	/56

The page numbers in parentheses indicate where in this book you can find the beginning of specific instruction about the various skills and fields and about the types of questions you encountered in the Simulated Test. In mathematics, however, the items in the chart are classified as Skills, Applications, or Problem Solving. In the chapters in Unit VII of this book, the three item types are covered in different levels:

Skills items are covered in Level 1,
Applications items are covered in Level 2;
Problem Solving items are covered in Level 3.

For example, the skills needed to solve Item 4 are covered in Level 3 of Chapter 6 in Unit VII. To locate in which chapter arithmetic items are addressed, reread the problem to see what kind of numbers (whole numbers, fractions, and so forth) are used and then go to the designated level of the appropriate chapter.

Answers and Explanations

Introduction

In the Answers and Explanations section, you will find answers to all the questions in these sections of the book:

- Previews
- Lesson Exercises
- Reviews
- Chapter Quizzes
- Practice Items
- Simulated Tests

You will discover that the Answers and Explanations section is a valuable study tool. It not only tells you the correct answer, but explains why each answer is correct. It also points out the reading skill that is required to answer each question successfully.

Even if you get a question right, it will help to review the explanation. The explanation will reinforce your understanding of the question and the material it was based on. Because you might have guessed a correct answer or answered correctly for the wrong reason, it can't hurt to review explanations. It might help a lot.

INSTRUCTION
UNIT 1 Writing Skills, Part I: Grammar

Chapter 1 Usage

Skill 1

Preview

1. Americans buy $3 billion worth of pet food every year. (Change *buys* to *buy* to agree with *Americans*.)
2. Correct.
3. Across the plain race hundreds of zebras. (Change *race* to *races* to agree with *hundreds*.)
4. There are three different shapes of leaves on the sassafras tree. (Change *is* to *are* to agree with *shapes*.)
5. Both cattle and horses crave salt. (Change *craves* to *crave* to agree with *cattle and horses*.)

Lesson 1

1. Weather conditions change rapidly in the summer months in the Midwest. (Change *changes* to *change* to agree with *conditions*.)
2. Both were eligible for the sweepstakes prize. (Change *was* to *were* to agree with *Both*.)
3. Effective speaking requires practice and determination. (Change *require* to *requires* to agree with *speaking*.)
4. Correct.
5. Correct.
6. The team is practicing on the field. (Change *are* to *is* to agree with *team*, which in this case is describing individuals working together as a unit.)
7. Somebody has the list of vacant apartments. (Change *have* to *has* to agree with *somebody*.)
8. Listening skills need to be taught in grade school. (Change *needs* to *need* to agree with *skills*.)
9. Measles is a serious disease if not treated properly. (Change *are* to *is* to agree with *Measles*, a singular noun that looks plural.)
10. The pair of pants is torn near the seam. (Change *were* to *was* to agree with *pair*.)

Lesson 2

1. The greatest verified age is 113 years. (Change *are* to *is* to agree with *age*.)
2. Clarity ~~in writing and speaking~~ is essential to success. (Change *are* to *is* to agree with *Clarity*.)
3. Correct.
4. Mark Twain's stories ~~of Mississippi River life~~ have fascinated many people. (Change *has* to *have* to agree with *stories*.)
5. The rabbit, ~~along with the antelope,~~ sees in a full circle without having to move its head. (Change *see* to *sees* to agree with *rabbit*.)

Lesson 3

1. At the meeting were the president and his advisors. (In subject-verb order this sentence reads, *The president and his advisors were at the meeting*. Change *was* to *were* to agree with *president and his advisors*.)
2. At the foot of the cave were the hibernating bears. (In subject-verb order this sentence reads, *The hibernating bears were at the foot of the cave*. Change *was* to *were* to agree with *bears*.)
3. Were the fireworks on the Fourth of July as spectacular as last year's? (Reworded as a statement in subject-verb order, this sentence reads, *The fireworks ~~on the Fourth of July~~ were as spectacular as last year's*. Change *was* to *were* to agree with *fireworks*.)
4. Correct. (This sentence does not have inverted structure. The verb, *are*, immediately follows the subject, *we*.)
5. Do the whales of the Pacific Ocean migrate every year? (Reworded as a statement in subject-verb order, this sentence reads, *The whales of the Pacific Ocean do migrate every year*. Change *Does* to *Do* to agree with *whales*.)

Lesson 4

1. There are approximately 2.5 million Americans audited by the IRS each year. (Subject—*Americans*; verb—*are audited*)
2. There are more than 2 billion pencils manufactured in the United states each year. (Subject—*pencils*; verb—*are manufactured*)
3. Here is the stack of new books from the library. (Subject—*stack*; verb—*is*)
4. Correct. (Subject—*site*; verb—*is*)
5. There is a type of shark that averages 5 inches in length when fully grown. (Subject—*type*; verb—*is*)

Lesson 5

1. Correct.
2. Neither Neptune nor Uranus *is* visible without a telescope.
3. Either the zoo or the art museums *were* my choice for a day's vacation.
4. Not only a checking account but also a savings account *was* required for a free gift.
5. Both Prince Charles and Prince Andrew of England *are* married.

Skill 1 Review

1. There are more than 155 million telephones in the United States. (Subject—*telephones*; verb—*are*)
2. The various buttons on the telephone in my office produce different tones. (Subject—*buttons*; verb—*produce*)
3. The orchestra gives pop concerts every Saturday night. (Subject—*orchestra*; verb—*gives*)
4. This television station employs eleven announcers. (Subject—*station*; verb—*employs*)
5. Parsley, a member of the herb family, was used by the ancient Romans. (Subject—*parsley*; verb—*was used*)
6. Were Mark Twain's manuscripts the first to be typewritten? (Subject—*manuscripts*; verb—*were*)
7. Correct. (Subject—*line*; verb—*is*)
8. Neither Alexander Graham Bell nor Thomas Edison was the first to design the telephone. (Subject—*Bell, Edison*; verb—*was*)
9. Peanuts provide more protein, minerals, and vitamins than beef and liver. (Subject—*Peanuts*; verb—*provide*)
10. The first railroad in the United States was the Baltimore and Ohio, which began to carry passengers in 1830. (Subject—*railroad*; verb—*was*)

Skill 2

Preview

1. He *had known* about the early settlement of Louisiana by French colonists.
2. Correct.
3. When we spoke about American Indian cultures, we *mentioned* differences in language.
4. In the last 20 years, many people *learned* to use computers. OR In the last 20 years, many people *have learned* to use computers.
5. After a meteor lands on Earth, it *becomes* a meteorite.

Lesson 1

1. Consumers spent more money on motor vehicles than on furniture and household equipment.
2. The largest single cause of errors in business is illegible handwriting.
3. The immigrants brought ideas and customs from their native countries.
4. The average heart pumps four liters of blood per minute.
5. The Union Jack is the nickname of the British flag.
6. It had taken 70 years to complete the Capitol building in Washington, D.C.
7. By July 1969, the United States had begun to withdraw troops from South Vietnam.
8. Farmers have spoken before Congress about the difficulties small farm owners face.
9. The water level of the Mississippi River has risen this year.
10. Scientists have drawn conclusions about prehistoric animals by studying fossils.

Lesson 2

1. The first electric elevator *was installed* in New York City in 1889.
2. Next year, construction workers *will build* a new amusement park on the island.
3. Correct.
4. Recently, scientists *studied* a supernova in the southern sky.
5. In 1916, a Model T Ford *cost* less than $400.

Lesson 3

Hippopotamuses secrete a thick, reddish film. It *resembles* blood in color and texture, but it *is* not blood. In fact, it does not have any blood in it. The secretion *keeps* the animals' hides from drying out. Hippos *need* this protection when they are out of water. When the animals are hot or in pain, the flow increases. The fluid also *becomes* a darker red.

Lesson 4

1. There was a water shortage during the summer, and the city council enacted strict conservation measures.
2. As oil prices fall, the nation increases its consumption of gasoline.
3. Most people supported a change in tax laws, so Congress passed new legislation.
4. We learned in biology class that enzymes play an important part in digestion.
5. As soon as the tide rises, ships will be able to enter the harbor.

Skill 2 Review

1. Tea *was* the favorite drink of the early American colonists.
2. When scientists make new discoveries, they *publish* papers about their findings. OR When scientists *made* new discoveries, they published papers about their findings.
3. A tidal wave broke the dam, and water *flooded* the village.
4. A museum *was built* inside the base of the Statue of Liberty.
5. Correct.
6. The words "The reports of my death are greatly exaggerated" *were written* by Mark Twain.
7. Cowhands *wore* leather leggings over their trousers before riding their horses.
8. Tomorrow, the president *will discuss* arms control agreements.
9. Passengers on the Concorde, a French aircraft, *have ridden* faster than the speed of sound.
10. An ostrich can outrun a horse, but it *cannot* fly.

Skill 3

Preview

1. Correct.
2. Tin or copper will turn to black powder when it is finely ground. (Change *they are* to *it is*. Subjects joined by *or* use a singular pronoun. A singular pronoun, in turn, uses a singular verb.)
3. We must be aware of our skills or we will not advance in our professions. (Change *you* to *we* to eliminate unnecessary pronoun shift.)
4. The giant squid continues to grow as long as it lives. (Change *they live* to *it lives* to agree in number with *squid*.)
5. Romans owned many chariots; these chariots were banned from the streets of Rome during daylight hours. (Substitute *these chariots* for *they* to eliminate ambiguous pronoun reference.)

Lesson 1

1. Many mothers make clothing for their children. (Change *her* to *their* to agree with the plural antecedent *mothers*.)
2. A senator or a member of Congress must campaign for his [or *her*] election to office. (Change *their* to *his* [or *her*] to agree with the singular antecedents, *senator* and *member*, joined by *and*.)
3. Everyone should be required to wear his [or *her*] seat belt. (Change *their* to *his* [or *her*] to agree with the singular pronoun *everyone*.)
4. Correct. (*Them* and *they*, both of which are plural, refer to *tools*.)
5. New Zealand and Australia sent their ambassadors to the United States. (Change *its* to *their* to agree with the antecedents *New Zealand* and *Australia*, which are joined by *and*.)

Lesson 2

1. Dreams are important to our emotional health as well as our physical health. OR Dreams are important to *your* emotional health as well as your physical health.
2. Correct.
3. You should not take a driving test if you are not prepared for it.
4. When *you* fall in love, you might have a temporary change in personality.
5. A man who is afraid to try will not accomplish much until *he* changes *his* thinking.

Lesson 3

1. King James I of England was one of the first people who said that smoking was harmful to one's health. (*Who* refers to a person.)
2. Correct.

UNIT I: WRITING SKILLS, PART 1: GRAMMAR   Ch. 1, Skill 3, Lesson 4—Chapter 1 Quiz   A-5

3. In *Macbeth*, the characters whom I enjoyed the most were Banquo and Macduff. (I enjoyed *them* most.)
4. The cowbird is a bird that lays its eggs in the nests of other birds. (*That* refers to an animal.)
5. Correct.

Lesson 4

1. Although the movie won an award, the *public* did not enjoy it as much as the movie reviewers did. (*They* might also be replaced by *the audience, the viewers,* and so on.)
2. Many people oppose the government's plan to increase the sales tax.
3. Steadily dropping temperatures forced the cancellation of the outdoor barbecue.
4. A recent news article said that more countries were asking for military aid.
5. Some people work more than eight hours a day, but doing so is against many union rules.

Lesson 5

1. Shakespeare wrote many interesting plays about English kings. OR Shakespeare wrote many plays about interesting subjects, including English kings.
2. Because of the president's controversial remarks, he and the secretary of state held a news conference. OR Because of the secretary of state's controversial remarks, he and the president held a news conference.
3. The teacher explained to the students that she, the student, needed to finish the project before the end of the semester. OR The teacher explained to the student that she, the teacher, needed to finish her project before the end of the semester.
4. One of the scouts told the scoutmaster that he, the scoutmaster, was lost. OR One of the scouts told the scoutmaster that he, the scout, was lost.
5. Some people read their horoscopes, which have a great deal of influence, every day. OR Some people, who have a great deal of influence, read their horoscopes every day.

Skill 3 Review

1. When quartz crystals were discovered, they were thought to be ice that could not melt. (Change *it was* to *they were* to agree with the antecedent, *crystals*.)
2. My nephew, whom I taught to ski, recently entered an amateur competition. (*I taught him to ski* can be substituted; therefore, *whom* is the correct choice.)
3. He dislikes eating in restaurants where he has to serve himself. (Change *yourself* to *himself* to eliminate the pronoun shift.)
4. Several of my friends have taught themselves to use a word processor. (Change *himself* to *themselves* to agree with the antecedent *several*.)
5. Tennessee and Missouri are the only states which (or that) are bordered by eight other states. (*Who* refers to people or animals. *Which* or *that* refers to things.)
6. In many states, you need to take a vision test before you are issued a driver's license. (Change *we* to *you* to avoid pronoun shift.)
7. Correct.
8. The boss informed the employee that she, the employee, would no longer be working for the company. OR The boss informed the employee that she, the boss, would no longer be working for the company. (Reword to eliminate ambiguous pronoun reference.)
9. Yesterday, I had a blood test. I also had a booster shot, which made me feel weak. (Reword to eliminate ambiguous pronoun reference.)
10. Fish make sounds by grinding their teeth. (Change *its* to *their*, a plural pronoun that agrees with the plural antecedent, *Fish*.)

Chapter 1 Quiz

1. Several of our country's presidents have never held any other elective office. (Change *has* to *have* to agree with the plural subject, *Several*.)
2. We spend one-third of our life asleep, and we dream about one-fifth of that time. (Change *you* to *we* to eliminate the pronoun shift.)
3. Long ago, the Belgians really invented the French-fried potato. (Change *invents* to *invented* to match the past-tense word clue, *Long ago*.)
4. Correct.
5. John Adams, who was the first U.S. president to live in the White House, moved there in the year 1800. (Change *whom* to *who* because *He was the first . . .* fits.)
6. At the crack of dawn were heard the crows of the rooster. (Change *was* to *were* to match the plural subject, *crows*.)
7. Generally, a person between the ages of five and fifteen is the healthiest. (Change *are* to *is* to match the singular subject, *person*.)
8. People of ancient times washed themselves with ashes and water. (Change *himself* to *themselves* so that the pronoun agrees with its antecedent, *people*.)
9. The first aircraft carrier was built in 1918 by the British. (Change *was build* to *was built*, the correct past-participle form of the verb.)
10. By next week, I probably will be very good at hitting volleys. (Change *am* to *will be* to match the future-tense word clue, *By next week*.)
11. There are seven red stripes in the United States flag. (Change *is* to *are* to agree with the plural subject, *stripes*.)
12. All the gods of ancient Rome parallel those of Greece. (Change *parallels* to *parallel* to agree with the plural subject, *All*.)
13. In 1491, James IV of Scotland signed a law that prohibited the playing of golf. (Change *signs* to *signed* to match the past-tense word clue, *In 1491*.)
14. This morning I got out of bed and showered before the alarm rang. (Change *rung* to *rang*, the correct past-tense form of the verb.)
15. Correct.
16. If we were interested in studying mountains, we would study orography. OR If you were interested in studying mountains, you would study orography. (Eliminate pronoun shift.)
17. I dislike returning merchandise to that store because the clerks give me a hard time. (Correct vague pronoun reference by replacing *they*, which has no clear antecedent.)
18. George Custer had become a general by the age of 23. (Change *had became* to *had become*, the correct past-participle form of the verb.)

19. Another interesting fact is that bird's-nest soup is really made from birds' nests. (Change *are* to *is* to agree with the singular subject, *soup*.)
20. Here is one of the newest electronic games on the market today. (Change *are* to *is* to agree with the singular subject, *one*.)

Chapter 2 Sentence Structure

Skill 1

Preview

There may be more than one correct way to edit some sentences.

1. Napoleon conquered Italy by the time he was 26. (Drop *who*, which makes this a sentence fragment.)
2. David never went to camp. He worked during the summer months. (This is a run-on sentence. Add a period or a semicolon after *camp*.)
3. Correct.
4. There are 20,000 television commercials each year for children, and 7,000 of them advertise sugared breakfast cereals. (This is a comma splice. One way to change this is to add the word *and* after *children*.)
5. A ten-gallon hat really holds less than a gallon. (This is a sentence fragment. Add a subject.)

Lesson 1

There may be more than one correct way to edit some sentences.

1. Dogs sweat through the pads of their feet. (Add a subject.)
2. The Fox River flows into Green Bay, Wisconsin. (Make *flowing* the main verb by changing its form.)
3. Correct.
4. A snowstorm with low temperatures and severe winds is a blizzard. (Add a verb and words to complete the meaning.)
5. When the hurricane reached land, huge waves and floods damaged the town. (Add words to complete the meaning.)

Lesson 2

1. A crocodile cannot move its tongue. Its tongue is rooted to the base of its mouth.
2. Dry ice does not melt. It evaporates.
3. The first coin minted in the United States was a silver dollar. It was issued on October 15, 1794.
4. The bark of the redwood tree is fireproof. A fire may take place inside the tree.
5. Cork comes from the bark of trees. It takes more than ten years to produce one layer of cork.

Lesson 3

There may be more than one correct way to edit some sentences.

1. An anteater is almost six feet long, but its mouth is only an inch wide.
2. Great Britain has few natural resources; therefore, foreign trade is important to its economy.
3. Correct.
4. The parachute was invented before the airplane; it was designed to help people jump from burning buildings.
5. More than 500 kinds of grass grow in Texas. The largest city in Texas is Houston. (Separate sentences are appropriate because the two ideas are not closely related.)
6. Thyme grows well in dry soil, and many gardeners grow this herb.
7. Tomato plants need sunlight, but they can be grown in almost any soil.
8. Correct.
9. The invention of the steam engine made fast river travel possible; moreover, it encouraged the expansion of railroads.
10. In 1953 the first color television broadcasts were made; however, few homes had color sets then.

Skill 1 Review

There may be more than one correct way to edit some sentences.

1. The Soviet Union is the largest country in the world; Canada is the second largest. (Or use a period, a semicolon and a connecting word, or a comma and a connecting word.)
2. Honey is the only food that does not spoil; it has been found in the tombs of ancient Egyptians. (Or use a period, a semicolon and a connecting word, or a comma and a connecting word.)
3. Correct.
4. There are professional tea tasters as well as wine tasters. (Add words to the sentence fragment to make the idea complete.)
5. The A&P was the first established chain-store business; it was established in 1842. (Or use a period, a semicolon and a connecting word, or a comma and a connecting word.)
6. The white shark is always hungry; therefore, its appetite is never satisfied. (Use a comma after a connecting word that is used with a semicolon.)
7. More Italians live in New York City than in Rome; more Irish live in New York City than in Dublin. (Or use a period, a semicolon and a connecting word, or a comma and a connecting word.)
8. More than one-third of the world's pineapples comes from Hawaii. (Add a verb and other words to the sentence fragment to make the idea complete.)
9. Theodore Roosevelt was the first president to ride in a car; Andrew Jackson was the first president to ride in a railroad train. (Or use a period, a semicolon and a connecting word, or a comma and a connecting word.)
10. Type O is the most common blood type in the world; type AB is the rarest. (Or use a period, a semicolon and a connecting word, or a comma and a connecting word.)

Skill 2

Preview

1. When you pay your full credit-card balance, you may not have to pay interest. (Add a comma after *balance*.)
2. Laser beams are being used in eye surgery because they make the surgery safer. (Use only one connector. *Because* expresses the relationship between the two ideas in the sentence.)
3. Babe Ruth holds the record for hitting the most home runs in a 154-game season, for he hit a total of 60. (Substitute a more appropriate word for *next*, which does not correctly show the relationship between ideas.)
4. The first president to be born in the United States was Martin Van Buren. He was born in 1782. On the other hand, the earlier

presidents were born in the colonies, for the United States of America came into existence in 1776. (The original sentence has too many ideas. Divide the sentence into smaller units of information. This is one of several correct ways of doing so.)
5. Correct.

Lesson 1

1. Amendments have been added to our Constitution; for example, the income-tax amendment was added in 1913. (Use a coordinator that shows an example or a reason.)
2. Correct.
3. The Klondike is a region of northwest Canada. The United States and Canada have remained allies. (Divide these ideas into two sentences because they are not closely related.)
4. Cortez introduced horses to the American continent, and he brought them in his conquest of Mexico in 1519. (Change the coordinator *but* to *and* because the second idea is added information.)
5. You might think that the cuttlefish is a fish, but it actually is a mollusk. It has sucker-bearing arms, and it ejects an inklike fluid. This fluid can be used in drawing. (The original sentence has too many ideas. Divide the sentence into smaller units of information. This is one of several correct ways of doing so.)

Lesson 2

1. Although stress and anxiety are often associated with the fear of failure, they can also occur as a result of success. (When using a subordinator [*although*], do not use a coordinator [*but*].)
2. While Ms. Cintron was taking a course in word processing, she continued to use her office typewriter. (Use a comma after a subordinate idea that comes first in the sentence.)
3. The shortage of trained computer personnel is not limited to top-level jobs. The Japanese continue to compete for sales. (Divide these ideas into two sentences because they are not closely related.)
4. Because running improves the efficiency of the lungs and strengthens the heart, doctors advise many patients to take part in this activity. (Use only one

subordinator. *Because* expresses a reason why.)
5. Correct.

Lesson 3

1. Elise purchased a camera and two rolls of film.
2. Miss Levitt's apartment is small and cozy. (Or use *but*.)
3. Terry Ohlsen enjoys baseball but does not enjoy hockey.
4. The surgeon and the therapist are examining the X-rays. (Use a plural verb with the plural subject.)
5. The senator proposed a tax cut and persuaded other senators to vote for it.

Skill 2 Review

1. As long as you order from the catalog, you will receive a 10-percent discount. (A comma follows a subordinate idea at the beginning of a sentence.)
2. Marco Polo was an early Italian world traveler; in fact, he was probably the first westerner to visit China. (Change *nevertheless* to a coordinator that shows an example.)
3. Correct.
4. The Dead Sea has no outlet, and the water is so salty that fish cannot live in it. (Change the coordinator to a word that adds an idea.)
5. Depression affects your well-being because it affects your ability to handle daily responsibilities. (No comma is needed when the subordinate idea comes last in the sentence.)
6. Foxes do not hunt in bands, for they prefer to hunt alone. (Choose a coordinator that gives a reason.)
7. Alaska and Hawaii were granted statehood in 1959. I am originally from Nebraska. (Divide these ideas into two sentences because they are not closely related.)
8. Before the Salk and Sabin vaccines were developed, polio was a national health problem. (Use only one subordinator. *Before* is the better choice because it describes the order of events.)
9. The Revolutionary War lasted about seven years. It began soon after the Declaration of Independence was signed; however, the peace treaty was not signed until January 21, 1783. (The original sentence has too many ideas. Divide the sentence

into smaller units of information. This is one of several correct ways of doing so.)
10. Unless we explore safe, new energy sources, our energy crisis will continue. (When using a subordinator [*unless*], do not also use a coordinator [*or*].)

Skill 3

Preview

1. As we turned the corner, the baseball stadium came into view. (Add a word to the modifier that tells who turned the corner.)
2. He hopes that he can finish college in three years and then visit Europe. (Change *to visit* to *visit*. *Visit* must be parallel to *finish*.)
3. Correct.
4. Vacationing in Arizona, Mr. and Mrs. Bohl were surprised at the heat. (Move the modifier closer to the words being modified.)
5. She is tall, slim, and brown-eyed. (Parallel structure requires that related items be expressed in the same form.)

Lesson 1

There may be more than one correct way to edit some sentences.

1. I have bills to pay because I purchased furniture on credit. (Eliminate or change words that make the sentence unclear.)
2. Correct.
3. I am certain that I saw a meteor fall. (Avoid wordiness.)
4. A ruby is red, and it is usually round. (Avoid wordiness.)
5. After visiting the Middle East, Senator Brown conferred with the president. OR After the president visited the Middle East, Senator Brown conferred with him. (Avoid unclear pronoun reference.)

Lesson 2

There may be more than one correct way to edit some sentences.

1. Walking through the White House, you might be overtaken by a feeling of awe.
2. He bought a minivan with power steering from a friend.
3. Correct.
4. Whistler painted his mother sitting in a rocking chair.
5. As we entered the theater, the curtain was just beginning to rise.

Lesson 3

1. His latest movie was exciting, informative, and interesting. (Change *had a lot of interest* to *interesting* for parallel structure.)
2. Correct.
3. Remedies used in the fourteenth century to eliminate the Black Plague included killing all swallows, smoking tobacco, and wearing packets of arsenic. (Change *wear* to *wearing* for parallel structure.)
4. At the age of 35, Dr. Cott had achieved neither success nor fame. (Change *to be famous* to *fame* for parallel structure.)
5. Inventing wax paper, developing the electric light, and designing the motion-picture camera were some of Thomas Edison's important contributions. (Change *to design* to *designing* for parallel structure.)

Skill 3 Review

1. Developed in the sixteenth century, the Yo-Yo was originally designed to be a weapon; it weighed four pounds and had a 20-foot cord. (Move the modifier closer to the words being modified.)
2. During the Middle Ages, German men went to the barber to get a shave and to take a bath. (Change *taking* to *to take* for parallel structure.)
3. There is an old car in that shed; the car needs a coat of paint. OR In that shed, which needs a coat of paint, there is an old car.
4. Correct.
5. During the peace demonstration, the building was surrounded. (Avoid wordiness. *On all sides* is unnecessary after *surrounded*, which means "enclosed on all sides.")
6. Correct.
7. Staring at the bulldozer, we saw the last wall of the old building fall. (Add a word, such as *we*, that can logically be modified by *staring*.)
8. Doctors recommend plenty of sleep, an adequate diet, and regular exercise for their patients. (Change *to exercise regularly* to *regular exercise* for parallel structure.)
9. At the beginning of the trip, Vincent felt nervous. (Avoid wordiness; *at first* is unnecessary after *At the beginning*.)
10. I would rather read the newspaper than watch the news on television. (Change *watching* to *watch* for parallel structure.)

Chapter 2 Quiz

There may be more than one correct way to edit a sentence.

1. The white area on an archery target is worth one point, and the red area is worth seven points. (Use a comma after the first complete idea in a compound sentence.)
2. Although deaf, dumb, and blind, Helen Keller spoke English, German, and French. (Place the modifiers close to the words being modified.)
3. Bruce Jenner was an American Olympic decathlon winner in 1976. (Add words to the sentence fragment to make a complete idea.)
4. Willa showed the canary in the cage to her friend. (Place *in the cage* closer to the word being modified, *canary*.)
5. The George Washington Bridge joins New York and New Jersey; the Oakland Bridge joins Oakland and San Francisco. (Eliminate the comma splice.)
6. Excited by the applause, the actors gave an even better performance. (Reword the sentence so that *Excited* is closer to the word it modifies, *actors*.)
7. Devil's Island is an island located off the coast of South America. (Add words to the sentence fragment to make a complete idea.)
8. The members of the debating team were instructed to be organized, to be prepared, and to speak clearly. (Change *speak* to *to speak* for parallel structure.)
9. The Pacific is the largest and the deepest ocean. (Eliminate the comma, since this is not a compound sentence.)
10. Correct.
11. Millie wears glasses for reading, but she does not need them for traveling. (Eliminate the run-on sentence.)
12. That is why I cannot attend the meeting. (Avoid wordiness.)
13. After the Salk vaccine was successfully tested, it was distributed nationally in 1955. (Use a comma after the subordinate idea when it comes first in a sentence.)
14. Excavating, ordering materials, and bidding for contracts are part of a contractor's job. (Change *to make bids* to *bidding* for parallel structure.)
15. Canberra is the capital city of Australia; however, many people think that Sydney is. (Change the coordinator *also* to *however*. The coordinator must show contrast of ideas.)
16. John Kennedy was the first Catholic to become president. He was also the youngest elected president. (Eliminate the run-on sentence.)
17. Wiley Post made the first solo airplane flight around the world. I do not like to fly. (Separate these ideas into two sentences. They are not closely related.)
18. It is wonderful that Americans are becoming more informed about their health. (Change the wording of the sentence to correct unclear pronoun reference.)
19. Although it is thought that most people have credit cards, fewer than three in ten actually own one. (Use only one subordinator. *Although* expresses contrast.)
20. By wearing the glass slipper, Cinderella was able to be identified by the prince. (Move the modified word closer to the phrase that modifies it.)

Chapter 3 Mechanics

Skill 1

Preview

1. There are twelve players on a Canadian football team. (Capitalize proper adjectives.)
2. The Acme Packing Company provided uniforms for the first Green Bay Packers football team. (Capitalize the names of companies.)
3. Weather forecasters are predicting a mild winter this year. (Do not capitalize the seasons.)
4. In 1643, the Puritans enacted a law in England that made the singing of Christmas carols a crime. (Capitalize the names of holidays.)
5. Correct.

UNIT I: WRITING SKILLS, PART 1: GRAMMAR

Ch. 3, Skill 1, Lesson 1—Ch. 3, Skill 2, Lesson 3 **A-9**

Lesson 1

1. In Boston, the Red Sox play in Fenway Park. (Capitalize the names of places.)
2. The largest privately owned ranch in the United States is Parker Ranch in Hawaii. (Capitalize the names of places.)
3. In 1915, a British ship, the *Lusitania*, was sunk by a German submarine. (Capitalize proper adjectives and the names of ships, planes, and other vehicles.)
4. Correct.
5. The founder of the American Red Cross Society was Clara Barton.

Lesson 2

1. Many laws regulating big business were passed under President Theodore Roosevelt. (Capitalize *president* when it is used with a name.)
2. Many best-selling children's books have been written by Dr. Seuss. (Capitalize abbreviations of titles.)
3. Correct.
4. Correct.
5. Disneyland is located at 1313 Harbor Boulevard in Anaheim, California. (Capitalize the names of streets.)

Lesson 3

1. Sadie Hawkins Day falls on the first Saturday after November 11. (Capitalize the days of the week.)
2. The first official day of summer is June 22. (Do not capitalize the seasons.)
3. The attack on Pearl Harbor occurred during World War II. (Capitalize historical events.)
4. During the Renaissance, great art and literature were developed in Europe. (Capitalize historical periods.)
5. Correct.

Skill 1 Review

1. The famous carol "Silent Night" was written the day before Christmas in 1818. (Capitalize the names of holidays.)
2. A popular soda was invented in 1886 in a drug store at 107 Marietta Street in Atlanta, Georgia. (Capitalize the names of streets and states.)
3. The first steam engine, built by John Fitch, was a toy train. (*Steam engine* is a common noun, not a proper noun, and therefore should not be capitalized.)
4. The average American spends about one year of his or her life talking on the telephone. (Capitalize proper nouns.)
5. We decided to go to Texas during our summer vacation. (*Summer vacation* is a common noun; the names of the seasons are not capitalized.)
6. On October 31, the streets were crowded with children in Halloween costumes. (Capitalize the months and the names of holidays.)
7. During the Civil War, General Grant and General Lee led the opposing armies. (*Civil War* should be capitalized because it is a historical event; *general* should be capitalized because it is a title; *Grant* and *Lee* should be capitalized because they are the names of people.)
8. We arrived at the observation deck of the World Trade Center at 4:00 P.M. (Capitalize the names of the buildings and the abbreviations *A.M.* and *P.M.*)
9. Correct.
10. The Stone Age probably ended between 10,000 and 8,000 B.C. (Capitalize historical periods and the abbreviations *B.C.* and *A.D.*)

Skill 2

Preview

1. The three softest minerals are talc, gypsum, and calcite. (Do not use a comma before the first item in a series.)
2. Correct.
3. To celebrate the Fourth of July, thousands of tourists visited the Statue of Liberty. (Use a comma to set off an introductory phrase.)
4. Many government buildings are protected by highly trained, dependable guard dogs. (Use a comma to separate two adjectives that describe the same noun.)
5. Bill Gore, an Englishman, once yodeled continuously for five hours and three minutes. (Use a comma before and after a sentence interrupter.)

Lesson 1

1. Avoid buying toys that have sharp points and unfinished surfaces. (Do not use commas when there are fewer than three items in a series.)
2. The exhausted, courageous, and relieved runner crossed the finish line. (Do not use a comma between the last adjective in a series and the word it modifies.)
3. Correct. (Commas are not used when coordinating words join items in a series.)
4. The words *beginner*, *novice*, *intermediate*, and *expert* are used to classify the abilities of cross-country skiers. (Do not use a comma before the first item in a series.)
5. The three color words in the English language that have no rhyme are *orange*, *silver*, and *purple*. (Do not use a comma before the first item in a series.)

Lesson 2

The rule that governs all of these sentences is that a comma precedes the coordinator in a compound sentence.

1. The name *Chang* is the most common last name in the world, but many people mistakenly think *Smith* is more common.
2. Correct.
3. The Mississippi River is the longest river in the United States, and it is the nation's most important inland waterway.
4. Antibiotics are extremely helpful in fighting disease, but some people develop a tolerance to them.
5. A new bus route was created, and commuting time for many people was reduced greatly.

Lesson 3

1. After years of training, professional divers learn to land in water that is only 12 feet deep. (Use a comma after an introductory phrase.)
2. Nevertheless, it is important to set goals for yourself throughout your life. (Use a comma after an introductory word.)
3. Covering eight acres of ground, the Goodyear airship hangar is the largest hangar in the world. (Use a comma after an introductory phrase.)
4. No, I did not know that astronauts must not be more than six feet tall. (Use a comma after an introductory word.)
5. Students and faculty, I am proud to announce the winners of the scholarship contest. (Use a comma

after names or words of direct address.)

Lesson 4

1. A caterpillar, I believe, has more than 2000 muscles. (Use commas to set off a sentence interrupter.)
2. *E*, by the way, is the most frequently used letter in the English alphabet. (Use commas to set off a sentence interrupter).
3. The nursery rhyme "Old King Cole" is based on a real king who ruled England about 2000 years ago. (Commas are not used if a word or phrase that describes a noun is essential to the meaning of the sentence.)
4. Correct.
5. Charles Dickens, the British novelist, never graduated from grade school. (Use commas to set off sentence interrupters.)

Lesson 5

1. Colorful flowers and many kinds of vegetation cover some deserts after a rainfall. (Do not use a comma with a compound subject; do not use a comma between the subject and verb of a sentence.)
2. Decisions in a democracy are made according to majority rule, but majority rule does not mean that the majority can do whatever it wants. (Do not use a comma after a coordinator that joins two complete sentences.)
3. The six coins currently minted in the United States are the penny, nickel, dime, quarter, 50-cent piece, and silver dollar. (Do not use a comma before the first item in a series.)
4. Correct.
5. Before being named the Cleveland Indians, the team was known as the Spiders. (Do not use a comma between the subject and verb of a sentence.)

Skill 2 Review

1. If you need to reduce the amount of salt in your diet, you should not eat canned vegetables or dill pickles or olives. (Do not use commas when items in a series are joined by coordinators.)
2. The oldest stained-glass window in the world was made almost one thousand years ago, and it can be found in Bavaria, Germany. (Use a comma before a coordinator in a compound sentence.)

3. There are, for example, plants that consist of only one cell. (Use commas to set off sentence interrupters.)
4. Correct.
5. Ellen, please have your report ready by 10:00 A.M. today. (Use a comma following a name used in direct address.)
6. Many people change jobs because of a need to perform interesting, fulfilling, and challenging work. (Do not use a comma between an adjective and the word it describes.)
7. The monkey wrench, named after Charles Moncke, is a useful tool. (Use commas to set off sentence interrupters.)
8. According to scientists, gold exists on Mercury, Venus, and Mars. (Do not use a comma between the subject and verb of a sentence.)
9. Discovered in 1891 in Arizona, Barringer Crater is the largest crater ever formed by a meteor that crashed into Earth. (Use a comma to set off an introductory phrase.)
10. Healthy snack foods include carrots, cauliflower, cucumbers, green peppers, and spinach. (Do not use a comma before the first item in a series.)

Skill 3

Preview

1. Eating too many carrots can make a *person's* skin turn orange.
2. Delicate crystal can *break* easily.
3. The swallow used small twigs to build *its* nest.
4. Correct.
5. The Germans built many of *their* castles along the Rhine River.

Lesson 1

1. Recent *discoveries* in medicine have changed the way people live.
2. In many *cities*, trolleys used to run along main streets.
3. Correct.
4. The candidates *running* for office appeared to have similar views.
5. Many families are *preparing* their children for school by helping them learn to read.

Lesson 2

1. One fourth of *India's* people live in cities.

2. The telephone *company's* employees attended a training course.
3. Earth's rotation on *its* axis causes day and night.
4. Correct.
5. One of *Texas's* most popular tourist attractions is the Alamo.

Lesson 3

1. If *you're* suffering from islomania, you have an irresistible attraction for islands.
2. Some of the company's employees think *they're* overworked.
3. *Don't* believe that Swiss steak originated in Switzerland; it was invented in the United States.
4. *It's* true that Thomas Jefferson was the first president to serve spaghetti at a state dinner.
5. Correct.

Lesson 4

1. We visited the *Capitol* building as part of our *course* in United States government.
2. Correct.
3. The principal spoke *to* the students who had already completed their studies.
4. The *plane* passed over the Rocky Mountains.
5. Receiving a *minor* compliment can *alter* the way you feel about yourself.

Lesson 5

1. change *acomodate* to *accomodate*
   change *acheivement* to *achievement*
   change *batchelor* to *bachelor*
2. change *beleive* to *believe*
   change *compell* to *compel*
   change *congradulate* to *congratulate*
3. change *corporel* to *corporal*
   change *desireable* to *desirable*
4. change *endevor* to *endeavor*
   change *exhorbitant* to *exorbitant*
   change *facillity* to *facility*
5. change *Febuary* to *February*
   change *guarrantee* to *guarantee*
   change *humerous* to *humorous*
6. change *journel* to *journal*
7. change *maintainence* to *maintenance*
   change *mispelled* to *misspelled*
   change *occassional* to *occasional*
   change *pamflet* to *pamphlet*
8. change *pleasent* to *pleasant*
   change *reciept* to *receipt*
   change *resistence* to *resistance*

9. change *supress* to *suppress*
   change *sylable* to *syllable*
   change *truley* to *truly*
10. change *unecessary* to *unnecessary*
    change *variaty* to *variety*
    change *Wensday* to *Wednesday*

Skill 3 Review

1. Would you *believe* that Russian dressing was invented in the United States?
2. On June 6, 1933, a drive-in theater, the first of *its* kind, opened in Camden, New Jersey.
3. John Jeffries was the first American to keep thorough records of *weather* conditions in our country.
4. Time-management courses teach you how not to *waste* your time.
5. Correct.
6. Asking for someone's *advice* may be the first step toward forming a friendship.
7. People *usually* forget a foreign language if they do not speak it for a long time.
8. *Weren't* Lewis and Clark famous explorers of the western region of the United States?
9. He didn't mind *keeping* his promise.
10. A presidential proclamation stated that Thomas *Jefferson's* birthday would be observed on April 13 every year.

Chapter 3 Quiz

1. The United States imports more oil *than* any other country. (Use *than* to show comparison.)
2. In the Soviet Union, World War II is called the *Great Patriotic War.* (Capitalize historical events.)
3. According to the U.S. Department of Agriculture, the average American eats 1425 pounds of food each year. (Set off introductory phrases with a comma.)
4. Soup is the last course in an authentic *Chinese* meal. (Capitalize proper adjectives.)
5. The spice *caraway* was first used in the country Turkey. (Do not capitalize common nouns.)
6. Correct.
7. Japan's largest automakers are Toyota, Nissan, Isuzu, Mitsubishi, Honda, and Mazda. (Do not use a comma before the first item in a series.)
8. South America's largest country is Brazil. (Use "s" to show possession in a singular noun.)
9. The world's tallest building, the Sears Tower, is located in Chicago, Illinois. (Set off a sentence interrupter by using commas.)
10. There are 42 gallons in a barrel of oil. (Do not use a comma between the subject and the verb of a sentence.)
11. The United States Air Force Academy is located in Colorado. (Capitalize proper nouns.)
12. P.T. Barnum and his circus began *their* first tour of the United States in 1835. (Replace *they're* with the possessive pronoun *their*.)
13. Pluto, Mickey Mouse's dog, was first called Rover. (Use commas to set off a sentence interrupter.)
14. China has only one time zone, but the Soviet Union has eleven. (Use a comma before the coordinator in a compound sentence.)
15. Julius Caesar was assassinated on March 15, 44 *B.C.* (Capitalize *A.D.* and *B.C.*)
16. The first daily television newscast was broadcast on NBC on February 16, 1948. (Change the spelling *dayly* to *daily*.)
17. Correct.
18. The Secret Service was created by an act of Congress on *June 23*, 1860. (Capitalize the months of the year.)
19. The Mason-Dixon Line was established to settle a dispute between Maryland and Pennsylvania. (Do not use a comma with fewer than three items in a series.)
20. You *don't* get rid of a bad temper by losing it. (Change the spelling of *do'nt* to *don't*.)

Chapter 4 Editing Paragraphs

Lesson 1

1. **(1)** *change were to was*   The singular subject, *item*, requires a singular verb, *was*.
2. **(4)** *meeting. Some*   This is a run-on sentence. Alternative (4) divides the run-on sentence into two smaller, complete sentences.
3. **(5)** *No correction is necessary*
4. **(1)** *add a comma after Jones*   Commas are used to set off sentence interrupters. *An exceptional worker* gives you added information about Ms. Jones.
5. **(2)** *however*   A transition that shows contrast is needed. The intent of the sentence is to show a problem between the number of working women and the salaries they earn.

Lesson 2

1. **(3)** *Mechanics/Punctuation/Sentence Revision.* Use a comma after an introductory dependent clause.
2. **(5)** *No correction is necessary*
3. **(2)** *Mechanics/Contractions/Sentence Correction. It's* is the contraction for *it is.*
4. **(3)** *Sentence Structure/Comma Splice/Sentence Revision.* Change the comma-splice sentence into two smaller, complete sentences.
5. **(4)** *Sentence Structure/Parallel Structure/Sentence Revision.* All items in a listing must be in the same form.

Lesson 3

1. **(4)** *Usage/Pronoun Reference/Sentence Correction.* Pronouns must agree with their subjects. *Their* refers to *people.*
2. **(2)** *Usage/Subject-Verb Agreement/Sentence Revision. Are* agrees with the subject *examples.*
3. **(1)** *Sentence Structure/Combining/Construction Shift.* Combining the sentences this way shows that one idea is a result of the other.
4. **(4)** *Usage/Verb Tense/Sentence Correction.* The clue (1960) to the tense in the sentence shows past-tense meaning.
5. **(2)** *Usage/Verb Form/Sentence Correction.* The past-participle form of the verb should be used with the helping verb.

Lesson 4

1. **(3)** *Sentence Structure/Run-on Sentence/Sentence Correction.* This run-on sentence should be divided into shorter sentences.
2. **(1)** *Sentence Structure/Combining/Construction Shift.* The combination of sentences illustrates cause and effect.
3. **(4)** *Sentence Structure/Parallel Form/Sentence Correction.* All the

Ch. 4, Lesson 5—Chapter 4 Quiz

items that are listed in a series should be in the same form.
4. **(4)** *Sentence Structure/Clarity/Sentence Revision.* The parts of a compound sentence must be separated by punctuation. Using a semicolon is one way to do this.
5. **(1)** *Sentence Structure/Sentence Fragment/Sentence Correction.* The word *because* makes this group of words dependent upon another idea.

Lesson 5

1. **(2)** *Mechanics/Punctuation/Sentence Correction.* A comma should follow a phrase that introduces a sentence.
2. **(1)** *Mechanics/Spelling/Sentence Correction. Affects* is a verb, *effects* is a noun.
3. **(5)** *Mechanics/Punctuation/Sentence Revision.* This sentence has an excessive number of commas. *To develop awareness* explains the word *way* and should not be separated from it.
4. **(2)** *Mechanics/Punctuation/Sentence Correction.* When only two items appear in a series and are joined by a connecting word, a comma is not necessary.
5. **(5)** *Mechanics/Capitalization/Sentence Correction.* Capitalize the name of a country.

Lesson 6

1. **(4)** *Mechanics/Capitalization/Sentence Correction.* Days of the week are always capitalized.
2. **(2)** *Mechanics/Punctuation/Sentence Revision.* Use a comma after a phrase that introduces a sentence.
3. **(4)** *Usage/Pronoun Reference/Sentence Correction.* Use the pronoun *themselves* to refer to the children.
4. **(3)** *Sentence Structure/Modification/Sentence Revision.* Closely related sentences may be joined together with a semicolon and without the use of a connecting word.
5. **(3)** *Mechanics/Posessives/Sentence Revision.* The budget belongs to a parent; therefore, ownership is shown by the use of an apostrophe.

Chapter 4 Quiz

1. Sentence-correction items
   Sentence-revision items
   Construction-shift items
2. 1. e; 2. a; 3. d; 4. b; 5. c
3. 1. Read; 2. Reflect; 3. Revise; 4. Reread; 5. Record
4. **(1)** *Mechanics/Punctuation/Sentence Revision.* Punctuation is not needed because the word *because* introduces a sentence fragment at the end of the sentence.
5. **(5)** *Mechanics/Punctuation/Sentence Revision.* Words that interrupt a sentence are set off from the rest of the sentence with commas.
6. **(3)** *Usage/Verb Form/Sentence Correction.* Do not change the verb tense in the paragraph.
7. **(3)** *Sentence Structure/Parallel Structure/Sentence Revision.* All the items in a series must be expressed in the same form in order to balance the sentence.
8. **(2)** *Mechanics/Spelling/Sentence Correction.* This is a commonly misspelled word.
9. **(1)** *Mechanics/Capitalization/Sentence Correction.* Government, in this case, is not a proper noun; therefore, it should not be capitalized.
10. **(1)** *Sentence Structure/Combining/Construction Shift.* This word tells how the officers can help the detained person.
11. **(4)** *Usage/Subject-Verb Agreement/Sentence Correction.* To correct the subject-verb agreement, *rights*, a plural noun, needs *are*, a singular verb.
12. **(2)** *Usage/Verb Tense/Sentence Correction.* This whole passage is written in the present tense. The present tense should be used consistently.
13. **(4)** *Usage/Pronoun Reference/Sentence Revision.* The word *which* refers to the agencies, not to the words *Some people.*
14. **(3)** *Usage/Contractions/Construction Shift.* Alternative (1) does not reflect the shift from singular (agency) to plural (agencies). The apostrophe takes the place of the letter *o*, which is left out of *do not.*
15. **(4)** *Usage/Coordinators/Construction Shift.* The other alternatives change the meaning of the original sentence. Use a comma and the coordinator *and* to combine these two sentences.
16. **(5)** *Sentence Structure/Comma Splice/Sentence Revision.* Use a conjunction and a comma to separate the two independent ideas.
17. **(3)** *Usage/Sequence of Tenses/Sentence Correction.* The verbs in all parts of a sentence should agree. Both verbs in this sentence should be in the present tense.
18. **(5)** *No correction is necessary*
19. **(3)** *Sentence Structure/Parallel Form/Sentence Correction.* The past tense *made introductions* is changed to *make introductions* to maintain the parallel structure of the sentence.
20. **(2)** *Usage/Verb Form/Sentence Correction.* The plural verb *require* should agree with the plural subject *all.*

UNIT III Reading Strategies

Chapter 1 A Strategy for Reading

Lesson 1

Previewing helps you understand what you will later read by allowing you to develop a mental map of the reading material.

1. *Application/Reading Skills.* Predictor Tests are located before the instruction units.
2. *Analysis/Reading Skills.* You would turn to Social Studies Practice Items. That section is organized by subject area; Simulated Test is not.
3. *Application/Reading Skills.* The answers to Simulated Tests are located after answers to GED Practice Items.

Lesson 2

When you preview a lesson, you should look over its important elements—the title, highlighted words, illustrations, and the exercise items.

1. (4) *Comprehension/Reading Skills.* The words *How do scientists acquire . . .* indicate that the passage will be about methods used by scientists.
2. *Application/Reading Skills.* The words in dark print are **hypothesis, prediction, experiment, evidence, valid, statistics,** and **probability.** Dark print draws your attention to their importance.
3. *Application/Reading Skills.* There are three items in the exercise. None are multiple choice items.

Lesson 3

When you preview a test item, you note the directions; the form of the passage; how many items are based on the material; the form of the answer choices; and any titles, labels, captions, and highlighted words.

1. *Application/Reading Skills.* The words *Items 3 to 5* show that there are three items in the set.
2. *Comprehension/Reading Skills.* The graph compares salaries of men and women.
3. *Comprehension/Reading Skills.* The numbers at the bottom of the graph are the years the graph reports about.
4. *Comprehension/Reading Skills.* The numbers on the right report median earnings.

Lesson 4

Questioning as you read a lesson involves turning clues you notice or statements you read into questions, predicting answers, and reading further to check predictions. Questioning promotes active reading and, therefore, better comprehension.

1. *Comprehension/Reading Skills.* Sample answer: How do you define a scientific fact?
2. *Evaluation/Reading Skills.* The prediction is not supported by the paragraph. An example is provided of a "scientific fact" that turned out not to be true.
3. *Analysis/Reading Skills.* Using an example from astronomy, the third paragraph implies that as instruments improve, scientists may make new observations that change their beliefs about what is true.

Lesson 5

You question a test item by rewording the question(s), reading the passage with your question(s) in mind, making predictions about answers, and checking your predictions. Questioning while you read test items improves the accuracy of your answers.

1. *Application/Reading Skills.* Sample answer: Are bananas yellow because they absorb (reflect, transmit) yellow light?
2. *Application/Reading Skills.* Sample answer: Why does something have a particular color?
3. *Application/Reading Skills.* Sample answer: How do transparent objects acquire color?

Chapter 1 Quiz

1. *Comprehension/Reading Skills.* (a), (b), (d).
2. *Comprehension/Reading Skills.* (1) Look at the title of the lesson; (2) Read the question that follows the title; (3) Glance at the lesson as a whole and notice its form. (Does it contain a list? a graph? a poem? a cartoon?) (4) Skim the lesson for prominent words and phrases: Are words repeated? in dark print? in labels? in captions? (5) Glance at the exercises for quick clues to form and topic. (how many? multiple choice? short answer? prominent words?)
3. *Comprehension/Reading Skills.* (a), (d).
4. *Application/Reading Skills.* After each chapter title is an objective that lists what you will find in the chapter.
5. *Application/Reading Skills.* There is always a lesson title followed by a question.
6. *Application/Reading Skills.* Five.
7. (2) *Application/Reading Skills.* The word *economics* is repeated throughout the lesson.
8. *Application/Reading Skills.* You would look at the question in Item 7.
9. *Comprehension/Reading Skills.* Other questions are those you might make up yourself.
10. (1) *Comprehension/Reading Skills.* Putting an idea into your own words often helps you understand and remember it.

Chapter 2 Reading for Answers

Lesson 1

The four levels of questions on the GED are comprehension, application, analysis, and evaluation. Recognizing the kind of thinking a question requires helps you identify the correct answer.

1. (2) *Comprehension/Reading Skills.* GED items will test your understanding and your ability to use and judge ideas.
2. *Comprehension/Reading Skills.* (1) d; (2) c; (3) b; (4) a.
3. *Comprehension/Reading Skills.* Knowing what a question asks you to do helps you to arrive at the best answer.

A-13

Lesson 2

Preview the passage and the item(s) following it. For each item, read the question, determine its type, reword it, and predict its answer, if possible. Read the passage to check your prediction(s), reconstruct the passage, reread the question(s), and select the best answer(s).

1. *Comprehension/Reading Skills.* Previewing: briefly looking at the organization of an item.
2. *Comprehension/Reading Skills.* If you read the question first and note its level, you have an idea of what information to look for as you read the passage or examine the graphic.
3. *Comprehension/Reading Skills.* (1) previewing; (2) questioning while reading; (3) reconstructing; (4) rereading.
4. **(3)** *Comprehension/Reading Skills.* Following the steps can take more time, but using them will help you get more answers correct.

Lesson 3

You can tell that an item is at the comprehension level if it asks you to restate an idea, summarize information, or identify an implication. To answer a comprehension item, predict the answer, read to check your prediction, and choose the best alternative.

1. **(3)** *Comprehension/Reading Skills.* Comprehension questions may also require you to restate an idea or to figure out implications.
2. **(3)** *Comprehension/Reading Skills.* Once you recognize a comprehension question, you should think about what the material means.
3. **(b); (c); (d).** *Comprehension/Reading Skills.* No GED items ask you simply to repeat facts. Items that ask you to judge whether statements are true are not comprehension items.
4. *Application/Reading Skills.* (A) Yes, you are asked to summarize the author's concern as it is expressed in the passage. (B) Sample answer: What bothers the author about current Disney movies is that they do not have ___. (C) **(2)** The point of the passage is that newer Disney productions fail to capture the "magic" (creativity) of the Disney classics.

Lesson 4

You can tell that an item is an application item if it asks you to use information in a new situation. Application items require you to comprehend and to transfer ideas to a new context.

1. **(4)** *Comprehension/Reading Skills.* Application questions require more than comprehension. Application items ask you to apply a principle to a new problem, choose a new situation that parallels one already described, or identify ideas that are or are not consistent with those already presented.
2. *Application/Reading Skills.* This is an application question.
3. *Application/Reading Skills.* This is a comprehension question.
4. *Analysis/Reading Skills.* (a) The wording *Which one of the following . . . would be most likely* asks you to apply your understanding of the table. (b) The table does not specifically mention the workers listed in the choices. (c) You should pay special attention to the *losers* section of the table. (d) You would use your background knowledge about what happens when people lose their jobs; such people need retraining for new jobs. You would also use your own understanding that "footwear" includes "shoes." (e) You would choose alternative (5) because the other choices list jobs that are either not mentioned in the table or are in industries that have gained jobs.

Lesson 5

You can tell that an item is an analysis item if it asks you to look at how different pieces of information or different ideas are related or organized. Comprehension questions require you to demonstrate that you understand information; analysis questions require you to see or to show how different parts of an idea are related or organized.

1. *Comprehension/Reading Skills.* Answers should resemble any *two* of the following:
Which of the statements is most likely based on facts (rather than on opinions or hypotheses)? Which of the statements is a conclusion (rather than a supporting statement)? Which of the following is an unstated assumption? How does the author's style relate to the effect of the writing? [for Interpreting Literature and the Arts, only]
2. *Application/Reading Skills* (1) comprehension; (2) application; (3) analysis. Each thinking level can require you to think at the previous level(s) as well.
3. **(4)** *Analysis/Reading Skills.* To answer this question you must distinguish Bryant's hypothesis from conclusions that are not his—(2) and (5)—and from facts, both correct (1) and incorrect (3).
4. *Application/Reading Skills.* You know that Item 3 is an analysis item because it asks you to distinguish a hypothesis from facts and conclusions.

Lesson 6

Evaluation items ask you to judge whether information or methods are accurate, valid, or effective. Evaluation questions are the only kind that require you to make a judgment.

1. **(3)** *Comprehension/Reading Skills.* Evaluation questions require you to judge the material provided, not to express your opinion of the material.
2. **(1)** *Comprehension/Reading Skills.* You will usually be asked to find the idea that is most accurate, clear, valid, or relevant based on the information you are given.
3. *Application/Reading Skills.* (1) d; (2) b; (3) a; (4) c
4. *Comprehension/Reading Skills.* (a) The question asks you to find the statement that is *best supported* by information in the graph. (b) *Analysis/Reading Skills.* Choice (3) is contradicted by the graph: immigration was highest between 1901 and 1910. (c) **(4)** *Evaluation/Reading Skills.* The graph shows that the number of immigrants has risen during each of the past several decades. Since immigrants, like everyone else, need jobs, the information supports the idea that more immigrants mean more job competition.

Lesson 7

To answer any item, follow all the steps for active reading. With nonmultiple-choice items, pay special

UNIT III: READING STRATEGIES   Ch. 2, Lesson 8—Ch. 3, Lesson 2   A-15

attention to the form of the question and the kind of answer that it requires. With multiple-choice questions, concentrate on predicting the correct answer and look for your prediction among the choices.

1. *Comprehension/Reading Skills.* The diagram on the left shows thermal energy being reflected from a planet without atmosphere. The diagram on the right shows thermal energy being reflected and some remaining near a planet with atmosphere.
2. **(1); (2); and (3).**
   Evaluation/Reading Skills. You can eliminate (1) because the arrow representing reflected light is the same in both diagrams. Since you know Earth is a planet you can eliminate (2); the diagram on the left shows the planet without atmosphere losing its thermal energy. You can eliminate (3) because the amount of sunlight hitting the planet is the same in both diagrams.
3. **(5)** *Evaluation/Reading Skills.* The diagrams say nothing about thermal energy near the sun.
4. *Comprehension/Reading Skills.* Planet. You need to know that Earth is a planet so that you can apply the information in the diagrams to what happens on Earth.

Lesson 8

You should use the Answer Key to check your answers in order to reward yourself for correct answers or to get help in figuring out what mistakes you made if you provided incorrect answers.

1. **(5)** *Comprehension/Reading Skills.* Answer Key entries for short-answer questions contain the level of the question, a short answer, and an explanation.
2. *Comprehension/Reading Skills.* Evaluation is the skill required for answering those items.
3. *Application/Reading Skills.* If you missed several evaluation questions, you should review Lesson 6 in Chapter 2.

Chapter 2   Quiz

1. *Analysis/Reading Skills.* Like previous chapters, Chapter 3 contains an objective, lessons, lesson exercises, and a chapter quiz.
2. *Comprehension/Reading Skills.* Sample answer: In what ways was the South different as a result of this invention?
3. *Comprehension/Reading Skills.* (a) true; (b) true; (c) false [60% of the literature and the arts items will be comprehension questions.]; (d) false [All four levels of questions are found in this book.]
4. (a) *Comprehension/Reading Skills.* After the preview, read while questioning. (b) *Application/Reading Skills.* You could draw a sketch of the brain and label its parts. (c) *Comprehension/Reading Skills.* Reconstructing such a passage would help you understand and remember what and where parts of the brain are.
5. *Comprehension/Reading Skills.* a. **(2)** b. In the "Population Density" column you find that the U.S. has 60 people per square mile and that Japan has 793.
6. a. **(4)** *Application/Reading Skills.* Viscous. b. *Comprehension/Reading Skills.* Glass; maple syrup.
7. *Comprehension/Reading Skills.* The entry for a multiple-choice item tells which of the five choices is correct. The entry for a nonmultiple-choice item is in whatever form the directions require: short answer, sentence, paragraph, diagram, or other form.
8. *Analysis/Reading Skills.* Except for the composition in the Writing Skills section, GED items are in multiple-choice format.
9. **(4)** *Application/Reading Skills/Analysis.* Sample explanation: The phrase *a certain age* indicates that the speaker is elderly.
10. *Application/Reading Skills.* Answers will vary.

Chapter 3   The Three "Reading Tests"

Lesson 1

1. *Comprehension/Reading Skills.* Only one item, Item 31, is based on the passage.
2. *Comprehension/Reading Skills.* Blood pressure. The phrase *blood pressure* is repeated throughout the passage and item.
3. *Comprehension/Reading Skills.* Two
4. *Application/Reading Skills.* Sample wording: Why does your body have to maintain fluid balance?
5. *Application/Reading Skills.* Sample answer: Suppose a doctor discovered that several patients had high blood pressure even after going on a salt-free diet. If the doctor were to give them medicine, what effect would be desired?
6. *Analysis/Reading Skills.* You need to understand the relationships between fluid, blood pressure, excretion, and salt. You are asked to supply a cause, given the desired effect of reducing blood pressure.
7. *Analysis/Reading Skills.* Three; (1) is wrong because eating salt can raise blood pressure. Since the patients whose blood pressure remains high have been on a salt-free diet already, (2) would not work. If patients urinated or sweated less, (3) and (4), their bodies would hold fluids, and their blood pressures would rise further.

Lesson 2

The steps in reading test items are previewing, questioning, reconstructing, choosing an answer, and reviewing the choice.

1. **(1)** *Application/Reading Skills.* An elevator is a small, enclosed space.
2. **(2)** *Application/Reading Skills.* Standing on a chair is standing at a height.
3. *Comprehension/Reading Skills.* Sample answer: "Some Statistics About Central America"
4. *Comprehension/Reading Skills.* The "Population" column gives the total population of each country and the percentage of the population living in rural areas.
5. *Comprehension/Reading Skills.* El Salvador has a per capita annual income of $750.
6. *Comprehension/Reading Skills.* False. You must read the column heading carefully. Fifty-nine percent of the people in El Salvador are illiterate, unable to read or write.
7. *Comprehension/Reading Skills.* Costa Ricans have the highest per capita income and longest life

expectancy of those shown on the chart.

Lesson 3

Because there are so few words in most graphic material, it is important to pay close attention to them. Comprehending a graphic requires that you first understand it as whole and that you then concentrate on a small piece of information.

1. **(5)** *Literal Comprehension, Specific/Reading Skills.* The evidence is in line 4.
2. **(2)** *Literal Comprehension, Global/Reading Skills.* The evidence is in lines 7, 14–15.
3. **(2)** *Inferential Comprehension, Specific/Reading Skills.* The main evidence is in lines 12–13.
4. **(1)** *Inferential Comprehension, Global/Reading Skills.* Even though why the man laughs is never explained, each time he laughs he refers to the fact that the narrator is a beginner.
5. *Literal Comprehension, Specific/Reading Skills.* The evidence is in line 4.

7. *Analysis/Reading Skills.* Capital letters show who is speaking. Words in italics tell what the speakers are doing.
8. **(4)** *Inferential Comprehension, Global/Reading Skills.* Evidence from the whole passage provides clues.
9. **(5)** *Application/Reading Skills.* To explain *why* a certain line in literature is effective, you must analyze it. To be able to analyze it, you must first comprehend what it means.
10. *Comprehension/Reading Skills.* It is easier and faster to look for your prediction among the alternatives than it is to have to narrow down five choices to one.

Chapter 3 Quiz

On the literature test there are four kinds of comprehension items; application items often require applying a point of view; analysis items require looking at how a writer conveys ideas. There are no evaluation questions.

1. *Comprehension/Reading Skills.* Air pollutants.
2. *Comprehension/Reading Skills.* Sample wording: occur in the concentrations of air pollutants as time passes?
3. *Comprehension/Reading Skills.* Air pollutants are measured in parts per million parts of air.
4. *Comprehension/Reading Skills.* The time period shown runs from 5 A.M. to 10 P.M., in one-hour segments.
5. *Comprehension/Reading Skills.* A rise shows an increase in the concentration of air pollutants as time passes. A fall shows a decrease. A level line shows a constant concentration.
6. Lines should connect archeologist, past, and other societies; anthropologist, present, and other societies; and sociologist, present, and own society.

UNIT IV Social Studies

Chapter 1
Introduction

Lesson 1

Social studies includes history, geography, economics, political science, and behavioral science. These different fields are related in that they all deal with aspects of people and society.

1. *(4) Application.* Nutrition is the concern of the biologial sciences.
2. *Application.* (1) History of Political Science (2) Geography (3) Economics (5) Psychology.
3. *Analysis.* People who study history often do so to learn how past events can help them understand and perhaps solve present-day and future situations.
4. *Application.* This type of analysis would belong in anthropology.

Lesson 2

Some types of graphs are circle graphs, bar graphs, and line graphs.

1. *Comprehension.* The approximate production was 23 million barrels per day.
2. *Analysis.* Oil production declined.
3. *Comprehension.* The average income is $21,000 per year.
4. *Analysis.* The graph seems to indicate that more education leads to higher salaries.

Chapter 1 Quiz

1. *Comprehension.* Psychology is the study of the mind, sociology is the study of people within society, and anthropology is the study of the history of a culture. These are all behavioral sciences.
2. *Analysis.* Economics and political science often affect each other. For example, imports and exports of consumer goods are often controlled by government policy.
3. *Analysis.* The physical geography of a country can affect its economy. For example, in a mountainous area with low annual rainfall, farming is difficult. (Answer might also mention the need for irrigation to aid farmers.)
4. *Application.* This report might involve all branches of social studies. History, behavioral science (anthropology and sociology), and cultural geography would almost certainly be involved. Some content on political and economic systems is probably likely as well.
5. *Application.* (a) history, political science (b) behavioral science (psychology, sociology) (c) sociology, economics
6. *Comprehension.* The size of each portion reflects the percentage of each category. The portions that represent equal percentages (38%) are the same size.
7. *Evaluation.* No, it cannot. The graph shows energy uses but gives no information about energy waste.
8. *Comprehension.* The time line covers the years from 1776 to 1830.
9. *(1) Application.* The timeline shows when nine different nations were established in South America. The timeline begins after the seventeenth century, so it is not useful for topic (2) or topic (3).
10. *Analysis.* The fight for independence of the Spanish and Portuguese colonies in South America came soon after the American and French revolutions. The time line suggests, that the fight for equality and freedom of the Americans and the French similarly inspired the colonists in South America.

Chapter 2 American History

Lesson 1

The New England Town meeting in government and the emphasis on individualism in daily life exemplified the influence of the desire for freedom.

1. *(4) Comprehension.* These people came to the New World, above all, to find religious freedom.
2. *Comprehension.* In the Mayflower Compact the Pilgrims agreed to self-government and majority rule in the Plymouth Colony.
3. *Analysis.* Individualism is in evidence in many ways—especially, perhaps, in our acceptance of the individual's right to decide on a career, to choose to worship or not worship, and generally to live as he or she wants as long as the rights of others are not adversely affected.

Lesson 2

The inadequecies of the Articles of Confederation—made evident, for example, by Shays' Rebellion—prompted the states to adopt a stronger central government.

1. *Analysis.* Britain's participation in the French and Indian War created a large war debt. The British government taxed the colonies to pay off the debt. To show their displeasure, the colonists dumped shiploads of tea, which was heavily taxed, into Boston Harbor.
2. *Analysis.* Each state would tax the others' products to make its own locally-produced products more attractive. This could lead to friction between states because each could try to block the others' imports.
3. *Analysis.* The plan to have the same number of representatives from each state would have been unfair to the largest states, which would have been under-represented given the greater size of their populations. The plan to have representation based on population would have been unfair to the small states, which would

A-17

have had a lesser voice in government. The compromise adopted was to have two houses of Congress, each reflecting one of the plans.

Lesson 3

With economic growth, the North and the South developed along different lines and therefore had different needs and different stances on issues. Territorial expansion repeatedly raised the issue of whether or not slavery should be extended. Sectionalism intensified until the South seceded and the war began.

1. *(3) Application.* This situation can be similar to sectionalism, in that each group has different interests and seeks to further those interests.
2. *Analysis.* Natural resources can influence the development of a region. The South had better cropland and a mild climate, so its economy was agricultural. The North developed an economy based on manufacturing and shipping, making use of water power from its rivers and the natural harbors along its coast.
3. *Comprehension.* The South seceded from the Union because it felt, especially with the election of Abraham Lincoln in 1860, that its interests were no longer represented by the federal government.

Lesson 4

As jobs in industry became more plentiful, many people left the rural areas and moved to the cities.

1. *Comprehension.* (a) State legislation that legalized segregation.
(b) A farmer who works another farmer's land for a portion of the crops.
(c) An organization to help farmers get reforms.
(d) Advances in technology and the resulting increases in industrial production.
(e) A worker's organization formed to protect employees from mistreatment.

2. *Comprehension.* Southern blacks gained very little in terms of racial equality and generally worked as sharecroppers.
3. *Comprehension.* The United States became a more urban nation because the technological advances of the Industrial Revolution created factory jobs in cities. These jobs attracted foreign immigrants and American farmers.
4. *Application.* Like migrant workers today, immigrants (1880–1910) received low wages and often worked under poor conditions.

Lesson 5

During the first half of the twentieth century, the Progressive Movement and New Deal legislation significantly improved the life of Americans. Laws were passed to, among other things, eliminate monopolies, protect consumers, and stabilize the economy.

1. *Comprehension.* (1)-(c), (2)-(a), (3)-(e), (4)-(b), (5)-(d).
2. *Comprehension.* (a) assist
(b) prevent
(c) assist
(d) assist

Lesson 6

During the first half of this century, American foreign policy alternated between isolationism and internationalism.

1. *Comprehension.* (1)-(c), (2)-(a), (3)-(b).
2. *Comprehension.* The United States entered World War I when Germany sank unarmed American ships.
3. *Analysis.* United States isolationism of the 1930s, together with the European policy of appeasement, allowed the Axis powers to absorb neighboring countries and expand the scope of their aggressions.

Lesson 7

The United States tried to counteract the Soviet expansion policy by providing aid to countries threatened by Communism.

1. *Comprehension.* The purpose of NATO is to provide the United States and Western Europe with a common military defense against the Soviet Union and its allies.
2. *Comprehension.* The containment doctrine seeks to block Soviet expansion.
3. *Comprehension.* Relations during the cold war involved superpower confrontation while relations during periods of detente show superpower cooperation.

Lesson 8

Issues the United States has faced have included civil rights, poverty, abuse of power, environmental quality, space exploration, and inflation.

1. *Comprehension.* The first piece of legislation promoting integration in the United States after World War II was the Civil Rights Act of 1964.
2. *Application.* The Watergate scandal, including the cover-up attempted by the executive branch, made many people concerned about central government's abuse of power.
3. *Evaluation.* Pioneers faced dangers from illness, hostile Indians, and natural disasters. Although the territory they explored was less different from their environment, they lacked the modern technological means of navigation and communications that present-day astronauts have. Essentially the astronauts and pioneers both faced the challenges of the unknown.

Chapter 2 Quiz

1. *Application.* The Pilgrims would not have agreed. They had to leave England in order to be individuals; that is, to practice their religion freely.
2. *Comprehension.* Federalists wanted a strong central government and supported the Constitution; anti-Federalists feared a strong central government and initially opposed the Constitution.
3. *Analysis.* The compromises in the development of the Constitution created a strong central government but did not give it complete power. The states kept certain powers, and the provision for states' representation in the federal government assured a balance of control.
4. *Analysis.* TRUE. The South seceded from the Union because differences between the regions had grown throughout the nineteenth century to the point that, when Lincoln was elected president, the South felt its interests were no longer represented by the federal government. Slavery was only one of the issues on which the North and South differed, and debate had centered on the extension of slavery into new territories, not on its existence per se.
5. (3) *Comprehension.* The main point of the passage is the effect of Ida Tarbell's writings. The other choices give details rather than the main idea.
6. (2) *Evaluation.* The passage mentions that Ida Tarbell wrote about the practices and methods of such monopolies as the Standard Oil Trust Company. The other choices go beyond what can be concluded from the passage.
7. (4) *Analysis.* Unfair railroad rates for small companies constituted an abuse specifically described in the passage. The other choices do not relate to abuses mentioned.
8. *Analysis.* Farms were ruined and could not produce enough food for the millions who were going hungry. Also, farmers who left their land often went to the cities, which were already overburdened with unemployed workers.
9. *Comprehension.* To free Cuba from Spanish rule to protect American interests in Cuba.
10. *Comprehension.* Civil rights legislation was needed in the 1960s because of continuing racial injustices and discrimination in areas such as employment, voting, and housing.

Chapter 3
Geography

Lesson 1

Physical geography and cultural geography are two major fields in the study of geography.

1. (2) *Comprehension.* All the other alternatives refer to physical geography. Alternative (2) refers to cultural geography.
2. *Application. Migration*—the movement of people from one area to another.
3. *Analysis.* Because Austin has the lowest population density, it could probably handle a surge in population. Based on the graph, Baltimore, with the highest density, would probably be least able to absorb a population increase.
4. *Evaluation.* FALSE. The population density of an area gives no indication of the ethnic composition of the area.

Lesson 2

The types of temperate climates are marine, continental, and highlands.

1. *Analysis.* One day's weather conditions is not always indicative of the climate. The Barnetts should have visited the area a few times and studied weather patterns in the area to get an overall idea of the climate, rather than a brief picture of the weather.
2. *Comprehension.* Climate depends on temperature, wind, and precipitation over a long period of time. Climates differ mostly according to the amount of heat they get from the sun.
3. *Comprehension.* (a) polar—B,F (least direct rays) (b) tropical—A,D (most direct rays) (c) temperate—C,E (moderate amount of rays)
4. *Application.* (a) Winnipeg, Manitoba—continental temperate (b) Vancouver, British Columbia—marine temperate

Lesson 3

The earth has two types of natural resources: renewable resources—those that can be replaced—and nonrenewable resources—those that cannot be replaced.

1. (3) *Comprehension.* The natural supplies of metal ores cannot be replaced once they are depleted; they are nonrenewable.
2. *Analysis.* Fish are a renewable resource if handled properly. If too many fish are caught, they cannot reproduce and eventually the supply vanishes. This affects the fishing industry, processing plants, the trucking companies in the area, as well as other related industries. Also, if the waterways are not kept clean, the fish become poisoned or die off completely, which in turn wipes out the fishing and dependent industries.
3. *Analysis.* Hydroelectric power uses a renewable resources—water. Fossil fuels such as coal, ore, and natural gas are nonrenewable. If energy use becomes too great, the supplies of these fuels will disappear.
4. (2) *Evaluation.* The last paragraph mentions the dangers of some chemical pesticides. These pesticides not only kill insects but they also seep into the soil and can become mixed in with the underground water supply. Natural methods of farming and pest control avoid many of the dangers involved in using these harmful chemicals.

Chapter 3 Quiz

1. *Comprehension.* (a) cultural geography (b) physical geography (c) cultural geography
2. *Application.* Regions around seaports usually have dense populations because seaports are centers of trade and commerce. In agricultural regions, since most of the land is used for growing crops, populations are less dense.
3. *Comprehension.* Dry weather is a short period, such as a few days, without rain or snow. A dry climate is one in which there is little precipitation over a period of many years.
4. *Analysis.* The climate of an area depends on sunlight, temperature,

wind, and precipitation. An area that has moderate temperature would be conducive to physical activity. Areas that have extreme weather conditions can hinder physical activity.
5. *Analysis.* FALSE. The equatorial areas have very little seasonal change because the angle of the sun's rays remains the same throughout the year; it is always hot. The temperate climates have four distinct seasons.
6. *Comprehension.* Pierre is closest to 44° north latitude, 100° west longitude.
7. *Application.* By looking at this map, a researcher would note the large areas set aside as Indian reservations. This would indicate a great potential for interaction between the Indian population and the other residents.
8. *Evaluation.* FALSE. Even though large areas of South Dakota are reservations, the map gives no information about population. Land size does not automatically relate to population size.
9. *Analysis.* Once nonrenewable resources are used up, they are gone forever. This would affect all aspects of our lives, for example, transportation, home life, food production. By finding substitutes for these resources, we can help preserve them and maintain our lives once the supplies are gone.
10. *Analysis.* Each part of the environment depends on the others. If the waters are polluted by industrial waste, the water plants die. Then the fish die or are poisoned. Birds eat the poisoned fish and become poisoned themselves. All this has an effect on our food and water supply. Industry benefits us by producing consumer goods, but it must also help by protecting the environment.

Chapter 4
Economics

Lesson 1

Under communism, government owns all businesses and makes all production decisions. The government controls some basic industries and public utilities in socialist countries. Under capitalism, the government involvement in the economy is considerably more limited.

1. *Application.* Wealth would be most unevenly distributed under a capitalist system since the government's regulation of production and wages is very limited.
2. **(3)** *Comprehension.* A communist government would be the most likely to set wages for workers since communism is the most tightly regulated of the three types of economic systems.
3. *Analysis.* The regulation of industries that produce food and drugs is important to protect the public from products that might not meet standards of quality or safety.
4. *Analysis.* The profit motive operates most strongly in a capitalist economic system since businesses may produce and charge what they want. Since production, prices, and wages are not subject to many regulations, businesses compete with one another to make the greatest profit.

Lesson 2

Generally, the demand for a product increases when the price goes down, and the demand decreases when the price goes up.

1. *Comprehension.* The demand for hand calculators is elastic if a decrease in price results in an increase in demand.
2. **(3)** *Application.* Consumers will probably buy more meat products other than beef in response to the increased cost of beef.
3. *Analysis.* Making certain standard features optional would enable the automobile maker to reduce its production costs. Eliminating some standard features might not have the same negative effect on demand that an increase in prices would have.

Lesson 3

Natural resources, labor, and capital are needed to operate any business.

1. *Comprehension.* (1)-(b), (2)-(d), (3)-(c), (4)-(a).
2. *Analysis.* A society that is not highly industrialized would require more labor to produce its goods than a highly industrialized society. Industrialized societies have more capital in the way of machinery and tools to produce goods.
3. **(2)** *Comprehension.* Since capital is equipment or machinery used by businesses to produce their products, bakery ovens are considered capital.
4. *Comprehension.* Stockholders in a corporation receive dividends from the corporation.

Lesson 4

Personal income taxes and social security taxes are the government's main sources of revenue.

1. *Analysis.* (1)-(c), (2)-(b), (3)-(a), (4)-(d).
2. *Analysis.* The state can borrow money by selling bonds; it can increase income taxes or other types of taxes; or it can reduce spending in other areas to permit the construction of new schools.
3. *Evaluation.* No, the argument is not valid. As the government continues to borrow money, the interest it owes increases. Eventually, interest payments would be so great that the government would be unable to finance its operations.

Lesson 5

The Federal Reserve Bank can increase interest rates during inflationary periods. Raising interest rates makes it more difficult for businesses and industries to borrow money, and thus the supply of money decreases.

1. *Analysis.* TRUE. Lowering interest rates would make it easier for businesses to borrow money. If businesses and individuals have more money to spend, production and consumption of goods increase.
2. *Comprehension.* The Gross National Product is the value of all goods and services produced in one year. The Consumer Price Index is the average price of essential goods and services.
3. **(2)** *Evaluation.* Although the graph shows a steady increase in the Gross National Product, it is

UNIT IV: SOCIAL STUDIES — Ch 4, Lesson 6—Ch 5, Lesson 2 — A-21

invalid to assume the GNP can never decrease (choice 1). Similarly, one cannot use the data to predict the GNP in the year 2000 (choice 3).

4. *Application.* Since the value of money decreases during inflationary periods, the value of money put aside in savings accounts decreases over time. As prices go up, savers will be able to buy fewer items with their savings than when they first earned the money.

Lesson 6

Countries sometimes have to take measures to create a protected market if imports threaten domestic industries.

1. **(1)** *Application.* The only action that would not affect trade is choice 1. Choice 2 would affect trade by making imported television sets less attractive economically. An increase in the price of automobiles made in the U.S. (choice 3) could cause both a decrease in exports and an increase in imports. An increase in domestic oil production (choice 5) would result in a decrease in the amount of oil the United States needs to import.
2. *Comprehension.* The regution of foreign trade is necessary to protect national economies. Completely unrestricted trade would make certain industries especially vulnerable to competition from foreign countries.
3. *Application.* Country B would raise the tariff on the product coming from Country A so that it would not be more desirable than the homemade product.

Chapter 4   Quiz

1. *Application.* The company can lower the price of its product to encourage more consumers to buy it.
2. *Comprehension.* The federal government can increase taxes or reduce spending to reduce the size of its debt.
3. **(b)**, **(c)**, and **(d)** *Comprehension.*

Providing low-cost loans to workforce. Public works projects provide employment for people. By lowering the amount of cash reserves that banks must keep on hand, more money is available for loans.

4. **(3)** *Analysis.* People who live on fixed incomes would be most hurt economically by inflation since the value of money decreases over time.
5. *Analysis.* A protected market is created when tariffs are imposed on imported goods. Manufacturers at home generally favor protected markets because they limit competition from foreign industries. Consumers, on the other hand, benefit from free markets since the choice of available goods is greater.
6. *Analysis.* Because demand will be high, farmers should be able to obtain their price without payments from the government. These should no longer be necessary.
7. *Comprehension.* Under communism, industries are owned by the government and production decisions are made by the government. In socialist economies, individuals own many businesses, but the government exercises a great deal of control in basic industries. Under capitalism, individuals own and operate most businesses.
8. **(1)** *Application.* Since machinery, tools, and equipment are capital, hospitals that join in the purchase of medical equipment do so to save capital expenses.
9. *Analysis.* Australia, New Guinea, and New Zealand; Asia; the United States and Canada; and Europe must import petroleum from other regions since their consumption is greater than their production.
10. *Evaluation.* Although it can be reasonably inferred from the graph that the export of petroleum is an important source of revenue for the Middle East, a projection about future revenues cannot be made. It is possible that other regions of the world could find or develop new petroleum deposits, which would reduce the exports from the Middle East. In the long run, the Middle East will not be able to depend on petroleum since the world's supply of this natural resource is limited.

Chapter 5   Political Science

Lesson 1

The Declaration of Independence expresses a belief in the basic equality of all individuals and the rights of every individual to "life, liberty, and the pursuit of happiness."

1. *Comprehension.* (1)-(b), (2)-(d), (3)-(c), (4)-(a).
2. *Application.* The actions of the English Parliament established a constitutional monarchy. Although England continued to be ruled by monarchs, Parliament put limits on the power of the English monarchy.
3. **(2)** *Application.* In a representative democracy, citizens express their approval or disapproval of government through the process of elections.

Lesson 2

A bicameral congress was established as a compromise between conflicting opinions about representation in the federal government. In the House of Representatives, representation is determined by state population; in the Senate, the states are equally represented.

1. *Comprehension.* In 1974, the House of Representatives' Judiciary Committee voted to recommend three articles of impeachment against Richard Nixon. By this action, the legislative branch of government was checking the executive branch of government.
2. *Comprehension.* Under the Articles of Confederation, the central government could not make laws without the approval of all the states, nor could it intervene in disputes between states. The lack of a President or a national court system was also a limitation.
3. *Analysis.* If representation were determined only according to

Lesson 3

The federal system provides for the sharing of power between the federal government and the states by delegating specific powers to the federal government, granting reserved power to the states, and assigning concurrent powers to both the federal and state governments.

1. *Application.* (1)-(a), (2)-(c), (3)-(b).
2. *Comprehension.* Before a proposed amendment to the Constitution can become law, it must be passed by Congress and ratified by three fourths of the state legislatures.
3. **(2)** *Application.* A state's right to regulate commerce within its borders is a reserved power.

Lesson 4

While the President is elected through the electoral college, representatives and senators are elected directly by popular vote. The President is elected to a four-year term. Representatives are elected to two-year terms; senators are elected to six-year terms.

1. *Application.* In a representative democracy, citizens choose representatives rather than participate directly in government. Primary elections illustrate representative democracy in that people elect delegates to vote for presidential candidates rather than voting directly for the candidates.
2. **(2)** *Comprehension.* The House of Representatives selects the President if no candidate wins a majority of electoral votes.
3. *Analysis.* As the ratio of a state's population to the nation's population changes, a state gains or loses representatives in the House of Representatives.

percentage of the overall population, heavily populated states would have a greater voice than states with small populations. If representation were equal for all states regardless of size, heavily populated states, which contribute more proportionally to the nation as a whole, would be under-represented. The bicameral system fairly represents both small states and large ones.

Chapter 5 Quiz

1. **(2)** *Evaluation.* Choice (1) is incorrect because history has shown that the original Constitution was not perfect. Choices (3) and (4) are both true, but they are examples of, not reasons for, the strict requirements. Choice (5) is a true statement that has no bearing on the question.
2. *Comprehension.* A form of government in which one person or a small group of people has total authority is called a dictatorship (or totalitarian).
3. *Analysis.* Because the United States has a large population, representative democracy is the only workable form of democracy. Direct democracy is only feasible if a political unit is small enough to permit all citizens or voters to meet together to make decisions.
4. *Application.* Like the Federalists, the Democratic party prefers a strong central government. Like the anti-Federalists, the Republican party promotes states' rights.
5. *Analysis.* In the House of Representatives, the votes of the people count more directly since representation is apportioned by state population. Since each state has an equal number of senators, on the other hand, the Senate as a body is more concerned with national interests than with representing popular opinion. The fact that senators are elected to a longer term of office (six years) than representatives (two years) enables them to shape programs and policies of long-range interest.
6. *Analysis.* No. Reagan received 59% of the popular vote in 1984. Because he had a majority of the popular vote in 49 states, all the electors from those states cast their ballots for Reagan in the electoral college.
7. *Evaluation.* Since the amendment was proposed, it is possible that two-thirds of the state legislatures approved the proposal. Since it was not ratified, less than three-fourths of the state legislatures approved ratification.
8. **(1)** *Application.* Delegated powers are those powers that are specifically assigned to the federal government.
9. *Comprehension.* (a) J, (b) E, (c) L, (d) L, (e) E, (f) J, (g) E, (h) L, (i) L.
10. *Analysis.* The administration of public school systems is one of the reserved powers of the states. In its 1954 decision, the Supreme Court ruled that the federal guarantee of equal protection under the law was more important than the states' autonomy in the area of education.

Chapter 6
Behavioral Science

Lesson 1

The three behavioral sciences are psychology, the study of individual behavior; sociology, the study of group behavior; and anthropolgy, the study of different cultures.

1. *Comprehension.* (a) behavioral sciences (b) behavior (c) psychology, sociology, anthropology
2. *Application.* (a) psychology (b) anthropology (c) sociology (d) psychology
3. *Application.* The psychologist is compiling a case study. This type of research is used when a great deal of specific, detailed information is needed about a person.
4. *Analysis.* The variable that was different between the groups was probably size of family.

Lesson 2

Operant conditioning uses reinforcement—either positive or negative—to teach behavior and the consequences of certain behavior.

1. *Application.* (a) This is an example of classical conditioning. (b) Counter-conditioning can be used to help people change undesirable behavior, such as overeating.

UNIT IV: SOCIAL STUDIES   Ch 6, Lesson 2—Chapter 6 Quiz   A-23

2. *Application.* **(2)** This is an example of punishment.
3. *Comprehension.* FALSE. Some behavior, such as coughing, is an automatic response to a stimulus. This type of automatic behavior is called a reflex and is not learned.
4. *Comprehension.* B. F. Skinner used the method of conditioning that depended on rewarding desirable behavior. Rewarding is similar to positive reinforcement.

Lesson 3

Sociologists often try to learn about how a society is structured, how its members behave toward one another, what rules they follow, and what changes occur over time.

1. *Comprehension.* **(2)** Heredity is the genetic transmission of characteristics and not part of the process of socialization. Family, school, and television all expose the individual to the society's norms.
2. *Comprehension.* (a) social interaction (b) status (c) social institutions (d) deviant behavior
3. *Application.* Three possible role expectations for parents might be affection, fairness, and guidance.
4. *Application.* (a) *Norm:* applauding after a performance; *Deviant:* applauding at a funeral (b) *Norm:* laughing at a humorous passage in a book; *Deviant:* laughing at a handicapped person (c) *Norm:* wearing a coat during a blizzard; *Deviant:* wearing a coat in a swimming pool

Lesson 4

Types of interaction that take place within a group include conflict, competition, cooperation, and accommodation.

1. *Application.* (a) This situation involves competition. Many are trying for a goal that only one can achieve. (b) This situation involves cooperation. Both parties are contributing to a shared goal (c) This is an example of accommodation. Both parties give up something to attain a mutual goal.
2. *Comprehension.* Recurrent groups are groups that are fairly constant, such as the local chapter of the Red Cross or a board of directors. Transitory groups only come together once such as a group at a block party or people on an airplane.
3. *Application.* (a) P, (b) S, (c) P, (d) S. Brothers and sisters are part of a family with whom an individual has continuous contact and deep relationships. No brother or sister can be replaced. In a similar way, especially for some adolescents, a gang functions like a family with continuous, close contact among members. A class or a team, however, is a temporary, loosely connected group whose members can be replaced.

Lesson 5

Physical anthropology studies the physical characteristics of humans and human evolution and adaptation. Cultural anthropology studies human cultures as they exist today and as they developed over time.

1. *Application.* Cultural; physical.
2. *Comprehension.* (a) cultural diffusion (b) clan (c) taboo
3. *Analysis.* The Chinatown community can be called a subculture because it has its own cultural features—its own rituals, taboos, and accepted behaviors—in addition to those in general American society.
4. *Application.* (a), (c), and (d) are examples of rituals in our society. The other behaviors either promote good health or are a one-time response to a special situation.

Chapter 6   Quiz

1. *Application.* This type of research is called a controlled experiment. Possible characteristics are economic background, living conditions, one- or two-parent family.
2. *Application.* Both positive reinforcement and negative reinforcement are types of operant conditioning. An example of positive reinforcement would be a bonus for one month of perfect attendance. An example of negative reinforcement would be a stern warning from a supervisor in the case of repeated lateness.
3. *Analysis.* A sociologist would say that Anita is experiencing role conflict. Conflicting expectations are associated with her role as a friend and her role as an employee.
4. *Comprehension.* FALSE. Proper socialization teaches us how to conform to and live within society's rules. Deviant behavior strays from the norm; therefore, it can't be called the result of proper socialization.
5. *Evaluation.* The values of immigrant parents usually are retained when they come to the United States. These values may often differ from American values. The American-born children of these parents learn the values of their own peers, which often conflict with the "old-country" ways.
6. *Comprehension.* **(4)** The other choices are all part of anthropology.
7. *Evaluation.* FALSE. No set pattern is shown in the graph; therefore, no predictions can be made; more information is needed.
8. *Application.* The graph shows that during the period studied there was a significant drop in the number of those below poverty level. The sociologist might want to see whether the change in the graph was associated with improved morale
9. *Analysis.* **(2)** In this way, smoking (an undesirable learned behavior) is associated with feeling ill (unpleasantness).
10. *Analysis.* The cities of the United States have many cultures represented in them. The habits and customs of these different cultures become familiar to all residents of the cities and become part of their daily lives. For example, consider how common such foods as pizza, tacos, and egg rolls have become.

UNIT V Science

Chapter 1
Introduction

Lesson 1

Science is the body of knowledge about every natural phenomenon. It includes the nature and the behavior of matter and energy in all forms and locations. The word also means the methods and the procedures by which this knowledge is obtained. Scientists study natural phenomena in order to add to our knowledge of them.

1. *Comprehension/Science.* Phenomena are facts or events perceived by the senses.
2. *Application/Science.* (1) *Earth Science.* Mountains are part of the structure of Earth. (2) *Physics.* Light is a form of energy. (3) *Biology.* Living things pass traits on to descendants. (4) *Chemistry.* Such study is about the composition of and the interactions in matter. (5) *Biology and Chemistry.* This is an example of the overlapping of two areas. There is a branch of science known as *biochemistry.*

Lesson 2

Scientists test scientific ideas by making observations and by performing experiments. Mathematics is used in much of their work.

1. *Application/Science.* In dealing with such large numbers, the biologist had to use *statistics*. Because 15 of 100 do not make it, each bird's probability of safe arrival is 85 percent. On the basis of the data, the conclusion is valid.
2. *Analysis/Science.* The "if" part of the statement is the hypothesis: *If there is a tenth planet in the solar system*. The "then" part is the prediction: *then the orbits of some of the other planets will be affected by it.*
3. *Evaluation/Science.* In order to flower, this plant needs the amount of sunlight it receives in late spring and early summer. It will not flower in less sunlight or more sunlight than that.

Lesson 3

Scientists prove the validity of their work by conducting experiments that are repeatable. They test only one variable at a time and use controls in their experiments.

1. *Comprehension/Science.* Repeatability is the production of the results by separate, identical experiments. A variable is the condition that is changed in an experiment to determine the effect of the change. Controls are the factors that remain constant throughout an experiment.
2. *Evaluation/Science.* The hypothesis should be considered to have been refuted, at least temporarily, because several repetitions failed to confirm the first results.
3. *Application/Science.* He changed two conditions at once—temperature and ingredients.
4. *Application/Science.* Put wet tea leaves on the soil of five of the plants but not on the others. In all other ways, treat all the plants exactly alike.

Lesson 4

A scientific fact is a conclusion supported by the best evidence now available.

1. *Comprehension/Science.* Part A presents the ancient, Earth-centered view. The planets, the moon, and the sun were believed to orbit Earth. Part B shows the solar system according to current knowledge.
2. *Application/Science.* (1) is not a fact: there are not enough data to support any conclusion. (2) is not a fact and is actually a false statement. (3) and (4) are facts supported by data from experiments.
3. **(3)** *Evaluation/Science.* A prediction may be based on a hypothesis rather than on scientific facts. The identification of scientific facts may be based on new evidence, observation, or experimentation (which includes repeatability).
4. *Analysis/Science.* The use of instruments greatly improves a scientist's powers of observation and measurement, giving a more complete picture.

Chapter 1 Quiz

1. *Comprehension/Science.* The steps in the scientific method are observation, hypothesis, experimentation, gathering evidence, conclusion.
2. *Application/Science.* **A.** *Physics.* This is an example of energy acting on matter. **B.** *Biology.* This is an example of the functions of living things. **C.** *Chemistry.* This is an example of the interactions in matter.
3. *Analysis/Science.* In **B** and **C**, something is caused to happen to see what the results will be; so these are experiments. **A** and **D** are observations because things and processes are being looked at, not changed or caused.
4. *Analysis/Science.* New evidence may come along to cast doubt on any scientific theory, no matter how long held or how well established. All scientific knowledge is, in this sense, temporary.
5. *Comprehension/Science.* The chart shows that wheat and oats were the most affected.
6. *Analysis/Science.* Alfalfa—the chart shows large variations from one soil to another. But within each soil type, the differences based on the fertilizer are small.
7. *Application/Science.* The output of corn varies very little with either the soil or the fertilizer.
8. *Evaluation/Science.* It would not recommend the fertilizer since yields actually declined or increased very little after application.
9. *Evaluation/Science.* The fertilizer inhibits plant growth.
10. *Application/Science.* They must be able to repeat the experiment and obtain similar results.

Chapter 2 Biology

Lesson 1

Biology is the study of life and all it involves.

1. *Analysis/Biology.* A scientist could not conclude that the objects are alive based on the information given. To be considered alive, the

A-24

objects would also need the ability to grow, the ability to reproduce, and the ability to respond to the environment.
2. *Application/Biology*. A pencil is not alive because it does not have all the characteristics of life. It cannot grow, it cannot reproduce, it cannot use energy, and it cannot respond to the environment. It can move, but only when you move it. Living things can move themselves.
3. *Comprehension/Biology*. Applications of biology to your life might include the use of medical knowledge to cure an illness, the use of improved crops and animals as food, or the lessening of pollution in your area due to studies of the effects of pollution on living things.
4. *Analysis/Biology*. Biology can provide knowledge about an endangered animal's behavior, diet, and survival needs. This knowledge can be used to help protect the animal.

Lesson 2

Evidence for the principle of the unity of life includes the fact that all living things carry on life functions in a similar way and that all share a common basic structure, the cell.

1. **(5)** *Comprehension/Biology*. An organism is defined in the lesson as an independent living thing. Of the choices listed, only the worm fits this category.
2. *Analysis/Biology*. The function of the flagellum is probably to propel those one-celled organisms that have it, since those without it usually cannot move on their own.
3. *Analysis/Biology*. Plants have cell walls and chloroplasts that make food, both of which animals lack. From this information and what you know about plants and animals, you can deduce that one reason they are in different groups is because plants make their own food, while animals must obtain food from their own environment.

Lesson 3

The basic functions necessary for life for a cell are absorption, digestion, synthesis, cellular respiration, excretion, response, and reproduction.

1. *Comprehension/Biology*. A cell must be capable of absorption in order to take in food, water, and other materials necessary for life.
2. *Comprehension/Biology*. The cell membrane is involved in absorbing raw materials for the cell and excreting waste materials.
3. *Analysis/Biology*. The photosynthesis process, by which plant cells capture the energy they need from the sun, is also the only source of energy for animal cells. An animal cell obtains this energy when the animal eats a plant or a plant-eating animal.
4. **(4)** *Comprehension/Biology*. Cellular respiration takes place in the mitochondrion, so this is the organelle in which energy is released from foods for the cell's use.
5. *Analysis/Biology*. Since one gram of fat stores twice as much energy as one gram of carbohydrate, it is more efficient for the body to store extra food (energy) as fat.

Lesson 4

The difference between the two types of reproduction is that in mitosis all of the daughter cell's chromosomes are from the mother cell, while in sexual reproduction half of the chromosomes in the fertilized egg come from the mother and half come from the father.

1. *Application/Biology*. A blueprint is to a house as genes are to a cell or an organism. Genes carry the directions for how the cell will be built, just as a blueprint does.
2. *Comprehension/Biology*. The daughter shares the trait of light skin color with both parents. She shares the trait of brown hair color with just one parent. Neither parent shares her trait of blue eye color.
3. *Application/Biology*. The daughter's dark hair color is a dominant trait. Her blue eye color is recessive trait. Her skin color is neither dominant nor recessive.
4. *Analysis/Biology*. Two people with brown eyes can have a blue-eyed child if each carries one recessive gene for blue eyes and each passes that gene on to the child.
5. *Analysis/Biology*. Since the trait for light-colored hair is recessive, it is not possible for two parents with light-colored hair to have a dark-haired child. In each parent, both genes would have to be for light-colored hair, and there would be no way for the child to receive even a single gene for dark hair.

Lesson 5

Species change over time through natural selection because those organisms that best suit life in their environment are the ones that survive. These organisms then pass on favorable variations to their offspring. Over time, a new species may result.

1. *Analysis/Biology*. Being much taller enables the animal to reach plant leaves that are too high for other animals. The taller animal thus has a protected food supply to help it survive.
2. *Comprehension/Biology*. If the animal fails to reproduce, its genetic variation will not be passed on to the next generation and will have no effect on the species.
3. *Analysis/Biology*. Because of genetic factors such as physical strength or unusual immunity, some insects are usually able to withstand a pesticide. These survivors then reproduce and pass on their characteristics to the new generation, and soon the majority of the species population can withstand the pesticide. At this point, a new pesticide is needed.
4. *Application/Biology*. Nothing in the theory of natural selection suggests that learned behavior can be passed along genetically. Only genetic variations can be transmitted to a new generation.
5. *Analysis/Biology*. Selective breeding is different from natural selection in that the first is deliberate and brought about by humans, while the second is brought about through interactions with the environment.

Lesson 6

In an ecosystem, the nonliving environment supplies the living things with the minerals, gases, energy, and water necessary for life. The living things continuously cycle energy and matter through producers to consumers to decomposers.

1. *Application/Biology*. The grass is a producer in this ecosystem, providing food and oxygen for the rabbit.
2. *Comprehension/Biology*. If all the bacteria suddenly died, plant and

animal matter would begin to build up. Plants would lack some of the nutrients they need for life. In time all life would die, since animals depend on plants for nutrition.
3. *Application/Biology.* The fox's role is that of a secondary consumer, since the fox ate a primary consumer.
4. *Evaluation/Biology.* Consumers are probably not essential members of an ecosystem, since the producers and decomposers could continue their life cycles without them. On the other hand, a lack of consumers might lead to overpopulation.
5. **(2)** *Comprehension/Biology.* When animals are easier to catch and eat, their death rate increases.

Chapter 2 Quiz

1. *Comprehension/Biology.* Not every offspring will necessarily have round seeds. In the parent plant with wrinkled seeds, both genes must be for wrinkled seeds. Consequently, every offspring is sure to receive one wrinkled-seed gene. In the parent plant with round seeds, both genes may be for round seeds. In this case, every offspring will receive a round-seed gene. This gene, even in the presence of a wrinkled-seed gene, will produce offspring with round seeds. However, the round-seeded parent may instead have one gene for round seeds and one gene for wrinkled seeds. In this case, some offspring may receive a wrinkled-seed gene. This gene, combined with the wrinkled-seed gene from the other parent, will produce offspring with wrinkled seeds.
2. **(4)** *Evaluation/Biology.* Parent plants with round seeds that produce offspring with round seeds may each have both genes for round seeds. However, each parent may instead have one gene for round seeds and one gene for wrinkled seeds. For now, all that is certain is that each parent has at least one gene for round seeds, and at least one round-seed gene had been passed on to each offspring.

3. **(2)** *Application/Biology.* The fish have linked one event, the tapping, with a second event, the arrival of food, and produce a response geared to that second event. Choices 1 and 4 are examples of trial and error learning. Choice 3 is an inherited behavior. Choice 5 is an example of the use of reasoning.
4. *Analysis/Biology.* The passage states that only inherited behaviors are passed on through the genes. Learned behaviors are not passed on to offspring and are thus unlikely to play any role in evolution.
5. *Comprehension/Biology.* The fox and rabbit populations rise and fall in cycles that are directly related. Whenever the rabbit population is increasing, more foxes can find food and the fox population also begins rising. In time, the growing number of predator foxes causes the rabbit population to drop. Still later, this drop in the number of rabbits makes food scarce and causes the fox population to start declining as well.
6. **(3)** *Evaluation/Biology.* As the graph shows, the cycles of increase and decrease in the two populations are directly related to each other: A rise in the number of rabbits is followed by a rise in the number of foxes, and so on until the whole cycle begins again. Choices 1 and 2 are incorrect because neither one takes into account the relationship between the increases and decreases of the two populations. Choices 4 and 5 are incorrect because human intervention is not needed to keep the rabbit and fox populations in balance.
7. *Analysis/Biology.* The time period shown on the graph must extend for many months or even years. That amount of time is required for the rabbit and fox populations to respond to changing conditions and to produce the offspring that periodically increase the total number of animals.
8. **(5)** *Application/Biology.* When the zebra population starts decreasing, the decline in the food supply will in time cause a decrease in the number of lions. Choices 1, 2, and 3 are incorrect because they predict an increase or no change. Choice 4 is wrong because the decrease in the lion population will not begin until sometime after the zebra population starts declining.
9. **(3)** *Analysis/Biology.* In South America, the poisonous toads compete with nonpoisonous ones for food and space, but no species has an advantage because all must contend with predators. However, in Florida, the poisonous toads would be free of predators, and, as a result, they most likely would increase very rapidly in number. They would soon start taking away food and space from the native toads, and these species' existence might be endangered. None of the other answer choices have any basis in the passage.
10. *Application/Biology.* The "wing" structures provide the maple tree with a particularly effective seed dispersal technique. The winged seeds are picked up by the wind and carried long distances. When a seed lands in a favorable environment, it sprouts and grows into a new tree.

Chapter 3
Earth Science

Lesson 1

The four areas of earth science are geology, meteorology, oceanography, and astronomy.

1. Predicting the weather involves knowledge of meteorology.
2. To help find new oil deposits you would hire a geologist.
3. Oceanographers would be most interested in maps of the temperature and movement of ocean water.
4. Astronomers discovered mountains on Venus.
5. Answers will vary. You could mention a benefit of geology, meteorology, astronomy, and/or oceanography. For example, benefits of geology include gasoline and plastics, both of which are made from oil. A benefit of meteorology is the daily weather forecast.

Lesson 2

At the center of the earth is a molten core. Above the core is a mantle of

UNIT V: SCIENCE Ch. 3, Lesson 3—Chapter 3 Quiz **A-27**

solid rock. At the surface are thin layers of continental crust and ocean crust.

1. *Analysis/Earth Science.* The earth's rotation is the spin it makes around its axis. The earth's revolution is the path it takes around the sun. A rotation is completed in one day. A revolution is completed in one year.
2. *Analysis/Earth Science.* The decks of the ship disappear from sight before the sails because the Earth is round. If it were flat, both would disappear at the same rate.
3. *Evaluation/Earth Science.* The direction to the geographic South Pole will not be exactly straight behind you, although the pole will be in that general direction. The reason is that compasses are oriented to Earth's magnetic poles, not its geographic poles.

Lesson 3

The theory of plate tectonics is the idea that the earth's outer shell is made up of plates that interact to produce earthquakes, volcanoes, mountains, and new crust. The theory is important because it explains many of the changes that occur on Earth's surface.

1. *Comprehension/Earth Science.* One of Earth's plates may move under another, two plates may move away from each other, or two plates may slide past each other.
2. *Comprehension/Earth Science.* Since obsidian forms from lava, it is an igneous rock.
3. *Application/Earth Science.* If a cliff is suddenly raised eight feet, probably an earthquake occurred, since the breaking of rock would cause the rock to snap suddenly into a new position.
4. *Comprehension/Earth Science.* The pictures demonstrate sideways slippage. The road before movement is an unbroken line, whereas after movement the left half has moved up in the picture and the right half has moved down.
5. (1) *Evaluation/Earth Science.* Only choice 1 would prove that the two cities are moving in relation to each other. Choices 2, 3, and 4 prove nothing about the movement of the two plates.

Lesson 4

The biosphere is the general term for all the parts of the Earth that support life, including the various land surfaces, the bodies of water, and the atmosphere.

1. (4) *Analysis/Earth Science.* Solar energy in the form of heat causes water to evaporate from the oceans into the atmosphere, setting the water cycle in motion.
2. *Application/Earth Science.* Because of the Gulf Stream, which brings warm water from the tropics, the climate of Great Britain is considerably milder than the climate of Canada directly across the Atlantic to the west.
3. *Analysis/Earth Science.* Life on land would be impossible if the water cycle were disrupted and no rain fell. No land plants could survive, and without plants all land animals would die.
4. *Analysis/Earth Science.* A toxic chemical allowed to enter a lake could pass into the ground water and spread across a wide area. Eventually the chemical could appear in well water drawn from the contaminated ground water.

Lesson 5

The four things that interact to create the earth's weather system are the atmosphere, the sun, the land, and the oceans.

1. *Analysis/Earth Science.* Coastal regions tend to have more moderate temperatures because they are affected by the oceans, which warm up and cool down more slowly than land does.
2. *Analysis/Earth Science.* On a hot day, the land heats up faster than the ocean. Warm air over the land rises, while cooler air over the ocean flows inland to take its place.
3. *Application/Earth Science.* The "bumpiness" is caused by warm air currents rising from the hot desert. These currents are especially strong on sunny days.
4. (5) *Application/Earth Science.* The earth's rotation pushes winds to the right or east in the Northern Hemisphere, which is where the United States is located.

Lesson 6

The solar system is the group of planets and their moons that circle the sun. It is important to us because our Earth is one of the planets in the system and because the sun is the source of all our energy.

1. (4) *Comprehension/Earth Science.* A galaxy is a group of stars.
2. *Comprehension/Earth Science.* If the sun were suddenly removed, its gravitational pull would no longer affect the Earth. The Earth would move in a straight line in whatever direction it was traveling at that moment.
3. *Analysis/Earth Science.* The Martian year is longer than an Earth year since Mars is farther than Earth from the sun and thus follows a longer orbit.
4. *Evaluation/Earth Science.* The effect of the moon on the ocean is evidence of the law of gravity. It shows that the moon's gravity is acting on the earth, just as the earth's gravity is acting on the moon.

Chapter 3   Quiz

1. (3) *Application/Earth Science.* Only choice 3 is an example of an exposed rock or mineral (in this case, metal) being broken up and also chemically changed into another substance; i.e., rust. In the other choices, rock is being broken up into small pieces but not chemically changed.
2. *Comprehension/Earth Science.* If you walked north along the river, you would be heading upstream because you would be crossing points of higher and higher elevation.
3. (2) *Evaluation/Earth Science.* A contour line joins points of the same elevation. Consequently, no contour line can ever cross another. Choice 1 is true of this map, but not of all contour maps. Choice 3 is false of this map: the "V's" point upstream. Choice 4 is false because contour lines on a hill will form a circle, as shown on the map. Choice 5 is false because contour lines are very close together where the land is steep.
4. *Analysis/Earth Science.* According to the passage, when

moist air crosses a mountain range, the moisture will condense and fall before it reaches the far side of the range. Consequently, the area of greatest rainfall is likely to be the mountain slopes, especially those facing the direction from which moist air generally approaches.

5. *(5) Application/Earth Science.* In California, moist air moving inland from the Pacific Ocoean will be traveling from west to east. Consequently, the driest area will be to the east of the mountains, on the side facing away from the moist Pacific Air.

6. *(3) Analysis/Earth Science.* According to the passage, the hydrogen fuel needed for nuclear fusion is readily available on Earth in water. Alternatives A and B are both true because water is both easier to locate and less likely to run out than the oil and gas deposits currently used as energy sources.

7. *Application/Earth Science.* The passage states that when plates collide, mountain chains are raised at the point of collision. The Himalaya Mountains extend all along the boundary between two huge land masses: India to the south and the rest of Asia to the north. As a result, the most likely explanation for these mountains is that they were formed by the collision of two plates: one that holds India and one that holds the rest of Asia.

8. *(2) Evaluation/Earth Science.* The fact that rock formations at the edges of many continents match formations at the edges of other continents would provide powerful evidence that at one time those continents were all joined together. Choices 1 and 4 indicate that mountains have been formed at many times and in many places from other landforms. Choice 3 indicates that birds travel freely across the oceans. Choice 5 indicates that Antarctica's climate was different in the past from what it is today.

9. *Comprehension/Earth Science.* Since the Pacific plate is moving Hawaii and the other islands toward a new location northwest of the "hot spot," that spot will eventually be located southeast of the island of Hawaii (even though the spot itself will not move.)

Therefore, the new volcano will be located off the southeast coast of Hawaii.

10. *(2) Analysis/Earth Science.* According to the passage, the Pacific plate is moving to the northwest, but there is no indication that the "hot spot" is moving. Instead, it seems to be staying in one place, even though the motion of the islands may give the illusion that the spot is moving to the southeast. The spot remains stationary, creating islands one after the other as the plate moves slowly above it.

Chapter 4 Chemistry

Lesson 1

The atom is made up of a nucleus, with protons and neutrons, surrounded by a cloud of electrons. An element is composed of the same type of atoms. A compound is formed of atoms of different elements bonded together.

1. *Comprehension/Chemistry.* Yes, the two hydrogen atoms bond to form a molecule because any atoms chemically bonded form a molecule.
2. *Application/Chemistry.* Each atom would still be gold. Since gold is an element, it cannot be broken down into further substances, even when separated into atoms.
3. *Analysis/Chemistry.* Fluorine probably forms bonds easily because it lacks only one electron to fill its outer energy level.

Lesson 2

A chemical equation shows exactly what takes place during a chemical reaction, representing the changes in bonding and energy.

1. *Comprehension/Chemistry.* A balanced chemical equation expresses the fact that during a reaction, atoms are rearranged to form new substances, but they do not disappear. This is a consequence of the law of conservation of matter.
2. *Comprehension/Chemistry.* The symbol for oxygen is O; the formula for oxygen gas, a two-atom molecule, is O_2.
3. *Application/Chemistry.* $2H_2O_2 \rightarrow 2H_2O + O_2$

Lesson 3

Two of the reasons that chemical reactions take place are the tendency toward entropy and the tendency of matter to go from a state of higher energy to a state of lower energy.

1. *Analysis/Chemistry.* The change in energy during a chemical reaction doesn't affect the total energy in the universe because the energy has simply changed from one form to another; for example, from heat energy to chemical bond energy.
2. *Application/Chemistry.* Exothermic, because energy is given off and used by the body.
3. *Application/Chemistry.* Endothermic, because the plant uses sunlight energy during photosynthesis to complete the reaction.
4. *(4) Evaluation/Chemistry.* In both examples the disorder in the system has increased, while the energy has increased or stayed the same.
5. *Comprehension/Chemistry.* The word "energy" belongs on the left side because the reaction absorbs energy as it occurs.

Lesson 4

An acid is a compound that contains hydrogen. A base contains hydroxide. A salt is formed from part of the acid and part of the base during a neutralization reaction.

1. *Application/Chemistry.* It is a base because any pH above 7 indicates a base.
2. *Application/Chemistry.* Lemons contain the stronger acid because their pH is lower than that of apples on the scale, so taste more sour.
3. *Application/Chemistry.* A strong acid could be made safe to discard through the use of a neutralization reaction. The products of the reaction, salt and water, would not cause damage.

Chapter 4 Quiz

1. *Analysis/Chemistry.* The mass of the carbon dioxide must be greater than the mass of the diamond. When the diamond was burned, the carbon in the diamond combined with the pure oxygen to from the carbon dioxide, a compound. This

UNIT V: SCIENCE — Chapter 4 Quiz — Ch. 5, Lesson 3 — A-29

compound must have a greater mass than one of its components.

2. *Comprehension/Chemistry.* Temperatures are likely to be lowest inside the top of the fractionating tower since the petroleum vapors grow increasingly cooler as they rise within the tower.

3. *Comprehension/Chemistry.* Fuel oil must have a higher condensation temperature since it condenses further down in the tower than kerosene. The hydrocarbons that make up the kerosene must cool to a lower temperature before they will condense.

4. *Analysis/Chemistry.* The hydrocarbons in each product of the refining process are likely to have the same (or a very similar) number of carbon atoms per molecule. The different types of hydrocarbons have different numbers of carbon atoms, and the refining process separates the types from each other.

5. *Application/Chemistry.* The burning of natural gas is an exothermic reaction since heat energy is released in the process.

6. *Analysis/Chemistry.* Neon, a noble gas, does not easily form compounds with other elements since it already has a complete outer energy level. It has no need to achieve a complete energy level by bonding with other atoms.

7. *Application/Chemistry.* The pure substance is salt, a compound with a definite chemical composition. Carbonated water is a mixture of water and carbon dioxide. Air is a mixture of gases.

8. *Application/Chemistry.* The mixtures are sweetened coffee and seawater. Sweetened coffee consists of sugar and coffee dissolved in water. Seawater consists of a variety of minerals dissolved in water. Pure water (a compound) is a pure substance.

9. (5) *Evaluation/Chemistry.* Observations B and C would support the conclusion that orange juice is an acid. The other observations have no bearing upon whether orange juice is an acid or a base.

10. (3) *Evaluation/Chemistry.* Only C describes an example of the natural trend toward entropy in matter. Choice A is evidence for the principle that matter tends to move from a state of higher energy to a state of lower energy. Choice B simply illustrates that matter may change its state as temperature varies.

Chapter 5 Physics

Lesson 1

A physical change is a change in the physical properties of matter such as color, odor, density, boiling and melting point, solubility in water, and hardness. A chemical change is a change in the chemical composition of matter.

1. *Application/Physics.* This is a proof of Boyle's Law, since the volume decreases as pressure on the gas increases.

2. *Application/Physics.* Its volume will increase, since as the temperature rises, volume increases according to Charles's Law.

3. *Application/Physics.* The size (volume) of the balloon will decrease as temperature decreases, according to Charles's Law.

4. *Application/Physics.* The pressure of the gas in your tires increases as temperatures increase in the summer, according to the Pressure versus Temperature Law.

5. (4) *Application/Physics.* Choice 4 is a chemical change. All the others are physical changes in which matter changes state or undergoes mixing but does not change in chemical composition.

Lesson 2

Machines make work easier by reducing the amount of energy needed to do work.

1. *Application/Physics.* (a) Arrow A represents the effort force; Arrow B represents the fulcrum; Arrow C represents the resistance. When cutting, you exert force at the handles; the scissors pivot around the center, where the two blades are connected; the resistance is the object that is being cut. (b) A pair of scissors is a first-class lever because the fulcrum is in the middle.

2. *Application/Physics.* Yes, it is a machine because it does the work of cutting objects.

3. *Application/Physics.* Kinetic, potential, kinetic. When the child is in motion, he is using kinetic energy. When the child is motionless at the top of his swing, he is exhibiting stored, or potential, energy.

4. *Analysis/Physics.* If work ÷ force = distance, if distance decreases, force increases. In a wheel and axle, the distance through which force is applied decreases—from the radius of the wheel to the radius of the axle. Therefore, the force is increased.

5. (2) *Comprehension/Physics.* Friction is the force that opposes the motion of an object. In this case, most of the friction is caused by the ball's surface rubbing against the floor's surface.

Lesson 3

The behavior of a moving object is governed by Newton's three laws of motion. These laws are as follows: (1) Every object at rest will stay at rest, and every object in motion with constant speed in a straight line will stay in motion, unless some force acts on the object to change that motion. (2) The acceleration of an object is directly proportional to the net force on the object and inversely proportional to the mass of the object. The acceleration is in the same direction as the net external force. (3) For every force there is an equal and opposite force.

1. *Application/Physics.* This is an example of an equal and opposite reaction to a force, or the third law of motion.

2. (3) *Comprehension/Physics.* The two cars' speeds are the same, but since they are traveling in different directions, their velocities are different.

3. *Application/Physics.* This makes use of the second law of motion, since by reducing the mass of a car but applying the same amount of force, the engineer will automatically increase the acceleration.

4. *Analysis/Physics.* When we walk across the floor, our feet exert a backward and downward force. The floor in turn exerts a forward and upward force, according to the third law of motion. (The floor's friction keeps our feet from slipping out from under us, as would happen when walking on a smooth piece of ice.)

Ch. 4, Lesson 1—Chapter 5 Quiz

5. *Evaluation/Physics.* Since the first law of motion states that an object in motion will continue in a straight line unless acted on by some force, the fact that the planets travel in a curved path proves they are being acted upon by some force, in this case the sun's gravity.

Lesson 4

A wave is a transmission of a disturbance that repeats itself across space and during time. All waves have a wave speed, a wavelength, a frequency, and an amplitude.

1. **(2)** *Comprehension/Physics.* The more dense the material, the greater will be the speed of sound through it.
2. *Application/Physics.* Waves traveling near the ground would be faster, since an increase in temperature increases the speed of a sound wave.
3. **(4)** *Evalutaion/Physics.* It would be helpful to chill the medium, since decreased temperature decreases the speed of the waves. Using air as the medium would be helpful because sound travels relatively slowly through air.
4. *Analysis/Physics.* The decrease in density would tend to make the sound travel more slowly, while the increase in temperature would tend to make the sound travel faster. If the sound actually travels more slowly, the decrease in density must have a greater effect than the increase in temperature.

Lesson 5

Electricity and magnetism are related in that an electric current can cause a magnetic field, and a changing magnetic field can generate electricity.

1. *Comprehension/Physics.* An electric motor changes electrical energy into kinetic or mechanical energy. An electric generator produces electric energy through the use of a changing magnetic field.
2. *Comprehension/Physics.* Yes, this substance is a magnet, because all the electrons are rotating in the same direction, counterclockwise.
3. *Application/Physics.* Lightning is a form of static electricity since it is caused by friction and discharges in a single bolt.
4. *Comprehension/Physics.* Since opposite poles attract each other, the tip of the compass must be a south pole because it is attracted to a north pole.

Chapter 5 Quiz

1. **(1)** *Comprehension/Physics.* If pressure and temperature are equal, a solid is more dense than a gas because it has more atoms packed into the same amount of volume.
2. *Analysis/Physics.* No, because an electron moving at a constant velocity in an unchanging direction is not accelerating, and thus is not producing electromagnetic radiation.
3. *Comprehension/Physics.* Drawing A represents a laser because its waves are in phase. Drawing B represents ordinary white light because its waves are out of phase.
4. **(4)** *Analysis/Physics.* According to the figure, incoherent light tends to spread out, while the coherent laser light is shooting straight out.
5. *Application/Physics.* The woman is not doing work since she is not moving an object.
6. *Analysis/Physics.* The magnetic field will cease to exist as soon as the wire is disconnected. The magnetic field exists only as long as electric current is flowing through the wire.
7. *Application/Physics.* The electromagnet's strength would be increased, since the magnets in the nail would contribute their magnetism to the magnetic field already present from the electric current.
8. **(5)** *Application/Physics.* A sound wave usually travels more quickly the denser the matter is. Water, a liquid, is denser than air, a mixture of gases, so the underwater swimmer hears the sound before the swimmer on the surface. The loudness of a sound (choices 1 and 4) has nothing to do with its speed. The frequency (choice 3) affects its pitch, not its speed. Choice 2 is irrelevant information, since both air and water are matter.
9. *Evaluation/Physics.* The experiment does not support the student's conclusion, which in fact is false. The fact that the rock hit the ground first shows only that the friction of the air slows the feather more than it does the rock. A true conclusion would be that the effect of friction on moving objects varies with the shape of the object.
10. *Evaluation/Physics.* The sailor is incorrect. According to the first law of motion, a moving object will keep moving unless some outside force acts to stop it. In the sailboat's case, this outside force is the friction between the moving boat and the water. If the wind stops, the sailboat will keep moving for a certain distance, but the force of friction will slow it down and then stop it.

UNIT VI Interpreting Literature and the Arts

Chapter 1
Introduction to Literature and Commentary on the Arts

Lesson 1

The chief characteristics of literature are that (1) it addresses subjects or ideas of universal interest and (2) it achieves an excellence of expression that gives the reader pleasure as well as information.

1. *Literal Comprehension, Global/Literature.* FALSE. A recipe, for example, may be very easy to understand, but it is not literature. The two greatest characteristics of literature are its ability to deal with universal concepts and its excellence in expression of those concepts.
2. *Literal Comprehension, Global/Literature.* The four genres discussed in the lesson are nonfiction, fiction, drama, and poetry.
3. *Application/Literature.* A magazine article generally should not be considered literature, especially if it deals with a "how-to" kind of topic. The writing is meant primarily to inform. Furthermore, the writing deals with a specific topic with a limited appeal, not with an idea of broad, permanent interest that will last far into the future.

Lesson 2

Commentary can summarize or provide readers with information about art. It can analyze or show the reader how a given work or kind of art achieves a particular effect. It also can evaluate, or make judgments about the value of, a given work or kind of art.

1. *Application/Commentary.* The article and the essay might be considered commentary. The interview is an example of nonfiction literature or just general-interest reading; the story is an example of fiction literature.
2. *Literal Comprehension, Global/Commentary.* Possible topics for a review could include an exhibition of paintings at a museum, a new production of a famous play, a concert, or the unveiling of a new statue.
3. *Inferential Comprehension, Global/Commentary.* Two critics can differ greatly and still write good commentary. If they present their views clearly and support their views well, both critics will have written effectively.

Chapter 1 Quiz

1. (2) *Application/Literature.* The purpose of traveling directions is to inform a limited audience of readers about a subject of temporary interest. The other choices—even song lyrics (Choice [4]) and a biography (Choice [5])—might deal with ideas of universal interest. In addition, all of the other choices might be appreciated for their excellence of expression. Traveling directions probably would not have that quality.
2. *Analysis/Commentary.* Television shows could be mentioned in a number of ways. It is most likely that they would be mentioned as examples to illustrate a broader subject concerning trends in television viewing—for example, the reasons for a rise in the popularity of sitcoms or the effectiveness of the work of a team of writers in several dramatic series.
3. *Application/Literature.* The writing comes from a work of literature. It deals with democracy, an idea of universal interest, and there is an excellence to its expression. Unlike commentary, it deals with a political idea, not with the merits of art.
4. (4) *Literal Comprehension, Global/Literature.* The author never gives a definite answer; rather, he spends part of his explanation showing what democracy means in a variety of situations—for example, in the ability to vote in secret (line 8) and to express one's views in a letter to the editor (line 10).
5. *Application/Literature.* The author clearly cares a great deal about democracy and probably would take great pains to guarantee its continued existence. It is reasonable, therefore, to believe that the author would be willing to fight for democracy, if necessary.

Chapter 2 Nonfiction

Lesson 1

Nonfiction literature has factual material as its subject matter. It is about actual people, events, or situations.

1. *Analysis/Nonfiction.* Both passages are concerned with ideas of permanent or universal interest. Passage A is broadly concerned with the process of growing up. Passage B expresses beliefs about the value of a human life. Universal themes such as these distinguish nonfiction literature from nonfiction works that are not considered literature.
2. *Analysis/Nonfiction.* Passage B is an example of nonfiction because it is an individual's recollection of an event that actually took place.
3. *Literal Comprehension, Global/Nonfiction.* Parents and schools sometimes hold competing, even conflicting, values. They compete with each other to earn children's acceptance of the values they hold.

Lesson 2

You can often discover the main idea of a nonfiction work by looking for the sentence that states the main idea directly.

1. *Literal Comprehension, Global/Fiction.* FALSE. Although the author discusses education in the United States, her topic is the conflicting roles of families and schools in shaping the lives and values of children.
2. *Literal Comprehension, Specific/Nonfiction.* "Gait" refers to the prisoner's manner of walking.

A-31

3. *Literal Comprehension, Specific/Nonfiction.* The prisoner states in lines 17–18. "But parents see kids as special individuals; the school inevitably sees them as part of a group."
4. *Literal Comprehension, Specific/Nonfiction.* The prisoner stepped aside to avoid a puddle.
5. *Literal Comprehension, Specific/Nonfiction.* Schools taught immigrant children how to speak English; they taught urban skills to people from the country, and they taught everyone "American" ways.

Lesson 3

The point of view tells whether the author addresses his or her readers and subject matter directly or indirectly. Surrounding words and sentences, or the context, can give clues to the implied meaning of a reading passage.

1. *Inferential Comprehension, Global/Nonfiction.* When the author writes in lines 19–22, "He and we were a party of men . . ." and "one of us would be gone," he conveys his attitude that the prisoner is no different from any of the other men.
2. *Inferential Comprehension, Global/Nonfiction.* TRUE. The author's belief is implied by her statement that "School is the essential but scary halfway house between the home and the world." The author also generally implies that standards used to judge children at school represent standards used by the outside world.
3. **(3)** *Inferential Comprehension, Global/Nonfiction.* The numerous details about the prisoner's appearance and movements enable the reader to conclude that the author is an observant person. Nothing in the passage pertains to the guilt or innocence of the prisoner, eliminating choice (1). Similarly, the prisoner's attitude toward his fate (choice [2]) and the author's position (choice [4]) cannot be inferred from the material in the passage.

Lesson 4

If you understand the principle behind a particular belief of an author, you can often predict the author's belief about another subject.

1. **(3)** *Application/Nonfiction.* Choice (3) would be the most likely event to create a conflict between a school and the parents of a student. The author makes the point that parents and schools often disagree about *basic* values and beliefs. Choice (3) is the only one that concerns values.
2. **(2)** *Application/Nonfiction.* The author of Passage B would agree with the second statement.
3. *Application/Nonfiction.* The author of Passage B would agree with John Donne's statement. The quotation from John Donne expresses Donne's belief in a common bond uniting all humanity. The author of Passage B expressed his belief that all individuals are linked by a common bond also. Like Donne, he views the loss of another's life as diminishing his own world.

Lesson 5

Authors use certain kinds of words and sentences—or a particular style—to express their ideas. They decide on a particular tone—or way of expressing their feelings—to address their readers.

1. *Analysis/Nonfiction.* The author of Passage B narrates an event in a way that resembles the telling of a story. His underlying purpose, however, is to convince the readers of the truth of his belief that a human life is sacred and should never be destroyed.
2. *Analysis/Nonfiction.* Passage A is more informal in style and tone than Passage B. The use of words and expressions such as "kids" instead of "children" and the author's occasional prefacing of a statement with "I suppose" contribute to an informal tone and style.
3. *Analysis/Nonfiction.* FALSE. An author may use an informal tone as a way of capturing a reader's interest or attention. An informal tone does not necessarily mean that the author does not view his or her subject matter seriously.

Chapter 2 Quiz

1. **(3)** *Literal Comprehension, Global/Nonfiction.* The author states directly in the first sentence that "language is the single human trait . . . setting us apart from all the rest of life." He makes this point again when he refers to language as the "biologically specific activity of human beings."
2. **(2)** *Inferential Comprehension, Specific/Nonfiction.* The expression "more and more disturbingly" suggests that the author has reached his conclusions about humanity with some reluctance. They apparently contradicted previously held beliefs or assumptions.
3. *Literal Comprehension, Global/Nonfiction.* The author's use of the word "we" indicates a first-person point of view.
4. **(3)** *Analysis/Nonfiction.* The use of the phrase "more and more disturbingly" (line 1) indicates the seriousness with which the author approaches his subject. The rest of the passage is written in a sincere manner from the author's personal perspective (which is therefore not "detached"). While the author may be compassionate, there is nothing in the passage to emphasize this trait.
5. *Literal Comprehension, Specific/Nonfiction.* No. The author states in the first line that she left Arkansas "for good" when she was thirteen.
6. *Inferential Comprehension, Global/Nonfiction.* The author's family owned the store and she spent a great deal of time there, perhaps helping her family by working there.
7. **(2)** *Analysis/Nonfiction.* In the last sentence of the passage, the author mentions the "promise of magic mornings," reinforcing her impression of the store each morning as "an unopened present from a stranger."
8. *Application/Nonfiction.* TRUE. The author's strong feeling about the store as a place that represented a warm family environment would be transferred to a home lived in for a long time.
9. *Analysis/Nonfiction.* The sentence "Whenever I walked into the Store, I sensed that it was tired" (lines 7–8) and the following sentence, in which the author refers to the "slow pulse" of the store (line 9), shows that she thinks of the store as having a life of its own.

UNIT VI: INTERPRETING LITERATURE AND THE ARTS — Ch. 3, Lesson 1—Ch. 3, Lesson 5 — A-33

10. *Inferential Comprehension, Specific/Nonfiction.* Because of the variety of the items mentioned, it can be assumed that the store was a general store.

Chapter 3 Fiction

Lesson 1

The basic difference between fiction and nonfiction is that the main focus of nonfiction is on fact whereas the main focus of fiction is on imagination.

1. *Literal Comprehension, Global/Fiction.* TRUE. The author refers to World War I, a historical event. Particular reference is made to the souvenirs that might be collected by a soldier in that war.
2. *Literal Comprehension, Specific/Fiction.* The two characters who converse are Marian and the nurse. An unnamed woman, a minor character, clears her throat late in the passage.
3. *Analysis/Fiction.* Both are examples of realistic fiction. The characters, setting, and plot are all very true to life.

Lesson 2

An author includes plot, or the sequence of events, in a story; setting, or a time and location in which a story takes place; and characters, or people who take part in the plot. The author may even appear as a character in a story by making use of a first-person observer point of view.

1. *Literal Comprehension, Specific/Fiction.* The term refers to the potted plant that Marian is carrying.
2. *Literal Comprehension, Specific/Fiction.* Father leaves a "trail of souvenirs"—so many that a long box is needed to store them all. The boy refers to them as Father's "treasures." In the last line of the passage, the boy states that Mother has a lower opinion of the collectibles.
3. *Literal Comprehension, Global/Fiction.* The scene takes place during the winter. The author refers to the "winter sunlight" that shines on the building when Marian arrives.
4. *Literal Comprehension, Global/Fiction.* Passage A makes use of a first-person point of view. The narrator is a first-person participant.
5. *Literal Comprehension, Global/Fiction.* Marian, a Campfire Girl, comes to the Old Ladies' Home, hoping to do a good deed that will earn her three points. The nurse, learning that "any" of the ladies "will do," takes her down the hall in search of a candidate. She makes her decision when she hears a patient clearing her throat. That noise frightens Marian.

Lesson 3

Apart from offering direct information, an author might have characters say or do things that reveal information. The conflicts within a story also can reveal information that is not immediately obvious.

1. *Inferential Comprehension, Specific/Fiction.* The comparison is made to illustrate Father's habit of collecting war souvenirs. It can be assumed that the magpie is also known for its collecting habits.
2. *Inferential Comprehension, Specific/Fiction.* The simile brings to the reader's mind a cold, colorless image. It could be inferred that something about the inside of the Old Ladies' Home is also cold and colorless—perhaps the way in which the patients are treated.
3. *Inferential Comprehension, Global/Fiction.* Taken as a whole, the passage gives the impression of a lack of human compassion. It might be expected that by the end of the story, one or more characters will have learned that people of all ages deserve love and respect.
4. *Inferential Comprehension, Global/Fiction.* The first and third figures are negative. A howling wolf is a gloomy or frightening thought. Scrooge, a literary character, was a miser who did not care for the needy. The second figure is positive. The image of a sailing ship—especially a golden one—speaks of power and even majesty.

Lesson 4

If you could determine from a passage a character's values, motives, fears, and so on, you might be able to predict his or her reactions to events beyond those in the plot.

1. *Application/Fiction.* The boy might feel a sense of loss, but he probably would not mourn. He considers his father as a visitor who brings him gifts, like Santa Claus; however, he also hints that his father makes things, "uncomfortable" (line 8). He might miss the presents if the man were killed, but he wouldn't miss the intrusions.
2. *Application/Fiction.* TRUE. The author presents a bleak view of nursing-home life and probably would welcome any program that "humanized" its elderly recipients.
3. *Application/Fiction.* Marian makes it clear that she is visiting only to earn points in the Campfire Girls. An adult with that attitude would want a career in which he or she could move ahead quickly, not a service career in which skill might never be recognized.

Lesson 5

An author's distinctive style can affect the reader in a number of ways. For example, vivid description can create strong mental images. Also, the author's choice of a simple style or a complex style can influence whether a reader views the story as simple or complex. Purpose also can affect the reader in many ways. For example, if an author's purpose is to entertain, the reader may be moved to laughter. If the purpose is to move the reader to action, the author may attempt to make the reader feel anger about the subject of the work. Irony can be a subtle but effective way of moving the reader to think twice about the author's purpose.

1. *Analysis/Fiction.* To the narrator, Father is a "big figure." He is compared to Santa Claus, a childhood favorite. The narrator also mentions climbing into bed with his parents and a childlike fascination with shaving. Most important, he spends considerable time describing Father's box of war souvenirs as if it were a treasure chest or a toy chest.
2. *Analysis/Fiction.* The passage indicates an unpleasant experience. As Marian talks with the nurse and walks down the hall, the overall impression is unhappy. Then, the noise that determines whom she

will meet is an unnatural, inhuman noise—a noise that frightens her and makes her want to run away. Even if the meeting turns out well, Marian goes into it with a feeling of dread.

3. *Analysis/Fiction.* FALSE. A child might share many of the narrator's attitudes, but a child would not understand why the author has chosen to talk about them. The insights about childhood that the author wants to reveal are beyond a child's understanding. A child would not respond to the subtleties of the family relationships that the author describes. Although the story is about a child, its complexities indicate that it is meant to be responded to by adults.

4. *Analysis/Fiction.* If a fear of the dark were a major characteristic of the adult, the reader might expect the character to overcome that fear (the second event) during the story. It would be ironic, or unexpected, if the adult were forced to undergo a prolonged period of darkness—as in a blackout (the first event), entrapment in a cave, or even blindness (the third event).

Chapter 3 Quiz

1. (2) *Literal Comprehension, Specific/Fiction.* The man explains to the girl that "Anis del Toro" is a drink (line 12).
2. *Inferential Comprehension, Global/Fiction.* TRUE. Their conversational style is that of people who are well acquainted; for example, the girl says with assurance that the man has never seen a white elephant (line 7). The comment "That's all we do. . ." (line 35) also indicates a continuing relationship.
3. *Analysis/Fiction.* The author describes a countryside from which the vitality has vanished. Everything is brown (not green), dry, and "white in the sun," possibly like bleached bones. That description provides an atmosphere for the two main characters. It quickly becomes apparent that their relationship, too, is "brown and dry"; its vitality has gone, leaving them disenchanted with each other.

4. *Literal Comprehension, Global/Fiction.* The characters interact primarily through dialogue; in fact, the passage is almost entirely conversation.
5. *Analysis/Fiction.* At first, the simile seems quite clever; the girl is proud of herself for having thought of it (lines 32–33). The image would seem to be positive, referring to the power and majesty of the elephant. However, it can be taken as a negative image as well. A "white elephant" is a gift that nobody wants—a gift that brings more unhappiness than happiness. The author may be suggesting that the girl unknowingly uses the simile to express her unhappiness with the "fine time" that she is supposed to be having.
6. (5) *Inferential Comprehension, Specific/Fiction.* The remark is made after the girl finds that she doesn't like Anis del Toro, after all. It has been a disappointment; and she uses the occasion to complain about "everything." A negative remark, it provokes an argument, which the man tries to settle by saying "Well, let's try to have a fine time" (line 31). Both of them seem only to go through the motions of enjoying their trip.
7. *Inferential Comprehension, Specific/Fiction.* TRUE. On this occasion she badgers the man to approve of her witty remark. Earlier in the passage, her desire to try Anis del Toro also seems motivated, in part, by her wish to have the man think well of her sophisticated tastes.
8. *Literal Comprehension, Global/Fiction.* The narrator is third person. There is no reference to "I," either as a participant or as an observer.
9. (3) *Application/Fiction.* In the lines mentioned, the girl equates "having a fine time" with "being amused." She then says to the man, "That's all we do, isn't it—look at things and try new drinks?" (lines 35–36). The man agrees. "Having a fine time," then, seems to be based on filling the senses (sight and taste, at least) with new experiences. Most of the choices given are based on "old" experiences—old friends (Choice [1]), old family (Choice [4]), old music (Choice [5]), and old history or art (Choice [2]). Only Choice (3) indicates an experience that is new and that is designed primarily to fill the senses.
10. *Analysis/Fiction.* The audience would have to be fairly mature; children, for example, would not understand why the man and girl talk to each other as they do. The audience would not need a lot of prior knowledge; the only unfamiliar term ("Anis del Toro") is explained by one of the characters. The sentence structure is fairly simple, and the descriptions are brief and clear. The story could be appreciated by a wide range of adults.

Chapter 4 Drama

Lesson 1

Drama is storytelling that is based upon written dialogue and stage directions.

1. *Literal Comprehension, Global/Drama.* Drama, unlike other forms of literature, is written to be performed by actors before an audience.
2. *Analysis/Drama.* Passages A and B are not examples of fiction because they are written in the form of a play, including 1) stage directions, 2) characters' names, and 3) dialogue.
3. *Literal Comprehension, Global/Drama.* Passage A. Passage A uses stage directions almost every time a new character speaks; Passage B uses them in only three places.

Lesson 2

In fiction, the author can describe a character's movements and expressions. In a dramatic work, the playwright uses stage directions to illustrate the dialogue and help bring the characters and plot to life.

1. *Literal Comprehension, Specific/Drama.* He is a chauffeur. In line 6, Walter says, "I drive a man around in his limousine."
2. *Literal Comprehension, Specific/Drama.* Lady Bracknell is Gwendolen's mother. Jack says he

UNIT VI: INTERPRETING LITERATURE AND THE ARTS   Ch. 4, Lesson 3—Chapter 4 Quiz   **A-35**

wants to "take advantage of Lady Bracknell's temporary absence," and Gwendolen replies that he should since, "Mamma has a way of coming back suddenly into a room."
3. *Literal Comprehension, Global/Drama.* Gwendolen thinks his name is Ernest. She addresses Jack near the end of the passage as "My own Ernest."

Lesson 3

Reading a play can be more difficult than reading a story because the playwright cannot use description in the same way. The reader of a play must use the dialogue and the actors' movements to understand the plot and the characters.

1. *Inferential Comprehension, Global/Drama.* TRUE. The stage directions indicate that the characters are sitting on and moving around a sofa.
2. *Inferential Comprehension, Global/Drama.* FALSE. The dialogue in the passage shows that Jack loves Gwendolen. It must be assumed that Jack has other reasons for using a false name.
3. *Inferential Comprehension, Specific/Drama.* Walter is black. Since he talks about seeing "white boys in restaurants," you can infer that he is black. Also, Mama's reference to lynching would imply that the family is black.
4. *Inferential Comprehension, Specific/Drama.* First, Gwendolen states that she is "never wrong." Then she says, "my ideal has always been to love someone of the name of Ernest." That she would base her love on so small a reason as a name suggests that Gwendolen is a superficial, or shallow, person.
5. *Inferential Comprehension, Global/Drama.* The playwright implies that they often come into conflict because they look at the world in different ways. Walter's mother thinks that life is freedom and is grateful for what she has. Walter thinks that life is money and is dissatisfied with what he has.

Lesson 4

The subject of a play is very often one that a reader can apply to other settings and situations.

1. *Application/Drama.* Most likely, Walter's mother would be unhappy. To Mama, money is not as important as being satisfied with your life. She probably would rather see Walter enjoying his work.
2. *Application/Drama.* Since Gwendolen thinks names are so important, she probably would be very upset if she had to change her own name. She might feel that she would have to change her personality to fit her new name.
3. *Application/Drama.* In lines 3–4, Mama shows that she feels very strong about family; she also refers to her grown son as "baby." (line 11) She probably would stay with her family.
4. *Application/Drama.* TRUE. Since Gwendolen cares more about a person's name than about the kind of person he is, she probably cares more about appearances—the coat with the designer label—than about substance—the more useful coat.

Lesson 5

Playwrights depend on dialogue and gestures to reveal characters' personalities and convey meaning. They also depend on setting and figurative language to give further insight to the themes of the play.

1. *Analysis/Drama.* Mama's words, "Once upon a time freedom used to be life," emphasize the basic difference between Mama and Walter. Mama has done without both money and freedom and knows that freedom is more important to life. The playwright uses these lines to illustrate these beliefs.
2. *Analysis/Drama.* The playwright uses the exchange of words in lines 28–35 to show Gwendolen's rigid attitude toward the name Ernest and to help the reader feel Jack's uneasiness about his deception. These two characterizations lay the path for the conflict to follow.
3. *Analysis/Drama.* TRUE. Walter walks back and forth across the stage and finally kneels next to his mother, suggesting he is upset or agitated.
4. *Analysis/Drama.* The playwright uses language such as "the edge of my days" and "looming blank space—full of *nothing*" to indicate

that Walter thinks his future is empty of hope and promise. It helps the reader feel Walter's unhappiness and frustration.

Chapter 4   Quiz

1. *Literal Comprehension, Specific/Drama.* Business (line 18). Julia says, toward the end of the passage, "But you haven't an idea yet of how exciting *business* can be."
2. *Inferential Comprehension, Global/Drama.* He wants to stop working for a while and try to find himself. Julia says to Johnny that it is "inconceivable" that he could stand not working, and Johnny tells her, "I'm after—all that's in me, all I am."
3. **(3)** *Inferential Comprehension, Specific/Drama.* Johnny tries to explain to Julia why he wants to take a break from work. When she doesn't understand him and says that making money is a "thrill," he stares at her because he hasn't seen this side of her before.
4. *Literal Comprehension, Global/Drama.* TRUE. Throughout the passage, Julia uses words such as, "inconceivable," "unthinkable," and "what's the matter with you" in reaction to Johnny's ideas and plans.
5. **(4)** *Analysis/Drama.* Johnny is trying to explain his feelings to Julia and she is not understanding him. He is diappointed that the woman he loves cannot express that feeling toward him and does not seem willing to listen to his ideas.
6. *Inferential Comprehension, Specific/Drama.* Since both Laurie and Nora speak to each other about "Daddy" and "Mom" without identifying them further, we can infer that Laurie and Nora are sisters. (lines 9–15)
7. *Inferential Comprehension, Specific/Drama.* Nora's lines to Laurie about privacy and Laurie's response suggest that the sisters have a conflict about sharing a bedroom.
8. *Application/Drama.* It is possible that the girls would not have felt the need for a house of their own

if they had their own bedrooms and, in turn, more privacy. However, they still might have felt the need for themselves and their mother to be self-sufficient.

9. *Literal Comprehension, Specific/Drama.* Only their mother is alive. Their father has died, as indicated in line 9.
10. *Application/Drama.* Nora misses her father very much and is worried that her Uncle Jack will be making an important decision for her (lines 8–9). She probably would not be as upset if she could discuss her problem with both parents since she indicates that her relationship with her father was a close one.

Chapter 5 Poetry

Lesson 1

Poetry has a unique form; its arrangement of lines is quite different from that of prose. The rhyme and rhythm in many poems are special qualities as well. However, the most distinctive element of poetry is its use of compact language. More than any other genre, poetry expresses important ideas in a very limited space and using a rather exacting form.

1. *Literal Comprehension, Global/Poetry.* Rather than drawing its strength from factual information, poetry relies on the creativity of the poet's imagination. As such, it is classified as imaginative literature.
2. *Literal Comprehension, Global/Poetry.* The first statement is FALSE. Some poems have characters and action, though many do not. The second statement is TRUE. Poets can arrange the placement and length of lines as they choose. The third statement is also TRUE. Many poems rhyme, though some do not.
3. *Inferential Comprehension, Global/Poetry.* Both poems deal with ideas and feelings. Poem A perhaps sounds more factual, but factual details appear in Poem B as well. Poem A may have a greater impact on the reader's emotions; Poem B may have a greater impact on the reader's senses.

Lesson 2

If the meaning of a poem is expressed literally, you can find a line in which it is stated. Sometimes the title can provide information about the literal meaning; so, too, can some details.

1. *Literal Comprehension, Specific/Poetry.* The boy could be made dizzy by the smell of the whiskey on his father's breath (lines 1–2).
2. *Literal Comprehension, Specific/Poetry.* FALSE. Although the mother frowns at the proceedings (lines 7–8), the waltzing continues until the boy is put to bed (lines 15–16).
3. *Literal Comprehension, Specific/Poetry.* In lines 7–8, the moon is described as "warning," "worn," "broken," and "tired."
4. *Literal Comprehension, Global/Poetry.* The singing does not come from birds (line 3); rather, it comes from insects. In the lines that follow, the poet refers to the noise of grasshoppers and locusts and to the chorus of "voices of little insects" (line 9).

Lesson 3

Unstated information can add various other levels of meaning to a poem. In particular, some details and most figurative language can give the reader new insights into the subject of the poem and can provide the reader with conclusions that are not stated directly.

1. *Inferential Comprehension, Specific/Poetry.* There are several indications that the boy is not enjoying the "waltz." The mention of "whiskey on your breath" (line 1) makes the reader wonder if the father is drunk. The "mother's countenance" that "Could not unfrown itself" (lines 7–8) adds to the reader's suspicion. The father also seems to be somewhat careless in the way he holds his son (the "missed" step causing a a "scraped" ear [lines 11–12]). Finally, the idea that the boy is holding on only because he is afraid to let go is suggested ("I hung on like death" [line 3]; "Still clinging" [line 16]).
2. *Inferential Comprehension, Specific/Poetry.* The boy says in line 3, "But I hung on like death." It is as if the boy is saying, "I hung on for dear life" or "I hung on so hard that only death could have loosened my grasp."
3. *Inferential Comprehension, Specific/Poetry.* The poet describes the harvested fields as "fields that rest" (line 14).
4. *Inferential Comprehension, Global/Poetry.* Of the choices given, *sad* and *nostalgic* best describe the poet's feeling. She is sad that the signs of summer soon will be gone, and she seems to be missing them even before they have disappeared.

Lesson 4

The poet's feelings about the subject of the poem and about related matters are indicated through the theme and through specific details in the poem. Sometimes those feelings are stated; sometimes they are implied. Once those feelings are understood, they can be applied to situations outside the poem, and the reader can make assumptions about a poet's reactions to real-life situations.

1. *Application/Poetry.* The father probably would not make a good business executive. His implied drinking problem would probably hurt his performance on the job. He might be better suited as a manual laborer. The details that the poet provides about the man's hands—that they are scraped (lines 9–10) and caked with dirt (line 14) indicate that hard physical labor is the kind of work he knows best.
2. *Application/Poetry.* The poet looks with fondness upon the things of nature. She seems sad that the natural way of things—in this case, the coming of winter—soon will take those things from her. Similarly, many parents look with sadness upon their children's approaching adulthood, knowing that the natural way of things—in this case, growing up—soon will make the happiness of childhood only a memory.
3. *Application/Poetry.* She probably would not fear death. The poem indicates that she understands and accepts the natural order of things. The two words she uses to describe winter—*snow-hushed* and *heavy*—are not words that indicate fear. If she were dying, the poet probably would think fondly of the world that she would be leaving behind,

but she probably would accept her death peacefully.

Lesson 5

A poet could use a wide variety of techniques to create a given mood. The use of stanzas or the choice of line length could create a flowing or a fragmented feeling. The regularity or lack of rhyme could create a similar effect. A number of devices of sound could impress the reader with a sense of the atmosphere of the poem, as well.

1. *Analysis/Poetry.* The poet wants the summer to linger and would like to make its special qualities last as long as possible. The lengthened lines might reflect her wish for lengthened summer days.
2. *Application/Poetry.* The third stanza would be labled *E F E F*; the fourth stanza would be labeled *G H G H*.
3. *Application/Poetry.* Poem B makes greater use of alliteration. Some examples can be found in the repeated "S" sound in the first stanza (Summer . . . scentless . . . singing . . . insects . . . Ceaseless . . . insistent) emphasizes the endurance of summerlike days. The "H" sound in line 12 ("Snow-hushed and heavy") is a breathy, quieting sound, like the silence of snow itself. The "M" sound in line 13 ("murmur your mute benediction") extends the murmuring sound that the poet describes.
4. *Application/Poetry.* Since it is a vowel sound that is repeated in those words, the words are examples of assonance.

Chapter 5 Quiz

1. **(4)** *Inferential Comprehension, Global/Poetry.* The poet considers dreams to be very important. The repeated "Hold fast to dreams" in each stanza emphasizes that dreams are to be treasured. The urgency in the poet's "voice" is followed by his warning of what will happen if his plea is not heard. If there is a sense of despair (Choice [2]), it is only a prediction of how the poet (and the reader) would feel if dreams were let go.
2. *Analysis/Poetry* FALSE. Both poems depend heavily upon the use of figurative language, but metaphor, not simile, is the figure that dominates both poems.
3. *Literal Comprehension, Global/Poetry.* Poem 2 is a lyric poem. Although it begins with an event (the sight of the spider at work), it focuses on exploring the poet's thoughts, not on telling a story.
4. *Literal Comprehension, Specific/Poetry.* In the first stanza of Poem 2, the author tells of watching a spider that is sending out filaments in an attempt to spin a web. The sight stirs him to think how people seek to do a different kind of "spinning."
5. **(1)** *Inferential Comprehension, Global/Poetry.* The metaphors present the image of life cut short or not lived to its fullest. If people choose to let go of their dreams, the poet says, they will be setting aside something that is essential to their ability to grow, even if that growth is only a growth in the imagination.
6. *Analysis/Poetry.* The repetition of *filament* imitates the repeated, unceasing work of the spider. The poet describes this work in line 5 as "Ever unreeling. . .ever tirelessly speeding."
7. *Inferential Comprehension, Specific/Poetry.* TRUE. All three figures refer to establishing a "foothold" in the "measureless oceans of space" that surround the soul.
8. **(2)** *Inferential Comprehension, Global/Poetry.* Point by point, the poet draws parallels between the spider's attempts to seek a foundation for its web and his soul's attempts to seek a foundation that will connect the "spheres" of its existence. He says that, like the spider, his soul will keep searching until he finds a foundation that satisfies him.
9. *Application/Poetry.* In Poem 1, "dreams die" (line 2) is an example of alliteration, as are "vacant vast" (line 3) and "soul . . . stand . . . Surrounded" (lines 6–7) in Poem 2.
10. *Application/Poetry.* The poet might see some value in organized religion as one kind of "bridge" that his soul could build to give his life meaning. However, he probably would not promote one religion over another as the "right" one. He seems to say that whatever satisfactory foundation the soul can find is the "right" one.

Chapter 6
Commentary

Lesson 1

Any subject dealing with the arts—literary arts, visual arts, or performing arts—is appropriate subject matter for commentary. Commentary can focus on a single work of art, as in a review, or it can discuss a broader subject in the arts, as in an essay.

1. *Literal Comprehension, Global/Commentary.* Passage B is a review of Eugene McCarthy's memoirs, *Up 'Til Now.*
2. *Literal Comprehension, Global/Commentary.* The author of Passage A compares novels with films. In particular, he compares the kind of "whodunit" novel made famous by Agatha Christie with the kind of "whodunit" movie he loved as a child.
3. *Literal Comprehension, Global/Commentary.* The visual arts are not discussed in either passage. Passage A discusses the literary arts (novels) and the peforming arts (film); Passage B discusses the literary arts (biography/memoirs)

Lesson 2

Since one of the chief purposes of commentary is to evaluate, or pass judgment, about art, it is important that the author's opinion be clear. In most pieces of commentary, therefore, the author's opinion will be stated and supported in an obvious way.

1. *Literal Comprehension, Specific/Commentary.* The author compares the writing styles of Agatha Christie and Noam Chomsky. He says that he has "difficulty plowing through" them (lines 11–12).
2. *Literal Comprehension, Global/Commentary.* Among the people and movements that the critic mentions to illustrate McCarthy's apparent change of

attitudes are Common Cause (line 8), congressional reformers (lines 8–9), and members of Congress whose attendance records are high (line 9).
3. *Literal Comprehension, Specific/Commentary.* Speaking of McCarthy's interesting way of expressing his recollections, the critic writes, "In fact, if there is a disappointment in *Up 'Til Now*, it is that one wishes he had told more" (lines 14–15).
4. *Literal Comprehension, Global/Commentary.* Some of the main elements of such movies are a "necessary" drawing-room scene, in which most of the mystery is explained (lines 15–16), "humorously elegant" circumstances (line 17), "foolish" characters (line 18), and "unbelievable" plots (line 18). When these movies are true to the novels from which they are taken, they will have an unexpected ending (lines 4–7). Many contain "bloodless, humdrum slayings" (line 25); some include a scene in which characters are watched through a peephole in a portrait (lines 25–27).

Lesson 3

A critic's bias will help to form his or her opinion about the subject at hand. Therefore, knowing something about a critic's biases will help the reader to understand why a critic holds a certain opinion. Objectivity can strengthen a critic's argument and make it easier for the reader to accept the critic's opinion.

1. *Inferential Comprehension, Global/Commentary.* The main idea of Passage A is that the author enjoys the "Christie"-style movie "whodunit," even though he knows it falls short of what most critics would consider great filmmaking.
2. *Inferential Comprehension, Specific/Commentary.* The critic recalls going to the movies with his friends as a child (lines 21–27). In the last sentence, he admits that they did not watch great films, "but in my day 10-year-olds would rather turn to salt in their seats than walk out of any movie in the middle." He suggests that he learned to love these movies by watching so many of them—and that he watched so many of them, in part, because of peer pressure to sit through the entire movie.
3. *Inferential Comprehension, Specific/Commentary.* The critic states, ". . . McCarthy has not written one of those thick, boring tell-all memoirs" (lines 12–13). The critic seems to be biased against most memoirs, having come across so many that he feels are too long, too boring, and too sensational ("tell-all").
4. *Inferential Comprehension, Specific/Commentary.* The key term in the critic's statement is *plain literacy*. The speaking style was *plain*—clear and straightforward. There was also a *literacy* to it—it had some of the excellence of expression associated with good literature. Thus the third choice is the most appropriate one.

Lesson 4

Ideas in a passage of commentary could be applied in a number of ways. For example, the main idea in a passage about one kind of art could be considered for another kind of art. Similarly, ideas about human behavior could be suggested in settings outside the world of art to see if they still held true.

1. *Application/Commentary.* The author of Passage B says that McCarthy ". . .gives everyone something to disagree with. That is probably why he did not make it to the very top in American politics" (lines 31–33). The implication is that he might have been more successful if he had been more agreeable. Of the choices given, the first would probably create disagreements. The author of Passage B would therefore probably agree with the second choice since compromise would be more likely to calm down opposing forces and make them more agreeable.
2. *Application/Commentary.* He probably gets along well with children because he remembers very well what it is like to be a child. In the final paragraph of Passage A, the author tells of his childhood experiences at the movies, and his memories seem to be fond ones. A person who can keep childhood memories fresh is more likely to get along well with children than one who cannot.
3. *Application/Commentary.* The two critics probably have different tastes in television shows. The author of Passage A makes the point that he enjoys the movies that have been popular, even though they fail to meet high critical standards. It can be assumed that he would feel the same way about some television shows. On the other hand, the author of Passage B reveals his bias against "thick, boring, tell-all memoirs," which are the kind that usually are very popular. Because one critic seems to find value in popular appeal whereas the other does not, it is doubtful that they would find much in common in television programming.

Lesson 5

Probably the most effective technique that a critic can use is a well-organized argument. If the argument has a strong structure, the opinion will be clear and well supported, and a conclusion usually will "wrap up" the author's thoughts. Readers are more likely to agree with a critic if they can follow the critic's argument. Authors of commentary also adopt a tone, or attitude, when they write, and they present their ideas within the context of that tone. Different tones affect readers in different ways; for example, negative comments in a serious tone have a different affect from negative comments in a playful tone. Finally, the word choice, or diction, of an author should support the tone and argument in the commentary.

1. *Analysis/Commentary.* The words that best describe the tone of Passage A are *informal* and *nostalgic*. The author is friendly toward his readers, even taking them into his confidence when discussing his childhood. He looks back fondly upon that childhood and admits that his memories have influenced his continued love for "whodunit" movies.
2. *Analysis/Commentary.* Passage B concludes with this comment: "Still, as Mr. McCarthy . . . would remind us, don't expect too much" (lines 34–35). The lack of idealism—in fact, the cynicism—in that comment mirrors what the author has said about McCarthy

earlier in the review—namely, that he has turned aside from many of the idealistic goals with which he was associated in the 1960s.
3. *Analysis/Commentary.* The words all begin with *over-*. Each one refers to a kind of excess. Taken together, however, the impact of all the excesses is almost overwhelming. The reader is hit so hard with this list of words that he or she is likely to ask whether McCarthy just might be right in his analysis. The reader would possibly want to read *Up 'Til Now* to find out what else he has said about these things.

Chapter 6 Quiz

1. *Literal Comprehension, Specific/Commentary.* The critic states that the quotation marks "imply that Terkel reserves judgment as to how 'good' World War II really was" (lines 10–11).
2. *Inferential Comprehension, Specific/Commentary.* TRUE. The passage opens with the comment "Solemn-minded historians speak ill of oral history, at least when it's published in book form." This is the very kind of work that *"The Good War"* is. As such, it probably would get a negative reaction from professional historians.
3. **(3)** *Analysis/Commentary.* By first showing the strengths of the oral tradition—that in the hands of the right person, oral history has a special "weight and perspective" (lines 5–6)—the critic then can go on to stress the value of "The Good War," a specific work of oral history that has been prepared by "a master interviewer and editor" (line 5).
4. *Literal Comprehension, Specific/Commentary.* The critic believes that *"The Good War"* is different because Studs Terkel, the editor, has asked the people that he has interviewed not only to tell about their wartime experiences but also to comment about the value of the war itself (lines 12–14).
5. *Literal Comprehension, Global/Commentary.* This passage is an example of a review. The critic discusses a specific work of art rather than a subject concerning the arts in a more general way.
6. **(5)** *Inferential Comprehension, Global/Commentary.* The critic addresses the difference in opinion over the past 30 years. Originally, the Seagram Building was considered beautiful—"a revelation" (line 2). Today, however, it is seen mostly as "severe and inhuman" (line 27). Choices (1), (2), (3), and (4) are opinions that might have been held at a given time over the past 30 years. Choice (5), however, summarizes an idea that is true throughout the passage—that tastes change.
7. *Analysis/Commentary.* The recollections strengthen the point—that the Seagram Building was originally considered beautiful—by showing how excited people once were about working there. The memories demonstrate that the opinion did not come from the critic or any other single person; rather, it was a widely held view.
8. *Literal Comprehension, Global/Commentary.* FALSE. The critic never gives his own opinion. He reports on the opinions held by other people.
9. **(1)** *Application/Commentary.* The critic discusses how a style that at one moment seems wonderful can be looked down upon at the next moment. In planning a monument, which would be intended to be meaningful for a long time, he probably would want to avoid a design that was so contemporary that it would pass out of fashion in only a few years (Choice [1]). Choice (2) is not addressed in the passage; the other choices relate to designs that could pass out of fashion quickly.
10. *Analysis/Commentary.* The tone is somewhat formal and quite impartial; the critic never states his own opinion about the Seagram Building. He also seems to keep his audience at something of a distance, never taking them into his confidence. The tone suits the passage well, for it probably is best to be impartial when discussing several opinions as equally valid.

UNIT VII Mathematics

Chapter 1 Whole Numbers

Level 1 Preview

1. 1281
   323
   217
   + 89
   1910

2. 2196
   − 328
   1868

3. 206
   × 38
   7828

4. 28)588 21
   56
   28
   28
   0

5. 34)1462 43
   136
   102
   102
   0

Lesson 1

1. 1029
   328
   + 16
   1373

2. 1632
   149
   + 28
   1809

3. 1619
   419
   + 8
   2046

4. 16,725
   4 692
   + 309
   21,726

5. 18,263
   5 901
   830
   + 76
   25,070

Lesson 2

1. 1059
   − 328
   731

2. 216
   − 98
   118

3. 1005
   − 426
   579

4. 13,328
   − 8,379
   4,949

5. 219
   − 37
   182

Lesson 3

1. 234
   × 12
   468
   234
   2808

2. 53
   × 4
   212

3. 321
   × 44
   1284
   1284
   14,124

4. 205
   × 37
   1435
   615
   7585

5. 140
   × 2
   280

6. 532
   × 108
   4256
   5320
   57,456

7. 604
   × 79
   5436
   4228
   47,716

8. 397
   × 45
   1985
   1588
   17,865

9. 3028
   × 16
   18168
   3028
   48,448

10. 163
    × 129
    1467
    326
    163
    21,027

Lesson 4

1. 40)1440 36
   120
   240
   240
   0

2. 27)1556 57 r 17
   135
   206
   189
   17

3. 34)7084 200 r 12
   68
   284
   272
   12

4. 204)19,584 96
   18 36
   1 224
   1 224
   0

5. 196)5096 26
   392
   1176
   1176
   0

Level 1 Review

1. $550
   300
   75
   + 35
   $960

2. 328,509
   + 213,694
   542,203

3. $40
   − 28
   $12

4. 92,984
   − 82,478
   10,506

5. 54
   × 16
   324
   54
   864

6. 28)5684 203
   56
   08
   00
   84
   84
   0

7. 3062
   × 208
   24496
   61240
   636,896

8. 50)2250 45
   200
   250
   250
   0

9. $140
   − 65
   $ 75

10. 603)31,356 52
    30 15
    1 206
    1 206
    0

Level 2

Lesson 1

1. **260**
2. **1850**
3. **13,260**
4. **116,890**
5. **47,910**
6. **1000**
7. **10,000**
8. **13,000**
9. **111,000**
10. **117,000**

Lesson 2

1. $d = rt$
   $= (600)(8)$
   $= 4800$ miles

2. $d = rt$
   $= (6)(15)$
   $= 90$ miles

3. $c = nr$
   $= (28)($2)$
   $= 56

A-40

UNIT VII: MATHEMATICS

Ch. 1, Level 2, Lesson 2 — Ch. 1, Level 3, Lesson 1   A-41

4. $c = nr$
 $= (12)(\$3)$
 $= \$36$

5. $c = nr$
 $= (14)(\$1)$
 $= \$14$

Lesson 3

1. $8 \times 8 = \mathbf{64}$
2. $15 \times 15 = \mathbf{225}$
3. $7 \times 7 \times 7 = \mathbf{343}$
4. $10 \times 10 \times 10 = \mathbf{1000}$
5. $3 \times 3 \times 3 \times 3 = \mathbf{81}$
6. **6**
 $6 \times 6 = 36$
7. **9**
 $9 \times 9 = 81$
8. **15**
 $15 \times 15 = 225$
9. **20**
 $20 \times 20 = 400$
10. **25**
 $25 \times 25 = 625$

Lesson 4

1. $P = 4s$
 $= 4(45)$
 $= \mathbf{180\ feet}$

2. $P = 2l + 2w$
 $= (2 \times 36) + (2 \times 12)$
 $= (72) + (24)$
 $= \mathbf{96\ inches}$

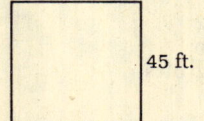

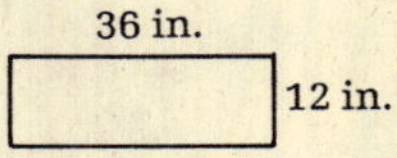

45 ft. (square)

36 in. × 12 in. (rectangle)

3. $P = a + b + c$
 $= 5 + 6 + 5$
 $= \mathbf{16\ feet}$

4. $A = lw$
 $= (16)(12)$
 $= \mathbf{192\ square\ feet}$

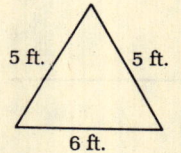

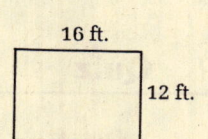

Triangle: 5 ft., 5 ft., 6 ft.

Rectangle: 16 ft. × 12 ft.

5. $A = \tfrac{1}{2}bh$
 $= \tfrac{1}{2}(20 \times 18)$
 $= \tfrac{1}{2}(360)$
 $= \mathbf{180\ square\ feet}$

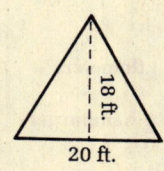

Triangle: 18 ft. high, 20 ft. base

Lesson 5

1. $V = lwh$
 $= (20)(7)(5)$
 $= \mathbf{700\ cubic\ inches}$

2. $V = lwh$
 $= (14)(10)(7)$
 $= \mathbf{980\ cubic\ yards}$

3. $V = s^3$
 $= 6 \times 6 \times 6$
 $= \mathbf{216\ cubic\ inches}$

4. $V = s^3$
 $= 10 \times 10 \times 10$
 $= \mathbf{1000\ cubic\ feet}$

5. $V = s^3$
 $= 8 \times 8 \times 8$
 $= \mathbf{512\ cubic\ yards}$

Lesson 6

1. 90
 85
 80
 75
 + 65
 ─────
 395

 $395 \div 5 = \mathbf{79}$

2. $63
 62
 58
 + 33
 ─────
 $216

 $216 \div 4 = \mathbf{\$54}$

3. 10
 9
 + 8
 ────
 27

 $27 \div 3 = \mathbf{9\ pounds}$

4. 68 78 81 **84** 86 90 92

5. 5 ft. 1 in.   5 ft. 4 in.   **5 ft. 6 in.**   5 ft. 9 in.   6 ft. 1 in.

Level 2   Review

1. $12,500; $12,000

2. $d = rt$
 $= 12(8)$
 $= \mathbf{96\ miles}$

3. $3 \times 3 \times 3 \times 3 = \mathbf{81}$

4. **11**
 $11 \times 11 = 121$

5. $P = 2l + 2w$
 $= (2 \cdot 72) + (2 \cdot 42)$
 $= (144) + (84)$
 $= \mathbf{228\ inches}$

6. $A = lw$
 $= (15)(12)$
 $= \mathbf{180\ square\ feet}$

7. $V = lwh$
 $= (24)(12)(12)$
 $= \mathbf{3456\ cubic\ inches}$

8. $V = s^3$
 $= 4 \times 4 \times 4$
 $= \mathbf{64\ cubic\ feet}$

9. $110
 85
 80
 80
 + 75
 ─────
 430

 $430 \div 5 = \mathbf{\$86}$

10. $75 $80 **$80** $85 $110

Level 3

Lesson 1

1. $18
 9
 + 7
 ────
 $34

2. $50
 − 34
 ─────
 $16

3. $16,500
 − 2,100
 ──────
 $14,400

4. 300
 × 4
 ─────
 $1200

5. $1200
 − 480
 ─────
 $ 720

$1,200
12)$14,400

4. $A = lw$
 $= (28)(13)$
 $= \mathbf{364\ square\ yards}$

 $A = lw$
 $= (12)(4)$
 $= \mathbf{48\ square\ yards}$

 364
 − 48
 ─────
 316 square yards

5. $A = s^2$
 $= (15)(15)$
 $= \mathbf{225\ square\ feet}$

 $A = s^2$
 $= (5)(5)$
 $= \mathbf{25\ square\ feet}$

 225
 − 25
 ─────
 200 square feet

A-42 Ch. 1, Level 3, Lesson 2—Chapter 1 Quiz

Lesson 2

1. 2 feet 9 inches rounds to 3 feet

      4 shelves
   3)$\overline{12}$

2.   400
   × 20
 8000 passengers

3.   300
  × 20
 6000 offspring

4.   **90 shares**
 1000)$\overline{90,000}$

5.   1000
 ×   30
 30,000 voters

Lesson 3

1. $8 per hour, part-time
 − 4 per hour, work-study
 $4 per hour more

2.   part-time   work-study
 ($8 × 30 hours) − ($4 × 40 hours)
    240   −   160
 $80 difference

3. ($4 × 40 hours per week × 50 weeks) + ($40 × 30 credits)
   (160   ×   50)   +   (1200)
        8000   +   1200
 $9200 per year

4. $2 per day × 5 days per week × 50 weeks
   (2   ×   5)   ×   50
     10   ×   50
 $500 per year

5.   part-time   work-study
 ($8 × 30 × 50) − ($2 × 5 × 50)   ($4 × 40 × 50) + ($40 × 30)
  (240 × 50) −   (10 × 50)   160 × 50 +   1200
   12,000   −   500   8000   +   1200
     $11,500 $9200
 Part-time job net income is higher.

Lesson 4

1. 52($145 + $85)
2. (76 + 67 + 65 + 74 + 77 + 75 + 70) ÷ 7
3. (48 × $252) − $8600
4. ($18,542 − $3286) ÷ 52
5. $A = lw$
   (3 × 2 × 12)$4

Level 3 Review

1. $550,000
     400,000
  + 270,000
  $1,220,000

    $1,500,000
  − 1,220,000
  $ 280,000

2. $1575
  − 250
  $1325

    $ 265
 5)$\overline{1325}$
   10
   32
   30
    25
    25

---

3. $262 $648
   155   − 555
    75   **$ 93**
    35
 + 28
 $555

4. 460 × 2 = 920
   390 × 3 = 1170
   520 × 4 = 2080
      2080
      1170
  + 920
  4170 calories

5. 460 × 3 = 1380
   520 × 2 = 1040
      1380
  − 1040
   340 calories

6. 630 × 2 = 1260
      3340
  − 1260
    2080

     4 hours
 520)$\overline{2080}$
    2080
       0

7. $A = lw$
   = (12)(10)
   = 120
  $A = lw$
   = (3)(2)
   = 6
  $A = lw$
   = (2)(1)
   = 2
     6
   + 2
     8
   120
  − 8
  112 square centimeters

8. $A = lw$
   = (14 + 10 + 8)(16)
   = (32)(16)
   = **512 square feet**
  $A = lw$
   = (10)(8)
   = **80 square feet**
    512
  + 80
  592 tiles

9. (15 × $4) + (20 × $5)

10. (2 × 25) + (3 × 28) + (30)

Chapter 1 Quiz

1.   628
   385
   305
 + 255
 1573 kilometers

2. $40
  − 28
  $12

3.   40
  × 15
 600 people

4.   **80 hamburgers**
 75)$\overline{6000}$
   600
     00
     00

5. **2230 miles**
   $d = rt$
     = (53)(42)
     = 2226, or 2230

6. 8 quarts = 2 gallons
   $c = nr$
     = (2)($3)
     = **$6**

7. **125**
   5 × 5 × 5 = 125

8. **9**
   9 × 9 = 81

9. $P = 2l + 2w$
   = (2 × 43) + (2 × 18)
   = (86) + (36)
   = **122 yards**

10. $A = s^2$
    = 15 × 15
    = **225 square feet**

UNIT VII: MATHEMATICS   Chapter 1 Quiz—Ch. 2, Level 1, Lesson 4   **A-43**

11. $V = lwh$
    $= (8)(4)(3)$
    = **96 cubic feet**

12. $A = lw$
    $= (15)(12)$
    = **180 square feet**

13. $A = lw$
    $= (15 + 4)(12 + 4)$
    $= (19)(16)$
    $= 304$ square feet

    304
    $\underline{-180}$
    124 square feet

14. $A = lw$
    $= (18)(22 - 8)$
    $= (18)(14)$
    $= 252$

    $A = lw$
    $= (9)(8)$
    $= 72$

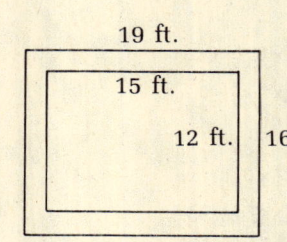

    252
    $\underline{+\ \ 72}$
    324 square feet

15. $A = lw$
    $= (100)(60)$
    $= 6000$ square feet

    6000
    $\underline{\times\ \ \ \ \$8}$
    $48,000

16. 2900
    $\underline{-2100}$
    800 calories

17. 2700
    2100
    2000
    $\underline{+\ 1700}$
    8500

    2125 calories
    $4 \overline{)8500}$

18. $\$450$
    $\underline{-\ \ \ 50}$
    $\$400$

    $40
    $10\overline{)400}$

19. $4 \times 2 = 8$ pounds
    $c = nr$
    $= (8)(\$4)$
    $= \$32$

20. $(52 \times \$125) + (12 \times \$350)$

Chapter 2   Fractions

Level 1   Preview

1. $\frac{1}{4} = \frac{5}{20}$
   $\frac{4}{5} = \frac{16}{20}$
   $\underline{+\ \frac{7}{10} = \frac{14}{20}}$
   $\frac{35}{20} = 1\frac{15}{20} = \mathbf{1\frac{3}{4}}$

2. $\frac{14}{15} = \frac{14}{15}$
   $\underline{-\ \frac{3}{5} = \frac{9}{15}}$
   $\frac{5}{15} = \mathbf{\frac{1}{3}}$

3. $2\frac{5}{8} \times \frac{5}{9}$
   $\frac{\cancel{21}^7}{8} \times \frac{5}{\cancel{9}_3} = \frac{35}{24} = \mathbf{1\frac{11}{24}}$

4. $\frac{6}{11} \div \frac{21}{22}$
   $\frac{\cancel{6}^2}{\cancel{11}_1} \times \frac{\cancel{22}^2}{\cancel{21}_7} = \mathbf{\frac{4}{7}}$

5. $4\frac{1}{5} \div 1\frac{13}{15}$
   $\frac{21}{5} \div \frac{28}{15}$
   $\frac{\cancel{21}^3}{\cancel{5}_1} \times \frac{\cancel{15}^3}{\cancel{28}_4} = \frac{9}{4} = \mathbf{2\frac{1}{4}}$

Lesson 1

1. $\frac{5 \div 5}{20 \div 5} = \mathbf{\frac{1}{4}}$
2. $\frac{6 \div 3}{9 \div 3} = \mathbf{\frac{2}{3}}$
3. $\frac{4 \div 4}{24 \div 4} = \mathbf{\frac{1}{6}}$
4. $\frac{56 \div 7}{63 \div 7} = \mathbf{\frac{8}{9}}$
5. $\frac{15 \div 3}{21 \div 3} = \mathbf{\frac{5}{7}}$

Lesson 2

1. $\frac{1 \times 3}{4 \times 3} = \mathbf{\frac{3}{12}}$
2. $\frac{1 \times 10}{2 \times 10} = \mathbf{\frac{10}{20}}$
3. $\frac{2 \times 3}{5 \times 3} = \mathbf{\frac{6}{15}}$
4. $\frac{5 \times 4}{8 \times 4} = \mathbf{\frac{20}{32}}$
5. $\frac{5 \times 6}{6 \times 6} = \mathbf{\frac{30}{36}}$
6. $\frac{7 \times 3}{9 \times 3} = \mathbf{\frac{21}{27}}$
7. $\frac{2 \times 8}{3 \times 8} = \mathbf{\frac{16}{24}}$
8. $\frac{5 \times 5}{6 \times 5} = \mathbf{\frac{25}{30}}$
9. $\frac{3 \times 5}{7 \times 5} = \mathbf{\frac{15}{35}}$
10. $\frac{5 \times 5}{12 \times 5} = \mathbf{\frac{25}{60}}$

Lesson 3

1. $7\overline{)7}^{\,\mathbf{1}}$
2. $4\overline{)28}^{\,\mathbf{7}}$
3. $10\overline{)22}^{\,2\frac{2}{10} = \mathbf{2\frac{1}{5}}}$
4. $9\overline{)66}^{\,7\frac{3}{9} = \mathbf{7\frac{1}{3}}}$
5. $8\overline{)54}^{\,6\frac{6}{8} = \mathbf{6\frac{3}{4}}}$
6. $1\frac{1}{2} = \frac{(1 \times 2) + 1}{2} = \mathbf{\frac{3}{2}}$
7. $2\frac{5}{6} = \frac{(2 \times 6) + 5}{6} = \mathbf{\frac{17}{6}}$
8. $8\frac{3}{7} = \frac{(8 \times 7) + 3}{7} = \mathbf{\frac{59}{7}}$
9. $4\frac{2}{5} = \frac{(4 \times 5) + 2}{5} = \mathbf{\frac{22}{5}}$
10. $5\frac{11}{12} = \frac{(5 \times 12) + 11}{12} = \mathbf{\frac{71}{12}}$

Lesson 4

1. $\frac{1}{3} = \frac{1 \times 3}{3 \times 3} = \mathbf{\frac{3}{9}}$
   $\frac{2}{9} = \frac{2 \times 1}{9 \times 1} = \mathbf{\frac{2}{9}}$

2. $\frac{2}{5} = \frac{2 \times 8}{5 \times 8} = \mathbf{\frac{16}{40}}$
   $\frac{3}{8} = \frac{3 \times 5}{8 \times 5} = \mathbf{\frac{15}{40}}$

3. $\frac{3}{4} = \frac{3 \times 3}{4 \times 3} = \mathbf{\frac{9}{12}}$
   $\frac{5}{6} = \frac{5 \times 2}{6 \times 2} = \mathbf{\frac{10}{12}}$

4. $\frac{1}{4} = \frac{1 \times 5}{4 \times 5} = \mathbf{\frac{5}{20}}$
   $\frac{7}{10} = \frac{7 \times 2}{10 \times 2} = \mathbf{\frac{14}{20}}$

5. $\frac{2}{3} = \frac{2 \times 8}{3 \times 8} = \mathbf{\frac{16}{24}}$
   $\frac{5}{8} = \frac{5 \times 3}{8 \times 3} = \mathbf{\frac{15}{24}}$

6. $\frac{2}{3} = \frac{2 \times 10}{3 \times 10} = \mathbf{\frac{20}{30}}$
   $\frac{9}{10} = \frac{9 \times 3}{10 \times 3} = \mathbf{\frac{27}{30}}$
   $\frac{11}{15} = \frac{11 \times 2}{15 \times 2} = \mathbf{\frac{22}{30}}$

A-44 Ch. 2, Level 1, Lesson 4 — Ch. 2, Level 1, Lesson 8INSTRUCTION

7. $\frac{1}{3} = \frac{1 \times 8}{3 \times 8} = \frac{8}{24}$

$\frac{5}{6} = \frac{5 \times 4}{6 \times 4} = \frac{20}{24}$

$\frac{7}{8} = \frac{7 \times 3}{8 \times 3} = \frac{21}{24}$

8. $\frac{1}{2} = \frac{1 \times 20}{2 \times 20} = \frac{20}{40}$

$\frac{3}{8} = \frac{3 \times 5}{8 \times 5} = \frac{15}{40}$

$\frac{2}{5} = \frac{2 \times 8}{5 \times 8} = \frac{16}{40}$

9. $12\frac{2}{3} = 12\frac{8}{12} = 11\frac{8}{12} + \frac{12}{12} = 11\frac{20}{12}$
$\underline{- \ 6\frac{3}{4} = \ 6\frac{9}{12} \ \ \ = \ \ 6\frac{9}{12}}$
$5\frac{11}{12}$

9. $\frac{1}{4} = \frac{1 \times 15}{4 \times 15} = \frac{15}{60}$

$\frac{4}{5} = \frac{4 \times 12}{5 \times 12} = \frac{48}{60}$

$\frac{5}{6} = \frac{5 \times 10}{6 \times 10} = \frac{50}{60}$

10. $\frac{5}{6} = \frac{5 \times 28}{6 \times 28} = \frac{140}{168}$

$\frac{5}{7} = \frac{5 \times 24}{7 \times 24} = \frac{120}{168}$

$\frac{5}{8} = \frac{5 \times 21}{8 \times 21} = \frac{105}{168}$

10. $13\frac{1}{8} = 13\frac{3}{24} = 12\frac{3}{24} + \frac{24}{24} = 12\frac{27}{24}$
$\underline{- \ 4\frac{7}{12} = \ \ 4\frac{14}{24} = \ \ \ \ \ \ \ 4\frac{14}{24}}$
$8\frac{13}{24}$

Lesson 5

1. $\frac{3}{5}$
$\underline{+\frac{1}{5}}$
$\frac{4}{5}$

2. $\frac{7}{12}$
$\underline{+\frac{11}{12}}$
$\frac{18}{12} = 1\frac{6}{12} = \mathbf{1\frac{1}{2}}$

Lesson 7

1. $\frac{3}{4} \times \frac{1}{4} = \frac{3}{16}$

2. $\frac{5}{2} \times \frac{1}{8} = \frac{5}{16}$

3. $6\frac{3}{8}$
$\underline{+7\frac{3}{8}}$
$13\frac{6}{8} = \mathbf{13\frac{3}{4}}$

4. $4\frac{7}{10}$
$\underline{+3\frac{3}{10}}$
$7\frac{10}{10} = \mathbf{8}$

3. $\frac{2}{3} \times \frac{5}{6} \times \frac{1}{8} = \frac{10}{72} = \frac{5}{36}$

4. $\frac{3}{4} \times 8$
$\frac{3}{1} \times \frac{2}{1} = \frac{6}{1} = \mathbf{6}$

5. $\frac{1}{2} = \frac{4}{8}$
$\underline{+\frac{3}{8} = \frac{3}{8}}$
$\frac{7}{8}$

6. $\frac{2}{3} = \frac{8}{12}$
$\underline{+\frac{3}{4} = \frac{9}{12}}$
$\frac{17}{12} = \mathbf{1\frac{5}{12}}$

5. $2\frac{1}{2} \times \frac{4}{5}$
$\frac{1}{1} \times \frac{2}{1} = \frac{2}{1} = \mathbf{2}$

6. $2\frac{1}{4} \times 3\frac{1}{3}$
$\frac{3}{2} \times \frac{10}{3} = \frac{15}{2} = \mathbf{7\frac{1}{2}}$

7. $\frac{1}{2} = \frac{6}{12}$
$\frac{1}{4} = \frac{3}{12}$
$\underline{+\frac{5}{6} = \frac{10}{12}}$
$\frac{19}{12} = \mathbf{1\frac{7}{12}}$

8. $4\frac{1}{6} = 4\frac{4}{24}$
$\underline{+8\frac{3}{8} = 8\frac{9}{24}}$
$12\frac{13}{24}$

7. $1\frac{2}{3} \times 9$
$\frac{5}{1} \times \frac{3}{1} = \frac{15}{1} = \mathbf{15}$

8. $1\frac{1}{6} \times \frac{3}{7} \times 4\frac{2}{3}$
$\frac{1}{3} \times \frac{1}{7} \times \frac{7}{1} = \frac{7}{3} = \mathbf{2\frac{1}{3}}$

9. $7\frac{2}{3} = 7\frac{4}{6}$
$\underline{+6\frac{1}{2} = 6\frac{3}{6}}$
$13\frac{7}{6} = \mathbf{14\frac{1}{6}}$

10. $3\frac{4}{5} = 3\frac{12}{15}$
$\underline{+\frac{13}{15} = \frac{13}{15}}$
$3\frac{25}{15} = 4\frac{10}{15} = \mathbf{4\frac{2}{3}}$

9. $3\frac{1}{5} \times 6 \times 1\frac{1}{4}$
$\frac{4}{1} \times \frac{6}{1} \times \frac{5}{4} = \frac{24}{1} = \mathbf{24}$

10. $1\frac{1}{11} \times \frac{11}{12}$
$\frac{12}{11} \times \frac{11}{12} = \frac{1}{1} = \mathbf{1}$

Lesson 6

1. $\frac{8}{9}$
$\underline{-\frac{7}{9}}$
$\frac{1}{9}$

2. $\frac{7}{16}$
$\underline{-\frac{3}{16}}$
$\frac{4}{16} = \mathbf{\frac{1}{4}}$

Lesson 8

1. $\frac{1}{3} \div \frac{3}{4}$
$\frac{1}{3} \times \frac{4}{3} = \frac{4}{9}$

2. $\frac{4}{5} \div \frac{7}{10}$
$\frac{4}{1} \times \frac{2}{7} = \frac{8}{7} = \mathbf{1\frac{1}{7}}$

3. $9\frac{3}{4}$
$\underline{-3\frac{1}{4}}$
$6\frac{2}{4} = \mathbf{6\frac{1}{2}}$

4. $\frac{2}{3} = \frac{4}{6}$
$\underline{-\frac{1}{6} = \frac{1}{6}}$
$\frac{3}{6} = \mathbf{\frac{1}{2}}$

3. $8 \div \frac{1}{2}$
$\frac{8}{1} \times \frac{2}{1} = \frac{16}{1} = \mathbf{16}$

4. $\frac{5}{6} \div 10$
$\frac{1}{6} \times \frac{1}{10} = \mathbf{\frac{1}{12}}$

5. $6\frac{4}{5} = 6\frac{8}{10}$
$\underline{-2\frac{1}{2} = 2\frac{5}{10}}$
$4\frac{3}{10}$

6. $7\frac{2}{5}$
$\underline{- \ 5}$
$2\frac{2}{5}$

5. $1\frac{2}{3} \div 3$
$\frac{5}{3} \times \frac{1}{3} = \mathbf{\frac{5}{9}}$

6. $\frac{3}{5} \div 5\frac{1}{4}$
$\frac{3}{5} \div \frac{21}{4}$
$\frac{1}{5} \times \frac{4}{7} = \mathbf{\frac{4}{35}}$

7. $11 \ = 10\frac{6}{6}$
$\underline{- \ 2\frac{5}{6} = \ 2\frac{5}{6}}$
$8\frac{1}{6}$

8. $8\frac{2}{5} = 7\frac{2}{5} + \frac{5}{5} = 7\frac{7}{5}$
$\underline{-1\frac{4}{5} \ \ \ \ \ \ \ \ \ \ = 1\frac{4}{5}}$
$6\frac{3}{5}$

7. $5\frac{1}{3} \div 4$
$\frac{16}{3} \times \frac{1}{4} = \frac{4}{3} = \mathbf{1\frac{1}{3}}$

8. $5 \div 4\frac{1}{6}$
$\frac{5}{1} \times \frac{6}{25} = \frac{6}{5} = \mathbf{1\frac{1}{5}}$

9. $3\frac{1}{2} \div 4\frac{5}{8}$
$\frac{7}{2} \times \frac{8}{37} = \mathbf{\frac{28}{37}}$

10. $2\frac{2}{3} \div 1\frac{1}{5}$
$\frac{8}{3} \times \frac{5}{6} = \frac{20}{9} = \mathbf{2\frac{2}{9}}$

UNIT VII: MATHEMATICS

Level 1   Review

1. $\dfrac{21 \div 3}{36 \div 3} = \dfrac{7}{12}$

2. $7\dfrac{3}{4} = \dfrac{(7 \times 4) + 3}{4} = \dfrac{31}{4}$

3. $\begin{aligned} \dfrac{2}{3} &= \dfrac{16}{24} \\ +\dfrac{5}{8} &= \dfrac{15}{24} \\ \hline \dfrac{31}{24} &= 1\dfrac{7}{24} \end{aligned}$

4. $\begin{aligned} 5\dfrac{7}{12} &= 5\dfrac{7}{12} \\ 3\dfrac{1}{6} &= 3\dfrac{2}{12} \\ +7\dfrac{2}{3} &= 7\dfrac{8}{12} \\ \hline & 15\dfrac{17}{12} = 16\dfrac{5}{12} \end{aligned}$

5. $\begin{aligned} 5\dfrac{6}{7} &= 5\dfrac{30}{35} \\ -2\dfrac{2}{5} &= 2\dfrac{14}{35} \\ \hline & 3\dfrac{16}{35} \end{aligned}$

6. $\begin{aligned} 9\dfrac{2}{3} &= 9\dfrac{6}{9} = 8\dfrac{6}{9} + \dfrac{9}{9} = 8\dfrac{15}{9} \\ -4\dfrac{7}{9} &= 4\dfrac{7}{9} \phantom{= 8\dfrac{6}{9} + \dfrac{9}{9}} = 4\dfrac{7}{9} \\ \hline & 4\dfrac{8}{9} \end{aligned}$

7. $\dfrac{4}{5} \times 2\dfrac{1}{2}$

   $\dfrac{\cancel{4}^{2}}{\cancel{5}_{1}} \times \dfrac{\cancel{5}^{1}}{\cancel{2}_{1}} = \dfrac{2}{1} = 2$

8. $4\dfrac{3}{8} \times \dfrac{4}{7} \times 3$

   $\dfrac{\cancel{35}^{5}}{\cancel{8}_{2}} \times \dfrac{\cancel{4}^{1}}{\cancel{7}_{1}} \times \dfrac{3}{1} = \dfrac{15}{2} = 7\dfrac{1}{2}$

9. $5 \div \dfrac{10}{11}$

   $\dfrac{\cancel{5}^{1}}{1} \times \dfrac{11}{\cancel{10}_{2}} = \dfrac{11}{2} = 5\dfrac{1}{2}$

10. $\dfrac{11}{12} \div 2\dfrac{4}{9}$

    $\dfrac{\cancel{11}^{1}}{\cancel{12}_{4}} \times \dfrac{\cancel{9}^{3}}{\cancel{22}_{2}} = \dfrac{3}{8}$

Level 2

Lesson 1

1. $\begin{aligned} & 12 \text{ inches per foot} \\ & \underline{\times 12 \text{ feet}} \\ & \mathbf{144 \text{ inches}} \end{aligned}$

2. $\begin{aligned} & 24 \text{ ounces} \\ & \overline{16 \text{ ounces per pound}} \\ & = 1\dfrac{8}{16} = \mathbf{1\dfrac{1}{2} \text{ pounds}} \end{aligned}$

3. $\begin{aligned} & 10 \text{ quarts} \\ & \overline{4 \text{ quarts per gallon}} \\ & = 2\dfrac{2}{4} = \mathbf{2\dfrac{1}{2} \text{ gallons}} \end{aligned}$

4. $\begin{aligned} & 45 \text{ minutes} \\ & \overline{60 \text{ minutes per hour}} \\ & = \mathbf{\dfrac{3}{4} \text{ hour}} \end{aligned}$

5. $\dfrac{1}{4}$ year $\times$ 12 months per year

   $\dfrac{1}{\cancel{4}_{1}} \times \dfrac{\cancel{12}^{3}}{1} = \dfrac{3}{1} = \mathbf{3 \text{ months}}$

6. $1\dfrac{1}{2}$ pints $\times$ 16 ounces per pint

   $\dfrac{\cancel{3}^{3}}{\cancel{2}_{1}} \times \dfrac{\cancel{16}^{8}}{1} = \mathbf{24 \text{ ounces}}$

7. $\begin{aligned} & 80 \text{ hours} \\ & \overline{24 \text{ hours per day}} \\ & = 3\dfrac{8}{24} = \mathbf{3\dfrac{1}{3} \text{ days}} \end{aligned}$

8. $\dfrac{5}{6}$ minute $\times$ 60 seconds per minute

   $\dfrac{5}{\cancel{6}_{1}} \times \dfrac{\cancel{60}^{10}}{1} = \dfrac{50}{1} = \mathbf{50 \text{ seconds}}$

9. $2\dfrac{1}{2}$ miles $\times$ 5280 feet per mile

   $\dfrac{5}{2} \times \dfrac{5280}{1} = \mathbf{13{,}200 \text{ feet}}$

10. $\begin{aligned} & 400 \text{ square rods} \\ & \overline{160 \text{ square rods per acre}} \\ & = 2\dfrac{80}{160} = \mathbf{2\dfrac{1}{2} \text{ acres}} \end{aligned}$

Lesson 2

1. $\dfrac{7}{8} = \dfrac{7 \times 3}{8 \times 3} = \dfrac{21}{24}$

   $\dfrac{5}{12} = \dfrac{5 \times 2}{12 \times 2} = \dfrac{10}{24}$

2. $\dfrac{3}{5} = \dfrac{3 \times 4}{5 \times 4} = \dfrac{12}{20}$

   $\dfrac{3}{4} = \dfrac{3 \times 5}{4 \times 5} = \dfrac{15}{20}$

3. $\dfrac{9}{10} = \dfrac{9 \times 3}{10 \times 3} = \dfrac{27}{30}$

   $\dfrac{13}{15} = \dfrac{13 \times 2}{15 \times 2} = \dfrac{26}{30}$

4. $\dfrac{2}{3} = \dfrac{2 \times 7}{3 \times 7} = \dfrac{14}{21}$

   $\dfrac{5}{7} = \dfrac{5 \times 3}{7 \times 3} = \dfrac{15}{21}$

5. $\dfrac{2}{11} = \dfrac{2 \times 6}{11 \times 6} = \dfrac{12}{66}$

   $\dfrac{1}{6} = \dfrac{1 \times 11}{6 \times 11} = \dfrac{11}{66}$

6. $\dfrac{1}{3} = \dfrac{1 \times 7}{3 \times 7} = \dfrac{7}{21}$

   $\dfrac{3}{7} = \dfrac{3 \times 3}{7 \times 3} = \dfrac{9}{21}$

7. $\dfrac{1}{2} = \dfrac{1 \times 13}{2 \times 13} = \dfrac{13}{26}$

   $\dfrac{6}{13} = \dfrac{6 \times 2}{13 \times 2} = \dfrac{12}{26}$

8. $\dfrac{5}{8} = \dfrac{5 \times 3}{8 \times 3} = \dfrac{15}{24}$

   $\dfrac{7}{12} = \dfrac{7 \times 2}{12 \times 2} = \dfrac{14}{24}$

9. $\dfrac{3}{14}, \dfrac{1}{4}, \dfrac{15}{28}, \dfrac{5}{7}$

   $\dfrac{5}{7} = \dfrac{5 \times 4}{7 \times 4} = \dfrac{20}{28}$

   $\dfrac{3}{14} = \dfrac{3 \times 2}{14 \times 2} = \dfrac{6}{28}$

   $\dfrac{1}{4} = \dfrac{1 \times 7}{4 \times 7} = \dfrac{7}{28}$

   $\dfrac{15}{28} = \dfrac{15 \times 1}{28 \times 1} = \dfrac{15}{28}$

10. $\dfrac{1}{6}, \dfrac{4}{9}, \dfrac{1}{2}, \dfrac{2}{3}$

    $\dfrac{4}{9} = \dfrac{4 \times 2}{9 \times 2} = \dfrac{8}{18}$

    $\dfrac{2}{3} = \dfrac{2 \times 6}{3 \times 6} = \dfrac{12}{18}$

    $\dfrac{1}{2} = \dfrac{1 \times 9}{2 \times 9} = \dfrac{9}{18}$

    $\dfrac{1}{6} = \dfrac{1 \times 3}{6 \times 3} = \dfrac{3}{18}$

Lesson 3

1. John $\dfrac{30}{54} = \dfrac{5}{9}$, Roger $\dfrac{27}{63} = \dfrac{3}{7}$, Sam $\dfrac{12}{48} = \dfrac{1}{4}$, Victoria $\dfrac{9}{24} = \dfrac{3}{8}$, Vincent $\dfrac{22}{55} = \dfrac{2}{5}$, William $\dfrac{32}{72} = \dfrac{4}{9}$, Zachary $\dfrac{9}{36} = \dfrac{1}{4}$

2. **Vincent** $\left(\dfrac{2}{5}\right)$ = Alberto $\left(\dfrac{2}{5}\right)$

   Sam $\left(\dfrac{1}{4}\right)$ = Zachary $\left(\dfrac{1}{4}\right)$

3. **Victoria** $\dfrac{3}{8} = \dfrac{3}{8}$

   Zachary $\dfrac{1}{4} = \dfrac{2}{8}$

4. **Elizabeth**

   $\dfrac{1}{2} = \dfrac{1 \times 28}{2 \times 28} = \dfrac{28}{56}$

   Roger

   $\dfrac{3}{7} = \dfrac{3 \times 8}{7 \times 8} = \dfrac{24}{56}$

   Victoria

   $\dfrac{3}{8} = \dfrac{3 \times 7}{8 \times 7} = \dfrac{21}{56}$

   Sam

   $\dfrac{1}{4} = \dfrac{1 \times 14}{4 \times 14} = \dfrac{14}{56}$

5. **Vincent**

   $\dfrac{2}{5} = \dfrac{2 \times 9}{5 \times 9} = \dfrac{18}{45}$

   William

   $\dfrac{4}{9} = \dfrac{4 \times 5}{9 \times 5} = \dfrac{20}{45}$

   John

   $\dfrac{5}{9} = \dfrac{5 \times 5}{9 \times 5} = \dfrac{25}{45}$

Lesson 4

1. $\dfrac{10}{22} = \dfrac{5}{11}$

2. $\dfrac{10}{6} = \dfrac{5}{3}$

3. $\dfrac{2000}{3000} = \dfrac{2}{3}$

4. $2 + 1 + 1 = 4$
$\dfrac{2}{4} = \dfrac{1}{2}$

5. $100 - 20 = 80$
$\dfrac{80}{100} = \dfrac{4}{5}$

Lesson 5

1. $2 + 1 + 1 = 4$
$\dfrac{1}{4}$

2. $2 + 3 + 4 = 9$
$\dfrac{3}{9} = \dfrac{1}{3}$

3. $15 + 20 = 35$
$\dfrac{15}{35} = \dfrac{3}{7}$

4. $5 + 3 + 2 - 1 = 9$
$\dfrac{2}{9}$

5. $20 - 3 = 17$
$\dfrac{17}{20}$

Level 2 Review

1. $n = c/r$
$= \dfrac{18}{3}$
$= \textbf{6 yards}$

2. $6\tfrac{1}{2}$ gallons × 8 pints per gallon
$\dfrac{13}{2} \times \dfrac{8}{1} = \textbf{52 pints}$

3. $\dfrac{24 \text{ ounces}}{16 \text{ ounces per pound}}$
$= 1\tfrac{8}{16} = \textbf{1}\tfrac{1}{2}$ **pounds**

4. $P = 4s$
$= 4 \times 5\tfrac{1}{4}$
$= \dfrac{4}{1} \times \dfrac{21}{4}$
$= \textbf{21 feet}$

5. The area of one bed:
$A = lw$
$= 7\tfrac{1}{3} \times 3\tfrac{1}{2}$
$= \dfrac{22}{3} \times \dfrac{7}{2}$
$= \dfrac{77}{3} = 25\tfrac{2}{3}$

The area of four beds:
$25\tfrac{2}{3} \times 4$
$\dfrac{77}{3} \times \dfrac{4}{1}$
$\dfrac{308}{3} = \textbf{102}\tfrac{2}{3}$ **square feet**

6. $\dfrac{1}{6}, \dfrac{1}{2}, \dfrac{5}{8}, \dfrac{2}{3}$

$\dfrac{2}{3} = \dfrac{2 \times 8}{3 \times 8} = \dfrac{16}{24}$

$\dfrac{5}{8} = \dfrac{5 \times 3}{8 \times 3} = \dfrac{15}{24}$

$\dfrac{1}{6} = \dfrac{1 \times 4}{6 \times 4} = \dfrac{4}{24}$

$\dfrac{1}{2} = \dfrac{1 \times 12}{2 \times 12} = \dfrac{12}{24}$

7. $100 - 75 = 25$
$\dfrac{25}{100} = \dfrac{1}{4}$

8. $15 + 13 = 28$
$\dfrac{15}{28}$

9. Add to find the total number of members: 80. There are 5 members who are 6 feet or more.
$\dfrac{5}{80} = \dfrac{1}{16}$

10. Add to find the number of members less than 6 feet: 75. There are 15 members who are 5 feet 4 inches or less.
$\dfrac{15}{75} = \dfrac{1}{5}$

Level 3

Lesson 1

1. (4)
$\dfrac{60 + 24 + 12 \text{ ounces}}{32 \text{ ounces per quart}}$

2. (2)
$\dfrac{120 \text{ hours}}{24 \text{ hours per day}}$ $\dfrac{2880 \text{ minutes}}{1440 \text{ minutes per day}}$

3. (3)
$\dfrac{\text{number of even numbers}}{\text{total number of numbers}}$

4. (2)
$\dfrac{\text{total feet}}{3 \text{ feet per yard}}$
$\dfrac{8 \times 2\tfrac{1}{4} \text{ total feet}}{3 \text{ feet per yard}}$
$\dfrac{8 \times 2\tfrac{1}{4}}{3} \times \text{rate}$

5. (3)
(cost per cubic yard × number of cubic yards) + delivery charge

Lesson 2

1. $\dfrac{8 \text{ feet}}{3 \text{ feet per yard}} = 2\tfrac{2}{3}$ yards
$A = lw$
$= 2\tfrac{2}{3} \times 2$
$= \dfrac{8}{3} \times \dfrac{2}{1}$
$= \dfrac{16}{3} = \textbf{5}\tfrac{1}{3}$ **square yards**

2. $\tfrac{1}{4}$ foot × 12 inches per foot $= \dfrac{12}{4} = 3$ inches
$A = s^2$
$= 3^2 = \textbf{9 square inches}$

3. $\dfrac{9 \text{ inches}}{12 \text{ inches per foot}} = \tfrac{3}{4}$ foot
$\tfrac{2}{3}$ yard × 3 feet per yard $= \dfrac{6}{3} = 2$ feet
$P = a + b + c$
$2\tfrac{3}{4} = 2\tfrac{3}{4}$
$+ 1\tfrac{1}{2} = 1\tfrac{2}{4}$
$3\tfrac{5}{4} = \textbf{4}\tfrac{1}{4}$ **feet**

UNIT VII: MATHEMATICS Ch. 2, Level 3, Lesson 2—Chapter 2 Quiz

4. $\frac{1}{2}$ foot × 12 inches per foot = $\frac{12}{2}$ = 6 inches
   $A = \frac{1}{2}bh$
   $= \frac{(11 \times 6)}{2}$
   $= \frac{66}{2} = \frac{33}{1} =$ **33 square inches**

5. $\frac{18 \text{ inches}}{12 \text{ inches per foot}} = 1\frac{1}{2}$ feet
   $V = lwh$
   $= 2 \times 1\frac{1}{2} \times \frac{3}{4}$
   $= \frac{2}{1} \times \frac{3}{2} \times \frac{3}{4}$
   $= \frac{9}{4} = 2\frac{1}{4}$ **cubic feet**

Lesson 3

1. Total tiles
   $5 \times 20 = 100$
   Tiles used
   $3\frac{1}{2} \times 20$
   $\frac{7}{2} \times \frac{20}{1} = 70$
   Tiles left
   $100 - 70 =$ **30 tiles**
   Extraneous: **cost**

2. $1\frac{1}{2} = 1\frac{4}{8} = \frac{4}{8} + \frac{8}{8} = \frac{12}{8}$
   $- \frac{5}{8} = \frac{5}{8} = \frac{5}{8}$
   $\frac{7}{8}$ **pound**
   Extraneous: **3-inch nails bought and used; price**

3. $\frac{50 \text{ minutes}}{60 \text{ minutes per hour}} = \frac{5}{6}$ hour
   1 hour 10 minutes = $1 + \frac{10 \text{ minutes}}{60 \text{ minutes per hour}} = 1\frac{1}{6}$ hours
   $\frac{3}{4} = \frac{9}{12}$
   $\frac{5}{6} = \frac{10}{12}$
   $2\frac{1}{2} = 2\frac{6}{12}$
   $1\frac{1}{2} = 1\frac{6}{12}$
   $+ 1\frac{1}{6} = 1\frac{2}{12}$
   $4\frac{33}{12} = 6\frac{9}{12} = 6\frac{3}{4}$ **hours**
   Extraneous: **number of trees; travel time**

4. $\frac{5}{55} = \frac{1}{11}$
   Extraneous: **bottle refund**

5. $3 \times 1\frac{1}{4} \times 4$
   $\frac{3}{1} \times \frac{5}{4} \times \frac{4}{1} =$ **15 cups**
   Extraneous: **amount of water conditioner and bleach used**

Level 3   Review

1. (3)
   $\left(42 \times \frac{2}{7}\right)$ gives cost to employee

2. (4)
   2000 − 1500 gives amount paid in taxes

3. (2)
   $\left(1\frac{1}{2} \times 4 \text{ quarts per gallon}\right) + \frac{14}{2}$ pints per quart

4. (4)
   1 foot = 12 inches
   $P = a + b + c$
   $= 3\frac{1}{2} + 3\frac{1}{2} + 3\frac{1}{2}$
   Find perimeter in feet, then divide by 12.

5. $2\frac{2}{3}$ yards × 3 feet per yard = $\frac{8}{3} \times 3 = 8$ feet
   $A = lw$
   $= 8 \times 3$
   $= 24$
   $= 24$ square feet
   $\frac{2}{3}$ yard × 3 feet per yard = $\frac{2}{3} \times 3 = 2$ feet
   $A = lw$
   $= 4 \times 2$
   $= 8$ square feet
   $\frac{8}{24} = \frac{1}{3}$

6. $1\frac{1}{2}$ feet × 12 inches per foot = 18 inches
   $A = lw$
   $= 18 \times 9$
   = **162 square inches**

7. 35 hours × 2 winders × 5 coils per hour = 350 coils
   $\frac{1}{35} \times 350$
   $\frac{1}{35} \times \frac{350}{1} =$ **10 bad coils**

8. $8\frac{3}{4} \times 200$
   $\frac{35}{4} \times \frac{200}{1} = \frac{1750}{1} = 1750$ feet
   $12\frac{70}{140} = 12\frac{1}{2}$ **spools**
   140)1750
      140
      350
      280
       70

9. $8\frac{3}{4} \times 5$
   $\frac{35}{4} \times \frac{5}{1} = \frac{175}{4} = 43\frac{3}{4}$ **feet**

10. Wire costs 10 cents per foot; all other materials cost $11\frac{1}{2}$ cents; coil winders earn $15 per hour.

Chapter 2   Quiz

1. a. **Cord C** = $28\frac{1}{2}$ feet. $1\frac{1}{2}$ rods × $16\frac{1}{2}$ feet per rod = $24\frac{3}{4}$ feet

   b. **Cord A** = 290 inches. $1\frac{1}{2}$ rods = $24\frac{3}{4}$ feet × 12 inches per foot = 297 inches.

   c. **Cord B** = $8\frac{1}{4}$ yards. $1\frac{1}{2}$ rods × $5\frac{1}{2}$ yards per rod = $8\frac{1}{4}$ yards.

A-48 Chapter 2 Quiz

2. 6,500,000 cubic miles $\times \frac{9}{10}$

   $\frac{\overset{650,000}{\cancel{6,500,000}}}{1} \times \frac{9}{\underset{1}{\cancel{10}}} = \frac{5,850,000}{1} =$ **5,850,000 cubic miles**

3. 20 gallons $\times \frac{1}{4}$

   $\frac{20}{1} \times \frac{1}{4} = \frac{20}{4} = 5$ gallons

   $16\frac{1}{2}$ miles per gallon $\times$ 5 gallons

   $\frac{33}{2} \times \frac{5}{1} = \frac{165}{2} =$ **$82\frac{1}{2}$ miles**

4. $\begin{aligned} 7\frac{1}{2} &= 7\frac{2}{4} \\ 6\frac{3}{4} &= 6\frac{3}{4} \\ +9\frac{1}{4} &= 9\frac{1}{4} \\ \hline 22\frac{6}{4} &= 23\frac{2}{4} = 23\frac{1}{2} \text{ hours} \end{aligned}$

   $\begin{aligned} 30 &= 29\frac{2}{2} \\ -23\frac{1}{2} &= 23\frac{1}{2} \\ \hline &\mathbf{6\tfrac{1}{2} \text{ hours, or 6 hours 30 minutes}} \end{aligned}$

5. $\$3000 \times \frac{5}{6}$ $\$3000$

   $\frac{\overset{500}{\cancel{3000}}}{1} \times \frac{5}{\underset{1}{\cancel{6}}} = \frac{2500}{1} = \$2500$ $\underline{-2500}$ $\$\,500$

6. $\frac{1}{4}, \frac{5}{12}, \frac{2}{3}, \frac{7}{9}$

   $\frac{1}{4} = \frac{1 \times 9}{4 \times 9} = \frac{9}{36}$

   $\frac{5}{12} = \frac{5 \times 3}{12 \times 3} = \frac{15}{36}$

   $\frac{2}{3} = \frac{2 \times 12}{3 \times 12} = \frac{24}{36}$

   $\frac{7}{9} = \frac{7 \times 4}{9 \times 4} = \frac{28}{36}$

7. $\frac{\text{Fiction}}{\text{All books}}$ $\frac{25}{25+30} = \frac{25}{55} = \frac{\mathbf{5}}{\mathbf{11}}$

8. a. $\begin{aligned} 8\frac{1}{2} &= 8\frac{6}{12} \\ 2\frac{1}{4} &= 2\frac{3}{12} \\ 1\frac{3}{4} &= 1\frac{9}{12} \\ 1\frac{2}{3} &= 1\frac{8}{12} \\ +\frac{1}{3} &= \frac{4}{12} \\ \hline 12\frac{30}{12} &= 14\frac{6}{12} = \mathbf{14\tfrac{1}{2}\text{ cups}} \end{aligned}$

   b. $14\frac{1}{2}$ cups

      2 cups per pint

      $14\frac{1}{2} \div 2$

      $\frac{29}{2} \times \frac{1}{2} = \frac{29}{4} = \mathbf{7\tfrac{1}{4}\text{ pints}}$

   c. $7\frac{1}{4}$ pints

      2 pints per quart

      $7\frac{1}{4} \div 2$

      $\frac{29}{4} \times \frac{1}{2} = \frac{29}{8} = \mathbf{3\tfrac{5}{8}\text{ quarts}}$

9. $\frac{\text{dry}}{\text{liquid}}$ $\frac{14\tfrac{1}{2}}{3+1} = \frac{14\tfrac{1}{2}}{4}$

10. $3\frac{5}{8}$ quarts = 3 quarts + $\frac{5}{8}$ quart

    $\frac{5}{8}$ quart $= \frac{5}{8} \times 32$ ounces per quart

              $= \frac{5}{\underset{1}{\cancel{8}}} \times \frac{\overset{4}{\cancel{32}}}{1}$

              = 20 ounces

    3 quarts 20 ounces

11. $7\frac{1}{3} \times \frac{5}{6}$

    $\frac{22}{3} \times \frac{5}{6} = \frac{55}{9} = 6\frac{1}{9}$ feet

    $\begin{aligned} 7\frac{1}{3} &= 7\frac{3}{9} \\ -6\frac{1}{9} &= 6\frac{1}{9} \\ \hline &\mathbf{1\tfrac{2}{9}\text{ feet}} \end{aligned}$

12. area of one board

    $\frac{4 \text{ inches}}{12 \text{ inches per foot}} = \frac{1}{3}$

    $A = lw$

       $= 6\frac{1}{2} \times \frac{1}{3}$

       $= \frac{13}{2} \times \frac{1}{3} = \frac{13}{6} = 2\frac{1}{6}$ square feet

    area of four boards

    $2\frac{1}{6} \times 4$

    $\frac{13}{6} \times 4 = \frac{52}{6} = \mathbf{8\tfrac{2}{3}\text{ square feet}}$

13. $\frac{18 \text{ cents per yard}}{3 \text{ feet per yard}}$

    $\frac{18}{3} = \mathbf{6 \text{ cents per foot}}$

14. $\begin{aligned} 2\frac{3}{4} &= 2\frac{18}{24} \\ 4\frac{1}{3} &= 4\frac{8}{24} \\ 5\frac{3}{8} &= 5\frac{9}{24} \\ +2\frac{7}{8} &= 2\frac{21}{24} \\ \hline 13\frac{56}{24} &= 15\frac{8}{24} = 15\frac{1}{3} \end{aligned}$

    $15\frac{1}{3}$ feet

    3 feet per yard

    $15\frac{1}{3} \div 3$

    $\frac{46}{3} \times \frac{1}{3} = \frac{46}{9} = \mathbf{5\tfrac{1}{9}\text{ yards}}$

15. $A = \frac{1}{2}bh$

    $= \left(1\frac{1}{3} \times \frac{1}{2}\right) \div 2$

    $= \left(\frac{4}{3} \times \frac{1}{2}\right) \div 2$

    $= \frac{2}{3} \div 2$

    $= \frac{\overset{1}{\cancel{2}}}{3} \times \frac{1}{\underset{1}{\cancel{2}}} = \frac{\mathbf{1}}{\mathbf{3}} \text{ square foot}$

16. $\frac{14 \text{ feet}}{3 \text{ feet per yard}} = \frac{14}{3} = 4\frac{2}{3}$ yards

    2 yards 1 foot = $2 + \frac{1 \text{ foot}}{3 \text{ feet per yard}} = 2\frac{1}{3}$ yards

    $V = lwh$

    $= 4\frac{2}{3} \times 2\frac{1}{3} \times 1$

    $= \frac{14}{3} \times \frac{7}{3} \times \frac{1}{1} = \frac{98}{9} = \mathbf{10\tfrac{8}{9}\text{ cubic yards}}$

UNIT VII: MATHEMATICS   Chapter 2 Quiz—Ch. 3, Level 1, Lesson 3   **A-49**

17. bicycling $5\frac{2}{3} \times 60 = \frac{17}{3} \times \frac{60}{1}^{20} = $ **340 calories**

    driving $2\frac{1}{4} \times 60 = \frac{9}{4} \times \frac{60}{1}^{15} = $ **135 calories**

    gardening $3\frac{3}{4} \times 60 = \frac{15}{4} \times \frac{60}{1}^{15} = $ **225 calories**

    jogging $6\frac{1}{12} \times 60 = \frac{73}{12} \times \frac{60}{1}^{5} = $ **365 calories**

    reading $1\frac{1}{2} \times 60 = \frac{3}{2} \times \frac{60}{1}^{30} = $ **90 calories**

    watching TV $1\frac{1}{2} \times 60 = \frac{3}{2} \times \frac{60}{1}^{30} = $ **90 calories**

    office work $2\frac{1}{4} \times 60 = \frac{9}{4} \times \frac{60}{1}^{15} = $ **135 calories**

18. jogging
    $45 \times 6\frac{1}{12}$
    $\frac{45}{1} \times \frac{73}{12} = \frac{3285}{12} = 273\frac{3}{4}$

    gardening
    $30 \times 3\frac{3}{4}$
    $\frac{30}{1} \times \frac{15}{4} = \frac{450}{4} = 112\frac{1}{2}$

    watching TV
    $45 + 30 = 75$ minutes
    $75 \times 1\frac{1}{2}$
    $\frac{75}{1} \times \frac{3}{1} = \frac{225}{2} = 112\frac{1}{2}$

    jogging $273\frac{3}{4} = 273\frac{3}{4}$
    gardening $112\frac{1}{2} = 112\frac{2}{4}$
    $\quad 385\frac{5}{4} = 386\frac{1}{4}$

    jogging and
    gardening $386\frac{1}{4} = 385\frac{5}{4}$
    watching TV $-112\frac{1}{2} = 112\frac{2}{4}$
    $\quad 273\frac{3}{4}$ **calories**

19. $1\frac{1}{2}$ hours $\times$ 60 minutes per hour = 90 minutes

    bicycling
    $90 \times 5\frac{2}{3}$
    $\frac{90}{1}^{30} \times \frac{17}{3} = 510$

    driving and office work
    $90 \times 2\frac{1}{4}$
    $\frac{90}{1} \times \frac{9}{4} = \frac{810}{4} = 202\frac{1}{2}$

    bicycling $510 = 509\frac{2}{2}$
    driving and
    office work $-202\frac{1}{2} = 202\frac{1}{2}$
    $\quad 307\frac{1}{2}$ **calories**

20. $\frac{3}{35} \times 365$
    $\frac{3}{35}^{7} \times \frac{365}{1}^{73} = \frac{219}{7} = 31\frac{2}{7}$ **pounds**

Chapter 3   Decimals

Level 1   Preview

1. **.0007, or 0.0007**
2. $\begin{array}{r} .730 \\ .600 \\ +.431 \\ \hline 1.761 \end{array}$
3. $\begin{array}{r} .790 \\ -.124 \\ \hline .666 \end{array}$ **or 0.666**

4. $\begin{array}{r} 4.3 \\ \times 2.5 \\ \hline 215 \\ 86 \\ \hline 10.75 \end{array}$
5. **.13, or 0.13**
   $9.7 \overline{)1.2{,}61}$
   97
   291
   291
   $\overline{0}$

Lesson 1

1. **c**   2. **e**   3. **d**   4. **b**   5. **a**

6. **7.013**   7. **.0027**   8. **10.000203**   9. **.13**   10. **300.7**

Lesson 2

1. $\begin{array}{r} .190 \\ .800 \\ +.326 \\ \hline 1.316 \end{array}$
2. $\begin{array}{r} \$.73 \\ .26 \\ +.11 \\ \hline \$1.10 \end{array}$
3. $\begin{array}{r} .0590 \\ .0700 \\ +.0694 \\ \hline .1984 \end{array}$, **or 0.1984**

4. $\begin{array}{r} 12.000 \\ .073 \\ +.380 \\ \hline 12.453 \end{array}$
5. $\begin{array}{r} 39.600 \\ .800 \\ +.007 \\ \hline 40.407 \end{array}$
6. $\begin{array}{r} .700 \\ -.006 \\ \hline .694 \end{array}$, **or 0.694**

7. $\begin{array}{r} 30.0 \\ -.8 \\ \hline 29.2 \end{array}$
8. $\begin{array}{r} 39.1 \\ -.2 \\ \hline 38.9 \end{array}$
9. $\begin{array}{r} \$86.30 \\ -23.00 \\ \hline \$63.30 \end{array}$

10. $\begin{array}{r} 5.004 \\ -1.999 \\ \hline 3.005 \end{array}$

Lesson 3

1. $\begin{array}{r} 9.6 \\ \times 23 \\ \hline 288 \\ 192 \\ \hline 220.8 \end{array}$
2. $\begin{array}{r} .72 \\ \times .3 \\ \hline .216 \end{array}$**, or 0.216**
3. $\begin{array}{r} .705 \\ \times 5 \\ \hline 3.525 \end{array}$

4. $\begin{array}{r} 1.029 \\ \times .884 \\ \hline 4116 \\ 8232 \\ 8232 \\ \hline .909636 \end{array}$**, or 0.909636**
5. **15.08**
   $5\overline{)75.4}$
   5
   $\overline{25}$
   25
   $\overline{40}$
   40
   $\overline{0}$
6. **5.12**
   $14\overline{)71.68}$
   70
   $\overline{16}$
   14
   $\overline{28}$
   28
   $\overline{0}$

7. **.00062, or 0.00062**
   $13\overline{).00806}$
   78
   $\overline{26}$
   26
   $\overline{0}$
8. **.15, or 0.15**
   $6\overline{).90}$
   6
   $\overline{30}$
   30
   $\overline{0}$

A-50 Ch. 3, Level 1, Lesson 3 – Ch. 3, Level 2, Lesson 6   INSTRUCTION

9. 1100., or 1100   10.   1.23
   .18.)198.00   .5.).6.15
        18   5
        ──   ──
        18   1 1
        18   1 0
        ──   ──
         0   15
                                 15
                                 ──
                                  0

Lesson 4

1. $.9 = \frac{9}{10}$ 2. $18.375 = 18 + \frac{375}{1000} = 18 + \frac{375 \div 125}{1000 \div 125} = 18\frac{3}{8}$

3. $7.08 = 7 + \frac{8}{100} = 7 + \frac{8 \div 4}{100 \div 4} = 7\frac{2}{25}$ 4. $6.4 = 6 + \frac{4}{10} = 6 + \frac{4 \div 2}{10 \div 2} = 6\frac{2}{5}$

5. $.85 = \frac{85}{100} = \frac{85 \div 5}{100 \div 5} = \frac{17}{20}$ 6.   .875
                                                                            8)7.00
                                                                              6 4
                                                                              ──
                                                                               60
                                                                               56
                                                                               ──
                                                                                40
                                                                                40
                                                                                ──
                                                                                 0

7. $.44\frac{4}{9}$ rounded to .44, or 0.44   8.   .8, or 0.8
    9)4.00   10)8.00
      3 6   8 0
      ──   ──
       40   0
       36
       ──
        4

9. $.46\frac{10}{15}$ rounded to .47, or 0.47   10. .45, or 0.45
    15)7.00   20)9.00
       6 0   8 0
       ──   ──
       1 00   1 00
         90   1 00
         ──   ──
         10   0

Level 1 Review

1. (4)   2. 72.016   3. $\frac{625}{1000} = \frac{5}{8}$ 4. $7\frac{96}{100} = 7\frac{24}{25}$

5.   .16   6. 9.790   7. 6.0000   8. 97.5
   25)4.00   9.000   −.4192   × .56
      2 5   +.938   ──────   ─────
      ──   ──────   5.5808   5850
      1 50   19.728   4875
      1 50   ─────
      ──   54.600
        0

9. .0023, or 0.0023   10. .56, or 0.56
    19).0437   .89.)49.84
        38   44 5
        ──   ──
        57   5 34
        57   5 34
        ──   ──
         0   0

Level 2

Lesson 1

1. .9④9 → .9 or 0.9   2. .③71 → .4 or 0.4   3. 1.⑤35 → 1.5

4. 10.⓪61 → 10.1   5. 78.③94 → 78.4   6. 5.8⑤62 → 5.86

7. .7⑥44 → .76   8. 23.7①31 → 23.71

9. .5⑨59 → .60 or 0.60   10. 8.1①06 → 8.11

Lesson 2

1. ($10.80 per hour)(7.25 hours)   2. $72.89 ÷ 3.7 meters
       (78.3000)   **$19.70 per meter**
       $78.30

3. ($119,583.54) + ($142,468.45) + ($186,294.36)
       $448,446.35

4. 976.9 liters − 374.2 liters   5. ($.89 per mile)(195 miles)
       602.7 liters   **$173.55**

Lesson 3

1. (17.21 m)(1000 mm per m)   2. 3764 cm ÷ 100 cm per m
       17,210 mm   **37.64 m**

3.   (.7 l)(100 cl per l)   4.   17 cg ÷ 100 cg per g
       70 cl   **.17 g**

5. (1.85 kg)(1000 g per kg)
       1850 g

Lesson 4

1. $r = d/2$ 2. $C = \pi d$ 3. $A = \pi r^2$
    $= 6/2$ $= 3.14(6)$ $= (3.14)(3)^2$
    = 3 inches   **= 18.84 inches** $= (3.14)(9)$
                                           = 28.26 square inches

4. $C = \pi d$ 5. $A = \pi r^2$
    $= (3.14)(10 \times 2)$ $= (3.14)(10)^2$
    $= (3.14)(20)$ $= (3.14)(100)$
    = 62.8 inches   **= 314 square inches**

Lesson 5

1. $V = \pi r^2 h$ 2. $V = \pi r^2 h$
    $= (3.14)(6 \times 6)(6)$ $= (3.14)(4/2)^2(12)$
    $= (3.14)(36)(6)$ $= (3.14)(2 \times 2)(12)$
    = 678.24 cubic inches $= (3.14)(4)(12)$
                                     = 150.72 cubic feet

3. $V = \pi r^2 h$ 4. $V = \pi r^2 h$
    $= (3.14)(10 \times 10)(7.5)$ $= (3.14)(.5 \times .5)(1)$
    $= (3.14)(100)(7.5)$ $= (3.14)(.25)(1)$
    = 2355 cubic meters   **= .785 cubic yards**

5. $V = \pi r^2 h$
    $= (3.14)(8 \times 8)(20)$
    = 4019.2 cubic centimeters

Lesson 6

1. .510   2. .9010   3. .40
    .501   .9001   .04

4. .7910 .7901 .7900 .7091   5. .6310 .6301 .6300 .6031

UNIT VII: MATHEMATICS   Ch. 3, Level 2 Review—Chapter 3 Quiz   **A-51**

Level 2   Review

1. 3.14①56 → **3.142**   2. 1.7 inches − .3 inch
                                    1.4 inches

3. ($22.50 per hour)(9.5 hours)
       213.750
       $213.75

4. $\sqrt{144}$ = 12, so $\sqrt{1.44}$ = **1.2**
         two   one
         places   place

5. 7.7 km × 1000 m per km   6. .681 .680 .600 .068
       7700 m

7. $A = \frac{1}{2}bh$ 8. $A = \pi r^2$
      = (19.4 × 3.6) ÷ 2   = (3.14)(9 × 9)
      = (69.84) ÷ 2   = (3.14)(81)
      = 34⑨92 → **34.9 square feet**   = 254.3̲4 → **254 square inches**

9. $V = \pi r^2 h$ 10. $c = nr$
      = (3.14)(10 ÷ 2)²(10)
      = (3.14)(5 × 5)(10) $r = \frac{c}{n}$
      = (3.14)(25)(10)
      = **785 cubic inches**   = $\frac{\$132.00}{60}$
                                     = **$2.20**

Level 3

Lesson 1

1.   (d = rt) + (d = rt)   2.   (d = rt) − (d = rt)
      (50 × 3.4) + (45 × 3.4)   (72.65 × 3.5) − (70.89 × 3.5)
       170   +   153   254.275   −   248.115
              323 miles   **6.16 miles**

3. 15 minutes = .25 hour   4.   (d = rt) + (d = rt)
       (d = rt) + (d = rt)   (3.5 × 1.5) + (8.53 × 1.5)
      (7.1 × .25) + (6.92 × .25)   5.25   +   12.795
       1.775   +   1.73   **18.045 miles**
            3.505 miles

5. 15 min. = .25 hr., 30 min. = .5 hr.
       (d = rt) − (d = rt) + (d = rt)
      (54 × .25) − (47 × .25) + (51 × .5)
       13.5   −   11.75   +   25.5
        1.75   +   25.5
              27.25 miles

Lesson 2

1. Insufficient data: **the number of days they saved**.

2. $A = \pi r^2$
      = (3.14)(6.3/2)²
      = (3.14)(3.15 × 3.15)
      = (3.14)(9.9225)
      = 31.15̲665 → **31.2 square inches**

3. Insufficient data: **the number of feet per truckload**.

4. Insufficient data: **the weight of the televisions and stereos**.

---

5. $10.00 − [($3.99 + $.24) + 3($1.19 + $.07)]
      10.00 − [4.23 + 3(1.26)]
      10.00 − [4.23 + 3.78]
      10.00 −   8.01
         $1.99

Level 3   Review

1. (70.8 ÷ 232) − (70.5 ÷ 235)   2. (74.4 ÷ 218) − (74.0 ÷ 230)
      (.30517) −   (.3)   (.34128) − (.32173)
       .3052   −   .3   .3413   −   .3217
      .0052 quadrillion BTUs   **.0196 quadrillion BTUs**

3.   18(78.9 ÷ 225)
          18(.35066)
          18(.3507)
      6.3126 quadrillion BTUs

4. 1976 (74.4 ÷ 218) = .34128 − .3413
    1977 (76.3 ÷ 220) = .34681 − .3468
    1978 (78.1 ÷ 223) = .35022 − .3502
    1979 (78.9 ÷ 225) = .35066 − .3507
    1980 (76.0 ÷ 228) = .33333 − .3333
    1981 (74.0 ÷ 230) = .32173 − .3217
    1982 (70.8 ÷ 232) = .30517 − .3052
    1983 (70.5 ÷ 235) = .3   − .3000
    .3507 − .3000
      .0507 quadrillion BTUs

5.   (d = rt) + (d = rt)   6.   (d = rt) − (d = rt)
      (6.7 × .25) + (5.9 × .25)   (6.9 × 1.25) − (6.1 × 1.25)
       1.675   +   1.475   8.625   −   7.625
            3.15 miles   **1 mile**

7. (3)   8. (5) Insufficient data: **the
    30 feet = 10 yards   cost of the material for
    $3.25(V = lwh) + $50   the blouses**.
    3.25(10 × 8 × 1.5) + 50
       3.25(120)   + 50
       (390.00)   + 50
          $440.00

9. $.57[102.6 + (9.6 × 14)]
    .57[102.6 +   134.4]
         $135 per pig

10. (3) $24,000 ÷ 12 = $2000 monthly income
    $450 + $75 + $225 = − 750 monthly expenses
                         $1250

     $\frac{1250}{2000} = \frac{1250 ÷ 250}{2000 ÷ 250} = \frac{5}{8}$ $\begin{array}{r}.625\\8)\overline{5.000}\\\underline{4\,8}\\20\\\underline{16}\\40\\\underline{40}\\0\end{array}$

Chapter 3   Quiz

1.   114.682   2.   60.010
    + 70.530   − 8.951
     185.212   **51.059**

A-52 Chapter 3 Quiz — Ch. 4, Level 1, Lesson 2

3. **1 min. 37.60 sec., 1 min. 37.52 sec., 1 min. 36.68 sec., 1 min. 13.36 sec.**

4. **1984, 1972, 1980, 1960, 1968, 1976, 1964**

5. $\dfrac{\$125.35 + \$56.76 + \$14.60 + \$9.85}{4} + \$20$
   $\dfrac{206.56}{4} \qquad\qquad + 20$
   $\quad 51.64 \qquad\qquad\quad + 20$
   $\qquad\qquad\qquad\qquad \mathbf{\$71.64}$

6. (3.9 yards × 3 feet per yard)$3.65
   (11.7)3.65
   42.705 → **$42.71**

7. $\dfrac{\frac{1}{2}(8 - 3.4)}{8}$
   $\dfrac{\frac{1}{2}(4.6)}{8}$
   $\dfrac{2.3}{8}$

8. 5(7.25 × $22.40) − $242
   5(162.40) − 242
   812 − 242
   $570

9. $33 \div 13\frac{3}{4}$
   33 ÷ 13.75
   2.4 pages per hour

10. $\dfrac{10 \times 75}{(10 \times 100) + (5 \times 50) + (10 \times 75)}$
    $\dfrac{750}{(1000) + (250) + (750)} = \dfrac{750}{2000} = \dfrac{750 \div 250}{2000 \div 250} = \dfrac{3}{8} = 8\overline{)3.00}^{.375}$

11. $c = nr$
    $= (A = lw)(\$9.50)$
    $= \left(\dfrac{14.25}{3} \times \dfrac{12.75}{3}\right)(9.50)$
    $= (4.75 \times 4.25)(9.50)$
    $= (20.1875)(9.50)$
    $= 191.78125$ — **$191.78**

12. **Tank A**
    $V = \pi r^2 h$
    $= (3.14)(5 \times 5)(6.2)$
    $= (3.14)(25)(6.2)$
    $= \mathbf{486.7\ ft^3}$
    Tank B
    $V = \pi r^2 h$
    $= (3.14)(4.5 \times 4.5)(6.9)$
    $= (3.14)(20.25)(6.9)$
    $= \mathbf{438.7365\ ft^3}$

13. $A = lw$
    $= 19.6 \times 6.6$
    $= 129.36$
    $= 129\tfrac{36}{100} = 129\tfrac{9}{25}$ **square inches**

14. $V = s^3$
    $= (.5 \times 100)^3 \qquad \div 20$
    $= (50)^3 \qquad\qquad \div 20$
    $= (50 \times 50 \times 50) \div 20$
    $= 125{,}000 \qquad\quad \div 20$
    $= \mathbf{6250\ cubic\ centimeters}$

15. $C = \pi d$
    $= (3.14)(2 \times .4)$
    $= (3.14)(.8)$
    $= \mathbf{2.512\ yards}$

16. (16,400 × .001) − (1087 × .001)
    16.4 − 1.087
    15.313 feet

17. 12(1087 × .03)
    12(32.61)
    391.32 inches

18. (186,000 × .00001) − (186,000 × .000001)
    1.86 − .186
    1.674 miles

19. $(d = rt) - (d = rt) + (d = rt)$
    $(53 \times 1.5) - (52 \times .5) + (49 \times 2)$
    $79.5 - 26 + 98$
    151.5 miles

20. $(d = rt) + \quad (d = rt)$
    $(85 \times .5) + \left[\left(85 \times \tfrac{3}{4}\right) \times .5\right]$
    $(85 \times .5) + [(85 \times .75) \times .5]$
    $(85 \times .5) + \quad [63.75 \times .5]$
    $42.5 + \quad 31.875$
    74.375 miles

Chapter 4 — Percents

Level 1 Preview

1. .137 = .13.7 = **13.7%**
2. $\dfrac{17}{20} = 17 \div 20 = .85 = .85. = \mathbf{85\%}$

3. $p = rb$
   $= 37.5\% \times 104$
   $= .375 \times 104$
   $= \mathbf{39}$

4. $r = p \div b$
   $= 68 \div 153$
   $= .444$
   $= 44.4\% → \mathbf{44\%}$

5. $b = p \div r$
   $= 37 \div 16\tfrac{2}{3}\%$
   $= 37 \div \tfrac{1}{6}$
   $= 37 \times \tfrac{6}{1}$
   $= \mathbf{222}$

Lesson 1

1. 29% = 29.% = .29. = **.29**
2. 3% = 3.% = .03. = **.03**
3. $1\tfrac{7}{10}\% = 1.7\% = .01.7 = \mathbf{.017}$
4. .07% = .00.07 = **.0007**
5. 3.09% = .03.09 = **.0309**
6. 7.13 = 7.13. = **713%**
7. .0396 = .03.96 = **3.96%**
8. .8 = .80. = **80%**
9. 30.001 = 30.00.1 = **3000.1%**
10. .05 = .05. = **5%**

Lesson 2

1. $96\% = \dfrac{96 \div 4}{100 \div 4} = \dfrac{24}{25}$

2. $37\tfrac{1}{2}\% = 37.5\% = \dfrac{37.5}{100} = \dfrac{375}{1000}$
   $\dfrac{375 \div 125}{1000 \div 125} = \dfrac{3}{8}$

3. $62.5\% = \dfrac{62.5}{100} = \dfrac{625 \div 125}{1000 \div 125} = \dfrac{5}{8}$

4. $56\tfrac{1}{4}\% = \dfrac{56.25}{100} = \dfrac{5625}{10{,}000}$
   $\dfrac{5625 \div 625}{10{,}000 \div 625} = \dfrac{9}{16}$

5. $18.75\% = \dfrac{18.75}{100} = \dfrac{1875 \div 625}{10{,}000 \div 625} = \dfrac{3}{16}$

6. $\dfrac{3}{15} = \dfrac{3}{15} \times \dfrac{100}{1} = \dfrac{300}{15} = \mathbf{20\%}$

7. $\dfrac{1}{8} = \dfrac{1}{8} \times \dfrac{100}{1} = \dfrac{100}{8} = \mathbf{12.5\%}$

UNIT VII: MATHEMATICS Ch. 4, Level 1, Lesson 2 – Ch. 4, Level 2, Lesson 2   A-53

8. $\frac{15}{16} = \frac{15}{16} \times \frac{100}{1} = \frac{1500}{16} =$ **93.75%**

9. $\frac{11}{40} = \frac{11}{40} \times \frac{100}{1} = \frac{1100}{40} =$ **27.5%**   10. $\frac{4}{5} = \frac{4}{5} \times \frac{100}{1} = \frac{400}{5} =$ **80%**

Lesson 3

1. **.3, or .30; 30%**   2. **.8, or .80; 80%**
3. **.833; 83.3%**   4. **.625; 62.5%**
5. **.5, or .50; 50%**   6. **.75; 75%**
7. **.333; 33.3%**   8. **.4, or .40; 40%**
9. **.167; 16.7%**   10. **.875; 87.5%**

Lesson 4

1. $p = rb$
   $= 16\frac{2}{3}\% \times 102$
   $= \frac{1}{6} \times 102$
   $=$ **17**

2. $p = rb$
   $= 87\frac{1}{2}\% \times 776$
   $= \frac{7}{8} \times 776$
   $=$ **679**

3. $p = rb$
   $= 90\% \times 81$
   $= .9 \times 81$
   $=$ **72.9**

4. $p = rb$
   $= 10\% \times 79$
   $= .1 \times 79$
   $=$ **7.9**

5. $p = rb$
   $= 66\frac{2}{3}\% \times 351$
   $= \frac{2}{3} \times 351$
   $=$ **234**

Lesson 5

1. $r = p \div b$
   $= 52 \div 65$
   $= .8$
   $=$ **80%**

2. $r = p \div b$
   $= 85 \div 102$
   $= .83\frac{1}{3}$
   $=$ **83$\frac{1}{3}$%**

3. $r = p \div b$
   $= 98 \div 112$
   $= .875$
   $=$ **87.5%**

4. $r = p \div b$
   $= 55 \div 275$
   $= .2$
   $=$ **20%**

5. $r = p \div b$
   $= 234.9 \div 87$
   $= 2.7$
   $=$ **270%**

Lesson 6

1. $b = p \div r$
   $= 1195 \div 62.5\%$
   $= 1195 \div .625$
   $=$ **1912**

2. $b = p \div r$
   $= 259 \div 87\frac{1}{2}\%$
   $= 259 \div \frac{7}{8}$
   $=$ **296**

3. $b = p \div r$
   $= 200 \div 166\frac{2}{3}\%$
   $= 200 \div \frac{5}{3}$
   $=$ **120**

4. $b = p \div r$
   $= 285 \div 19\%$
   $= 285 \div .19$
   $=$ **1500**

5. $b = p \div r$
   $= 3737 \div 37\%$
   $= 3737 \div .37$
   $=$ **10,100**

Level 1 Review

1. $3.4\% = .03.4 =$ **.034**
2. $17.05 = 17.05 =$ **1705%**
3. $3.75\% = \frac{3.75}{100} = \frac{375}{10,000}$
   $\frac{375 \div 125}{10,000 \div 125} = \frac{3}{80}$
4. $\frac{11}{40} = \frac{11}{40} \times \frac{100}{1} = \frac{1100}{40} =$ **27.5%**

5. $p = rb$
   $= 115\% \times 360$
   $= 1.15 \times 360$
   $=$ **414**

6. $p = rb$
   $= 3.78\% \times 1500$
   $= .0378 \times 1500$
   $=$ **56.7**

7. $r = p \div b$
   $= 18 \div 128$
   $= .1406$
   $= 14.06\% \rightarrow$ **14%**

8. $r = p \div b$
   $= 600 \div 96$
   $= 6.25$
   $=$ **625%**

9. $b = p \div r$
   $= 176 \div 160\%$
   $= 176 \div 1.6$
   $=$ **110**

10. $b = p \div r$
    $= 7 \div 1\frac{3}{4}\%$
    $= 7 \div 1.75\%$
    $= 7 \div .0175$
    $=$ **400**

Level 2

Lesson 1

1. $p = rb$
   $= 12\% \times 9850$
   $= .12 \times 9850$
   $=$ **1182 widgets**

2. $p = rb$
   $= 8\% \times \$5999$
   $= .08 \times 5999$
   $=$ **$479.92**

3. $p = rb$
   $= 70\% \times 2400$
   $= .7 \times 2400$
   $=$ **1680 calories**

4. $p = rb$
   $= 12\% \times 3,005,000$
   $= .12 \times 3,005,000$
   $=$ **360,600 people**

5. $r = p \div b$
   $= 9 \div 15$
   $= .6$
   $=$ **60%**

6. $r = p \div b$
   $= 65 \div 52$
   $= 1.25$
   $=$ **125%**

7. $r = p \div b$
   $= \$341,550 \div \$297,000$
   $= 1.15$
   $=$ **115%**

8. $b = p \div r$
   $= \$12,150 \div 10\%$
   $= 12,150 \div .1$
   $=$ **$121,500**

9. $b = p \div r$
   $= 35 \div 83\frac{1}{3}\%$
   $= 35 \div \frac{5}{6}$
   $=$ **42 applications**

10. $b = p \div r$
    $= 81 \div 90\%$
    $= 81 \div .9$
    $=$ **90 assemblies**

Lesson 2

1. $i = prt$
   $= \$5000 \times 9\% \times 2 \text{ years}$
   $= 5000 \times .09 \times 2$
   $=$ **$900**

2. $i = prt$
   $= \$1750 \times 12\% \times 1 \text{ year}$
   $= 1750 \times .12 \times 1$
   $=$ **$210**

3. $i = prt$
   $= \$200 \times 11\% \times 9 \text{ months}$
   $= 200 \times .11 \times \frac{9}{12}$
   $= 200 \times .11 \times .75$
   $=$ **$16.50**

4. $i = prt$
   $= \$750 \times 18\% \times 30 \text{ months}$
   $= 750 \times .18 \times \frac{30}{12}$
   $= 750 \times .18 \times 2.5$
   $=$ **$337.50**

5. $i = prt$
   $= \$2000 \times 7\frac{1}{2}\% \times 2 \text{ years}$
   $= 2000 \times .075 \times 2$
   $=$ **$300**

A-54 Ch. 4, Level 2 Review — Ch. 4, Level 3 Review   INSTRUCTION

Level 2 Review

1. $p = p \div b$
   $= 75\% \times 25{,}000$
   $= .75 \times 25{,}000$
   $= \mathbf{18{,}750 \text{ convertibles}}$

2. $r = p \div b$
   $= 26{,}000{,}000 \div 61{,}600{,}000$
   $= .422$
   $= 42.2\% \rightarrow \mathbf{42\%}$

3. $b = p \div r$
   $= 156{,}000{,}000 \div 38\%$
   $= 156{,}000{,}000 \div .38$
   $= \mathbf{410{,}526{,}310 \text{ automobiles}}$

4. $p = rb$
   $= 37\frac{1}{2}\% \times \$88{,}000{,}000$
   $= \frac{3}{8} \times \$88{,}000{,}000$
   $= \mathbf{\$33{,}000{,}000}$

5. $r = p \div b$
   $= 38{,}500{,}000 \div 175{,}000{,}000$
   $= .22$
   $= \mathbf{22\%}$

6. $b = p \div r$
   $= \$40 \div 266\frac{2}{3}\%$
   $= 40 \div \frac{8}{3}$
   $= \mathbf{\$15}$

7. $p = rb$
   $= 54\% \times 160{,}000{,}000$
   $= .54 \times 160{,}000{,}000$
   $= \mathbf{86{,}400{,}000 \text{ people}}$

8. $r = p \div b$
   $= \$83{,}000{,}000 \div \$65{,}000{,}000$
   $= 1.2769$
   $= 127.69\% \rightarrow \mathbf{128\%}$

9. $i = prt$
   $= \$250 \times 18\% \times 6 \text{ months}$
   $= 250 \times .18 \times \frac{6}{12}$
   $= 250 \times .18 \times .5$
   $= \mathbf{\$22.50}$

10. $i = prt$
    $= \$4500 \times 7\frac{1}{2}\% \times 2 \text{ years}$
    $= 4500 \times 7.5\% \times 2$
    $= 4500 \times .075 \times 2$
    $= \mathbf{\$675}$

Level 3

Lesson 1

1. $\$10 + \$23 = \$33$
   $\$50 - \$33 = \$17$
   $r = p \div b$
   $= 17 \div 50$
   $= .34$
   $= \mathbf{34\%}$

2. $b = p \div r$
   $= \$220 \div 55\%$
   $= 220 \div .55$
   $= \$400$
   $\$400 - \$220 = \mathbf{\$180}$

3. $b = p \div r$
   $= 135 \div 18\%$
   $= 135 \div .18$
   $= 750 \text{ total voters}$

   $p = rb$
   $= 20\% \times 750$
   $= .2 \times 750$
   $= 150 \text{ petitioners}$

   150
   $\underline{-\ 135}$
   $\mathbf{15 \text{ signatures}}$

4. $b = p \div r$
   $= \$68.75 \div 2\frac{1}{2}\%$
   $= 68.75 \div 2.5\%$
   $= 68.75 \div .025$
   $= \$2750$

   $\$2750.00$
   $\underline{-\ \ \ 68.75}$
   $\mathbf{\$2681.25}$

5. $b = p \div r$
   $= 18 \div 12\%$
   $= 18 \div .12$
   $= 150 \text{ pounds}$

   150
   $\underline{-\ 18}$
   $\mathbf{132 \text{ pounds}}$

Lesson 2

1. $17{,}572 - 15{,}280 = 2292$
   $r = p \div b$
   $= 2292 \div 15{,}280$
   $= .15$
   $= \mathbf{15\%}$

2. $\$71{,}326 - \$66{,}298 = \$5028$
   $r = p \div b$
   $= \$5028 \div \$71{,}326$
   $= .0705$
   $= 7.05\% \rightarrow \mathbf{7\%}$

3. $3{,}120{,}000 - 2{,}590{,}000 = 530{,}000$
   $r = p \div b$
   $= 530{,}000 \div 2{,}590{,}000$
   $= .2046$
   $= 20.46\% \rightarrow \mathbf{20\%}$

4. $\$15.00 - \$9.00 = \$6.00$
   $r = p \div b$
   $= \$6 \div \$15.00$
   $= .4$
   $= \mathbf{40\%}$

5. $\$115 - \$46 = \$69$
   $r = p \div b$
   $= \$69 \div \$46$
   $= 1.5$
   $= \mathbf{150\%}$

Level 3 Review

1. **1965** $1214 + 1162 + 278 + 495 + 244 = 3393$
   $r = p \div b = 1214 \div 3393$
   $= .3577 = 35.77\% \rightarrow \mathbf{36\%}$

   1970 $1144 + 1099 + 496 + 377 + 314 = 3430$
   $r = p \div b = 1144 \div 3430$
   $= .3335 = 33.35\% \rightarrow \mathbf{33\%}$

   1975 $5292 + 5492 + 987 + 991 + 858 = 13{,}620$
   $r = p \div b = 5292 \div 13{,}620$
   $= .3885 = 38.85\% \rightarrow \mathbf{39\%}$

   1980 $6660 + 9759 + 1126 + 2864 + 1288 = 21{,}697$
   $r = p \div b = 6660 \div 21{,}697$
   $= .3069 = 30.69\% \rightarrow \mathbf{31\%}$

2. **1965**
   $r = p \div b$
   $= 244 \div 3393$
   $= .0719 = 7.19\% \rightarrow \mathbf{7\%}$

   1970
   $r = p \div b$
   $= 314 \div 3430$
   $= .0915 = 9.15\% \rightarrow \mathbf{9\%}$

   1975
   $r = p \div b$
   $= 858 \div 13{,}620$
   $= .0629 = 6.29\% = \mathbf{6\%}$

   1980
   $r = p \div b$
   $= 1288 \div 21{,}697$
   $= .0593 = 5.93\% = \mathbf{6\%}$

3. **Wheat**
   $1214 - 1144 = 70$
   $r = p \div b$
   $= 70 \div 1214$
   $= .0576$
   $= 5.76\% \rightarrow \mathbf{6\% \text{ decrease}}$

   Feed Grains
   $1162 - 1099 = 63$
   $r = p \div b$
   $= 63 \div 1162$
   $= .0542$
   $= 5.42\% \rightarrow \mathbf{5\% \text{ decrease}}$

   Fodders
   $496 - 278 = 218$
   $r = p \div b$
   $= 218 \div 278$
   $= .7841$
   $= 78.41\% \rightarrow \mathbf{78\% \text{ increase}}$

   Cotton
   $495 - 377 = 118$
   $r = p \div b$
   $= 118 \div 495$
   $= .2383$
   $= 23.83\% \rightarrow \mathbf{24\% \text{ decrease}}$

   Rice
   $314 - 244 = 70$
   $r = p \div b$
   $= 70 \div 244$
   $= .2868$
   $= 28.68\% \rightarrow \mathbf{29\% \text{ increase}}$

UNIT VII: MATHEMATICS

4. $6660 + 9759 + 1126 + 2864 + 1288 = 21{,}697$
   $r = p \div b$
   $= 9759 \div 21{,}697$
   $= .4497$
   $= 44.97\% \rightarrow \mathbf{45\%}$

5. Cotton
   $991 - 377 = 614$
   $r = p \div b$
   $= 614 \div 377$
   $= 1.628$
   $= 162.8\% \rightarrow \mathbf{163\%\ increase}$

   Rice
   $858 - 314 = 544$
   $r = p \div b$
   $= 544 \div 314$
   $= 1.732$
   $= 173.2\% \rightarrow \mathbf{173\%\ increase}$

6. $7{,}900{,}000 - 7{,}070{,}000 = 830{,}000$
   $r = p \div b$
   $= 830{,}000 \div 7{,}900{,}000$
   $= .1051$
   $= 10.51\% \rightarrow \mathbf{11\%}$

7. $b = p \div r$
   $= 1500 \div \tfrac{2}{3}$
   $= 2250$
   $2250 - 1500 = \mathbf{750\ calories}$

8. $\$9000 - \$3600 = \$5400$
   $r = p \div b$
   $= \$5400 \div \$9000$
   $= .6$
   $= \mathbf{60\%}$

9. $100\% - 75\% = 25\%$
   $b = p \div r$
   $= 312 \div 25\%$
   $= 312 \div .25$
   $= \mathbf{1248\ people}$

10. CreditCharge
    $i = prt$
    $= \$150 \times 16.9\% \times 1$
    $= 150 \times .169 \times 1$
    $= \$25.35$
    $\$25.35 + \$65 = \$90.35$

    SavingCard Gold
    $i = prt$
    $= \$150 \times 18\% \times 1$
    $= 150 \times .18 \times 1$
    $= \$27$
    $\$27 + \$60 = \$87$

    PrestigePlatinum
    $i = prt$
    $= \$150 \times 21.9\% \times 1$
    $= 150 \times .219 \times 1$
    $= \$32.85$
    $\$32.85 + \$50 = \mathbf{\$82.85}$

    Colossal Card
    $i = prt$
    $= \$150 \times 20\% \times 1$
    $= 150 \times .2 \times 1$
    $= \$30$
    $\$30 + \$55 = \$85$

Chapter 4 Quiz

1. $.0075 = .00.75 = \mathbf{.75\%\ or\ \tfrac{3}{4}\%}$

2. $31\tfrac{1}{4}\% = 31.25\% = \dfrac{31.25}{100} = \dfrac{3125 \div 625}{10{,}000 \div 625} = \mathbf{\tfrac{5}{16}}$

3. $p = rb$
   $= 21.8\% \times 146$
   $= .218 \times 146$
   $= \mathbf{31.828}$

4. $p = rb$
   $= 5\tfrac{1}{2}\% \times 600$
   $= 5.5\% \times 600$
   $= .055 \times 600 = 33$
   $600 - 33 = \mathbf{567}$

5. $p = rb$
   $= 7\tfrac{1}{2}\% \times \$78.70$
   $= 7.5\% \times 78.70$
   $= .075 \times 78.70$
   $= 5.902 \rightarrow \$5.90$
   $\$78.70 + \$5.90 = \mathbf{\$84.60}$

6. $r = p \div b$
   $= 51 \div 357$
   $= .1428$
   $= 14.28\% \rightarrow \mathbf{14\%}$

---

7. $b = p \div r$
   $= 300 \div 28\tfrac{3}{8}\%$
   $= 300 \div .28375$
   $= 1057.26 \rightarrow 1057$
   $1057 - 300 = \mathbf{757\ miles}$

8. $i = prt$
   $= \$2500 \times 7\tfrac{1}{2}\% \times 18\ \text{months}$
   $= 2500 \times 7.5\% \times \dfrac{18}{12}$
   $= 2500 \times .075 \times 1.5$
   $= \mathbf{\$281.25}$

9. $\$15.00 \div 100 = \$.15\ \text{per pound}$
   $r = p \div b$
   $= \$.15 \div \$.39$
   $= .3846$
   $= 38.46\% \rightarrow \mathbf{38\%}$

10. $340 - 51 = 289$
    $r = p \div b$
    $= 289 \div 340$
    $= .85$
    $= \mathbf{85\%}$

11. $b = p \div r$
    $= 3819 \div 57\%$
    $= 3819 \div .57$
    $= \mathbf{6700\ candidates}$

12. $p = rb$
    $= 36\% \times 50\ \text{states}$
    $= .36 \times 50$
    $= 18$
    $50 - 18 = \mathbf{32\ states}$

13. $r = p \div b$
    $= \$1443.75 \div \$17{,}500$
    $= .0825$
    $= \mathbf{8.25\%\ or\ 8\tfrac{1}{4}\%}$

14. Plan 1
    $\$130 \times 18 = \$2340$
    $p = rb$
    $= 2\% \times \$2340$
    $= .02 \times 2340$
    $= \$46.80$
    $\$2340 - \$46.80 = \$2293.20$

    Plan 2
    $\$1000 + (\$1000 \times 12)$
    $\$1000 + \$1200 = \mathbf{\$2200}$

    Plan 3
    $\$104 \times 23 = \$2392$

    Plan 4
    $\$105 \times 24 = 2520$
    $p = rb$
    $= 12\tfrac{1}{2}\% \times \$2520$
    $= \tfrac{1}{8} \times 2520$
    $= \$315$
    $\$2520 - \$315 = \$2205$

    Plan 5
    $\$500 + (\$87.50 \times 24)$
    $\$500 + \$2100 = \$2600$

15. $p = rb$
    $= 17.9\% \times 29{,}000$
    $= .179 \times 29{,}000$
    $= 5191$
    $29{,}000 - 5191 = \mathbf{23{,}809\ spectators}$

16. Group A
    $\$2153$
    1201
    747
    $+\ 2441$
    $\overline{\$6542}$
    $r = p \div b$
    $= \$2441 \div \$6542$
    $= .373$
    $= 37.3\%$

    Group B
    $\$1870$
    1197
    732
    $+\ 2697$
    $\overline{\$6496}$
    $r = p \div b$
    $= \$2697 \div \$6496$
    $= .415$
    $= 41.5\%$

    Group C
    $\$1482$
    1331
    772
    $+\ 2672$
    $\overline{\$6257}$
    $r = p \div b$
    $= \$2672 \div \$6257$
    $= .427$
    $= 42.7\%$

    Group D
    $\$1416$
    1539
    732
    $+\ 2883$
    $\overline{\$6570}$
    $r = p \div b$
    $= \$2883 \div \$6570$
    $= .439$
    $= \mathbf{43.9\%}$

    Group E
    $\$1544$
    1791
    734
    $+\ 3016$
    $\overline{\$7085}$
    $r = p \div b$
    $= \$3016 \div \$7085$
    $= .426$
    $= 42.6\%$

A-56 Chapter 4 Quiz—Ch. 5, Lesson 2

17. **Group A**
$r = p \div b$
$= \$1201 \div \$6542$
$= .1836$
$= \mathbf{18.36\%}$

   Group B
$r = p \div b$
$= \$1197 \div \$6496$
$= .1843$
$= \mathbf{18.43\%}$

   Group C
$r = p \div b$
$= \$1331 \div \$6257$
$= .2127$
$= \mathbf{21.27\%}$

   Group D
$r = p \div b$
$= \$1539 \div \$6570$
$= .2342$
$= \mathbf{23.42\%}$

   Group E
$r = p \div b$
$= \$1791 \div \$7085$
$= .2528$
$= \mathbf{25.28\%}$

18. **Group A**
$r = p \div b$
$= \$3354 \div \$6542$
$= .5127$
$= \mathbf{51.27\%}$

   $\begin{array}{r}\$2153\\+\ 1201\\\hline\$3354\end{array}$

   Group B
$r = p \div b$
$= \$3067 \div \$6496$
$= .4721$
$= \mathbf{47.21\%}$

   $\begin{array}{r}\$1870\\+\ 1197\\\hline\$3067\end{array}$

   Group C
$r = p \div b$
$= \$2813 \div \$6257$
$= .4496$
$= \mathbf{44.96\%}$

   $\begin{array}{r}\$1482\\+\ 1331\\\hline\$2813\end{array}$

   Group D
$r = p \div b$
$= \$2955 \div \$6570$
$= .4498$
$= \mathbf{44.98\%}$

   $\begin{array}{r}\$1416\\+\ 1539\\\hline\$2955\end{array}$

   Group E
$r = p \div b$
$= \$3335 \div \$7085$
$= .4707$
$= \mathbf{47.07\%}$

   $\begin{array}{r}\$1544\\+\ 1791\\\hline\$3335\end{array}$

19. **Group A**
$r = p \div b$
$= \$1948 \div \$6542$
$= .2978$
$= \mathbf{29.78\%}$

   $\begin{array}{r}\$1201\\+\ \ 747\\\hline\$1948\end{array}$

   Group B
$r = p \div b$
$= \$1929 \div \$6496$
$= .297$
$= \mathbf{29.7\%}$

   $\begin{array}{r}\$1197\\+\ \ 732\\\hline\$1929\end{array}$

   Group C
$r = p \div b$
$= \$2103 \div \$6257$
$= .3361$
$= \mathbf{33.61\%}$

   $\begin{array}{r}\$1331\\+\ \ 772\\\hline\$2103\end{array}$

   Group D
$r = p \div b$
$= \$2271 \div \$6570$
$= .3457$
$= \mathbf{34.57\%}$

   $\begin{array}{r}\$1539\\+\ \ 732\\\hline\$2271\end{array}$

   Group E
$r = p \div b$
$= \$2525 \div \$7085$
$= .3564$
$= \mathbf{35.64\%}$

   $\begin{array}{r}\$1791\\+\ \ 734\\\hline\$2525\end{array}$

20. **Group D**
$r = p \div b$
$= \$6570 \div \$17{,}000$
$= .3864$
$= \mathbf{38.64\%}$

   Group E
$r = p \div b$
$= \$7085 \div \$19{,}000$
$= .3729$
$= \mathbf{37.29\%}$

Chapter 5 Graphs

Preview

1. **9 billion pounds of milk**

2. $\begin{array}{l}\$.10 \text{ machinery \& vehicles}\\ \ \ .06 \text{ financial assets}\\ \ \ .05 \text{ livestock \& poultry}\\ \ \ .03 \text{ crops stored}\\ +\ .03 \text{ household furnishings}\\ \hline \$.27 \end{array}$

   $\begin{array}{r}\$.73 \text{ real estate}\\ -\ .27\\ \hline \mathbf{\$.46}\end{array}$

3. $\begin{array}{r}25{,}000{,}000 \ \ 1982\\ -\ 5{,}000{,}000 \ \ 1970\\ \hline 20{,}000{,}000\end{array}$

   $r = p \div b$
$= 20{,}000{,}000 \div 5{,}000{,}000$
$= 4 = \mathbf{400\%}$

4. $\begin{array}{r}\$35{,}000{,}000{,}000 \ \ 1984\\ -\ 15{,}000{,}000{,}000 \ \ 1983\\ \hline \mathbf{\$20{,}000{,}000{,}000}\end{array}$

5. $\begin{array}{r}\$26{,}000{,}000{,}000\\ 20{,}000{,}000{,}000\\ 20{,}000{,}000{,}000\\ 27{,}000{,}000{,}000\\ 32{,}000{,}000{,}000\\ 20{,}000{,}000{,}000\\ 30{,}000{,}000{,}000\\ 25{,}000{,}000{,}000\\ 15{,}000{,}000{,}000\\ +\ 35{,}000{,}000{,}000\\ \hline \$250{,}000{,}000{,}000 \end{array}$ $\div$ 10 years = **$25,000,000,000 per year**

Lesson 1

1. **$1 billion**

2. 1975—$5 billion + $4 billion = **$9 billion**
   1982—$15 billion + $10 billion = **$25 billion**

3. $20 billion + $14 billion = $34 billion
   $r = p \div b$
$= \$14 \text{ billion} \div \$34 \text{ billion}$
$= .4117 = \mathbf{41.17\%}$

4. $\begin{array}{r}\$15 \text{ billion} \ \ 1982\\ -\ 5 \text{ billion} \ \ 1975\\ \hline \mathbf{\$10 \text{ billion}}\end{array}$

5. $\begin{array}{r}\$14.0 \text{ billion} \ \ 1984\\ -\ 7.5 \text{ billion} \ \ 1980\\ \hline \mathbf{\$6.5 \text{ billion}}\end{array}$

Lesson 2

1. $\begin{array}{r}\$.73\\+\ .06\\\hline\$.79\end{array}$

   $\begin{array}{r}100\\\times\ .79\\\hline \mathbf{79\%}\end{array}$

2. **Machinery and vehicles**

   10¢ = 2 × 5¢

UNIT VII: MATHEMATICS Ch. 5, Lesson 2 — Ch. 6, Level 1, Lesson 1

3. $1.00 − ($.05 + $.03)
    = $1.00 − $.08 = $.92

    $\begin{array}{r} 100 \\ \times\ .92 \\ \hline \textbf{92\%} \end{array}$

4. $.10 + $.03 = $.13

    $\dfrac{13}{100}$

5. $b = p \div r$
    $= \$49{,}000{,}000{,}000 \div .05$
    $= \textbf{\$980{,}000{,}000{,}000 or \$980 billion}$

Lesson 3

1. **5 million**   2. **1981**

3. $\begin{array}{r} 34{,}000{,}000\ 1984 \\ -\ 29{,}000{,}000\ 1983 \\ \hline 5{,}000{,}000 \end{array}$ 4. $\dfrac{5{,}000{,}000}{25{,}000{,}000} = \dfrac{1}{5}$

5. $\begin{array}{r} 34{,}000{,}000\ 1984 \\ -\ 5{,}000{,}000\ 1970 \\ \hline 29{,}000{,}000 \end{array}$ $r = p \div b$
    $= 29{,}000{,}000 \div 5{,}000{,}000$
    $= 5.8 = \textbf{580\%}$

Lesson 4

1. **30 oil wells**   2. **5 gas wells**

3. $\begin{array}{r} 40\ \text{oil wells} \\ +\ 15\ \text{gas wells} \\ \hline \textbf{55 wells} \end{array}$ 4. **1982 and 1984**

5. 1974 — 15 oil wells − 5 gas wells = 10 wells
   1976 — 20 oil wells − 10 gas wells = 10 wells
   1978 — 20 oil wells − 15 gas wells = 5 wells
   1980 — 30 oil wells − 15 gas wells = 15 wells
   1982 — 40 oil wells − 20 gas wells = 20 wells
   1984 — 40 oil wells − 15 gas wells = 25 wells

Chapter 5 Quiz

1. $8.5 \times 2 =$ **17 million metric tons**

2. PRC — $10 \times 2 = 20$ million metric tons
   FRG — $2.5 \times 2 = 5$ million metric tons
   $20 \div 5 =$ **4 times**

3. Brazil — $\dfrac{1.5}{2} = \dfrac{15 \div 5}{20 \div 5} = \dfrac{3}{4}$
   France

4. United States — $8.5 \times 2 = 17$ million metric tons
   Soviet Union — $6.5 \times 2 = 13$ million metric tons
   PRC   — $10 \times 2 = 20$ million metric tons

    $\begin{array}{r} 17\ \text{million metric tons} \\ +\ 13\ \text{million metric tons} \\ \hline 30\ \text{million metric tons} \end{array}$ $r = p \div b$
    $= 30\ \text{million} \div 20\ \text{million}$
    $= 1.5 = \textbf{150\%}$

5. $8.5 \times 2 = 17$ million metric tons
   17 tons × 2000 kilograms per metric ton =
   34 billion kilograms
   $34{,}000{,}000{,}000 \div 226{,}500{,}000 = 150.11 \rightarrow$
   150 kilograms per person

6. $9.7\% + 10\% + 18\% + 18.4\% =$ **56.1%**

7. **no children** — $49.9\% − 43.1\% = 6.8$ point increase
   four or more children — $9.7\% − 3.2\% = 6.5$ point decrease
   three children — $10\% − 7.2\% = 2.8$ point decrease
   two children — $19\% − 18\% = 1$ point increase
   one child — $20.7\% − 18.4\% = 2.3$ point increase

8. no children — $49.9\% − 43.1\% = 6.8$ point increase
   four or more children — $9.7\% − 3.2\% = 6.5$ point decrease
   three children — $10\% − 7.2\% = 2.8$ point decrease
   two children — $19\% − 18\% = 1$ point increase
   one child — $20.7\% − 18.4\% = 2.3$ point increase

9. 1960 — $10\% + 9.7\% = 19.7\%$ $\begin{array}{r} 19.7\% \\ -\ 10.4 \\ \hline 9.3\% \end{array}$
   1984 — $7.2\% + 3.2\% = 10.4\%$

10. $62{,}000{,}000 \times .499 =$ **30,938,000 families**

11. **1980**   12. **1965 to 1970**

13. $460{,}000 − 320{,}000 = 140{,}000 \rightarrow$ **100,000**

14. $400{,}000 − 200{,}000 = 200{,}000$
    $r = p \div b$
    $= 200{,}000 \div 200{,}000$
    $= 1 = \textbf{100\%}$

15. $\begin{array}{r} 100\%\ \text{prison increase} \\ -\ 13\%\ \text{general increase} \\ \hline \textbf{77\%} \end{array}$ 16. **millions of pounds**

17. **1979**   18. **1979 to 1983**

19. $\begin{array}{r} 800\ \text{million pounds} \\ -\ 500\ \text{million pounds} \\ \hline \textbf{300 million pounds} \end{array}$ 20. $\begin{array}{r} 600\ \text{million pounds} \\ 400\ \text{million pounds} \\ +\ 100\ \text{million pounds} \\ \hline \textbf{1100 million pounds} \end{array}$

Chapter 6 Algebra

Level 1 Preview

1. **D**
   $\dfrac{^+3}{2} = {}^+1.5$

2. $(^+8) + (^-4) − (^-10) + (^+3) = (^+8) + (^-4) + (^+10) + (^+3)$
   $(^+8) + (^+10) + (^+3) = {}^+21$ positive total
   $(^-4) = {}^-4$ negative total
   $(^+21) + (^-4) = {}^+\textbf{17}$

3. $\dfrac{^-6}{1} \cdot \dfrac{3}{8} = {}^-2\tfrac{1}{4}$ 4. $18c^2a − 4c^2a = {}^+\textbf{14}\boldsymbol{c^2 a}$

5. $(^+20) \div (^-2) = {}^-10$
   $5 − 3 = 2$
   $^-\boldsymbol{10a^2}$

Lesson 1

1. **D**   2. **A**   3. **E**   4. **B**   5. **C**

Lesson 2

1. $4 + 8 = 12$
   $(^+4) + (^+8) = {}^+12$
2. $10 + 20 = 30$
   $(^-10) + (^-20) = {}^-30$
3. $16 - 14 = 2$
   $(^+14) + (^-16) = {}^-2$
4. $13 - 9 = 4$
   $(^-9) + (^+13) = {}^+4$
5. $(^+4) + (^+6) = {}^+10$
   $(^-2) = {}^-2$
   $(^+10) + (^-2) = {}^+8$
6. $(^+3) + (^+7) = {}^+10$
   $(^-15) + (^-6) = {}^-21$
   $(^+10) + (^-21) = {}^-11$
7. $(^+4) + (^+8) = {}^+12$
8. $(^-9) + (^-6) = {}^-15$
9. $(^-13) + (^-3) + (^-16) = {}^-32$
10. $(^+3) + (^+2) + (^+20) = {}^+25$

Lesson 3

1. $3 \times 9 = 27$
   $(^+3)(^-9) = {}^-27$
2. $5 \times 5 = 25$
   $^-5(^-5) = {}^+25$
3. $7 \times 9 = 63$
   $^+7 \cdot {}^+9 = {}^+63$
4. $50 \div 5 = 10$
   $(^+50) \div (^-5) = {}^-10$
5. $17 \times 8 = 136$
   $(17)(^-8) = {}^-136$
6. $104 \div 13 = 8$
   $\dfrac{(104)}{(^-13)} = {}^-8$
7. $40 \div 10 = 4$
   $\dfrac{^-40}{^+10} = {}^-4$
8. $18 \div 10 = 1.8$
   $\dfrac{(^-6)(^-3)}{10} = {}^+1.8$
9. $2 \times 4 \times 5 \times 3 = 120$
   $(^-2)(4)(^-5)(^-3) = {}^-120$
10. $6 \times 1 \times 2 \times 3 = 36 \div 2 = 18$
    $(6)(^+1)(^-2)(^+3) = {}^-36 \div 2 = {}^-18$

Lesson 4

1. $19 + 7 = 26$
   $19x + 7x = 26x$
2. $4 + 13 = 17$
   $(4b^2) + (13b^2) = 17b^2$
3. $2 + 1 = 3$
   $(2abc) + (abc) = 3abc$
4. $13 - 4 = 9$
   $(13n^2) - (4n^2) = 9n^2$
5. $(^-8) - (^+4) = {}^-12$
   $(^-8s^3) - (^+4s^3) = {}^-12s^3$
6. $(^+13) - (^-13) = {}^+26$
   $(^+13b^2c^2) - (^-13b^2c^2) = {}^+26b^2c^2$
7. $(^-9.5) + (10.2) - (1) = {}^-.3$
   $(^-9.5a) + (10.2a) - (a) = {}^-.3a$
8. $(8) - (^+3) + (^-14) = {}^-9$
   $(8st) - (^+3st) + (^-14st) = {}^-9st$
9. $(1) - (^-4) - (4) = 1$
   $c - (^-4c) - 4c = c$
10. $(10) + (1) - (^-9) = 20$
    $(10p^2q^3) + (p^2q^2) - (^-9p^2q^2) = 20p^2q^2$

Lesson 5

1. $2 \times 2 = 4$
   $t^3 \times t^2 = t^5$
   $2t^3 \cdot 2t^2 = 4t^5$
2. $3 \times 5 = 15$
   $ab \times ab^2 = a^2b^3$
   $(3ab)(5ab^2) = 15a^2b^3$
3. $(^-3)(4)(^-3) = {}^+36$
   $(x)(xy)(y) = x^2y^2$
   $(^-3x)(4xy)(^-3y) = {}^+36x^2y^2$
4. $1 \div 1 = 1$
   $(y^4) \div (y^2) = y^2$
   $\dfrac{y^4}{y^2} = y^2$
5. $^-6 \div 2 = {}^-3$
   $s^6 \div s^2 = s^4$
   $\dfrac{^-6s^6}{2s^2} = {}^-3s^4$
6. $32 \div {}^-8 = {}^-4$
   $x^5 \div x^3 = x^2$
   $(32x^5) \div (^-8x^3) = {}^-4x^2$
7. $\dfrac{2a \cdot 2b}{4ab} = \dfrac{4ab}{4ab} = 1$
8. $\dfrac{6(3x^6y^4z^6)}{3(4x^4y^4z^3)} = \dfrac{18x^6y^4z^6}{12x^4y^4z^3}$
   $18 \div 12 = 1.5$
   $x^6y^4z^6 \div x^4y^4z^3 = x^2z^3$
   $\dfrac{6(3x^6y^4z^6)}{3(4x^4y^4z^3)} = 1.5x^2z^3$
9. $4.5 \times 2.7 = 12.15$
   $a^2b^3 \cdot b^2c = a^2b^5c$
   $(4.5a^2b^3)(2.7b^2c) = 12.15a^2b^5c$
10. $20 \div {}^-2 = -10$
    $x^2 \div x^3 = x^{-1}$
    $\dfrac{20x^2}{^-2x^3} = {}^-10x^{-1}$

Level 1 Review

1. B
   $\dfrac{^-4}{2} = {}^-2$
2. $(^-4) + (^-2) + (^-1) = (^-7)$ negative total
   $(^+3) = (^+3)$ positive total
   $(^-7) + (^+3) = (^-4)$
3. $(^+5) + (^-3) + (^+4) + (^+2)$
   $(^+5) + (^+4) + (^+2) = (^+11)$
   $(^-3) = (^-3)$
   $(^+11) + (^-3) = {}^+8$
4. $(^-13) - (^+5) = (^-13) + (^-5) = {}^-18$
5. $(8) + (1) + (^-6) = {}^+3$
   $(8m^2n) + (m^2n) + (^-6m^2n) = 3m^2n$
6. $9 \times 2 = 18$
   $x^2y \times xy^2 = x^3y^3$
   $(9x^2y)(2xy^2) = 18x^3y^3$
7. $6 \times 5 \times 2 = 60$
   $(^-6)(^+5)(^-2) = {}^+60$
8. $54 \div 9 = 6$
   $\dfrac{54}{^-9} = {}^-6$
9. $(^-9) - (^-7) = (^-9) + (^+7) = {}^-2$
   $(^-9abc) - (^-7abc) = {}^-2abc$
10. $^-6 \div 24 = {}^-.25$
    $s^4t^3 \div st^2 = s^3t$
    $\dfrac{^-6s^4t^3}{24st^2} = {}^-.25s^3t$

Level 2

Lesson 1

1. $\dfrac{9x}{9} = \dfrac{72}{9}$
   $x = 8$
   $9 \cdot 8 = 72$
2. $g + 20 = 64$
   $ - 20 -20$
   $g = 44$
   $44 + 20 = 64$
3. $c - 14 = 39$
   $ + 14 + 14$
   $c = 53$
   $53 - 14 = 39$
4. $\dfrac{5}{1} \times \dfrac{b}{5} = 30 \times \dfrac{5}{1}$
   $b = 150$
   $\dfrac{150}{5} = 30$

UNIT VII: MATHEMATICS Ch. 6, Level 2, Lesson 1 — Ch. 6, Level 2 Review **A-59**

5. $32 = y + 7$
   $\underline{-7 \quad -7}$
   $25 = y$
   $32 = 25 + 7$

6. $\frac{2}{1} \times \frac{1}{2}x = 6 \times \frac{2}{1}$
   $x = 12$
   $\frac{1}{2} \cdot 12 = 6$

3. $8n - n = n + 3$
   $7n = n + 3$
   $\underline{-n \quad -n}$
   $\frac{6n}{6} = \frac{3}{6}$
   $n = \frac{1}{2}$

4. $6n + 11 = 3n - 4$
   $\underline{-3n \quad -3n}$
   $3n + 11 = ^-4$
   $\underline{-11 \quad -11}$
   $\frac{3n}{3} = \frac{^-15}{3}$
   $n = ^-5$

7. $42 = x - 1$
   $\underline{+1 \quad +1}$
   $43 = x$
   $42 = 43 - 1$

8. $b + 16 = 40$
   $\underline{-16 \quad -16}$
   $b = 24$
   $24 + 16 = 40$

5. $12 = \frac{n}{8}$
   $8 \times 12 = \frac{n}{8} \times 8$
   $96 = n$

9. $\frac{1}{4}k = 24$
   $\frac{4}{1} \cdot \frac{1}{4}k = 24 \cdot \frac{4}{1}$
   $k = 96$
   $\frac{1}{4} \cdot 96 = 24$

10. $x - 18 = 108$
    $\underline{+18 \quad +18}$
    $x = 126$
    $126 - 18 = 108$

Lesson 5

1. $\quad 3t + 4$
   $\quad\;\; t - 6$
   $\underline{-18t - 24}$
   $3t^2 + 4t$
   $\overline{3t^2 - 14t - 24}$

2. $\quad x - 6$
   $\quad\; x + 6$
   $\underline{+6x - 36}$
   $x^2 - 6x$
   $\overline{x^2 \quad\;\; - 36}$

Lesson 2

1. $3n + 5n = 40$
   $\frac{8n}{8} = \frac{40}{8}$
   $n = 5$

2. $8t + 12 = 2t - 6$
   $\underline{-2t \quad\;\; -2t}$
   $6t + 12 = ^-6$
   $\underline{-12 \quad -12}$
   $\frac{6t}{6} = \frac{^-18}{6}$
   $t = -3$

3. $\quad 2b - 3$
   $\quad\; 3b - 4$
   $\underline{-8b + 12}$
   $6b^2 - 9b$
   $\overline{6b^2 - 17b + 12}$

4. $\quad c + 3$
   $\quad\; c - 3$
   $\underline{-3c - 9}$
   $c^2 + 3c$
   $\overline{c^2 \quad\;\; - 9}$

3. $2(y + 10) = 38$
   $2y + 20 = 38$
   $\underline{-20 \quad -20}$
   $\frac{2y}{2} = \frac{18}{2}$
   $y = 9$

4. $3x - 4 - x = 16$
   $2x - 4 = 16$
   $\underline{+4 \quad +4}$
   $\frac{2x}{2} = \frac{20}{2}$
   $x = 10$

5. $\quad 4a + 6$
   $\quad\; 2a - 3$
   $\underline{-12a - 18}$
   $8a^2 + 12a$
   $\overline{8a^2 \quad\;\; - 18}$

5. $9s - 27 = 3s + 27$
   $\underline{-3s \quad\;\; -3s}$
   $6s - 27 = 27$
   $\underline{+27 \quad +27}$
   $\frac{6s}{6} = \frac{54}{6}$
   $s = 9$

Level 2 Review

1. $\frac{w}{8} = 16$
   $\frac{8}{1} \times \frac{1}{8}w = 16 \times \frac{8}{1}$
   $w = 128$

2. $3n - \frac{1}{2}n = 10$
   $\frac{2}{5} \times \frac{5}{2}n = 10 \times \frac{2}{5}$
   $n = 4$

Lesson 3

1. $4y - 10 \geq 14$
   $\underline{+10 \quad +10}$
   $\frac{4y}{4} \geq \frac{24}{4}$
   $y \geq 6$

2. $5t + 2 > 12$
   $\underline{-2 \quad -2}$
   $\frac{5t}{5} > \frac{10}{5}$
   $t > 2$

3. $3x - 24 = x + 2\frac{1}{2}$
   $\underline{-x \quad\;\; -x}$
   $2x - 24 = 2\frac{1}{2}$
   $\underline{+24 \quad +24}$
   $\frac{2x}{2} = \frac{26\frac{1}{2}}{2}$
   $x = 13\frac{1}{4}$

4. $\frac{2}{3}b + 62 = 4(b + 3)$
   $\frac{2}{3}b + 62 = 4b + 12$
   $\underline{-\frac{2}{3}b \quad\;\; -\frac{2}{3}b}$
   $62 = 3\frac{1}{3}b + 12$
   $\underline{-12 \quad\;\; -12}$
   $\frac{3}{10} \times 50 = \frac{10}{3}b \times \frac{3}{10}$
   $15 = b$

3. $9v - 2 \leq 25$
   $\underline{+2 \quad +2}$
   $\frac{9v}{9} \leq \frac{27}{9}$
   $v \leq 3$

4. $13d - 4 > 22$
   $\underline{+4 \quad +4}$
   $\frac{13d}{13} > \frac{26}{13}$
   $d > 2$, no

5. $8d + 4 \geq 20$
   $\underline{-4 \quad -4}$
   $\frac{8d}{8} \geq \frac{16}{8}$
   $d \geq 2$

6. $12y - 12 < 12$
   $\underline{+12 \quad +12}$
   $\frac{12y}{12} < \frac{24}{12}$
   $y < 2$

5. $5m + 3 \geq 33$
   $\underline{-3 \quad -3}$
   $\frac{5m}{5} \geq \frac{30}{5}$
   $m \geq 6$, yes

7. $\frac{n - 14}{7}$

8. $10x - 3 = 2x + 29$
   $\underline{-2x \quad\;\; -2x}$
   $8x - 3 = 29$
   $\underline{+3 \quad\;\; +3}$
   $\frac{8x}{8} = \frac{32}{8}$
   $x = 4$

Lesson 4

1. $3n + 5n = 24$
   $\frac{8n}{8} = \frac{24}{8}$
   $n = 3$

2. $n = \frac{5}{6}n + 11$
   $\underline{-\frac{5}{6}n \quad -\frac{5}{6}n}$
   $\frac{6}{1} \times \frac{1}{6}n = +11 \times 6$
   $n = 66$

9. $\quad 4b - 3$
   $\underline{\times\; 2b + 4}$
   $16b - 12$
   $8b^2 - 6b$
   $\overline{8b^2 + 10b - 12}$

10. $\quad x - 9$
    $\underline{\times\; x + 9}$
    $9x - 81$
    $x^2 - 9x$
    $\overline{x^2 \quad\;\; - 81}$

A-60 Ch. 6, Level 3, Lesson 1 – Chapter 6 Quiz

Level 3

Lesson 1

1. $\frac{8}{120} = \frac{x}{195}$
    $8 \times 195 = 120x$
    $\frac{1560}{120} = \frac{120x}{120}$
    $13 = x$

2. $\frac{\frac{1}{2}}{20} = \frac{3}{x}$
    $\frac{1}{2}x = 3 \times 20$
    $\frac{2}{1} \times \frac{1}{2}x = 60 \times \frac{2}{1}$
    $x = 120$ miles

3. $\frac{1\frac{1}{2}}{\frac{2}{3}} = \frac{x}{2}$
    $1\frac{1}{2} \times 2 = \frac{2}{3}x$
    $\frac{3}{\frac{2}{3}} = \frac{\frac{2}{3}x}{\frac{2}{3}}$
    $4\frac{1}{2} = x$

4. $\frac{4}{11} = \frac{x}{33}$
    $4 \times 33 = 11x$
    $132 = 11x$
    $12 = x$

5. $\frac{2}{5} = \frac{3000}{x}$
    $2x = 3000 \times 5$
    $\frac{2x}{2} = \frac{15,000}{2}$
    $x = 7500$

    3000
    $+ 7500$
    $\overline{10,500}$

Lesson 2

1. (3)

2. (3)
   $x + (x + 65) + 115 =$ total weight
   $(2x + 180) \div 3$

3. (2)
   $x - \frac{1}{3}x - 175$
   $\frac{2}{3}x - 175$

4. (2)

5. (3)

Level 3 Review

1. $x + 18 = 4(x + 3)$
    $x + 18 = 4x + 12$
    $\underline{-x \qquad\quad -x}$
    $18 = 3x + 12$
    $\underline{-12 \qquad -12}$
    $\frac{6}{3} = \frac{3x}{3}$
    $2 = x$
    $5 = x + 3$

2. $x + (x + 3) + 2(x + 3) = 13$
    $x + (x + 3) + 2x + 6 = 13$
    $4x + 9 = 13$
    $\underline{\quad -9 \quad -9}$
    $\frac{4x}{4} = \frac{4}{4}$
    $x = 1$
    $2(x + 3) = 8$

3. $3x - x = 24$
    $\frac{2x}{2} = \frac{24}{2}$
    $x = 12$
    $3x = 36$

4. $115x + 2(65) + 105 = 580$
    $115x + 130 + 105 = 580$
    $115x + 235 = 580$
    $\underline{\qquad\quad -235 \quad -235}$
    $\frac{115x}{115} = \frac{345}{115}$
    $x = 3$

5. $105 + 2(105) + 2(75) + 2x = 735$
    $105 + 210 + 150 + 2x = 735$
    $465 + 2x = 735$
    $\underline{\quad -465 \qquad -465}$
    $\frac{2x}{2} = \frac{270}{2}$
    $x = 135$
    boiled ham

6. $2(65) + 4x = 470$
    $130 + 4x = 470$
    $\underline{-130 \qquad -130}$
    $\frac{4x}{4} = \frac{340}{4}$
    $x = 85$
    roast beef

7. (1)

8. (1)

---

9. 1 quart = 32 ounces
    $2 \times 32 = 64$
    $\frac{64}{\$.96} = \frac{1}{x}$
    $64x = 1 \times .96$
    $\frac{64x}{64} = \frac{.96}{64}$
    $x = \$.015$

10. $\frac{9}{70} = \frac{630}{x}$
    $9x = 70 \times 630$
    $\frac{9x}{9} = \frac{44,100}{9}$
    $x = 4900$

Chapter 6   Quiz

1. **C**
    $\frac{7}{6} = 1\frac{1}{6}$

2. $(^+14) - (^-4) + (^-8) - (^+2)$
    $(^+14) + (^+4) + (^-8) + (^-2)$
    $(^+18) + (^-10) = {}^+8$

3. $\frac{1}{3} \times 18 \times 4 \times 3 = 72$
    $\left(\frac{^+1}{3}\right)(^-18)(^+4)(^-3) = {}^+72$

4. $72 \div 6 = 12$
    $\frac{72}{^-6} = {}^-12$

5. $^-10 \times {}^+4 \times {}^-3 = {}^+120$
    $m^2 \times m \times m^3 = m^6$
    $n^2 \times n \times n^2 = n^5$
    $^+120m^6n^5$

6. $46 - 3b = 7b + 6$
    $\underline{\quad + 3b \quad\quad + 3b}$
    $46 = 10b + 6$
    $\underline{-6 \qquad\quad -6}$
    $\frac{40}{10} = \frac{10b}{10}$
    $4 = b$

7. $8x + 5 = 3(x - 5)$
    $8x + 5 = 3x - 15$
    $\underline{-3x \quad\quad -3x}$
    $5x + 5 = -15$
    $\underline{\quad -5 \quad\quad -5}$
    $\frac{5x}{5} = \frac{-20}{5}$
    $x = {}^-4$

8. $12n + 3 \geq 2n + 23$
    $\underline{-2n \qquad -2n}$
    $10n + 3 \geq 23$
    $\underline{\quad -3 \qquad -3}$
    $\frac{10n}{10} \geq \frac{20}{10}$
    $n \geq 2$

9. $\frac{2}{3}w + 14 < 26$
    $\underline{\quad -14 \quad -14}$
    $\frac{3}{2} \times \frac{2}{3}w < 12 \times \frac{3}{2}$
    $w < 18$

10. $\frac{1}{2}n - 8$

11. $5n - 16 = 3n + 2$
    $\underline{-3n \qquad -3n}$
    $2n - 16 = 2$
    $\underline{\quad + 16 \quad + 16}$
    $\frac{2n}{2} = \frac{18}{2}$
    $n = 9$

12. $3n - \frac{1}{2}n + 6 = 16$
    $2\frac{1}{2}n + 6 = 16$
    $\underline{\qquad -6 \quad -6}$
    $2n = 10$
    $\frac{2}{5} \times \frac{5}{2}n = 10 \times \frac{2}{5}$
    $n = 4$

13. $\quad 4c - 8$
     $\quad 2c + 6$
     $+ 24c - 48$
     $8c^2 - 16c$
     $\overline{8c^2 + 8c - 48}$

14. $\frac{8a^2b^3}{2a^2b^2} - \frac{2a^3b^2}{2a^2b^2} + \frac{6a^4b^4}{2a^2b^2} = 2a^2b^2(4b - a + 3a^2b^2)$

15. $x + (x + 3) + (x + 3 + 2) = 17$
    $3x + 8 = 17$
    $\underline{\quad -8 \quad -8}$
    $\frac{3x}{3} = \frac{9}{3}$
    $x = 3$

UNIT VII: MATHEMATICS Chapter 6 Quiz—Ch. 7, Level 2, Lesson 2 **A-61**

16. $x + 2x + 3x = \$480$
    $\dfrac{6x}{6} = \dfrac{480}{6}$
    $x = \$80$
    $3x = \$240$

17. $x + 2x + 8x = \$990$
    $\dfrac{11x}{11} = \dfrac{990}{11}$
    $x = \$90$
    $8x = \$720$

18. $\dfrac{2}{2.5} = \dfrac{x}{25}$
    $2.5x = 50$
    $x = 20$

19. (3)
    $x + 3x + 30$
    $4x + 30$

20. (2)
    $x + (x + 3) + 2(x + 3)$
    $x + (x + 3) + (2x + 6)$
    $4x + 9$

Chapter 7 Geometry

Level 1 Preview

1. a. **right**
   b. **90°**

2. **70°**
   $180° - 110° = 70°$

3. $\angle b$, $\angle f$, and $\angle g$

4. **52°**
   $180° - 76° = 104°$
   $104° \div 2 = 52°$

5. **50°**
   45 180
   $\underline{+\,85}$ $\underline{-\,130}$
   130 $\,50$

Lesson 1

1. **right**   2. **reflex**   3. **reflex**
4. **straight** 5. **acute**   6. **obtuse**
7. **acute**   8. **straight** 9. **right**
10. **reflex**

Lesson 2

1. a. **acute**   2. $\angle f$ 3. $\angle a$, $\angle e$, and $\angle h$
   b. **obtuse**
   c. **obtuse**

4. **65°**
   $180° - 115° = 65°$

5. **65°**
   $180° - 115° = 65°$

Lesson 3

1. a. **50°**
   $\angle B + \angle C = 90°$
   $90° - 40° = 50°$
   b. **right**

2. a. **100°**
   $45° + 35° = 80°$
   $180° - 80° = 100°$
   b. **scalene**

3. **54°**
   $180° - 72° = 108°$
   $\dfrac{108°}{2} = 54°$

4. a. **60°**
   $55° + 65° = 120°$
   $180° - 120° = 60°$
   b. **scalene**

5. a. **34°**
   $120° + 26° = 146°$
   $180° - 146° = 34°$
   b. **scalene**

Level 1 Review

1. A = **right** B = **acute** C = **obtuse** D = **straight**

2. **40°**
   $90° - 50° = 40°$

3. **supplementary**

4. **85°**
   $\angle k = \angle m$

5. $\angle d$, $\angle e$, and $\angle h$

6. **180°**

7. **75°**
   $32° + 73° = 105°$
   $180° - 105° = 75°$

8. **52°**
   $64° + 64° = 128°$
   $180° - 128° = 52°$

9. **130°**
   $23° + 4° = 27°$
   $23° + 27° = 50°$
   $180° - 50° = 130°$

10. **135°**
    $\angle J = \angle L$
    $\angle L = \dfrac{90°}{2} = 45°$
    $180° - 45° = 135°$

Level 2

Lesson 1

1. Yes. Because two pairs of corresponding angles are equal, the other corresponding angles are equal, and the triangles are in proportion to one another.

2. $6\tfrac{2}{3}$ **feet**
   $\dfrac{10}{12} = \dfrac{x}{8}$
   $\dfrac{12x}{12} = \dfrac{80}{12}$
   $x = 6\tfrac{2}{3}$

3. **18 feet**
   $\dfrac{6}{24} = \dfrac{x}{72}$
   $\dfrac{24x}{24} = \dfrac{432}{24}$
   $x = 18$

4. **60 feet**
   GI corresponds to IK.
   GH corresponds to JK.
   $\dfrac{25}{100} = \dfrac{15}{x}$
   $\dfrac{25x}{25} = \dfrac{1500}{25}$
   $x = 60$

5. **4 feet**
   Triangle ABC is similar to triangle DEC.
   $AC = 4 + 8 = 12$
   $\dfrac{6}{12} = \dfrac{x}{8}$
   $\dfrac{12x}{12} = \dfrac{48}{12}$
   $x = 4$

Lesson 2

1. **15 inches**
   $a^2 + b^2 = c^2$
   $12^2 + 9^2 = c^2$
   $144 + 81 = c^2$
   $\sqrt{225} = \sqrt{c^2}$
   $15 = c$

2. **6 feet**
   $a^2 + b^2 = c^2$
   $8^2 + b^2 = 10^2$
   $64 + b^2 = 100$
   $\underline{-\,64 -\,64}$
   $\sqrt{b^2} = \sqrt{36}$
   $b = 6$

A-62 Ch. 7, Level 2, Lesson 2 — Ch. 7, Level 3, Lesson 2   INSTRUCTION

3. **30 feet**
   $a^2 + b^2 = c^2$
   $40^2 + b^2 = 50^2$
   $1600 + b^2 = 2500$
   $ -1600 -1600$
   $\sqrt{b^2} = \sqrt{900}$
   $b = 30$

4. **25 miles**
   $a^2 + b^2 = c^2$
   $20^2 + 15^2 = c^2$
   $400 + 225 = c^2$
   $\sqrt{625} = \sqrt{c^2}$
   $25 = c$

3. **15 inches**
   $a^2 + b^2 = c^2$
   $a^2 + 8^2 = 17^2$
   $a^2 + 64 = 289$
   $ -64 -64$
   $a^2 = 225$
   $\sqrt{a^2} = \sqrt{225}$
   $a = 15$

4. **35°**
   $\angle GIH = 90° - 55° = 35°$
   $\angle GIH = \angle JIK$
   $\angle JIK = 35°$

5. **20 feet**
   $a^2 + b^2 = c^2$
   $16^2 + 12^2 = c^2$
   $256 + 144 = c^2$
   $\sqrt{400} = \sqrt{c^2}$
   $20 = c$

5. **13 miles**
   $a^2 + b^2 = c^2$
   $12^2 + 5^2 = c^2$
   $144 + 25 = c^2$
   $169 = c^2$
   $\sqrt{169} = \sqrt{c^2}$
   $13 = c$

6. $A = (^-4, ^+6)$
   $B = (^-2, ^+3)$
   $C = (^+4, ^+5)$
   $D = (^-3, ^-4)$
   $E = (0, ^-2)$
   $F = (^+4, ^-3)$

Lesson 3

1. $A = (^+5, ^+4)$ 2. $B = (^+2, ^+3)$ 3. $C = (^-3, ^+5)$

4. $D = (^-5, ^+2)$ 5. $E = (^-2, 0)$ 6. $F = (^-3, ^-3)$

7. $G = (^+4, ^-2)$ 8. $H = (^+5, ^-6)$ 9. $(0, ^+4)$

10. $(^+4, 0)$

Lesson 4

1. **7**
   $A = 3$ spaces left of the y-axis
   $B = 4$ spaces right of the y-axis
   $3 + 4 = 7$ spaces

2. **7**
   $C = 3$ spaces left of the y-axis
   $D = 4$ spaces right of the y-axis
   $3 + 4 = 7$ spaces

3. **9**
   $B = 5$ spaces above the x-axis
   $D = 4$ spaces below the x-axis
   $5 + 4 = 9$ spaces

4. **8**
   $A = 5$ spaces above the x-axis
   Line $y = -3 = 3$ spaces below the x-axis
   $5 + 3 = 8$ spaces

5. **13**
   $E: (^-6, ^-2); F: (6, 3)$
   $d = \sqrt{(x_2 - x_1)^2 + (y_2 - y_1)^2}$
   $= \sqrt{(6 - (^-6))^2 + (3 - (^-2))^2}$
   $= \sqrt{(12)^2 + (5)^2}$
   $= \sqrt{144 + 25}$
   $= \sqrt{169} = 13$

7. **8**
   $T = 1$ space above the x-axis
   $V = 7$ spaces below the x-axis
   $1 + 7 = 8$ total spaces

8. $(0, ^-3)$
   on the y-axis (0),
   3 spaces below the x-axis ($^-3$)

9. $d = \sqrt{(x_2 - x_1)^2 + (y_2 - y_1)^2}$
   $= \sqrt{(4 - 0)^2 + (4 - 1)^2}$
   $= \sqrt{(4)^2 + (3)^2}$
   $= \sqrt{16 + 9}$
   $= \sqrt{25}$
   $= 5$

10. $(^+2, 0)$

Level 3

Lesson 1

1. $\frac{2}{5}$
   $\frac{1 - 3}{0 - 5} = \frac{^-2}{^-5} = \frac{2}{5}$

2. $^-4$
   $\frac{^-2 - 2}{3 - 2} = \frac{^-4}{1} = ^-4$

3. $\frac{2}{3}$
   $\frac{2 - (^-2)}{4 - (^-2)} = \frac{4}{6} = \frac{2}{3}$

4. $^-1\frac{2}{5}$
   $\frac{^-5 - 2}{2 - (^-3)} = \frac{^-7}{5} = ^-1\frac{2}{5}$

5. $^-1$
   $\frac{4 - 0}{3 - 4} = \frac{4}{^-1} = ^-1$

Lesson 2

1. If $x = 3$, $y = ^-3$. If $x = 1$, $y = 1$. If $x = 2$, $y = ^-1$.

2. Line F shows the equation $y = -2x + 3$.

3. If $x = 4$, $y = 0$. If $x = 2$, $y = ^-1$. If $x = ^-4$, $y = ^-4$.

4. Line I shows the equation $y = \frac{1}{2}x - 2$.

5. $(0, ^-2)$

Level 2   Review

1. **Yes**
   In triangle ABC:
   $\angle A = 35°$, $\angle B = 90°$,
   $\angle C = 55°$.
   In triangle DEF:
   $\angle D = 35°$, $\angle E = 90°$,
   $\angle F = 55°$.
   Triangles that have equal corresponding angles are similar.

2. **15 feet**
   $\frac{20}{60} = \frac{5}{x}$
   $\frac{20x}{20} = \frac{300}{20}$
   $x = 15$

UNIT VII: MATHEMATICS   Ch. 7, Level 3 Review — Chapter 7 Quiz   A-63

Level 3 Review

1. **1**
   $(^-2, ^-6)(5, 1)$
   $m = \dfrac{y_2 - y_1}{x_2 - x_1}$
   $= \dfrac{1 - ^-6}{5 - ^-2}$
   $= \dfrac{1 + 6}{5 + 2}$
   $= \dfrac{7}{7} = 1$

2. **$^-2$**
   $(^-3, 7)(3, ^-5)$
   $m = \dfrac{y_2 - y_1}{x_2 - x_1}$
   $= \dfrac{^-5 - 7}{3 - ^-3} = \dfrac{^-12}{6} = ^-2$

3. Line *B* shows the equation $y = x - 2$.

4. Line *A* shows the equation $y = -x + 1$.

5. Line *C* shows the equation $y = x - 3$.

6. **$^-1$**
   $(^-3, 4)(3, ^-2)$
   $m = \dfrac{y_2 - y_1}{x_2 - x_1}$
   $= \dfrac{^-2 - 4}{3 - ^-3}$
   $= \dfrac{^-6}{6}$
   $= ^-1$

7. **1**
   $(0, ^-3)(2, ^-1)$
   $m = \dfrac{y_2 - y_1}{x_2 - x_1}$
   $= \dfrac{^-1 - ^-3}{2 - 0}$
   $= \dfrac{2}{2}$
   $= 1$

8. **line *A***
   $y = -x + 1$
   $3 = -(^-2) + 1$
   $3 = 2 + 1$
   $3 = 3$

9. **line *C***
   $y = x - 3$
   $^-4 = ^-1 - 3$
   $^-4 = ^-4$

10. **$\dfrac{1}{3}$**
    Bottom of ramp: $(x_1, y_1) = (0, 0)$
    Top of ramp: $(x_2, y_2) = (18, 6)$
    $m = \dfrac{y_2 - y_1}{x_2 - x_1}$
    $= \dfrac{6 - 0}{18 - 0}$
    $= \dfrac{6}{18}$
    $= \dfrac{1}{3}$

4. **55°**
   $\angle BAC = 90° - 35°$
   $\angle BAC = 55°$

5. **65°**
   $\angle a = \angle e$
   $\angle e + \angle f = 180°$
   $\angle f = 180° - 115°$
   $\angle f = 65°$

6. **45°**
   $80° + 55° = 135°$
   $180° - 135° = 45°$

7. **35°**
   $180° - 110° = 70°$
   $70° \div 2 = 35°$ in each angle

8. **two triangles with equal angles are similar.**
   $\angle C = 180° - 120° = 60°$
   $\angle E = 85°$
   $\angle D = 180° - 145° = 35°$
   $\angle A = \angle D = 35°$
   $\angle E = \angle B = 85°$
   $\angle C = \angle F = 60°$

9. **5 miles**
   $c^2 = a^2 + b^2$
   $c^2 = 3^2 + 4^2$
   $c^2 = 9 + 16$
   $c^2 = 25$
   $c = \sqrt{25}$
   $c = 5$

10. **D**
    Point *D* is 2 spaces to the right of the *y*-axis and $= ^+2$ and 3 spaces below the *x*-axis and $= ^-3$.

11. **61**
    $(-2, 3)(4, -2)$
    $d = \sqrt{(4 - (-2))^2 + (^-2 - 3)^2}$
    $d = \sqrt{(6)^2 + (-5)^2}$
    $d = \sqrt{36 + 25}$
    $d = \sqrt{61}$

12. **line *GH***

13. **$-\dfrac{7}{5}$**
    $m = \dfrac{y_2 - y_1}{x_2 - x_1}$
    $m = \dfrac{^-5 - 2}{2 - (^-3)}$
    $m = \dfrac{^-7}{2 + 3}$
    $m = \dfrac{^-7}{5} = -\dfrac{7}{5}$

14. **54 feet tall**
    $\dfrac{6}{2} = \dfrac{x}{18}$
    $\dfrac{2x}{2} = \dfrac{108}{2}$
    $54 = x$

15. Line *A* shows the equation $y = x - 7$.

16. Line *B* shows the equation $y = 2x - 4$.

17. **line *A***

18. **$\dfrac{1}{2}$**
    $(0, 0)(10, 5)$
    $m = \dfrac{y_2 - y_1}{x_2 - x_1}$
    $= \dfrac{5 - 0}{10 - 0}$
    $= \dfrac{5}{10}$
    $= \dfrac{1}{2}$

19. **26 miles**
    $c^2 = a^2 + b^2$
    $c^2 = 10^2 + 24^2$
    $c^2 = 100 + 576$
    $c^2 = 676$
    $c = 26$

20. **20 inches**
    $c^2 = a^2 + b^2$
    $c^2 = 12^2 + 16^2$
    $c^2 = 144 + 256$
    $c^2 = 400$
    $c = 20$

Chapter 7 Quiz

1. acute

2. reflex

3. **101°**
   180
   $\underline{-79}$
   101

PRACTICE

PRACTICE ITEMS 1
Writing Skills, Part I: Grammar

1. **(3)** *Mechanics/Spelling/Sentence Correction.* Decided is spelled with a soft *c*, not an *s*.
2. **(1)** *Usage/Verb Form/Sentence Correction.* The plural subject, questions, requires a plural verb, are.
3. **(3)** *Mechanics/Capitalization/Sentence Correction.* Since technical describes a general type of paper and is not a proper name, it should not be capitalized.
4. **(4)** *Sentence Structure/Sentence Fragment/Sentence Revision.* The sentence fragment is corrected by providing a subject, you, and verb phrase, will have to buy.
5. **(5)** *Sentence Structure/Parallelism/Sentence Revision.* The two equivalent ideas about computer uses should be expressed in the same form: playing, drawing.
6. **(1)** *Usage/Verb Form/Sentence Correction.* Because Sentence 7 begins with Maybe you want, which is conditional, the verb in Sentence 8 must be in the conditional form, would choose.
7. **(2)** *Mechanics/Punctuation/Sentence Revision.* No comma is used to set off a phrase when it is essential to meaning: with teaching programs.
8. **(3)** *Usage/Verb Tense/Sentence Revision.* The phrase, If you plan, is subjunctive and clues you to the need for the conditional verb form, should ask.
9. **(2)** *Usage/Pronoun Reference/Construction Shift.* You will be ready to ask a computer dealer for help in finding the computer that meets your needs once you have considered what these needs are. The rewritten form clears up the vague reference, it.
10. **(4)** *Sentence Structure/Clarity—Dangling Modifier/Construction Shift.* Someday you may be writing a business letter to accompany your application for a job. Your letter, not you, will accompany your application.
11. **(1)** *Sentence Structure/Sentence Fragment/Sentence Correction.* The insertion of a subject and verb, You may not know, corrects the fragment.
12. **(4)** *Sentence Structure/Run-on Sentence/Sentence Correction.* The period corrects the run-on by forming two sentences, each able to stand alone.
13. **(1)** *Mechanics/Punctuation/Construction Shift.* Research shows that, when in doubt about a choice of greeting, you should avoid the phrases Dear Sirs and Gentlemen. The rewritten form reads more smoothly.
14. **(3)** *Usage/Subject-Verb Agreement/Sentence Correction.* The subject, study, and verb, was done, must agree despite the interrupting phrases between them.
15. **(4)** *Usage/Subject-Verb Agreement/Sentence Revision.* The singular subject, none, requires a singular verb, was chosen.
16. **(3)** *Usage/Verb Tense/Sentence Correction.* To remain consistent with the rest of the paragraph, the past tense should be used to describe the study.
17. **(5)** *Mechanics/Spelling/Sentence Correction.* Difference is spelled correctly, and the sentence contains no errors in usage or punctuation.
18. **(1)** *Usage/Ambiguous Pronoun Reference/Construction Shift.* Perhaps masculine greetings annoy female employers. The rewritten form clears up the ambiguous reference, they and them.
19. **(4)** *Sentence Structure/Improper Subordination/Sentence Revision.* It is incorrect to use because of before a subject-verb structure.
20. **(5)** *Mechanics/Capitalization/Sentence Correction.* Here, user group is only the general name of a type of group. You would capitalize a proper name, such as Kingston User Group.
21. **(4)** *Mechanics/Punctuation/Sentence Correction.* The comma only confuses the reader by separating advantages from the phrase essential to its meaning.
22. **(1)** *Sentence Structure/Modification/Construction Shift.* Having borrowed a program, you may be able to make and keep a copy. The rewritten form is simpler.
23. **(1)** *Mechanics/Spelling/Sentence Correction.* Another is one word.
24. **(5)** *Sentence Structure/Comma Splice/Sentence Revision.* The two sentences can stand alone and should be separated by a period.
25. **(4)** *Usage/Pronoun Shift/Sentence Revision.* The pronoun, you, has been used throughout the paragraph, and so should continue to be used.
26. **(5)** *Usage/Relative Pronoun/Sentence Revision.* The most effective version eliminates the awkward phrase, that is nearest.
27. **(5)** *Usage/Subject-Verb Agreement/Sentence Correction.* No correction is necessary.
28. **(5)** *Sentence Structure/Parallelism/Sentence Correction.* Parallel ideas should be expressed in the same form: the money you save, the knowledge you gain, the friends you make.
29. **(3)** *Mechanics/Spelling/Sentence Correction.* Remember the silent *t* in often.
30. **(2)** *Sentence Structure/Comma Splice/Sentence Revision.* A period is needed to separate the two independent clauses (dealers add and dealers may charge) into sentences.
31. **(4)** *Usage/Subject-Verb Agreement/Sentence Revision.* The singular subject, it, takes a singular verb, makes.
32. **(3)** *Sentence Structure/Sentence Fragment/Sentence Correction.* The fragment is corrected by insertion of a verb, may come.

33. **(3)** *Usage/Verb Tense/Sentence Correction.* The present tense is needed because ongoing tests are being described here and elsewhere in the paragraph.
34. **(2)** *Usage/Vague Pronoun Reference/Construction Shift.* After the car is driven at 35 miles per hour into a wall, the dummies' condition is examined. The rewritten version makes clear which condition is examined.
35. **(2)** *Mechanics/Punctuation/Sentence Revision.* Do not use a comma to separate phrases joined by or.
36. **(4)** *Sentence Structure/Run-on/Sentence Revision.* The period corrects the run-on. Each of the subject-verb structures, *you will travel* and *you do not want*, should stand alone.
37. **(5)** *Mechanics/Capitalization/Sentence Correction.* American is a proper adjective referring to the United States, whereas *foreign* describes other countries generally.
38. **(2)** *Sentence Structure/Sentence Fragment/Sentence Correction.* The subject, *jobs*, requires a verb to correct the fragment. Changing *involving* to *involve* supplies the verb.
39. **(5)** *Sentence Structure/Sentence Fragment/Sentence Revision.* The fragment is corrected by supplying a verb, *is*, for *example*, which becomes the subject.
40. **(4)** *Mechanics/Capitalization/Sentence Correction.* U.S. Park Service is the proper name of an organization and needs to be capitalized.
41. **(4)** *Sentence Structure/Modification/Construction Shift.* Since many applicants take the test, only those with excellent scores become finalists. The rewritten form avoids the awkward repetition of *finalists*.
42. **(2)** *Usage/Wrong Relative Pronoun/Sentence Correction.* Few refers to people and requires the pronoun *who*.
43. **(2)** *Usage/Pronoun Shift/Sentence Revision.* Use of the pronoun *you* is inconsistent with the rest of the paragraph.
44. **(1)** *Mechanics/Spelling/Sentence Correction.* Remember that *y* in *day* is changed to *i* in *daily*.
45. **(3)** *Usage/Ambiguous Reference/Construction Shift.* Rangers must relabel changing displays in park museums. The rewritten form clears up the ambiguous *they* and *them*.
46. **(4)** *Mechanics/Punctuation/Sentence Revision.* Elements in a series are separated by commas: writing, typing, filling out.
47. **(1)** *Mechanics/Punctuation/Sentence Revision.* Put a comma before the word *but* when it separates two ideas that could stand alone.
48. **(2)** *Usage/Subject-Verb Agreement/Sentence Revision.* The plural subject, *computers*, requires a plural verb, *have arrived*.
49. **(1)** *Usage/Verb Tense/Sentence Correction.* The present tense, *use*, is consistent with the tense found throughout the paragraph.
50. **(4)** *Sentence Structure/Clarity—Subordination/Construction Shift.* Others take advantage of programs that teach about the machine, *itself*. The new form is more simple and clear.
51. **(5)** *Mechanics/Punctuation/Sentence Correction.* GED is the abbreviation for the name of a particular test and needs to be capitalized.
52. **(5)** *Sentence Structure/Run-on/Sentence Correction.* There are no run-ons or other errors to be corrected.
53. **(4)** *Usage/Verb Form-Tense/Sentence Revision.* The phrase *If you ask* is a clue that the conditional tense can be used with the subject, *librarian*.
54. **(4)** *Mechanics/Punctuation/Sentence Correction.* Set off an introductory clause with a comma.
55. **(4)** *Sentence Structure/Parallelism/Sentence Revision.* Computers have changed *appearances* and *uses*. Use the same form for equivalent ideas.

PRACTICE ITEMS 1
Writing Skills, Part II: Essay-writing

How to Score Your Essay

To score your essay, compare it with the following model essays. These model essays received scores of 3 and 5 respectively.

Compare your essay with the 3 model essay. If it is as good as the 3 model essay, then assign your essay a score of 3. If it is not as good as the 3 model essay, then refer back to the answer key for the Writing Skills Predictor Test and use the descriptions of the 1 and 2 model essays to evaluate your essay. It should be easy to assign a score to your essay if you compare your essay with these model essays and their character-trait analyses.

If your essay is better than the 3 model essay, compare it to the model essay that received a 5. If it is better than the 3, but not as good as the 5, score your essay a 4. Give your essay a 5 if it is as good as the second model. If your essay is better than the 5 model, then score your essay a 6.

In addition, look at the notes and character-trait analyses that accompany the model essays. Those comments explain the strengths and weaknesses of the essays.

Model Essay—Holistic Score 3

States the point of view.

I don't think that forcing people to retire is a good idea. Many people are good at there work even if there really old. This is not a good law because a lot of people would not be treated right by this law.

Elaborates on the point of view with a good example. Run-on sentences make this example less effective.

Just because someone is older doesn't mean that they can't do a good job if they weren't doing a good job they would be fired for doing a bad job but this law would fire people just because of there age instead of because of the kind of job they were doing.

Haphazard listing of ideas about the topic.

It is good to have older people on the job. Older people know lots of things that younger people don't know and they have lots of experiences too. Its unfair to make people retire when they don't want to. Maybe they could be good for there companys. Maybe they could help there companys. But if they retire they can't show what they can do. They can show that they can do a good job. Younger workers need jobs but older workers need jobs too. Maybe some day older people won't have to retire because of the law. Its not fair.

Restates the point of view.

Character-Trait Analysis
1. The organization is poor. Better paragraphing would help this essay.
2. The point of view is clear in the opening, but the restated point of view in the conclusion is weak.
3. The supporting examples are too general. The example in the first paragraph is good, but the run-on sentence structure takes away from the impact of the underlying area. The examples in the second paragraph are simply a haphazard listing of ideas.
4. There are many problems with accepted English usage that interfere with the essay's effectiveness.

Model Essay—Holistic Score 5

States the point of view and the reason the writer holds it.

I am opposed to requirements that employees retire when they reach a particular age. Such retirement rules are both unfair and unfounded.

Restates one reason for point of view and supports the reason by explaining it.

In many cases, people are not ready to retire when the rules say they must. After having spent much of their adult lives working, these people find that their jobs are an important part of their daily lives. It is unfair to tell such loyal employees that they must give up their livelihood merely because they have reached a specific age.

Restates the second reason for the point of view and supports it by explaining it with two examples.

Arguments for setting such a specified age are often unfounded. It is not necessarily true that younger workers can do a job better than older ones. For example, sometimes the best management decisions are made by people who have the advantage of long experience within a company. If eyesight or hearing is important on a job, let one's performance on vision or hearing tests, not one's date of birth, determine whether one keeps working.

Summarizes and elaborates on the point of view. First, presents possible reason behind contrasting opinion. Then suggests new alternatives for action based on the writer's point of view.

I believe that the real reason many employers set a mandatory retirement age is that they find it cheaper to hire young employees at beginning wages than to continue paying higher salaries to older workers. If more money were spent hiring new personnel to retrain older employees, rather than to replace them, everyone would benefit. Older workers could share their valuable experience, younger workers could share their new job skills, and the company could benefit from the increased productivity of both groups. Hopefully, the day will soon come when more employers will recognize how unjust and unrealistic mandatory retirement is.

Character-Trait Analysis
1. The organization is very good.
2. The point of view is clear and consistent throughout the essay.
3. The point of view is supported by good examples, but the examples are not as specific as they could be. They do not paint a vivid picture for the reader in the way that a 6 essay would.
4. The essay is easy to read. It has few problems with accepted English usage and flows smoothly.

PRACTICE ITEMS 2
Social Studies

1. **(4)** *Comprehension/History.* The states were represented in Congress, and the executive consisted of a committee of states. Choice (1) is not discussed in the passage. Choices (2), (3), and (5) are all contradicted by the passage.

2. **(2)** *Comprehension/History.* Congress lacked many powers, and the executive existed only as a committee of states. Choice (1) is incorrect, since it was the states themselves, and not the central government, that essentially held the power in the first place. Nothing is said about choice (3), choice (4), or choice (5). In fact, choice (3) is unlikely, since the executive was a weak committee of states, as is choice (4), since the national government did not have the power to tax.

3. **(3)** *Analysis/History.* Lacking the power to levy taxes, Congress found itself unable to pay off the Continental Army. (Eventually the needed money was obtained from banks.) Choice (3) is incorrect because the new government lacked the power to raise an army. When the rebellion in question (Shays' rebellion) occurred, the state of Massachusetts had to fend for itself. Choice (2) and choice (4) are wrong, since Congress couldn't regulate international trade. Choice (5) is not addressed in the passage.

4. **(2)** *Comprehension/History.* The documents trampled beneath Jackson's feet and the presidential veto clutched in his hand suggest that the cartoonist felt that Jackson was abusing his powers of office.

5. **(2)** *Analysis/History.* The passage states that there was distrust among the major powers. Therefore, it is logical that each wanted, by means of the veto, to protect its interests from possibly undesirable moves of the others that might be supported by a majority vote of the Security Council. Choice (1) and choice (5) are therefore incorrect. There is nothing in the passage to support choice (3) or choice (4) as an explanation for the veto.

6. **(2)** *Comprehension/History.* Both plans imposed restrictions on certain former Confederates. And both required acceptance of the ban against slavery. (The congressional plan actually went much further, requiring acceptance of black citizenship and voting rights as well.) Choice (1) is not mentioned in the discussion of presidential Reconstruction. Choice (3) is incorrect because the only reference to blacks in the discussion of the presidential plan regards the abolition of slavery. The return of property is mentioned only under the presidential plan and the assumption of debts is not discussed, so choice (4) is invalid. Choice (5) is not described in the passage.

7. **(3)** *Analysis/History.* The Ten Percent Plan did not require that blacks be given the vote and it restored the vote to most ex-Confederates. As the electorate was therefore essentially the same as before the Civil War, the passage of laws restricting black rights could be expected and did occur. For this same reason, choices (1) and (4) are unlikely. Choice (2) was specifically barred by the Ten Percent Plan. Choice (5) is not supported by the passage.

8. **(4)** *Evaluation/History.* Inclusion of freed blacks in the electorate of reconstructed states and acceptance of Fourteenth Amendment citizenship requirements for blacks were major provisions of the congressional plan. Choices (1) and (5) are incorrect, since Congress took a punitive stance toward these sectors of Southern society. Choices (2) and (3) are not discussed in the passage.

9. **(5)** *Evaluation/History.* The conclusion that America's neutrality policy would likely fail is justified by the fact that Uncle Sam is shown precariously walking a tightrope and having difficulty with his balancing act. The lack of cooperation from Britain and Germany also supports this conclusion. And a close examination of the goods Uncle Sam is trading suggests that the United States is already departing from strict neutrality: The allies are receiving war material (guns) while Germany is only receiving cotton. Choice (1) and choice (2) are neither confirmed nor denied by the cartoon. Choice (3) is not supported by this cartoon since Uncle Sam is shown bringing goods to Europe himself. Choice (4) is wrong because the John Bull figure representing Great Britain shouts his intention to search U.S. goods for contraband and suggests Britain's unwillingness to have the United States trade with Germany.

10. **(5)** *Comprehension/History.* Choice (5) is the most comprehensive and accurate statement about the content of the passage. Choice (1), choice (2), and choice (4) contain only partial statements of the content of the passage. Choice (3) is incorrect because it is too general.

11. **(5)** *Analysis/History.* An inflationary policy is precisely what farmers wanted. They would benefit from such a policy in two ways. The prices of their crops would rise. And since the dollar would be worth less, while their debts would remain fixed, farmers would find it easier to repay these debts. Since inflation would have reduced the value of existing savings, thereby decreasing the number of potential investors, and would have raised prices of

goods, those who were on fixed incomes, had savings, needed investors, or wanted lower priced goods would all have been hurt. As a result, choices (1), (2), (3), and (4) are incorrect.

12. **(1)** *Analysis/History.* The introduction of more gold into the U.S. economy had the same effect the coinage of more silver would have had: It increased the money supply and thus had inflationary consequences. Note that the passage says advocates of free silver were helped by the discovery of gold. Choice (2) is wrong since the cost of living increases during an inflationary period. Choice (4) is wrong since people on fixed incomes pay more during an inflationary period but do not earn more. Neither choice (3) nor choice (5) is discussed in the passage.

13. **(2)** *Analysis/History.* The colonists felt that their hundred-year tradition of self-government was being denied by Parliament. They were not yet ready to declare independence. Thus choice (1) is incorrect. They were claiming their traditional rights as Englishmen, so choice (4) is wrong. Choices (3) and (5) are not discussed in the passage, nor can they be inferred from the material presented in it.

14. **(4)** *Comprehension/History.* The figures representing Soviet and American leaders are trying to put the cork of arms control back into the nuclear bottle; that is, they are to limit the arms race. The figure representing the Third World is trying to pull the cork from the bottle, in other words, to release nuclear power to be used for Third World armaments.

15. **(2)** *Evaluation/History.* As more Third World and other countries develop nuclear capabilities, the problem of arms control naturally becomes much more difficult. Choice (1) is contradicted by the cartoon. There is nothing in the cartoon to support choices (3) or (4). Choice (5) is not supported because the figure on the right is merely a symbol used by the cartoonist in making his point; in fact, some Third World nations do have nuclear capabilities.

16. **(3)** *Analysis/History.* Guarantees of Cuban independence under the Teller Amendment were violated by provisions of the Platt Amendment, which gave the United States control over Cuban foreign policy, etc. For this reason, choice (1) is false. Choice (2) is incorrect since both amendments relate to the role of the United States in Cuba after the Spanish-American War. There is nothing in the passage to support choice (4) or choice (5), both of which are false.

17. **(2)** *Evaluation/History.* The provisions of the Platt Amendment, which gave the United States the right to intervene in Cuba and to have a naval base there, suggest that the United States was interested in exerting its influence in Cuba and the rest of the Caribbean. For this reason choice (1) is incorrect; the trend was toward imperialism. Choice (3) is not supported by the passage; in fact, Latin American nations generally opposed U.S. controls over the Cuban economy and government as inconsistent with Cuban independence. Neither choice (4) nor choice (5) is supported by the passsge.

18. **(1)** *Analysis/Geography.* As the northwest is forest land that lacks any agriculture, it is likely to have a low population density. In fact, it is part of the Amazon Region, which is very thinly populated.

19. **(4)** *Evaluation/Geography* Since the map shows that half of Brazil is chiefly forest and that only a small strip is intensively cultivated, it is possible to conclude that much of Brazil's land remains underused. None of the other choices can be supported by the map.

20. **(5)** *Application/Geography.* The statement in choice (5) described Chicago as linking two parts of the United States. All the other statements in one way or another involve a city linking a country with the outside world.

21. **(4)** *Comprehension/Geography.* The passage indicates that the main reason there's a water distribution problem is that the hydrologic cycle doesn't distribute water evenly. Droughts are just one factor in the uneven distribution, so choice (1) is incomplete. Choices (2) and (3) exacerbate the problem but are not its main cause. Nothing is said to support the relevance of choice (5).

22. **(5)** *Analysis/Geography.* The difference between the Eastern and Western states is that in the latter evaporation exceeds precipitation, that is, the water supply is less. As a consequence, these states need to use irrigation extensively in farming. The concentration of agriculture in the Western states has occurred despite, not because of, the water distribution patterns, so choice (3) is incorrect. Choice (2) is contradicted by the passage, and choice (1) is unlikely in view of the passage. There is nothing in the passage related to choice (4).

23. **(1)** *Evaluation/Geography.* The hydrologic cycle determines the Earth's water supply and its essential distribution. Nothing is said to suggest that there are other sources of water. The statements in the other choices, in contrast, are all supported in the passage.

24. **(4)** *Comprehension/Geography.* West Street was built on the landfill developed in 1965. It did not yet exist in 1850. In contrast Water Street would still have afforded a view of the river; the Stock Exchange is built on the original land; and the landfill that permitted the extension of Broad Street to Water Street, and of Fulton Street to its present-day length, was developed in 1800.

25. **(2)** *Comprehension/Geography.* The presence of mountains that break up regions and the absence of rivers that unify them result in the problem of geographic isolation. The regions in a country are isolated from one another, and this hinders development. Choice (4) is only part of the problem. None of the other choices are supported by the passage.

26. **(2)** *Application/Economics.* A situation in which three firms dominate the market for a product is an example of an oligopoly.

27. **(3)** *Application/Economics.* In combining to regulate production in order to increase prices the oil-producing nations were acting as a cartel.

28. **(4)** *Application/Economics.* In formally combining the various firms into a single organization, John D. Rockefeller created a

trust. (The Standard Oil Trust and similar organizations were soon eliminated by legislation.)

29. **(1)** *Application/Economics*. The situation described is a monopoly. For the reason mentioned in the description, utilities are the one kind of monopoly allowed.

30. **(4)** *Comprehension/Economics*. In each of the years in the graph, government outlays are greater than government revenues; this is precisely what creates the budget deficit. Choice (3) is therefore incorrect. Choices (1) and (2) are incorrect, since revenues and outlays both steadily increase over the period shown in the graph. There is nothing in the graph to support choice (5).

31. **(5)** *Comprehension/Economics*. The largest deficits would occur where there are the biggest differences between outlays and revenues. These are associated with the 1980s, and therefore with the Reagan administration.

32. **(3)** *Application/Economics*. Since the number of service jobs is increasing, while the number of manufacturing jobs is decreasing, it should in general be more advisable to pursue a job in the service sector. With the exception of textile worker, all the careers mentioned are in the service sector.

33. **(4)** *Analysis/Economics*. The passage states that U.S. manufacturing companies have been losing some of their market to foreign competitors. The clearest example of this is choice (4), which involves an American family selecting an imported car, rather than a domestic one. Note that choice (5) does not involve other countries, choice (2) does not involve the manufacturing sector, and choice (3), although perhaps bad for American workers, does not imply diminished competitiveness of the American manufacturer.

34. **(5)** *Evaluation/Economics*. The passage points out that the new technologies allow manufacturers to make their operations more efficient. By being more efficient, they are able to produce more goods with fewer workers. This fact contradicts choice (1), as does the statement in the passage that the new technologies often require service workers. Choices (2), (3), and (4) are nowhere implied in the passage.

35. **(4)** *Evaluation/Economics*. The fact that U.S. companies compete with foreign companies means that economic developments overseas will likely affect the American work force. The passage indicates that both developments in American society, such as the growing number of old people, and technological changes have led to more service jobs. The passage also says that business decisions will have important repercussions for the health of manufacturing and, by implication, for the work force. Government legislation may or may not affect number and kinds of jobs; nothing is said in the passage, however.

36. **(2)** *Comprehenion/Economics*. The sources in choice (1), choice (4), and choice (5) showed increases. The source in choice (3) showed a more moderate decrease than that in choice (2).

37. **(3)** *Analysis/Economics*. With fewer new houses under construction and more abandoned buildings, the property tax base would shrink. Choice (1) is incorrect since income taxes increased. In other words, unemployment may or may not have risen, but even if it did, this didn't lead to a decline in income tax as a source of revenue. Choice (2) would involve revenues from toll roads, which are not given as a separate category in this graph. Choice (4) is incorrect because sales and gross receipt taxes increased, indicating increased purchasing. Choice (5) is wrong because federal outlays increased.

38. **(2)** *Comprehension/Political Science*. That bills become law when the president signs them is strongly suggested by the discussion of bills as proposed laws that the president may either sign or veto. Choice (1) is not implied in the passage, especially since the one comparison of presidents and governors indicates that governors possess a power presidents lack. Choice (3) is incorrect; although presidents may propose laws, nothing is implied in the passage. Choice (4) is wrong since the president has the choice of signing bills or vetoing them. Choice (5) is contradicted by the discussion of the item veto, which the president lacks.

39. **(4)** *Evaluation/Political Science*. The president exerts considerable influence on the legislative process even though he lacks an item veto. As indicated in the passage, fear of a veto may shape the legislation Congress passes for the president to sign. Choice (1) is not supported by the passage. Choice (2) is incorrect since pocket vetoes occur when Congress has adjourned and cannot override a veto. Choice (3) is neither confirmed nor denied by the content of the paragraph. Choice (5) is wrong; presidents will sign important bills *despite* riders, not because of them.

40. **(5)** *Evaluation/Political Science*. If the young, uneducated, poor, and minorities fail to vote, then a significant portion of the population is underrepresented in government. Choice (1) is incorrect since the poor, who presumably need the most help from government, are less likely than others to vote. Choice (2) and choice (3) are false because voting is related to education, income, etc. Choice (4) is an opinion, neither confirmed nor denied by the passage.

41. **(2)** *Comprehension/Political Science*. Public opinion is flexible and changing. Therefore, the statement in choice (2) is in direct contradiction to the strict constructionist perspective.

42. **(5)** *Evaluation/Political Science*. Choice (5) is taken from *McCulloch v. Maryland*, the classic statement of the loose constructionist position. All the other choices are quotes from strict constructionists and express their philosophy, as defined in the passage.

43. **(2)** *Evaluation/Political Science*. Choice (2) is correct because the House in effect indicts; that is, impeachment proceedings determine whether there is enough evidence for a formal accusation against an official, or grounds for a trial to be held. Thus choice (3) is incorrect. There is no evidence to support choice (1). Choice (4) is contradicted by

PRACTICE ITEMS Test 2: Social Studies A-71

the passage, which indicates that removal upon a verdict of guilty is obligatory, not optional. Choice (5) is also contradicted by the passage, as only a small number of individuals have been impeached in the nation's two-hundred-year history.

44. **(5)** *Comprehension/Political Science.* The passage mentions that officials must be accused of "high crimes and misdemeanors." Thus, incompetency is not grounds for impeachment, nor are political opposition or "disloyalty" to Congress, as is also shown by the acquittal of President Johnson. Choices (1), (2), and (4) are therefore wrong. Choice (3) is also incorrect since the impeachment process does not apply to Congress.

45. **(5)** *Comprehension/Political Science.* PAC contributions tripled while contributions from other sources didn't even double. Therefore, the statement in choice (5) is inaccurate.

46. **(5)** *Evaluation/Political Science.* As of the last year in the graph, PAC contributions accounted for a far larger share of congressional campaign monies than they had in the past. Choice (1) cannot be determined from the graph, since even in the last year shown, three-quarters of contributions came from sources other than PAC. Choices (2) and (3) are opinions for which the graph offers no information. Choice (4) is also an opinion that is not directly supported by the data.

47. **(2)** *Application/Political Science.* Choice (2) is correct, as it involves voting on a measure. Choice (1) describes the initiative, another form of participation, in which the voters can actually propose—rather than simply vote on—laws. Choice (3) illustrates recall, or removal by the electorate of public officials. Choice (4) is an example of a primary. Choice (5) is the act of a private citizen or pressure group, aimed at the national level.

48. **(1)** *Application/Political Science.* By prohibiting a member of Congress from holding any other position in government during his or her term of office, this article of the Constitution is ensuring that the legislative power is separated from other powers of government.

49. **(5)** *Application/Political Science.* Because the Senate has the right to support or reject the president's treaties and appointments, it is sharing—and limiting—an executive power.

50. **(3)** *Application/Political Science.* The prohibition and creating noble titles is consistent with the principle of republicanism, which rejects an aristocracy.

51. **(2)** *Application/Political Science.* The process of constitutional amendment, as spelled out by the Constitution, involves a sharing of power between the national legislature and the state legislatures.

52. **(1)** *Application/Behavioral Science.* The passage emphasizes that each child is different and that parents' responses to these differences, from infancy on, will affect the way a child develops. Therefore, it is important that parents get to know their infants. There is nothing in the passage to support any of the other choices.

53. **(3)** *Evaluation/Behavioral Science.* The passage states that individuals have a certain temperament from the time they are infants (nature) but that the way they develop will also depend on parents' response (nurture).

54. **(4)** *Evaluation/Behavioral Science.* The hypothesis in choice (4) would be tested by asking people for their opinions. None of the other hypotheses could be tested in this way. The hypotheses in choices (1) and (2), for example, could not be tested by a survey because they concern people's unconscious or undesired behavior.

55. **(2)** *Evaluation/Behavioral Science.* The right-hand side of the graph supports the idea that the decrease in household size is continuing. Choice (1) is therefore incorrect. Choice (3) is contradicted by the drop in household size during the 1930s. Neither choice (4) nor choice (5) can be supported on the basis of the information in the graph.

56. **(3)** *Analysis/Behavioral Science.* A decrease in immigration would not necessarily lead to a decrease in household size. And immigration has *not* steadily decreased over the period shown in the graph. All the other choices are demographic changes that would logically contribute to—and have in fact contributed to—the decline in household size.

57. **(5)** *Application/Behavioral Science.* As the average household size decreases, large economy packages become less appropriate for many households. All other choices may or may not be good advice, but they have nothing to do with the graph.

58. **(3)** *Analysis/Behavioral Science.* The decline in household size is in keeping with an emphasis on personal freedom, since such an emphasis might lead adults to decide to live alone, couples to have fewer or no children, etc. Emphasis on the values stated in the other choices would, if anything, contribute to *increased* household size.

59. **(4)** *Application/Behavioral Science.* The article indicates that television has contributed to the focus on personality by allowing voters to see the candidates and react to personal traits. Only choice (4) involves a personal trait.

60. **(4)** *Analysis/Behavioral Science.* The conclusion of the research is essentially that in today's elections, the personality of the candidates is quite important to voters. The statements in choice (2) and choice (4) support this conclusion. The statement in choice (1) is a hypothesis offered as a partial explanation for the conclusion. The statement in choice (3) is not relevant to the research.

61. **(4)** *Evaluation/Behavioral Science.* The surveys mentioned in the article document the decline in the number of voters who vote a straight ticket. The statement in choice (2) is presented as speculation by researchers, not as fact. None of the other choices are presented in the article.

62. **(3)** *Evaluation/Behavioral Science.* It can be argued that by failing to focus on candidates' stands, their voting records, and their political philosophies, voters are not as informed as they should be, since a healthy democracy requires informed and knowledgeable voters. Choice (2) is incorrect because, although the article states that television has

contributed to the focus on personality rather than issues, it does not claim that the media is exerting excessive influence. Choice (4) is incorrect because the declining importance of party affiliation is in no way equivalent to the failure of the two-party system. The statements in choice (1) and choice (5) are not discussed in the article.

63. **(2)** *Analysis/Behavioral Science.* Although advertising is often not thought of as propaganda, it in fact fits all aspects of the definition of "propaganda." Choices (1) and (4) are not necessarily true, and they are not supported by the passage. Choice (3) is contradicted by the passage. Choice (5) is a matter of opinion, and not a fact.

64. **(3)** *Comprehension/Behavioral Science.* The table shows that 73 percent of children whose mothers worked full time, and 71 percent of children whose mothers worked part time, prefer that their mothers work, while 67 percent of children whose mother's didn't work preferred that their mothers stay home. None of the other choices are supported by the table.

PRACTICE ITEMS 3
Science

1. **(3)** *Analysis/Biology*. Hemoglobin bonds with oxygen where oxygen is plentiful. Oxygen enters the blood through the lungs, so the lungs would be where the most hemoglobin would become bound to oxygen.

2. **(1)** *Comprehension/Biology*. Both parents have to pass on the gene for the sickle-cell trait for the offspring to develop sickle-cell anemia. Therefore, there is no chance that the children of a carrier and a person with normal hemoglobin will have the disease.

3. **(2)** *Evaluation/Biology*. If the single-dominant-gene theory were correct, then a sickle-cell gene passed on from either parent would cause the disease in any child that inherited it. Yet it was never the case that where only one parent showed the trait, a child developed the anemia. The fact that disproved the theory was that both parents always showed signs of the sickle-cell trait.

4. **(1)** *Analysis/Biology*. A person who suffers from sickle-cell anemia must carry two genes for the disease. The normal person has two genes for normal hemoglobin. The diseased person will always pass on the gene for sickle cell, and the other will always pass on the normal gene. Each of their children will have one of each, making them all carriers of the sickle-cell trait.

5. **(3)** *Evaluation/Biology*. (1) and (4) are true, but do not support the theory. If (2) and (5) were true, they would provide evidence against the theory. Thus, the statement that the malarial parasite rarely can establish itself in persons with the sickle-cell trait best supports the theory.

6. **(2)** *Application/Biology*. The other behaviors must all be learned. However, the ability to blink is inherited. It is a reflex behavior that people are born with.

7. **(5)** *Comprehension/Biology*. The other choices were the same for both the front yard and the back yard. However, when the homeowner raked the front yard, she would have loosened the soil, increasing the erosion rate. The seeds were probably washed away in the sudden rainstorm.

8. **(4)** *Application/Biology*. By concentrating on growing food grains, a country with a limited amount of farmland could feed a large number of people more efficiently. Eating food grains instead of livestock would mean taking energy directly from the bottom of the food pyramid, eliminating the energy loss involved in raising livestock.

9. **(4)** *Comprehension/Biology*. The results of the experiment indicates that a well-watered, well-lit, pinched-back marigold will yield the best results. None of the other choices include all three factors.

10. **(4)** *Comprehension/Biology*. The fruit surrounds the seed and provides a food supply for the plant, just as we use the apple fruit for food.

11. **(1)** *Analysis/Biology*. Since the allergy is to pollen grains, and pollen is the plants' sperm, the allergy would most likely flare up during the plants' reproductive season.

12. **(2)** *Analysis/Biology*. Genetic variation tends to be an advantage in species survival, so pollen grains that help increase genetic variation give the species an advantage. Choices (1) and (4) would work against genetic variation. Choice (3) may or may not be true; it is difficult to assess. Choice (5) would be an advantage for a seed, but a pollen grain that traveled too far might not find another plant stigma to fertilize.

13. **(3)** *Analysis/Biology*. Choices (1) and (2) are not covered in the passage. Choice (4) is false; the plants do not become seeds first. Choice (5) is also false; if the offspring are genetic copies of the parent, they will grow into flowering plants like the parent. Choice (3) is correct because the plants are produced from a single parent, and are exact genetic copies of it.

14. **(2)** *Evaluation/Biology*. The other choices are all possible uses. Choice (2) is not a possible use because the plants reproduce so quickly that they would clog up the waterways, making boating difficult.

15. **(4)** *Analysis/Biology*. The fact that the animal cannot move around during hibernation could decrease its chances for survival, since it is unable to escape from predators.

16. **(5)** *Evaluation/Biology*. Both hibernation and estivation are a response to extremes in temperature; in the first case, cold, in the second case, heat.

17. **(1)** *Analysis/Biology*. By studying the figure, you will see that Adenine always pairs with Thymine, Thymine always pairs with Adenine, Cytosine always pairs with Guanine, and Guanine always pairs with Cytosine. Thus, if you know the sequence of the bases on the first strand, you can quickly deduce the order of the bases on the complementary strand.

18. **(5)** *Analysis/Biology*. Because food is brought to the animal, it can survive without moving. Choices (2) and (4) describe plant nutrition, not animal nutrition. There is no basis for choice (3) in the passage.

19. **(4)** *Analysis/Biology*. A balanced vegetarian diet supplies all the necessary vitamins for proper nutrition. By examining the source column, this becomes evident.

20. **(1)** *Evaluation/Biology*. Although deficiencies in other vitamins might cause similar symptoms, vitamin A is the only vitamin listed that has an effect on eye health.

21. **(3)** *Comprehension/Biology.* The peak of the graph for both years is between 20 to 24 years, indicating that the largest share of births are to women between these ages.

22. **(3)** *Evaluation/Biology.* In each year, the two age groups (15–19 and 30–31) each accounted for roughly 15 percent of total births. Therefore, whatever the total number of births in each year, the number for the younger age group was about the same as the number for the older group. If the younger mothers were more likely than the older ones to give birth to boys, the actual number of boys born to the younger mothers was most likely greater than the number born to the older mothers. None of the other conclusions is supported by the information.

23. **(5)** *Evaluation/Biology.* The graphs from 1970 and 1980 are fairly close together, so the age group with the largest share of births was the same for both years. Some of the other choices may be true, but the graph does not offer enough information to confirm them. Choice (4) is probably not true; even though the share of births to women aged 20 to 24 was roughly the same for the two years, the actual number of births most likely was different.

24. **(1)** *Application/Biology.* Air-popped popcorn is high in fiber and low in fat. If unsalted, it is a good snack food. Choices (2), (4), and (5) all contain sugar and may contain high levels of fat. Choice (3) is usually high in both sodium and fat.

25. **(4)** *Application/Biology.* The best choice, per the guidelines, is a food high in protein, low in fat, and low in sodium. Six ounces of plain yogurt best fits that profile.

26. **(2)** *Application/Biology.* The best choice, per the guidelines, is a cereal that is a good source of protein and carbohydrates, and low in sugars. The other choices are all fairly high in sugars, although they are good sources of protein and carbohydrates.

27. **(1)** *Analysis/Biology.* The fact that the group are vegetarians means that they have less variety in their diet, since they do not eat fish, meat, or poultry.

28. **(1)** *Evaluation/Biology.* You should advise your friend to quit this diet. Besides violating guidelines 1 and 4, it is also likely to be high in fat, since meat is generally high in fat. (In the extreme case, a diet that overemphasizes protein can lead to ketosis, a change in the body's chemical balance, which can cause death.)

29. **(3)** *Evaluation/Biology.* The fact that the fox population becomes smaller and then larger in response to similar changes in the lemming population indicates that there is a natural balance between prey and predator.

30. **(3)** *Comprehension/Biology.* Drugs, like nutrients and oxygens, diffuse across the placenta into the embryo's blood.

31. **(4)** *Application/Biology.* The other choices could be true of many different organisms. Choice (4) is specific enough to indicate a common ancestor.

32. **(4)** *Comprehension/Earth Science.* According to the passage, the moon's shadow affects only a very small area of Earth. This area is on Earth's daylight side, so choice (1) is wrong. The moon is between the sun and Earth, so choice (3) is wrong.

33. **(4)** *Comprehension/Earth Science.* Both Florida and Delaware are in a coastal plain region. Therefore, the answer is choice (4).

34. **(5)** *Application/Earth Science.* Colorado, Arizona, Nevada, and Idaho are all either mountains or plateaus, so a city in any of these states would not be likely to be suitable. Only Baton Rouge, in a state that is all coastal plains, would definitely be suitable.

35. **(2)** *Analysis/Earth Science.* Water coming off the western slopes of the Appalachian Mountains naturally flows from higher elevations to lower elevations. Some flows into the Great Lakes. The rest, blocked by mountains from the Atlantic Ocean and Pacific Ocean, flows into rivers that descend from the interior plains to the coastal plains and eventually enter the Gulf of Mexico.

36. **(3)** *Evaluation/Earth Science.* Both the Midwestern states and the Atlantic coast states are plains regions. If these states are noted for farming, then these plains regions must have large areas of rich soil.

37. **(3)** *Evaluation/Earth Science.* Of the different types of stars, red stars are coolest, cooler even than red-orange stars. Our sun is much cooler than the hottest stars, but hotter than the coolest ones, so choice (2) is wrong. Nothing in the chart supports choice (1).

38. **(3)** *Comprehension/Earth Science.* Since earth scientists use light-years to measure distances in space, the answer is choice (3). Despite the name, light-years are not used to measure time.

39. **(5)** *Comprehension/Earth Science.* The article states that the star system closest to Earth is more than four light-years away. According to the definition of a light-year, the light from this star system would take more than four years to reach the Earth.

40. **(3)** *Analysis/Earth Science.* Since you are seeing light that left the star 100 years ago, you are seeing the star as it appeared at that time. Choice (5) is wrong because the passage states that some distant stars are more than 12 billion light-years away.

41. **(4)** *Analysis/Earth Science.* In the last paragraph, the passage states that some distant star systems are more than 12 billion light-years away. This means that the light from those star systems would take more than 12 billion years to reach us. The passage goes on to say that the light from those star systems must have started traveling toward Earth long before Earth was even formed. Thus the age of Earth must be considerably less than 12 billion years.

42. **(4)** *Evaluation/Earth Science.* Since one light-year equals 9.5 trillion kilometers, four light-years must equal 4 × 9.5 trillion, or 38 trillion kilometers. Since the galaxies are four light-years apart, it would required a trip of 38 trillion kilometers to travel between them.

43. **(3)** *Application/Earth Science.* Of the cities listed, only Sydney, Australia, is south of the equator and has a location described in "south latitude."

44. **(4)** *Analysis/Earth Science.* It is the opinion of some scientists that the Earth's supply of petroleum will last only until the year 2020. Thus the statement that the world's petroleum will be gone by 2021 represents an opinion.

45. **(5)** *Analysis/Chemistry*. Water is produced as this peptide linkage is formed, so if the reaction is typical, water is always produced. Choices (1), (2), (3) are not covered in the equation. Choice (4) is false, because the two amino acids have different numbers of atoms.
46. **(2)** *Evaluation/Chemistry*. If an enzyme's shape is related to its function, then changing its shape will change its ability to bind with other molecules, thereby changing its function. Choices (1), (3), and (5) are false. Choice (4) is not covered in the passage.
47. **(4)** *Application/Chemistry*. Adding the atoms on the left and right sides will show that for choice (1) there are one too many H (hydrogen) atoms on the right side. For choice (2) there are one too few of both oxygen and hydrogen atoms on the right side. For choice (3) the right side lacks two H's and one O. Choice (4) has equal numbers on both sides. Choice (5) has one too few H's on the right side.
48. **(4)** *Application/Chemistry*. The charge on the atom would be +2, since the loss of two electrons makes the total charge +10 +(−8) = +2.
49. **(5)** *Application/Chemistry*. If the reaction proceeds as shown in the graph, the product, CO_2, will have less energy than the reactants, graphite and oxygen. This is because burning is a reaction that gives off energy; it is thus the opposite of endothermic, so choice (1) is wrong.
50. **(3)** *Analysis/Chemistry*. The change in energy level from point D to point B shows a loss in energy involved in the creation of the product XY. Since the reaction involves burning, this is the energy given off by the fire as heat and light.
51. **(2)** *Evaluation/Chemistry*. In the experiment, the chemist took advantage of the different boiling temperatures to separate the substances in the mixture. The substances were not combined chemically, so choice (1) is wrong. Boiling is not a chemical reaction, so choice (4) is wrong. Nothing in the experiment supports choice (5).
52. **(1)** *Analysis/Chemistry*. Since carbon dioxide causes bread to rise, and since carbon dioxide is formed when sodium bicarbonate reacts with an acid, bread dough must contain at least one ingredient that is an acid.
53. **(1)** *Comprehension/Chemistry*. Scientists use the decay of carbon-14 to date ancient organisms. If this decay did not take place at a constant rate, it could not be used as a standard of measurement.
54. **(4)** *Application/Chemistry*. It would take two half-lives for the amount of carbon-14 to be reduced to one-fourth the original amount. Since one half-life is equal to 5730 years, two times that amount is 11,460 years.
55. **(2)** *Application/Chemistry*. Thirty-two days represents four half-lives. The idoine would be reduced to 20 grams, then 10 grams, then 5 grams, then 2.5 grams.
56. **(1)** *Analysis/Chemistry*. Because scientists compare the amount of carbon-14 present in the remains of an organism with the amount present in the living organism, it can be inferred that they know how much carbon-14 was present in the living organism.
57. **(3)** *Application/Physics*. Since the car travels 150 miles in 3 hours, velocity = distance/time = 150/3 = 50 miles per hour.
58. **(4)** *Comprehension/Physics*. The passage states that when popcorn is heated, the water in the kernel changes into steam, then the steam expands to pop the kernel.
59. **(5)** *Analysis/Physics*. It is the heating of the popcorn that makes the water change into steam and the steam expand. Raising the temperature would make the water turn to steam faster.
60. **(4)** *Evaluation/Physics*. The article states that as the steam gets hotter, pressure builds up inside the kernel. Therefore, the relationship illustrated is that as temperature increases, pressure increases.
61. **(2)** *Analysis/Physics*. Since water in the kernels is what makes popcorn pop, it is most likely that the kernels will no longer pop because the water inside has dried up.
62. **(4)** *Application/Physics*. Rearranging the molecules in the bar will cause the magnetic domains to be arranged randomly, resulting in unmagnetized iron. Choices (1), (2), and (3) are incorrect because all would mean the bar is still a magnet, and it is unlikely the domains would retain an aligned arrangement after being heated and cooled. There is no evidence for choice (5).
63. **(5)** *Comprehension/Physics*. The mass of the water is 100 grams, and the temperature change is +15°. The change in calories would be 100 grams × 15°, or +1500 calories.
64. **(2)** *Comprehension/Physics*. Since pressure increases up the side of the graph and temperature increases from left to right across the graph, the straight diagonal line clearly shows that pressure steadily increases as temperature increases.
65. **(3)** *Application/Physics*. A can of aerosol spray contains gas under pressure. When thrown into a fire, the can gets hot and the temperature of the gas increases. This temperature increase causes a rise in pressure, which then produces an explosion. Choices (1), (2), and (5) all deal with the relationship between temperature and volume, not temperature and pressure. Choice (4) is irrelevant.
66. **(5)** *Analysis/Physics*. Pressure will increase as temperature increases only as long as the gas is kept at a constant volume—for example, inside the sealed container. If the sealed container were suddenly opened, some of the gas could escape, and the pressure of the gas would decrease.

PRACTICE ITEMS 4
Interpreting Literature and the Arts

1. **(2)** *Literal Comprehension, Global/Nonfiction.* The author wonders if his high scores mean only that he is very good at answering the kinds of questions that writers of intelligence tests like to ask (lines 11–17). He also states that his intelligence "is not absolute but is a function of the society" in which he lives (lines 37–38). The adequacy of intelligence tests is called into question throughout the passage.
2. **(4)** *Inferential Comprehension, Specific/Nonfiction.* The author is discussing tests that attempt to measure intelligence. Of his score on that aptitude test, he says that scores like that make him feel complacent about his intelligence (lines 9–11). It can be assumed that the aptitude test that he took in the army was an intelligence tests.
3. **(1)** *Application/Nonfiction.* In lines 18–27, the author compares his kind of "intelligence" with that of an auto-repair man. He states that in their respective fields, both are intelligent. He speculates that he would flunk a test written by "anyone but an academician." He seems to think that aptitude tests should measure intelligence in a given field, and one can assume that he would want to see such tests devised by those who are experienced in that field.
4. **(5)** *Analysis /Nonfiction.* The author's use of questions such as "What is intelligence, anyway?" (line 1) and his simple, straightforward sentences give the passage a conversational style.
5. **(3)** *Literal Comprehension, Global/Nonfiction.* Throughout the passage, the author tells us that decisions should not be based on what others think or even on a person's own memories, but on each person's idea of what is best. The author makes statements that contradict choices (1), (4), and (5). The author does not discuss how to begin trusting oneself [choice (2)].
6. **(4)** *Inferential Comprehension, Specific/Nonfiction.* The author is trying to illustrate his belief that past events and deeds should remain, or be "buried," in the past.
7. **(2)** *Literal Comprehension, Global/Nonfiction.* The author states that it is hard to follow your own ideas "because you will always find those who think they know what is your duty better than you know it" (lines 5–7). The author also says "The other terror that scares us from self-trust is our consistency; a reverence for our past act or word . . ." (lines 15–17).
8. **(3)** *Application/Nonfiction.* The attitude presented in this essay would be appropriate for a drug and alcohol abuse workshop where participants are encouraged to ignore peer pressure. Young artists might also be helped by knowing that their own personal style is as valid as that of an existing art style.
9. **(4)** *Literal Comprehension, Specific/Nonfiction.* The authors are talking about eliminating farm-produced foods and creating all food products from chemicals.
10. **(3)** *Inferential Comprehension, Global/Nonfiction.* Food production would not be a natural process, but rather an artifical process requiring factory operation. The chemicals and artificial substances used in the production of these synthetic foods might be very harmful to other parts of the environment.
11. **(2)** *Application/Nonfiction.* These authors feel that agriculture is a costly, inefficient industry. They might wish to do away with natural fibers used in clothing and create a clothing industry that uses only synthetic fibers.
12. **(2)** *Analysis/Nonfiction.* In the final paragraph, the authors state "The society of the future gains on all fronts: economic, social and also moral . . ." The preceding portion of the passage was spent illustrating this belief. The overall tone of the passage, therefore, is optimistic.
13. **(3)** *Literal Comprehension, Global/Fiction.* There are specific references throughout the passage to indicate this answer: line 19—"Indian Curios"; line 31—"pseudo-Navajo"; line 56—"a fat Navajo."
14. **(5)** *Inferential Comprehension, Specific/Fiction.* The paragraph states that Chee's "lips tightened," indicating that he became tense. Also, the phrase, "bearing down on them, scowling" shows us the negative way in which Chee views old Man Fat.
15. **(3)** *Analysis/Fiction.* Chee feels that Red Sands is an ugly place. The description of Red Sands as "sprawled in mushroom growth" highlights this feeling. "Sprawled" gives the reader a sense of disorganization and "mushroom growth" suggests the unpleasant characteristics of mushrooms (damp, moldy, etc.).
16. **(2)** *Application/Fiction.* Through the sympathetic portrayal of Chee, the authors present their love for the land and their respect for those who work the land. The authors most likely would want to help farmers keep their farms.
17. **(3)** *Inferential Comprehension, Specific/Fiction.* Verkhovensky was explaining that the mainstream population already believed in many of the socialist ideas. Therefore, it would be easier to win support for socialist causes.
18. **(4)** *Literal Comprehension, Global/Fiction.* Even though they may be socialists [choice (1)], these people indirectly weaken the framework of society, which the socialists saw as being beneficial to their revolution.
19. **(2)** *Inferential Comprehension, Global/Fiction.* By having

Verkhovensky present himself as a crook and by having him "praise" the corrupt people in the society, the author shows the irony of the situation: these "bad" people believe they are working for a "good" cause that will help society.

20. **(4)** *Literal Comprehension, Specific/Fiction.* The teachers pull their students into the socialist circle by teaching them to break away from their families, their religions, and their beliefs.

21. **(4)** *Literal Comprehension, Specific/Fiction.* Grandfather was telling his children and grandchildren not to surrender, as he had done.

22. **(5)** *Inferential Comprehension, Global/Fiction.* Grandfather felt that he had betrayed his people by not fighting for his rights when he was younger.

23. **(3)** *Application/Fiction.* Because he was not one to oppose authority, Grandfather most likely would not become a union member [choice (1)]. However, he would feel comfortable overcoming a boss "with yesses" in a service position.

24. **(5)** *Analysis/Fiction.* Death-bed scenes are often used to add drama to a situation. By using this setting, the author has created an additional sense of urgency about his grandfather's words.

25. **(5)** *Literal Comprehension, Global/Drama.* Caligula already rules over a kingdom [choice (2)] but wants more. He wants to be "above the gods," have the moon in his hands (rule over nature), and to give society "the gift of equality."

26. **(5)** *Analysis/Drama.* Caesonia disagrees with Caligula and is shown in the passage to become more and more upset by his remarks. The author's inclusion of the phrase "a man's heart from growing old" sheds light on Caesonia's fear for Caligula's increasing indifference to what the word is really like.

27. **(4)** *Inferential Comprehension, Specific/Drama.* Caesonia disagrees with Caligula and knows that he is heading for trouble. By using the word "imploring" in the stage directions, the playwright illustrates the urgency of her speech.

28. **(3)** *Literal Comprehension, Specific/Drama.* Although Ken's body is no longer functioning properly, his thinking processes are. Because so many machines keep him alive, he feels like the "thinking" part of a giant machine.

29. **(1)** *Inferential Comprehension, Global/Drama.* Ken believes that his moral attitudes about his own death are as important as Dr. Scott's attitudes about keeping him alive. He feels that Dr. Scott should respect his beliefs and allow him to die.

30. **(5)** *Inferential Comprehension, Global/Drama.* The characters disagree on a very basic point—a patient's right to die. At the end of this passage, Ken is still questioning Dr. Scott about this issue, which suggests that their conflict will continue.

31. **(1)** *Literal Comprehension, Global/Poetry.* In lines 18-19, the mother says "For I'se still goin', honey,/I'se still climbin'." Although the mother has had a hard life, she wants her son to know that she is not going to stop struggling.

32. **(3)** *Inferential Comprehension, Global/Poetry.* In line 14, the mother tells her son not to turn back, which suggests that he had already begun his journey through life and is finding the road difficult. He might be tempted to quit, but her words are intended to give him the encouragement he needs to continue.

33. **(3)** *Analysis/Poetry.* The mother wants to give her son the strength to continue his life by telling him that even though life has been difficult for her, she still keeps trying and keeps on climbing.

34. **(5)** *Literal Comprehension, Global/Poetry.* Line 7 states that the man was reading a book.

35. **(4)** *Inferential Comprehension, Specific/Poetry.* The poet implies that the man was hungry for knowledge and that the world was nourishing to his spirit.

36. **(2)** *Analysis/Poetry.* Even though the poem is about reading, the tone of the poem is neither literary [choice (1)] nor educational [choice (5)]. Instead it tells us about the happiness the man gets from reading.

37. **(3)** *Literal Comprehension, Global/Commentary.* The statistics given in lines 22–27 support this conclusion.

38. **(1)** *Inferential Comprehension, Specific/Commentary.* Programs that would show "prosocial behavior" would be good role models.

39. **(4)** *Application/Commentary.* The author of the passage is more interested in the effect that watching television has on children than in how the content of the programs on television affects children. The author would therefore by most interested in how the actual experience of reading has an impact on people. Choices (1), (2), and (3) are all questions concerned with the content of books. Choice (5) questions the relationship between two different types of experiences; there is no evidence in the passage that the author would be concerned with this type of question.

40. **(1)** *Analysis/Commentary.* The author makes extensive use of statistics but does not quote from any authors or offer any examples (ironic or otherwise). Her style is marked particularly by factual reporting and question-raising in which no figurative language is used.

41. **(4)** *Analysis/Commentary.* The use of statistics and a newspaper style of reporting would be inappropriate in a letter to a friend.

42. **(2)** *Literal Comprehension, Global/Commentary.* Graham felt that classical ballet did not reflect the way people were living, so she created a style of dance that did.

43. **(5)** *Inferential Comprehension, Specific/Commentary.* "Extraneous" tells the reader that there was nothing unnecessary or irrelevant about Graham's style of dance. Even though it differs from ballet, it had its own rules.

44. **(3)** *Application/Commentary.* Jazz, which also became popular in the 1920s, often has a "nervous, sharp, and zigzag" feel to it, and it is also uniquely American; it would be an appropriate type of music for Graham's choreography.

45. **(3)** *Analysis/Commentary.* Because the Colorado River was responsible for carving out the Grand Canyon, any comparison to it suggests a very mighty force.

PRACTICE ITEMS 5
Mathematics

1. **(4)** *Arithmetic/Problem Solving.*
   7 hours 45 minutes × 7 = 49 hours 315 minutes
   $\frac{315}{60}$ = 5 hours 15 minutes
   Total sleeping time = 54 hours 15 minutes

2. **(1)** *Arithmetic/Skills.*
   $\frac{12,766}{52}$ – 245.50

3. **(5)** *Arithmetic/Problem Solving.*
   1 pound 9 ounces × 24 = 24 pounds 216 ounces
   $\frac{216}{16}$ = 13 pounds 8 ounces
   Total pounds = 37 pounds 8 ounces

4. **(2)** *Arithmetic/Problem Solving.*
   (.79 – .30) = cost per dozen
   To find unit cost, divide by 12.

5. **(4)** *Arithmetic/Problem Solving.*
   d = rt
   1 hour 45 minutes = 1.75 hours
   1.75 × 12 = 21

6. **(3)** *Arithmetic/Problem Solving.*
   Change minutes into hours, multiply each rate by its time, and add the two products together.

7. **(3)** *Arithmetic/Applications.*
   i = prt
   Interest = 11.896 (principal) × .077 (rate) × 3 (time)

8. **(1)** *Arithmetic/Problem Solving.*
   Dealer financing costs:
       8888 × .06 × 4 = 2133.12
       8888 + 2133.12 = 11,021.12
   Rebate with bank financing costs:
       8888 – 1000 = 7888
       7888 × .11 × 3 = 2603.04
       7888 + 2603.04 = 10,491.04
   Savings:
       11,021.12 – 10,491.04 = 530.08

9. **(2)** *Arithmetic/Applications.*
   i = prt
   i = 7985 × .095 × 3
   i = 2275.73

10. **(4)** *Arithmetic/Problem Solving.*
    i = prt
    i = 7985 × .08 × 4
    i = 2555.2
    7985 + 2555.2 = 10,540.20

11. **(4)** *Arithmetic/Problem Solving.*
    p = 2l + 2w
    2(27) + 2(32) = 118
    Subtract 24 feet for the garage:
    118 – 24 = 94

12. **(5)** *Arithmetic/Problem Solving.*
    The area behind the garage is not clearly defined.

13. **(3)** *Arithmetic/Problem Solving.*
    A = πr²
    Radius of pool = 3 feet   6 inches = .5 feet   Radius of cover = 3.5 feet
    3.14 × 3.5 × 3.5 = 38.47

14. **(4)** *Arithmetic/Skills.*
    ⁻10 + 5 = ⁻5

15. **(3)** *Arithmetic/Problem Solving.*
    V = πr²h
    Volume of one can:
    3.14 × 1 × 1 × 5 = 15.7
    15.7 × 6 = 94.2

16. **(4)** *Arithmetic/Problem Solving.*
    A $\frac{1}{4} = \frac{2}{8}$
    B $\frac{1}{2} = \frac{4}{8}$
    C $\frac{1}{8} = \frac{1}{8}$
    D $\frac{7}{8} = \frac{7}{8}$
    E $\frac{3}{4} = \frac{6}{8}$

17. **(2)** *Arithmetic/Problem Solving.*
    9 × .05 = .45
    13 × .03 = .39
    1 × .40 = .40
    7 × .06 = .42

18. **(5)** *Arithmetic/Problem Solving.*
    Note both the title of the graph and the label on the y axis.

19. **(3)** *Arithmetic/Applications.*
    4 × 4 × 4 = 64

20. **(5)** *Arithmetic/Problem Solving.*
    1.86×10^5 = 186,000
    186,000 × 60 = 11,160,000

PRACTICE ITEMS

Test 5: Mathematics A-79

21. **(4)** *Arithmetic/Problem Solving.*
    7973 + 8638 = 16,611 children
    $\frac{16,611}{6,780}$ = 2.45 children per household

22. **(2)** *Arithmetic/Problem Solving.*
    $\frac{1}{4}$ of 15,000,000 = 3,750,000
    $\frac{400}{3,750,000} = \frac{1}{9375}$

23. **(1)** *Arithmetic/Problem Solving.*
    i = prt
    6 mo = ½ yr
    50,000 × .06 × $\frac{1}{2}$ = 1500

24. **(5)** *Arithmetic/Applications.*
    d = rt
    d = 4 × 2 × 7
    d = 56

25. **(4)** *Arithmetic/Applications.*
    P = a + b + c
    P = 75 + 100 + 125
    P = 300

26. **(3)** *Arithmetic/Applications.*
    A = ½bh
    A = $\frac{1}{2}$ × 28 × 18.5
    A = 259

27. **(5)** *Arithmetic/Problem Solving.*
    No correlation can be made between the two given figures.

28. **(2)** *Arithmetic/Problem Solving.*
    85.43 × .45 = 38.4435

29. **(4)** *Algebra/Problem Solving.*
    $\frac{25}{45} = \frac{5}{9}$
    $\frac{5}{9} = \frac{4000}{x}$
    5x = 36,000
    x = 7200

30. **(1)** *Algebra/Problem Solving.*
    Four times the number of adults' tickets plus 2.5 times the number of children's tickets equals the total receipts.
    4·a = number of adult tickets
    2.5·c = number of children's tickets
    4a + 2.5c = total receipts

31. **(2)** *Algebra/Problem Solving.*
    The insurance company will pay a percent of the amount shown by the expression (r − 200).
    .8(r − 200) equals 80% of that amount.

32. **(5)** *Algebra/Problem Solving.*
    s = cost of the dinette set at full price
    $\frac{c}{2}$ = one-half the regular price of the couch
    $s + \frac{c}{2}$ = total cost
    Only the couch is at half price.

33. **(5)** *Algebra/Problem Solving.*
    The expression (f + 1) equals the number of friends plus Albert.

34. **(4)** *Algebra/Problem Solving.*
    6% = .06
    .06 of the annual income is divided by 5.

35. **(4)** *Algebra/Problem Solving.*
    w = warm-up time
    2w = aerobic-exercise time
    $\frac{5w}{8}$ = cool-down time
    The sum of the three times equals 60 minutes.

36. **(2)** *Algebra/Problem Solving.*
    The total cost of the gifts plus the sales tax on them must be $37. If 5g equals the gifts, then .06(5g) equals the amount of sales tax that would be charged on them.

37. **(5)** *Algebra/Problem Solving.*
    If r = rye seed, then $\frac{r}{24} = \frac{9}{4}$, and r = 54.
    54 + 24 = 78

38. **(3)** *Algebra/Problem Solving.*
    Let c = more expensive call.
    $\frac{c}{3}$ + .50 = 3.95
    $\frac{c}{3}$ = 3.45
    c = 10.35

39. **(1)** *Algebra/Problem Solving.*
    Let s = sales.
    .18s + 200 = 483.68
    .18s = 283.68
    s = 1576

40. **(4)** *Algebra/Problem Solving.*
    A 30 × 40 = 1200
    B 35 × 15 =   525
    C 40 × 42 = 1680
    D 45 × 32 = 1440
    E 37 × 37 = 1369

41. **(4)** *Algebra/Problem Solving.*
    Set up a ratio.
    If r = revolutions, then 33.45 = 297:r.
    33r = 13,365
    r = 405

42. **(1)** *Algebra/Problem Solving.*
    f = cost of flowers
    f = cost of gown
    4f = cost of food

43. **(1)** *Algebra/Applications.*
    Because the x coefficient is positive 1, the only possible solution is (x − 6)(x + 7).

44. **(3)** *Algebra/Applications.*
    Use the distributive property:
    (y + 9)(y − 5) = y^2 − 5y + 9y − 45
    Simplify to get y^2 + 4y − 45.

A-80 Test 5: Mathematics

45. **(5)** *Algebra/Applications.*
Factor out to $(p-4)(p+3)=0$, or substitute the values for p.

46. **(4)** *Algebra/Skills.*
Subtract exponents: $2-(-1)=3$.

47. **(4)** *Geometry/Skills.*
Angle a and angle b are supplementary angles.
$180-54=126$

48. **(1)** *Geometry/Applications.*
To make it perpendicular, it should measure 90° in relation to the ground.
$90-76=14$

49. **(1)** *Geometry/Skills.*
The sum of the angles of a triangle equals 180°
$151+25+4=180$

50. **(3)** *Geometry/Applications.*
Use line EI coordinates $H(3, 0)$ and $G(0, 1)$:
$m = \dfrac{y_2 - y_1}{x_2 - x_1}$
$m = \dfrac{1-0}{0-3} = \dfrac{1}{-3}$
$m = -\dfrac{1}{3}$

51. **(2)** *Geometry/Applications.*
$K = (-3, -2); H = (3, 0)$
$-3 + 3 = 0; \dfrac{0}{2} = 0$
$-2 + 0 = -2; \dfrac{-2}{2} = -1$

52. **(5)** *Geometry/Applications.*
$H = (3, 0); F = (-12, 5)$
$d = \sqrt{(x_2 - x_1)^2 + (y_2 - y_1)^2}$
$-12 - 3 = -15; \; -15 \times -15 = 225$
$5 - 0 = 5; \; 5 \times 5 = 25$
$225 + 25 = 250$
$d = \sqrt{250}$

53. **(3)** *Geometry/Problem Solving.*
Use the Pythagorean relationship:
$c^2 = a^2 + b^2$
$9 \times 9 = 81; \; 12 \times 12 = 144$
$144 + 81 = 225$
$\sqrt{225} = 15$

54. **(2)** *Geometry/Problem Solving.*
Use the ratio 6:9 = 8:width, where w = width.
$9 \times 8 = 72$
$\dfrac{72}{6} = 12$

55. **(44)** *Geometry/Skills.*
The roof forms an isosceles triangle that has equal base angles.
The sum of the three angles is 180°
$180 - 66 = 114$
$\dfrac{114}{2} = 57$

56. **(1)** *Geometry/Problem Solving.*
The distance equals the square root of the difference between the Mt. Burn–Mt. Blue distance and the Mt. Burn–Mt. Green distance.
$a^2 + b^2 = c^2$
$125 \times 125 = 15{,}625$
$75 \times 75 = 5625$
$15{,}625 - 5625 = 10{,}000$
$\sqrt{10{,}000} = 100$

SIMULATION

SIMULATED TEST 1

Writing Skills, Part I: Grammar

1. **(5)** *Usage/Verb Tense/Sentence Revision.* Word clues in the rest of the paragraph indicate that present perfect tense should be used for consistency's sake.
2. **(4)** *Sentence Structure/Parallelism/Sentence Correction.* Express equivalent ideas in the same form. You should think about two things, your *choice* and *use* of credit cards.
3. **(1)** *Usage/Pronoun Shift/Sentence Correction.* Don't shift pronouns within a sentence. Before *you* apply for a card (implied *you*), find out each company's charge.
4. **(4)** *Sentence Structure/Sentence Fragment/Sentence Revision.* Correct the sentence fragment by providing a complete verb, *is* added, for the subject, *charge*.
5. **(5)** *Usage/Pronoun Reference, Agreement with Antecedent/Construction Shift.* When considering different cards, think about how widely each card is accepted. The new construction eliminates the vague *it*, which did not agree with *different cards*.
6. **(3)** *Mechanics/Capitalization/Sentence Correction.* Sierra Club is the proper name of an organization and needs to be capitalized.
7. **(2)** *Mechanics/Spelling/Sentence Correction.* Specified contains a soft *c*.
8. **(3)** *Mechanics/Punctuation/Sentence Revision.* Use a comma to separate an introductory clause from the main subject-verb structure. *Once you do choose a card* comes before (implied *you*) *put* and should be set off with a comma.
9. **(5)** *Sentence Structure/Comma Splice/Sentence Revision.* Two complete ideas are incorrectly joined by a comma. The error is corrected by making one idea dependent on the other.
10. **(1)** *Sentence Structure/Subordination, Coordination/Construction Shift.* It may be inconvenient to write a thank-you note after a job interview, but the effort *is worth the bother*. The new construction preserves the meaning of the original.
11. **(2)** *Usage/Pronoun Reference, Wrong Relative Pronoun/Sentence Correction.* Who refers to people; which refers to things.
12. **(5)** *Mechanics/Spelling/Sentence Correction.* Ability is spelled correctly. Since *others* is a plural and not a possessive here, it requires no apostrophe.
13. **(5)** *Mechanics/Punctuation/Construction Shift.* The note that is clear, concise, and effectively written shows that the writer has good communication skills. Separate items in a series with commas.
14. **(4)** *Sentence Structure/Modification, Dangling Modifier/Sentence Revision.* The thank-you note, not the interviewer, arrives in the mail. Make sure that the modifier stands close to the person or thing involved in the action.
15. **(3)** *Usage/Subject-Verb Agreement/Sentence Revision.* Singular nouns joined by *or* are considered a singular subject and require a singular verb: *he or she thinks.*
16. **(1)** *Sentence Structure/Improper Subordination/Sentence Correction.* The new construction is clearer and less awkward than the original. (The phrase *such that* usually modifies a noun: *Her temper was such that he didn't dare ask.*)
17. **(4)** *Usage/Pronoun Shift/Sentence Correction.* You, not one, is the pronoun used throughout the paragraph.
18. **(2)** *Usage/Verb Tense/Sentence Correction.* The future tense, not the past, is consistent with the use in the rest of the paragraph. The writer is telling you what will happen if you write the note.
19. **(3)** *Sentence Structure/Comma Splice/Sentence Correction.* Two complete ideas are incorrectly joined by a comma. The error is corrected by forming two sentences.
20. **(5)** *Usage/Subject-Verb Agreement, Connectives Other Than And/Sentence Correction.* Despite the connecting phrase, *like other agencies*, the subject is singular, *The Internal Revenue Service*, and requires a singular verb, *uses*.
21. **(4)** *Sentence Structure/Run-on/Sentence Correction.* Two complete subject-verb structures are incorrectly joined without proper punctuation. The error is corrected by forming two separate sentences.
22. **(3)** *Mechanics/Capitalization/Sentence Correction.* New York City is the complete name of a place and, as such, should be capitalized.
23. **(1)** *Mechanics/Spelling/Sentence Correction.* Service contains a soft *c*.
24. **(2)** *Mechanics/Punctuation/Sentence Correction.* Use commas to set off defining phrases. *Data base means not just computerized library but computerized library for storing large amounts of information.*
25. **(4)** *Usage/Verb Tense Errors/Sentence Revision.* Present tense is consistent with use throughout the paragraph. The

A-81

plural subject, *kinds*, requires a plural verb, *are*.

26. **(2)** *Sentence Structure/Parallelism/Sentence Revision*. The connector, *and*, joins sentence elements of equal importance. The elements should be expressed in similar form. *Your employer sends . . . and the Department of Motor Vehicles sends. . . .*

27. **(2)** *Sentence Structure/Subordination/Construction Shift*. *The computer searches the data base for information that should be reported on your tax forms.* The new construction effectively combines the two sentences, while stating clearly both the subject, *computer*, and the verb, *searches*.

28. **(4)** *Sentence Structure/Sentence Fragment/Sentence Revision*. The revised form corrects the sentence fragment by providing the singular subject with the singular verb, *is processed*, required by the either/or construction.

29. **(5)** *Usage/Vague Pronoun Reference/Construction Shift*. *One fortunate result has been a rise in the number of people taking the GED Tests in order to become eligible for further education.* The new construction eliminates the vague reference to *it*.

30. **(1)** *Mechanics/Overuse of Commas/Sentence Correction*. The comma confuses the reader by separating the subject, *result*, from the verb, *has been*.

31. **(2)** *Sentence Structure/Sentence Fragment/Sentence Correction*. The sentence fragment is corrected by supplying a verb, *reports*, which agrees with the subject, *American Council on Education*.

32. **(4)** *Usage/Verb Tense Errors/Sentence Revision*. The present tense of the verb, *advertise*, is consistent with the tense used throughout the paragraph.

33. **(3)** *Sentence Structure/Parallelism/Sentence Revision*. Express equivalent ideas in similar form. The three things you can avoid wasting are *time*, *energy*, and *money*.

34. **(1)** *Mechanics/Spelling/Sentence Correction*. *Don't* is the contraction for *do not*. The apostrophe takes the place of the missing *o*.

35. **(3)** *Sentence Structure/Comma Splice/Sentence Revision*. Two complete ideas are incorrectly joined by a comma. A semicolon—such as the words *and, but, or, nor, for,* and *yet*—can be used to mark the dividing point between two such complete ideas.

36. **(3)** *Usage/Subject-Verb Agreement, Either-Or/Sentence Correction*. When the neither/nor construction is used, the verb agrees with the noun or pronoun closer to it: *anyone else needs*.

37. **(5)** *Mechanics/Capitalization/Sentence Correction*. As part of an address, *Circle* is properly capitalized.

38. **(1)** *Sentence Structure/Improper Subordination/Sentence Correction*. Although the improper phrase, *something what*, is sometimes heard, *that* is the connector required here.

39. **(3)** *Usage/Ambiguous, Vague Pronoun Reference/Construction Shift*. *Many workers change jobs, either by choice or necessity.* The new construction eliminates the vague references to *they* and *it*. The revised version reads more smoothly.

40. **(4)** *Mechanics/Punctuation/Sentence Revision*. Use a comma to set off the introductory clause from the subject, *many job hunters*.

41. **(5)** *Usage/Verb Tense Errors/Sentence Revision*. The present tense should be used to remain consistent with usage throughout the paragraph.

42. **(2)** *Sentence Structure/Clarity, Modification/Construction Shift*. *Although it may be fairly easy to get a service job, it is often difficult to find career ladders, steps for working up to higher wages, within service jobs.* Meaning is made clearer by defining *career ladders* within the sentence.

43. **(2)** *Mechanics/Capitalization/Sentence Correction*. Capitalize titles of people when they come before names; don't capitalize career names.

44. **(2)** *Usage/Subject-Verb Agreement, Interrupting Phrase/Sentence Correction*. Despite the interrupting phrase between the subject and the verb, the singular subject, *problem*, requires a singular verb, *is*.

45. **(5)** *Sentence Structure/Modification/Sentence Revision*. Place a description close to what it modifies. The phrase, *who serve them*, describes employees, not jobs.

46. **(2)** *Mechanics/Spelling/Sentence Correction*. All the forms of *attempt* have *tempt* within them.

47. **(5)** *Usage/Pronoun Shift/Sentence Revision*. Keep pronouns consistent within a sentence. The writer addressed the last two sentences of the paragraph to *you*, the reader.

48. **(5)** *Usage/Ambiguous Pronoun Reference, Agreement with Antecedent/Sentence Revision*. The revised sentence eliminates the ambiguous *they*.

49. **(2)** *Mechanics/Punctuation/Sentence Correction*. Use a comma to separate the introductory element from the subject, *physicians*.

50. **(4)** *Mechanics/Capitalization/Sentence Correction*. Capitalize a title when it comes before someone's name.

51. **(3)** *Sentence Structure/Improper Subordination/Sentence Revision*. Don't confuse *because of* (a preposition) with *because* (a conjunction). *Because of* precedes a noun, as in this sentence.

52. **(5)** *Sentence Structure/Modification, Run-on/Sentence Correction.* The sentence is not a run-on. The phrase *about people with similar symptoms*, modifies *information* and could not stand alone.

53. **(1)** *Usage/Subject-Verb Agreement, Inverted Structure/Sentence Correction*. Even if the usual order of subject followed by verb is reversed, the plural subject, *doctors*, requires a plural verb, *do*.

54. **(3)** *Usage/Verb Tense Errors/Sentence Revision*. The present tense is consistent with that used throughout the rest of the paragraph.

55. **(1)** *Sentence Structure/Coordination, Subordination/Construction Shift*. *Putting medical records into data bases is just one of many ways doctors can use computers to provide improved health care.* The new construction effectively shows the relationship of ideas in the sentence, while the original simply strings ideas together with *and*.

SIMULATED TEST 1
Writing Skills, Part II: Essay-writing

How to Score Your Essay

To score your essay, compare it with the following model essays. These model essays received scores of 3 and 5 respectively.

Compare your essay with the 3 model essay. If it is as good as the 3 model essay, then assign your essay a score of 3. If it is not as good as the 3 model essay, then refer back to the answer key for the Writing Skills Predictor Test and use the descriptions of the 1 and 2 model essays to evaluate your essay. It should be easy to assign a score to your essay if you compare your essay with these model essays and their character-trait analyses.

If your essay is better than the 3 model essay, compare it to the model essay that received a 5. If it is better than the 3, but not as good as the 5, score your essay a 4. Give your essay a 5 if it is as good as the second model. If your essay is better than the 5 model, then score your essay a 6.

In addition, look at the notes and character-trait analyses that accompany the model essays. Those comments explain the strengths and weaknesses of the essays.

Model Essay—Holistic Score 3

Introduces subject but point of view is not clearly stated. Repetitous statements, lists of ideas and undeveloped examples on the subject do not provide an adequate explanation of the effect of technology on the writer's free time activities. Point of view is stated in the conclusion.

Technology affects how I spend my free time. Like when I come home from work, there are lots of things to do with it. In the living room I have a video cassete recorder hooked up to the TV set. Near them is a small personal computer. On the other side of the room is a stereo. It sits between two bookcases. After I eat if there is nothing on TV I'll go out and rent a movie and play it on the VCR. If its busy and I can't find anything to rent, I'll come home and play video games on the computer or listen to the stereo. Playing computer games is getting really boring. Ive got sports games like baseball games and space games and aliens games but once you figure them out theyre not fun to play anymore. I have to get more software if I want to play anything new on the computer but when I do the same thing will happen again and I'll have to buy more. That is how they get you. New technology sounds good at first but it gets expensive to use and it keeps costing money all the time.

Character-Trait Analysis

1. The essay is not organized. it is a choppy account of the writer's activities after work. It *lists* the technological products used by the writer but the essay does not explain how technology has affected the writer's choice of free time activities. In the essay's conclusion we are told that the writer does not enjoy the expense involved in using modern technology but we are not told *why* the writer feels this way. A more effective essay would explain how the writer feels about the effect of technology on his/her free time and *why* the writer feels this way.

2. The essay's listing of products and repetitious sentence structure make this essay less effective than it could be. An essay with specific examples, explanation of the writer's point of view, and varied sentence structure would be more interesting and effective.

3. There are errors in spelling, punctuation, sentence structure, and accepted English usage that detract from the essay's effectiveness.

Model Essay—Holistic Score 5

Introduces subject and states point of view.

Technology has affected how I spend my free time in many ways. Primarily, it has enhanced my enjoyment in doing some, otherwise, old-fashioned activities.

Elaborates on point of view with specific examples. Note contrasts between playing piano with and without modern technology.

For example, I have an electronic keyboard in addition to a regular piano. Whenever I have some free time, I like to practice playing the piano. This is not any different from what I did before I bought the electronic piano. What is different is that, now, I can use these skills on the electronic keyboard as well. The electronic keyboard can sound like a regular piano but it can also play rhythms and other special effects. With it I can sound like a one-man band! I really enjoy being able to play requests for different types of music whenever we have parties and family get-togethers.

Technology has not really changed my choice of free time activities, I still enjoy the piano and watch television with my family. But technology has provided me with different ways of enjoying those activities.

Character-Trait Analysis
1. The essay is organized effectively.
2. The point of view is clearly stated in the introduction and summarized in the conclusion.
3. The first example supports the writer's stated point of view. However, the second example of *watching old movies at home on cable* TV would be more effective if the home vs. movie theater aspect of it were stressed instead of the before and after cable aspect.
4. The essay is easy to read. The sentence structure is awkward in places but it does not interfere with the essay's overall effectiveness.

SIMULATED TEST 2
Social Studies

1. **(3)** *Evaluation/History.* The various inventions in choice (3) are examples of western resourcefulness and innovation. The developments in choices (1) and (4) are examples of interdependence and cooperation that would, if anything, contradict Turner's notion of individualism. The developments in choice (2) and choice (5) are essentially irrelevant to Turner's thesis.

2. **(4)** *Analysis/History.* Distrust of the East, while it may have existed, would not have promoted nationalism in the West. Quite the contrary, it would have encouraged regionalism. Choices (1), (2), (3), and (5) all offer reasons that historians frequently cite for western nationalism: In most instances, frontier people had not yet developed local traditions; they needed access to the rest of the nation which only national funding and policies could provide; they required organized military defense from hostile Indians; and they resented the influence of faraway European powers and focused instead on their own country's virtues and power.

3. **(4)** *Analysis/Economics.* If there is a trade deficit and the amount of money earned from exports becomes closer to the amount of money spent on imports, then the trade deficit would be reduced. This occurs in the graph in 1981. Choice (1) is incorrect, as the graph shows imports increasing at the same time as exports. Choice (2) and choice (3) are incorrect because the deficit existed between 1981 and 1983, when imports decreased, and between 1983 and 1985, when exports increased. Choice (5) is incorrect because the difference between exports and imports would be a trade <u>surplus</u> in the event that exports were higher than imports.

4. **(3)** *Application/Behavioral Science.* The fact that Manifest Destiny included a concept of the United States as having a "civilizing" influence is indicative of the element of ethnocentrism involved in this policy. The other policies described either explicitly reject or do not involve ethnocentrism.

5. **(4)** *Comprehension/Behavioral Science.* The passage centers on the evidently widespread feeling of alienation among the American public. The statements in choice (1) and choice (3) are necessary background. The statement in choice (2) provides an important detail; that in choice (5) an interpretation.

6. **(5)** *Comprehension/Behavioral Science.* The passage indicates that alienation had been fairly low, climbed steadily and reached high levels with Watergate, and never really declined since. The graph in choice (5) most accurately describes this sequence.

7. **(3)** *Application/Behavioral Science.* The passage ties the feeling of alienation to a sense of remoteness from decisionmaking processes. Regular meetings involving citizens and officials would be one way of attacking this sense of remoteness. None of the other alternatives suggested would serve the function. Failure to vote, for example, would probably stem from alienation, in which case to get more of the public to vote it would be necessary to first deal with the alienation. A high-level commission would not involve the public, and press coverage, as suggested by the comment on Watergate, would just increase the feeling of alienation without dealing with it.

8. **(4)** *Evaluation/Political Science.* Choice (4) is supported by the comparison between bureaucracy in Jefferson's time, when the federal government did relatively little, and modern bureaucracy and by the rapid growth of bureaucracy from the mid-1920s to the mid-1970s, a period during which the federal government came to assume significantly more responsibility. None of the other choices are supported by the passage. If anything, Kaufman's finding that many new agencies were added in areas where agencies already existed might contradict the statements in choices (1) and (5) by suggesting that the bureaucracy is inefficient and that it involves extensive specialization of function.

9. **(4)** *Evaluation/History.* Contrary to what the isolationist, whose feet are dry for the moment, may think, it is a small boat and all who are in it must bail out water or sink. Although it is Europe that has the leak, the United States and Europe would sink or swim together; therefore, U.S. aid is crucial. Choice (1) may or may not be true; however, it is not the topic of the cartoon. There is nothing in the cartoon to support choice (2), choice (3), or choice (5).

10. **(3)** *Comprehension/Political Science.* The passage states that the number of electors depends on the size of the congressional delegation. This, in turn, depends in large part on population. Therefore, the more populous states have more electors and more influence. The other choices are false and cannot be supported by the discussion in the passage.

11. **(5)** *Comprehension/Political Science.* Choice (5) is correct since the Electoral College is a two-stage election system and therefore indirect. That is, the people vote for electors, who then cast their ballots for the candidates. Choice (1) refers to the mechanics of casting a vote. Choice (2) is the process of direct election, where voters' ballots directly determine the winner of an election. Choice (3) and choice

A-85

(4) are part of the nominating process.

12. **(2)** *Analysis/Political Science.* The passage implies that the framers felt that selection of the president was too important to be entrusted to the people. They were also afraid to give too much power to Congress. They therefore created the Electoral College. The statements in the other choices are factually correct but are not supported by the material contained in the passage.

13. **(3)** *Application/Economics.* The passage emphasizes the importance of innovation, and research and development is the process through which innovations emerge. The fact that fewer patents are being applied for merely points to a lack of U.S. research and development activities. Therefore, the recommendations in choices (2), (4), and (5) may or may not make sense; however, they are not supported by the discussion in the passage.

14. **(5)** *Comprehension/History.* By consulting the map and the legend it can be seen that several states were contested. The statements in all the other choices are contradicted by the map and legend.

15. **(2)** *Analysis/History.* Had even the contested state with the fewest votes (Oregon, with 3) been assigned to the Democrats, Tilden would have won the electoral, as well as the popular, vote. Therefore choice (1) is incorrect. Choice (4) is implicitly contradicted by the closeness of the election. Choice (3) is wrong since, as is indicated by the blank areas on the map, the territories did not participate in the election. The map does not support choice (5); note that Tilden won New York's 35 electoral votes.

16. **(3)** *Application/Geography.* In order to make room for large-scale farming, the Europeans cleared the land by cutting down the forests.

17. **(5)** *Application/Geography.* Because Manhattan is an island, and is already completely developed, the only way to make more land available is by creating it. Manhattan's shorelines have been extended by filling in parts of the rivers that surround it, thus creating extra land on which to build.

18. **(1)** *Application/Geography.* The Southeast Asian farmers' problem is not one of water supply, because there is plenty of water. The problem is one of keeping the water in place to form ponds in which the rice can grow. This problem is solved by terracing the mountains in such a way that the water will remain on the slopes and not drain away.

19. **(2)** *Application/Geography.* To solve the problem of seasonal drought, the Aswan Dam has been built on the Nile. This dam ensures that there will be a steady supply of water throughout the year, instead of too much at one time and not enough at another. Farmlands are connected to the artificial lake by a network of canals.

20. **(4)** *Application/Geography.* Reformation is an attempt to restore an environment that has been damaged by human activities.

21. **(4)** *Comprehension/Economics.* The figures for the country as a whole were 11.4 percent for small-business-dominated areas. The corresponding figures for services industries—12.6 percent and 5.5 percent—come extremely close to these overall figures.

22. **(1)** *Evaluation/Economics.* Despite variations, all industries with both small- and large-business-dominated areas show larger percent increases in job growth in the small-business-dominated areas. However, it is not possible to judge on the basis of the chart alone whether small businesses created more jobs than large businesses, since the figures are not for small versus large businesses but for small-versus large-business-dominated areas. If large-business-dominated areas had more employees initially, a smaller percentage increase could in fact mean more jobs created than a larger percentage increase for small-business-dominated areas with fewer employees. Thus choice (3) is incorrect. The statement in choice (5) cannot be supported for the same reason: The 18.9 percent gain in small-business-dominated areas might actually mean fewer jobs created than were lost with the 10.2 percent decrease in the large-business-dominated areas. Choice (4) is incorrect, since large- and small-business-dominated areas are separate areas and not in competition. Nothing in the chart supports choice (2).

23. **(4)** *Comprehension/Political Science.* The passage discusses how the new testing and monitoring technology has made privacy in the workplace an important concern. Choices (1) and (3) are too general to accurately state the purpose of the passage. Since the passage is discussing the problems involved in the use of technology, choice (2) is wrong. Choice (5) is incorrect because the passage discusses employers, not the government, as using the technology.

24. **(4)** *Analysis/Political Science.* As the opening sentences of the passage imply, breakthroughs in testing and monitoring technology have positive as well as negative features. They may, for example, be useful for such purposes as the detection and apprehension of criminals. In addition, once technologies are available, it is difficult to ban their use. Thus choice (3) is the least appropriate and likely response to this threat to privacy. In contrast, the public can seek various ways to limit the technology's use and abuse, which is why choices (1), (2), (3), and (5) are more likely responses.

25. **(2)** *Evaluation/Political Science.* Choice (2) is correct because these tests and monitoring devices may be seen as unauthorized searches and may yield incriminating evidence. The other choices are inappropriate to the situation described in the passage.

26. **(3)** *Comprehension/Economics.* The passage treats advertising and packaging and labeling as psychological tools of competition; that is, as ways of attracting consumers' attention to a product and giving the product a "different" and desirable image. Thus choice (3) is correct. Choice (4) and choice (5), concerning advertising and differentiation, each refer to only one aspect of what is discussed.

27. **(5)** *Analysis/History.* If large businesses made deals with one another at the public's expense,

this implies that there was in all likelihood a lack of competition in many industries. Thus, government action came in the form of antitrust laws. Choice (1) is therefore incorrect. Choices (2), (3), and (4) would all promote, rather than regulate, business.

28. **(4)** *Comprehension/Geography.* The only reason suggested in the passage is the fact that the Arctic Ocean separates the Soviet Union from North America. Choice (1) is incorrect because the military bases are the result, not the cause, of the Arctic's perceived importance to national security.

29. **(5)** *Comprehension/Economics.* The passage mentions that Japan has moved out of areas in which it can no longer realistically compete and has invested heavily in areas with potential for the future. The statements in choices (1), (2), and (3) are all explicitly contradicted by the passage. Nothing is said to support the statement in choice (4).

30. **(4)** *Evaluation/History.* High prices for food result from middlemen, speculators, and monopolists who make profits from the farmers' crops, leaving farmers little to show for their efforts. There is little or no evidence in the cartoon to support the other choices.

31. **(2)** *Application/History.* Monopolies, including railroad lines, which charged farmers high rates to ship their produce to markets in the East, are shown in the cartoon as the source of the farmers' misfortunes. Therefore, based on the cartoon, what farmers most need are laws to regulate the railroads and other large companies. None of the problems that the other choices would address are depicted in the cartoon.

32. **(4)** *Analysis/Political Science.* The passage states that the United States would be able to reach Soviet and Eastern European targets even if its missiles are removed from European soil. This implies that the United States has long-range bombers and missiles. Choices (1) and (3) are opinions neither confirmed nor denied in the passage. Choice (2) is wrong because the passage indicates that the Soviet and Warsaw Pact military resources remain greater than those of NATO. Choice (5) is not supported by the passage and is in fact a position the United States abandoned upon entering World War II.

33. **(5)** *Analysis/Political Science.* Both the presence of U.S. nuclear weapons in Europe and the discussion of removing those weapons in view of U.S. long-range capacity to defend Europe are based on the idea that Western European security depends on U.S. nuclear weapons. Warsaw pact troops outnumber NATO troops. Whether the statements in choices (3) and (4) are true or not cannot be verified from the passage. However, the passage does make clear that these are not the strategic hypotheses underlying the U.S. commitment to NATO. The statement in choice (1) directly contradicts the idea of a U.S. commitment to NATO.

34. **(2)** *Comprehension/Political Science.* The passage discusses early and more recent consideration of removal of U.S. nuclear arms from Europe. Choice (1) is incorrect, as the passage is not taking a position on the issue. Choices (3) and (5) are incorrect, as neither Soviet strategy nor numbers of missiles are discussed. Relative troop strength is mentioned, but primarily as information needed for discussion of the larger topic. Thus choice (4) is also incorrect.

35. **(1)** *Evaluation/Political Science.* Removal of all nuclear weapons from an area would reduce the chance of atomic warfare in that area but not eliminate it, as indicated by the fact that countries can hit targets from great distances. Choice (5) is incorrect, as there are other nuclear weapons in Europe; the passage mentions Western and Eastern stockpiles. There is nothing in the passage to support any of the other choices.

36. **(1)** *Evaluation/History.* The passage states that, through an unprecedented series of programs, the government would restore the economy and protect the nation against future depressions. Choice (2) is wrong because the idea of rugged individualism and self-help tend to preclude the idea of aid from the government. Choice (4) is not supported by the passage, since the New Deal programs are discussed as attempts to help business and the economy. As the immediate and long-term effects of New Deal programs are not discussed, neither choice (3) nor choice (5) is supported by the passage.

37. **(3)** *Analysis/History.* This explanation most closely draws together the information presented in the passage and shows how the economy embarked on a downward spiral. Choice (1) contradicts business decisions described in the passage. There is no information given to support either choice (2) or choice (4). The statement in choice (5), taken from the passage, is an effect of the depression, not a cause.

38. **(4)** *Application/History.* The Works Progress Administration, which provided jobs for 8 million people, is the best example of a relief measure, although it may have also contributed to the goal of recovery. Choice (1) was a classic example of a much-needed reform. Choice (2) was an example of a recovery act. Choices (3) and (5) were also examples of New Deal reforms.

39. **(2)** *Comprehension/Behaviorial Science.* Inspection of the graph shows that the steepest five-year decline was associated with 1960–1965, during which time the birthrate dropped from about 24 per 1,000 people to about 19 per 1,000 people. The statements in the other choices are not accurate descriptions of the graph.

40. **(3)** *Evaluation/Behavioral Science.* The graph shows that the birthrate was low between 1965 and 1980, especially when compared to that for 1945–1960. Because this cohort has fewer individuals, they will probably experience less competition for jobs, admission into colleges, housing, etc. Thus choice (3) is correct, and choices (1) and (4) are wrong. Choices (2) and (5) may or may not be factually correct; they are not supported by the information in the graph.

41. **(2)** *Evaluation/Behavioral Science.* Relative to other periods in the graph, present birthrates are low, and low birthrates mean that a relatively small proportion

of the population will be reaching childbearing age in the decades to come. Thus the birthrate—that is, the number of births per 1,000 people in the population—will probably be low.

42. **(1)** *Comprehension/Economics.* Aircraft and auto engines would be included in the "machinery and equipment" category, which is the largest category in the U.S. exports graph.

43. **(4)** *Evaluation/Economics.* The graphs give U.S. import and export totals and percentage breakdowns of both imports and exports by category. The calculations required in choices (1), (2), (3), and (5) can all be made on the basis of this information. In contrast, there is no way to determine which U.S. industries are most hurt by competition from imports.

44. **(2)** *Evaluation/Economics.* Choice (1) is supported by the total dollar amounts, which show that U.S. imports exceed exports in value while the opposite is true of Japan. Choices (3) and (5) are also supported, as Japanese exports consist almost entirely of manufactured goods while imports consist mainly of fuels, raw materials, and foods. The United States has a wider range of both imports and exports. The fact that U.S. exports include significant quantities of food, raw materials, and even fuels, whereas Japanese exports do not, supports the statement in choice (4). Given its small land surface, Japan must import food and raw materials. It relies on money earned from exports in order to do so. Thus the graphs may contradict, and certainly do not support, choice (2).

45. **(3)** *Application/History.* This selection from the Fourteen Points comes closest to restating Hay's goals since it also emphasizes territorial integrity and free trade. Choice (1) was an informal arrangement of spheres of influence which Hay protested in China. Choice (2) also represents restraints on international trade that Hay would have opposed. Choice (5) treated Latin America as an American sphere of influence and thus also contradicted Hay's policy.

46. **(1)** *Analysis/History.* Roosevelt's deal through an exchange of notes with British officials can only be described as an executive agreement, which the president, having primary responsibility for foreign affairs, may enter into. The other choices can all be eliminated. Choice (2) requires the advice and consent of the Senate. Choice (3) has no relevance to negotiations with another government. Choice (4) is wrong because no declaration of war was involved. Choice (5) is not the best answer because it does not explain where the president got the authority to make a trade with Britain. It only indicates that once made, and executive agreement is, like any other act of the federal government, considered law.

47. **(3)** *Application/History.* Among the choices presented, this is the only one that involves another executive agreement, that is, a direct agreement between the president of the United States and the leaders of another country. In Choice (1), Carter acted as a facilitator, helping the leaders of other countries get together. The SALT Treaty, mentioned in choice (2), was submitted to the Senate. Choice (4) did not yield any concrete results, or agreements. Choice (5) is an example of the president acting as commander-in-chief.

48. **(2)** *Evaluation/Behavioral Science.* The passage mentions that gift giving occurs between social groups in conjunction with social events and that a group that receives a gift must give something in return. From this it can be concluded that gift exchange serves largely to maintain relationships among groups. Thus choice (5) is incorrect; although "showing off" may be a secondary purpose, it is by no means the primary one. As the passage indicates that groups often deliberately attempt to return gifts of greater value than the gifts they receive, choice (1) and choice (3) must both be wrong. As gift giving occurs among all sorts of social groups and on all sorts of occasions, choice (4) is also wrong.

49. **(2)** *Comprehension/Geography.* The map shows that Cincinnati had temperatures in the 70s and no rain on May 25, 1987. All of the other cities experienced some precipitation.

50. **(5)** *Application/Behavioral Science.* Even those who do not agree with the particular rule believe it to be legitimate because it has been approved by a majority, as required by the Constitution.

51. **(3)** *Application/Behavioral Science.* Public support from the law stems from support for the leader.

52. **(4)** *Application/Behavioral Science.* The group members are actually breaking the rule of the larger society in obeying the rule of their group. They do so because the resolution is based on a value principle in which they believe, namely, nonviolence.

53. **(1)** *Application/Behavioral Science.* The people support the proclamation naming the son king because this is the way it has always been done. The line of succession is established by tradition.

54. **(3)** *Application/Behavioral Science.* The description focuses on the leader. Although choice (2)—emotion—may also be a factor, belief in the leader's vision would seem to stem utlimately from faith in the leader.

55. **(5)** *Application/History.* The example in choice (5) is the historical extension of Calhoun's doctrine, and it took a Civil War to ultimately deny this extremist states' rights position. The other choices are incorrect because in each case the entity rejecting the act, treaty, etc., is using powers it has been given. For example, the Constitution allows the Senate to reject treaties. Only the case of secession follows Calhoun's logic that a state has the right to overturn an act of the federal government.

56. **(2)** *Analysis/History.* Since poor housing and schools existed before the riots occurred, the Johnson administration's efforts to improve housing and education through the War on Poverty and Great Society programs did not have a quick and significant impact. There is nothing in the cartoon to suggest the statement in choice (1). Choice (2) may or may not have contributed to the riots; however, it is not addressed

57. **(1)** *Analysis/Behavioral Science.* Although factually correct, choice (4) simply restates the pattern in the graphs. Choice (1) offers an explanation for this pattern: The reason children know more about their mother's parents than their father's parents is that they tend to be closer to, and talk more with, their mother than their father. Choice (2) is incorrect as it would explain a pattern opposite from that found in the graphs. Choice (3) is an incorrect factual statement about the graphs; the graphs show that children do know about their grandparents. For this reason, choice (5) is also incorrrect.

58. **(5)** *Analysis/Economics.* The chart shows that as the amount of the loan still outstanding goes down, interest paid during the year goes down as well. That is, yearly payments remain the same but an even greater share will consist of principal. Thus choice (2) and choice (3) are incorrect: The amount of total payments during a year is always the same, and very little principal is repaid during the early years of repayment. Choice (4) is also wrong because, as shown in the chart, total interest paid exceeds the principal (at $1,158 per year, payments at the end of 20 years total over $20,000 and the loan was for $10,000). Choice (1) is incorrect, because the chart shows that equity is calculated by adding payments of principal to date.

59. **(2)** *Evaluation/History.* White settlers, for sport and profit, killed off the buffalo, on which the Plains Indians depended for most of their life necessities. The settlers expected a nomadic people to live in a confined area and farm the land. It can therefore be concluded that the white settlers failed to understand or respect Indian culture. None of the statements in the other choices can be confirmed on the basis of the passage.

60. **(3)** *Analysis/Political Science.* Choice (3) is supported by the sharp increases in actual and projected Social Security payments, which are granted to people over the age of 65. Steep increases in Aid to Families With Dependent Children would not necessarily mean a high overall birth rate, and the increases in the graph are not steep, so choice (1) is incorrect. Choice (2) cannot be determined from any of the curves on the graph. Choice (4) is not be supported by the military retirement data; data on enlistments is needed. Choice (5) is contradicted by the rise in Medicare costs. Note that the Medicare rise provides further support for choice (3), as Medicare is health insurance for retired people.

61. **(4)** *Evaluation/Political Science.* Choice (4) is consistent with the spending levels for Social Security and Medicare as compared to Aid to Families With Dependent Children. Although the aging of the population is one reason for the sharp increases in Social Security and Medicare spending; the budget is also affected by the relative strength of different constituencies and interest groups. Choices (1), (2), and (3) are not substantiated by the information in the graph. Choice (5) is an opinion that is not verified by the data.

62. **(4)** *Application/Economics.* Only firefighters' services are a public consumer good/service. A car and a tax preparer's services are private consumer goods/services. A factory building is a private capital good. A highway system, although public, is a capital—not a consumer—good.

63. **(1)** *Application/Economics.* GNP is a total figure; therefore it does not indicate breakdown by kind of good or service. It provides no information about how goods and services are distributed.

64. **(4)** *Analysis/History.* As the passage indicates, Watergate badly shook the public's trust in government. Ford stated that in pardoning Nixon, he hoped to put the Watergate episode behind the nation so that the country might be able to move on. There is nothing in the passage to support any of the other choices.

SIMULATED TEST 3
Science

1. **(3)** *Application/Biology.* The facts that the amoeba consists of one cell and that it exhibits signs of independent life eliminate the other choices.
2. **(3)** *Application/Biology.* The fact that the heart is made up of tissues eliminates choices (1) and (2). The fact that it does not include any organs eliminates choice (4). The fact that it does not function on its own eliminates choice (5). The heart is a group of different tissues that work together, so it is classified as an organ.
3. **(4)** *Application/Biology.* Organelles carry out life processes for the cell.
4. **(2)** *Application/Biology.* A chemical compound is nonliving matter composed of atoms.
5. **(5)** *Application/Biology.* The fact that a dog is an independent being eliminates choices (1), (2), and (3). The fact that it is composed of many cells eliminates choice (4), leaving multicellular organism as the only choice.
6. **(2)** *Analysis/Biology.* Little rain falls in the desert, so plants need to conserve whatever water they can. Since transpiration takes place through the leaves, having few leaves would decrease the rate of transpiration and thus conserve water for the cactus.
7. **(3)** *Evaluation/Biology.* Both plants and animals transpire, or give off moisture, so increasing the numbers of both would increase the relative humidity in a room.
8. **(1)** *Application/Biology.* A low water level in the blood is an internal environmental change that stimulates the hypothalamus to cause you to feel thirsty. The sun may be part of the stimulus that lowers your blood's water level, but it is not what actually causes you to feel thirsty.
9. **(5)** *Application/Earth Science.* Since Snowcap Mountain rises into the upper two-thirds of the troposphere, cold temperatures and noticably less oxygen could be a problem.
10. **(3)** *Comprehension/Earth Science.* The correct response is (3) because it gives not only the correct order of events but also a logical sequence in which one step leads to another. Choice (1) is incorrect because it is water heated by the sun, not the heat alone, that is circulated through the house. Choices (2) and (5) lack a logical link between the heating of the water and the obtainment of warm air. Choice (4) by-passes the whole idea of heating the house.
11. **(1)** *Application/Earth Science.* A solar collector should be painted black on the inside to absorb maximum sunlight; it should have a clear covering to prevent heat loss while allowing the rays to pass through; and it should be surrounded on the sides by an insulating material. White or shiny metal containers would reflect too much sunlight; a clear glass container would transmit, rather than absorb, the light. Lack of a cover or insulating material would allow too much heat to be lost to the surroundings.
12. **(3)** *Analysis/Earth Science.* Since pump A pumps the cooled water from the tank back to the collector, it is probably the cause of the problem. If pump B were defective, the water level in the tank would be low. The fan and heat exchangers do not really affect the water levels.
13. **(5)** *Evaluation/Earth Science.* Water is heated in a boiler and also in a solar collector. If you answered choice (2), you confused the idea of a heating device with the fuel that runs it. The sun is to a solar heating system as fuel for the boiler is to a hot-water heating system.
14. **(1)** *Analysis/Biology.* If the orange and yellow colors are visible only after the chlorophyll decays, and the chlorophyll is necessary for photosynthesis, then the tree is not carrying on photosynthesis after its leaves change color.
15. **(2)** *Comprehension/Biology.* The passage is about the pros and cons of a particular program to manage a wolf population. There is disagreement between backers and opponents of the program, which indicates controversy.
16. **(1)** *Evaluation/Biology.* The fact that the prey populations decreased in large numbers in those years supports the argument that these populations are headed for extinction. Choice (4) is irrelevant to the argument. Choices (2), (3), and (5) support the position of the program's opponents.
17. **(4)** *Comprehension/Biology.* One of Darwin's conclusions was that individuals with favorable variations are more likely to survive and reproduce than others of their species.
18. **(5)** *Comprehension/Biology.* Darwin did not know about the existence of genes and thus could not have known that natural selection acts on genetic variations.
19. **(5)** *Analysis/Biology.* Lamarck's belief that acquired traits could be passed on to offspring is considered incorrect because these traits are not recorded in the genes. Only genetic variations are passed on to offspring.
20. **(1)** *Analysis/Biology.* Since natural selection operates through reproduction, the speed at which the species reproduces would most determine the speed at which evolution takes place. The other choices describe conditions that may affect evolution, but not necessarily the speed with which it occurs.
21. **(1)** *Evaluation/Biology.* Since

bigger, stronger muscles with exercise are an acquired trait, Lamarck might have used it to support his theory.
22. **(2)** *Application/Physics.* The correct response is (2) because the gain and loss of magnetism with electric current would be very useful in picking up and dropping pieces of metal.
23. **(4)** *Comprehension/Biology.* The rat is the smallest mammal listed, so it has the shortest life expectancy.
24. **(3)** *Evaluation/Biology.* The evidence supports the generalization that inhaling the smoke of others is a health hazard. Choice (2) is false. Choices (1), (4), and (5) are true but are not concerned with passive smoking.
25. **(4)** *Analysis/Earth Science.* Statements (1) and (5) are opinions. Statements (2) and (3) are presented in the passage as facts. The idea that ozone can cause cancer is a hypothesis that is currently being tested.
26. **(2)** *Application/Chemistry.* Of all the elements listed, sodium has the lowest atomic number (11) and atomic mass (22.9898). Therefore, if a relatively heavy metallic substance is needed, of the elements listed, sodium is the least likely choice.
27. **(4)** *Evaluation/Chemistry.* The elements listed are all located in the same vertical column ("group") in the table. Similarity of chemical and physical properties is clearly one of the principles determining the structure of the table, so choice (5) is wrong. Choices (1), (2), and (3) can be seen to be wrong by examination of the table.
28. **(4)** *Application/Physics.* The arrow flies upward in a straight line until gravity, an outside force, causes it to change direction and fall back to the ground. Choices (1) and (3) describe objects at rest that are set in motion. Choice (2) describes an object that changes speed but not direction. Choice (5) illustrates another law of motion: for every action there is an equal and opposite reaction.
29. **(3)** *Comprehension/Earth Science.* Since carbonated water consists of carbon dioxide dissolved in water, it would have the same effect on limestone as rainwater mixed with carbon dioxide. The dissolving of sulfur dioxide gas in rainwater is similar to the dissolving of carbon dioxide in rainwater, but no mention is made in choice (4) of the sulfuric acid having a corrosive effect on an object.
30. **(5)** *Application/Chemistry.* Cleaning the silver immediately would remove any sulfur-containing foods such as egg yolk. Keeping it in an air-tight container would prevent contact with the hydrogen sulfide in the atmosphere.
31. **(3)** *Comprehension/Physics.* The idea that heat is a fluid was part of the caloric theory. Heat is a form of energy. Like all forms of energy, it is invisible—only the results it produces are visible.
32. **(5)** *Application/Physics.* Because the temperature difference between the cold milk and the desired temperature is twice as great as the temperature difference between the hot milk and the desired temperature, the hot and cold milk should be mixed in a 2:1 ratio. If the hot and cold milk are mixed in equal amounts, the final temperature of the mixture will be about 55°C.
33. **(2)** *Analysis/Physics.* The correct response is (2) because motion produces heat as kinetic energy is converted into heat energy. Choice (4) is incorrect because the rope is not in motion. Choices (1), (3), and (5) are incorrect because the rope is not the source of the heat.
34. **(4)** *Evaluation/Physics.* If energy of motion can be converted into heat, then energy must be able to change from one form to another. Choices (3) and (5) relate to the misconceptions of heat that were part of the caloric theory. Choices (1) and (2) are incorrect because the passage included no quantitative discussion of molecular energy.
35. **(3)** *Evaluation/Earth Science.* According to the diagram, all stars begin life by passing through the main sequence. Then they take different pathways depending upon their mass. Nothing conclusive is shown by the diagram with respect to length of life or distance traveled by stars, or to the energy contained in any particular type of star.
36. **(4)** *Analysis/Physics.* Choice (4) results in momentum that is one-and-one-half times as great as the original momentum. The momentum in choices (1) and (2) remains constant. The momentum in choices (3) and (5) decreases.
37. **(3)** *Comprehension/Biology.* According to the diagram, 25 percent of the offspring of one pair of pink flowers are likely to be red. Therefore, of the 16 offspring of four pairs of pink flowers, 25 percent, or four flowers, are likely to be red.
38. **(4)** *Application/Biology.* The red flower would yield two red genes, and the white flower would yield two white genes. AA + aa yields Aa, Aa, Aa, and Aa, or 100 percent pink flowers, since the Aa genotype produces a pink flower.
39. **(2)** *Comprehension/Biology.* The pink genotype is Aa and the red genotype is AA, so half the flowers would have the genotype AA and the other half would have the genotype Aa.
40. **(1)** *Evaluation/Biology.* If either gene were dominant, one would determine the trait when crossed with the other. However, a flower with one red gene and one white gene is neither red nor white but pink.
41. **(5)** *Evaluation/Biology.* If skin color is inherited in a way similar to that shown for flower color in the diagram, then dark skin color may be considered analogous to a red flower, and light skin color to a white flower. Thus neither the gene for dark skin color nor the one for light skin color is dominant. If one percent has dark-colored skin and one has light-colored skin, all the children will have skin colors between dark and light.
42. **(3)** *Comprehension/Earth Science.* Although one paragraph of the passage discusses possible reasons for Earth's magnetism, the main purpose of the passage is to discuss the magnetic properties of Earth in general. Use of an iron bar magnet simply provides an opening illustration.
43. **(1)** *Comprehension/Earth Science.* The fact that the magnetosphere contains charged particles, and the idea that Earth's magnetism may be caused by bands of electric current, suggest that a

relationship exists between electricity and magnetism.

44. **(2)** *Analysis/Earth Science.* A compass would point to Earth's magnetic, not geographic, north pole. Thus a person using a compass must take into account the "error" of the compass in locating true north.

45. **(4)** *Analysis/Earth Science.* The idea that Earth's magnetism is caused by bands of electric current is presented as a possible explanation for Earth's magnetic behavior. Therefore it is a hypothesis. The other choices all represent statements that can be verified as fact or established theory.

46. **(4)** *Evaluation/Earth Science.* Statements about the locations of the poles are backed up by geographical data. Choices (2) and (3) are supported by the opening demonstration of the bar magnet, as well as by detailed information about the magnetosphere. Recent ideas about the cause of Earth's magnetism are stated but not supported by data.

47. **(4)** *Application/Chemistry.* In this reaction, the sodium and hydrogen exchange places: HCl + NaOH → NaCl + HOH. Thus the procedure is a double replacement reaction.

48. **(2)** *Application/Chemistry.* Water is broken down into oxygen and hydrogen: $H_2O \rightarrow O_2 + H_2$.

49. **(3)** *Application/Chemistry.* The zinc replaces the hydrogen in sulfuric acid to form zinc sulfate: $Zn + H_2SO_4 \rightarrow ZnSO_4 + H_2$.

50. **(5)** *Application/Chemistry.* Because sodium is less active than lithium, it cannot replace lithium in lithium chloride. Thus no reaction occurs.

51. **(3)** *Analysis/Biology.* Statements A and C could be chemically proven. B and D are the opinions of the author of the article.

52. **(5)** *Analysis/Physics.* As the train passed by, you would hear sound waves that were less compressed. As a result, the whistle would sound lower in pitch than it did before the train passed by.

53. **(1)** *Comprehension/Biology.* The red blood cell is the only substance of this group that is not a foreign substance and thus will not provoke an attack by the immune system.

54. **(3)** *Application/Biology.* The energy from one molecule of glucose can be used to make as many as 36 molecules of ATP, so divide 36 by 3 (the number of ATP molecules formed for every atom of oxygen used) to get 12, the number of oxygen atoms needed to use the energy in one molecule of glucose.

55. **(4)** *Analysis/Biology.* In the muscle cells ADP is being converted into ATP and back into ADP. Furthermore, this process is occurring without the use of oxygen, so it is considered to be anaerobic respiration.

56. **(4)** *Analysis/Biology.* There is nothing in the passage about a difference in reuse of ADP, speed of energy release, type of carbohydrates, or individual differences among cells regarding anaerobic versus aerobic respiration, which eliminates choices (2), (3), (4), and (5). The presence of free oxygen is a difference between aerobic and anaerobic respiration, and thus seems likely to have something to do with the greater yield of energy.

57. **(5)** *Application/Biology.* The passage is concerned with biology in that it discusses how cells obtain energy; it is concerned with chemistry in that it discusses how certain molecules and atoms change and combine; and it is concerned with physics in that it discusses changes in energy. There is no mention of the concerns of earth science.

58. **(2)** *Evaluation/Biology.* If the first living organisms evolved in an atmosphere without oxygen, then it is likely that anaerobic respiration evolved earlier than aerobic respiration, since these organisms would have needed to obtain energy in the absence of oxygen. This eliminates choice (1). Choices (3), (4), and (5) are irrelevant information.

59. **(5)** *Analysis/Biology.* There is no information contained in the graph regarding the brain location or the size of the two cortexes, so choices (1), (2), and (4) are eliminated. Choice (3) is false because the cortexes each receive signals from the same body parts. Thus choice (5) is correct because a body part such as the lips, which are moved often, has more space devoted to it in both cortexes than the trunk, which is used less often.

60. **(4)** *Comprehension/Physics.* Because the angle of reflection equals the angle of incidence, the total angle between the line of incidence and the line of reflection would be 50° + 50° or 100°.

61. **(1)** *Analysis/Physics.* The apparent bending of the straw is caused by the bending of light waves as they pass from air to water. This is the only choice that correctly relates to the information provided.

62. **(5)** *Analysis/Chemistry.* Choice (1) is a statement of fact. Choice (2) is incorrect because the author does not imply that the industries are careless in the burning of fuels. Choices (3) and (4) are facts that can be verified by measurement and analysis.

63. **(1)** *Analysis/Biology.* As the diagrams show, a plant cell and a bacterium both have a cell wall, a cell membrane, and at least one chromosome, which eliminates choices (2), (3), and (4). Only a plant cell has chloroplasts, so choice (5) would not tell you that your cell is a bacterium. However, a plant cell has a nucleus and a bacterium does not, so choice (1) would immediately tell you that the cell is a bacterium.

64. **(3)** *Analysis/Chemistry.* Depending upon the structure of the molecule, the formula C_2H_6O can represent either ethanol or ethyl ether—two very different compounds. Thus a structural formula, rather than a molecular formula, is needed to determine the arrangement of atoms in a molecule.

65. **(4)** *Evaluation/Biology.* Choice (4) would indicate that the female cowbird listens to the dialect in choosing her mate. Her rejection of newcomers and young cowbirds could be based on other reasons, such as smell or appearance, eliminating choices (1) and (3). Choices (2) and (5) do not support the hypothesis because learning the dialect could serve other biological purposes, such as communicating the location of food.

66. **(3)** *Evaluation/Physics.* In a rainbow, the white light from the sun is split apart into its many component wavelengths, each of which appears as a different color. Choice (4) is incorrect because infrared and other normally invisible types of light are not visible in a rainbow. Choice (5) is incorrect because the rainbow effect is created not by the bending of light but by the separation of the different wavelengths. Choices (1) and (2) are not addressed by the passage.

SIMULATED TEST 4
Interpreting Literature and the Arts

1. **(5)** *Inferential Comprehension, Global/Fiction.* The Evertons have left their home in San Francisco for a place that they have never seen and know little about. The author explains that they have done this to "weave chance and hope into a fabric that would clothe them as long as they lived" (lines 37–39). Their motive is not to find adventure (Choices [1] and [3]), nor to get away from the sadness of society (Choices [2] and [4]), but to pursue a rather unrealistic goal.
2. **(3)** *Literal Comprehension, Specific/Fiction.* Ibarra is described as lacking telegram services (lines 42–43). Also, when the Evertons are asked about airport facilities and lighting for the house, they avoid answering (lines 43–50).
3. **(2)** *Inferential Comprehension, Specific/Fiction.* Memories can be compared to corks left out of bottles because, after a while, they "swell" and "no longer fit" reality (line 60). The Evertons base their vision of Ibarra on a great-aunt's memories of it, never imagining that those memories may have been exaggerated or otherwise distorted.
4. **(3)** *Analysis/Fiction.* A story told in the present tense expresses the immediacy of the here and now. The author's choice of the present tense makes the Everton's travels unfold before the reader's eyes as though they happen at the moment of reading.
5. **(5)** *Literal Comprehension, Global/Poetry.* If the fog acts like a cat, then its movements are slow and stealthy. The fog "moves on" (line 6) rather than stays (Choice [2]). It also is not described as swift (Choice [1]) or dark (Choice [3]). The "shapes" of feet (line 2) and haunches (line 5) are figurative rather than literal (Choice [4]).
6. **(3)** *Inferential Comprehension, Specific/Poetry.* The "little cat feet" can be interpreted in several ways, but the fog would not hold soot (Choice [4]). Pedestrians (Choice [5]) are not mentioned. The wisps of mist are probably the "feet."
7. **(4)** *Analysis/Poetry.* The poet concentrates on the image of the moving fog, not on the way the fog feels. The fog moves silently and slowly, as a cat walks.
8. **(4)** *Literal Comprehension, Global/Drama.* Illingworth's advice to Gerald is primarily in response to Gerald's question "But it is very difficult to get into society, isn't it?" (lines 10–11).
9. **(3)** *Analysis/Drama.* The author's views are stated by Illingworth, who finds no serious purpose to society at all. He presents "the best society" as a group of people who need only to be fed, amused, or shocked (lines 12–15). According to him, being a member of such a society ensures that one will not have to pursue any serious goal in life.
10. **(1)** *Inferential Comprehension, Global/Drama.* It is implied throughout the passage that "society" is concerned largely with its own amusement and entertainment. From the beginning of the passage, Gerald's concerns about the proper way to wear a tie and to talk indicate that a concern for fashion and manners characterizes the "society" that Gerald admires and Illingworth laughs at.
11. **(4)** *Literal Comprehension, Global/Commentary.* The topic of boxing is discussed throughout. The book that is being reviewed is titled *On Boxing*.
12. **(1)** *Inferential Comprehension, Specific/Commentary.* Oates has written that her "feminist preconception" about boxing shaped her view of boxing as an expression of violence. By stating that she later became more sympathetic (lines 46–47), she implies that her original views of boxing were negative.
13. **(1)** *Analysis/Commentary.* Oates first compares boxing to the arts in her discussion of the role of the referee (lines 28–29). She then considers boxing as theater (lines 35–38). Her quotation of Emily Dickinson (lines 58–60) implies a comparison between the impact of great art and of a great boxing match.
14. **(4)** *Literal Comprehension, Specific/Commentary.* The term is used to refer to the Greco-Roman origins of boxing, which Oates mentions as part of the "history lesson" in *On Boxing*.
15. **(5)** *Application/Commentary.* Oates expresses her belief that boxing is an outlet for aggression that cannot be directed toward any "legitimate objects" in society (line 42). However, she also views aggression as "inevitable and quite natural" (line 48). It is likely that Oates believes that competitive instincts are natural and that school sports provide a healthy outlet for these instincts.
16. **(5)** *Literal Comprehension, Global/Poetry.* The poem begins with "I think it must be lonely to be God" (line 1) and ends with "Perhaps sometimes He tires of being great/In solitude" (lines 23–25). Throughout the poem, consideration is given to the thought that God and humans cannot feel close to each other.
17. **(3)** *Inferential Comprehension, Specific/Poetry.* The poet says that despite these seeming shows of worship, "Nobody loves a master" (line 2).
18. **(4)** *Application/Poetry.* Nothing is said in the poem about social programs (Choice [2]), about church involvement in political matters (Choice [3]), or about missionary work (Choice [5]). What is said concerns the great separation between people and

A-94

God. A church that offered elaborate, dignified services (Choice [1]) probably would only widen the gap. A church whose members were "friends of God," however, might keep God from feeling "lonely."

19. **(5)** *Literal Comprehension, Specific/Fiction.* In repeating the story of his offer to buy the horse, the rancher explains that Joe's answer was "Ain't my horse" (line 53).

20. **(1)** *Inferential Comprehension, Global/Fiction.* The Indians want to keep secret the reason for the killing of the horse. Although the mission priest believes that the event has "dark, pagan significance" (Choice [3]), there is no evidence in the passage to support his view.

21. **(2)** *Application/Fiction.* The cultural ritual of killing the horse is similar to the cultural ritual of a bullfight. To someone outside the tradition, the event may seem to be distasteful. (Choice [3] is the only other event that might arouse distaste, but it does not produce nearly as strong a reaction as bullfighting does for most people.) Like Joe's killing of the horse, the killing of the bull and the entire bullfight has great cultural significance.

22. **(2)** *Analysis/Fiction.* It is ironic that a character with the name of Joe Walking Wolf should be lame. The fact is revealed in line 31. None of the other choices is supported in the passage.

23. **(3)** *Literal Comprehension, Specific/Nonfiction.* The speaker explains the term by saying that Estebita's voice "could be heard by everyone" (lines 5–6).

24. **(1)** *Inferential Comprehension, Global/Nonfiction.* The speaker specifically mentions his "will to survive" and his "determination" (lines 13–14). The passage as a whole focuses on how he found ways to cope with the ordeal of his imprisonment.

25. **(4)** *Application/Nonfiction.* The passage shows that the speaker is able to adapt to a harsh environment; he is not the kind of person to give up (Choice [2]). Just as he figured out ways to preserve his physical fitness and his mental concentration in prison, so would he probably figure out how to feed and shelter himself on a desert island.

26. **(3)** *Analysis/Nonfiction.* Although the speaker may have felt some anger and frustration over his situation (Choice [5]), he gives the reader a picture of prison life through the use of concrete, descriptive details. These details include a mention of Estebita's storytelling, descriptions of the physical and mental exercises the speaker performed, and information about the physical appearance of the prison.

27. **(5)** *Inferential Comprehension, Global/Drama.* That Ramirez is angry with the social worker can be seen in his words and in the stage directions. His remark to "Mr. Palm-Beach-Suit" is meant as an insult, and the social worker takes it as such (line 18). That Ramirez resents the social worker's superior attitude can be seen in comments such as "Every night we give thanks to you" (lines 21–22) and the angry closing line "I got no change" (line 38).

28. **(3)** *Inferential Comprehension, Specific/Drama.* There is no evidence for Choices (1), (2), or (5) in the passage. Ramirez cares about Candido's education (lines 29–31), but the education is free (line 20). He explains that he has helped to take care of Candido by giving him a job that will help with his family's expenses (lines 9–11). It is right after that explanation that he identifies himself as "one of the fathers" (lines 11–12).

29. **(1)** *Application/Drama.* The social worker is not a compassionate man. In the passage, he makes no attempt to help the family; instead, he criticizes Ramirez. Choices (2) and (5) contrast strongly with the kinds of comments he makes to Ramirez. Instead, his attitude is summed up in "You people always give us a hard time" (lines 35–36). The social worker is quick to group people together and label them unkindly. Choice (1) is the same kind of comment, referring to the stereotypical view that Hispanics are "lazy."

30. **(4)** *Inferential Comprehension, Specific/Fiction.* Elena's deepest wish is to do something meaningful with her life. As she explains when speaking of "one's proper place," "Each of you . . . knows what he is working for." Her "proper place" is not necessarily in her social class (Choice [1]) or with a respectable family (Choice [3]), but in a productive task that would give her life a purpose.

31. **(5)** *Inferential Comprehension, Global/Fiction.* Elena sees the benefits of being healthy and productive. Concerning her own situation, she states, "I should prefer the hardest labor to such a condition" (lines 14–16). She does not despise wealth in general (Choice [1]); she merely states that wealth does not guarantee happiness. She is not embarrassed by her own wealth (Choice [3]). If she resents her husband (Choice [4]), it is for caring too much for the in-laws who have refused to forgive them for marrying.

32. **(5)** *Literal Comprehension, Specific/Fiction.* Elena says of her "illness," "I get no sleep; continual headache gives me no peace . . . I am weak all over" (lines 11–14).

33. **(4)** *Analysis/Fiction.* The author mentions young and old, male and female in the group of peasants. All hear what Elena speaks of as a lesson—that not everyone who looks wealthy is satisfied with life (lines 48–50).

34. **(4)** *Literal Comprehension, Global/Nonfiction.* The topic—referred to throughout as a "dream," as "faith," and as a "hope"—appears most boldly at the end of the passage. There Dr. King describes a scene of people of all different backgrounds—"all of God's children" (line 37)—joined together.

35. **(2)** *Analysis/Nonfiction.* "I have a dream" is in harmony with "let freedom ring" (Choice [1]) one is the cause, the other is the effect. Never in the passage does Dr. King refer to historical dreamers (Choice [3]), plead for peaceful rather than violent solutions (Choice [4]), or indicate that the "dream" is for the future rather than the present (Choice [5]). Repetition is a technique that can underscore the importance of the material repeated. Dr. King's "dream" is the reason for continuing with his work despite "the difficulties and frustrations

of the moment" (lines 2–3); thus, it is not surprising that he repeats "I have a dream" and related words such as "faith" and "hope."

36. **(2)** *Literal Comprehension, Specific/Nonfiction.* Choices (1), (3), (4), and (5) all can be found in lines 14–25.

37. **(5)** *Analysis/Fiction.* The passage is about political changes within society, not religious feelings within the individual (thus eliminating Choices [1], [2], and [4]). According to Dr. King, these changes can be accomplished when people work together (lines 20–21, thus eliminating Choice [3]). Nevertheless, singing—and particularly religious singing—is part of his listener's heritage. To inspire his audience to feel the passion he feels about political matters, he appeals to their spiritual passion.

38. **(2)** *Literal Comprehension, Global/Commentary.* The critic points out that the Beatles were quite concerned with melody, harmony, and poetry (lines 5–9). Heavy metal, on the other hand, seems to care more "about sound, not music" (line 20). Although some of the other choices may be true, only Choice (2) is the focus of the passage as a whole.

39. **(3)** *Inferential Comprehension, Specific/Commentary.* The comment appears immediately after the critic comments, "And in most pop rock, synthesized handclaps and artificial impulses . . . take the place of melody and harmony" (lines 50–55). The reference to a "barren landscape" is his prediction that current trends in pop music probably will not change. Society still may be interested in music (Choice [2]), but it will be music of a different order.

40. **(4)** *Analysis/Commentary.* Choices (1), (2), (3), and (5) are affectionate endorsements of the Beatles but are not the highest praise in the passage. In lines 21–25, the critic compares *musica divina* (church music) to *musica vulgaris* (secular music) after comparing the Beatles music to heavy metal. He implies that as *musica divina* was considered the more noble music of a past era, so the Beatles' music should be considered the more noble music of the present era.

41. **(1)** *Analysis/Commentary.* The critic does not attempt to support his view by referring to authorities on music or by arguing against those who may like heavy metal. Rather, he uses historical references to recall nostalgically the impact that the Beatles originally made. He also gives frequent examples—especially of the aspects of heavy metal that he finds distasteful.

42. **(5)** *Application/Commentary.* The recent dominance of special-effects technology in movies can be compared to the increasing importance of musical-effects technology in pop songs. It could be argued that both kinds of technologies replace natural "effects" with something artificial and thus hurt the media in which they are used.

43. **(5)** *Literal Comprehension, Specific/Nonfiction.* The poacher's reason for hunting rhinos is summed up in the statement "The prize is the rhino's horn" (lines 38–39) and explained in the rest of that paragraph.

44. **(3)** *Inferential Comprehension, Global/Nonfiction.* The threats to the American wildlife population are discussed throughout the passage. Given the problems of poaching (lines 22–24) and takeover of wilderness areas for human use (line 1), the future looks grim for African wildlife. The author seems to side with the "pessimists [who] predict that wild Africa will soon become little more than a string of glorified safari parks as the true wilderness shrivels and the animals die out" (lines 12–16).

45. **(4)** *Analysis/Nonfiction.* The author uses statistics to describe the impact of poaching on the rhino population (lines 24–29). The big-game hunter Robin Hurt is quoted as an authority (lines 7–11). An example of figurative language is the description of the rhino as "a lumbering prehistoric tank" (line 4).

SIMULATED TEST 5
Mathematics

1. **(4)** *Arithmetic/Applications.*
   $V = \pi r^2 h$
   $= 3.14 \times 1.5 \times 1.5 \times 4$
   $= 28.26$

2. **(4)** *Arithmetic/Problem Solving.*
   55 minutes $= \frac{55}{60}$
   $d = rt$
   $= 87.8 \times \frac{55}{60}$
   $= \frac{4829}{60}$
   $= 80.48$, rounded to 80.5

3. **(3)** *Arithmetic/Problem Solving.*
   Total MPG = 105.2
   $\frac{105.2}{5} = 21.04$

4. **(5)** *Algebra/Problem Solving.*
   $.65u$ gives 65% of the units.

5. **(2)** *Algebra/Problem Solving.*
   If a = size of apartment:
   $3a + 75 = 1500$
   $3a = 1425$
   $a = 475$

6. **(2)** *Geometry/Skills.*
   Angles a and e are equal, angles c and e are supplementary; therefore, angles a and c are supplementary.

7. **(2)** *Arithmetic/Applications.*
   Add the sides that need railing.
   $12 + 21 + 24 + 10 = 67$ ft.

8. **(5)** *Arithmetic/Problem Solving.*
   Divide the deck into two rectangular areas, then add.
   $A = lw$
   $A = 21 \times 12$
   $= 252$

   $A = 13 \times 12$
   $= 156$
   $252 + 156 = 408$

9. **(1)** *Arithmetic/Applications.*
   $\frac{180}{24} = 7.5$

10. **(3)** *Arithmetic/Applications.*
    $i = prt$
    $= 588 \times .15 \times 1$
    $= 88.20$

11. **(4)** *Arithmetic/Problem Solving.*
    Total purchases = 218.37
    3 months = .25
    $i = prt$
    $= 218.37 \times .18 \times .25$
    $= 9.82665$ rounded to 9.83
    $218.37 + 9.83 = 228.20$

12. **(1)** *Arithmetic/Problem Solving.*
    $689 - 25 = 664$
    $i = prt; p = \frac{i}{rt}$
    $p = \frac{664}{.10 \times 1}$
    $= 6640$

13. **(3)** *Arithmetic/Problem Solving.*
    $i = prt; p = \frac{i}{rt}$
    $p = \frac{84}{(.16 \times .75)}$
    $= 700$

14. **(1)** *Arithmetic/Problem Solving.*
    Sales tax collected:
    A .09
    B .06
    C .10
    D .15

15. **(4)** *Geometry/Applications.*
    Use points $E\,(^-2, ^-8)$ and $F\,(1, 4)$:
    $m = \frac{y_2 - y_1}{x_2 - x_1}$
    $= \frac{4 - {}^-8}{1 - {}^-2}$
    $= \frac{12}{3}$
    $= 4$

16. **(3)** *Geometry/Applications.*
    $C = (^-3, ^-5)$
    $D = (11, 9)$
    $\frac{(x_1 + x_2)}{2}, \frac{(y_1 + y_2)}{2}$
    $\frac{(^-3 + 11)}{2}, \frac{(^-5 + 9)}{2}$
    $(4, 2)$

17. **(4)** *Geometry/Applications.*
    $(0,0)$ and $(9, ^-3)$
    $d = \sqrt{(x_2 - x_1)^2 + (y_2 - y_1)^2}$
    $= \sqrt{(9 - 0)^2 + (^-3 - 0)^2}$
    $= \sqrt{(9)^2 + (^-3)^2}$
    $= \sqrt{81 + 9}$
    $= \sqrt{90}$

A-98   Test 5: Mathematics   Simulation

18. **(3)** *Algebra/Applications.*
    $(z + 7)(z - 1) = z^2 - z + 7z - 7$
    Simplify to $z^2 + 6z - 7$.

19. **(1)** *Algebra/Problem Solving.*
    $\frac{t}{5}$ gives the average weight of the team.

20. **(1)** *Geometry/Problem Solving.*
    Use the Pythagorean relationship:
    $c^2 = a^2 + b^2$
    $ = (3)^2 + (4)^2$
    $ = 9 + 16$
    $ = 25$
    $c = 5$

21. **(5)** *Arithmetic/Problem Solving.*
    No correlation can be made between the amount of coal mined and the amount used.

22. **(1)** *Arithmetic/Problem Solving.*
    12.7% produced by hydroelectric power
    $2{,}310{,}000 \times .127 = 293{,}370$

23. **(3)** *Arithmetic/Problem Solving.*
    Amount produced by other methods, 5%; by oil, 5%
    $.5:5 = 1:10$

24. **(2)** *Arithmetic/Applications.*
    $C = \pi d$
    $ = 3.14 \times 24$
    $ = 75.36$

25. **(5)** *Arithmetic/Problem Solving.*
    While ¾ of the city's area is located inside the beltway, the question fails to say what part of the area inside the beltway is part of the city.

26. **(4)** *Algebra/Applications.*
    Factor to $(s - 3)(s - 6)$, or use the substitution method.

27. **(5)** *Algebra/Problem Solving.*
    The cost of mailing the packages would be 10p. Her change would equal $20 minus the mailing cost.

28. **(2)** *Geometry/Problem Solving.*
    Find the difference in the height of the buildings:
    $747 - 387 = 360$
    Use the Pythagorean relationship:
    $c^2 = a^2 + b^2$
    $ = (360)^2 + (480)^2$
    $ = 129{,}600 + 230{,}400$
    $ = 360{,}000$
    $c = 600$

29. **(1)** *Geometry/Problem Solving.*
    $6:21 = 4:s$
    $6s = 84$
    $s = 14$

30. **(5)** *Arithmetic/Problem Solving.*
    Convert 3 hours to seconds:
    $60 \times 60 \times 3 = 10{,}800$
    Ratio of computer speed: Robin's speed $= 1:10{,}800$

31. **(1)** *Geometry/Skills.*
    Angle a is the angle formed by the interaction of the wall and the shelf.

32. **(1)** *Algebra/Problem Solving.*
    If r = riding time:
    $2r + 5 = 45$
    $2r = 40$
    $r = 20$

33. **(1)** *Algebra/Problem Solving.*
    $\frac{3s}{7} = \frac{3}{7}$ of the salary
    Rent is ¯25 that amount.

34. **(3)** *Arithmetic/Problem Solving.*
    3.6 billion $= 3.6 \times 10^9$
    36 million $= .036 \times 10^9$
    $3.6 - .036 = 3.564$

35. **(3)** *Arithmetic/Problem Solving.*
    Total deposits $= 895.57$
    Total withdrawals $= 1128.90$
    $1215 + 895.57 - 1128.90 = 981.67$

36. **(4)** *Arithmetic/Problem Solving.*
    Find the areas of both the triangular part and the rectangular part of the wall, then add.
    Triangular area:
    $A = \tfrac{1}{2}bh$
    $ = .5 \times 15 \times 5$
    $ = 37.5$
    Rectangular area:
    $A = lw$
    $ = 15 \times 12$
    $ = 180$
    $180 + 37.5 = 217.5$

37. **(4)** *Arithmetic/Problem Solving.*
    Convert the cost of siding per square foot to cost per square yard:
    9 sq. ft. = 1 sq. yd.
    $9 \times 1.75 = 15.75$
    $15.75 - .75 = 15.00$

38. **(4)** *Arithmetic/Problem Solving.*
    $.045 =$ the amount of sales tax charged
    $1.045(5.78) =$ the total cost
    Divide by 48 to get the unit cost.

39. **(2)** *Geometry/Skills.*
    The triangle formed by the rake is an isosceles triangle. Angle b is the second base angle and measure 55 degrees.
    $55 + 55 = 110$
    $180 - 110 = 70$

40. **(2)** *Arithmetic/Problem Solving.*
    $1{,}750 \times 7 = 12{,}250$
    $\frac{12{,}250}{2{,}000} = 6$ remainder 250

41. **(2)** *Algebra/Skills.*
    Divide coefficients; subtract exponents.

42. **(4)** *Algebra/Problem Solving.*
    Let w = water:
    $1:3 = 18:w$
    $w = 54$

43. **(4)** *Arithmetic/Problem Solving.*
    $V = lwh$
    $ = 4 \times 4 \times 8$
    $ = 2^2 \times 2^2 \times 2^3$
    Add exponents to get 2^7.

44. **(3)** *Algebra/Problem Solving.*
    $d = rt$
    $ = 50m$

45. **(1)** *Arithmetic/Problem Solving.*
    45 minutes = .75 hour
    $d = rt$
    $ = 11 \times .75 \times 5$
    $ = 41.25$

46. **(3)** *Arithmetic/Skills.*
    $80 \times 23 = 1840$

47. **(4)** *Algebra/Applications.*
    $^+4$ and $^-6$ are the only two factors of 24 that would give ^-2c.

48. **(3)** *Geometry/Skills.*
    The sum of the angles in a triangle is 180°. Notice the triangle that is formed by extending the line made by the fishing pole to the ground.
    $ 90 + 30 = 120$
    $ 180 - 120 = 60$

49. **(1)** *Algebra/Problem Solving.*
    $>$ means greater than
    t must be greater than 347 for the light patterns to change.

50. **(4)** *Algebra/Problem Solving.*
    $c + e$ = total attendance
    $75 + 49$ = total events
    Attendance divided by events gives the average.

51. **(1)** *Algebra/Problem Solving.*
    $q + b$ = total amount of money she made.
    Dividing the total by 52 gives the average weekly salary.

52. **(5)** *Arithmetic/Problem Solving.*
    Since the problem does not give the number of people who left early, the chances for those people who stayed cannot be calculated.

53. **(5)** *Arithmetic/Problem Solving.*
    The problem does not give information about how many days each employee missed.

54. **(3)** *Arithmetic/Applications.*
    $A = \pi r^2$
    $ = 3.14 \times 3 \times 3$
    $ = 28.26$

55. **(4)** *Arithmetic/Problem Solving.*
    7 hr. 15 min. $\times$ 22 = 154 hr. 330 min.
    $\frac{330}{60} = 5.5$
    $154 + 5.5 = 159$ hr. 30 min.

56. **(3)** *Arithmetic/Problem Solving.*
    $3 \times 8 = 24$ hr.
    $\frac{15,000,000}{24} = 625,000$